We[illegible]
OPERATIONS MAN[illegible]MENT

Operations Management is important, exciting, challe[illegible]
look!

Important, because it's concerned with creating all of the proc[illegible] which we depend. Exciting, because it's at the centre of so m[illegible] the world of business. Challenging, because the solutions that [illegible] globally and responsibly within society and the environment. And everywhere, because every service and product that you use – the cereal you eat at breakfast, the chair you sit on, and the radio station you listen to while you eat – is the result of an operation or process.

Our aim in writing *Operations Management* is to give you a **comprehensive understanding** of the issues and techniques of operations management, and to **help you get a great final result** in your course. Here's how you might make the most of the text:

- Get ahead with the latest developments – from the up-to-the-minute *Operations in practice* features in every chapter to the focus on corporate social responsibility in the final chapter – these **put you at the cutting edge**.
- Use the *Worked examples* and *Problems and applications* to improve your use of key quantitative and qualitative techniques, and work your way to **better grades in your assignments and exams**.
- Follow up on the recommended readings at the end of each chapter. They're specially selected to enhance your learning and **give you an edge** in your course work.

And in particular, look out for the references to **MyOMLab** in the text, and log on to **www.myomlab.com*** where you can

- check and reinforce your understanding of key concepts using self-assessment questions, audio summaries, animations video clips and more;
- practice your problem-solving with feedback, guided solutions and a limitless supply of questions!

We want *Operations Management* to give you what you need: a comprehensive view of the subject, an ambition to put that into practice, and – of course – success in your studies. So, read on and good luck!

Nigel Slack
Stuart Chambers
Robert Johnston

* P.S. In order to **log in to MyOMLab**, you'll need to **register with the access code** included with all new copies of the book.

Further reading in Operations Management

Take your study and interest in operations management further with these leading textbooks written by the same team of expert authors.

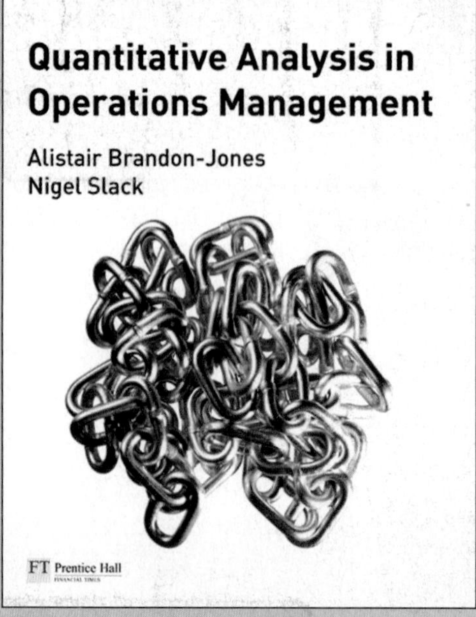

OPERATIONS MANAGEMENT

Sixth Edition

Nigel Slack

Stuart Chambers

Robert Johnston

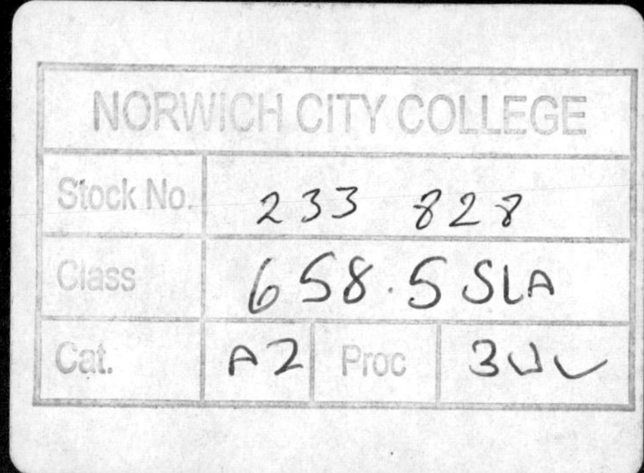

Financial Times Prentice Hall is an imprint of

PEARSON

Harlow, England • London • New York • Boston • San Francisco • Toronto • Sydney • Singapore • Hong Kong
Tokyo • Seoul • Taipei • New Delhi • Cape Town • Madrid • Mexico City • Amsterdam • Munich • Paris • Milan

Pearson Education Limited

Edinburgh Gate
Harlow
Essex CM20 2JE
England

and Associated Companies throughout the world

Visit us on the World Wide Web at:
www.pearsoned.co.uk

First published under the Pitman Publishing imprint 1995
Second edition (Pitman Publishing) 1998
Third edition 2001
Fourth edition 2004
Fifth edition 2007
Sixth edition 2010

ISBN: 978-0-273-73046-0

British Library Cataloguing-in-Publication Data
A catalogue record for this book is available from the British Library

Library of Congress Cataloging-in-Publication Data
Slack, Nigel.
Operations management / Nigel Slack, Stuart Chambers, Robert Johnston. – 6th ed.
p. cm.
ISBN 978-0-273-73046-0 (pbk.)
1. Production management. I. Chambers, Stuart. II. Johnston, Robert, 1953– III. Title.
TS155.S562 2010
658.5–dc22

10 9 8 7 6 5 4 3 2 1
14 13 12 11 10

Typeset in 10/12pt Minion by 35
Printed and bound by Rotolito Lombarda, Italy

The publisher's policy is to use paper manufactured from sustainable forests.

Brief contents

Contents

Guide to 'operations in practice', examples, short cases and case studies

Chapter	*Location*	*Company/example*	*Region*	*Sector/activity*	*Company size*
Chapter 1 Operations management	p. 3	IKEA	Global	Retail	Large
	p. 8	Acme Whistles	UK	Manufacturing	Small
	p. 9	Oxfam	Global	Charity	Large
	p. 14	Prêt A Manger	Europe/USA	Retail	Medium
	p. 21	Formule 1	Europe	Hospitality	Large
	p. 21	Mwagusi Safari Lodge	Tanzania	Hospitality	Small
	p. 27	Concept Design Services	UK	Design/manufacturing/ distribution	Medium
Chapter 2 Operations performance	p. 33	A tale of two terminals	Dubai and UK	Transport	Large
	p. 41	Lower Hurst Farm	UK	Agricultural	Small
	p. 43	Accident recovery	General	Healthcare	Medium
	p. 44	Dabbawalas hit 99.9999% dependability	India	General service	Large
	p. 47	BBC	Global	Media	Large
	p. 49	Aldi	Europe	Retail	Large
	p. 51	Hon Hai Precision Industry	Taiwan/China	Manufacturing	Large
	p. 57	Mutiara Beach Resort, Penang	Malaysia	Hospitality	Medium
Chapter 3 Operations strategy	p. 61	Two operations strategies: Flextronics and Ryanair	Global/Europe	Manufacturing service/ transport	Large
	p. 68	Giordano	Asia	Retail	Large
	p. 74	Amazon what exactly is your core competence?	Global	Retail/business services	Large
	p. 77	Sometimes any plan is better than no plan	Europe	Military	Large
	p. 80	Long Ridge Gliding Club	UK	Sport	Small
Chapter 4 Process design	p. 87	McDonalds	USA	Quick service	Large
	p. 90	Daimler-Chrysler, Smart car	France	Auto manufacturing	Large
	p. 107	Heathrow	UK	Transport	Large
	p. 109	The Central Evaluation Unit (European Union Directorate)	Belgium	Non-governmental organization	Large
Chapter 5 The design of products and services	p. 113	Airbus A380	Europe	Aerospace	Large
	p. 116	Dyson	Global	Design/manufacturing	Large
	p. 120	Square water melons	Japan	Retail/Agriculture	Various
	p. 122	Daniel Hersheson	UK	Hairdressing	Small
	p. 125	Art Attack!	UK	Media	Small
	p. 135	Chatsworth House	UK	Tourism	Medium
Chapter 6 Supply network design	p. 139	Dell	Global	Computer manufacturing	Large
	p. 145	Hon Hai, Quanta and Compal	Taiwan	Computer manufacturing	Large
	p. 147	Tata Nano	India	Manufacturing	Large
	p. 149	Tesco	Thailand	Retail	Large
	p. 151	High-tech subcontracting	India/China	Research and development	Medium/large
	p. 162	Disneyland Paris	France	Entertainment	Large

Chapter	*Location*	*Company/example*	*Region*	*Sector/activity*	*Company size*
Chapter 7 Layout and flow	p. 178	Tesco	Global	Retail	Large
	p. 180	Surgery	UK	Healthcare	Medium
	p. 185	Yamaha	Japan	Piano manufacturing	Large
	p. 186	Cadbury	UK	Entertainment and manufacturing	Large
	p. 203	Weldon Hand Tools	UK	Manufacturing	Large
Chapter 8 Process technology	p. 207	Airlines	All	Airlines	Large
	p. 210	Robots	All	Security	Various
	p. 211	Yo! Sushi	UK	Restaurants	Medium
	p. 213	IBM	USA	Disaster recovery	Large
	p. 218	Farming	Netherlands	Agriculture	Medium
	p. 220	QB House	Asia	Hairdressing	Medium
	p. 224	SVT (Sveriges Television)	Sweden	Media	Large
	p. 230	Rochem Ltd	UK	Food processing	Medium
Chapter 9 People, jobs and organization	p. 234	W.L. Gore and Associates	Global	Manufacturing and research	Large
	p. 237	Google	Global	e-services	Large
	p. 247	McDonalds	UK	Restaurants	Large
	p. 250	Lloyds TSB	Europe	Banking	Large
	p. 256	Service Adhesives	Europe	Manufacturing	Large
Chapter 10 The nature of planning and control	p. 269	BMW dealership	UK	Service and repair	Medium
	p. 273	Air France	Global	Airline	Large
	p. 281	Accident and Emergency	All	Healthcare	Large
	p. 286	Chicken salad sandwich (Part 1)	All	Food processing	Large
	p. 292	Robert Wiseman Dairies	UK	Milk distribution	Large
	p. 294	Air traffic control	All	Air travel	Medium
Chapter 11 Capacity planning and control	p. 298	Britvic	Europe	Distribution	Large
	p. 304	Seasonal products and services	All	Various	Various
	p. 309	British Airways London Eye	UK	Tourism	Medium
	p. 310	Lettuce growing	Europe	Agriculture	Large
	p. 315	Seasonal products and services	UK/Global	Food processing/media	Large
	p. 317	Greetings cards	All	Design	Large
	p. 326	Madame Tussauds, Amsterdam	Netherlands	Tourism	Medium
	p. 328	Holly Farm	UK	Agriculture/ entertainment	Small
Chapter 12 Inventory planning and control	p. 341	UK National Blood Service	UK	Healthcare	Large
	p. 348	Croft Port	Europe	Beverages	Large
	p. 356	The Howard Smith Paper Group	UK	Distribution service	Large
	p. 369	Trans-European Plastic	France	Manufacturing	Large
Chapter 13 Supply chain planning and control	p. 374	Siemens	Europe	Service and manufacturing	Large
	p. 379	Ford Motor Company	Global	Auto manufacturing	Large
	p. 384	Levi Straus & Co	Global	Garment design/ retailing	Large
	p. 385	TDG	Europe	Logistics services	Large
	p. 397	Northern Foods	Europe	Food services	Large
	p. 398	Seven-Eleven Japan	Japan	Retail	Large
	p. 401	H&M, Benetton and Zara	Global	Design/manufacturing/ distribution/retail	Large

Chapter	*Location*	*Company/example*	*Region*	*Sector/activity*	*Company size*
Chapter 14 Enterprise Resource Planning	p. 407	Rolls Royce	Global	Aerospace	Large
	p. 410	SAP	Global	IT services	Large
	p. 411	Chicken salad sandwich (Part 2)	All	Food processing	Small
	p. 414	SAP	Global	IT services	Large
	p. 417	What a waste	US	Waste management	Large
	p. 418	Psycho Sports Ltd	All	Manufacturing	Small
Chapter 15 Lean synchronization	p. 430	Toyota Motor Company	Global	Auto manufacturing	Large
	p. 440	Hospitals	UK	Healthcare	Medium/large
Chapter 16 Project planning and control	p. 458	The Millau Bridge	France	Construction	Large
	p. 465	The National Trust	UK	Heritage	Various
	p. 47	Access HK	Hong Kong	Charity	Small
	p. 488	United Photonics Malaysia Sdn Bhd	Malaysia	Research and development	Medium
Chapter 17 Quality management	p. 496	Four Seasons Hotel	Global/UK	Hospitality	Large
	p. 499	Tea and Sympathy	USA	Hospitality	Small
	p. 500	Magic Moments	UK	Photography services	Small
	p. 505	Vitacress	Europe	Agriculture	Large
	p. 507	Surgical Statistics	US	Healthcare	Various
	p. 512	IBM	Canada	IT services	Large
	p. 516	Rendall Graphics	Canada	Manufacturing	Medium
Chapter 18 Improvement	p. 541	Heineken International (Part I)	Netherlands	Brewery	Large
	p. 548	Erdington	UK	Beverage	Large
	p. 556	Xchanging	Europe	Process outsourcing	Large
	p. 565	Geneva Construction and Risk (GCR)	Europe	Insurance	Large
Chapter 19 Risk management	p. 572	Cadburys Salmonella outbreak	Global	Confectionary	Large
	p. 575	Not what you want to hear	USA	Airline	Large
	p. 577	Viruses, threats and 30 years of spam	Global	Internet	Various
	p. 592	Otis Elevators	Global	Facilities services	Large
	p. 597	Chernobyl	Ukraine	Power generation	Large
Chapter 20 Organizing for improvement	p. 602	Taxing Quality	Denmark	Public service	Large
	p. 620	Heineken International (Part II)	Netherlands	Brewery	Large
	p. 622	Work-Out at GE	Global	Various	?Large
	p. 626	Singapore Libraries	Singapore	?	?
Chapter 21 Corporate social responsibility (CSR)	p. 635	Ecological footprints	All	All	All
	p. 638	HP Recycling Program	Global	Manufacturing	Large
	p. 642	The Gap between perception, reality and intention	Global	Retail	Large
	p. 649	CSR as it is presented	Various	Various	Various

Making the most of this book and MyOMLab

Check your understanding

Each chapter opens with a set of **Key questions** to identify major topics. **Summary answers** conclude the chapter. You can check your understanding of each chapter by taking the **Sample tests of self-assessment questions** on MyOMLab at **www.myomlab.com**.

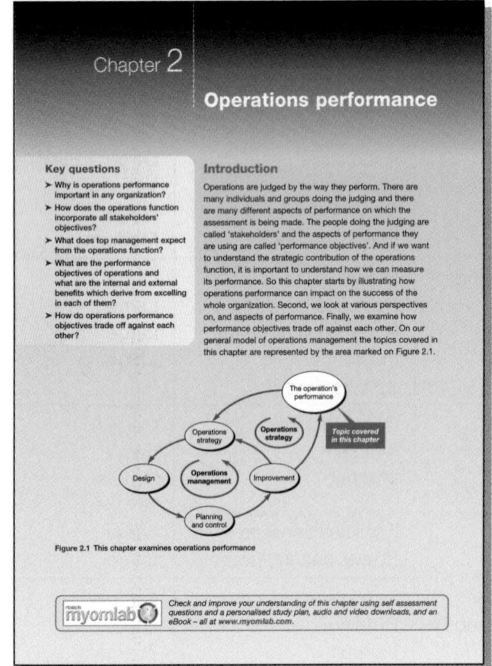

Chapter 2

Operations performance

Key questions

- ➤ Why is operations performance important in any organization?
- ➤ How does the operations function incorporate all stakeholders' objectives?
- ➤ What does top management expect from the operations function?
- ➤ What are the performance objectives of operations and what are the internal and external benefits which derive from excelling in each of them?
- ➤ How do operations performance objectives trade off against each other?

Introduction

Operations are judged by the way they perform. There are many individuals and groups doing the judging and there are many different aspects of performance on which the assessment is being made. The people doing the judging are called 'stakeholders' and the aspects of performance they are using are called 'performance objectives'. And if we want to understand the strategic contribution of the operations function, it is important to understand how we can measure its performance. So this chapter starts by illustrating how operations performance can impact on the success of the whole organization. Second, we look at various perspectives on, and aspects of performance. Finally, we examine how performance objectives trade off against each other. On our general model of operations management the topics covered in this chapter are represented by the area marked on Figure 2.1.

Figure 2.1 This chapter examines operations performance

myomlab *Check and improve your understanding of this chapter using self assessment questions and a personalised study plan, audio and video downloads, and an eBook – all at www.myomlab.com.*

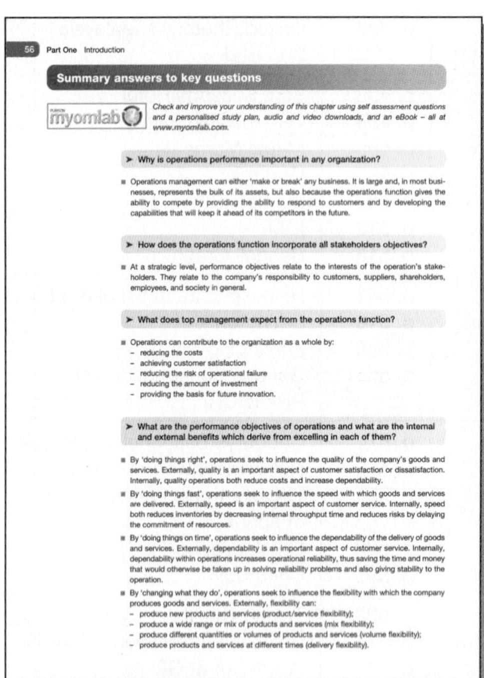

56 Part One Introduction

Summary answers to key questions

myomlab *Check and improve your understanding of this chapter using self assessment questions and a personalised study plan, audio and video downloads, and an eBook – all at www.myomlab.com.*

➤ Why is operations performance important in any organization?

- Operations management can either 'make or break' any business. It is large and, in most businesses, represents the bulk of its assets, but also because the operations function gives the ability to compete by providing the ability to respond to customers and by developing the capabilities that will keep it ahead of its competitors in the future.

➤ How does the operations function incorporate all stakeholders objectives?

- At a strategic level, performance objectives relate to the interests of the operation's stakeholders. They relate to the company's responsibility to customers, suppliers, shareholders, employees, and society in general.

➤ What does top management expect from the operations function?

- Operations can contribute to the organization as a whole by:
  - reducing the costs
  - achieving customer satisfaction
  - reducing the risk of operational failure
  - reducing the amount of investment
  - providing the basis for future innovation.

➤ What are the performance objectives of operations and what are the internal and external benefits which derive from excelling in each of them?

- By 'doing things right', operations seek to influence the quality of the company's goods and services. Externally, quality is an important aspect of customer satisfaction or dissatisfaction. Internally, quality operations both reduce costs and increase dependability.
- By 'doing things fast', operations seek to influence the speed with which goods and services are delivered. Externally, speed is an important aspect of customer service. Internally, speed both reduces inventories by decreasing internal throughput time and reduces risks by delaying the commitment of resources.
- By 'doing things on time', operations seek to influence the dependability of the delivery of goods and services. Externally, dependability is an important aspect of customer service. Internally, dependability within operations increases operational reliability, thus saving the time and money that would otherwise be taken up in solving reliability problems and also giving stability to the operation.
- By 'changing what they do', operations seek to influence the flexibility with which the company produces goods and services. Externally, flexibility can:
  - produce new products and services (product/service flexibility);
  - produce a wide range or mix of products and services (mix flexibility);
  - produce different quantities or volumes of products and services (volume flexibility);
  - produce products and services at different times (delivery flexibility).

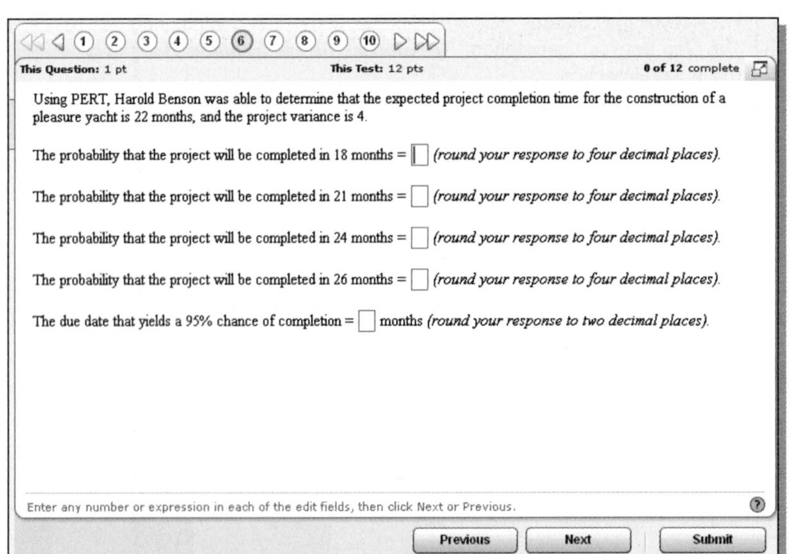

Practice makes perfect

Worked examples show how quantitative and qualitative techniques can be used in operations management. **Problems and applications** at the end of the chapter allow you to apply these techniques, and you can get more practice as well as guided solutions from the **Study plan** on MyOMLab at **www.myomlab.com**.

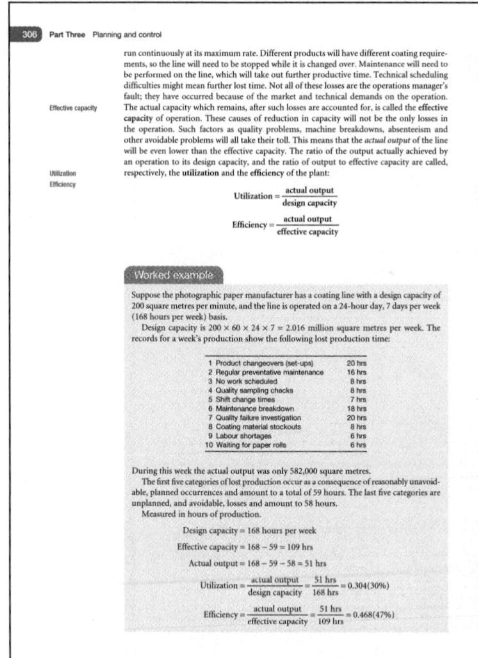

306 Part Three Planning and control

run continuously at its maximum rate. Different products will have different coating requirements, so the line will need to be stopped while it is changed over. Maintenance will need to be performed on the line, which will take out further productive time. Technical scheduling difficulties might mean further lost time. Not all of these losses are the operations manager's fault; they have occurred because of the market and technical demands on the operation. The actual capacity which remains, after such losses are accounted for, is called the **effective capacity** of operation. These causes of reduction in capacity will not be the only losses in the operation. Such factors as quality problems, machine breakdowns, absenteeism and other avoidable problems will all take their toll. This means that the *actual output* of the line will be even lower than the effective capacity. The ratio of the output actually achieved by an operation to its design capacity, and the ratio of output to effective capacity are called, respectively, the **utilization** and the **efficiency** of the plant:

Effective capacity

Utilization

Efficiency

$$\text{Utilization} = \frac{\text{actual output}}{\text{design capacity}}$$

$$\text{Efficiency} = \frac{\text{actual output}}{\text{effective capacity}}$$

Worked example

Suppose the photographic paper manufacturer has a coating line with a design capacity of 200 square metres per minute, and the line is operated on a 24-hour day, 7 days per week (168 hours per week) basis.

Design capacity is 200 × 60 × 24 × 7 = 2.016 million square metres per week. The records for a week's production show the following lost production time:

1 Product changeovers (set-ups)	20 hrs
2 Regular preventative maintenance	16 hrs
3 No work scheduled	8 hrs
4 Quality sampling checks	8 hrs
5 Shift change times	7 hrs
6 Maintenance breakdown	18 hrs
7 Quality failure investigation	20 hrs
8 Coating material stockouts	8 hrs
9 Labour shortages	6 hrs
10 Waiting for paper rolls	6 hrs

During this week the actual output was only 582,000 square metres.

The first five categories of lost production occur as a consequence of reasonably unavoidable, planned occurrences and amount to a total of 59 hours. The last five categories are unplanned, and avoidable, losses and amount to 58 hours.

Measured in hours of production.

$$\text{Design capacity} = 168 \text{ hours per week}$$

$$\text{Effective capacity} = 168 - 59 = 109 \text{ hrs}$$

$$\text{Actual output} = 168 - 59 - 58 = 51 \text{ hrs}$$

$$\text{Utilization} = \frac{\text{actual output}}{\text{design capacity}} = \frac{51 \text{ hrs}}{168 \text{ hrs}} = 0.304(30\%)$$

$$\text{Efficiency} = \frac{\text{actual output}}{\text{effective capacity}} = \frac{51 \text{ hrs}}{109 \text{ hrs}} = 0.468(47\%)$$

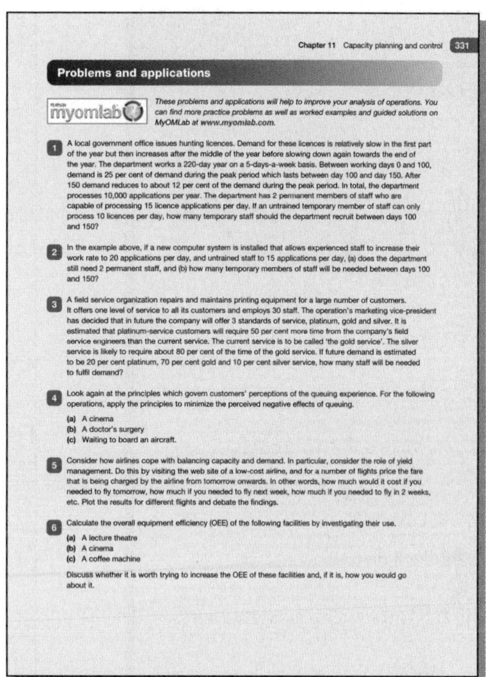

Chapter 11 Capacity planning and control 331

Problems and applications

These problems and applications will help to improve your analysis of operations. You can find more practice problems as well as worked examples and guided solutions on MyOMLab at www.myomlab.com.

1. A local government office issues hunting licences. Demand for these licences is relatively slow in the first part of the year but then increases after the middle of the year before slowing down again towards the end of the year. The department works a 220-day year on a 5-days-a-week basis. Between working days 0 and 100, demand is 25 per cent of demand during the peak period which lasts between day 100 and day 150. After 150 demand reduces to about 12 per cent of the demand during the peak period. In total, the department processes 10,000 applications per year. The department has 2 permanent members of staff who are capable of processing 15 licence applications per day. If an untrained temporary member of staff can only process 10 licences per day, how many temporary staff should the department recruit between days 100 and 150?

2. In the example above, if a new computer system is installed that allows experienced staff to increase their work rate to 20 applications per day, and untrained staff to 15 applications per day, (a) does the department still need 2 permanent staff, and (b) how many temporary members of staff will be needed between days 100 and 150?

3. A field service organization repairs and maintains printing equipment for a large number of customers. It offers one level of service to all its customers and employs 30 staff. The operation's marketing vice-president has decided that in future the company will offer 3 standards of service, platinum, gold and silver. It is estimated that platinum-service customers will require 50 per cent more time from the company's field service engineers than the current service. The current service is to be called 'the gold service'. The silver service is likely to require about 80 per cent of the time of the gold service. If future demand is estimated to be 20 per cent platinum, 70 per cent gold and 10 per cent silver service, how many staff will be needed to fulfil demand?

4. Look again at the principles which govern customers' perceptions of the queuing experience. For the following operations, apply the principles to minimize the perceived negative effects of queuing.
   (a) A cinema
   (b) A doctor's surgery
   (c) Waiting to board an aircraft.

5. Consider how airlines cope with balancing capacity and demand. In particular, consider the role of yield management. Do this by visiting the web site of a low-cost airline, and for a number of flights price the fare that is being charged by the airline from tomorrow onwards. In other words, how much would it cost if you needed to fly tomorrow, how much if you needed to fly next week, how much if you needed to fly in 2 weeks, etc. Plot the results for different flights and debate the findings.

6. Calculate the overall equipment efficiency (OEE) of the following facilities by investigating their use.
   (a) A lecture theatre
   (b) A cinema
   (c) A coffee machine

   Discuss whether it is worth trying to increase the OEE of these facilities and, if it is, how you would go about it.

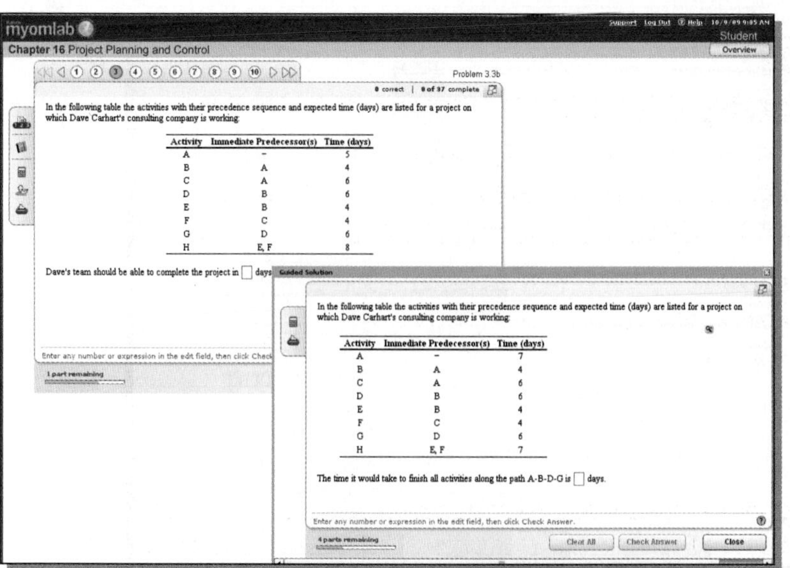

Making the most of this book and MyOMLab (continued)

Analyse operations in action

The **Operations in practice** and **Case study** features in each chapter illustrate and encourage you to analyse operations management in action. You can see and hear more about how theory is applied in practice in the animations and video clips in the **Multimedia library** in MyOMLab at **www.myomlab.com**.

298 Part Three Planning and control

Operations in practice Britvic – delivering drinks to demand[1]

Britvic is amongst Europe's leading soft-drink manufacturers, a major player in a market consuming nearly ten billion litres a year. Annually, Britvic bottles, distributes and sells over 1 billion litres of ready-to-drink soft drinks in around 400 different flavours, shapes and sizes, including brands such as Pepsi, Tango, Robinsons, Aqua Libra, Purdey's and J2O. Every year, Britvic produce enough cans of soft drinks to stretch three times around the world, so it has to be a high-volume and high-speed business. Its six UK factories contain factory lines producing up to 1,500 cans a minute, with distribution organized on a giant scale. At the centre of its distribution network is a National Distribution Centre (NDC) located at Lutterworth, UK. It is designed to operate 24 hours a day throughout the year, handling up to 620 truckloads of soft drinks daily and, together with a national network of 12 depots, it has to ensure that 250,000 outlets in the UK receive their orders on time. Designed and built in collaboration with Wincanton, a specialist supply chain solutions company, which now manages Britvic's NDC, it is capable of holding up to 140 million cans in its 50,000-pallet 'High Bay' warehouse. All information, from initial order to final delivery, is held electronically. Loads are scanned at Britvic factories and fed into the *'Business Planning and Control System'* that creates a schedule of receipts. This information is then fed to the *Warehouse Management System* and when hauliers arrive at the NDC, data are passed over to the *Movement Control System* that controls the retrieval of pallets from the High Bay.

Over the year Britvic distribute over 100 million cases. However, the demand pattern for soft drinks is seasonal, with short-term changes caused by both weather and marketing campaigns. Furthermore, Britvic's service policy of responding whenever customers want them to deliver has a dramatic impact on the NDC and its capacity planning. *'Our busiest periods are during the summer and in the run-up to Christmas, where we expect over 200 trailers in and out each day – that equates to about 3 million cases per week. In the quiet periods, especially after Christmas, we have less than a million cases per week'* (Distribution Manager).

Not only is demand on the NDC seasonal in a general sense, it can vary from 2,000 pallets one day, to 6,000 the next, as a result of short-term weather patterns and variable order patterns from large customers (supermarkets). Given the lack of space in the High Bay, it is not possible to simply stock up for the busy periods, so flexibility and efficiency are the keys to success.

The NDC uses a number of methods to cope with demand fluctuation. Most importantly is the use and development of technology both within the NDC and out in Britvic's supply chain. High levels of throughput and the ability to respond quickly to demand fluctuations depend on the use of integrated information technology linked to automated 'High Bay' handling technology. *'Without the automation this plant simply couldn't function. You realize how much you need this system when it breaks down! The other day, multiple errors in the system meant that in the space of 6 hours we went from being ahead to having 50 loads waiting to be processed. That equates to 1,350 pallets or nearly 4 million cans.'*

Human resource management is also key in managing capacity. Every morning the shift manager receives orders for the day, although further orders can be placed at any time during the day. The order information allows the multi-skilled workforce to be allocated effectively. The daily meetings also allow any problems to be addressed and dealt with before they become critical. Finally, by outsourcing the NDC management to Wincanton, the site is able to second employees from other Wincanton-owned sites when demand is high. *'Our other sites around the country have different peaks and troughs throughout the year which helps us utilize employee numbers.'*

Chapter 1 Operations management 27

Case study
Design house partnerships at Concept Design Services[6]

'I can't believe how much we have changed in a relatively short time. From being an inward-looking manufacturer, we became a customer-focused "design and make" operation. Now we are an integrated service provider. Most of our new business comes from the partnerships we have formed with design houses. In effect, we design products jointly with specialist design houses that have a well-known brand, and offer them a complete service of manufacturing and distribution. In many ways we are now a "business-to-business" company rather than a "business-to-consumer" company.' (Jim Thompson, CEO, Concept Design Services (CDS))

CDS had become one of Europe's most profitable homeware businesses. Originally founded in the 1960s, the company had moved from making industrial mouldings, mainly in the aerospace sector, and some cheap 'homeware' items such as buckets and dustpans, sold under the 'Focus' brand name, to making very high-quality (expensive) stylish homewares with a high 'design value'.

The move into 'Concept' products

The move into higher-margin homeware had been masterminded by Linda Fleet, CDS's Marketing Director, who had previously worked for a large retail chain of paint and wallpaper retailers. *'Experience in the decorative products industry had taught me the importance of fashion and product development, even in mundane products such as paint. Premium-priced colours and new textures would become popular for one or two years, supported by appropriate promotion and features in lifestyle magazines. The manufacturers and retailers who created and supported these products were dramatically more profitable than those who simply provided standard ranges. Instinctively, I felt that this must also apply to homeware. We decided to develop a whole coordinated range of such items, and to open up a new distribution network for them to serve up-market stores, kitchen equipment and speciality retailers. Within a year of launching our first new range of kitchen homeware under the "Concept" brand name, we had over 3000 retail outlets signed up, provided with point-of-sale display facilities. Press coverage generated an enormous interest which was reinforced by the product placement on several TV cookery and "lifestyle" programmes. We soon developed an entirely new market and within two years "Concept" products were providing over 75 per cent of our revenue and 90 per cent of our profits. The price realization of Concept products is many times higher than for the Focus range. To keep ahead we launched new ranges at regular intervals.'*

The move to the design house partnerships

'Over the last four years, we have been designing, manufacturing and distributing products for some of the more prestigious design houses. This sort of business is likely to grow, especially in Europe where the design houses appreciate our ability to offer a full service. We can design products in conjunction with their own design staff and offer them a level of manufacturing expertise they can't get elsewhere. More significantly, we can offer a distribution service which is tailored to their needs. From the customer's point of view the distribution arrangements appear to belong to the design house itself. In fact they are based exclusively on our own call centre, warehouse and distribution resources.'

The most successful collaboration was with Villessi, the Italian designers. Generally it was CDS's design expertise which was attractive to 'design house' partners. Not only did CDS employ professionally respected designers, they had also acquired a reputation for being able to translate difficult technical designs into manufacturable and saleable →

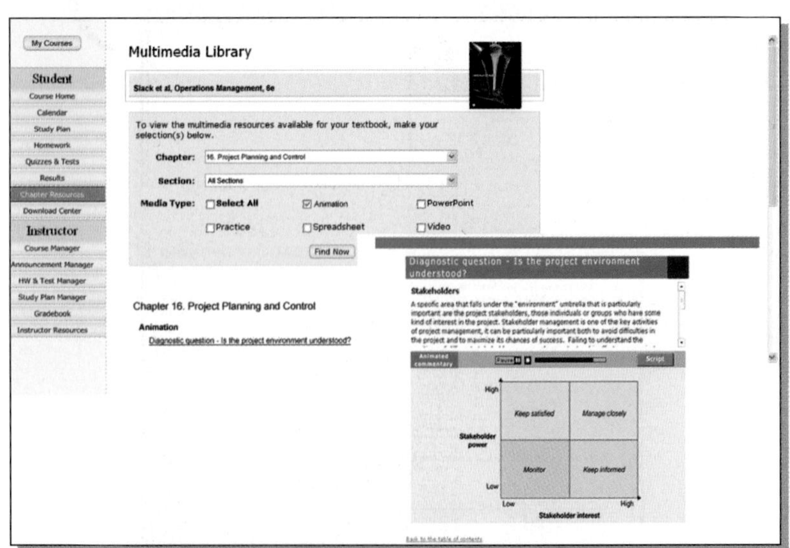

Take a different view

Critical commentaries, together with **Further reading** and **Useful websites** at the end of each chapter, show a diversity of viewpoint and encourage you to think critically about operations management. You can find the **Useful websites** in the **Multimedia library** of MyOMLab at **www.myomlab.com**.

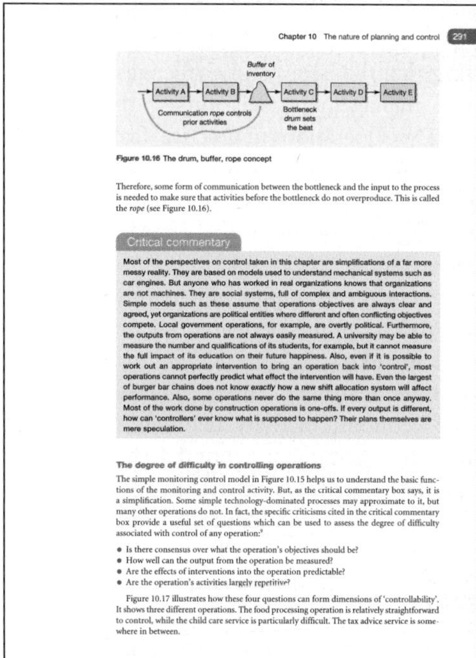

Chapter 10 The nature of planning and control 291

Figure 10.16 The drum, buffer, rope concept

Therefore, some form of communication between the bottleneck and the input to the process is needed to make sure that activities before the bottleneck do not overproduce. This is called the *rope* (see Figure 10.16).

Critical commentary

Most of the perspectives on control taken in this chapter are simplifications of a far more messy reality. They are based on models used to understand mechanical systems such as car engines. But anyone who has worked in real organizations knows that organizations are not machines. They are social systems, full of complex and ambiguous interactions. Simple models such as these assume that operations objectives are always clear and agreed, yet organizations are political entities where different and often conflicting objectives compete. Local government operations, for example, are overtly political. Furthermore, the outputs from operations are not always easily measured. A university may be able to measure the number and qualifications of its students, for example, but it cannot measure the full impact of its education on their future happiness. Also, even if it is possible to work out an appropriate intervention to bring an operation back into 'control', most operations cannot perfectly predict what effect the intervention will have. Even the largest of burger bar chains does not know *exactly* how a new shift allocation system will affect performance. Also, some operations never do the same thing more than once anyway. Most of the work done by construction operations is one-offs. If every output is different, how can 'controllers' ever know what is supposed to happen? Their plans themselves are mere speculation.

The degree of difficulty in controlling operations

The simple monitoring control model in Figure 10.15 helps us to understand the basic functions of the monitoring and control activity. But, as the critical commentary box says, it is a simplification. Some simple technology-dominated processes may approximate to it, but many other operations do not. In fact, the specific criticisms cited in the critical commentary box provide a useful set of questions which can be used to assess the degree of difficulty associated with control of any operation:[9]

- Is there consensus over what the operation's objectives should be?
- How well can the output from the operation be measured?
- Are the effects of interventions into the operation predictable?
- Are the operation's activities largely repetitive?

Figure 10.17 illustrates how these four questions can form dimensions of 'controllability'. It shows three different operations. The food processing operation is relatively straightforward to control, while the child care service is particularly difficult. The tax advice service is somewhere in between.

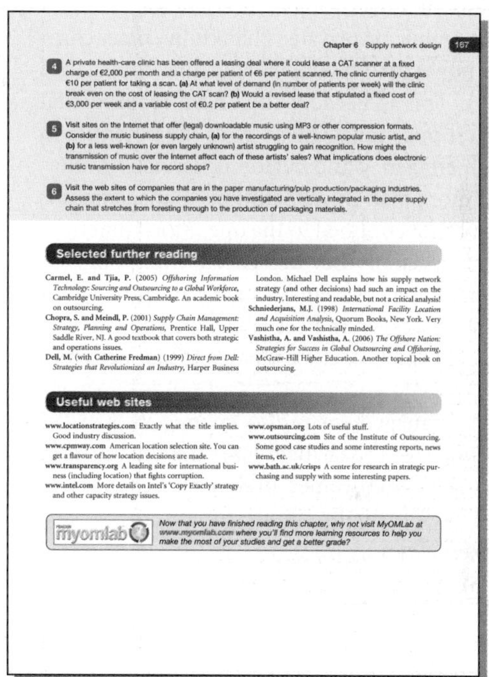

Chapter 6 Supply network design 167

4 A private health-care clinic has been offered a leasing deal where it could lease a CAT scanner at a fixed charge of €2,000 per month and a charge per patient of €6 per patient scanned. The clinic currently charges €10 per patient for taking a scan. **(a)** At what level of demand (in number of patients per week) will the clinic break even on the cost of leasing the CAT scan? **(b)** Would a revised lease that stipulated a fixed cost of €3,000 per week and a variable cost of €0.2 per patient be a better deal?

5 Visit sites on the Internet that offer (legal) downloadable music using MP3 or other compression formats. Consider the music business supply chain, **(a)** for the recordings of a well-known popular music artist, and **(b)** for a less well-known (or even largely unknown) artist struggling to gain recognition. How might the transmission of music over the Internet affect each of these artists' sales? What implications does electronic music transmission have for record shops?

6 Visit the web sites of companies that are in the paper manufacturing/pulp production/packaging industries. Assess the extent to which the companies you have investigated are vertically integrated in the paper supply chain that stretches from foresting through to the production of packaging materials.

Selected further reading

Carmel, E. and Tjia, P. (2005) *Offshoring Information Technology: Sourcing and Outsourcing to a Global Workforce*, Cambridge University Press, Cambridge. An academic book on outsourcing.

Chopra, S. and Meindl, P. (2001) *Supply Chain Management: Strategy, Planning and Operations*, Prentice Hall, Upper Saddle River, NJ. A good textbook that covers both strategic and operations issues.

Dell, M. (with **Catherine Fredman**) (1999) *Direct from Dell: Strategies that Revolutionized an Industry*, Harper Business London. Michael Dell explains how his supply network strategy (and other decisions) had such an impact on the industry. Interesting and readable, but not a critical analysis!

Schniederjans, M.J. (1998) *International Facility Location and Acquisition Analysis*, Quorum Books, New York. Very much one for the technically minded.

Vashistha, A. and Vashistha, A. (2006) *The Offshore Nation: Strategies for Success in Global Outsourcing and Offshoring*, McGraw-Hill Higher Education. Another topical book on outsourcing.

Useful web sites

www.locationstrategies.com Exactly what the title implies. Good industry discussion.

www.cpmway.com American location selection site. You can get a flavour of how location decisions are made.

www.transparency.org A leading site for international business (including location) that fights corruption.

www.intel.com More details on Intel's 'Copy Exactly' strategy and other capacity strategy issues.

www.opsman.org Lots of useful stuff.

www.outsourcing.com Site of the Institute of Outsourcing. Some good case studies and some interesting reports, news items, etc.

www.bath.ac.uk/crisps A centre for research in strategic purchasing and supply with some interesting papers.

myomlab *Now that you have finished reading this chapter, why not visit MyOMLab at www.myomlab.com where you'll find more learning resources to help you make the most of your studies and get a better grade?*

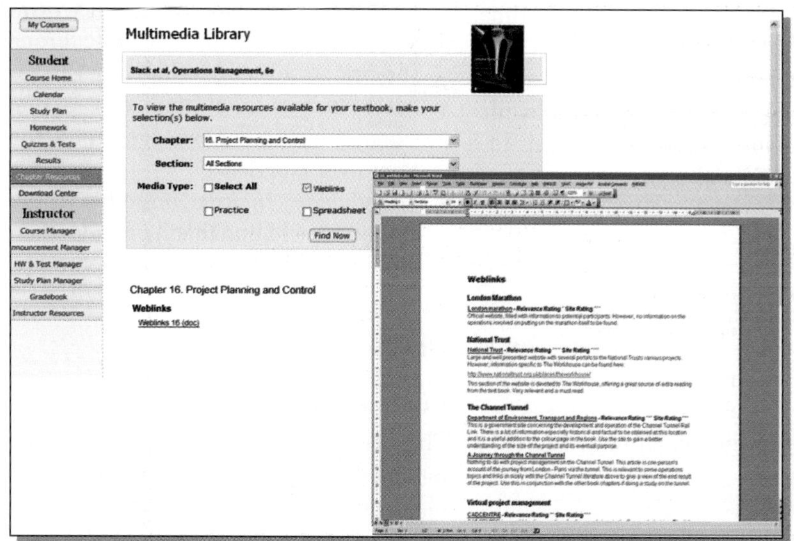

Preface

Introduction

Operations management is *important*. It is concerned with creating the services and products upon which we all depend. And all organizations produce some mixture of services and products, whether that organization is large or small, manufacturing or service, for profit or not for profit, public or private. Thankfully, most companies have now come to understand the importance of operations. This is because they have realized that effective operations management gives the potential to improve both efficiency and customer service simultaneously. But more than this, operations management is *everywhere*, it is not confined to the operations function. All managers, whether they are called Operations or Marketing or Human Resources or Finance, or whatever, manage processes and serve customers (internal or external). This makes, at least part of their activities 'operations'.

Operations management is also *exciting*. It is at the centre of so many of the changes affecting the business world – changes in customer preference, changes in supply networks brought about by internet-based technologies, changes in what we want to do at work, how we want to work, where we want to work, and so on. There has rarely been a time when operations management was more topical or more at the heart of business and cultural shifts.

Operations management is also *challenging*. Promoting the creativity which will allow organizations to respond to so many changes is becoming the prime task of operations managers. It is they who must find the solutions to technological and environmental challenges, the pressures to be socially responsible, the increasing globalization of markets and the difficult-to-define areas of knowledge management.

The aim of this book

This book provides a clear, authoritative, well structured and interesting treatment of operations management as it applies to a variety of businesses and organizations. The text provides both a logical path through the activities of operations management and an understanding of their strategic context.

More specifically, this text is:

- *Strategic* in its perspective. It is unambiguous in treating the operations function as being central to competitiveness.
- *Conceptual* in the way it explains the reasons why operations managers need to take decisions.
- *Comprehensive* in its coverage of the significant ideas and issues which are relevant to most types of operation.
- *Practical* in that the issues and challenges of making operations management decisions *in practice* are discussed. The 'Operations in practice' feature, which starts every chapter, the short cases that appear through the chapters, and the case studies at the end of each chapter, all explore the approaches taken by operations managers in practice.
- *International* in the examples which are used. There are over 120 descriptions of operations practice from all over the world.
- *Balanced* in its treatment. This means we reflect the balance of economic activity between service and manufacturing operations. Around seventy-five per cent of examples are from service organizations and twenty-five percent from manufacturing.

Who should use this book?

Anyone who is interested in how services and products are created.

- *Undergraduates* on business studies, technical or joint degrees should find it sufficiently structured to provide an understandable route through the subject (no prior knowledge of the area is assumed).
- *MBA students* should find that its practical discussions of operations management activities enhance their own experience.
- *Postgraduate students* on other specialist masters degrees should find that it provides them with a well-grounded and, at times, critical approach to the subject.

Distinctive features

Clear structure

The structure of the book uses a model of operations management which distinguishes between design, planning and control, and improvement.

Illustrations-based

Operations management is a practical subject and cannot be taught satisfactorily in a purely theoretical manner. Because of this we have used examples and 'boxed' short cases which explain some issues faced by real operations.

Worked examples

Operations management is a subject that blends qualitative and quantitative perspectives; 'worked examples' are used to demonstrate how both types of technique can be used.

Critical commentaries

Not everyone agrees about what is the best approach to the various topics and issues with operations management. This is why we have included 'critical commentaries' that pose alternative views to the one being expressed in the main flow of the text.

Summary answers to key questions

Each chapter is summarized in the form of a list of bullet points. These extract the essential points which answer the key question posed at the beginning of each chapter.

Case studies

Every chapter includes a case study suitable for class discussion. The cases are usually short enough to serve as illustrations, but have sufficient content also to serve as the basis of case sessions.

Problems and applications

Every chapter includes a set of problem type exercises. These can be used to check out your understanding of the concepts illustrated in the worked examples. There are also activities that support the learning objectives of the chapter that can be done individually or in groups.

Selected further reading

Every chapter ends with a short list of further reading which takes the topics covered in the chapter further, or treats some important related issues. The nature of each further reading is also explained.

Useful websites

A short list of web addresses is included in each chapter for those who wish to take their studies further.

To the Instructor ...

Teaching and learning resources for the 6th edition

New for the sixth edition

We have a regular opportunity to listen to the views of users of the book and are always keen to receive feedback. Our research for the 6th edition resulted in maintaining the successful structure of previous editions and incorporating the following key changes:

- An even greater emphasis has been placed on the idea of 'process management', making the subject more relevant to every functional areas of the organization.
- A whole new chapter on Corporate Social Responsibility (CSR) has been added, and reflects a greater emphasis on this issue throughout the book.
- The 'Operations in Practice' sections that are used to introduce the topic at the beginning of each chapter have been refreshed.
- The Worked examples have been extended to provide a better balance between qualitative and quantitative-based techniques.
- Many of the cases at the end of the chapter and short cases are new (but the old ones are still available on the web site), and provide an up-to-date selection of operations issues.
- The 'Problems' and 'Study activities' sections have been merged. This makes each chapter more compact.
- The book has been visually redesigned to aid learning.

Instructor's resources

A completely new instructor's manual is available to lecturers adopting this textbook, together with PowerPoint presentations for each chapter and a Testbank of assessment questions. Visit **www.pearsoned.co.uk/slack** to access these.

In addition a new Operations in Practice DVD is now available. Please contact your local Pearson Education Sales Consultant (**www.pearsoned.co.uk/replocator**) for further details and to request a copy.

Finally, and most importantly, a new set of online resources to enable students to check their understanding, practice key techniques and improve their problem-solving skills now accompanies the book. Please see below for details of MyOMLab.

The key to greater understanding and better grades in Operations Management!

MyOMLab for instructors

MyOMLab is designed to save you time in preparing and delivering assignments and assessments for your course, and to enable your students to study independently and at their own pace. Using MyOMLab, you can take advantage of:

- A wide range of engaging resources, including video, powerpoint slides and animated models with audio commentary.
- Hundreds of self-assessment questions, including algorithmically-generated quantitative values which make for a different problem every time.
- A Homework feature, allowing you to assign work for your students to prepare for your next class or seminar.
- A Gradebook which tracks students' performance on sample tests as well as assessments of your own design.

If you'd like to learn more or find out how MyOMLab could help you, please contact your local Pearson sales consultant at **www.pearsoned.co.uk/replocator** or visit **www.myomlab.com**.

To the Student . . .
Making the most of this book

All academic textbooks in business management are, to some extent, simplifications of the messy reality which is actual organizational life. Any book has to separate topics, in order to study them, which in reality are closely related. For example, technology choice impacts on job design which in turn impacts on quality control; yet we have treated these topics individually. The first hint therefore in using this book effectively is to look out for all the links between the individual topics. Similarly with the sequence of topics, although the chapters follow a logical structure, they need not be studied in this order. Every chapter is, more or less, self-contained. Therefore study the chapters in whatever sequence is appropriate to your course or your individual interests. But because each part has an introductory chapter, those students who wish to start with a brief 'overview' of the subject may wish first to study Chapters 1, 4, 10 and 18 and the chapter summaries of selected chapters. The same applies to revision – study the introductory chapters and summary answers to key questions.

The book makes full use of the many practical examples and illustrations which can be found in all operations. Many of these were provided by our contacts in companies, but many also come from journals, magazines and newspapers. So if you want to understand the importance of operations management in everyday business life look for examples and illustrations of operations management decisions and activities in newspapers and magazines. There are also examples which you can observe every day. Whenever you use a shop, eat a meal in a restaurant, borrow a book from the library or ride on public transport, consider the operations management issues of all the operations for which you are a customer.

The case exercises and study activities are there to provide an opportunity for you to think further about the ideas discussed in the chapters. Study activities can be used to test out your understanding of the specific points and issues discussed in the chapter and discuss them as a group, if you choose. If you cannot answer these you should revisit the relevant parts of the chapter. The case exercises at the end of each chapter will require some more thought. Use the questions at the end of each case exercise to guide you through the logic of analysing the issue treated in the case. When you have done this individually try to discuss your analysis with other course members. Most important of all, every time you analyse one of the case exercises (or any other case or example in operations management) start off your analysis with the two fundamental questions:

- How is this organization trying to compete (or satisfy its strategic objectives if a not-for-profit organization)?,
- What can the operation do to help the organization compete more effectively?

The key to greater understanding and better grades in Operations Management!

MyOMLab for students

MyOMLab has been developed to help students make the most of their studies in operations management. Visit the MyOMLab at **www.myomlab.com** to find valuable teaching and learning material including:

- Self-assessment questions and a personalized Study Plan to diagnose areas of strength and weakness, direct students' learning, and improve results.
- Unlimited practice on quantitative techniques and solving problems.
- Audio downloads, animated models and electronic flashcards to aid exam revision.
- Video clips and short cases to illustrate operations management in action.

Ten steps to getting a better grade in operations management

I could say that the best rule for getting a better grade is to be good. I mean really, really good! But, there are plenty of us who, while fairly good, don't get as good a grade as we really deserve. So, if you are studying operations management, and you want a really good grade, try following these simple steps:

Step 1 Practice, practice, practice. Use the Key questions and the Problems and applications to check your understanding. Use the Study plan feature in MyOMLab and practice to master the topics which you find difficult.

Step 2 Remember a few **key models**, and apply them wherever you can. Use the diagrams and models to describe some of the examples that are contained within the chapter. You can also use the revision pod casts on MyOMLab.

Step 3 Remember to use both **quantitative and qualitative analysis.** You'll get more credit for appropriately mixing your methods: use a quantitative model to answer a quantitative question and vice versa, but qualify this with a few well chosen sentences. Both the chapters of the book, and the exercises on MyOMLab, incorporate qualitative and quantitative material.

Step 4 There's always a ***strategic* objective** behind any operational issue. Ask yourself, 'Would a similar operation with a different strategy do things differently?' Look at the Short cases, Case studies, and Operations in practice pieces in the book.

Step 5 Research widely around the topic. Use websites that you trust – we've listed some good websites at the end of each chapter and on MyOMLab. You'll get more credit for using references that come from genuine academic sources.

Step 6 Use **your own experience.** Every day, you're experiencing an opportunity to apply the principles of operations management. Why is the queue at the airport check-in desk so long? What goes on behind the 'hole in the wall' of your bank's ATM machines? Use the videos on MyOMLab to look further at operations in practice.

Step 7 Always answer the question. Think 'What is really being asked here? What topic or topics does this question cover?' Find the relevant chapter or chapters, and search the Key questions at the beginning of each chapter and the Summary at the end of each chapter to get you started.

Step 8 Take account of the three tiers of accumulating marks for your answers.

(a) First, demonstrate your knowledge and understanding. Make full use of the text and MyOMLab to find out where you need to improve.
(b) Second, show that you know how to illustrate and apply the topic. The Short cases, Case studies and 'Operations in practice' sections, combined with those on MyOMLab, give you hundreds of different examples.
(c) Third, show that you can discuss and analyse the issues critically. Use the Critical commentaries within the text to understand some of the alternative viewpoints.

Generally, if you can do (a) you will pass; if you can do (a) and (b) you will pass well, and if you can do all three, you will pass with flying colours!

Step 9 Remember not only **what** the issue is about, but also **understand why**! Read the text and apply your knowledge on MyOMLab until you really understand why the concepts and techniques of operations management are important, and what they contribute to an organisation's success. Your new-found knowledge will stick in your memory, allow you to develop ideas, and enable you to get better grades.

Step 10 Start now! Don't wait until two weeks before an assignment is due. Log on (**www.myomlab.com**), read on, and GOOD LUCK!

Nigel Slack

About the authors

Nigel Slack is the Professor of Operations Management and Strategy at Warwick University. Previously he has been Professor of Service Engineering at Cambridge University, Professor of Manufacturing Strategy at Brunel University, a University Lecturer in Management Studies at Oxford University and Fellow in Operations Management at Templeton College, Oxford.

He worked initially as an industrial apprentice in the hand-tool industry and then as a production engineer and production manager in light engineering. He holds a Bachelor's degree in Engineering and Master's and Doctor's degrees in Management, and is a chartered engineer. He is the author of many books and papers in the operations management area, including *The Manufacturing Advantage*, published by Mercury Business Books, 1991, and *Making Management Decisions* (with Steve Cooke), 1991, published by Prentice Hall, *Service Superiority* (with Robert Johnston), published in 1993 by EUROMA and *Cases in Operations Management* (with Robert Johnston, Alan Harrison, Stuart Chambers and Christine Harland) third edition published by Financial Times Prentice Hall in 2003, *The Blackwell Encyclopedic Dictionary of Operations Management* (with Michael Lewis) published by Blackwell in 2005, *Operations Strategy* together with Michael Lewis, the second edition published by Financial Times Prentice Hall in 2008 and *Perspectives in Operations Management (Volumes I to IV)* also with Michael Lewis, published by Routledge in 2003. He has authored numerous academic papers and chapters in books. He also acts as a consultant to many international companies around the world in many sectors, especially financial services, transport, leisure and manufacturing. His research is in the operations and manufacturing flexibility and operations strategy areas.

Stuart Chambers is a Principle Teaching Fellow at Warwick Business School, where he has been since 1988. He began his career as an undergraduate apprentice at Rolls Royce Aerospace, graduating in mechanical engineering, and then worked in production and general management with companies including Tube Investments and the Marley Tile Company. In his mid-thirties and seeking a career change, he studied for an MBA, and then took up a three-year contract as a researcher in manufacturing strategy. This work enabled him to help executives develop the analyses, concepts and practical solutions required for them to develop manufacturing strategies. Several of the case studies prepared from this work have been published in an American textbook on manufacturing strategy. In addition to lecturing on a range of operations courses at the Business School and in industry, he undertakes consultancy in a diverse range of industries and is co-author of several operations management books.

Robert Johnston is Professor of Operations Management at Warwick Business School and its Deputy Dean. He is the founding editor of the *International Journal of Service Industry Management* and he also serves on the editorial board of the *Journal of Operations Management* and the *International Journal of Tourism and Hospitality Research*. He is the author of the market leading text, *Service Operations Management* (with Graham Clark), now in its 3rd edition (2008), published by Financial Times Prentice Hall. Before moving to academia Dr Johnston held several line management and senior management posts in a number of service organizations in both the public and private sectors. He continues to maintain close and active links with many large and small organizations through his research, management training and consultancy activities. As a specialist in service operations, his research interests include service design, service recovery, performance measurement and service quality. He is the author or co-author of many books, as well as chapters in other texts, numerous papers and case studies.

Acknowledgements

During the preparation of the fifth edition of this book, the authors conducted a number of 'faculty workshops' and the many useful comments from these sessions have influenced this and the other books for the 'Warwick group'. Our thanks go to everyone who attended these sessions and other colleagues. We thank Pär Åhlström of Stockholm School of Economics and Alistair Brandon-Jones of Bath University for assistance well beyond the call of duty, Alan Betts of ht2.org for case writing help and support, and Shirley Johnston for case writing help and support. Also, Professor Sven Åke Hörte of Lulea University of Technology, Eamonn Ambrose of University College, Dublin, Colin Armistead of Bournemouth University, Ran Bhamra, Loughbrough University, Ruth Boaden of Manchester Business School, Peter Burcher of Aston University, John K Christiansen of Copenhagen Business School, Philippa Collins of Heriot-Watt University, Henrique Correa of Rollins College, Florida, Paul Coughlan, Trinity College Dublin, Simon Croom, University of San Diego, Stephen Disney, Cardiff University, Doug Davies of University of Technology, Sydney, Tony Dromgoole of the Irish Management Institute, Dr J.A.C. de Haan of Tilburg University, Carsten Dittrich, University of Southern Denmark, David Evans of Middlesex University, Paul Forrester of Keele University, Keith Goffin, Cranfield University, Ian Graham of Edinburgh University, Alan Harle of Sunderland University, Norma Harrison of Macquarie University, Catherine Hart of Loughborough Business School, Chris Hillam of Sunderland University, Ian Holden of Bristol Business School, Matthias Holweg, Cambridge University, Mickey Howard, Bath University, Brian Jefferies of West Herts College, Tom Kegan of Bell College of Technology, Hamilton, Denis Kehoe, Liverpool University, Mike Lewis, Bath University, Peter Long of Sheffield Hallam University, John Maguire of the University of Sunderland, Charles Marais of the University of Pretoria, Roger Maull, Exeter University, Bart McCarthy, Nottingham University, Harvey Maylor of Cranfield University, John Meredith Smith of EAP, Oxford, Michael Milgate of Macquarie University, Keith Moreton of Staffordshire University, Chris Morgan, Cranfield University, Adrian Morris of Sunderland University, Steve New, Oxford University, John Pal of Manchester Metropolitan University, Peter Race of Henley College, Reading University, Ian Sadler of Victoria University, Richard Small, Supply Network Solutions, Andi Smart, Exeter University, Amrik Sohal of Monash University, Alex Skedd of Northumbria Business School, Martin Spring of Lancaster University, Dr Ebrahim Soltani of the University of Kent, R. Stratton of Nottingham Trent University, Dr Nelson Tang of the University of Leicester, David Twigg of Sussex University, Helen Valentine of the University of the West of England, Professor Roland van Dierdonck of the University of Ghent, Dirk Pieter van Donk of the University of Groningen and Peter Worthington.

Our academic colleagues in the Operations Management Group at Warwick Business School also helped, both by contributing ideas and by creating a lively and stimulating work environment. Our thanks go to Jannis Angelis, Nicola Burgess, Dan Chicksand, Michaelis Giannakis, Zoe Radnor, Michael Shulver, Rhian Silvestro, Nick Wake, Dick Wheeler, Helen Walker, and Paul Walley. We are also grateful to many friends, colleagues and company contacts. In particular thanks for help with this edition goes to Philip Godfrey and Cormac Campbell and their expert colleagues at OEE, David Garman and Carol Burnett of The Oakwood Partnership, Clive Buesnel of Xchanging, Hans Mayer and Tyko Persson of Nestlé, Peter Norris and Mark Fisher of the Royal Bank of Scotland, John Tyley of Lloyds TSB, Joanne Chung of Synter BMW, Michael Purtill of Four Seasons Hotel Group, Catherine Pyke and Nick Fudge of Lower Hurst Farm, Johan Linden of SVT, John Matthew of HSPG, Dan McHugh of Credit Swiss First Boston, David Nichol of Morgan Stanley, Leigh Rix of The National Trust, and Simon Topman of Acme Whistles. Mary Walton is coordinator to our group at Warwick Business School. Her continued efforts at keeping us organized (or as organized as we are capable of being) are always appreciated, but never more so than when we were engaged on 'the book'.

We were lucky to receive continuing professional and friendly assistance from a great publishing team. Especial thanks to Matthew Walker, Elizabeth Wright and Colin Reed.

Finally, all six editions were organized, and largely word processed by Angela Slack. It was, yet again, an heroic effort. To Angela – our thanks.

Nigel Slack
Stuart Chambers
Robert Johnston

Publisher's acknowledgements

We are grateful to the following for permission to reproduce copyright material:

Figures

Figure 15.11 from *'Strategies for implemeting JIT' in Just in Time Manufacture* IFS/Springer-Verlag (Voss, C.A., and Harrison, A. 1987) Springer; Figure 17.4 adapted from A conceptual model of service quality and implications for future research, *Journal of Marketing*, vol. 49, Fall, pp. 41–50 (Parasuraman, A. et al. 1985), American Marketing Association.

Tables

Table 8.1 after E-commerce and its impact on operations management, *International Journal of Production Economics*, 75, pp. 185–97 (Gunasekaran, A., Marri, H.B., McGaughey, R.E. and Nebhwani, M.D. 2002), Elsevier; Table S9.2 adapted from Adapted from Barnes, Frank C. (1983) 'Principles of Motion Economy: Revisited, Reviewed, and Restored', Proceedings of the Southern Management Association Annual Meeting (Atlanta, G.A. 1983), p. 298.

In some instances we have been unable to trace the owners of copyright material, and we would appreciate any information that would enable us to do so.

Photographs

The publisher would like to thank the following for their kind permission to reproduce their photographs:

3 **Alamy Images:** Neil Cannon. 7 **Alamy Images:** Chris Rout (c); Golden Pixels/LLC (b). **Corbis:** Claudio Peri/epa (br). **Getty Images:** Siri Stafford (tl). **Rex Features:** Action Press (t). 8 **ACME.** 9 **Rex Features:** Brian Rasic. 14 **Alamy Images:** Alex Segre. 27 **Alamy Images:** Adrian Sherratt. 33 **Alamy Images:** Craig Ingram. 34 **Rex Features:** Jurgen Hasenkopf. 41 **Alamy Images:** David Hoffman Photo Library (tl); Stuart Pearce (b). **Courtesy of Arup:** (cr). **Honda:** (tr). **Rex Features:** Per Lindgren. 42 **Alamy Images:** David Hoffman Photo Library (cl). **Rex Features:** Per Lindgren (bl). 43 **Corbis:** Bernardo Bucci. 44 **Alamy Images:** David Hoffman Photo Library (tl). **Getty Images:** AFP (b). **Rex Features:** Per Lindgren (cl). 46 **Alamy Images:** David Hoffman Photo Library. **Rex Features:** Per Lindgren (bl). 47 **BBC Photo Library:** Jeff Overs. 49 **Alamy Images:** Bildagentur-online (b); David Hoffman Photo Library (tl). **Rex Features:** Per Lindgren (cl). 57 **Alamy Images:** Tim Graham. 61 **Corbis:** Thomas White (b); Ulrich Perrey/epa (t). 68 **Alamy Images:** Rob Crandell. 74 **Alamy Images:** Bernhard Classen. 87 **Getty Images:** AFP. 90 **Getty Images.** 92 **Corbis:** Construction Photography (cr); Heinz von Heyenaber (br). 93 **Getty Images:** Burje/Triolo Productions (tr). **Rex Features:** Richard Jones (cr). 94 **Alamy Images:** Directphoto.org (t). **Getty Images:** David Sacks (b). 95 **© The Royal Bank of Scotland Group plc.** 107 **Alamy Images:** Michael Jones. 113 **Rex Features:** Action Press. 116 **Alamy Images:** Adrian Sherratt. 120 **Getty Images.** 122 **Photographers Direct:** Martin Karius. 139 **Corbis:** Gianni Giansanti/Sygma. 145 **Rex Features:** Image Source. 147 **Getty Images:** AFP. 151 **Getty Images:** AFP. 162 **Corbis:** Jacques Langevin. 178 **Alamy Images:** British Retail Photography. 186 **Cadbury World:** (t). **Corbis:** Marijan Murat/epa (b). 207 **Rex Features:** Action Press. 210 **Corbis:** Yiorgos Karahalis. 211 **YO! Sushi:** Jonathan Roberts. 213 **Rex Features.** 216 **Rex Features.** 220 **Photographers Direct:** Andy Maluche. 224 **SVT Bengt O Nordin.** 230 **Press Association Images:** ECKEHARD SCHULZ/AP. 234 **Alamy Images:** Ashley Cooper. 237 **Alamy Images:** David Hancock. 247 **Corbis:** Reuters. 248 **Getty Images.** 250 **Rex Features:** Voisin Phanie. 251 **Getty Images:** Williams & Hirakawa. 269 **© BMW Group.** 273 **Getty Images:** AFP. 281 **Alamy Images:** Ian Miles/Flashpoint Pictures. 292 **Robert Wiseman Dairies.** 294 **Courtesy of Arup.** 298 **Wincanton.** 304 **Alamy Images:** Medical-on-Line. 309 **British Airways.** 310 **Corbis:** G Flayols/Photocuisine. 317 **Press Association Images:** Orlin Wagner/AP. 341 **Alamy Images:** Van Hilversum. 356 **Howard Smith Paper Group.** 369 **Alamy Images:** Archive Berlin Fotoagentur GmbH. 374 **Alamy Images:** Imagebroker. 379 **Getty Images:** Getty Images News. 384 **Corbis:** Joes Luis Pelaez. 385 **TDG Logistics.** 387 **Virgin Atlantic.** 398 **Getty Images:** AFP. 402 **Press Association Images:** JAVA/ABACA. 407 **© Rolls-Royce plc.** 410 **Courtesy of SAP (UK) Limited.** 414 **Alamy Images:** Bon Appetit. 417 **Alamy Images:** A T Willett. 418 **Corbis:** Mark Cooper. 430 **Corbis:** Denis Balihoudr. 440 **Rex Features:** Burger/Phanie. 458 **Corbis:** Jane-Philippe Arles/Reuters. 465 **Alamy Images:** Oleksandr Ivanchenko. 475 **Image courtesy of Silicon Graphics, Inc. © 2003 Silicon Graphics, Inc. Used.** 488 **Corbis:** Eric K K Yu. 496 **Four Seasons Hotels:** Robert Miller. 499 **Corbis:** Eleanor Bentall. 500 **Alamy Images:** Les Gibbons. 505 **Alamy Images:** Daniel Jones. 541 **Getty Images.** 548 **Rex Features:** Dan Tuffs. 556 **Rex Features:** Charles Knight. 572 **Science Photo Library Ltd:** Simon Fraser. 577 **Alamy Images:** Imagina Photography. 592 **Alamy Images:** Dinodia Images. 602 **Rex Features:** Action Press. 622 **Getty Images:** Paul Vismara. 633 **Rex Features:** Design Pics Inc. 638 **Photographers Direct:** Awe Inspiring Images. 642 **Alamy Images:** PSL Images. 649 **Corbis:** Ultraf.

All other images © Nigel Slack, Stuart Chambers and Robert Johnston

Every effort has been made to trace the copyright holders and we apologise in advance for any unintentional omissions. We would be pleased to insert the appropriate acknowledgement in any subsequent edition of this publication.

Key operations questions

Chapter 1 **Operations management**

- What is operations management?
- Why is operations management important in all types of organization?
- What is the input–transformation–output process?
- What is the process hierarchy?
- How do operations processes have different characteristics?
- What are the activities of operations management?

Chapter 2 **Operations performance**

- Why is operations performance important in any organization?
- How does the operations function incorporate all stakeholders' objectives?
- What does top management expect from the operations function?
- What are the performance objectives of operations and what are the internal and external benefits which derive from excelling in each of them?
- How do operations performance objectives trade off against each other?

Chapter 3 **Operations strategy**

- What is strategy and what is operations strategy?
- What is the difference between a 'top-down' and a 'bottom-up' view of operations strategy?
- What is the difference between a 'market requirements' and an 'operations resources' view of operations strategy?
- How can an operations strategy be put together?

Part One
INTRODUCTION

This part of the book introduces the idea of the operations function in different types of organization. It identifies the common set of objectives to which operations managers aspire in order to serve their customers, and it explains how operations can have an important strategic role.

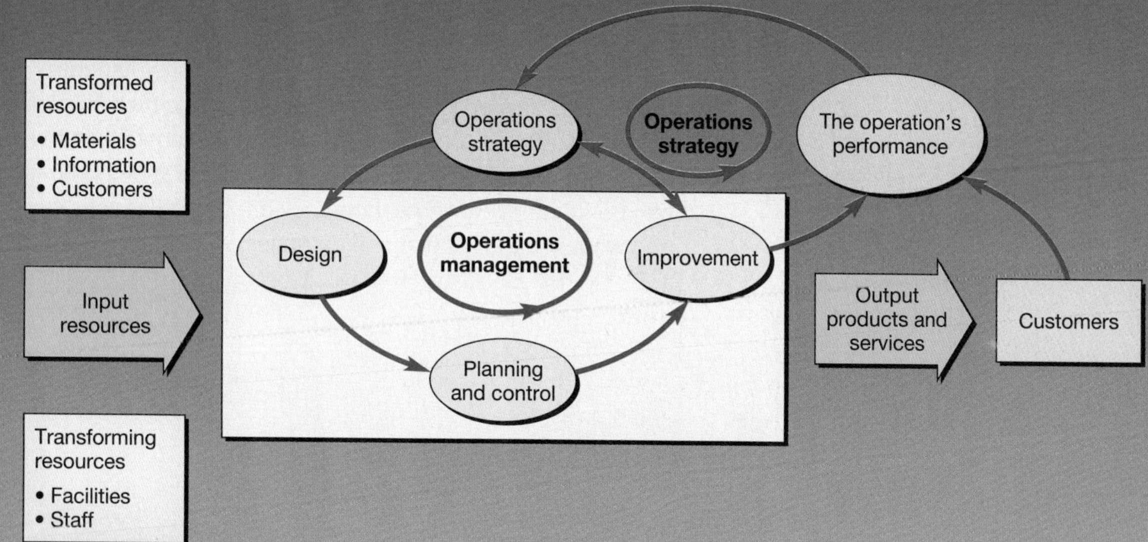

Chapter 1

Operations management

Key questions

- What is operations management?
- Why is operations management important in all types of organization?
- What is the input–transformation–output process?
- What is the process hierarchy?
- How do operations processes have different characteristics?
- What are the activities of operations management?

Introduction

Operations management is about how organizations produce goods and services. Everything you wear, eat, sit on, use, read or knock about on the sports field comes to you courtesy of the operations managers who organized its production. Every book you borrow from the library, every treatment you receive at the hospital, every service you expect in the shops and every lecture you attend at university – all have been produced. While the people who supervised their 'production' may not always be called operations managers that is what they really are. And that is what this book is concerned with – the tasks, issues and decisions of those operations managers who have made the services and products on which we all depend. This is an introductory chapter, so we will examine what we mean by 'operations management', how operations processes can be found everywhere, how they are all similar yet different, and what it is that operations managers do.

Operations in practice IKEA[1]

(All chapters start with an 'Operations in practice' example that illustrates some of the issues that will be covered in the chapter.)

Love it or hate it, IKEA is the most successful furniture retailer ever. With 276 stores in 36 countries, it has managed to develop its own special way of selling furniture. The stores' layout means customers often spend two hours in the store – far longer than in rival furniture retailers. IKEA's philosophy goes back to the original business, started in the 1950s in Sweden by Ingvar Kamprad. He built a showroom on the outskirts of Stockholm where land was cheap and simply displayed suppliers' furniture as it would be in a domestic setting. Increasing sales soon allowed IKEA to start ordering its own self-designed products from local manufacturers. But it was innovation in its operations that dramatically reduced its selling costs. These included the idea of selling furniture as self-assembly flat packs (which reduced production and transport costs) and its 'showroom–warehouse' concept which required customers to pick the furniture up themselves from the warehouse (which reduced retailing costs). Both of these operating principles are still the basis of IKEA's retail operations process today.

Stores are designed to facilitate the smooth flow of customers, from parking, moving through the store itself, to ordering and picking up goods. At the entrance to each store large notice-boards provide advice to shoppers. For young children, there is a supervised children's play area, a small cinema, and a parent and baby room so parents can leave their children in the supervised play area for a time. Parents are recalled via the loudspeaker system if the child has any problems. IKEA 'allow customers to make up their minds in their own time' but 'information points' have staff who can help. All furniture carries a ticket with a code number which indicates its location in the warehouse. (For larger items customers go to the information desks for assistance.) There is also an area where smaller items are displayed, and can be picked directly. Customers then pass through the warehouse where they pick up the items viewed in the showroom. Finally, customers pay at the checkouts, where a ramped conveyor belt moves purchases up to the checkout staff. The exit area has service points and a loading area that allows customers to bring their cars from the car park and load their purchases.

Behind the public face of IKEA's huge stores is a complex worldwide network of suppliers, 1,300 direct suppliers, about 10,000 sub-suppliers, wholesale and transport operations include 26 Distribution Centres. This supply network is vitally important to IKEA. From purchasing raw materials, right through to finished products arriving in its customers' homes, IKEA relies on close partnerships with its suppliers to achieve both ongoing supply efficiency and new product development. However, IKEA closely controls all supply and development activities from IKEA's home town of Älmhult in Sweden.

Source: Alamy Images

But success brings its own problems and some customers became increasingly frustrated with overcrowding and long waiting times. In response IKEA in the UK launched a £150 m programme to 'design out' the bottlenecks. The changes included:

- Clearly marked in-store short cuts allowing customers who just want to visit one area, to avoid having to go through all the preceding areas.
- Express checkout tills for customers with a bag only rather than a trolley.
- Extra 'help staff' at key points to help customers.
- Redesign of the car parks, making them easier to navigate.
- Dropping the ban on taking trolleys out to the car parks for loading (originally implemented to stop vehicles being damaged).
- A new warehouse system to stop popular product lines running out during the day.
- More children's play areas.

IKEA spokeswoman Nicki Craddock said: *'We know people love our products but hate our shopping experience. We are being told that by customers every day, so we can't afford not to make changes. We realized a lot of people took offence at being herded like sheep on the long route around stores. Now if you know what you are looking for and just want to get in, grab it and get out, you can.'*

→

Operations management is a vital part of IKEA's success

IKEA shows how important operations management is for its own success and the success of any type of organization. Of course, IKEA understands its market and its customers. But, just as important, it knows that the way it manages the network of operations that design, produce and deliver its products and services must be right for its market. No organization can survive in the long term if it cannot supply its customers effectively. And this is essentially what operations management is about – designing, producing and delivering products and services that satisfy market requirements. For any business, it is a vitally important activity. Consider just some of the activities that IKEA's operations managers are involved in.

- Arranging the store's layout to gives smooth and effective flow of customers (called process design)
- Designing stylish products that can be flat-packed efficiently (called product design)
- Making sure that all staff can contribute to the company's success (called job design)
- Locating stores of an appropriate size in the most effective place (called supply network design)
- Arranging for the delivery of products to stores (called supply chain management)
- Coping with fluctuations in demand (called capacity management)
- Maintaining cleanliness and safety of storage area (called failure prevention)
- Avoiding running out of products for sale (called inventory management)
- Monitoring and enhancing quality of service to customers (called quality management)
- Continually examining and improving operations practice (called operations improvement).

And these activities are only a small part of IKEA's total operations management effort. But they do give an indication, first of how operations management should contribute to the businesses success, and second, what would happen if IKEA's operations managers failed to be effective in carrying out any of its activities. Badly designed processes, inappropriate products, poor locations, disaffected staff, empty shelves, or forgetting the importance of continually improving quality, could all turn a previously successful organization into a failing one. Yet, although the relative importance of these activities will vary between different organizations, operations managers in all organizations will be making the same *type* of decision (even if *what* they actually decide is different).

What is operations management?

Operations management
Operations function
Operations managers

Operations management is the activity of managing the resources which produce and deliver products and services. The **operations function** is the part of the organization that is responsible for this activity. Every organization has an operations function because every organization produces some type of products and/or services. However, not all types of organization will necessarily call the operations function by this name. (Note that we also use the shorter terms 'the operation' and 'operations' interchangeably with the 'operations function'). **Operations managers** are the people who have particular responsibility for managing some, or all, of the resources which compose the operations function. Again, in some organizations the operations manager could be called by some other name. For example, he or she might be called the 'fleet manager' in a distribution company, the 'administrative manager' in a hospital, or the 'store manager' in a supermarket.

Operations in the organization

Three core functions

The operations function is central to the organization because it produces the goods and services which are its reason for existing, but it is not the only function. It is, however, one of the **three core functions** of any organization. These are:

- the marketing (including sales) function – which is responsible for *communicating* the organization's products and services to its markets in order to generate customer requests for service;

- the product/service development function – which is responsible for *creating* new and modified products and services in order to generate future customer requests for service;
- the operations function – which is responsible for *fulfilling* customer requests for service through the production and delivery of products and services.

Support functions

In addition, there are the **support functions** which enable the core functions to operate effectively. These include, for example:

- the accounting and finance function – which provides the information to help economic decision-making and manages the financial resources of the organization;
- the human resources function – which recruits and develops the organization's staff as well as looking after their welfare.

Remember that different organizations will call their various functions by different names and will have a different set of support functions. Almost all organizations, however, will have the three core functions, because all organizations have a fundamental need to sell their services, satisfy their customers and create the means to satisfy customers in the future. Table 1.1 shows the activities of the three core functions for a sample of organizations.

Broad definition of operations

In practice, there is not always a clear division between the three core functions or between core and support functions. This leads to some confusion over where the boundaries of the operations function should be drawn. In this book we use a relatively **broad definition of operations**. We treat much of the product/service development, technical and information systems activities and some of the human resource, marketing, and accounting and finance activities as coming within the sphere of operations management. We view the operations function as comprising all the activities necessary for the day-to-day fulfilment of customer requests. This includes sourcing products and services from suppliers and transporting products and services to customers.

Working effectively with the other parts of the organization is one of the most important responsibilities of operations management. It is a fundamental of modern management that functional boundaries should not hinder efficient internal processes. Figure 1.1 illustrates some of the relationships between operations and some other functions in terms of the flow of information between them. Although it is not comprehensive, it gives an idea of the nature of each relationship. However, note that the support functions have a different relationship with operations than operations has with the other core functions. Operations management's responsibility to support functions is primarily to make sure that they understand operations' needs and help them to satisfy these needs. The relationship with the other two core functions is more equal – less of '*this is what we want*' and more '*this is what we can do currently – how do we reconcile this with broader business needs?*'

Table 1.1 The activities of core functions in some organizations

Core functional activities	*Internet service provider (ISP)*	*Fast food chain*	*International aid charity*	*Furniture manufacturer*
Marketing and sales	Promote services to users and get registrations Sell advertising space	Advertise on TV Devise promotional materials	Develop funding contracts Mail out appeals for donations	Advertise in magazines Determine pricing policy Sell to stores
Product/service development	Devise new services and commission new information content	Design hamburgers, pizzas, etc. Design décor for restaurants	Develop new appeals campaigns Design new assistance programmes	Design new furniture Coordinate with fashionable colours
Operations	Maintain hardware, software and content Implement new links and services	Make burgers, pizzas etc. Serve customers Clear away Maintain equipment	Give service to the beneficiaries of the charity	Make components Assemble furniture

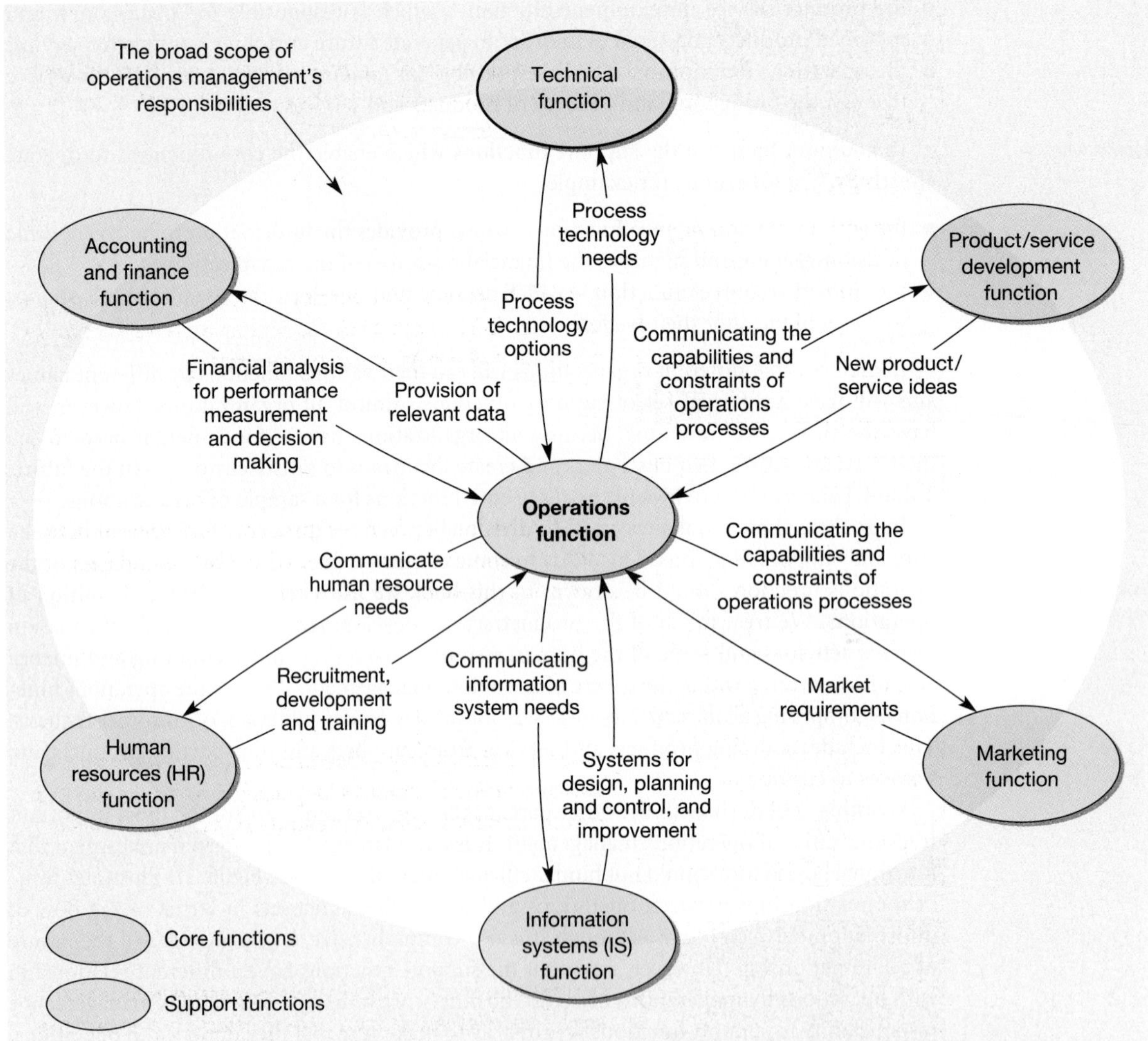

Figure 1.1 The relationship between the operations function and other core and support functions of the organization

Operations management is important in all types of organization

In some types of organization it is relatively easy to visualize the operations function and what it does, even if we have never seen it. For example, most people have seen images of automobile assembly. But what about an advertising agency? We know vaguely what they do – they produce the advertisements that we see in magazines and on television – but what is their operations function? The clue lies in the word 'produce'. Any business that produces something, whether tangible or not, must use resources to do so, and so must have an operations activity. Also the automobile plant and the advertising agency do have one important element in common: both have a higher objective – to make a profit from producing their products or services. Yet not-for-profit organizations also use their resources to produce services, not to make a profit, but to serve society in some way. Look at the following examples of what operations management does in five very different organizations and some common themes emerge.

Source: Rex Features

Automobile assembly factory – *Operations management uses machines to efficiently assemble products that satisfy current customer demands*

Source: Getty Images

Physician (general practitioner) – *Operations management uses knowledge to effectively diagnose conditions in order to treat real and perceived patient concerns*

Source: Alamy Images

Management consultant – *Operations management uses people to effectively create the services that will address current and potential client needs*

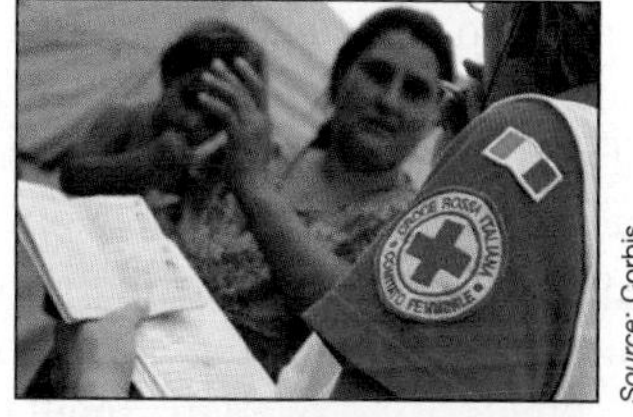

Source: Corbis

Disaster relief charity – *Operations management uses our and our partners' resources to speedily provide the supplies and services that relieve community suffering*

Source: Alamy Images

Advertising agency – *Operations management uses our staff's knowledge and experience to creatively present ideas that delight clients and address their real needs*

Start with the statement from the 'easy to visualize' automobile plant. Its summary of what operations management did was that . . . *'Operations management uses machines to efficiently assemble products that satisfy current customer demands.'* The statements from the other organizations were similar, but used slightly different language. Operations management used, not just machines but also . . . *'knowledge, people, "our and our partners' resources"'* and *'our staff's experience and knowledge'*, to *efficiently* (or *effectively*, or *creatively*) *assemble* (or *produce, change, sell, move, cure, shape*, etc.) *products* (or *services* or *ideas*) *that satisfy* (or *match* or *exceed* or *delight*) *customers'* (or *clients'* or *citizens'* or *society's*) *demands* (or *needs* or *concerns* or even *dreams*). So whatever terminology is used there is a common theme and a common purpose to how we can visualize the operations activity in any type of organization: small or large, manufacturing or service, public or private, profit or not-for-profit. Operations management uses *resources* to *appropriately create outputs* that *fulfil defined market requirements. See* Figure 1.2. However, although the essential nature and purpose of operations management is the same in every type of organization, there are some special issues to consider, particularly in smaller organizations and those whose purpose is to maximize something other than profit.

Operations management uses . . .

resources		appropriately	create	outputs		fulfil	defined	market	requirements
			produce						
experience			change				potential	citizens'	
people		effectively	sell	ideas		match	perceived	client	dreams
machines	to	efficiently	assemble	products	that	satisfy	current	customer	demands
knowledge		creatively	move	services		exceed	emerging	society	needs
partners		etc.	cure	etc.		delight	real	etc.	concerns
etc.			shape			etc.	etc.		etc.
			etc.						

Figure 1.2 **Operations management uses resources to appropriately create outputs that fulfil defined market requirements**

Operations management in the smaller organization

The role of operations management in smaller organizations often overlaps significantly with other functions

Operations management is just as important in small organizations as it is in large ones. Irrespective of their size, all companies need to produce and deliver their products and services efficiently and effectively. However, in practice, managing operations in a small or medium-size organization has its own set of problems. Large companies may have the resources to dedicate individuals to specialized tasks but smaller companies often cannot, so people may have to do different jobs as the need arises. Such an informal structure can allow the company to respond quickly as opportunities or problems present themselves. But decision making can also become confused as individuals' roles overlap. Small companies may have exactly the same operations management issues as large ones but they can be more difficult to separate from the mass of other issues in the organization. However, small operations can also have significant advantages; the short case on Acme Whistles illustrates this.

Short case
Acme Whistles[2]

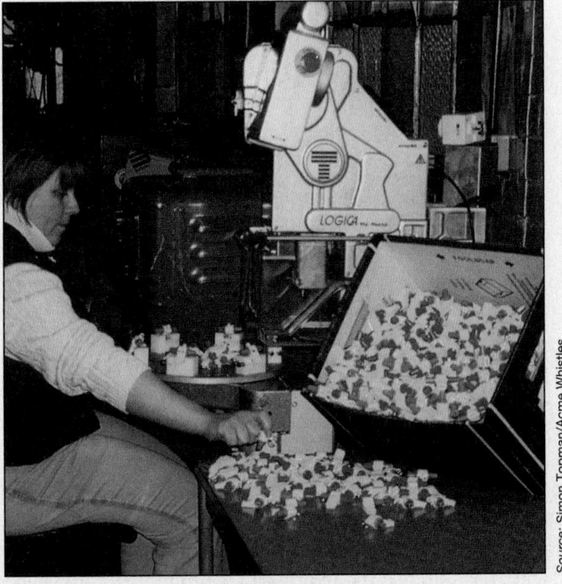

Source: Simon Topman/Acme Whistles

Acme Whistles can trace its history back to 1870 when Joseph Hudson decided he had the answer to the London Metropolitan Police's request for something to replace the wooden rattles that were used to sound the alarm. So the world's first police whistle was born. Soon Acme grew to be the premier supplier of whistles for police forces around the world. *'In many ways'*, says Simon Topman, owner and Managing Director of the company, *'the company is very much the same as it was in Joseph's day. The machinery is more modern, of course, and we have a wider variety of products, but many of our products are similar to their predecessors. For example, football referees seem to prefer the traditional snail-shaped whistle. So, although we have dramatically improved the performance of the product, our customers want it to look the same. We have also maintained the same manufacturing tradition from those early days. The original owner insisted on personally blowing every single whistle before it left the factory. We still do the same, not by personally blowing them, but by using an air line, so the same tradition of quality has endured.'*

The company's range of whistles has expanded to include sports whistles (they provide the whistles for the soccer World Cup), distress whistles, (silent) dog whistles, novelty whistles, instrumental whistles (used by all of the world's top orchestras), and many more types. *'We are always trying to improve our products'*, says Simon, *'it's a business of constant innovation. Sometimes I think that after 130 years surely there is nothing more to do, but we always find some new feature to incorporate. Of course, managing the operations in a small company is very different to working in a large one. Everyone has much broader jobs; we cannot afford the overheads of having specialist people in specialized roles. But this relative informality has a lot of advantages. It means that we can maintain our philosophy of quality amongst everybody in the company, and it means that we can react very quickly when the market demands it.'* Nor is the company's small size any barrier to its ability to innovate. *'On the contrary'*, says Simon, *'there is something about the culture of the company that is extremely important in fostering innovation. Because we are small we all know each other and we all want to contribute something to the company. It is not uncommon for employees to figure out new ideas for different types of whistle. If an idea looks promising, we will put a small and informal team together to look at it further. It is not unusual for people who have been with us only a few months to start wanting to make innovations. It's as though something happens to them when they walk through the door of the factory that encourages their natural inventiveness.'*

Operations management in not-for-profit organizations

Operations decisions are the same in commercial and not-for-profit organizations

Terms such as *competitive advantage*, *markets* and *business*, which are used in this book, are usually associated with companies in the for-profit sector. Yet operations management is also relevant to organizations whose purpose is not primarily to earn profits. Managing the operations in an animal welfare charity, hospital, research organization or government department is essentially the same as in commercial organizations. **Operations have to take the same decisions** – how to produce products and services, invest in technology, contract out some of their activities, devise performance measures, and improve their operations performance and so on. However, the strategic objectives of not-for-profit organizations may be more complex and involve a mixture of political, economic, social and environmental objectives. Because of this there may be a greater chance of operations decisions being made under conditions of conflicting objectives. So, for example, it is the operations staff in a children's welfare department who have to face the conflict between the cost of providing extra social workers and the risk of a child not receiving adequate protection. Nevertheless the vast majority of the topics covered in this book have relevance to all types of organization, including non-profit, even if the context is different and some terms may have to be adapted.

Short case
Oxfam International[3]

Source: Rex Features

Oxfam International is a confederation of 13 like-minded organizations based around the world that, together with partners and allies, work directly with communities seeking to ensure that poor people can improve their lives and livelihoods and have a say in decisions that affect them. With an annual expenditure that exceeds US$700 million, Oxfam International focuses its efforts in several areas, including development work, long-term programmes to eradicate poverty and

combat injustice, emergency relief delivering immediate life-saving assistance to people affected by natural disasters or conflict, helping to build their resilience to future disasters, campaigning and raising public awareness of the causes of poverty, encouraging ordinary people to take action for a fairer world, and advocacy and research that pressures decision-makers to change policies and practices that reinforce poverty and injustice.

All of Oxfam International's activities depend on effective and professional operations management. For example, Oxfam's network of charity shops, run by volunteers, is a key source of income. The shops sell donated items and handcrafts from around the world giving small-scale producers fair prices, training, advice and funding. Supply chain management and development is just as central to the running of these shops as it is to the biggest commercial chain of stores. The operations challenges involved in Oxfam's ongoing 'Clean Water' exercise are different but certainly no less important. Around 80 per cent of diseases and over one-third of deaths in the developing world are caused by contaminated water and Oxfam has a particular expertise in providing clean water and sanitation facilities. The better their coordinated efforts of identifying potential projects, working with local communities, providing help and education, and helping to providing civil engineering expertise, the more effective Oxfam is at fulfilling its objectives.

More dramatically, Oxfam International's response to emergency situations, providing humanitarian aid where it is needed, must be fast, appropriate and efficient. Whether the disasters are natural or political, they become emergencies when the people involved can no longer cope. In such situations, Oxfam, through its network of staff in local offices, is able to advise on what and where help is needed. Indeed, local teams are often able to provide warnings of impending disasters, giving more time to assess needs and coordinate a multi-agency response. The organization's headquarters in Oxford in the UK provides advice, materials and staff, often deploying emergency support staff on short-term assignments. Shelters, blankets and clothing can be flown out at short notice from the Emergencies Warehouse. Engineers and sanitation equipment can also be provided, including water tanks, latrines, hygiene kits and containers. When an emergency is over, Oxfam continues to work with the affected communities through their local offices to help people rebuild their lives and livelihoods. In an effort to improve the timeliness, effectiveness and appropriateness of its response to emergencies, Oxfam recently adopted a more systematic approach to evaluating the successes and failures of its humanitarian work. Real-time evaluations, which seek to assess and influence emergency response programmes in their early stages, were implemented during the response to floods in Mozambique and South Asia, the earthquake in Peru, Hurricane Felix in Nicaragua and the conflicts in Uganda. These exercises provided Oxfam's humanitarian teams with the opportunity to gauge the effectiveness of their response, and make crucial adjustments at an early stage if necessary. The evaluations highlighted several potential improvements. For example, it became evident that there was a need to improve preparation ahead of emergencies, as well as the need to develop more effective coordination planning tools. It was also decided that adopting a common working approach with shared standards would improve the effectiveness of their response to emergencies. Oxfam also emphasizes the importance of the role played by local partners in emergencies. They are often closer to, and more in tune with, affected communities, but may require additional support and empowerment to scale up their response and comply with the international humanitarian standards.

The new operations agenda

Modern business pressures have changed the operations agenda

The business environment has a significant impact on what is expected from operations management. In recent years there have been new pressures for which the operations function has needed to develop responses. Table 1.2 lists some of these **business pressures** and the operations responses to them. These operations responses form a major part of a *new agenda* for operations. Parts of this agenda are trends which have always existed but have accelerated, such as globalization and increased cost pressures. Part of the agenda involves seeking ways to exploit new technologies, most notably the Internet. Of course, the list in Table 1.2 is not comprehensive, nor is it universal. But very few businesses will be unaffected by at least some of these concerns. When businesses have to cope with a more challenging environment, they look to their operations function to help them respond.

Table 1.2 Changes in the business environment are shaping a new operations agenda

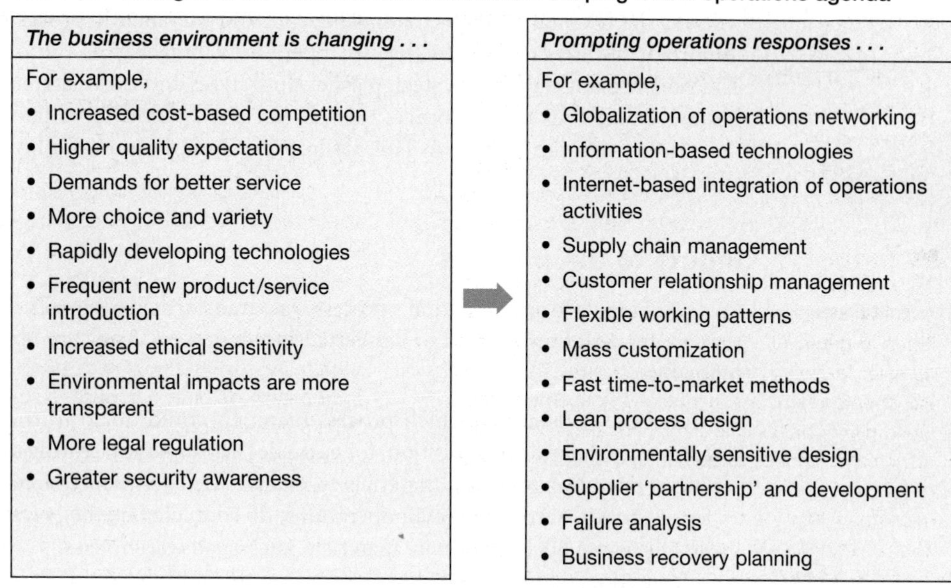

The business environment is changing . . .	*Prompting operations responses . . .*
For example, • Increased cost-based competition • Higher quality expectations • Demands for better service • More choice and variety • Rapidly developing technologies • Frequent new product/service introduction • Increased ethical sensitivity • Environmental impacts are more transparent • More legal regulation • Greater security awareness	For example, • Globalization of operations networking • Information-based technologies • Internet-based integration of operations activities • Supply chain management • Customer relationship management • Flexible working patterns • Mass customization • Fast time-to-market methods • Lean process design • Environmentally sensitive design • Supplier 'partnership' and development • Failure analysis • Business recovery planning

The input–transformation–output process

Transformation process model

Input resources

Outputs of goods and services

All operations produce products and services by changing *inputs* into *outputs* using an 'input-transformation-output' process. Figure 1.3 shows this general **transformation process model.** Put simply, operations are processes that take in a set of **input resources** which are used to transform something, or are transformed themselves, into **outputs of products and services.** And although all operations conform to this general input–transformation–output model, they differ in the nature of their specific inputs and outputs. For example, if you stand far enough away from a hospital or a car plant, they might look very similar, but move closer and clear differences do start to emerge. One is a manufacturing operation producing 'products', and the other is a service operation producing 'services' that change the physiological or psychological condition of patients. What is inside each operation will also be

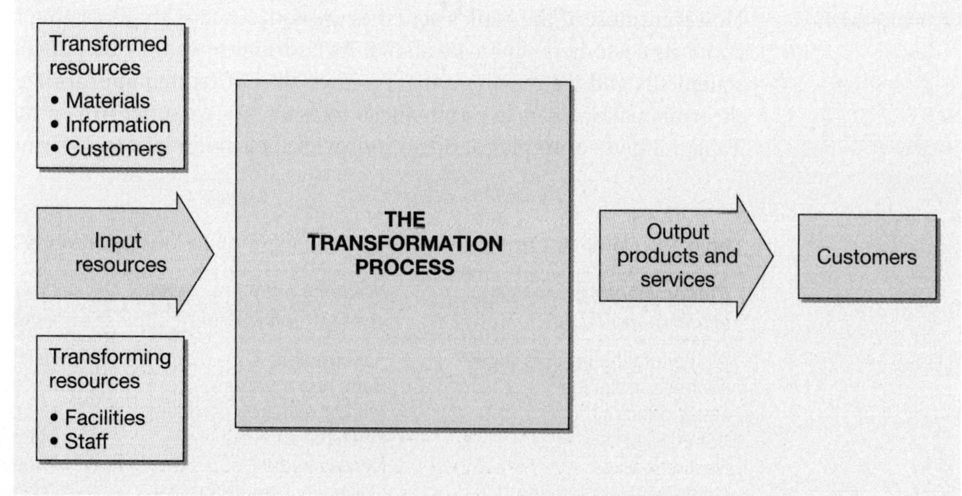

Figure 1.3 All operations are input–transformation–output processes

different. The motor vehicle plant contains metal-forming machinery and assembly processes, whereas the hospital contains diagnostic, care and therapeutic processes. Perhaps the most important difference between the two operations, however, is the nature of their inputs. The vehicle plant transforms steel, plastic, cloth, tyres and other materials into vehicles. The hospital transforms the customers themselves. The patients form part of the input to, and the output from, the operation. This has important implications for how the operation needs to be managed.

Inputs to the process

Transformed resources

One set of inputs to any operation's processes are **transformed resources**. These are the resources that are treated, transformed or converted in the process. They are usually a mixture of the following:

- **Materials** – operations which process materials could do so to transform their *physical properties* (shape or composition, for example). Most manufacturing operations are like this. Other operations process materials to change their *location* (parcel delivery companies, for example). Some, like retail operations, do so to change the *possession* of the materials. Finally, some operations *store* materials, such as in warehouses.
- **Information** – operations which process information could do so to transform their *informational properties* (that is the purpose or form of the information); accountants do this. Some change the *possession* of the information, for example market research companies sell information. Some *store* the information, for example archives and libraries. Finally, some operations, such as telecommunication companies, change the *location* of the information.
- **Customers** – operations which process customers might change their *physical properties* in a similar way to materials processors: for example, hairdressers or cosmetic surgeons. Some *store* (or more politely *accommodate*) customers: hotels, for example. Airlines, mass rapid transport systems and bus companies transform the *location* of their customers, while hospitals transform their *physiological state.* Some are concerned with transforming their *psychological state*, for example most entertainment services such as music, theatre, television, radio and theme parks.

Material inputs
Customer inputs
Information inputs

Often one of these is dominant in an operation. For example, a bank devotes part of its energies to producing printed statements of accounts for its customers. In doing so, it is processing **inputs of material** but no one would claim that a bank is a printer. The bank is also concerned with processing **inputs of customers**. It gives them advice regarding their financial affairs, cashes their cheques, deposits their cash, and has direct contact with them. However, most of the bank's activities are concerned with processing **inputs of information** about its customers' financial affairs. As customers, we may be unhappy with badly printed statements and we may be unhappy if we are not treated appropriately in the bank. But if the bank makes errors in our financial transactions, we suffer in a far more fundamental way. Table 1.3 gives examples of operations with their dominant transformed resources.

Table 1.3 Dominant transformed resource inputs of various operations

Predominantly processing inputs of materials	*Predominantly processing inputs of information*	*Predominantly processing inputs of customers*
All manufacturing operations	Accountants	Hairdressers
Mining companies	Bank headquarters	Hotels
Retail operations	Market research company	Hospitals
Warehouses	Financial analysts	Mass rapid transport
Postal services	News service	Theatres
Container shipping line	University research unit	Theme parks
Trucking companies	Telecoms company	Dentists

Transforming resources

The other set of inputs to any operations process are **transforming resources.** These are the resources which act upon the transformed resources. There are two types which form the 'building blocks' of all operations:

Facilities

Staff

- **facilities** – the buildings, equipment, plant and process technology of the operation;
- **staff** – the people who operate, maintain, plan and manage the operation. (Note that we use the term 'staff' to describe all the people in the operation, at any level.)

The exact nature of both facilities and staff will differ between operations. To a five-star hotel, its facilities consist mainly of 'low-tech' buildings, furniture and fittings. To a nuclear-powered aircraft carrier, its facilities are 'high-tech' nuclear generators and sophisticated electronic equipment. Staff will also differ between operations. Most staff employed in a factory assembling domestic refrigerators may not need a very high level of technical skill. In contrast, most staff employed by an accounting company are, hopefully, highly skilled in their own particular 'technical' skill (accounting). Yet although skills vary, all staff can make a contribution. An assembly worker who consistently misassembles refrigerators will dissatisfy customers and increase costs just as surely as an accountant who cannot add up. The balance between facilities and staff also varies. A computer chip manufacturing company, such as Intel, will have significant investment in physical facilities. A single chip fabrication plant can cost in excess of $4 billion, so operations managers will spend a lot of their time managing their facilities. Conversely, a management consultancy firm depends largely on the quality of its staff. Here operations management is largely concerned with the development and deployment of consultant skills and knowledge.

Outputs from the process

Tangibility

Although products and services are different, the distinction can be subtle. Perhaps the most obvious difference is in their respective **tangibility**. Products are usually tangible. You can physically touch a television set or a newspaper. Services are usually intangible. You cannot touch consultancy advice or a haircut (although you can often see or feel the results of these services). Also, services may have a shorter stored life. Products can usually be stored, at least for a time. The life of a service is often much shorter. For example, the service of 'accommodation in a hotel room for tonight' will perish if it is not sold before tonight – accommodation in the same room tomorrow is a different service.

Most operations produce both products and services

'Pure' products

'Pure' service

Facilitating services

Facilitating products

Some operations produce just products and others just services, but most operations produce a mixture of the two. Figure 1.4 shows a number of operations (including some described as examples in this chapter) positioned in a spectrum from **'pure' product** producers to **'pure' service** producers. Crude oil producers are concerned almost exclusively with the product which comes from their oil wells. So are aluminium smelters, but they might also produce some services such as technical advice. Services produced in these circumstances are called **facilitating services.** To an even greater extent, machine tool manufacturers produce facilitating services such as technical advice and applications engineering. The services produced by a restaurant are an essential part of what the customer is paying for. It is both a manufacturing operation which produces meals and a provider of service in the advice, ambience and service of the food. An information systems provider may produce software 'products', but primarily it is providing a service to its customers, with **facilitating products**. Certainly, a management consultancy, although it produces reports and documents, would see itself primarily as a service provider. Finally, pure services produce no products, a psychotherapy clinic, for example. Of the short cases and examples in this chapter, Acme Whistles is primarily a product producer, although it can give advice or it can even design products for individual customers. Pret A Manger both manufactures and serves its sandwiches to customers. IKEA subcontracts the manufacturing of its products before selling them, and also offers some design services. It therefore has an even higher service content.

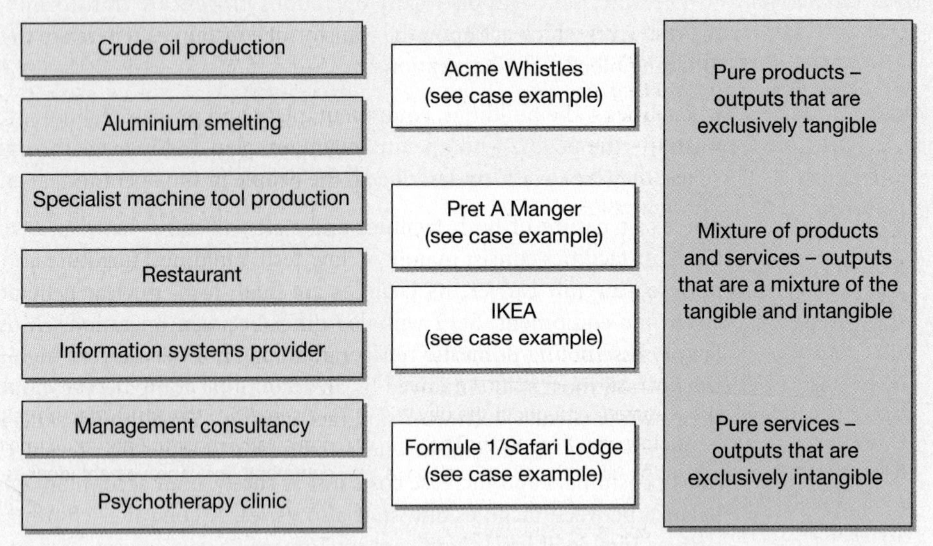

Figure 1.4 The output from most types of operation is a mixture of goods and services

Formule 1 and the safari park (see later) are close to being pure services, although they both have some tangible elements such as food.

Services and products are merging

Increasingly the distinction between services and products is both difficult to define and not particularly useful. Information and communications technologies are even overcoming some of the consequences of the intangibility of services. Internet-based retailers, for example, are increasingly 'transporting' a larger proportion of their services into customers' homes. Even the official statistics compiled by governments have difficulty in separating products and services. Software sold on a disc is classified as a product. The same software sold over the Internet is a service. Some authorities see the essential purpose of all businesses, and therefore operations processes, as being to 'service customers'. Therefore, they argue, **all operations are service providers** which may produce products as a part of serving their customers. Our approach in this book is close to this. We treat operations management as being important for all organizations. Whether they see themselves as manufacturers or service providers is very much a secondary issue.

All operations are service providers

Short case
Pret A Manger[4]

Source: Alamy Images

Described by the press as having *'revolutionized the concept of sandwich making and eating'*, Pret A Manger opened their first shop in the mid-1980s, in London. Now they have over 130 shops in UK, New York, Hong Kong and Tokyo. They say that their secret is to focus continually on quality – not just of their food, but in every aspect of their operations practice. They go to extraordinary lengths to avoid the chemicals and preservatives common in most 'fast' food, say the company. *'Many food retailers focus on extending the shelf life of their food, but that's of no interest to us. We maintain our edge by selling food that simply can't be beaten for freshness. At the end of the day, we give whatever we haven't sold to charity to help feed those who would otherwise go hungry. When we were just starting out, a big supplier tried to sell us coleslaw that lasted sixteen days. Can you imagine! Salad that lasts sixteen days? There and then we decided Pret would stick to wholesome fresh food – natural stuff. We have not changed that policy.'*

The first Pret A Manger shop had its own kitchen where fresh ingredients were delivered first thing every morning, and food was prepared throughout the day. Every Pret shop since has followed this model. The team members serving on the tills at lunchtime will have been making sandwiches in the kitchen that morning. The company rejected the idea of a huge centralized sandwich factory even though it could significantly reduce costs. Pret also own and manage all their shops directly so that they can ensure consistently high standards in all their shops. *'We are determined never to forget that our hard-working people make all the difference. They are our heart and soul. When they care, our business is sound. If they cease to care, our business goes down the drain. In a retail sector where high staff turnover is normal, we're pleased to say our people are much more likely to stay around! We work hard at building great teams. We take our reward schemes and career opportunities very seriously. We don't work nights (generally), we wear jeans, we party!'* Customer feedback is regarded as being particularly important at Pret. Examining customers' comments for improvement ideas is a key part of weekly management meetings, and of the daily team briefs in each shop.

The processes hierarchy

So far we have discussed operations management, and the input–transformation–output model, at the level of 'the operation'. For example, we have described 'the whistle factory', 'the sandwich shop', 'the disaster relief operation', and so on. But look inside any of these operations. One will see that all operations consist of a collection of processes (though these processes may be called 'units' or 'departments') interconnecting with each other to form a network. Each process acts as a smaller version of the whole operation of which it forms a part, and transformed resources flow between them. In fact within any operation, the mechanisms that actually transform inputs into outputs are these **processes**. A process is 'an arrangement of resources that produce some mixture of products and services'. They are the 'building blocks' of all operations, and they form an 'internal network' within an operation. Each process is, at the same time, an **internal supplier** and an **internal customer** for other processes. This 'internal customer' concept provides a model to analyse the internal activities of an operation. It is also a useful reminder that, by treating internal customers with the same degree of care as external customers, the effectiveness of the whole operation can be improved. Table 1.4 illustrates how a wide range of operations can be described in this way.

Processes

Internal supplier

Internal customer

Within each of these processes is another network of individual units of resource such as individual people and individual items of process technology (machines, computers, storage facilities, etc.). Again, transformed resources flow between each unit of transforming resource. So any business, or operation, is made up of a network of processes and any process is made up of a network of resources. But also any business or operation can itself be viewed as part of a greater network of businesses or operations. It will have operations that supply it with the products and services it needs and unless it deals directly with the end-consumer, it will supply customers who themselves may go on to supply their own customers. Moreover, any operation could have several suppliers and several customers and may be in competition with other operations producing similar services to those it produces itself. This network of operations is called the **supply network.** In this way the input–transformation–output model can be used at a number of different 'levels of analysis'. Here we have used the idea to **analyse businesses at three levels**, the process, the operation and the supply network. But one could define many different 'levels of analysis', moving upwards from small to larger processes, right up to the huge supply network that describes a whole industry.

Supply network

Operations can be analysed at three levels

Table 1.4 Some operations described in terms of their processes

Operation	*Some of the operation's inputs*	*Some of the operation's processes*	*Some of the operation's outputs*
Airline	Aircraft Pilots and air crew Ground crew Passengers and freight	Check passengers in Board passengers Fly passengers and freight around the world Care for passengers	Transported passengers and freight
Department store	Goods for sale Sales staff Information systems Customers	Source and store goods Display goods Give sales advice Sell goods	Customers and goods 'assembled' together
Police	Police officers Computer systems Information systems Public (law-abiding and criminals)	Crime prevention Crime detection Information gathering Detaining suspects	Lawful society, public with a feeling of security
Frozen food manufacturer	Fresh food Operators Processing technology Cold storage facilities	Source raw materials Prepare food Freeze food Pack and freeze food	Frozen food

Hierarchy of operations

This idea is called the **hierarchy of operations** and is illustrated for a business that makes television programmes and videos in Figure 1.5. It will have inputs of production, technical and administrative staff, cameras, lighting, sound and recording equipment, and so on. It transforms these into finished programmes, music, videos, etc. At a more macro level, the business itself is part of a whole supply network, acquiring services from creative agencies, casting agencies and studios, liaising with promotion agencies, and serving its broadcasting company customers. At a more micro level within this overall operation there are many individual processes: workshops manufacturing the sets; marketing processes that liaise with potential customers; maintenance and repair processes that care for, modify and design technical equipment; production units that shoot the programmes and videos; and so on. Each of these individual processes can be represented as a network of yet smaller processes, or even individual units of resource. So, for example, the set manufacturing process could consist of four smaller processes: one that designs the sets, one that constructs them, one that acquires the props, and one that finishes (paints) the set.

Critical commentary

The idea of the internal network of processes is seen by some as being over-simplistic. In reality the relationship between groups and individuals is significantly more complex than that between commercial entities. One cannot treat internal customers and suppliers exactly as we do external customers and suppliers. External customers and suppliers usually operate in a free market. If an organization believes that in the long run it can get a better deal by purchasing goods and services from another supplier, it will do so. But internal customers and suppliers are not in a 'free market'. They cannot usually look outside either to purchase input resources or to sell their output goods and services (although some organizations are moving this way). Rather than take the 'economic' perspective of external commercial relationships, models from organizational behaviour, it is argued, are more appropriate.

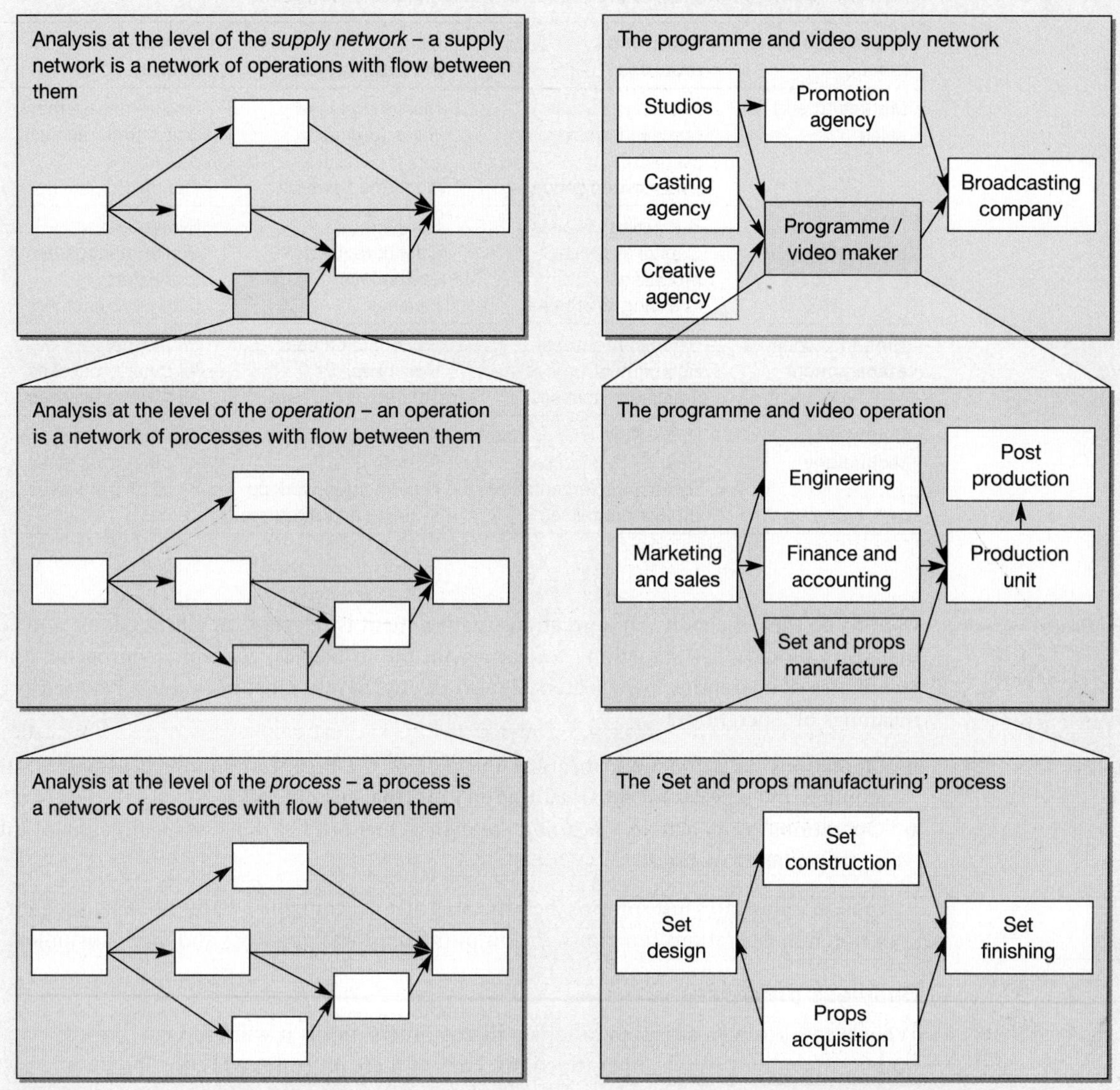

Figure 1.5 Operations and process management requires analysis at three levels: the supply network, the operation, and the process

Operations management is relevant to all parts of the business

All functions manage processes

The example in Figure 1.5 demonstrates that it is not just the operations function that manages processes; **all functions manage processes**. For example, the marketing function will have processes that produce demand forecasts, processes that produce advertising campaigns and processes that produce marketing plans. These processes in the other functions also need managing using similar principles to those within the operations function. Each function will have its 'technical' knowledge. In marketing, this is the expertise in designing and shaping marketing plans; in finance, it is the technical knowledge of financial reporting. Yet each will also have a 'process management' role of producing plans, policies, reports and services. The implications of this are very important. Because all managers have some responsibility for managing processes, they are, to some extent, operations managers. They all should want to give good service to their (often internal) customers, and they all will

Table 1.5 Some examples of processes in non-operations functions

Organizational function	*Some of its processes*	*Outputs from its process*	*Customer(s) for its outputs*
Marketing and sales	Planning process Forecasting process Order taking process	Marketing plans Sales forecasts Confirmed orders	Senior management Sales staff, planners, operations Operations, finance
Finance and accounting	Budgeting process Capital approval processes Invoicing processes	Budgets Capital request evaluations Invoices	Everyone Senior management, requesters External customers
Human resources management	Payroll processes Recruitment processes Training processes	Salary statements New hires Trained employees	Employees All other processes All other processes
Information technology	Systems review process Help desk process System implementation project processes	System evaluation Advice Implemented working systems and aftercare	All other processes All other processes All other processes

All managers, not just operations managers, manage processes

want to do this efficiently. So, **operations management is relevant for all functions**, and all managers should have something to learn from the principles, concepts, approaches and techniques of operations management. It also means that we must distinguish between two meanings of 'operations':

Operations as a function

Operations as an activity

- **'Operations' as a function**, meaning the part of the organization which produces the products and services for the organization's external customers;
- **'Operations' as an activity**, meaning the management of the processes within any of the organization's functions.

Table 1.5 illustrates just some of the processes that are contained within some of the more common non-operations functions, the outputs from these processes and their 'customers'.

Business processes

'End-to-end' business processes

Business process re-engineering

Whenever a business attempts to satisfy its customers' needs it will use many processes, in both its operations and its other functions. Each of these processes will contribute some part to fulfilling customer needs. For example, the television programme and video production company, described previously, produces two types of 'product'. Both of these products involve a slightly different mix of processes within the company. The company decides to re-organize its operations so that each product is produced from start to finish by a dedicated process that contains all the elements necessary for its production, as in Figure 1.6. So customer needs for each product are entirely fulfilled from within what is called an **'end-to-end' business process**. These often cut across conventional organizational boundaries. Reorganizing (or 're-engineering') process boundaries and organizational responsibilities around these business processes is the philosophy behind **business process re-engineering** (BPR) which is discussed further in Chapter 18.

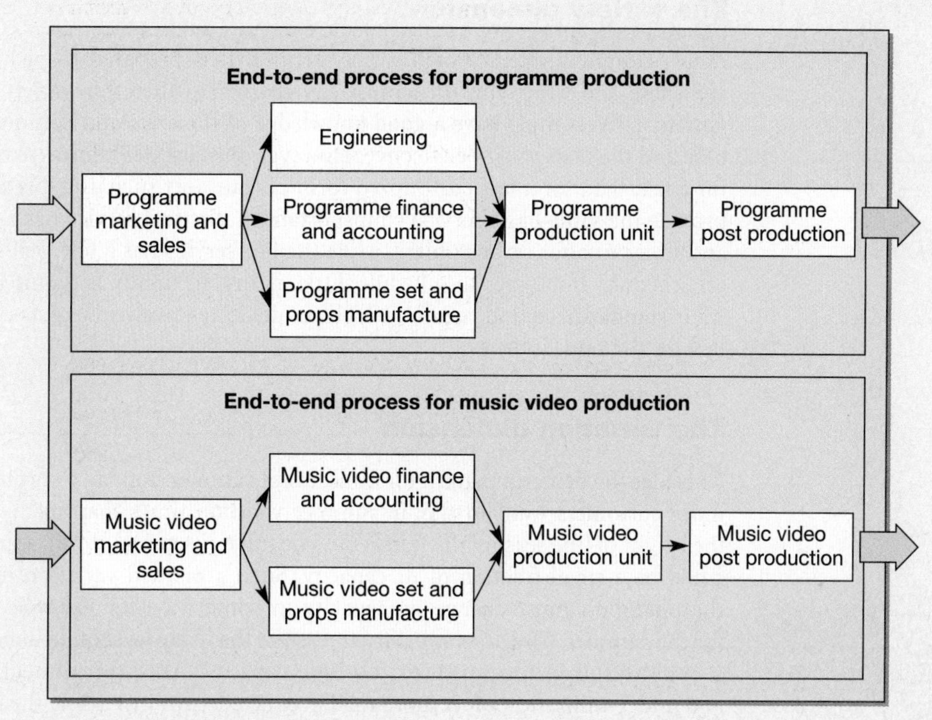

Figure 1.6 The television and video company divided into two 'end-to-end' business processes, one dedicated to producing programmes and the other dedicated to producing music videos

Operations processes have different characteristics

Although all operations processes are similar in that they all transform inputs, they do differ in a number of ways, four of which, known as the four Vs, are particularly important:

Volume
Variety
Variation
Visibility

- The **volume** of their output;
- The **variety** of their output;
- The **variation** in the demand for their output;
- The degree of **visibility** which customers have of the production of their output.

The volume dimension

Repeatability
Systematization

Let us take a familiar example. The epitome of high-volume hamburger production is McDonald's, which serves millions of burgers around the world every day. Volume has important implications for the way McDonald's operations are organized. The first thing you notice is the **repeatability** of the tasks people are doing and the **systematization** of the work where standard procedures are set down specifying how each part of the job should be carried out. Also, because tasks are systematized and repeated, it is worthwhile developing specialized fryers and ovens. All this gives *low unit costs*. Now consider a small local cafeteria serving a few 'short-order' dishes. The range of items on the menu may be similar to the larger operation, but the volume will be far lower, so the repetition will also be far lower and the number of staff will be lower (possibly only one person) and therefore individual staff are likely to perform a wider range of tasks. This may be more rewarding for the staff, but less open to systematization. Also it is less feasible to invest in specialized equipment. So the cost per burger served is likely to be higher (even if the price is comparable).

The variety dimension

A taxi company offers a high-variety service. It is prepared to pick you up from almost anywhere and drop you off almost anywhere. To offer this variety it must be relatively *flexible*. Drivers must have a good knowledge of the area, and communication between the base and the taxis must be effective. However, the cost per kilometre travelled will be higher for a taxi than for a less customized form of transport such as a bus service. Although both provide the same basic service (transportation), the taxi service has a high variety of routes and times to offer its customers, while the bus service has a few well-defined routes, with a set schedule. If all goes to schedule, little, if any, flexibility is required from the operation. All is **standardized** and regular, which results in relatively low costs compared with using a taxi for the same journey.

Standardized

The variation dimension

Consider the demand pattern for a successful summer holiday resort hotel. Not surprisingly, more customers want to stay in summer vacation times than in the middle of winter. At the height of 'the season' the hotel could be full to its capacity. Off-season demand, however, could be a small fraction of its capacity. Such a marked variation in demand means that the operation must change its capacity in some way, for example, by hiring extra staff for the summer. The hotel must try to predict the likely level of demand. If it gets this wrong, it could result in too much or too little capacity. Also, recruitment costs, overtime costs and under-utilization of its rooms all have the effect of increasing the hotel's costs operation compared with a hotel of a similar standard with level demand. A hotel which has relatively level demand can plan its activities well in advance. Staff can be scheduled, food can be bought and rooms can be cleaned in a *routine* and *predictable* manner. This results in a high utilization of resources and unit costs which are likely to be lower than those in hotels with a highly variable demand pattern.

The visibility dimension

Visibility means process exposure

High received variety

Customer contact skills

Visibility is a slightly more difficult dimension of operations to envisage. It refers to how much of the operation's activities its customers experience, or how much the operation is **exposed** to its customers. Generally, customer-processing operations are more exposed to their customers than material- or information-processing operations. But even customer-processing operations have some choice as to how visible they wish their operations to be. For example, a retailer could operate as a high-visibility 'bricks and mortar', or a lower-visibility web-based operation. In the 'bricks and mortar', high-visibility operation, customers will directly experience most of its 'value-adding' activities. Customers will have a relatively *short waiting tolerance*, and may walk out if not served in a reasonable time. Customers' perceptions, rather than objective criteria, will also be important. If they perceive that a member of the operation's staff is discourteous to them, they are likely to be dissatisfied (even if the staff member meant no discourtesy), so high-visibility operations require staff with good customer contact skills. Customers could also request goods which clearly would not be sold in such a shop, but because the customers are actually in the operation they can ask what they like! This is called **high received variety**. This makes it difficult for high-visibility operations to achieve high productivity of resources, so they tend to be relatively high-cost operations. Conversely, a web-based retailer, while not a pure low-contact operation, has far lower visibility. Behind its web site it can be more 'factory-like'. The *time lag* between the order being placed and the items ordered by the customer being retrieved and dispatched does not have to be minutes as in the shop, but can be hours or even days. This allows the tasks of finding the items, packing and dispatching them to be *standardized* by staff who need few **customer contact skills**. Also, there can be relatively *high staff utilization*. The web-based organization can also centralize its operation

Short case
Two very different hotels

Formule 1

Hotels are high-contact operations – they are staff-intensive and have to cope with a range of customers, each with a variety of needs and expectations. So, how can a highly successful chain of affordable hotels avoid the crippling costs of high customer contact? Formule 1, a subsidiary of the French Accor group, manages to offer outstanding value by adopting two principles not always associated with hotel operations – standardization and an innovative use of technology. Formule 1 hotels are usually located close to the roads, junctions and cities which make them visible and accessible to prospective customers. The hotels themselves are made from state-of-the-art volumetric prefabrications. The prefabricated units are arranged in various configurations to suit the characteristics of each individual site. All rooms are nine square metres in area, and are designed to be attractive, functional, comfortable and soundproof. Most important, they are designed to be easy to clean and maintain. All have the same fittings, including a double bed, an additional bunk-type bed, a wash basin, a storage area, a working table with seat, a wardrobe and a television set. The reception of a Formule 1 hotel is staffed only from 6.30 am to 10.00 am and from 5.00 pm to 10.00 pm. Outside these times an automatic machine sells rooms to credit card users, provides access to the hotel, dispenses a security code for the room and even prints a receipt. Technology is also evident in the washrooms. Showers and toilets are automatically cleaned after each use by using nozzles and heating elements to spray the room with a disinfectant solution and dry it before it is used again. To keep things even simpler, Formule 1 hotels do not include a restaurant as they are usually located near existing restaurants. However, a continental breakfast is available, usually between 6.30 am and 10.00 am, and of course on a 'self-service' basis!

Mwagusi Safari Lodge

The Mwagusi Safari Lodge lies within Tanzania's Ruaha National Park, a huge undeveloped wilderness, whose beautiful open landscape is especially good for seeing elephant, buffalo and lion. Nestled into a bank of the Mwagusi Sand River, this small exclusive tented camp overlooks a watering hole in the riverbed. Its ten tents are within thatched bandas (accommodation), each furnished comfortably in the traditional style of the camp. Each banda has an en-suite bathroom with flush toilet and a hot shower. Game viewing can be experienced even from the seclusion of the veranda. The sight of thousands of buffalo flooding the riverbed below the tents and dining room banda is not uncommon, and elephants, giraffes, and wild dogs are frequent uninvited guests to the site. There are two staff for each customer, allowing individual needs and preferences to be met quickly at all times. Guest numbers vary throughout the year, occupancy being low in the rainy season from January to April, and full in the best game viewing period from September to November. There are game drives and walks throughout the area, each selected for individual customers' individual preferences. Drives are taken in specially adapted open-sided four-wheel-drive vehicles, equipped with reference books, photography equipment, medical kits and all the necessities for a day in the bush. Walking safaris, accompanied by an experienced guide can be customized for every visitor's requirements and abilities. Lunch can be taken communally, so that visitors can discuss their interests with other guides and managers. Dinner is often served under the stars in a secluded corner of the dry riverbed.

on one (physical) site, whereas the 'bricks and mortar' shop needs many shops close to centres of demand. Therefore, the low-visibility web-based operation will have lower costs than the shop.

Mixed high- and low-visibility processes

Some operations have both high- and low-visibility processes within the same operation. In an airport, for example: some activities are totally 'visible' to its customers such as information desks answering people's queries. These staff operate in what is termed a **front-office** environment. Other parts of the airport have little, if any, customer 'visibility', such as the baggage handlers. These rarely-seen staff perform the vital but low-contact tasks, in the **back-office** part of the operation.

Front office

Back office

The implications of the four Vs of operations processes

All four dimensions have implications for the cost of creating the products or services. Put simply, high volume, low variety, low variation and low customer contact all help to keep processing costs down. Conversely, low volume, high variety, high variation and high customer contact generally carry some kind of cost penalty for the operation. This is why the volume dimension is drawn with its 'low' end at the left, unlike the other dimensions, to keep all the 'low cost' implications on the right. To some extent the position of an operation in the **four dimensions** is determined by the demand of the market it is serving. However, most operations have some discretion in moving themselves on the dimensions. Figure 1.7 summarizes the implications of such positioning.

'Four Vs' analysis of processes

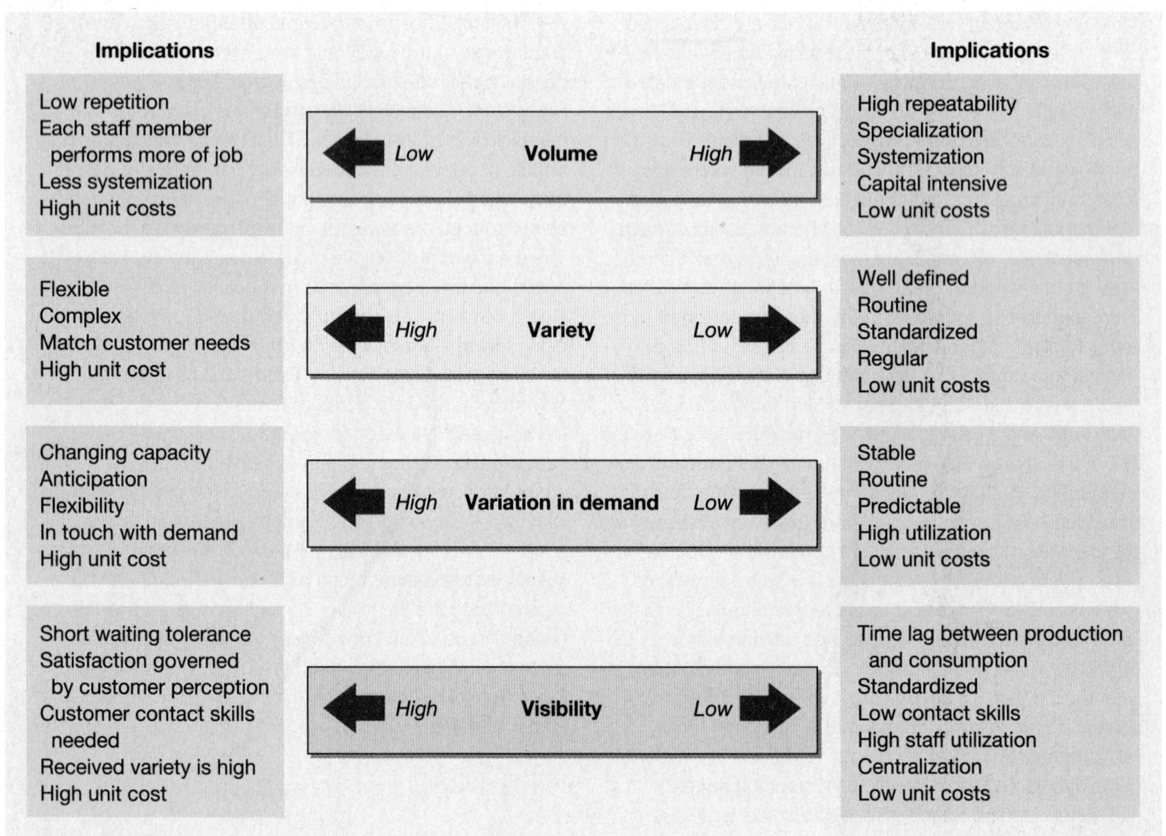

Figure 1.7 A typology of operations

Worked example

Figure 1.8 illustrates the different positions on the dimensions of the Formule 1 hotel chain and the Mwagusi Safari Lodge (*see* the short case on 'Two very different hotels'). Both provide the same basic service as any other hotel. However, one is of a small, intimate nature with relatively few customers. Its variety of services is almost infinite in the sense that customers can make individual requests in terms of food and entertainment. Variation is high and customer contact, and therefore visibility, is also very high (in order to ascertain customers' requirements and provide for them). All of this is very different from Formule 1, where volume is high (although not as high as in a large city-centre hotel), variety of service is strictly limited, and business and holiday customers use the hotel at different times, which limits variation. Most notably, though, customer contact is kept to a minimum. The Mwagusi Safari Lodge hotel has very high levels of service but provides them at a high cost (and therefore a high price). Conversely, Formule 1 has arranged its operation in such a way as to minimize its costs.

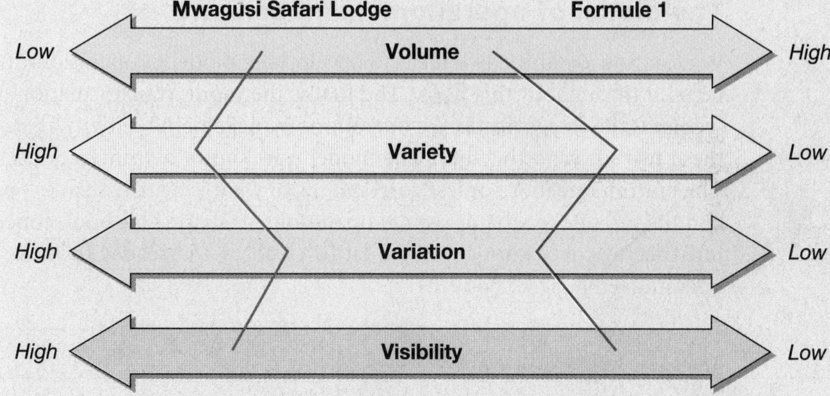

Figure 1.8 Profiles of two operations

The activities of operations management

Operations managers have some responsibility for all the activities in the organization which contribute to the effective production of products and services. And while the exact nature of the operations function's responsibilities will, to some extent, depend on the way the organization has chosen to define the boundaries of the function, there are some general classes of activities that apply to all types of operation.

- **Understanding the operation's strategic performance objectives.** The first responsibility of any operations management team is to understand what it is trying to achieve. This means understanding how to judge the performance of the operation at different levels, from broad and strategic to more operational performance objectives. This is discussed in Chapter 2.
- **Developing an operations strategy for the organization.** Operations management involves hundreds of minute-by-minute decisions, so it is vital that there is a set of general principles which can guide decision-making towards the organization's longer-term goals. This is an operations strategy and is discussed in Chapter 3.

- **Designing the operation's products, services and processes.** Design is the activity of determining the physical form, shape and composition of products, services and processes. It is a crucial part of operations managers' activities and is discussed in Chapters 4 to 9.
- **Planning and controlling the operation.** Planning and control is the activity of deciding what the operations resources should be doing, then making sure that they really are doing it. Chapters 10 to 17 explain various planning and control activities.
- **Improving the performance of the operation.** The continuing responsibility of all operations managers is to improve the performance of their operation. Chapters 18 to 20 describes improvement activities.
- **The social responsibilities of operations management.** It is increasingly recognized by many businesses that operations managers have a set of broad societal responsibilities and concerns beyond their direct activities. The general term for these aspects of business responsibility is 'corporate social responsibility' or CSR. It should be of particular interest to operations managers, because their activities can have a direct and significant effect on society. This is discussed in Chapter 21.

The model of operations management

Operations activities define operations management and operations strategy

We can now combine two ideas to develop the model of operations management which will be used throughout this book. The first is the input–transformation–output model and the second is the categorization of operations management's activity areas. Figure 1.9 shows how these two ideas go together. The model now shows two interconnected loops of **activities**. The bottom one more or less corresponds to what is usually seen as operations management, and the top one to what is seen as operations strategy. This book concentrates on the former but tries to cover enough of the latter to allow the reader to make strategic sense of the operations manager's job.

Critical commentary

The central idea in this introductory chapter is that all organizations have operations processes which produce products and services and all these processes are essentially similar. However, some believe that by even trying to characterize processes in this way (perhaps even by calling them 'processes') one loses or distorts their nature, depersonalizes or takes the 'humanity' out of the way in which we think of the organization. This point is often raised in not-for-profit organizations, especially by 'professional' staff. For example the head of one European 'Medical Association' (a doctors' trade union) criticized hospital authorities for expecting a *'sausage factory service based on productivity targets'*.[5] No matter how similar they appear on paper, it is argued, a hospital can never be viewed in the same was a factory. Even in commercial businesses, professionals, such as creative staff, often express discomfort at their expertise being described as a 'process'.

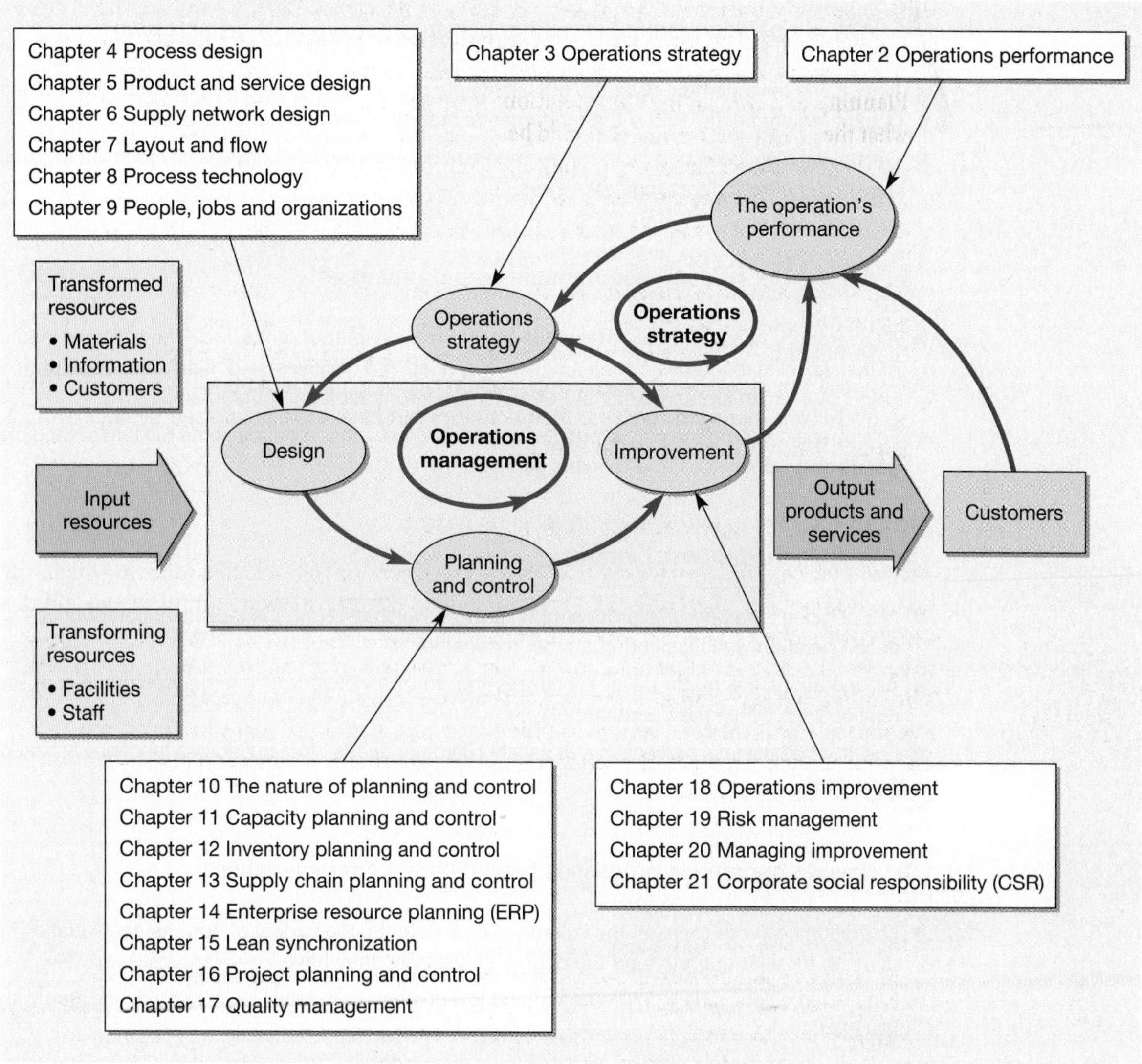

Chapter 4 Process design
Chapter 5 Product and service design
Chapter 6 Supply network design
Chapter 7 Layout and flow
Chapter 8 Process technology
Chapter 9 People, jobs and organizations

Chapter 3 Operations strategy

Chapter 2 Operations performance

The operation's performance

Transformed resources
- Materials
- Information
- Customers

Operations strategy

Operations strategy

Design

Operations management

Improvement

Input resources

Planning and control

Output products and services

Customers

Transforming resources
- Facilities
- Staff

Chapter 10 The nature of planning and control
Chapter 11 Capacity planning and control
Chapter 12 Inventory planning and control
Chapter 13 Supply chain planning and control
Chapter 14 Enterprise resource planning (ERP)
Chapter 15 Lean synchronization
Chapter 16 Project planning and control
Chapter 17 Quality management

Chapter 18 Operations improvement
Chapter 19 Risk management
Chapter 20 Managing improvement
Chapter 21 Corporate social responsibility (CSR)

Figure 1.9 **A general model of operations management and operations strategy**

Summary answers to key questions

Check and improve your understanding of this chapter using self assessment questions and a personalised study plan, audio and video downloads, and an eBook – all at ***www.myomlab.com.***

➤ What is operations management?

- Operations management is the activity of managing the resources which are devoted to the production and delivery of products and services. It is one of the core functions of any business, although it may not be called operations management in some industries.
- Operations management is concerned with managing processes. And all processes have internal customers and suppliers. But all management functions also have processes. Therefore, operations management has relevance for all managers.

➔

➤ Why is operations management important in all types of organization?

- Operations management uses the organization's resources to create outputs that fulfil defined market requirements. This is the fundamental activity of any type of enterprise.
- Operations management is increasingly important because today's business environment requires new thinking from operations managers.

➤ What is the input–transformation–output process?

- All operations can be modelled as input–transformation–output processes. They all have inputs of transforming resources, which are usually divided into 'facilities' and 'staff', and transformed resources, which are some mixture of materials, information and customers.
- Few operations produce only products or only services. Most produce some mixture of tangible goods or products and less tangible services.

➤ What is the process hierarchy?

- All operations are part of a larger supply network which, through the individual contributions of each operation, satisfies end-customer requirements.
- All operations are made up of processes that form a network of internal customer–supplier relationships within the operation.
- End-to-end business processes that satisfy customer needs often cut across functionally based processes.

➤ How do operations processes have different characteristics?

- Operations differ in terms of the volume of their outputs, the variety of outputs, the variation in demand for their outputs, and the degree of 'visibility' they have.
- High volume, low variety, low variation and low customer 'visibility' are usually associated with low cost.

➤ What are the activities of operations management?

- Responsibilities include understanding relevant performance objectives, setting an operations strategy, the design of the operation (products, services and processes), planning and controlling the operation, and the improvement of the operation over time.
- Operations managers also have a set of broad societal responsibilities. These are generally called 'corporate social responsibility' or CSR objectives.

Case study
Design house partnerships at Concept Design Services[6]

'I can't believe how much we have changed in a relatively short time. From being an inward-looking manufacturer, we became a customer-focused "design and make" operation. Now we are an integrated service provider. Most of our new business comes from the partnerships we have formed with design houses. In effect, we design products jointly with specialist design houses that have a well-known brand, and offer them a complete service of manufacturing and distribution. In many ways we are now a "business-to-business" company rather than a "business-to-consumer" company.' (Jim Thompson, CEO, Concept Design Services (CDS))

CDS had become one of Europe's most profitable homeware businesses. Originally founded in the 1960s, the company had moved from making industrial mouldings, mainly in the aerospace sector, and some cheap 'homeware' items such as buckets and dustpans, sold under the 'Focus' brand name, to making very high-quality (expensive) stylish homewares with a high 'design value'.

Source: Alamy/Adrian Sherratt

The move into 'Concept' products

The move into higher-margin homeware had been masterminded by Linda Fleet, CDS's Marketing Director, who had previously worked for a large retail chain of paint and wallpaper retailers. *'Experience in the decorative products industry had taught me the importance of fashion and product development, even in mundane products such as paint. Premium-priced colours and new textures would become popular for one or two years, supported by appropriate promotion and features in lifestyle magazines. The manufacturers and retailers who created and supported these products were dramatically more profitable than those who simply provided standard ranges. Instinctively, I felt that this must also apply to homeware. We decided to develop a whole coordinated range of such items, and to open up a new distribution network for them to serve up-market stores, kitchen equipment and speciality retailers. Within a year of launching our first new range of kitchen homeware under the* "Concept" *brand name, we had over 3000 retail outlets signed up, provided with point-of-sale display facilities. Press coverage generated an enormous interest which was reinforced by the product placement on several TV cookery and "lifestyle" programmes. We soon developed an entirely new market and within two years "Concept" products were providing over 75 per cent of our revenue and 90 per cent of our profits. The price realization of Concept products is many times higher than for the* Focus *range. To keep ahead we launched new ranges at regular intervals.'*

The move to the design house partnerships

'Over the last four years, we have been designing, manufacturing and distributing products for some of the more prestigious design houses. This sort of business is likely to grow, especially in Europe where the design houses appreciate our ability to offer a full service. We can design products in conjunction with their own design staff and offer them a level of manufacturing expertise they can't get elsewhere. More significantly, we can offer a distribution service which is tailored to their needs. From the customer's point of view the distribution arrangements appear to belong to the design house itself. In fact they are based exclusively on our own call centre, warehouse and distribution resources.'

The most successful collaboration was with Villessi, the Italian designers. Generally it was CDS's design expertise which was attractive to 'design house' partners. Not only did CDS employ professionally respected designers, they had also acquired a reputation for being able to translate difficult technical designs into manufacturable and saleable →

products. Design house partnerships usually involved relatively long lead times but produced unique products with very high margins, nearly always carrying the design house's brand. *'This type of relationship plays to our strengths. Our design expertise gains us entry to the partnership but we are soon valued equally for our marketing, distribution and manufacturing competence.'* (Linda Fleet, Marketing Director)

Manufacturing operations

All manufacturing was carried out in a facility located 20 km from head office. Its moulding area housed large injection-moulding machines, most with robotic material handling capabilities. Products and components passed to the packing hall, where they were assembled and inspected. The newer more complex products often had to move from moulding to assembly and then back again for further moulding. All products followed the same broad process route but with more products needing several progressive moulding and assembly stages, there was an increase in 'process flow recycling' which was adding complexity. One idea was to devote a separate cell to the newer and more complex products until they had 'bedded in'. This cell could also be used for testing new moulds. However, it would need investment in extra capacity that would not always be fully utilized. After manufacture, products were packed and stored in the adjacent distribution centre.

'When we moved into making the higher-margin Concept products, we disposed of most of our older, small injection-moulding machines. Having all larger machines allowed us to use large multi-cavity moulds. This increased productivity by allowing us to produce several products, or components, each machine cycle. It also allowed us to use high-quality and complex moulds which, although cumbersome and more difficult to change over, gave a very high-quality product. For example, with the same labour we could make three items per minute on the old machines, and 18 items per minute on the modern ones using multi-moulds. That's a 600 per cent increase in productivity. We also achieved high-dimensional accuracy, excellent surface finish, and extreme consistency of colour. We could do this because of our expertise derived from years making aerospace products. Also, by standardizing on single large machines, any mould could fit any machine. This was an ideal situation from a planning perspective, as we were often asked to make small runs of Concept *products at short notice.'* (Grant Williams, CDS Operations Manager)

Increasing volume and a desire to reduce cost had resulted in CDS subcontracting much of its Focus products to other (usually smaller) moulding companies. *'We would never do it with any complex or design house partner products, but it should allow us to reduce the cost of making basic products while releasing capacity for higher-margin ones. However, there have been quite a few 'teething problems'. Coordinating the production schedules is currently a problem, as is agreeing quality standards. To some extent it's our own fault. We didn't realize that subcontracting was a skill in its own right. And although we have got over some of the problems, we still do not have a satisfactory relationship with all of our subcontractors.'* (Grant Williams, CDS Operations Manager)

Planning and distribution services

The distribution services department of the company was regarded as being at the heart of the company's customer service drive. Its purpose was to integrate the efforts of design, manufacturing and sales by planning the flow of products from production, through the distribution centre, to the customer. Sandra White, the Planning Manager, reported to Linda Fleet and was responsible for the scheduling of all manufacturing and distribution, and for maintaining inventory levels for all the warehoused items. *'We try to stick to a preferred production sequence for each machine and mould so as to minimize set-up times by starting on a light colour, and progressing through a sequence to the darkest. We can change colours in 15 minutes, but because our moulds are large and technically complex, mould changes can take up to three hours. Good scheduling is important to maintain high plant utilization. With a higher variety of complex products, batch sizes have reduced and it has brought down average utilization. Often we can't stick to schedules. Short-term changes are inevitable in a fashion market. Certainly better forecasts would help . . . but even our own promotions are sometimes organized at such short notice that we often get caught with stockouts. New products in particular are difficult to forecast, especially when they are "fashion" items and/or seasonal. Also, I have to schedule production time for new product mould trials; we normally allow 24 hours for the testing of each new mould received, and this has to be done on production machines. Even if we have urgent orders, the needs of the designers always have priority.'* (Sandra White)

Customer orders for Concept and design house partnership products were taken by the company's sales call centre located next to the warehouse. The individual orders would then be dispatched using the company's own fleet of medium and small distribution vehicles for UK orders, but using carriers for the Continental European market. A standard delivery timetable was used and an 'express delivery' service was offered for those customers prepared to pay a small delivery premium. However, a recent study had shown that almost 40 per cent of express deliveries were initiated by the company rather than customers. Typically this would be to fulfil deliveries of orders containing products out of stock at the time of ordering. The express delivery service was not required for *Focus* products because almost all deliveries were to five large customers. The size of each order was usually very large, with deliveries to customers' own distribution depots. However, although the organization of Focus delivery was relatively straightforward, the consequences of failure were large. Missing a delivery meant upsetting a large customer.

Challenges for CDS

Although the company was financially successful and very well regarded in the homeware industry, there were a number of issues and challenges that it knew it would have to address. The first was the role of the design department and its influence over new product development.

New product development had become particularly important to CDS, especially since they had formed alliances with design houses. This had led to substantial growth in both the size and the influence of the design department, which reported to Linda Fleet. *'Building up and retaining design expertise will be the key to our future. Most of our growth is going to come from the business which will be bought in through the creativity and flair of our designers. Those who can combine creativity with an understanding of our partners' business and design needs can now bring in substantial contracts. The existing business is important of course, but growth will come directly from these people's capabilities.'* (Linda Fleet)

But not everyone was so sanguine about the rise of the design department. *'It is undeniable that relationships between the designers and other parts of the company have been under strain recently. I suppose it is, to some extent, inevitable. After all, they really do need the freedom to design as they wish. I can understand it when they get frustrated at some of the constraints which we have to work under in the manufacturing or distribution parts of the business. They also should be able to expect a professional level of service from us. Yet the truth is that they make most of the problems themselves. They sometimes don't seem to understand the consequences or implications of their design decisions or the promises they make to the design houses. More seriously they don't really understand that we could actually help them do their job better if they cooperated a bit more. In fact, I now see some of our design house partners' designers more than I do our own designers. The Villessi designers are always in my factory and we have developed some really good relationships.'* (Grant Williams)

The second major issue concerned sales forecasting, and again there were two different views. Grant Williams was convinced that forecasts should be improved. *'Every Friday morning we devise a schedule of production and distribution for the following week. Yet, usually before Tuesday morning, it has had to be significantly changed because of unexpected orders coming in from our customers' weekend sales. This causes tremendous disruption to both manufacturing and distribution operations. If sales could be forecast more accurately we would achieve far high utilization, better customer service, and I believe, significant cost savings.'*

However, Linda Fleet saw things differently. *'Look, I do understand Grant's frustration, but after all, this is a fashion business. By definition it is impossible to forecast accurately. In terms of month-by-month sales volumes we are in fact pretty accurate, but trying to make a forecast for every week end every product is almost impossible to do accurately. Sorry, that's just the nature of the business we're in. In fact, although Grant complains about our lack of forecast accuracy, he always does a great job in responding to unexpected customer demand.'*

Jim Thompson, the Managing Director, summed up his view of the current situation. *'Particularly significant has been our alliances with the Italian and German design houses. In effect we are positioning ourselves as a complete service partner to the designers. We have a world-class design capability together with manufacturing, order processing, order-taking and distribution services. These abilities allow us to develop genuinely equal partnerships which integrate us into the whole industry's activities.'*

Linda Fleet also saw an increasing role for collaborative arrangements. *'It may be that we are seeing a fundamental change in how we do business within our industry. We have always seen ourselves as primarily a company that satisfies consumer desires through the medium of providing good service to retailers. The new partnership arrangements put us more into the "business-to-business" sector. I don't have any problem with this in principle, but I'm a little anxious as to how much it gets us into areas of business beyond our core expertise.'*

The final issue which was being debated within the company was longer-term, and particularly important. *'The two big changes we have made in this company have both happened because we exploited a strength we already had within the company. Moving into Concept products was only possible because we brought our high-tech precision expertise that we had developed in the aerospace sector into the homeware sector where none of our new competitors could match our manufacturing excellence. Then, when we moved into design house partnerships we did so because we had a set of designers who could command respect from the world-class design houses with whom we formed partnerships. So what is the next move for us? Do we expand globally? We are strong in Europe but nowhere else in the world. Do we extend our design scope into other markets, such as furniture? If so, that would take us into areas where we have no manufacturing expertise. We are great at plastic injection moulding, but if we tried any other manufacturing processes, we would be no better than, and probably worse than, other firms with more experience. So what's the future for us?'* (Jim Thompson, CEO CDS).

Questions

1 Why is operations management important in CDS?

2 Draw a 4 Vs profile for the company's products and services.

3 What would you recommend to the company if they asked you to advise them in improving their operations?

Problems and applications

These problems and applications will help to improve your analysis of operations. You can find more practice problems as well as worked examples and guided solutions on MyOMLab at ***www.myomlab.com.***

1. Read the short case on Pret A Manger and **(a)** identify the processes in a typical Pret A Manger shop together with their inputs and outputs, **(b)** Pret A Manger also supplies business lunches (of sandwiches and other take-away food). What are the implications for how it manages its processes within the shop? **(c)** What would be the advantages and disadvantages if Pret A Manger introduced 'central kitchens' that made the sandwiches for a number of shops in an area? (As far as we know, they have no plans to do so.)

2. Compare and contrast Acme Whistles and Pret A Manger in terms of the way that they will need to manage their operations.

3. Visit a furniture store (other than IKEA) and a sandwich or snack shop (other than Pret A Manger). Observe how each shop operates, for example, where customers go, how staff interact with them, how big it is, how the shop has chosen to use its space, what variety of products it offers, and so on. Talk with the staff and managers if you can. Think about how the shops you have visited are similar to IKEA and Pret A Manger, and how they differ. Then consider the question, *'What implications do the differences between the shops you visited and the two described in Chapter 1 have for their operations management?'*

4. Visit and observe three restaurants, cafés or somewhere that food is served. Compare them in terms of the Volume of demand that they have to cope with, the Variety of menu items they service, the Variation in demand during the day, week and year, and the Visibility you have of the preparation of the food. Think about and discuss the impact of volume, variety, variation and visibility on the day-to-day management of each of the operations and consider how each operation attempts to cope with its volume, variety, variation and visibility.

5. (Advanced) Find a copy of a financial newspaper (*Financial Times*, *Wall Street Journal*, *Economist*, etc.) and identify one company which is described in the paper that day. Using the list of issues identified in Table 1.1, what do you think would be the *new operations agenda* for that company?

Selected further reading

Chase, R.B., Jacobs, F.R. and Aquilano, N.J. (2004) *Operations Management for Competitive Advantage* (10th edn), McGraw-Hill/Irwin, Boston. There are many good general textbooks on operations management. This was one of the first and is still one of the best, though written very much for an American audience.

Chopra, S., Deshmukh, S., Van Mieghem, J., Zemel, E. and Anupindi, R. (2005) *Managing Business Process Flows: Principles of Operations Management*, Prentice-Hall, NJ. Takes a 'process' view of operations. Mathematical but rewarding.

Hammer, M. and Stanton, S. (1999) How process enterprises really work, *Harvard Business Review*, Nov–Dec. Hammer is one of the gurus of process design. This paper is typical of his approach.

Heizer, J. and Render, B. (2006) *Operations Management* (8th edn), Prentice Hall, New Jersey. Another good US authored general text on the subject.

Johnston, R. and Clark, G. (2008) *Service Operations Management* (3rd edn), Financial Times-Prentice Hall, Harlow. What can we say! A great treatment of service operations from the same stable as this textbook.

Slack, N. and Lewis, M.A. (eds) (2005) *The Blackwell Encyclopedic Dictionary of Operations Management* (2nd edn), Blackwell Business, Oxford. For those who like technical descriptions and definitions.

Useful web sites

www.opsman.org Useful materials and resources.

www.iomnet.org The Institute of Operations Management site. One of the main professional bodies for the subject.

www.poms.org A US academic society for production and operations management. Academic, but some useful material, including a link to an encyclopaedia of operations management terms.

www.sussex.ac.uk/users/dt31/TOMI/ One of the longest-established portals for the subject. Useful for academics and students alike.

www.ft.com Useful for researching topics and companies.

www.journaloperationsmanagement.org The home site for the best known operations management journal. A bit academic, but some pages are useful.

Now that you have finished reading this chapter, why not visit MyOMLab at ***www.myomlab.com*** *where you'll find more learning resources to help you make the most of your studies and get a better grade?*

Chapter 2

Operations performance

Key questions

- ➤ Why is operations performance important in any organization?
- ➤ How does the operations function incorporate all stakeholders' objectives?
- ➤ What does top management expect from the operations function?
- ➤ What are the performance objectives of operations and what are the internal and external benefits which derive from excelling in each of them?
- ➤ How do operations performance objectives trade off against each other?

Introduction

Operations are judged by the way they perform. There are many individuals and groups doing the judging and there are many different aspects of performance on which the assessment is being made. The people doing the judging are called 'stakeholders' and the aspects of performance they are using are called 'performance objectives'. And if we want to understand the strategic contribution of the operations function, it is important to understand how we can measure its performance. So this chapter starts by illustrating how operations performance can impact on the success of the whole organization. Second, we look at various perspectives on, and aspects of performance. Finally, we examine how performance objectives trade off against each other. On our general model of operations management the topics covered in this chapter are represented by the area marked on Figure 2.1.

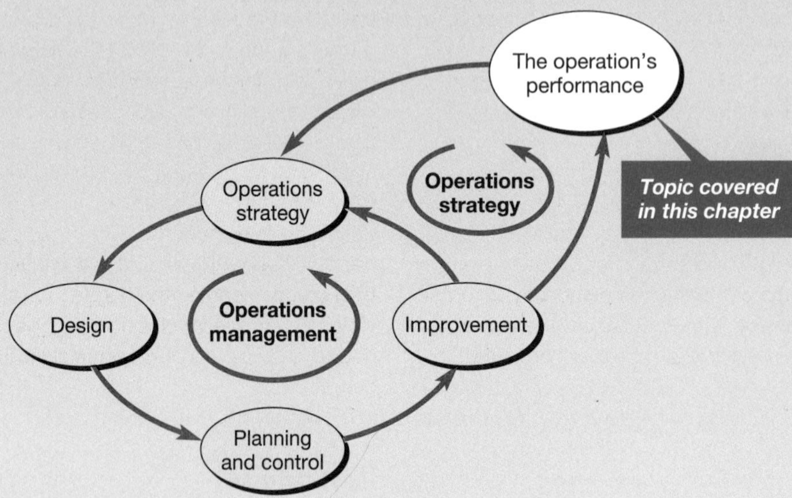

Figure 2.1 This chapter examines operations performance

Operations in practice A tale of two terminals[1]

On 15 April 2008 British Airways (BA) announced that two of its most senior executives, its director of operations and its director of customer services, would leave the company. They were paying the price for the disastrous opening of British Airways' new Terminal 5 at London's Heathrow airport. The opening of the £4.3bn terminal, said BA's boss, Willie Walsh, with magnificent understatement, 'was not the company's finest hour'. The chaos at the terminal on its opening days made news around the world and was seen by many as one of the most public failures of basic operations management in the modern history of aviation. 'It's a terrible, terrible PR nightmare to have hanging over you', said David Learmount, an aviation expert. 'Somebody who may have been a faithful customer and still not have their luggage after three weeks, is not good for their [BA's] image. The one thing that's worse than having a stack of 15,000 bags is adding 5,000 a day to that heap.' According to a BA spokeswoman it needed an extra 400 volunteer staff and courier companies to wade through the backlog of late baggage. So the new terminal that had opened on 27 March could not even cope with BA's full short-haul service until 8 April (two hundred flights in and out of T5 were cancelled in its first three days). This delayed moving its long-haul operations to the new building from Terminal 4 as scheduled on 30 April, which, in turn, disrupted the operations of other airlines, many of which were scheduled to move into Terminal 4 once BA had moved its long-haul flights from there. Sharing the blame with BA was the British Airports Authority (BAA) which was already suffering criticism from passenger groups, airlines and businesses for allegedly poor performance. BAA's non-executive chairman, Sir Nigel Rudd, said he was 'bitterly disappointed' about the opening of the terminal. 'It was clearly a huge embarrassment to the company, me personally, and the board. Nothing can take away that failure. We had all believed genuinely that it would be a great opening, which clearly it wasn't.'

Yet it all should have been so different. T5 took more than six years and around 60,000 workers to build. And it's an impressive building. It is Europe's largest free-standing structure. It was also keenly anticipated by travellers and BA alike. Willie Walsh has said that the terminal 'will completely change his passengers' experience'. He was right, but not in the way he imagined! So what went wrong? As is often the case with major operations failures, it was not one thing, but several interrelated problems (all of which could have been avoided). Press reports initially blamed glitches with the state-of-the-art baggage handling system

Source: Alamy Images

that consisted of 18 km of conveyor belts and was (theoretically) capable of transporting 12,000 bags per hour. And indeed the baggage handling system did experience problems which had not been exposed in testing. But BAA, the airport operator, doubted that the main problem was the baggage system itself. The system had worked until it became clogged with bags that were overwhelming BA's handlers loading them onto the aircraft. Partly this may have been because staff were not sufficiently familiar with the new system and its operating processes, but handling staff had also suffered delays getting to their new (and unfamiliar) work areas, negotiating (new) security checks and finding (again, new) car parking spaces. Also, once staff were 'airside' they had problems logging in. The cumulative effect of these problems meant that the airline was unable to get ground handling staff to the correct locations for loading and unloading bags from the aircraft, so baggage could not be loaded onto aircraft fast enough, so baggage backed up, clogging the baggage handling system, which in turn meant closing baggage check-in and baggage drops, leading eventually to baggage check-in being halted.

However, not every airline underestimates the operational complexity of airport processes. During the same year that Terminal 5 at Heathrow was suffering queues, lost bags and bad publicity, Dubai International Airport's Terminal 3 opened quietly with little publicity and fewer problems. Like T5, it is also huge and designed to impress. Its new shimmering facilities are solely dedicated to Emirates Airline. Largely built underground (20 metres beneath the taxiway area) the multi-level environment reduces passenger walking by using 157 elevators, 97 escalators and 82 moving walkways. Its underground baggage handling system is

Source: Rex Features

the deepest and the largest of its kind in the world with 90 km of baggage belts handling around 15,000 items per hour, with 800 RFID (see Chapter 8) read/write stations for 100% accurate tracking. Also like T5 it handles about 30 million passengers a year.

But one difference between the two terminals was that Dubai's T3 could observe and learn lessons from the botched opening of Heathrow's Terminal 5. Paul Griffiths, the former head of London's Gatwick Airport, who is now Dubai Airport's chief executive, insisted that his own new terminal should not be publicly shamed in the same way. 'There was a lot of arrogance and hubris around the opening of T5, with all the . . . publicity that BA generated', Mr Griffiths says. 'The first rule of customer service is under-promise and over-deliver because that way you get their loyalty. BA was telling people that they were getting a glimpse of the future with T5, which created expectation and increased the chances of disappointment. Having watched the development of T5, it was clear that we had to make sure that everyone was on-message. We just had to bang heads together so that people realized what was at stake. We knew the world would be watching and waiting after T5 to see whether T3 was the next big terminal fiasco. We worked very hard to make sure that didn't happen.'

Paul Griffiths was also convinced that Terminal 3 should undergo a phased programme with flights added progressively, rather than a 'big bang' approach where the terminal opened for business on one day. 'We exhaustively tested the terminal systems throughout the summer . . . We continue to make sure we're putting large loads on it, week by week, improving reliability. We put a few flights in bit by bit, in waves rather than a big bang.' Prior to the opening he also said that Dubai Airports would never reveal a single opening date for its new Terminal 3 until all pre-opening test programmes had been completed. 'T3 opened so quietly', said one journalist, 'that passengers would have known that the terminal was new only if they had touched the still-drying paint.'

Operations performance is vital for any organization

Operations management is a 'make or break' activity

It is no exaggeration to view operations management as being able to either '**make or break**' any business. This is not just because the operations function is large and, in most businesses, represents the bulk of its assets and the majority of its people, but because the operations function gives the ability to compete by providing the ability to respond to customers and by developing the capabilities that will keep it ahead of its competitors in the future. For example, operations management principles and the performance of its operations function proved hugely important in the Heathrow T5 and Dubai T3 launches. It was a basic failure to understand the importance of operations processes that (temporarily) damaged British Airways' reputation. It was Dubai's attention to detail and thorough operational preparation that avoided similar problems. Figure 2.2 illustrates just some of the positive and the negative effects that operations management can have.

How operations can affect profits

Operations management can significantly affect profitability

The way operations management performs its activities can have a very significant effect on a business. Look at how it can influence the **profitability** of a company. Consider two information technology (IT) support companies. Both design, supply, install and maintain IT systems for business clients. Table 2.1 shows the effect that good operations management could have on a business's performance.

Company A believes that the way it produces and delivers its services can be used for long-term competitive advantage. Company B, by contrast, does not seem to be thinking about how its operations can be managed creatively in order to add value for its customers

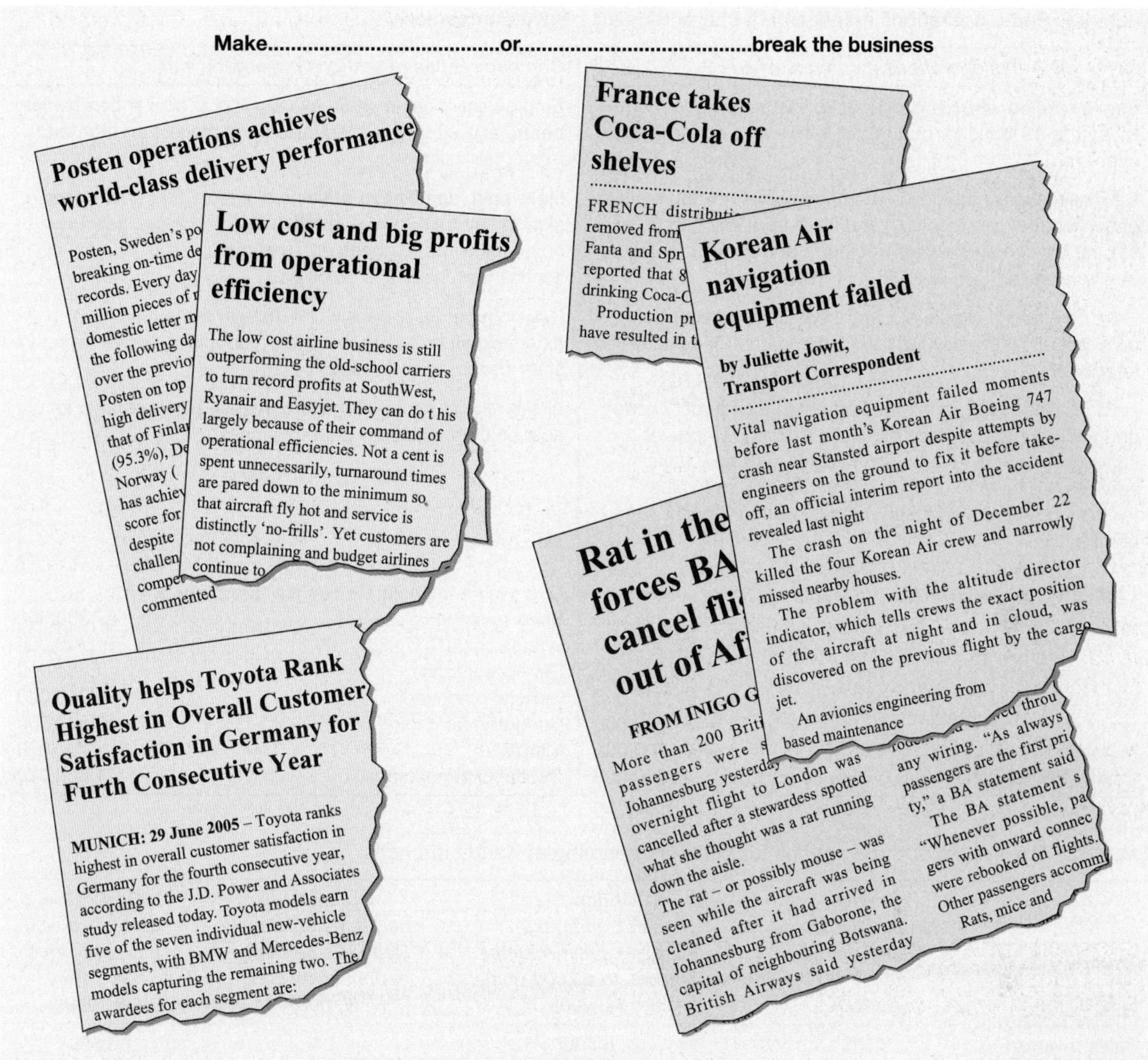

Figure 2.2 Operations management can 'make or break' any business

and sustain its own profitability. Company A is paying its service engineers higher salaries, but expects them to contribute their ideas and enthusiasm to the business without excessive supervision. Perhaps this is why Company A is 'wasting' less of its expenditure on overheads. Its purchasing operations are also spending less on buying in the computer hardware that it installs for its customers, perhaps by forming partnerships with its hardware suppliers. Finally, Company A is spending its own money wisely by investing in 'appropriate rather than excessive' technology of its own.

So, operations management can have a very significant impact on a business's financial performance. Even when compared with the contribution of other parts of the business, the contribution of operations can be dramatic. Consider the following example. Kandy Kitchens currently produce 5,000 units a year. The company is considering three options for boosting its earnings. Option 1 involves organizing a sales campaign that would involve spending an extra €100,000 in purchasing extra market information. It is estimated that sales would rise by 30 per cent. Option 2 involves reducing operating expenses by 20 per cent through forming improvement teams that will eliminate waste in the firm's operations. Option 3 involves investing €70,000 in more flexible machinery that will allow the company to respond faster to customer orders and therefore charge 10 per cent extra for this 'speedy service'. Table 2.2 illustrates the effect of these three options.

Table 2.1 Some operations management characteristics of two companies

Company A has operations managers who . . .	*Company B has operations managers who . . .*
Employ skilled, enthusiastic people, and encourage them to contribute ideas for cutting out waste and working more effectively.	Employ only people who have worked in similar companies before and supervise them closely to make sure that they 'earn their salaries'.
Carefully monitor their customers' perception of the quality of service they are receiving and learn from any examples of poor service and always apologize and rectify any failure to give excellent service.	Have rigid 'completion of service' sheets that customers sign to say that they have received the service, but they never follow up to check on customers' views of the service that they have received.
Have invested in simple but appropriate systems of their own that allow the business to plan and control its activities effectively.	Have bought an expensive integrative system with extensive functionality, because 'you might as well invest in state-of-the-art technology'.
Hold regular meetings where staff share their experiences and think about how they can build their knowledge of customer needs and new technologies, and how their services will have to change in the future to add value for their customers and help the business to remain competitive.	At the regular senior managers' meeting always have an agenda item entitled 'Future business'.
Last year's financial details for Company A: Sales revenue = €10,000,000 Wage costs = €2,000,000 Supervisor costs = €300,000 General overheads = €1,000,000 Bought-in hardware = €5,000,000 Margin = €1,700,000 Capital expenditure = €600,000	**Last year's financial details for Company B:** Sales revenue = €9,300,000 Wages costs = €1,700,000 Supervisor costs = €800,000 General overheads = €1,300,000 Bought-in hardware = €6,500,000 Margin = €700,000 Capital expenditure = €1,500,000

Table 2.2 The effects of three options for improving earning at Kandy Kitchens

	Original (sales volume = 50,000 units) (€, 000)	*Option 1 – sales campaign Increase sales volumes by 30% to 65,000 units (€, 000)*	*Option 2 – operations efficiency Reduce operating expenses by 20% (€, 000)*	*Option 3 – 'speedy service' Increase price by 10% (€, 000)*
Sales revenue	5,000	6,500	5,000	5,500
Operating expenses	4,500	5,550	3,800	4,500
EBIT*	500	1,000	1,200	1,000
Investment required		100		70

*EBIT = Earnings before interest and tax = Net sales – Operating expenses. It is sometimes called 'Operating profit'.

Increasing sales volume by 30 per cent certainly improves the company's sales revenue, but operating expenses also increase. Nevertheless, earnings before investment and tax (EBIT) rise to €1,000,000. But reducing operating expenses by 20 per cent is even more effective, increasing EBIT to €1,200,000. Furthermore, it requires no investment to achieve this. The third option involves improving customer service by responding more rapidly to customer orders. The extra price this will command improves EBIT to €1,000,000 but requires an investment of €70,000. Note how options 2 and 3 involve operations management in changing the way the company operates. Note also how, potentially, reducing operating costs and improving customer service can equal and even exceed the benefits that come from improving sales volume.

So if operations performance has such a significant effect on the whole organization, it follows that any organization needs some way of assessing the performance of its operations function and its operations management. We shall look at three perspectives on operations performance, from macro to micro. First, we examine how each of the organization's stakeholders may view operations performance. Next, we consider what top management may

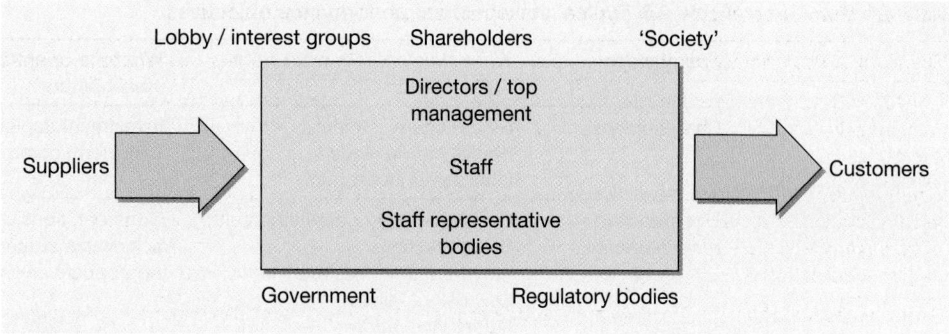

Figure 2.3 Stakeholder groups with a *'legitimate interest in the operation's activities'*

expect of the operations function. Finally, we look at a common set of more detailed operations performance objectives.

The 'stakeholder' perspective on operations performance

Operations may attempt to satisfy a wide range of stakeholders

All operations have a **stakeholders.** Stakeholders are the people and groups that have a legitimate interest in the operation's activities. Some stakeholders are internal, for example the operation's employees; others are external, for example customers, society or community groups, and a company's shareholders. Some external stakeholders have a direct commercial relationship with the organization, for example suppliers and customers; others do not, for example, industry regulators. In not-for-profit operations, these stakeholder groups can overlap. So, voluntary workers in a charity may be employees, shareholders and customers all at once. However, in any kind of organization, it is a responsibility of the operations function to understand the (sometimes conflicting) objectives of its stakeholders and set its objectives accordingly.

Figure 2.3 illustrates just some of the stakeholder groups that would have an interest in how an organization's operations function performs. But although each of these groups, to different extents, will be interested in operations performance, they are likely to have very different views of which aspect of performance is important. Table 2.3 identifies typical stakeholder requirements. But stakeholder relationships are not just one-way. It is also useful to consider what an individual organization or business wants of the stakeholder groups themselves. Some of these requirements are also illustrated in Table 2.3.

Corporate social responsibility (CSR)

Strongly related to the stakeholder perspective of operations performance is that of corporate social responsibility (generally known as CSR). According to the UK government's definition, *'CSR is essentially about how business takes account of its economic, social and environmental impacts in the way it operates – maximizing the benefits and minimizing the downsides. . . . Specifically, we see CSR as the voluntary actions that business can take, over and above compliance with minimum legal requirements, to address both its own competitive interests and the interests of wider society.'* A more direct link with the stakeholder concept is to be found in the definition used by Marks and Spencer, the UK-based retailer. *'Corporate Social Responsibility . . . is listening and responding to the needs of a company's stakeholders. This includes the requirements of sustainable development. We believe that building good relationships with employees, suppliers and wider society is the best guarantee of long-term success. This is the backbone of our approach to CSR.'*

The issue of how broader social performance objectives can be included in operations management's activities is of increasing importance, from both an ethical and a commercial point of view. It is treated again at various points throughout this book, and the final chapter (Chapter 21) is devoted entirely to the topic.

Table 2.3 Typical stakeholders' performance objectives

Stakeholder	*What stakeholders want from the operation*	*What the operation wants from stakeholders*
Shareholders	Return on investment Stability of earnings Liquidity of investment	Investment capital Long-term commitment
Directors/top management	Low/acceptable operating costs Secure revenue Well-targeted investment Low risk of failure Future innovation	Coherent, consistent, clear and achievable strategies Appropriate investment
Staff	Fair wages Good working conditions Safe work environment Personal and career development	Attendance Diligence/best efforts Honesty Engagement
Staff representative bodies e.g. trade unions	Conformance with national agreements Consultation	Understanding Fairness Assistance in problem solving
Suppliers of materials, services, equipment, etc.	Early notice of requirements Long-term orders Fair price On-time payment	Integrity of delivery, quality and volume Innovation Responsiveness Progressive price reductions
Regulators e.g. financial regulators	Conformance to regulations Feedback on effectiveness of regulations	Consistency of regulation Consistency of application of regulations Responsiveness to industry concerns
Government: local, national, regional	Conformance to legal requirements Contribution to (local/national/regional) economy	Low/simple taxation Representation of local concerns Appropriate infrastructure
Lobby groups e.g. environmental lobby groups	Alignment of the organization's activities with whatever the group is promoting	No unfair targeting Practical help in achieving stakeholder aims (if the organization wants to achieve them)
Society	Minimize negative effects from the operation (noise, traffic, etc.) and maximize positive effects (jobs, local sponsorship, etc.)	Support for organization's plans

Critical commentary

The dilemma with using this wide range of stakeholders to judge performance is that organizations, particularly commercial companies, have to cope with the conflicting pressures of maximizing profitability on one hand, with the expectation that they will manage in the interests of (all or part of) society in general with accountability and transparency. Even if a business wanted to reflect aspects of performance beyond its own immediate interests, how is it to do it? According to Michael Jensen of Harvard Business School, '*At the economy-wide or social level, the issue is this: If we could dictate the criterion or objective function to be maximized by firms (and thus the performance criterion by which corporate executives choose among alternative policy options), what would it be? Or, to put the issue even more simply: How do we want the firms in our economy to measure their own performance? How do we want them to determine what is better versus worse?*'[2] He also holds that using stakeholder perspectives gives undue weight to narrow special interests that want to use the organization's resources for their own ends. The stakeholder perspective gives them a spurious legitimacy which '*undermines the foundations of value-seeking behavior*'.

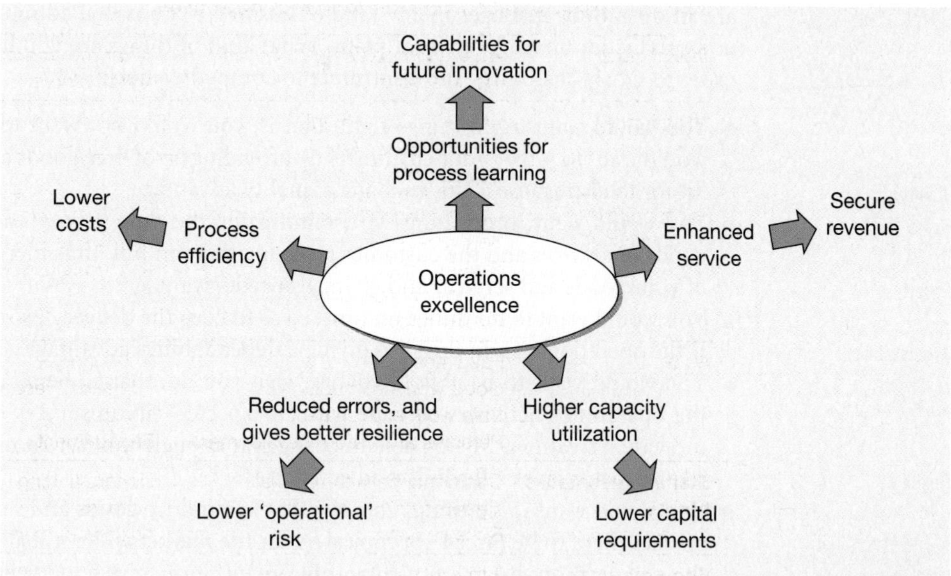

Figure 2.4 Operations can contribute to competitiveness through low costs, high levels of service (securing revenue), lower operational risk, lower capital requirements, and providing the capabilities that determine future innovation

Top management's performance objectives for operations

Operations can have a significant impact on strategic success

Of all stakeholder groups, it is the organization's top management who can have the most immediate impact on its performance. They represent the interests of the owners (or trustees, or electorate, etc.) and therefore are the direct custodians of the organization's basic purpose. They also have responsibility for translating the broad objectives of the organization into a more tangible form. So what should they expect from their operations function? Broadly they should expect all their operations managers to contribute to the success of the organization by using its resources effectively. To do this it must be creative, innovative and energetic in improving its processes, products and services. In more detail, effective operations management can give five types of advantage to the business (see Figure 2.4):

Operations management can reduce costs

Operations management can increase revenue

Operations management can reduce risk

Operations management can reduce the need for investment

Operations management can enhance innovation

- It can reduce the **costs** of producing products and services, and being efficient.
- It can achieve customer satisfaction through good quality and service.
- It can reduce the risk of operational failure, because well designed and well run operations should be less likely to fail, and if they do they should be able to recover faster and with less disruption (this is called *resilience*).
- It can reduce the amount of **investment** (sometimes called *capital employed*) that is necessary to produce the required type and quantity of products and services by increasing the effective capacity of the operation and by being innovative in how it uses its physical resources.
- It can provide the basis for *future* **innovation** by learning from its experience of operating its processes, so building a solid base of operations skills, knowledge and capability within the business.

The five operations performance objectives

Five basic 'performance objectives'

Broad stakeholder objectives form the backdrop to operations decision-making, and top management's objectives provide a strategic framework, but running operations at an operational day-to-day level requires a more tightly defined set of objectives. These are the **five basic 'performance objectives'** and they apply to all types of operation. Imagine that you are an operations manager in any kind of business – a hospital administrator, for example, or a production manager at a car plant. What kind of things are you likely to want to do in order to satisfy customers and contribute to competitiveness?

Quality

- You would want to do things right; that is, you would not want to make mistakes, and would want to satisfy your customers by providing error-free goods and services which are 'fit for their purpose'. This is giving a **quality** advantage.

Speed

- You would want to do things fast, minimizing the time between a customer asking for goods or services and the customer receiving them in full, thus increasing the availability of your goods and services and giving a **speed** advantage.

Dependability

- You would want to do things on time, so as to keep the delivery promises you have made. If the operation can do this, it is giving a **dependability** advantage.

Flexibility

- You would want to be able to change what you do; that is, being able to vary or adapt the operation's activities to cope with unexpected circumstances or to give customers individual treatment. Being able to change far enough and fast enough to meet customer requirements gives a **flexibility** advantage.

Cost

- You would want to do things cheaply; that is, produce goods and services at a cost which enables them to be priced appropriately for the market while still allowing for a return to the organization; or, in a not-for-profit organization, give good value to the taxpayers or whoever is funding the operation. When the organization is managing to do this, it is giving a **cost** advantage.

The next part of this chapter examines these five performance objectives in more detail by looking at what they mean for four different operations: a general hospital, an automobile factory, a city bus company and a supermarket chain.

The quality objective

Quality is a major influence on customer satisfaction or dissatisfaction

Quality is consistent conformance to customers' expectations, in other words, 'doing things right', but the things which the operation needs to do right will vary according to the kind of operation. All operations regard quality as a particularly important objective. In some ways quality is the most visible part of what an operation does. Furthermore, it is something that a customer finds relatively easy to judge about the operation. Is the product or service as it is supposed to be? Is it right or is it wrong? There is something fundamental about quality. Because of this, it is clearly **a major influence on customer satisfaction or dissatisfaction**. A customer perception of high-quality products and services means customer satisfaction and therefore the likelihood that the customer will return. Figure 2.5 illustrates how quality could be judged in four operations.

Quality inside the operation

When quality means consistently producing services and products to specification it not only leads to external customer satisfaction, but makes life easier inside the operation as well.

Quality reduces costs. The fewer mistakes made by each process in the operation, the less time will be needed to correct the mistakes and the less confusion and irritation will be spread. For example, if a supermarket's regional warehouse sends the wrong goods to the supermarket, it will mean staff time, and therefore cost, being used to sort out the problem.

Quality increases dependability. Increased costs are not the only consequence of poor quality. At the supermarket it could also mean that goods run out on the supermarket shelves with a resulting loss of revenue to the operation and irritation to the external customers. Sorting the problem out could also distract the supermarket management from giving attention to

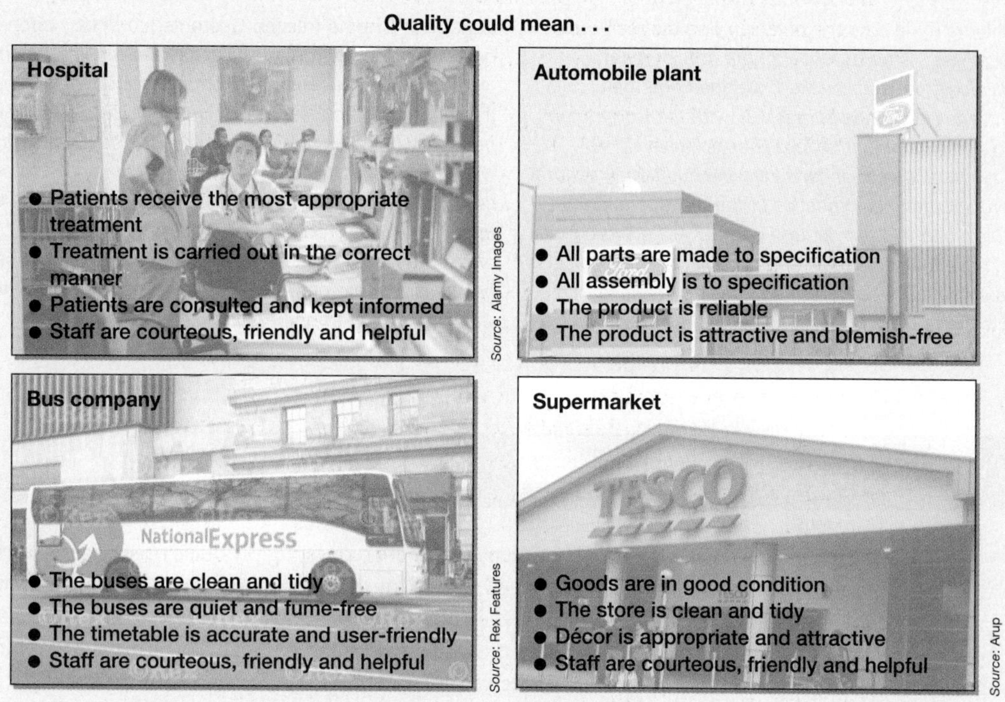

Figure 2.5 Quality means different things in different operations

the other parts of the supermarket operation. This in turn could result in further mistakes being made. So, quality (like the other performance objectives, as we shall see) has both an external impact which influences customer satisfaction and an internal impact which leads to stable and efficient processes.

Short case
Organically good quality[3]

'Organic farming means taking care and getting all the details right. It is about quality from start to finish. Not only the quality of the meat that we produce but also quality of life and quality of care for the countryside.' Nick Fuge is the farm manager at Lower Hurst Farm located within the Peak District National Park of the UK. He has day-to-day responsibility for the well-being of all the livestock and the operation of the farm on strict organic principles. The 85-hectare farm has been producing high-quality beef for almost 20 years but changed to fully organic production in 1998. Organic farming is a tough regime. No artificial fertilizers, genetically modified feedstuff or growth-promoting agents are used. All beef sold from the farm is home-bred and can be traced back to the animal from which it came. *'The quality of the herd is most important'*, says Nick, *'as is animal care. Our customers trust us to ensure that the cattle are organically and humanely reared, and slaughtered in a manner that minimizes any distress.*

If you want to understand the difference between conventional and organic farming, look at the way we use veterinary help. Most conventional farmers use veterinarians like an emergency service to put things right when there is a problem with an animal. The amount we pay for veterinary assistance is lower because we try to avoid problems with the animals from the start. We use veterinaries as consultants to help us in preventing problems in the first place.'

→

Catherine Pyne runs the butchery and the mail-order meat business. *'After butchering, the cuts of meat are individually vacuum-packed, weighed and then blast-frozen. We worked extensively with the Department of Food and Nutrition at Oxford Brooks University to devise the best way to encapsulate the nutritional, textural and flavoursome characteristics of the meat in its prime state. So, when you defrost and cook any of our products you will have the same tasty and succulent eating qualities associated with the best fresh meat.'* After freezing, the products are packed in boxes, designed and labelled for storage in a home freezer. Customers order by phone or through the Internet for next-day delivery in a special 'mini-deep-freeze' reusable container which maintains the meat in its frozen state. *'It isn't just the quality of our product which has made us a success'*, says Catherine. *'We give a personal and inclusive level of service to our customers that makes them feel close to us and maintains trust in how we produce and prepare the meat. The team of people we have here is also an important aspect of our business. We are proud of our product and feel that it is vitally important to be personally identified with it.'*

The speed objective

Speed means the elapsed time between customers requesting products or services and receiving them. Figure 2.6 illustrates what speed means for the four operations. The main benefit to the operation's (external) customers of speedy delivery of goods and services is that the faster they can have the product or service, the more likely they are to buy it, or the more they will pay for it, or the greater the **benefit they receive** (see the short-case 'When speed means life or death').

Speed increases value for some customers

Speed inside the operation

Inside the operation, speed is also important. Fast response to external customers is greatly helped by speedy decision-making and speedy movement of materials and information inside the operation. And there are other benefits.

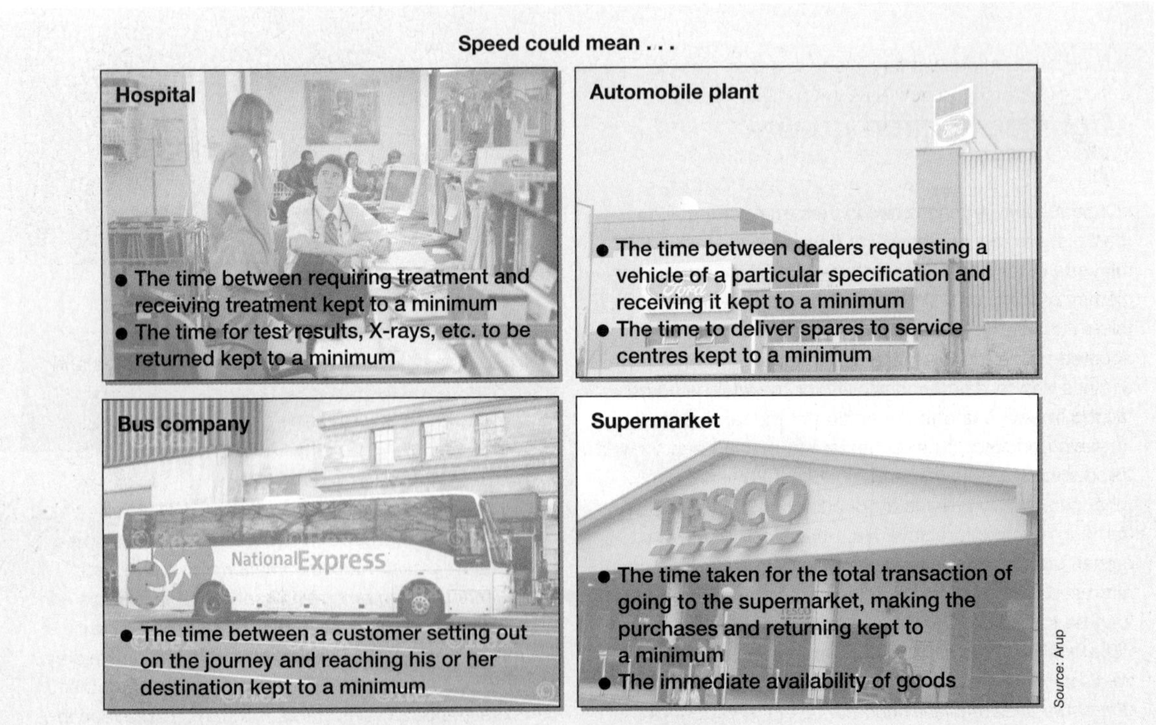

Figure 2.6 Speed means different things in different operations

Speed reduces inventories. Take, for example, the automobile plant. Steel for the vehicle's door panels is delivered to the press shop, pressed into shape, transported to the painting area, coated for colour and protection, and moved to the assembly line where it is fitted to the automobile. This is a simple three-stage process, but in practice material does not flow smoothly from one stage to the next. First, the steel is delivered as part of a far larger batch containing enough steel to make possibly several hundred products. Eventually it is taken to the press area, pressed into shape, and again waits to be transported to the paint area. It then waits to be painted, only to wait once more until it is transported to the assembly line. Yet again, it waits by the trackside until it is eventually fitted to the automobile. The material's journey time is far longer than the time needed to make and fit the product. It actually spends most of its time waiting as stocks (inventories) of parts and products. The longer items take to move through a process, the more time they will be waiting and the higher inventory will be. This is an important idea which will be explored in Chapter 15 on lean operations.

Speed reduces risks. Forecasting tomorrow's events is far less of a risk than forecasting next year's. The further ahead companies forecast, the more likely they are to get it wrong. The faster the throughput time of a process the later forecasting can be left. Consider the automobile plant again. If the total throughput time for the door panel is six weeks, door panels are being processed through their first operation six weeks before they reach their final destination. The quantity of door panels being processed will be determined by the forecasts for demand six weeks ahead. If instead of six weeks, they take only one week to move through the plant, the door panels being processed through their first stage are intended to meet demand only one week ahead. Under these circumstances it is far more likely that the number and type of door panels being processed are the number and type which eventually will be needed.

Short case
When speed means life or death[4]

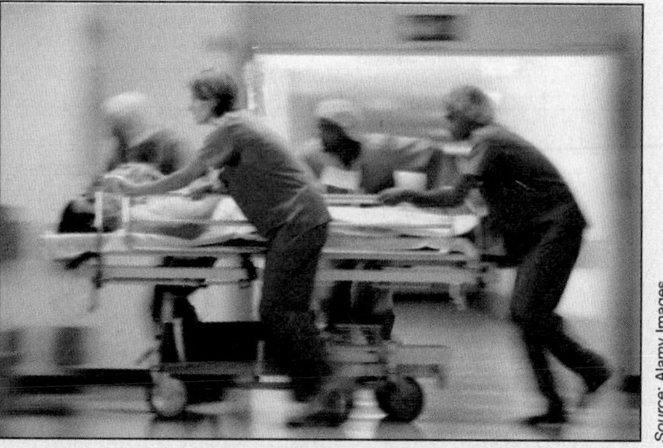

Source: Alamy Images

Of all the operations which have to respond quickly to customer demand, few have more need of speed than the emergency services. In responding to road accidents especially, every second is critical. The treatment you receive during the first hour after your accident (what is called the 'golden hour') can determine whether you survive and fully recover or not. Making full use of the golden hour means speeding up three elements of the total time to treatment – the time it takes for the emergency services to find out about the accident, the time it takes them to travel to the scene of the accident, and the time it takes to get the casualty to appropriate treatment.

Alerting the emergency services immediately is the idea behind Mercedes-Benz's TeleAid system. As soon as the vehicle's airbag is triggered, an on-board computer reports through the mobile phone network to a control centre (drivers can also trigger the system manually if not too badly hurt), satellite tracking allows the vehicle to be precisely located and the owner identified (if special medication is needed). Getting to the accident quickly is the next hurdle. Often the fastest method is by helicopter. When most rescues are only a couple of minutes' flying time back to the hospital speed can really saves lives. However, it is not always possible to land a helicopter safely at night (because of possible overhead wires and other hazards) so conventional ambulances will always be needed, both to get paramedics quickly to accident victims and to speed them to hospital. One increasingly common method of ensuring that ambulances arrive quickly at the accident site is to position them, not at hospitals, but close to where accidents are likely to occur. Computer analysis of previous accident data helps to select the ambulance's waiting position, and global positioning systems help controllers to mobilize the nearest unit. At all times a key requirement for fast service is effective communication between all who are involved in each stage of the emergency. Modern communications technology can play an important role in this.

The dependability objective

Dependability is judged over time

Dependability means doing things in time for customers to receive their goods or services exactly when they are needed, or at least when they were promised. Figure 2.7 illustrates what dependability means in the four operations. Customers might only judge the dependability of an operation after the product or service has been delivered. Initially this may not affect the likelihood that customers will select the service – they have already 'consumed' it. Over **time**, however, dependability can override all other **criteria.** No matter how cheap or fast a bus service is, if the service is always late (or unpredictably early) or the buses are always full, then potential passengers will be better off calling a taxi.

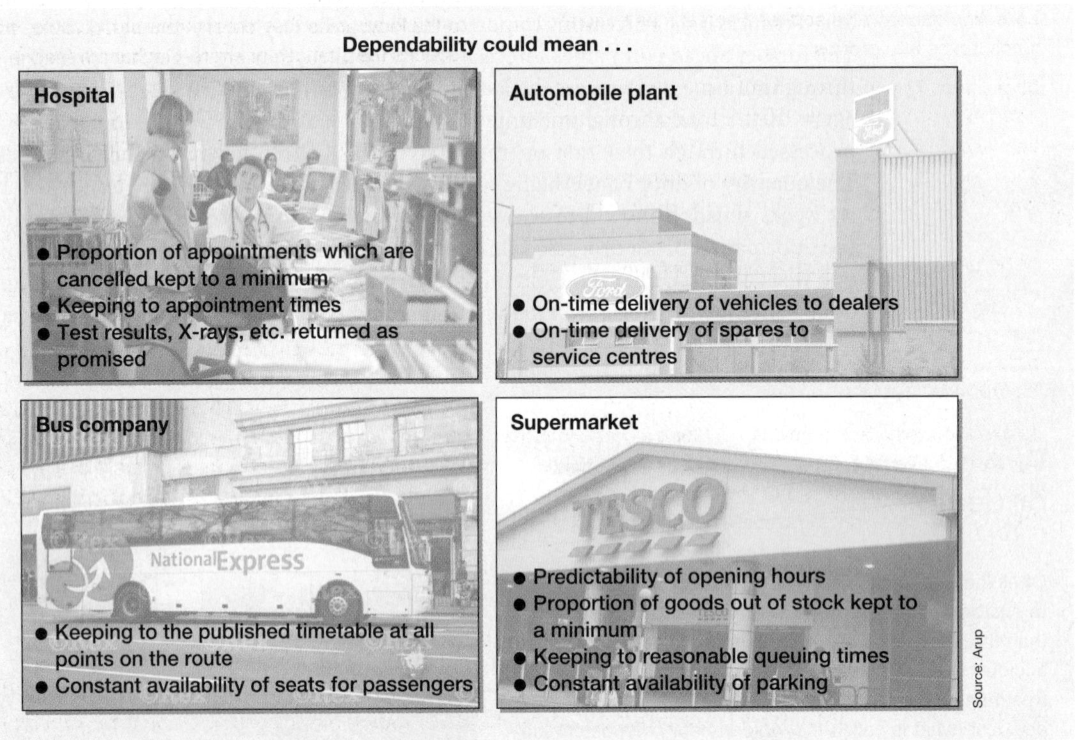

Figure 2.7 Dependability means different things in different operations

Short case
Dabbawalas hit 99.9999% dependability[5]

Mumbai is India's most densely populated city, and every working day its millions of commuters crowd onto packed trains for an often lengthy commute to their workplaces. Going home for lunch is not possible, so many office workers have a cooked meal sent either from their home, or from a caterer. It is Mumbai's 5,000-strong dabbawala collective that provides this service, usually for a monthly fee. The meal is cooked in the morning (by family or caterer), placed in regulation dabbas or tiffin (lunch) boxes and delivered to each individual worker's office at lunch time. After lunch the boxes are collected and returned so that they can be re-sent the next day. 'Dabbawala' means 'one who carries a box', or more colloquially, 'lunch box delivery man'. This is how the service works:

7am–9am The dabbas (boxes) are collected by dabbawalas on bicycles from nearly 200,000 suburban homes or from the dabba makers and taken to railway stations. The dabbas have distinguishing marks on them, using colours and symbols (necessary because many dabbawalas are barely literate). The dabbawala then takes them to a designated sorting place, where he and other collecting dabbawalas sort (and sometimes bundle) the lunch boxes into groups.

9am–11am The grouped boxes are put in the coaches of trains, with markings to identify the destination of the box (usually there is a designated car for the boxes). The markings include the rail station where the boxes are to be unloaded and the building address where the box has to be delivered. This may involve boxes being sorted at intermediary stations, with each single dabba changing hands up to four times.

10am–12midday Dabbas taken into Mumbai using the otherwise under-utilized capacity on commuter trains in the mid-morning.

11am–12midday Arrive downtown Mumbai where dabbas are handed over to **local dabbawalas**, who distribute them to more locations where there is more sorting and loading on to handcarts, bicycles and dabbawalas.

12midday–1pm Dabbas are delivered to appropriate office locations.

2pm Process moves into reverse, after lunch, when the empty boxes are collected from office locations and returned to suburban stations.

6pm Empty dabbas sent back to the respective houses.

The service has a remarkable record of almost flawlessly reliable delivery, even on the days of severe weather such as Mumbai's characteristic monsoons. Dabbawalas all receive the same pay and at both the receiving and the sending ends, are known to the customers personally, so are trusted by customers. Also, they are well accustomed to the local areas they collect from or deliver to, which reduces the chances of errors. Raghunath Medge, the president of the Bombay Tiffin Box Supply Charity Trust, which oversees the dabbawallas, highlights the importance of their hands-on operations management. *'Proper time management is our key to success. We do everything to keep the customer happy and they help in our marketing.'* There is no system of documentation. The success of the operation depends on teamwork and human ingenuity. Such is the dedication and commitment of the barefoot delivery men (there are only a few delivery women) that the complex logistics operation works with only three layers of management. Although the service remains essentially low-tech, with the barefoot delivery men as the prime movers, the dabbawalas now use some modern technology, for example they now allow booking for delivery through SMS and their web site, (www.mydabbawala.com).

Dependability inside the operation

Inside the operation internal customers will judge each other's performance partly by how reliable the other processes are in delivering material or information on time. Operations where internal dependability is high are more effective than those which are not, for a number of reasons.

Dependability saves time. Take, for example, the maintenance and repair centre for the city bus company. If the centre runs out of some crucial spare parts, the manager of the centre will need to spend time trying to arrange a special delivery of the required parts and the resources allocated to service the buses will not be used as productively as they would have been without this disruption. More seriously, the fleet will be short of buses until they can be repaired and the fleet operations manager will have to spend time rescheduling services. So, entirely due to the one failure of dependability of supply, a significant part of the operation's time has been wasted coping with the disruption.

Dependability saves money. Ineffective use of time will translate into extra cost. The spare parts might cost more to be delivered at short notice and maintenance staff will expect to be paid even when there is not a bus to work on. Nor will the fixed costs of the operation, such as heating and rent, be reduced because the two buses are not being serviced. The rescheduling of buses will probably mean that some routes have inappropriately sized buses and some services could have to be cancelled. This will result in empty bus seats (if too large a bus has to be used) or a loss of revenue (if potential passengers are not transported).

Dependability gives stability. The disruption caused to operations by a lack of dependability goes beyond time and cost. It affects the 'quality' of the operation's time. If everything in an operation is always perfectly dependable, a level of trust will have built up between the different parts of the operation. There will be no 'surprises' and everything will be predictable. Under such circumstances, each part of the operation can concentrate on improving its own area of responsibility without having its attention continually diverted by a lack of dependable service from the other parts.

The flexibility objective

Flexibility means being able to change in some way

Flexibility means being able to **change** the operation in some way. This may mean changing what the operation does, how it is doing it, or when it is doing it. Specifically, customers will need the operation to change so that it can provide four types of requirement:

Product/service flexibility

- **product/service flexibility** – the operation's ability to introduce new or modified products and services;

Mix flexibility

- **mix flexibility** – the operation's ability to produce a wide range or mix of products and services;

Volume flexibility

- **volume flexibility** – the operation's ability to change its level of output or activity to produce different quantities or volumes of products and services over time;

Delivery flexibility

- **delivery flexibility** – the operation's ability to change the timing of the delivery of its services or products.

Figure 2.8 gives examples of what these different types of flexibility mean to the four different operations.

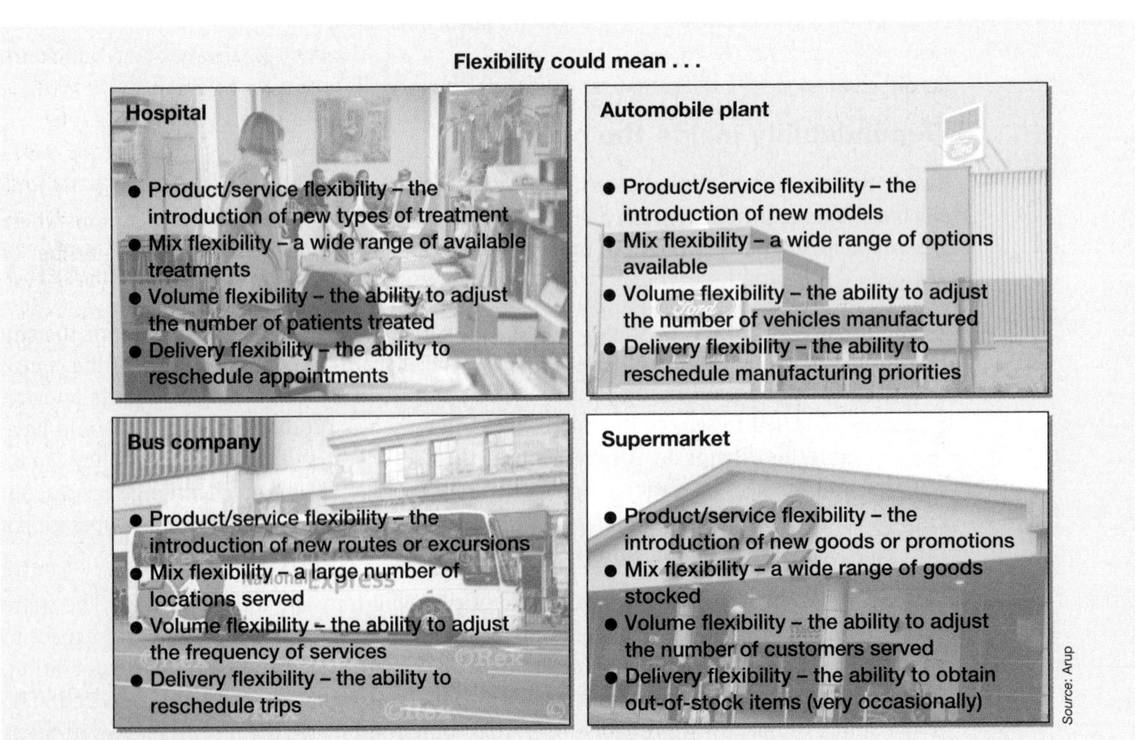

Figure 2.8 Flexibility means different things in different operations

Short case

Flexibility and dependability in the newsroom[6]

Source: BBC/Jeff Overs

Television news is big business. Satellite and cable, as well as developments in terrestrial transmission, have all helped to boost the popularity of 24-hour news services. But news perishes fast. A daily newspaper delivered one day late is practically worthless. This is why broadcasting organizations like the BBC have to ensure that up-to-date news is delivered on time, every time. The BBC's ability to achieve high levels of dependability is made possible by the technology employed in news gathering and editing. At one time news editors would have to schedule a video-taped report to start its countdown five seconds prior to its broadcasting time. With new technology the video can be started from a freeze-frame and will broadcast the instant the command to play is given. The team have faith in the dependability of the process. In addition, technology allows them the flexibility to achieve dependability, even when news stories break just before transmission. In the hours before scheduled transmission, journalists and editors prepare an 'inventory' of news items stored electronically. The presenter will prepare his or her commentary on the autocue and each item will be timed to the second. If the team needs to make a short-term adjustment to the planned schedule, the news studio's technology allows the editors to take broadcasts live from journalists at their locations, on satellite 'takes', directly into the programme. Editors can even type news reports directly onto the autocue for the presenter to read as they are typed – nerve-racking, but it keeps the programme on time.

Mass customization

Mass customization

One of the beneficial external effects of flexibility is the increased ability of operation to do different things for different customers. So, high flexibility gives the ability to produce a high variety of products or services. Normally high variety means high cost (see Chapter 1). Furthermore, high-variety operations do not usually produce in high volume. Some companies have developed their flexibility in such a way that products and services are customized for each individual customer. Yet they manage to produce them in a high-volume, mass-production manner which keeps costs down. This approach is called **mass customization.** Sometimes this is achieved through flexibility in design. For example, Dell is one of the largest volume producers of personal computers in the world, yet allows each customer to 'design' (albeit in a limited sense) their own configuration. Sometimes flexible technology is used to achieve the same effect. For example, Paris Miki, an up-market eyewear retailer which has the largest number of eyewear stores in the world, uses its own 'Mikissimes Design System' to capture a digital image of the customer and analyse facial characteristics. Together with a list of customers' personal preferences, the system then recommends a particular design and displays it on the image of the customer's face. In consultation with the optician the customer can adjust shapes and sizes until the final design is chosen. Within the store the frames are assembled from a range of pre-manufactured components and the lenses ground and fitted to the frames. The whole process takes around an hour.

Agility

Agility

Judging operations in terms of their **agility** has become popular. Agility is really a combination of all the five performance objectives, but particularly flexibility and speed. In addition, agility implies that an operation and the supply chain of which it is a part (supply chains are described in Chapter 6) can respond to uncertainty in the market. Agility means responding to market requirements by producing new and existing products and services fast and flexibly.

Flexibility inside the operation

Developing a flexible operation can also have advantages to the internal customers within the operation.

Flexibility speeds up response. Fast service often depends on the operation being flexible. For example, if the hospital has to cope with a sudden influx of patients from a road accident, it clearly needs to deal with injuries quickly. Under such circumstances a flexible hospital which can speedily transfer extra skilled staff and equipment to the Accident and Emergency department will provide the fast service which the patients need.

Flexibility saves time. In many parts of the hospital, staff have to treat a wide variety of complaints. Fractures, cuts or drug overdoses do not come in batches. Each patient is an individual with individual needs. The hospital staff cannot take time to 'get into the routine' of treating a particular complaint; they must have the flexibility to adapt quickly. They must also have sufficiently flexible facilities and equipment so that time is not wasted waiting for equipment to be brought to the patient. The time of the hospital's resources is being saved because they are flexible in 'changing over' from one task to the next.

Flexibility maintains dependability. Internal flexibility can also help to keep the operation on schedule when unexpected events disrupt the operation's plans. For example, if the sudden influx of patients to the hospital requires emergency surgical procedures, routine operations will be disrupted. This is likely to cause distress and considerable inconvenience. A flexible hospital might be able to minimize the disruption by possibly having reserved operating theatres for such an emergency, and being able to bring in medical staff quickly that are 'on call'.

The cost objective

Low cost is a universally attractive objective

To the companies which compete directly on price, cost will clearly be their major operations objective. The lower the cost of producing their goods and services, the lower can be the price to their customers. Even those companies which do not compete on price will be interested in keeping costs low. Every euro or dollar removed from an operation's cost base is a further euro or dollar added to its profits. Not surprisingly, **low cost is a universally attractive objective**. The short-case 'Everyday low prices at Aldi' describes how one retailer keeps its costs down. The ways in which operations management can influence cost will depend largely on where the operation costs are incurred. The operation will spend its money on staff (the money spent on employing people), facilities, technology and equipment (the money spent on buying, caring for, operating and replacing the operation's 'hardware') and materials (the money spent on the 'bought-in' materials consumed or transformed in the operation). Figure 2.9 shows typical cost breakdowns for the hospital, car plant, supermarket and bus company.

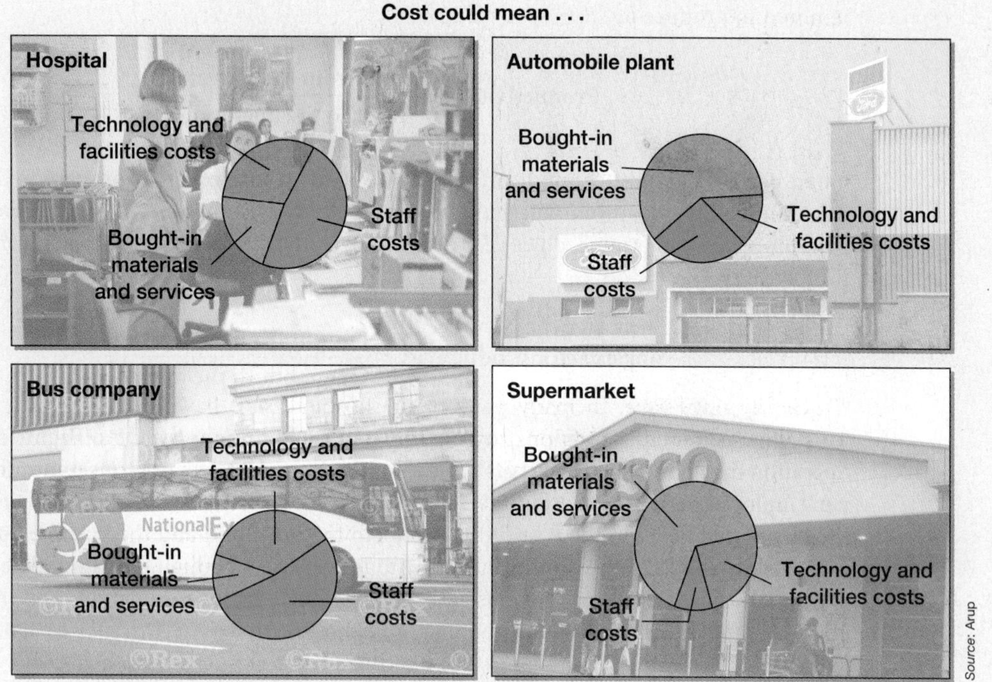

Figure 2.9 Cost means different things in different operations

Keeping operations costs down

All operations have an interest in keeping their costs as low as is compatible with the levels of quality, speed, dependability and flexibility that their customers require. The measure that is most frequently used to indicate how successful an operation is at doing this is

Short case
Everyday low prices at Aldi[7]

Aldi is an international 'limited assortment' supermarket specializing in 'private label', mainly food products. It has carefully focused its service concept and delivery system to attract customers in a highly competitive market. The company believes that its unique approach to operations management make it 'virtually impossible for competitors to match our combination of price and quality'.

Aldi operations challenge the norms of retailing. They are deliberately simple, using basic facilities to keep down overheads. Most stores stock only a limited range of goods (typically around 700 compared with 25,000 to 30,000 stocked by conventional supermarket chains). The private label approach means that the products have been produced according to Aldi quality specifications and are only sold in Aldi stores. Without the high costs of brand marketing and advertising and with Aldi's formidable purchasing power, prices can be 30 per cent below their branded equivalents. Other cost-saving practices include open carton displays which eliminate the need for special shelving, no grocery bags to encourage reuse as well as saving costs, and using a 'cart rental' system which requires customers to return the cart to the store to get their coin deposit back.

Productivity

productivity. **Productivity** is the ratio of what is produced by an operation to what is required to produce it.

$$\textbf{Productivity} = \frac{\textbf{Output from the operation}}{\textbf{Input to the operation}}$$

Often partial measures of input or output are used so that comparisons can be made. So, for example, in the automobile industry productivity is sometimes measured in terms of the number of cars produced per year per employee. This is called a **single-factor measure of productivity.**

Single-factor productivity

$$\textbf{Single-factor productivity} = \frac{\textbf{Output from the operation}}{\textbf{One input to the operation}}$$

This allows different operations to be compared excluding the effects of input costs. One operation may have high total costs per car but high productivity in terms of number of cars per employee per year. The difference between the two measures is explained in terms of the distinction between the cost of the inputs to the operation and the way the operation is managed to convert inputs into outputs. Input costs may be high, but the operation itself is good at converting them to goods and services. Single-factor productivity can include the effects of input costs if the single input factor is expressed in cost terms, such as 'labour costs'. Total factor productivity is the measure that includes all input factors.

$$\textbf{Multi-factor productivity} = \frac{\textbf{Output from the operation}}{\textbf{All inputs to the operation}}$$

Worked example

A health-check clinic has five employees and 'processes' 200 patients per week. Each employee works 35 hours per week. The clinic's total wage bill is £3,900 and its total overhead expenses are £2,000 per week. What are the clinic's single-factor labour productivity and its multi-factor productivity?

$$\text{Labour productivity} = \frac{200}{5} = 40 \text{ patients/employee/week}$$

$$\text{Labour productivity} = \frac{200}{(5 \times 35)} = 1.143 \text{ patients/labour hour}$$

$$\text{Multi-factor productivity} = \frac{200}{(3900 + 2000)} = 0.0339 \text{ patient/£}$$

Improving productivity

One obvious way of improving an operation's productivity is to reduce the cost of its inputs while maintaining the level of its outputs. This means reducing the costs of some or all of its transformed and transforming resource inputs. For example, a bank may choose to locate its call centres to a place where its facility-related costs (for example, rent), are cheaper. A software developer may relocate its entire operation to India or China where skill labour is available at rates significantly less than in European countries. A computer manufacturer may change the design of its products to allow the use of cheaper materials. Productivity can also be improved by making better use of the inputs to the operation. For example, garment manufacturers attempt to cut out the various pieces of material that make up the garment by positioning each part on the strip of cloth so that material wastage is minimized. All operations are increasingly concerned with cutting out waste, whether it is waste of materials, waste of staff time, or waste through the under-utilization of facilities.

Short case

Being cheap is our speciality[8]

Hon Hai Precision Industry is sometimes called the biggest company you have never heard of. Yet it is one of the world's largest contract electronics manufacturers who produce many of the world's computer, consumer electronics and communications products for customers such as Apple, Dell, Nokia and Sony. Since it was founded in 1974, the company's growth has been phenomenal. It is now the world's biggest contract manufacturer for the electronics industry. Why? Because it can make these products cheaper than its rivals. In fact, the company is known for having an obsession with cutting its costs. Unlike some of its rivals, it has no imposing headquarters. The company is run from a five-storey concrete factory in a grimy suburb of Taipei and its annual meeting is held in the staff canteen. 'Doing anything else would be spending your money. Cheap is our speciality', says chairman Terry Gow, and he is regarded as having made Hon Hai the most effective company in his industry at controlling costs. The extra business this has brought has enabled the company to achieve economies of scale above those of its competitors. It has also expanded into making more of the components that go into its products than its competitors. Perhaps most significantly, Hon Hai has moved much of its manufacturing into China and other low-cost areas with plants in South-East Asia, Eastern Europe and Latin America. In China alone, it employs 100,000 people, and with wages rates as low as one-fifth of those in Taiwan many of Hon Hai's competitors have also shifted their production into China.

Source: Empics

Cost reduction through internal effectiveness

All performance objectives affect cost

Our previous discussion distinguished between the benefits of each performance objective to externally and internally. Each of the various performance objectives has several internal effects, but **all of them affect cost**. So, one important way to improve cost performance is to improve the performance of the other operations objectives (see Figure 2.10).

- High-quality operations do not waste time or effort having to re-do things, nor are their internal customers inconvenienced by flawed service.
- Fast operations reduce the level of in-process inventory between and within processes, as well as reducing administrative overheads.
- Dependable operations do not spring any unwelcome surprises on their internal customers. They can be relied on to deliver exactly as planned. This eliminates wasteful disruption and allows the other micro-operations to operate efficiently.
- Flexible operations adapt to changing circumstances quickly and without disrupting the rest of the operation. Flexible micro-operations can also change over between tasks quickly and without wasting time and capacity.

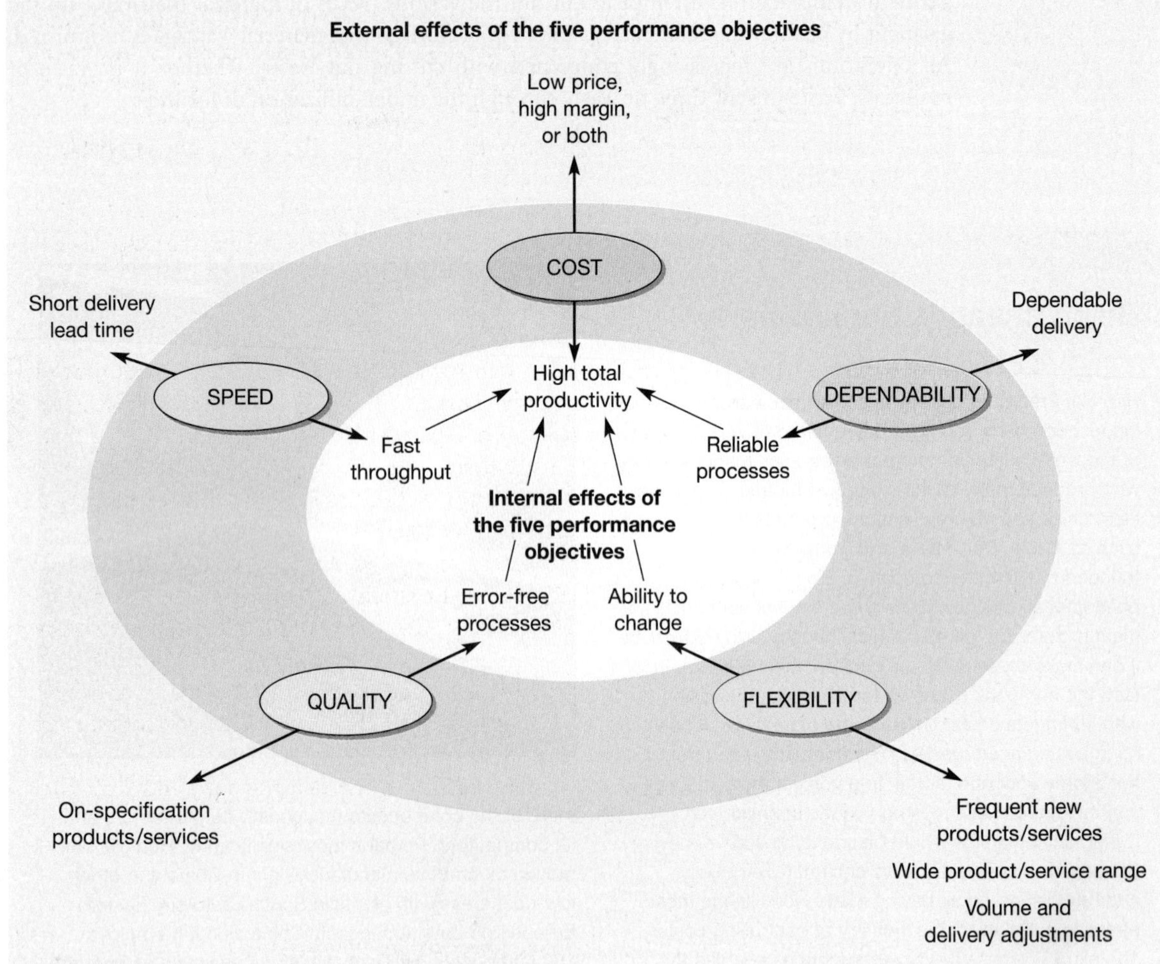

Figure 2.10 Performance objectives have both external and internal effects. Internally, cost is influenced by the other performance objectives

Worked example

Slap.com is an Internet retailer of speciality cosmetics. It orders products from a number of suppliers, stores them, packs them to customers' orders, and then dispatches them using a distribution company. Although broadly successful, the business is very keen to reduce its operating costs. A number of suggestions have been made to do this. There are as follows:

- Make each packer responsible for his or her own quality. This could potentially reduce the percentage of mis-packed items from 0.25 per cent to near zero. Repacking an item that has been mis-packed costs €2 per item.
- Negotiate with suppliers to ensure that they respond to delivery requests faster. It is estimated that this would cut the value of inventories held by slap.com by €1,000,000.
- Institute a simple control system that would give early warning if the total number of orders that should be dispatched by the end of the day actually is dispatched in time. Currently one per cent of orders is not packed by the end of the day and therefore has to be sent by express courier the following day. This costs an extra €2 per item.

Because demand varies through the year, sometimes staff have to work overtime. Currently the overtime wage bill for the year is €150,000. The company's employees have indicated that they would be willing to adopt a flexible working scheme where extra hours could be worked when necessary in exchange for having the hours off at a less busy time and receiving some kind of extra payment. This extra payment is likely to total €50,000 per year.

If the company dispatches 5 million items every year and if the cost of holding inventory is 10 per cent of its value, how much cost will each of these suggestions save the company?

Analysis

Eliminating mis-packing would result in an improvement in quality. 0.25 per cent of 5 million items are mis-packed currently. This amounts to 12,500 items per year. At €2 repacking charge per item, this is a cost of €25,000 that would be saved.

Getting faster delivery from suppliers helps reduce the amount of inventory in stock by €1,000,000. If the company is paying 10 per cent of the value of stock for keeping it in storage the saving will be €1,000,000 × 0.1 = €100,000.

Ensuring that all orders are dispatched by the end of the day increases the dependability of the company's operations. Currently, 1 per cent are late, in other words, 50,000 items per year. This is costing €2 × 50,000 = €100,000 per year which would be saved by increasing dependability.

Changing to a flexible working hours system increases the flexibility of the operation and would cost €50,000 per year, but it saves €150,000 per year. Therefore, increasing flexibility could save €100,000 per year.

So, in total, by improving the operation's quality, speed, dependability and flexibility, a total of €325,000 can be saved.

The polar representation of performance objectives

Polar representation

A useful way of representing the relative importance of performance objectives for a product or service is shown in Figure 2.11(a). This is called the **polar representation** because the scales which represent the importance of each performance objective have the same origin. A line describes the relative importance of each performance objective. The closer the line is to the common origin, the less important is the performance objective to the operation. Two

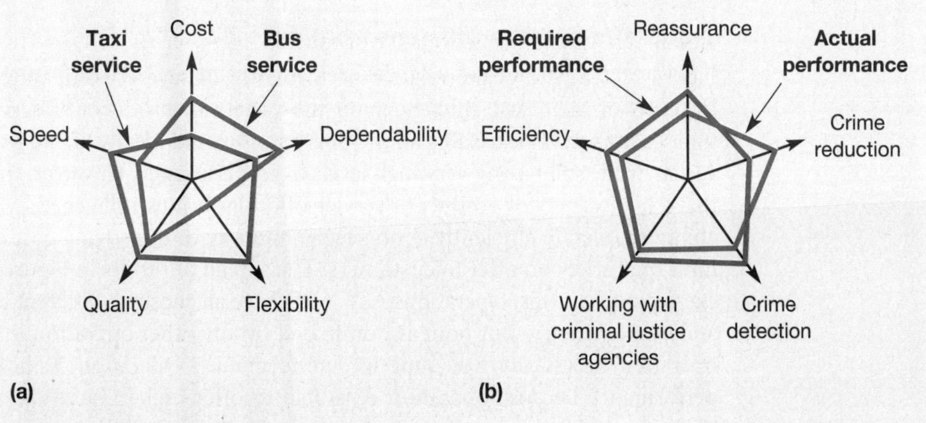

Figure 2.11 Polar representations of (a) the relative importance of performance objectives for a taxi service and a bus service, and (b) a police force targets and performance

services are shown, a taxi and a bus service. Each essentially provides the same basic service, but with different objectives. The differences between the two services are clearly shown by the diagram. Of course, the polar diagram can be adapted to accommodate any number of different performance objectives. For example, Figure 2.11(b) shows a proposal for using a polar diagram to assess the relative performance of different police forces in the UK.[9] Note that this proposal uses three measures of quality (reassurance, crime reduction and crime detection), one measure of cost (economic efficiency), and one measure of how the police force develops its relationship with 'internal' customers (the criminal justice agencies). Note also that actual performance as well as required performance is marked on the diagram.

Trade-offs between performance objectives

Earlier we examined how improving the performance of one objective inside the operation could also improve other performance objectives. Most notably, better quality, speed, dependability and flexibility can improve cost performance. But externally this is not always the case. In fact there may be a *'trade-off'* between performance objectives. In other words improving the performance of one performance objective might only be achieved by sacrificing the performance of another. So, for example, an operation might wish to improve its cost efficiencies by reducing the variety of products or services that it offers to its customers. '*There is no such thing as a free lunch*' could be taken as a summary of this approach. Probably the best-known summary of the **trade-off** idea comes from Professor Wickham Skinner, who said:

There can be a trade-off between an operation's performance objectives

'most managers will readily admit that there are compromises or trade-offs to be made in designing an airplane or truck. In the case of an airplane, trade-offs would involve matters such as cruising speed, take-off and landing distances, initial cost, maintenance, fuel consumption, passenger comfort and cargo or passenger capacity. For instance, no one today can design a 500-passenger plane that can land on an aircraft carrier and also break the sound barrier. Much the same thing is true in [operations]'.[10]

But there are two views of trade-offs. The first emphasizes 'repositioning' performance objectives by trading off improvements in some objectives for a reduction in performance in others. The other emphasizes increasing the 'effectiveness' of the operation by overcoming trade-offs so that improvements in one or more aspects of performance can be achieved without any reduction in the performance of others. Most businesses at some time or other will adopt both approaches. This is best illustrated through the concept of the 'efficient frontier' of operations performance.

Trade-offs and the efficient frontier

Figure 2.12(a) shows the relative performance of several companies in the same industry in terms of their cost efficiency and the variety of products or services that they offer to their customers. Presumably all the operations would ideally like to be able to offer very high variety while still having very high levels of cost efficiency. However, the increased complexity that a high variety of product or service offerings brings will generally reduce the operation's ability to operate efficiently. Conversely, one way of improving cost efficiency is to severely limit the variety on offer to customers. The spread of results in Figure 2.12(a) is typical of an exercise such as this. Operations A, B, C, D have all chosen a different balance between variety and cost efficiency. But none is dominated by any other operation in the sense that another operation necessarily has 'superior' performance. Operation X, however, has an inferior performance because operation A is able to offer higher variety at the same level of cost efficiency and operation C offers the same variety but with better cost efficiency. The convex line on which operations A, B, C and D lie is known as the '**efficient frontier**'. They may choose to position themselves differently (presumably because of different market strategies)

The efficient frontier

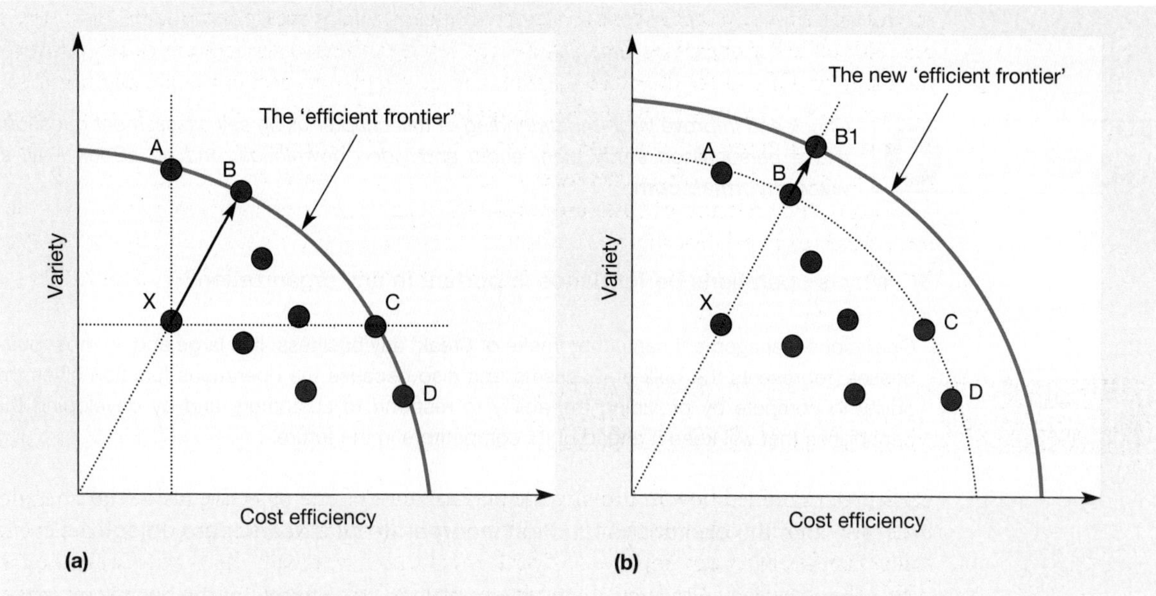

Figure 2.12 The efficient frontier identifies operations with performances that dominate other operations' performance

but they cannot be criticized for being ineffective. Of course, any of these operations that lie on the efficient frontier may come to believe that the balance they have chosen between variety and cost efficiency is inappropriate. In these circumstances they may choose to reposition themselves at some other point along the efficient frontier. By contrast, operation X has also chosen to balance variety and cost efficiency in a particular way but is not doing so effectively. Operation B has the same ratio between the two performance objectives but is achieving them more effectively.

However, a strategy that emphasizes increasing effectiveness is not confined to those operations that are dominated, such as operation X. Those with a position on the efficient frontier will generally also want to improve their operations effectiveness by overcoming the trade-off that is implicit in the efficient frontier curve. For example, suppose operation B in Figure 2.12(b) wants to improve both its variety and its cost efficiency simultaneously and move to position B1. It may be able to do this, but only if it adopts operations improvements that extend the efficient frontier. For example, one of the decisions that any supermarket manager has to make is how many checkout positions to open at any time. If too many checkouts are opened then there will be times when the checkout staff do not have any customers to serve and will be idle. The customers, however, will have excellent service in terms of little or no waiting time. Conversely, if too few checkouts are opened, the staff will be working all the time but customers will have to wait in long queues. There seems to be a direct trade-off between staff utilization (and therefore cost) and customer waiting time (speed of service). Yet even the supermarket manager might, for example, allocate a number of 'core' staff to operate the checkouts but also arrange for those other staff who are performing other jobs in the supermarket to be trained and 'on call' should demand suddenly increase. If the manager on duty sees a build-up of customers at the checkouts, these other staff could quickly be used to staff checkouts. By devising a flexible system of staff allocation, the manager can both improve customer service and keep staff utilization high.

This distinction between positioning on the efficient frontier and increasing operations effectiveness by extending the frontier is an important one. Any business must make clear the extent to which it is expecting the operation to reposition itself in terms of its performance objectives and the extent to which it is expecting the operation to improve its effectiveness in several ways simultaneously.

Summary answers to key questions

Check and improve your understanding of this chapter using self assessment questions and a personalised study plan, audio and video downloads, and an eBook – all at ***www.myomlab.com****.*

➤ Why is operations performance important in any organization?

- Operations management can either 'make or break' any business. It is large and, in most businesses, represents the bulk of its assets, but also because the operations function gives the ability to compete by providing the ability to respond to customers and by developing the capabilities that will keep it ahead of its competitors in the future.

➤ How does the operations function incorporate all stakeholders objectives?

- At a strategic level, performance objectives relate to the interests of the operation's stakeholders. They relate to the company's responsibility to customers, suppliers, shareholders, employees, and society in general.

➤ What does top management expect from the operations function?

- Operations can contribute to the organization as a whole by:
  - reducing the costs
  - achieving customer satisfaction
  - reducing the risk of operational failure
  - reducing the amount of investment
  - providing the basis for future innovation.

➤ What are the performance objectives of operations and what are the internal and external benefits which derive from excelling in each of them?

- By 'doing things right', operations seek to influence the quality of the company's goods and services. Externally, quality is an important aspect of customer satisfaction or dissatisfaction. Internally, quality operations both reduce costs and increase dependability.
- By 'doing things fast', operations seek to influence the speed with which goods and services are delivered. Externally, speed is an important aspect of customer service. Internally, speed both reduces inventories by decreasing internal throughput time and reduces risks by delaying the commitment of resources.
- By 'doing things on time', operations seek to influence the dependability of the delivery of goods and services. Externally, dependability is an important aspect of customer service. Internally, dependability within operations increases operational reliability, thus saving the time and money that would otherwise be taken up in solving reliability problems and also giving stability to the operation.
- By 'changing what they do', operations seek to influence the flexibility with which the company produces goods and services. Externally, flexibility can:
  - produce new products and services (product/service flexibility);
  - produce a wide range or mix of products and services (mix flexibility);
  - produce different quantities or volumes of products and services (volume flexibility);
  - produce products and services at different times (delivery flexibility).

Internally, flexibility can help speed up response times, save time wasted in changeovers, and maintain dependability.

- By 'doing things cheaply', operations seek to influence the cost of the company's goods and services. Externally, low costs allow organizations to reduce their price in order to gain higher volumes or, alternatively, increase their profitability on existing volume levels. Internally, cost performance is helped by good performance in the other performance objectives.

➤ How do operations performance objectives trade off against each other?

- Trade-offs are the extent to which improvements in one performance objective can be achieved by sacrificing performance in others. The 'efficient frontier' concept is a useful approach to articulating trade-offs and distinguishes between repositioning performance on the efficient frontier and improving performance by overcoming trade-offs.

Case study
Operations objectives at the Penang Mutiara[11]

There are many luxurious hotels in the South-East Asia region but few can compare with the Penang Mutiara, a 440-room top-of-the-market hotel which nestles in the lush greenery of Malaysia's Indian Ocean Coast. Owned by Pernas–OUE of Malaysia and managed by Singapore Mandarin International Hotels, the hotel's General Manager is under no illusions about the importance of running an effective operation. *'Managing a hotel of this size is an immensely complicated task'*, he says. *'Our customers have every right to be demanding. They expect first class service and that's what we have to give them. If we have any problems with managing this operation, the customer sees them immediately and that's the biggest incentive for us to take operations performance seriously. Our quality of service just has to be impeccable. This means dealing with the basics. For example, our staff must be courteous at all times and yet also friendly towards our guests. And of course they must have the knowledge to be able to answer guests' questions. The building and equipment – in fact all the hardware of the operation – must support the luxury atmosphere which we have created in the hotel. Stylish design and top-class materials not only create the right impression but, if we choose them carefully, are also durable so the hotel still looks good over the years. Most of all, though, quality is about anticipating our guests' needs, thinking ahead so you can identify what will delight or irritate a guest.'* The hotel tries to anticipate guests' needs in a number of ways. For example, if guests have been to the hotel before, staff avoid their having to repeat the information they gave on the previous visit. Reception staff simply check to see if guests have stayed before, retrieve the information and take them straight to their room without irritating delays. Quality of service also means helping

Source: Alamy Images

guests sort out their own problems. If the airline loses a guest's luggage en route to the hotel, for example, he or she will arrive at the hotel understandably irritated. *'The fact that it is not us who have irritated them is not really the issue. It is our job to make them feel better.'*

Speed, in terms of fast response to customers' requests is something else that is important. *'A guest just should not be kept waiting. If a guest has a request, he or she has that request now so it needs to be sorted out now. This is not always easy but we do our best. For example, if every guest in the hotel tonight decided to call room service and request a meal instead of going to the restaurants, our room service department would obviously be grossly overloaded and customers would have to wait an unacceptably long time before the meals were brought up to their rooms. We cope with this by keeping a close watch on how demand for room service is building up. If we think it's going to get*

above the level where response time to customers would become unacceptably long, we will call in staff from other restaurants in the hotel. Of course, to do this we have to make sure that our staff are multi-skilled. In fact we have a policy of making sure that restaurant staff can always do more than one job. It's this kind of flexibility which allows us to maintain fast response to the customer.'

Dependability is also a fundamental principle of a well-managed hotel. *'We must always keep our promises. For example, rooms must be ready on time and accounts must be ready for presentation when a guest departs; the guests expect a dependable service and anything less than full dependability is a legitimate cause for dissatisfaction.'* It is on the grand occasions, however, when dependability is particularly important in the hotel. When staging a banquet, for example, everything has to be on time. Drinks, food, entertainment have to be available exactly as planned. Any deviation from the plan will very soon be noticed by customers. *'It is largely a matter of planning the details and anticipating what could go wrong. Once we've done the planning we can anticipate possible problems and plan how to cope with them, or better still, prevent them from occurring in the first place.'*

Flexibility means a number of things to the hotel. First of all it means that they should be able to meet a guest's requests. *'We never like to say NO!. For example, if a guest asks for some Camembert cheese and we don't have it in stock, we will make sure that someone goes to the supermarket and tries to get it. If, in spite of our best efforts, we can't get any we will negotiate an alternative solution with the guest. This has an important side-effect – it greatly helps us to maintain the motivation of our staff. We are constantly being asked to do the seemingly impossible – yet we do it, and our staff think it's great. We all like to be part of an organization which is capable of achieving the very difficult, if not the impossible.'* Flexibility in the hotel also means the ability to cope with the seasonal fluctuations in demand. They achieve this partly by using temporary part-time staff. In the back-office parts of the hotel this isn't a major problem. In the laundry, for example, it is relatively easy to put on an extra shift in busy periods by increasing staffing levels. However, this is more of a problem in the parts of the hotel that have direct contact with the customer. *'New temporary staff can't be expected to have the same customer contact skills as our more regular staff. Our solution to this is to keep the temporary staff as far in the background as we possibly can and make sure that our skilled, well-trained staff are the ones who usually interact with the customer. So, for example, a waiter who would normally take orders, service the food, and take away the dirty plates would in peak times restrict his or her activities to taking orders and serving the food. The less skilled part of the job, taking away the plates, could be left to temporary staff.'*

As far as cost is concerned, around 60 per cent of the hotel's total operating expenses go on food and beverages, so one obvious way of keeping costs down is by making sure that food is not wasted. Energy costs, at 6 per cent of total operating costs, are also a potential source of saving. However, although cost savings are welcome, the hotel is very careful never to compromise the quality of its service in order to cut costs. *'It is impeccable customer service which gives us our competitive advantage, not price. Good service means that our guests return again and again. At times, around half our guests are people who have been before. The more guests we have, the higher is our utilization of rooms and restaurants, and this is what really keeps cost per guest down and profitability reasonable. So in the end we've come full circle: it's the quality of our service which keeps our volumes high and our costs low.'*

Questions

1 Describe how you think the hotel's management will:
  - **(a)** Make sure that the way it manages the hotel is appropriate to the way it competes for business;
  - **(b)** Implement any change in strategy;
  - **(c)** Develop its operation so that it drives the long-term strategy of the hotel.

2 The case describes how quality, speed, dependability, flexibility and cost impact on the hotel's external customers. Explain how each of these performance objectives might have internal benefits.

Problems and applications

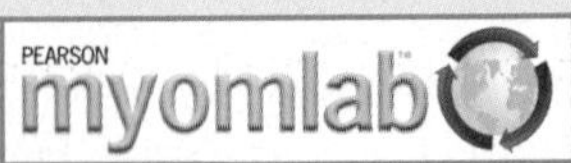

These problems and applications will help to improve your analysis of operations. You can find more practice problems as well as worked examples and guided solutions on MyOMLab at ***www.myomlab.com****.*

The 'forensic science' service of a European country has traditionally been organized to provide separate forensic science laboratories for each police force around the country. In order to save costs, the government has decided to centralize this service in one large central facility close to the country's capital. What do you think are the external advantages and disadvantages of this to the stakeholders of the operation? What do you think are the internal implications to the new centralized operation that will provide this service?

2 A publishing company plans to replace its four proofreaders who look for errors in manuscripts with a new scanning machine and one proofreader in case the machine breaks down. Currently the proofreaders check 15 manuscripts every week between them. Each is paid €80,000 per year. Hiring the new scanning machine will cost €5,000 each calendar month. How will this new system affect the proofreading department's productivity?

3 Bongo's Pizzas has a service guarantee that promises you will not pay for your pizza if it is delivered more than 30 minutes from the order being placed. An investigation shows that 10 per cent of all pizzas are delivered between 15 and 20 minutes from order, 40 per cent between 20 and 25 minutes from order, 40 per cent between 25 and 30 minutes from order, 5 per cent between 30 and 35 minutes from order, 3 per cent between 35 and 40 minutes from order, and 2 per cent over 40 minutes from order. If the average profit on each pizza delivered on time is €1 and the average cost of each pizza delivered is €5, is the fact that Bongo's does not charge for 10 per cent of its pizzas a significant problem for the business? How much extra profit per pizza would be made if 5 minutes was cut from all deliveries?

4 *Step 1.* Look again at the figures in the chapter which illustrate the meaning of each performance objective for the four operations. Consider the bus company and the supermarket, and in particular consider their external customers.

Step 2. Draw the relative required performance for both operations on a polar diagram.

Step 3. Consider the internal effects of each performance objective. For both operations, identify how quality, speed, dependability and flexibility can help to reduce the cost of producing their services.

5 Visit the web sites of two or three large oil companies such as Exxon, Shell, Elf, etc. Examine how they describe their policies towards their customers, suppliers, shareholders, employees and society at large. Identify areas of the company's operations where there may be conflicts between the needs of these different stakeholder groups. Discuss or reflect on how (if at all) such companies try and reconcile these conflicts.

Selected further reading

Bourne, M., Kennerley, M. and Franco, M. (2005) Managing through measures: a study of the impact on performance, *Journal of Manufacturing Technology Management*, vol. 16, issue 4, 373–95. What it says on the tin.

Kaplan, R.S. and Norton, D.P. (2005) The Balanced Scorecard: measures that drive performance, *Harvard Business Review*, Jul/Aug. The latest pronouncements on the Balanced Scorecard approach (which we cover in Chapter 18).

Neely, A. (ed.) (2002) *Business Performance Measurement: Theory and Practice*, Cambridge University Press, Cambridge. A collection of papers on the details of measuring performance objectives.

Pine, B.J. (1993) *Mass Customization*, Harvard Business School Press, Boston. The first substantial work on the idea of mass customization. Still a classic.

Waddock, S. (2003) Stakeholder performance implications of corporate responsibility, *International Journal of Business Performance Management*, vol. 5, numbers 2–3, 114–24. An introduction to stakeholder analysis.

Useful web sites

www.aom.pac.edu/bps/ General strategy site of the American Academy of Management.

www.cranfield,ac.uk/som Look for the 'Best factory awards' link. Manufacturing, but interesting.

www.opsman.org Lots of useful stuff.

www.worldbank.org Global issues. Useful for international operations strategy research.

www.weforum.org Global issues, including some operations strategy ones.

www.ft.com Great for industry and company examples.

Now that you have finished reading this chapter, why not visit MyOMLab at ***www.myomlab.com*** *where you'll find more learning resources to help you make the most of your studies and get a better grade?*

Chapter 3

Operations strategy

Key questions

- What is strategy and what is operations strategy?
- What is the difference between a 'top-down' and a 'bottom-up' view of operations strategy?
- What is the difference between a 'market requirements' and an 'operations resources' view of operations strategy?
- How can an operations strategy be put together?

Introduction

No organization can plan in detail every aspect of its current or future actions, but all organizations need some strategic direction and so can benefit from some idea of where they are heading and how they could get there. Once the operations function has understood its role in the business and after it has articulated its performance objectives, it needs to formulate a set of general principles which will guide its decision-making. This is the operations strategy of the company. Yet the concept of 'strategy' itself is not straightforward; neither is operations strategy. This chapter considers four perspectives, each of which goes partway to illustrating the forces that shape operations strategy. Figure 3.1 shows the position of the ideas described in this chapter in the general model of operations management.

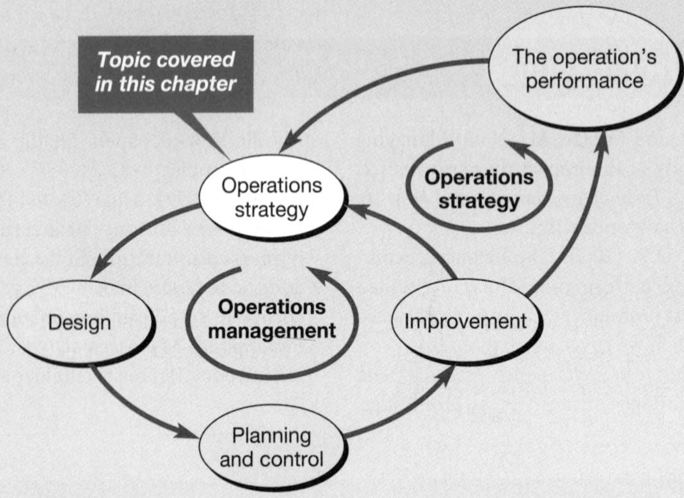

Figure 3.1 This chapter examines operations strategy

Check and improve your understanding of this chapter using self assessment questions and a personalised study plan, audio and video downloads, and an eBook – all at ***www.myomlab.com****.*

Operations in practice Two operations strategies: Flextronics and Ryanair[1]

The two most important attributes of any operations strategy are first that it aligns operations activities with the strategy of the whole organization, and second that it gives clear guidance. Here are two examples of very different businesses and very different strategies which nonetheless meet both criteria.

Source: Corbis

Ryanair is today Europe's largest low-cost airline (LCAs) and whatever else can be said about its strategy, it does not suffer from any lack of clarity. It has grown by offering low-cost basic services and has devised an operations strategy which is in line with its market position. The efficiency of the airline's operations supports its low-cost market position. Turnaround time at airports is kept to a minimum. This is achieved partly because there are no meals to be loaded onto the aircraft and partly through improved employee productivity. All the aircraft in the fleet are identical, giving savings through standardization of parts, maintenance and servicing. It also means large orders to a single aircraft supplier and therefore the opportunity to negotiate prices down. Also, because the company often uses secondary airports landing and service fees are much lower. Finally, the cost of selling its services is reduced where possible.

Ryanair has developed its own low-cost Internet booking service. In addition, the day-to-day experiences of the company's operations managers can also modify and refine these strategic decisions. For example, Ryanair changed its baggage handling contractors at Stansted airport in the UK after problems with misdirecting customers' luggage. The company's policy on customer service is also clear. *'We patterned Ryanair after Southwest Airlines, the most consistently profitable airline in the US'*, says Michael O'Leary, Ryanair's Chief Executive. *'Southwest founder Herb Kelleher created a formula for success that works by flying only one type of airplane – the 737, using smaller airports, providing no-frills service on-board, selling tickets directly to customers and offering passengers the lowest fares in the market. We have adapted his model for our marketplace and are now setting the low-fare standard for Europe. Our customer service'*, says O'Leary, *'is about the most well defined in the world. We guarantee to give you the lowest air fare. You get a safe flight. You get a normally on-time flight. That's the package. We don't, and won't, give you anything more. Are we going to say sorry for our lack of customer service? Absolutely not. If a plane is cancelled, will we put you up in a hotel overnight? Absolutely not. If a plane is delayed, will we give you a voucher for a restaurant? Absolutely not.'*

Flextronics is a global company based in Singapore that lies behind such well-known brand names as Nokia and Dell, which are increasingly using electronic manufacturing services (EMS) companies, such as Flextronics, which specialize in providing the outsourced design, engineering, manufacturing and logistics operations for the big brand names. It is amongst the biggest of those EMS suppliers that offer the broadest worldwide capabilities, from design to end-to-end vertically integrated global supply chain services. Flextronics' operations strategy must balance their customers' need for low costs (electronic goods are often sold in a fiercely competitive market) with their need for responsive and flexible service (electronics markets can also be volatile). The company achieves this in number of ways. First, it has an extensive network of design, manufacturing and logistics facilities in the world's major electronics markets, giving them significant scale and the flexibility to move activities to the most appropriate location to serve customers. Second, Flextronics offers vertical integration capabilities that simplify global product

Source: Corbis

development and supply processes, moving a product from its initial design through volume production, test, distribution, and into post-sales service, responsively and efficiently. Finally, Flextronics has developed integrated industrial parks to exploit fully the advantages of their global, large-scale, high-volume capabilities. Positioned in low-cost regions, yet close to all major world markets, Flextronics industrial parks can significantly reduce the cost of production. Locations include Gdansk in Poland, Hungary, Guadalajara in Mexico, Sorocaba in Brazil, Chennai in India and Shanghai in China. Flextronics own suppliers are encouraged to locate within these parks, from which products can be produced on-site and shipped directly from the industrial park to customers, greatly reducing freight costs of incoming components and outgoing products. Products not produced on-site can be obtained from Flextronics' network of regional manufacturing facilities located near the industrial parks. Using this strategy, Flextronics says it can provide cost-effective delivery of finished products within 1–2 days of orders.

What is strategy and what is operations strategy?

Surprisingly, 'strategy' is not particularly easy to define. Linguistically the word derives from the Greek word '*strategos*' meaning 'leading an army'. And although there is no direct historical link between Greek military practice and modern ideas of strategy, the military metaphor is powerful. Both military and business strategy can be described in similar ways, and include some of the following.

- Setting broad objectives that direct an enterprise towards its overall goal.
- Planning the path (in general rather than specific terms) that will achieve these goals.
- Stressing long-term rather than short-term objectives.
- Dealing with the total picture rather than stressing individual activities.
- Being detached from, and above, the confusion and distractions of day-to-day activities.

Strategic decisions

Here, by '**strategic decisions**' we mean those decisions which are widespread in their effect on the organization to which the strategy refers, define the position of the organization relative to its environment, and move the organization closer to its long-term goals. But 'strategy' is more than a single decision; it is the *total pattern of the decisions* and actions that influence the long-term direction of the business. Thinking about strategy in this way helps us to discuss an organization's strategy even when it has not been explicitly stated. Observing the total pattern of decisions gives an indication of the *actual* strategic behaviour.

Operations strategy

'Operations' is not the same as 'operational'

The content and process of operations strategy

Operations strategy concerns the pattern of strategic decisions and actions which set the role, objectives and activities of the operation. The term 'operations strategy' sounds at first like a contradiction. How can 'operations', a subject that is generally concerned with the day-to-day creation and delivery of goods and services, be strategic? 'Strategy' is usually regarded as the opposite of those day-to-day routine activities. But **'*operations*' is not the same as '*operational*'**. 'Operations' are the resources that create products and services. 'Operational' is the opposite of strategic, meaning day-to-day and detailed. So, one can examine both the operational ***and*** the strategic aspects of operations. It is also conventional to distinguish between the **'content' and the 'process'** of operations strategy. The *content* of operations strategy is the specific decisions and actions which set the operations role, objectives and activities. The *process* of operations strategy is the method that is used to make the specific 'content' decisions.

From implementing to supporting to driving strategy

Most businesses expect their operations strategy to improve operations performance over time. In doing this they should be progressing from a state where they are contributing very little to the competitive success of the business through to the point where they are directly responsible for its competitive success. This means that they should be able to, in turn, master the skills to first 'implement', then 'support', and then 'drive' operations strategy.

Implement strategy

Implementing business strategy. The most basic role of operations is to **implement strategy**. Most companies will have some kind of strategy but it is the operation that puts it into practice. You cannot, after all, touch a strategy; you cannot even see it; all you can see is how the operation behaves in practice. For example, if an insurance company has a strategy of moving to an entirely online service, its operations function will have to supervise the design of all the processes which allow customers to access online information, issue quotations, request further information, check credit details, send out documentation and so on. Without effective implementation even the most original and brilliant strategy will be rendered totally ineffective.

Support strategy

Supporting business strategy. **Support strategy** goes beyond simply implementing strategy. It means developing the capabilities which allow the organization to improve and refine its strategic goals. For example, a mobile phone manufacturer wants to be the first in the market with new product innovations so its operations need to be capable of coping with constant innovation. It must develop processes flexible enough to make novel components, organize its staff to understand the new technologies, develop relationships with its suppliers which help them respond quickly when supplying new parts, and so on. The better the operation is at doing these things, the more support it is giving to the company's strategy.

Drive strategy

Driving business strategy. The third, and most difficult, role of operations is to **drive strategy** by giving it a unique and long-term advantage. For example, a specialist food service company supplies restaurants with frozen fish and fish products. Over the years it has built up close relationships with its customers (chefs) as well as its suppliers around the world (fishing companies and fish farms). In addition it has its own small factory which develops and produces a continual stream of exciting new products. The company has a unique position in the industry because its exceptional customer relationships, supplier relationship and new product development are extremely difficult for competitors to imitate. In fact, the whole company's success is based largely on these unique operations capabilities. The operation drives the company's strategy.

Hayes and Wheelwright's four stages of operations contribution

The four-stage model of operations contribution

The ability of any operation to play these roles within the organization can be judged by considering the organizational aims or aspirations of the operations function. Professors Hayes and Wheelwright of Harvard University,[2] developed a **four-stage model** which can be used to evaluate the role and contribution of the operations function. The model traces the progression of the operations function from what is the largely negative role of stage 1 operations to its becoming the central element of competitive strategy in excellent stage 4 operations. Figure 3.2 illustrates the four stages.

Stage 1: Internal neutrality. This is the very poorest level of contribution by the operations function. It is holding the company back from competing effectively. It is inward-looking and, at best, reactive with very little positive to contribute towards competitive success. Paradoxically, its goal is 'to be ignored' (or 'internally neutral'). At least then it isn't holding the company back in any way. It attempts to improve by 'avoiding making mistakes'.

Stage 2: External neutrality. The first step of breaking out of stage 1 is for the operations function to begin comparing itself with similar companies or organizations in the outside market (being 'externally neutral'). This may not immediately take it to the 'first division' of companies in the market, but at least it is measuring itself against its competitors' performance and trying to implement 'best practice'.

Stage 3: Internally supportive. Stage 3 operations are amongst the best in their market. Yet, stage 3 operations still aspire to be clearly and unambiguously the very best in the market.

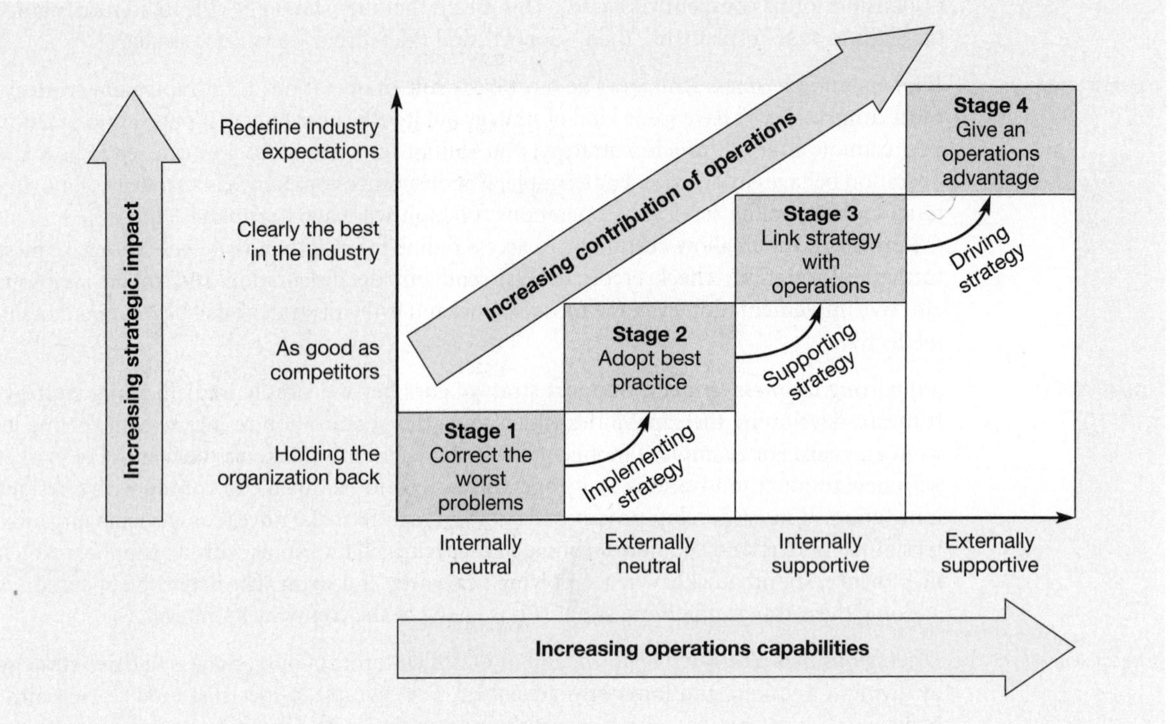

Figure 3.2 The four-stage model of operations contribution

They achieve this by gaining a clear view of the company's competitive or strategic goals and supporting it by developing appropriate operations resources. The operation is trying to be 'internally supportive' by providing a credible operations strategy.

Stage 4: Externally supportive. Yet Hayes and Wheelwright suggest a further stage – stage 4, where the company views the operations function as providing the foundation for its competitive success. Operations looks to the long term. It forecasts likely changes in markets and supply, and it develops the operations-based capabilities which will be required to compete in future market conditions. Stage 4 operations are innovative, creative and proactive and are driving the company's strategy by being 'one step ahead' of competitors – what Hayes and Wheelwright call 'being externally supportive'.

Critical commentary

The idea that operations can have a leading role in determining a company's strategic direction is not universally supported. Both Hayes and Wheelwright's stage 4 of their four-stage model and the concept of operations 'driving' strategy do not only imply that it is possible for operations to take such a leading role, but are explicit in seeing it as a 'good thing'. A more traditional stance taken by some authorities is that the needs of the market will always be pre-eminent in shaping a company's strategy. Therefore, operations should devote all their time to understanding the requirements of the market (as defined by the marketing function within the organization) and devote themselves to their main job of ensuring that operations processes can actually deliver what the market requires. Companies can only be successful, they argue, by positioning themselves in the market (through a combination of price, promotion, product design and managing how products and services are delivered to customers) with operations very much in a 'supporting' role. In effect, they say, Hayes and Wheelwright's four-stage model should stop at stage 3. The issue of an 'operations resource' perspective on operations strategy is discussed later in the chapter.

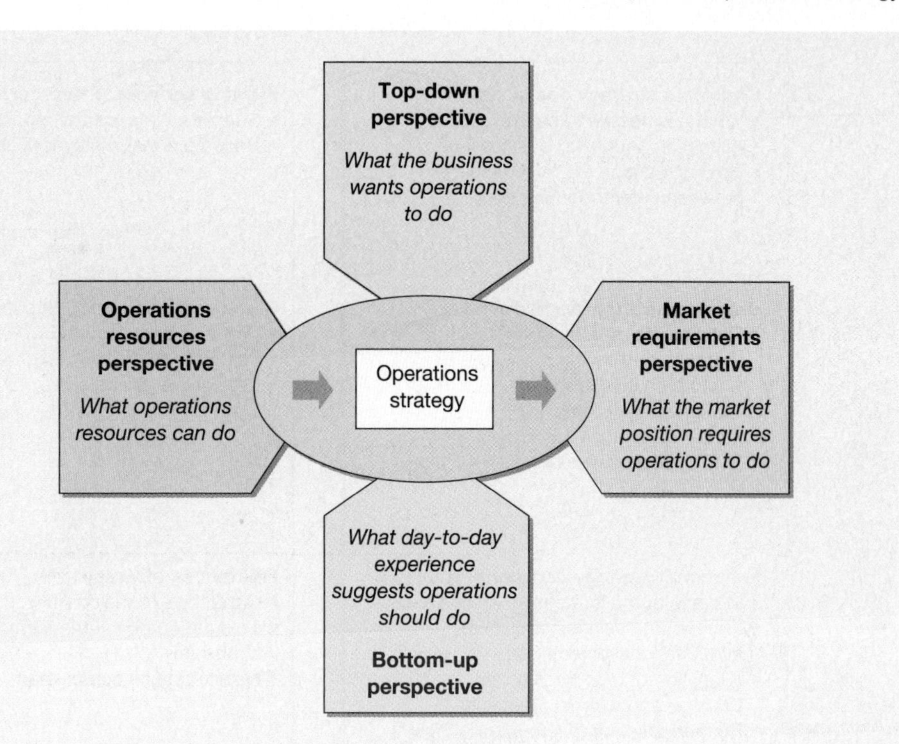

Figure 3.3 The four perspectives on operations strategy

Perspectives on operations strategy

Different authors have slightly different views and definitions of operations strategy. Between them, four 'perspectives' emerge:[3]

Top-down

Bottom-up

Market requirements

Operations resource capabilities

- Operation strategy is a **top-down** reflection of what the whole group or business wants to do.
- Operations strategy is a **bottom-up** activity where operations improvements cumulatively build strategy.
- Operations strategy involves translating **market requirements** into operations decisions.
- Operations strategy involves exploiting the **capabilities of operations resources** in chosen markets.

None of these four perspectives alone gives the full picture of what operations strategy is. But together they provide some idea of the pressures which go to form the content of operations strategy. We will treat each in turn (*see* Figure 3.3).

The 'top-down' and 'bottom-up' perspectives

Top-down strategies

Corporate strategy

Business strategy

A large corporation will need a strategy to position itself in its global, economic, political and social environment. This will consist of decisions about what types of business the group wants to be in, what parts of the world it wants to operate in, how to allocate its cash between its various businesses, and so on. Decisions such as these form the **corporate strategy** of the corporation. Each business unit within the corporate group will also need to put together its own business strategy which sets out its individual mission and objectives. This **business strategy** guides the business in relation to its customers, markets and competitors, and also the

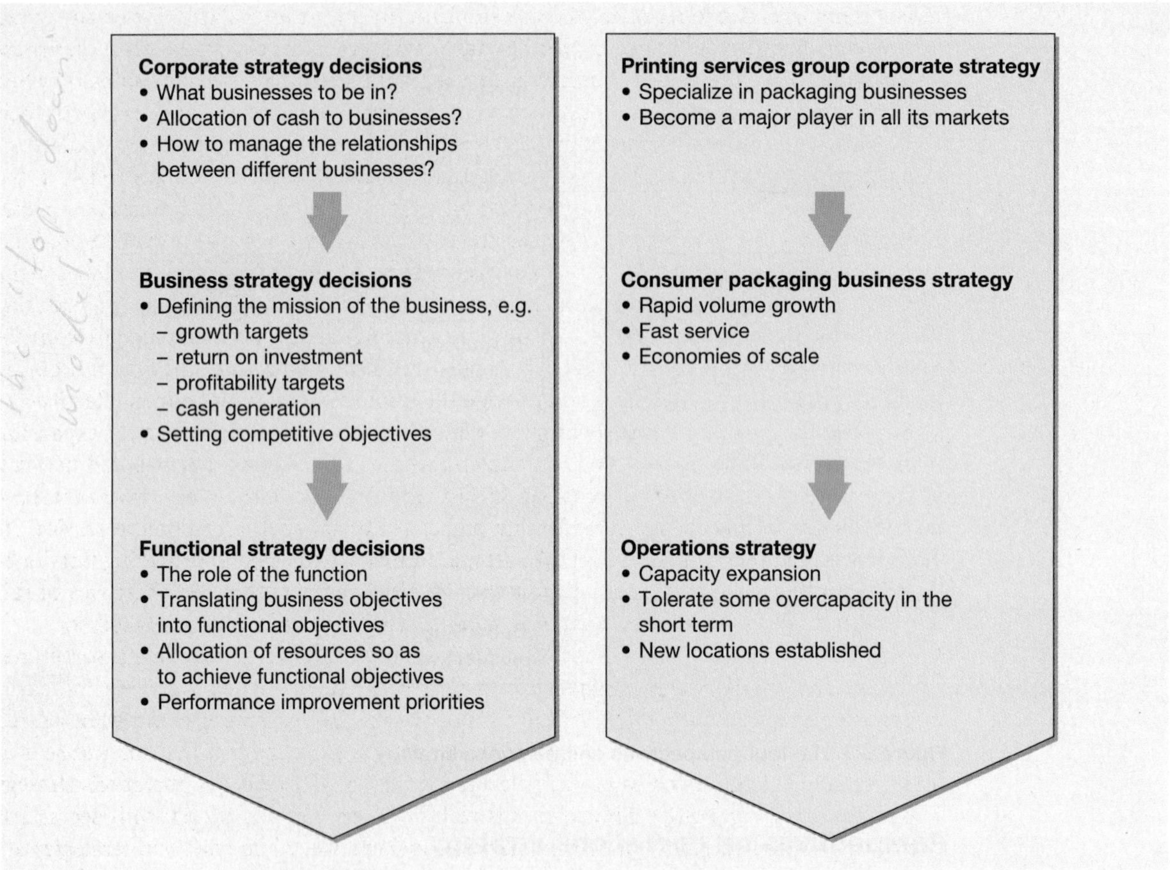

Corporate strategy decisions	Printing services group corporate strategy
• What businesses to be in? • Allocation of cash to businesses? • How to manage the relationships between different businesses?	• Specialize in packaging businesses • Become a major player in all its markets
Business strategy decisions	**Consumer packaging business strategy**
• Defining the mission of the business, e.g. – growth targets – return on investment – profitability targets – cash generation • Setting competitive objectives	• Rapid volume growth • Fast service • Economies of scale
Functional strategy decisions	**Operations strategy**
• The role of the function • Translating business objectives into functional objectives • Allocation of resources so as to achieve functional objectives • Performance improvement priorities	• Capacity expansion • Tolerate some overcapacity in the short term • New locations established

Figure 3.4 The top-down perspective of operations strategy and its application to the printing services group

Functional strategy

strategy of the corporate group of which it is a part. Similarly, within the business, **functional strategies** need to consider what part each function should play in contributing to the strategic objectives of the business. The operations, marketing, product/service development and other functions will all need to consider how best they should organize themselves to support the business's objectives.

So, one perspective on operations strategy is that it should take its place in this hierarchy of strategies. Its main influence, therefore, will be whatever the business sees as its strategic direction. For example, a printing services group has a company which prints packaging for consumer products. The group's management figures that, in the long term, only companies with significant market share will achieve substantial profitability. Its corporate objectives therefore stress market dominance. The consumer packaging company decides to achieve volume growth, even above short-term profitability or return on investment. The implication for operations strategy is that it needs to expand rapidly, investing in extra capacity (factories, equipment and labour) even if it means some excess capacity in some areas. It also needs to establish new factories in all parts of its market to offer relatively fast delivery. The important point here is that different business objectives would probably result in a very different operations strategy. The role of operations is therefore largely one of implementing or 'operationalizing' business strategy. Figure 3.4 illustrates this strategic hierarchy, with some of the decisions at each level and the main influences on the strategic decisions.

'Bottom-up' strategies

The 'top-down' perspective provides an orthodox view of how functional strategies *should* be put together. But in fact the relationship between the levels in the strategy hierarchy is more complex than this. Although it is a convenient way of thinking about strategy, this hierarchical model is not intended to represent the way strategies are always formulated. When any group is reviewing its corporate strategy, it will also take into account the circumstances, experiences and capabilities of the various businesses that form the group. Similarly, businesses, when reviewing their strategies, will consult the individual functions within the business about their constraints and capabilities. They may also incorporate the ideas which come from each function's day-to-day experience. Therefore an alternative view to the top-down perspective is that many strategic ideas emerge over time from operational experience. Sometimes companies move in a particular strategic direction because the ongoing experience of providing products and services to customers at an operational level convinces them that it is the right thing to do. There may be no high-level decisions examining alternative strategic options and choosing the one which provides the best way forward. Instead, a general consensus emerges from the operational level of the organization. The 'high-level' strategic decision-making, if it occurs at all, may confirm the consensus and provide the resources to make it happen effectively.

Suppose the printing services company described previously succeeds in its expansion plans. However, in doing so it finds that having surplus capacity and a distributed network of factories allows it to offer an exceptionally fast service to customers. It also finds that some customers are willing to pay considerably higher prices for such a responsive service. Its experiences lead the company to set up a separate division dedicated to providing fast, high-margin printing services to those customers willing to pay. The strategic objectives of this new division are not concerned with high-volume growth but with high profitability.

Emergent strategies

This idea of strategy being shaped by operational level experience over time is sometimes called the concept of **emergent strategies**.[4] Strategy is gradually shaped over time and based on real-life experience rather than theoretical positioning. Indeed, strategies are often formed in a relatively unstructured and fragmented manner to reflect the fact that the future is at least partially unknown and unpredictable (*see* Figure 3.5). This view of operations strategy is perhaps more descriptive of how things really happen, but at first glance it seems less useful in providing a guide for specific decision-making. Yet while emergent strategies are less easy to categorize, the principle governing a bottom-up perspective is clear: shape the operation's objectives and action, at least partly, by the knowledge it gains from its day-to-day activities. The key virtues required for shaping strategy from the bottom up are an ability to learn from experience and a philosophy of continual and incremental improvement.

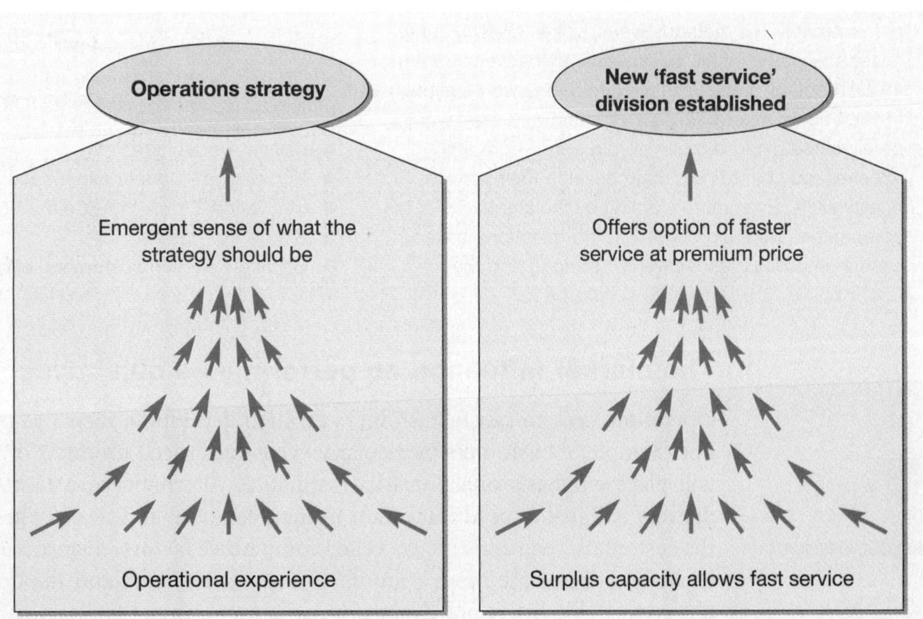

Figure 3.5 The 'bottom-up' perspective of operations strategy and its application to the printing services company

The market requirements and operations resources perspectives

Market-requirements-based strategies

One of the obvious objectives for any organization is to satisfy the requirements of its markets. No operation that continually fails to serve its markets adequately is likely to survive in the long term. And although understanding markets is usually thought of as the domain of the marketing function, it is also of importance to operations management. Without an understanding of what markets require, it is impossible to ensure that operations is achieving the right priority between its performance objectives (quality, speed, dependability, flexibility and cost). For example, the short case Giordano describes a company that designed its operations to fit what it saw as a market that was starting to prioritize quality of service.

Short case
Giordano

Source: Alamy Images

With a vision that explicitly states its ambition to be *'the best and the biggest world brand in apparel retailing'*, Giordano is setting its sights high. Yet it is the company that changed the rules of clothes retailing in the fast-growing markets around Hong Kong, China, Malaysia and Singapore, so industry experts take its ambitions seriously. Before Giordano, up-market shops sold high-quality products and gave good service. Cheaper clothes were piled high and sold by sales assistants more concerned with taking the cash than smiling at customers. Jimmy Lai, founder and Chief Executive of Giordano Holdings, changed all that. He saw that unpredictable quality and low levels of service offered an opportunity in the casual clothes market. Why could not value and service, together with low prices, generate better profits? His methods were radical. Overnight he raised the wages of his salespeople by between 30 and 40 per cent, all employees were told they would receive at least 60 hours of training a year and new staff would be allocated a 'big brother' or 'big sister' from among experienced staff to help them develop their service quality skills. Even more startling by the standards of his competitors, Mr Lai brought in a 'no-questions-asked' exchange policy irrespective of how long ago the garment had been purchased. Staff were trained to talk to customers and seek their opinion on products and the type of service they would like. This information would be immediately fed back to the company's designers for incorporation into their new products. How Giordano achieved the highest sales per square metre of almost any retailer in the region and its founding operations principles are summarized in its 'QKISS' list.

- Quality – do things right.
- Knowledge – update experience and share knowledge.
- Innovation – think 'outside the box'.
- Simplicity – less is more.
- Service – exceed customers' expectations.

The market influence on performance objectives

Operations seek to satisfy customers through developing their five performance objectives. For example, if customers particularly value low-priced products or services, the operation will place emphasis on its cost performance. Alternatively, a customer emphasis on fast delivery will make speed important to the operation, and so on. These factors which define the customers' requirements are called **competitive factors.**[5] Figure 3.6 shows the relationship between some of the more common competitive factors and the operation's performance objectives. This list is not exhaustive; whatever competitive factors are important to customers should influence the priority of each performance objective. Some organizations put considerable effort into bringing an idea of their customers' needs into the operation.

Competitive factors

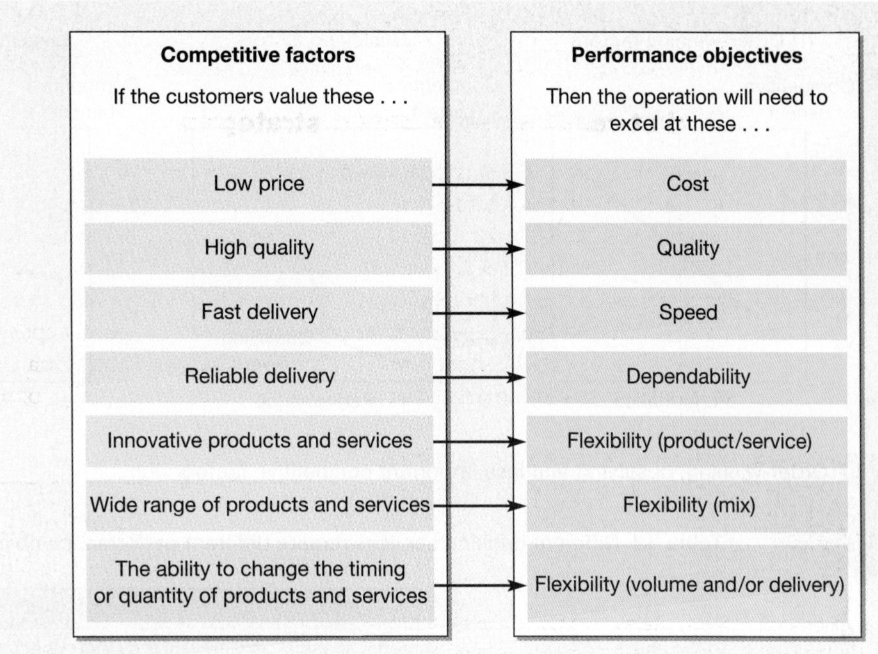

Figure 3.6 Different competitive factors imply different performance objectives

Order-winning and qualifying objectives

Order-winning factors

Qualifying factors

Less important factors

A particularly useful way of determining the relative importance of competitive factors is to distinguish between 'order-winning' and 'qualifying' factors.[6] **Order-winning factors** are those things which directly and significantly contribute to winning business. They are regarded by customers as key reasons for purchasing the product or service. Raising performance in an order-winning factor will either result in more business or improve the chances of gaining more business. **Qualifying factors** may not be the major competitive determinants of success, but are important in another way. They are those aspects of competitiveness where the operation's performance has to be above a particular level just to be considered by the customer. Performance below this 'qualifying' level of performance will possibly disqualify the company from being considered by many customers. But any further improvement above the qualifying level is unlikely to gain the company much competitive benefit. To order-winning and qualifying factors can be added **less important factors** which are neither order-winning nor qualifying. They do not influence customers in any significant way. They are worth mentioning here only because they may be of importance in other parts of the operation's activities.

Figure 3.7 shows the difference between order-winning, qualifying and less important factors in terms of their utility or worth to the competitiveness of the organization. The curves illustrate the relative amount of competitiveness (or attractiveness to customers) as the operation's performance at the factor varies. Order-winning factors show a steady and significant increase in their contribution to competitiveness as the operation gets better at providing them. Qualifying factors are 'givens'; they are expected by customers and can severely disadvantage the competitive position of the operation if it cannot raise its performance above the qualifying level. Less important objectives have little impact on customers no matter how well the operation performs in them.

Different customer needs imply different objectives

If, as is likely, an operation produces goods or services for more than one customer group, it will need to determine the order-winning, qualifying and less important competitive factors for each group. For example, Table 3.1 shows two 'product' groups in the banking industry.

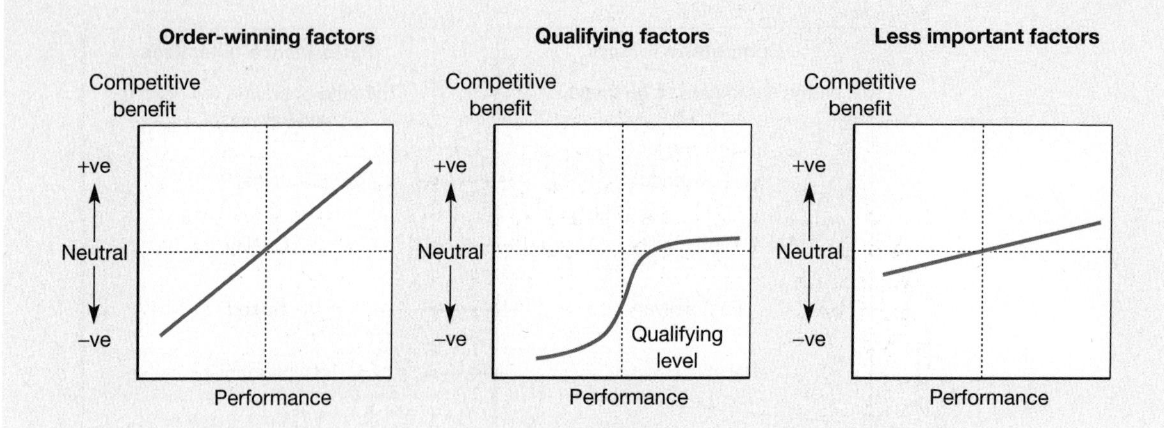

Figure 3.7 Order-winning, qualifying and less important competitive factors

Table 3.1 Different banking services require different performance objectives

	Retail banking	*Corporate banking*
Products	Personal financial services such as loans and credit cards	Special services for corporate customers
Customers	Individuals	Businesses
Product range	Medium but standardized, little need for special terms	Very wide range, many need to be customized
Design changes	Occasional	Continual
Delivery	Fast decisions	Dependable service
Quality	Means error-free transactions	Means close relationships
Volume per service type	Most services are high-volume	Most services are low-volume
Profit margins	Most are low to medium, some high	Medium to high
Competitive factors		
Order winners	Price Accessibility Speed	Customization Quality of service Reliability
Qualifiers	Quality Range	Speed Price
Less important		Accessibility
Internal performance objectives	Cost Speed Quality	Flexibility Quality Dependability

Here the distinction is drawn between the customers who are looking for banking services for their private and domestic needs (current accounts, overdraft facilities, savings accounts, mortgage loans, etc.) and those corporate customers who need banking services for their (often large) organizations. These latter services would include such things as letters of credit, cash transfer services and commercial loans.

Worked example

'It is about four years now since we specialized in the small-to-medium firms market. Before that we also used to provide legal services for anyone who walked in the door. So now we have built up our legal skills in many areas of corporate and business law. However, within the firm, I think we could focus our activities even more. There seem to be two types of assignment that we are given. About forty per cent of our work is relatively routine. Typically these assignments are to do with things like property purchase and debt collection. Both these activities involve a relatively standard set of steps which can be automated or carried out by staff without full legal qualifications. Of course, a fully qualified lawyer is needed to make some decisions; however, most work is fairly routine. Customers expect us to be relatively inexpensive and fast in delivering the service. Nor do they expect us to make simple errors in our documentation, in fact if we did this too often we would lose business. Fortunately our customers know that they are buying a standard service and don't expect it to be customized in any way. The problem here is that specialist agencies have been emerging over the last few years and they are starting to undercut us on price. Yet I still feel that we can operate profitably in this market and anyway, we still need these capabilities to serve our other clients. The other sixty per cent of our work is for clients who require far more specialist services, such as assignments involving company merger deals or major company restructuring. These assignments are complex, large, take longer, and require significant legal skill and judgement. It is vital that clients respect and trust the advice we give them across a wide range of legal specialisms. Of course they assume that we will not be slow or unreliable in preparing advice, but mainly it's trust in our legal judgement which is important to the client. This is popular work with our lawyers. It is both interesting and very profitable. But should I create two separate parts to our business, one to deal with routine services and the other to deal with specialist services? And, what aspects of operations performance should each part be aiming to excel at?' (Managing Partner, Branton Legal Services)

Analysis

Table 3.2 has used the information supplied above to identify the order winners, qualifiers and less important competitive factors for the two categories of service. As the Managing Partner suspects, the two types of service are very different. Routine services must be relatively inexpensive and fast, whereas the clients for specialist services must trust the quality of advice and range of legal skills available in the firm. The customers for routine services do not expect errors and those for specialist services assume a basic level of dependability and speed. These are the qualifiers for the two categories of service. Note that qualifiers are not 'unimportant'. On the contrary, failure to be 'up to standard' at them can lose the firm business. However, it is the order winner that attracts new business. Most significantly, the performance objectives which each operations partner should stress are very different. Therefore there does seem to be a case for separating the sets of resources (e.g. lawyers and other staff) and processes (information systems and procedures) that produce each type of service.

Table 3.2 Competitive factors and performance objectives for the legal firm

Service category	*Routine services*	*Specialist services*
Examples	Property purchase Debt collection	Company merger deals Company restructuring
Order winner	Price Speed	Quality of service Range of skills
Qualifiers	Quality (conformance)	Dependability Speed
Less important	Customization	Price
Operations partners should stress	Cost Speed Quality	Quality of relationship Legal skills Flexibility

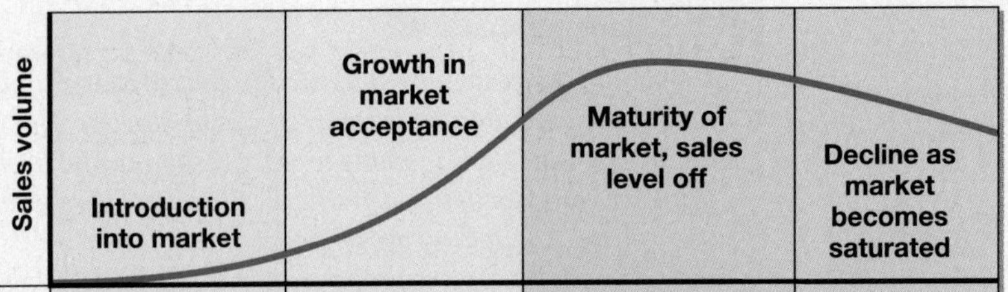

Sales volume	Introduction into market	Growth in market acceptance	Maturity of market, sales level off	Decline as market becomes saturated
Customers	Innovators	Early adopters	Bulk of market	Laggards
Competitors	Few/none	Increasing numbers	Stable number	Declining number
Likely order winners	Product/service specification	Availability	Low price Dependable supply	Low price
Likely qualifiers	Quality Range	Price Range	Range Quality	Dependable supply
Dominant operations performance objectives	Flexibility Quality	Speed Dependability Quality	Cost Dependability	Cost

Figure 3.8 The effects of the product/service life cycle on operations performance objectives

The product/service life cycle influence on performance objectives

Product/service life cycles

One way of generalizing the behaviour of both customers and competitors is to link it to the life cycle of the products or services that the operation is producing. The exact form of **product/service life cycles** will vary, but generally they are shown as the sales volume passing through four stages – introduction, growth, maturity and decline. The important implication of this for operations management is that products and services will require operations strategies in each stage of their life cycle (*see* Figure 3.8).

Introduction stage. When a product or service is first introduced, it is likely to be offering something new in terms of its design or performance, with few competitors offering the same product or service. The needs of customers are unlikely to be well understood, so the operations management needs to develop the flexibility to cope with any changes and be able to give the quality to maintain product/service performance.

Growth stage. As volume grows, competitors may enter the growing market. Keeping up with demand could prove to be the main operations preoccupation. Rapid and dependable response to demand will help to keep demand buoyant, while quality levels must ensure that the company keeps its share of the market as competition starts to increase.

Maturity stage. Demand starts to level off. Some early competitors may have left the market and the industry will probably be dominated by a few larger companies. So operations will be expected to get the costs down in order to maintain profits or to allow price cutting, or both. Because of this, cost and productivity issues, together with dependable supply, are likely to be the operation's main concerns.

Decline stage. After time, sales will decline with more competitors dropping out of the market. There might be a residual market, but unless a shortage of capacity develops the market will continue to be dominated by price competition. Operations objectives continue to be dominated by cost.

The operations resources perspective

Resource-based view

The fourth and final perspective we shall take on operations strategy is based on a particularly influential theory of business strategy – the **resource-based view** (RBV) of the firm.[7] Put simply, the RBV holds that firms with an 'above-average' strategic performance are likely to have gained their sustainable competitive advantage because of the core competences (or capabilities) of their resources. This means that the way an organization inherits, or acquires, or develops its operations resources will, over the long term, have a significant impact on its strategic success. Furthermore, the impact of its 'operations resource' capabilities will be at least as great as, if not greater than, that which it gets from its market position. So understanding and developing the capabilities of operations resources, although often neglected, is a particularly important perspective on operations strategy.

Resource constraints and capabilities

No organization can merely choose which part of the market it wants to be in without considering its ability to produce products and services in a way that will satisfy that market. In other words, the constraints imposed by its operations must be taken into account. For example, a small translation company offers general translation services to a wide range of customers who wish documents such as sales brochures to be translated into another language. A small company, it operates an informal network of part-time translators who enable the company to offer translation into or from most of the major languages in the world. Some of the company's largest customers want to purchase their sales brochures on a 'one-stop shop' basis and have asked the translation company whether it is willing to offer a full service, organizing the design and production, as well as the translation, of export brochures. This is a very profitable market opportunity; however, the company does not have the resources, financial or physical, to take it up. From a market perspective, it is good business; but from an operations resource perspective, it is not feasible.

However, the operations resource perspective is not always so negative. This perspective may identify *constraints* to satisfying some markets but it can also identify *capabilities* which can be exploited in other markets. For example, the same translation company has recently employed two new translators who are particularly skilled at web site development. To exploit this, the company decides to offer a new service whereby customers can transfer documents to the company electronically, which can then be translated quickly. This new service is a 'fast response' service which has been designed specifically to exploit the capabilities within the operations resources. Here the company has chosen to be driven by its resource capabilities rather than the obvious market opportunities.

Intangible resources

An operations resource perspective must start with an understanding of the resource capabilities and constraints within the operation. It must answer the simple questions, what do we have, and what can we do? An obvious starting point here is to examine the transforming and transformed resource inputs to the operation. These, after all, are the 'building blocks' of the operation. However, merely listing the type of *resources* an operation has does not give a complete picture of what it can do. Trying to understand an operation by listing its resources alone is like trying to understand an automobile by listing its component parts. To describe it more fully, we need to describe how the component parts form the internal mechanisms of the motor car. Within the operation, the equivalent of these mechanisms is its *processes*. Yet, even for an automobile, a technical explanation of its mechanisms still does not convey everything about its style or 'personality'. Something more is needed to describe these. In the same way, an operation is not just the sum of its processes. In addition, the operation has some **intangible resources**. An operation's intangible resources include such things as its relationship with suppliers, the reputation it has with its customers, its knowledge of its process technologies and the way its staff can work together in new product and service development. These intangible resources may not always be obvious within the

Intangible resources

Short case
Amazon, what exactly is your core competence?[8]

Source: Alamy Images

The founder and boss of Amazon, Jeff Bezos, was at a conference speaking about the company's plans. Although Amazon was generally seen as an Internet book retailer and then a more general Internet retailer, Jeff Bezos was actually pushing three of Amazon's 'utility computing' services. These were: a company that provides cheap access to online computer storage, a company that allows program developers to rent computing capacity on Amazon systems, and a service that connects firms with other firms that perform specialist tasks that are difficult to automate. The problem with online retailing, said Bezos, is its seasonality. At peak times, such as Christmas, Amazon has far more computing capacity than it needs for the rest of the year. At low points it may be using as little as 10 per cent of its total capacity. Hiring out that spare capacity is an obvious way to bring in extra revenue. In addition, Amazon had developed a search engine, a video download business, a service (Fulfilment By Amazon) that allowed other companies to use Amazon's logistics capability including the handling of returned items, and a service that provided access to Amazon's 'back-end' technology.

Amazon's apparent redefinition of its strategy was immediately criticized by some observers. 'Why not', they said, 'stick to what you know, focus on your core competence of Internet retailing?' Bezos's response was clear. 'We *are* sticking to our core competence; this is what we've been doing for the last 11 years. The only thing that's changed is that we are exposing it for [the benefit of] others.' At least for Jeff Bezos, Amazon is not so much an Internet retailer as a provider of Internet-based technology and logistics services.

operation, but they are important and have real value. It is these intangible resources, as well as its tangible resources, that an operation needs to deploy in order to satisfy its markets. The central issue for operations management, therefore, is to ensure that its pattern of strategic decisions really does develop appropriate capabilities within its resources and processes.

Structural and infrastructural decisions

Structure
Infrastructure

A distinction is often drawn between the strategic decisions which determine an operation's **structure** and those which determine its **infrastructure**. An operation's structural decisions are those which we have classed as primarily influencing design activities, while infrastructural decisions are those which influence the workforce organization and the planning and control, and improvement activities. This distinction in operations strategy has been compared to that between 'hardware' and 'software' in computer systems. The hardware of a computer sets limits to what it can do. In a similar way, investing in advanced technology and building more or better facilities can raise the potential of any type of operation. Within the limits which are imposed by the hardware of a computer, the software governs how effective the computer actually is in practice. The most powerful computer can only work to its full potential if its software is capable of exploiting its potential. The same principle applies with operations. The best and most costly facilities and technology will only be effective if the operation also has an appropriate infrastructure which governs the way it will work on a day-to-day basis. Table 3.3 illustrates both structural and infrastructural decision areas, arranged to correspond approximately to the chapter headings used in this book. The table also shows some typical questions which each strategic decision area should be addressing.

Table 3.3 Structural and infrastructural strategic decision areas

Structural strategic decisions	*Typical questions which the strategy should help to answer*
New product/service design	How should the operation decide which products or services to develop and how to manage the development process?
Supply network design	Should the operation expand by acquiring its suppliers or its customers? If so, what customers and suppliers should it acquire? How should it develop the capabilities of its customers and suppliers? What capacity should each operation in the network have? What number of geographically separate sites should the operation have and where should they be located? What activities and capacity should be allocated to each plant?
Process technology	What types of process technology should the operation be using? Should it be at the leading edge of technology or wait until the technology is established?
Infrastructural strategic decisions	*Typical questions which the strategy should help to answer*
Job design and organization	What role should the people who staff the operation play in its management? How should responsibility for the activities of the operations function be allocated between different groups in the operation? What skills should be developed in the staff of the operation?
Planning and control	How should the operation forecast and monitor the demand for its products and services? How should the operation adjust its activity levels in response to demand fluctuations? What systems should the operation use to plan and control its activities? How should the operation decide the resources to be allocated to its various activities?
Inventory	How should the operation decide how much inventory to have and where it is to be located? How should the operation control the size and composition of its inventories?
Supplier development	How should the operation choose its suppliers? How should it develop its relationship with its suppliers? How should it monitor its suppliers' performance?
Improvement	How should the operation's performance be measured? How should the operation decide whether its performance is satisfactory? How should the operation ensure that its performance is reflected in its improvement priorities? Who should be involved in the improvement process? How fast should the operation expect improvement in performance to be? How should the improvement process be managed?
Failure prevention, risk and recovery	How should the operation maintain its resources so as to prevent failure? How should the operation plan to cope with a failure if one occurs?

The process of operations strategy

The process of strategy formulation is concerned with 'how' operations strategies are put together. It is important because, although strategies will vary from organization to organization, they are usually trying to achieve some kind of alignment, or 'fit', between what the market wants, and what the operation can deliver, and how that 'alignment' can be sustained over time. So the process of operations strategy should both satisfy market requirements through appropriate operations resources, *and also* develop those resources in the long term so that they can provide competitive capabilities in the longer term that are sufficiently powerful to achieve sustainable competitive advantage.

There are many 'formulation processes' which are, or can be, used to formulate operations strategies. Most consultancy companies have developed their own frameworks, as have several academics. Typically, these formulation processes include the following elements:

- A process which formally links the total organization strategic objectives (usually a business strategy) to resource-level objectives.
- The use of competitive factors (called various things such as order winners, critical success factors, etc.) as the translation device between business strategy and operations strategy.
- A step which involves judging the relative importance of the various competitive factors in terms of customers' preferences.
- A step which includes assessing current achieved performance, usually as compared against competitor performance levels.
- An emphasis on operations strategy formulation as an iterative process.
- The concept of an 'ideal' or 'greenfield' operation against which to compare current operations. Very often the question asked is: 'If you were starting from scratch on a greenfield site, how, ideally, would you design your operation to meet the needs of the market?' This can then be used to identify the differences between current operations and this ideal state.
- A 'gap-based' approach. This is a well-tried approach in all strategy formulation which involves comparing what is required of the operation by the marketplace against the levels of performance the operation is currently achieving.

What should the formulation process be trying to achieve?

So what should any operations strategy be trying to achieve? Clearly, it should provide a set of actions that, with hindsight, have provided the 'best' outcome for the organization. But that really does not help us. What do we mean by 'the best', and what good is a judgement that can only be applied in hindsight? Yet, even if we cannot assess the 'goodness' of a strategy for certain in advance, we can check it out for some attributes that could stop it being a success. First, is the operations strategy comprehensive? Second, is there is internal coherence between the various actions it is proposing? Third, do the actions being proposed as part of the operations strategy correspond to the appropriate priority for each performance objective? Fourth, does the strategy prioritize the most critical activities or decisions?

Comprehensive

The notion of 'comprehensiveness' is a critical first step in seeking to achieve an effective operations strategy. Business history is littered with world-class companies that simply failed to notice the potential impact of, for instance, new process technology or emerging changes in their supply network. Also, many strategies have failed because operations have paid undue attention to only one key decision area.

Coherence

As a comprehensive strategy evolves over time, different tensions will emerge that threaten to pull the overall strategy in different directions. This can result in a loss of coherence. Coherence is when the choices made in each decision area do not pull the operation in different directions. For example, if new flexible technology is introduced which allows products or services to be customized to individual clients' needs, it would be 'incoherent' to devise an organization structure which did not enable the relevant staff to exploit the technology because it would limit the effective flexibility of the operation. For the investment in flexible technology to be effective, it must be accompanied by an organizational structure which deploys the organization's skills appropriately, a performance measurement system which acknowledges that flexibility must be promoted, a new product/service development policy which stresses appropriate types of customization, a supply network strategy which develops suppliers and customers to understand the needs of high-variety customization, a capacity strategy which deploys capacity where the customization is needed, and so on. In other words, all the decision areas complement and reinforce each other in the promotion of that particular performance objective.

Correspondence

Equally, an operation has to achieve a correspondence between the choices made against each of the decision areas and the relative priority attached to each of the performance objectives. In other words, the strategies pursued in each decision area should reflect the true priority of each performance objective. So, for example, if cost reduction is the main organizational objective for an operation, then its process technology investment decisions might err towards the purchase of 'off-the-shelf' equipment from a third-party supplier. This would reduce the capital cost of the technology and may also imply lower maintenance and running costs. Remember, however, that making such a decision will also have an impact on other performance objectives. An off-the-shelf piece of equipment may not, for example, have the flexibility that more 'made-to-order' equipment has. Also, the other decision areas must correspond with the same prioritization of objectives. If low cost is really important then one would expect to see capacity strategies which exploit natural economies of scale, supply network strategies which reduce purchasing costs, performance measurement systems which stress efficiency and productivity, continuous improvement strategies which emphasize continual cost reduction, and so on.

Criticality

In addition to the difficulties of ensuring coherence between decision areas, there is also a need to include financial and competitive priorities. Although all decisions are important and a comprehensive perspective should be maintained, in practical terms some resource or requirement intersections will be more critical than others. The judgement over exactly which intersections are particularly critical is very much a pragmatic one which must be based on the particular circumstances of an individual firm's operations strategy. It is therefore difficult to generalize as to the likelihood of any particular intersections being critical. However, in practice, one can ask revealing questions such as, 'If flexibility is important, of all the decisions we make in terms of our capacity, supply networks, process technology, or development and organization, which will have the most impact on flexibility?' This can be done for all performance objectives, with more emphasis being placed on those having the highest priority. Generally, when presented with a framework such as the operations strategy matrix, executives can identify those intersections which are particularly significant in achieving alignment.

Short case
Sometimes any plan is better than no plan[9]

There is a famous story that illustrates the importance of having some kind of plan, even if hindsight proves it to be the wrong plan. During manoeuvres in the Alps, a detachment of Hungarian soldiers got lost. The weather was severe and the snow was deep. In these freezing conditions, after two days of wandering, the soldiers gave up hope and became reconciled to a frozen death on the mountains. Then, to their delight, one of the soldiers discovered a map in his pocket. Much cheered by this discovery, the soldiers were able to escape from the mountains. When they were safe back at their headquarters, they discovered that the map was not of the Alps at all, but of the Pyrenees. The moral of the story? A plan (or a map) may not be perfect but it gives a sense of purpose and a sense of direction. If the soldiers had waited for the right map they would have frozen to death. Yet their renewed confidence motivated them to get up and create opportunities.

Implementation

A large number of authors, writing about all forms of strategy, have discussed the importance of effective implementation. This reflects an acceptance that no matter how sophisticated the intellectual and analytical underpinnings of a strategy, it remains only a document until it has been implemented. Ken Platts of Cambridge University has written about the nature of the operations strategy formulation process. His generic description of the **process** is referred to as the five Ps.

The five Ps of operations strategy formulation

1 *Purpose.* As with any form of project management, the more clarity that exists around the ultimate goal, the more likely it is that the goal will be achieved. In this context, a shared understanding of the motivation, boundaries and context for developing the operations strategy is crucial.
2 *Point of entry.* Linked with the above point, any analysis, formulation and implementation process is potentially politically sensitive and the support that the process has from within the hierarchy of the organization is central to the implementation success.
3 *Process.* Any formulation process must be explicit. It is important that the managers who are engaged in putting operations strategies together actively think about the process in which they are participating.
4 *Project management.* There is a cost associated with any strategy process. Indeed one of the reasons why operations have traditionally not had explicit strategies relates to the difficulty of releasing sufficient managerial time. The basic disciplines of project management such as resource and time planning, controls, communication mechanisms, reviews and so on, should be in place.
5 *Participation.* Intimately linked with the above points, the selection of staff to participate in the implementation process is also critical. So, for instance, the use of external consultants can provide additional specialist expertise, the use of line managers (and indeed staff) can provide 'real-world' experience and the inclusion of cross-functional managers (and suppliers etc.) can help to integrate the finished strategy.

Critical commentary

The argument has been put forward that strategy does not lend itself to a simple 'stage model' analysis that guides managers in a step-by-step manner through to the eventual 'answer' that is a final strategy. Therefore, the models put forward by consultants and academics are of very limited value. In reality, strategies (even those that are made deliberately, as opposed to those that simply 'emerge') are the result of very complex organizational forces. Even descriptive models such as the five Ps described above can do little more than sensitize managers to some of the key issues that they should be taking into account when devising strategies. In fact, it is argued that articulating the 'content' of operation strategy that is more useful than adhering to some over-simplistic description of a strategy process.

Summary answers to key questions

*Check and improve your understanding of this chapter using self assessment questions and a personalised study plan, audio and video downloads, and an eBook – all at **www.myomlab.com**.*

➤ What is strategy and what is operations strategy?

- Strategy is the total pattern of decisions and actions that position the organization in its environment and that are intended to achieve its long-term goals.
- Operations strategy concerns the pattern of strategic decisions and actions which set the role, objectives and activities of the operation.
- Operations strategy has content and process. The content concerns the specific decisions which are taken to achieve specific objectives. The process is the procedure which is used within a business to formulate its strategy.

➤ What is the difference between a 'top-down' and a 'bottom-up' view of operations strategy?

- The 'top-down' perspective views strategic decisions at a number of levels. Corporate strategy sets the objectives for the different businesses which make up a group of businesses. Business strategy sets the objectives for each individual business and how it positions itself in its marketplace. Functional strategies set the objectives for each function's contribution to its business strategy.
- The 'bottom-up' view of operations strategy sees overall strategy as emerging from day-to-day operational experience.

➤ What is the difference between a 'market requirements' and an 'operations resource' view of operations strategy?

- A 'market requirements' perspective of operations strategy sees the main role of operations as satisfying markets. Operations performance objectives and operations decisions should be primarily influenced by a combination of customers' needs and competitors' actions. Both of these may be summarized in terms of the product/service life cycle.
- The 'operations resource' perspective of operations strategy is based on the resource-based view (RBV) of the firm and sees the operation's core competences (or capabilities) as being the main influence on operations strategy. Operations capabilities are developed partly through the strategic decisions taken by the operation. Strategic decision areas in operations are usually divided into structural and infrastructural decisions. Structural decisions are those which define an operation's shape and form. Infrastructural decisions are those which influence the systems and procedures that determine how the operation will work in practice.

➤ How can an operations strategy be put together?

- There are many different procedures which are used by companies, consultancies and academics to formulate operations strategies. Although differing in the stages that they recommend, many of these models have similarities.
- Any operations strategy process should result in strategies that are comprehensive and coherent, provide correspondence, and prioritize the most critical activities or decisions.

Case study
Long Ridge Gliding Club[10]

Long Ridge Gliding Club is a not-for-profit organization run by its members. The large grass airfield is located on the crest of a ridge about 400 metres above sea level. It is an ideal place to practise ridge soaring and cross-country flying. The gliders are launched using a winch machine which can propel them from a standing start to around 110 kilometres per hour (70 mph), 300 metres above the airfield, in just five seconds. The club is housed in a set of old farm buildings with simple but comfortable facilities for members. A bar and basic catering services are provided by the club steward and inexpensive bunk-rooms are available for club members wishing to stay overnight.

The club has a current membership of nearly 150 pilots who range in ability from novice to expert. While some members have their own gliders, the club has a fleet of three single-seater and three twin-seater gliders available to its members. The club also offers trial flights to members of the public. (In order to provide insurance cover they actually sell a three-month membership with a 'free' flight at the start.) These 'casual flyers' can book flights in advance or just turn up and fly on a first-come, first-served basis. The club sells trial-flight gift vouchers which are popular as birthday and Christmas presents. The club's brochure and web site encourage people to:

> *'Experience the friendly atmosphere and excellent facilities and enjoy the thrill of soaring above Long Ridge's dramatic scenery. For just £70 you could soon be in the air. Phone now or just turn up and our knowledgeable staff will be happy to advise you. We have a team of professional instructors dedicated to make this a really memorable experience.'*

The average flight for a trial lesson is around 10 minutes. If the conditions are right the customer may be lucky and get a longer flight although at busy times the instructors may feel under pressure to return to the ground to give another lesson. Sometimes when the weather is poor, low cloud and wind in the wrong direction, almost not fit for flying at all, the instructors still do their best to get people airborne but they are restricted to a 'circuit': a takeoff, immediate circle and land. This only takes two minutes. Circuits are also used to help novice pilots practise landings and takeoffs. At the other end of the scale many of the club's experienced pilots can travel long distances and fly back to the airfield. The club's record for the longest flight is 755 kilometres, taking off from the club's airfield and landing back on the same airfield eight hours later, never having touched the ground. (They take sandwiches and drinks and a bottle they can use to relieve themselves!)

The club has three part-time employees: a club steward, an office administrator and a mechanic. In the summer months the club also employs a winch driver (for launching the gliders) and two qualified flying instructors. Throughout the whole year essential tasks such as maintaining the gliders, getting them out of the hangar and towing them to the launch point, staffing the winches, keeping the flying log, bringing back gliders, and providing look-out cover is undertaken on a voluntary basis by club members. It takes a minimum of five experienced people (club members) to be able to launch one glider. The club's membership includes ten qualified instructors who, together with the two paid summer instructors, provide instruction in two-seater gliders for the club's members and the casual flyers.

When club members come to fly they are expected to arrive by 9.30 am and be prepared to stay all day to help each other and any casual flyers get airborne while they wait their turn to fly. On a typical summer's day there might be ten club members requiring instruction plus four casual flyers and also six members with their own gliders who have to queue up with the others for a launch hoping for a single long-distance flight. In the winter months there would typically be six members, one casual flyer and six experienced pilots. Club members would hope to have three flights on a good day, with durations of between two and forty (average ten) minutes per flight depending on conditions. However, if the weather conditions change they may not get a flight. Last year there were 180 days when flying took place, 140 in the 'summer' season and 40 in the 'winter'. Club members are charged an £8.00 winch fee each time they take to the air. In addition, if they are using one of the club's gliders, they are charged 50p per minute that they are in the air.

Bookings for trial flights and general administration are dealt with by the club's administrator who is based in a cabin close to the car park and works most weekday mornings from 9.00 am to 1.00 pm. An answerphone takes messages at other times. The launch point is out of sight and 1.5 km from the cabin but a safe walking route is signposted. Club members can let themselves onto the airfield and drive to the launch point. At the launch point the casual flyers might have to stand and wait for some time until a club member has time to find out what they want. Even when a flight has been pre-booked casual flyers may then be kept waiting, on the exposed and often windy airfield, for up to two hours before their flight, depending on how many club members are present. Occasionally they will turn up for a pre-booked trial flight and will be turned away because either the weather is unsuitable or there are not enough club members to get a glider into the air. The casual flyers are encouraged to help out with the routine tasks but often seem reluctant to do so. After their flight they are left to find their own way back to their cars.

Income from the casual flyers is seen to be small compared to membership income and launch fees but the club's management committee views casual flying as a 'loss leader' to generate club memberships which are £350 per annum. The club used to generate a regular surplus of around £10,000 per year which is used to upgrade the gliders and other facilities. However, insurance costs have risen dramatically due to their crashing and severely damaging four gliders during the last two years. Two of the accidents resulted in the deaths of one member and one casual flyer and serious injuries to three other members.

The club's committee is under some pressure from members to end trial flights because they reduce the number of flights members can have in a day. Some members have complained that they sometimes spend most of their day working to get casual flyers into the air and miss out on flying themselves. Although they provide a useful source of income for the hard-pressed club (around 700 were sold in the previous year), only a handful have been converted into club memberships.

Questions

1 Evaluate the service to club members and casual flyers by completing a table similar to Table 3.1.

2 Chart the five performance objectives to show the differing expectations of club members and casual flyers and compare these with the actual service delivered.

3 What advice would you give to the chairman?

Problems and applications

These problems and applications will help to improve your analysis of operations. You can find more practice problems as well as worked examples and guided solutions on MyOMLab at ***www.myomlab.com****.*

1 Explain how the four perspectives of operations strategy would apply to Ryanair and Flextronics.

2 Compare the operations strategies of Ryanair and a full-service airline such as British Airways or KLM.

3 What do you think are the qualifying and order-winning factors for (a) a top of the range Ferrari, and (b) a Renault Clio?

4 What do you think are the qualifying or order-winning factors for IKEA described in Chapter 1?

5 Search the Internet site of Intel, the best-known microchip manufacturer, and identify what appear to be its main structural and infrastructural decisions in its operations strategy.

6 **(Advanced)** McDonald's has come to epitomize the 'fast-food' industry. When the company started in the 1950s it was the first to establish itself in the market. Now there are hundreds of 'fast-food' brands in the market competing in different ways. Some of the differences between these fast-food chains are obvious. For example, some specialize in chicken products, others in pizza, and so on. However, some differences are less obvious. Originally, McDonald's competed on low price, fast service and a totally standardized service offering. They also offered a very narrow range of items on their menu. Visit a McDonald's restaurant and deduce what you believe to be its most important performance objectives. Then try and identify two other chains which appear to compete in a slightly different way. Then try to identify how these differences in the relative importance of competitive objectives must influence the structural and infrastructural decisions of each chain's operations strategy.

Selected further reading

Boyer, K.K., Swink, M. and Rosenzweig, E.D. (2006) Operations strategy research in the POMS Journal, *Production and Operations Management*, vol. 14, issue 4. A survey of recent research in the area.

Hayes, R.H., Pisano, G.P., Upton, D.M. and Wheelwright, S.C. (2005) *Operations, Strategy, and Technology: Pursuing the Competitive Edge*, Wiley. The gospel according to the Harvard school of operations strategy. Articulate, interesting and informative.

Slack, N. and Lewis, M. (2008) *Operations Strategy*, 2nd edn, Financial Times Prentice Hall, Harlow. What can we say – just brilliant!

Useful web sites

www.aom.pac.edu/bps/ General strategy site of the American Academy of Management.

www.cranfield,ac.uk/som Look for the 'Best factory awards' link. Manufacturing, but interesting.

www.opsman.org Lots of useful stuff.

www.worldbank.org Global issues. Useful for international operations strategy research.

www.weforum.org Global issues, including some operations strategy ones.

www.ft.com Great for industry and company examples.

*Now that you have finished reading this chapter, why not visit MyOMLab at **www.myomlab.com** where you'll find more learning resources to help you make the most of your studies and get a better grade?*

Key operations questions

Chapter 4 **Process design**

- ➤ What is process design?
- ➤ What objectives should process design have?
- ➤ How do volume and variety affect process design?
- ➤ How are processes designed in detail?

Chapter 5 **The design of products and services**

- ➤ Why is good product and service design important?
- ➤ What are the stages in product and service design?
- ➤ Why should product and service design and process design be considered interactively?

Chapter 6 **Supply network design**

- ➤ Why should an organization take a total supply network perspective?
- ➤ What is involved in configuring a supply network?
- ➤ Where should an operation be located?
- ➤ How much capacity should an operation plan to have?

Chapter 7 **Layout and flow**

- ➤ What is layout?
- ➤ What are the basic layout types used in operations?
- ➤ What type of layout should an operation choose?
- ➤ What is layout design trying to achieve?
- ➤ How should each basic layout type be designed in detail?

Chapter 8 **Process technology**

- ➤ What is process technology?
- ➤ How does one gain an understanding of process technologies?
- ➤ How are process technologies evaluated?
- ➤ How are process technologies implemented?

Chapter 9 **People, jobs and organization**

- ➤ Why are people issues so important in operations management?
- ➤ How do operations managers contribute to human resource strategy?
- ➤ What forms can organization designs take?
- ➤ What is the role of recruitment and development?
- ➤ How do we go about designing jobs?
- ➤ How are work times allocated?

Part Two
DESIGN

All operations managers are designers, because design is the process of satisfying people's requirements through the shaping or configuring products, services, and processes. This part of the book looks at how managers can manage the design of the products and services they produce and the processes that produce them. At the most strategic level 'design' means shaping the network of operations that supply products and services. At a more operational level it means the arrangement of the processes, technology and people that constitute operations processes.

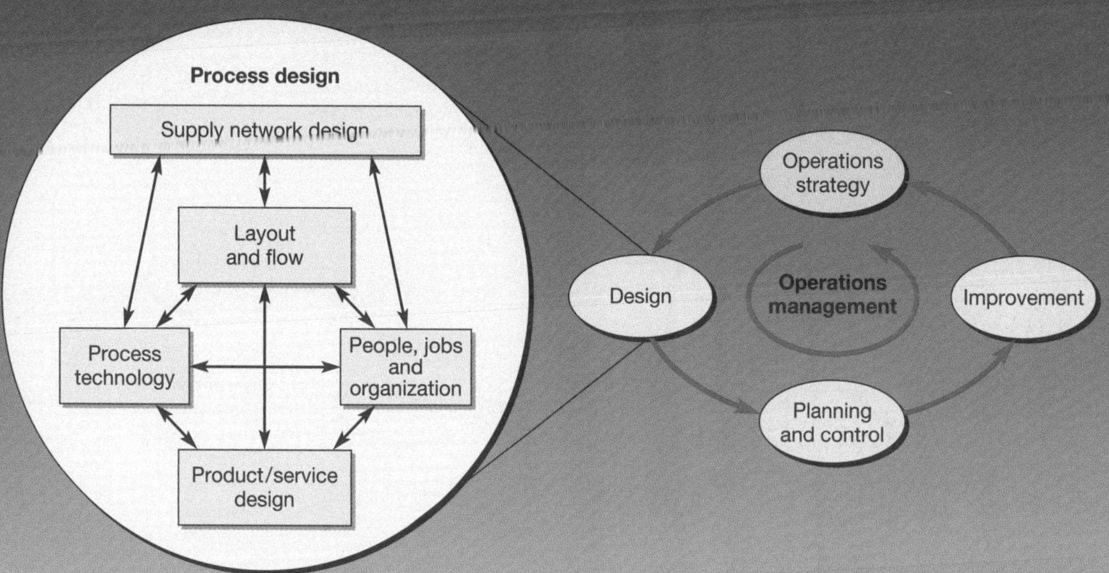

Chapter 4

Process design

Key questions

- ➤ What is process design?
- ➤ What objectives should process design have?
- ➤ How do volume and variety affect process design?
- ➤ How are processes designed in detail?

Introduction

Say you are a 'designer' and most people will assume that you are someone who is concerned with how a product looks. But the design activity is much broader than that and while there is no universally recognized definition of 'design', we take it to mean 'the process by which some functional requirement of people is satisfied through the shaping or configuration of the resources and/or activities that compose a product, or a service, or the transformation process that produces them'. All operations managers are designers. When they purchase or rearrange the position of a piece of equipment, or when they change the way of working within a process, it is a design decision because it affects the physical shape and nature of their processes. This chapter examines the design of processes. Figure 4.1 shows where this topic fits within the overall model of operations management.

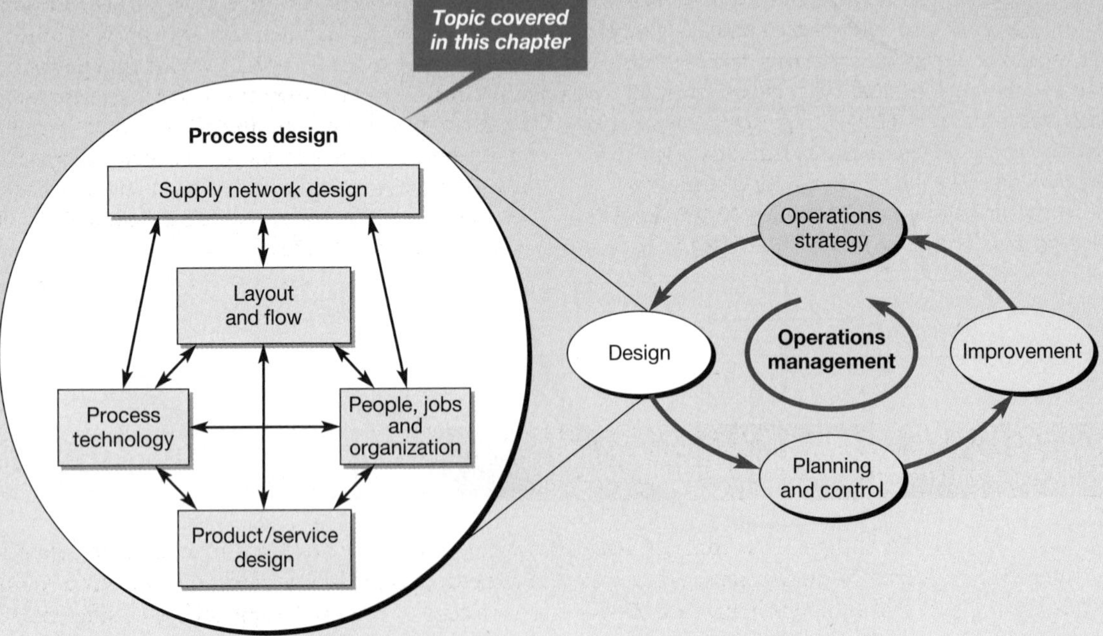

Figure 4.1 This chapter examines process design

*Check and improve your understanding of this chapter using self assessment questions and a personalised study plan, audio and video downloads, and an eBook – all at **www.myomlab.com**.*

Operations in practice Fast-food drive-throughs[1]

The quick-service restaurant (QSR) industry reckons that the very first drive-through dates back to 1928 when Royce Hailey first promoted the drive-through service at his Pig Stand restaurant in Los Angeles. Customers would simply drive by the back door of the restaurant where the chef would come out and deliver the restaurant's famous 'Barbequed Pig' sandwiches. Today, drive-through processes are slicker and faster. They are also more common. In 1975, McDonald's did not have any drive-throughs, but now more than 90 per cent of its US restaurants incorporate a drive-through process. In fact 80 per cent of recent fast-food growth has come through the growing number of drive-throughs. Says one industry specialist, *'There are a growing number of customers for whom fast-food is not fast enough. They want to cut waiting time to the very minimum without even getting out of their car. Meeting their needs depends on how smooth we can get the process.'*

The competition to design the fastest and most reliable drive-through process is fierce. Starbucks drive-throughs have strategically placed cameras at the order boards so that servers can recognize regular customers and start making their order even before it's placed. Burger King has experimented with sophisticated sound systems, simpler menu boards and see-through food bags to ensure greater accuracy (no point in being fast if you don't deliver what the customer ordered). These details matter. McDonald's reckon that their sales increase one per cent for every six seconds saved at a drive-through, while a single Burger King restaurant calculated that its takings increased by 15,000 dollars a year each time it reduced queuing time by one second.

Source: Getty Images

Menu items must be easy to read and understand. Designing 'combo meals' (burger, fries and a cola), for example, saves time at the ordering stage. Perhaps the most remarkable experiment in making drive-through process times slicker is being carried out by McDonald's in the USA. On California's central coast 150 miles from Los Angeles, a call centre takes orders remotely from 40 McDonald's outlets around the country. The orders are then sent back to the restaurants through the Internet and the food is assembled only a few metres from where the order was placed. It may only save a few seconds on each order, but that can add up to extra sales at busy times of the day. But not everyone is thrilled by the boom in drive-throughs. People living in the vicinity may complain of the extra traffic they attract and the unhealthy image of fast food combined with a process that does not even make customers get out of their car, is, for some, a step too far.

What is process design?

Design happens before creation

To 'design' is to conceive the looks, arrangement, and workings of something *before it is created*. In that sense it is a conceptual exercise. Yet it is one which must deliver a solution that will work in practice. Design is also an activity that can be approached at different levels of detail. One may envisage the general shape and intention of something before getting down to defining its details. This is certainly true for process design. At the start of the process design activity it is important to understand the design objectives, especially at first, when the overall shape and nature of the process is being decided. The most common way of doing this is by positioning it according to its volume and variety characteristics. Eventually the details of the process must be analysed to ensure that it fulfils its objectives effectively.

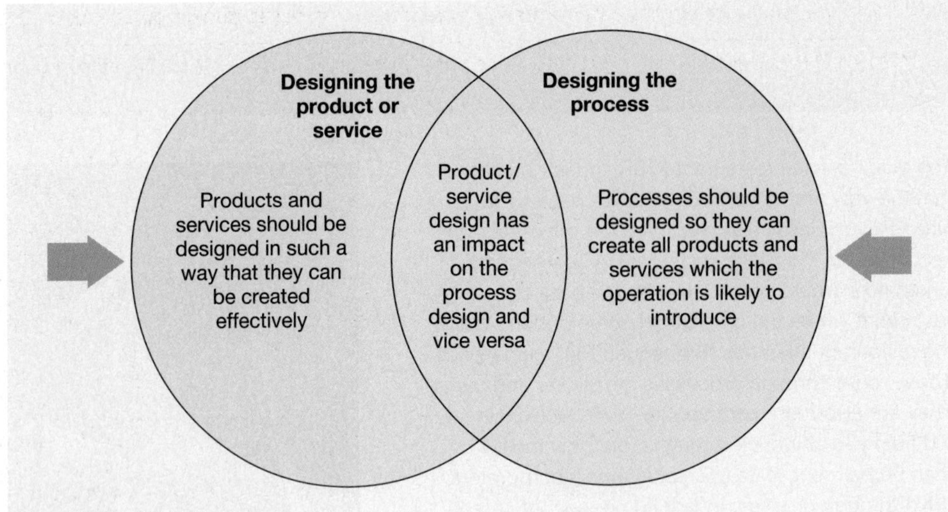

Figure 4.2 **The design of products/services and processes are interrelated and should be treated together**

Yet, it is often only through getting to grips with the detail of a design that the feasibility of its overall shape can be assessed. But don't think of this as a simple sequential process. There may be aspects concerned with the objectives or the broad positioning of the process that will need to be modified following its more detailed analysis.

Process design and product/service design are interrelated

Often we will treat the design of products and services, on the one hand, and the design of the processes which make them, on the other, as though they were separate activities. Yet they are clearly interrelated. It would be foolish to commit to the detailed design of any product or service without some consideration of how it is to be produced. Small changes in the design of products and services can have profound implications for the way the operation eventually has to produce them. Similarly, the design of a process can constrain the freedom of product and service designers to operate as they would wish (*see* Fig. 4.2). This holds good whether the operation is producing products or services. However, the overlap between the two design activities is generally greater in operations which produce **services**. Because many services involve the customer in being part of the transformation process, the service, as far as the customer sees it, cannot be separated from the process to which the customer is subjected. Overlapping product and process design has implications for the organization of the design activity, as will be discussed in Chapter 5. Certainly, when product designers also have to make or use the things which they design, it can concentrate their minds on what is important. For example, in the early days of flight, the engineers who designed the aircraft were also the test pilots who took them out on their first flight. For this reason, if no other, safety was a significant objective in the design activity.

Process design and product/service design should be considered together

What objectives should process design have?

The whole point of process design is to make sure that the performance of the process is appropriate for whatever it is trying to achieve. For example, if an operation competed primarily on its ability to respond quickly to customer requests, its processes would need to be designed to give fast throughput times. This would minimize the time between customers

Table 4.1 The impact of strategic performance objectives on process design objectives and performance

Operations performance objective	*Typical process design objectives*	*Some benefits of good process design*
Quality	• Provide appropriate resources, capable of achieving the specification of product of services • Error-free processing	• Products and services produced 'on-specification' • Less recycling and wasted effort within the process
Speed	• Minimum throughput time • Output rate appropriate for demand	• Short customer waiting time • Low in-process inventory
Dependability	• Provide dependable process resources • Reliable process output timing and volume	• On-time deliveries of products and services • Less disruption, confusion and rescheduling within the process
Flexibility	• Provide resources with an appropriate range of capabilities • Change easily between processing states (what, how, or how much is being processed)	• Ability to process a wide range of products and services • Low cost/fast product and service change • Low cost/fast volume and timing changes • Ability to cope with unexpected events (e.g. supply or a processing failure)
Cost	• Appropriate capacity to meet demand • Eliminate process waste in terms of – excess capacity – excess process capability – in-process delays – in-process errors – inappropriate process inputs	• Low processing costs • Low resource costs (capital costs) • Low delay and inventory costs (working capital costs)

requesting a product or service and their receiving it. Similarly, if an operation competed on low price, cost-related objectives are likely to dominate its process design. Some kind of logic should link what the operation as a whole is attempting to achieve and the **performance objectives** of its individual processes. This is illustrated in Table 4.1.

Process design should reflect process objectives

Operations performance objectives translate directly to process design objectives as shown in Table 4.1. But, because processes are managed at a very operational level, process design also needs to consider a more 'micro' and detailed set of objectives. These are largely concerned with flow through the process. When whatever are being 'processed' enter a process they will progress through a series of activities where they are 'transformed' in some way. Between these activities they may dwell for some time in inventories, waiting to be transformed by the next activity. This means that the time that a unit spends in the process (its throughput time) will be longer than the sum of all the transforming activities that it passes through. Also the resources that perform the processes activities may not be used all the time because not all units will necessarily require the same activities and the capacity of each resource may not match the demand placed upon it. So neither the units moving through the process, nor the resources performing the activities may be fully utilized. Because of this the way that units leave the process is unlikely to be exactly the same as the way they arrive at the process. It is common for more 'micro' performance flow objectives to be used that describe process flow performance. For example:

Throughput rate

- **Throughput rate** (or flow rate) is the rate at which units emerge from the process, i.e. the number of units passing through the process per unit of time.

Throughput time

- **Throughput time** is the average elapsed time taken for inputs to move through the process and become outputs.

Work in process

- The number of units in the process (also called the '**work in process**' or in-process inventory), as an average over a period of time.

Utilization

- The **utilization** of process resources is the proportion of available time that the resources within the process are performing useful work.

Environmentally sensitive design

With the issues of environmental protection becoming more important, both process and product/service designers have to take account of 'green' issues. In many developed countries, legislation has already provided some basic standards which restrict the use of toxic materials, limit discharges to air and water, and protect employees and the public from immediate and long-term harm. Interest has focused on some fundamental issues:

- *The sources of inputs* to a product or service. (Will they damage rainforests? Will they use up scarce minerals? Will they exploit the poor or use child labour?)
- *Quantities and sources of energy* consumed in the process. (Do plastic beverage bottles use more energy than glass ones? Should waste heat be recovered and used in fish farming?)
- *The amounts and type of waste material* that are created in the manufacturing processes. (Can this waste be recycled efficiently, or must it be burnt or buried in landfill sites? Will the waste have a long-term impact on the environment as it decomposes and escapes?)
- *The life of the product itself.* It is argued that if a product has a useful life of, say, twenty years, it will consume fewer resources than one that only lasts five years, which must therefore be replaced four times in the same period. However, the long-life product may require more initial inputs, and may prove to be inefficient in the latter part of its use, when the latest products use less energy or maintenance to run.
- *The end-of-life of the product.* (Will the redundant product be difficult to dispose of in an environmentally friendly way? Could it be recycled or used as a source of energy? Could it still be useful in third-world conditions? Could it be used to benefit the environment, such as old cars being used to make artificial reefs for sea life?)

Short case
Ecologically smart[2]

Source: Getty Images

When Daimler-Chrysler started to examine the feasibility of the Smart town car, the challenge was not just to examine the economic feasibility of the product but also to build in environmental sensitivity to the design of the product and the process that was to make it. This is why environmental protection is now a fundamental part of all production activities in its 'Smartville' plant at Hambach near France's border with Germany. The product itself is designed on environmentally compatible principles. Even before assembly starts, the product's disassembly must be considered. In fact the modular construction of the Smart car helped to guarantee economical dismantling at the end of its life. This also helps with the recycling of materials. Over 85 per cent of the Smart's components are recyclable and recycled material is used in its initial construction. For example, the Smart's instrument panel comprises 12 per cent recycled plastic material. Similarly, production processes are designed to be ecologically sustainable. The plant's environmentally friendly painting technique allows less paint to be used while maintaining a high quality of protection. It also involves no solvent emission and no hazardous waste, as well as the recycling of surplus material. But it is not only the use of new technology that contributes to the plant's ecological credentials. Ensuring a smooth and efficient movement of materials within the plant also saves time, effort and, above all, energy. So, traffic flow outside and through the building has been optimized, buildings are made accessible to suppliers delivering to the plant, and conveyor systems are designed to be loaded equally in both directions so as to avoid empty runs. The company even claims that the buildings themselves are a model for ecological compatibility. No construction materials contain formaldehyde or CFCs and the outside of the buildings are lined with 'TRESPA', a raw material made from European timber that is quick to regenerate.

Designers are faced with complex trade-offs between these factors, although it is not always easy to obtain all the information that is needed to make the 'best' choices. For example, it is relatively straightforward to design a long-life product, using strong material, over-designed components, ample corrosion protection, and so on. But its production might use more materials and energy and it could create more waste on disposal. To help make more rational decisions in the design activity, some industries are experimenting with ***life cycle analysis***. This technique analyses all the production inputs, the life-cycle use of the product and its final disposal, in terms of total energy used (and more recently, of all the emitted wastes such as carbon dioxide, sulphurous and nitrous gases, organic solvents, solid waste, etc.). The inputs and wastes are evaluated at *every* stage in its creation, beginning with the extraction or farming of the basic raw materials. The short case 'Ecologically smart' demonstrates that it is possible to include ecological considerations in all aspects of product and process design.

Life cycle analysis

Process types – the volume–variety effect on process design

In Chapter 1 we saw how processes in operations can range from producing a very high volume of products or services (for example, a food canning factory) to a very low volume (for example, major project consulting engineers). Also they can range from producing a very low variety of products or services (for example, in an electricity utility) to a very high variety (as, for example, in an architects' practice). Usually the two dimensions of volume and variety go together. Low-volume operations processes often have a high variety of products and services, and high-volume operations processes often have a narrow variety of products and services. Thus there is a continuum from low volume and high variety through to high volume and low variety, on which we can position operations. Different operations, even those in the same operation, may adopt different types of processes. Many manufacturing plants will have a large area, organized on a 'mass-production' basis, in which it makes its high-volume 'best-selling' products. In another part of the plant it may also have an area where it makes a wide variety of products in much smaller volumes. The design of each of these processes is likely to be different. Similarly, in a medical service, compare the approach taken during mass medical treatments, such as large-scale immunization programmes, with that taken for a transplant operation where the treatment is designed specifically to meet the needs of one person. These differences go well beyond their differing technologies or the processing requirements of their products or services. They are explained by the fact that no one type of process design is best for all types of operation in all circumstances. The differences are explained largely by the different **volume–variety positions** of the operations.

Volume–variety positions

Process types

The position of a process on the volume–variety continuum shapes its overall design and the general approach to managing its activities. These 'general approaches' to designing and managing processes are called **process types**. Different terms are sometimes used to identify process types depending on whether they are predominantly manufacturing or service processes, and there is some variation in the terms used. For example, it is not uncommon to find the 'manufacturing' terms used in service industries. Figure 4.3 illustrates how these 'process types' are used to describe different positions on the volume–variety spectrum.

Process types

Project processes

Project processes

Project processes are those which deal with discrete, usually highly customized products. Often the timescale of making the product or service is relatively long, as is the interval between the completion of each product or service. So low volume and high variety are characteristics of project processes. The activities involved in making the product can be ill-defined and uncertain, sometimes changing during the production process itself. Examples of project

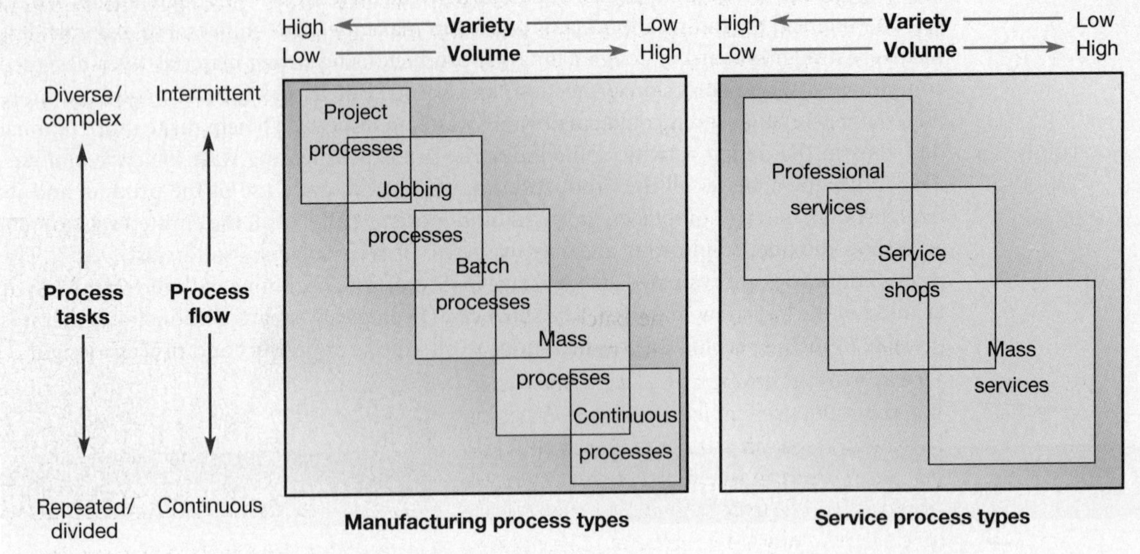

Figure 4.3 Different process types imply different volume–variety characteristics for the process

processes include shipbuilding, most construction companies, movie production companies, large fabrication operations such as those manufacturing turbo generators, and installing a computer system. The essence of project processes is that each job has a well-defined start and finish, the time interval between starting different jobs is relatively long and the transforming resources which make the product will probably have been organized especially for each product. The process map for project processes will almost certainly be complex, partly because each unit of output is so large with many activities occurring at the same time and partly because the activities in such processes often involve significant discretion to act according to professional judgement.

Source: Corbis

The major construction site shown in this picture is a project process. Each 'product' (project) is different and poses different challenges to those running the process (civil engineers).

Jobbing processes

Jobbing processes

Jobbing processes also deal with very high variety and low volumes. Whereas in project processes each product has resources devoted more or less exclusively to it, in jobbing processes each product has to share the operation's resources with many others. The resources of the operation will process a series of products but, although all the products will require the same kind of attention, each will differ in its exact needs. Examples of jobbing processes include many precision engineers such as specialist toolmakers, furniture restorers, bespoke tailors, and the printer who produces tickets for the local social event. Jobbing processes produce more

Source: Corbis

This craftsperson is using general purpose wood-cutting technology to make a product for an individual customer. The next product he makes will be different (although it may be similar), possibly for a different customer.

and usually smaller items than project processes but, like project processes, the degree of repetition is low. Many jobs will probably be 'one-offs'. Again, any process map for a jobbing process could be relatively complex for similar reasons to project processes. However, jobbing processes usually produce physically smaller products and, although sometimes involving considerable skill, such processes often involve fewer unpredictable circumstances.

Batch processes

Batch processes

Batch processes can often look like jobbing processes, but batch does not have quite the degree of variety associated with jobbing. As the name implies, each time batch processes produce a product they produce more than one. So each part of the operation has periods when it is repeating itself, at least while the 'batch' is being processed. The size of the batch could be just two or three, in which case the batch process would differ little from jobbing, especially if each batch is a totally novel product. Conversely, if the batches are large, and especially if the products are familiar to the operation, batch processes can be fairly repetitive. Because of this, the batch type of process can be found over a wide range of volume and variety levels. Examples of batch processes include machine tool manufacturing, the production of some special gourmet frozen foods, and the manufacture of most of the component parts which go into mass-produced assemblies such as automobiles.

Source: Getty Images

In this kitchen, food is being prepared in batches. All batches go through the same sequence (preparation, cooking, storing), but each batch is a different dish.

Mass processes

Mass processes

Mass processes are those which produce goods in high volume and relatively narrow variety – narrow, that is, in terms of the fundamentals of the product design. An automobile plant, for example, might produce several thousand variants of car if every option of engine size, colour, extra equipment, etc. is taken into account. Yet essentially it is a mass operation because the different variants of its product do not affect the basic process of production. The activities in the automobile plant, like all mass operations, are essentially repetitive and largely predictable. Examples of mass processes include the automobile plant, a television factory, most food processes and DVD production. Several variants of a product could be produced on a mass process such as an assembly line, but the process itself is unaffected. The equipment used at each stage of the process can be designed to handle several different types of components loaded into the assembly equipment. So, provided the sequence of components in the equipment is synchronized with the sequence of models moving through the process, the process seems to be almost totally repetitive.

Source: Rex Features

This automobile plant is everyone's' idea of a mass process. Each product is almost (but not quite) the same, and is made in large quantities.

Continuous processes

Continuous processes

Continuous processes are one step beyond mass processes insomuch as they operate at even higher volume and often have even lower variety. They also usually operate for longer periods of time. Sometimes they are literally continuous in that their products are inseparable, being produced in an endless flow. Continuous processes are often associated with relatively inflexible, capital-intensive technologies with highly predictable flow. Examples of continuous processes include petrochemical refineries, electricity utilities, steel making and some paper making. There are often few elements of discretion in this type of process and although products may be stored during the process, the predominant characteristic of most continuous processes is of smooth flow from one part of the process to another. Inspections are likely to form part of the process, although the control applied as a consequence of those inspections is often automatic rather than requiring human discretion.

Source: Alamy Images

This continuous water treatment process almost never stops (it only stops for maintenance) and performs a narrow range of tasks (filters impurities). Often we only notice the process if it goes wrong!

Professional services

Professional services

Professional services are defined as high-contact organizations where customers spend a considerable time in the service process. Such services provide high levels of customization, the service process being highly adaptable in order to meet individual customer needs. A great deal of staff time is spent in the front office and contact staff are given considerable discretion in servicing customers. Professional services tend to be people-based rather than equipment-based, with emphasis placed on the process (how the service is delivered) rather than the 'product' (what is delivered). Professional services include management consultants, lawyers' practices, architects, doctors' surgeries, auditors, health and safety inspectors and some computer field service operations. A typical example would be OEE, a consultancy that sells the problem-solving expertise of its skilled staff to tackle clients' problems. Typically, the problem will first be discussed with clients and the boundaries of the project defined. Each 'product' is different, and a high proportion of work takes place at the client's premises, with frequent contact between consultants and the client.

Here consultants are preparing to start a consultancy assignment. They are discussing how they might approach the various stages of the assignment, from understanding the real nature of the problem through to the implementation of their recommended solutions. This is a process map, although a very high level one. It guides the nature and sequence of the consultants' activities.

Service shops

Service shops

Service shops are characterized by levels of customer contact, customization, volumes of customers and staff discretion, which position them between the extremes of professional and mass services (see next paragraph). Service is provided via mixes of front- and back-office activities. Service shops include banks, high-street shops, holiday tour operators, car rental companies, schools, most restaurants, hotels and travel agents. For example, an equipment hire and sales organization may have a range of products displayed in front-office outlets, while back-office operations look after purchasing and administration. The front-office staff have

Source: Getty Images

The health club shown in the picture has front-office staff who can give advice on exercise programmes and other treatments. To maintain a dependable service the staff need to follow defined processes every day.

some technical training and can advise customers during the process of selling the product. Essentially the customer is buying a fairly standardized product but will be influenced by the process of the sale which is customized to the customer's individual needs.

Mass services

Mass services

Mass services have many customer transactions, involving limited contact time and little customization. Such services may be equipment-based and 'product'-oriented, with most value added in the back office and relatively little judgement applied by front-office staff. Staff are likely to have a closely defined division of labour and to follow set procedures. Mass services include supermarkets, a national rail network, an airport, telecommunications services, libraries, television stations, the police service and the enquiry desk at a utility. For example, rail services such as Virgin Trains in the UK or SNCF in France all move a large number of passengers with a variety of rolling stock on an immense infrastructure of railways. Passengers pick a journey from the range offered. One of the most common types of mass service is the call centres used by almost all companies that deal directly with consumers. Coping with a very high volume of enquiries requires some kind of structuring of the process of communicating with customers. This is often achieved by using a carefully designed enquiry process (sometimes known as a 'script').

Source: © Royal Bank of Scotland Group plc

This is an account management centre for a large retail bank. It deals with thousands of customer requests every day. Although each customer request is different, they are all of the same type – involving customers' accounts.

Critical commentary

Although the idea of process types is useful insomuch as it reinforces the, sometimes important, distinctions between different types of process, it is in many ways simplistic. In reality there is no clear boundary between process types. For example, many processed foods are manufactured using mass-production processes but in batches. So, a 'batch' of one type of cake (say) can be followed by a 'batch' of a marginally different cake (perhaps with different packaging), followed by yet another, etc. Essentially this is still a mass process, but not quite as pure a version of mass processing as a manufacturing process that only makes one type of cake. Similarly, the categories of service processes are likewise blurred. For example, a specialist camera retailer would normally be categorized as a service shop, yet it also will give, sometimes very specialized, technical advice to customers. It is not a professional service like a consultancy of course, but it does have elements of a professional service process within its design. This is why the volume and variety characteristics of a process are sometimes seen as being a more realistic way of describing processes. The product–process matrix described next adopts this approach.

The product–process matrix

Making comparisons between different processes along a spectrum which goes, for example, from shipbuilding at one extreme to electricity generation at the other has limited value. No one grumbles that yachts are so much more expensive than electricity. The real point is that because the different process types overlap, organizations often have a choice of what type of process to employ. This choice will have consequences to the operation, especially in terms of its cost and flexibility. The classic representation of how cost and flexibility vary with process choice is the **product–process matrix** that comes from Professors Hayes and Wheelwright of Harvard University.[3] They represent process choices on a matrix with the

Product–process matrix

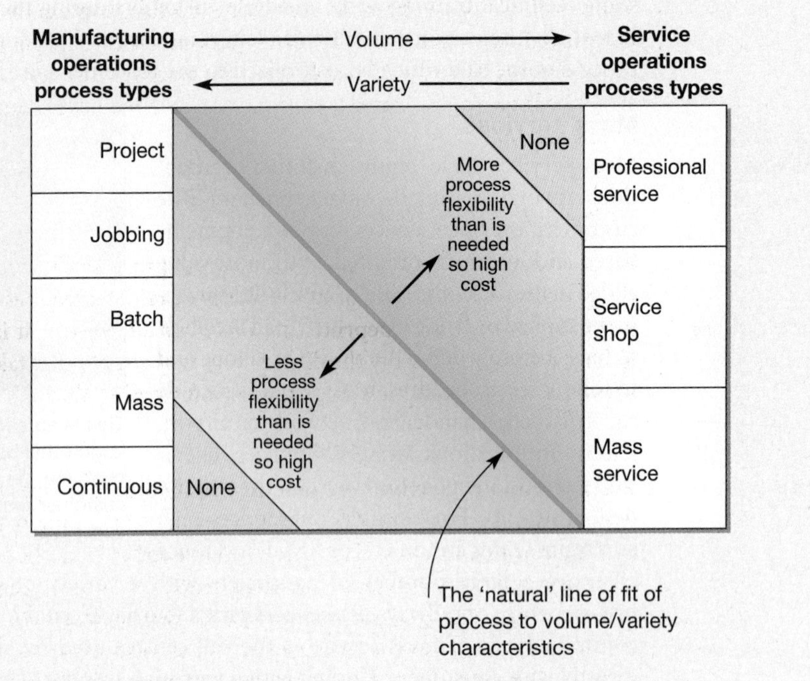

Figure 4.4 Deviating from the 'natural' diagonal on the product–process matrix has consequences for cost and flexibility

Source: Based on Hayes and Wheelwright[4]

The 'natural' diagonal

volume–variety as one dimension, and process types as the other. Figure 4.4 shows their matrix adapted to fit with the terminology used here. Most operations stick to **the 'natural' diagonal** of the matrix, and few, if any, are found in the extreme corners of the matrix. However, because there is some overlap between the various process types, operations might be positioned slightly off the diagonal.

The diagonal of the matrix shown in Figure 4.4 represents a 'natural' lowest cost position for an operation. Operations which are on the right of the 'natural' diagonal have processes which would normally be associated with lower volumes and higher variety. This means that their processes are likely to be more flexible than seems to be warranted by their actual volume–variety position. Put another way, they are not taking advantage of their ability to standardize their processes. Because of this, their costs are likely to be higher than they would be with a process that was closer to the diagonal. Conversely, operations that are on the left of the diagonal have adopted processes which would normally be used in a higher-volume and lower-variety situation. Their processes will therefore be 'over-standardized' and probably too inflexible for their volume–variety position. This lack of flexibility can also lead to high costs because the process will not be able to change from one activity to another as efficiently as a more flexible process.

Detailed process design

After the overall design of a process has been determined, its individual activities must be configured. At its simplest this detailed design of a process involves identifying all the individual activities that are needed to fulfil the objectives of the process and deciding on the sequence in which these activities are to be performed and who is going to do them.

There will, of course, be some constraints on this. Some activities must be carried out before others and some activities can only be done by certain people or machines. Nevertheless, for a process of any reasonable size, the number of alternative process designs is usually large. Because of this, process design is often done using some simple visual approach such as **process mapping**.

Process mapping

Process mapping

Process mapping simply involves describing processes in terms of how the activities within the process relate to each other. There are many techniques which can be used for *process mapping* (or **process blueprinting**, or **process analysis**, as it is sometimes called). However, all the techniques identify the different *types of* activity that take place during the process and show the flow of materials or people or information through the process.

Process blueprinting

Process analysis

Process mapping symbols

Process mapping symbols

Process mapping symbols are used to classify different types of activity. And although there is no universal set of symbols used all over the world for any type of process, there are some that are commonly used. Most of these derive either from the early days of 'scientific' management around a century ago (see Chapter 9) or, more recently, from information system flowcharting. Figure 4.5 shows the symbols we shall use here.

These symbols can be arranged in order, and in series or in parallel, to describe any process. For example, the retail catering operation of a large campus university has a number of outlets around the campus selling sandwiches. Most of these outlets sell 'standard' sandwiches that are made in the university's central kitchens and transported to each outlet every day. However, one of these outlets is different; it is a kiosk that makes more expensive 'customized' sandwiches to order. Customers can specify the type of bread they want and a very wide combination of different fillings. Because queues for this customized service are becoming excessive, the catering manager is considering redesigning the process to speed it up. This new process design is based on the findings from a recent student study of the current process which proved that 95 per cent of all customers ordered only two types of bread (soft roll and Italian bread) and three types of protein filling (cheese, ham and chicken). Therefore the six 'sandwich bases' (2 types of bread × 3 protein fillings) could be prepared

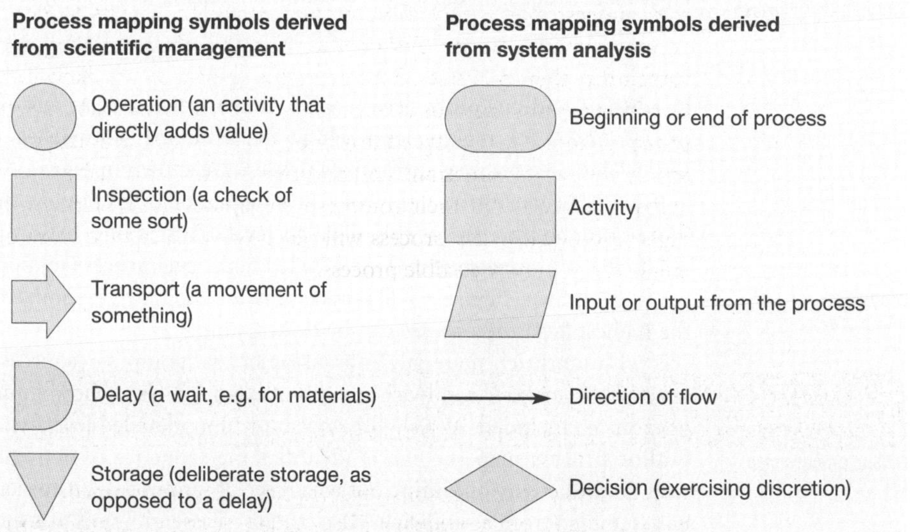

Figure 4.5 Some common process mapping symbols

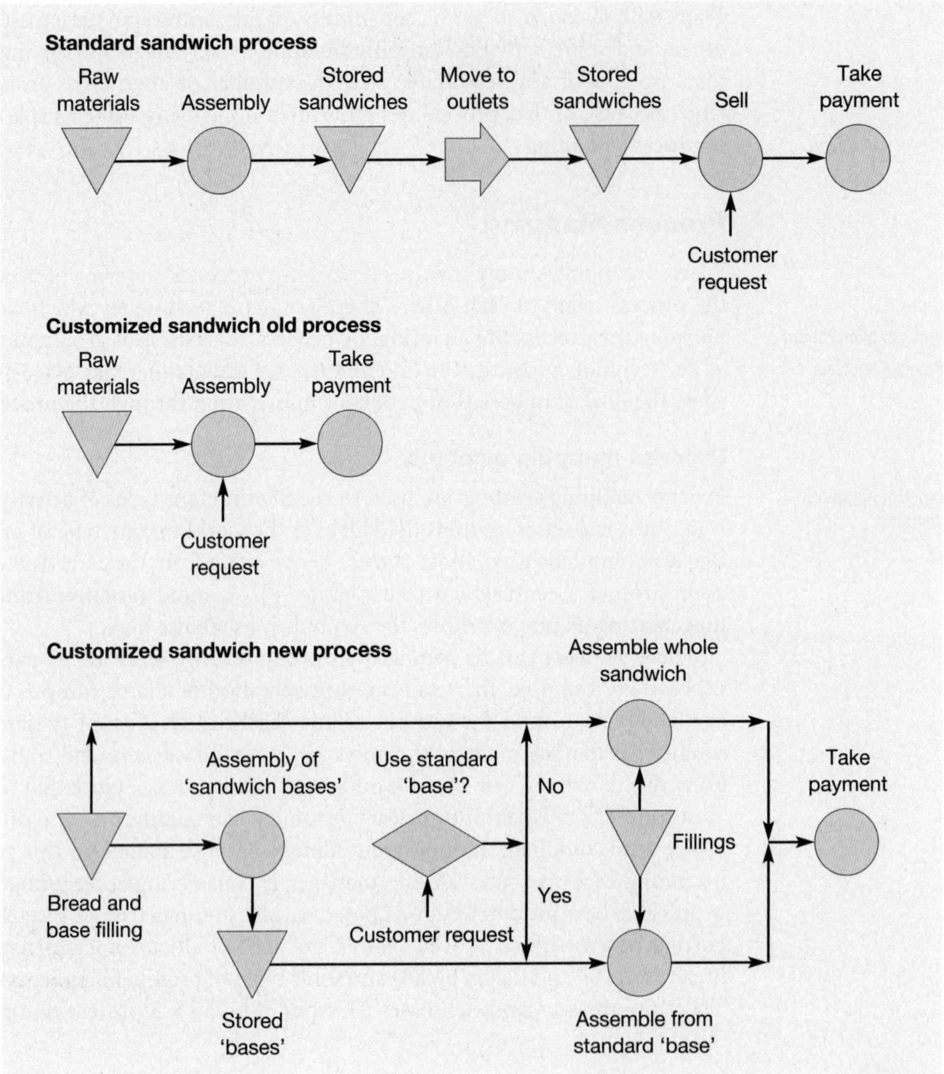

Figure 4.6 Process maps for three sandwich making and selling processes

in advance and customized with salad, mayonnaise, etc. as customers ordered them. The process maps for making and selling the standard sandwiches, the current customized sandwiches and the new customized process are shown in Figure 4.6.

Note how the introduction of some degree of discretion in the new process makes it more complex to map at this detailed level. This is one reason why processes are often mapped at a more aggregated level, called **high-level process mapping**, before more detailed maps are drawn. Figure 4.7 illustrates this for the new customized sandwich operation. At the highest level the process can be drawn simply as an input–transformation–output process with sandwich materials and customers as its input resources and satisfied customers 'assembled' to their sandwich as outputs. No details of how inputs are transformed into outputs are included. At a slightly lower, or more detailed level, what is sometimes called an **outline process map** (or chart) identifies the sequence of activities but only in a general way. So the activity of finding out what type of sandwich a customer wants, deciding if it can be assembled from a sandwich 'base' and then assembling it to meet the customer's request, is all contained in the general activity 'assemble as required'. At the more detailed level, all the activities are shown (we have shown the activities within 'assemble as required').

High-level process mapping

Outline process map

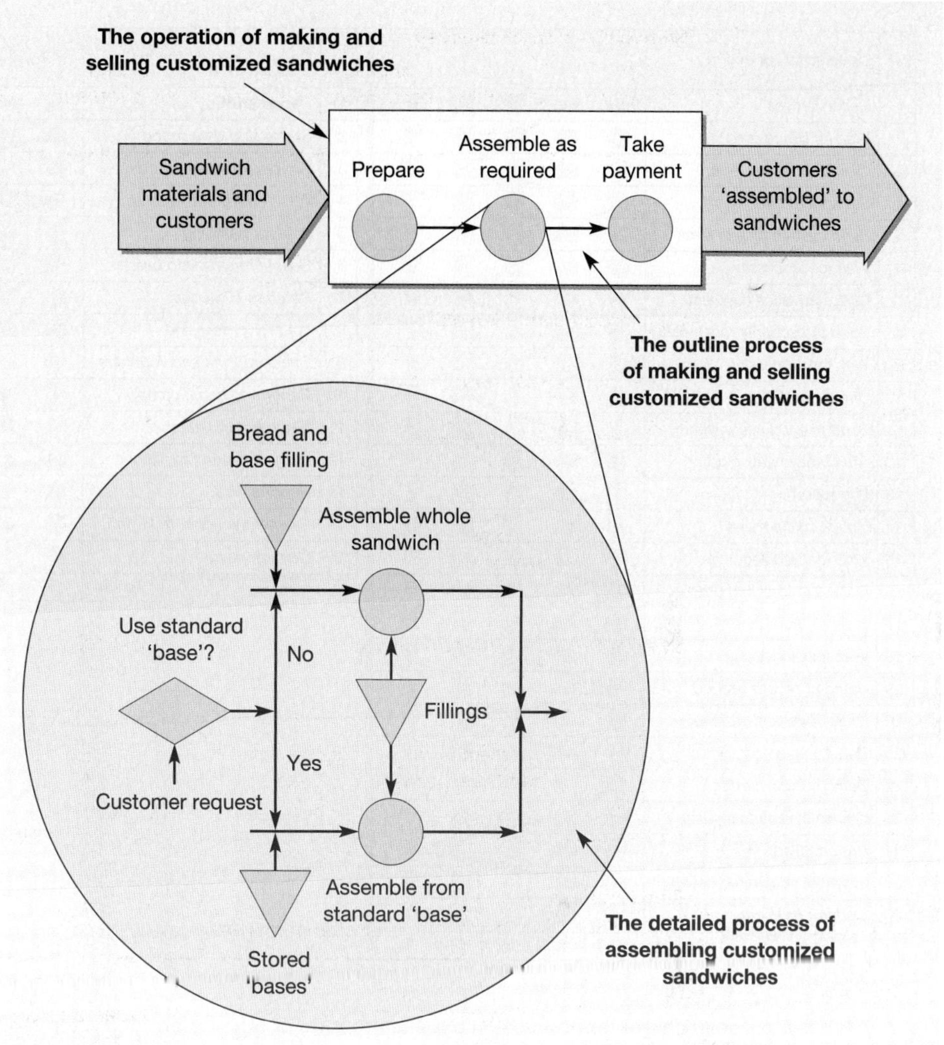

Figure 4.7 The new customized sandwich process mapped at three levels

Using process maps to improve processes

One significant advantage of mapping processes is that each activity can be systematically challenged in an attempt to improve the process. For example, Figure 4.8 shows the flow process chart which Intel Corporation, the computer chip company, drew to describe its method of processing expense reports (claims forms). It also shows the process chart for the same process after critically examining and improving the process. The new process cut the number of activities from 26 down to 15. The accounts payable's activities were combined with the cash-receipt's activities of checking employees' past expense accounts (activities 8, 10 and 11) which also eliminated activities 5 and 7. After consideration, it was decided to eliminate the activity of checking items against company rules, because it seemed '*more trouble than it was worth*'. Also, logging the batches was deemed unnecessary. All this combination and elimination of activities had the effect of removing several 'delays' from the process. The end-result was a much-simplified process which reduced the staff time needed to do the job by 28 per cent and considerably speeded up the whole process.

In the case of the customized sandwich process, the new design was attempting to offer as wide a range of sandwiches as were previously offered, without the slow service of the old

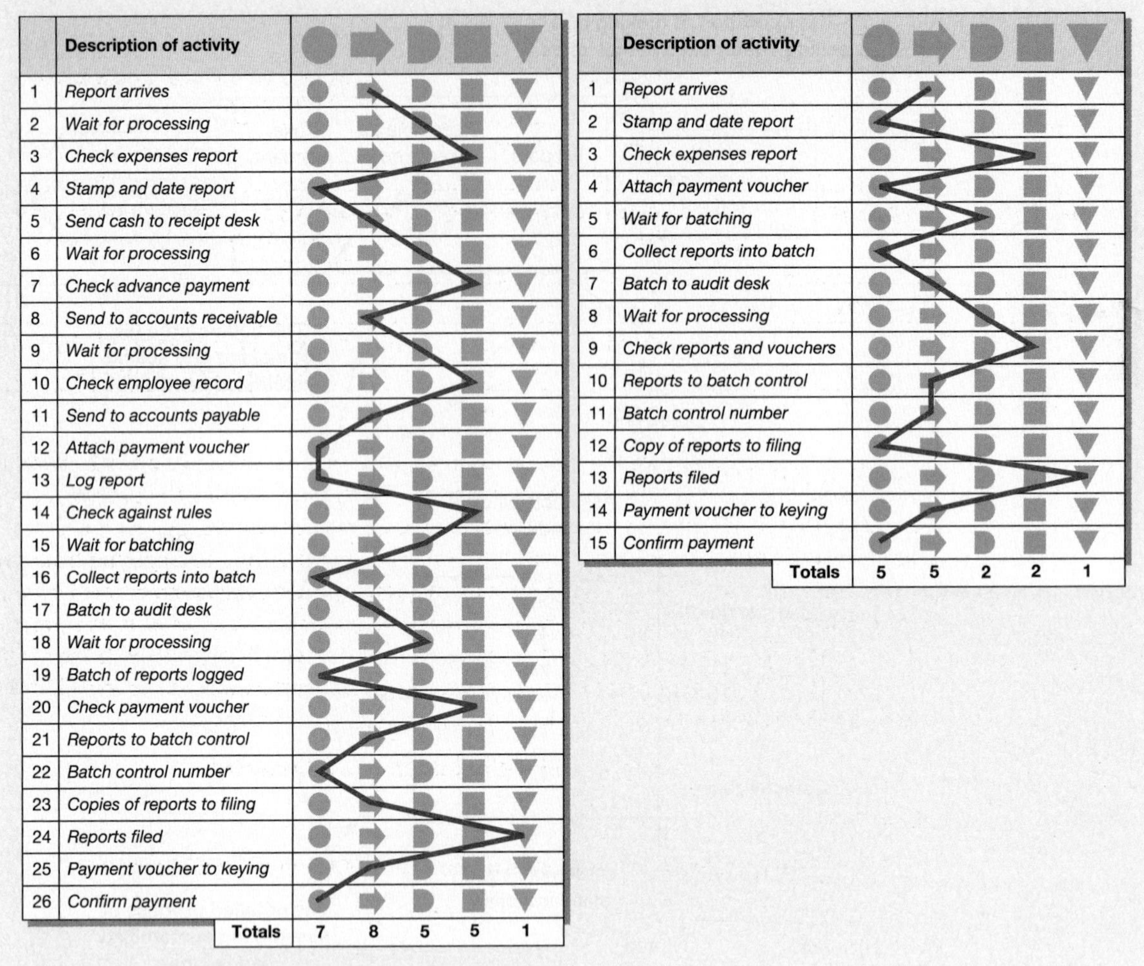

	Description of activity	●	➡	D	■	▼
1	*Report arrives*		➡			
2	*Wait for processing*			D		
3	*Check expenses report*				■	
4	*Stamp and date report*	●				
5	*Send cash to receipt desk*		➡			
6	*Wait for processing*			D		
7	*Check advance payment*				■	
8	*Send to accounts receivable*		➡			
9	*Wait for processing*			D		
10	*Check employee record*				■	
11	*Send to accounts payable*		➡			
12	*Attach payment voucher*	●				
13	*Log report*	●				
14	*Check against rules*				■	
15	*Wait for batching*			D		
16	*Collect reports into batch*	●				
17	*Batch to audit desk*		➡			
18	*Wait for processing*			D		
19	*Batch of reports logged*	●				
20	*Check payment voucher*				■	
21	*Reports to batch control*		➡			
22	*Batch control number*	●				
23	*Copies of reports to filing*		➡			
24	*Reports filed*					▼
25	*Payment voucher to keying*		➡			
26	*Confirm payment*	●				
	Totals	7	8	5	5	1

	Description of activity	●	➡	D	■	▼
1	*Report arrives*		➡			
2	*Stamp and date report*	●				
3	*Check expenses report*				■	
4	*Attach payment voucher*	●				
5	*Wait for batching*			D		
6	*Collect reports into batch*	●				
7	*Batch to audit desk*		➡			
8	*Wait for processing*			D		
9	*Check reports and vouchers*				■	
10	*Reports to batch control*		➡			
11	*Batch control number*		➡			
12	*Copy of reports to filing*	●				
13	*Reports filed*					▼
14	*Payment voucher to keying*		➡			
15	*Confirm payment*	●				
	Totals	5	5	2	2	1

Figure 4.8 Flow process charts for processing expense reports at Intel before and after improving the process

process. In other words, it was maintaining similar levels of flexibility (to offer the same variety) while improving the speed of service. The new process would probably also increase the efficiency of the process because the sandwich 'bases' could be assembled during periods of low demand. This would balance the load on staff and so cost performance would improve. The quality of the sandwiches would presumably not suffer, although pre-assembling the sandwich bases may detract from the fresh appearance and taste. The dependability of the new process is less easy to assess. With the old process the time between requesting a sandwich and its delivery was long but reasonably predictable. The new process, however, will deliver fairly quickly 95 per cent of the time but take longer if the sandwich is non-standard. Table 4.2 summarizes the performance of the new design.

Throughput, cycle time and work-in-process

The new customized sandwich process has one indisputable advantage over the old process: it is faster in the sense that customers spend less time in the process. The additional benefit this brings is a reduction in cost per customer served (because more customers can be served without increasing resources). Note, however, that the total amount of work needed to make and sell a sandwich has not reduced. All the new process has done is to move some of the work to a less busy time. So the **work content** (the total amount of work required to produce a unit of output) has not changed but customer **throughput time** (the time for a unit to move through the process) has improved.

Work content

Throughput time

Table 4.2 Assessing the performance of the new customized sandwich process

Performance objective	*Change with new process*	*Comments*
Quality	No change?	Check to make sure that sandwich bases do not deteriorate in storage
Speed	Faster for 95 per cent of customers	
Dependability	Less predictable delivery time	Need to manage customer expectations regarding delivery time for non-standard sandwiches
Flexibility	No change	
Cost	Potentially lower cost	Need to forecast the number of each type of sandwich 'base' to pre-assemble

For example, suppose that the time to assemble and sell a sandwich (the work content) using the old process was two minutes and that two people were staffing the process during the busy period. Each person could serve a customer every two minutes, therefore every two minutes two customers were being served, so on average a customer is emerging from the process every minute. This is called the **cycle time** of the process, the average time between units of output emerging from the process. When customers join the queue in the process they become **work-in-process** (or work-in-progress) sometimes written as WIP. If the queue is ten people long (including that customer) when the customer joins it, he or she will have to wait ten minutes to emerge from the process. Or put more succinctly:

Cycle time

Work-in-process

$$\textbf{Throughput time} = \textbf{Work-in-process} \times \textbf{Cycle time}$$

In this case,

$$10 \text{ minutes wait} = 10 \text{ people in the system} \times 1 \text{ minute per person}$$

Little's law

This mathematical relationship (throughput time = work-in-process × cycle time) is called **Little's law**. It is simple but very useful, and it works for any stable process. For example, suppose it is decided that, when the new process is introduced, the average number of customers in the process should be limited to around ten and the maximum time a customer is in the process should be on average four minutes. If the time to assemble and sell a sandwich (from customer request to the customer leaving the process) in the new process has reduced to 1.2 minutes, how many staff should be serving?

Little's law

Putting this into Little's law:

$$\text{Throughput time} = 4 \text{ minutes}$$

and

$$\text{Work-in-progress, WIP} = 10$$

So, since

$$\text{Throughput time} = \text{WIP} \times \text{Cycle time}$$

$$\text{Cycle time} = \frac{\text{Throughput time}}{\text{WIP}}$$

$$\text{Cycle time for the process} = \frac{4}{10} = 0.4 \text{ minute}$$

That is, a customer should emerge from the process every 0.4 minute, on average.

Given that an individual can be served in 1.2 minutes,

$$\text{Number of servers required} = \frac{1.2}{0.4} = 3$$

In other words, three servers would serve three customers in 1.2 minutes. Or one customer in 0.4 minute.

Worked example

Mike was totally confident in his judgement, *'You'll never get them back in time'*, he said. *'They aren't just wasting time, the process won't allow them to all have their coffee and get back for 11 o'clock.'* Looking outside the lecture theatre, Mike and his colleague Dick were watching the 20 business people who were attending the seminar queuing to be served coffee and biscuits. The time was 10.45 and Dick knew that unless they were all back in the lecture theatre at 11 o'clock there was no hope of finishing his presentation before lunch. *'I'm not sure why you're so pessimistic'*, said Dick. *'They seem to be interested in what I have to say and I think they will want to get back to hear how operations management will change their lives.'* Mike shook his head. *'I'm not questioning their motivation'*, he said, *'I'm questioning the ability of the process out there to get through them all in time. I have been timing how long it takes to serve the coffee and biscuits. Each coffee is being made fresh and the time between the server asking each customer what they want and them walking away with their coffee and biscuits is taking 48 seconds. Remember that, according to Little's law, throughput equals work-in-process multiplied by cycle time. If the work-in-process is the 20 managers in the queue and cycle time is 48 seconds, the total throughput time is going to be 20 multiplied by 0.8 minute which equals 16 minutes. Add to that sufficient time for the last person to drink their coffee and you must expect a total throughput time of a bit over 20 minutes. You just haven't allowed long enough for the process.'* Dick was impressed. *'Err . . . what did you say that law was called again?'* *'Little's law'*, said Mike.

Worked example

Every year it was the same. All the workstations in the building had to be renovated (tested, new software installed, etc.) and there was only one week in which to do it. The one week fell in the middle of the August vacation period when the renovation process would cause minimum disruption to normal working. Last year the company's 500 workstations had all been renovated within one working week (40 hours). Each renovation last year took on average 2 hours and 25 technicians had completed the process within the week. This year there would be 530 workstations to renovate but the company's IT support unit had devised a faster testing and renovation routine that would only take on average $1\frac{1}{2}$ hours instead of 2 hours. How many technicians will be needed this year to complete the renovation processes within the week?

Last year:

$$\text{Work-in-progress (WIP)} = 500 \text{ workstations}$$

$$\text{Time available } (T_t) = 40 \text{ hours}$$

$$\text{Average time to renovate} = 2 \text{ hours}$$

$$\text{Therefore throughput rate } (T_r) = \tfrac{1}{2} \text{ hour per technician}$$

$$= 0.5N$$

where N = Number of technicians

Little's law:

$$\text{WIP} = T_t \times T_r$$
$$500 = 40 \times 0.5N$$
$$N = \frac{500}{40 \times 0.5}$$
$$= 25 \text{ technicians}$$

This year:

$$\text{Work-in-progress (WIP)} = 530 \text{ workstations}$$
$$\text{Time available} = 40 \text{ hours}$$
$$\text{Average time to renovate} = 1.5 \text{ hours}$$
$$\text{Throughput rate } (T_r) = 1/1.5 \text{ per technician}$$
$$= 0.67N$$

where N = Number of technicians

Little's law:

$$\text{WIP} = T_t \times T_r$$
$$530 = 40 \times 0.67N$$
$$N = \frac{530}{40 \times 0.67}$$
$$= 19.88 \text{ technicians}$$

Throughput efficiency

This idea that the throughput time of a process is different from the work content of whatever it is processing has important implications. What it means is that for significant amounts of time no useful work is being done to the materials, information or customers that are progressing through the process. In the case of the simple example of the sandwich process described earlier, customer throughput time is restricted to 4 minutes, but the work content of the task (serving the customer) is only 1.2 minutes. So, the item being processed (the customer) is only being 'worked on' for 1.2/4 = 30 per cent of its time. This is called the **throughput efficiency** of the process.

Throughput efficiency

$$\textbf{Percentage throughput efficiency} = \frac{\textbf{Work content}}{\textbf{Throughput time}} \times 100$$

In this case the throughput efficiency is very high, relative to most processes, perhaps because the 'items' being processed are customers who react badly to waiting. In most material and information transforming processes, throughput efficiency is far lower, usually in single percentage figures.

Worked example

A vehicle licensing centre receives application documents, keys in details, checks the information provided on the application, classifies the application according to the type of licence required, confirms payment and then issues and mails the licence. It is currently processing an average of 5,000 licences every 8-hour day. A recent spot check found 15,000 applications that were 'in progress' or waiting to be processed. The sum of all activities that are required to process an application is 25 minutes. What is the throughput efficiency of the process?

→

$$\text{Work-in-progress} = 15{,}000 \text{ applications}$$

$$\text{Cycle time} = \text{Time producing}$$

$$\frac{\text{Time producing}}{\text{Number produced}} = \frac{8 \text{ hours}}{5{,}000} = \frac{480 \text{ minutes}}{5{,}000} = 0.096 \text{ minute}$$

From Little's law,

$$\text{Throughput time} = \text{WIP} \times \text{Cycle time}$$

$$\text{Throughput time} = 15{,}000 \times 0.096$$

$$= 1{,}440 \text{ minutes} = 24 \text{ hours} = 3 \text{ days of working}$$

$$\text{Throughput efficiency} = \frac{\text{Work content}}{\text{Throughput time}} = \frac{25}{1{,}440} = 1.74 \text{ per cent}$$

Although the process is achieving a throughput time of 3 days (which seems reasonable for this kind of process) the applications are only being worked on for 1.7 per cent of the time they are in the process.

Value-added throughput efficiency

The approach to calculating throughput efficiency that is described above assumes that all the 'work content' is actually needed. Yet we have already seen from the Intel expense report example that changing a process can significantly reduce the time that is needed to complete the task. Therefore, work content is actually dependent upon the methods and technology used to perform the task. It may be also that individual elements of a task may not be considered 'value-added'. In the Intel expense report example the new method eliminated some steps because they were 'not worth it', that is, they were not seen as adding value. So, **value-added throughput efficiency** restricts the concept of work content to only those tasks that are actually adding value to whatever is being processed. This often eliminates activities such as movement, delays and some inspections.

Value-added throughput efficiency

For example, if in the licensing worked example, of the 25 minutes of work content only 20 minutes were actually adding value, then

$$\text{Value-added throughput efficiency} = \frac{20}{1{,}440} = 1.39 \text{ per cent}$$

Workflow[5]

When the transformed resources in a process is information (or documents containing information), and when information technology is used to move, store and manage the information, process design is sometimes called 'workflow' or 'workflow management'. It is defined as 'the automation of procedures where documents, information or tasks are passed between participants according to a defined set of rules to achieve, or contribute to, an overall business goal'. Although workflow may be managed manually, it is almost always managed using an IT system. The term is also often associated with business process re-engineering (see Chapter 1 and Chapter 18). More specifically, workflow is concerned with the following:

- Analysis, modelling, definition and subsequent operational implementation of business processes;
- The technology that supports the processes;
- The procedural (decision) rules that move information or documents through processes;
- Defining the process in terms of the sequence of work activities, the human skills needed to perform each activity and the appropriate IT resources.

The effects of process variability

So far in our treatment of process design we have assumed that there is no significant variability either in the demand to which the process is expected to respond or in the time taken for the process to perform its various activities. Clearly, this is not the case in reality. So, it is important to look at the variability that can affect processes and take account of it.

Process variability

There are many reasons why **variability** occurs in processes. These can include: the late (or early) arrival of material, information or customers, a temporary malfunction or breakdown of process technology within a stage of the process, the recycling of 'mis-processed' materials, information or customers to an earlier stage in the process, variation in the requirements of items being processed. All these sources of variation interact with each other, but result in two fundamental types of variability.

- Variability in the demand for processing at an individual stage within the process, usually expressed in terms of variation in the inter-arrival times of units to be processed.
- Variation in the time taken to perform the activities (i.e. process a unit) at each stage.

To understand the effect of arrival variability on process performance it is first useful to examine what happens to process performance in a very simple process as arrival time changes under conditions of no variability. For example, the simple process shown in Figure 4.9 is composed of one stage that performs exactly 10 minutes of work. Units arrive at the process at a constant and predictable rate. If the arrival rate is one unit every 30 minutes, then the process will be utilized for only 33.33% of the time, and the units will never have to wait to be processed. This is shown as point A on Figure 4.9. If the arrival rate increases to one arrival every 20 minutes, the utilization increases to 50%, and again the units will not have to wait to be processed. This is point B on Figure 4.9. If the arrival rate increases to one arrival every 10 minutes, the process is now fully utilized, but, because a

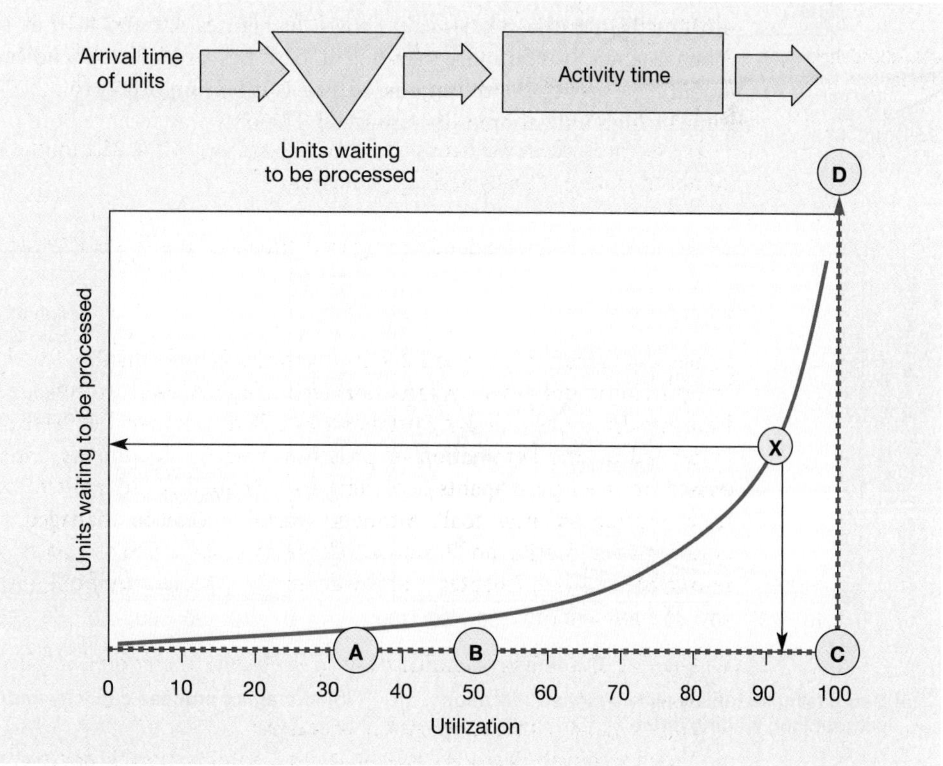

Figure 4.9 The relationship between process utilization and number of units waiting to be processed for constant, and variable, arrival and process times

unit arrives just as the previous one has finished being processed, no unit has to wait. This is point C on Figure 4.9. However, if the arrival rate ever exceeded one unit every 10 minutes, the waiting line in front of the process activity would build up indefinitely, as is shown as point D in Figure 4.9. So, in a perfectly constant and predictable world, the relationship between process waiting time and utilization is a rectangular function as shown by the red dotted line in Figure 4.9.

However, when arrival and process times are variable, then sometimes the process will have units waiting to be processed, while at other times the process will be idle, waiting for units to arrive. Therefore the process will have both a 'non-zero' average queue and be under-utilized in the same period. So, a more realistic point is that shown as point X in Figure 4.9. If the average arrival time were to be changed with the same variability, the blue line in Figure 4.9 would show **the relationship between average waiting time and process utilization.** As the process moves closer to 100% utilization the higher the average waiting time will become. Or, to put it another way, the only way to guarantee very low waiting times for the units is to suffer low process utilization.

The relationship between average waiting time and process utilization is a particularly important one

The greater the variability in the process, the more the waiting time utilization deviates from the simple rectangular function of the 'no variability' conditions that was shown in Figure 4.9. A set of curves for a typical process is shown in Figure 4.10(a). This phenomenon has important implications for the design of processes. In effect it presents three options to process designers wishing to improve the waiting time or utilization performance of their processes, as shown in Figure 4.10(b):

- Accept long average waiting times and achieve high utilization (point X);
- Accept low utilization and achieve short average waiting times (point Y); or
- Reduce the variability in arrival times, activity times, or both, and achieve higher utilization and short waiting times (point Z).

To analyse processes with both inter-arrival and activity time variability, queuing or 'waiting line' analysis can be used. This is treated in the supplement to Chapter 11. But, do not dismiss the relationship shown in Figures 4.9 and 4.10 as some minor technical phenomenon. It is far more than this. It identifies an important choice in process design that could have strategic implications. Which is more important to a business, fast throughput time or high utilization of its resources? The only way to have both of these simultaneously

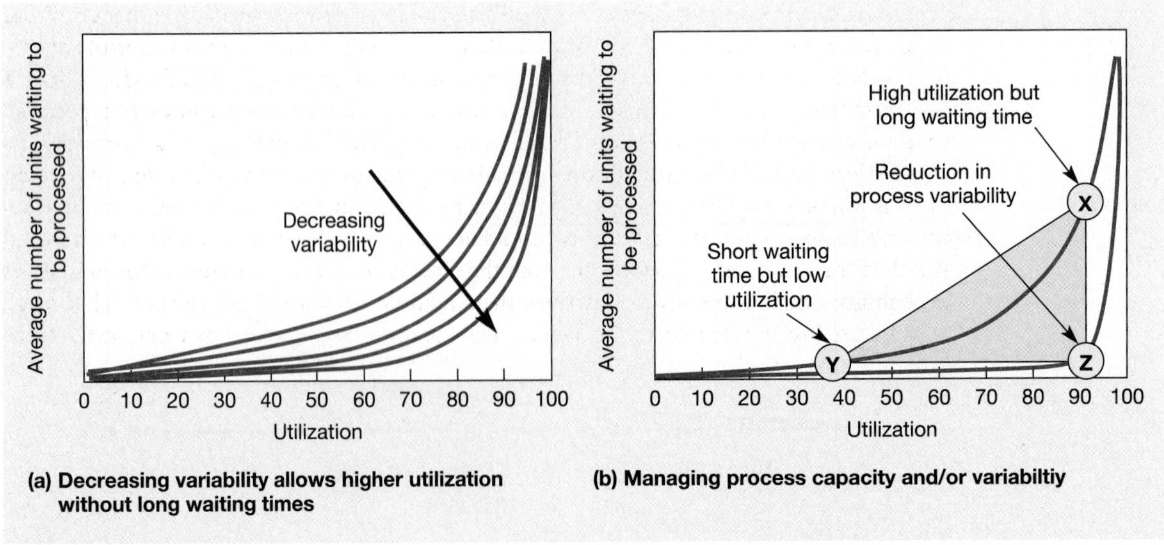

Figure 4.10 The relationship between process utilization and number of units waiting to be processed for variable arrival and activity times

is to reduce variability in its processes, which may itself require strategic decisions such as limiting the degree of customization of products or services, or imposing stricter limits on how products or services can be delivered to customers, and so on. It also demonstrates an important point concerned with the day-to-day management of process – the only way to absolutely guarantee a hundred per cent utilization of resources is to accept an infinite amount of work-in-progress and/or waiting time.

Short case

Heathrow delays caused by capacity utilization[6]

Source: Alamy Images

It may be the busiest international airport in the world, but it is unlikely to win any prizes for being the most loved. Long delays, overcrowding and a shortage of capacity has meant that Heathrow is often a cause of frustration to harassed passengers. Yet to the airlines it is an attractive hub. Its size and location give it powerful 'network effects'. This means that it can match incoming passengers with outgoing flights to hundreds of different cities. Actually it is its attractiveness to the airlines that is one of its main problems. Heathrow's runways are in such demand that they are almost always operating at, or close to, their maximum capacity. In fact, its runways operate at 99% of capacity. This compares with about 70% at most other large airports. This means that the slightest variability (bad weather or an unscheduled landing such as a plane having to turn back with engine trouble) causes delays, which in turn cause more delays. (See Figure 4.10 for the theoretical explanation of this effect.) The result is that a third of all flights at Heathrow are delayed by at least 15 minutes. This is poor when compared with other large European airports such as Amsterdam and Frankfurt, which have 21% and 24% of flights delayed respectively.

Simulation in design

Designing processes often involves making decisions in advance of the final process being created, and so the designer is often not totally sure of the consequences of his or her decisions. To increase their own confidence in their design decision, however, they will probably try to *simulate* how the process might work in practice. In some ways simulation is one of the most fundamental approaches to decision-making. Children play games and 'pretend' so as to extend their experience of novel situations; likewise, managers can gain insights and explore possibilities through the formalized 'pretending' involved in using simulation models. These **simulation models** can take many forms. In designing the various processes within a football stadium, the architect could devise a computer-based 'model' which would simulate the movement of people through the stadium's various processes according to the probability distribution which describes their random arrival and movement. This could then be used to predict where the layout might become overcrowded or where extra space might be reduced.

Simulation models

Summary answers to key questions

*Check and improve your understanding of this chapter using self assessment questions and a personalised study plan, audio and video downloads, and an eBook – all at **www.myomlab.com.***

➤ What is process design?

- Design is the activity which shapes the physical form and purpose of both products and services and the processes that produce them.
- This design activity is more likely to be successful if the complementary activities of product or service design and process design are coordinated.

➤ What objectives should process design have?

- The overall purpose of process design is to meet the needs of customers through achieving appropriate levels of quality, speed, dependability, flexibility and cost.
- The design activity must also take account of environmental issues. These include examination of the source and suitability of materials, the sources and quantities of energy consumed, the amount and type of waste material, the life of the product itself, and the end-of-life state of the product.

➤ How do volume and variety affect process design?

- The overall nature of any process is strongly influenced by the volume and variety of what it has to process.
- The concept of process types summarizes how volume and variety affect overall process design.
- In manufacturing, these process types are (in order of increasing volume and decreasing variety) project, jobbing, batch, mass and continuous processes. In service operations, although there is less consensus on the terminology, the terms often used (again in order of increasing volume and decreasing variety) are professional services, service shops and mass services.

➤ How are processes designed in detail?

- Processes are designed initially by breaking them down into their individual activities. Often common symbols are used to represent types of activity. The sequence of activities in a process is then indicated by the sequence of symbols representing activities. This is called 'process mapping'. Alternative process designs can be compared using process maps and improved processes considered in terms of their operations performance objectives.
- Process performance in terms of throughput time, work-in-progress, and cycle time are related by a formula known as Little's law: throughput time equals work-in-progress multiplied by cycle time.
- Variability has a significant effect on the performance of processes, particularly the relationship between waiting time and utilization.

Case study
The Central Evaluation Unit

The Central Evaluation Unit (CEU) of the XIII Directorate evaluated applications from academics bidding for research grants available under the 'cooperation and foundations' scheme of the European Union. This scheme distributed relatively small grants (less than €100,000) to fund the early stages of cooperative research between universities in the European Union. Based in Brussels, the CEU's objectives were to make decisions that were consistently in line with directory guide rules, but also to give as speedy a response as possible to applicants. All new applications are sent to the CEU's applications processing unit (CEUPU) by University Liaison Officers (ULOs) who were based at around 150 universities around the EU. Any academic who wanted to apply for a grant needed to submit an application form (downloadable online) and other signed documentation through the local ULO. The CEUPU employs three 'checkers' with three support and secretarial staff, a pool of twelve clerks who are responsible for data entry and filing, ten auditors (staff who prepare and issue the grant approval documents), and a special advisor (who is a senior ex-officer employed part-time to assess non-standard applications).

Véronique Fontan was the manager in charge of the Central Evaluation Unit's applications processing unit (CEUPU). She had been invited by the Directory chief executive, Leda Grumman, to make a presentation to senior colleagues about the reasons for the success of her unit. The reason for her invitation to the meeting was, first, that the systems used for handling new grant applications were well proven and robust, and, secondly, that her operation was well known for consistently meeting, and in many cases exceeding, its targets.

Véronique set a day aside to collect some information about the activities of the CEUPU. She first reviewed her monthly management reports. The information system provided an update of number of applications (by week, month and year), the number and percentage of applications approved, number and percentage of those declined, the cumulative amount of money allocated, and the value of applications processed during the month. These reports identified that the Unit dealt with about 200 to 300 applications per week (the Unit operated a five-day 35-hour week) and all the Unit's financial targets were being met. In addition most operational performance criteria were being exceeded. The targets for turnaround of an application, from receipt of an application to the applicant being informed (excluding time spent waiting for additional information from ULOs) was 40 working days. The average time taken by the CEUPU was 36 working days. Accuracy had never been an issue as all files were thoroughly assessed to ensure that all the relevant and complete data were collected before the applications were processed. Staff productivity was high and there was always plenty of work waiting for processing at each section. A cursory inspection of the sections' in-trays revealed about 130 files in each with just two exceptions. The 'receipt' clerks' tray had about 600 files in it and the checkers' tray contained about 220 files.

Source: © Getty Images

Processing grant applications

The processing of applications is a lengthy procedure requiring careful examination by checkers trained to make assessments. All applications arriving at the Unit are placed in an in-tray. The incoming application is then opened by one of the eight 'receipt' clerks who will check that all the necessary forms have been included in the application. This is then placed in an in-tray pending collection by the coding staff. The two clerks with special responsibility for coding allocate a unique identifier to each application and code the information on the application into the information system.

The application is then given a front sheet, a pro forma, with the identifier in the top left corner. The files are then placed in a tray on the senior checker's secretary's desk. As a checker becomes available, the senior secretary provides the next job in the line to the checker. In the case of about half of the applications, the checker returns the file to the checkers' secretaries to request the collection of any information that is missing or additional information that is required. The secretaries then write to the applicant and return the file to the 'receipt' clerks who place the additional information into the file as it arrives. Once the file is complete it is returned to the checkers for a decision on

the grant application. The file is then taken to auditors who prepare the acceptance or rejection documents.

These documents are then sent, with the rest of the file, to the two 'dispatch' clerks who complete the documents and mail them to the ULO for delivery to the academic who made the application. Each section, clerical, coding, checkers, secretarial, auditing or issuing, have trays for incoming work. Files are taken from the bottom of the pile when someone becomes free to ensure that all documents are dealt with in strict order.

Véronique's confidence in her operation was somewhat eroded when she asked for comments from some university liaison officers and staff. One ULO told her of frequent complaints about the delays over the processing of the applications and she felt there was a danger of alienating some of the best potential applicants to the point where they 'just would not bother applying'. A second ULO complained that when he telephoned to ascertain the status of an application, the CEUPU staff did not seem to know where it was or how long it might be before a decision would be made. Furthermore he felt that this lack of information was eroding his relationship with potential applicants, some of whom had already decided to apply elsewhere for research funding. Véronique reviewed the levels of applications over the last few years which revealed a decline of five per cent last year and two per cent the year before that on the number of applications made. Véronique then spent about ten minutes with four of the clerks. They said their work was clear and routine, but their life was made difficult by university liaison officers who rang in expecting them to be able to tell them the status of an application they had submitted. It could take them hours, sometimes days, to find any individual file. Indeed, two of the 'receipt' clerks now worked full-time on this activity. They also said that university liaison officers frequently complained that decision-making seemed to be unusually slow, given the relatively small amounts of money being applied for. Véronique wondered whether, after all, she should agree to make the presentation.

Questions

1 Analyse and evaluate the processing of new applications at the CEUPU:
   - Create a process map for new applications
   - Calculate the time needed to process an individual application cycle time for the process
   - Calculate the number of people involved in the processing of an application
   - Explain why it is difficult to locate an individual file.

2 Summarize the problems of the CEUPU process.

3 What suggestions would you make to Véronique to improve her process?

Problems and applications

*These problems and applications will help to improve your analysis of operations. You can find more practice problems as well as worked examples and guided solutions on MyOMLab at **www.myomlab.com**.*

1 Read again the description of fast-food drive-through processes at the beginning of this chapter. (a) Draw a process map that reflects the types of process described. (b) What advantage do you think is given to McDonald's through its decision to establish a call centre for remote order-taking for some of its outlets?

2 A laboratory process receives medical samples from hospitals in its area and then subjects them to a number of tests that take place in different parts of the laboratory. The average response time for the laboratory to complete all its tests and mail the results back to the hospital (measured from the time that the sample for analysis arrives) is 3 days. A recent process map has shown that, of the 60 minutes that are needed to complete all the tests, the tests themselves took 30 minutes, moving the samples between each test area took 10 minutes, and double-checking the results took a further 20 minutes. What is the throughput efficiency of this process? What is the value-added throughput efficiency of the process? (State any assumptions that you are making.) If the process is rearranged so that all the tests are performed in the same area, thus eliminating the time to move between test areas, and the tests themselves are improved to halve the amount of time needed for double-checking, what effect would this have on the value-added throughput efficiency?

3 A regional government office that deals with passport applications is designing a process that will check applications and issue the documents. The number of applications to be processed is 1,600 per week and the time available to process the applications is 40 hours per week. What is the required cycle time for the process?

4 For the passport office, described above, the total work content of all the activities that make up the total task of checking, processing and issuing a passport is, on average, 30 minutes. How many people will be needed to meet demand?

5 The same passport office has a 'clear desk' policy that means that all desks must be clear of work by the end of the day. How many applications should be loaded onto the process in the morning in order to ensure that every one is completed and desks are clear by the end of the day? (Assume a 7.5-hour (450-minute) working day.)

6 Visit a drive-through quick-service restaurant and observe the operation for half an hour. You will probably need a stop watch to collect the relevant timing information. Consider the following questions.

(a) Where are the bottlenecks in the service (in other words, what seems to take the longest time)?
(b) How would you measure the efficiency of the process?
(c) What appear to be the key design principles that govern the effectiveness of this process?
(d) Using Little's law, how long would the queue have to be before you think it would be not worth joining the queue?

Selected further reading

Chopra, S., Anupindi, R., Deshmukh, S.D., Van Mieghem, J.A. and Zemel, E. (2006) *Managing Business Process Flows*, Prentice-Hall, Upper Saddle River NJ. An excellent, although mathematical, approach to process design in general.

Hammer, M. (1990) Reengineering work: don't automate, obliterate, *Harvard Business Review*, July–August. This is the paper that launched the whole idea of business processes and process management in general to a wider managerial audience. Slightly dated but worth reading.

Hopp, W.J. and Spearman, M.L. (2001) *Factory Physics*, 2nd edn, McGraw-Hill. Very technical so don't bother with it if you aren't prepared to get into the maths. However, there is some fascinating analysis, especially concerning Little's law.

Smith, H. and Fingar, P. (2003) *Business Process Management: The Third Wave*, Meghan-Kiffer Press, Tampa, Fla. A popular book on process management from a BPR perspective.

Useful web sites

www.bpmi.org Site of the Business Process Management Initiative. Some good resources including papers and articles.

www.bptrends.com News site for trends in business process management generally. Some interesting articles.

www.bls.gov/oes/ US Department of Labor employment statistics.

www.fedee.com/hrtrends Federation of European Employers guide to employment and job trends in Europe.

www.iienet.org The American Institute of Industrial Engineers site. This is an important professional body for process design and related topics.

www.opsman.org Lots of useful stuff.

www.waria.com A Workflow and Reengineering Association web site. Some useful topics.

*Now that you have finished reading this chapter, why not visit MyOMLab at **www.myomlab.com** where you'll find more learning resources to help you make the most of your studies and get a better grade?*

Chapter 5 The design of products and services

Key questions

- ➤ Why is good product and service design important?
- ➤ What are the stages in product and service design?
- ➤ Why should product and service design and process design be considered interactively?

Introduction

Products and services are often the first thing that customers see of a company, so they should have an impact. And although operations managers may not have direct responsibility for product and service design, they always have an indirect responsibility to provide the information and advice upon which successful product or service development depends. But, increasingly, operations managers are expected to take a more active part in product and service design. Unless a product, however well designed, can be produced to a high standard, and unless a service, however well conceived, can be implemented, the design can never bring its full benefits. Figure 5.1 shows where this chapter fits into the overall operations model.

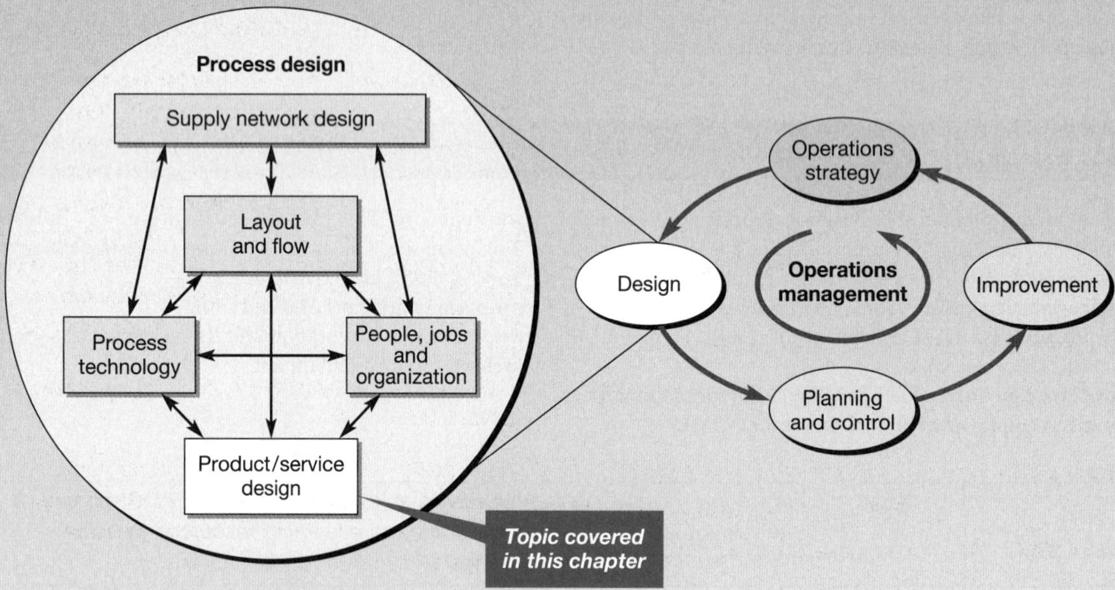

Figure 5.1 This chapter examines product and service design

Check and improve your understanding of this chapter using self assessment questions and a personalised study plan, audio and video downloads, and an eBook – all at ***www.myomlab.com****.*

Operations in practice The troubled history of the Airbus A380[1]

It is perhaps inevitable that a major new and complex product like a passenger aircraft will experience a few problems during its development. But the history of the Airbus A380 was a long and incident-packed journey from drawing board to reality that illustrates the dangers when the design activity goes wrong. This is the story in brief.

1991 – Airbus consults with international airlines about their requirements for a super-large passenger aircraft.

January 1993 – Airbus rival Boeing says it has begun studies into 'very large' commercial aircraft.

June 1993 – Boeing decides not to go for a super-large passenger aircraft, but instead to focus on designing smaller 'jumbos'. Airbus and its partners set up the A3XX team to start the 'super-jumbo' project.

1996 – Airbus forms its 'Large Aircraft' Division. Because of the size of the aircraft, it is decided to develop specially designed engines rather than adapt existing models.

2000 – The commercial launch of the A3XX (later to be named the A380).

2002 – Work starts on manufacturing the aircraft's key components.

February 2004 – Rolls-Royce delivers the first Airbus engines to the assembly plant in Toulouse.

April 2004 – The first Airbus wings are completed in the North Wales factory. London's Heathrow airport starts to redevelop its facilities so that it can accommodate the new aircraft.

May 2004 – Assembly begins in the Toulouse plant.

December 2004 – EADS reveals the project is €1.45 billion over budget, and will now cost more than €12 billion.

January 2005 – Airbus unveils the A380 to the world's press and European leaders.

27 April 2005 – The aircraft makes its maiden flight, taking off in Toulouse and circling the Bay of Biscay for four hours before returning to Toulouse. A year of flight-testing and certification work begins.

June 2005 – Airbus announces that the plane's delivery schedule will slip by six months.

March 2006 – The plane passes important safety tests involving 850 passengers and 20 crew safely leaving the aircraft in less than 80 seconds with half the exits blocked.

Source: Rex Features

July 2006 – The A380 suffers another production delay. Airbus now predicts a delay of a further six to seven months. This causes turmoil in the boardrooms of both Airbus and its parent company EADS. The company's directors are accused of suppressing the news for months before revealing it to shareholders. It leads to the resignations of Gustav Humbert, Airbus' chief executive, Noel Forgeard, EADS co-chief executive, and Charles Campion, the A380 programme manager.

October 2006 – Airbus infuriates customers by announcing yet a further delay for the A380, this time of a whole year. The first plane is now forecast to enter commercial service around twenty months later than had been originally planned. The delays will cost Airbus another estimated €4.8 billion over the next four years. The company announces a drastic cost-cutting plan to try to recoup some of the losses. The Power8 programme is intended to 'reduce costs, save cash and develop new products faster'. It wants to increase productivity by 20% and reduce overheads by 30%.

October 2007 – The super-jumbo eventually takes off in full service as a commercial airliner for Singapore Airlines. It wins rave reviews from both airlines and passengers – even if it is two years late!

So what caused the delays? First, the A380 was the most complex passenger jet ever to be built. Second, the company was notorious for its internal rivalries, its constant need to balance work between its French and German plants so that neither country had too obvious an advantage, constant political infighting, particularly by the French and German governments, and frequent changes of management. According to one insider, 'the underlying reason for the mess we were in was the

hopeless lack of integration [between the French and German sides] within the company'. Even before the problems became evident to outsiders, critics of Airbus claimed that its fragmented structure was highly inefficient and prevented it from competing effectively. Eventually it was this lack of integration between design and manufacturing processes that was the main reason for the delays to the aircraft's launch. During the early design stages the firm's French and German factories had used incompatible software to design the 500 km of wiring that each plane needs. Eventually, to resolve the cabling problems, the company had to transfer two thousand German staff from Hamburg to Toulouse. Processes that should have been streamlined had to be replaced by temporary and less efficient ones, described by one French union official as a *'do-it-yourself system'*. Feelings ran high on the shopfloor, with tension and arguments between French and German staff. *'The German staff will first have to succeed at doing the work they should have done in Germany'*, said the same official. Electricians had to resolve the complex wiring problems, with the engineers having to adjust the computer blueprints as they modified them so they could be used on future aircraft. *'Normal installation time is two to three weeks'*, said Sabine Klauke, a team leader. *'This way it is taking us four months.'* Mario Heinen, who ran the cabin and fuselage cross-border division, admitted the pressure to keep up with intense production schedules and the overcrowded conditions made things difficult. *'We have been working on these initial aircraft in a handmade way. It is not a perfectly organized industrial process.'* But, he claimed, there was no choice. *'We have delivered five high-quality aircraft this way. If we had left the work in Hamburg, to wait for a new wiring design, we would not have delivered one by now.'* But the toll taken by these delays was high. The improvised wiring processes were far more expensive than the planned 'streamlined' processes and the delay in launching the aircraft meant two years without the revenue that the company had expected.

But Airbus was not alone. Its great rival, Boeing, was also having problems. Engineers' strikes, supply chain problems and mistakes by its own design engineers had further delayed its '787 Dreamliner' aircraft. Specifically, fasteners used to attach the titanium floor grid, to the composite 'barrel' of the fuselage had been wrongly located, resulting in 8,000 fasteners having to be replaced. By 2009 it looked as if the Boeing aircraft was also going to be two years late. At the same time, Airbus had finally moved to what it called 'wave 2' production where the wiring harnesses that caused the problem were fitted automatically, instead of manually.

Why is good design so important?

Good design satisfies customers, communicates the purpose of the product or service to its market, and brings financial rewards to the business. The objective of good design, whether of products or services is to satisfy customers by meeting their actual or anticipated needs and expectations. This, in turn, enhances the competitiveness of the organization. Product and service design, therefore, can be seen as starting and ending with the customer. So the design activity has one overriding objective: to provide products, services and processes which will satisfy the operation's customers. *Product* designers try to achieve aesthetically pleasing designs which meet or exceed customers' expectations. They also try to design a product which performs well and is reliable during its lifetime. Further, they should design the product so that it can be manufactured easily and quickly. Similarly, service designers try to put together a service which meets, or even exceeds, customer expectations. Yet at the same time the service must be within the capabilities of the operation and be delivered at reasonable cost.

Good design enhances profitability

In fact, the business case for putting effort into good product and service design is overwhelming according to the UK Design Council.[2] Using design throughout the business ultimately boosts the bottom line by helping create better products and services that compete on value rather than price. **Design** helps businesses connect strongly with their customers by anticipating their real needs. That in turn gives them the ability to set themselves apart in increasingly tough markets. Furthermore, using design both to generate new ideas and turn them into reality allows businesses to set the pace in their markets and even create new ones rather than simply responding to the competition.

Critical commentary

Remember that not all new products and services are created in response to a clear and articulated customer need. While this is usually the case, especially for products and services that are similar to (but presumably better than) their predecessors, more radical innovations are often brought about by the innovation itself creating demand. Customers don't usually know that they need something radical. For example, in the late 1970s people were not asking for microprocessors, they did not even know what they were. They were improvised by an engineer in the USA for a Japanese customer who made calculators. Only later did they become the enabling technology for the PC and after that the innumerable devices that now dominate our lives.

What is designed in a product or service?

All products and services can be considered as having three aspects:

Concept
Package
Process

- a **concept**, which is the understanding of the nature, use and value of the service or product;
- a **package** of 'component' products and services that provide those benefits defined in the concept;
- the **process** defines the way in which the component products and services will be created and delivered.

The concept

Designers often talk about a 'new concept'. This might be a concept car specially created for an international show or a restaurant concept providing a different style of dining. The concept is a clear articulation of the outline specification including the nature, use and value of the product or service against which the stages of the design (see later) and the resultant product and/or service can be assessed. For example, a new car, just like existing cars, will have an underlying concept, such as an economical two-seat convertible sports car, with good road-holding capabilities and firm, sensitive handling, capable of 0–100 kph in 7 seconds and holding a bag of golf clubs in the boot. Likewise a concept for a restaurant might be a bold and brash dining experience aimed at the early 20s market, with contemporary décor and music, providing a range of freshly made pizza and pasta dishes.

Although the detailed design and delivery of the concept requires designers and operations managers to carefully design and select the components of the package and the processes by which they will be created or delivered, it is important to realize that customers are buying more than just the package and process; they are buying into the particular concept. Patients consuming a pharmaceutical company's products are not particularly concerned about the ingredients contained in the drugs they are using nor about the way in which they were made, they are concerned about the notion behind them, how they will use them and the benefits they will provide for them. Thus the articulation, development and testing of the concept is a crucial stage in the design of products and services.

The package of products and services

Normally the word 'product' implies a tangible physical object, such as a car, washing machine or watch, and the word 'service' implies a more intangible experience, such as an evening at a restaurant or a nightclub. In fact, as we discussed in Chapter 1, most, if not all, operations produce a combination of products *and* services. The purchase of a car includes the car itself and the services such as 'warranties', 'after-sales services' and 'the services of the person selling the car'. The restaurant meal includes products such as 'food' and 'drink' as well as services such as 'the delivery of the food to the table and the attentions of the waiting staff'. It is this collection of products and services that is usually referred to as the 'package' that customers buy. Some of the products or services in the package are **core**, that is they are fundamental to the purchase and could not be removed without destroying the nature of the package. Other parts will serve to enhance the core. These are **supporting goods and services**. In the case of the car, the leather trim and guarantees are supporting goods and services. The core good is the car itself. At the restaurant, the meal itself is the core. Its provision and preparation are important but not absolutely necessary (in some restaurants you might serve and even cook the meal yourself). By changing the core, or adding or subtracting supporting goods and services, organizations can provide different packages and in so doing create quite different concepts. For instance, engineers may wish to add traction control and four-wheel drive to make the two-seater sports car more stable, but this might conflict with the concept of an 'economical' car with 'sensitive handling'.

Core products and services

Supporting products and services

The process

The package of components which make up a product, service or process are the 'ingredients' of the design; however, designers need to design the way in which they will be created and delivered to the customer – this is process design. For the new car the assembly line has to be designed and built which will assemble the various components as the car moves down the line. New components such as the cloth roof need to be cut, stitched and trimmed. The gear box needs to be assembled. And, all the products need to be sourced, purchased and delivered as required. All these and many other manufacturing processes, together with the service processes of the delivery of cars to the showrooms and the sales processes have to be designed to support the concept. Likewise in the restaurant, the manufacturing processes of food purchase, preparation and cooking need to be designed, just like the way in which the customers will be processed from reception to the bar or waiting area and to the table and the way in which the series of activities at the table will be performed in such a way as to deliver the agreed concept.

Short case
Spangler, Hoover and Dyson[3]

In 1907 a janitor called Murray Spangler put together a pillowcase, a fan, an old biscuit tin and a broom handle. It was the world's first vacuum cleaner. One year later he sold his patented idea to William Hoover whose company went on to dominate the vacuum cleaner market for decades, especially in its United States homeland. Yet between 2002 and 2005 Hoover's market share dropped from 36 per cent to 13.5 per cent. Why? Because a futuristic-looking and comparatively expensive rival product, the Dyson vacuum cleaner, had jumped from nothing to over 20 per cent of the market. In fact, the Dyson product dates back to 1978 when James Dyson noticed how the air filter in the spray-finishing room of a company where he had been working was constantly clogging with powder particles (just like a vacuum cleaner bag clogs with dust). So he designed and built an industrial cyclone tower, which removed the powder particles by exerting centrifugal forces. The question intriguing him was, *'Could the same principle work in a domestic vacuum cleaner?'* Five years and

Source: Alamy Images

James Dyson

five *thousand* prototypes later he had a working design, since praised for its 'uniqueness and functionality'. However, existing vacuum cleaner manufacturers were not as impressed – two rejected the design outright. So Dyson started making his new design himself. Within a few years Dyson cleaners were, in the UK, outselling the rivals that had once rejected them. The aesthetics and functionality of the design help to keep sales growing in spite of a higher retail price. To Dyson, good *'is about looking at everyday things with new eyes and working out how they can be made better. It's about challenging existing technology'*.

Dyson engineers have taken this technology one stage further and developed core separator technology to capture even more microscopic dirt. Dirt now goes through three stages of separation. Firstly, dirt is drawn into a powerful outer cyclone. Centrifugal forces fling larger debris, such as pet hair and dust particles, into the clear bin at 500 Gs (the maximum G-force the human body can take is 8 Gs). Second, a further cyclonic stage, the core separator, removes dust particles as small as 0.5 microns from the airflow – particles so small you could fit 200 of them on this full stop. Finally, a cluster of smaller, even faster cyclones generate centrifugal forces of up to 150,000 G – extracting particles as small as mould and bacteria.

The design activity is itself a process

The design activity is one of the most important operations processes

Producing designs for products, services is itself a process which conforms to the input–transformation–output model described in Chapter 1. It therefore has to be designed and managed like any other **process**. Figure 5.2 illustrates the design activity as an input–transformation–output diagram. The transformed resource inputs will consist mainly of information in the form of market forecasts, market preferences, technical data, and so on. Transforming resource inputs includes operations managers and specialist technical staff, design equipment and software such as computer-aided design (CAD) systems (*see* later) and simulation packages. One can describe the objectives of the design activity in the same way as we do any transformation process. All operations satisfy customers by producing their services and goods according to customers' desires for quality, speed, dependability, flexibility and cost. In the same way, the design activity attempts to produce designs to the same objectives.

The stages of design – from concept to specification

Concept generation
Screening
Preliminary design
Evaluation and improvement
Prototyping and final design

Fully specified designs rarely spring, fully formed, from a designer's imagination. To get to a final design of a product or service, the design activity must pass through several key stages. These form an approximate sequence, although in practice designers will often recycle or backtrack through the stages. We will describe them in the order in which they usually occur, as shown in Figure 5.3. First, comes the **concept generation** stage that develops the overall concept for the product or service. The concepts are then **screened** to try to ensure that, in broad terms, they will be a sensible addition to its product/service portfolio and meet the concept as defined. The agreed concept has then to be turned into a **preliminary design** that then goes through a stage of **evaluation and improvement** to see if the concept can be served better, more cheaply or more easily. An agreed design may then be subjected to **prototyping and final design**.

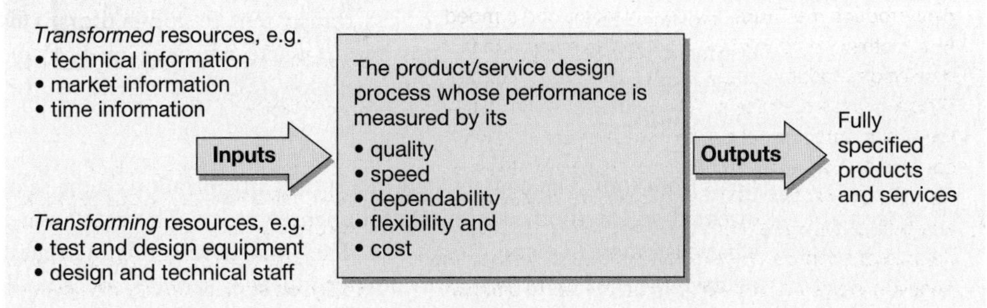

Figure 5.2 The design activity is itself a process

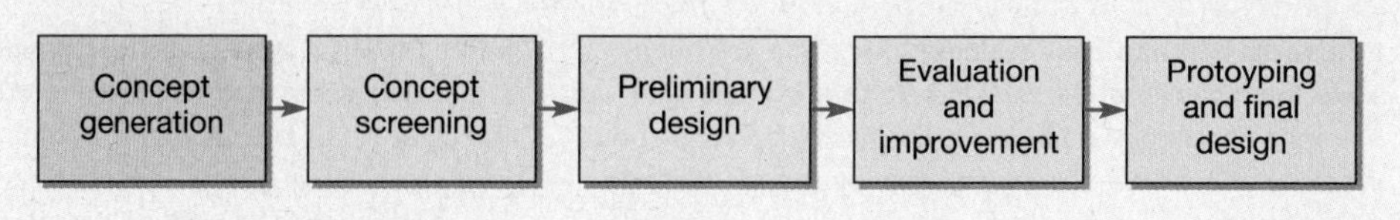

Figure 5.3 The stages of product/service design

Concept generation

The ideas for new product or service concepts can come from sources outside the organization, such as customers or competitors, and from sources within the organization, such as staff (for example, from sales staff and front-of-house staff) or from the R&D department.

Ideas from customers. Marketing, the function generally responsible for identifying new product or service opportunities may use many market research tools for gathering data from customers in a formal and structured way, including questionnaires and interviews. These techniques, however, usually tend to be structured in such a way as only to test out ideas or check products or services against predetermined criteria. Listening to the customer, in a less structured way, is sometimes seen as a better means of generating new ideas. **Focus groups**, for example, are one formal but unstructured way of collecting ideas and suggestions from customers. A focus group typically comprises seven to ten participants who are unfamiliar with each other but who have been selected because they have characteristics in common that relate to the particular topic of the focus group. Participants are invited to 'discuss' or 'share ideas with others' in a permissive environment that nurtures different perceptions and points of view, without pressurizing participants. The group discussion is conducted several times with similar types of participants in order to identify trends and patterns in perceptions.

Focus groups

Listening to customers. Ideas may come from customers on a day-to-day basis. They may write to complain about a particular product or service, or make suggestions for its improvement. Ideas may also come in the form of suggestions to staff during the purchase of the product or delivery of the service. Although some organizations may not see gathering this information as important (and may not even have mechanisms in place to facilitate it), it is an important potential source of ideas.

Ideas from competitor activity. All market-aware organizations follow the activities of their competitors. A new idea may give a competitor an edge in the marketplace, even if it is only a temporary one, then competing organizations will have to decide whether to imitate, or alternatively to come up with a better or different idea. Sometimes this involves **reverse engineering**, that is taking apart a product to understand how a competing organization has made it. Some aspects of services may be more difficult to reverse-engineer (especially back-office services) as they are less transparent to competitors. However, by consumer-testing a service, it may be possible to make educated guesses about how it has been created. Many service organizations employ 'testers' to check out the services provided by competitors.

Reverse engineering

Ideas from staff. The contact staff in a service organization or the salesperson in a product-oriented organization could meet customers every day. These staff may have good ideas about what customers like and do not like. They may have gathered suggestions from customers or have ideas of their own as to how products or services could be developed to meet the needs of their customers more effectively.

Research and development

Ideas from research and development. One formal function found in some organizations is **research and development** (R&D). As its name implies, its role is twofold. Research usually means attempting to develop new knowledge and ideas in order to solve a particular problem or to grasp an opportunity. Development is the attempt to try to utilize and operationalize the ideas that come from research. In this chapter we are mainly concerned with the 'development' part of R&D – for example, exploiting new ideas that might be afforded by new materials or new technologies. And although 'development' does not sound as exciting as 'research', it often requires as much creativity and even more persistence. Both creativity and persistence took James Dyson (see the short case earlier) from a potentially good idea to a workable technology. One product has commemorated the persistence of its development engineers in its company name. Back in 1953 the Rocket Chemical Company set out to create a rust-prevention solvent and degreaser to be used in the aerospace industry. Working in their lab in San Diego, California, it took them 40 attempts to get the water-displacing formula worked out. So that is what they called the product. WD-40 literally stands for water displacement, fortieth attempt. It was the name used in the lab book. Originally used to protect the outer skin of the Atlas missile from rust and corrosion, the product worked so well that employees kept taking cans home to use for domestic purposes. Soon after, the product was launched, with great success, into the consumer market.

Open-sourcing – using a 'development community'[4]

Not all 'products' or services are created by professional, employed designers for commercial purposes. Many of the software applications that we all use, for example, are developed by an open community, including the people who use the products. If you use Google, the Internet search facility, or use Wikipedia, the online encyclopaedia, or shop at Amazon, you are using open-source software. The basic concept of open-source software is extremely simple. Large communities of people around the world, who have the ability to write software code, come together and produce a software product. The finished product is not only available to be used by anyone or any organization for free but is regularly updated to ensure it keeps pace with the necessary improvements. The production of open-source software is very well organized and, like its commercial equivalent, is continuously supported and maintained. However, unlike its commercial equivalent, it is absolutely free to use. Over the last few years the growth of open-source has been phenomenal with many organizations transitioning over to using this stable, robust and secure software. With the maturity open-source software now has to offer, organizations have seen the true benefits of using free software to drive down costs and to establish themselves on a secure and stable platform. Open-source has been the biggest change in software development for decades and is setting new open standards in the way software is used.

The open nature of this type of development also encourages compatibility between products. BMW, for example, was reported to be developing an open-source platform for vehicle electronics. Using an open-source approach, rather than using proprietary software, BMW can allow providers of 'infotainment' services to develop compatible, plug-and-play applications. '*We were convinced we had to develop an open platform that would allow for open software since the speed in the infotainment and entertainment industry requires us to be on a much faster track*', said Gunter Reichart, BMW vice-president of driver assistance, body electronics and electrical networks. '*We invite other OEMs to join with us, to exchange with us. We are open to exchange with others.*'

Short case
Square watermelons![5]

Source: Getty Images

It sounds like a joke, but it is a genuine product innovation motivated by a market need. It's green, it's square and it comes originally from Japan. It's a square watermelon! Why square? Because Japanese grocery stores are not large and space cannot be wasted. Similarly a round watermelon does not fit into a refrigerator very conveniently. There is also the problem of trying to cut the fruit when it kept rolling around. So an innovative farmer from Japan's south-western island of Shikoku solved the problem devised with the idea of making a cube-shaped watermelon which could easily be packed and stored. But there is no genetic modification or clever science involved in growing watermelons. It simply involves placing the young fruit into wooden boxes with clear sides. During its growth, the fruit naturally swells to fill the surrounding shape. Now the idea has spread from Japan. *'Melons are among the most delicious and refreshing fruit around but some people find them a problem to store in their fridge or to cut because they roll around,'* said Damien Sutherland, the exotic fruit buyer from Tesco, the UK supermarket. 'We've seen samples of these watermelons and they literally stop you in their tracks because they are so eye-catching. These square melons will make it easier than ever to eat because they can be served in long strips rather than in the crescent shape.' But not everyone liked the idea. Comments on news web sites included: *'Where will engineering everyday things for our own unreasonable convenience stop? I prefer melons to be the shape of melons!'*, *'They are probably working on straight bananas next!'*, and *'I would like to buy square sausages, then they would be easier to turn over in the frying pan Round sausages are hard to keep cooked all over.'*

Concept screening

Not all concepts which are generated will necessarily be capable of further development into products and services. Designers need to be selective as to which concepts they progress to the next design stage. The purpose of the concept-screening stage is to take the flow of concepts and evaluate them. Evaluation in design means assessing the worth or value of each design option, so that a choice can be made between them. This involves assessing each concept or option against a number of **design criteria**. While the criteria used in any particular design exercise will depend on the nature and circumstances of the exercise, it is useful to think in terms of three broad categories of design criteria:

Design criteria

Feasibility

- The **feasibility** of the design option – can we do it?
  - Do we have the skills (quality of resources)?
  - Do we have the organizational capacity (quantity of resources)?
  - Do we have the financial resources to cope with this option?

Acceptability

- The **acceptability** of the design option – do we want to do it
  - Does the option satisfy the performance criteria which the design is trying to achieve? (These will differ for different designs.)
  - Will our customers want it?
  - Does the option give a satisfactory financial return?

Vulnerability

- The **vulnerability** of each design option – do we want to take the risk? That is,
  - Do we understand the full consequences of adopting the option?
  - Being pessimistic, what could go wrong if we adopt the option? What would be the consequences of everything going wrong? (This is called the 'downside risk' of an option.)

Figure 5.4 illustrates this classification of design criteria.

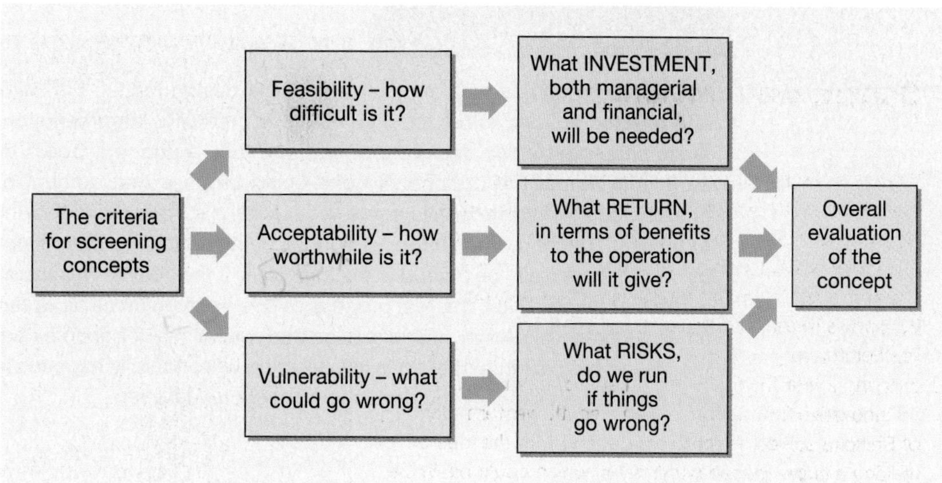

Figure 5.4 Broad categories of evaluation criteria for assessing concepts

The design 'funnel'

Applying these evaluation criteria progressively reduces the number of options which will be available further along in the design activity. For example, deciding to make the outside casing of a camera case from aluminium rather than plastic limits later decisions, such as the overall size and shape of the case. This means that the uncertainty surrounding the design reduces as the number of alternative designs being considered decreases. Figure 5.5 shows what is sometimes called the **design funnel**, depicting the progressive reduction of design options from many to one. But reducing design uncertainty also impacts on the cost of changing one's mind on some detail of the design. In most stages of design the cost of changing a decision is bound to incur some sort of rethinking and recalculation of costs. Early on in the design activity, before too many fundamental decisions have been made, the costs of change are relatively low. However, as the design progresses the interrelated and cumulative decisions already made become increasingly expensive to change.

Design funnel

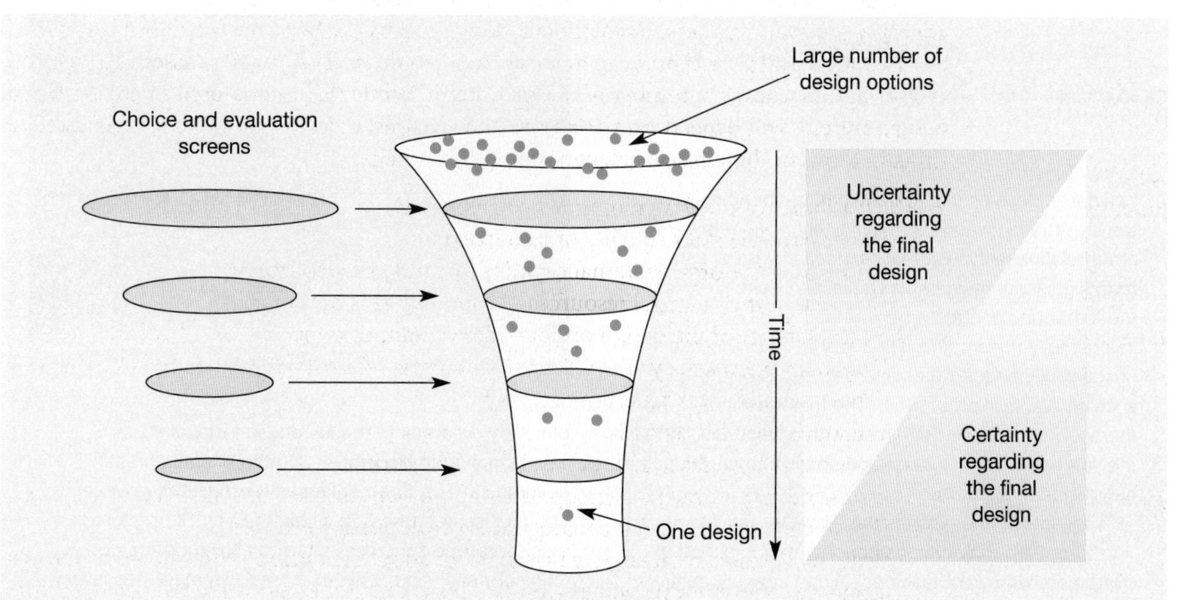

Figure 5.5 The design funnel – progressively reducing the number of possibilities until the final design is reached

Critical commentary

Not everyone agrees with the concept of the design funnel. For some it is just too neat and ordered an idea to reflect accurately the creativity, arguments and chaos that sometimes characterize the design activity. First, they argue, managers do not start out with an infinite number of options. No one could process that amount of information – and anyway, designers often have some set solutions in their mind, looking for an opportunity to be used. Second, the number of options being considered often *increases* as time goes by. This may actually be a good thing, especially if the activity was unimaginatively specified in the first place. Third, the real process of design often involves cycling back, often many times, as potential design solutions raise fresh questions or become dead ends. In summary, the idea of the design funnel does not describe what actually happens in the design activity. Nor does it necessarily even describe what *should* happen.

Balancing evaluation with creativity

Creativity is important in product/service design

The systematic process of evaluation is important but it must be balanced by the need for design creativity. **Creativity** is a vital ingredient in effective design. The final quality of any design of product or service will be influenced by the creativity of its designers. Increasingly, creativity is seen as an essential ingredient not just in the design of products and services, but also in the design of operations processes. Partly because of the fast-changing nature of many industries, a lack of creativity (and consequently of innovation) is seen as a major risk. For example, '*It has never been a better time to be an industry revolutionary. Conversely, it has never been a more dangerous time to be complacent . . . The dividing line between being a leader and being a laggard is today measured in months or a few days, and not in decades.*'[2] Of course, creativity can be expensive. By its nature it involves exploring sometimes unlikely possibilities. Many of these will die as they are proved to be inappropriate. Yet, to some extent, the process of creativity depends on these many seemingly wasted investigations. As Art Fry, the inventor of 3M's Post-it note products, said: '*You have to kiss a lot of frogs to find the prince. But remember, one prince can pay for a lot of frogs.*'

Short case
The Daniel Hersheson Blowdry Bar at Top Shop[6]

Source: Photographers Direct

Even at the chic and stylish end of the hairdressing business, close as it is to the world of changing fashion trends, true innovation and genuinely novel new services are a relative rarity. Yet real service innovation can reap significant rewards as Daniel and Luke Hersheson, the father and son team behind the Daniel Hersheson salons, fully understand. The Hersheson brand has successfully bridged the gaps between salon, photo session and fashion catwalk. The team first put themselves on the fashion map with a salon in London's Mayfair followed by a salon and spa in Harvey Nichols's flagship London store.

Their latest innovation is the 'Blowdry Bar at Top Shop'. This is a unique concept that is aimed at customers who want fashionable and catwalk quality styling at an affordable price without the full 'cut and blow-dry' treatment. The Hersheson Blowdry Bar was launched in December 2006 to ecstatic press coverage in Top Shop's flagship Oxford Circus store. The four-seater pink pod within the Top Shop store is a scissors-free zone dedicated to styling on the go. Originally seen as a walk-in, no-appointment-necessary format, demand has proved to be so high that an appointment system has been implemented to avoid disappointing customers. Once in the pod, customers can choose from a tailor-made picture menu of nine fashion styles with names like 'The Super Straight', 'The Classic Big and Bouncy' and 'Wavy Gravy'. Typically, the wash and blow-dry takes around 30 minutes. *'It's just perfect for a client who wants to look that bit special for a big night out but who doesn't want a full cut'*, says Ryan Wilkes, one of the stylists at the Blowdry Bar. *'Some clients will "graduate" to become regular customers at the main Daniel Hersheson salons. I have clients who started out using the Blowdry Bar but now also get their hair cut with me in the salon.'*

Partnering with Top Shop is an important element in the design of the service, says Daniel Hersheson, *'We are delighted to be opening the UK's first blow-dry bar at Top Shop. Our philosophy of constantly relating hair back to fashion means we will be perfectly at home in the most creative store on the British high street.'* Top Shop also recognizes the fit. *'The Daniel Hersheson Blowdry Bar is a really exciting service addition to our Oxford Circus flagship and offers the perfect finishing touch to a great shopping experience at Top Shop'*, says Jane Shepherdson, Brand Director of Top Shop.

But the new service has not just been a success in the market; it also has advantages for the operation itself. *'It's a great opportunity for young stylists not only to develop their styling skills, but also to develop the confidence that it takes to interact with clients'*, says George Northwood, Manager of Daniel Hersheson's Mayfair salon. *'You can see a real difference after a trainee stylist has worked in the Blowdry Bar. They learn how to talk to clients, to understand their needs, and to advise them. It's the confidence that they gain that is so important in helping them to become fully qualified and successful stylists in their own right.'*

Preliminary design

Having generated an acceptable, feasible and viable product or service concept the next stage is to create a preliminary design. The objective of this stage is to have a first attempt at both specifying the component products and services in the *package*, and defining the *processes* to create the package.

Specify the components of the package

Component (or product) structure

The first task in this stage of design is to define exactly what will go into the product or service: that is, specifying the components of the package. This will require the collection of information about such things as the *constituent component parts* which make up the product or service package and the **component (or product) structure**, the order in which the component parts of the package have to be put together. For example the components for a remote mouse for a computer may include, upper and lower casings, a control unit and packaging, which are themselves made up of other components. The product structure shows how these components fit together to make the mouse (*see* Fig. 5.6).

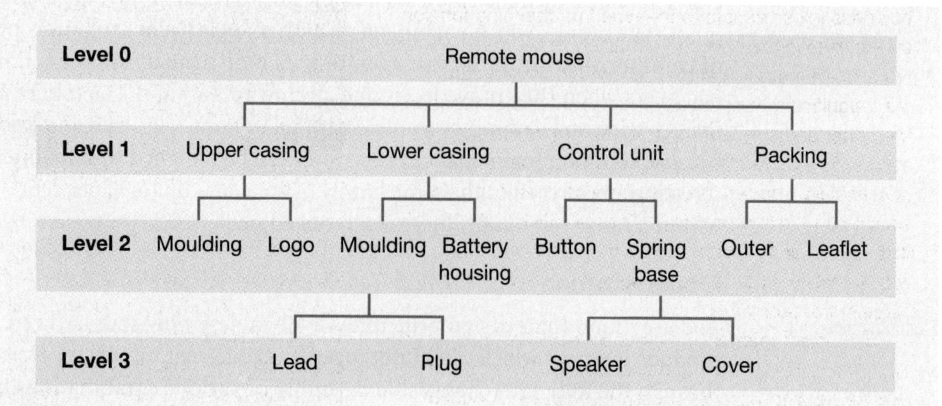

Figure 5.6 The component structure of a remote mouse

Reducing design complexity

Simplicity is usually seen as a virtue amongst designers of products and services. The most elegant design solutions are often the simplest. However, when an operation produces a variety of products or services (as most do) the range of products and services considered as a whole can become complex, which, in turn, increases costs. Designers adopt a number of approaches to reducing the inherent complexity in the design of their product or service range. Here we describe three common approaches to complexity reduction – standardization, commonality and modularization.

Standardization

Standardization

Operations sometimes attempt to overcome the cost penalties of high variety by **standardizing** their products, services or processes. This allows them to restrict variety to that which has real value for the end-customer. Often it is the operation's outputs which are standardized. Examples of this are fast-food restaurants, discount supermarkets and telephone-based insurance companies. Perhaps the most common example of standardization is the clothes which most of us buy. Although everybody's body shape is different, garment manufacturers produce clothes in only a limited number of sizes. The range of sizes is chosen to give a reasonable fit for most body shapes. To suit all their potential customers and/or to ensure a perfect fit, garment manufacturers would have to provide an infeasibly large range of sizes. Alternatively, they would need to provide a customized service. Both solutions would have a significant impact on cost. This control of variety is an important issue with most companies. A danger facing established operations is that they allow variety to grow excessively. They are then faced with the task of *variety reduction*, often by assessing the real profit or contribution of each product or service. Many organizations have significantly improved their profitability by careful variety reduction. In order to overcome loss of business, customers may be offered alternative products or services which provide similar value.

Commonality

Using common elements within a product or service can also simplify design complexity. Using the same components across a range of automobiles is a common practice. Likewise, standardizing the format of information inputs to a process can be achieved by using appropriately designed forms or screen formats. The more different products and services can be based on common components, the less complex it is to produce them. For example, the European aircraft maker Airbus has designed its new generation of jetliners with a high degree of **commonality**. Airbus developed full design and operational commonality with the introduction of fly-by-wire technology on its civil aircraft in the late 1980s. This meant that ten aircraft models ranging from the 100-seat A318 through to the world's largest aircraft, the 555-seat A380, feature virtually identical flight decks, common systems and similar handling characteristics. In some cases, such as the entire A320 family, the aircraft even share the same 'pilot-type rating', which enables pilots with a single licence to fly any of them. The advantages of commonality for the airline operators include a much shorter training time for pilots and engineers when they move from one aircraft to another. This offers pilots the possibility of flying a wide range of routes from short-haul to ultra-long-haul and leads to greater efficiencies because common maintenance procedures can be designed with maintenance teams capable of servicing any aircraft in the same family. Also, when up to 90 per cent of all parts are common within a range of aircraft, there is a reduced need to carry a wide range of spare parts.

Commonality

Modularization

Modularization

The use of **modular** design principles involves designing standardized 'sub-components' of a product or service which can be put together in different ways. It is possible to create wide choice through the fully interchangeable assembly of various combinations of a smaller number of standard sub-assemblies; computers are designed in this way, for example. These standardized modules, or sub-assemblies, can be produced in higher volume, thereby reducing their cost.

Similarly, the package holiday industry can assemble holidays to meet a specific customer requirement, from pre-designed and purchased air travel, accommodation, insurance, and so on. In education also there is an increasing use of modular courses which allow 'customers' choice but permit each module to have economical volumes of students. The short case 'Customizing for kids' describes an example of modularization in TV programme production.

Short case
Customizing for kids[7]

Reducing design complexity is a principle that applies just as much to service as to manufactured products. For example, television programmes are made increasingly with a worldwide market in mind. However, most television audiences around the world have a distinct preference for programmes which respect their regional tastes, culture and of course language. The challenge facing global programme makers therefore is to try and achieve the economies which come as a result of high volume production while allowing programmes to be customized for different markets. For example, take the programme *Art Attack*! made for the Disney Channel, a children's TV channel shown around the world. In 2001 two hundred and sixteen episodes of the show were made in six different language versions. About 60 per cent of each show is common across all versions. Shots without speaking or where the presenter's face is not visible are shot separately. For example, if a simple cardboard model is being made all versions will share the scenes where the presenter's hands only are visible. Commentary in the appropriate language is over-dubbed onto the scenes which are edited seamlessly with other shots of the appropriate presenter. The final product will have the head and shoulders of Brazilian, French, Italian, German, or Spanish presenters flawlessly mixed with the same pair of (British) hands constructing the model. The result is that local viewers in each market see the show as their own. Even though presenters are flown into the UK production studies, the cost of making each episode is only about one third of producing separate programmes for each market.

Define the process to create the package

The product/service structure and bill-of-materials specifies what goes into a product. It is around this stage in the design process where it is necessary to examine how a process could put together the various components to create the final product or service. At one time this activity would have been delayed until the very end of the design process. However, this can cause problems if the designed product or service cannot be produced to the required quality and cost constraints. For now, what is important to understand is that processes should at least be examined in outline well before any product or service design is finalized. We outlined some of the basic ideas behind process design. The techniques of process mapping (see Chapter 4) can be used during this stage.

Design evaluation and improvement

The purpose of this stage in the design activity is to take the preliminary design and see if it can be improved before the product or service is tested in the market. There are a number of techniques that can be employed at this stage to evaluate and improve the preliminary design. Here we treat three which have proved particularly useful:

- Quality function deployment (QFD)
- Value engineering (VE)
- Taguchi methods.

Quality function deployment[8]

Quality function deployment

The key purpose of **quality function deployment** (QFD) is to try to ensure that the eventual design of a product or service actually meets the needs of its customers. Customers may not have been considered explicitly since the concept generation stage, and therefore it is

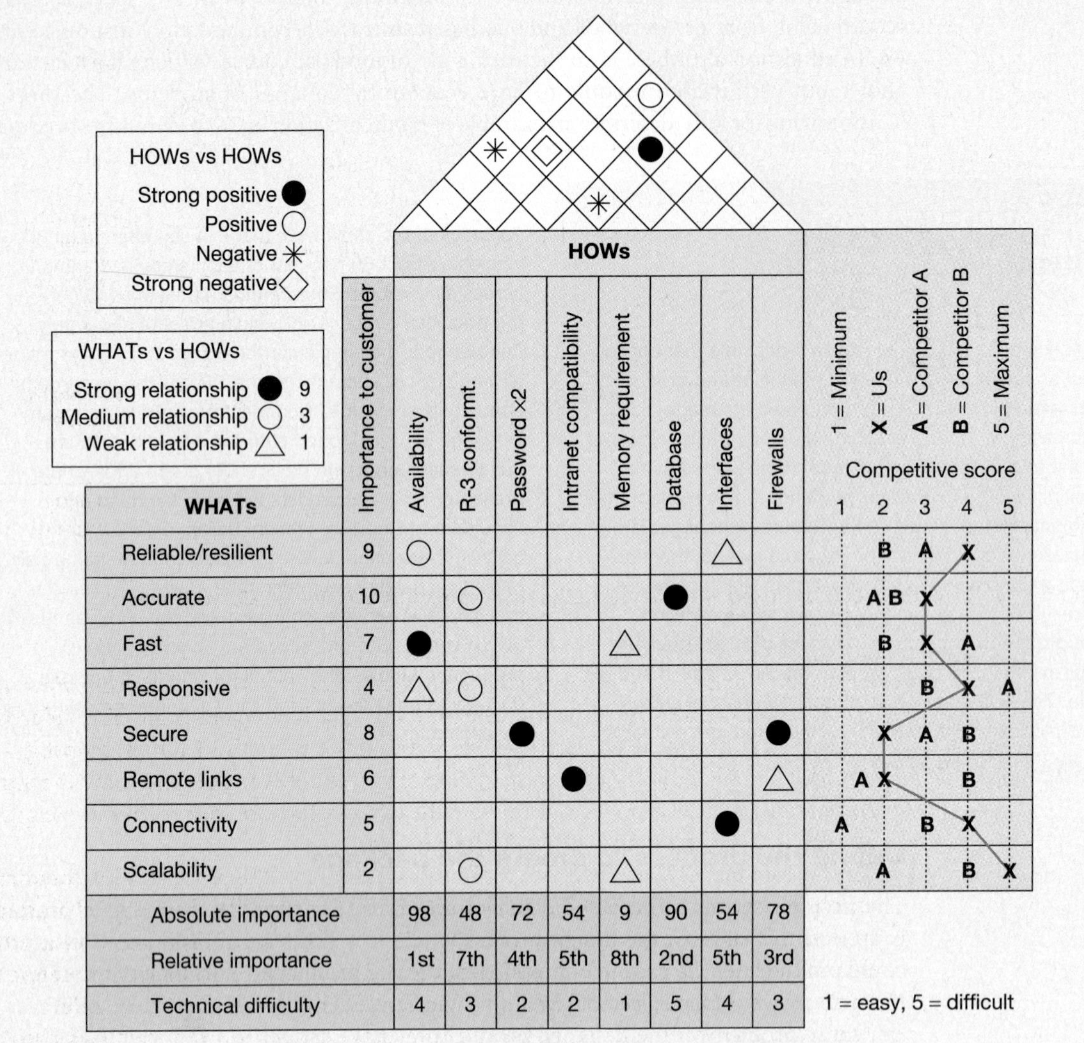

Figure 5.7 A QFD matrix for an information system product

appropriate to check that what is being proposed for the design of the product or service will meet their needs. It is a technique that was developed in Japan at Mitsubishi's Kobe shipyard and used extensively by Toyota, the motor vehicle manufacturer, and its suppliers. It is also known as the 'house of quality' (because of its shape) and the 'voice of the customer' (because of its purpose). The technique tries to capture *what* the customer needs and *how* it might be achieved. Figure 5.7 shows an example of quality function deployment being used in the design of a new information system product. The QFD matrix is a formal articulation of how the company sees the relationship between the requirements of the customer (the *whats*) and the design characteristics of the new product (the *hows*). The matrix contains various sections, as explained below:

- The *whats*, or 'customer requirements', is the list of competitive factors which customers find significant. Their relative importance is scored, in this case on a 10-point scale, with *accurate* scoring the highest.
- The competitive scores indicate the relative performance of the product, in this case on a 1 to 5 scale. Also indicated are the performances of two competitor products.
- The *hows*, or 'design characteristics' of the product, are the various 'dimensions' of the design which will operationalize customer requirements within the product or service.

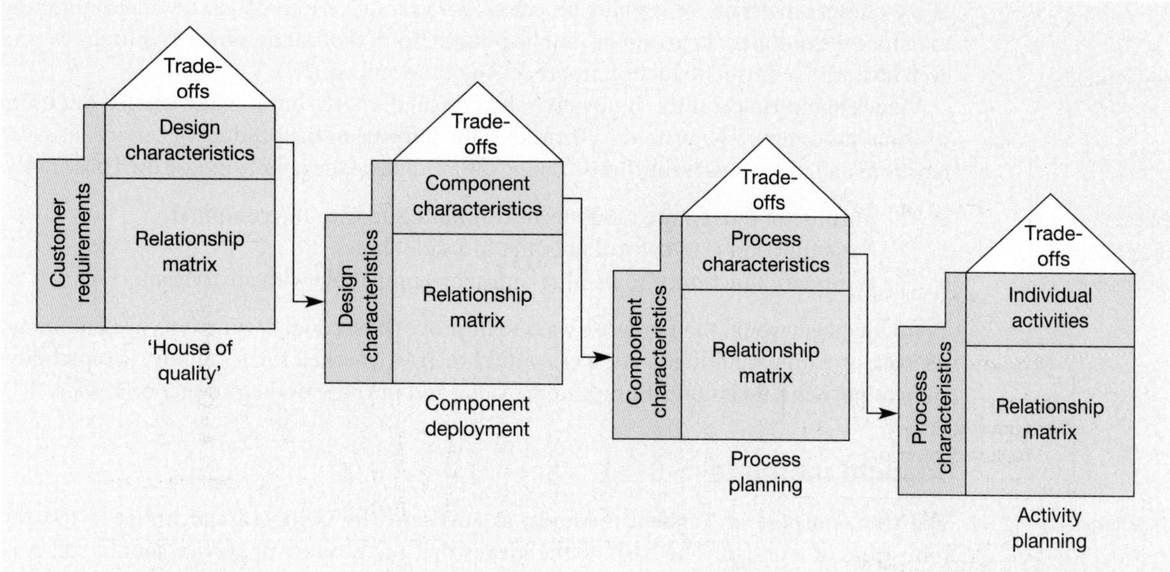

Figure 5.8 QFD matrices can be linked with the 'hows' of one matrix forming the 'whats' of the next

- The central matrix (sometimes called the 'relationship matrix') represents a view of the interrelationship between the *whats* and the *hows*. This is often based on value judgements made by the design team. The symbols indicate the strength of the relationship – for example, the relationship between the ability to link remotely to the system and the intranet compatibility of the product is strong. All the relationships are studied, but in many cases, where the cell of the matrix is blank, there is none.
- The bottom box of the matrix is a technical assessment of the product. This contains the absolute importance of each design characteristic. [For example, the design characteristic 'interfaces' has a relative importance of $(9 \times 5) + (1 \times 9) = 54$.] This is also translated into a ranked relative importance. In addition, the degree of technical difficulty to achieve high levels of performance in each design characteristic is indicated on a 1 to 5 scale.
- The triangular 'roof' of the 'house' captures any information the team has about the correlations (positive or negative) between the various design characteristics.

Although the details of QFD may vary between its different variants, the principle is generally common, namely to identify the customer requirements for a product or service (together with their relative importance) and to relate them to the design characteristics which translate those requirements into practice. In fact, this principle can be continued by making the *hows* from one stage become the *whats* of the next (*see* Fig. 5.8). Some experienced users of QFD have up to four linked matrices in this way. If engineering or process trade-offs need to be made at a later stage, the interrelated houses enable the effect on customer requirements to be determined.

Value engineering

Value engineering

The purpose of **value engineering** is to try to reduce costs, and prevent any unnecessary costs, before producing the product or service. Simply put, it tries to eliminate any costs that do not contribute to the value and performance of the product or service. ('Value analysis' is the name given to the same process when it is concerned with cost reduction after the product or service has been introduced.) Value-engineering programmes are usually conducted by project teams consisting of designers, purchasing specialists, operations managers and financial analysts. The chosen elements of the package are subject to rigorous scrutiny, by analysing their function and cost, then trying to find any similar components that could do the same job at lower cost. The team may attempt to reduce the number of components, or use cheaper materials, or simplify processes. For example, Motorola used value engineering to reduce the number of parts in its mobile phones from 'thousands' down to 'hundreds' and even less, with a drastic reduction in processing time and cost.

Value engineering requires innovative and critical thinking, but it is also carried out using a formal procedure. The procedure examines the purpose of the product or service, its basic functions and its secondary functions. Taking the example of the remote mouse used previously:

Purpose
Basic functions
Secondary functions

- The **purpose** of the remote mouse is to communicate with the computer.
- The **basic function** is to control presentation slide shows.
- The **secondary function** is to be plug-and-play-compatible with any system.

Team members would then propose ways to improve the secondary functions by combining, revising or eliminating them. All ideas would then be checked for feasibility, acceptability, vulnerability and their contribution to the value and purpose of the product or service.

Taguchi methods

Taguchi methods

The main purpose of **Taguchi methods**, as advocated by Genichi Taguchi,[9] is to test the robustness of a design. The basis of the idea is that the product or service should still perform in extreme conditions. A telephone, for example, should still work even when it has been knocked onto the floor. Although one does not expect customers to knock a telephone to the floor, this does happen, and so the need to build strength into the casing should be considered in its design. Likewise, a pizza parlour should be able to cope with a sudden rush of customers and a hotel should be able to cope with early arrivals. Product and service designers therefore need to brainstorm to try to identify all the possible situations that might arise and check that the product or service is capable of dealing with those that are deemed to be necessary and cost-effective. In the case of an adventure holiday, for example, service designers need to plan for such contingencies as:

- foul weather – the need for bad-weather alternatives;
- equipment failure – the provision of enough equipment to cover for maintenance;
- staff shortages – flexible working to allow cover from one area to another;
- accidents – the ability to deal with an accident without jeopardizing the other children in the group, with easily accessible first-aid equipment, and using facilities and equipment that are easy to clean and unlikely to cause damage to children;
- illness – the ability to deal with ill children who are unable to take part in an activity.

The task is then to achieve a design which can cope with all these uncertainties. The major problem designers face is that the number of design factors which they could vary to try to cope with the uncertainties, when taken together, is very large. For example, in designing the telephone casing there could be many thousands of combinations of casing size, casing shape, casing thickness, materials, jointing methods, etc. Performing all the investigations (or experiments, as they are called in the Taguchi technique) to try to find a combination of design factors which gives an optimum design can be a lengthy process. The Taguchi procedure is a statistical procedure for carrying out relatively few experiments while still being able to determine the best combination of design factors. Here 'best' means the lowest cost and the highest degree of uniformity.

Prototyping and final design

At around this stage in the design activity it is necessary to turn the improved design into a prototype so that it can be tested. It may be too risky to go into full production of the telephone, or the holiday, before testing it out, so it is usually more appropriate to create a prototype. Product prototypes include everything from clay models to computer simulations. Service prototypes may also include computer simulations but also the actual implementation of the service on a pilot basis. Many retailing organizations pilot new products and services in a small number of stores in order to test customers' reaction to them. Increasingly, it is

Virtual prototype

possible to store the data that define a product or service in a digital format on computer systems, which allows this **virtual prototype** to be tested in much the same way as a physical prototype. This is a familiar idea in some industries such as magazine publishing, where images and text can be rearranged and subjected to scrutiny prior to them existing in any physical form. This allows them to be amended right up to the point of production without incurring high costs. Now this same principle is applied to the prototype stage in the design of three-dimensional physical products and services. Virtual-reality-based simulations allow businesses to test new products and services as well as visualize and plan the processes that will produce them. Individual component parts can be positioned together virtually and tested for fit or interference. Even virtual workers can be introduced into the prototyping system to check for ease of assembly or operation.

Computer-aided design (CAD)

CAD

CAD systems provide the computer-aided ability to create and modify product drawings. These systems allow conventionally used shapes such as points, lines, arcs, circles and text, to be added to a computer-based representation of the product. Once incorporated into the design, these entities can be copied, moved about, rotated through angles, magnified or deleted. The designs thus created can be saved in the memory of the system and retrieved for later use. This enables a library of standardized drawings of parts and components to be built up. The simplest CAD systems model only in two dimensions in a similar way to a conventional engineering 'blueprint'. More sophisticated systems model products in three dimensions. The most obvious advantage of CAD systems is that their ability to store and retrieve design data quickly, as well as their ability to manipulate design details, can considerably increase the productivity of the design activity. In addition to this, however, because changes can be made rapidly to designs, CAD systems can considerably enhance the flexibility of the design activity, enabling modifications to be made much more rapidly. Further, the use of standardized libraries of shapes and entities can reduce the possibility of errors in the design.

Skunkworks[10]

Encouraging creativity in design, while at the same time recognizing the constraints of everyday business life, has always been one of the great challenges of industrial design. One well-known approach to releasing the design and development creativity of a group has been called a 'Skunkworks'. This is usually taken to mean a small team who are taken out of their normal work environment and granted freedom from their normal management activities and constraints. It was an idea that originated in the Lockheed aircraft company in the 1940s, where designers were set up outside the normal organizational structure and given the task of designing a high-speed fighter plane. The experiment was so successful that the company continued with it to develop other innovative products.

Skunkworks

Since that time many other companies have used a similar approach, although '**Skunkworks**' is a registered trademark of Lockheed Martin Corporation. Motorola's mobile phone 'Razr' was designed and developed in a Skunkworks-like special laboratory that the company set up, well away from its main Research and Development site in Illinois. Even the décor and layout of the laboratory were different: open-plan and with lots of bright colours. Something similar is reportedly used by Malaysia Airlines to tackle wider business issues, not just 'design' assignments.

The benefits of interactive design

Earlier we made the point that in practice it is a mistake to separate the design of products and services from the design of the processes which will produce them. Operations managers should have some involvement from the initial evaluation of the concept right through to the

Interactive design

Interactive design can shorten time to market

production of the product or service and its introduction to the market. Merging the design of products/services and the processes which create them is sometimes called **interactive design**. Its benefits come from the reduction in the elapsed time for the whole design activity, from concept through to market introduction. This is often called the **time to market** (TTM). The argument in favour of reducing time to market is that doing so gives increased competitive advantage. For example, if it takes a company five years to develop a product from concept to market, with a given set of resources, it can introduce a new product only once every five years. If its rival can develop products in three years, it can introduce its new product, together with its (presumably) improved performance, once every three years. This means that the rival company does not have to make such radical improvements in performance each time it introduces a new product, because it is introducing its new products more frequently. In other words, shorter TTM means that companies get more opportunities to improve the performance of their products or services.

If the development process takes longer than expected (or even worse, longer than competitors') two effects are likely to show. The first is that the costs of development will increase. Having to use development resources, such as designers, technicians, subcontractors, and so on, for a longer development period usually increases the costs of development. Perhaps more seriously, the late introduction of the product or service will delay the revenue from its sale (and possibly reduce the total revenue substantially if competitors have already got to the market with their own products or services). The net effect of this could be not only a considerable reduction in sales but also reduced profitability – an outcome which could considerably extend the time before the company breaks even on its investment in the new product or service. This is illustrated in Figure 5.9.

A number of factors have been suggested which can significantly reduce time to market for a product or service, including the following:

- simultaneous development of the various stages in the overall process;
- an early resolution of design conflict and uncertainty;
- an organizational structure which reflects the development project.

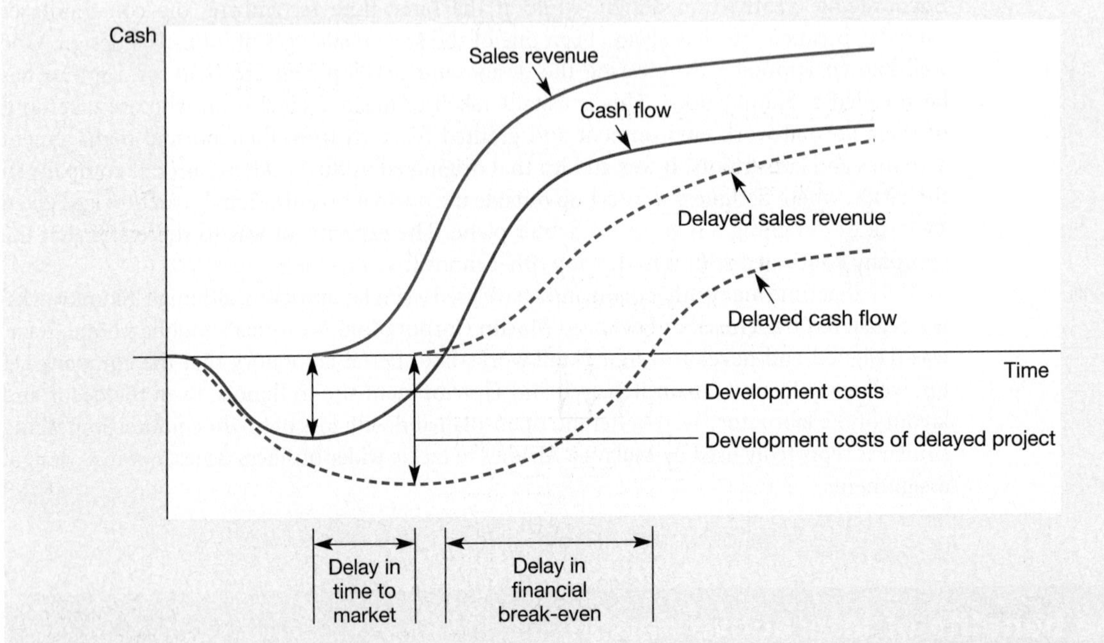

Figure 5.9 Delay in the time to market of new products and services not only reduces and delays revenues, it also increases the costs of development. The combination of both these effects usually delays the financial break-even point far more than the delay in the time to market

Simultaneous development

Sequential approach to design

Earlier in the chapter we described the design process as essentially a set of individual, predetermined stages. Sometimes one stage is completed before the next one commences. This step-by-step, or **sequential**, approach has traditionally been the typical form of product/service development. It has some advantages. It is easy to manage and control design projects organized in this way, since each stage is clearly defined. In addition, each stage is completed before the next stage is begun, so each stage can focus its skills and expertise on a limited set of tasks. The main problem of the sequential approach is that it is both time-consuming and costly. When each stage is separate, with a clearly defined set of tasks, any difficulties encountered during the design at one stage might necessitate the design being halted while responsibility moves back to the previous stage. This sequential approach is shown in Figure 5.10(a).

Simultaneous or concurrent approach to design

Simultaneous (or concurrent) engineering

Yet often there is really little need to wait until the absolute finalization of one stage before starting the next. For example, perhaps while generating the concept, the evaluation activity of screening and selection could be started. It is likely that some concepts could be judged as 'non-starters' relatively early on in the process of idea generation. Similarly, during the screening stage, it is likely that some aspects of the design will become obvious before the phase is finally complete. Therefore, the preliminary work on these parts of the design could be commenced at that point. This principle can be taken right through all the stages, one stage commencing before the previous one has finished, so there is **simultaneous or concurrent** work on the stages (*see* Fig. 5.10(b)). (Note that simultaneous development is often called **simultaneous (or concurrent) engineering** in manufacturing operations.)

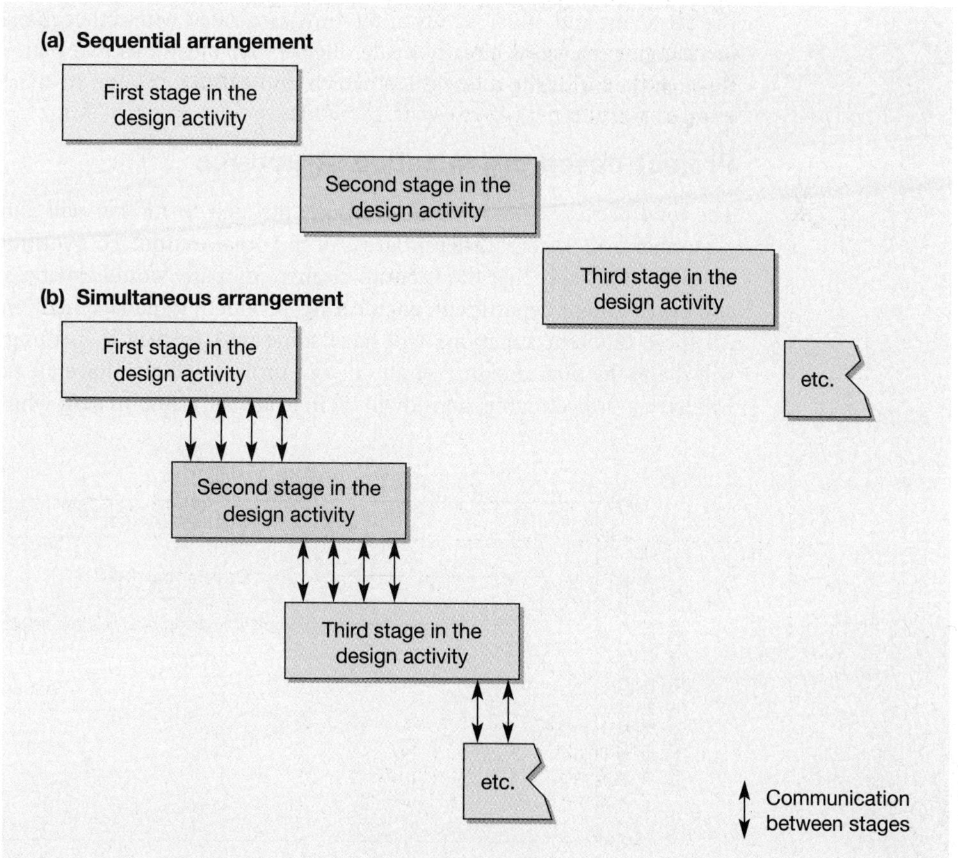

Figure 5.10 (a) Sequential arrangement of the stages in the design activity; (b) simultaneous arrangement of the stages in the design activity

Early conflict resolution

Characterizing the design activity as a whole series of decisions is a useful way of thinking about design. However, a decision, once made, need not totally and utterly commit the organization. For example, if a design team is designing a new vacuum cleaner, the decision to adopt a particular style and type of electric motor might have seemed sensible at the time the decision was made but might have to be changed later, in the light of new information. It could be that a new electric motor becomes available which is clearly superior to the one initially selected. Under those circumstances the designers might very well want to change their decision.

There are other, more avoidable, reasons for designers changing their minds during the design activity, however. Perhaps one of the initial design decisions was made without sufficient discussion among those in the organization who have a valid contribution to make. It may even be that when the decision was made there was insufficient agreement to formalize it, and the design team decided to carry on without formally making the decision. Yet subsequent decisions might be made as though the decision had been formalized. For example, suppose the company could not agree on the correct size of electric motor to put into its vacuum cleaner. It might well carry on with the rest of the design work while further discussions and investigations take place on what kind of electric motor to incorporate in the design. Yet much of the rest of the product's design is likely to depend on the choice of the electric motor. The plastic housings, the bearings, the sizes of various apertures, and so on, could all be affected by this decision. Failure to resolve these conflicts and/or decisions early on in the process can prolong the degree of uncertainty in the total design activity. In addition, if a decision is made (even implicitly) and then changed later on in the process, the costs of that change can be very large. However, if the design team manages to resolve conflict early in the design activity, this will reduce the degree of uncertainty within the project and reduce the extra cost and, most significantly, time associated with either managing this uncertainty or changing decisions already made. Figure 5.11 illustrates two patterns of design changes through the life of the total design, which imply different time-to-market performances.

Project-based organization structures

The total process of developing concepts through to market will almost certainly involve personnel from several different areas of the organization. To continue the vacuum cleaner example, it is likely that the vacuum cleaner company would involve staff from its research and development department, engineering, production management, marketing and finance. All these different functions will have some part to play in making the decisions which will shape the final design. Yet any design project will also have an existence of its own. It will have a project name, an individual manager or group of staff who are championing the

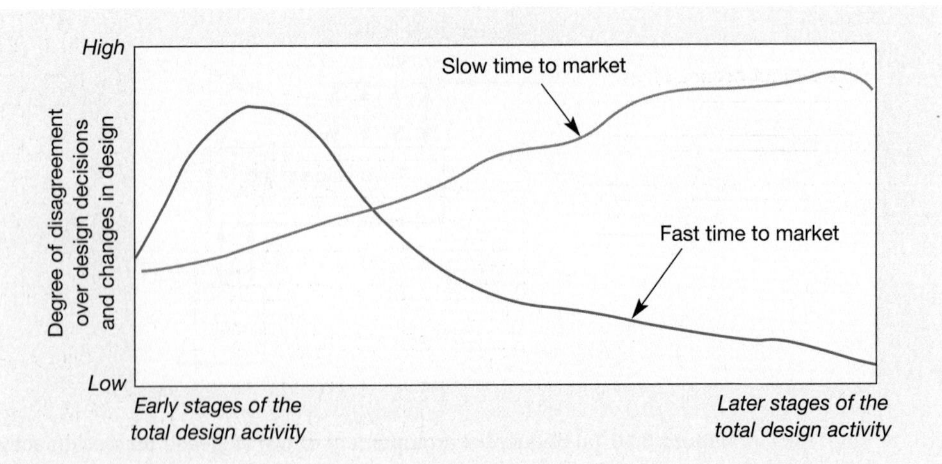

Figure 5.11 Sorting out problems early saves greater disruption later in the design activity

project, a budget and, hopefully, a clear strategic purpose in the organization. The organizational question is which of these two ideas – the various organizational functions which contribute to the design or the design project itself – should dominate the way in which the design activity is managed?

Functional design organization

Project design organization

Task force

Matrix organization

Before answering this, it is useful to look at the range of organizational structures which are available – from **pure functional** to **pure project** forms. In a pure functional organization, all staff associated with the design project are based unambiguously in their functional groups. There is no project-based group at all. They may be working full-time on the project but all communications and liaison are carried out through their functional manager. The project exists because of agreement between these functional managers. At the other extreme, all the individual members of staff from each function who are involved in the project could be moved out of their functions and perhaps even physically relocated to a **task force** dedicated solely to the project. The task force could be led by a project manager who might hold all the budget allocated to the design project. Not all members of the task force necessarily have to stay in the team throughout the development period, but a substantial core might see the project through from start to finish. Some members of a design team may even be from other companies. In between these two extremes there are various types of **matrix organization** with varying emphasis on these two aspects of the organization (*see* Fig. 5.12). Although the 'task force' type of organization, especially for small projects, can sometimes be a little cumbersome, it seems to be generally agreed that, for substantial projects at least, it is more effective at reducing overall time to market.[11]

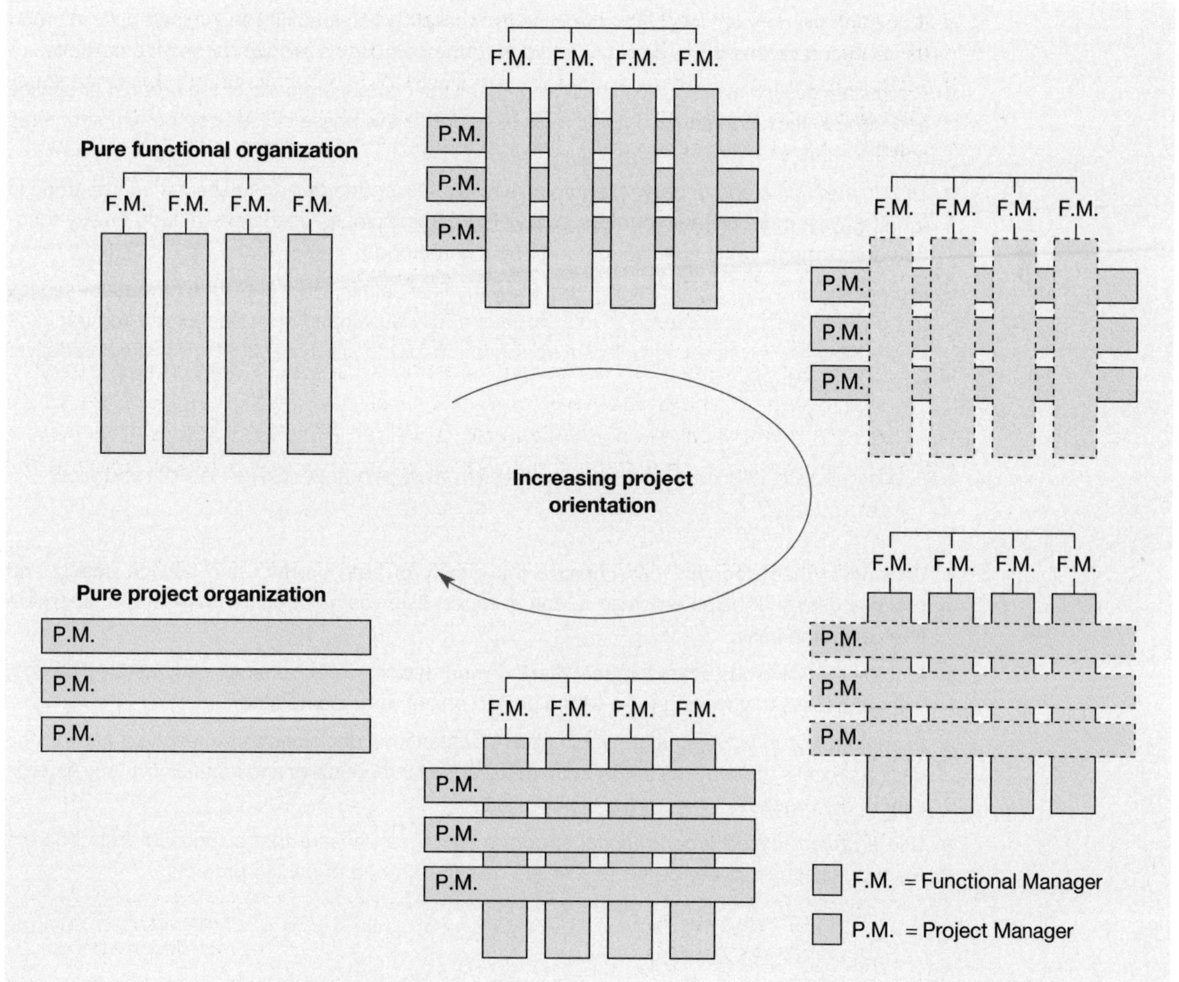

Figure 5.12 Organization structures for the design activity

Summary answers to key questions

*Check and improve your understanding of this chapter using self assessment questions and a personalised study plan, audio and video downloads, and an eBook – all at **www.myomlab.com**.*

➤ Why is good product and service design important?

- Good design makes good business sense because it translates customer needs into the shape and form of the product or service and so enhances profitability.
- Design includes formalizing three particularly important issues: the concept, package and process implied by the design.
- Design is a process that itself must be designed according to the process design principles described in the previous chapter.

➤ What are the stages in product and service design?

- *Concept generation* transforms an idea for a product or service into a concept which captures the nature of the product or service and provides an overall specification for its design.
- *Screening* the concept involves examining its feasibility, acceptability and vulnerability in broad terms to ensure that it is a sensible addition to the company's product or service portfolio.
- *Preliminary design* involves the identification of all the component parts of the product or service and the way they fit together. Typical tools used during this phase include component structures and flow charts.
- *Design evaluation and improvement* involve re-examining the design to see if it can be done in a better way, more cheaply or more easily. Typical techniques used here include quality function deployment, value engineering and Taguchi methods.
- *Prototyping and final design* involve providing the final details which allow the product or service to be produced. The outcome of this stage is a fully developed specification for the package of products and services, as well as a specification for the processes that will make and deliver them to customers.

➤ Why should product and service design and process design be considered interactively?

- Looking at them together can improve the quality of both product and service design and process design. It helps a design 'break even' on its investment earlier than would otherwise have been the case.
- Employ *simultaneous development* where design decisions are taken as early as they can be, without necessarily waiting for a whole design phase to be completed.
- Ensure early *conflict resolution* which allows contentious decisions to be resolved early in the design process, thereby not allowing them to cause far more delay and confusion if they emerge later in the process.
- Use a *project-based organizational structure* which can ensure that a focused and coherent team of designers is dedicated to a single design or group of design projects.

Case study
Chatsworth – the adventure playground decision

Chatsworth, the home of the 12th Duke and Duchess of Devonshire, is one of the finest and most palatial houses in the UK, set in over 1,000 acres of parkland in the Peak District National Park in central England. The original house was built over 400 years ago and rebuilt starting in the 17th century. The house is vast, with 175 rooms, lit by over 2,000 light bulbs, and with a roof that covers 1.3 acres. Chatsworth's many rooms are full of treasures including famous works of art by painters including Rembrandt, and tapestries, sculptures, valuable furniture, musical instruments and even 63 antique clocks which need winding every day. The gardens cover over 105 acres with over five miles of footpaths that guide visitors past fountains, small and large (the largest is 28 metres high), cascades, streams and ponds, all of which are fed by gravity from four large artificial lakes on the moors above the grounds. The gardens are a mix of formal and informal areas. There are sculptures, statues, rock gardens, a maze and garden views that constantly change with the seasons, all managed and maintained by a team of 20 gardeners. Both the house and gardens are open from March to December and are just two of the experiences available to visitors. Others include the orangery gift shop, restaurant and farm shop, which are open all year round, and the surrounding parkland which is open to visitors for walking, picnics and swimming in the river. The whole estate is owned and managed by an independent charity.

Close to the house and gardens, with a separate admission charge, is the farmyard and adventure playground. The farmyard is a popular attraction for families and provides close encounters with a variety of livestock including pigs, sheep, cows, chickens and fish. The staff provide daily milking demonstrations and animal handling sessions. The woodland adventure playground is accessed through the farmyard and is one of the largest in the country with a range of frames, bridges, high-level walkways, swings, chutes and slides.

Simon Seligman is the Promotions and Education Manager at Chatsworth. As head of marketing he is closely involved in the design and development of new services and facilities. He explained the way they do this at Chatsworth. *'It is a pretty abstract and organic process. Looking back over the last 25 years we either take occasional great leaps forward or make frequent little shuffles. The little shuffles tend to be organic changes usually in response to visitor feedback. The great leaps forward have been the few major changes that we decided we wanted to bring about.'*

One of those great leaps forward was the decision to replace the children's adventure playground attached to the farmyard. Simon explained, *'The existing adventure playground was clearly coming to the end of its life and it*

was time to make a decision about what to do with it. It was costing us about £18,000 each winter to maintain it and these costs were increasing year on year. We believed we could get a better one for around £100,000. The trustees asked me, the deputy estate manager with line responsibility for the farmyard and the farmyard manager to form a group and put forward a report to the trustees setting out all the options. We asked ourselves several detailed questions and some fundamental ones too, such as why are we replacing it, and should we replace it at all. We came up with four options, remove it, do nothing, replace with similar, replace with substantially better.'

It was felt that removing the playground altogether was a realistic option. The Duke and Duchess had a view that Chatsworth should be true to its roots and traditions. Whereas one could make an argument for a farmyard being part of a country estate, an adventure playground was considered to fit less well. The downside would be that the lack of an adventure playground, which is a big attraction for families with young children, could have an impact on visitor numbers. However, there would be a saving in terms of site maintenance.

The 'do nothing' option would entail patching up the playground each year and absorbing the increasing maintenance costs. This could be a low-impact option, in the short term at least. However, it was felt that this option would simply delay the replace or remove decision by five years at most. The current playground was no longer meeting international safety standards so this could be a good opportunity to replace the playground with something 

similar. It was estimated that a like-for-like replacement would cost around £100,000. Replacing the playground with a substantially better one would entail a much greater cost but could have an impact on visitor numbers. Simon and his team keep a close eye on their competitors and visit them whenever they can. They reported that several other attractions had first-rate adventure playgrounds. Installing a substantially better playground could provide an opportunity for Chatsworth to leapfrog over them and provide something really special.

'We tried to cost out all four alternatives and estimate what we thought the impact on visitor numbers might be. We presented an interim report to the Duke and the other trustees. We felt that maintaining the status quo was inappropriate and a like-for-like replacement was expensive, especially given that it would attract little publicity and few additional visitors. We strongly recommended two options: either remove the playground or go for a great leap forward. The trustees asked us to bear in mind the "remove" option and take a closer look at the "substantially better" option.'

Three companies were asked to visit the site, propose a new adventure playground and develop a site plan and initial design to a budget of £150,000. All three companies provided some outline proposals for such a figure but they all added that for £200,000 they could provide something really quite special. Furthermore, the team realized that they would have to spend some additional money putting in a new ramp and a lift into the farmyard at an estimated £50,000. It was starting to look like a very expensive project. Simon takes up the story, *'One of the companies came along with a complete idea for the site based on water, which is a recurring theme in the garden at Chatsworth. They had noticed the stream running through the playground and thought it could make a wonderful feature. They told us they were reluctant to put up a single solution but wanted to work with us, really engage with us, to explore what would really work for us and how it could be achieved. They also wanted to take us to visit their German partner who made all the major pieces of equipment. So, over the next few months, together, we worked up a complete proposal for a state-of-the-art adventure playground, including the structural changes in the farmyard. The budget was £250,000. To be honest, it was impossible to know what effect this would have on visitor numbers, so in the end we put in a very conservative estimate that suggested that we would make the investment back in seven years. Over the next few years we reckon the playground led to an increase in visitor numbers of 85,000 per year and so we recouped our investment in just three years.'*

Questions

1 What do you think make up the concept, package and process for the adventure playground?

2 Describe the four options highlighted in the case in terms of their feasibility, acceptability and vulnerability.

3 What does the concept of interactive design mean for a service such as the adventure playground described here?

Problems and applications

*These problems and applications will help to improve your analysis of operations. You can find more practice problems as well as worked examples and guided solutions on MyOMLab at **www.myomlab.com**.*

1 How would you evaluate the design of this book?

2 A company is developing a new web site that will allow customers to track the progress of their orders. The web site developers charge €10,000 for every development week and it is estimated that the design will take 10 weeks from the start of the design project to the launch of the web site. Once launched, it is estimated that the new site will attract extra business that will generate profits of €5,000 per week. However, if the web site is delayed by more than 5 weeks, the extra profit generated would reduce to €2,000 per week. How will a delay of 5 weeks affect the time when the design will break even in terms of cash flow?

3 How can the concept of modularization be applied to package holidays sold through an online travel agent?

4 One product where a very wide range of product types is valued by customers is that of domestic paint. Most people like to express their creativity in the choice of paints and other home-decorating products that they use in their homes. Clearly, offering a wide range of paint must have serious cost implications for the companies which manufacture, distribute and sell the product. Visit a store which sells paint and get an idea of the range of products available on the market. How do you think paint manufacturers and retailers manage to design their products and services so as to maintain high variety but keep costs under control?

5 Design becomes particularly important at the interface between products or services and the people that use them. This is especially true for internet-based services. Consider two types of web site:

(a) those which are trying to sell something such as Amazon.com, and

(b) those which are primarily concerned with giving information, for example bbc.co.uk.

For each of these categories, what seems to constitute 'good design'? Find examples of particularly good and particularly poor web design and explain what makes them good or bad.

Selected further reading

Bangle, C. (2001) The ultimate creativity machine: how BMW turns art into profit, *Harvard Business Review*, Jan, 47–55. A good description of how good aesthetic design translates into business success.

Bruce, M. and Bessant, J. (2002) *Design in Business: Strategic Innovation through Design*, Financial Times Prentice Hall and The Design Council. Probably one of the best overviews of design in a business context available today.

Bruce, M. and Cooper, R. (2000) *Creative Product Design: A Practical Guide to Requirements Capture Management*, Wiley, Chichester. Exactly what it says.

Goldstein, S.M., Johnston, R., Duffy, J. and Raod, J. (2002) The service concept: the missing link in service design research? *Journal of Operations Management* volume 20, issue 2, April, 121–34. Readable.

The Industrial Designers Society of America (2003) *Design Secrets: Products: 50 Real-Life Projects Uncovered (Design Secrets)*, Rockport Publishers Inc, Gloucester, Mass. Very much a practitioner book with some great examples.

Lowe, A. and Ridgway, K. (2000) A user's guide to quality function deployment, *Engineering Management Journal*, June. A good overview of QFD explained in straightforward non-technical language.

Useful web sites

www.cfsd.org.uk The centre for sustainable design's site. Some useful resources, but obviously largely confined to sustainability issues.

www.conceptcar.co.uk A site devoted to automotive design. Fun if you like new car designs!

www.betterproductdesign.net A site that acts as a resource for good design practice. Set up by Cambridge University and the Royal College of Art. Some good material that supports all aspects of design.

www.ocw.mit.edu/OcwWeb/Sloan-School-of-Management Good source of open courseware from MIT.

www.design-council.org.uk Site of the UK's Design Council. One of the best sites in the world for design-related issues.

www.nathan.com/ed/glossary/#ED

www.opsman.org Lots of useful stuff.

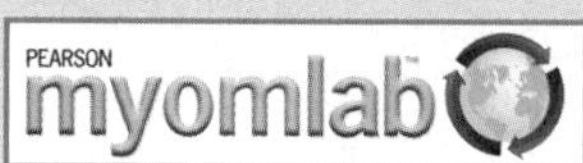

*Now that you have finished reading this chapter, why not visit MyOMLab at **www.myomlab.com** where you'll find more learning resources to help you make the most of your studies and get a better grade?*

Chapter 6

Supply network design

Key questions

- Why should an organization take a total supply network perspective?
- What is involved in configuring a supply network?
- Where should an operation be located?
- How much capacity should an operation plan to have?

Introduction

No operation exists in isolation. Every operation is part of a larger and interconnected network of other operations. This *supply network* will include suppliers and customers. It will also include suppliers' suppliers and customers' customers, and so on. At a strategic level, operations managers are involved in 'designing' the shape and form of their network. Network design starts with setting the network's strategic objectives. This helps the operation to decide how it wants to influence the overall shape of its network, the location of each operation, and how it should manage its overall capacity within the network. This chapter treats all these strategic design decisions in the context of supply networks (*see* Figure 6.1).

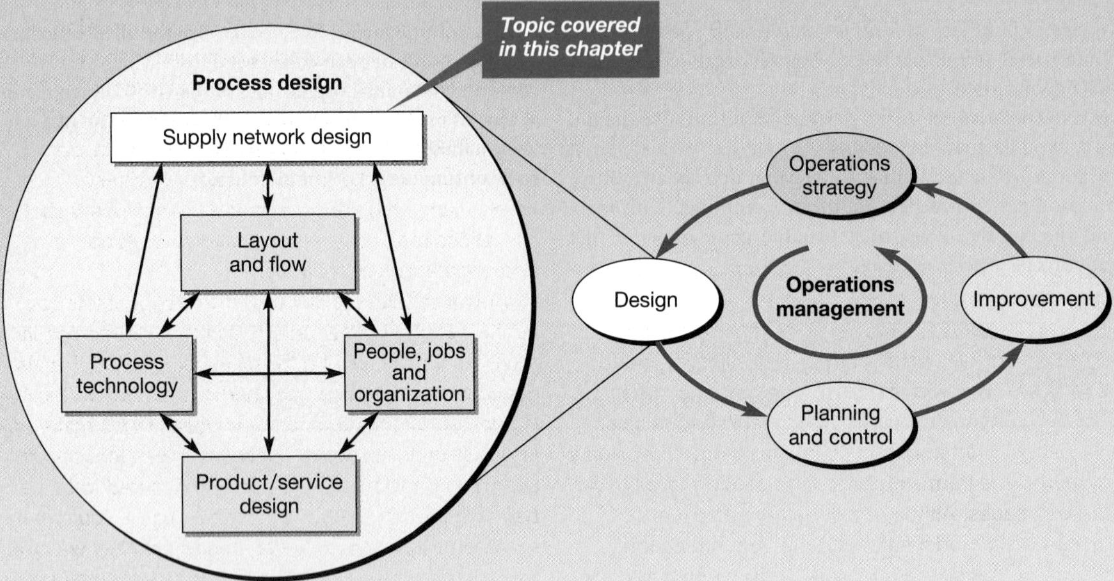

Figure 6.1 This chapter examines supply network design

*Check and improve your understanding of this chapter using self assessment questions and a personalised study plan, audio and video downloads, and an eBook – all at **www.myomlab.com**.*

Operations in practice Dell: no operating model lasts forever[1]

When he was a student at the University of Texas at Austin, Michael Dell's sideline of buying unused stock of PCs from local dealers, adding components, and re-selling the now higher-specification machines to local businesses was so successful he quit university and founded a computer company which was to revolutionize the industry's supply network management. But his fledgling company was just too small to make its own components. Better, he figured to learn how to manage a network of committed specialist component manufacturers and take the best of what was available in the market. Dell says that his commitment to outsourcing was always done for the most positive of reasons. '*We focus on how we can coordinate our activities to create the most value for customers*'. Yet Dell still faced a cost disadvantage against its far bigger competitors, so they decided to sell its computers direct to its customers, bypassing retailers. This allowed the company to cut out the retailer's (often considerable) margin, which in turn allowed Dell to offer lower prices. Dell also realized that cutting out the link in the supply network between them and the customer also provided them with significant learning opportunities by offering an opportunity to get to know their customers' needs far more intimately. This allowed them to forecast based on the thousands of customer contact calls every hour. It also allowed them to talk with customers about what they really want from their machines. Most importantly it allowed Dell to learn how to run its supply chain so that products could move through the supply chain to the end-customer in a fast and efficient manner, reducing Dell's level of inventory and giving Dell a significant cost advantage.

However, what is right at one time may become a liability later on. Two decades later Dell's growth started to slow down. The irony of this is that, what had been one of the company's main advantages, its direct sales model using the Internet and its market power to squeeze price reductions from suppliers, were starting to be seen as disadvantages. Although the market had changed, Dell's operating model had not. Some commentators questioned Dell's size. How could a $56 billion company remain lean, sharp, and alert? Other commentators pointed out that Dell's rivals had also now learnt to run efficient supply chains ('Getting a 20-year competitive advantage from your knowledge of how to run supply chains isn't too bad.') However, one of the main factors was seen as the shift in the nature of the market itself.

Source: Corbis/Gianni Giansanti/Sygma

Sales of PCs to business users had become largely a commodity business with wafer-thin margins, and this part of the market was growing slowly compared to the sale of computers to individuals. Selling computers to individuals provided slightly better margins than the corporate market, but they increasingly wanted up-to-date computers with a high design value, and most significantly, they wanted to see, touch and feel the products before buying them. This was clearly a problem for a company like Dell which had spent 20 years investing in its telephone- and later, internet-based sales channels. What all commentators agreed on was that in the fast-moving and cut-throat computer business, where market requirements could change overnight, operations resources must constantly develop appropriate new capabilities.

However, Michael Dell says it could regain its spot as the world's number one PC maker by switching its focus to consumers and the developing world. He also conceded that the company had missed out on the boom in supplying computers to home users – who make up just 15% of its revenues – because it was focused on supplying businesses. *'Let's say you wanted to buy a Dell computer in a store nine months ago – you'd have searched a long time and not found one. Now we have over 10,000 stores that sell our products.'* He rejected the idea that design was not important to his company, though he accepted that it had not been a top priority when all the focus was on business customers. *'As we've gone to the consumer we've been paying quite a bit more attention to design, fashion, colors, textures and materials.'*

The supply network perspective

Supply network

Supply side

Demand side

First-tier

Second-tier

Immediate supply network

Total supply network

A **supply network** perspective means setting an operation in the context of all the other operations with which it interacts, some of which are its suppliers and its customers. Materials, parts, other information, ideas and sometimes people all flow through the network of customer–supplier relationships formed by all these operations. On its **supply side** an operation has its suppliers of parts, or information, or services. These suppliers themselves have their own suppliers who in turn could also have suppliers, and so on. On the **demand side** the operation has customers. These customers might not be the final consumers of the operation's products or services; they might have their own set of customers. On the supply side is a group of operations that directly supply the operation; these are often called **first-tier** suppliers. They are supplied by **second-tier** suppliers. However, some second-tier suppliers may also supply an operation directly, thus missing out a link in the network. Similarly, on the demand side of the network, 'first-tier' customers are the main customer group for the operation. These in turn supply 'second-tier' customers, although again the operation may at times supply second-tier customers directly. The suppliers and customers who have direct contact with an operation are called its **immediate supply network**, whereas all the operations which form the network of suppliers' suppliers and customers' customers, etc., are called the **total supply network.**

Figure 6.2 illustrates the total supply network for two operations. First is a plastic homeware (kitchen bowls, food containers, etc.) manufacturer. Note that on the demand side the

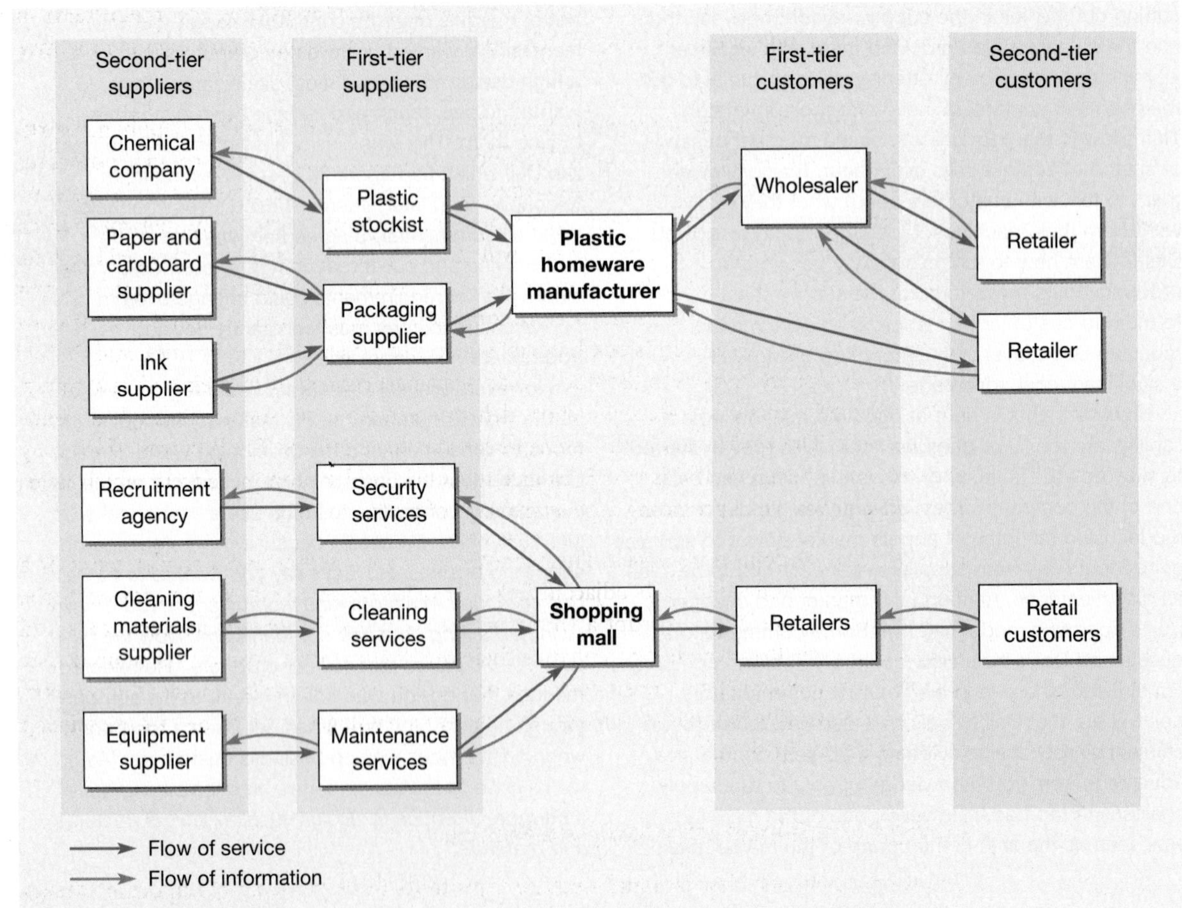

Figure 6.2 Operations network for a plastic homeware company and a shopping mall

homeware manufacturer supplies some of its basic products to wholesalers which supply retail outlets. However, it also supplies some retailers directly with 'made-to-order' products. Along with the flow of goods in the network from suppliers to customers, each link in the network will feed back orders and information to its suppliers. When stocks run low, the retailers will place orders with the wholesaler or directly with the manufacturer. The wholesaler will likewise place orders with the manufacturer, which will in turn place orders with its suppliers, which will replenish their own stocks from their suppliers. It is a two-way process with goods flowing one way and information flowing the other. It is not only manufacturers that are part of a supply network. The second (service) operation, an operation which manages an enclosed shopping mall, also has suppliers and customers that themselves have their own suppliers and customers. Figure 6.2 shows the supply network for an operation which manages an enclosed shopping mall.

Why consider the whole supply network?

There are three important reasons for taking a supply network perspective:

It helps an understanding of competitiveness. Immediate customers and immediate suppliers, quite understandably, are the main concern to competitively minded companies. Yet sometimes they need to look beyond these immediate contacts to understand why customers and suppliers act as they do. Any operation has only two options if it wants to understand its ultimate customers' needs at the end of the network. It can rely on all the intermediate customers and customers' customers, etc., which form the links in the network between the company and its end-customers. Alternatively, it can look beyond its immediate customers and suppliers. Relying on one's immediate network is seen as putting too much faith in someone else's judgement of things which are central to an organization's own competitive health.

Downstream

Upstream

It helps identify significant links in the network. The key to understanding supply networks lies in identifying the parts of the network which contribute to those performance objectives valued by end-customers. Any analysis of networks must start, therefore, by understanding the **downstream** end of the network. After this, the **upstream** parts of the network which contribute most to end-customer service will need to be identified. But they will not be equally significant. For example, the important end-customers for domestic plumbing parts and appliances are the installers and service companies that deal directly with domestic consumers. They are supplied by 'stock holders' which must have all parts in stock and deliver them fast. Suppliers of parts to the stock holders can best contribute to their end-customers' competitiveness partly by offering a short delivery lead time but mainly through dependable delivery. The key players in this example are the stock holders. The best way of winning end-customer business in this case is to give the stock holder prompt delivery which helps keep costs down while providing high availability of parts.

It helps focus on long-term issues. There are times when circumstances render parts of a supply network weaker than its adjacent links. A major machine breakdown, for example, or a labour dispute might disrupt a whole network. Should its immediate customers and suppliers exploit the weakness to enhance their own competitive position, or should they tolerate the problems, and hope the customer or supplier will eventually recover? A long-term supply-network view would be to weigh the relative advantages to be gained from assisting or replacing the weak link.

Design decisions in supply networks

The supply-network view is useful because it prompts three particularly important design decisions. These are the most strategic of all the design decisions treated in this part of the book. It is necessary to understand them at this point, however, because, as well as having a particularly significant impact on the strategy of the organization, they set the context in which all other process design decisions are made. The three decisions are:

Outsourcing
Vertical integration
Do or buy

Location

Long-term capacity management

1 How should the network be configured? This means, first, how can an operation influence the shape which the network might take? Second, how much of the network should the operation own? This may be called the **outsourcing, vertical integration** or **do-or-buy** decision.
2 Where should each part of the network be located? If the homeware company builds a new factory, should it be close to its suppliers or close to its customers, or somewhere in between? This decision is called the operations **location** decision.
3 What physical capacity should each part of the network have? How large should the homeware factory be? Should it expand in large-capacity steps or small ones? These type of decisions are called **long-term capacity management** decisions.

Note that all three of these decisions rely on assumptions regarding the level of future demand. The supplement to this chapter explores forecasting in more detail. Also, in Chapter 13, we will cover the more operational day-to-day issues of managing operations networks. In this chapter we deal with these three related strategic decisions.

Configuring the supply network

Changing the shape of the supply network

Even when an operation does not directly own, or even control, other operations in its network, it may still wish to change the shape of the network. This involves attempting to manage network behaviour by reconfiguring the network so as to change the scope of the activities performed in each operation and the nature of the relationships between them. Reconfiguring a supply network sometimes involves parts of the operation being merged – not necessarily in the sense of a change of ownership of any parts of an operation, but rather in the way responsibility is allocated for carrying out activities. The most common example of network reconfiguration has come through the many companies that have recently reduced the number of direct suppliers. The complexity of dealing with many hundreds of suppliers may both be expensive for an operation and (sometimes more important) prevent the operation from developing a close relationship with a supplier. It is not easy to be close to hundreds of different suppliers.

Disintermediation

Disintermediation

Another trend in some supply networks is that of companies within a network bypassing customers or suppliers to make contact directly with customers' customers or suppliers' suppliers. 'Cutting out the middlemen' in this way is called **disintermediation**. An obvious example of this is the way the Internet has allowed some suppliers to 'disintermediate' traditional retailers in supplying goods and services to consumers. So, for example, many services in the travel industry that used to be sold through retail outlets (travel agents) are now also available direct from the suppliers. The option of purchasing the individual components of a vacation through the web sites of the airline, hotel, car hire company, etc., is now easier for consumers. Of course, they may still wish to purchase an 'assembled' product from retail travel agents which can have the advantage of convenience. Nevertheless the process of disintermediation has developed new linkages in the supply network.

Co-opetition

One approach to thinking about supply networks sees any business as being surrounded by four types of players: suppliers, customers, competitors and complementors. Complementors enable one's products or services to be valued more by customers because they can also have the complementor's products or services, as opposed to when they have yours alone. Competitors are the opposite: they make customers value your product or service less when they can have their product or service, rather than yours alone. Competitors can also be complementors and vice versa. For example, adjacent restaurants may see themselves as competitors for customers' business. A customer standing outside and wanting a meal will choose between the two of them. Yet, in another way they are complementors. Would that customer have come to this part of town unless there was more than one restaurant to choose from? Restaurants, theatres, art galleries and tourist attractions generally, all cluster together in a form of cooperation to increase the total size of their joint market. It is important to distinguish between the way companies cooperate in increasing the total size of a market and the way in which they then compete for a share of that market. Customers and suppliers, it is argued, should have 'symmetric' roles. Harnessing the value of suppliers is just as important as listening to the needs of customers. Destroying value in a supplier in order to create it in a customer does not increase the value of the network as a whole. So, pressurizing suppliers will not necessarily add value. In the long term it creates value for the total network to find ways of increasing value for suppliers and well as customers. All the players in the network, whether they are customers, suppliers, competitors or complementors, can be both friends and enemies at different times. The term used to capture this idea is '**co-opetition**'.[2]

Co-opetition

In-house or outsource? Do or buy? The vertical integration decision

No single business does everything that is required to produce its products and services. Bakers do not grow wheat or even mill it into flour. Banks do not usually do their own credit checking: they retain the services of specialist credit checking agencies that have the specialized information systems and expertise to do it better. This process is called 'outsourcing' and has become an important issue for most businesses. This is because, although most companies have always outsourced some of their activities, a larger proportion of direct activities are now being bought from suppliers. Also many indirect processes are now being outsourced. This is often referred to as 'business process outsourcing' (BPO). Financial service companies in particular are starting to outsource some of their more routine back-office processes. In a similar way many processes within the human resource function from simply payroll services through to more complex training and development processes, are being outsourced to specialist companies. The processes may still be physically located where they were before, but the staff and technology are managed by the outsourcing service provider. The reason for doing this is often primarily to reduce cost. However, there can sometimes also be significant gains in the quality and flexibility of service offered. '*People talk a lot about looking beyond cost cutting when it comes to outsourcing companies' human resource functions*', says Jim Madden, CEO of Exult, the California-based specialist outsourcing company, '*I don't believe any company will sign up for this [outsourcing] without cost reduction being part of it, but for the clients whose human resource functions we manage, such as BP, and Bank of America, it is not just about saving money.*'

The outsourcing debate is just part of a far larger issue which will shape the fundamental nature of any business. Namely, what should the scope of the business be? In other words, what should it do itself and what should it buy in? This is often referred to as the 'do-or-buy decision' when individual components or activities are being considered, or 'vertical integration' when it is the ownership of whole operations that is being decided. Vertical integration is the extent to which an organization owns the network of which it is a part. It usually involves an organization assessing the wisdom of acquiring suppliers or customers. Vertical integration can be defined in terms of three factors.[3]

1 *The direction of vertical integration.* Should an operation expand by buying one of its suppliers or by buying one of its customers? The strategy of expanding on the supply side of the network is sometimes called 'backward' or 'upstream' vertical integration,

and expanding on the demand side is sometimes called 'forward' or 'downstream' vertical integration.

2 *The extent of vertical integration.* How far should an operation take the extent of its vertical integration? Some organizations deliberately choose not to integrate far, if at all, from their original part of the network. Alternatively, some organizations choose to become very vertically integrated.

3 *The balance among stages.* How exclusive should the relationship be between operations. A totally balanced network relationship is one where one operation produces only for the next stage in the network and totally satisfies its requirements. Less than full balance allows each operation to sell its output to other companies or to buy in some of its supplies from other companies.

Making the outsourcing / vertical integration decision

Whether it is referred to as do-or-buy, vertical integration or no vertical integration, in-house or outsourced supply, the choice facing operations is rarely simple. Organizations in different circumstances with different objectives are likely to take different decisions. Yet the question itself is relatively simple, even if the decision itself is not: 'Does in-house or outsourced supply in a particular set of circumstances give the appropriate performance objectives that it requires to compete more effectively in its markets?' For example, if the main performance objectives for an operation are dependable delivery and meeting short-term changes in customers' delivery requirements, the key question should be: 'How does in-house or outsourcing give better dependability and delivery flexibility performance?' This means judging two sets of opposing factors – those which give the potential to improve performance and those which work against this potential being realized. Table 6.1 summarizes some arguments for in-house supply and outsourcing in terms of each performance objective.

Table 6.1 How in-house and outsourced supply may affect an operation's performance objectives

Performance objective	*'Do it yourself' in-house supply*	*'Buy it in' outsourced supply*
Quality	The origins of any quality problems are usually easier to trace in-house and improvement can be more immediate but there can be some risk of complacency.	Supplier may have specialized knowledge and more experience, also may be motivated through market pressures, but communication more difficult.
Speed	Can mean synchronized schedules which speeds throughput of materials and information, but if the operation has external customers, internal customers may be low-priority.	Speed of response can be built into the supply contract where commercial pressures will encourage good performance, but there may be significant transport/delivery delays.
Dependability	Easier communications can help dependability, but, if the operation also has external customers, internal customers may receive low priority.	Late-delivery penalties in the supply contract can encourage good delivery performance, but organizational barriers may inhibit in communication.
Flexibility	Closeness to the real needs of a business can alert the in-house operation to required changes, but the ability to respond may be limited by the scale and scope of internal operations.	Outsource suppliers may be larger with wider capabilities than in-house suppliers and have more ability to respond to changes, but may have to balance conflicting needs of different customers.
Cost	In-house operations do not have to make the margin required by outside suppliers so the business can capture the profits which would otherwise be given to the supplier, but relatively low volumes may mean that it is difficult to gain economies of scale or the benefits of process innovation.	Probably the main reason why outsourcing is so popular. Outsourced companies can achieve economies of scale and they are motivated to reduce their own costs because it directly impacts on their profits, but costs of communication and coordination with supplier need to be taken into account.

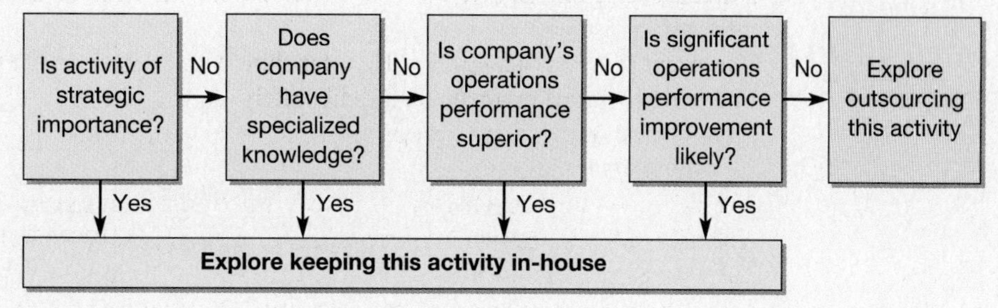

Figure 6.3 The decision logic of outsourcing

Deciding whether to outsource

Outsourcing is a strategic decision

Although the effect of outsourcing on the operation's performance objective is important, there are other factors that companies take into account when deciding if outsourcing an activity is a sensible option. For example, if an activity has long-term **strategic importance** to a company, it is unlikely to outsource it. For example, a retailer might choose to keep the design and development of its web site in-house even though specialists could perform the activity at less cost because it plans to move into web-based retailing at some point in the future. Nor would a company usually outsource an activity where it had specialized skills or knowledge. For example, a company making laser printers may have built up specialized knowledge in the production of sophisticated laser drives. This capability may allow it to introduce product or process innovations in the future. It would be foolish to 'give away' such capability. After these two more strategic factors have been considered the company's operations performance can be taken into account. Obviously if its operations performance is already too superior to any potential supplier, it would be unlikely to outsource the activity. But also even if its performance was currently below that of potential suppliers, it may not outsource the activity if it feels that it could significantly improve its performance. Figure 6.3 illustrates this decision logic.

Short case
Behind the brand names[4]

Source: Rex Features

The market for notebook computers is a fast-evolving and competitive one. Brands such as Dell, Sony, Fujitsu and Apple as well as many smaller brands vie for customers' attention. Yet few who buy these products know that the majority of the world's notebooks, including most of those sold by the big names, are made by a small number of Taiwanese and Korean manufacturers. Taiwanese firms alone make around 60 per cent of all notebooks in the world, including most of Dell, Compaq and Apple machines. And this group of Taiwanese manufacturers is dominated by Hon Hai, Quanta and Compal. In a market with unremitting technological innovation and fierce price competition, it makes sense to outsource production to companies that can achieve the economies that come with high-volume manufacture as well develop the expertise which enables new designs to be put into production without the cost overruns and delays which could ruin a new product launch. However, the big brand names are keen to defend their products' performance. Dell, for example, admits that a major driver of its outsourcing policy is the requirement to keep costs at a competitive level, but says that it can ensure product quality and performance through its relationship with its suppliers. *'The production lines are set up by Dell and managed by Dell'*, says Tony Bonadero, Director of Product Marketing for Dell's laptop range. Dell also imposes strict quality control and manages the overall design of the product.

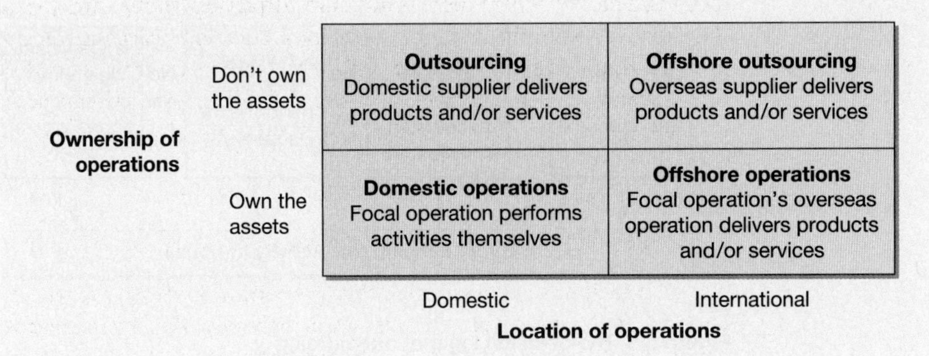

Figure 6.4 Offshoring and outsourcing are related but different

Outsourcing and offshoring

Two supply network strategies that are often confused are those of outsourcing and offshoring. Outsourcing means deciding to buy-in products or services rather than perform the activities in-house. Off-shoring means obtaining products and services from operations that are based outside one's own country. Of course, one may both outsource and offshore as illustrated in Figure 6.4. Offshoring is very closely related to outsourcing and the motives for each may be similar. Offshoring to a lower-cost region of the world is usually done to reduce an operation's overall costs as is outsourcing to a supplier that has greater expertise or scale or both.[5]

Critical commentary

In many instances there has been fierce opposition to companies outsourcing some of their processes. Trade unions often point out that the only reason that outsourcing companies can do the job at lower cost is that they either reduce salaries or reduce working conditions, or both. Furthermore, they say, flexibility is only achieved by reducing job security. Employees who were once part of a large and secure corporation could find themselves as far less secure employees of a less benevolent employer with a philosophy of permanent cost-cutting. Even some proponents of outsourcing are quick to point out the problems. There can be significant obstacles, including understandable resistance from staff who find themselves 'outsourced'. Some companies have also been guilty of 'outsourcing a problem'. In other words, having failed to manage a process well themselves, they ship it out rather than face up to why the process was problematic in the first place. There is also evidence that, although long-term costs can be brought down when a process is outsourced, there may be an initial period when costs rise as both sides learn how to manage the new arrangement.

The location of capacity

It was reputedly Lord Sieff, one-time boss of Marks and Spencer, the UK-based retail organization, who said, '*There are three important things in retailing – location, location and location*', and any retailing operation knows exactly what he meant. Get the location wrong and it can have a significant impact on profits, or service. For example, mislocating a fire service station can slow down the average journey time of the fire crews in getting to the fires;

locating a factory where there is difficulty attracting labour with appropriate skills will affect the effectiveness of the factory's operations. Location decisions will usually have an effect on an operation's costs as well as its ability to serve its customers (and therefore its revenues). Also, location decisions, once taken, are difficult to undo. The costs of moving an operation can be hugely expensive and the risks of inconveniencing customers very high. No operation wants to move very often.

Reasons for location decisions

Not all operations can logically justify their location. Some are where they are for historical reasons. Yet even the operations that are 'there because they're there' are implicitly making a decision not to move. Presumably their assumption is that the cost and disruption involved in changing location would outweigh any potential benefits of a new location. Two stimuli often cause organizations to change locations: changes in demand for their goods and services, and changes in supply of their inputs.

Changes in demand. A change in location may be prompted by customer demand shifting. For example, as garment manufacture moved to Asia, suppliers of zips, threads, etc. started to follow them. Changes in the volume of demand can also prompt relocation. To meet higher demand, an operation could expand its existing site, or choose a larger site in another location, or keep its existing location and find a second location for an additional operation; the last two options will involve a location decision. High-visibility operations may not have the choice of expanding on the same site to meet rising demand. A dry cleaning service may attract only marginally more business by expanding an existing site because it offers a local, and therefore convenient, service. Finding a new location for an additional operation is probably its only option for expansion.

Changes in supply. The other stimulus for relocation is changes in the cost, or availability, of the supply of inputs to the operation. For example, a mining or oil company will need to relocate as the minerals it is extracting become depleted. A manufacturing company might choose to relocate its operations to a part of the world where labour costs are low, because the equivalent resources (people) in its original location have become relatively expensive. Sometimes a business might choose to relocate to release funds if the value of the land it occupies is worth more than an alternative, equally good, location.

Short case
The Tata Nano finds a new home[6]

Source: Getty Images

Finding a suitable site for any operation can be a political as well as an economic problem. It certainly was when Tata, the Indian company, unveiled its plans for the Nano in 2007. Named the '1 lakh car' (in India one lakh means 100,000), it would be the cheapest car in the world, with the basic model priced at 100,000 rupees, or $2,500, excluding taxes. The price was about half of existing low-cost cars. And the site chosen by Tata was equally bold. It was to be made at Singur, in the Indian state of West Bengal, a populous state with Calcutta (now called Kolkata) as its capital. Although the Communist Party had ruled the state for four decades, the West Bengal government was keen to encourage the Nano plant. It would bring much-needed jobs and send a message that the state welcomed inward investment. In fact, it had won the plant against stiff competition from rival states.

Controversially, the state government had expropriated land for the factory using an old law dating from 1894, which requires private owners to sell land for a 'public purpose'. The government justified this action by pointing out that over 13,000 people had some kind of claim to parts of the land required for the new plant. Tata could not be expected to negotiate, one by one, with all of them. Also financial compensation was offered at significantly above market rates. Unfortunately about 2,250 people refused to accept the offered compensation. The political opposition organized mass protests in support of the farmers who did not want to move. They blocked roads, threatened staff and even assaulted an employee of a Tata supplier. In response, Ratan Tata, chairman of the Tata group, threatened to move the Nano plant from the state if the company really was not wanted, even though the company had already invested 15 billion rupees in the project. Eventually, exasperated with being caught in the 'political crossfire', Tata said it would abandon its factory in the state. Instead, the company selected a location in Gujarat, one of India's most industrialized states, which quickly approved even more land than the West Bengal site.

The objectives of the location decision

The aim of the location decision is to achieve an appropriate balance between three related objectives:

Spatially variable costs

- the **spatially variable costs** of the operation (spatially variable means that something changes with geographical location);
- the service the operation is able to provide to its customers;
- the revenue potential of the operation.

In for-profit organizations the last two objectives are related. The assumption is that the better the service the operation can provide to its customers, the better will be its potential to attract custom and therefore generate revenue. In not-for-profit organizations, revenue potential might not be a relevant objective and so cost and customer service are often taken as the twin objectives of location. In making decisions about where to locate an operation, operations managers are concerned with minimizing spatially variable costs and maximizing revenue and customer service. Location affects both of these but not equally for all types of operation. For example, with most products, customers may not care very much where they were made. Location is unlikely to affect the operation's revenues significantly. However, the costs of the operation will probably be very greatly affected by location. Services, on the other hand, often have both costs and revenues affected by location. The location decision for any operation is determined by the relative strength of supply-side and demand-side factors (*see* Fig. 6.5).

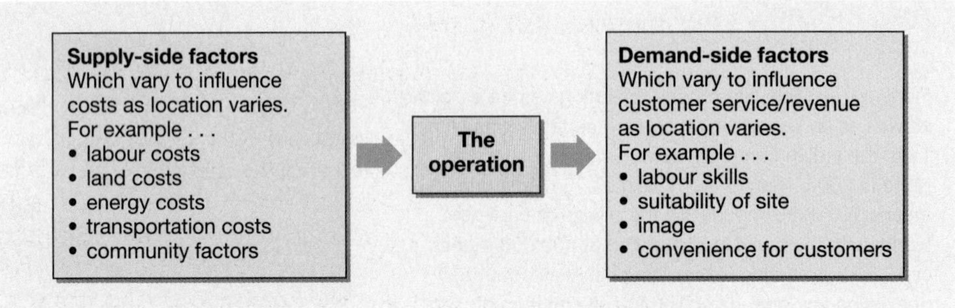

Figure 6.5 Supply-side and demand-side factors in location decisions

Short case
Tesco Thailand[7]

Tesco is an international retailer with sales in excess of £50 billion, operating around 4,000 stores worldwide, employing almost half a million people and serving millions of customers each week. It sells a wide range of items including groceries, petrol, financial services, electrical goods, household items, toys and even furniture. Although based in the UK Tesco now trades all over the world. One of its big successes is Thailand, where it has 476 stores and employs over 36,000 people. Tesco's expansion strategy is founded on the need to provide quality products, convenient locations and opening hours and value for money. The company has come to realize that international markets need differing local approaches, with local supply chains, different store formats and sensitivity to local traditions. So how does Tesco (branded 'Tesco Lotus' in Thailand) adapt its operating practice to local conditions?

Some things are relatively straightforward. For example, those stores with limited opening hours open at 9.09 precisely, as Thais believe these numbers bring good fortune. Other things are based on a thorough understanding of local customers. They discovered that around 5% of their customers were actually small family-run stores taking advantage of Tesco's lower prices. Rather than discourage this they developed their 'Club Pack' products that shopkeepers could break up and sell in their own stores at a good profit. They also investigated the shopping experience their Thai customers really want. '*We started out by asking our customers what they want our stores to sell and look like. From the responses that we received, we realized that the optimal solution would be best delivered by Tesco Lotus constructing its own malls*' (Mrs Veena Arunyakasem, Mall and Media Director, Tesco Lotus).

So, they developed two new concepts, the Lifestyle Shopping Mall and Community Mall. Lifestyle Shopping Malls contain the flagship hypermarket stores and other shops, including restaurants and banks, promoting high-quality local brands rather than expensive imported brands. '*These "lifestyle shopping malls" provide better service and increased convenience to our customers. The biggest beneficiaries will be our upcountry customers who have previously lived a long way from the nearest cinema*' (Gwyn Sundhagul, Tesco Lotus Director and Chief Marketing Officer).

Community Malls are smaller and emphasize easy access to local neigbourhoods.

Other local developments take account of cultural sensitivities. Thais greatly admire individuals and organizations that help the poor. So Tesco set up 'Tesco for Thais', a non-profit charitable foundation.

The green agenda is also important in Thailand and large organizations are expected to lead the way. In 2004 Tesco opened its first 'green' superstore in Bangkok. This store includes a range of energy-saving initiatives including recycling and the use of rainwater, with its air conditioning run by solar panels, the size of three football pitches, on the roof.

Supply-side influences

Labour costs. The costs of employing people with particular skills can vary between different areas in any country, but are likely to be more significant when international comparisons are made. Labour costs can be expressed in two ways. The 'hourly cost' is what firms have to pay workers on average per hour. However, the 'unit cost' is an indication of the labour cost per unit of production. This includes the effects both of productivity differences between countries and of differing currency exchange rates. Exchange rate variation can cause unit costs to change dramatically over time. Yet in spite of this, labour costs exert a major influence on the location decision, especially in some industries such as clothing, where labour costs as a proportion of total costs are relatively high.

Land costs. The cost of acquiring the site itself is sometimes a relevant factor in choosing a location. Land and rental costs vary between countries and cities. At a more local level, land costs are also important. A retail operation, when choosing 'high-street' sites, will pay a particular level of rent only if it believes it can generate a certain level of revenue from the site.

Energy costs. Operations which use large amounts of energy, such as aluminium smelters, can be influenced in their location decisions by the availability of relatively inexpensive energy. This may be direct, as in the availability of hydroelectric generation in an area, or indirect, such as low-cost coal which can be used to generate inexpensive electricity.

Transportation costs. Transportation costs include both the cost of transporting inputs from their source to the site of the operation, and the cost of transporting goods from the site to customers. Whereas almost all operations are concerned to some extent with the former, not all operations transport goods to customers; rather, customers come to them (for example, hotels). Even for operations that do transport their goods to customers (most manufacturers, for example), we consider transportation as a supply-side factor because as location changes, transportation costs also change. Proximity to sources of *supply* dominates the location decision where the cost of transporting input materials is high or difficult. Food processing and other agriculture-based activities, for example, are often carried out close to growing areas. Conversely, transportation to *customers* dominates location decisions where this is expensive or difficult. Civil engineering projects, for example, are constructed mainly where they will be needed.

Community factors. Community factors are those influences on an operation's costs which derive from the social, political and economic environment of its site. These include:

- local tax rates
- capital movement restrictions
- government financial assistance
- government planning assistance
- political stability
- local attitudes to 'inward investment'
- language
- local amenities (schools, theatres, shops, etc.)
- availability of support services
- history of labour relations and behaviour
- environmental restrictions and waste disposal
- planning procedures and restrictions.

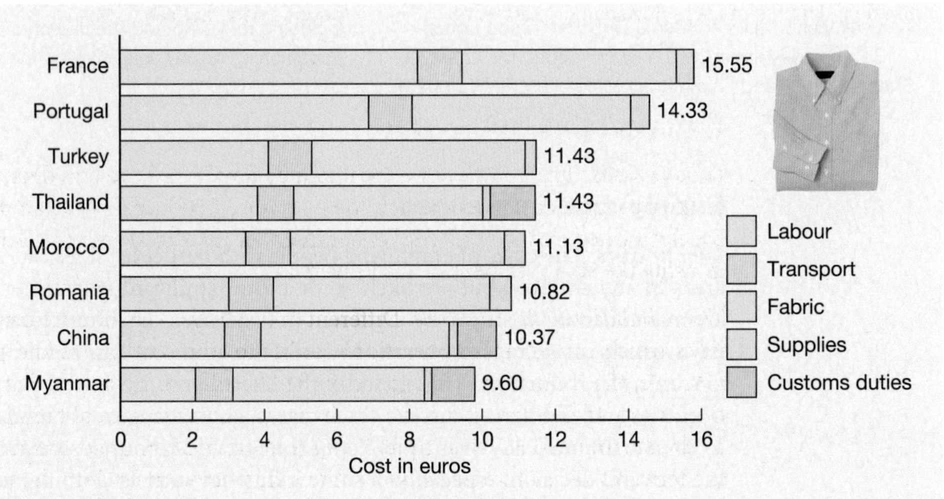

Figure 6.6 A major influence in where businesses locate is the cost of operating at different locations. But, total operating cost depends on more than wage costs, or even total labour costs (which includes allowances for different productivity rates). The chart illustrates what makes up the cost of shirts sold in France. Remember, the retailer will often sell the item for more than double the cost[8]

Short case

Developing nations challenge Silicon Valley[9]

Source: Getty Images/AFP

Similar companies with similar needs often cluster together in the same location. For example, knitted garment manufacturers dominate parts of Northern Italy. Perhaps the most famous location cluster is in the area south of San Francisco known as Silicon Valley, acknowledged as the most important intellectual and commercial hub of high-tech business. Yet Silicon Valley is being challenged by up-and-coming locations, especially in developing countries. Here are two examples.

Bangalore in India has for many years been attractive in the computer industry. Back in the 1980s the area attracted software code-writing business from Western multinationals attracted by the ready availability of well-educated, low-cost English-speaking software technicians. Now the area has attracted even more, and even more sophisticated, business. Companies such as Intel, Sun Microsystems, Texas Instruments and Cisco have a presence in the area and are using their Bangalore development centres to tackle cutting-edge projects. The biggest draw is still India's pool of high-quality, low-cost software engineers. Each year Bangalore alone graduates 25,000 computer science engineers, almost the number who graduate in the entire USA. More significantly, the average wage of a top-class graduate software engineer is around one fifth of that in the USA. Nor is there any lack of multinational experience. For years Western (especially US) high-tech companies have employed senior Indian-born engineers. Equipped with Silicon Valley experience, some of these engineers are happy to return home to manage development teams.

The high-tech research and development activities around **Shanghai** in China do not have the pedigree of those in India, but are increasingly seen as significant in the global technology industry. *'Over the next ten years, China will become a ferociously formidable competitor for companies that run the entire length of the technology food chain'*, according to Michael J. Moritz, a Californian venture-capital firm specializing in high-tech businesses. And although most industry commentators admit that China has far to go, the combination of the availability of a highly skilled and well-educated workforce, often at even lower cost than in India, together with the Chinese government encouragement of joint ventures with multinationals is seen as a big impetus to high-tech growth. Multinationals such as Alkatel, the French telecom giant, and Matsushita, Japan's largest consumer electronics company, as well as chip manufacturer Intel are all investing in research and development facilities.

Demand-side influences

Labour skills. The abilities of a local labour force can have an effect on customer reaction to the products or services which the operation produces. For example, 'science parks' are usually located close to universities because they hope to attract companies that are interested in using the skills available at the university.

The suitability of the site itself. Different sites are likely to have different intrinsic characteristics which can affect an operation's ability to serve customers and generate revenue. For example, the location of a luxury resort hotel which offers up-market holiday accommodation is very largely dependent on the intrinsic characteristics of the site. Located next to the beach, surrounded by waving palm trees and overlooking a picturesque bay, the hotel is very attractive to its customers. Move it a few kilometres away into the centre of an industrial estate and it rapidly loses its attraction.

Image of the location. Some locations are firmly associated in customers' minds with a particular image. Suits from Savile Row (the centre of the up-market bespoke tailoring district in London) may be no better than high-quality suits made elsewhere but, by locating its operation there, a tailor has probably enhanced its reputation and therefore its revenue. The product and fashion design houses of Milan and the financial services in the City of London also enjoy a reputation shaped partly by that of their location.

Convenience for customers. Of all the demand-side factors, this is, for many operations, the most important. Locating a general hospital, for instance, in the middle of the countryside may have many advantages for its staff, and even perhaps for its costs, but it clearly would be very inconvenient to its customers. Those visiting the hospital would need to travel long distances. Because of this, general hospitals are located close to centres of demand. Similarly with other public services and restaurants, stores, banks, petrol filling stations etc., location determines the effort to which customers have to go in order to use the operation.

Locations which offer convenience for the customer are not always obvious. In the 1950s Jay Pritzker called into a hotel at Los Angeles airport for a coffee. He found that, although the hotel was full, it was also for sale. Clearly there was customer demand but presumably the hotel could not make a profit. That is when he got the idea of locating luxury hotels which could command high revenues at airports where there was always demand. He called his hotel chain Hyatt; it is now one of the best-known hotel chains in the world.

Location techniques

Although operations managers must exercise considerable judgement in the choice of alternative locations, there are some systematic and quantitative techniques which can help the decision process. We describe two here – the **weighted-score** method and the **centre-of-gravity** method.

Weighted-score method
Centre-of-gravity method

Weighted-score method

The procedure involves, first of all, identifying the criteria which will be used to evaluate the various locations. Second, it involves establishing the relative importance of each criterion and giving weighting factors to them. Third, it means rating each location according to each criterion. The scale of the score is arbitrary. In our example we shall use 0 to 100, where 0 represents the worst possible score and 100 the best.

Worked example

An Irish company which prints and makes specialist packaging materials for the pharmaceutical industry has decided to build a new factory somewhere in the Benelux countries so as to provide a speedy service for its customers in continental Europe. In order to choose a site it has decided to evaluate all options against a number of criteria, as follows:

- the cost of the site;
- the rate of local property taxation;
- the availability of suitable skills in the local labour force;
- the site's access to the motorway network;
- the site's access to the airport;
- the potential of the site for future expansion.

After consultation with its property agents the company identifies three sites which seem to be broadly acceptable. These are known as sites A, B and C. The company also investigates each site and draws up the weighted-score table shown in Table 6.2. It is important to remember that the scores shown in Table 6.2 are those which the manager has given as an indication of how each site meets the company's needs specifically. Nothing is necessarily being implied regarding any intrinsic worth of the locations. Likewise, the weightings are an indication of how important the company finds each criterion in the circumstances it finds itself. The 'value' of a site for each criterion is then calculated by multiplying its score by the weightings for each criterion.

For location A, its score for the 'cost-of-site' criterion is 80 and the weighting of this criterion is 4, so its value is 80 × 4 = 320. All these values are then summed for each site to obtain its total weighted score.

Table 6.2 indicates that location C has the highest total weighted score and therefore would be the preferred choice. It is interesting to note, however, that location C has the lowest score on what is, by the company's own choice, the most important criterion – cost of the site. The high total weighted score which location C achieves in other criteria, however, outweighs this deficiency. If, on examination of this table, a company cannot accept what appears to be an inconsistency, then either the weights which have been given to each criterion, or the scores that have been allocated, do not truly reflect the company's preference.

Table 6.2 Weighted-score method for the three sites

Criteria	*Importance weighting*	*Scores*		
			Sites	
		A	*B*	*C*
Cost of the site	4	80	65	60
Local taxes	2	20	50	80
Skills availability	1	80	60	40
Access to motorways	1	50	60	40
Access to airport	1	20	60	70
Potential for expansion	1	75	40	55
Total weighted scores		585	580	605*

*Preferred option.

The centre-of-gravity method

The centre-of-gravity method is used to find a location which minimizes transportation costs. It is based on the idea that all possible locations have a 'value' which is the sum of all transportation costs to and from that location. The best location, the one which minimizes costs, is represented by what in a physical analogy would be the weighted centre of gravity of all points to and from which goods are transported. So, for example, two suppliers, each sending 20 tonnes of parts per month to a factory, are located at points A and B. The factory must then assemble these parts and send them to one customer located at point C. Since point C receives twice as many tonnes as points A and B (transportation cost is assumed to be directly related to the tonnes of goods shipped) then it has twice the weighting of point A or B. The lowest transportation cost location for the factory is at the centre of gravity of a (weightless) board where the two suppliers' and one customer's locations are represented to scale and have weights equivalent to the weightings of the number of tonnes they send or receive.

Worked example

A company which operates four out-of-town garden centres has decided to keep all its stocks of products in a single warehouse. Each garden centre, instead of keeping large stocks of products, will fax its orders to the warehouse staff who will then deliver replenishment stocks to each garden centre as necessary.

The location of each garden centre is shown on the map in Figure 6.7. A reference grid is superimposed over the map. The centre-of-gravity coordinates of the lowest-cost location for the warehouse, $\bar{x}$ and $\bar{y}$, are given by the formulae:

$$\bar{x} = \frac{\sum x_i V_i}{\sum V_i}$$

→

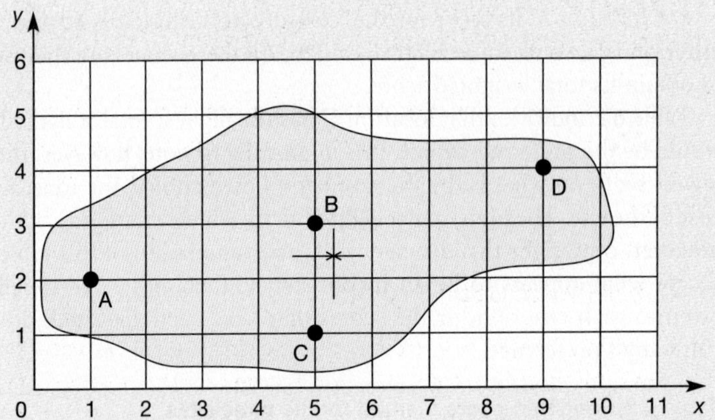

Figure 6.7 Centre-of-gravity location for the garden centre warehouse

and

$$\bar{y} = \frac{\Sigma y_i V_i}{\Sigma V_i}$$

where

x_i = the x coordinate of source or destination i
y_i = the y coordinate of source or destination i
V_i = the amount to be shipped to or from source or destination i.

Each of the garden centres is of a different size and has different sales volumes. In terms of the number of truck loads of products sold each week, Table 6.3 shows the sales of the four centres.

Table 6.3 The weekly demand levels (in truck loads) at each of the four garden centres

	Sales per week (truck loads)
Garden centre A	5
Garden centre B	10
Garden centre C	12
Garden centre D	8
Total	35

In this case

$$\bar{x} = \frac{(1 \times 5) + (5 \times 10) + (5 \times 12) + (9 \times 8)}{35} = 5.34$$

and

$$\bar{y} = \frac{(2 \times 5) + (3 \times 10) + (1 \times 12) + (4 \times 8)}{35} = 2.4$$

So the minimum cost location for the warehouse is at point (5.34, 2.4) as shown in Figure 6.7. That is, at least, theoretically. In practice, the optimum location might also be influenced by other factors such as the transportation network. So if the optimum location was at a point with poor access to a suitable road or at some other unsuitable location (in a residential area or the middle of a lake, for example) then the chosen location will need to be adjusted. The technique does go some way, however, towards providing an indication of the area in which the company should be looking for sites for its warehouse.

Long-term capacity management

The next set of supply network decisions concern the size or capacity of each part of the network. Here we shall treat capacity in a general long-term sense. The specific issues involved in measuring and adjusting capacity in the medium and short terms are examined in Chapter 11.

The optimum capacity level

Most organizations need to decide on the size (in terms of capacity) of each of their facilities. An air-conditioning unit company, for example, might operate plants each of which has a capacity (at normal product mix) of 800 units per week. At activity levels below this, the average cost of producing each unit will increase because the fixed costs of the factory are being covered by fewer units produced. The total production costs of the factory have some elements which are fixed – they will be incurred irrespective of how much, or little, the factory produces. Other costs are variable – they are the costs incurred by the factory for each unit it produces. Between them, the fixed and variable costs make up the total cost at any output level. Dividing this cost by the output level itself will give the theoretical average cost of producing units at that output rate. This is the green line shown as the theoretical unit cost curve for the 800-unit plant in Figure 6.8. However, the actual average cost curve may be different from this line for a number of reasons:

Fixed-cost breaks

- All fixed costs are not incurred at one time as the factory starts to operate. Rather they occur at many points (called **fixed-cost breaks**) as volume increases. This makes the theoretically smooth average cost curve more discontinuous.
- Production levels may be increased above the theoretical capacity of the plant, by using prolonged overtime, for example, or temporarily subcontracting some parts of the work.
- There may be less obvious cost penalties of operating the plant at levels close to or above its nominal capacity. For example, long periods of overtime may reduce productivity levels as well as costing more in extra payments to staff; operating plant for long periods with reduced maintenance time may increase the chances of breakdown, and so on. This usually means that average costs start to increase after a point which will often be lower than the theoretical capacity of the plant.

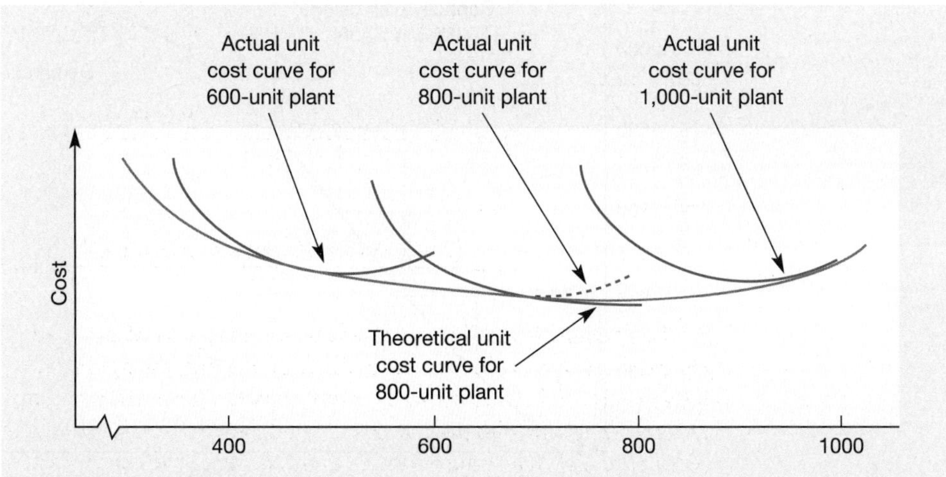

Figure 6.8 Unit cost curves for individual plants of varying capacities and the unit cost curve for this type of plant as its capacity varies

The blue dotted line in Figure 6.8 shows this effect. The two other blue lines show similar curves for a 600-unit plant and a 1,000-unit plant. Figure 6.8 also shows that a similar relationship occurs between the average-cost curves for plants of increasing size. As the nominal capacity of the plants increases, the lowest-cost points at first reduce. There are two main reasons for this:

- The fixed costs of an operation do not increase proportionately as its capacity increases. An 800-unit plant has less than twice the fixed costs of a 400-unit plant.
- The capital costs of building the plant do not increase proportionately to its capacity. An 800-unit plant costs less to build than twice the cost of a 400-unit plant.

Economies of scale

Diseconomies of scale

These two factors, taken together, are often referred to as **economies of scale**. However, above a certain size, the lowest-cost point may increase. In Figure 6.8 this happens with plants above 800 units capacity. This occurs because of what are called the **diseconomies of scale**, two of which are particularly important. First, transportation costs can be high for large operations. For example, if a manufacturer supplies its global market from one major plant in Denmark, materials may have to be brought in to, and shipped from, several countries. Second, complexity costs increase as size increases. The communications and coordination effort necessary to manage an operation tends to increase faster than capacity. Although not seen as a direct cost, it can nevertheless be very significant.

Scale of capacity and the demand–capacity balance

Large units of capacity also have some disadvantages when the capacity of the operation is being changed to match changing demand. For example, suppose that the air-conditioning unit manufacturer forecasts demand increase over the next three years, as shown in Figure 6.9, to level off at around 2,400 units a week. If the company seeks to satisfy all demand by building three plants, each of 800 units capacity, the company will have substantial amounts of over-capacity for much of the period when demand is increasing. Over-capacity means low capacity utilization, which in turn means higher unit costs. If the company builds smaller plants, say 400-unit plants, there will still be over-capacity but to a lesser extent, which means higher capacity utilization and possibly lower costs.

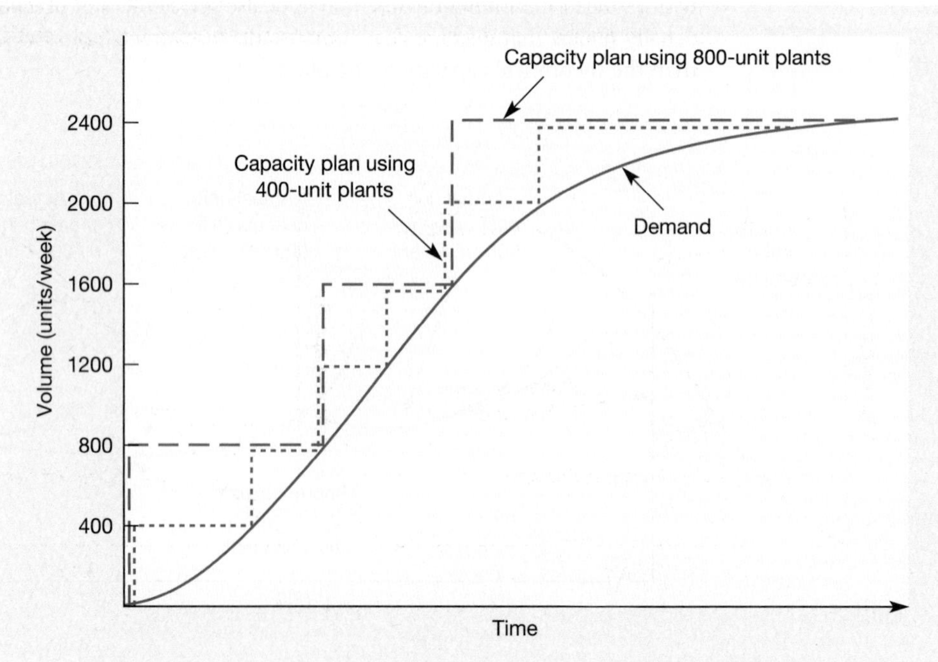

Figure 6.9 The scale of capacity increments affects the utilization of capacity

Balancing capacity

As we discussed in Chapter 1, all operations are made up of separate processes, each of which will itself have its own capacity. So, for example, the 800-unit air-conditioning plant may not only assemble the products but may also manufacture the parts from which they are made, pack, store and load them in a warehouse and distribute them to customers. If demand is 800 units per week, not only must the assembly process have a capacity sufficient for this output, but the parts manufacturing processes, warehouse and distribution fleet of trucks must also have sufficient capacity. For the network to operate efficiently, all its stages must have the same capacity. If not, the capacity of the network as a whole will be limited to the capacity of its slowest link.

The timing of capacity change

Changing the capacity of an operation is not just a matter of deciding on the best size of a capacity increment. The operation also needs to decide when to bring 'on-stream' new capacity. For example, Figure 6.10 shows the forecast demand for the new air-conditioning unit. The company has decided to build 400-unit-per-week plants in order to meet the growth in demand for its new product. In deciding *when* the new plants are to be introduced the company must choose a position somewhere between two extreme strategies:

Capacity leading

- **capacity leads** demand – timing the introduction of capacity in such a way that there is always sufficient capacity to meet forecast demand;

Capacity lagging

- **capacity lags** demand – timing the introduction of capacity so that demand is always equal to or greater than capacity.

Figure 6.10(a) shows these two extreme strategies, although in practice the company is likely to choose a position somewhere between the two. Each strategy has its own advantages and disadvantages. These are shown in Table 6.4. The actual approach taken by any company will depend on how it views these advantages and disadvantages. For example, if the company's access to funds for capital expenditure is limited, it is likely to find the delayed capital expenditure requirement of the capacity-lagging strategy relatively attractive.

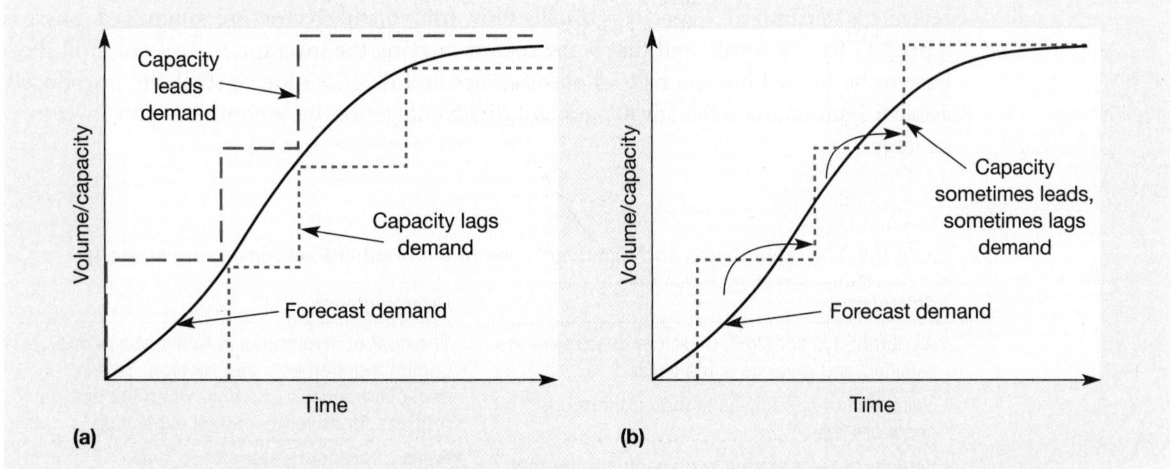

Figure 6.10 (a) Capacity-leading and capacity-lagging strategies, (b) Smoothing with inventories means using the excess capacity in one period to produce inventory that supplies the under-capacity period

Table 6.4 The arguments for and against pure leading and pure lagging strategies of capacity timing

Advantages	*Disadvantages*
Capacity-leading strategies	
Always sufficient capacity to meet demand, therefore revenue is maximized and customers satisfied	Utilization of the plants is always relatively low, therefore costs will be high
Most of the time there is a 'capacity cushion' which can absorb extra demand if forecasts are pessimistic	Risks of even greater (or even permanent) over-capacity if demand does not reach forecast levels
Any critical start-up problems with new plants are less likely to affect supply to customers	Capital spending on plant early
Capacity-lagging strategies	
Always sufficient demand to keep the plants working at full capacity, therefore unit costs are minimized	Insufficient capacity to meet demand fully, therefore reduced revenue and dissatisfied customers
Over-capacity problems are minimized if forecasts are optimistic	No ability to exploit short-term increases in demand
Capital spending on the plants is delayed	Under-supply position even worse if there are start-up problems with the new plants

'Smoothing' with inventory

The strategy on the continuum between pure leading and pure lagging strategies can be implemented so that no inventories are accumulated. All demand in one period is satisfied (or not) by the activity of the operation in the same period. Indeed, for customer-processing operations there is no alternative to this. A hotel cannot satisfy demand in one year by using rooms which were vacant the previous year. For some materials- and information-processing operations, however, the output from the operation which is not required in one period can be stored for use in the next period. The economies of using inventories are fully explored in Chapter 12. Here we confine ourselves to noting that inventories can be used to obtain the advantages of both capacity leading and capacity lagging. Figure 6.10(b) shows how this can be done. Capacity is introduced such that demand can always be met by a combination of production and inventories, and capacity is, with the occasional exception, fully utilized. This may seem like an ideal state. Demand is always met and so revenue is maximized. Capacity is usually fully utilized and so costs are minimized. There is a price to pay, however, and that is the cost of carrying the inventories. Not only will these have to be funded but the risks of obsolescence and deterioration of stock are introduced. Table 6.5 summarizes the advantages and disadvantages of the 'smoothing-with-inventory' strategy.

Table 6.5 The advantages and disadvantages of a smoothing-with-inventory strategy

Advantages	*Disadvantages*
All demand is satisfied, therefore customers are satisfied and revenue is maximized	The cost of inventories in terms of working capital requirements can be high. This is especially serious at a time when the company requires funds for its capital expansion
Utilization of capacity is high and therefore costs are low	
Very short-term surges in demand can be met from inventories	Risks of product deterioration and obsolescence

Worked example

A business process outsourcing (BPO) company is considering building some processing centres in India. The company has a standard call centre design that it has found to be the most efficient around the world. Demand forecasts indicate that there is already demand from potential clients to fully utilize one process centre that would generate $10 million of business per quarter (3-month period). The forecasts also indicate that by quarter 6 there will be sufficient demand to fully utilize one further processing centre. The costs of running a single centre are estimated to be $5 million per quarter and the lead time between ordering a centre and it being fully operational is two quarters. The capital costs of building a centre is $10 million, $5 million of which is payable before the end of the first quarter after ordering, and $5 million payable before the end of the second quarter after ordering. How much funding will the company have to secure on a quarter-by-quarter basis if it decides to build one processing centre as soon as possible and a second processing centre to be operational by the beginning of quarter 6?

Analysis

The funding required for a capacity expansion such as this can be derived by calculating the amount of cash coming in to the operation each time period, then subtracting the operating and capital costs for the project each time period. The cumulative cash flow indicates the funding required for the project. In Table 6.6 these calculations are performed for eight quarters. For the first two quarters there is a net cash outflow because capital costs are incurred by no revenue is being earned. After that, revenue is being earned but in quarters four and five this is partly offset by further capital costs for the second processing centre. However, from quarter six onwards the additional revenue from the second processing centre brings the cash flow positive again. The maximum funding required occurs in quarter two and is $10 million.

Table 6.6 The cumulative cash flow indicating the funding required for the project

	Quarters							
	1	*2*	*3*	*4*	*5*	*6*	*7*	*7*
Sales revenue ($ millions)	0	0	10	10	10	20	20	20
Operating costs ($ millions)	0	0	−5	−5	−5	−10	−10	−10
Capital costs ($ millions)	−5	−5	−0	−5	−5	0	0	0
Required cumulative funding ($ millions)	−5	−10	−5	−5	−5	+5	+15	+25

Break-even analysis of capacity expansion

Fixed-cost breaks are important in determining break-even points

An alternative view of capacity expansion can be gained by examining the cost implications of adding increments of capacity on a break-even basis. Figure 6.11 shows how increasing capacity can move an operation from profitability to loss. Each additional unit of capacity results in a ***fixed-cost break*** that is a further lump of expenditure which will have to be incurred before any further activity can be undertaken in the operation. The operation is unlikely to be profitable at very low levels of output. Eventually, assuming that prices are greater than marginal costs, revenue will exceed total costs. However, the level of profitability at the point where the output level is equal to the capacity of the operation may not be sufficient to absorb all the extra fixed costs of a further increment in capacity. This could make the operation unprofitable in some stages of its expansion.

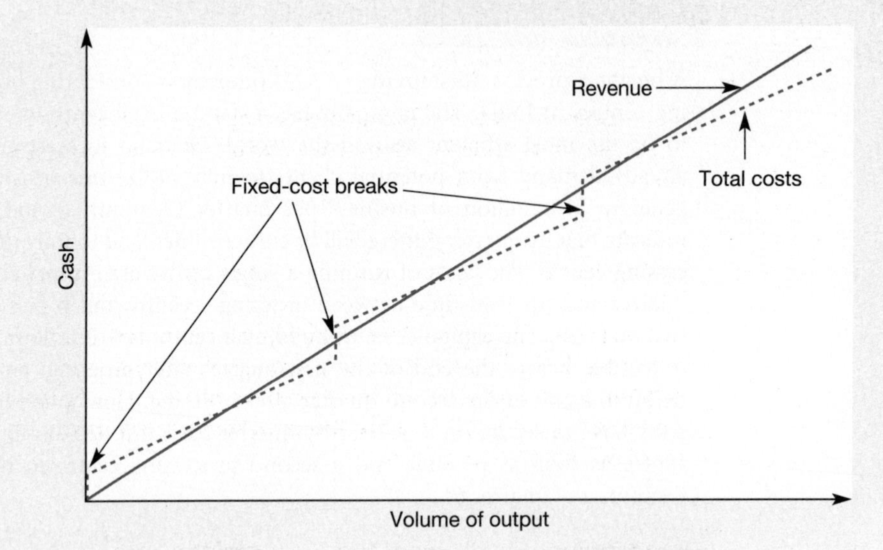

Figure 6.11 Repeated incurring of fixed costs can raise total costs above revenue

Worked example

A specialist graphics company is investing in a new machine which enables it to make high-quality prints for its clients. Demand for these prints is forecast to be around 100,000 units in year 1 and 220,000 units in year 2. The maximum capacity of each machine the company will buy to process these prints is 100,000 units per year. They have a fixed cost of €200,000 per year and a variable cost of processing of €1 per unit. The company believe they will be able to charge €4 per unit for producing the prints.

Question

What profit are they likely to make in the first and second years?

Year 1 demand = 100,000 units; therefore company will need one machine
Cost of manufacturing = fixed cost for one machine + variable cost × 100,000
= €200,000 + (€1 × 100,000)
= €300,000
Revenue = demand × price
= 100,000 × €4
= €400,000
Therefore profit = €400,000 – €300,000
= €100,000

Year 2 demand = 220,000; therefore company will need three machines
Cost of manufacturing = fixed cost for three machines + variable cost × 220,000
= (3 × €200,000) + (€1 × 220,000)
= €820,000
Revenue = demand × price
= 220,000 × €4
= €880,000
Therefore profit = €880,000 – €820,000
= €60,000

Note: the profit in the second year will be lower because of the extra fixed costs associated with the investment in the two extra machines.

Summary answers to key questions

*Check and improve your understanding of this chapter using self assessment questions and a personalised study plan, audio and video downloads, and an eBook – all at **www.myomlab.com**.*

➤ Why should an organization take a total supply network perspective?

- The main advantage is that it helps any operation to understand how it can compete effectively within the network. This is because a supply network approach requires operations managers to think about their suppliers and their customers *as operations*. It can also help to identify particularly significant links within the network and hence identify long-term strategic changes which will affect the operation.

➤ What is involved in configuring a supply network?

- There are two main issues involved in configuring the supply network. The first concerns the overall shape of the supply network. The second concerns the nature and extent of *outsourcing* or *vertical integration*.
- Changing the shape of the supply network may involve reducing the number of suppliers to the operation so as to develop closer relationships, any bypassing or disintermediating operations in the network.
- Outsourcing or vertical integration concerns the nature of the ownership of the operations within a supply network. The direction of vertical integration refers to whether an organization wants to own operations on its supply side or demand side (backwards or forwards integration). The extent of vertical integration relates to whether an organization wants to own a wide span of the stage in the supply network. The balance of vertical integration refers to whether operations can trade with only their vertically integrated partners or with any other organizations.

➤ Where should an operation be located?

- The stimuli which act on an organization during the location decision can be divided into supply-side and demand-side influences. Supply-side influences are the factors such as labour, land and utility costs which change as location changes. Demand-side influences include such things as the image of the location, its convenience for customers and the suitability of the site itself.

➤ How much capacity should an operation plan to have?

- The amount of capacity an organization will have depends on its view of current and future demand. It is when its view of future demand is different from current demand that this issue becomes important.
- When an organization has to cope with changing demand, a number of capacity decisions need to be taken. These include choosing the optimum capacity for each site, balancing the various capacity levels of the operation in the network, and timing the changes in the capacity of each part of the network.
- Important influences on these decisions include the concepts of economy and diseconomy of scale, supply flexibility if demand is different from that forecast, and the profitability and cash-flow implications of capacity timing changes.

Case study
Disneyland Resort Paris (abridged)[10]

In August 2006, the company behind Disneyland Resort Paris reported a 13 per cent rise in revenues, saying that it was making encouraging progress with new rides aimed at getting more visitors. *'I am pleased with year-to-date revenues and especially with third quarter's, as well as with the success of the opening of Buzz Lightyear Laser Blast, the first step of our multi-year investment program. These results reflect the group's strategy of increasing growth through innovative marketing and sales efforts as well as a multi-year investment program. This performance is encouraging as we enter into the important summer months'*, said Chairman and Chief Executive Karl L. Holz. Yet it hadn't always been like that. The 14-year history of Disneyland Paris had more ups and downs than any of its rollercoasters. From 12 April 1992 when EuroDisney opened, through to this more optimistic report, the resort had been subject simultaneously to both wildly optimistic forecasts and widespread criticism and ridicule. An essay on one critical Internet site (called 'An Ugly American in Paris') summarized the whole venture in this way. *'When Disney decided to expand its hugely successful theme park operations to Europe, it brought American management styles, American cultural tastes, American labor practices, and American marketing pizzazz to Europe. Then, when the French stayed away in droves, it accused them of cultural snobbery.'*

Source: Corbis/Jacques Langevin

The 'magic' of Disney

Since its founding in 1923, The Walt Disney Company had striven to remain faithful in its commitment to *'Producing unparalleled entertainment experiences based on its rich legacy of quality creative content and exceptional storytelling'*. In the Parks and Resorts division, according to the company's description, customers could experience the 'Magic of Disney's beloved characters'. It was founded in 1952, when Walt Disney formed what is now known as 'Walt Disney Imagineering' to build Disneyland in Anaheim, California. By 2006, Walt Disney Parks and Resorts operated or licensed 11 theme parks at five Disney destinations around the world. They were: Disneyland Resort, California, Walt Disney World Resort, Florida, Tokyo Disney Resort, Disneyland Resort Paris, and their latest park, Hong Kong Disneyland. In addition, the division operated 35 resort hotels, two luxury cruise ships and a wide variety of other entertainment offerings. But perhaps none of its ventures had proved to be as challenging as its Paris Resort.

Service delivery at Disney resorts and parks

The core values of the Disney company and, arguably, the reason for its success, originated in the views and personality of Walt Disney, the company's founder. He had what some called an obsessive focus on creating images, products and experiences for customers that epitomized fun, imagination and service. Through the 'magic' of legendary fairytale and story characters, customers could escape the cares of the real world. Different areas of each Disney Park are themed, often around various 'lands' such as Frontierland, and Fantasyland. Each land contains attractions and rides, most of which are designed to be acceptable to a wide range of ages. Very few rides are 'scary' when compared to many other entertainment parks. The architectural styles, décor, food, souvenirs and cast costumes were all designed to reflect the theme of the 'land', as were the films and shows. And although there were some regional differences, all the theme parks followed the same basic set-up. The terminology used by the company reinforced its philosophy of consistent entertainment. Employees, even those working 'backstage', were called 'cast members'. They did not wear uniforms but 'costumes', and rather than being given a job they were 'cast in a role'. All park visitors were called 'guests'.

Disney employees were generally relatively young, often of school or college age. Most were paid hourly on tasks that could be repetitive even though they usually involved constant contact with customers. Yet, employees were still expected to maintain a high level of courtesy and work performance. All cast members were expected to conform to strict dress and grooming standards. Applicants to become cast members were screened for qualities such as how well they responded to questions, how well they listened to their peers, how they smiled and used body language, and whether they had an 'appropriate attitude'. Disney parks had gained a reputation for their obsession with delivering a high level of service and experience through attention to operations detail. All parks employed queue management techniques such as providing information and entertainment for visitors, who were also seen as having a role within the park. They were not merely spectators or passengers on the rides, they were considered to be participants in a play. Their needs and desires were analysed and met through frequent interactions with staff (cast members). In this way they could be drawn into the illusion that they were actually part of the fantasy.

Disney's stated goal was to exceed their customers' expectations every day. Service delivery was mapped and continuously refined in the light of customer feedback and the staff induction programme emphasized the company's quality assurance procedures and service standards based on the four principles of safety, courtesy, show and efficiency. Parks were kept fanatically clean. The same Disney character never appears twice within sight – how could there be two Mickeys? Staff were taught that customer perceptions are both the key to customer delight, but also are extremely fragile. Negative perceptions can be established after only one negative experience. Disney university-trained their employees in their strict service standards as well as providing the skills to operate new rides as they were developed. Staff recognition programmes attempted to identify outstanding service delivery performance as well as 'energy, enthusiasm, commitment, and pride'. All parks contained phones connected to a central question hotline for employees to find the answer to any question posed by customers.

Tokyo Disneyland

Tokyo Disneyland, opened in 1982, was owned and operated by the Oriental Land Company. Disney had designed the park and advised on how it should be run and it was considered a great success. Japanese customers revealed a significant appetite for American themes and American brands, and already had a good knowledge of Disney characters. Feedback was extremely positive with visitors commenting on the cleanliness of the park and the courtesy and the efficiency of staff members. Visitors also appreciated the Disney souvenirs because giving gifts is deeply embedded in the Japanese culture. The success of the Tokyo Park was explained by one American living in Japan. 'Young Japanese are very clean-cut. They respond well to Disney's clean-cut image, and I am sure they had no trouble filling positions. Also, young Japanese are generally comfortable wearing uniforms, obeying their bosses, and being part of a team. These are part of the Disney formula. Also, Tokyo is very crowded and Japanese here are used to crowds and waiting in line. They are very patient. And above all, Japanese are always very polite to strangers.'

Disneyland Paris

By 2006 Disneyland Paris consisted of three parks: the Disney Village, Disneyland Paris itself and the Disney Studio Park. The Village was composed of stores and restaurants; the Disneyland Paris was the main theme park; and Disney Studio Park has a more general movie-making theme. At the time of the European park's opening more than two million Europeans visited the US Disney parks. The company's brand was strong and it had over half a century of translating the Disney brand into reality. The name 'Disney' had become synonymous with wholesome family entertainment that combined childhood innocence with high-tech 'Imagineering'.

Initially, as well as France, Germany, Britain, Italy and Spain were all considered as possible locations, though Germany, Britain and Italy were soon discarded from the list of potential sites. The decision soon came to a straight contest between the Alicante area of Spain, which had a similar climate to Florida for a large part of the year and the Marne-la-Vallée area just outside Paris. Certainly, winning the contest to host the new park was important for all the potential host countries. The new park promised to generate more than 30,000 jobs. The major advantage of locating in Spain was the weather. However, the eventual decision to locate near Paris was thought to have been driven by a number of factors that weighed more heavily with Disney executives. These included the following:

- There was a suitable site available just outside Paris.
- The proposed location put the park within a 2-hour drive for 17 million people, a 4-hour drive for 68 million people, a 6-hour drive for 110 million people and a 2-hour flight for a further 310 million or so.
- The site also had potentially good transport links. The Channel Tunnel that was to connect England with France was due to open in 1994. In addition, the French autoroutes network and the high-speed TGV network could both be extended to connect the site with the rest of Europe.
- Paris was already a highly attractive vacation destination.
- Europeans generally take significantly more holidays each year than Americans (five weeks of vacation as opposed to two or three weeks).
- Research indicated that 85% of French people would welcome a Disney park.
- Both national and local government in France were prepared to give significant financial incentives (as were the Spanish authorities), including an offer to invest in local infrastructure, reduce the rate of value added tax on goods sold in the park, provide subsidized loans, and value the land artificially low to help reduce taxes. Moreover, the French government was prepared to expropriate land from local farmers to smooth the planning and construction process.

Early concerns that the park would not have the same sunny, happy feel in a cooler climate than Florida were allayed by the spectacular success of Disneyland Tokyo in a location with a similar climate to Paris, and construction started in August 1988. But from the announcement that the park would be built in France, it was subject to a wave of criticism. One critic called the project a 'cultural Chernobyl' because of how it might affect French cultural values. Another described it as *'a horror made of cardboard,*

plastic, and appalling colours; a construction of hardened chewing-gum and idiot folklore taken straight out of comic books written for obese Americans'. However, as some commentators noted, the cultural arguments and anti-Americanism of the French intellectual elite did not seem to reflect the behaviour of most French people, who 'eat at McDonald's, wear Gap clothing, and flock to American movies'.

Designing Disneyland Resort Paris

Phase 1 of the Euro Disney Park was designed to have 29 rides and attractions and a championship golf course together with many restaurants, shops, live shows and parades as well as six hotels. Although the park was designed to fit in with Disney's traditional appearance and values, a number of changes were made to accommodate what was thought to be the preferences of European visitors. For example, market research indicated that Europeans would respond to a 'wild west' image of America. Therefore, both rides and hotel designs were made to emphasize this theme. Disney was also keen to diffuse criticism, especially from French left-wing intellectuals and politicians, that the design of the park would be too 'Americanized' and would become a vehicle for American 'cultural imperialism'. To counter charges of American imperialism, Disney gave the park a flavour that stressed the European heritage of many of the Disney characters, and increased the sense of beauty and fantasy. They were, after all, competing against Paris's exuberant architecture and sights. For example, Discoveryland featured storylines from Jules Verne, the French author. Snow White (and her dwarfs) was located in a Bavarian village. Cinderella was located in a French inn. Even Peter Pan was made to appear more 'English Edwardian' than in the original US designs.

Because of concerns about the popularity of American 'fast food', Euro Disney introduced more variety into its restaurants and snack bars, featuring foods from around the world. In a bold publicity move, Disney invited a number of top Paris chefs to visit and taste the food. Some anxiety was also expressed concerning the different 'eating behaviour' between Americans and Europeans. Whereas Americans preferred to 'graze', eating snacks and fast meals throughout the day, Europeans generally preferred to sit down and eat at traditional meal times. This would have a very significant impact on peak demand levels on dining facilities. A further concern was that in Europe (especially French) visitors would be intolerant of long queues. To overcome this, extra diversions such as films and entertainments were planned for visitors as they waited in line for a ride.

Before the opening of the park, Euro Disney had to recruit and train between 12,000 and 14,000 permanent and around 5,000 temporary employees. All these new employees were required to undergo extensive training in order to prepare them to achieve Disney's high standard of customer service as well as understand operational routines and safety procedures. Originally, the company's objective was to hire 45 per cent of its employees from France, 30 per cent from other European countries, and 15 per cent from outside of Europe. However, this proved difficult and when the park opened around 70 per cent of employees were French. Most cast members were paid around 15 per cent above the French minimum wage.

An information centre was opened in December 1990 to show the public what Disney was constructing. The 'casting centre' was opened on 1 September 1991 to recruit the 'cast members' needed to staff the park's attractions. But the hiring process did not go smoothly. In particular, Disney's grooming requirements that insisted on a 'neat' dress code, a ban on facial hair, set standards for hair and finger nails, and an insistence on 'appropriate undergarments' proved controversial. Both the French press and trade unions strongly objected to the grooming requirements, claiming they were excessive and much stricter than was generally held to be reasonable in France. Nevertheless, the company refused to modify its grooming standards. Accommodating staff also proved to be a problem, when the large influx of employees swamped the available housing in the area. Disney had to build its own apartments as well as rent rooms in local homes just to accommodate its employees. Notwithstanding all the difficulties, Disney did succeed in recruiting and training all its cast members before the opening.

The park opens

The park opened to employees, for testing during late March 1992, during which time the main sponsors and their families were invited to visit the new park, but the opening was not helped by strikes on the commuter trains leading to the park, staff unrest, threatened security problems (a terrorist bomb had exploded the night before the opening) and protests in surrounding villages that demonstrated against the noise and disruption from the park. The opening day crowds, expected to be 500,000, failed to materialize, however, and at close of the first day only 50,000 people had passed through the gates. Disney had expected the French to make up a larger proportion of visiting guests than they did in the early days. This may have been partly due to protests from French locals who feared their culture would be damaged by Euro Disney. Also, all Disney parks had traditionally been alcohol-free. To begin with, Euro Disney was no different. However, this was extremely unpopular, particularly with French visitors who like to have a glass of wine or beer with their food. But whatever the cause the low initial attendance was very disappointing for the Disney Company.

It was reported that, in the first 9 weeks of operation, approximately 1,000 employees left Euro Disney, about one half of whom 'left voluntarily'. The reasons cited for leaving varied. Some blamed the hectic pace of work and the long hours that Disney expected. Others mentioned the 'chaotic' conditions in the first few weeks. Even Disney conceded that conditions had been tough immediately after the park opened. Some leavers blamed Disney's apparent difficulty in understanding 'how Europeans work'. '*We can't just be told what to do, we ask questions and don't all think the same*.' Some visitors who had experience of the American parks commented that the standards of service were noticeably below what would be acceptable in America. There were reports that some cast members were failing to meet Disney's normal service standard: '*even on the opening weekend some clearly couldn't care less . . . My overwhelming impression . . . was that they were out of their depth. There is much more to being a cast member than endlessly saying "Bonjour". Apart from having a detailed knowledge of the site, Euro Disney staff have the anxiety of not knowing in what language they are going to be addressed . . . Many were struggling.*'

It was also noticeable that different nationalities exhibited different types of behaviour when visiting the park. Some nationalities always used the waste bins while others were more likely to drop litter on the floor. Most noticeable were differences in queuing behaviour. Northern Europeans tend to be disciplined and content to wait for rides in an orderly manner. By contrast some Southern European visitors '*seem to have made an Olympic event out of getting to the ticket taker first*'. Nevertheless, not all reactions were negative. European newspapers also quoted plenty of positive reaction from visitors, especially children. Euro Disney was so different from the existing European theme parks, with immediately recognizable characters and a wide variety of attractions. Families who could not afford to travel to the United States could now interact with Disney characters and 'sample the experience at far less cost'.

The next 15 years

By August 1992 estimates of annual attendance figures were being drastically cut from 11 million to just over 9 million. EuroDisney's misfortunes were further compounded in late 1992 when a European recession caused property prices to drop sharply, and interest payments on the large start-up loans taken out by EuroDisney forced the company to admit serious financial difficulties. Also the cheap dollar resulted in more people taking their holidays in Florida at Walt Disney World. At the first anniversary of the park's opening, in April 1993, Sleeping Beauty's Castle was decorated as a giant birthday cake to celebrate the occasion; however, further problems were approaching. Criticized for having too few rides, the roller coaster 'Indiana Jones and the Temple of Peril' was opened in July. This was the first Disney roller coaster that included a 360-degree loop, but just a few weeks after opening emergency brakes locked on during a ride, causing some guest injuries. The ride was temporarily shut down for investigations. Also in 1993 the proposed Euro Disney phase 2 was shelved due to financial problems. This meant Disney MGM Studios Europe and 13,000 hotel rooms would not be built to the original 1995 deadline originally agreed upon by the Walt Disney Company. However, Discovery Mountain, one of the planned phase 2 attractions, did get approval.

By the start of 1994 rumours were circulating that the park was on the verge of bankruptcy. Emergency crisis talks were held between the banks and backers with things coming to a head during March when Disney offered the banks an ultimatum. It would provide sufficient capital for the park to continue to operate until the end of the month, but unless the banks agreed to restructure the park's $1bn debt, the Walt Disney Company would close the park, and walk away from the whole European venture, leaving the banks with a bankrupt theme park and a massive expanse of virtually worthless real estate. Michael Eisner, Disney's CEO, announced that Disney was planning to pull the plug on the venture at the end of March 1994 unless the banks were prepared to restructure the loans. The banks agreed to Disney's demands.

In May 1994 the connection between London and Marne La Vallée was completed, along with a TGV link, providing a connection between several major European cities. By August the park was starting to find its feet at last, and all of the park's hotels were fully booked during the peak holiday season. Also, in October, the park's name was officially changed from EuroDisney to 'Disneyland Paris' in order to '*show that the resort now was named much more like its counterparts in California and Tokyo*'. The end-of-year figures for 1994 showed encouraging signs despite a 10% fall in attendance caused by the bad publicity over the earlier financial problems. For the next few years new rides continued to be introduced. 1995 saw the opening of the new roller coaster, 'Space Mountain de la Terre à la Lune', and Euro Disney did announce its first annual operating profit in November 1995. New attractions were added steadily, but in 1999 the planned Christmas and New Year celebrations are disrupted when a freak storm caused havoc, destroying the Mickey Mouse glass statue that had just been installed for the Lighting Ceremony and many other attractions.

Disney's 'Fastpass' system was introduced in 2000: a new service that allowed guests to use their entry passes to gain a ticket at certain attractions and return at the time stated and gain direct entry to the attraction without queuing. Two new attractions were also opened, 'Indiana Jones et la Temple du Peril' and 'Tarzan le Recontre' starring a cast of acrobats along with Tarzan, Jane and all their jungle friends with music from the movie in different European languages. In 2001 the 'ImagiNations Parade' is replaced by the 'Wonderful World of Disney Parade' which receives some criticism for being 'less than spectacular' with only 8 parade floats. Also Disney's 'California Adventure' was opened in California. The Paris resort's 10th anniversary saw the opening of the new Walt Disney Studios Park attraction, based on a similar attraction in Florida that had already proved to be a success.

André Lacroix from Burger King was appointed as CEO of Disneyland Resort Paris in 2003, to 'take on the challenge 

of a failing Disney park in Europe and turn it around'. Increasing investment, he refurbished whole sections of the park and introduced the Jungle Book Carnival in February to increase attendance during the slow months. By 2004 attendance had increased but the company announced that it was still losing money. And even the positive news of 2006, although generally well received still left questions unanswered. As one commentator put it, 'Would Disney, the stockholders, the banks, or even the French government make the same decision to go ahead if they could wind the clock back to 1987? Is this a story of a fundamentally flawed concept, or was it just mishandled?'

Questions

1 What markets are the Disney resorts and parks aiming for?

2 Was Disney's choice of the Paris site a mistake?

3 What aspects of their parks' design did Disney change when it constructed Euro Disney?

4 What did Disney *not* change when it constructed Euro Disney?

5 What were Disney's main mistakes from the conception of the Paris resort through to 2006?

Problems and applications

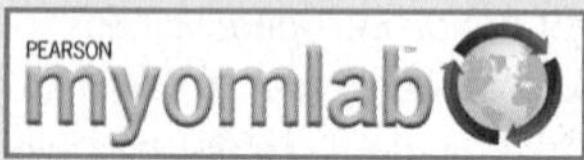

These problems and applications will help to improve your analysis of operations. You can find more practice problems as well as worked examples and guided solutions on MyOMLab at ***www.myomlab.com****.*

1 A company is deciding between two locations (Location A and Location B). It has six location criteria, the most important being the suitability of the buildings that are available in each location. About half as important as the suitability of the buildings are the access to the site and the supply of skills available locally. Half as important as these two factors are the potential for expansion on the sites and the attractiveness of the area. The attractiveness of the buildings themselves is also a factor, although a relatively unimportant one, rating one half as important as the attractiveness of the area. Table 6.7 indicates the scores for each of these factors, as judged by the company's senior management. What would you advise the company to do?

Table 6.7 The scores for each factor in the location decision as judged by the company's senior management

	Location A	*Location B*
Access	4	6
Expansion	6	5
Attractiveness (area)	10	6
Skills supply	5	7
Suitability of buildings	8	7
Attractiveness of buildings	4	6

2 A company which assembles garden furniture obtains its components from three suppliers. Supplier A provides all the boxes and packaging material; supplier B provides all metal components; and supplier C provides all plastic components. Supplier A sends one truckload of the materials per week to the factory and is located at the position (1,1) on a grid reference which covers the local area. Supplier B sends four truckloads of components per week to the factory and is located at point (2,3) on the grid. Supplier C sends three truckloads of components per week to the factory and is located at point (4,3) on the grid. After assembly, all the products are sent to a warehouse which is located at point (5,1) on the grid. Assuming there is little or no waste generated in the process, where should the company locate its factory so as to minimize transportation costs? Assume that transportation costs are directly proportional to the number of truckloads of parts, or finished goods, transported per week.

3 A rapid-response maintenance company serves its customers who are located in four industrial estates. Estate A has 15 customers and is located at grid reference (5,7). Estate B has 20 customers and is located at grid reference (6,3). Estate C has 15 customers and is located at grid reference (10,2) but these customers are twice as likely to require service as the company's other customers. Estate D has 10 customers and is located at grid reference (12,3). At what grid reference should the company be looking to find a suitable location for its service centre?

4 A private health-care clinic has been offered a leasing deal where it could lease a CAT scanner at a fixed charge of €2,000 per month and a charge per patient of €6 per patient scanned. The clinic currently charges €10 per patient for taking a scan. **(a)** At what level of demand (in number of patients per week) will the clinic break even on the cost of leasing the CAT scan? **(b)** Would a revised lease that stipulated a fixed cost of €3,000 per week and a variable cost of €0.2 per patient be a better deal?

5 Visit sites on the Internet that offer (legal) downloadable music using MP3 or other compression formats. Consider the music business supply chain, **(a)** for the recordings of a well-known popular music artist, and **(b)** for a less well-known (or even largely unknown) artist struggling to gain recognition. How might the transmission of music over the Internet affect each of these artists' sales? What implications does electronic music transmission have for record shops?

6 Visit the web sites of companies that are in the paper manufacturing/pulp production/packaging industries. Assess the extent to which the companies you have investigated are vertically integrated in the paper supply chain that stretches from foresting through to the production of packaging materials.

Selected further reading

Carmel, E. and Tjia, P. (2005) *Offshoring Information Technology: Sourcing and Outsourcing to a Global Workforce*, Cambridge University Press, Cambridge. An academic book on outsourcing.

Chopra, S. and Meindl, P. (2001) *Supply Chain Management: Strategy, Planning and Operations,* Prentice Hall, Upper Saddle River, NJ. A good textbook that covers both strategic and operations issues.

Dell, M. (with **Catherine Fredman**) (1999) *Direct from Dell: Strategies that Revolutionized an Industry,* Harper Business London. Michael Dell explains how his supply network strategy (and other decisions) had such an impact on the industry. Interesting and readable, but not a critical analysis!

Schniederjans, M.J. (1998) *International Facility Location and Acquisition Analysis*, Quorum Books, New York. Very much one for the technically minded.

Vashistha, A. and Vashistha, A. (2006) *The Offshore Nation: Strategies for Success in Global Outsourcing and Offshoring*, McGraw-Hill Higher Education. Another topical book on outsourcing.

Useful web sites

www.locationstrategies.com Exactly what the title implies. Good industry discussion.

www.cpmway.com American location selection site. You can get a flavour of how location decisions are made.

www.transparency.org A leading site for international business (including location) that fights corruption.

www.intel.com More details on Intel's 'Copy Exactly' strategy and other capacity strategy issues.

www.opsman.org Lots of useful stuff.

www.outsourcing.com Site of the Institute of Outsourcing. Some good case studies and some interesting reports, news items, etc.

www.bath.ac.uk/crisps A centre for research in strategic purchasing and supply with some interesting papers.

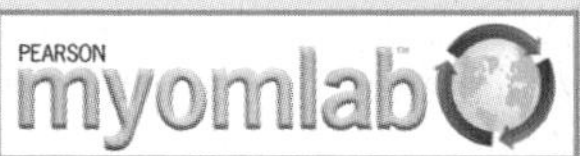

Now that you have finished reading this chapter, why not visit MyOMLab at ***www.myomlab.com*** *where you'll find more learning resources to help you make the most of your studies and get a better grade?*

Supplement to Chapter 6 Forecasting

Introduction

Some forecasts are accurate. We know exactly what time the sun will rise at any given place on earth tomorrow or one day next month or even next year. Forecasting in a business context, however, is much more difficult and therefore prone to error. We do not know precisely how many orders we will receive or how many customers will walk through the door tomorrow, next month, or next year. Such forecasts, however, are necessary to help managers make decisions about resourcing the organization for the future.

Forecasting – knowing the options

Simply knowing that demand for your goods or services is rising or falling is not enough in itself. Knowing the rate of change is likely to be vital to business planning. A firm of lawyers may have to decide the point at which, in their growing business, they will have to take on another partner. Hiring a new partner could take months so they need to be able to forecast when they expect to reach that point and then when they need to start their recruitment drive. The same applies to a plant manager who will need to purchase new plant to deal with rising demand. She may not want to commit to buying an expensive piece of machinery until absolutely necessary but in enough time to order the machine and have it built, delivered, installed and tested. The same is so for governments whether planning new airports or runway capacity or deciding where and how many primary schools to build.

The first question is to know how far you need to look ahead and this will depend on the options and decisions available to you. Take the example of a local government where the number of primary-age children (5–11-year-olds) is increasing in some areas and declining in other areas within its boundaries. It is legally obliged to provide school places for all such children. Government officials will have a number of options open to them and they may each have different lead times associated with them. One key step in forecasting is to know the possible options and the lead times required to bring them about (see Table S6.1).

Table S6.1 Options available and lead time required for dealing with changes in numbers of schoolchildren

Options available	*Lead time required*
Hire short-term teachers	Hours
Hire staff	↓
Build temporary classrooms	↓
Amend school catchment areas	↓
Build new classrooms	↓
Build new schools	Years

1 Individual schools can hire (or lay off) short-term (supply) teachers from a pool not only to cover for absent teachers but also to provide short-term capacity while teachers are hired to deal with increases in demand. Acquiring (or dismissing) such temporary cover may only require a few hours' notice. (This is often referred to as short-term capacity management.)
2 Hiring new (or laying off existing) staff is another option but both of these may take months to complete. (Medium-term capacity management.)
3 A shortage of accommodation may be fixed in the short to medium term by hiring or buying temporary classrooms. It may only take a couple of weeks to hire such a building and equip it ready for use.
4 It may be possible to amend catchment areas between schools to try to balance an increasing population in one area against a declining population in another. Such changes may require lengthy consultation processes.
5 In the longer term new classrooms or even new schools may have to be built. The planning, consultation, approval, commissioning, tendering, building and equipping process may take 1 to 5 years depending on the scale of the new build. (Long-term capacity planning – see Chapter 6.)

Knowing the range of options managers can then decide the timescale for their forecasts; indeed several forecasts might be needed for the short term, medium term and long term.

In essence forecasting is simple

In essence forecasting is easy. To know how many children may turn up in a local school tomorrow you can use the number that turned up today. In the long term in order to forecast how many primary-aged children will turn up at a school in five years' time one need simply look at the birth statistics for the current year for the school's catchment area, see Figure S6.1.

However, such simple extrapolation techniques are prone to error and indeed such approaches have resulted in some local governments committing themselves to building schools which 5 or 6 years later, when complete, had few children and other schools bursting at the seams with temporary classrooms and temporary teachers, often resulting in falling morale and declining educational standards. The reason why such simple approaches are prone to problems is that there are many contextual variables (see Figure S6.2) which will have a potentially significant impact on, for example, the school population five years hence. For example:

1 One minor factor in developed countries, though a major factor in developing countries, might be the death rate in children between birth and 5 years of age. This may be dependent upon location with a slightly higher mortality rate in the poorer areas compared to the more affluent areas.
2 Another more significant factor is immigration and emigration as people move into or out of the local area. This will be affected by housing stock and housing developments and the ebb and flow of jobs in the area and the changing economic prosperity in the area.

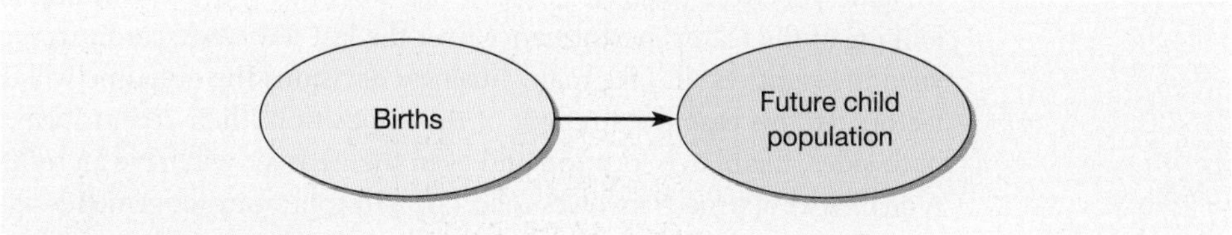

Figure S6.1 Simple prediction of future child population

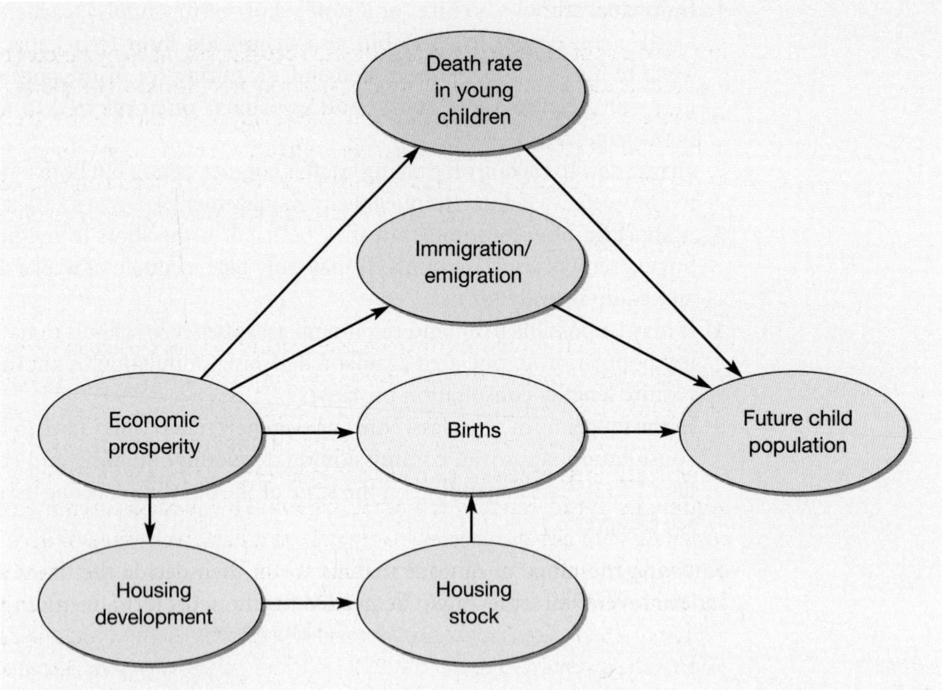

Figure S6.2 Some of the key causal variables in predicting child populations

3 One key factor which has an impact on the birth rate in an area is the amount and type of the housing stock. City-centre tenement buildings tend to have a higher proportion of children per dwelling, for example, than suburban semi-detached houses. So, not only will existing housing stock have an impact on the child population but so also will the type of housing developments under construction, planned and proposed.

Approaches to forecasting

Qualitative forecasting

Quantitative forecasting

There are two main approaches to forecasting. Managers sometimes use **qualitative** methods based on opinions, past experience and even best guesses. There is also a range of qualitative forecasting techniques available to help managers evaluate trends and causal relationships and make predictions about the future. Also, **quantitative forecasting** techniques can be used to model data. Although no approach or technique will result in an accurate forecast a combination of qualitative and quantitative approaches can be used to great effect by bringing together expert judgements and predictive models.

Qualitative methods

Imagine you were asked to forecast the outcome of a forthcoming football match. Simply looking at the teams' performance over the last few weeks and extrapolating it is unlikely to yield the right result. Like many business decisions the outcome will depend on many other factors. In this case the strength of the opposition, their recent form, injuries to players on both sides, the match location and even the weather will have an influence on the outcome. A qualitative approach involves collecting and appraising judgements, options, even best guesses as well as past performance from 'experts' to make a prediction. There are several ways this can be done: a panel approach, the Delphi method and scenario planning.

Panel approach

Just as panels of football pundits gather to speculate about likely outcomes so too do politicians, business leaders, stock market analysts, banks and airlines. The panel acts like a focus group allowing everyone to talk openly and freely. Although there is the great advantage of several brains being better than one, it can be difficult to reach a consensus, or sometimes the views of the loudest or highest status may emerge (the bandwagon effect). Although more reliable than one person's views the panel approach still has the weakness that everybody, even the experts, can get it wrong.

Delphi method

Delphi methods

Perhaps the best-known approach to generating forecasts using experts is the **Delphi method.** This is a more formal method which attempts to reduce the influences from procedures of face-to-face meetings. It employs a questionnaire, e-mailed or posted to the experts. The replies are analysed and summarized and returned, anonymously, to all the experts. The experts are then asked to re-consider their original response in the light of the replies and arguments put forward by the other experts. This process is repeated several more times to conclude with either a consensus or at least a narrower range of decisions. One refinement of this approach is to allocate weights to the individuals and their suggestions based on, for example, their experience, their past success in forecasting, other people's views of their abilities. The obvious problems associated with this method include constructing an appropriate questionnaire, selecting an appropriate panel of experts and trying to deal with their inherent biases.[1]

Scenario planning

Scenario planning

One method for dealing with situations of even greater uncertainty is **scenario planning.** This is usually applied to long-range forecasting, again using a panel. The panel members are usually asked to devise a range of future scenarios. Each scenario can then be discussed and the inherent risks considered. Unlike the Delphi method scenario planning is not necessarily concerned with arriving at a consensus but looking at the possible range of options and putting plans in place to try to avoid the ones that are least desired and taking action to follow the most desired.

Quantitative methods

Time series analysis
Causal modelling

There are two main approaches to qualitative forecasting, **time series analysis** and **causal modelling** techniques.

Time series examine the pattern of past behaviour of a single phenomenon over time taking into account reasons for variation in the trend in order to use the analysis to forecast the phenomenon's future behaviour.

Causal modelling is an approach which describes and evaluates the complex cause–effect relationships between the key variables (such as in Figure S6.2).

Time series analysis

Simple time series plot a variable over time by removing underlying variations with assignable causes use extrapolation techniques to predict future behaviour. The key weakness with this approach is that it simply looks at past behaviour to predict the future ignoring causal variables which are taken into account in other methods such as causal modelling or qualitative techniques. For example, suppose a company is attempting to predict the future sales of a product. The past three years' sales, quarter by quarter, are shown in Figure S6.3(a). This series of past sales may be analysed to indicate future sales. For instance, underlying the series might be a linear upward trend in sales. If this is taken out of the data, as in Figure S6.3(b), we are left with a cyclical seasonal variation. The mean deviation of each quarter from the trend line can now be taken out, to give the average seasonality deviation. What remains is

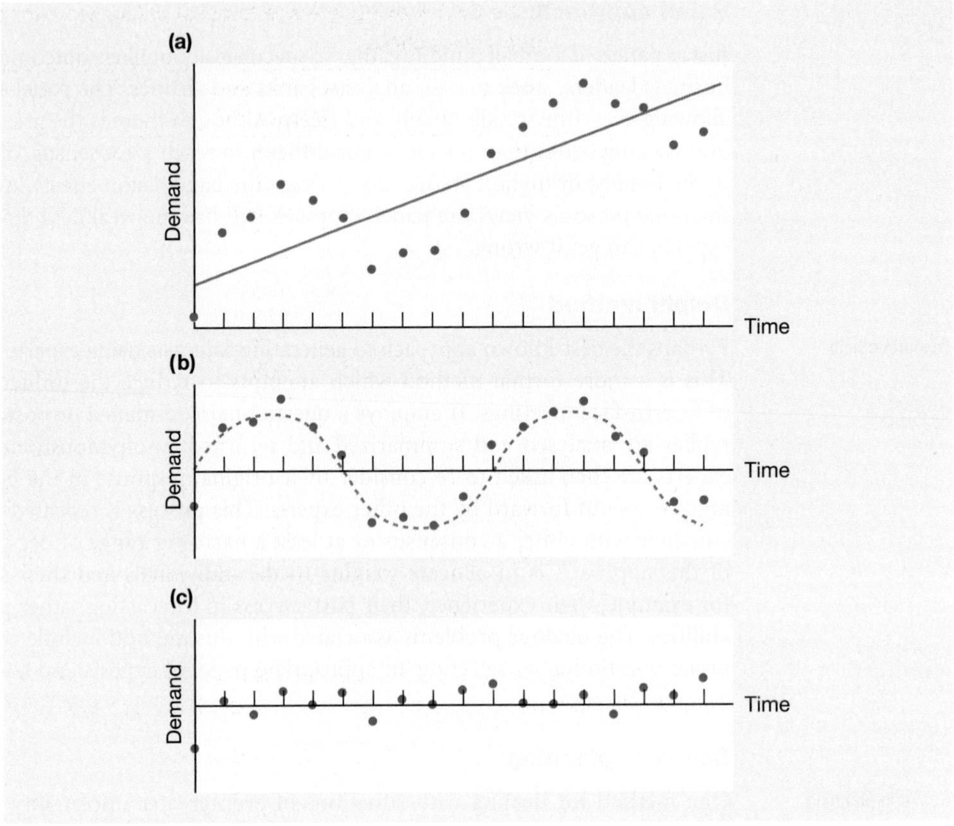

Figure S6.3 Time series analysis with (a) trend, (b) seasonality and (c) random variation

the random variation about the trends and seasonality lines, Figure S6.3(c). Future sales may now be predicted as lying within a band about a projection of the trend, plus the seasonality. The width of the band will be a function of the degree of random variation.

Forecasting unassignable variations

The random variations which remain after taking out trend and seasonal effects are without any known or assignable cause. This does not mean that they do not have a cause, however, but just that we do not know what it is. Nevertheless, some attempt can be made to forecast it, if only on the basis that future events will, in some way, be based on past events. We will examine two of the more common approaches to forecasting which are based on projecting forward from past behaviour. These are:

Moving-average forecasting

Exponentially smoothed forecasting

- **moving-average forecasting;**
- **exponentially smoothed forecasting.**

Moving-average forecasting

The moving-average approach to forecasting takes the previous *n* periods' actual demand figures, calculates the average demand over the *n* periods, and uses this average as a forecast for the next period's demand. Any data older than the *n* periods plays no part in the next period's forecast. The value of *n* can be set at any level, but is usually in the range 4 to 7.

Example – Eurospeed parcels

Table S6.2 shows the weekly demand for Eurospeed, a Europe-wide parcel delivery company. It measures demand, on a weekly basis, in terms of the number of parcels which it is given to deliver (irrespective of the size of each parcel). Each week, the next week's demand is

Table S6.2 Moving-average forecast calculated over a four-week period

Week	*Actual demand (thousands)*	*Forecast*
20	63.3	
21	62.5	
22	67.8	
23	66.0	
24	67.2	64.9
25	69.9	65.9
26	65.6	67.7
27	71.1	66.3
28	68.8	67.3
29	68.4	68.9
30	70.3	68.5
31	72.5	69.7
32	66.7	70.0
33	68.3	69.5
34	67.0	69.5
35		68.6

forecast by taking the moving average of the previous four weeks' actual demand. Thus if the forecast demand for week t is F_t and the actual demand for week t is A_t, then

$$F_t = \frac{A_{t-2} + A_{t-3} + A_{t-4}}{4}$$

For example, the forecast for week 35:

$$F_{35} = \frac{(72.5 + 66.7 + 68.3 + 67.0)}{4}$$

$$= 68.6$$

Exponential smoothing

There are two significant drawbacks to the moving-average approach to forecasting. First, in its basic form, it gives equal weight to all the previous n periods which are used in the calculations (although this can be overcome by assigning different weights to each of the n periods). Second, and more important, it does not use data from beyond the n periods over which the moving average is calculated. Both these problems are overcome by *exponential smoothing*, which is also somewhat easier to calculate. The exponential smoothing approach forecasts demand in the next period by taking into account the actual demand in the current period and the forecast which was previously made for the current period. It does so according to the formula

$$F_t = \alpha A_{t-1} + (1 - x)F_{t-1}$$

where α = the smoothing constant.

The smoothing constant α is, in effect, the weight which is given to the last (and therefore assumed to be most important) piece of information available to the forecaster. However, the other expression in the formula includes the forecast for the current period which included the previous period's actual demand, and so on. In this way all previous data has a (diminishing) effect on the next forecast.

Table S6.3 shows the data for Eurospeed's parcels forecasts using this exponential smoothing method, where $\alpha = 0.2$. For example, the forecast for week 35 is:

$$F_{35} = 0.2 \times 67.0 + 0.8 \times 68.3 = 68.04$$

Table S6.3 Exponentially smoothed forecast calculated with smoothing constant α = 0.2

Week (*t*)	*Actual demand (thousands)* (*A*)	*Forecast* ($F_t = \alpha A_{t-1} + (1 - \alpha)F_{t-1}$) ($\alpha = 0.2$)
20	63.3	60.00
21	62.5	60.66
22	67.8	60.03
23	66.0	61.58
24	67.2	62.83
25	69.9	63.70
26	65.6	64.94
27	71.1	65.07
28	68.8	66.28
29	68.4	66.78
30	70.3	67.12
31	72.5	67.75
32	66.7	68.70
33	68.3	68.30
34	67.0	68.30
35		68.04

The value of α governs the balance between the *responsiveness* of the forecasts to changes in demand, and the *stability* of the forecasts. The closer α is to 0 the more forecasts will be dampened by previous forecasts (not very sensitive but stable). Figure S6.4 shows the Eurospeed volume data plotted for a four-week moving average, exponential smoothing with α = 0.2 and exponential smoothing with α = 0.3.

Causal models

Causal models often employ complex techniques to understand the strength of relationships between the network of variables and the impact they have on each other. Simple regression models try to determine the 'best fit' expression between two variables. For example, suppose an ice-cream company is trying to forecast its future sales. After examining previous demand,

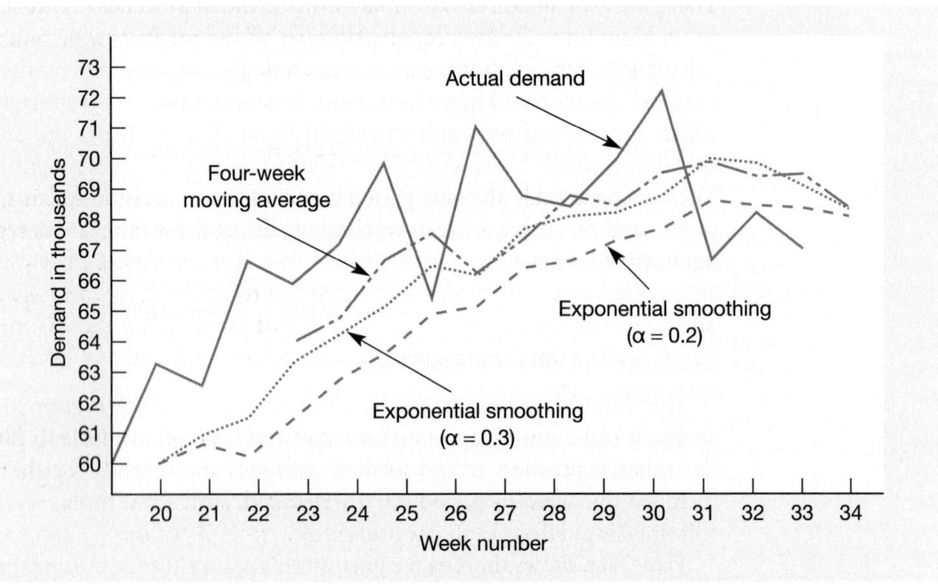

Figure S6.4 **A comparison of a moving-average forecast and exponential smoothing with the smoothing constant α = 0.2 and 0.3**

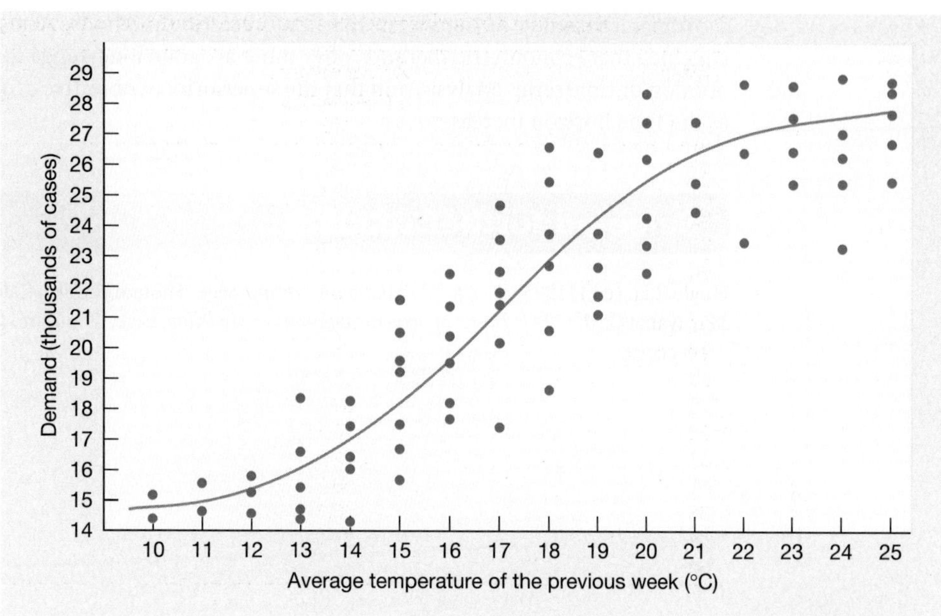

Figure S6.5 Regression line showing the relationship between the previous week's average temperature and demand

it figures that the main influence on demand at the factory is the average temperature of the previous week. To understand this relationship, the company plots demand against the previous week's temperatures. This is shown in Figure S6.5. Using this graph, the company can make a reasonable prediction of demand, once the average temperature is known, provided that the other conditions prevailing in the market are reasonably stable. If they are not, then these other factors which have an influence on demand will need to be included in the regression model, which becomes increasingly complex.

These more complex networks comprise many variables and relationships each with their own set of assumptions and limitations. While developing such models and assessing the importance of each of the factors and understanding the network of interrelationships is beyond the scope of this text, many techniques are available to help managers undertake this more complex modelling and also feed back data into the model to further refine and develop it, in particular structural equation modelling.

The performance of forecasting models

Forecasting models are widely used in management decision-making, and indeed most decisions require a forecast of some kind, yet the performance of this type of model is far from impressive. Hogarth and Makridakis,[2] in a comprehensive review of the applied management and finance literature, show that the record of forecasters using both judgement and sophisticated mathematical methods is not good. What they do suggest, however, is that certain forecasting techniques perform better under certain circumstances. In short-term forecasting there is:

> *considerable inertia in most economic and natural phenomena. Thus the present states of any variables are predictive of the short-term future (i.e. three months or less). Rather simple mechanistic methods, such as those used in time series forecasts, can often make accurate short-term forecasts and even out-perform more theoretically elegant and elaborate approaches used in econometric forecasting.*[3]

Long-term forecasting methods, although difficult to judge because of the time lapse between the forecast and the event, do seem to be more amenable to an objective causal approach. In a comparative study of long-term market forecasting methods, Armstrong and Grohman[4] conclude that econometric methods offer more accurate long-range forecasts than do expert opinion or time series analysis, and that the superiority of objective causal methods improves as the time horizon increases.

Selected further reading

Hoyle R.H. (ed.) (1995) *Structural Equation Modeling*, Sage, Thousand Oaks, California. For the specialist.

Maruyama G.M. (1997) *Basics of Structural Equation Modeling*, Sage, Thousand Oaks, California. For the specialist.

Chapter 7

Layout and flow

Key questions

- What is 'layout'?
- What are the basic layout types used in operations?
- What type of layout should an operation choose?
- How should each basic layout type be designed in detail?

Introduction

The layout of an operation is concerned with the physical location of its transforming resources. This means deciding where to put all the facilities, machines, equipment and staff in the operation. Layout is often the first thing most of us would notice on entering an operation because it governs its appearance. It also determines the way in which transformed resources – the materials, information and customers – flow through the operation. Relatively small changes in goods in a supermarket, or changing rooms in a sports centre, or the position of a machine in a factory, can affect the flow through the operation which, in turn, affects the costs and general effectiveness of the operation. Figure 7.1 shows the facilities layout activity in the overall model of design in operations.

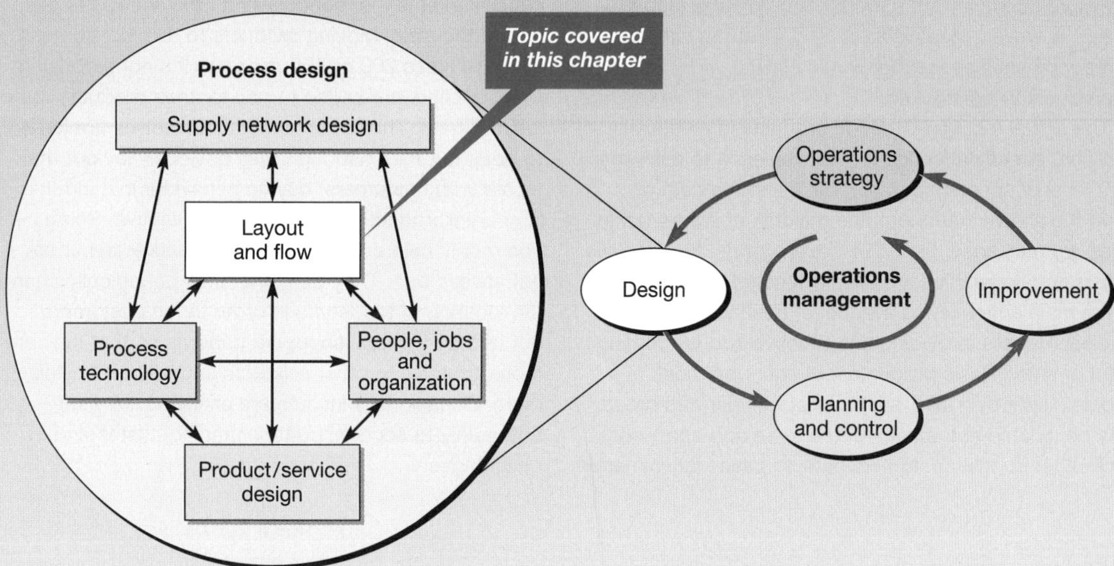

Figure 7.1 This chapter examines layout and flow

*Check and improve your understanding of this chapter using self assessment questions and a personalised study plan, audio and video downloads, and an eBook – all at **www.myomlab.com**.*

Operations in practice Tesco's store flow processes[1]

Source: Alamy Images

Successful supermarkets, like Tesco, know that the design of their stores has a huge impact on profitability. They must maximize their revenue per square metre and minimize the costs of operating the store, while keeping customers happy. At a basic level, supermarkets have to get the amount of space allocated to the different areas right. Tesco's 'One in front' campaign, for example, tries to avoid long waiting times by opening additional tills if more than one customer is waiting at a checkout. Tesco also uses technology to understand exactly how customers flow through their stores. The 'Smartlane' system from Irisys, a specialist in intelligent infrared technologies, counts the number and type of customers entering the store (in family or other groups known as 'shopping units'), tracks their movement using infrared sensors, and predicts the likely demand at the checkouts up to an hour in advance. The circulation of customers through the store must be right and the right layout can make customers buy more. Some supermarkets put their entrance on the left-hand side of a building with a layout designed to take customers in a clockwise direction around the store. Aisles are made wide to ensure a relatively slow flow of trolleys so that customers pay more attention to the products on display (and buy more). However, wide aisles can come at the expense of reduced shelf space that would allow a wider range of products to be stocked.

The actual location of all the products is a critical decision, directly affecting the convenience to customers, their level of spontaneous purchase and the cost of filling the shelves. Although the majority of supermarket sales are packaged, tinned or frozen goods, the displays of fruit and vegetables are usually located adjacent to the main entrance, as a signal of freshness and wholesomeness, providing an attractive and welcoming point of entry. Basic products that figure on most people's shopping lists, such as flour, sugar and bread, may be located at the back of the store and apart from each other so that customers have to pass higher-margin items as they search. High-margin items are usually put at eye level on shelves (where they are more likely to be seen) and low-margin products lower down or higher up. Some customers also go a few paces up an aisle before they start looking for what they need. Some supermarkets call the shelves occupying the first metre of an aisle 'dead space' – not a place to put impulse-bought goods. But the prime site in a supermarket is the 'gondola-end', the shelves at the end of the aisle. Moving products to this location can increase sales 200 or 300 per cent. It's not surprising that suppliers are willing to pay for their products to be located here. The supermarkets themselves are keen to point out that, although they obviously lay out their stores with customers' buying behaviour in mind, it is counterproductive to be too manipulative. Some commonly held beliefs about supermarket layout are not always true. They deny that they periodically change the location of foodstuffs in order to jolt customers out of their habitual shopping patterns so that they are more attentive to other products and end up buying more. Occasionally layouts are changed, they say, but mainly to accommodate changing, tastes and new ranges.

What is layout?

The 'layout' of an operation or process means how its transformed resources are positioned relative to each other and how its various tasks are allocated to these transforming resources. Together these two decisions will dictate the pattern of flow for transformed resources as they progress through the operation or process (see Figure 7.2). It is an important decision because, if the layout proves wrong, it can lead to over-long or confused flow patterns, customer queues, long process times, inflexible operations, unpredictable flow and high cost. Also, re-laying out an existing operation can cause disruption, leading to customer dissatisfaction or lost operating time. So, because the **layout decision** can be difficult and expensive, operations managers are reluctant to do it too often. Therefore layout must start with a full appreciation of the objectives that the layout should be trying to achieve. However, this is only the starting point of what is a multi-stage process which leads to the final physical layout of the operation.

The layout decision is relatively infrequent but important

What makes a good layout?

To a large extent the objectives of any layout will depend on the strategic objectives of the operation, but there are some general objectives which are relevant to all operations:

- *Inherent safety*. All processes which might constitute a danger to either staff or customers should not be accessible to the unauthorized.
- *Length of flow*. The flow of materials, information or customers should be appropriate for the operation. This usually means minimizing the distance travelled by transformed resources. However, this is not always the case (in a supermarket, for example).
- *Clarity of flow*. All flow of materials and customers should be well signposted, clear and evident to staff and customers alike.
- *Staff conditions*. Staff should be located away from noisy or unpleasant parts of the operation.
- *Management coordination*. Supervision and communication should be assisted by the location of staff and communication devices.
- *Accessibility*. All machines and facilities should be accessible for proper cleaning and maintenance.
- *Use of space*. All layouts should use space appropriately. This usually means minimizing the space used, but sometimes can mean achieving an impression of spacious luxury, as in the entrance lobby of a high-class hotel.
- *Long-term flexibility*. Layouts need to be changed periodically. A good layout will have been devised with the possible future needs of the operation in mind.

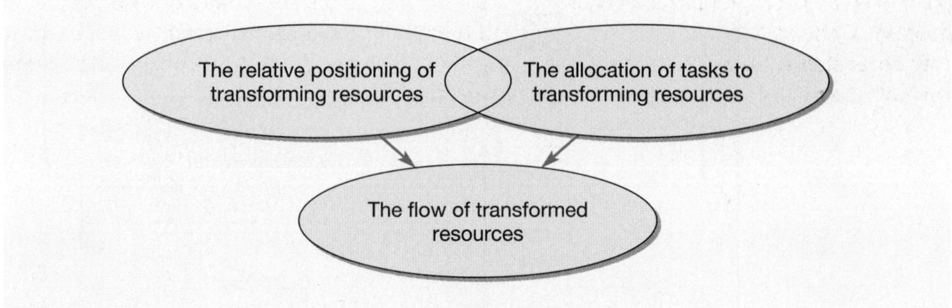

Figure 7.2 Layout involves the relative positioning of transformed resources within operations and processes and the allocation of tasks to the resources, which together dictate the flow of transformed resources through the operation or process

The basic layout types

Basic layout type

Most practical layouts are derived from only four **basic layout types**. These are:

Fixed-position layout
Functional layout
Cell layout
Product layout

- **fixed-position layout**
- **functional layout**
- **cell layout**
- **product layout.**

Layout is related to process type

Layout is influenced by process types

Process 'types' (described in Chapter 4) represent the broad approaches to the organization of processes and activities. Layout is a narrower, but related concept. It is the physical manifestation of a process type, but there is often some overlap between **process types** and the layouts that they could use. As Table 7.1 indicates, a process type does not necessarily imply only one particular basic layout.

Fixed-position layout

Fixed-position layout is in some ways a contradiction in terms, since the transformed resources do not move between the transforming resources. Instead of materials, information or customers flowing through an operation, the recipient of the processing is stationary and the equipment, machinery, plant and people who do the processing move as necessary. This could be because the product or the recipient of the service is too large to be moved conveniently, or it might be too delicate to move, or perhaps it could object to being moved; for example:

- *Motorway construction* – the product is too large to move.
- *Open-heart surgery* – patients are too delicate to move.
- *High-class service restaurant* – customers would object to being moved to where food is prepared.
- *Shipbuilding* – the product is too large to move.
- *Mainframe computer maintenance* – the product is too big and probably also too delicate to move, and the customer might object to bringing it in for repair.

Table 7.1 The relationship between process types and basic layout types

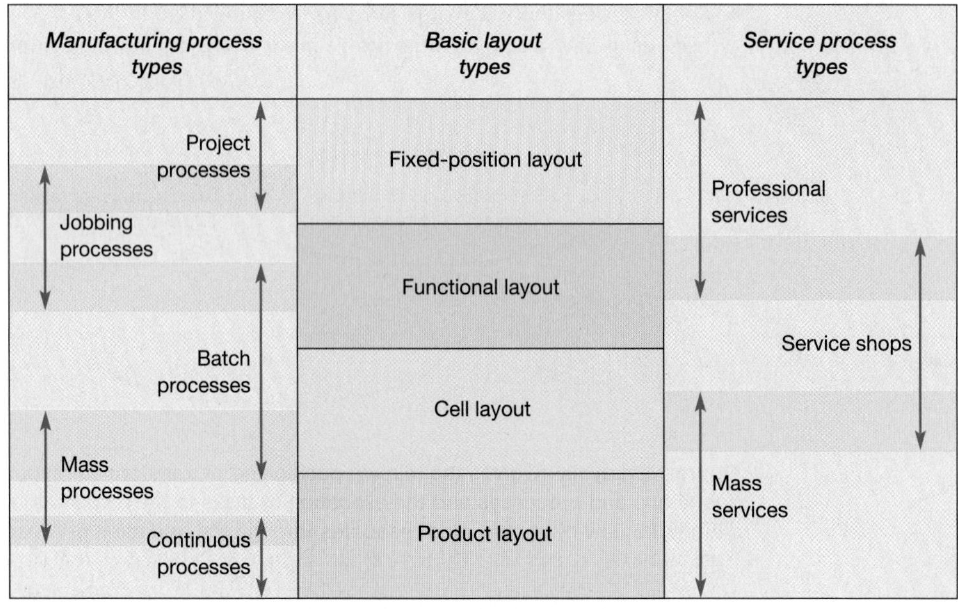

A construction site is typical of a fixed-position layout in that there is a limited amount of space which must be allocated to the various transforming resources. The main problem in designing this layout will be to allocate areas of the site to the various contractors so that they have adequate space, they can receive and store their deliveries of materials, they can have access to their parts of the project without interfering with each other's movements, they minimize movement, and so on.

Short case
'Factory flow' helps surgery productivity[2]

Even surgery can be seen as a process, and like any process, it can be improved. Normally patients remain stationary with surgeons and other theatre staff performing their tasks around the patient. But this idea has been challenged by John Petri, an Italian consultant orthopaedic surgeon at a hospital in Norfolk in the UK. Frustrated by spending time drinking tea while patients were prepared for surgery, he redesigned the process so now he moves continually between two theatres. While he is operating on a patient in one theatre, his anaesthetist colleagues are preparing a patient for surgery in another theatre. After finishing with the first patient, the surgeon 'scrubs up', moves to the second operating theatre, and begins the surgery on the second patient. While he is doing this the first patient is moved out of the first operating theatre and the third patient is prepared. This method of overlapping operations in different theatres allows the surgeon to work for five hours at a time rather than the previous standard three-and-a-half-hour session. *'If you were running a factory'*, says the surgeon, *'you wouldn't allow your most important and most expensive machine to stand idle. The same is true in a hospital.'* Currently used on hip and knee replacements, this layout would not be suitable for all surgical procedures. But, since its introduction the surgeon's waiting list has fallen to zero and his productivity has doubled. *'For a small increase in running costs we are able to treat many more patients'*, said a spokesperson for the hospital management. *'What is important is that clinicians . . . produce innovative ideas and we demonstrate that they are effective.'*

Assembly line surgery

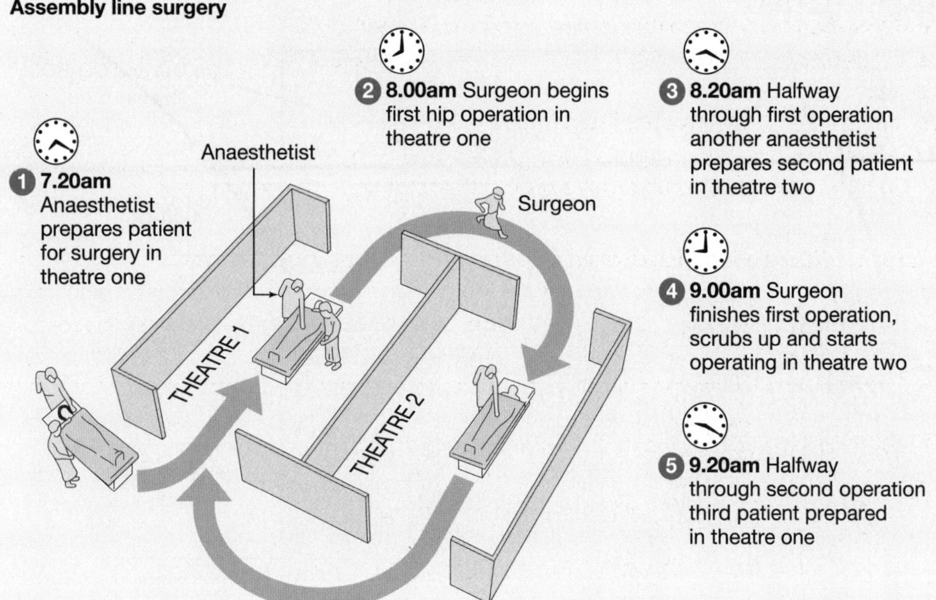

Figure 7.3 Assembly line surgery

Functional layout

Functional layout is so called because it conforms to the needs and convenience of the functions performed by the transforming resources within the processes. (Confusingly, functional layout is also referred to as 'process layout' but this term is being superseded.)

In functional layout, similar resources or processes are located together. This may be because it is convenient to group them together, or that the utilization of transforming resources is improved. It means that when materials, information or customers flow through the operation, their route is determined according to their needs. Different products or customers will have different needs and therefore take different routes. Usually this makes the flow pattern in the operation very complex. Examples of functional layouts include:

- *Hospital* – some processes (e.g. X-ray machines and laboratories) are required by several types of patient; some processes (e.g. general wards) can achieve high staff- and bed-utilization.
- *Machining the parts which go into aircraft engines* – some processes (e.g. heat treatment) need specialist support (heat and fume extraction); some processes (e.g. machining centres) require the same technical support from specialist setter–operators; some processes (e.g. grinding machines) get high machine utilization as all parts which need grinding pass through a single grinding section.
- *Supermarket* – some products, such as tinned goods, are convenient to restock if grouped together. Some areas, such as those holding frozen vegetables, need the common technology of freezer cabinets. Others, such as the areas holding fresh vegetables, might be together because that way they can be made to look attractive to customers (see the opening short case).

Figure 7.4 shows a functional layout in a university library. The various areas – reference books, enquiry desk, journals, and so on – are located in different parts of the operation. The customer is free to move between the areas depending on his or her requirements. The

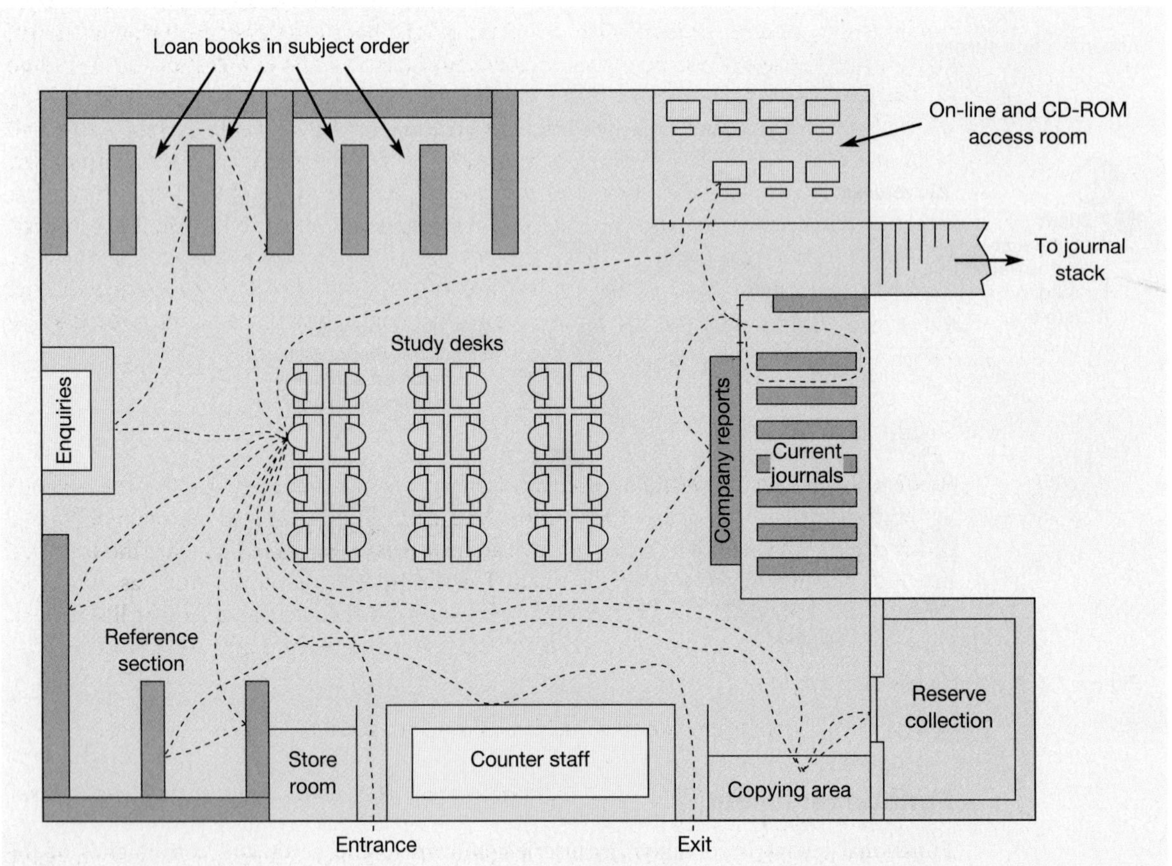

Figure 7.4 An example of a functional layout in a library showing the path of just one customer

figure also shows the route taken by one customer on one visit to the library. If the routes for the customers were superimposed on the plan, the pattern of the traffic between the various parts of the operation would be revealed. The density of this traffic flow is an important piece of information in the detailed design of this type of layout. Changing the location of the various areas in the library will change the pattern of flow for the library as a whole.

Cell layout

A cell layout is one where the transformed resources entering the operation are pre-selected (or pre-select themselves) to move to one part of the operation (or cell) in which all the transforming resources, to meet their immediate processing needs, are located. After being processed in the cell, the transformed resources may go on to another cell. In effect, cell layout is an attempt to bring some order to the complexity of flow which characterizes functional layout. Examples of cell layouts include:

- *Some laptop assembly* – within a contract manufacturer's factory, the assembly of different laptop brands may be done in a special area dedicated to that one brand that has special requirements such as particularly high quality levels.
- *'Lunch' products area in a supermarket* – some customers use the supermarket just to purchase sandwiches, savoury snacks, etc. for their lunch. These products may be located together so that these customers do not have to search around the store.
- *Maternity unit in a hospital* – customers needing maternity attention are a well-defined group who can be treated together and who are unlikely to need the other facilities of the hospital at the same time that they need the maternity unit.

Shop-within-a-shop

Although the idea of cell layout is often associated with manufacturing, the same principle can be, and is, used in services. In Figure 7.5 the ground floor of a department store is shown, comprising displays of various types of goods in different parts of the store. In this sense the predominant layout of the store is a functional layout. However, some 'themed' products may be put together, such as in the sports shop. This area is a **shop-within-a-shop** which will stock sports clothes, sports shoes, sports bags, sports books and videos, sports equipment and energy drinks, which are also located elsewhere in the store. They have been located in the 'cell' not because they are similar goods (shoes, books and drinks would not usually be located together) but because they are needed to satisfy the needs of a particular type of customer. Enough customers come to the store to buy 'sports goods' in particular to devote an area specifically for them. Also, customers intending to buy sports shoes might also be persuaded to buy other sports goods if they are placed in the same area.

Product layout

Line layout

Product layout involves locating the transforming resources entirely for the convenience of the transformed resources. Each product, piece of information or customer follows a prearranged route in which the sequence of activities that are required matches the sequence in which the processes have been located. The transformed resources 'flow' as in a 'line' through the process. This is why this type of layout is sometimes called flow or **line layout**. Flow is predictable and therefore relatively easy to control. Examples of product layout include:

- *Automobile assembly* – almost all variants of the same model require the same sequence of processes.
- *Loan application processing* – all applications require the same sequence of clerical and decision-making activities.
- *Self-service cafeteria* – generally the sequence of customer requirements (starter, main course, dessert, drink) is common to all customers, but layout also helps control customer flow.

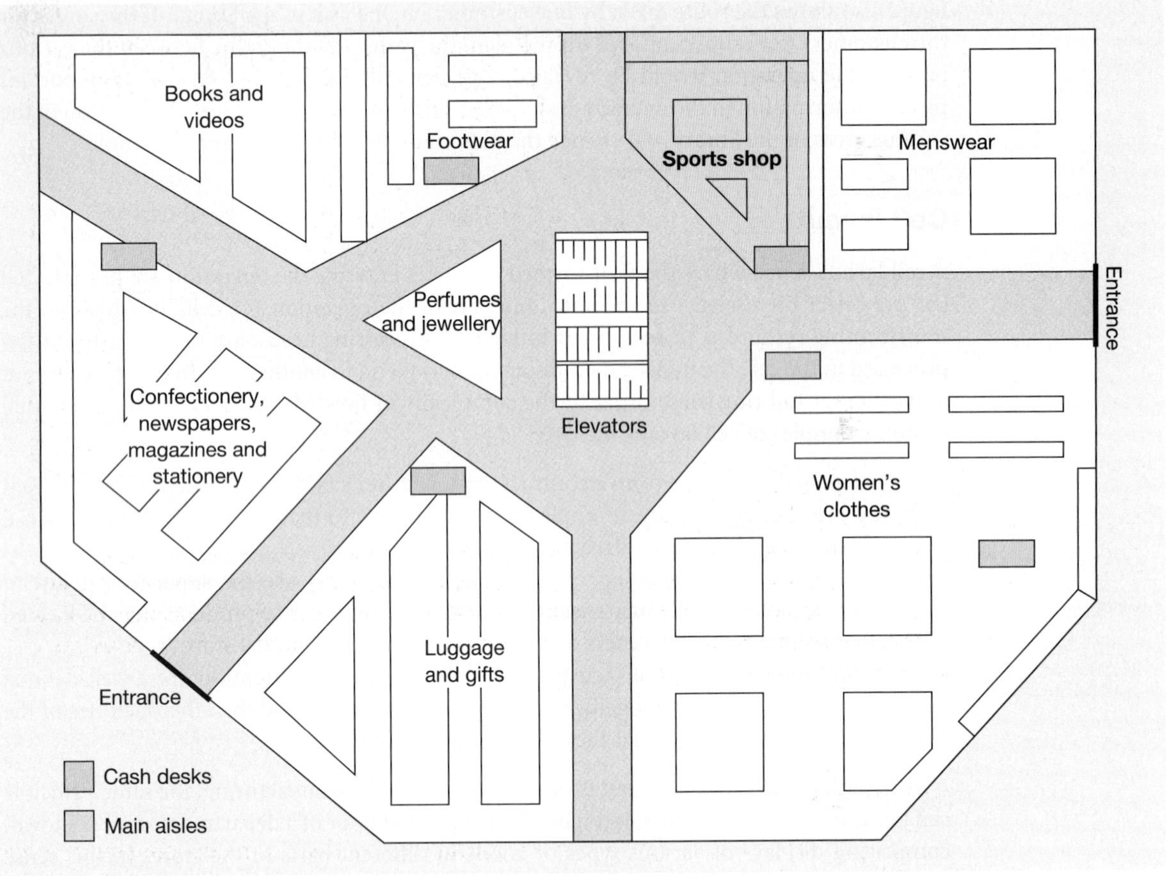

Figure 7.5 The ground floor plan of a department store showing the sports goods shop-within-a-shop retail 'cell'

Figure 7.6 shows the sequence of processes in a paper-making operation. Such an operation would use product layout. Gone are the complexities of flow which characterized functional layouts, and to a lesser extent cell layouts, and although different types of paper are produced in this operation, all types have the same processing requirements.

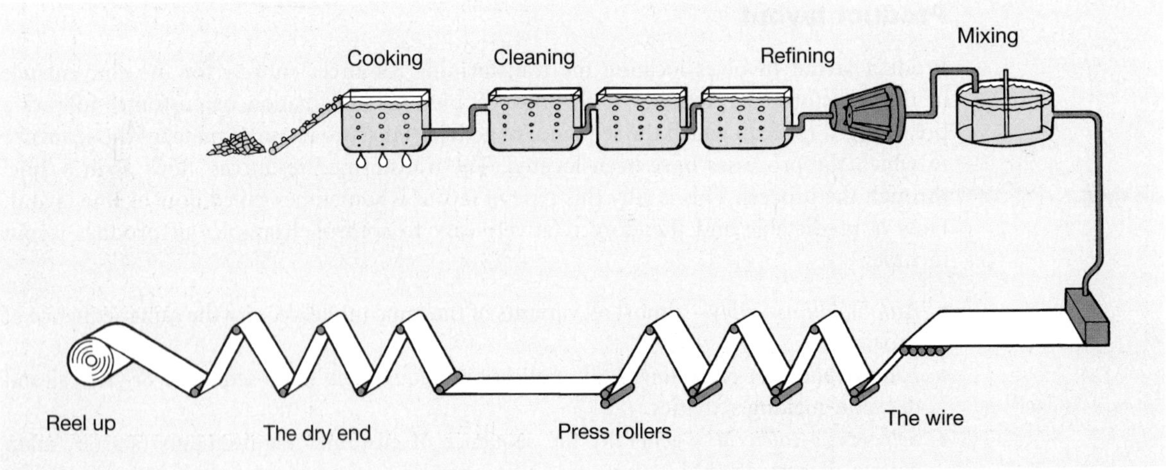

Figure 7.6 The sequence of processes in paper-making; each process will be laid out in the same sequence

Short case
Yamaha tunes its assembly lines

The Yamaha Corporation of Japan, founded in 1887, has grown to become the world's largest manufacturer of musical instruments, as well as producing a whole variety of other goods, from semiconductors and robots through to sporting goods and furniture. In recent years it has developed a reputation for product diversification, an understanding of new markets and, especially, innovative manufacturing methods. For example, it was one of the first piano manufacturers to make up-market grand pianos using assembly line techniques (the picture shows grand pianos being assembled in the same way as motor vehicles). Traditionally, grand pianos (as opposed to the less expensive and better-selling upright pianos) were made using individual build methods which relied on craft skills. The main advantage of this was that skilled workers could accommodate individual variations in the (often inconsistent) materials from which the piano is made. Each individual piano would be constructed around the idiosyncrasies of the material to make a product unique in its tone and tuning. Not so with Yamaha, which, although making some of the highest-quality pianos in the world, emphasizes consistency and reliability, as well as richness of tone.

Mixed layouts

Many operations either design themselves hybrid layouts which combine elements of some or all of the basic layout types, or use the 'pure' basic layout types in different parts of the operation. For example, a hospital would normally be arranged on functional-layout principles, each department representing a particular type of process (the X-ray department, the surgical theatres, the blood-processing laboratory, and so on). Yet within each department, quite different layouts are used. The X-ray department is probably arranged in a functional layout, the surgical theatres in a fixed-position layout, and the blood-processing laboratory in a product layout. Another example is shown in Figure 7.7. Here a restaurant complex is

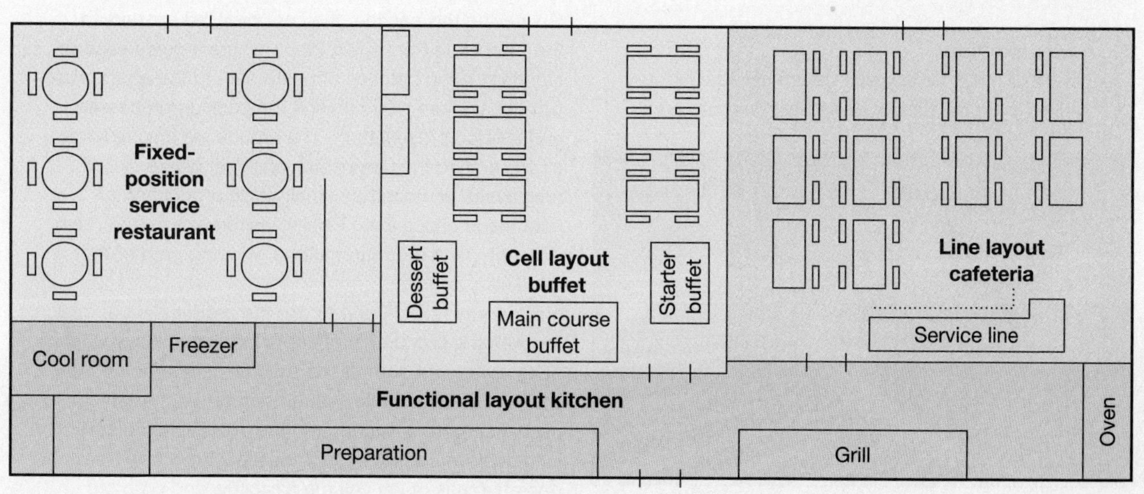

Figure 7.7 A restaurant complex with all four basic layout types

shown with three different types of restaurant and the kitchen which serves them all. The kitchen is arranged in a functional layout, the traditional service restaurant is arranged in a fixed-position layout, the buffet restaurant is arranged in a cell-type layout, while in the cafeteria restaurant, all customers take the same route when being served with their meal. They may not take the opportunity to be served with every dish but they move through the same sequence of processes.

Short case
Chocolate and customers flow through Cadbury's[3]

Flow of chocolate

In the famous Cadbury's chocolate factory at Bourneville, on the outskirts of Birmingham, UK, chocolate products are manufactured to a high degree of consistency and efficiency. Production processes are based on a *product layout*. This has allowed Cadbury's engineers to develop and procure machinery to meet the technical and capacity requirements of each stage of the process. Consider, for example, the production of Cadbury's Dairy Milk bars. First, the standard liquid chocolate is prepared from cocoa beans, fresh milk and sugar using specialized equipment, connected together with pipes and conveyors. These processes operate continuously, day and night, to ensure consistency of both the chocolate itself and the rate of output. Next, the liquid is pumped through heated pipework to the moulding department, where it is automatically dispensed into a moving line of precision-made plastic moulds which form the chocolate bars and vibrate them to remove any trapped air bubbles. The moulds are continuously conveyed into a large refrigerator, allowing sufficient time for the chocolate to harden. The next stage inverts the moulds and shakes out the moulded bars. These then pass directly to a set of highly automated wrapping and packing machines, from where they go to the warehouse.

Flow of customers

Cadbury also has a large visitor centre called 'Cadbury World' alongside the factory (linked to a viewing area which looks onto the packaging area described above). Cadbury World is a permanent exhibition devoted entirely to chocolate and the part Cadbury has played in its fascinating history. Because most of the attractions are indoors, with limited circulation space, the main exhibition and demonstration areas are designed to allow a smooth flow of customers, where possible avoiding bottlenecks and delays. The design is also a 'product' layout with a single route for all customers. Entry to the Exhibition Area is by timed ticket, to ensure a constant flow of input customers, who are free to walk around at their preferred speed, but are constrained to keep to the single track through the sequence of displays. On leaving this section, they are directed upstairs to the Chocolate Packaging Plant, where a guide escorts standard-sized batches of customers to the appropriate positions where they can see the packing processes and a video presentation. The groups are then led down to and around the Demonstration Area, where skilled employees demonstrate small-scale production of handmade chocolates. Finally, visitors are free to roam unaccompanied through a long, winding path of the remaining exhibits.

Source: Cadbury World

Customers being processed

Source: Cadbury World

Chocolate being processed

Cadbury has chosen to use the product layout design for both the production of chocolates and the processing of its visitors. In both cases, volumes are large and the variety offered is limited. Sufficient demand exists for each standard 'product', and the operations objective is to achieve consistent high quality at low cost. Neither operation has much volume flexibility, and both are expensive to change.

What type of layout should an operation choose?

The volume and variety characteristics of an operation will influence its layout

The importance of flow to an operation will depend on its **volume and variety characteristics.** When volume is very low and variety is relatively high, 'flow' is not a major issue. For example, in telecommunications satellite manufacture, a fixed-position layout is likely to be appropriate because each product is different and because products 'flow' through the operation very infrequently, so it is just not worth arranging facilities to minimize the flow of parts through the operation. With higher volume and lower variety, flow becomes an issue. If the variety is still high, however, an entirely flow-dominated arrangement is difficult because there will be different flow patterns. For example, the library in Figure 7.4 will arrange its different categories of books and its other services partly to minimize the average distance its customers have to 'flow' through the operation. But, because its customers' needs vary, it will arrange its layout to satisfy the majority of its customers (but perhaps inconvenience a minority). When the variety of products or services reduces to the point where a distinct 'category' with similar requirements becomes evident but variety is still not small, cell layout could become appropriate, as in the sports goods cell in Figure 7.5. When variety is relatively small and volume is high, flow can become regularized and a product-based layout is likely to be appropriate, as in an assembly plant (see Figure 7.8).

Selecting a layout type

The volume–variety characteristics of the operation will, to a large extent, narrow the choice down to one or two layout options. The decision as to which layout type to adopt will be influenced by an understanding of their relative advantages and disadvantages. Table 7.2 shows some of the more significant advantages and disadvantages associated with each layout

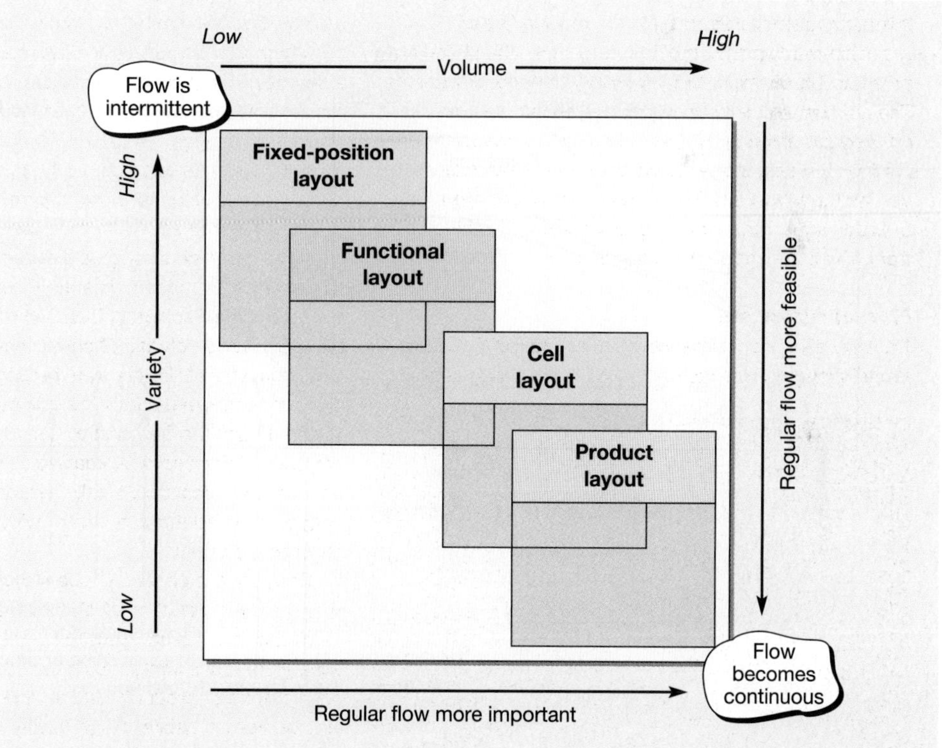

Figure 7.8 The volume–variety process position of an operation influences its layout and, in turn, the flow of transformed resources

Table 7.2 The advantages and disadvantages of the basic layout types

	Advantages	*Disadvantages*
Fixed-position	Very high mix and product flexibility Product or customer not moved or disturbed High variety of tasks for staff	Very high unit costs Scheduling of space and activities can be difficult Can mean much movement of plant and staff
Functional	High mix and product flexibility Relatively robust in the case of disruptions Relatively easy supervision of equipment or plant	Low facilities utilization Can have very high work-in-progress or customer queuing Complex flow can be difficult to control
Cell	Can give a good compromise between cost and flexibility for relatively high-variety operations Fast throughput Group work can result in good motivation	Can be costly to rearrange existing layout Can need more plant and equipment Can give lower plant utilization
Product	Low unit costs for high volume Gives opportunities for specialization of equipment Materials or customer movement is convenient	Can have low mix flexibility Not very robust if there is disruption Work can be very repetitive

type. It should be stressed, however, that the type of operation will influence their relative importance. For example, a high-volume television manufacturer may find the low-cost characteristics of a product layout attractive, but an amusement theme park may adopt the same layout type primarily because of the way it 'controls' customer flow.

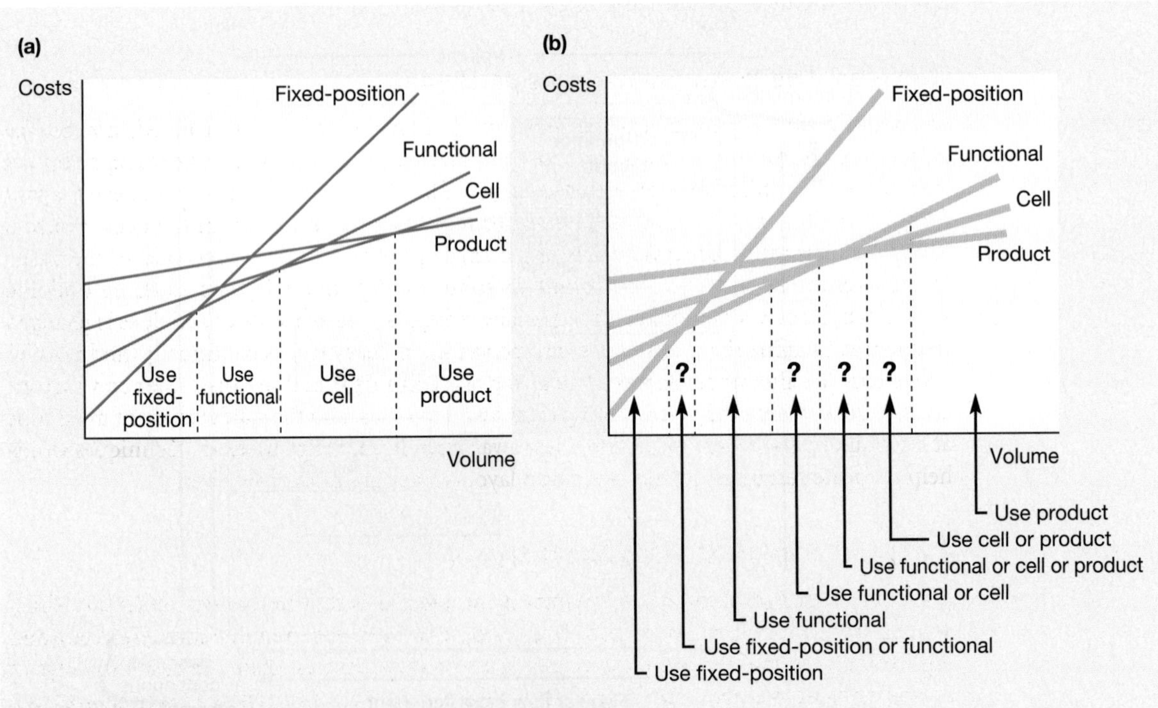

Figure 7.9 (a) The basic layout types have different fixed- and variable-cost characteristics which seem to determine which one to use. (b) In practice the uncertainty about the exact fixed and variable costs of each layout means the decision can rarely be made on cost alone

Of all the characteristics of the various layout types, perhaps the most generally significant are the unit cost implications of layout choice. This is best understood by distinguishing between the fixed- and variable-cost elements of adopting each layout type. For any particular product or service, the fixed costs of physically constructing a fixed-position layout are relatively small compared with any other way of producing the same product or service. However, the variable costs of producing each individual product or service are relatively high compared to the alternative layout types. Fixed costs then tend to increase as one moves from fixed-position, through functional and cell, to product layout. Variable costs per product or service tend to decrease, however. The total costs for each layout type will depend on the volume of products or services produced and are shown in Figure 7.9(a). This seems to show that for any volume there is a lowest-cost basic layout. However, in practice, the cost analysis of layout selection is rarely as clear as this. The exact cost of operating the layout is difficult to forecast and will probably depend on many often-difficult-to-predict factors. Rather than use lines to represent the cost of layout as volume increases, broad bands, within which the real cost is likely to lie, are probably more appropriate (*see* Fig. 7.9(b)). The discrimination between the different layout types is now far less clear. There are ranges of volume for which any of two or three layout types might provide the lowest operating cost. The less certainty there is over the costs, the broader the cost 'bands' will be, and the less clear the choice will be. The probable costs of adopting a particular layout need to be set in the broader context of advantages and disadvantages in Table 7.2.

Detailed design of the layout

Once the basic layout type has been decided, the next step is to decide the detailed design of the layout. Detailed design is the act of operationalizing the broad principles which were implicit in the choice of the basic layout type.

Detailed design in fixed-position layout

In fixed-position arrangements the location of resources will be determined, not on the basis of the flow of transformed resources, but on the convenience of transforming resources themselves. The objective of the detailed design of fixed-position layouts is to achieve a layout for the operation which allows all the transforming resources to maximize their contribution to the transformation process by allowing them to provide an effective 'service' to the transformed resources. The detailed layout of some fixed-position layouts, such as building sites, can become very complicated, especially if the planned schedule of activities is changed frequently. Imagine the chaos on a construction site if heavy trucks continually (and noisily) drove past the site office, delivery trucks for one contractor had to cross other contractors' areas to get to where they were storing their own materials, and the staff who spent most time at the building itself were located furthest away from it. Although there are techniques which help to locate resources on fixed-position layouts, they are not widely used.

Detailed design in functional layout

The detailed design of functional layouts is complex, as is flow in this type of layout. Chief among the factors which lead to this complexity is the very large number of different options. For example, in the very simplest case of just two work centres, there are only two ways of arranging these *relative to each other*. But there are six ways of arranging three centres and 120 ways of arranging five centres. This relationship is a factorial one. For N centres there are factorial N ($N!$) different ways of arranging the centres, where:

$$N! = N \times (N-1) \times (N-2) \times \ldots \times (1)$$

So for a relatively simple functional layout with, say, 20 work centres, there are $20! = 2.433 \times 10^{18}$ ways of arranging the operation. This **combinatorial complexity** of functional layouts makes optimal solutions difficult to achieve in practice. Most functional layouts are designed by a combination of intuition, common sense and systematic trial and error.

Combinatorial complexity

The information for functional layouts

Before starting the process of detailed design in functional layouts there are some essential pieces of information which the designer needs:

- The area required by each work centre;
- The constraints on the shape of the area allocated to each work centre;
- The degree and direction of flow between each work centre (for example, number of journeys, number of loads or cost of flow per distance travelled);
- The desirability of work centres being close together or close to some fixed point in the layout.

Flow record chart

The degree and direction of flow are usually shown on a **flow record chart** like that shown in Figure 7.10(a) which records in this case the number of loads transported between departments. This information could be gathered from routeing information, or where flow is more random, as in a library for example, the information could be collected by observing

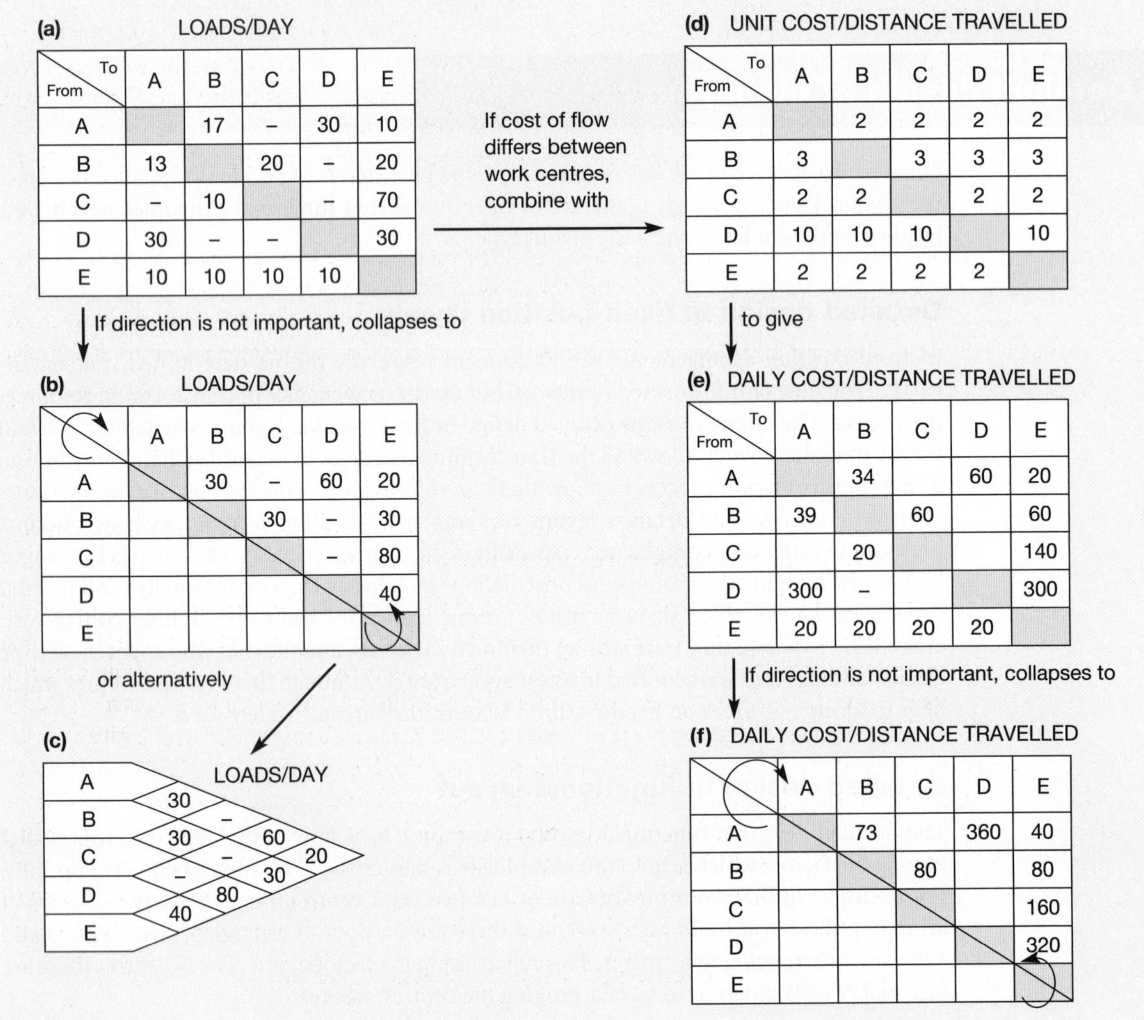

Figure 7.10 Collecting information in functional layout

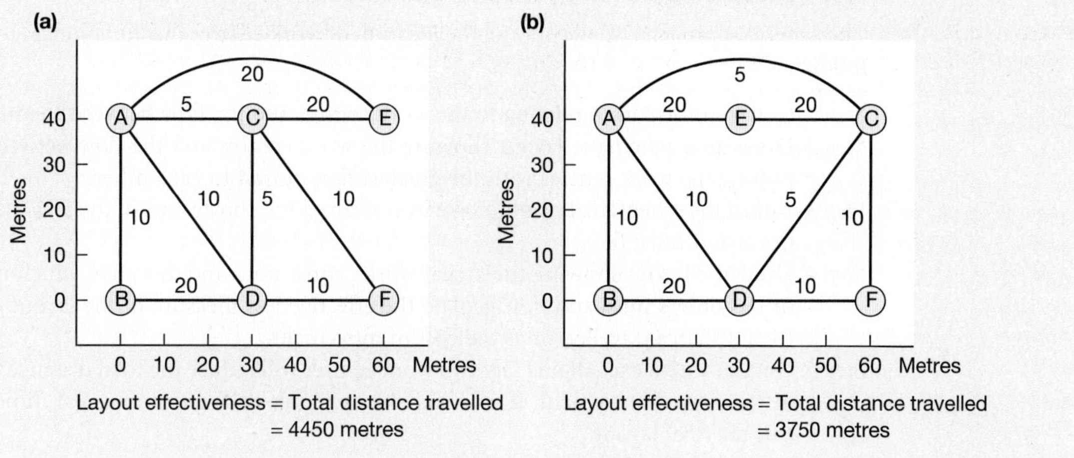

Figure 7.11 (a) and (b) The objective of most functional layouts is to minimize the cost associated with movement in the operation, sometimes simplified to minimizing the total distance travelled

the routes taken by customers over a typical period of time. If the direction of the flow between work centres makes little difference to the layout, the information can be collapsed as shown in Figure 7.10(b), an alternative form of which is shown in Figure 7.10(c). There may be significant differences in the costs of moving materials or customers between different work centres. For example, in Figure 7.10(d) the unit cost of transporting a load between the five work centres is shown. Combining the unit cost and flow data gives the cost-per-distance-travelled data shown in Figure 7.10(e). This has been collapsed as before into Figure 7.10(f).

Minimizing distance travelled

In most examples of functional layout, the prime objective is to minimize the costs to the operation which are associated with flow through the operation. This usually means minimizing the total distance travelled in the operation. For example, Figure 7.11(a) shows a simple six-centre functional layout with the total number of journeys between centres each day. The effectiveness of the layout, at this simple level, can be calculated from:

$$\text{Effectiveness of layout} = \sum F_{ij} D_{ij} \text{ for all } i \neq j$$

where

F_{ij} = the flow in loads or journeys per period of time from work centre i to work centre j
D_{ij} = the distance between work centre i and work centre j.

The lower the effectiveness score, the better the layout. In this example the total of the number of journeys multiplied by the distance for each pair of departments where there is some flow is 4,450 metres. This measure will indicate whether changes to the layout improve its effectiveness (at least in the narrow terms defined here). For example, if centres C and E are exchanged as in Figure 7.11(b) the effectiveness measure becomes 3,750, showing that the new layout now has reduced the total distance travelled in the operation. These calculations assume that all journeys are the same in that their cost to the operation is the same. In some operations this is not so, however. For example, in the hospital some journeys involving healthy staff and relatively fit patients would have little importance compared with other journeys where very sick patients need to be moved from the operating theatres to intensive-care wards. In these cases a cost (or difficulty) element is included in the measure of layout effectiveness:

$$\text{Effectiveness of layout} = \sum F_{ij} D_{ij} C_{ij} \text{ for all } i \neq j$$

where

C_{ij} is the cost per distance travelled of making a journey between departments i and j.

The general functional layout design method

The general approach to determining the location of work centres in a functional layout is as follows:

Step 1 Collect information relating to the work centres and the flow between them.
Step 2 Draw up a schematic layout showing the work centres and the flow between them, putting the work centres with the greatest flow closest to each other.
Step 3 Adjust the schematic layout to take into account the constraints of the area into which the layout must fit.
Step 4 Draw the layout showing the actual work centre areas and distances which materials or customers must travel. Calculate the effectiveness measure of the layout either as total distance travelled or as the cost of movement.
Step 5 Check to see if exchanging any two work centres will reduce the total distance travelled or the cost of movement. If so, make the exchange and return to step 4. If not, make this the final layout.

Worked example

Rotterdam Educational Group (REG) is a company which commissions, designs and manufactures education packs for distance-learning courses and training. It has leased a new building with an area of 1,800 square metres, into which it needs to fit 11 'departments'. Prior to moving into the new building it has conducted an exercise to find the average number of trips taken by its staff between the 11 departments. Although some trips are a little more significant than others (because of the loads carried by staff) it has been decided that all trips will be treated as being of equal value.

Step 1 – Collect information

The areas required by each department together with the average daily number of trips between departments are shown in the flow chart in Figure 7.12. In this example the direction of flow is not relevant and very low flow rates (less than five trips per day) have not been included.

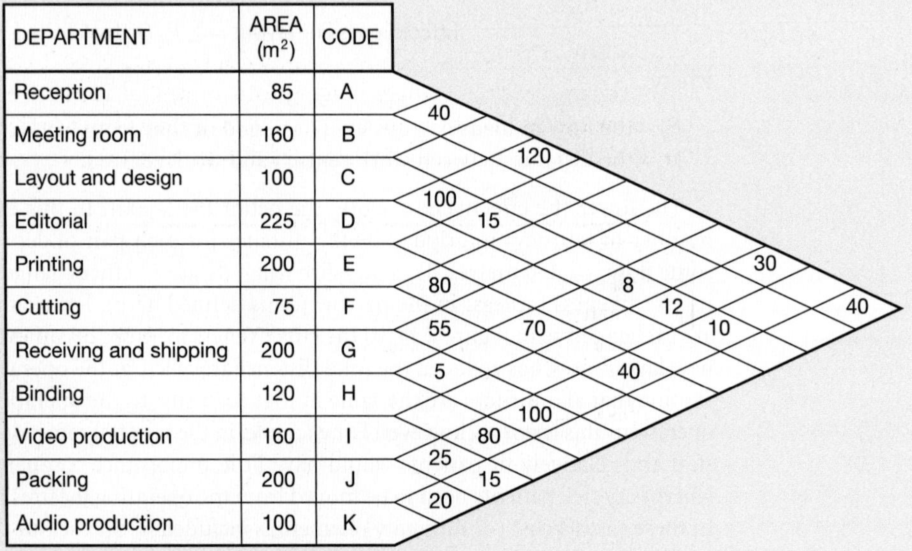

DEPARTMENT	AREA (m^2)	CODE
Reception	85	A
Meeting room	160	B
Layout and design	100	C
Editorial	225	D
Printing	200	E
Cutting	75	F
Receiving and shipping	200	G
Binding	120	H
Video production	160	I
Packing	200	J
Audio production	100	K

Dimensions of the building = 30 metres × 60 metres

Figure 7.12 Flow information for Rotterdam Educational Group

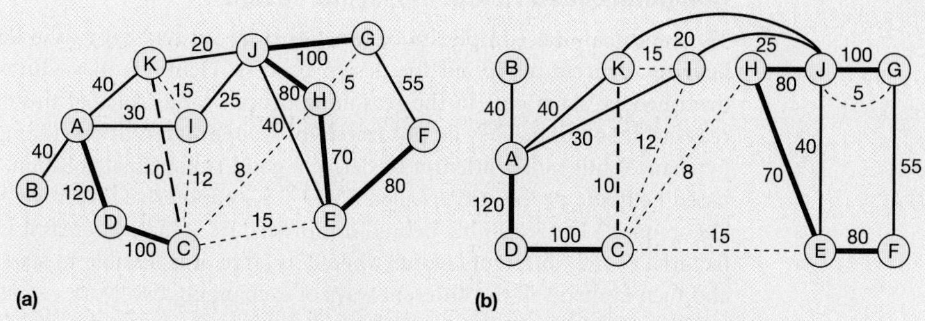

Figure 7.13 (a) Schematic layout placing centres with high traffic levels close to each other, (b) schematic layout adjusted to fit building geometry

Step 2 – Draw schematic layout

Figure 7.13(a) shows a schematic arrangement of departments. The thickest lines represent high flow rates between 70 and 120 trips per day; the medium lines are used for flow rates between 20 and 69 trips per day; and the thinnest lines are for flow rates between 5 and 19 trips per day. The objective here is to arrange the work centres so that those with the thick lines are closest together. The higher the flow rate, the shorter the line should be.

Step 3 – Adjust the schematic layout

If departments were arranged exactly as shown in Figure 7.13(a), the building which housed them would be of an irregular, and therefore high-cost, shape. The layout needs adjusting to take into account the shape of the building. Figure 7.13(b) shows the departments arranged in a more ordered fashion which corresponds to the dimensions of the building.

Step 4 – Draw the layout

Figure 7.14 shows the departments arranged with the actual dimensions of the building and occupying areas which approximate to their required areas. Although the distances between the centroids of departments have changed from Figure 7.14 to accommodate their physical shape, their relative positions are the same. It is at this stage that a quantitative expression of the cost of movement associated with this relative layout can be calculated.

Step 5 – Check by exchanging

The layout in Figure 7.14 seems to be reasonably effective but it is usually worthwhile to check for improvement by exchanging pairs of departments to see if any reduction in total flow can be obtained. For example, departments H and J might be exchanged, and the total distance travelled calculated again to see if any reduction has been achieved.

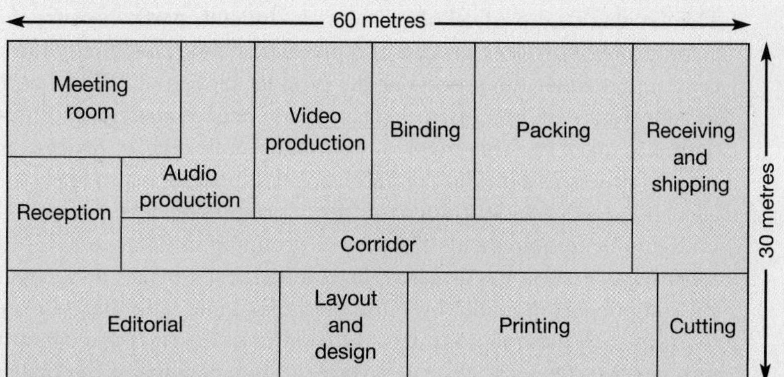

Figure 7.14 Final layout of building

→

Computer-aided functional layout design

Heuristic procedures

The combinatorial complexity of functional layout has led to the development of several **heuristic procedures** to aid the design process. Heuristic procedures use what have been described as 'short cuts in the reasoning process' and 'rules of thumb' in the search for a reasonable solution. They do not search for an optimal solution (though they might find one by chance) but rather attempt to derive a good suboptimal solution. One such computer-based heuristic procedure is called **CRAFT** (Computerized Relative Allocation of Facilities Technique).[4] The reasoning behind this procedure is that, whereas it is infeasible to evaluate factorial N ($N!$) different layouts when N is large, it is feasible to start with an initial layout and then evaluate all the different ways of exchanging two work centres.

CRAFT

There are

$$\frac{N!}{2!(N-2)!}$$

possible ways of exchanging 2 out of N work centres. So for a 20-work-centre layout, there are 190 ways of exchanging 2 work centres.

Three inputs are required for the CRAFT heuristic: a matrix of the flow between departments; a matrix of the cost associated with transportation between each of the departments; and a spatial array showing an initial layout. From these:

- the location of the centroid of each department is calculated;
- the flow matrix is weighted by the cost matrix, and this weighted flow matrix is multiplied by the distances between departments to obtain the total transportation costs of the initial layout;
- the model then calculates the cost consequence of exchanging every possible pair of departments.

The exchange giving the most improvement is then fixed, and the whole cycle is repeated with the updated cost flow matrix until no further improvement is made by exchanging two departments.

Detailed design in cell layout

Figure 7.15 shows how a functional layout has been divided into four cells, each of which has the resources to process a 'family' of parts. In doing this the operations management has implicitly taken two interrelated decisions regarding:

- the extent and nature of the cells it has chosen to adopt;
- which resources to allocate to which cells.

Production flow analysis

Cluster analysis

Production flow analysis

The detailed design of cellular layouts is difficult, partly because the idea of a cell is itself a compromise between process and product layout. To simplify the task, it is useful to concentrate on either the process or the product aspects of cell layout. If cell designers choose to concentrate on processes, they could use **cluster analysis** to find which processes group naturally together. This involves examining each type of process and asking which other types of processes a product or part using that process is also likely to need. One approach to allocating tasks and machines to cells is **production flow analysis** (PFA), which examines both product requirements and process grouping simultaneously. In Figure 7.16(a) a manufacturing operation has grouped the components it makes into eight families – for example, the components in family 1 require machines 2 and 5. In this state the matrix does not seem to exhibit any natural groupings. If the order of the rows and columns is changed, however, to move the crosses as close as possible to the diagonal of the matrix which goes from top left to bottom right, then a clearer pattern emerges. This is illustrated in Figure 7.16(b) and shows that the machines could conveniently be grouped together in three cells, indicated on the diagram as cells A, B and C. Although this procedure is a particularly useful way to

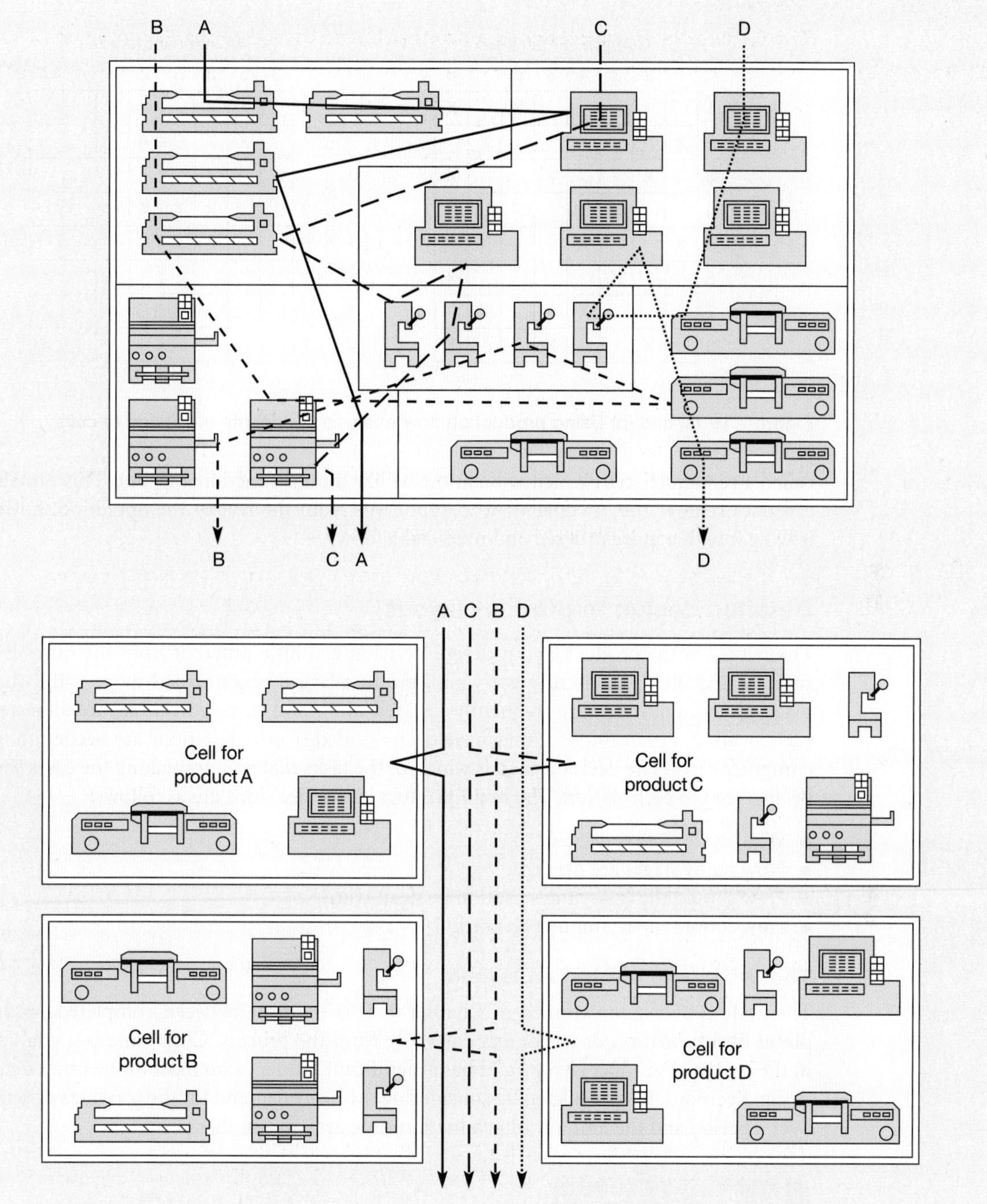

Figure 7.15 Cell layout groups processes together which are necessary for a family of products

allocate machines to cells, the analysis is rarely totally clean. This is the case here where component family 8 needs processing by machines 3 and 8 which have been allocated to cell B. There are some partial solutions for this. More machines could be purchased and put into cell A. This would clearly solve the problem but requires investing capital in a new machine which might be under-utilized. Or, components in family 8 could be sent to cell B after they have been processed in cell A (or even in the middle of their processing route if necessary). This solution avoids the need to purchase another machine but it conflicts partly with the basic idea of cell layout – to achieve a simplification of a previously complex flow. Or, if there are several components like this, it might be necessary to devise a special cell for them (usually

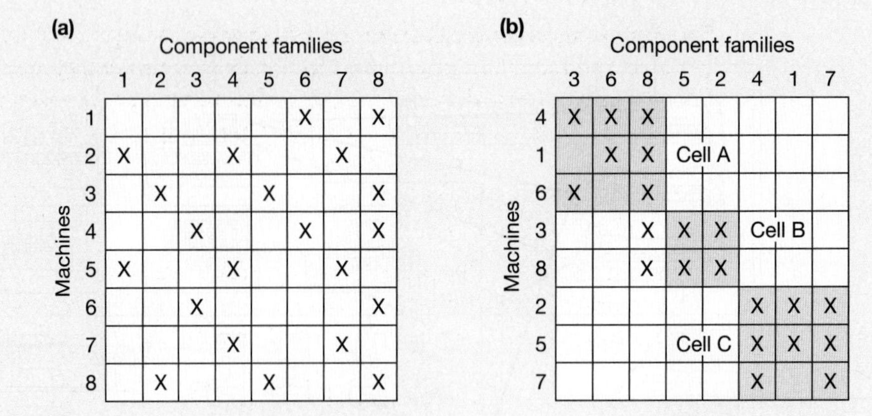

Figure 7.16 (a) and (b) Using production flow analysis to allocate machines to cells

Remainder cell

called a **remainder cell**) which will almost be like a mini-functional layout. This remainder cell does remove the 'inconvenient' components from the rest of the operation, however, leaving it with a more ordered and predictable flow.

Detailed design in product layout

The nature of the product layout design decision is a little different from the other layout types. Rather than 'where to place what', product layout is concerned more with 'what to place where'. Locations are frequently decided upon and then work tasks are allocated to each location. For example, it may have been decided that four stations are needed to make computer cases. The decision then is which of the tasks that go into making the cases should be allocated to each station. The main product layout decisions are as follows:

- What cycle time is needed?
- How many stages are needed?
- How should the task-time variation be dealt with?
- How should the layout be balanced?

The cycle time of product layouts

Cycle time

The **cycle time** was mentioned in Chapter 4. It is the time between completed products, pieces of information or customers emerging from the process. Cycle time is a vital factor in the design of product layouts and has a significant influence on most of the other detailed design decisions. It is calculated by considering the likely demand for the products or services over a period and the amount of production time available in that period.

Worked example

Suppose the regional back-office operation of a large bank is designing an operation which will process its mortgage applications. The number of applications to be processed is 160 per week and the time available to process the applications is 40 hours per week.

$$\text{Cycle time for the layout} = \frac{\text{time available}}{\text{number to be processed}} = \frac{40}{160} = \frac{1}{4}\text{ hour}$$

$$= 15 \text{ minutes}$$

So the bank's layout must be capable of processing a completed application once every 15 minutes.

The number of stages

Total work content

The next decision concerns the number of stages in the layout and depends on the cycle time required and the total quantity of work involved in producing the product or service. This latter piece of information is called the **total work content**. The larger the total work content and the smaller the required cycle time, the more stages will be necessary.

Worked example

Suppose the bank in the previous example calculated that the average total work content of processing a mortgage application is 60 minutes. The number of stages needed to produce a processed application every 15 minutes can be calculated as follows:

$$\text{Number of stages} = \frac{\text{total work content}}{\text{required cycle time}}$$

$$= \frac{60 \text{ minutes}}{15 \text{ minutes}}$$

$$= 4 \text{ stages}$$

If this figure had not emerged as a whole number it would have been necessary to round it up to the next largest whole number. It is difficult (although not always impossible) to hire fractions of people to staff the stages.

Task-time variation

Imagine a line of four stages, each contributing a quarter of the total work content of processing the mortgage, and passing the documentation on to the next stage every 15 minutes. In practice, of course, the flow would not be so regular. Each station's allocation of work might on average take 15 minutes, but almost certainly the time will vary each time a mortgage application is processed. This is a general characteristic of all repetitive processing (and indeed of all work performed by humans) and can be caused by such factors as differences between each product or service being processed along the line (in the mortgage-processing example, the time some tasks require will vary depending on the personal circumstances of the person applying for the loan), or slight variations in coordination and effort on the part of staff performing the task. This variation can introduce irregularity into the flow along the line, which in turn can lead to both periodic queues at the stages and lost processing time. It may even prove necessary to introduce more resources into the operation to compensate for the loss of efficiency resulting from work-time variation.

Balancing work-time allocation

Line balancing

One of the most important design decisions in product layout is that of **line balancing**. In the mortgage-processing example we have assumed that the 15 minutes of work content are allocated equally to the four stations. This is nearly always impossible to achieve in practice and some imbalance in the work allocation results. Inevitably this will increase the effective cycle time of the line. If it becomes greater than the required cycle time, it may be necessary to devote extra resources, in the shape of a further stage, to compensate for the imbalance. The effectiveness of the line-balancing activity is measured by **balancing loss**. This is the time wasted through the unequal allocation of work as a percentage of the total time invested in processing the product or service.

Balancing loss

Balancing techniques[5]

Precedence diagram

There are a number of techniques available to help in the line-balancing task. Again, in practice, the most useful (and most used) 'techniques' are the relatively simple such as the **precedence diagram**. This is a representation of the ordering of the elements which compose the total work content of the product or service. Each element is represented by a circle. The circles are connected by arrows which signify the ordering of the elements. Two rules apply when constructing the diagram:

- the circles which represent the elements are drawn as far to the left as possible;
- none of the arrows which show the precedence of the elements should be vertical.

The precedence diagram, either using circles and arrows or transposed into tabular form, is the most common starting point for most balancing techniques. We do not treat the more complex of these techniques here but it is useful to describe the general approach to balancing product layouts.

Worked example

In Figure 7.17 the work allocations in a four-stage line are illustrated. The total amount of time invested in producing each product or service is four times the cycle time because, for every unit produced, all four stages have been working for the cycle time. When the work is equally allocated between the stages, the total time invested in each product or service produced is $4 \times 2.5 = 10$ minutes. However, when work is unequally allocated, as illustrated, the time invested is $3.0 \times 4 = 12$ minutes, i.e. 2.0 minutes of time, 16.67 per cent of the total, is wasted.

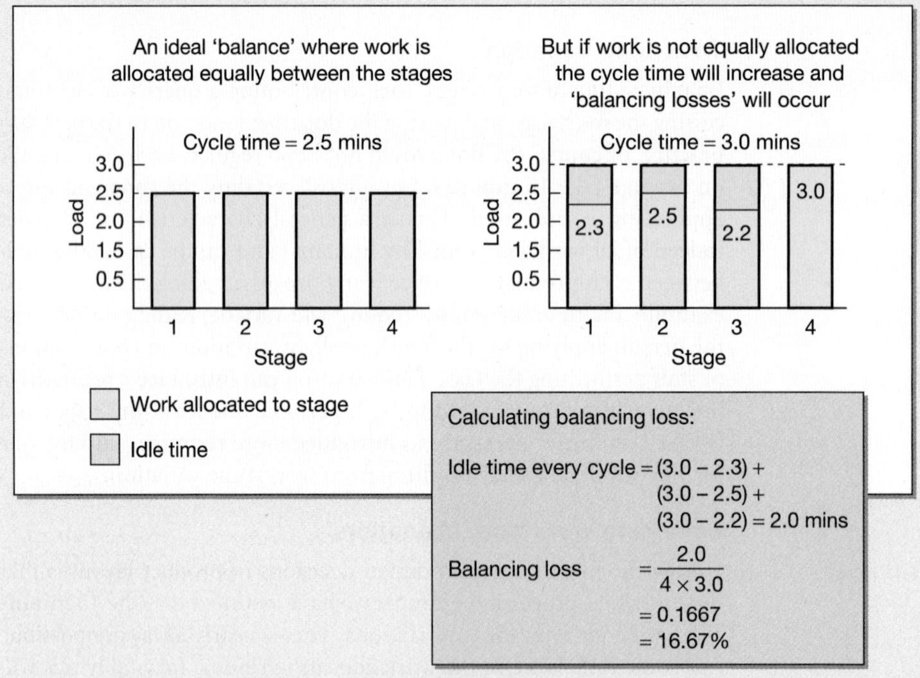

Figure 7.17 Balancing loss is that proportion of the time invested in processing the product or service which is not used productively

This general approach is to allocate elements from the precedence diagram to the first stage, starting from the left, in order of the columns until the work allocated to the stage is as close to, but less than, the cycle time. When that stage is as full of work as is possible without exceeding the cycle time, move on to the next stage, and so on, until all the work elements are allocated. The key issue is how to select an element to be allocated to a stage when more than one element could be chosen. Two heuristic rules have been found to be particularly useful in deciding this:

- Simply choose the largest that will 'fit' into the time remaining at the stage.
- Choose the element with the most 'followers': that is the highest number of elements which can only be allocated when that element has been allocated.

Worked example

Karlstad Kakes (KK) is a manufacturer of speciality cakes, which has recently obtained a contract to supply a major supermarket chain with a speciality cake in the shape of a space rocket. It has been decided that the volumes required by the supermarket warrant a special production line to perform the finishing, decorating and packing of the cake. This line would have to carry out the elements shown in Figure 7.18, which also shows the precedence diagram for the total job. The initial order from the supermarket is for 5,000 cakes a week and the number of hours worked by the factory is 40 per week. From this:

$$\text{The required cycle time} = \frac{40 \text{ hrs} \times 60 \text{ mins}}{5{,}000} = 0.48 \text{ min}$$

$$\text{The required number of stages} = \frac{1.68 \text{ min (the total work content)}}{0.48 \text{ min (the required cycle time)}} = 3.5 \text{ stages}$$

This means four stages.

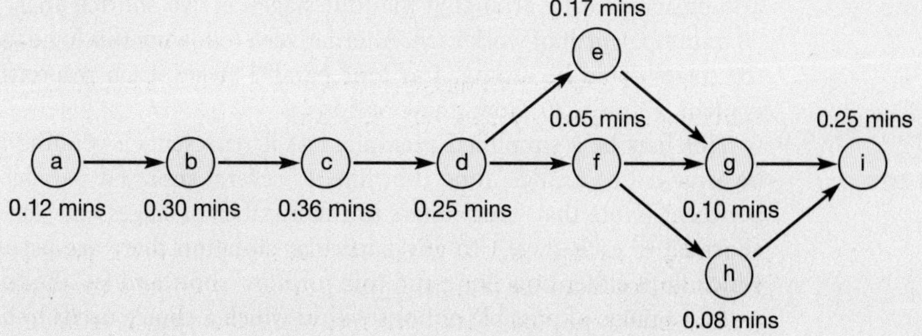

Figure 7.18 Element listing and precedence diagram for Karlstad Kakes

→

Working from the left on the precedence diagram, elements a and b can be allocated to stage 1. Allocating element c to stage 1 would exceed the cycle time. In fact, only element c can be allocated to stage 2 because including element d would again exceed the cycle time. Element d can be allocated to stage 3. Either element e or element f can also be allocated to stage 3, but not both, or the cycle time would be exceeded. Following the 'largest element' heuristic rule, element e is chosen. The remaining elements then are allocated to stage 4. Figure 7.19 shows the final allocation and the balancing loss of the line.

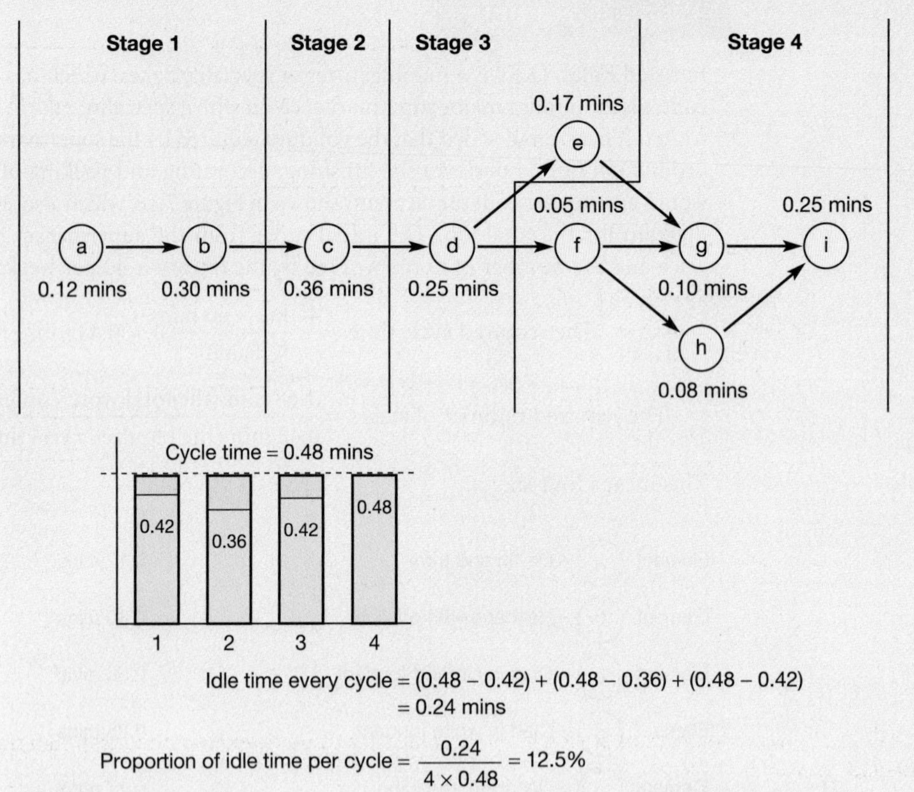

Figure 7.19 Allocation of elements to stages and balancing loss for Karlstad Kakes

Arranging the stages

All the stages necessary to fulfil the requirements of the layout may not be arranged in a sequential 'single line'. Return to the mortgage-processing example, which requires four stages working on the task to maintain a cycle time of one processed application every 15 minutes. The conventional arrangement of the four stages would be to lay them out in one line, each stage having 15 minutes' worth of work. However, nominally, the same output rate could also be achieved by arranging the four stages as two shorter lines, each of two stages with 30 minutes' worth of work each. Alternatively, following this logic to its ultimate conclusion, the stages could be arranged as four parallel stages, each responsible for the whole work content. Figure 7.20 shows these options.

Long thin
Short fat

This may be a simplified example, but it represents a genuine issue. Should the layout be arranged as a single **long thin** line, as several **short fat** parallel lines, or somewhere in between? (Note that 'long' refers to the number of stages and 'fat' to the amount of work allocated to each stage.) In any particular situation there are usually technical constraints which limit either how 'long and thin' or how 'short and fat' the layout can be, but there is usually a range of possible options within which a choice needs to be made. The advantages of each extreme of the long thin to short fat spectrum are very different and help to explain why different arrangements are adopted.

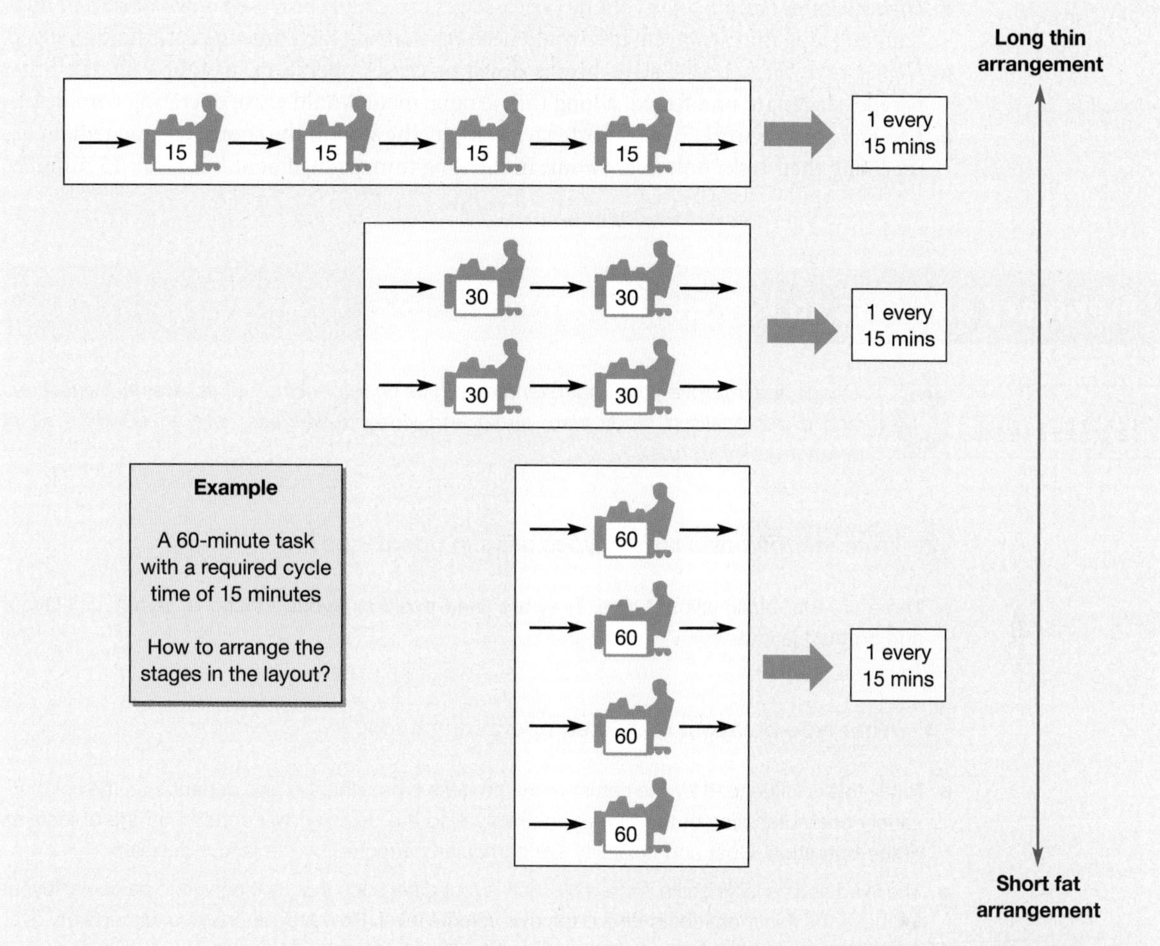

Figure 7.20 The arrangement of stages in product layout can be described on a spectrum from 'long thin' to 'short fat'

The advantages of the long thin arrangement

These include:

- *Controlled flow of materials or customers* – which is easy to manage.
- *Simple materials handling* – especially if a product being manufactured is heavy, large or difficult to move.
- *Lower capital requirements.* If a specialist piece of equipment is needed for one element in the job, only one piece of equipment would need to be purchased; on short fat arrangements every stage would need one.
- *More efficient operation.* If each stage is only performing a small part of the total job, the person at the stage will have a higher proportion of direct productive work as opposed to the non-productive parts of the job, such as picking up tools and materials.

This latter point is particularly important and is fully explained in Chapter 9 when we discuss job design.

The advantages of the short fat arrangement

These include:

- *Higher mix flexibility.* If the layout needs to process several types of product or service, each stage or line could specialize in different types.

- *Higher volume flexibility*. As volume varies, stages can simply be closed down or started up as required; long thin arrangements would need rebalancing each time the cycle time changed.
- *Higher robustness*. If one stage breaks down or ceases operation in some way, the other parallel stages are unaffected; a long thin arrangement would cease operating completely.
- *Less monotonous work*. In the mortgage example, the staff in the short fat arrangement are repeating their tasks only every hour; in the long thin arrangement it is every 15 minutes.

Summary answers to key questions

Check and improve your understanding of this chapter using self assessment questions and a personalised study plan, audio and video downloads, and an eBook – all at ***www.myomlab.com.***

➤ What are the basic layout types used in operations?

- There are four basic layout types. They are fixed-position layout, functional layout, cell layout and product layout.

➤ What type of layout should an operation choose?

- Partly this is influenced by the nature of the process type, which in turn depends on the volume–variety characteristics of the operation. Partly also the decision will depend on the objectives of the operation. Cost and flexibility are particularly affected by the layout decision.
- The fixed and variable costs implied by each layout differ such that, in theory, one particular layout will have the minimum costs for a particular volume level. However, in practice, uncertainty over the real costs involved in layout makes it difficult to be precise on which is the minimum-cost layout.

➤ What is layout design trying to achieve?

- In addition to the conventional operations objectives which will be influenced by the layout design, factors of importance include the length and clarity of customer, material or information flow; inherent safety to staff and/or customers; staff comfort; accessibility to staff and customers; the ability to coordinate management decisions; the use of space; and long-term flexibility.

➤ How should each basic layout type be designed in detail?

- In fixed-position layout the materials or people being transformed do not move but the transforming resources move around them. Techniques are rarely used in this type of layout, but some, such as resource location analysis, bring a systematic approach to minimizing the costs and inconvenience of flow at a fixed-position location.
- In functional layout all similar transforming resources are grouped together in the operation. The detailed design task is usually (although not always) to minimize the distance travelled by the transformed resources through the operation. Either manual or computer-based methods can be used to devise the detailed design.
- In cell layout the resources needed for a particular class of product are grouped together in some way. The detailed design task is to group the products or customer types such that convenient cells can be designed around their needs. Techniques such as production flow analysis can be used to allocate products to cells.

- In product layout, the transforming resources are located in sequence specifically for the convenience of products or product types. The detailed design of product layouts includes a number of decisions, such as the cycle time to which the design must conform, the number of stages in the operation, the way tasks are allocated to the stages in the line, and the arrangement of the stages in the line. The cycle time of each part of the design, together with the number of stages, is a function of where the design lies on the 'long thin' to 'short fat' spectrum of arrangements. This position affects costs, flexibility, robustness and staff attitude to work. The allocation of tasks to stages is called line balancing, which can be performed either manually or through computer-based algorithms.

Case study
Weldon Hand Tools

Weldon Hand Tools, one of the most successful of the European hand tool manufacturers, decided to move into the 'woodworking' tools market. Previously its products had been confined to car maintenance, home decorating and general hand tools. One of the first products which it decided to manufacture was a general-purpose 'smoothing plane', a tool which smoothes and shapes wood. Its product designers devised a suitable design and the company's work measurement engineers estimated the time it would take in standard minutes (the time to perform the task plus allowances for rest etc.) to perform each element in the assembly process. The marketing department also estimated the likely demand (for the whole European market) for the new product. Its sales forecast is shown in Table 7.3.

The marketing department was not totally confident of its forecast, however. *'A substantial proportion of demand is likely to be export sales, which we find difficult to predict. But whatever demand does turn out to be, we will have to react quickly to meet it. The more we enter these parts of the market, the more we are into impulse buying and the more sales we lose if we don't supply.'*

This plane was likely to be the first of several similar planes. A further model had already been approved for launch about one year after this, and two or three further models were in the planning stage. All the planes were similar, merely varying in length and width.

Table 7.3 Sales forecast for smoothing plane

Time period	*Volume*
Year 1	
1st quarter	98,000 units
2nd quarter	140,000 units
3rd quarter	140,000 units
4th quarter	170,000 units
Year 2	
1st quarter	140,000 units
2nd quarter	170,000 units
3rd quarter	200,000 units
4th quarter	230,000 units

Designing the manufacturing operation

It has been decided to assemble all planes at one of the company's smaller factory sites where a whole workshop is unused. Within the workshop there is plenty of room for expansion if demand proves higher than forecast. All machining and finishing of parts would be performed at the main factory and the parts shipped to the smaller site where they would be assembled at the available workshop. An idea of the assembly task can be gained from the partially exploded view of the product (*see* Fig. 7.21). Table 7.4 gives the 'standard time' for each element of the assembly task. Some of the tasks are described as 'press' operations. These use a simple mechanical press that applies sufficient force for simple bending, riveting or force-fitting operations. This type of press is not an expensive or sophisticated piece of technology.

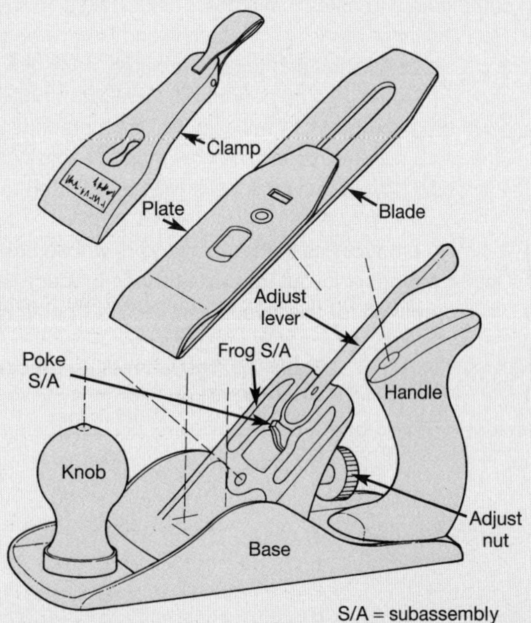

Figure 7.21 Partially exploded view of the new plane

Table 7.4 Standard times for each element of assembly task in standard minutes (SM)

Element	*Time in standard minutes (SM)*
Press operations	
Assemble poke subassembly	0.12
Fit poke subassembly to frog	0.10
Rivet adjusting lever to frog	0.15
Press adjusting nut screw to frog	0.08
TOTAL PRESS OPERATIONS	0.45
Bench operations	
Fit adjusting nut to frog	0.15
Fit frog screw to frog	0.05
Fit knob to base	0.15
Fit handle to base	0.17
Fit frog subassembly to base	0.15
Assemble blade subassembly	0.08
Assemble blade subassembly, clamp and label to base and adjust	0.20
Make up box and wrap plane, pack and stock	0.20
TOTAL ASSEMBLY AND PACK TIME	1.60

Costs and pricing

The standard costing system at the company involves adding a 150 per cent overhead charge to the direct labour cost of manufacturing the product, and the product would retail for the equivalent of around €35 in Europe where most retailers will sell this type of product for about 70–120 per cent more than they buy it from the manufacturer.

Questions

1. How many staff should the company employ?
2. What type of facilities and technology will the company need to buy in order to assemble this product?
3. Design a layout for the assembly operation (to include the fly press work) including the tasks to be performed at each part of the system.
4. How would the layout need to be adjusted as demand for this and similar products builds up?

Problems and applications

These problems and applications will help to improve your analysis of operations. You can find more practice problems as well as worked examples and guided solutions on MyOMLab at ***www.myomlab.com****.*

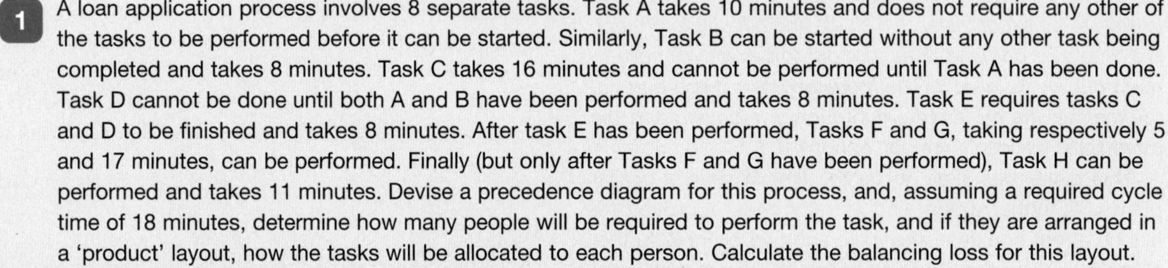

1 A loan application process involves 8 separate tasks. Task A takes 10 minutes and does not require any other of the tasks to be performed before it can be started. Similarly, Task B can be started without any other task being completed and takes 8 minutes. Task C takes 16 minutes and cannot be performed until Task A has been done. Task D cannot be done until both A and B have been performed and takes 8 minutes. Task E requires tasks C and D to be finished and takes 8 minutes. After task E has been performed, Tasks F and G, taking respectively 5 and 17 minutes, can be performed. Finally (but only after Tasks F and G have been performed), Task H can be performed and takes 11 minutes. Devise a precedence diagram for this process, and, assuming a required cycle time of 18 minutes, determine how many people will be required to perform the task, and if they are arranged in a 'product' layout, how the tasks will be allocated to each person. Calculate the balancing loss for this layout.

2 A simple product has 8 elements (a to h) whose times and immediate predecessors are shown in Table 7.5. Devise a product layout that will produce products at a rate of at least 6 products an hour. How many people will be required for this layout, and what will be its balancing loss?

Table 7.5 The immediate predecessors table for a simple product

Task	*Time (mins)*	*Immediate predecessor task*
a	5	–
b	4	a
c	3	b
d	4	b
e	2	c
f	6	c
g	3	d, e, f
h	4	g

Table 7.6 Flow of materials

	D1	*D2*	*D3*	*D4*	*D5*	*D6*	*D7*	*D8*
D1	\	30						
D2	10	\	15	20				
D3		5	\	12	2		15	
D4		6		\	10	20		
D5				8	\	8	10	12
D6	3				2	\	30	
D7	3					13	\	2
D8				10	6		15	\

3 The flow of materials through eight departments is shown in Table 7.6. Assuming that the direction of the flow of materials is not important, construct a relationship chart, a schematic layout and a suggested layout, given that each department is the same size and the eight departments should be arranged four along each side of a corridor.

4 Sketch the layout of your local shop, coffee bar or sports hall reception area. Observe the area and draw onto your sketch the movements of people through the area over a sufficient period of time to get over 20 observations. Assess the flow in terms of volume, variety and type of layout.

5 Revisit the opening short case in this chapter that examines some of the principles behind supermarket layout. Then visit a supermarket and observe people's behaviour. You may wish to try and observe which areas they move slowly past and which areas they seem to move past without paying attention to the products. (You may have to exercise some discretion when doing this; people generally don't like to be stalked round the supermarket too obviously.) Try and verify, as far as you can, some of the principles that were outlined in the opening short case. If you were to redesign the supermarket what would you recommend?

Selected further reading

This is a relatively technical chapter and, as you would expect, most books on the subject are technical. Here are a few of the more accessible.

Karlsson, C. (1996) Radically new production systems, *International Journal of Operations and Production Management*, vol. 16, no. 11. An interesting paper because it traces the development of Volvo's factory layouts over the years.

Meyers, F.E. and Stephens, M.P. (2000) *Manufacturing Facilities Design and Material Handling*, Prentice-Hall, Upper Saddle River, NJ. Exactly what it says, thorough.

Meller, R.D. and Kai-Yin Gau (1996) The facility layout problem: recent and emerging trends and perspectives, *Journal of Manufacturing Systems*, vol. 15, issue 5, 351–66. A review of the literature in the area.

Useful web sites

www.bpmi.org Site of the Business Process Management Initiative. Some good resources including papers and articles.

www.bptrends.com News site for trends in business process management generally. Some interesting articles.

www.iienet.org The American Institute of Industrial Engineers site. They are an important professional body for process design and related topics.

www.waria.com A Workflow and Reengineering Association web site. Some useful topics.

www.strategosinc.com/plant_layout_elements Some useful briefings, mainly in a manufacturing context.

www.opsman.org Lots of useful stuff.

*Now that you have finished reading this chapter, why not visit MyOMLab at **www.myomlab.com** where you'll find more learning resources to help you make the most of your studies and get a better grade?*

Chapter 8

Process technology

Key questions

- ➤ What is process technology?
- ➤ How does one gain an understanding of process technologies?
- ➤ How are process technologies evaluated?
- ➤ How are process technologies implemented?

Introduction

Advances in process technology have radically changed many operations over the last two or three decades. And all indications are that the pace of technological development is not slowing down. Few operations have been unaffected by this because all operations use some kind of process technology, whether it is a simple Internet link or the most complex and sophisticated of automated factories. But whatever the technology, all operations managers need to understand what emerging technologies can do, in broad terms how they do it, what advantages the technology can give and what constraints it might impose on the operation. Figure 8.1 shows where the issues covered in this chapter relate to the overall model of operations management activities.

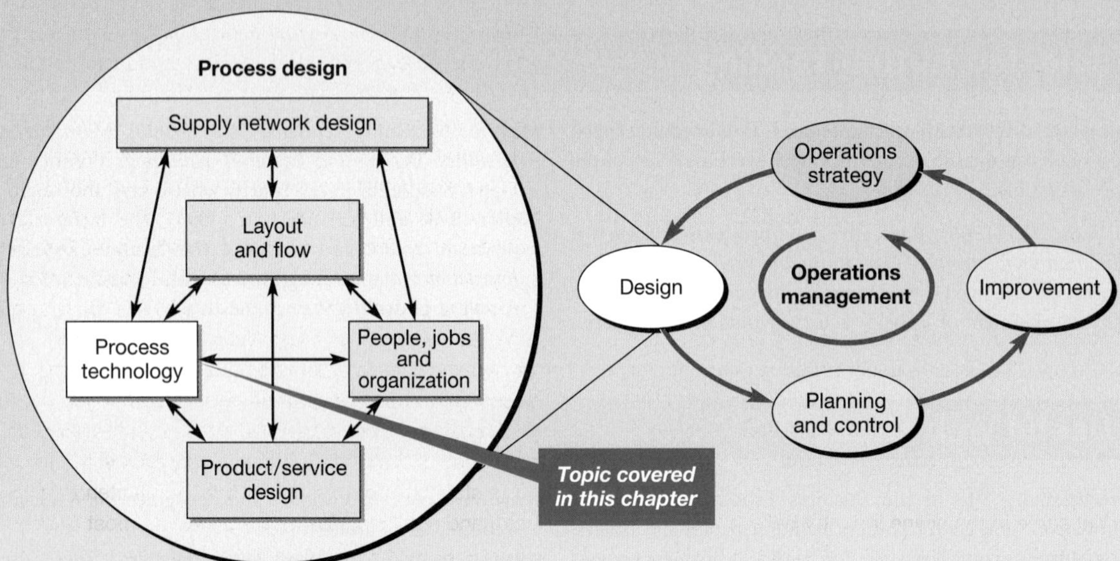

Figure 8.1 This chapter examines process technology

*Check and improve your understanding of this chapter using self assessment questions and a personalised study plan, audio and video downloads, and an eBook – all at **www.myomlab.com**.*

Operations in practice Who's in the cockpit?[1]

Modern aircraft fly on automatic pilot for most of their time, certainly more than most passengers realize. *'Most people are blissfully unaware that when an aircraft lands in mist or fog, it is a computer that is landing it'*, says Paul Jackson of *Jane's All the World's Aircraft*. *'It is the only sensible thing to do'*, agrees Ken Higgins of Boeing, *'When autopilots can do something better than a human pilot, we obviously use auto pilots.'* Generally this means using autopilots to do two jobs. First, they can take control of the plane during the long and (for the pilot) monotonous part of the flight between take-off and landing. Automatic pilots are not prone to the tedium or weariness which can affect humans and which can cause pilot error. The second job is to make landings, especially when visibility is poor because of fog or light conditions. The autopilot communicates with automatic equipment on the ground which allows the aircraft to be landed, if necessary, under conditions of zero visibility. In fact, automatic landings when visibility is poor are safer than when the pilot is in control. Even in the unlikely event of one of an aircraft's two engines failing an autopilot can land the plane safely. This means that on some flights, the autopilot is switched on within seconds of the aircraft wheels leaving the ground and then remains in charge throughout the flight and the landing. One of the few reasons not to use the autopilot is if the pilot is training or needs to log up the required number of landings to keep licensed.

As yet, commercial flights do not take-off automatically, mainly because it would require airports and airlines to invest in extra guidance equipment which would be expensive to develop and install. Also take-off is technically more complex than landing. More things could go wrong and some situations (for example, an engine failure during take-off) require split-second decision-making from the pilot. Industry analysts agree that it would be technically feasible to develop automatic take-off technology that met required safety standards but it could be prohibitively expensive.

Yet some in the airline industry believe that technology could be developed to the point where commercial flights can do without a pilot on the aircraft entirely. This is not as far-fetched as it seems. In April 2001 the Northrop Grumman Global Hawk, an 'unmanned aerial vehicle' (UAV), completed the first entirely unmanned flight across the Pacific when it took off from California and landed nearly twenty-four hours later in South Australia. The Global Hawk made the journey without any human intervention whatsoever. *'We made a historic flight with two clicks of the mouse'*, said Bob Mitchell of Northrop Grumman. The first mouse click told the aircraft to take off; the second, made after landing, told it to switch off its engine. UAVs are used for military reconnaissance purposes but enthusiasts point out that most aircraft breakthroughs, such as the jet engine and radar, were developed for military use before they found civilian applications. However, even the enthusiasts admit that there are some significant problems to overcome before pilotless aircraft could become commonplace. The entire commercial flight infrastructure from air traffic control through to airport control would need to be restructured, a wholly automatic pilotless aircraft would have to be shown to be safe, and perhaps most important, passengers would have to be persuaded to fly in them. If all these objections could be overcome, the rewards are substantial. Airlines' largest single cost is the wages of its staff (far more than fuel costs or maintenance cost) and of all staff, pilots are by far the most costly. Automated flights would cut costs significantly, but no one is taking bets on it happening soon!

Source: Rex Features

What is process technology?

Process technology

In this chapter, we discuss **process technology** – the machines, equipment and devices that *create* and/or *deliver* the goods and services. Process technology ranges from milking machines to marking software, from body scanners to bread ovens, from mobile phones to milling machines. Disney World uses flight simulation technologies to create the thrill of space travel on its rides, just one in a long history of Disney Corporation and its 'imagineers' using technology to engineer the experience for their customers. In fact, process technology is pervasive in all types of operations. Without it many of the products and services we all purchase would be less reliable, take longer to arrive and arrive unexpectedly, only be available in a limited variety, and be more expensive. Process technology has a very significant effect on quality, speed, dependability, flexibility and cost. That is why it is so important to operations managers, and that is why we devote a whole chapter to it. Even when technology seems peripheral to the actual creation of goods and services, it can play a key role in *facilitating* the direct transformation of inputs to an operation. For example, the computer systems which run planning and control activities, accounting systems and stock control systems can be used to help managers and operators control and improve the processes. This type of technology is called **indirect process technology**. It is becoming increasingly important. Many businesses spend more on the computer systems which control their processes than they do on the direct process technology which acts on its material, information or customers.

Indirect process technology

Integrating technologies

In this chapter, we distinguish between material, information and customer processing technologies, but this is only for convenience because many newer technologies process combinations of materials, staff and customers. These technologies are called **integrating technologies**. **Electronic point of sale** (EPOS) technology, for example, processes shoppers, products and information. Figure 8.2 illustrates examples of processing technology, some of which primarily process one type of transformed resource and others that integrate the processing of more than one transformed resources.

Integrating technologies

Electronic point of sale

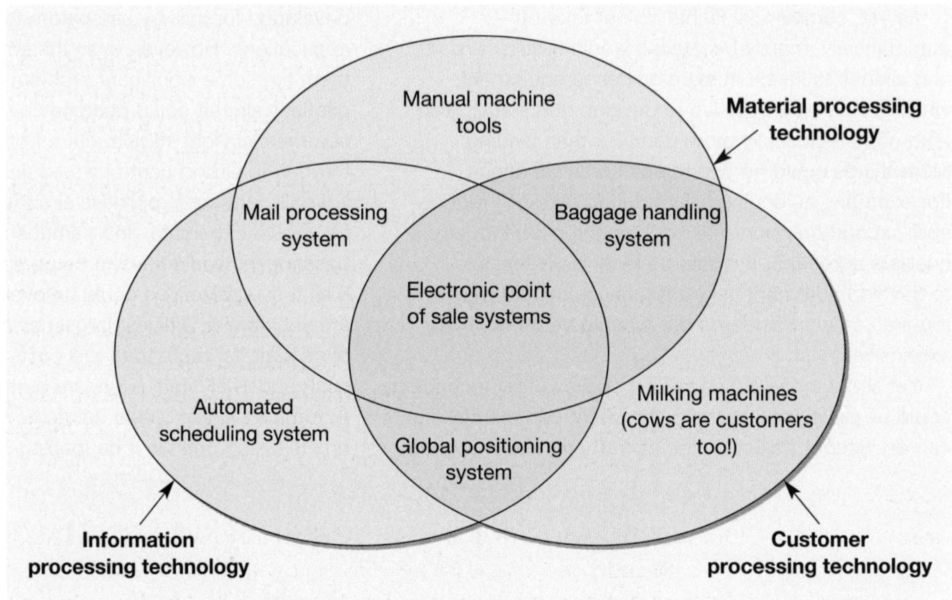

Figure 8.2 Process technologies can be classified by the transformed resource that they process (material, information or customer processing), but many technologies integrate more than one transformed resource

Operations management and process technology

Operations managers are continually involved in the management of process technology. They do not need to be experts in engineering, computing, biology, electronics or whatever constitutes the core science of the technology, but they should be able to do three things. First, they need to understand the technology to the extent that they are able to articulate what the technology should be able to do. Second, they should be able to evaluate alternative technologies and share in the decisions of which technology to choose. Third, they must implement the technology so that it can reach its full potential in contributing to the performance of the operation as a whole. These are the three issues which this chapter deals with.

Understanding process technologies

Operations managers do not need to be experts but do need to know the principles behind the technology

Understanding process technology does not (necessarily) mean knowing the details of the science and engineering embedded in the technology. But it does mean knowing enough about the **principles behind the technology** to be comfortable in evaluating some technical information, capable of dealing with experts in the technology and confident enough to ask relevant questions, such as:

- What does the technology do which is different from other similar technologies?
- How does it do it? That is, what particular characteristics of the technology are used to perform its function?
- What benefits does using the technology give to the operation?
- What constraints or risks does using the technology place on the operation?

In the rest of this section we (briefly) look at some of the more significant material, information and customer processing technologies. Our discussion of any of these technologies could be expanded into a whole book. Here we confine ourselves to answering (also briefly) the four questions posed earlier.

Materials-processing technology

Technological advances have meant that the ways in which metals, plastics, fabric and other materials are processed have improved over time. Generally it is the initial forming and shaping of materials at the start, and the handling and movement through the manufacturing process that has been most affected by technology advances. Assembling parts to make products, although far more automated that once it was, presents more challenges. Here are just some of the technologies that have helped to transform material processing industries.

Computer numerically controlled machine tools

Computer numerically controlled machine tools (CNC) are machine tools that use computers to control their actions, rather than control by human hand. *What does the technology do?* Performs the same types of metal cutting and forming operations which have always been done, but with control provided by a computer. *How does it do it?* Programmed computer-stored instructions activate the physical controls in the machine tool. *What benefits does it give?* Precision, accuracy, optimum use of cutting tools which maximizes their life, and higher labour productivity. *What constraints or risks does it impose?* Higher capital cost than manual technology. Needs programming skills.

Robots

Robots. *What does the technology do?* Primarily used for handling materials, for example, loading and unloading work pieces onto a machine, for processing where a tool is gripped by the robot, and for assembly where the robot places parts together. Some robots have some limited sensory feedback through vision control and touch control. *How does it do it?* Through a programmable and computer-controlled (sometimes multi-jointed) arm with an effector end-piece which will depend on the task being performed. *What benefits does it give?* Can be used where conditions are hazardous or uncomfortable for humans, or where tasks are highly repetitive. Performs repetitive tasks at lower cost than using humans and gives greater accuracy and repeatability. *What constraints or risks does it impose?* Although the sophistication of robotic movement is increasing, their abilities are still more limited than popular images of robot-driven factories suggest. Not always good at performing tasks which require delicate sensory feedback or sophisticated judgement.

Short case
Robots reduce the risks[2]

Source: Corbis/Yiorgos Karahalis

Robots, long used for repetitive and heavy activities, are also increasingly used to tackle dangerous ones. Robots were used during the clear-up operation amongst the rubble of the Twin Towers in New York. *'Enough people have died here'*, said a spokesperson for the emergency services. *'We don't want to risk anyone.'* Likewise, bomb disposal squads have developed specialized robots which can take at least some of the risk from what remains a hazardous job. Another job where robots reduce the risk is in decommissioning spent nuclear power stations. It is an agonizingly slow process which in many countries will take well over 100 years to complete. It is also a delicate and potentially dangerous process for those involved. This is why robots are used where possible to move, dismantle and manipulate hazardous radioactive material. Robots are also used for controlled-circuit television inspections as well as the pumping and removal of radioactive sludge. For example, at BNFL's Windscale plant in the UK, remote-controlled robotic crushers are being used to dismantle the plant's pile chimneys, and in nearby Sellafield a floating robot is draining and dismantling a tank of highly radioactive liquid waste.

Automated guided vehicles

Automated guided vehicles (AGVs). *What does the technology do?* Small, independently powered vehicles move materials between operations. Can be used as mobile workstations; for example, truck engines can be assembled on AGVs, which move between assembly stations. AGVs are also used in warehouses, in libraries to move books, in offices to move mail and even in hospitals to transport samples. *How do they do it?* They are often guided by cables buried in the floor of the operation and receive instructions from a central computer. *What benefits do they give?* Independent movement, flexibility of routeing and long-term flexibility of use. *What constraints or risks do they impose?* Capital cost considerably higher than alternative (conveyor) systems.

Flexible manufacturing systems

Flexible manufacturing systems (FMSs). *What does the technology do?* Completely manufactures a range of components (occasionally whole simple products) without significant human intervention during the processing. So, an FMS is not a single technology as such, but one that has integrated several technologies such as CNC 'workstations', loading/unloading facilities, transport/materials handling facilities and a computer control system, to realize a potential that is greater than the sum of its parts. The flexibility of each of the individual technologies combine to make an FMS (at least in theory) an extremely versatile manufacturing technology. *How does it do it?* By integrating programmable technologies such as machine tools, materials handling devices and robots through centralized computer control. *What benefits does it give?* Faster throughput times, higher utilization of capital equipment, lower work-in-progress inventories, more consistent quality, higher long-term product flexibility. A sequence of products, each different but within the capability 'envelope' of the system, could be processed in the system in any order and without changeover delays between each product. The 'envelope of capability' concept is important here. Any collection of machines within an FMS must have some finite limits on the size and shape of the materials it can process. *What constraints or risks does it impose?* Very high capital costs with uncertain payback, needs programming skills, and can be vulnerable to tool breakage (which can stop the whole system).

Short case
YO! Sushi[3]

YO! Sushi are sushi restaurants with an accent on style. They also employ technology to create their unique atmosphere. Prepared dishes are circulated around the sitting area on a moving conveyor. Customers simply take what they want as they pass by. In fact, this idea goes back to 1958 when Yoshiaki Shiraishi saw beer bottles moving down an Asahi brewery conveyor. Wanting to cut overheads in his restaurant, he developed the idea of the rotating conveyor belt. Originally known as 'satellite-turning-around-sushi' (rough translation), he calculated that the dishes should move at a rate of 8 centimetres per second. No more, no less. Any slower and customers get bored and the food may dry out. Any faster and customers do not have time to decide and the food may fly off the belt. At YO! Sushi tables also have personal metred beer taps but also a one-metre-high automated moving trolley, which, stocked with drinks, glides gently through the eating area inciting customers to 'stop me if you wish'.

Source: YO! Sushi/Jonathan Roberts

A moving belt used to serve customers at YO! Sushi restaurant

Computer integrated manufacturing

Computer integrated manufacturing (CIM). *What does the technology do?* Coordinates the whole process of manufacturing and manufactures a part, component or product. *How does it do it?* Connects and integrates the information technology which forms the foundation of design technology (CAD), manufacturing technology (flexible manufacturing centres or systems), materials handling (AGVs or robots) and the immediate management of these activities (scheduling, loading, monitoring). *What benefits does it give?* Fast throughput times, flexibility when compared with other previous 'hard' technologies, the potential for largely unsupervised manufacture. *What constraints or risks does it impose?* Extremely high capital costs, formidable technical problems of communications between the different parts of the system, and some vulnerability to failure and breakdown.

Information-processing technology

Information technology

Information-processing technology, or just **information technology** (IT), is the most common single type of technology within operations, and includes any device which collects, manipulates, stores or distributes information. Often organizational and operational issues are the main constraints in applying information technology because managers are unsure how best to use the potential in the technology. The following quotation gives some idea of how fast information technology is changing:

> *'The rate of progress in information technology has been so great that if comparable advances had been made in the automotive industry, you could buy a Jaguar that would travel at the speed of sound, go 600 miles on a thimble of gas and cost only $2!'*[7]

Here we will examine just some of the types of (and developments in) IT that are having, or could have, a significant impact on operations management.

Networked information technology

When used in IT, networking means two or more computers or devices linked together in some way so that data can be shared between them. The 'network' is, in effect, a combination of computer hardware and computer software that can be categorized in terms of the geographic area that it covers. So, at the micro level, a desk-area network (DAN), extends over a single desk. At the macro level a wide-area network (WAN) covers a large physical distance. Even the Internet itself could be classified as the largest WAN, covering the whole world. In between these extremes are local-area networks (LANs), wireless local-area networks (WLANs), campus-area networks (CANs), wide-area networks (WANs), metropolitan-area networks (MANs) and so on. The LAN and the WAN were the original categories. The others have emerged as technology has evolved. A LAN connects networked computers and devices a relatively short distance such as within an office, department or home. Sometimes one building may contain more than one smaller LAN, and sometimes a LAN will span a group of nearby buildings. Whatever its scope, a LAN is usually controlled by a single person or organization. WANs, by contrast, are geographically dispersed collection of LANs, and are not usually owned by a single organization but have some kind of collective or distributed ownership and management. A router is used to connect LANs to a WAN. A wireless local-area network is a LAN based on 'Wi-Fi' wireless network technology that uses radio waves to transmit information.

Computers can be connected through wired or wireless networks. Originally almost all businesses networks used wired (Ethernet) connections; more recently wireless networking is being widely used. Whereas wired networking relies on copper or fibre-optic cabling between network devices, wireless networks use radio waves (or microwaves) to connect computers. The advantages of a wireless network, when compared with a wired network, include mobility and the elimination of cables. However, wireless networks may suffer from radio interference due to weather, other wireless devices, and signal deterioration when obstructed by walls.

Networks can have two types of overall design, depending on the relationship between the computers – client–server and peer-to-peer. Client–server networks feature centralized server computers that store data, such as files, e-mails, web pages and applications. The client program makes a 'service request' from a server program. The server program then fulfils the request. The client–server model in networks provides an efficient method of connecting programs that are physically in different locations, which is why this type of relationship is generally used in business. It is one of the central ideas underpinning network computing. For example, if one company wanted to check what it had ordered from a supplier, a client program in its computer sends a request to a server program at its supplier. That program may send the request to its own client program, which, in turn, may send a request to a database server in another part of its organization to retrieve the customer's account details. These account details are then sent back to its own client program, which in turn sends it back to the customer. By contrast, a peer-to-peer network connects computers, all of which tend to have the same, or similar, functions or capabilities and either party can initiate a communication session. Peer-to-peer networks are much more commonly used for domestic purposes.

So, returning to our four questions. *What do networks do?* Allow decentralized computers and devices to communicate with each other and with shared devices over a varying distance. *How do they do it?* Through a hard-wired, or wireless, network and shared communication protocols. *What benefits do they give?* Flexibility, easy access to other users, shared databases and applications software. *What constraints do they impose*? Wired network installation costs can be high, while wireless networks may have security issues.

The Internet, intranets and extranets

World Wide Web

In 1989 a computer scientist called Tim Berners-Lee who was working at CERN, Geneva (Europe's particle physics laboratory) wrote a paper entitled 'Information management: a proposal'. Little did he realize that his idea would blossom into the **World Wide Web**. This, and the **Internet**, has been the most influential technology in the last several decades. In practical terms most of us think of the Internet as the provider of services such as the ability to browse the World Wide Web. The World Wide Web (WWW) provides a 'distributed hypermedia/hypertext' system, where elements of stored pages are identified as links allowing users to transfer to another page of information, which in turn had hypertext links to other pages, and so on. An **intranet** uses the same technologies as the Internet, but does so in order to provide a computer network that is private. Its purpose is to allow secure sharing of information to any part of an organization, its systems and its staff. It may be as simple as an internal web site. Alternatively, it could be a more complex arrangement that communicates with an organization's operating systems. **Extranets**, by contrast, link organizations together through secure business networks using Internet technology. They are used primarily for various aspects of supply chain management (*see* Chapter 13). They tend to be cheaper to set up and cheaper to maintain than the commercial trading networks which preceded them. For example, details of orders placed with suppliers, orders received from customers, payments to suppliers and payments received from customers can all be transmitted through the extranet. Banks and other financial institutions can also be incorporated into these networks. The use of networks in this way is often called electronic data interchange (EDI).

Intranet

Extranets

Again, returning to our four questions for the Internet, intranets and extranets. *What do they do?* Allow companies to use networks to exchange information electronically, publicly or securely. *How do they do it?* By connecting through networks, allowing businesses, customers, suppliers and banks to exchange trading information. *What advantages do they give?* Almost unimaginably significant (potentially!), allowing many applications (see Table 8.1) such as electronic data interchange (EDI). *What constraints do they impose?* Costs of setting up networks can be high for a small firm, yet is now a prerequisite for doing business. There can be problems in integrating networks into internal systems.

Short case

Recovering from Hurricane Katrina[4]

One would expect that IBM, one of the world's foremost technology companies, would be an early adopter of many technologies. For example, when it wanted to consult with its employees over restating the company's core set of values, it organized a 72-hour online real-time chat session. It also opened an online suggestions box called 'Think Place' where ideas are posted for everyone to see (and possibly improve upon). This type of internal communications technology not only promotes collaboration, it can also help when fast response is a priority. For example, along with other companies, IBM suffered technical problems after Hurricane Katrina struck New Orleans and the surrounding area. Using its 'Blue Pages Plus' expertise located on its corporate intranet it identified the people who had the potential to solve its problems within the space of a few hours. It also set up a wiki (a web page that can be edited by anyone who has access) that it used as a virtual meeting room. This enabled a group of IBM experts from the US, Germany and the UK to solve the problems within a few days.

Source: Rex Features

E-business and m-business

E-business

E-commerce

Reach

Richness

The use of internet-based technology, either to support existing business processes or to create entirely new business opportunities, has come to be known as **e-business**. The most obvious impact has been on those operations and business processes that are concerned with the buying and selling activity (**e-commerce**). The Internet provided a whole new channel for communicating with customers. The advantage of Internet selling was that it increased both **reach** (the number of customers who could be reached and the number of items they could be presented with) and **richness** (the amount of detail which could be provided concerning both the items on sale and customers' behaviour in buying them). Traditionally, selling involved a trade-off between reach and richness. The Internet effectively overcame this trade-off. However, the Internet had equally powerful implications for the ongoing provision of services. Figure 8.3 illustrates the relative cost to a retail bank of providing its services using different channels of communication. With cost savings of this magnitude, internet-based services have become the preferred medium for many operations.[5] Table 8.1 illustrates just a few of the applications of e-business to operations management.

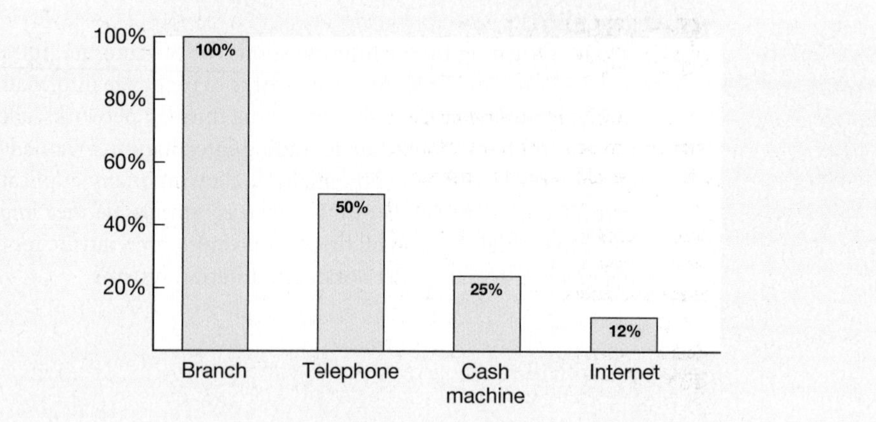

Figure 8.3 Average transaction cost for bank 'technologies'

Table 8.1 Some applications of e-business to operations management[6]

Organizational tasks	*E-business applications and/or contributions*	*E-business tools and systems*
Design	Customer feedback, research on customer requirements, product design, quality function deployment, data mining and warehousing	WWW-integrated CAD, Hyperlinks, 3D navigation, Internet for data and information exchange
Purchasing	Ordering, fund transfer, supplier selection	EDI, Internet purchasing, EFT
Supplier development	Partnership, supplier development	WWW-assisted supplier selection, communication using Internet (e-mails), research on suppliers and products with WWW and intelligent agents
Human resource management	E-recruiting, benefit selection and management, training and education using WWW	E-mails, interactive web sites, WWW-based multimedia applications
Production	Production planning and control, scheduling, inventory management, quality control	B2B e-business, MRP, ERP, SAP, BAAN, Peoplesoft, IBM e-business (web-integrated)
Marketing/sales and customer service	Product promotion, new sales channels, direct savings, reduced cycle time, customer services, Internet sales, selection of distribution channels, transportation, scheduling, third-party logistics	B2B e-business, Internet ordering, web site for the company, electronic funds transfer, online TPS, bar-coding system, ERP, WWW-integrated inventory management, Internet delivery of products and services
Warehousing	Inventory management, forecasting, scheduling of work force	EDI, EFT, WWW-integrated inventory management

M-business

Mobile business (**M-business**) is any transaction, involving the transfer of ownership or rights to use goods and services, which is initiated and/or completed by using mobile access to computer-mediated networks with the help of an electronic device[7].' Or, more generally, the ability to conduct commerce using a mobile device (e.g. a mobile phone, a PDA or a laptop) while on the move. Just look at the cards and other personal information that you carry around; almost all the information can be carried on a mobile telephone: credit cards, membership cards, cash, pre-paid transport or parking fees, and so on. There are two main benefits from m-commerce, selling a product or service, for example, micro-payments, location-based m-commerce and improving productivity, for example by supplying mobile workers with up-to-date information in order to deliver an effective service, or allowing mobile workers who are gathering time-critical information (reports, photographs, etc.) to capture and transmit it.

Although e- and m-business are rather large topics to review effectively in four questions, it is possible to summarize their impact. *What do they do?* Allow internal and external sharing of business information. *How do they do it?* By connecting individual computers, computer-based operating systems and mobile devices through area networks and wireless telecommunications networks by means of internet-based technology. *What advantages do they give?* Connectivity! It allows communication between business and personal activities. *What constraints do they impose?* Same as for the Internet, plus some extra security concerns for m-business.

Decision support systems (DSSs) and expert systems (ESs)

Decision support system

A **decision support system** is one which provides information with the direct objective of aiding or supporting managerial decision-making. It does this by storing relevant information, processing it and presenting it in such a way as to be appropriate to the decision being made. In this way, it supports managers by helping them to understand the nature of decisions and their consequences, but it does not actually make the decision itself. Often DSSs are used for 'what if' analyses which explore the (often financial) consequences of changing operations practice. **Expert systems** take the idea of DSSs one stage further in that they attempt to 'solve' problems that would normally be solved by humans. The key part of an ES is its 'inference engine' which performs the reasoning or formal logic on the rules that have been defined as governing the decision. These rules are called the 'knowledge base' of the ES (which is why ESs are also called knowledge-based systems). There have been many attempts to utilize the idea of an ES in operations management. Table 8.2 illustrates some of the decision areas and questions which have been treated. However, although authorities agree that ESs will become far more important in the future of operations management, not all applications so far have been totally successful. Return to our four questions. *What do they do?* Provide information to assist decision-making (DSS) or make operational decisions (ES). *How do they do it?* Use data storage, models and presentation formats to structure information and present consequences of decisions (DSS) and by mimicking human decision-making using data, knowledge bases and an inference engine (ES). *What benefits do they give?* Speed and sophistication of decision-making (DSS) and can take routine decision-making out of human hands (ES). *What constraints do they impose?* Can be expensive to model human decision-making, can lead to 'over-analysis' and is dependent on quality of data and models.

Expert systems

Automatic identification technologies

Bar code

Back in 1973 the Universal Product Code or **bar code** was developed that enabled a part or product type to be identified when read by a bar code scanner. Now bar codes are used to speed up checkout operations in most large supermarkets. However, they also have a role to play in many of the stages in the supply chain that delivers products into retail outlets. During manufacture and in warehouses bar codes are used to keep track of products passing through processes. But bar codes do have some disadvantages. It is sometimes difficult to align the item so that the bar code can be read conveniently, items can only be scanned one by one, most significantly, the bar code only identifies the *type* of item not a specific item itself. That is, the code identifies that an item is, say, a can of one type of drink rather than one specific

Table 8.2 Examples of the application of expert systems in operations management[8]

Decision area	*Typical issues*	*Some current applications*
Capacity planning	What is a reasonable size for a facility? What is the workforce size for our operation system?	PEP, CAPLAN
Facility location	Where is the best geographic site to locate the operation?	FADES
Facility layout	How should we arrange equipment in our facility site?	CRAFT, CORELAP, WORKPLACE DESIGNER
Aggregate planning	What should be the output rates and staffing levels for this quarter?	PATRIARCH, CAPLANLITE
Product design	Does the design of the product fit the firm's capability to produce it?	XCON, CDX
Scheduling	Which customers or jobs should receive top priority?	ISIS, MARS
Quality management	How do we best achieve our quality goals? Is the process capable of meeting the specifications?	PL DEFT
Inventory control	How much inventory do we need in our store? How should we control it?	IVAN, LOGIX, RIM
Maintenance	Where do we have a problem in our equipment? What kind of measures should we take to control or remove this problem?	DELTA/CATS

Radio-frequency identification (RFID)

can. Yet these drawbacks can be overcome through the use of **radio frequency identification** (RFID). Here an electronic product code (ePC) that is a unique number, 96 bits long, is embedded in a memory chip or smart tag. These tags are put on individual items so that each item has its own unique identifying code. At various points during its manufacture, distribution, storage and sale each smart tag can be scanned by a wireless radio frequency 'reader'. This can transmit the item's embedded identify code to a network such as the Internet (see Figure 8.4). RFID could help operations save significant amounts of money in lost, stolen or wasted products by helping manufacturers, distribution companies and retailers to pinpoint exactly where every item is in the supply chain. So, for example, if a product had to be recalled because of a health-risk scare, the exact location of every potentially dangerous product

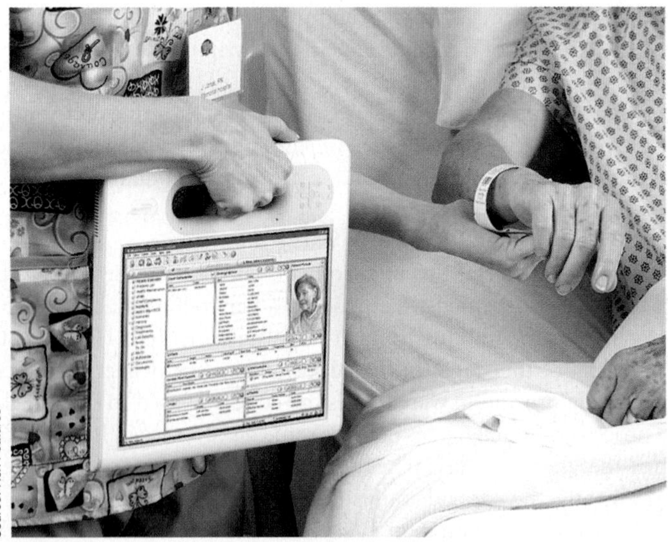

Source: Rex Features

Some hospitals now use RFID technology to improve patients' safety. Patients are given an arm band with an RFID chip. This contains all data on the patient's health history, required medication, allergies and so on. It helps to prevent patients being given inappropriate treatment.

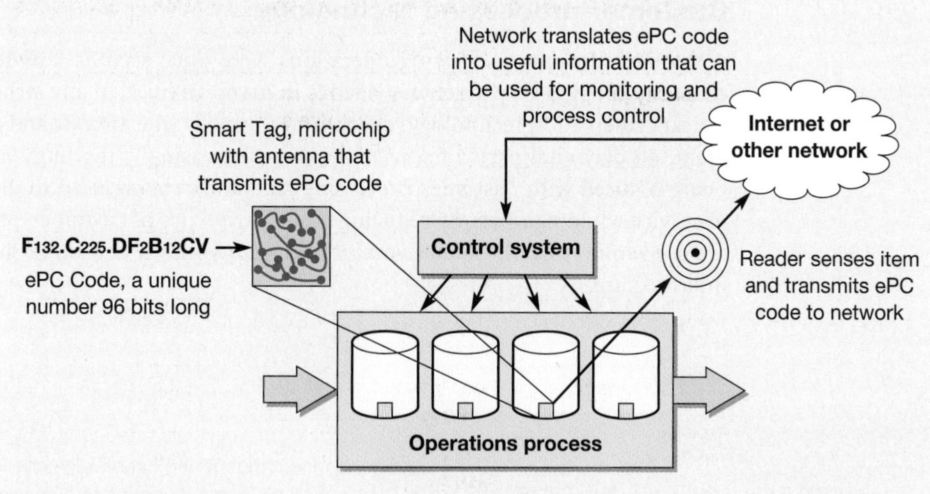

Figure 8.4 Using radio-frequency identification for control of operations processes

could be immediately identified. Shoppers could easily scan products to learn more about its characteristics and features while they are in the store; waiting at checkout counters could be eliminated because items will be scanned automatically by readers; the bill could even be automatically debited from your personal account as you leave the store. There are also potential benefits in tracking products after they leave the store. Data on how customers use products could be collected automatically and accurate recycling of waste materials would be made considerably easier. However, there are significant issues regarding customer privacy in extending data capture from products beyond the checkout.

Critical commentary

The idea of Auto-ID opens up many ethical issues. People see its potential and its dangers in very different ways. Take the following two statements.

> *'We are on the brink of a revolution of "smart products" that will interconnect everyday objects, consumers and manufacturers in a dynamic cycle of world commerce. . . . The vision of the Auto-ID centre is to create a universal environment in which computers understand the world without help from human beings.'*

> *'Supermarket cards and other retail surveillance devices are merely the opening volley of the marketers' war against consumers. If consumers fail to oppose these practices now our long-term prospects may look like something from a dystopian science-fiction novel. . . . though many Auto-ID proponents appear focused on inventory and supply chain efficiency, others are developing financial and consumer applications that, if adopted, will have chilling effects on consumers' ability to escape the oppressive surveillance of manufacturers, retailers, and marketers. Of course, government and law enforcement will be quick to use the technology to keep tabs on citizens as well.'*

It is this last issue which particularly scares some civil liberties activists. Keeping track of items within a supply chain is a relatively uncontentious issue. Keeping track of items when those items are identified with a particular individual going about their everyday lives, is far more problematic. So, beyond the checkout for every arguably beneficial application there is also potential for misuse. For example, smart tags could drastically reduce theft because items could automatically report when they are stolen, their tags serving as a homing device pinpoint their exact location. But, similar technology could be used to trace any citizen, honest or not.

Customer-processing technology

Although, customer-processing operations were once seen as 'low-technology', now process technology is very much in evidence in many services. In any airline flight, for example, e-ticket reservation technology, check-in technology, the aircraft and its in-flight entertainment, all play vital parts in service delivery. Increasingly, the human element of service is being reduced with customer-processing technology being used to give an acceptable level of service while significantly reducing costs. Two types of customer-processing technologies are used to do this: those that you interact with yourself and those that are operated by an intermediary.

Short case
Customers are not always human[9]

The first milking machines were introduced to grateful farmers over 100 years ago. Until recently, however, they could not operate without a human hand to attach the devices to the cows. This problem has been overcome by a consortium in the Netherlands which includes the Dutch government and several private firms. They hope that the 'robot milkmaid' will do away with the farmers' early morning ritual of milking. Each machine can milk between 60 and 100 cows a day and 'processes' the cows through a number of stages. Computer-controlled gates activated by transmitters around the cows' necks allow the cows to enter. The machine then checks their health, connects them to the milking machine and feeds them while they are being milked. If illness is detected in any cow, or if the machine for some reason fails to connect the milking cups to the cow after five attempts, automatic gates divert it into a special pen where the farmer can inspect it later. Finally, the machine ushers the cows out of the system. It also self-cleans periodically and can detect and reject any impure milk. Rather than herding all the cows in a 'batch' to the milking machine twice a day, the system relies on the cows being able to find their own way to the machine. Cows, it would appear, are creatures of habit. Once they have been shown the way to the machine a few times, they go there of their own volition because they know that it will relieve the discomfort in their udders, which grow heavier as they fill up. The cows may make the journey to the machine three or more times per day (*see* Fig. 8.5). Farmers also appear to be as much creatures of habit as their cows, however. Mr Riekes Uneken of Assen, the Dutch farmer who bought the very first robot milking machine, admitted, *'I have a bleeper if things go wrong. But I still like to get up early in the morning. I just like to see what goes on.'*

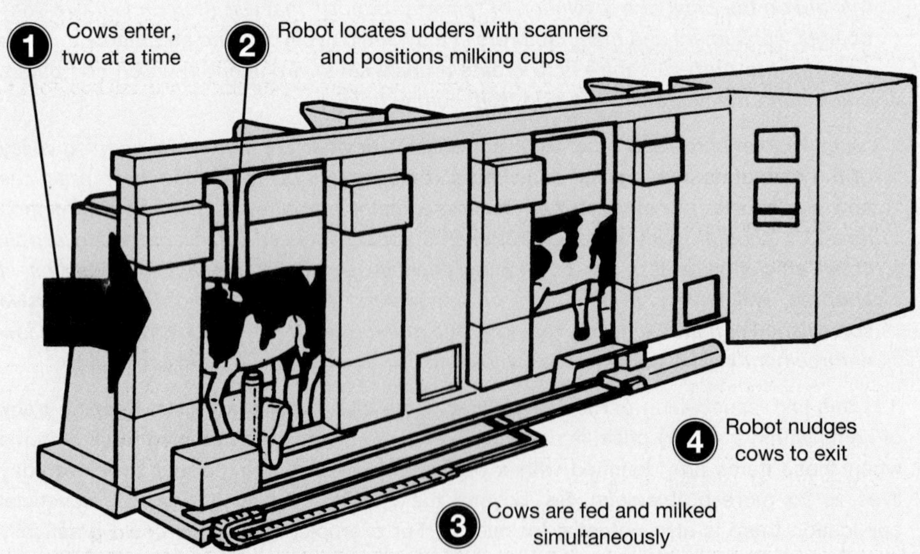

Figure 8.5 Cows are also customers

Technology involving customer interaction

Active interaction technology

Passive interaction technology

Hidden technologies

Cars, direct-dial telephones, Internet bookings and purchases, fitness equipment and automatic teller machines (ATMs – cash machines) are all examples of technology with which the customer interacts directly. In these cases, customers themselves are using **active interaction technology** to create the service. On an airline flight, for example, the passenger may choose to use the aircraft's entertainment facilities. This is likely to be an individual screen and headphones which can be used to view movies or listen to audio entertainment. The passenger might even make use of telecommunications equipment at the seat to book hotels or rent a car. In these cases, the customer takes control of the technology. Some customer-processing technology is **passive interactive technology**, for example being a 'passenger' in an aircraft, mass transport systems, moving walkways and lifts, cinemas and theme parks. This technology guides customers rather than the other way around. It 'processes' and controls customers by constraining their actions in some way. This helps to reduce variety in the operation. Some technology is 'aware' of customers but not the other way round, for example, security monitoring technologies in shopping malls or at national frontier customs areas. The objective of these **hidden technologies** is to track customers' movements or transactions in an unobtrusive way. Supermarkets, for example, can use bar-code scanner technologies (or RFID) to track the movement of customers around the store and indicate the relationship between the customers and their propensity to buy particular products.

The nature, benefits and constraints of interactive customer-processing technologies will vary, but generally the four questions that we have been using to understand technologies can be answered as follows. *What do they do?* Allow customers to control, or indirectly facilitate, some aspect of service. *How do they do it?* Through interfacing directly or indirectly between the functionality of the technology and the customer. *What benefits do they give?* Usually some combination of greater customer control, availability of service, speed of response, range of services and cost savings to the operation. *What constraints do they impose?* Active interaction technologies can allow customers 'visibility' of operational systems so must be secure and designed to facilitate navigation. Hidden technologies must be sensitive to customer privacy.

Interaction with technology through an intermediary

Book an airline flight on the Internet, and you are using direct customer-processing technology, but call or visit a travel agent and they will do it for you. You are 'using' technology through an intermediary. The benefits to the customer may be a more flexible service and the use of specialist knowledge. An intermediary dealing with the complex airline systems may be able to obtain better deals. In such cases, the customer may 'navigate' or guide the process but does not

Table 8.3 Types of customer processing technology

Type of interaction between the customers and the technology	*Examples*
Active interaction with the technology	Mobile phone services Internet-based ordering E-mail Cash machines
Passive interaction with the technology	Transport systems Theme park rides Automatic car wash
Hidden interaction with the technology	Security cameras Retail scanners Credit card tracking
Interaction with the technology through an intermediary	Call centre technology Travel shop's booking system

'drive' it. The technology may even be arranged to help customers navigate the process. Other examples of this kind of technology are the systems used in call centres, the customer support enquiry lines used by utilities, and some tracking systems in parcel delivery services.

Again, the nature, benefits and constraints of intermediated customer-processing technologies will vary, but generally the four questions can be answered as follows. *What do they do?* Allow the operation to facilitate some aspect of service. *How do they do it?* Through interfacing between the functionality of the technology and the customer using staff as intermediaries. *What benefits do they give?* Allow greater sophistication of customer response, and cost savings to the operation. *What constraints do they impose?* The technology is only as good as the staff who are the intermediaries. Also, customer interaction can seem formulaic, for example as in the 'script' screens used by call centres.

Short case
QB House speeds up the cut[10]

It was back in 1996 when Kuniyoshi Konishi became so frustrated by having to wait to get his hair cut and then pay over 3,000 yen for the privilege, decided that there must be a better way to offer this kind of service. *'Why not,'* he said, *'create a no-frills barber's shop where the customer could get a haircut in ten minutes at a cost of 1,000 yen (€7)?'* He realized that a combination of technology and process design could eliminate all non-essential elements from the basic task of cutting hair. How is this done? Well, first QB House's barbers never handle cash. Each shop has a ticket vending machine that accepts 1,000 yen bills (and gives no change!) and issues a ticket that the customer gives the barber in exchange for the hair cut. Second, QB House does not take reservations. The shops don't even have telephones. Therefore, no receptionist is needed, nor anyone to schedule appointments. Third, QB House developed a lighting system to indicate how long customers will have to wait. Electronic sensors under each seat in the waiting area and in each barber's chair track how many customers are waiting in the shop and different coloured lights are displayed outside the shop. Green lights indicate that there is no waiting, yellow lights indicate a wait of about 5 minutes, and red lights indicate that the wait may be around 15 minutes. This system can also keep track of how long it takes for each customer to be served. Fourth, QB has done away with the traditional Japanese practice of shampooing their customers after the haircut to remove any loose hairs. Instead, the barbers use QB House's own 'air wash' system where a vacuum cleaner hose is pulled down from the ceiling and used to vacuum the customer's hair clean. The QB House system has proved so popular that its shops (now over 200) can be found not only in Japan but in many other South East Asian countries such as Singapore, Malaysia and Thailand. Each year almost 4,000,000 customers experience QB House's 10-minute haircuts.

Source: Andy Maluche/Photographers Direct

Customer training

If customers are to have direct contact with technology, they must have some idea of how to operate it. Where customers have an active interaction with technology, the limitations of their understanding of the technology can be the main constraint on its use. For example, even some domestic technology such as video recorders cannot be used to their full potential by most owners. Other **customer-driven technologies** can face the same problem, with the important addition that if customers cannot use technologies such as ATMs, there are serious commercial consequences for a bank's customer service. Staff in manufacturing operations may require several years of training before they are given control of the technology they operate. Service operations may not have the same opportunity for **customer training**. Walley and Amin[11] suggest that the ability of the operation to train its customers in the use of its technology depends on three factors: complexity, repetition and the variety of tasks performed by the customer. If services are complex, higher levels of 'training' may be needed, for example, the technologies in theme parks and fast-food outlets rely on customers copying the behaviour of others. Frequency of use is important because the payback for the 'investment' in training will be greater if the customer uses the technology frequently. Also, customers may, over time, forget how to use the technology, but regular repetition will reinforce the training. Finally, training will be easier if the customer is presented with a low variety of tasks. For example, vending machines tend to concentrate on one category of product, so that the sequence of tasks required to operate the technology remains consistent.

Customer-driven technologies

Customer training

Evaluating process technologies

The most common technology-related decision in which operations managers will be involved is the choice between alternative technologies. It is an important decision because process technology can have a significant effect on the operation's long-term strategic capability; no one wants to change expensive technologies too frequently. This means that the characteristics of alternative technologies need to be evaluated so that they can be compared. Here we use three sets of criteria for evaluation.

- Does the technology fit the processing task for which it is intended?
- How does the technology improve the operation's performance?
- Does the technology give an acceptable financial return?

Does the process technology fit the processing task?

Different process technologies will be appropriate for different types of operations, not just because they process different transformed resources, but also because they do so at different levels of volume and variety. High-variety low-volume processes generally require process technology that is *general-purpose*, because it can perform the wide range of processing activities that high variety **demands**. High-volume low-variety processes can use technology that is more *dedicated* to its narrower range of processing requirements. Within the spectrum from general-purpose to dedicated-process technologies three dimensions in particular tend to vary with volume and variety. Figure 8.6 illustrates these three dimensions of process technology.

Technology should reflect the volume-variety requirements of the operation

- Its degree of 'automation'
- The capacity of the technology to process work, that is, its 'scale' or 'scalability'
- The extent to which it is integrated with other technologies; that is, its degree of 'coupling' or 'connectivity'.

The degree of automation of the technology

To some extent, all technology needs human intervention. It may be minimal, for example the periodic maintenance interventions in a petrochemical refinery. Conversely, the person who operates the technology may be the entire 'brains' of the process, for example the surgeon using keyhole surgery techniques. The ratio of technological to human effort it

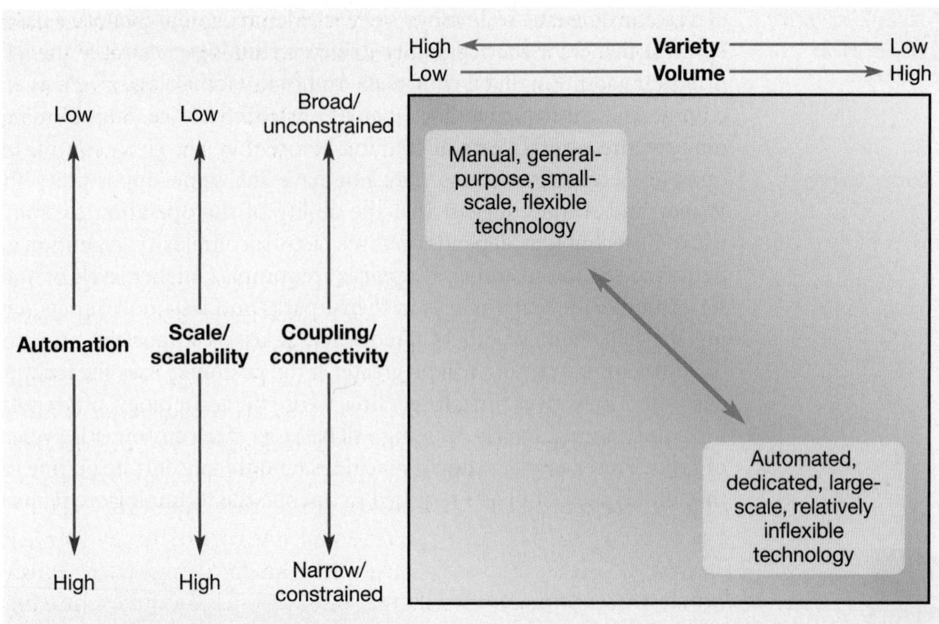

Figure 8.6 Different process technologies are important for different volume–variety combinations

Capital intensity

Automation of technology

employs is sometimes called the **capital intensity** of the process technology. Generally processes that have high variety and low volume will employ process technology with lower degrees of **automation** than those with higher volume and lower variety. For example, investment banks trade in highly complex and sophisticated financial 'derivatives', often customized to the needs of individual clients, and each may be worth millions of dollars. The back office of the bank has to process these deals to make sure that payments are made on time, documents are exchanged, and so on. Much of this processing will be done using relatively general-purpose technology such as spreadsheets. Skilled back-office staff are making the decisions rather than the technology. Contrast this with higher-volume, low-variety products, such as straightforward equity (stock) trades. Most of these products are simple and straightforward and are processed in very high volume of several thousand per day by 'automated' technology.

The scale or scalability of the technology

There is usually some discretion as to the scale of individual units of technology. For example, the duplicating department of a large office complex may decide to invest in a single, very large, fast copier, or alternatively in several smaller, slower copiers distributed around the operation's various processes. An airline may purchase one or two wide-bodied aircraft or a larger number of smaller aircraft. The advantage of large-scale technologies is that they can usually process items cheaper than small-scale technologies, but usually need high volume and can cope only with low variety. By contrast, the virtues of smaller-scale technology are often the nimbleness and flexibility that is suited to high-variety, lower-volume processing. For example, four small machines can between them produce four different products simultaneously (albeit slowly), whereas a single large machine with four times the output can produce only one product at a time (albeit faster). Small-scale technologies are also more robust. Suppose the choice is between three small machines and one larger one. In the first case, if one machine breaks down, a third of the capacity is lost, but in the second, capacity is reduced to zero. The advantages of large-scale technologies are similar to those of large-capacity increments discussed in Chapter 6.

The scale or scalability of technology

The equivalent to scale for some types of information processing technology is ***scalability***. By scalability we mean the ability to shift to a different level of useful capacity quickly and cost-effectively. Scalability is similar to absolute scale insomuch as it is influenced by the same volume–variety characteristics. IT scalability relies on consistent IT platform architecture and the high process standardization that is usually associated with high-volume and low-variety operations.

The coupling/connectivity of the technology

The coupling of technology

Coupling means the linking together of separate activities within a single piece of process technology to form an interconnected processing system. Tight coupling usually gives fast process throughput. For example, in an automated manufacturing system products flow quickly without delays between stages, and inventory will be lower – it can't accumulate when there are no 'gaps' between activities. Tight coupling also means that flow is simple and predictable, making it easier to keep track of parts when they pass through fewer stages, or information when it is automatically distributed to all parts of an information network. However, closely coupled technology can be both expensive (each connection may require capital costs) and vulnerable (a failure in one part of an interconnected system can affect the whole system). The fully integrated manufacturing system constrains parts to flow in a predetermined manner, making it difficult to accommodate products with very different processing requirements. So, coupling is generally more suited to relatively low variety and high volume. Higher variety processing generally requires a more open and unconstrained level of coupling because different products and services will require a wider range of processing activities.

How does the technology improve the operation's performance?

In Chapters 2 and 3, we identified the five operations *performance objectives*. So a sensible approach to evaluating the impact of any process technology on an operation is to assess how it affects the quality, speed, dependability, flexibility and cost performance of the operation. For example, consider a warehouse that stores spare parts which it packs and distributes to its customers. It is considering investing in a new 'retrieval and packing' system which converts sales orders into 'retrieval lists' and uses materials-handling equipment to automatically pick up the goods from its shelves and bring them to the packing area. The market requirements evaluation for this warehouse might be as follows:

- *Quality*. The impact on quality could be the fact that the computerized system is not prone to human error, which may previously have resulted in the wrong part being picked off the shelves.
- *Speed*. The new system may be able to retrieve items from the shelves faster than human operators can do safely.
- *Dependability*. This will depend on how reliable the new system is. If it is less likely to break down than the operators in the old system were likely to be absent (through illness etc.), then the new system may improve dependability of service.
- *Flexibility*. New service flexibility is not likely to be as good as the previous manual system. For example, there will be a physical limit to the size of products able to be retrieved by the automatic system, whereas people are capable of adapting to doing new things in new ways. Mix flexibility will also be poorer than was previously the case, for the same reason. Volume (and perhaps delivery) flexibility, however, could be better. The new system can work for longer hours when demand is higher than expected or deadlines are changed.
- *Cost*. The new system is certain to require fewer direct operatives to staff the warehouse, but will need extra engineering and maintenance support. Overall, however, lower labour costs are likely.

Short case
SVT programme investment in technology[12]

In the summer of 2000 the management of SVT (Sveriges Television) the Swedish public-service television company, decided to invest in a whole new type of digital news technology. At the same time they also decided to reorganize their news operations, move the whole news operation to a new building and, if that wasn't enough, launch its own new 24-hour news channel. This meant building a new studio facility for 11 shows (all in one huge room), moving 600 people, building control rooms, buying and constructing new news production hardware, and most significantly, investing $20 million in constructing a cutting-edge digital news production system without comparison in the world. The hardware for this was bought 'off the shelf' but SVT's own software staff coded the software. The system also allowed contributions from all regions of Sweden to be integrated into national and local news programmes. Together with the rebranding of the company's news and current affairs shows, it was the single biggest organizational development in the history of SVT.

For many, the most obvious result of the step change in the company's technology was to be the launch of its new 24-hour digital rolling news service. This finally launched on 10 September 2001. One day later it had to cope with the biggest news story that had broken for decades. To the relief of all, the new system coped. Now well bedded in, the system lets journalists create, store and share news clips easier and faster, with no video cassettes requiring physical handling. Broadcast quality has also improved because video cassettes were prone to breakdown. The atmosphere in the control room is much calmer. Finally, the number of staff necessary to produce the broadcast news has decreased and resources have been shifted into journalism.

Source: SVT Bengt O Nordin

SVT's new technology allows it to edit studio and pre-recorded material flexibly and easily

Does the technology give an acceptable financial return?

Assessing the financial value of investing in process technology is in itself a specialized subject. And while it is not the purpose of this book to delve into the details of financial analysis, it is important to highlight one important issue that is central to financial evaluation: while the benefits of investing in new technology can be spread over many years into the future, the costs associated with investing in the technology usually occur up-front. So we have to consider the **time value of money**. Simply, this means that receiving €1,000 now is better than receiving €1,000 in a year's time. Receiving €1,000 now enables us to invest the money so that it will be worth more than the €1,000 we receive in a year's time. Alternatively, reversing the logic, we can ask ourselves how much would have to be invested now to receive €1,000 in one year's time. This amount (lower than €1,000) is called the **net present value** of receiving €1,000 in one year's time.

Time value of money

Net present value

For example, suppose current interest rates are 10 per cent per annum; then the amount we would have to invest to receive €1,000 in one year's time is

$$€1{,}000 \times \frac{1}{(1.10)} = €909.10$$

So the present value of €1,000 in one year's time, *discounted for the fact that we do not have it immediately*, is €909.10. In two years' time, the amount we would have to invest to receive €1,000 is:

$$€1{,}000 \times \frac{1}{(1.10)} \times \frac{1}{(1.10)} = €1{,}000 \times \frac{1}{(1.10)^2} = €826.50$$

Discount rate

The rate of interest assumed (10 per cent in our case) is known as the **discount rate**. More generally, the present value of €x in n years' time, at a discount rate of r per cent, is:

$$€\frac{x}{(1 + r/100)}n$$

Worked example

The warehouse which we have been using as an example has been subjected to a costing and cost savings exercise. The capital cost of purchasing and installing the new technology can be spread over three years, and from the first year of its effective operation, overall operations cost savings will be made. Combining the cash that the company will have to spend and the savings that it will make, the cash flow year by year is shown in Table 8.4.

Table 8.4 Cash flows for the warehouse process technology

Year	*0*	*1*	*2*	*3*	*4*	*5*	*6*	*7*
Cash flow (€000s)	–300	30	50	400	400	400	400	0
Present value (discounted at 10%)	–300	27.27	41.3	300.53	273.21	248.37	225.79	0

However, these cash flows have to be discounted in order to assess their 'present value'. Here the company is using a discount rate of 10 per cent. This is also shown in Table 8.4. The effective life of this technology is assumed to be six years:

The total cash flow (sum of all the cash flows) = €1.38 million

However, the net present value (NPV) = €816,500

This is considered to be acceptable by the company.

Calculating discount rates, although perfectly possible, can be cumbersome. As an alternative, tables are usually used such as the one in Table 8.5.

So now the net present value, P = DF × FV

where

DF = the discount factor from Table 8.5
FV = future value

To use the table, find the vertical column and locate the appropriate discount rate (as a percentage). Then find the horizontal row corresponding to the number of years it will take to receive the payment. Where the column and the row intersect is the present value of €1. You can multiply this value by the expected future value, in order to find its present value.

Table 8.5 Present value of €1 to be paid in future

Years	*3.0%*	*4.0%*	*5.0%*	*6.0%*	*7.0%*	*8.0%*	*9.0%*	*10.0%*
1	€0.970	€0.962	€0.952	€0.943	€0.935	€0.926	€0.918	€0.909
2	€0.942	€0.925	€0.907	€0.890	€0.873	€0.857	€0.842	€0.827
3	€0.915	€0.889	€0.864	€0.840	€0.816	€0.794	€0.772	€0.751
4	€0.888	€0.855	€0.823	€0.792	€0.763	€0.735	€0.708	€0.683
5	€0.862	€0.822	€0.784	€0.747	€0.713	€0.681	€0.650	€0.621
6	€0.837	€0.790	€0.746	€0.705	€0.666	€0.630	€0.596	€0.565
7	€0.813	€0.760	€0.711	€0.665	€0.623	€0.584	€0.547	€0.513
8	€0.789	€0.731	€0.677	€0.627	€0.582	€0.540	€0.502	€0.467
9	€0.766	€0.703	€0.645	€0.592	€0.544	€0.500	€0.460	€0.424
10	€0.744	€0.676	€0.614	€0.558	€0.508	€0.463	€0.422	€0.386
11	€0.722	€0.650	€0.585	€0.527	€0.475	€0.429	€0.388	€0.351
12	€0.701	€0.626	€0.557	€0.497	€0.444	€0.397	€0.356	€0.319
13	€0.681	€0.601	€0.530	€0.469	€0.415	€0.368	€0.326	€0.290
14	€0.661	€0.578	€0.505	€0.442	€0.388	€0.341	€0.299	€0.263
15	€0.642	€0.555	€0.481	€0.417	€0.362	€0.315	€0.275	€0.239
16	€0.623	€0.534	€0.458	€0.394	€0.339	€0.292	€0.252	€0.218
17	€0.605	€0.513	€0.436	€0.371	€0.317	€0.270	€0.231	€0.198
18	€0.587	€0.494	€0.416	€0.350	€0.296	€0.250	€0.212	€0.180
19	€0.570	€0.475	€0.396	€0.331	€0.277	€0.232	€0.195	€0.164
20	€0.554	€0.456	€0.377	€0.312	€0.258	€0.215	€0.179	€0.149

Worked example

A health-care clinic is considering purchasing a new analysis system. The net cash flows from the new analysis system are as follows.

Year 1: –€10,000 (outflow of cash)
Year 2: €3,000
Year 3: €3,500
Year 4: €3,500
Year 5: €3,000

Assuming that the real discount rate for the clinic is 9%, using the net present value table (Table 8.6), demonstrate whether the new system would at least cover its costs. Table 8.6 shows the calculations. It shows that, because the net present value of the cash flow is positive, purchasing the new system would cover its costs, and will be (just) profitable for the clinic.

Table 8.6 Present value calculations for the clinic

Year	*Cash flow*	*Table factor*	*Present value*
1	(€10,000) ×	1.000 =	(€10,000.00)
2	€ 3,000 ×	0.917 =	€2,752.29
3	€ 3,500 ×	0.842 =	€2,945.88
4	€ 3,500 ×	0.772 =	€2,702.64
5	€ 3,000 ×	0.708 =	€2,125.28
	Net present value =		€526.09

Implementing process technology

Implementating process technology means organizing all the activities involved in making the technology work as intended. No matter how potentially beneficial and sophisticated the technology, it remains only a prospective benefit until it has been implemented successfully. So implementation is an important part of process technology management. Yet it is not always straightforward to make general points about the implementation process because it is very context-dependent. That is, the way one implements any technology will very much depend on its specific nature, the changes implied by the technology and the organizational conditions that apply during its implementation. In the remainder of this chapter we look at two particularly important issues that affect technology implementation: the idea of resource and process 'distance', and the idea that if anything can go wrong, it will.

Resource and process 'distance'

The degree of difficulty in the implementation of process technology will depend on the degree of novelty of the new technology resources and the changes required in the operation's processes. The less that the new technology resources are understood (influenced perhaps by the degree of innovation) the greater their 'distance' from the current technology resource base of the operation. Similarly, the extent to which an implementation requires an operation to modify its existing processes, the greater the 'process distance'. The greater the resource and process distance, the more difficult any implementation is likely to be. This is because such distance makes it difficult to adopt a systematic approach to analysing change and learning from mistakes. Those implementations which involve relatively little process or resource 'distance' provide an ideal opportunity for organizational learning. As in any classic scientific experiment, the more variables that are held constant, the more confidence you have in determining cause and effect. Conversely, in an implementation where the resource and process 'distance' means that nearly everything is 'up for grabs', it becomes difficult to know what has worked and what has not. More importantly, it becomes difficult to know why something has or has not worked.[13] This idea is illustrated in Figure 8.7.

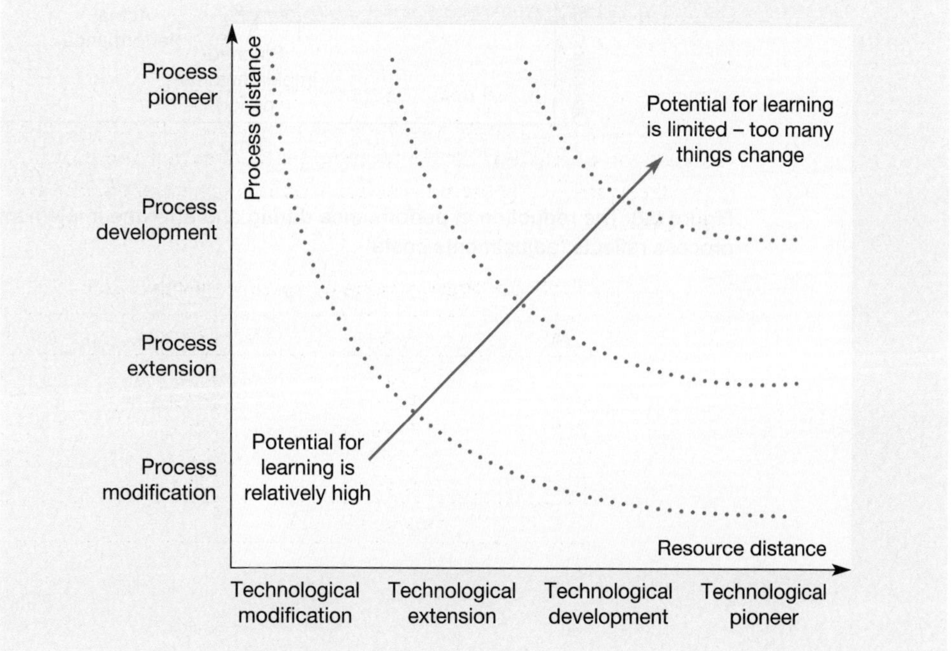

Figure 8.7 Learning potential depends on both technological resource and process 'distance'

Anticipating implementation problems

The implementation of any process technology will need to account for the 'adjustment' issues that almost always occur when making any organizational change. By adjustment issues we mean the losses that could be incurred before the improvement is functioning as intended. But estimating the nature and extent of any implementation issues is notoriously difficult. This is particularly true because more often than not, Murphy's law seems to prevail. This law is usually stated as, 'if anything can go wrong, it will'. This effect has been identified empirically in a range of operations, especially when new types of process technology are involved. Specifically discussing technology-related change (although the ideas apply to almost any implementation), Bruce Chew of Massachusetts Institute of Technology[14] argues that adjustment 'costs' stem from unforeseen mismatches between the new technology's capabilities and needs and the existing operation. New technology rarely behaves as planned and as changes are made their impact ripples throughout the organization. Figure 8.8 is an example of what Chew calls a 'Murphy curve'. It shows a typical pattern of performance reduction (in this case, quality) as a new process technology is introduced. It is recognized that implementation may take some time; therefore allowances are made for the length and cost of a 'ramp-up' period. However, as the operation prepares for the implementation, the distraction causes performance actually to deteriorate. Even after the start of the implementation this downward trend continues and it is only weeks, indeed maybe months, later that the old performance level is reached. The area of the dip indicates the magnitude of the adjustment costs, and therefore the level of vulnerability faced by the operation.

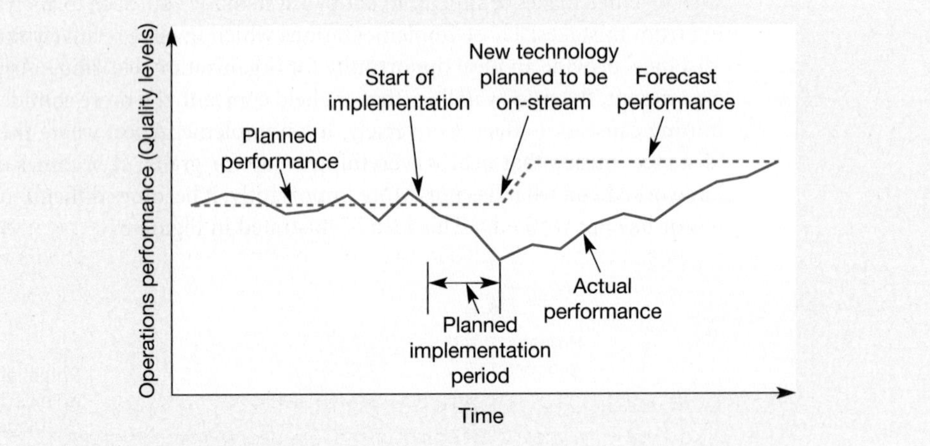

Figure 8.8 The reduction in performance during and after the implementation of a new process reflects 'adjustments costs'

Summary answers to key questions

Check and improve your understanding of this chapter using self assessment questions and a personalised study plan, audio and video downloads, and an eBook – all at ***www.myomlab.com.***

➤ What is process technology?

- Process technology is the machines, equipment or devices that help operations to create or deliver products and services. Indirect process technology helps to facilitate the direct creation of products and services.

➤ How does one gain an understanding of process technologies?

- Operations managers do not need to know the technical details of all technologies, but they do need to know the answers to the following questions. What does it do? How does it do it? What advantages does it give? What constraints does it impose?
- Material processing technologies which have had a particular impact include numerically controlled machine tools, robots, automated guided vehicles, flexible manufacturing systems and computer-integrated manufacturing systems.
- Information processing technologies which have had a particular impact include networks, such as local-area networks (LANs), wireless LANs and wide-area networks (WANs), the Internet, the World Wide Web and extranets. Other developments include RFID, management information systems, decision support systems and expert systems.
- There are no universally agreed classifications of customer-processing technologies, such as there are with materials- and information-processing technologies. The way we classify technologies here is through the nature of the interaction between customers, staff and the technology itself. Using this classification, technologies can be categorized into those with direct customer interaction and those which are operated by an intermediary.

➤ How are process technologies evaluated?

- All technologies should be appropriate for the activities that they have to undertake. In practice this means making sure that the degree of automation of the technology, the scale or scalability of the technology, and the degree of coupling or connectivity of the technology fit the volume and variety characteristics of the operation.
- All technologies should be evaluated by assessing the impact that the process technology will have on the operation's performance objectives (quality, speed, dependability, flexibility and cost).
- All technologies should be evaluated financially. This usually involves the use of some of the more common evaluation approaches, such as net present value (NPV).

➤ How are process technologies implemented?

- Implementating process technology means organizing all the activities involved in making the technology work as intended.
- The resource and process 'distance' implied by the technology implementation will indicate the degree of difficulty.
- It is necessary to allow for the adjustment costs of implementation.

Case study
Rochem Ltd

Dr Rhodes was losing his temper. *'It should be a simple enough decision. There are only two alternatives. You are only being asked to choose a machine!'*

The Management Committee looked abashed. Rochem Ltd was one of the largest independent companies supplying the food-processing industry. Its initial success had come with a food preservative used mainly for meat-based products and marketed under the name of 'Lerentyl'. Other products were subsequently developed in the food colouring and food container coating fields, so that now Lerentyl accounted for only 25 per cent of total company sales, which were now slightly over £10 million.

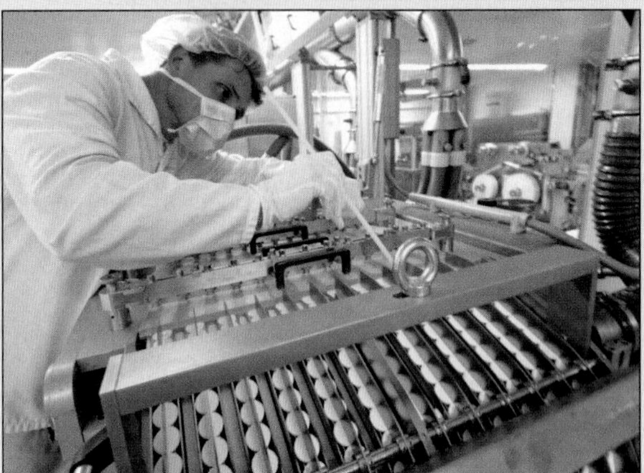

Source: Press Association Images

The decision

The problem over which there was such controversy related to the replacement of one of the process units used; to manufacture Lerentyl. Only two such units were used; both were 'Chemling' machines. It was the older of the two Chemling units which was giving trouble. High breakdown figures, with erratic quality levels, meant that output level requirements were only just being reached. The problem was: should the company replace the ageing Chemling with a new Chemling, or should it buy the only other plant on the market capable of the required process, the 'AFU' unit? The Chief Chemist's staff had drawn up a comparison of the two units, shown in Table 8.7.

The body considering the problem was the newly formed Management Committee. The committee consisted of the four senior managers in the firm: the Chief Chemist and the Marketing Manager, who had been with the firm since its beginning, together with the Production Manager and the Accountant, both of whom had joined the company only six months before.

What follows is a condensed version of the information presented by each manager to the committee, together with their attitudes to the decision.

The marketing manager

The current market for this type of preservative had reached a size of some £5 million, of which Rochem Ltd supplied approximately 48 per cent. There had, of late, been significant changes in the market – in particular, many of the users of preservatives were now able to buy products similar to Lerentyl. The result had been the evolution of a much more price-sensitive market than had previously been the case. Further market projections were somewhat uncertain. It was clear that the total market would not shrink (in volume terms) and best estimates suggested a market of perhaps £6 million within the next three or four years (at current prices). However, there were some people in the industry who believed that the present market only represented the tip of the iceberg.

Although the food preservative market had advanced by a series of technical innovations, 'real' changes in the basic product were now few and far between. Lerentyl was sold in either solid powder or liquid form, depending on

Table 8.7 A comparison of the two alternative machines

	CHEMLING	*AFU*
Capital cost	£590,000	£880,000
Processing costs	Fixed: £15,000/month Variable: £750/kg	Fixed: £40,000/month Variable: £600/kg
Design	105 kg/month	140 kg/month
Capacity	98 ± 0.7% purity	99.5 ± 0.2% purity
Quality	Manual testing	Automatic testing
Maintenance	Adequate but needs servicing	Not known – probably good
After-sales services	Very good	Not known – unlikely to be good
Delivery	Three months	Immediate

the particular needs of the customer. Prices tended to be related to the weight of chemical used, however. Thus, for example, the current average market price was approximately £1,050 per kg. There were, of course, wide variations depending on order size, etc.

'At the moment I am mainly interested in getting the right quantity and quality of Lerentyl each month and although Production has never let me down yet, I'm worried that unless we get a reliable new unit quickly, it soon will. The AFU machine could be on line in a few weeks, giving better quality too. Furthermore, if demand does increase (but I'm not saying it will), the AFU will give us the extra capacity. I will admit that we are not trying to increase our share of the preservative market as yet. We see our priority as establishing our other products first. When that's achieved, we will go back to concentrating on the preservative side of things.'

The chief chemist

The Chief Chemist was an old friend of John Rhodes and together they had been largely responsible for every product innovation. At the moment, the major part of his budget was devoted to modifying basic Lerentyl so that it could be used for more acidic food products such as fruit. This was not proving easy and as yet nothing had come of the research, although the Chief Chemist remained optimistic.

'If we succeed in modifying Lerentyl the market opportunities will be doubled overnight and we will need the extra capacity. I know we would be taking a risk by going for the AFU machine, but our company has grown by gambling on our research findings, and we must continue to show faith. Also the AFU technology is the way all similar technologies will be in the future. We have to start learning how to exploit it sooner or later.'

The production manager

The Lerentyl Department was virtually self-contained as a production unit. In fact, it was physically separate, located in a building a few yards detached from the rest of the plant. Production requirements for Lerentyl were currently at a steady rate of 190 kg per month. The six technicians who staffed the machines were the only technicians in Rochem who did all their own minor repairs and full quality control. The reason for this was largely historical since, when the firm started, the product was experimental and qualified technicians were needed to operate the plant. Four of the six had been with the firm almost from its beginning.

'It's all right for Dave and Eric [Marketing Manager and Chief Chemist] to talk about a big expansion of Lerentyl sales; they don't have to cope with all the problems if it doesn't happen. The fixed costs of the AFU unit are nearly three times those of the Chemling. Just think what that will do to my budget at low volumes of output. As I understand it, there is absolutely no evidence to show a large upswing in Lerentyl. No, the whole idea [of the AFU plant] is just too risky. Not only is there the risk. I don't think it is generally understood what the consequences of the AFU would mean. We would need twice the variety of spares for a start. But what really worries me is the staff's reaction. As fully qualified technicians they regard themselves as the elite of the firm; so they should, they are paid practically the same as I am! If we get the AFU plant, all their most interesting work, like the testing and the maintenance, will disappear or be greatly reduced. They will finish up as highly paid process workers.'

The accountant

The company had financed nearly all its recent capital investment from its own retained profits, but would be taking out short-term loans the following year for the first time for several years.

'At the moment, I don't think it wise to invest extra capital we can't afford in an attempt to give us extra capacity we don't need. This year will be an expensive one for the company. We are already committed to considerably increased expenditure on promotion of our other products and capital investment in other parts of the firm, and Dr Rhodes is not in favour of excessive funding from outside the firm. I accept that there might eventually be an upsurge in Lerentyl demand but, if it does come, it probably won't be this year and it will be far bigger than the AFU can cope with anyway, so we might as well have three Chemling plants at that time.'

Questions

1. How do the two alternative process technologies (Chemling and AFU) differ in terms of their scale and automation? What are the implications of this for Rochem?
2. Remind yourself of the distinction between feasibility, acceptability and vulnerability discussed in Chapter 4. Evaluate both technologies using these criteria.
3. What would you recommend the company should do?

Problems and applications

These problems and applications will help to improve your analysis of operations. You can find more practice problems as well as worked examples and guided solutions on MyOMLab at ***www.myomlab.com****.*

1. A new machine requires an investment of €500,000 and will generate profits of €100,000 for 10 years. Will the investment have a positive net present value assuming that a realistic interest is 6 per cent?

2. A local government housing office is considering investing in a new computer system for managing the maintenance of its properties. The system is forecast to generate savings of around £100,000 per year and will cost £400,000. It is expected to have a life of 7 years. The local authority expects its departments to use a discount rate of 0.3 to calculate the financial return on its investments. Is this investment financially worthwhile?

3. In the example above, the local government's finance officers have realized that their discount rate has been historically too low. They now believe that the discount rate should be doubled. Is the investment in the new computer system still worthwhile?

4. A new optical reader for scanning documents is being considered by a retail bank. The new system has a fixed cost of €30,000 per year and a variable cost of €2.5 per batch. The cost of the new scanner is €100,000. The bank charges €10 per batch for scanning documents and it believes that the demand for its scanning services will be 2,000 batches in year 1, 5,000 batches in year 2, 10,000 batches in year 3, and then 12,000 batches per year from year 4 onwards. If the realistic discount rate for the bank is 6 per cent, calculate the net present value of the investment over a 5-year period.

5. How do you think RFID could benefit operations process in (a) a hospital, (b) an airport, (c) a warehouse?

Selected further reading

Brain, M. (2001) Marshall Brain's *How Stuff Works*, Hungry Minds, NY. Exactly what it says. A lot of the 'stuff' is product technology, but the book also explains many process technologies in a clear and concise manner without sacrificing relevant detail.

Carr, N.G. (2000) Hypermediation: 'commerce and clickstream', *Harvard Business Review*, January–February. Written at the height of the Internet boom, it gives a flavour of how Internet technologies were seen.

Chew, W.B., Leonard-Barton, D. and Bohn, R.E. (1991) Beating Murphy's law, *Sloan Management Review*, vol. 5, Spring. One of the few articles that treats the issue of why everything seems to go wrong when any new technology is introduced. Insightful.

Cobham, D. and Curtis, G. (2004) *Business Information Systems: Analysis, Design and Practice*, Financial Times Prentice Hall, Harlow. A good solid text on the subject.

Evans, P. and Wurster, T. (1999) *Blown to Bits: How the New Economics of Information Transforms Strategy*, Harvard Business School Press, Boston. Interesting exposition of how Internet-based technologies can change the rules of the game in business.

Useful web sites

www.bpmi.org Site of the Business Process Management Initiative. Some good resources including papers and articles.

www.opsman.org Lots of useful stuff.

www.iienet.org The American Institute of Industrial Engineers site. An important professional body for technology, process design and related topics.

www.waria.com A Workflow and Reengineering Association web site. Some useful topics.

Now that you have finished reading this chapter, why not visit MyOMLab at ***www.myomlab.com*** *where you'll find more learning resources to help you make the most of your studies and get a better grade?*

Chapter 9

People, jobs and organization

Key questions

- Why are people issues so important in operations management?
- How do operations managers contribute to human resource strategy?
- What forms can organization designs take?
- How do we go about designing jobs?
- How are work times allocated?

Introduction

Operations management is often presented as a subject the main focus of which is on technology, systems, procedures and facilities – in other words the non-human parts of the organization. This is not true of course. On the contrary, the manner in which an organization's human resources are managed has a profound impact on the effectiveness of its operations function. In this chapter we look especially at the elements of human resource management which are traditionally seen as being directly within the sphere of operations management. These are, how operations managers contribute to human resource strategy, organization design, designing the working environment, job design, and the allocation of 'work times' to operations activities. The more detailed (and traditional) aspects of these last two elements are discussed further in the supplement to this chapter on Work Study. Figure 9.1 shows how this chapter fits into the overall model of operations activities.

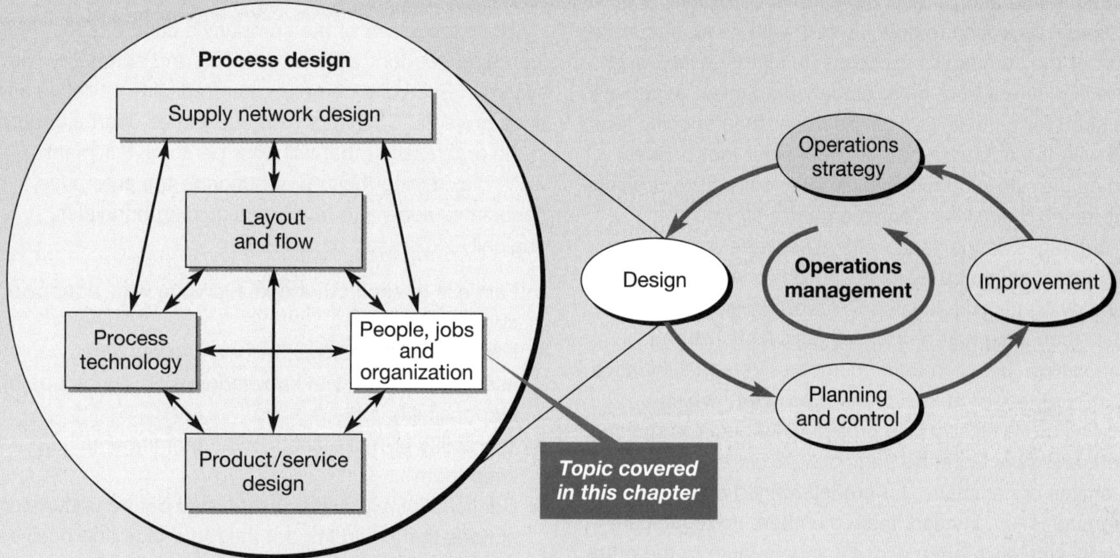

Figure 9.1 This chapter examines people, jobs and organization

*Check and improve your understanding of this chapter using self assessment questions and a personalised study plan, audio and video downloads, and an eBook – all at **www.myomlab.com**.*

Operations in practice W.L. Gore & Associates Inc[1]

Source: Alamy Images

Most famous for its high-performance fabrics such as GORE-TEX® Fabrics, Gore also has an enviable reputation as being one of the best companies to work for wherever it operates. In a recent 'Best companies to work for' list, its associates (the company does not use the term 'employees'), gave it the very top marks for 'feeling you can make a difference'. More than half of its Associates (staff) have been with the firm for at least a decade, a consequence of its philosophy ('to make money and have fun'), and its unique organizational culture and job design practices. Few in the company have any formal job titles, or job descriptions. There are no managers, only leaders and associates, people are paid 'according to their contribution' and staff help to determine each other's pay – ideas which seem revolutionary yet are based on the company's founding principles from over 50 years ago. Started by Bill and Vieve Gore in the basement of their home in Delaware, it has now become a global business with facilities in more than 45 locations around the world. Its skilled staff develop, manufacture and sell a range of innovative products, virtually all of which are based on just one material (expanded polytetrafluoroethylene) which was discovered by Bob Gore (the founder's son) in 1969. It now has approximately 8,000 associates in its four main divisions (textiles, electronic, medical and industrial products) and annual revenues of over $2 billion.

Gore's approach to how it works with its staff is at the heart of the company's success. On almost every level Gore is different from other global companies. Associates are hired for general work areas rather than specific jobs, and with the guidance of their 'sponsors' (not bosses) and as they develop experience, they commit to projects that match their skills. Teams organize around opportunities as they arise with associates committing to the projects that they have chosen to work on, rather than having tasks delegated to them. Project teams are small, focused, multi-disciplined, and foster strong relationships between team members. Personal initiative is encouraged, as is 'hands-on' innovation, which involves those closest to a project in its decision making. There are, says Gore, no traditional organizational charts, no chains of command, no predetermined channels of communication. Instead, team members communicate directly with each other and are accountable to the other members of their team. Groups are led by whoever is the most appropriate person at each stage of a project. Leaders are not appointed by senior management; they 'emerge' naturally by demonstrating special knowledge, skill or experience that advances a business objective.

Everyone's performance is assessed using a peer-level rating system. Even the Group's CEO (one of the few people with a title), Terri Kelly, 'emerged' in this way. When the previous CEO retired, no shortlist of preferred candidates was interviewed; instead, along with board discussions, a wide range of associates were invited to nominate people they would be willing to follow. *'We weren't given a list of names – we were free to choose anyone in the company',* she says. *'To my surprise, it was me.'*

The explicit aim of the company's culture is to 'combine freedom with cooperation and autonomy with synergy'. Everyone can earn the credibility to define and drive projects. Sponsors help associates chart a course in the organization that will offer personal fulfilment while maximizing their contribution to the enterprise. Associates adhere to four basic guiding principles, originally expressed by Bill Gore:

- Fairness to each other and everyone with whom we come in contact
- Freedom to encourage, help, and allow other associates to grow in knowledge, skill, and scope of responsibility
- The ability to make one's own commitments and keep them
- Consultation with other associates before undertaking actions that could impact the reputation and business directions of the company.

This degree of personal commitment and control by associates would not sit happily with a large 'corporate'-style organization. It is no surprise, then, that Gore have unusual notions of economies of scale.

Bill Gore believed in the need 'to divide so that you can multiply'. So when units grow to around 200 people, they are usually split up, with these small facilities organized in clusters or campuses. Ideally a dozen or so sites are close enough to permit good communication and knowledge exchange, but can still be intimate yet separate enough to promote a feeling of ownership. Bill Gore also believed that people come to work to be innovative and had a desire to invent great products. This, he said, *'would be the glue holding the company together'*, rather than the official procedures other companies rely on. And at Gore's Livingston plant in Scotland the story of 'the breathable bagpipes' is used to illustrate this type of creative innovation generated from the company's culture of trust that allows people to follow their passion. The story goes that an associate who worked in Gore's filter bags department at Livingstone was also a keen exponent of his national instrument – the bagpipes. By day he'd be working on filter systems, in the evening he'd play his bagpipes. It occurred to him that the physical properties of the product he was putting together during the day could make a synthetic bag for the pipes he played in the evening. Traditionally, bagpipes have a bag made from sheepskin or cow leather which fills up with moisture and becomes a smelly health hazard. He recognized that if you added GORE-TEX® Fabrics, it would be breathable and it would be dry. He put a prototype together, tried it, and it worked. So he decided to spend time developing it, created a team to develop it further, and now almost all Scottish bagpipes have a GORE-TEX® Pipe bag in them.

NB: GORE-TEX®, GORE® and designs are registered trade marks of W.L. Gore & Associates.

People in operations

To say that an organization's human resources are its greatest asset is something of a cliché. Yet it is worth reminding ourselves of the importance of human resources, especially in the operations function, where most 'human resources' are to be found. It follows that it is operations managers who are most involved in the leadership, development and organization of human resources. In this chapter we examine some of the issues that most directly affect, or are affected by, operations management; these are illustrated in Figure 9.2. But the influence of operations management on the organization's staff is not limited to the topics covered in this chapter. Almost everything discussed in this book has a 'people' dimension. Yet, in some chapters, the human perspective is particularly important. In addition to this chapter, Chapters 18 and 20, for example, are concerned largely with how the contribution of the operation's staff can be harnessed. In essence the issues covered in this chapter define how people go about their working lives. It positions their expectations of what is required of them, and it influences their perceptions of how they contribute to the organization. It defines their activities in relation to their work colleagues and it channels the flows of communication between different parts of the operation. But, of most importance, it helps to develop the culture of the organization – its shared values, beliefs and assumptions.

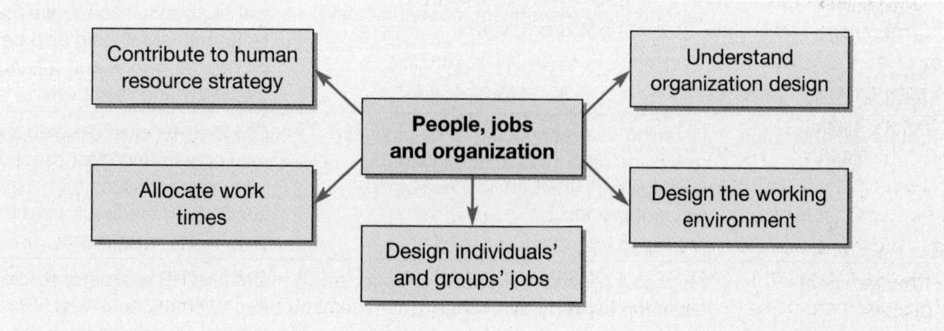

Figure 9.2 People in operations

Human resource strategy

Human resource strategy is the overall long-term approach to ensuring that an organization's human resources provide a strategic advantage. It involves two interrelated activities. First, identifying the number and type of people that are needed to manage, run and develop the organization so that it meets its strategic business objectives. Second, putting in place the programmes and initiatives that attract, develop and retain appropriate staff. It is an essential activity. Here is what Accenture, one of the top consultancies in the world, has to say about it.[2]

'Attention to people is more critical than ever . . . a company's workforce has become increasingly important to business success – so much so that most senior executives now view people and workforce issues as a critical competitive differentiator and one of their top agenda items. . . . A superior workforce – supported by highly effective, flexible and business-oriented HR and learning organizations – will be essential to achieving these objectives and taking greater strides toward high performance.'

Developing the specific details of an HR strategy is outside the scope of this book. Yet one set of issues is directly relevant, namely, how can operations managers make sure that they are well served by, and contribute to the strategy?

An influential contribution to the strategic role of HR comes from Dave Ulrich,[3] at the University of Michigan. His assumption is that traditional HR departments are often inadequate at fulfilling a meaningful strategic role. He proposes four elements to the HR activity: being 'strategic partner' to the business, administering HR procedures and processes, being an 'employee champion', and being a 'change agent'. Figure 9.3 illustrates these roles, and Table 9.1 explains each role and suggests how operations managers can be associated with each role.

It is important to recognize the interdependence of all the activities in Table 9.1. Managers may focus only on whatever of these activities currently demands attention. But, just as in

Table 9.1 Ulrich's HR roles and their relevance to operations managers

Human resources (HR) role	*What it involves*	*Relevance to operations management (OM)*
Strategic partner	Aligning HR and business strategy: 'organizational diagnosis', manpower planning, environmental monitoring, etc.	OM integrates operations strategy with HR strategy. OM both specifies its long-term skills requirements and relies on HR to supply / develop them informed by labour market forecasts, succession planning, etc.
Administrative expert	Running the organization's HR processes and 'shared services': payroll, appraisal, selection and recruitment, communication, etc.	OM is largely an 'internal customer' for HR's processes. OM must be clear in its requirements with agreed service levels mutually negotiated. Note that OM should also be able to advise HR on how to design and manage its processes efficiently and effectively.
Employee champion	Listening and responding to employees: 'providing resources to employees', conciliation, career advice, grievance procedures, etc.	OM and HR must develop a good working relationship and clear procedures to deal with any 'emergency' issues that arise. Also OM must be sensitive to feedback from HR on how it manages day-to-day operations.
Change agent	Managing transformation and change: 'ensuring capacity for change', management development, performance appraisal, organization development, etc.	OM and HR are jointly responsible for operations improvement activities. HR has a vital role in all the cultural, developmental and evaluation activities associated with improvement.

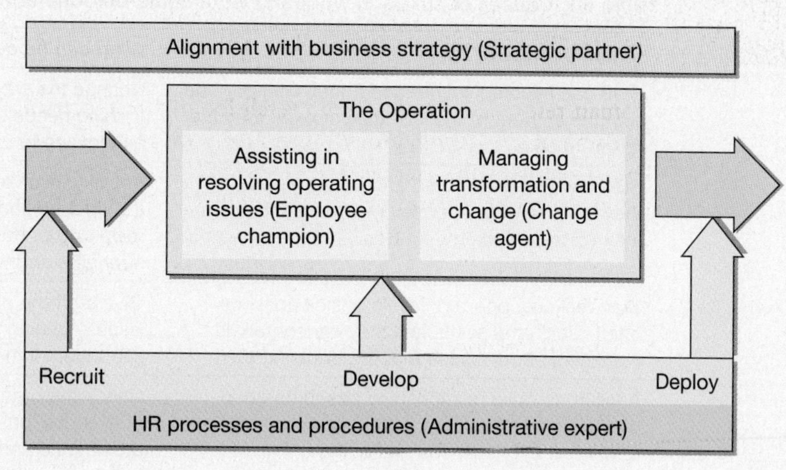

Figure 9.3 Human resource strategy

the operations function generally, people issues are inter-reliant. There is little point in attempting to, for example, develop a more egalitarian team-based structure and then fail to change the organization's training or reward procedures. This is why a strategic perspective aimed at identifying the relationship between all four roles is necessary, and why the first step in **developing an HR strategy** is to understand the organization's overall strategy. In particular, key questions are what are the implications of the strategy for human resources? And how can the people in the organization contribute to successfully achieving the strategy?

Short case
Is it 'googley'?[4]

Do a company's resources, particularly its people, come to reflect the vision and culture of the company? Some companies are keen to make sure that they do. For example, drivers on Highway 101 that passes through Silicon Valley, if they were paying attention, would have notice a billboard that read '[first 10-digit prime found in consecutive digits of e].com'. Those drivers with both the intellectual curiosity and the mathematical knowledge would have realized that the number in question is 7427466391, and is a sequence that starts at the 101st digit of the constant e (the base of the natural logarithm). Those that looked up the web site then found a mathematically more difficult riddle to solve. Solving that led to another web page where they were invited to submit their CVs to Google. It was one of Google's ideas for attracting the type of clever but inventive staff that they need, and also a way of further establishing Google as the type of company that has the quirky vision to make it attractive to such people. The tone of the billboard was, as its employees like to say, 'Googley – something that evokes a humble, cosmopolitan, different, toned down, classiness'. At a recent conference, instead of the rock music and flashing lights used by most firms to introduce their speakers, Google played Bach's Brandenburg Concerto No 3 and had a 'thought puzzle' placed on every seat. Whatever else it is, Google is an organization that thinks hard about what it is, what it wants to be, and how its people can sustain its position.

Source: Alamy Images

Table 9.2 Causes of stress at work and what could be done about it

Causes of stress	*What can be done about it*
Staff can become overloaded if they cannot cope with the amount of work or type of work they are asked to do	Change the way the job is designed, training needs and whether it is possible for employees to work more flexible hours
Staff can feel disaffected and perform poorly if they have no control or say over how and when they do their work	Actively involve staff in decision making, the contribution made by teams, and how reviewing performance can help identify strengths and weaknesses
Staff feel unsupported: levels of sick absence often rise if employees feel they cannot talk to managers about issues that are troubling them	Give staff the opportunity to talk about the issues causing stress, be sympathetic and keep them informed
A failure to build relationships based on good behaviour and trust can lead to problems related to discipline, grievances and bullying	Check the organization's policies for handling grievances, unsatisfactory performance, poor attendance and misconduct, and for tackling bullying and harassment
Staff will feel anxious about their work and the organization if they don't know their role and what is expected of them	Review the induction process, work out an accurate job description and maintain a close link between individual targets and organizational goals
Change can lead to huge uncertainty and insecurity	Plan ahead so change is not unexpected. Consult with employees so they have a real input, and work together to solve problems

Work-related stress

The idea that there is a link between human resource strategy and the incidence of stress at work is not new. Even some of the early 'scientific management' pioneers accepted that working arrangements should not result in conditions that promoted stress. Now it is generally accepted that stress can seriously undermine the quality of people's working lives and, in turn, their effectiveness of the workplace. Here stress is defined as 'the adverse reaction people have to excessive pressures or other types of demand placed on them'.[5] In addition to the obvious ethical reasons for avoiding work-related stress, there are also business-related benefits, such as the following.[6]

- Staff feel happier at work, their quality of working life is improved and they perform better.
- Introducing improvements is easier when 'stress' is managed effectively.
- Employment relations: problems can be resolved more easily.
- Attendance levels increase and sickness absence reduces.

Table 9.2 illustrates some of the causes of stress at work and what operations managers can do about it.

Organization design

There are many different ways of defining 'organization structure', here it is seen as the way in which tasks and responsibilities are divided into distinct groupings, and how the responsibility and coordination relationships between the groupings are defined. This includes the informal relationships which build up between groups as well as their more formal relationships.

Perspectives on organizations[7]

How we illustrate organizations says much about our underlying assumptions of what an 'organization' is and how it is supposed to work. For example, the illustration of an organization as a conventional 'organogram' implies that organizations are neat and controllable with unambiguous lines of accountability. But this is rarely the case. In fact taking such a mechanistic view may be neither appropriate nor desirable. Seeing an organization as though it was unambiguously machine-like is just one of several metaphors commonly used to understand organizations. One well-known analysis by Gareth Morgan proposes a number of 'images' or 'metaphors' which can be used to understand organizations as follows.

Organizations are machines – the resources within organizations can be seen as 'components' in a mechanism whose purpose is clearly understood. Relations within the organization are clearly defined and orderly, processes and procedures that should occur usually do occur, and the flow of information through the organization is predictable. Such mechanical metaphors appear to impose clarity on what is actually messy organizational behaviour. But, where it is important to impose clarity (as in much operations analysis) such a metaphor can be useful, and is the basis of the 'process approach' used in this and similar books.

Organizations are organisms – organizations are living entities. Their behaviour is dictated by the behaviour of the individual humans within them. Individuals, and their organizations, adapt to circumstances just as different species adapt to the environment. This is a particularly useful way of looking at organizations if parts of the environment (such as the needs of the market) change radically. The survival of the organization depends on its ability to exhibit enough flexibility to respond to its environment.

Organizations are brains – like brains, organizations process information and make decisions. They balance conflicting criteria, weigh up risks and decide when an outcome is acceptable. They are also capable of learning, changing their model of the world in the light of experience. This emphasis on decision making, accumulating experience and learning from that experience is important in understanding organizations. They consist of conflicting groups where power and control are key issues.

Organizations are cultures – an organization's culture is usually taken to mean its shared values, ideology, pattern of thinking and day-to-day ritual. Different organizations will have different cultures stemming from their circumstances and their history. A major strength of seeing organizations as cultures is that it draws attention to their shared 'enactment of reality'. Looking for the symbols and shared realities within an organization allows us to see beyond what the organization says about itself.

Organizations are political systems – organizations, like communities, are governed. The system of government is rarely democratic, but nor is it usually a dictatorship. Within the mechanisms of government in an organization are usually ways of understanding alternative philosophies, ways of seeking consensus (or at least reconciliation) and sometimes ways of legitimizing opposition. Individuals and groups seek to pursue their aims through the detailed politics of the organization. They form alliances, accommodate power relationships and manage conflict. Such a view is useful in helping organizations to legitimize politics as an inevitable aspect of organizational life.

Forms of organization structure

Most organization designs attempt to divide an organization into discrete parts which are given some degree of authority to make decisions within their part of the organization. All but the very smallest of organizations need to delegate decision making in this way, it allows specialization so decisions can be taken by the most appropriate people. The main issue is what dimension of specialization should be used when grouping parts of the organization together. There are three basic approaches to this:

- Group resources together according to their *functional purpose* – so, for example, sales, marketing, operations, research and development, finance, etc.
- Group resources together by the *characteristics of the resources themselves* – this may be done, for example, by clustering similar technologies together (extrusion technology, rolling, casting, etc.). Alternatively, it may be done by clustering similar skills together (audit, mergers and acquisitions, tax, etc.). It may also be done according to the resources required for particular products or services (chilled food, frozen food, canned food, etc.).
- Group resources together by the *markets* which the resources are intended to serve – again this may be done in various ways. Markets may be defined by location, with distinct geographical boundaries (North America, South America, Europe and Middle East, South East Asia, etc.). Alternatively, markets may be defined by the type of customer (small firms, large national firms, large multinational firms, etc.).

Within an organization, resources can be grouped in several different ways, and the lines of responsibility linking the resource clusters can also be configured in different ways. There are an almost infinite number of possible organizational structures. However, some pure types of organization have emerged that are useful in illustrating different approaches to organizational design, even if, in their pure form, they are rarely found.

The U-form organization. The unitary form, or U-form, organization clusters its resources primarily by their functional purpose. Figure 9.4(a) shows a typical U-form organization with a pyramid management structure, each level reporting to the managerial level above. Such structures can emphasize process efficiency above customer service and the ability to adapt to changing markets. The classic disease of such bureaucratic structures is that efficiency becomes an end in itself. Functions may even become primarily concerned with their own survival and power. But, the U-form keeps together expertise and can promote the creation

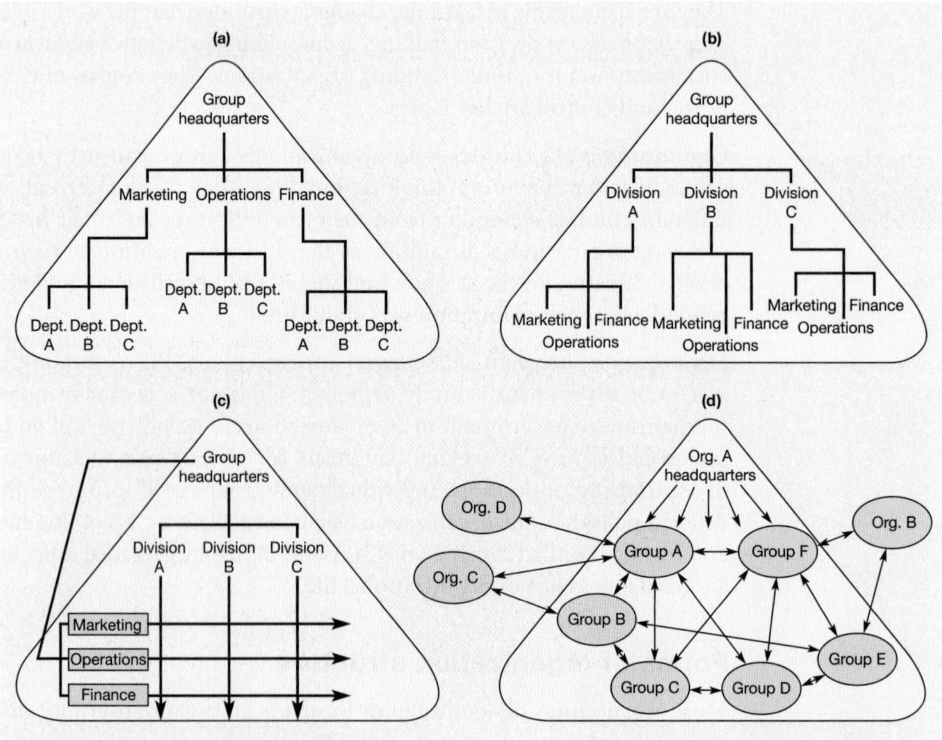

Figure 9.4 (a) U-form organizations give prominence to functional groupings of resources; (b) the M form separates the organization's resources into separate divisions; (c) matrix form structures the organization's resources so that they have two (or more) levels of responsibility; (d) N form organizations form loose networks internally between groups of resources and externally with other organizations

and sharing of technical knowledge. The problem then with the U-form organization is not so much the development of capabilities, but the flexibility of their deployment.

The M-form organization. This form of organizational structure emerged because the functionally based structure of the U-form was cumbersome when companies became large, often with complex markets. It groups together either the resources needed for each product or service group, or alternatively, those needed to serve a particular geographical market, in separate divisions. The separate functions such as operations may be distributed throughout the different divisions (see Figure 9.4(b)), which can reduce economies of scale and the operating efficiency of the structure. However, it does allow each individual division to focus on the specific needs of its markets.

Matrix forms. Matrix structures are a hybrid, usually combining the M-form with the U-form. In effect, the organization has simultaneously two different structures (see Figure 9.4(c)). In a matrix structure each resource cluster has at least two lines of authority, for example both to the division and to the functional groups. So, an operations manager may be directly responsible to his or her division head, while at the same time having a (sometimes weaker) reporting responsibility to the head of the operations function for the whole company. While a matrix organization ensures the representation of all interests within the company, it can be complex and sometimes confusing.

The N-form organization. The 'N' in N-form stand for 'network'. In N-form organizations, resources are clustered into groups as in other organizational forms, but with more delegation of responsibility for the strategic management of those resources. N-forms have relatively little hierarchical reporting and control. Each cluster of resources is linked to the others to form a network, with the relative strength of the relationships between clusters changing over time, depending on circumstances (see Figure 9.4(d)). Senior management set broad goals and attempt to develop a unifying culture but do not 'command and control' to the same extent as in other organization forms. They may, however, act to encourage any developments they see as beneficial to the organization as a whole.

Job design

In the remainder of this chapter we deal with three interrelated topics: the design of individuals' and groups' jobs, the allocation of work times to people's activities, and the design of the working environment. We look at them together because they are influenced by and use a, more or less, common set of concepts and frameworks. These are illustrated in Figure 9.5.

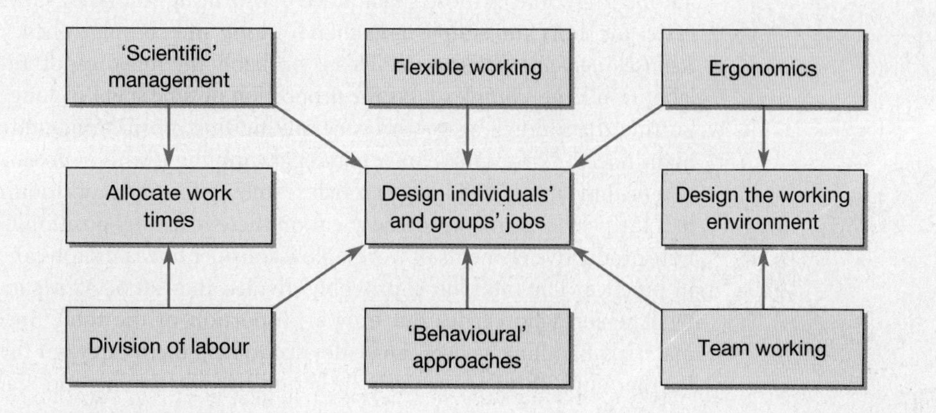

Figure 9.5 The main influences on job design, work time allocation and the design of the working environment

Job design

Job design is about how we structure each individual's jobs, the team to which they belong (if any), their workplace and their interface with the technology they use. It involves a number of separate yet related elements.

- *What tasks are to be allocated to each person in the operation?* Producing goods and services involves a whole range of different tasks which need to be divided between the people who staff the operation. Different approaches to the division of labour will lead to different task allocations.
- *What is the best method of performing each job?* Every job should have an approved (or best) method of completion. And although there are different ideas of what is 'best', it is generally the most efficient method but that fits the task, and does not unduly interfere with other tasks.
- *How long will it take and how many people will be needed?* Work measurement helps us calculate the time required to do a job, and therefore how many people will be needed.
- *How do we maintain commitment?* Understanding how we can encourage people and maintain job commitment is, arguably, the most important of the issues in job design. This is why behavioural approaches, including empowerment, teamwork and flexible working are at the core of job design.
- *What technology is available and how will it be used?* Many operational tasks require the use of technology. Not only does the technology need to be appropriately designed, but also so does the interface between the people and the hardware.
- *What are the environmental conditions of the workplace?* The conditions under which jobs are performed will have a significant impact on people's effectiveness, Although often considered a part of job design, we treat it separately in this chapter.

Task allocation – the division of labour

Division of labour

Any operation must decide on the balance between using specialists or generalists. This idea is related to the **division of labour** – dividing the total task down into smaller parts, each of which is accomplished by a single person or team. It was first formalized as a concept by the economist Adam Smith in his *Wealth of Nations* in 1746. Perhaps the epitome of the division of labour is the assembly line, where products move along a single path and are built up by operators continually repeating a single task. This is the predominant model of job design in most mass-produced products and in some mass-produced services (fast food, for example). There are some *real advantages* in division of labour:

- *It promotes faster learning.* It is obviously easier to learn how to do a relatively short and simple task than a long and complex one. This means that new members of staff can be quickly trained and assigned to their tasks when they are short and simple.
- *Automation becomes easier.* Dividing a total task into small parts raises the possibility of automating some of those small tasks. Substituting technology for labour is considerably easier for short and simple tasks than for long and complex ones.
- *Reduced non-productive work.* This is probably the most important benefit of division of labour. In large, complex tasks the proportion of time spent picking up tools and materials, putting them down again and generally finding, positioning and searching can be very high indeed. For example, one person assembling a whole motor-car engine would take two or three hours and involve much searching for parts, positioning, and so on. Around half the person's time would be spent on these reaching, positioning, finding tasks (called non-productive elements of work). Now consider how a motor-car engine is actually made in practice. The total job is probably divided into 20 or 30 separate stages, each staffed by a person who carries out only a proportion of the total. Specialist equipment and materials-handling devices can be devised to help them carry out their job more efficiently. Furthermore, there is relatively little finding, positioning and reaching involved in this simplified task. Non-productive work can be considerably reduced, perhaps to under 10 per cent, which would be very significant to the costs of the operation.

There are also serious drawbacks to highly divided jobs:

- *Monotony*. The shorter the task, the more often operators will need to repeat it. Repeating the same task, for example every 30 seconds, eight hours a day and five days a week, can hardly be called a fulfilling job. As well as any ethical objections, there are other, more obviously practical objections to jobs which induce such boredom. These include the increased likelihood of absenteeism and staff turnover, the increased likelihood of error and even the deliberate sabotage of the job.
- *Physical injury*. The continued repetition of a very narrow range of movements can, in extreme cases, lead to physical injury. The over-use of some parts of the body (especially the arms, hands and wrists) can result in pain and a reduction in physical capability. This is sometimes called repetitive strain injury (RSI).
- *Low flexibility*. Dividing a task up into many small parts often gives the job design a rigidity which is difficult to change under changing circumstances. For example, if an assembly line has been designed to make one particular product but then has to change to manufacture a quite different product, the whole line will need redesigning. This will probably involve changing every operator's set of tasks, which can be a long and difficult procedure.
- *Poor robustness*. Highly divided jobs imply materials (or information) passing between several stages. If one of these stages is not working correctly, for example because some equipment is faulty, the whole operation is affected. On the other hand, if each person is performing the whole of the job, any problems will only affect that one person's output.

Designing job methods – scientific management

Scientific management

Taylorism

The term **scientific management** became established in 1911 with the publication of the book of the same name by Fredrick Taylor (this whole approach to job design is sometimes referred to, pejoratively, as **Taylorism**). In this work he identified what he saw as the basic tenets of scientific management:[6]

- All aspects of work should be investigated on a scientific basis to establish the laws, rules and formulae governing the best methods of working.
- Such an investigative approach to the study of work is necessary to establish what constitutes a 'fair day's work'.
- Workers should be selected, trained and developed methodically to perform their tasks.
- Managers should act as the planners of the work (analysing jobs and standardizing the best method of doing the job) while workers should be responsible for carrying out the jobs to the standards laid down.
- Cooperation should be achieved between management and workers based on the 'maximum prosperity' of both.

Method study

Work measurement

Work study

The important thing to remember about scientific management is that it is not particularly 'scientific' as such, although it certainly does take an 'investigative' approach to improving operations. Perhaps a better term for it would be 'systematic management'. It gave birth to two separate, but related, fields of study, **method study**, which determines the methods and activities to be included in jobs, and **work measurement**, which is concerned with measuring the time that should be taken for performing jobs. Together, these two fields are often referred to as **work study** and are explained in detail in the supplement to this chapter.

Critical commentary

Even in 1915, criticisms of the scientific management approach were being voiced.[8] In a submission to the United States Commission on Industrial Relations, scientific management is described as:

→

- being in 'spirit and essence a cunningly devised speeding up and sweating system';
- intensifying the 'modern tendency towards specialization of the work and the task';
- condemning 'the worker to a monotonous routine';
- putting 'into the hands of employers an immense mass of information and methods that may be used unscrupulously to the detriment of workers';
- tending to 'transfer to the management all the traditional knowledge, the judgement and skills of workers';
- greatly intensifying 'unnecessary managerial dictation and discipline';
- tending to 'emphasize quantity of product at the expense of quality'.

Two themes evident in this early criticism do warrant closer attention. The first is that scientific management inevitably results in standardization of highly divided jobs and thus reinforces the negative effects of excessive division of labour previously mentioned. Second, scientific management formalizes the separation of the judgemental, planning and skilled tasks, which are done by 'management', from the routine, standardized and low-skill tasks, which are left for 'operators'. Such a separation, at the very least, deprives the majority of staff of an opportunity to contribute in a meaningful way to their jobs (and, incidentally, deprives the organization of their contribution). Both of these themes in the criticisms of scientific management lead to the same point: that the jobs designed under strict scientific management principles lead to low motivation among staff, frustration at the lack of control over their work, and alienation from the job.

Designing the human interface – ergonomic workplace design

Ergonomics

Ergonomics is concerned primarily with the physiological aspects of job design. Physiology is about the way the body functions. It involves two aspects: first, how a person interfaces with his or her immediate working area, second, how people react to environmental conditions. We will examine the second aspect of ergonomics later in this chapter. Ergonomics is sometimes referred to as **human factors** engineering or just 'human factors'. Both aspects are linked by two common ideas:

Human factors

- There must be a fit between people and the jobs they do. To achieve this fit there are only two alternatives. Either the job can be made to fit the people who are doing it, or, alternatively, the people can be made (or perhaps less radically, recruited) to fit the job. Ergonomics addresses the former alternative.
- It is important to take a 'scientific' approach to job design, for example collecting data to indicate how people react under different job design conditions and trying to find the best set of conditions for comfort and performance.

Anthropometric aspects

Many ergonomic improvements are primarily concerned with what are called the anthropometric aspects of jobs – that is, the aspects related to people's size, shape and other physical abilities. The design of an assembly task, for example, should be governed partly by the size and strength of the operators who do the job. The data which ergonomists use when doing this is called **anthropometric data**. Because we all vary in our size and capabilities, ergonomists are particularly interested in our range of capabilities, which is why anthropometric data is usually expressed in percentile terms. Figure 9.6 illustrates this idea. This shows the idea of size (in this case height) variation. Only 5 per cent of the population are smaller than the person on the extreme left (5th percentile), whereas 95 per cent of the population are smaller than the person on the extreme right (95th percentile). When this principle is applied to other dimensions of the body, for example arm length, it can be used to design work areas. Figure 9.6 also shows the normal and maximum work areas derived from anthropometric data. It would be inadvisable, for example, to place frequently used components or tools outside the maximum work area derived from the 5th percentile dimensions of human reach.

Anthropometric data

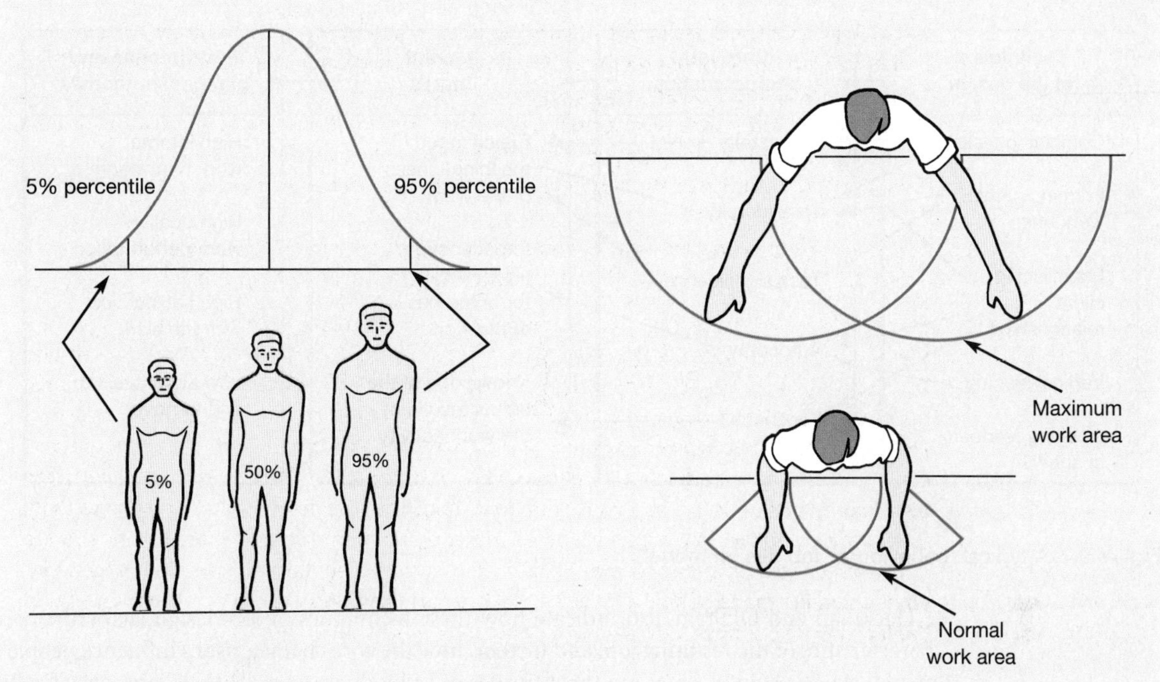

Figure 9.6 The use of anthropometric data in job design

Designing for job commitment – behavioural approaches to job design

Behavioural approach

Jobs which are designed purely on division of labour, scientific management or even purely ergonomic principles can alienate the people performing them. Job design should also take into account the desire of individuals to fulfil their needs for self-esteem and personal development. This is where motivation theory and its contribution to the **behavioural approach** to job design is important. This achieves two important objectives of job design. First, it provides jobs which have an intrinsically higher quality of working life – an ethically desirable end in itself. Second, because of the higher levels of motivation it engenders, it is instrumental in achieving better performance for the operation, in terms of both the quality and the quantity of output.[9] This approach to job design involves two conceptual steps: first, exploring how the various characteristics of the job affect people's motivation; second, exploring how individuals' motivation towards the job affects their performance at that job.

Typical of the models which underlie this approach to job design is that by Hackman and Oldham shown in Figure 9.7.[9] Here a number of 'techniques' of job design are recommended in order to affect particular core 'characteristics' of the job. These core characteristics of the job are held to influence various positive 'mental states' towards the job. In turn, these are assumed to give certain performance outcomes. In Figure 9.7 some of the 'techniques' (which Hackman and Oldham originally called 'implementing concepts') need a little further explanation:

- Combining tasks means increasing the number of activities allocated to individuals.
- Forming natural work units means putting together activities which make a coherent whole.
- Establishing client relationships means that staff make contact with their internal customers directly.
- Vertical loading means including 'indirect' activities (such as maintenance).
- Opening feedback channels means that internal customers feed back perceptions directly.

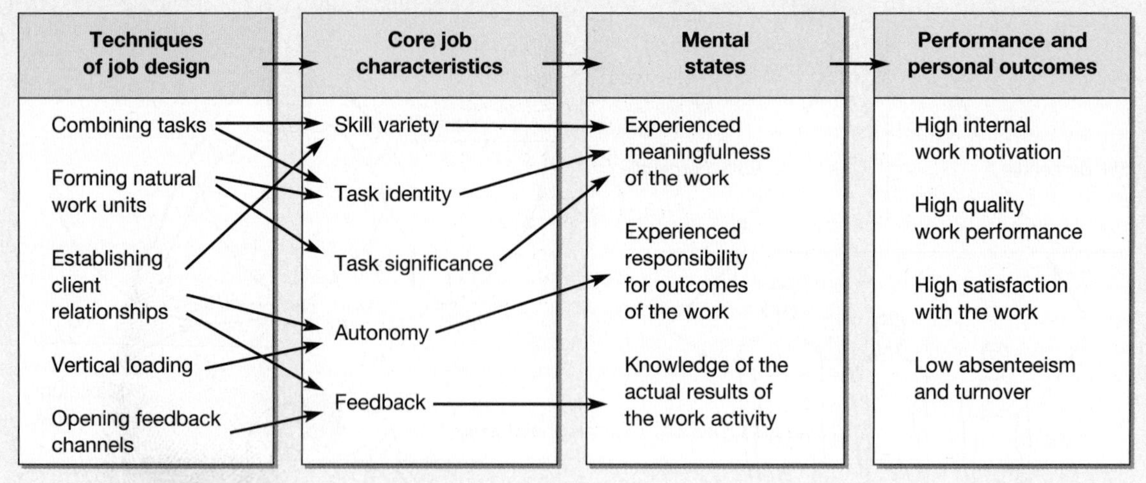

Figure 9.7 A typical 'behavioural' job design model

Hackman and Oldham also indicate how these techniques of job design shape the core characteristics of the resulting job, and further, how the core characteristics influence people's 'mental states'. Mental states are the attitudes of individuals towards their jobs, specifically, how meaningful they find the job, how much responsibility and control they feel they have over the way the job is done, and how much they understand about the results of their efforts. All of these mental states influence people's performance at their job in terms of their motivation, quality of work, satisfaction with their work, turnover and absenteeism.

Job rotation

Job rotation

If increasing the number of related tasks in the job is constrained in some way, for example by the technology of the process, one approach may be to encourage **job rotation**. This means moving individuals periodically between different sets of tasks to provide some variety in their activities. When successful, job rotation can increase skill flexibility and make a small contribution to reducing monotony. However, it is not viewed as universally beneficial either by management (because it can disrupt the smooth flow of work) or by the people performing the jobs (because it can interfere with their rhythm of work).

Job enlargement

Job enlargement

The most obvious method of achieving at least some of the objectives of behavioural job design is by allocating a larger number of tasks to individuals. If these extra tasks are broadly of the same type as those in the original job, the change is called **job enlargement**. This may not involve more demanding or fulfilling tasks, but it may provide a more complete and therefore slightly more meaningful job. If nothing else, people performing an enlarged job will not repeat themselves as often, which could make the job marginally less monotonous. So, for example, suppose that the manufacture of a product has traditionally been split up on an assembly-line basis into 10 equal and sequential jobs. If that job is then redesigned so as to form two parallel assembly lines of five people, the output from the system as a whole would be maintained but each operator would have twice the number of tasks to perform. This is job enlargement. Operators repeat themselves less frequently and presumably the variety of tasks is greater, although no further responsibility or autonomy is necessarily given to each operator.

Job enrichment

Job enrichment

Job enrichment, not only means increasing the number of tasks, but also allocating extra tasks which involve more decision making, greater autonomy and greater control over the job. For example, the extra tasks could include maintenance, planning and control, or monitoring

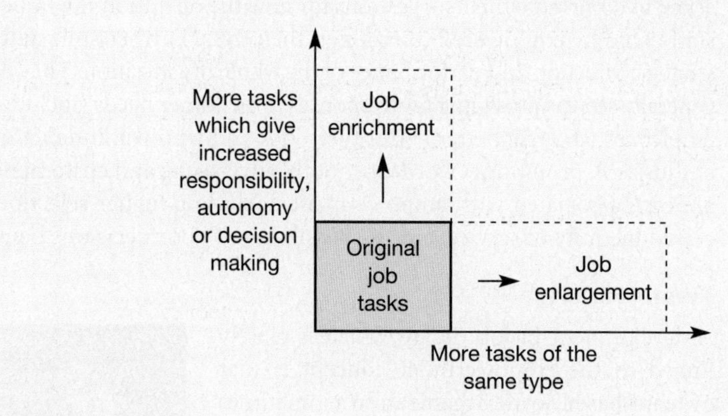

Figure 9.8 Job enlargement and job enrichment

quality levels. The effect is both to reduce repetition in the job and to increase autonomy and personal development. So, in the assembly-line example, each operator, as well as being allocated a job which is twice as long as that previously performed could also be allocated responsibility for carrying out routine maintenance and such tasks as record-keeping and managing the supply of materials. Figure 9.8 illustrates the difference between what are called 'horizontal' and 'vertical' changes. Broadly, horizontal changes are those which extend the variety of *similar* tasks assigned to a particular job. Vertical job changes are those which add responsibilities, decision making or autonomy to the job. Job enlargement implies movement only in the horizontal scale, whereas job enrichment certainly implies movement on the vertical scale and perhaps on both scales.

Short case
McDonald's lets families share job

Source: Corbis/Reuters

In what was thought to be the first contract of its type in the UK, McDonald's the quick-service restaurant chain, announced in 2005 that it was to allow family members to cover each other's jobs. Under the deal members of the same family working in the same outlet would be able to work each other's shifts without giving any prior notice or getting a manager's permission. The company said that it hoped the contracts would, *'encourage people to become fully trained and fully rotatable'*. But that the main aim was to, *'cut absenteeism and improve staff retention'*. *'It's great'*, said one McDonald's employee, *'Depending on how we feel in a morning, we decide which one of us wants to go in and work.'* Although the scheme is currently limited to family members only, McDonald's said that they might consider extending it to cover friends who work at the same restaurant.

Empowerment

Empowerment

Empowerment is an extension of the *autonomy* job characteristic prominent in the behavioural approach to job design. However, it is usually taken to mean more than autonomy. Whereas autonomy means giving staff the *ability* to change how they do their jobs, empowerment means giving staff the *authority* to make changes to the job itself, as well as how it is performed. This can be designed into jobs to different degrees.[10] At a minimum, staff could be asked to contribute their suggestions for how the operation might be improved. Going further, staff could be empowered to redesign their jobs. Further still, staff could be included in the strategic direction and performance of the whole organization. The *benefits* of empowerment are generally seen as providing fast responses to customer needs (including dissatisfied customers), employees who feel better about their jobs and who will interact with customers with more enthusiasm, promoting 'word-of-mouth' advertising and customer retention. However, there are *costs* associated with empowerment, including higher selection and training costs, perceived inequity of service and the possibility of poor decisions being made by employees.

Team-working

Team-based work organization

A development in job design which is closely linked to the empowerment concept is that of **team-based work organization** (sometimes called self-managed work teams). This is where staff, often with overlapping skills, collectively perform a defined task and have a high degree of discretion over how they actually perform the task. The team would typically control such things as task allocation between members, scheduling work, quality measurement and improvement, and sometimes the hiring of staff. To some extent most work has always been a group-based activity. The concept of teamwork, however, is more prescriptive and assumes a shared set of objectives and responsibilities. Groups are described as teams when the virtues of working together are being emphasized, such as the ability to make use of the various skills within the team. Teams may also be used to compensate for other organizational changes such as the move towards flatter organizational structures. When organizations have fewer managerial levels, each manager will have a wider span of activities to control. Teams which are capable of autonomous decision-making have a clear advantage in these circumstances. The benefits of teamwork can be summarized as:

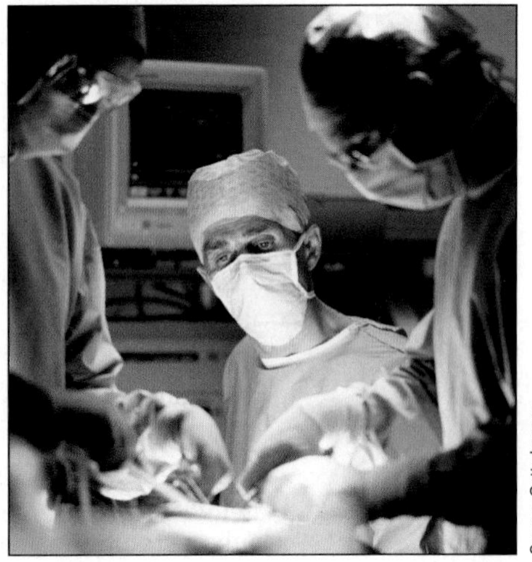

Source: Getty Images

- improving productivity through enhanced motivation and flexibility;
- improving quality and encouraging innovation;
- increasing satisfaction by allowing individuals to contribute more effectively;
- making it easier to implement technological changes in the workplace because teams are willing to share the challenges this brings.

Critical commentary

Teamwork is not only difficult to implement successfully, but it can also place undue stress on the individuals who form the teams. Some teams are formed because more radical solutions, such as total reorganization, are being avoided. Teams cannot compensate for badly designed organizational processes; nor can they substitute for management's responsibility to define how decisions should be made. Often teams are asked to make decisions but are given insufficient responsibility to carry them out. In other cases, teams may provide results, but at a price. The Swedish car maker Volvo introduced self-governing teams in the 1970s and 1980s which improved motivation and morale but eventually proved prohibitively expensive. Perhaps most seriously, teamwork is criticized for substituting one sort of pressure for another. Although teams may be autonomous, this does not mean they are stress-free. Top-down managerial control is often replaced by excessive peer pressure which is in some ways more insidious.

Flexible working

The nature of most jobs has changed significantly over the last 25 years. New technologies, more dynamic marketplaces, more demanding customers and a changed understanding of how individuals can contribute to competitive success have all had their impact. Also changing is our understanding of how home life, work and social life need to be balanced. Alternative forms of organization and alternative attitudes to work are being sought which allow, and encourage, a degree of flexibility in working practice which matches the need for flexibility in the marketplace. From an operations management perspective, three aspects of flexible working are significant: skills flexibility, time flexibility and location flexibility.

Multi-skilling

Skills flexibility. A flexible workforce that can move across several different jobs, could be deployed (or deploy themselves) in whatever activity is in demand at the time. In the short term staff at a supermarket may be moved from warehouse activities to shelf replenishment in the store to the checkout, depending on what is needed at the time. In the longer-term sense, **multi-skilling** means being able to migrate individuals from one skill set to another as longer-term demand trends become obvious. So, for example, an engineer who at one time maintained complex equipment by visiting the sites where such equipment was installed may now perform most of his or her activities by using remote computer diagnostics and 'helpline' assistance. The implication of job flexibility is that a greater emphasis must be placed on training, learning and knowledge management. Defining what knowledge and experience are required to perform particular tasks and translating these into training activities are clearly prerequisites for effective multi-skilling.

Flexi-time working

Annual hours

Time flexibility. Not every individual wants to work full-time. Many people, often because of family responsibilities, only want to work for part of their time, sometimes only during specific parts of the day or week (because of childcare responsibilities, etc.). Likewise, employers may not require the same number of staff at all times. They may, for example, need extra staff only at periods of heavy demand. Bringing both the supply of staff and the demand for their work together is the objective of 'flexible time' or **flexi-time working** systems. These may define a core working time for each individual member of staff and allow other times to be accumulated flexibly. Other schemes include **annual hours** schemes, one solution to the capacity management issue described in Chapter 11.

Teleworking

Location flexibility. The sectoral balance of employment has changed. The service sector in most developed economies now accounts for between 70 and 80 per cent of all employment. Even within the manufacturing sector, the proportion of people with indirect jobs (those not directly engaged in making products) has also increased significantly. One result of all this is that the number of jobs which are not 'location-specific' has increased. Location-specific means that a job must take place in one fixed location. So a shop worker must work in a shop and an assembly line worker must work on the assembly line. But many jobs could be performed at any location where there are communication links to the rest of the organization. The realization of this has given rise to what is known as **teleworking**, which is also known as 'using alternative workplaces' (AW), 'flexible working', 'home working', 'mobile working' and 'creating the virtual office'.

Critical commentary

There is always a big difference between what is technically possible and what is organizationally feasible. Mobile working does have its problems. In particular, those types that deny individuals the chance to meet with colleagues often face difficulties. Problems can include the following:

- *Lack of socialization* – offices are social places where people can adopt the culture of an organization as well as learn from each other. It is naïve to think that all knowledge can be codified and learnt formally at a distance.

→

- *Effectiveness of communication* – a large part of the essential communication we have with our colleagues is unplanned and face-to-face. It happens on 'chance meet' occasions, yet it is important in spreading contextual information as well as establishing specific pieces of information necessary to the job.
- *Problem-solving* – it is still often more efficient and effective informally to ask a colleague for help in resolving problems than formally to frame a request using communications technology.
- *It is lonely* – isolation amongst mobile or home workers is a real problem. For many of us, the workplace provides the main focus for social interaction. A computer screen is no substitute.

Short case

Flexible working at Lloyds TSB[11]

Source: Rex Features

Not too long ago in many organizations, employees were expected to work fixed hours. There was a fixed start time; miss it and you were late, and subject to some form of penalty. There was a fixed finish time; why would anyone want to work later than this 'for free'. And although there are some places where the vestiges of this attitude remain, many enterprises now understand the benefits of taking a more flexible attitude. Amongst the first large organizations to take flexible working seriously in Europe was Lloyds TSB Group, one of the UK's biggest banking groups, employing over 66,000 people worldwide and serving more than 16 million customers. The Group was prompted to take up flexible working because it was sensitive to the social and economic changes that were affecting, not only its customers, but its staff as well. People's lives were becoming more complex. There seemed to be clear benefits of adapting work patterns so they reflected its staff's needs and constraints and yet still offered the best quality and quantity of service to its customers. Recruiting and keeping talented and committed people, wanting to build a career in the Group, meant understanding and implementing the right balance between staff's individual needs, the business's requirement to control the costs of delivering service, and the customers' expectation of excellent service. So, to further its interest in flexible working, the Group researched its employees' views. The results showed that one of their main issues was trying to balance a demanding job with outside commitments, such as family and leisure. In response the Group introduced its flexible working policy. Called 'Work Options', it allowed staff to reconfigure their working activities by requesting a different working pattern from the conventional working day. This can be done in several ways. Sometimes it may simply involve starting and finishing earlier or later each day, while maintaining the same weekly hours. This could allow for other commitments such as childcare activities, or simply cater for working preferences. Also it could benefit the business. Customer demand does not necessarily follow a traditional working day. Varying staff work patterns could mean staffing is more closely aligned with actual customer demand. The business may also be able to extend staff without paying overtime premiums.

Job sharing is also used, where two members of staff share one job role. It suits the two staff, who may not want full-time employment, and the business can have two people's combined experience, skills and creativity. Job-sharing staff can also be more productive than full-time colleagues. As one Customer Service Manager at Lloyds TSB says, *'We have job-shared for nine years now. We cover a full working week between us with handover meetings every Tuesday morning. We talk about any issues that have arisen. We are very different characters and react in completely different ways to problems. However, we find our skills complement each other well. The bank benefits because it wouldn't get this from just one person.'* Another form of flexible working is 'compressed working', which allows staff to work a standard one or two weeks within a shorter timescale, for example by working more days a week, then taking extra time off to compensate. For example: *'I have worked a compressed week for five years. This means I can pursue the two hobbies I love, scuba diving and genealogy. I feel motivated, enthused and energized about my role in Lloyds TSB. I take my non-working day when it suits both me and the branch. My manager knows I will get the job done. It has transformed my work and my non-work life!'*

Working from home may also be an option. A Process Designer in Group Operations says: *'I have two children and my husband is self-employed. I work from home five days a week. I have been able to continue my career with the bank and deliver 100% commitment.'*

To some extent, the introduction of flexible working has been motivated by demographic and social changes. There are also increasing regulatory and legal requirements promoting working flexibility in some parts of the world. However, Lloyds TSB believes its ability to deal effectively with the need for flexibility makes good business sense. It helps to bolster its reputation as an employer of choice, and allows it to deliver differentiated levels of service; customers can deal with a skilled, friendly and enthusiastic member of staff, and the best staff are more likely to stay.

Designing the working environment – ergonomics

Source: Getty Images

One aspect of ergonomics is concerned with how a person interfaces with the physical aspects of his or her immediate working area, such as its dimensions; we examined this earlier. Here we look at how people interface with their working environment. By this we mean the temperature, lighting, noise environment, and so on. The immediate environment in which jobs take place will influence the way they are performed. Working conditions which are too hot or too cold, insufficiently illuminated or glaringly bright, excessively noisy or irritatingly silent, will all influence the way jobs are carried out. Many of these issues are often covered by **occupational health and safety** legislation which controls environmental conditions in workplaces throughout the world. A thorough understanding of this aspect of ergonomics is necessary to work within the guidelines of such legislation.

Occupational health and safety

Working temperature

Predicting the reactions of individuals to working temperature is not straightforward. Individuals vary in the way their performance and comfort vary with temperature. Furthermore, most of us judging 'temperature' will also be influenced by other factors such as humidity and air movement. Nevertheless, some general points regarding working temperatures provide guidance to job designers:[12]

- Comfortable temperature range will depend on the type of work being carried out, lighter work requiring higher temperatures than heavier work.
- The effectiveness of people at performing vigilance tasks reduces at temperatures above about 29 °C; the equivalent temperature for people performing light manual tasks is a little lower.
- The chances of accidents occurring increase at temperatures which are above or below the comfortable range for the work involved.

Illumination levels

The intensity of lighting required to perform any job satisfactorily will depend on the nature of the job. Some jobs which involve extremely delicate and precise movement, surgery for example, require very high levels of illumination. Other, less delicate jobs do not require such high levels. Table 9.3 shows the recommended illumination levels (measured in lux) for a range of activities.

Table 9.3 Examples of recommended lighting levels for various activities[2]

Activity	*Illuminance (lx)*
Normal activities in the home, general lighting	50
Furnace rooms in glass factory	150
General office work	500
Motor vehicle assembly	500
Proofreading	750
Colour matching in paint factory	1,000
Electronic assembly	1,000
Close inspection of knitwear	1,500
Engineering testing inspection using small instruments	3,000
Watchmaking and fine jewellery manufacture	3,000
Surgery, local lighting	10,000–50,000

Table 9.4 Noise levels for various activities

Noise	*Decibels (dB)*
Quiet speech	40
Light traffic at 25 metres	50
Large busy office	60
Busy street, heavy traffic	70
Pneumatic drill at 20 metres	80
Textile factory	90
Circular saw – close work	100
Riveting machine – close work	110
Jet aircraft taking off at 100 metres	120

Noise levels

The damaging effects of excessive noise levels are perhaps easier to understand than some other environmental factors. Noise-induced hearing loss is a well-documented consequence of working environments where noise is not kept below safe limits. The noise levels of various activities are shown in Table 9.4. When reading this list, bear in mind that the recommended (and often legal) maximum noise level to which people can be subjected over the working day is 90 decibels (dB) in the UK (although in some parts of the world the legal level is lower than this). Also bear in mind that the decibel unit of noise is based on a logarithmic scale, which means that noise intensity doubles about every 3 dB. In addition to the damaging effects of high levels of noise, intermittent and high-frequency noise can also affect work performance at far lower levels, especially on tasks requiring attention and judgement.[3]

Ergonomics in the office

As the number of people working in offices (or office-like workplaces) has increased, ergonomic principles have been applied increasingly to this type of work. At the same time, legislation has been moving to cover office technology such as computer screens and keyboards. For example, European Union directives on working with display screen equipment require organizations to assess all workstations to reduce the risks inherent in their use, plan work times for breaks and changes in activity and provide information and training for users. Figure 9.9 illustrates some of the ergonomic factors which should be taken into account when designing office jobs.

Allocate work times

Without some estimate of how long it takes to complete an activity, it would not be possible to know how much work to allocate to teams or individuals, to know when a task will be completed, to know how much it costs, to know if work is progressing according

Figure 9.9 Ergonomics in the office environment

to schedule, and many other vital pieces of information that are needed to manage any operation. Without some estimate of work times, operations managers are 'flying blind'. At the same time it does not need much thought before it becomes clear that measuring work times must be difficult to do with any degree of accuracy or confidence. The time you take to do any task will depend on how skilled you are at the task, how much experience you have, how energetic or motivated you are, whether you have the appropriate tools, what the environmental conditions are, how tired you are, and so on. So, at best, any 'measurement' of how long a task will, or should, take, will be an estimate. It will be our 'best guess' of how much time to allow for the task. That is why we call this process of estimating work times 'work time allocation'. We are allocating a time for completing a task because we need to do so for many important operations management decisions. For example, work times are needed for:

- Planning how much work a process can perform (its capacity).
- Deciding how many staff are needed to complete tasks.
- Scheduling individual tasks to specific people.
- Balancing work allocation in processes (see Chapter 7).
- Costing the labour content of a product or service.
- Estimating the efficiency or productivity of staff and/or processes.
- Calculating bonus payments (less important than it was at one time).

Notwithstanding the weak theoretical basis of work measurement, understanding the relationship between work and time is clearly an important part of job design. The advantage of structured and systematic work measurement is that it gives a common currency for the evaluation and comparison of all types of work. So, if work time allocation is important, how should it be done? In fact, there is a long-standing body of knowledge and experience in this area. This is generally referred to as '**work measurement**', although as we have said,

Work measurement

'measurement' could be regarded as indicating a somewhat spurious degree of accuracy. Formally, work measurement is defined as 'the process of establishing the time for a **qualified worker**, at a **defined level of performance**, to carry out a **specified job**'. Although not a precise definition, generally it is agreed that a *specified job* is one for which specifications have been established to define most aspects of the job. A *qualified worker* is 'one who is accepted as having the necessary physical attributes, intelligence, skill, education and knowledge to perform the task to satisfactory standards of safety, quality and quantity'. **Standard performance** is 'the rate of output which qualified workers will achieve without over-exertion as an average over the working day provided they are motivated to apply themselves to their work'.

Qualified worker

Defined level of performance

Specified job

Standard performance

The techniques of work measurement

At one time, work measurement was firmly associated with an image of the 'efficiency expert', 'time and motion' man or 'rate fixer', who wandered around factories with a stopwatch, looking to save a few cents or pennies. And although that idea of work measurement has (almost) died out, the use of a stopwatch to establish a basic time for a job is still relevant, and used in a technique called 'time study'. Time study and the general topic of work measurement are treated in the supplement to this chapter – work study.

As well as time study, there are other work measurement techniques in use. They include the following.

- **Synthesis from elemental data** is a work measurement technique for building up the time for a job at a defined level of performance by totalling element times obtained previously from the studies in other jobs containing the elements concerned or from synthetic data.
- **Predetermined motion-time systems (PMTS)** is a work measurement technique whereby times established for basic human motions (classified according to the nature of the motion and the conditions under which it is made) are used to build up the time for a job at a defined level of performance.
- **Analytical estimating** is a work measurement technique which is a development of estimating whereby the time required to carry out the elements of a job at a defined level of performance is estimated from knowledge and experience of the elements concerned.
- **Activity sampling** is a technique in which a large number of instantaneous observations are made over a period of time of a group of machines, processes or workers. Each observation records what is happening at that instant and the percentage of observations recorded for a particular activity or delay is a measure of the percentage of time during which that activity or delay occurs.

Synthesis from elemental data

Predetermined motion-time systems

Analytical estimating

Activity sampling

Critical commentary

The criticisms aimed at work measurement are many and various. Amongst the most common are the following:

- All the ideas on which the concept of a standard time is based are impossible to define precisely. How can one possibly give clarity to the definition of qualified workers, or specified jobs, or especially a defined level of performance?
- Even if one attempts to follow these definitions, all that results is an excessively rigid job definition. Most modern jobs require some element of flexibility, which is difficult to achieve alongside rigidly defined jobs.
- Using stopwatches to time human beings is both degrading and usually counter-productive. At best it is intrusive, at worst it makes people into 'objects for study'.
- The rating procedure implicit in time study is subjective and usually arbitrary. It has no basis other than the opinion of the person carrying out the study.
- Time study, especially, is very easy to manipulate. It is possible for employers to 'work back' from a time which is 'required' to achieve a particular cost. Also, experienced staff can 'put on an act' to fool the person recording the times.

Summary answers to key questions

Check and improve your understanding of this chapter using self assessment questions and a personalised study plan, audio and video downloads, and an eBook – all at ***www.myomlab.com****.*

➤ Why are people issues so important in operations management?

- Human resources are any organization's and therefore any operation's greatest asset. Often, most 'human resources' are to be found in the operations function.

➤ How do operations managers contribute to human resource strategy?

- Human resource strategy is the overall long-term approach to ensuring that an organization's human resources provide a strategic advantage. It involves identifying the number and type of people that are needed to manage, run and develop the organization so that it meets its strategic business objectives, and putting in place the programmes and initiatives that attract, develop and retain appropriate staff. It involves being a strategic partner, an administrative expert, an employee champion and a change agent.

➤ What forms can organization designs take?

- One can take various perspectives on organizations. How we illustrate organizations says much about our underlying assumptions of what an 'organization' is. For example, organizations can be described as machines, organisms, brains, cultures or political systems.
- There are an almost infinite number of possible organizational structures. Most are blends of two or more 'pure types', such as
  - The U-form
  - The M-form
  - Matrix forms
  - The N-form.

➤ How do we go about designing jobs?

- There are many influences on how jobs are designed. These include the following:
  - the division of labour
  - scientific management
  - method study
  - work measurement
  - ergonomics
  - behavioural approaches, including job rotation, job enlargement and job enrichment
  - empowerment
  - team-working, and
  - flexible working.

➤ How are work times allocated?

- The best-known method is time study, but there are other work measurement techniques, including:
  - Synthesis from elemental data
  - Predetermined motion-time systems (PMTS)
  - Analytical estimating
  - Activity sampling.

Case study
Service Adhesives tries again[13]

By Dr Ran Bhamra, Lecturer in Engineering Management, Loughborough University.

'I'm not sure why we've never succeeded in really getting an improvement initiative to take hold in this company. It isn't that we haven't been trying. TQM, Lean, even a limited attempt to adopt Six Sigma; we've tried them all. I guess that we just haven't yet found the right approach that fits us. That is why we're quite excited about what we saw at Happy Products' (James Broadstone, Operations Director, Service Adhesives Limited).

Service Adhesives Ltd was a mid-sized company founded over twenty years ago to produce specialist adhesives, mainly used in the fast-moving consumer goods (FMCG) business, where any adhesive had to be guaranteed 'non-irritating' (for example in personal care products) and definitely 'non-toxic' (for example in food-based products). Largely because of its patented adhesive formulation, and its outstanding record in developing new adhesive products, it has always been profitable. Yet, although its sales revenue had continued to rise, the last few years had seen a slowdown in the company's profit margins. According to Service Adhesives senior management there were two reasons for this: first, production costs were rising more rapidly than sales revenues, second, product quality, while acceptable, was no longer significantly better than competitors'. These issues had been recognized by senior management for a number of years and several improvement initiatives, focusing on product quality and process improvement, had attempted to reverse their declining position relative to competitors. However, none of the initiatives had fully taken hold and delivered as promised.

In recent years, Service Adhesives Ltd had tried to embrace a number of initiatives and modern operations philosophies such as TQM (Total Quality Management) and Lean; all had proved disappointing, with little resulting change within the business. It was never clear why these steps towards modern ways of working had not been successful. Some senior management viewed the staff as being of 'below-average' skills and motivation, and very reluctant to change. There was a relatively high staff turnover rate and the company had recently started employing short-term contract labour as an answer to controlling its fluctuating orders. The majority of the short-term staff were from eastern European Union member states such as Poland and the Czech Republic and accounted for almost 20% of the total shop-floor personnel. There had been some issues with temporary staff not adhering to quality procedures or referring to written material, all of which was written in English. Despite this, the company's management saw the use of migrant labour as largely positive: they were hard-working and provided an opportunity to save costs. However, there had been some tension between temporary and permanent employees over what was seen as a perceived threat to their jobs.

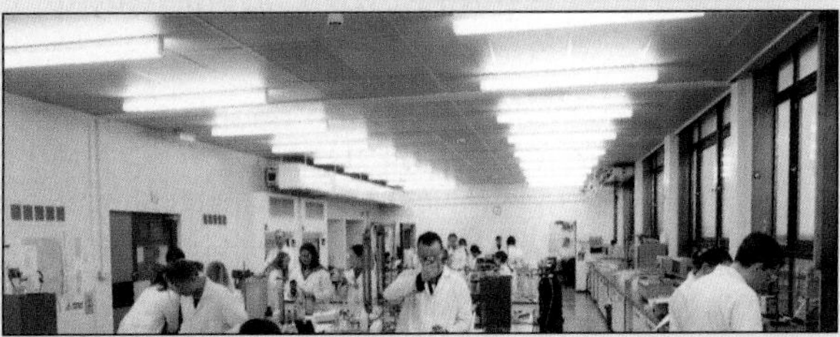

James Broadstone, the Operations Director of Service Adhesives, was particularly concerned about the failure of their improvement initiatives and organized a number of visits to other companies with similar profiles and also to a couple of Service Adhesives, customers. It was a visit to one of their larger customers, called (bizarrely) 'Happy Products' that had particularly enthused the senior management team. *'It was like entering another world. Their processes are different from ours, but not that different. But their plant was cleaner, the flow of materials seemed smoother, their staff seemed purposeful, and above all, it seemed efficient and a happy place to work. Everybody really did work as a team. I think we have a lot to learn from them. I'm sure that a team-based approach could be implemented just as successfully in our plant'* (James Broadstone).

Happy Products were a global company and the market leaders in their field. And although their various plants in different parts of the world had slightly different approaches to how they organized their production operations, the group as a whole had a reputation for excellent human resource management. The plant visited by Service Adhesives was in the third year of a five-year programme to introduce and embed a team-based work structure and culture. It had won the coveted international 'Best Plant in Division' award twice within three years. The clear driver of this success had been identified by the award-judging panel as its implementation of a team-based work structure. The Happy Products plant operated a three-shift system over a 24/7 operation cycle making diapers (nappies) and health-care products and was organized into three distinct product areas, each containing at least two production lines utilizing highly complex technology. Each production line was staffed by five operators (with additional support staff serving the whole plant). One operator was a team leader responsible for 'first-line management'. A second operator was a specially trained health and safety representative. A third was a trained quality representative who also liaised with the Quality Department. A fourth operator was a trained maintenance engineer, while a fifth was a non-specialist, 'floating' operator. The team had support from the production process engineering, quality and logistics departments.

Most problems encountered in the day-to-day operation of the line could be dealt with immediately, on the line. This ensured that production output, product quality and line efficiency were controlled exceptionally well. Individual team roles enabled team members to contribute and take great satisfaction in the knowledge that they played a key part in the success of the organization. The team specialist roles also gave the opportunity for networking with counterparts in other plants across the world. This international communication was encouraged and added to the sense of belonging and organizational goal orientation. Teams were also involved in determining annual performance targets for their specific areas. Annually, corporate strategy identified business direction, and developed performance requirements for each business division which, in turn, filtered down to individual plants. Plants devised strategic targets for their sections and the teams themselves created a list of projects and activities to meet (and hopefully exceed) targets. In this way the individual operator on the shop floor had direct influence over their future and the future of their business.

So impressed were Service Adhesives with what they perceived to be a world-class operation, that they decided that they should also consider following a similar path towards a team-based work organization. They were obviously missing the organizational 'cohesiveness' that their customer seemed to be demonstrating. Until that time, however, the management at Service Adhesives Ltd had prided themselves on their traditional, hierarchical organization structure. The organization had five layers of operational management from the plant director at the top to the shop floor operatives at the bottom. The chain of command was strictly enforced by operating procedures entwined with their long-established and comprehensive quality assurance system. Now, it seemed, a very different approach was needed. '*We are very interested in learning from the visit. We have to change the way we work and make some radical improvements to our organization's operational effectiveness. I have come to believe that we have fallen behind in our thinking. A new kind of organizational culture is needed for these challenging times and we must respond by learning from the best practice that we can find. We also must be seen by our customers as forward thinking. We have to prove that we are in the same league as the "big boys"*' (James Broadstone).

At the next top team meeting, Service formally committed itself to adopting a 'team-based organizational structure' with the aim of 'establishing a culture of improvement and operational excellence'.

Questions

1 Service Adhesives Ltd currently employs up to 20% of their workforce on short-term contracts. What effect will this have on the proposed team-based working structure?

2 In considering a transition from a traditional organizational work structure to a team-based work structure, what sort of barriers are Service Adhesives Ltd likely to encounter? Think about formal structures (e.g. roles and procedures) and informal structures (e.g. social groups and communication).

3 Senior management of Service Adhesives thought that the reason for ineffective improvement initiatives in the past was due mainly to the apparent lack of cohesion amongst the organization's human resource. Could a team-based work organization be the answer to their organizational difficulties? Why do think that previous initiatives at Super Supply had failed?

4 Employee empowerment is a key element of team-based working; what difficulties could Service Adhesives face in implementing empowerment?

Problems and applications

*These problems and applications will help to improve your analysis of operations. You can find more practice problems as well as worked examples and guided solutions on MyOMLab at **www.myomlab.com**.*

1 A hotel has two wings, an east wing and a west wing. Each wing has 4 'room service maids' working 7-hour shifts to service the rooms each day. The east wing has 40 standard rooms, 12 de luxe rooms and 5 suites. The west wing has 50 standard rooms and 10 de luxe rooms. The standard times for servicing rooms are as follows: standard rooms 20 standard minutes, de luxe rooms 25 standard minutes, and suites 40 standard minutes. In addition, an allowance of 5 standard minutes per room is given for any miscellaneous jobs such as collecting extra items for the room or dealing with customer requests. What is the productivity of the maids in each wing of the hotel? What other factors might also influence the productivity of the maids?

2 In the example above, one of the maids in the west wing wants to job-share with his partner, each working 3 hours per day. His colleagues have agreed to support him and will guarantee to service all the rooms in the west wing to the same standard each day. If they succeed in doing this, how has it affected their productivity?

3 *Step 1* – Make a sandwich (any type of sandwich, preferably one that you enjoy) and document the task you have to perform in order to complete the job. Make sure you include all the activities including the movement of materials (bread etc.) to and from the work surface.

Step 2 – So impressed were your friends with the general appearance of your sandwich that they have persuaded you to make one each for them every day. You have ten friends so every morning you must make ten identical sandwiches (to stop squabbling). How would you change the method by which you make the sandwiches to accommodate this higher volume?

Step 3 – The fame of your sandwiches had spread. You now decide to start a business making several different types of sandwich in high volume. Design the jobs of the two or three people who will help you in this venture. Assume that volumes run into at least 100 of three types of sandwich every day.

4 A little-known department of your local government authority has the responsibility for keeping the area's public lavatories clean. It employs ten people who each have a number of public lavatories that they visit and clean and report any necessary repairs every day. Draw up a list of ideas for how you would keep this fine body of people motivated and committed to performing this unpleasant task.

5 Visit a supermarket and observe the people who staff the checkouts.

(a) What kind of skills do people who do this job need to have?
(b) How many customers per hour are they capable of 'processing'?
(c) What opportunities exist for job enrichment in this activity?
(d) How would you ensure motivation and commitment amongst the staff who do this job?

Selected further reading

Apgar, M. (1998) The alternative workplace: changing where and how people work, *Harvard Business Review*, May–June. Interesting perspective on homeworking and teleworking amongst other things.

Argyris, C. (1998) Empowerment: the emperor's new clothes, *Harvard Business Review*, May–June. A critical but fascinating view of empowerment.

Bond, F.W. and Bunce, D. (2001) Job control mediates change in a work reorganization intervention for stress reduction, *Journal of Occupational Health Psychology*, vol. 6, 290–302.

Bridger, R. (2003) *Introduction to Ergonomics*, Taylor & Francis, London. Exactly what it says in the title, an introduction (but a good one) to ergonomics. A revised edition of a core textbook that gives a comprehensive introduction to ergonomics.

Hackman, R.J. and Oldham, G. (1980) *Work Redesign*, Addison-Wesley, Reading, Mass. Somewhat dated but, in its time, ground-breaking and certainly hugely influential.

Herzberg, F. (1987) One more time: how do you motivate employees? (with retrospective commentary), *Harvard Business Review*, vol. 65, no. 5. An interesting look back by one of the most influential figures in the behavioural approach to job design school.

Lantz, A. and Brav, A. (2007) Job design for learning in work groups, *Journal of Workplace Learning*, vol. 19, issue 5, 269–85.

Useful web sites

www.bpmi.org Site of the Business Process Management Initiative. Some good resources including papers and articles.

www.bptrends.com News site for trends in business process management generally. Some interesting articles.

www.bls.gov/oes/ US Department of Labor employment statistics.

www.fedee.com/hrtrends Federation of European Employers guide to employment and job trends in Europe.

www.waria.com A Workflow and Reengineering Association web site. Some useful topics.

www.opsman.org Lots of useful stuff.

Supplement to Chapter 9 Work study

Introduction

A tale is told of Frank Gilbreth (the founder of method study) addressing a scientific conference with a paper entitled 'The best way to get dressed in a morning'. In his presentation, he rather bemused the scientific audience by analysing the 'best' way of buttoning up one's waistcoat in the morning. Among his conclusions was that waistcoats should always be buttoned from the bottom upwards. (To make it easier to straighten his tie in the same motion; buttoning from the top downwards requires the hands to be raised again.) Think of this example if you want to understand scientific management and method study in particular. First of all, he is quite right. Method study and the other techniques of scientific management may often be without any intellectual or scientific validation, but by and large they work in their own terms. Second, Gilbreth reached his conclusion by a systematic and critical analysis of what motions were necessary to do the job. Again, these are characteristics of scientific management – detailed analysis and painstakingly systematic examination. Third (and possibly most important), the results are relatively trivial. A great deal of effort was put into reaching a conclusion that was unlikely to have any earth-shattering consequences. Indeed, one of the criticisms of scientific management, as developed in the early part of the twentieth century, is that it concentrated on relatively limited, and sometimes trivial, objectives.

The responsibility for its application, however, has moved away from specialist 'time and motion' staff to the employees who can use such principles to improve what they do and how they do it. Further, some of the methods and techniques of scientific management, as opposed to its philosophy (especially those which come under the general heading of 'method study'), can in practice prove useful in critically re-examining job designs. It is the practicality of these techniques which possibly explains why they are still influential in job design almost a century after their inception.

Method study in job design

Method study is a systematic approach to finding the best method. There are six steps:

1 Select the work to be studied.
2 Record all the relevant facts of the present method.
3 Examine those facts critically and in sequence.
4 Develop the most practical, economic and effective method.
5 Install the new method.
6 Maintain the method by periodically checking it in use.

Step 1 – Selecting the work to be studied

Most operations have many hundreds and possibly thousands of discrete jobs and activities which could be subjected to study. The first stage in method study is to select those jobs to be studied which will give the most return on the investment of the time spent studying them. This means it is unlikely that it will be worth studying activities which, for example, may soon be discontinued or are only performed occasionally. On the other hand, the types of job which should be studied as a matter of priority are those which, for example, seem to offer the greatest scope for improvement, or which are causing bottlenecks, delays or problems in the operation.

Step 2 – Recording the present method

There are many different recording techniques used in method study. Most of them:

- record the sequence of activities in the job;
- record the time interrelationship of the activities in the job; or
- record the path of movement of some part of the job.

Perhaps the most commonly used recording technique in method study is process mapping, which was discussed in Chapter 4. Note that we are here recording the present method of doing the job. It may seem strange to devote so much time and effort to recording what is currently happening when, after all, the objective of method study is to devise a better method. The rationale for this is, first of all, that recording the present method can give a far greater insight into the job itself, and this can lead to new ways of doing it. Second, recording the present method is a good starting point from which to evaluate it critically and therefore improve it. In this last point the assumption is that it is easier to improve the method by starting from the current method and then criticizing it in detail than by starting with a 'blank sheet of paper'.

Step 3 – Examining the facts

This is probably the most important stage in method study and the idea here is to examine the current method thoroughly and critically. This is often done by using the so-called 'questioning technique'. This technique attempts to detect weaknesses in the rationale for existing methods so that alternative methods can be developed (see Table S9.1). The approach

Table S9.1 The method study questioning technique

Broad question	*Detailed question*
The purpose of each activity (questions the fundamental need for the element)	What is done? Why is it done? What else could be done? What should be done?
The place in which each element is done (may suggest a combination of certain activities or operations)	Where is it done? Why is it done there? Where else could it be done? Where should it be done?
The sequence in which the elements are done (may suggest a change in the sequence of the activity)	When is it done? Why is it done then? When should it be done?
The person who does the activity (may suggest a combination and/or change in responsibility or sequence)	Who does it? Why does that person do it? Who else could do it? Who should do it?
The means by which each activity is done (may suggest new methods)	How is it done? Why is it done in that way? How else could it be done? How should it be done?

Table S9.2 The principles of motion economy

Broad principle	*How to do it*
Use the human body the way it works best	• Work should be arranged so that a natural rhythm can become automatic • Motion of the body should be simultaneous and symmetrical if possible • The full capabilities of the human body should be employed • Arms and hands as weights are subject to the physical laws and energy should be conserved • Tasks should be simplified
Arrange the workplace to assist performance	• There should be a defined place for all equipment and materials • Equipment, materials and controls should be located close to the point of use • Equipment, materials and controls should be located to permit the best sequence and path of motions • The workplace should be fitted both to the tasks and to human capabilities
Use technology to reduce human effort	• Work should be presented precisely where needed • Guides should assist in positioning the work without close operator attention • Controls and foot-operated devices can relieve the hands of work • Mechanical devices can multiply human abilities • Mechanical systems should be fitted to human use

Source: Adapted from Barnes, Frank C. (1983) Principles of motion economy: revisited, reviewed, and restored, *Proceedings of the Southern Management Association Annual Meeting* (Atlanta, GA 1983), p. 298.

may appear somewhat detailed and tedious, yet it is fundamental to the method study philosophy – everything must be critically examined. Understanding the natural tendency to be less than rigorous at this stage, some organizations use pro forma questionnaires, asking each of these questions and leaving space for formal replies and/or justifications, which the job designer is required to complete.

Step 4 – Developing a new method

The previous critical examination of current methods has by this stage probably indicated some changes and improvements. This step involves taking these ideas further in an attempt to:

- eliminate parts of the activity altogether;
- combine elements together;
- change the sequence of events so as to improve the efficiency of the job; or
- simplify the activity to reduce the work content.

Principles of motion economy

A useful aid during this process is a checklist such as the revised **principles of motion economy**. Table S9.2 illustrates these.

Steps 5 and 6 – Install the new method and regularly maintain it

The method study approach to the installation of new work practices concentrates largely on 'project managing' the installation process. It also emphasizes the need to monitor regularly the effectiveness of job designs after they have been installed.

Work measurement in job design

Basic times

Basic time

Terminology is important in work measurement. When a *qualified worker* is working on a *specified job* at *standard performance*, the time he or she takes to perform the job is called the **basic time** for the job. Basic times are useful because they are the 'building blocks' of time estimation. With the basic times for a range of different tasks, an operations manager can construct a time estimate for any longer activity which is made up of the tasks. The best-known technique for establishing basic times is probably time study.

Time study

Time study

Time study is, 'a work measurement technique for recording the times and rate of working for the elements of a specified job, carried out under specified conditions, and for analysing the data so as to obtain the time necessary for the carrying out of the job at a defined level of performance'. The technique takes three steps to derive the basic times for the elements of the job:

- observing and measuring the time taken to perform each element of the job;
- adjusting, or 'normalizing', each observed time;
- averaging the adjusted times to derive the basic time for the element.

Step 1 – Observing, measuring and rating

Rating

A job is observed through several cycles. Each time an element is performed, it is timed using a stopwatch. Simultaneously with the observation of time, a rating of the perceived performance of the person doing the job is recorded. **Rating** is, 'the process of assessing the worker's rate of working relative to the observer's concept of the rate corresponding to standard performance. The observer may take into account, separately or in combination, one or more factors necessary to carrying out the job, such as speed of movement, effort, dexterity, consistency, etc.' There are several ways of recording the observer's rating. The most common is on a scale which uses a rating of 100 to represent standard performance. If an observer rates a particular observation of the time to perform an element at 100, the time observed is the actual time which anyone working at standard performance would take.

Step 2 – Adjusting the observed times

The adjustment to normalize the observed time is:

$$\frac{\text{observed rating}}{\text{standard rating}}$$

where standard rating is 100 on the common rating scale we are using here. For example, if the observed time is 0.71 minute and the observed rating is 90, then:

$$\text{Basic time} = \frac{0.71 \times 90}{100} = 0.64 \text{ min}$$

Step 3 – Average the basic times

In spite of the adjustments made to the observed times through the rating mechanism, each separately calculated basic time will not be the same. This is not necessarily a function of inaccurate rating, or even the vagueness of the rating procedure itself; it is a natural phenomenon of the time taken to perform tasks. Any human activity cannot be repeated in *exactly* the same time on every occasion.

Standard times

Standard time

Allowances

The **standard time** for a job is an extension of the basic time and has a different use. Whereas the basic time for a job is a piece of information which can be used as the first step in estimating the time to perform a job under a wide range of conditions, standard time refers to the time *allowed* for the job under specific circumstances. This is because standard time includes **allowances** which reflect the rest and relaxation allowed because of the conditions under which the job is performed. So the standard time for each element consists principally of two parts, the basic time (the time taken by a qualified worker, doing a specified job at standard performance) and an allowance (this is added to the basic time to allow for rest, relaxation and personal needs).

Allowances

Allowances are additions to the basic time intended to provide the worker with the opportunity to recover from the physiological and psychological effects of carrying out specified work under specified conditions and to allow for personal needs. The amount of the allowance will depend on the nature of the job. The way in which relaxation allowance is calculated, and the exact allowances given for each of the factors which determine the extent of the allowance, vary between different organizations. Table S9.3 illustrates the allowance table used by one company which manufactures domestic appliances. Every job has an allowance of 10%; the table shows the further percentage allowances to be applied to each element of the job. In addition, other allowances may be applied for such things as unexpected contingencies, synchronization with other jobs, unusual working conditions, and so on.

Figure S9.1 shows how average basic times for each element in the job are combined with allowances (low in this example) for each element to build up the standard time for the whole job.

Table S9.3 An allowances table used by a domestic appliance manufacturer

Allowance factors	*Example*	*Allowance (%)*
Energy needed		
Negligible	none	0
Very light	0–3 kg	3
Light	3–10 kg	5
Medium	10–20 kg	10
Heavy	20–30 kg	15
Very heavy	Above 30 kg	15–30
Posture required		
Normal	Sitting	[illegible]
Erect	Standing	[illegible]
Continuously erect	Standing for long period[illegible]	[illegible]
Lying	On side, face or [illegible]	[illegible]
Difficult	Crouchin[illegible]	[illegible]
Visual fatigue		
Nearly continuous attention	[illegible]	[illegible]
Continuous attention wit[illegible]	[illegible]	[illegible]
Continu[illegible]	[illegible]	[illegible]

Job Pack 20 x pt # 7312A Location Packing Dept. Observer FWT

Element		Observation 1	2	3	4	5	6	7	8	9	10	Average basic time	Allowances	Element standard time
Make box	Observed time	0.71	0.71	0.71	0.69	0.75	0.68	0.70	0.72	0.70	0.68			
	Rating	90	90	90	90	80	90	90	90	90	90			
	Basic time	0.64	0.64	0.63	0.62	0.60	0.61	0.63	0.65	0.63	0.61	0.626	10%	0.689
Pack x 20	Observed time	1.30	1.32	1.25	1.33	1.33	1.28	1.32	1.32	1.30	1.30			
	Rating	90	90	100	90	90	90	90	90	90	90			
	Basic time	1.17	1.19	1.25	1.20	1.20	1.15	1.19	1.19	1.17	1.17	1.168	12%	1.308
Seal and secure	Observed time	0.53	0.55	0.55	0.56	0.53	0.53	0.60	0.55	0.49	0.51			
	Rating	90	90	90	90	90	90	85	90	100	100			
	Basic time	0.48	0.50	0.50	0.50	0.48	0.48	0.51	0.50	0.49	0.51	0.495	10%	0.545
Assemble outer,	Observed time	1.12	1.21	1.20	1.25	1.41	1.27	1.11	1.15	1.20	1.23			
fix and label	Rating	100	90	90	90	90	90	100	100	90	90			
	Basic time	1.12	1.09	1.08	1.13	1.27	1.14	1.11	1.15	1.08	1.21	1.138	12%	1.275
													Raw standard time	3.817
												Allowances for total job	5%	0.191
													Standard time for job	4.01 SM

Figure S9.1 Time study of a packing task – standard time for the whole task calculated

Worked example

Two work teams in the Monrovian Embassy have been allocated the task of processing visa applications. Team A processes applications from Europe, Africa and the Middle East. Team B processes applications from North and South America, Asia and Australasia. Team A has chosen to organize itself in such a way that each of its three team members processes an application from start to finish. The four members of Team B have chosen to split themselves into two sub-teams. Two open the letters and carry out the checks for a criminal record (no one who has been convicted of any crime other than a motoring offence can enter Monrovia), while the other two team members check for financial security (only people with more than Monrovian $1,000 may enter the country). The head of consular affairs is keen to find out if one of these methods of organizing the teams is more efficient than the other. The problem is that the mix of applications differs region by region. Team A typically processes around two business applications to every one tourist application. Team B processes around one business application to every two tourist applications.

A study revealed the following data:

Average standard time to process a business visa = 63 standard minutes

Average time to process a tourist visa = 55 standard minutes

Average weekly output from Team A is:
85.2 Business visas
39.5 Tourist visas

Average weekly output from Team B is:
53.5 Business visas
100.7 Tourist visas

All team members work a 40-hour week.

The efficiency of each team can be calculated by comparing the actual output in standard minutes and the time worked in minutes.

Team A processes:

$$(85.2 \times 63) + (39.5 \times 55) = 7{,}540.1 \text{ standard minutes of work}$$

$$\text{in } 3 \times 40 \times 60 \text{ minutes} = 7{,}200 \text{ minutes}$$

$$\text{So its efficiency} = \frac{7{,}540.1}{7{,}200} \times 100 = 104.72\%$$

Team B processes:

$$(53.5 \times 63) + (100.7 \times 55) = 8{,}909 \text{ standard minutes of work}$$

$$\text{in } 4 \times 40 \times 60 \text{ minutes} = 9{,}600 \text{ minutes}$$

$$\text{So its efficiency} = \frac{8{,}909}{9{,}600} \times 100 = 92.8\%$$

The initial evidence therefore seems to suggest that the way Team A has organized itself is more efficient.

Key operations questions

Chapter 10
The nature of planning and control

- What is planning and control?
- How do supply and demand affect planning and control?
- What are the activities of planning and control?

Chapter 11
Capacity planning and control

- What is capacity planning and control?
- How are demand and capacity measured?
- What are the alternative ways of coping with demand fluctuation?
- How can operations plan and control their capacity level?
- How can queuing theory be used to plan capacity?

Chapter 12
Inventory planning and control

- What is inventory?
- Why is inventory necessary?
- What are the disadvantages of holding inventory?
- How much inventory should an operation hold?
- When should an operation replenish its inventory?
- How can inventory be controlled?

Chapter 13
Supply chain planning and control

- What is supply chain management?
- What are the activities of supply chain management?
- What are the types of relationship between operations in supply chains?
- How do supply chains behave in practice?
- How can supply chains be improved?

Chapter 14
ERP

- What is ERP?
- How did ERP develop?
- How should ERP systems be implemented?

Chapter 15
Lean synchronization

- What is lean synchronization?
- How does lean synchronization eliminate waste?
- How does lean synchronization apply throughout the supply network?
- How does lean synchronization compare with other approaches?

Chapter 16
Project planning and control

- What is a project?
- What makes project management successful?
- How are projects planned and controlled?
- What is project planning and why is it important?
- How can the techniques of network planning help project management?

Chapter 17
Quality planning and control

- What is quality and why is it so important?
- How can quality problems be diagnosed?
- What steps lead towards conformance to specification?
- What is total quality management (TQM)?

Part Three
PLANNING AND CONTROL

The physical design of an operation should have provided the fixed resources which are capable of satisfying customers' demands. Planning and control are concerned with operating those resources on a day-to-day basis and ensuring availability of materials and other variable resources in order to supply the goods and services which fulfil customers' demands. This part of the book will look at several different aspects of planning and control, including some of the specialist approaches which are used in particular types of operations.

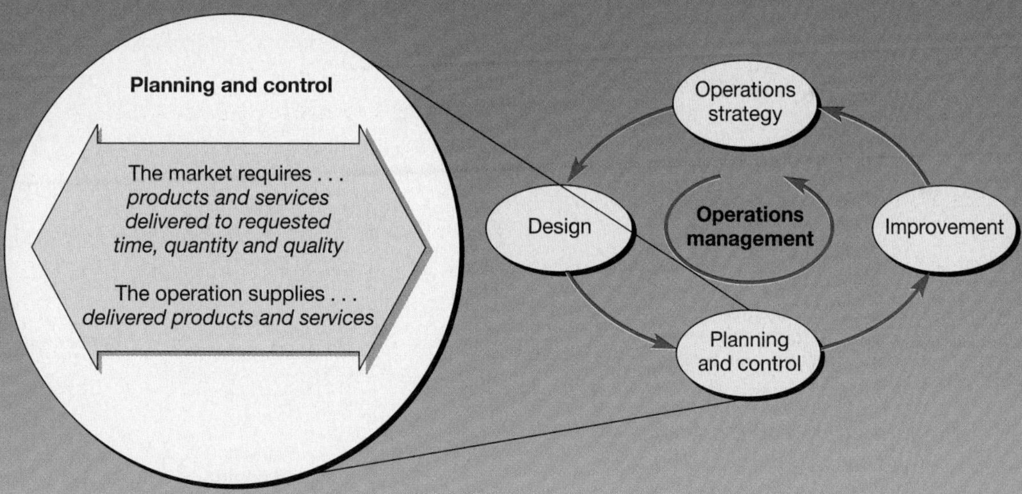

Chapter 10 The nature of planning and control

Key questions

- What is planning and control?
- How do supply and demand affect planning and control?
- What are the activities of planning and control?

Introduction

Within the constraints imposed by its design, an operation has to be run on an ongoing basis. 'Planning and control' is concerned with managing the ongoing activities of the operation so as to satisfy customer demand. All operations require plans and require controlling, although the degree of formality and detail may vary. This chapter introduces and provides an overview of some of the principles and methods of planning and control. Some of these, such as ERP (enterprise resources planning) and JIT (just-in-time), have been developed into more extensive concepts and these are examined in later chapters. Similarly, there are separate specialist tools to plan and control projects and a separate chapter is devoted to this area. In all cases, however, the different aspects of planning and control can be viewed as representing the reconciliation of supply with demand (*see* Figure 10.1).

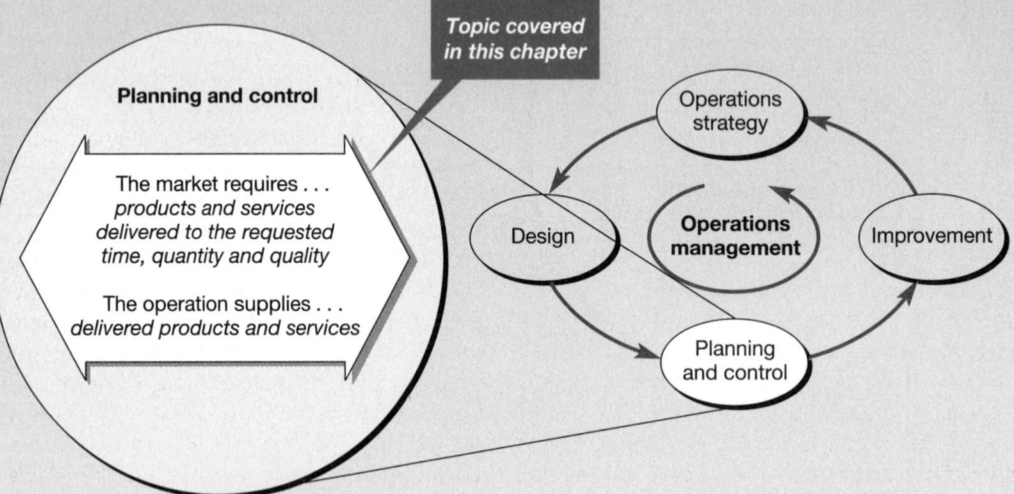

Figure 10.1 This chapter introduces planning and control

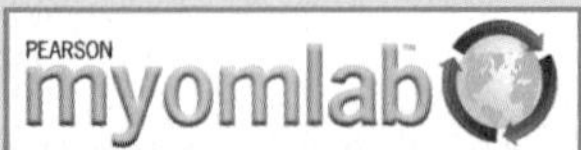

Check and improve your understanding of this chapter using self assessment questions and a personalised study plan, audio and video downloads, and an eBook – all at ***www.myomlab.com****.*

Operations in practice Joanne manages the schedule[1]

Joanne Cheung is the Senior Service Adviser at a premier BMW dealership. She and her team act as the interface between customers who want their cars serviced and repaired, and the 16 technicians who carry out the work in their state-of-the-art workshop. '*There are three types of work that we have to organize*', says Joanne. '*The first is performing repairs on customers' vehicles. They usually want this doing as soon as possible. The second type of job is routine servicing. It is usually not urgent so customers are generally willing to negotiate a time for this. The remainder of our work involves working on the pre-owned cars which our buyer has bought-in to sell on to customers. Before any of these cars can be sold they have to undergo extensive checks. To some extent we treat these categories of work slightly differently. We have to give good service to our internal car buyers, but there is some flexibility in planning these jobs. At the other extreme, emergency repair work for customers has to be fitted into our schedule as quickly as possible. If someone is desperate to have their car repaired at very short notice, we sometimes ask them to drop their car in as early as they can and pick it up as late as possible. This gives us the maximum amount of time to fit it into the schedule.*'

'*There are a number of service options open to customers. We can book short jobs in for a fixed time and do it while they wait. Most commonly, we ask the customer to leave the car with us and collect it later. To help customers we have ten loan cars which are booked out on a first-come first-served basis. Alternatively, the vehicle can be collected from the customer's home and delivered back there when it is ready. Our four drivers who do this are able to cope with up to twelve jobs a day.*'

'*Most days we deal with fifty to eighty jobs, taking from half-an-hour up to a whole day. To enter a job into our process all Service Advisers have access to the computer-based scheduling system. On-screen it shows the total capacity we have day-by-day, all the jobs that are booked in, the amount of free capacity still available, the number of loan cars available, and so on. We use this to see when we have the capacity to book a customer in, and then enter all the customer's details. BMW have issued "standard times" for all the major jobs. However, you have to modify these standard times a bit to take account of circumstances. That is where the Service Adviser's experience comes in.*'

Joanne has to balance the needs of customers and the constraints of the workshop

Source: © BMW Group

'*We keep all the most commonly used parts in stock, but if a repair needs a part which is not in stock, we can usually get it from the BMW parts distributors within a day. Every evening our planning system prints out the jobs to be done the next day and the parts which are likely to be needed for each job. This allows the parts staff to pick out the parts for each job so that the technicians can collect them first thing the next morning without any delay.*'

'*Every day we have to cope with the unexpected. A technician may find that extra work is needed, customers may want extra work doing, and technicians are sometimes ill, which reduces our capacity. Occasionally parts may not be available so we have to arrange with the customer for the vehicle to be rebooked for a later time. Every day up to four or five customers just don't turn up. Usually they have just forgotten to bring their car in so we have to rebook them in at a later time. We can cope with most of these uncertainties because our technicians are flexible in terms of the skills they have and also are willing to work overtime when needed. Also, it is important to manage customers' expectations. If there is a chance that the vehicle may not be ready for them, it shouldn't come as a surprise when they try and collect it.*'

What is planning and control?

Planning and control reconciles supply and demand

Planning and control is concerned with the reconciliation between what the market requires and what the operation's resources can deliver. **Planning and control** activities provide the systems, procedures and decisions which bring different aspects of supply and demand together. In this part of the book, the different aspects of supply and demand, and different circumstances under which supply and demand must be reconciled, are treated in each chapter. But in every case, the purpose is the same – to make a connection between supply and demand that will ensure that the operation's processes run effectively and efficiently and produce products and services as required by customers. Consider, for example, the way in which routine surgery is organized in a hospital. When a patient arrives and is admitted to the hospital, much of the planning for the surgery will already have happened. The operating theatre will have been reserved, and the doctors and nurses who staff the operating theatre will have been provided with all the information regarding the patient's condition. Appropriate preoperative and postoperative care will have been organized. All this will involve staff and facilities in different parts of the hospital. All must be given the same information and their activities coordinated. Soon after the patient arrives, he or she will be checked to make sure that the condition is as expected (in much the same way as material is inspected on arrival in a factory). Blood, if required, will be cross-matched and reserved, and any medication will be made ready (in the same way that all the different materials are brought together in a factory). Any last-minute changes may require some degree of replanning. For example, if the patient shows unexpected symptoms, observation may be necessary before the surgery can take place. Not only will this affect the patient's own treatment, but other patients' treatment may also have to be rescheduled (in the same way as machines will need rescheduling if a job is delayed in a factory). All these activities of scheduling, coordination and organization are concerned with the planning and control of the hospital.

The difference between planning and control

Planning concerns what should happen in the future

Control copes with changes

In this text we have chosen to treat planning and control together. This is because the division between planning and control is not clear, either in theory or in practice. However, there are some general features that help to distinguish between the two. **Planning** is a formalization of what is intended to happen at some time in the future. But a plan does not guarantee that an event will actually happen. Rather it is a statement of intention. Although plans are based on expectations, during their implementation things do not always happen as expected. Customers change their minds about what they want and when they want it. Suppliers may not always deliver on time, machines may fail, or staff may be absent through illness. **Control** is the process of coping with changes in these variables. It may mean that plans need to be redrawn in the short term. It may also mean that an 'intervention' will need to be made in the operation to bring it back 'on track' – for example, finding a new supplier that can deliver quickly, repairing the machine which failed, or moving staff from another part of the operation to cover for the absentees. Control makes the adjustments which allow the operation to achieve the objectives that the plan has set, even when the assumptions on which the plan was based do not hold true.

Long-, medium- and short-term planning and control

The nature of planning and control activities changes over time. In the very long term, operations managers make plans concerning what they intend to do, what resources they need, and what objectives they hope to achieve. The emphasis is on planning rather than control, because there is little to control as such. They will use forecasts of likely demand which are described in aggregated terms. For example, a hospital will make plans for '2,000 patients' without necessarily going into the details of the individual needs of those 2,000 patients. Similarly, the hospital might plan to have 100 nurses and 20 doctors but again without deciding on the specific attributes of the staff. Operations managers will be concerned mainly to achieve financial targets. Budgets will be put in place which identify its costs and revenue targets.

Medium-term planning and control is more detailed. It looks ahead to assess the overall demand which the operation must meet in a partially disaggregated manner. By this time, for example, the hospital must distinguish between different types of demand. The number of patients coming as accident and emergency cases will need to be distinguished from those requiring routine operations. Similarly, different categories of staff will have been identified and broad staffing levels in each category set. Just as important, contingencies will have been put in place which allow for slight deviations from the plans. These contingencies will act as 'reserve' resources and make planning and control easier in the short term.

In short-term planning and control, many of the resources will have been set and it will be difficult to make large changes. However, short-term interventions are possible if things are not going to plan. By this time, demand will be assessed on a totally disaggregated basis, with all types of surgical procedures treated as individual activities. More importantly, individual patients will have been identified by name, and specific time slots booked for their treatment. In making short-term interventions and changes to the plan, operations managers will be attempting to balance the quality, speed, dependability, flexibility and costs of their operation on an *ad hoc* basis. It is unlikely that they will have the time to carry out detailed calculations of the effects of their short-term planning and control decisions on all these objectives, but a general understanding of priorities will form the background to their decision making. Figure 10.2 shows how the control aspects of planning and control increase in significance closer to the date of the event.

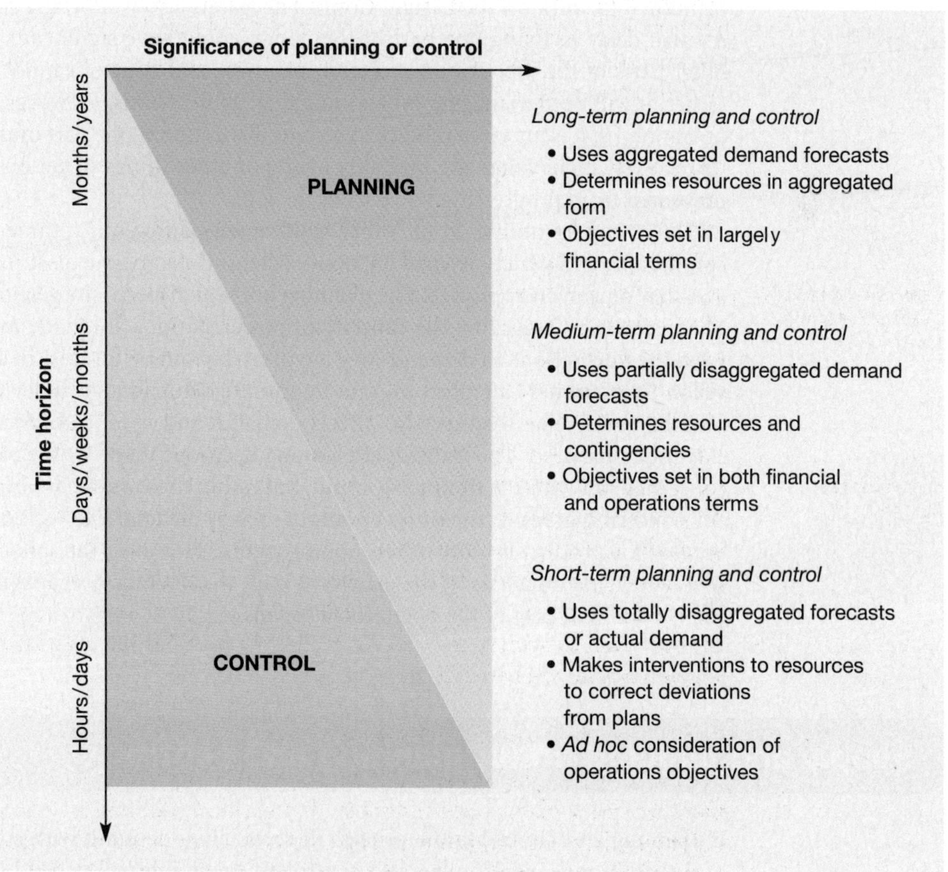

Figure 10.2 The balance between planning and control activities changes in the long, medium and short term

Table 10.1 The volume–variety effects on planning and control

Volume	*Variety*	*Customer responsiveness*	*Planning horizon*	*Major planning decision*	*Control decisions*	*Robustness*
Low	High	Slow	Short	Timing	Detailed	High
↓	↓	↓	↓	↓	↓	↓
High	Low	Fast	Long	Volume	Aggregated	Low

The volume–variety effect on planning and control

Operations which produce a high variety of products or services in relatively low volume will clearly have customers that require a different set of factors and use processes which have a different set of needs from those operations which create standardized products or services in high volume (*see* Table 10.1).

Take two contrasting operations – an architects' practice and an electricity utility. The architects' high variety means that their services will have little standardization, nor can they produce designs in advance of customers requesting them. Because of this, the time it will take to respond to customers' requests will be relatively slow. Customers will understand this and expect to be consulted extensively as to their needs. The details and requirements of each job will emerge only as each individual building is designed to the client's requirements, so planning occurs on a relatively short-term basis. The individual decisions which are taken in the planning process will usually concern the timing of activities and events – for example, when a design is to be delivered, when building should start, when each individual architect will be needed to work on the design. Control decisions also will be at a relatively detailed level. A small delay in fixing one part of the design could have significant implications in many other parts of the job. For an architect, planning and control cannot be totally routinized; rather, it will need managing on an individual project basis. However, the robustness of the operation (that is, its vulnerability to serious disruption if one part of the operation fails) will be relatively high. There are probably plenty of other things to get on with if an architect is prevented from progressing one part of the job.

The electricity utility, on the other hand, is very different. Volume is high, production is continuous, and variety is virtually non-existent. Customers expect instant 'delivery' whenever they plug in an appliance. The planning horizon in electricity generation can be very long. Major decisions regarding the capacity of power stations are made many years in advance. Even the fluctuations in demand over a typical day can be forecast in advance. Popular television programmes can affect minute-by-minute demand and these are scheduled weeks or months ahead. The weather also affects demand, and is more uncertain, but can to some extent be predicted. The individual planning decisions made by the electricity utility will be concerned not with the timing of output, but rather the volume of output. Control decisions will concern aggregated measures of output such as the total kilowatts of electricity generated, because the product is more or less homogeneous. However, the robustness of the operation is very low, insomuch as, if the generator fails, the operation's capability of supplying electricity from that part of the operation also fails.

Supply and demand affect planning and control

If planning and control is the process of reconciling demand with supply, then the nature of the decisions taken to plan and control an operation will depend on both the nature of demand and the nature of supply in that operation. In this section, we examine some differences in demand and supply which can affect the way in which operations managers plan and control their activities.

Short case
Operations control at Air France[2]

Source: Getty Images

'In many ways a major airline can be viewed as one large planning problem which is usually approached as many independent, smaller (but still difficult) planning problems. The list of things which need planning seems endless: crews, reservation agents, luggage, flights, through trips, maintenance, gates, inventory, equipment purchases. Each planning problem has its own considerations, its own complexities, its own set of time horizons, its own objectives, but all are interrelated.'

Air France has eighty flight planners working 24-hour shifts in their flight planning office at Roissy, Charles de Gaulle. Their job is to establish the optimum flight routes, anticipate any problems such as weather changes, and minimize fuel consumption. Overall the goals of the flight planning activity are first, and most important, safety followed by economy and passenger comfort. Increasingly powerful computer programs process the mountain of data necessary to plan the flights, but in the end many decisions still rely on human judgement. Even the most sophisticated expert systems only serve as support for the flight planners. Planning Air France's schedule is a massive job. Just some of the considerations which need to be taken into account include the following.

- *Frequency* – for each airport how many separate services should the airline provide?
- *Fleet assignment* – which type of plane should be used on each leg of a flight?
- *Banks* – at any airline hub where passengers arrive and may transfer to other flights to continue their journey, airlines like to organize flights into 'banks' of several planes which arrive close together, pause to let passengers change planes, and all depart close together. So, how many banks should there be and when should they occur?
- *Block times* – a block time is the elapsed time between a plane leaving the departure gate at an airport and arriving at its gate in the arrival airport. The longer the allowed block time the more likely a plane will be to keep to schedule even if it suffers minor delays. However, longer block times also mean fewer flights can be scheduled.
- *Planned maintenance* – any schedule must allow time for planes to have time at a maintenance base.
- *Crew planning* – pilot and cabin crew must be scheduled to allocate pilots to fly planes on which they are licensed and to keep within maximum 'on duty' times for all staff.
- *Gate plotting* – if many planes are on the ground at the same time there may be problems in loading and unloading them simultaneously.
- *Recovery* – many things can cause deviations from any plan in the airline industry. Allowances must be built in to allow for recovery.

For flights within and between Air France's 12 geographic zones, the planners construct a flight plan that will form the basis of the actual flight only a few hours later. All planning documents need to be ready for the flight crew who arrive two hours before the scheduled departure time. Being responsible for passenger safety and comfort, the captain always has the final say and, when satisfied, co-signs the flight plan together with the planning officer.

Uncertainty in supply and demand

Uncertainty makes both planning and control more difficult. Local village carnivals, for example, rarely work to plan. Events take longer than expected, some of the acts scheduled in the programme may be delayed *en route*, and some traders may not arrive. The event requires a good compère to keep it moving, keep the crowd amused, and in effect control the event. Demand may also be unpredictable. A fast-food outlet inside a shopping centre does not know how many people will arrive, when they will arrive and what they will order. It may be possible to predict certain patterns, such as an increase in demand over the lunch and tea-time periods, but a sudden rainstorm that drives shoppers indoors into the centre could significantly and unpredictably increase demand in the very short term. Conversely, other operations are reasonably predictable, and the need for control is minimal. For example, cable TV services provide programmes to a schedule into subscribers' homes. It is rare to change the programme plan. Demand may also be predictable. In a school, for example, once classes are fixed and the term or semester has started, a teacher knows how many pupils are in the class. A combination of uncertainty in the operation's ability to supply, and in the demand for its products and services, is particularly difficult to plan and control.

Dependent and independent demand

Some operations can predict demand with more certainty than others. For example, consider an operation providing professional decorating and refurbishment services which has as its customers a number of large hotel chains. Most of these customers plan the refurbishment and decoration of their hotels months or even years in advance. Because of this, the decoration company can itself plan its activities in advance. Its own demand is dependent upon the relatively predictable activities of its customers. By contrast, a small painter and decorator serves the domestic and small business market. Some business also comes from house construction companies, but only when their own painters and decorators are fully occupied. In this case, demand on the painting and decorating company is relatively unpredictable. To some extent, there is a random element in demand which is virtually independent of any factors obvious to the company.

Dependent demand

Dependent demand, then, is demand which is relatively predictable because it is dependent upon some factor which is known. For example, the manager who is in charge of ensuring that there are sufficient tyres in an automobile factory will not treat the demand for tyres as a totally random variable. He or she will not be totally surprised by the exact quantity of tyres which are required by the plant every day. The process of demand forecasting is relatively straightforward. It will consist of examining the manufacturing schedules in the car plant and deriving the demand for tyres from these. If 200 cars are to be manufactured on a particular day, then it is simple to calculate that 1,000 tyres will be demanded by the car plant (each car has five tyres) – demand is dependent on a known factor, the number of cars to be manufactured. Because of this, the tyres can be ordered from the tyre manufacturer to a delivery schedule which is closely in line with the demand for tyres from the plant (as in Fig. 10.3). In fact, the demand for every part of the car plant will be derived from

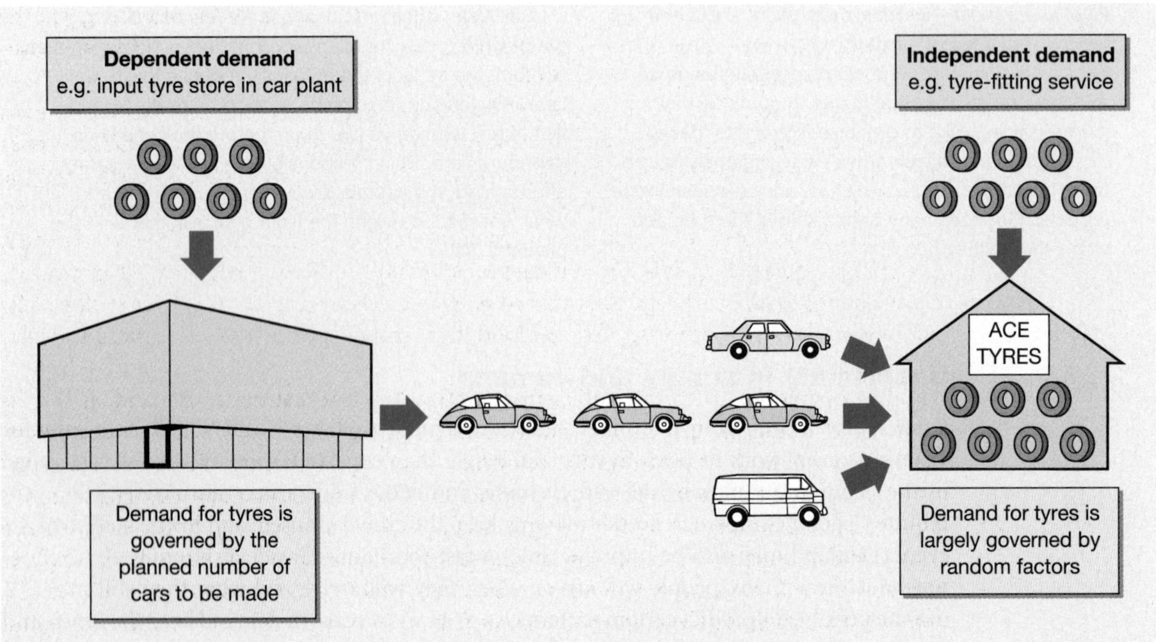

Figure 10.3 Dependent demand is derived from the demand for something else; independent demand is more random

the assembly schedule for the finished cars. Manufacturing instructions and purchasing requests will all be dependent upon this figure. Other operations will act in a dependent demand manner because of the nature of the service or product which they provide. For example, a jobbing dressmaker will not buy fabric and patterns and make up dresses in many different sizes just in case someone comes along and wants to buy one. Nor will a high-class restaurant begin to cook food just in case a customer arrives and requests it. In both these cases, a combination of risk and the perishability of the product or service prevents the operation from starting to create the goods or services until it has a firm order. Dependent demand planning and control concentrates on the consequences of the demand within the operation. Materials requirements planning, which is treated in Chapter 14, is one such dependent demand approach.

Independent demand

Some operations are subject to **independent demand**. They will supply demand without having any firm forward visibility of customer orders. For example, customers do not have to inform a supermarket when they are arriving and what they will buy. The supermarket takes its planning and control decisions based on its experience and understanding of the market, independent of what may actually happen. They run the risk of being out of stock of items when demand does not match their expectations. For example, the Ace Tyre Company, which operates a drive-in tyre replacement service, will need to manage a stock of tyres. In that sense it is exactly the same task that faced the manager of tyre stocks in the car plant. However, demand is very different for Ace Tyre. It cannot predict either the volume or the specific needs of customers. It must make decisions on how many and what type of tyres to stock, based on demand forecasts and in the light of the risks it is prepared to run of being out of stock. This is the nature of *independent demand planning and control*. It makes 'best guesses' concerning future demand, attempts to put the resources in place which can satisfy this demand, and attempts to respond quickly if actual demand does not match the forecast. Inventory planning and control, treated in Chapter 12, is typical of independent demand planning and control.

Responding to demand

Dependent and independent demand concepts are closely related to how the operation chooses to respond to demand. In conditions of dependent demand, an operation will only start the process of producing goods or services when it needs to. Each order triggers the planning and control activities to organize their production. For example, a specialist house-builder might only start the process of planning and controlling the construction of a house when requested to do so by the customer. The builder might not even have the resources to start building before the order is received. The material that will be necessary to build the house will be purchased only when the timing and nature of the house are certain. The staff and the construction equipment might also be 'purchased' only when the nature of demand is clear. In a similar way, a specialist conference organizer will start planning for an event only when specifically requested to do so by the clients. A venue will be booked, speakers organized, meals arranged and the delegates contacted only when the nature of the service is clear. The planning and control necessary for this kind of operation can be called **resource-to-order** planning and control.

Resource-to-order

Other operations might be sufficiently confident of the nature of demand, if not its volume and timing, to keep 'in stock' most of the resources it requires to satisfy its customers. Certainly it will keep its transforming resources, if not its transformed resources. However, it would still make the actual product or service only to a firm customer order. For example, a house builder who has standard designs might choose to build each house only when a customer places a firm order. Because the design of the house is relatively standard, suppliers of materials will have been identified, even if the building operation does not keep the items in stock itself. The equivalent in the conference business would be a conference centre which has its own 'stored' permanent resources (the building, staff, etc.) but only starts planning a conference when it has a firm booking. In both cases, the operations would need **create-to-order or make-to-order** planning and control.

Create-to-order and make-to-order

Some operations produce goods or services ahead of any firm orders 'to stock'. For example, some builders will construct pre-designed standard houses or apartments ahead of any firm demand for them. This will be done either because it is less expensive to do so or because it is difficult to create the goods or services on a one-off basis (it is difficult to make each apartment only when a customer chooses to buy one). If demand is high, customers may place requests for houses before they are started or during their construction. In this case, the customer will form a backlog of demand and must wait. The builder is also taking the risk, however, of holding a stock of unsold houses if buyers do not come along before they are finished. In fact, it is difficult for small builders to operate in this way, but less so for (say) a bottled cola manufacturer or other mass producer. The equivalent in the conference market would be a conference centre which schedules a series of events and conferences, programmed in advance and open to individual customers to book into or even turn up on the day. Cinemas and theatres usually work in this manner. Their performances are produced and supplied irrespective of the level of actual demand. Operations of this type will require **make-to-stock** planning and control.

Make-to-stock

P:D ratios[3]

P:D ratio

Another way of characterizing the graduation between resource-to-order planning and control and make-to-stock planning and control is by using a ***P:D* ratio**. This contrasts the total length of time customers have to wait between asking for the product or service and receiving it, demand time, *D*, and the total throughput time, *P*. Throughput time is how long the operation takes to obtain the resources, and produce and deliver the product or service.

P and *D* times depend on the operation

Some operations (called make-to-stock operations) produce their products and services in advance of any demand. For example, in an operation making consumer durables, demand time, *D*, is the sum of the times for transmitting the order to the company's warehouse or stock point, picking and packing the order and physically transporting it to the customer. Behind this visible order cycle, however, lie other cycles. Reduction in the finished goods stock will eventually trigger the decision to manufacture a replenishment batch. This 'produce' cycle involves scheduling work to the various stages in the manufacturing process. Behind the 'produce' cycle lies the 'obtain resources' cycle – the time for obtaining the input stocks. So, for this type of operation, the 'demand' time which the customer sees is very short compared with the total 'throughput' cycle. Contrast this with a resource-to-order operation. Here, *D* is the same as *P*. Both include the 'obtain resources', 'produce' and 'delivery' cycles. The produce-to-order operation lies in between these two (*see* Fig. 10.4).

P:D ratios indicate the degree of speculation

Reducing total throughput time *P* will have varying effects on the time the customer has to wait for demand to be filled. In resource-to-order operations, *P* and *D* are the same. Speeding up any part of *P* will reduce customer's waiting time, *D*. On the other hand, in 'produce-to-stock' operations, customers would only see reduced *D* time if the 'deliver' part of *P* were reduced. Also, in Figure 10.4, *D* is always shown as being smaller than *P*, which is the case for most companies. How much smaller *D* is than *P* is important because it indicates the proportion of the operation's activities which are speculative, that is, carried out on the expectation of eventually receiving a firm order for its efforts. The larger *P* is compared with *D*, the higher the proportion of speculative activity in the operation and the greater the risk the operation carries. The speculative element in the operation is not there only because *P* is greater than *D*, however; it is there because *P* is greater than *D* and demand cannot be forecast perfectly. With exact or close to exact forecasts, risk would be non-existent or very low, no matter how much bigger *P* was than *D*. Expressed another way: when *P* and *D* are equal, no matter how inaccurate the forecasts are, speculation is

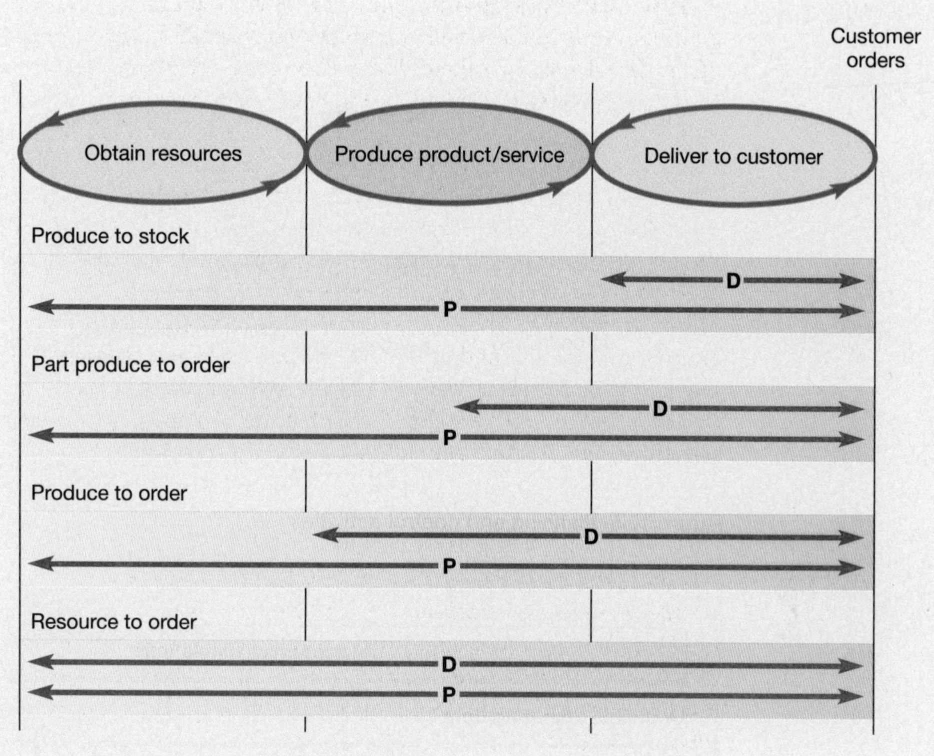

Figure 10.4 ***P* and *D* for the different types of planning and control**

eliminated because everything is made to a firm order (although bad forecasting will lead to other problems). Reducing the *P*:*D* ratio becomes, in effect, a way of taking some of the risk out of operations planning and control.

Planning and control activities

Planning and control requires the reconciliation of supply and demand in terms of volumes, timing and quality. In this chapter we will focus on an overview of the activities that plan and control volume and timing (most of this part of the book is concerned with these issues). There are four overlapping activities: loading, sequencing, scheduling, and monitoring and control (*see* Fig. 10.5). Some caution is needed when using these terms. Different organizations may use them in different ways, and even textbooks in the area adopt different definitions. For example, some authorities describe what we have called 'planning and control' as 'operations scheduling'. However, the terminology of planning and control is less important than understanding the basic ideas described in the remainder of this chapter.

Loading

Loading

Loading is the amount of work that is allocated to a work centre. For example, a machine on the shop floor of a manufacturing business is available, in theory, 168 hours a week. However, this does not necessarily mean that 168 hours of work can be loaded onto that machine. Figure 10.6 shows what erodes this available time. For some periods the machine cannot be worked; for example, it may not be available on statutory holidays and weekends. Therefore, the load put onto the machine must take this into account. Of the time that the machine is

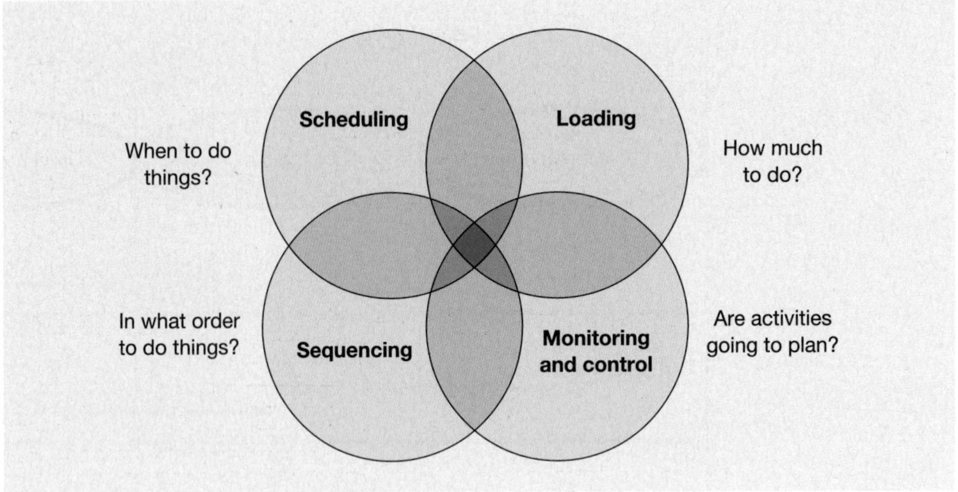

Figure 10.5 Planning and control activities

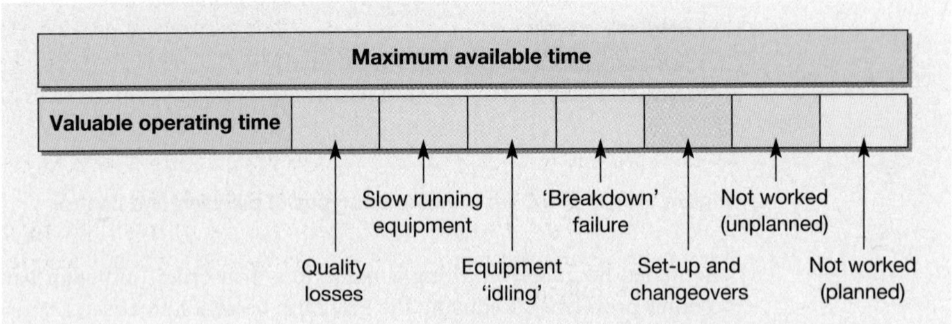

Figure 10.6 The reduction in the time available for valuable operating time

available for work, other losses further reduce the available time. For example, time may be lost while changing over from making one component to another. If the machine breaks down, it will not be available. If there is machine reliability data available, this must also be taken into account. Sometimes the machine may be waiting for parts to arrive or be 'idling' for some other reason. Other losses could include an allowance for the machine being run below its optimum speed (for example, because it has not been maintained properly) and an allowance for the 'quality losses' or defects which the machine may produce. Of course, many of these losses (shown in Figure 10.6) should be small or non-existent in a well-managed operation. However, the **valuable operating time** available for productive working, even in the best operations, can be significantly below the maximum time available. This idea is taken further in Chapter 11 when we discuss the measurement of capacity.

Valuable operating time

Finite and infinite loading

Finite loading

Finite loading is an approach which only allocates work to a work centre (a person, a machine, or perhaps a group of people or machines) up to a set limit. This limit is the estimate of capacity for the work centre (based on the times available for loading). Work over and above this capacity is not accepted. Figure 10.7 first shows how the load on the work centres is not allowed to exceed the capacity limit. Finite loading is particularly relevant for operations where:

- *it is possible to limit the load* – for example, it is possible to run an appointment system for a general medical practice or a hairdresser;

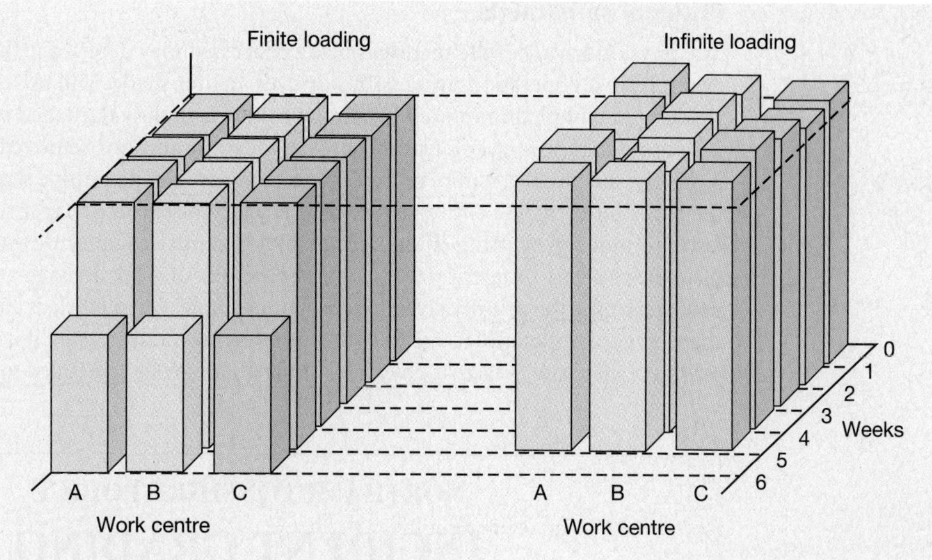

Figure 10.7 Finite and infinite loading of jobs on three work centres A, B and C. Finite loading limits the loading on the centres to their capacities, even if it means that jobs will be late. Infinite loading allows the loading on each centre to exceed its capacity to ensure that jobs will not be late

- *it is necessary to limit the load* – for example, for safety reasons only a finite number of people and weight of luggage are allowed on an aircraft;
- *the cost of limiting the load is not prohibitive* – for example, the cost of maintaining a finite order book at a specialist sports car manufacturer does not adversely affect demand, and may even enhance it.

Infinite loading

Infinite loading is an approach to loading work which does not limit accepting work, but instead tries to cope with it. The second diagram in Figure 10.7 illustrates this loading pattern where capacity constraints have not been used to limit loading so the work is completed earlier. Infinite loading is relevant for operations where:

- *it is not possible to limit the load* – for example, an accident and emergency department in a hospital should not turn away arrivals needing attention;
- *it is not necessary to limit the load* – for example, fast-food outlets are designed to flex capacity up and down to cope with varying arrival rates of customers. During busy periods, customers accept that they must queue for some time before being served. Unless this is extreme, the customers might not go elsewhere;
- *the cost of limiting the load is prohibitive* – for example, if a retail bank turned away customers at the door because a set amount were inside, customers would feel less than happy with the service.

In complex planning and control activities where there are multiple stages, each with different capacities and with a varying mix arriving at the facilities, such as a machine shop in an engineering company, the constraints imposed by finite loading make loading calculations complex and not worth the considerable computational power which would be needed.

Sequencing

Sequencing

Whether the approach to loading is finite or infinite, when work arrives, decisions must be taken on the order in which the work will be tackled. This activity is termed **sequencing**. The priorities given to work in an operation are often determined by some predefined set of rules, some of which are relatively complex. Some of these are summarized below.

Physical constraints

The physical nature of the materials being processed may determine the priority of work. For example, in an operation using paints or dyes, lighter shades will be sequenced before darker shades. On completion of each batch, the colour is slightly darkened for the next batch. This is because darkness of colour can only be added to and not removed from the colour mix. Similarly, the physical nature of the equipment used may determine sequence. For example, in the paper industry, the cutting equipment is set to the width of paper required. It is easier and faster to move the cutting equipment to an adjacent size (up or down) than it is to reset the machine to a very different size. Sometimes the mix of work arriving at a part of an operation may determine the priority given to jobs. For example, when fabric is cut to a required size and shape in garment manufacture, the surplus fabric would be wasted if it is not used for another product. Therefore, jobs that physically fit together may be scheduled together to reduce waste.

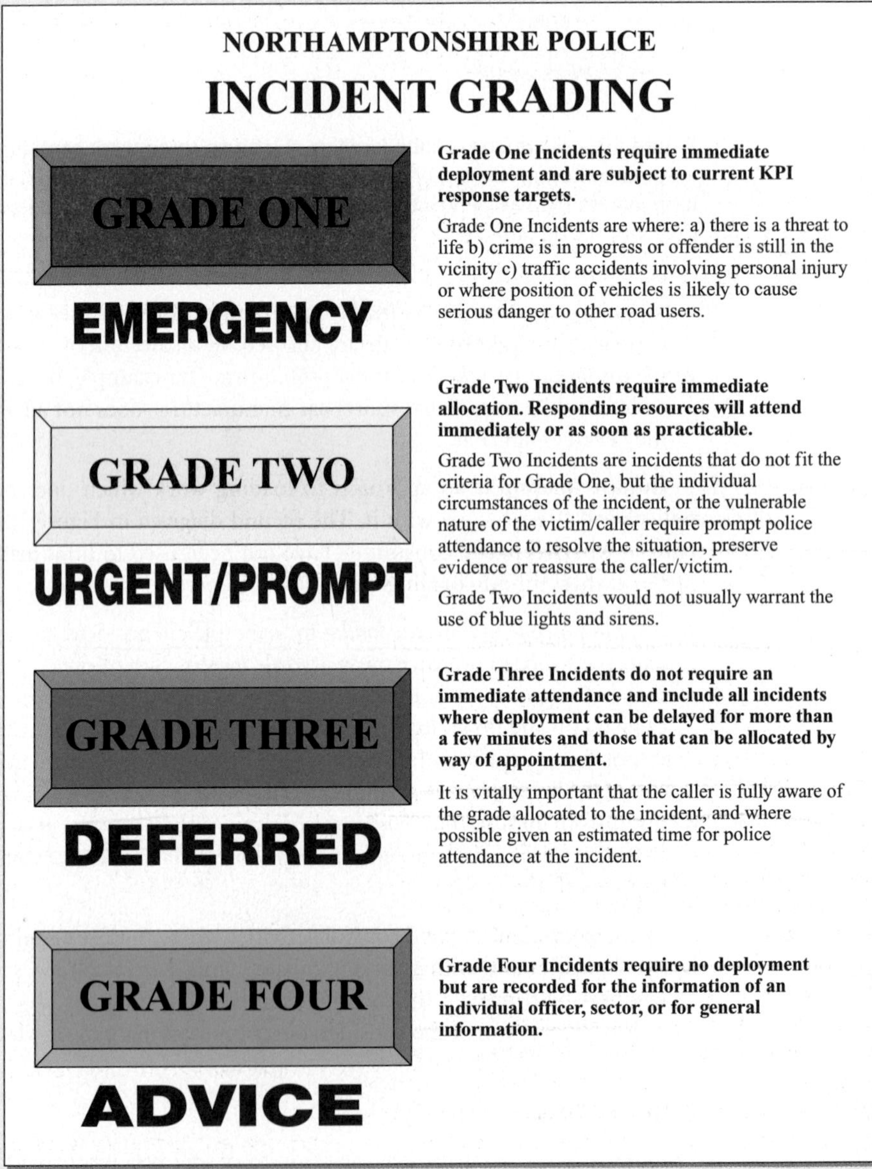

(Courtesy of Northamptonshire Police)

Figure 10.8 The call grading system for a police force

Customer priority

Customer priority sequencing

Operations will sometimes use **customer priority sequencing**, which allows an important or aggrieved customer, or item, to be 'processed' prior to others, irrespective of the order of arrival of the customer or item. This approach is typically used by operations whose customer base is skewed, containing a mass of small customers and a few large, very important customers. Some banks, for example, give priority to important customers. Similarly, in hotels, complaining customers will be treated as a priority because their complaint may have an adverse effect on the perceptions of other customers. More seriously, the emergency services often have to use their judgement in prioritizing the urgency of requests for service. For example, Figure 10.8 shows the priority system used by a police force. Here the operators receiving emergency and other calls are trained to grade the calls into one of five categories. The response by the police is then organized to match the level of priority. The triage system in hospitals operates in a similar way (*see* short case below). However, customer priority sequencing, although giving a high level of service to some customers, may erode the service given to many others. This may lower the overall performance of the operation if work flows are disrupted to accommodate important customers.

Due date (DD)

Due date sequencing

Prioritizing by due date means that work is sequenced according to when it is 'due' for delivery, irrespective of the size of each job or the importance of each customer. For example, a support service in an office block, such as a reprographic unit, will often ask when photocopies are required, and then sequence the work according to that due date. **Due date sequencing** usually improves the delivery reliability of an operation and improves average delivery speed. However, it may not provide optimal productivity, as a more efficient sequencing of work may reduce total costs. However, it can be flexible when new, urgent work arrives at the work centre.

Short case
The hospital triage system[4]

One of the hospital environments that is most difficult to schedule is the Accident and Emergency department, where patients arrive at random, without any prior warning, throughout the day. It is up to the hospital's reception and the medical staff to devise very rapidly a schedule which meets most of the necessary criteria. In particular, patients who arrive having had very serious accidents, or presenting symptoms of a serious illness, need to be attended to urgently. Therefore, the hospital will schedule these cases first. Less urgent cases – perhaps patients who are in some discomfort, but whose injuries or illnesses are not life-threatening – will have to wait until the urgent cases are treated. Routine non-urgent cases will have the lowest priority of all. In many circumstances, these patients will have to wait for the longest time, which may be many hours, especially if the hospital is busy. Sometimes these non-urgent cases may even be turned away if the hospital is too busy with more important cases. In situations where hospitals expect sudden influxes of patients, they have developed what is known as a triage system, whereby medical staff hurriedly sort through the patients who have arrived to determine which category of urgency each patient fits into. In this way a suitable schedule for the various treatments can be devised in a short period of time.

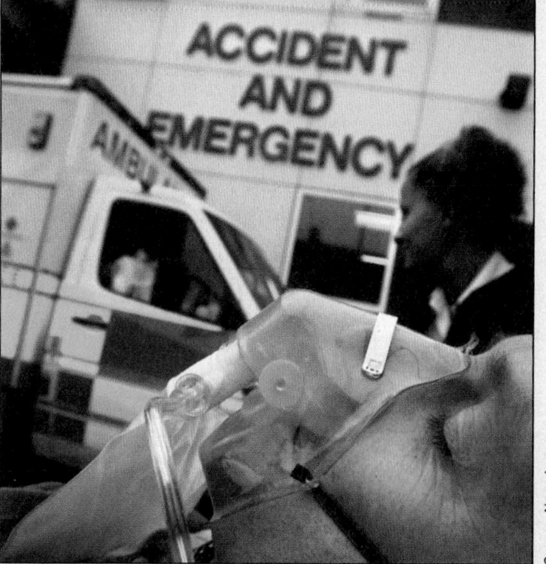

Source: Alamy Images

Last-in first-out (LIFO)

Last-in first-out sequencing

Last-in first-out (LIFO) is a method of sequencing usually selected for practical reasons. For example, unloading an elevator is more convenient on a LIFO basis, as there is only one entrance and exit. However, it is not an equitable approach. Patients at hospital clinics may be infuriated if they see newly arrived patients examined first. This sequencing rule is not determined for reasons of quality, flexibility or cost, and none of these performance objectives is well served by this method.

First-in first-out (FIFO)

First-in first-out sequencing

Some operations serve customers in exactly the sequence they arrive in. This is called **first-in first-out sequencing** (FIFO), or sometimes 'first come, first served' (FCFS). For example, UK passport offices receive mail, and sort it according to the day when it arrived. They work through the mail, opening it in sequence, and process the passport applications in order of arrival. Queues in theme parks may be designed so that one long queue snakes around the lobby area until the row of counters is reached. When customers reach the front of the queue, they are served at the next free counter.

Longest operation time (LOT)

Longest operation time sequencing

Operations may feel obliged to sequence their longest jobs first in the system called **longest operation time sequencing**. This has the advantage of occupying work centres for long periods. By contrast, relatively small jobs progressing through an operation will take up time at each work centre because of the need to change over from one job to the next. However, although longest operation time sequencing keeps utilization high, this rule does not take into account delivery speed, reliability or flexibility. Indeed, it may work directly against these performance objectives.

Shortest operation time first (SOT)

Shortest operation time sequencing

Most operations at some stage become cash-constrained. In these situations, the sequencing rules may be adjusted to tackle short jobs first in the system, called **shortest operation time sequencing**. These jobs can then be invoiced and payment received to ease cash-flow problems. Larger jobs that take more time will not enable the business to invoice as quickly. This has an effect of improving delivery performance, if the unit of measurement of delivery is jobs. However, it may adversely affect total productivity and can damage service to larger customers.

Judging sequencing rules

All five performance objectives, or some variant of them, could be used to judge the effectiveness of sequencing rules. However, the objectives of dependability, speed and cost are particularly important. So, for example, the following performance objectives are often used:

- Meeting 'due date' promised to customer (dependability);
- Minimizing the time the job spends in the process, also known as 'flow time' (speed);
- Minimizing work-in-progress inventory (an element of cost);
- Minimizing idle time of work centres (another element of cost).

Comparing the results from the three sequencing rules described in the worked example together with the two other sequencing rules described earlier and applied to the same problem, gives the results summarized in Table 10.2. The shortest operation time (SOT) rule resulted in both the best average time in process and the best (or least bad) in terms of average lateness. Although different rules will perform differently depending on the circumstances of the sequencing problem, in practice the SOT rule generally performs well.

Worked example

Steve Smith is a web site designer in a business school. Returning from his annual vacation (he finished all outstanding jobs before he left), five design jobs are given to him upon arrival at work. He gives them the codes A to E. Steve has to decide in which sequence to undertake the jobs. He wants both to minimize the average time the jobs are tied up in his office and, if possible, to meet the deadlines (delivery times) allocated to each job.

His first thought is to do the jobs in the order they were given to him, i.e. first-in first-out (FIFO):

Sequencing rule – first-in first-out (FIFO)

Sequence of jobs	*Process time (days)*	*Start time*	*Finish time*	*Due date*	*Lateness (days)*
A	5	0	5	6	0
B	3	5	8	5	3
C	6	8	14	8	6
D	2	14	16	7	9
E	1	16	17	3	14
	Total time in process	60		**Total lateness**	32
	Average time in process (total/5)	12		**Average lateness (total/5)**	6.4

Alarmed by the average lateness, Steve tries the due date (DD) rule:

Sequencing rule – due date (DD)

Sequence of jobs	*Process time (days)*	*Start time*	*Finish time*	*Due date*	*Lateness (days)*
E	1	0	1	3	0
B	3	1	4	5	0
A	5	4	9	6	3
D	2	9	11	7	4
C	6	11	17	8	9
	Total time in process	42		**Total lateness**	16
	Average time in process (total/5)	8.4		**Average lateness (total/5)**	3.2

Better! But Steve tries out the shortest operation time (SOT) rule:

Sequencing rule – shortest operation time (SOT)

Sequence of jobs	*Process time (days)*	*Start time*	*Finish time*	*Due date*	*Lateness (days)*
E	1	0	1	3	0
D	2	1	3	7	0
B	3	3	6	5	1
A	5	6	11	6	5
C	6	11	17	8	9
	Total time in process	38		**Total lateness**	16
	Average time in process (total/5)	7.6		**Average lateness (total/5)**	3.2

This gives the same degree of average lateness but with a lower average time in the process. Steve decides to use the SOT rule.

Table 10.2 Comparison of five sequencing decision rules

Rule	*Average time in process (days)*	*Average lateness (days)*
FIFO	12	6.4
DD	8.4	3.2
SOT	7.6	3.2
LIFO	8.4	3.8
LOT	12.8	7.4

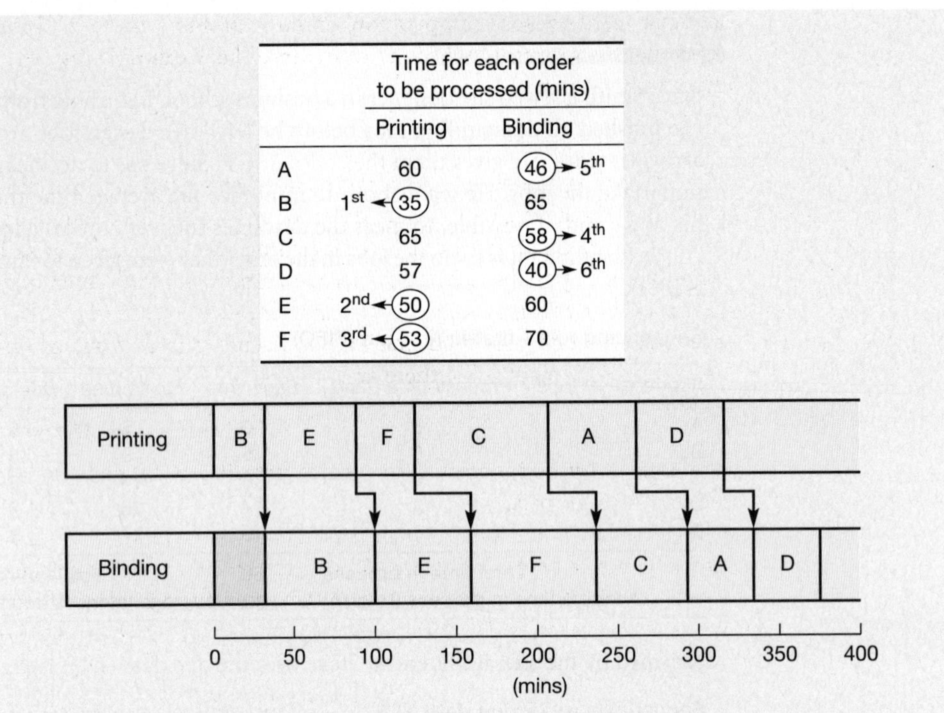

Figure 10.9 The application of Johnson's rule for scheduling *n* jobs through two work centres

Johnson's rule[5]

Johnson's rule

Johnson's rule applies to the sequencing of *n* jobs through two work centres. Figure 10.9 illustrates its use. In this case, a printer has to print and bind six jobs. The times for processing each job through the first (printing) and second (binding) work centres are shown in the figure. The rule is simple. First look for the smallest processing time. If that time is associated with the first work centre (printing in this case) then schedule that job first, or as near first as possible. If the next smallest time is associated with the second work centre then sequence that job last or as near last as possible. Once a job has been sequenced, delete it from the list. Carry on allocating jobs until the list is complete. In this particular case, the smallest processing time is 35 minutes for printing job B. Because this is at the first process (printing), job B is assigned first position in the schedule. The next smallest processing time is 40 minutes for binding (job D). Because this is at the second process (binding), it is sequenced last. The next lowest processing time, after jobs B and D have been struck off the list, is 46 minutes for binding job A. Because this is at the second work centre, it is sequenced as near last as possible, which in this case is fifth. This process continues until all the jobs have been sequenced. It results in a schedule for the two processes which is also shown in Figure 10.9.

Scheduling

Scheduling

Having determined the sequence that work is to be tackled in, some operations require a detailed timetable showing at what time or date jobs should start and when they should end – this is **scheduling**. Schedules are familiar statements of volume and timing in many consumer environments. For example, a bus schedule shows that more buses are put on routes at more frequent intervals during rush-hour periods. The bus schedule shows the time each bus is due to arrive at each stage of the route. Schedules of work are used in operations where some planning is required to ensure that customer demand is met. Other operations, such as rapid-response service operations where customers arrive in an unplanned way, cannot schedule the operation in a short-term sense. They can only respond at the time demand is placed upon them.

The complexity of scheduling[6]

The scheduling activity is one of the most complex tasks in operations management. First, schedulers must deal with several different types of resource simultaneously. Machines will have different capabilities and capacities; staff will have different skills. More importantly, the number of possible schedules increases rapidly as the number of activities and processes increases. For example, suppose one machine has five different jobs to process. Any of the five jobs could be processed first and, following that, any one of the remaining four jobs, and so on. This means that there are:

$$5 \times 4 \times 3 \times 2 = 120 \text{ different schedules possible}$$

More generally, for n jobs there are $n!$ (factorial n) different ways of scheduling the jobs through a single process.

We can now consider what impact there would be if, in the same situation, there was more than one type of machine. If we were trying to minimize the number of set-ups on two machines, there is no reason why the sequence on machine 1 would be the same as the sequence on machine 2. If we consider the two sequencing tasks to be independent of each other, for two machines there would be

$$120 \times 120 = 14{,}400 \text{ possible schedules of the two machines and five jobs.}$$

A general formula can be devised to calculate the number of possible schedules in any given situation, as follows:

$$\text{Number of possible schedules} = (n!)m$$

where n is the number of jobs and m is the number of machines.

In practical terms, this means that there are often many millions of feasible schedules, even for relatively small operations. This is why scheduling rarely attempts to provide an 'optimal' solution but rather satisfies itself with an 'acceptable' feasible one.

Forward and backward scheduling

Forward scheduling
Backward scheduling

Forward scheduling involves starting work as soon as it arrives. **Backward scheduling** involves starting jobs at the last possible moment to prevent them from being late. For example, assume that it takes six hours for a contract laundry to wash, dry and press a batch of overalls. If the work is collected at 8.00 am and is due to be picked up at 4.00 pm, there are more than six hours available to do it. Table 10.3 shows the different start times of each job, depending on whether they are forward- or backward-scheduled.

Table 10.3 The effects of forward and backward scheduling

Task	*Duration*	*Start time (backwards)*	*Start time (forwards)*
Press	1 hour	3.00 pm	1.00 pm
Dry	2 hours	1.00 pm	11.00 am
Wash	3 hours	10.00 am	8.00 am

The choice of backward or forward scheduling depends largely upon the circumstances. Table 10.4 lists some advantages and disadvantages of the two approaches. In theory, both materials requirements planning (MRP, *see* the supplement to Chapter 14) and just-in-time planning (JIT, *see* Chapter 15) use backward scheduling, only starting work when it is required. In practice, however, users of MRP have tended to allow too long for each task to be completed, and therefore each task is not started at the latest possible time. In comparison, JIT is started, as the name suggests, just in time.

Table 10.4 Advantages of forward and backward scheduling

Advantages of forward scheduling	*Advantages of backward scheduling*
High labour utilization – workers always start work to keep busy	Lower material costs – materials are not used until they have to be, therefore delaying added value until the last moment
Flexible – the time slack in the system allows unexpected work to be loaded	Less exposed to risk in case of schedule change by the customer Tends to focus the operation on customer due dates

Gantt charts

The most common method of scheduling is by use of the Gantt chart. This is a simple device which represents time as a bar, or channel, on a chart. Often the charts themselves are made up of long plastic channels into which coloured pieces of paper can be slotted to indicate what is happening with a job or a work centre. The start and finish times for activities can be indicated on the chart and sometimes the actual progress of the job is also indicated. The advantages of Gantt charts are that they provide a simple visual representation both of what should be happening and of what actually is happening in the operation. Furthermore, they can be used to 'test out' alternative schedules. It is a relatively simple task to represent alternative schedules (even if it is a far from simple task to find a schedule which fits all the resources satisfactorily). Figure 10.10 illustrates a Gantt chart for a specialist software developer. It indicates the progress of several jobs as they are expected to progress through five stages of the process. Gantt charts are not an optimizing tool, they merely facilitate the development of alternative schedules by communicating them effectively.

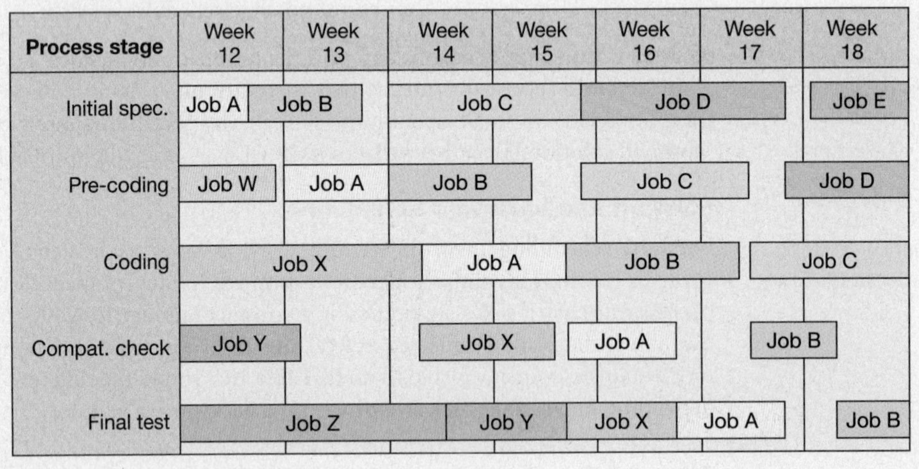

Figure 10.10 Gantt chart showing the schedule for jobs at each process stage

Short case
The life and times of a chicken salad sandwich – part one[7]

Pre-packed sandwiches are a growth product around the world as consumers put convenience and speed above relaxation and cost. But if you have recently consumed a pre-packed sandwich, think about the schedule of events which has gone into its making. For example, take a chicken salad sandwich. Less than 5 days ago, the chicken was on the farm unaware that it would never see another weekend. The Gantt chart schedule shown in Figure 10.11 tells the story of the sandwich, and (posthumously), of the chicken.

From the forecast, orders for non-perishable items are placed for goods to arrive up to a week in advance of their use. Orders for perishable items will be placed daily, a day or two before the items are required. Tomatoes,

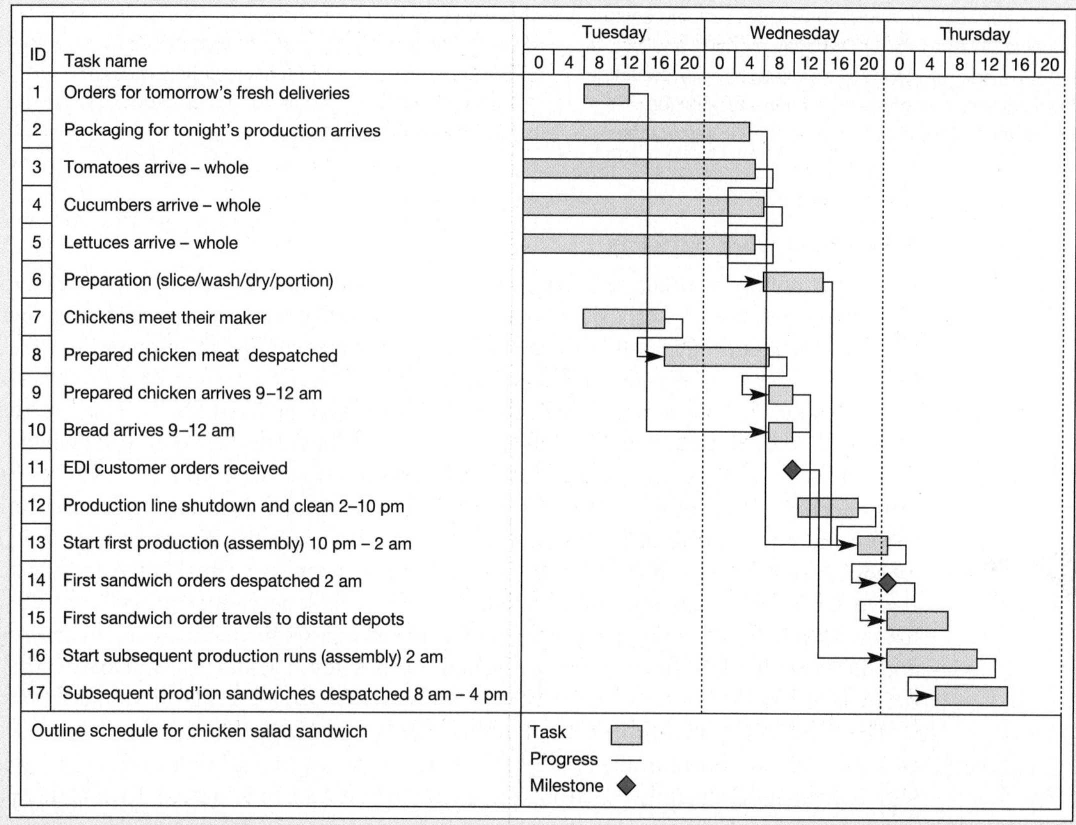

Figure 10.11 Simplified schedule for the manufacture and delivery of a chicken salad sandwich

cucumbers and lettuces have a three-day shelf life so may be received up to three days before production. Stock is held on a strict first-in-first-out (FIFO) basis. If today is (say) Wednesday, vegetables are processed that have been received during the last three days. This morning the bread arrived from a local bakery and the chicken arrived fresh, cooked and in strips ready to be placed directly in the sandwich during assembly. Yesterday (Tuesday) it had been killed, cooked, prepared and sent on its journey to the factory. By midday orders for tonight's production will have been received on the Internet. From 2.00 pm until 10.00 pm the production lines are closed down for maintenance and a very thorough cleaning. During this time the production planning team is busy planning the night's production run. Production for delivery to customers furthest away from the factory will have to be scheduled first. By 10 pm production is ready to start. Sandwiches are made on production lines. The bread is loaded onto a conveyor belt by hand and butter is spread automatically by a machine. Next the various fillings are applied at each stage according to the specified sandwich 'design', see Figure 10.12. After the filling has been assembled the top slice of bread is placed on the sandwich and

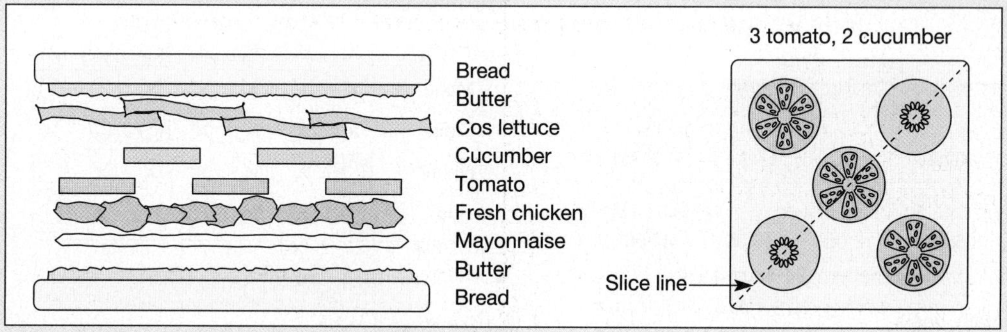

Figure 10.12 Design for a chicken salad sandwich

→

machine-chopped into two triangles, packed and sealed by machine. It is now early Thursday morning and by 2.00 am the first refrigerated lorries are already departing on their journeys to various customers. Production continues through until 2.00 pm on the Thursday, after which once again the maintenance and cleaning teams move in. The last sandwiches are dispatched by 4.00 pm on the Thursday. There is no finished goods stock.

Part two of the life and times of a chicken salad sandwich is in Chapter 14.

Scheduling work patterns

Where the dominant resource in an operation is its staff, then the schedule of work times effectively determines the capacity of the operation itself. The main task of scheduling, therefore, is to make sure that sufficient numbers of people are working at any point in time to provide a capacity appropriate for the level of demand at that point in time. This is often called staff **rostering**. Operations such as call centres, postal delivery, policing, holiday couriers, retail shops and hospitals will all need to schedule the working hours of their staff with demand in mind. This is a direct consequence of these operations having relatively high 'visibility' (we introduced this idea in Chapter 1). Such operations cannot store their outputs in inventories and so must respond directly to customer demand. For example, Figure 10.13 shows the scheduling of shifts for a small technical 'hot line' support service for a small software company. It gives advice to customers on their technical problems. Its service times are 4.00 hrs to 20.00 hrs on Monday, 4.00 hrs to 22.00 hrs Tuesday to Friday, 6.00 hrs to 22.00 hrs on Saturday, and 10.00 hrs to 20.00 hrs on Sunday. Demand is heaviest Tuesday to Thursday, starts to decrease on Friday, is low over the weekend and starts to increase again on Monday.

Rostering

The scheduling task for this kind of problem can be considered over different timescales, two of which are shown in Figure 10.13. During the day, working hours need to be agreed with individual staff members. During the week, days off need to be agreed. During the year, vacations, training periods and other blocks of time where staff are unavailable need to be agreed. All this has to be scheduled such that:

- capacity matches demand;
- the length of each shift is neither excessively long nor too short to be attractive to staff;
- working at unsocial hours is minimized;
- days off match agreed staff conditions (for example) in this example – staff prefer two consecutive days off every week;
- vacation and other 'time-off' blocks are accommodated;
- sufficient flexibility is built into the schedule to cover for unexpected changes in supply (staff illness) and demand (surge in customer calls).

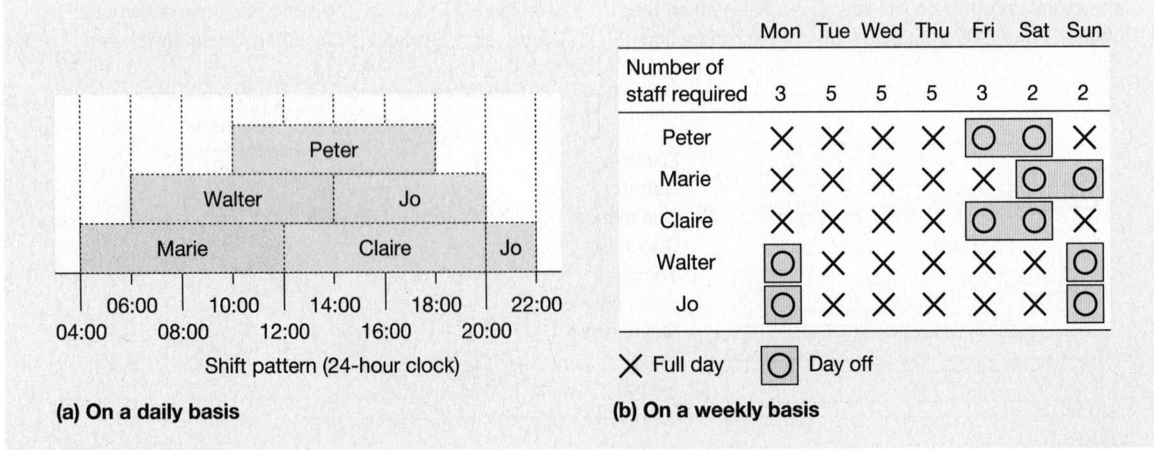

Figure 10.13 Shift scheduling in a home-banking enquiry service

Scheduling staff times is one of the most complex of scheduling problems. In the relatively simple example shown in Figure 10.13 we have assumed that all staff have the same level and type of skill. In very large operations with many types of skill to schedule and uncertain demand (for example a large hospital) the scheduling problem becomes extremely complex. Some mathematical techniques are available but most scheduling of this type is, in practice, solved using heuristics (rules of thumb), some of which are incorporated into commercially available software packages.

Monitoring and controlling the operation

Having created a plan for the operation through loading, sequencing and scheduling, each part of the operation has to be monitored to ensure that planned activities are indeed happening. Any deviation from the plans can then be rectified through some kind of intervention in the operation, which itself will probably involve some replanning. Figure 10.14 illustrates a simple view of control. The output from a work centre is monitored and compared with the plan which indicates what the work centre is supposed to be doing. Deviations from this plan are taken into account through a replanning activity and the necessary interventions made to the work centre which will (hopefully) ensure that the new plan is carried out. Eventually, however, some further deviation from planned activity will be detected and the cycle is repeated.

Push and pull control

Push control
Pull control

One element of control, then, is periodic intervention into the activities of the operation. An important decision is how this intervention takes place. The key distinction is between intervention signals which **push** work through the processes within the operation and those which **pull** work only when it is required. In a push system of control, activities are scheduled by means of a central system and completed in line with central instructions, such as an MRP system (*see* Chapter 14). Each work centre pushes out work without considering whether the succeeding work centre can make use of it. Work centres are coordinated by means of the central operations planning and control system. In practice, however, there are many reasons why actual conditions differ from those planned. As a consequence, idle time, inventory and queues often characterize push systems. By contrast, in a pull system of control, the pace and specification of what is done are set by the 'customer' workstation, which 'pulls' work from the preceding (supplier) workstation. The customer acts as the only 'trigger' for movement. If a request is not passed back from the customer to the supplier, the supplier cannot produce anything or move any materials. A request from a customer not only triggers production at the supplying stage, but also prompts the supplying stage to request a further delivery from its

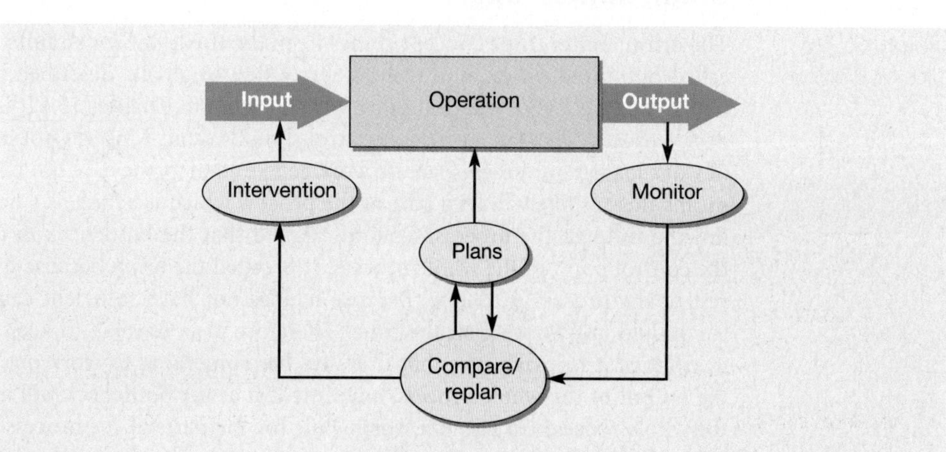

Figure 10.14 A simple model of control

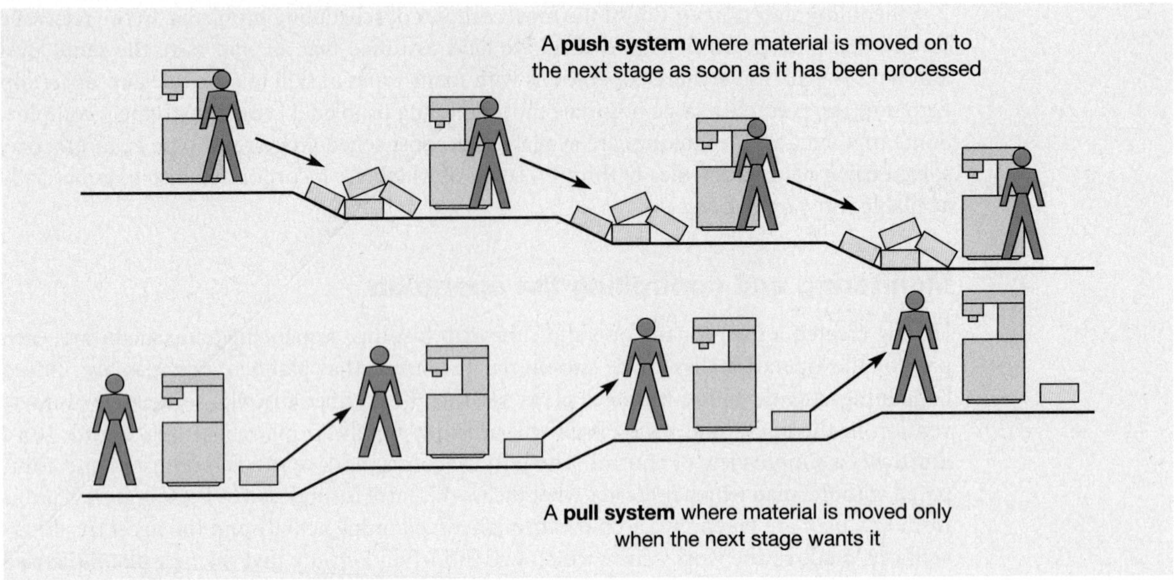

Figure 10.15 Push versus pull: the gravity analogy

own suppliers. In this way, demand is transmitted back through the stages from the original point of demand by the original customer.

The inventory consequences of push and pull

Understanding the differing principles of push and pull is important because they have different effects in terms of their propensities to accumulate inventory in the operation. Pull systems are far less likely to result in inventory build-up and are therefore favoured by JIT operations (*see* Chapter 15). To understand why this is so, consider an analogy: the 'gravity' analogy is illustrated in Figure 10.15. Here a push system is represented by an operation, each stage of which is on a lower level than the previous stage. When parts are processed by each stage, it pushes them down the slope to the next stage. Any delay or problem at that stage will result in the parts accumulating as inventory. In the pull system, parts cannot naturally flow uphill, so they can only progress if the next stage along deliberately pulls them forward. Under these circumstances, inventory cannot accumulate as easily.

Drum, buffer, rope

Drum, buffer, rope
Theory of constraints

The **drum, buffer, rope** concept comes from the **theory of constraints** (TOC) and a concept called optimized production technology (OPT) originally described by Eli Goldratt in his novel *The Goal*.[8] (We will deal more with his ideas in Chapter 15.) It is an idea that helps to decide exactly *where* in a process control should occur. Most do not have the same amount of work loaded onto each separate work centre (that is, they are not perfectly balanced. This means there is likely to be a part of the process which is acting as a bottleneck on the work flowing through the process. Goldratt argued that the bottleneck in the process should be the control point of the whole process. It is called the *drum* because it sets the 'beat' for the rest of the process to follow. Because it does not have sufficient capacity, a bottleneck is (or should be) working all the time. Therefore, it is sensible to keep a *buffer* of inventory in front of it to make sure that it always has something to work on. Because it constrains the output of the whole process, any time lost at the bottleneck will affect the output from the whole process. So it is not worthwhile for the parts of the process before the bottleneck to work to their full capacity. All they would do is produce work which would accumulate further along in the process up to the point where the bottleneck is constraining the flow.

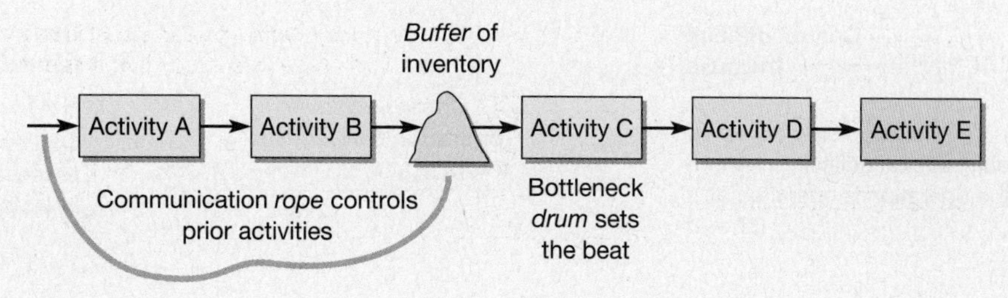

Figure 10.16 The drum, buffer, rope concept

Therefore, some form of communication between the bottleneck and the input to the process is needed to make sure that activities before the bottleneck do not overproduce. This is called the *rope* (see Figure 10.16).

Critical commentary

Most of the perspectives on control taken in this chapter are simplifications of a far more messy reality. They are based on models used to understand mechanical systems such as car engines. But anyone who has worked in real organizations knows that organizations are not machines. They are social systems, full of complex and ambiguous interactions. Simple models such as these assume that operations objectives are always clear and agreed, yet organizations are political entities where different and often conflicting objectives compete. Local government operations, for example, are overtly political. Furthermore, the outputs from operations are not always easily measured. A university may be able to measure the number and qualifications of its students, for example, but it cannot measure the full impact of its education on their future happiness. Also, even if it is possible to work out an appropriate intervention to bring an operation back into 'control', most operations cannot perfectly predict what effect the intervention will have. Even the largest of burger bar chains does not know *exactly* how a new shift allocation system will affect performance. Also, some operations never do the same thing more than once anyway. Most of the work done by construction operations is one-offs. If every output is different, how can 'controllers' ever know what is supposed to happen? Their plans themselves are mere speculation.

The degree of difficulty in controlling operations

The simple monitoring control model in Figure 10.15 helps us to understand the basic functions of the monitoring and control activity. But, as the critical commentary box says, it is a simplification. Some simple technology-dominated processes may approximate to it, but many other operations do not. In fact, the specific criticisms cited in the critical commentary box provide a useful set of questions which can be used to assess the degree of difficulty associated with control of any operation:[9]

- Is there consensus over what the operation's objectives should be?
- How well can the output from the operation be measured?
- Are the effects of interventions into the operation predictable?
- Are the operation's activities largely repetitive?

Figure 10.17 illustrates how these four questions can form dimensions of 'controllability'. It shows three different operations. The food processing operation is relatively straightforward to control, while the child care service is particularly difficult. The tax advice service is somewhere in between.

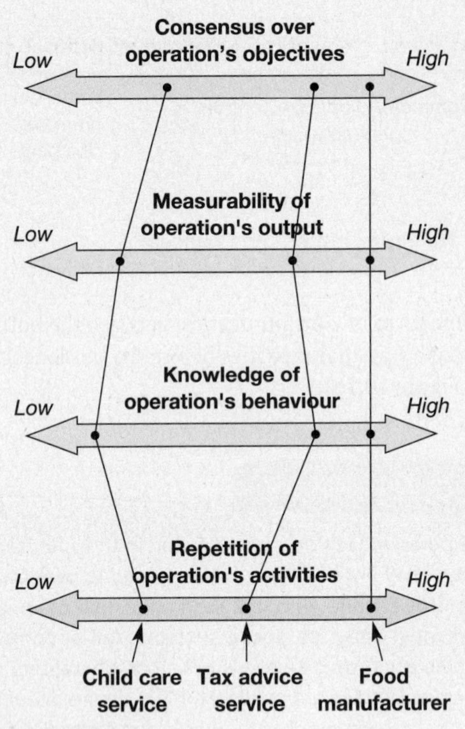

Figure 10.17 How easy is an operation to control?

Short case[10]
Routeing and scheduling helps milk processor gain an extra collection trip a day

Source: Robert Wiseman Dairies

Robert Wiseman Dairies is a major supplier of liquid milk, buying, producing and delivering to customers throughout Great Britain. The company's growth has been achieved through its strong relationship with farmer suppliers, ongoing investment in dairies and distribution depots, and excellent customer care. But, unless the company can schedule its collection and delivery activities effectively, both its costs and its customer service could suffer. This is why it uses a computerized routeing and scheduling system and a geographic information system to plan its transport operations. Previously the company's tankers completed two trips in a day – one involving offloading at locally based collection points, the other delivering direct to the company's factory. Now the same vehicles complete three round trips a day because of additional collections and a scheduling system (the TruckStops system).

Describing the change to its milk collection operations, group transport manager William Callaghan explains: *'The network of farms that supply our milk is constantly evolving, and we're finding that we now tend to deal with a smaller number of larger farms, often within a narrower radius. That gives us the opportunity to use our vehicles more economically, but it also means we need to keep updating our collection routes. In the past the company scheduled collections manually with the aid of maps, but we simply couldn't keep up with the complexity of the task with a manual system. In any case, TruckStops does the scheduling much more efficiently in a fraction of the time. One of the challenges in scheduling milk collection is that the vehicles start off each day empty, and ideally end up fully loaded. It's the exact reverse of a normal delivery operation.'*

The scheduling system has also proved invaluable in forward planning and 'first-cut' costing of collections from potential new suppliers. By using the system for progressive refinements to its regular schedules, Wiseman has been able to create what amount to 'look-up charts' that give approximate costs for collections from different locations.

Summary answers to key questions

*Check and improve your understanding of this chapter using self assessment questions and a personalised study plan, audio and video downloads, and an eBook – all at **www.myomlab.com**.*

➤ What is planning and control?

- Planning and control is the reconciliation of the potential of the operation to supply products and services, and the demands of its customers on the operation. It is the set of day-to-day activities that run the operation on an ongoing basis.
- A plan is a formalization of what is intended to happen at some time in the future. Control is the process of coping with changes to the plan and the operation to which it relates. Although planning and control are theoretically separable, they are usually treated together.
- The balance between planning and control changes over time. Planning dominates in the long term and is usually done on an aggregated basis. At the other extreme, in the short term, control usually operates within the resource constraints of the operation but makes interventions into the operation in order to cope with short-term changes in circumstances.

➤ How do supply and demand affect planning and control?

- The degree of uncertainty in demand affects the balance between planning and control. The greater the uncertainty, the more difficult it is to plan, and greater emphasis must be placed on control.
- This idea of uncertainty is linked with the concepts of dependent and independent demand. Dependent demand is relatively predictable because it is dependent on some known factor. Independent demand is less predictable because it depends on the chances of the market or customer behaviour.
- The different ways of responding to demand can be characterized by differences in the *P*:*D* ratio of the operation. The *P*:*D* ratio is the ratio of total throughput time of goods or services to demand time.

➤ What are the activities of planning and control?

- In planning and controlling the volume and timing of activity in operations, four distinct activities are necessary:
  - loading, which dictates the amount of work that is allocated to each part of the operation;
  - sequencing, which decides the order in which work is tackled within the operation;
  - scheduling, which determines the detailed timetable of activities and when activities are started and finished;
  - monitoring and control, which involve detecting what is happening in the operation, replanning if necessary, and intervening in order to impose new plans. Two important types are 'pull' and 'push' control. Pull control is a system whereby demand is triggered by requests from a work centre's (internal) customer. Push control is a centralized system whereby control (and sometimes planning) decisions are issued to work centres which are then required to perform the task and supply the next workstation. In manufacturing, 'pull' schedules generally have far lower inventory levels than 'push' schedules.
- The ease with which control can be maintained varies between operations.

Case study
Air traffic control – a world-class juggling act

Air traffic controllers have one of the most stressful jobs in the world. They are responsible for the lives of thousands of passengers who fly every day in and out of the world's airports. Over the last 15 years, the number of planes in the sky has doubled, leading to congestion at many airports and putting air traffic controllers under increasing pressure. The controllers battle to maintain 'separation standards' that set the distance between planes as they land and take off. Sheer volume pushes the air traffic controllers' skills to the limit. Jim Courtney, an air traffic controller at LaGuardia airport in New York, says: *'There are half a dozen moments of sheer terror in each year when you wish you did something else for a living.'*

Source: Arup

Error-free control is particularly important where people are being processed, as is the case for these air traffic controllers

New York – the world's busiest airspace

The busiest airspace in the world is above New York. Around 7,500 planes arrive and depart each day at New York's three airports, John F. Kennedy, LaGuardia and Newark. The three airports form a triangle around New York and are just 15 miles from each other. This requires careful coordination of traffic patterns, approach and take-off routes, using predetermined invisible corridors in the sky to keep the planes away from each other. If the wind changes, all three airports work together to change the flight paths.

Sophisticated technology fitted to most of the bigger planes creates a safety zone around the aircraft so that when two aircraft get near to each other their computers negotiate which is going to take action to avoid the other and then alerts the pilot who changes course. Smaller aircraft, without radar, rely upon vision and the notion of 'little plane, big sky'.

During its passage into or out of an airport, each plane will pass through the hands of about eight different controllers. The airspace is divided into sectors controlled by different teams of air traffic controllers. Tower controllers at each airport control planes landing and taking off together with ground controllers who manage the movement of the planes on the ground around the airport. The TRACON (Terminal Radar Approach Control) controllers oversee the surrounding airspace. Each New York air traffic controller handles about 100 landings and take-offs an hour, about one every 45 seconds.

TRACON controllers

The 60 TRACON controllers manage different sectors of airspace, with planes being handed over from one controller to the next. Each controller handles about 15 planes at a time, yet they never see them. All they see is a blip on a two-dimensional radar screen, which shows their aircraft type, altitude, speed and destination. The aircraft, however, are in three-dimensional airspace, flying at different altitudes and in various directions. The job of the approach controllers is to funnel planes from different directions into an orderly queue before handing each one over to the tower controllers for landing.

Tower controllers

The tower controllers are responsible for coordinating landing and taking off. Newark is New York's busiest airport. During the early morning rush periods, there can be 40 planes an hour coming into land, with about 60 wanting to take off. As a result there can be queues of up to 25 planes waiting to depart.

At LaGuardia, there are two runways that cross each other, one used for take-off and the other for landing. At peak times, air traffic controllers have to 'shoot the gap' – to get planes to take off in between the stream of landing aircraft, sometimes less than 60 seconds apart. Allowing planes to start their take-off as other planes are landing, using 'anticipated separation', keeps traffic moving and helps deal with increasing volumes of traffic. At peak times, controllers have to shoot the gap 80 times an hour.

Most airports handle a mixture of large and small planes, and tower controllers need to be able to calculate safe take-off intervals in an instant. They have to take into account aircraft type and capabilities in order to ensure that appropriate separations can be kept. The faster planes need to be given more space in front of them than the slower planes. Wake turbulence – mini-hurricanes which trail downstream of a plane's wing tips – is another major factor in determining how closely planes can follow each other. The larger the plane and the slower the plane, the greater the turbulence.

Besides the usual 'large' planes, controllers have to manage the small aircraft, business helicopters, traffic spotter planes and the many sightseeing planes flying over Manhattan, or up the Hudson towards the Statue of Liberty. The tower controllers have to control the movement of over 2,000 helicopters and light aircraft that fly through New York's airspace every day, being sure to keep them out of the airspace around each airport used by the arriving and departing aircraft.

Ground controllers

As an aircraft lands, it is handed over to the ground controllers who are responsible for navigating it through the maze of interconnecting taxiways found at most international airports. Some airport layouts mean that planes, having landed, have to cross over the runway where other planes are taking off in order to get to the terminal. All this needs careful coordination by the ground controllers.

Some pilots may be unfamiliar with airport layouts and need careful coaxing. Worse still is poor visibility, fog or low cloud. At Kennedy airport, the ground radar does not show aircraft type, so the controllers have to rely upon memory and constant checking of aircraft position by radio to ensure they know where each aircraft is at any time.

Stress

Dealing continually with so many aircraft movements means that controllers have but a split second to analyse and react to every situation, yet they need to be right 100 per cent of the time. Any small error or lapse in concentration can have catastrophic consequences. They can't afford to lose track of a single aircraft, because it may stray into someone else's airspace and into the path of another aircraft. If the computer projects that two planes are about to fly closer than three miles, the Conflict Alert buzzer sounds and the controllers have just seconds to make the right decision and then transmit it to the pilots. Sometimes problems arise in the planes themselves, such as an aircraft running short of fuel. Emergency landing procedures cover such eventualities. At Kennedy airport, they have about one such incident each day. As one controller remarked, *'It's like an enhanced video game, except you only have one life.'*

Questions

1 What does 'planning and control' mean to air traffic controllers?

2 What are the differing problems faced by TRACON, tower and ground controllers?

3 What sequencing rules do you think the tower controllers use?

Problems and applications

These problems and applications will help to improve your analysis of operations. You can find more practice problems as well as worked examples and guided solutions on MyOMLab at ***www.myomlab.com.***

1 Re-read the 'operations management in practice' at the beginning of the chapter, 'Joanne manages the schedule', and also the short case on Air France. What are the differences and what are the similarities between the planning and control tasks in these two operations?

2 A specialist sandwich retailer must order sandwiches at least 8 hours before they are delivered. When they arrive in the shop, they are immediately displayed in a temperature-controlled cabinet. The average time that the sandwiches spend in the cabinet is 6 hours. What is the *P:D* ratio for this retail operation?

3 It is the start of the week and Marie, Willy and Silvie have three jobs to complete. The three of them can work on these jobs in any order. Job A requires 4 hours of Marie's time, 5 hours of Willy's time and 3 hours of Silvie's time. Job B requires 2 hours of Marie's time, 8 hours of Willy's time and 7 hours of Silvie's time. Job C requires 10 hours of Marie's time, 4 hours of Willy's time and 5 hours of Silvie's time. Devise a schedule for Marie, Willy and Sylvie that details when they will be working on each job. (Assume that they work 7 hours per day.)

4 For the example above, what is the loading on Marie, Willy and Silvie? If all the jobs have to be finished within 2 days, how much extra time must each of them work?

5 *Step 1* – Make a list of all the jobs you have to do in the next week. Include in this list jobs relating to your work and/or study, jobs relating to your domestic life, in fact all the things you have to do.

Step 2 – Prioritize all these jobs on a 'most important' to 'least important' basis.

Step 3 – Draw up an outline schedule of exactly when you will do each of these jobs.

Step 4 – At the end of the week compare what your schedule said you *would* do with what you actually *have* done. If there is a discrepancy, why did it occur?

Step 5 – Draw up you own list of planning and control rules from your experience in this exercise in personal planning and control.

6 From your own experience of making appointments at your general practitioner's surgery, or by visiting whoever provides you with primary medical care, reflect on how patients are scheduled to see a doctor or nurse.

(a) What do you think planning and control objectives are for a general practitioner's surgery?
(b) How could your own medical practice be improved?

Selected further reading

Goldratt, E.Y. and Cox, J. (1984) *The Goal*, North River Press. Don't read this if you like good novels but do read it if you want an enjoyable way of understanding some of the complexities of scheduling. It particularly applies to the drum, buffer, rope concept described in this chapter and it also sets the scene for the discussion of OPT in Chapter 14.

Kehoe, D.F. and Boughton, N.J. (2001) New paradigms in planning and control across manufacturing supply chains – the utilization of Internet technologies, *International Journal of Operations and Production Management*, vol. 21, issue 5/6, 582–93.

Vollmann, T., Berry, W., Whybark, D.C. and Jacobs, F.R. (2004) *Manufacturing Planning and Control Systems for Supply Chain Management: The Definitive Guide for Professionals*, McGraw-Hill Higher Education. The latest version of the 'bible' of manufacturing planning and control.

Useful web sites

www.bpic.co.uk/ Some useful information on general planning and control topics.

www.apics.org. The American professional and education body that has its roots in planning and control activities.

www.opsman.org Lots of useful stuff.

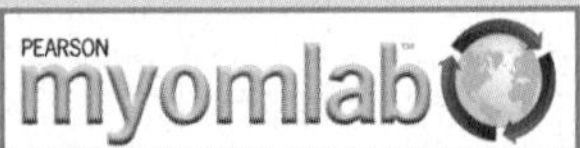

*Now that you have finished reading this chapter, why not visit MyOMLab at **www.myomlab.com** where you'll find more learning resources to help you make the most of your studies and get a better grade?*

Chapter 11

Capacity planning and control

Key questions

- What is capacity planning and control?
- How are demand and capacity measured?
- What are the alternative ways of coping with demand fluctuation?
- How can operations plan and control their capacity level?
- How can queuing theory be used to plan capacity?

Introduction

Providing the capability to satisfy current and future demand is a fundamental responsibility of operations management. Get the balance between capacity and demand right and the operation can satisfy its customers cost-effectively. Get it wrong and it will fail to satisfy demand, and have excessive costs. Capacity planning and control is also sometimes referred to as *aggregate* planning and control. This is because, at this level of the planning and control, demand and capacity calculations are usually performed on an aggregated basis which does not discriminate between the different products and services that an operation might produce. The essence of the task is to reconcile, at a general and aggregated level, the supply of capacity with the level of demand which it must satisfy (*see* Figure 11.1). This chapter also has a supplement that deals with analytical queuing models, one way of considering capacity planning and control, especially in some service operations.

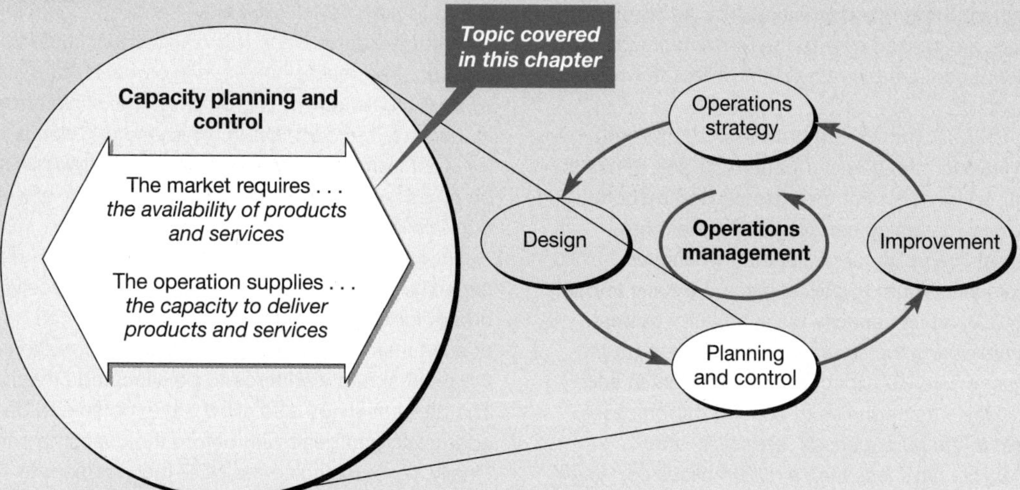

Figure 11.1 This chapter covers capacity planning and control

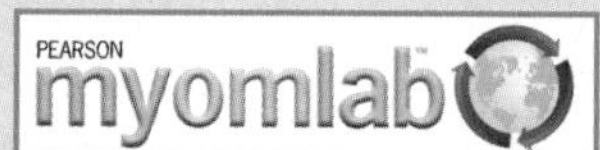

Check and improve your understanding of this chapter using self assessment questions and a personalised study plan, audio and video downloads, and an eBook – all at ***www.myomlab.com***.

Operations in practice Britvic – delivering drinks to demand[1]

Source: Wincanton

Britvic is amongst Europe's leading soft-drink manufacturers, a major player in a market consuming nearly ten billion litres a year. Annually, Britvic bottles, distributes and sells over 1 billion litres of ready-to-drink soft drinks in around 400 different flavours, shapes and sizes, including brands such as Pepsi, Tango, Robinsons, Aqua Libra, Purdey's and J2O. Every year, Britvic produce enough cans of soft drinks to stretch three times around the world, so it has to be a high-volume and high-speed business. Its six UK factories contain factory lines producing up to 1,500 cans a minute, with distribution organized on a giant scale. At the centre of its distribution network is a National Distribution Centre (NDC) located at Lutterworth, UK. It is designed to operate 24 hours a day throughout the year, handling up to 620 truckloads of soft drinks daily and, together with a national network of 12 depots, it has to ensure that 250,000 outlets in the UK receive their orders on time. Designed and built in collaboration with Wincanton, a specialist supply chain solutions company, which now manages Britvic's NDC, it is capable of holding up to 140 million cans in its 50,000-pallet 'High Bay' warehouse. All information, from initial order to final delivery, is held electronically. Loads are scanned at Britvic factories and fed into the *'Business Planning and Control System'* that creates a schedule of receipts. This information is then fed to the *Warehouse Management System* and when hauliers arrive at the NDC, data are passed over to the *Movement Control System* that controls the retrieval of pallets from the High Bay.

Over the year Britvic distribute over 100 million cases. However, the demand pattern for soft drinks is seasonal, with short-term changes caused by both weather and marketing campaigns. Furthermore, Britvic's service policy of responding whenever customers want them to deliver has a dramatic impact on the NDC and its capacity planning. *'Our busiest periods are during the summer and in the run-up to Christmas, where we expect over 200 trailers in and out each day – that equates to about 3 million cases per week. In the quiet periods, especially after Christmas, we have less than a million cases per week'* (Distribution Manager).

Not only is demand on the NDC seasonal in a general sense, it can vary from 2,000 pallets one day, to 6,000 the next, as a result of short-term weather patterns and variable order patterns from large customers (supermarkets). Given the lack of space in the High Bay, it is not possible to simply stock up for the busy periods, so flexibility and efficiency are the keys to success.

The NDC uses a number of methods to cope with demand fluctuation. Most importantly is the use and development of technology both within the NDC and out in Britvic's supply chain. High levels of throughput and the ability to respond quickly to demand fluctuations depend on the use of integrated information technology linked to automated 'High Bay' handling technology. *'Without the automation this plant simply couldn't function. You realize how much you need this system when it breaks down! The other day, multiple errors in the system meant that in the space of 6 hours we went from being ahead to having 50 loads waiting to be processed. That equates to 1,350 pallets or nearly 4 million cans.'*

Human resource management is also key in managing capacity. Every morning the shift manager receives orders for the day, although further orders can be placed at any time during the day. The order information allows the multi-skilled workforce to be allocated effectively. The daily meetings also allow any problems to be addressed and dealt with before they become critical. Finally, by outsourcing the NDC management to Wincanton, the site is able to second employees from other Wincanton-owned sites when demand is high. *'Our other sites around the country have different peaks and troughs throughout the year which helps us utilize employee numbers.'*

What is capacity management?

Capacity

The most common use of the word **capacity** is in the static, physical sense of the fixed *volume* of a container, or the space in a building. This meaning of the word is also sometimes used by operations managers. For example, a pharmaceutical manufacturer may invest in new 1,000-litre capacity reactor vessels, a property company purchases a 500-vehicle capacity city-centre car park, and a 'multiplex' cinema is built with 10 screens and a total capacity of 2,500 seats. Although these capacity measures describe the *scale* of these operations, they do not reflect the processing capacities of these investments. To do this we must incorporate a *time* dimension appropriate to the use of assets. So the pharmaceutical company will be concerned with the level of output that can be achieved using the 1,000-litre reactor vessel. If a batch of standard products can be produced every hour, the planned processing capacity could be as high as 24,000 litres per day. If the reaction takes four hours, and two hours are used for cleaning between batches, the vessel may only produce 4,000 litres per day. Similarly, the car park may be fully occupied by office workers during the working day, 'processing' only 500 cars per day. Alternatively, it may be used for shoppers staying on average only one hour, and theatre-goers occupying spaces for three hours in the evening. The processing capacity would then be up to 5,000 cars per day. Thus the definition of the capacity of an operation is the *maximum level of value-added activity over a period of time* that the process can achieve under normal operating conditions.

Capacity constraints

Capacity constraint

Many organizations operate at below their maximum processing capacity, either because there is insufficient demand completely to 'fill' their capacity, or as a deliberate policy, so that the operation can respond quickly to every new order. Often, though, organizations find themselves with some parts of their operation operating below their capacity while other parts are at their capacity 'ceiling'. It is the parts of the operation that are operating at their capacity 'ceiling' which are the **capacity constraint** for the whole operation. It is these parts of the operation that are pushed to their capacity ceiling that act as the constraint on the whole operation. For example, a retail superstore might offer a gift-wrapping service which at normal times can cope with all requests for its services without delaying customers unduly. At Christmas, however, the demand for gift wrapping might increase proportionally far more than the overall increase in custom for the store as a whole. Unless extra resources are provided to increase the capacity of this micro-operation, it could constrain the capacity of the whole store.

Planning and controlling capacity

Long-term capacity strategy

Capacity planning and control is the task of setting the effective capacity of the operation so that it can respond to the demands placed upon it. This usually means deciding how the operation should react to fluctuations in demand. We have faced this issue before in Chapter 6 where we examined long-term changes in demand and the alternative capacity strategies for dealing with the changes. These strategies were concerned with introducing (or deleting) major increments of physical capacity. We called this task **long-term capacity strategy**. In this chapter we are treating the shorter timescale where capacity decisions are being made largely within the constraints of the physical capacity limits set by the operation's long-term capacity strategy.

Medium- and short-term capacity

Medium term capacity planning and control

Having established long-term capacity, operations managers must decide how to adjust the capacity of the operation in the **medium term**. This usually involves an assessment of the demand forecasts over a period of 2–18 months ahead, during which time planned output can be varied, for example, by changing the number of hours the equipment is used. In practice, however, few forecasts are accurate, and most operations also need to respond to changes in demand which occur over a shorter timescale. Hotels and restaurants have unexpected and apparently random changes in demand from night to night, but also know from experience that certain days are on average busier than others. So operations managers also have to make **short-term capacity** adjustments, which enable them to flex output for a short period, either on a predicted basis (for example, bank checkouts are always busy at lunchtimes) or at short notice (for example, a sunny warm day at a theme park).

Short-term capacity planning and control

Aggregate demand and capacity

The important characteristic of capacity planning and control, as we are treating it here, is that it is concerned with setting capacity levels over the medium and short terms in **aggregated** terms. That is, it is making overall, broad capacity decisions, but is not concerned with all of the detail of the individual products and services offered. This is what 'aggregated' means – different products and services are bundled together in order to get a broad view of demand and capacity. This may mean some degree of approximation, especially if the mix of products or services being produced varies significantly (as we shall see later in this chapter). Nevertheless, as a first step in planning and control, aggregation is necessary. For example, a hotel might think of demand and capacity in terms of 'room nights per month', which ignores the number of guests in each room and their individual requirements, but is a good first approximation. A woollen knitwear factory might measure demand and capacity in the number of units (garments) it is capable of making per month, ignoring size, colour or style variations. Aluminium producers could use tonnes per month, ignoring types of alloy, gauge and batch size variation. The ultimate aggregation measure is money. For example, retail stores, which sell an exceptionally wide variety of products, use revenue per month, ignoring variation in spend, number of items bought, the gross margin of each item and the number of items per customer transaction. If all this seems very approximate, remember that most operations have sufficient experience of dealing with aggregated data to find it useful.

Aggregate planning and control

The objectives of capacity planning and control

The decisions taken by operations managers in devising their capacity plans will affect several different aspects of performance:

- *Costs* will be affected by the balance between capacity and demand (or output level if that is different). Capacity levels in excess of demand could mean under-utilization of capacity and therefore high unit cost.
- *Revenues* will also be affected by the balance between capacity and demand, but in the opposite way. Capacity levels equal to or higher than demand at any point in time will ensure that all demand is satisfied and no revenue lost.
- *Working capital* will be affected if an operation decides to build up finished goods inventory prior to demand. This might allow demand to be satisfied, but the organization will have to fund the inventory until it can be sold.
- *Quality* of goods or services might be affected by a capacity plan which involved large fluctuations in capacity levels, by hiring temporary staff for example. The new staff and the disruption to the routine working of the operation could increase the probability of errors being made.
- *Speed* of response to customer demand could be enhanced, either by the build-up of inventories (allowing customers to be satisfied directly from the inventory rather than having to wait for items to be manufactured) or by the deliberate provision of surplus capacity to avoid queuing.
- *Dependability* of supply will also be affected by how close demand levels are to capacity. The closer demand gets to the operation's capacity ceiling, the less able it is to cope with any unexpected disruptions and the less dependable its deliveries of goods and services could be.

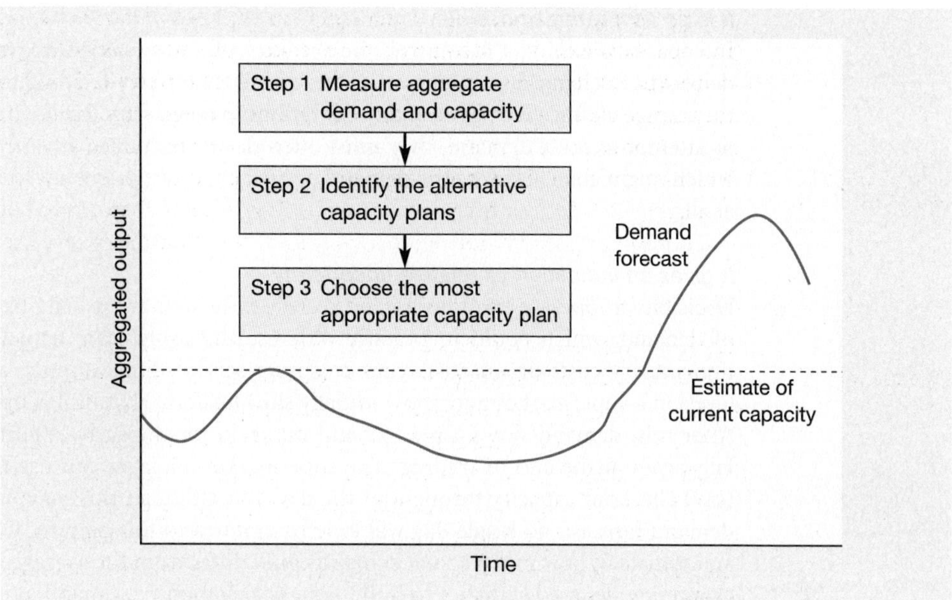

Figure 11.2 The steps in capacity planning and control

- *Flexibility*, especially volume flexibility, will be enhanced by surplus capacity. If demand and capacity are in balance, the operation will not be able to respond to any unexpected increase in demand.

The steps of capacity planning and control

The sequence of capacity planning and control decisions which need to be taken by operations managers is illustrated in Figure 11.2. Typically, operations managers are faced with a forecast of demand which is unlikely to be either certain or constant. They will also have some idea of their own ability to meet this demand. Nevertheless, before any further decisions are taken, they must have quantitative data on both capacity and demand. So the first step will be to *measure the aggregate demand and capacity* levels for the planning period. The second step will be to *identify the alternative capacity plans* which could be adopted in response to the demand fluctuations. The third step will be to *choose the most appropriate capacity plan* for their circumstances.

Measuring demand and capacity

Forecasting demand fluctuations

Forecasting is a key input to capacity planning and control

Although demand forecasting is usually the responsibility of the sales and/or marketing functions, it is a very important input into the **capacity planning and control** decision, and so is of interest to operations managers. After all, without an estimate of future demand it is not possible to plan effectively for future events, only to react to them. It is therefore important to understand the basis and rationale for these demand forecasts. (See the supplement on forecasting at the end of Chapter 6.) As far as capacity planning and control is concerned, there are three requirements from a demand forecast.

It is expressed in terms which are useful for capacity planning and control

If forecasts are expressed only in money terms and give no indication of the demands that will be placed on an operation's capacity, they will need to be translated into realistic expectations of demand, expressed in the same units as the capacity (for example, machine hours per year, operatives required, space, etc.).

It is as accurate as possible

In capacity planning and control, the accuracy of a forecast is important because, whereas demand can change instantaneously, there is a lag between deciding to change capacity and the change taking effect. Thus many operations managers are faced with a dilemma. In order to attempt to meet demand, they must often decide output in advance, based on a forecast which might change before the demand occurs, or worse, prove not to reflect actual demand at all.

It gives an indication of relative uncertainty

Decisions to operate extra hours and recruit extra staff are usually based on forecast levels of demand, which could in practice differ considerably from actual demand, leading to unnecessary costs or unsatisfactory customer service. For example, a forecast of demand levels in a supermarket may show initially slow business that builds up to a lunchtime rush. After this, demand slows, only to build up again for the early evening rush, and it finally falls again at the end of trading. The supermarket manager can use this forecast to adjust (say) checkout capacity throughout the day. But although this may be an accurate average demand forecast, no single day will exactly conform to this pattern. Of equal importance is an estimate of how much actual demand could differ from the average. This can be found by examining demand statistics to build up a distribution of demand at each point in the day. The importance of this is that the manager now has an understanding of when it will be important to have reserve staff, perhaps filling shelves, but on call to staff the checkouts should demand warrant it. Generally, the advantage of probabilistic forecasts such as this is that it allows operations managers to make a judgement between possible plans that would virtually guarantee the operation's ability to meet actual demand, and plans that minimize costs. Ideally, this judgement should be influenced by the nature of the way the business wins orders: price-sensitive markets may require a risk-avoiding cost minimization plan that does not always satisfy peak demand, whereas markets that value responsiveness and service quality may justify a more generous provision of operational capacity.

Seasonality of demand

Demand seasonality
Supply seasonality

In many organizations, capacity planning and control is concerned largely with coping with seasonal demand fluctuations. Almost all products and services have some **demand seasonality** and some also have **supply seasonality**, usually where the inputs are seasonal agricultural products – for example, in processing frozen vegetables. These fluctuations in demand or supply may be reasonably forecastable, but some are usually also affected by unexpected variations in the weather and by changing economic conditions. Figure 11.3 gives some examples of seasonality, and the short case 'Producing while the sun shines' discusses the sometimes unexpected link between weather conditions and demand levels.

Consider the four different types of operation described previously: a wool knitwear factor, a city hotel, a supermarket and an aluminium producer. Their demand patterns are shown in Figure 11.4. The woollen knitwear business and the city hotel both have seasonal sales demand patterns, but for different reasons: the woollen knitwear business because of climatic patterns (cold winters, warm summers) and the hotel because of demand from business people, who take vacations from work at Christmas and in the summer. The retail supermarket is a little less seasonal, but is affected by pre-vacation peaks and reduced sales during vacation periods. The aluminium producer shows virtually no seasonality, but is showing a steady growth in sales over the forecast period.

Weekly and daily demand fluctuations

Seasonality of demand occurs over a year, but similar predictable variations in demand can also occur for some products and services on a shorter cycle. The daily and weekly demand patterns of a supermarket will fluctuate, with some degree of predictability. Demand might be low in the morning, higher in the afternoon, with peaks at lunchtime and after work in the evening. Demand might be low on Monday and Tuesday, build up during the latter part

Figure 11.3 Many types of operation have to cope with seasonal demand

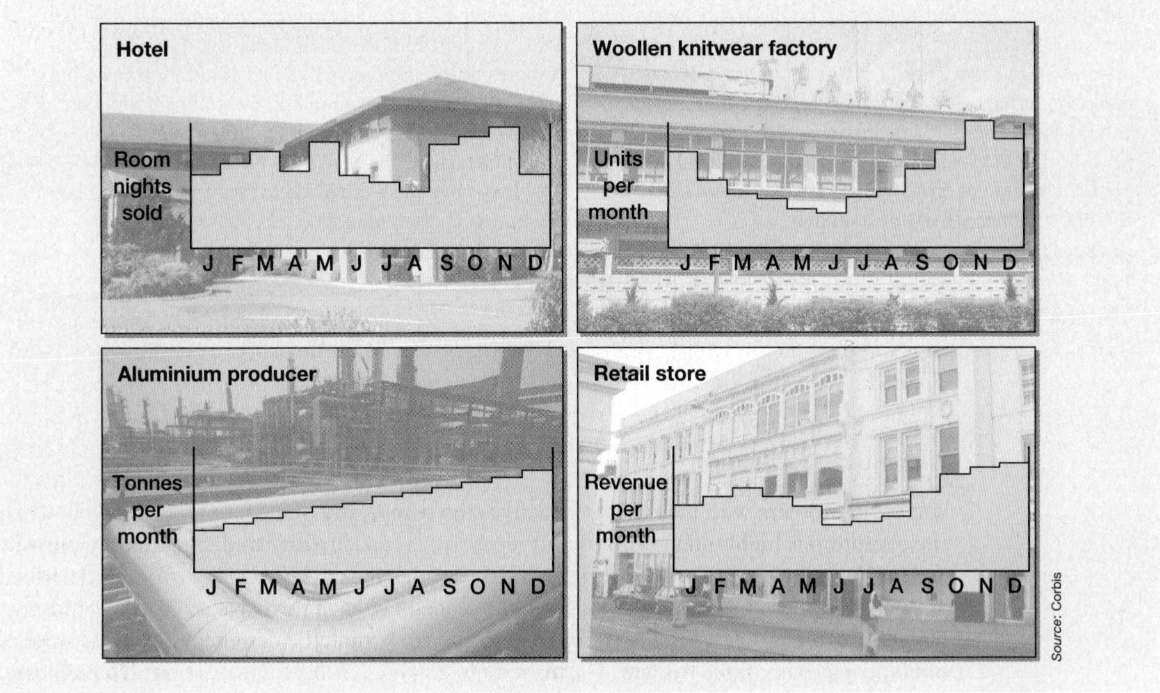

Figure 11.4 Aggregate demand fluctuations for four organizations

of the week and reach a peak on Friday and Saturday. Banks, public offices, telephone sales organizations and electricity utilities all have weekly and daily, or even hourly, demand patterns which require capacity adjustment. The extent to which an operation will have to cope with very short-term demand fluctuations is partly determined by how long its customers are prepared to wait for their products or services. An operation whose customers are incapable of, or unwilling to, wait will have to plan for very short-term demand fluctuations. Emergency services, for example, will need to understand the hourly variation in the demand for their services and plan capacity accordingly.

Short case
Producing while the sun shines[2]

Source: Alamy/Medical-on-line

The sales of some products are profoundly affected by the weather. Sunglasses, sunscreen, waterproof clothing and ice cream are all obvious examples. Yet the range of operations interested in weather forecasting has expanded significantly. Energy utilities, soft drink producers and fresh food producers and retailers are all keen to purchase the latest weather forecasts. But so are operations such as banking call centres and mobile phone operators. It would appear that the demand for telephone banking falls dramatically when the sun shines, as does the use of mobile phones. A motorway catering group was surprised to find that their sales of hot meals fell predictably by €110,000 per day for each degree temperature rise above 20 °C. Similarly, insurance companies have found it wise to sell their products when the weather is poor and likely customers are trapped indoors rather than relaxing outside in the sun, refusing to worry about the future. In the not-for-profit sector new understanding is being developed on the link between various illnesses and temperature. Here temperature is often used as a predictor of demand. So, for example, coronary thrombosis cases peak two days after a drop in temperature, for strokes the delay is around five days, while deaths from respiratory infections peak twelve days from a temperature drop. Knowing this, hospital managers can plan for changes in their demand.

Because of this, meteorological services around the world now sell increasingly sophisticated forecasts to a wide range of companies. In the UK, the Meteorological Office offers an internet-based service for its customers. It is also used to help insurance specialists price insurance policies to provide compensation against weather-related risk. Complex financial products called 'weather derivates' are now available to compensate for weather-related uncertainty. So, for example, an energy company could buy a financial option before winter where the seller pays the company a guaranteed sum of money if the temperature rises above a certain level. If the weather is mild and energy sales are low, the company gets compensation. If the weather is cold, the company loses the premium it has paid to the seller but makes up for it by selling more power at higher prices. However, as meteorologists point out, it is up to the individual businesses to use the information wisely. Only they have the experience to assess the full impact of weather on their operation. So, for example, supermarkets know that a rise in temperature will impact on the sales of cottage cheese (whereas, unaccountably, the sales of cottage cheese with pineapple chunks are not affected).

Measuring capacity

The main problem with measuring capacity is the complexity of most operations. Only when the operation is highly standardized and repetitive is capacity easy to define unambiguously. So if a television factory produces only one basic model, the weekly capacity could be described as 2,000 Model A televisions. A government office may have the capacity to print and post 500,000 tax forms per week. A fast ride at a theme park might be designed to process batches of 60 people every three minutes – a capacity to convey 1,200 people per hour. In each case, an **output capacity measure** is the most appropriate measure because the output from the operation does not vary in its nature. For many operations, however, the definition of capacity is not so obvious. When a much wider range of outputs places varying demands on the process, for instance, output measures of capacity are less useful. Here **input capacity measures** are frequently used to define capacity. Almost every type of operation could use a mixture of both input and output measures, but in practice, most choose to use one or the other (*see* Table 11.1).

Output capacity measure

Input capacity measures

Capacity depends on activity mix

The hospital measures its capacity in terms of its resources, partly because there is not a clear relationship between the number of beds it has and the number of patients it treats. If all

Table 11.1 Input and output capacity measures for different operations

Operation	*Input measure of capacity*	*Output measure of capacity*
Air-conditioner plant	Machine hours available	**Number of units per week**
Hospital	**Beds available**	Number of patients treated per week
Theatre	**Number of seats**	Number of customers entertained per week
University	**Number of students**	Students graduated per year
Retail store	**Sales floor area**	Number of items sold per day
Airline	**Number of seats available on the sector**	Number of passengers per week
Electricity company	Generator size	**Megawatts of electricity generated**
Brewery	Volume of fermentation tanks	**Litres per week**

Note: The most commonly used measure is shown in bold.

its patients required relatively minor treatment with only short stays in hospital, it could treat many people per week. Alternatively, if most of its patients required long periods of observation or recuperation, it could treat far fewer. Output depends on the mix of activities in which the hospital is engaged and, because most hospitals perform many different types of activities, output is difficult to predict. Certainly it is difficult to compare directly the capacity of hospitals which have very different activities.

Worked example

Suppose an air-conditioner factory produces three different models of air-conditioner unit: the de luxe, the standard and the economy. The de luxe model can be assembled in 1.5 hours, the standard in 1 hour and the economy in 0.75 hour. The assembly area in the factory has 800 staff hours of assembly time available each week.

If demand for de luxe, standard and economy units is in the ratio 2:3:2, the time needed to assemble 2 + 3 + 2 = 7 units is:

$$(2 \times 1.5) + (3 \times 1) + (2 \times 0.75) = 7.5 \text{ hours}$$

The number of units produced per week is:

$$\frac{800}{7.5} \times 7 = 746.7 \text{ units}$$

If demand changes to a ratio of de luxe, economy, standard units of 1:2:4, the time needed to assemble 1 + 2 + 4 = 7 units is:

$$(1 \times 1.5) + (2 \times 1) + (4 \times 0.75) = 6.5 \text{ hours}$$

Now the number of units produced per week is:

$$\frac{800}{6.5} \times 7 = 861.5 \text{ units}$$

Design capacity and effective capacity

The theoretical capacity of an operation – the capacity which its technical designers had in mind when they commissioned the operation – cannot always be achieved in practice. For example, a company coating photographic paper will have several coating lines which deposit thin layers of chemicals onto rolls of paper at high speed. Each line will be capable of running at a particular speed. Multiplying the maximum coating speed by the operating time of the plant gives the theoretical **design capacity** of the line. But in reality the line cannot be

Design capacity

run continuously at its maximum rate. Different products will have different coating requirements, so the line will need to be stopped while it is changed over. Maintenance will need to be performed on the line, which will take out further productive time. Technical scheduling difficulties might mean further lost time. Not all of these losses are the operations manager's fault; they have occurred because of the market and technical demands on the operation. The actual capacity which remains, after such losses are accounted for, is called the **effective capacity** of operation. These causes of reduction in capacity will not be the only losses in the operation. Such factors as quality problems, machine breakdowns, absenteeism and other avoidable problems will all take their toll. This means that the *actual output* of the line will be even lower than the effective capacity. The ratio of the output actually achieved by an operation to its design capacity, and the ratio of output to effective capacity are called, respectively, the **utilization** and the **efficiency** of the plant:

Effective capacity

Utilization

Efficiency

$$\text{Utilization} = \frac{\text{actual output}}{\text{design capacity}}$$

$$\text{Efficiency} = \frac{\text{actual output}}{\text{effective capacity}}$$

Worked example

Suppose the photographic paper manufacturer has a coating line with a design capacity of 200 square metres per minute, and the line is operated on a 24-hour day, 7 days per week (168 hours per week) basis.

Design capacity is 200 × 60 × 24 × 7 = 2.016 million square metres per week. The records for a week's production show the following lost production time:

1 Product changeovers (set-ups)	20 hrs
2 Regular preventative maintenance	16 hrs
3 No work scheduled	8 hrs
4 Quality sampling checks	8 hrs
5 Shift change times	7 hrs
6 Maintenance breakdown	18 hrs
7 Quality failure investigation	20 hrs
8 Coating material stockouts	8 hrs
9 Labour shortages	6 hrs
10 Waiting for paper rolls	6 hrs

During this week the actual output was only 582,000 square metres.

The first five categories of lost production occur as a consequence of reasonably unavoidable, planned occurrences and amount to a total of 59 hours. The last five categories are unplanned, and avoidable, losses and amount to 58 hours.

Measured in hours of production.

$$\text{Design capacity} = 168 \text{ hours per week}$$

$$\text{Effective capacity} = 168 - 59 = 109 \text{ hrs}$$

$$\text{Actual output} = 168 - 59 - 58 = 51 \text{ hrs}$$

$$\text{Utilization} = \frac{\text{actual output}}{\text{design capacity}} = \frac{51 \text{ hrs}}{168 \text{ hrs}} = 0.304(30\%)$$

$$\text{Efficiency} = \frac{\text{actual output}}{\text{effective capacity}} = \frac{51 \text{ hrs}}{109 \text{ hrs}} = 0.468(47\%)$$

Critical commentary

For such an important topic, there is surprisingly little standardization in how capacity is measured. Not only is a reasonably accurate measure of capacity needed for operations planning and control, it is also needed to decide whether it is worth investing in extra physical capacity such as machines. Yet not all practitioners would agree with the way in which design and effective capacity have been defined or measured in the previous worked example. For example, some would argue that the first five categories do *not* occur as 'a consequence of reasonably unavoidable, planned occurrences'. Product changeover set-ups can be reduced, allocating work in a different manner between processes could reduce the amount of time when no work is scheduled, even re-examining preventive maintenance schedules could lead to a reduction in lost time. One school of thought is that whatever capacity efficiency measures are used, they should be useful as diagnostic measures which can highlight the root causes of inefficient use of capacity. The idea of overall equipment effectiveness (OEE) described next is often put forward as a useful way of measuring capacity efficiencies.

Overall equipment effectiveness[3]

Overall equipment effectiveness

The **overall equipment effectiveness** (OEE) measure is an increasingly popular method of judging the effectiveness of operations equipment. It is based on three aspects of performance:

- *the time* that equipment is available to operate;
- *the quality* of the product or service it produces;
- *the speed,* or throughput rate, of the equipment.

Overall equipment effectiveness is calculated by multiplying an availability rate by a performance (or speed) rate multiplied by a quality rate. Figure 11.5 uses the same categories of 'lost' time as were used in Figure 10.5 in the previous chapter. Some of the reduction in available capacity of a piece of equipment (or any process) is caused by time losses such as set-up and changeover losses (when the equipment or process is being prepared for its next

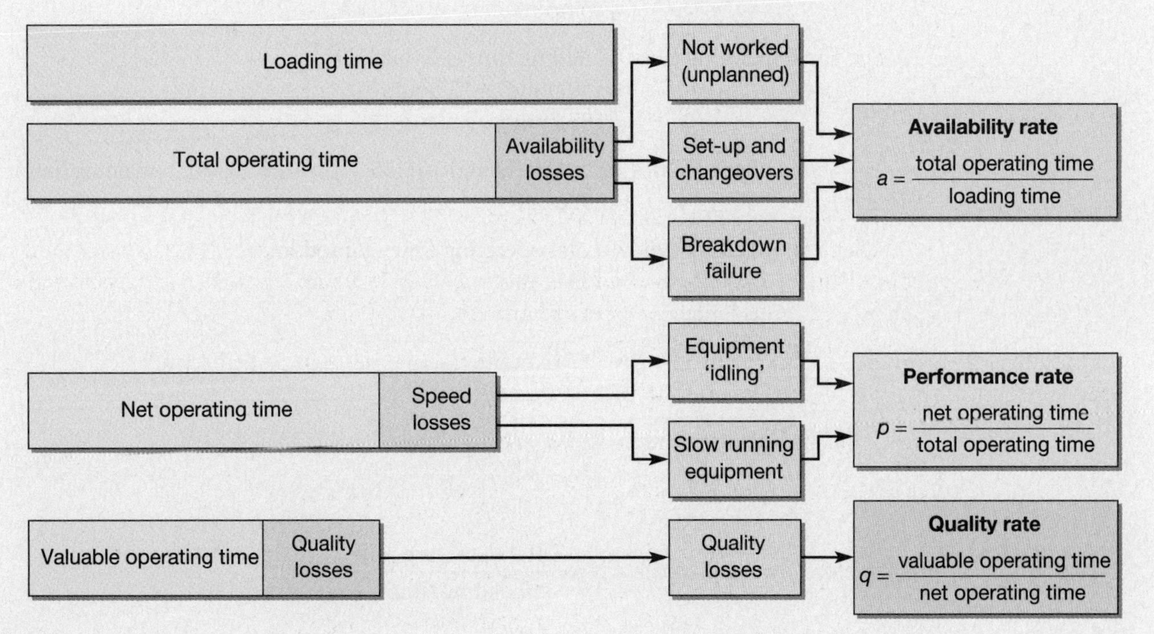

Figure 11.5 Operating equipment effectiveness

activity), and breakdown failures when the machine is being repaired. Some capacity is lost through speed losses such as when equipment is idling (for example when it is temporarily waiting for work from another process) and when equipment is being run below its optimum work rate. Finally, not everything processed by a piece of equipment will be error-free. So some capacity is lost through quality losses.

Taking the notation in Figure 11.5,

$$\text{OEE} = a \times p \times q$$

For equipment to operate effectively, it needs to achieve high levels of performance against all three of these dimensions. Viewed in isolation, these individual metrics are important indicators of plant performance, but they do not give a complete picture of the machine's *overall* effectiveness. This can only be understood by looking at the combined effect of the three measures, calculated by multiplying the three individual metrics together. All these losses to the OEE performance can be expressed in terms of units of time – the design cycle time to produce one good part. So, a reject of one part has an equivalent time loss. In effect, this means that an OEE represents the valuable operating time as a percentage of the design capacity.

Worked example

In a typical 7-day period, the planning department programmes a particular machine to work for 150 hours – its loading time. Changeovers and set-ups take an average of 10 hours and breakdown failures average 5 hours every 7 days. The time when the machine cannot work because it is waiting for material to be delivered from other parts of the process is 5 hours on average and during the period when the machine is running, it averages 90 per cent of its rated speed. Three per cent of the parts processed by the machine are subsequently found to be defective in some way.

$$\begin{aligned}
\text{Maximum time available} &= 7 \times 24 \text{ hours} \\
&= 168 \text{ hours}
\end{aligned}$$

$$\text{Loading time} = 150 \text{ hours}$$

$$\begin{aligned}
\text{Availability losses} &= 10 \text{ hours (set-ups)} + 5 \text{ hrs (breakdowns)} \\
&= 15 \text{ hours}
\end{aligned}$$

$$\begin{aligned}
\text{So, Total operating time} &= \text{Loading time} - \text{Availability} \\
&= 150 \text{ hours} - 15 \text{ hours} \\
&= 135 \text{ hours}
\end{aligned}$$

$$\begin{aligned}
\text{Speed losses} &= 5 \text{ hours (idling)} + ((135 - 5) \times 0.1)(10\% \text{ of remaining time}) \\
&= 18 \text{ hours}
\end{aligned}$$

$$\begin{aligned}
\text{So, Net operating time} &= \text{Total operating time} - \text{Speed losses} \\
&= 135 - 18 \\
&= 117 \text{ hours}
\end{aligned}$$

$$\begin{aligned}
\text{Quality losses} &= 117 \text{ (Net operating time)} \times 0.03 \text{ (Error rate)} \\
&= 3.51 \text{ hours}
\end{aligned}$$

$$\begin{aligned}
\text{So, Valuable operating time} &= \text{Net operating time} - \text{Quality losses} \\
&= 117 - 3.51 \\
&= 113.49 \text{ hours}
\end{aligned}$$

$$\begin{aligned}
\text{Therefore, availability rate} = a &= \frac{\text{Total operating time}}{\text{Loading time}} \\
&= \frac{135}{150} = 90\%
\end{aligned}$$

$$\text{and, performance rate} = p = \frac{\text{Net operating time}}{\text{Total operating time}}$$

$$= \frac{117}{135} = 86.67$$

$$\text{and quality rate} = q = \frac{\text{Valuable operating time}}{\text{Net operating time}}$$

$$= \frac{113.49}{117} = 97\%$$

$$\text{OEE } (a \times p \times q) = 75.6\%$$

Short case
British Airways London Eye

The British Airways London Eye is the world's largest observation wheel and one of the UK's most spectacular tourist attractions. The 32 passenger capsules, fixed on the perimeter of the 135 metre diameter rim, each hold 25 people. The wheel rotates continuously, so entry requires customers to step into the capsules which are moving at 0.26 metre per second, which is a quarter of normal walking speed. One complete 360 degree rotation takes 30 minutes, at the end of which the doors open and passengers disembark. Boarding and disembarkation are separated on the specially designed platform which is built out over the river. The attraction has a 'timed admissions booking system' (TABS) for both individual and group bookings. This allocates requests for 'flights' on the basis of half-hour time slots. At the time of writing, the BA London Eye is open every day except Christmas Day. Admission is from 10.00 am to 9.30 pm (for the 9.30 to 10.00 pm slot) in the summer, from the beginning of April to mid-September. For the rest of the year, the winter season, admission begins at 10.00 am, and last admissions are for the 5.30 to 6.00 pm slot.

Source: British Airways London Eye

The BA London Eye forecasts anticipated that 2.2 million passengers would fly the London Eye in 2000, excluding January, which was reserved for final testing and admission of invited guests only. An early press release told journalists that the London Eye would rotate an average of 6,000 revolutions per year.

The alternative capacity plans

With an understanding of both demand and capacity, the next step is to consider the alternative methods of responding to demand fluctuations. There are three 'pure' options available for coping with such variation:

Level capacity plan
Chase demand plan
Demand management

- Ignore the fluctuations and keep activity levels constant (**level capacity plan**).
- Adjust capacity to reflect the fluctuations in demand (**chase demand plan**).
- Attempt to change demand to fit capacity availability (**demand management**).

In practice, most organizations will use a mixture of all of these 'pure' plans, although often one plan might dominate. The Short case 'Seasonal salads' describes how one operation pursues some of these options.

Short case

Seasonal salads

Source: Corbis

Lettuce is an all-year-round ingredient for most salads, but both the harvesting of the crop and its demand are seasonal. Lettuces are perishable and must be kept in cold stores and transported in refrigerated vehicles. Even then the product only stays fresh for a maximum of a week. In most north European countries, demand continues throughout the winter at around half the summer levels, but outdoor crops cannot be grown during the winter months. Glasshouse cultivation is possible but expensive.

One of Europe's largest lettuce growers is G's Fresh Salads, based in the UK. Their supermarket customers require fresh produce to be delivered 364 days a year, but because of the limitations of the English growing season, the company has developed other sources of supply in Europe. It acquired a farm and packhouse in the Murcia region of south-eastern Spain, which provides the bulk of salad crops during the winter, transported daily to the UK by a fleet of refrigerated trucks. Further top-up produce is imported by air from around the world.

Sales forecasts are agreed with the individual supermarkets well in advance, allowing the planting and growing programmes to be matched to the anticipated level of sales. However, the programme is only a rough guide. The supermarkets may change their orders right up to the afternoon of the preceding day. Weather is a dominant factor. First, it determines supply – how well the crop grows and how easy it is to harvest. Second, it influences sales – cold, wet periods during the summer discourage the eating of salads, whereas hot spells boost demand greatly.

Figure 11.6 illustrates this. The Iceberg lettuce sales programme is shown, and compared with the actual English-grown and Spanish-grown sales. The fluctuating nature of the actual sales is the result of a combination of weather-related availability and supermarket demand. These do not always match. When demand is higher than expected, the picking rigs and their crews continue

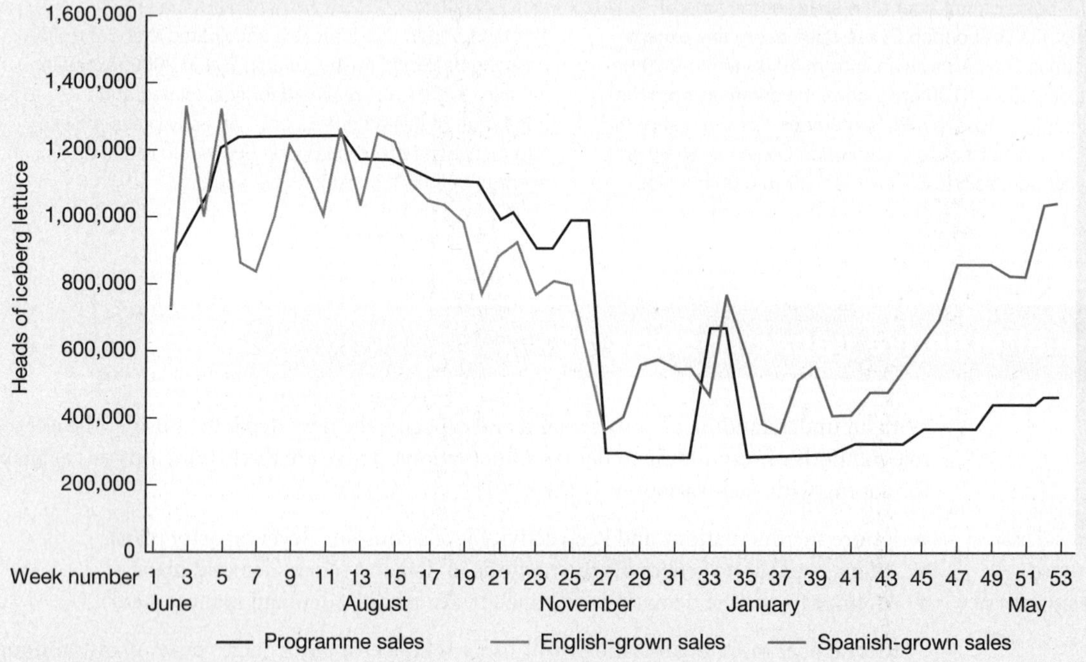

Figure 11.6 Typical year's iceberg lettuce sales

to work into the middle of night, under floodlights. Another capacity problem is the operation's staffing levels. It relies on temporary seasonal harvesting and packing staff to supplement the full-time employees for both the English and Spanish seasons. Since most of the crop is transported to the UK in bulk, a large permanent staff is maintained for packing and distribution in the UK. The majority of the Spanish workforce is temporary, with only a small number retained during the extremely hot summer to grow and harvest other crops such as melons.

The specialist lettuce harvesting machines (the 'rigs') are shipped over to Spain every year at the end of the English season, so that the company can achieve maximum utilization from all this expensive capital equipment. These rigs not only enable very high productivity of the pickers, but also ensure the best possible conditions for quality packing and rapid transportation to the cold stores.

Level capacity plan

In a level capacity plan, the processing capacity is set at a uniform level throughout the planning period, regardless of the fluctuations in forecast demand. This means that the same number of staff operate the same processes and should therefore be capable of producing the same aggregate output in each period. Where non-perishable materials are processed, but not immediately sold, they can be transferred to finished goods inventory in anticipation of sales at a later time. Thus this plan is feasible (but not necessarily desirable) for our examples of the woollen knitwear company and the aluminium producer (*see* Fig. 11.7).

Level capacity plans of this type can achieve the objectives of stable employment patterns, high process utilization, and usually also high productivity with low unit costs. Unfortunately, they can also create considerable inventory which has to be financed and stored. Perhaps the biggest problem, however, is that decisions have to be taken as to what to produce for inventory rather than for immediate sale. Will green woollen sweaters knitted in July still be fashionable in October? Could a particular aluminium alloy in a specific sectional shape still be sold months after it has been produced? Most firms operating this plan, therefore, give priority to only creating inventory where future sales are relatively certain and unlikely to be affected by changes in fashion or design. Clearly, such plans are not suitable for 'perishable' products, such as foods and some pharmaceuticals, for products where fashion changes rapidly and unpredictably (for example, popular music CDs, fashion garments), or for customized products.

A level capacity plan could also be used by the hotel and supermarket, although this would not be the usual approach of such organizations, because it usually results in a waste of staff resources, reflected in low productivity. Because service cannot be stored as inventory, a level capacity plan would involve running the operation at a uniformly high level of capacity

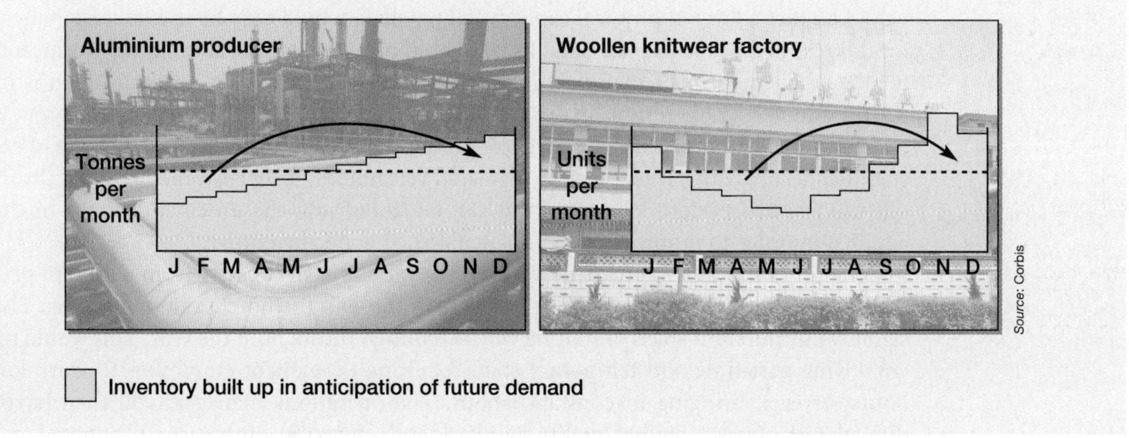

Figure 11.7 Level capacity plans which use anticipation inventory to supply future demand

Figure 11.8 Level capacity plans with under-utilization of capacity

availability. The hotel would employ sufficient staff to service all the rooms, to run a full restaurant, and to staff the reception even in months when demand was expected to be well below capacity. Similarly, the supermarket would plan to staff all the checkouts, warehousing operations, and so on, even in quiet periods (*see* Fig. 11.8).

Low utilization can make level capacity plans prohibitively expensive in many service operations, but may be considered appropriate where the opportunity costs of individual lost sales are very high. For example, in the high-margin retailing of jewellery and in (real) estate agents. It is also possible to set the capacity somewhat below the forecast peak demand level in order to reduce the degree of under-utilization. However, in the periods where demand is expected to exceed planned capacity, customer service may deteriorate. Customers may have to queue for long periods or may be 'processed' faster and less sensitively. While this is obviously far from ideal, the benefits to the organization of stability and productivity may outweigh the disadvantages of upsetting some customers.

Chase demand plan

The opposite of a level capacity plan is one which attempts to match capacity closely to the varying levels of forecast demand. This is much more difficult to achieve than a level capacity plan, as different numbers of staff, different working hours, and even different amounts of equipment may be necessary in each period. For this reason, pure chase demand plans are unlikely to appeal to operations which manufacture standard, non-perishable products. Also, where manufacturing operations are particularly capital-intensive, the chase demand policy would require a level of physical capacity, all of which would only be used occasionally. It is for this reason that such a plan is less likely to be appropriate for the aluminium producer than for the woollen garment manufacturer (*see* Fig. 11.9). A pure chase demand plan is more usually adopted by operations which cannot store their output, such as customer-processing operations or manufacturers of perishable products. It avoids the wasteful provision of excess staff that occurs with a level capacity plan, and yet should satisfy customer demand throughout the planned period. Where output can be stored, the chase demand policy might be adopted in order to minimize or eliminate finished goods inventory.

Sometimes it is difficult to achieve very large variations in capacity from period to period. If the changes in forecast demand are as large as those in the hotel example (*see* Fig. 11.10), significantly different levels of staffing will be required throughout the year. This would mean employing part-time and temporary staff, requiring permanent employees to work longer hours, or even bringing in contract labour. The operations managers will then have the difficult task of ensuring that quality standards and safety procedures are still adhered to, and that the customer service levels are maintained.

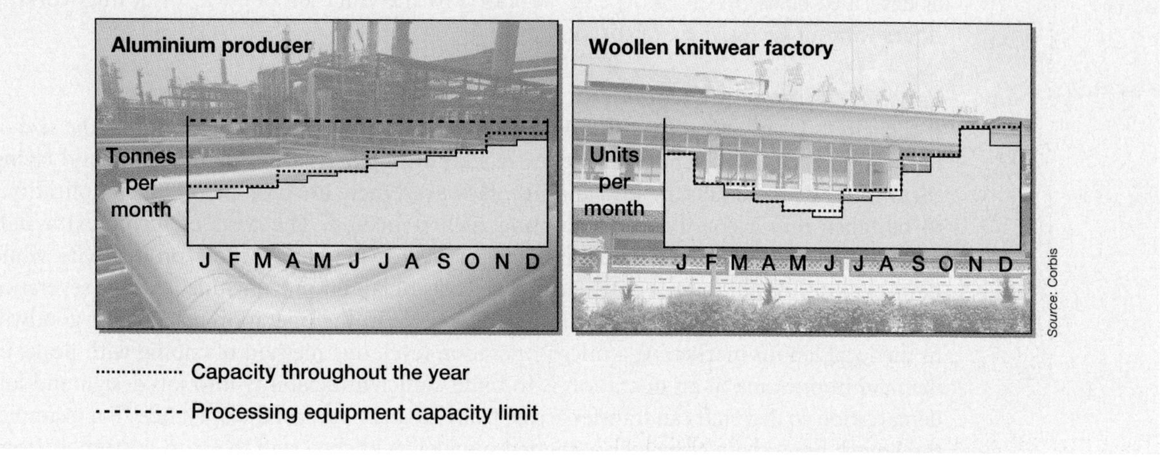

Figure 11.9 Chase demand capacity plans with changes in capacity which reflect changes in demand

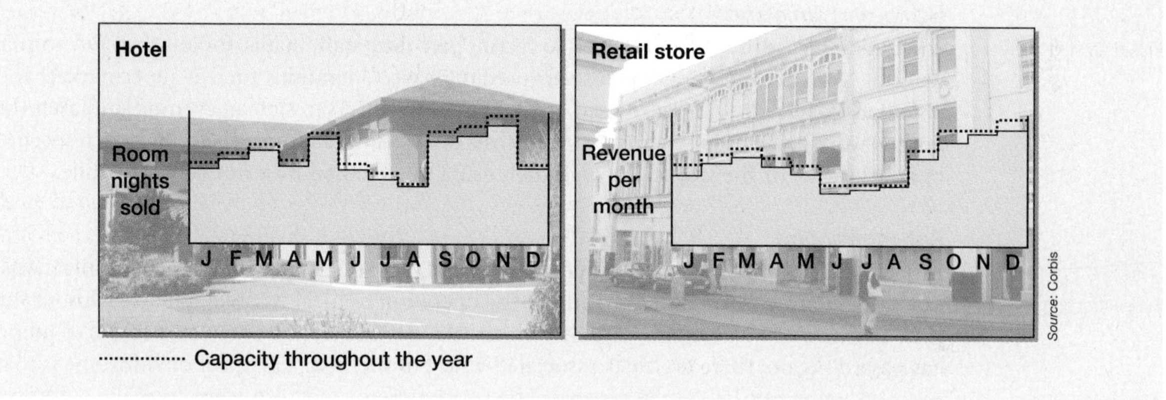

Figure 11.10 Chase demand capacity plans with changes in capacity which reflect changes in demand

Methods of adjusting capacity

The chase demand approach requires that capacity is adjusted by some means. There are a number of different methods for achieving this, although they may not all be feasible for all types of operation. Some of these methods are listed below.

Overtime and idle time

Often the quickest and most convenient method of adjusting capacity is by varying the number of productive hours worked by the staff in the operation. When demand is higher than nominal capacity, **overtime** is worked, and when demand is lower than nominal capacity the amount of time spent by staff on productive work can be reduced. In the latter case, it may be possible for staff to engage in some other activity such as cleaning or maintenance. This method is only useful if the timing of the extra productive capacity matches that of the demand. For example, there is little to be gained in asking a retail operation's staff to work extra hours in the evening if all the extra demand is occurring during their normal working period. The costs associated with this method are either the extra payment which is normally necessary to secure the agreement of staff to work overtime, or in the case of **idle time**, the costs of paying staff who are not engaged in direct productive work. Further, there might be costs associated with the fixed costs of keeping the operation heated, lit and secure over the extra period staff are working. There is also a limit to the amount of extra working time which any workforce can deliver before productivity levels decrease. **Annualized hours** approaches,

Overtime

Idle time

Annualized hours

as described below in the Short case 'Working by the year', are one way of flexing working hours without excessive extra costs.

Varying the size of the workforce

If capacity is largely governed by workforce size, one way to adjust it is to adjust the size of the workforce. This is done by hiring extra staff during periods of high demand and laying them off as demand falls, or **hire and fire**. However, there are cost and ethical implications to be taken into account before adopting such a method. The costs of hiring extra staff include those associated with recruitment, as well as the costs of low productivity while new staff go through the learning curve. The costs of lay-off may include possible severance payments, but might also include the loss of morale in the operation and loss of goodwill in the local labour market. At a micro-operation level, one method of coping with peaks in demand in one area of an operation is to build sufficient flexibility into job design and job demarcation so that staff can transfer across from less busy parts of the operation. For example, the French hotel chain Novotel has trained some of its kitchen staff to escort customers from the reception area up to their rooms. The peak times for registering new customers coincide with the least busy times in the kitchen and restaurant areas.

Hire and fire

Using part-time staff

A variation on the previous strategy is to recruit **part-time staff**, that is, for less than the normal working day. This method is extensively used in service operations such as supermarkets and fast-food restaurants but is also used by some manufacturers to staff an evening shift after the normal working day. However, if the fixed costs of employment for each employee, irrespective of how long he or she works, are high then using this method may not be worthwhile.

Part-time staff

Subcontracting

In periods of high demand, an operation might buy capacity from other organizations, called **subcontracting**. This might enable the operation to meet its own demand without the extra expense of investing in capacity which will not be needed after the peak in demand has passed. Again, there are costs associated with this method. The most obvious one is that subcontracting can be very expensive. The subcontractor will also want to make sufficient margin out of the business. A subcontractor may not be as motivated to deliver on time or to the desired levels of quality. Finally, there is the risk that the subcontractors might themselves decide to enter the same market.

Subcontracting

Critical commentary

To many, the idea of fluctuating the workforce to match demand, either by using part-time staff or by hiring and firing, is more than just controversial. It is regarded as unethical. It is any business's responsibility, they argue, to engage in a set of activities which are capable of sustaining employment at a steady level. Hiring and firing merely for seasonal fluctuations, which can be predicted in advance, is treating human beings in a totally unacceptable manner. Even hiring people on a short-term contract, in practice, leads to them being offered poorer conditions of service and leads to a state of permanent anxiety as to whether they will keep their jobs. On a more practical note, it is pointed out that, in an increasingly global business world where companies may have sites in different countries, those countries that allow hiring and firing are more likely to have their plants 'downsized' than those where legislation makes this difficult.

Manage demand plan

The most obvious mechanism of **demand management** is to **change demand** through price. Although this is probably the most widely applied approach in demand management, it is less common for products than for services. For example, some city hotels offer low-cost 'city break' vacation packages in the months when fewer business visitors are expected. Skiing and

Demand management
Change demand

camping holidays are cheapest at the beginning and end of the season and are particularly expensive during school vacations. Discounts are given by photo-processing firms during winter periods, but never around summer holidays. Ice cream is 'on offer' in many supermarkets during the winter. The objective is invariably to stimulate off-peak demand and to constrain peak demand, in order to smooth demand as much as possible. Organizations can also attempt to increase demand in low periods by appropriate advertising. For example, turkey growers in the UK and the USA make vigorous attempts to promote their products at times other than Christmas and Thanksgiving.

Short case
Working by the year[4]

One method of fluctuating capacity as demand varies throughout the year without many of the costs associated with overtime or hiring temporary staff is called the Annual Hours Work Plan. This involves staff contracting to work a set number of hours per year rather than a set number of hours per week. The advantage of this is that the amount of staff time available to an organization can be varied throughout the year to reflect the real state of demand. Annual hours plans can also be useful when supply varies throughout the year. For example, a UK cheese factory of Express Foods, like all cheese factories, must cope with processing very different quantities of milk at different times of the year. In spring and during early summer, cows produce large quantities of milk, but in late summer and autumn the supply of milk slows to a trickle. Before the introduction of annualized hours, the factory had relied on overtime and hiring temporary workers during the busy season. Now the staff are contracted to work a set number of hours a year with rotas agreed more than a year in advance and after consultation with the union. This means that at the end of July staff broadly know what days and hours they will be working up to September of the following year. If an emergency should arise, the company can call in people from a group of 'super crew' who work more flexible hours in return for higher pay but can do any job in the factory.

However, not all experiments with annualized hours have been as successful as that at Express Foods. In cases where demand is very unpredictable, staff can be asked to come in to work at very short notice. This can cause considerable disruption to social and family life. For example, at one news-broadcasting company, the scheme caused problems. Journalists and camera crew who went to cover a foreign crisis found that they had worked so many hours they were asked to take the whole of one month off to compensate. Since they had no holiday plans, many would have preferred to work.

Alternative products and services

Alternative products

Sometimes, a more radical approach is required to fill periods of low demand such as developing **alternative products** or services which can be produced on existing processes, but have different demand patterns throughout the year (see the Short case 'Getting the message' for an example of this approach). Most universities fill their accommodation and lecture theatres with conferences and company meetings during vacations. Ski resorts provide organized mountain activity holidays in the summer. Some garden tractor companies in the US now make snow movers in the autumn and winter. The apparent benefits of filling capacity in this way must be weighted against the risks of damaging the core product or service, and the operation must be fully capable of serving both markets. Some universities have been criticized for providing sub-standard, badly decorated accommodation which met the needs of impecunious undergraduates, but which failed to impress executives at a trade conference.

Mixed plans

Each of the three 'pure' plans is applied only where its advantages strongly outweigh its disadvantages. For many organizations, however, these 'pure' approaches do not match their required combination of competitive and operational objectives. Most operations managers are required simultaneously to reduce costs and inventory, to minimize capital investment, and yet to provide a responsive and customer-oriented approach at all times. For this reason, most organizations choose to follow a mixture of the three approaches. This can be best illustrated by the woollen knitwear company example (*see* Fig. 11.11). Here some of the peak demand has been brought forward by the company offering discounts to selected retail

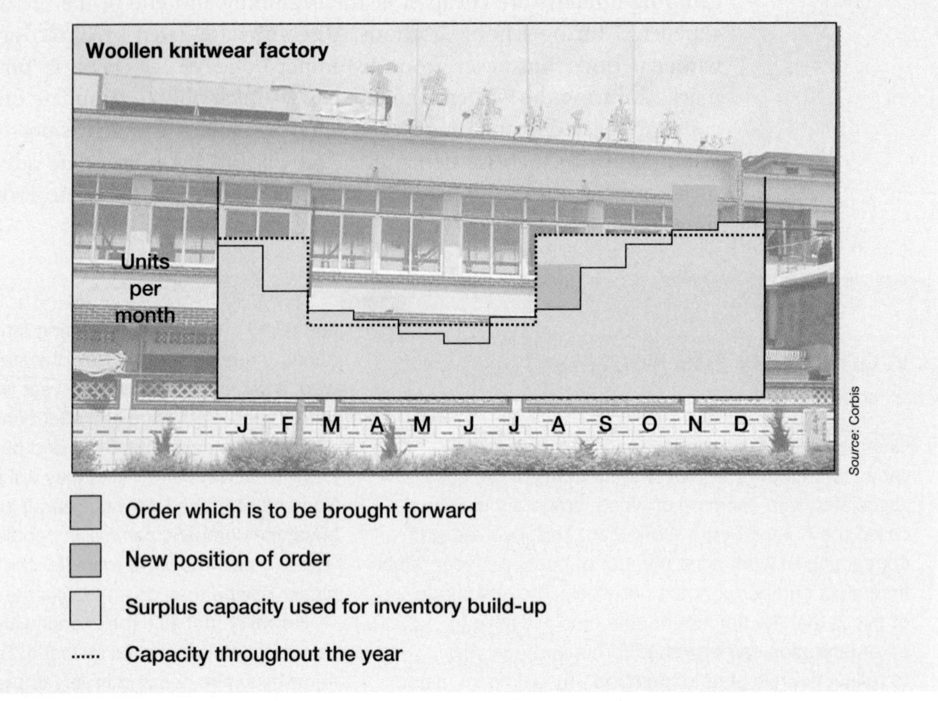

Figure 11.11 A mixed capacity plan for the woollen knitwear factory

customers (manage demand plan). Capacity has also been adjusted at two points in the year to reflect the broad changes in demand (chase demand plan). Yet the adjustment in capacity is not sufficient to avoid totally the build-up of inventories (level capacity plan).

Yield management

Yield management

In operations which have relatively fixed capacities, such as airlines and hotels, it is important to use the capacity of the operation for generating revenue to its full potential. One approach used by such operations is called **yield management**.[5] This is really a collection of methods, some of which we have already discussed, which can be used to ensure that an operation maximizes its potential to generate profit. Yield management is especially useful where:

- capacity is relatively fixed;
- the market can be fairly clearly segmented;
- the service cannot be stored in any way;
- the services are sold in advance;
- the marginal cost of making a sale is relatively low.

Airlines, for example, fit all these criteria. They adopt a collection of methods to try to maximize the yield (i.e. profit) from their capacity. These include the following:

- *Over-booking capacity.* Not every passenger who has booked a place on a flight will actually show up for the flight. If the airline did not fill this seat it would lose the revenue from it. Because of this, airlines regularly book more passengers onto flights than the capacity of the aircraft can cope with. If they over-book by the exact number of passengers who fail to show up, they have maximized their revenue under the circumstances. Of course, if more passengers show up than they expect, the airline will have a number of upset passengers to deal with (although they may be able to offer financial inducements for the passengers to take another flight). If they fail to over-book sufficiently, they will have empty seats. By studying past data on flight demand, airlines try to balance the risks of over-booking and under-booking.

Short case
Getting the message[6]

Source: Press Association Images

Companies which traditionally operate in seasonal markets can demonstrate some considerable ingenuity in their attempts to develop counter-seasonal products. One of the most successful industries in this respect has been the greetings card industry. Mother's Day, Father's Day, Halloween, Valentine's Day and other occasions have all been promoted as times to send (and buy) appropriately designed cards. Now, having run out of occasions to promote, greetings card manufacturers have moved on to 'non-occasion' cards, which can be sent at any time. These have the considerable advantage of being less seasonal, thus making the companies' seasonality less marked.

Hallmark Cards, the market leader in North America, has been the pioneer in developing non-occasion cards. Their cards include those intended to be sent from a parent to a child with messages such as 'Would a hug help?', 'Sorry I made you feel bad' and 'You're perfectly wonderful – it's your room that's a mess'. Other cards deal with more serious adult themes such as friendship ('You're more than a friend, you're just like family') or even alcoholism ('This is hard to say, but I think you're a much neater person when you're not drinking'). Now Hallmark Cards has founded a 'loyalty marketing group' that 'helps companies communicate with their customers at an emotional level'. It promotes the use of greetings cards for corporate use, to show that customers and employees are valued. Whatever else these products may be, they are not seasonal!

- *Price discounting.* At quiet times, when demand is unlikely to fill capacity, airlines will also sell heavily discounted tickets to agents who then themselves take the risk of finding customers for them. In effect, this is using the price mechanism to affect demand.
- *Varying service types.* Discounting and other methods of affecting demand are also adjusted depending on the demand for particular types of service. For example, the relative demand for first-, business- and economy-class seats varies throughout the year. There is no point discounting tickets in a class for which demand will be high. Yield management also tries to adjust the availability of the different classes of seat to reflect their demand. They will also vary the number of seats available in each class by upgrading or even changing the configuration of airline seats.

Choosing a capacity planning and control approach

Before an operation can decide which of the capacity plans to adopt, it must be aware of the consequences of adopting each plan in its own set of circumstances. Two methods are particularly useful in helping to assess the consequences of adopting particular capacity plans:

Cumulative representations

Queuing theory

- **cumulative representations** of demand and capacity;
- **queuing theory**.

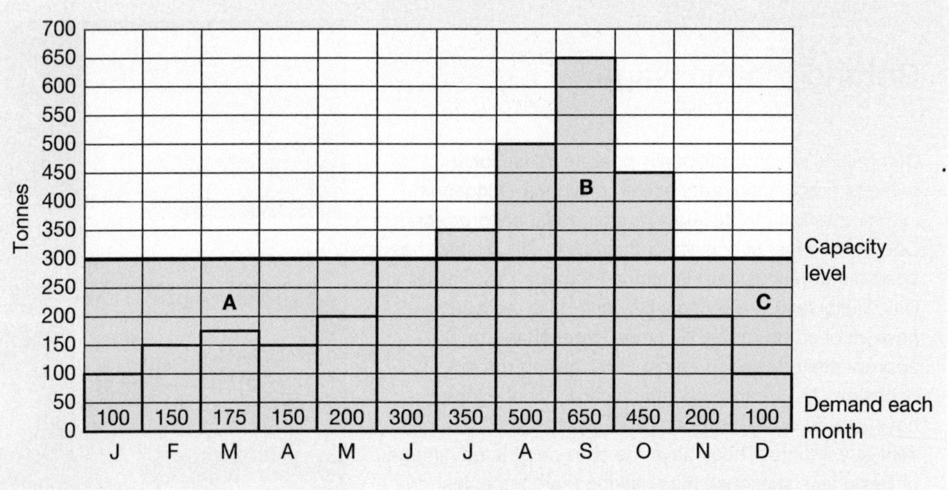

Figure 11.12 If the over-capacity areas (A+C) are greater than the under-capacity area (B), the capacity level seems adequate to meet demand. This may not necessarily be the case, however

Cumulative representations

Figure 11.12 shows the forecast aggregated demand for a chocolate factory which makes confectionery products. Demand for its products in the shops is greatest at Christmas. To meet this demand and allow time for the products to work their way through the distribution system, the factory must supply a demand which peaks in September, as shown. One method of assessing whether a particular level of capacity can satisfy the demand would be to calculate the degree of over-capacity below the graph which represents the capacity levels (areas A and C) and the degree of under-capacity above the graph (area B). If the total over-capacity is greater than the total under-capacity for a particular level of capacity, then that capacity could be regarded as adequate to satisfy demand fully, the assumption being that inventory has been accumulated in the periods of over-capacity. However, there are two problems with this approach. The first is that each month shown in Figure 11.12 may not have the same amount of productive time. Some months (August, for example) may contain vacation periods which reduce the availability of capacity. The second problem is that a capacity level which seems adequate may only be able to supply products *after* the demand for them has occurred. For example, if the period of under-capacity occurred at the beginning of the year, no inventory could have accumulated to meet demand. A far superior way of assessing capacity plans is first to plot demand on a *cumulative* basis. This is shown as the thicker line in Figure 11.13.

The cumulative representation of demand immediately reveals more information. First, it shows that although total demand peaks in September, because of the restricted number of available productive days, the peak demand per productive day occurs a month earlier in August. Second, it shows that the fluctuation in demand over the year is even greater than it seemed. The ratio of monthly peak demand to monthly lowest demand is 6.5:1, but the ratio of peak to lowest demand per productive day is 10:1. Demand per productive day is more relevant to operations managers, because productive days represent the time element of capacity.

The most useful consequence of plotting demand on a cumulative basis is that, by plotting capacity on the same graph, the feasibility and consequences of a capacity plan can be assessed. Figure 11.13 also shows a level capacity plan which produces at a rate of 14.03 tonnes per productive day. This meets cumulative demand by the end of the year. It would also pass our earlier test of total over-capacity being the same as or greater than under-capacity.

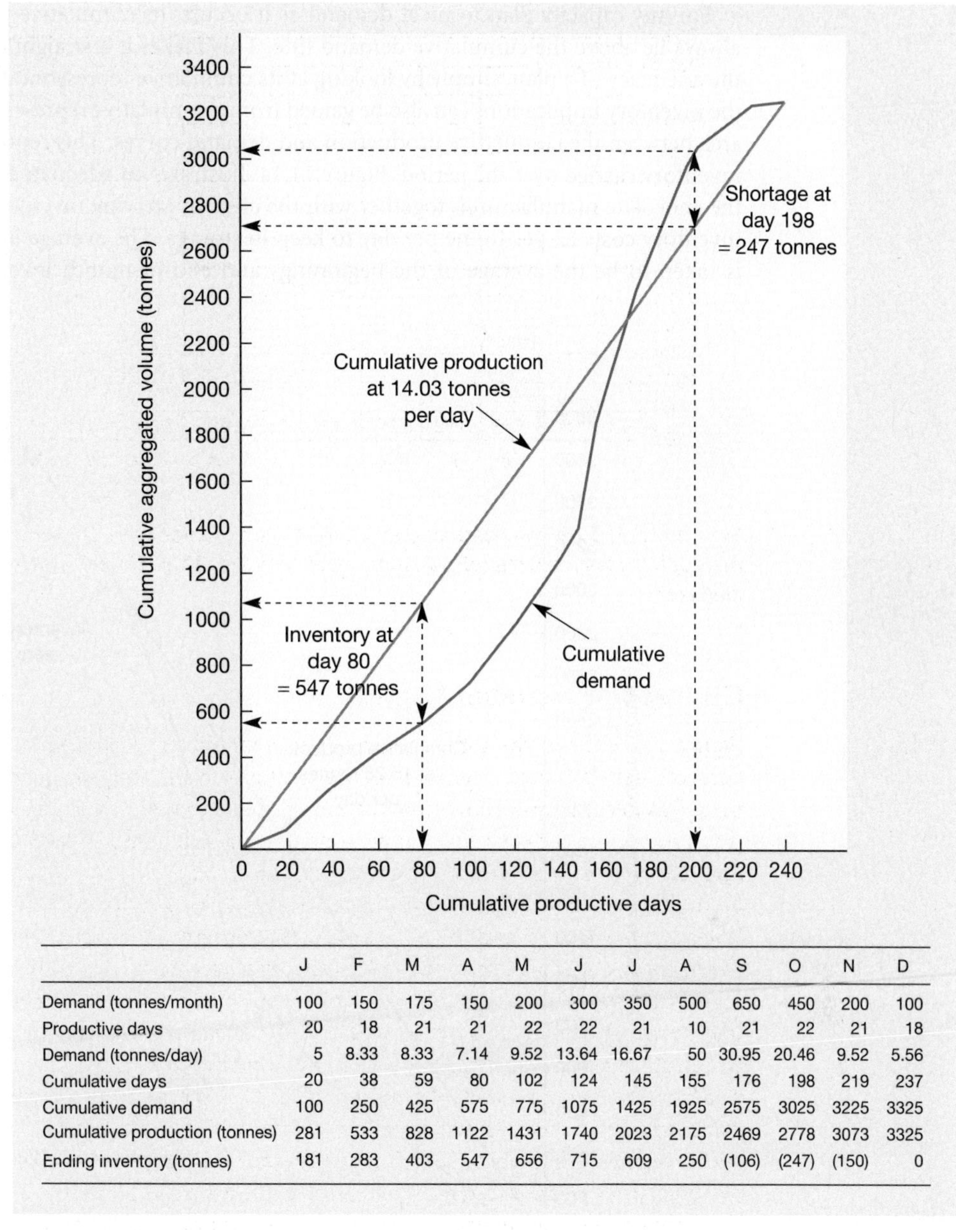

	J	F	M	A	M	J	J	A	S	O	N	D
Demand (tonnes/month)	100	150	175	150	200	300	350	500	650	450	200	100
Productive days	20	18	21	21	22	22	21	10	21	22	21	18
Demand (tonnes/day)	5	8.33	8.33	7.14	9.52	13.64	16.67	50	30.95	20.46	9.52	5.56
Cumulative days	20	38	59	80	102	124	145	155	176	198	219	237
Cumulative demand	100	250	425	575	775	1075	1425	1925	2575	3025	3225	3325
Cumulative production (tonnes)	281	533	828	1122	1431	1740	2023	2175	2469	2778	3073	3325
Ending inventory (tonnes)	181	283	403	547	656	715	609	250	(106)	(247)	(150)	0

Figure 11.13 A level capacity plan which produces shortages in spite of meeting demand at the end of the year

However, if one of the aims of the plan is to supply demand when it occurs, the plan is inadequate. Up to around day 168, the line representing cumulative production is above that representing cumulative demand. This means that at any time during this period, more product has been produced by the factory than has been demanded from it. In fact the vertical distance between the two lines is the level of inventory at that point in time. So by day 80, 1,122 tonnes have been produced but only 575 tonnes have been demanded. The surplus of production above demand, or inventory, is therefore 547 tonnes. When the cumulative demand line lies above the cumulative production line, the reverse is true. The vertical distance between the two lines now indicates the shortage, or lack of supply. So by day 198, 3,025 tonnes have been demanded but only 2,778 tonnes produced. The shortage is therefore 247 tonnes.

For any capacity plan to meet demand as it occurs, its cumulative production line must always lie above the cumulative demand line. This makes it a straightforward task to judge the adequacy of a plan, simply by looking at its cumulative representation. An impression of the inventory implications can also be gained from a cumulative representation by judging the area between the cumulative production and demand curves. This represents the amount of inventory carried over the period. Figure 11.14 illustrates an adequate level capacity plan for the chocolate manufacturer, together with the costs of carrying inventory. It is assumed that inventory costs £2 per tonne per day to keep in storage. The average inventory each month is taken to be the average of the beginning- and end-of-month inventory levels, and the

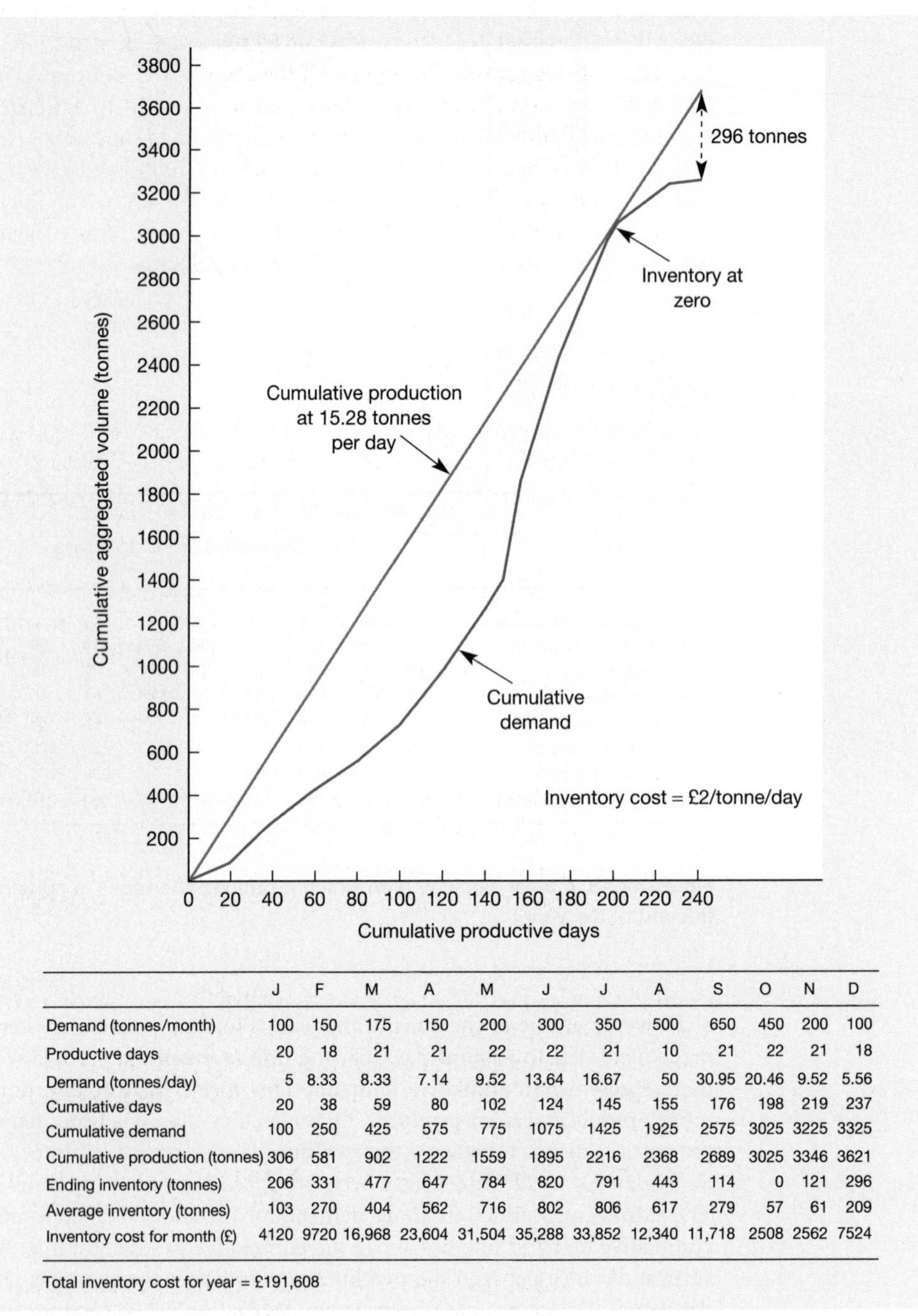

	J	F	M	A	M	J	J	A	S	O	N	D
Demand (tonnes/month)	100	150	175	150	200	300	350	500	650	450	200	100
Productive days	20	18	21	21	22	22	21	10	21	22	21	18
Demand (tonnes/day)	5	8.33	8.33	7.14	9.52	13.64	16.67	50	30.95	20.46	9.52	5.56
Cumulative days	20	38	59	80	102	124	145	155	176	198	219	237
Cumulative demand	100	250	425	575	775	1075	1425	1925	2575	3025	3225	3325
Cumulative production (tonnes)	306	581	902	1222	1559	1895	2216	2368	2689	3025	3346	3621
Ending inventory (tonnes)	206	331	477	647	784	820	791	443	114	0	121	296
Average inventory (tonnes)	103	270	404	562	716	802	806	617	279	57	61	209
Inventory cost for month (£)	4120	9720	16,968	23,604	31,504	35,288	33,852	12,340	11,718	2508	2562	7524

Total inventory cost for year = £191,608

Figure 11.14 A level capacity plan which meets demand at all times during the year

inventory-carrying cost each month is the product of the average inventory, the inventory cost per day per tonne and the number of days in the month.

Comparing plans on a cumulative basis

Chase demand plans can also be illustrated on a cumulative representation. Rather than the cumulative production line having a constant gradient, it would have a varying gradient representing the production rate at any point in time. If a pure demand chase plan was adopted, the cumulative production line would match the cumulative demand line. The gap between the two lines would be zero and hence inventory would be zero. Although this would eliminate inventory-carrying costs, as we discussed earlier, there would be costs associated with changing capacity levels. Usually, the marginal cost of making a capacity change increases with the size of the change. For example, if the chocolate manufacturer wishes to increase capacity by 5 per cent, this can be achieved by requesting its staff to work overtime – a simple, fast and relatively inexpensive option. If the change is 15 per cent, overtime cannot provide sufficient extra capacity and temporary staff will need to be employed – a more expensive solution which also would take more time. Increases in capacity of above 15 per cent might only be achieved by subcontracting some work out. This would be even more expensive. The cost of the change will also be affected by the point from which the change is being made, as well as the direction of the change. Usually, it is less expensive to change capacity towards what is regarded as the 'normal' capacity level than away from it.

Worked example

Suppose the chocolate manufacturer, which has been operating the level capacity plan as shown in Figure 11.15, is unhappy with the inventory costs of this approach. It decides to explore two alternative plans, both involving some degree of demand chasing.

Plan 1

- Organize and staff the factory for a 'normal' capacity level of 8.7 tonnes per day.
- Produce at 8.7 tonnes per day for the first 124 days of the year, then increase capacity to 29 tonnes per day by heavy use of overtime, hiring temporary staff and some subcontracting.
- Produce at 29 tonnes per day until day 194, then reduce capacity back to 8.7 tonnes per day for the rest of the year.

The costs of changing capacity by such a large amount (the ratio of peak to normal capacity is 3.33:1) are calculated by the company as being:

Cost of changing from 8.7 tonnes/day to 29 tonnes/day = £110,000
Cost of changing from 29 tonnes/day to 8.7 tonnes/day = £60,000

Plan 2

- Organize and staff the factory for a 'normal' capacity level of 12.4 tonnes per day.
- Produce at 12.4 tonnes per day for the first 150 days of the year, then increase capacity to 29 tonnes per day by overtime and hiring some temporary staff.
- Produce at 29 tonnes/day until day 190, then reduce capacity back to 12.4 tonnes per day for the rest of the year.

The costs of changing capacity in this plan are smaller because the degree of change is smaller (a peak to normal capacity ratio of 2.34:1), and they are calculated by the company as being:

Cost of changing from 12.4 tonnes/day to 29 tonnes/day = £35,000
Cost of changing from 29 tonnes/day to 12.4 tonnes/day = £15,000

→

Figure 11.15 illustrates both plans on a cumulative basis. Plan 1, which envisaged two drastic changes in capacity, has high capacity change costs but, because its production levels are close to demand levels, it has low inventory carrying costs. Plan 2 sacrifices some of the inventory cost advantage of Plan 1 but saves more in terms of capacity change costs.

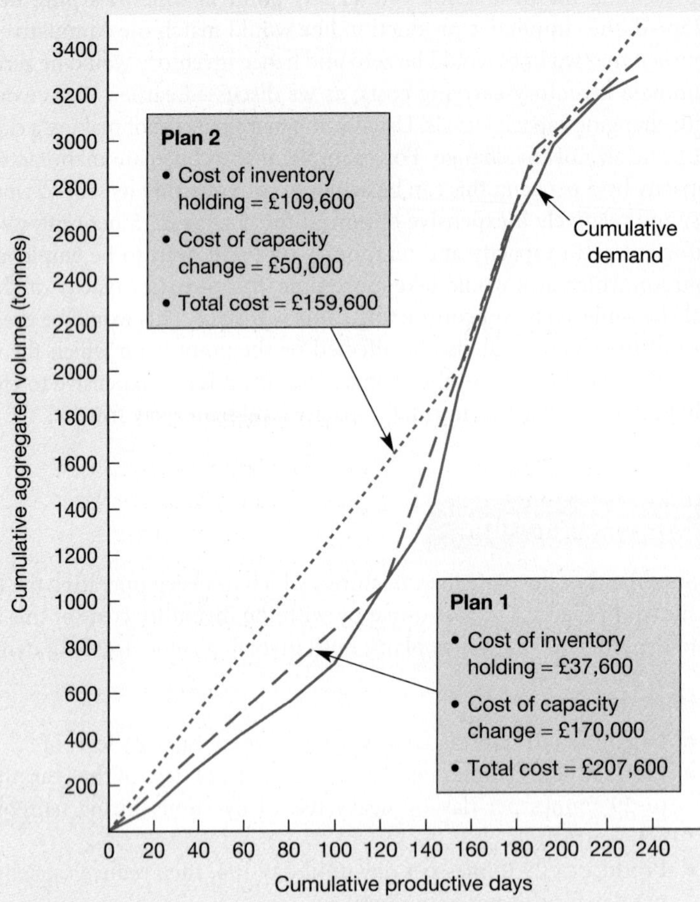

Figure 11.15 Comparing two alternative capacity plans

Capacity planning as a queuing problem

Cumulative representations of capacity plans are useful where the operation has the ability to store its finished goods as inventory. However, for operations where it is not possible to produce products and services *before* demand for them has occurred, a cumulative representation would tell us relatively little. The cumulative 'production' could never be above the cumulative demand line. At best, it could show when an operation failed to meets its demand. So the vertical gap between the cumulative demand and production lines would indicate the amount of demand unsatisfied. Some of this demand would look elsewhere to be satisfied, but some would wait. This is why, for operations which, by their nature, cannot store their output, such as most service operations, capacity planning and control is best considered using waiting or **queuing theory**.

Queuing theory

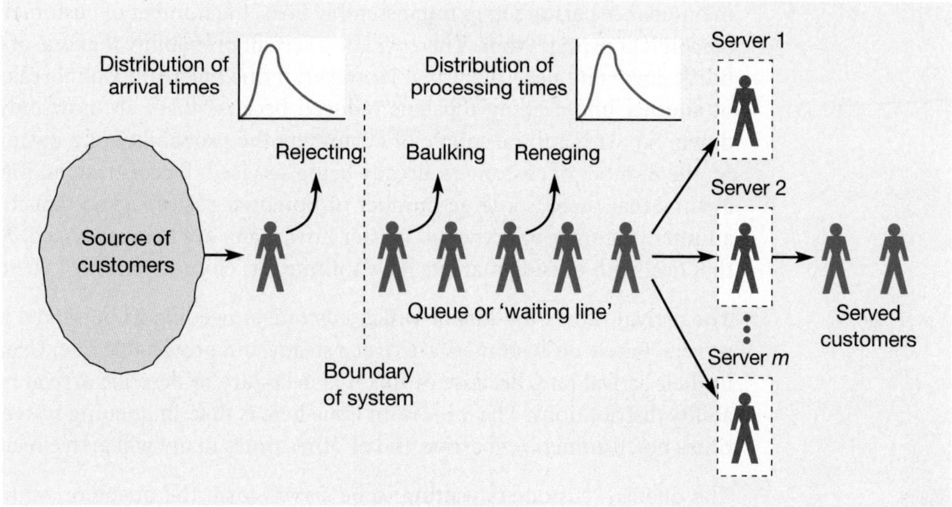

Figure 11.16 The general form of the capacity decision in queuing systems

Queuing or 'waiting line' management

When we were illustrating the use of cumulative representations for capacity planning and control, our assumption was that, generally, any production plan should aim to meet demand at any point in time (the cumulative production line must be above the cumulative demand line). Looking at the issue as a queuing problem (in many parts of the world queuing concepts are referred to as 'waiting line' concepts) accepts that, while sometime demand may be satisfied instantly, at other times customers may have to wait. This is particularly true when the arrival of individual demands on an operation are difficult to predict, or the time to produce a product or service is uncertain, or both. These circumstances make providing adequate capacity at all points in time particularly difficult. Figure 11.16 shows the general form of this capacity issue. Customers arrive according to some probability distribution and wait to be processed (unless part of the operation is idle); when they have reached the front of the queue, they are processed by one of the *n* parallel 'servers' (their processing time also being described by a probability distribution), after which they leave the operation. There are many examples of this kind of system. Table 11.2 illustrates some of these. All of these examples can be described by a common set of elements that define their queuing behaviour.

Calling population

The source of customers – sometimes called the **calling population** – is the source of supply of customers. In queue management 'customers' are not always human. 'Customers' could for example be trucks arriving at a weighbridge, orders arriving to be processed or machines waiting to be serviced, etc. The source of customers for queuing system can be either *finite* or *infinite*. A finite source has a known number of possible customers. For example, if one

Table 11.2 Examples of operations which have parallel processors

Operation	*Arrivals*	*Processing capacity*
Bank	Customers	Tellers
Supermarket	Shoppers	Checkouts
Hospital clinic	Patients	Doctors
Graphic artist	Commissions	Artists
Custom cake decorators	Orders	Cake decorators
Ambulance service	Emergencies	Ambulances with crews
Telephone switchboard	Calls	Telephonists
Maintenance department	Breakdowns	Maintenance staff

maintenance person serves four assembly lines, the number of customers for the maintenance person is known, i.e. four. There will be a certain probability that one of the assembly lines will break down and need repairing. However, if one line really does break down the probability of another line needing repair is reduced because there are now only three lines to break down. So, with a finite source of customers the probability of a customer arriving depends on the number of customers already being serviced. By contrast, an infinite customer source assume that there is a large number of potential customers so that it is always possible for another customer to arrive no matter how many are being serviced. Most queuing systems that deal with outside markets have infinite, or 'close-to-infinite', customer sources.

Arrival rate

The arrival rate is the rate at which customers needing to be served arrive at the server or servers. Rarely do customers arrive at a steady and predictable rate. Usually there is variability in their arrival rate. Because of this it is necessary to describe arrival rates in terms of probability distributions. The important issue here is that, in queuing systems, it is normal that at times no customers will arrive and at other times many will arrive relatively close together.

Queue

The queue – customers waiting to be served form the queue or waiting line itself. If there is relatively little limit on how many customers can queue at any time, we can assume that, for all practical purposes, an infinite queue is possible. Sometimes, however, there is a limit to how many customers can be in the queue at any one time.

Rejecting

Rejecting – if the number of customers in a queue is already at the maximum number allowed, then the customer could be rejected by the system. For example, during periods of heavy demand some web sites will not allow customers to access part of the site until the demand on its services has declined.

Baulking

Baulking – when a customer is a human being with free will (and the ability to get annoyed) he or she may refuse to join the queue and wait for service if it is judged to be too long. In queuing terms this is called baulking.

Reneging

Reneging – this is similar to baulking but here the customer has queued for a certain length of time and then (perhaps being dissatisfied with the rate of progress) leaves the queue and therefore the chance of being served.

Queue discipline

Queue discipline – this is the set of rules that determine the order in which customers waiting in the queue are served. Most simple queues, such as those in a shop, use a *first-come first-served* queue discipline. The various sequencing rules described in Chapter 10 are examples of different queue disciplines.

Servers

Servers – a server is the facility that processes the customers in the queue. In any queuing system there may be any number of servers configured in different ways. In Figure 11.16 servers are configured in parallel, but some may have servers in a series arrangement. For example, on entering a self-service restaurant you may queue to collect a tray and cutlery, move on to the serving area where you queue again to order and collect a meal, move on to a drinks area where you queue once more to order and collect a drink, and then finally queue to pay for the meal. In this case you have passed through four servers (even though the first one was not staffed) in a series arrangement. Of course, many queue systems are complex arrangements of series and parallel connections. There is also likely to be variation in how long it takes to process each customer. Even if customers do not have differing needs, human servers will vary in the time they take to perform repetitive serving tasks. Therefore processing time, like arrival time, is usually described by a probability distribution.

Balancing capacity and demand

The dilemma in managing the capacity of a queuing system is how many servers to have available at any point in time in order to avoid unacceptably long queuing times or unacceptably low utilization of the servers. Because of the probabilistic arrival and processing times, only rarely will the arrival of customers match the ability of the operation to cope with them. Sometimes, if several customers arrive in quick succession and require longer-than-average processing times, queues will build up in front of the operation. At other times, when customers arrive less frequently than average and also require shorter-than-average processing times, some of the servers in the system will be idle. So even when the average capacity (processing capability) of the operation matches the average demand (arrival rate) on the system, both queues and idle time will occur.

If the operation has too few servers (that is, capacity is set at too low a level), queues will build up to a level where customers become dissatisfied with the time they are having to wait, although the utilization level of the servers will be high. If too many servers are in place (that is, capacity is set at too high a level), the time which customers can expect to wait will not be long but the utilization of the servers will be low. This is why the capacity planning and control problem for this type of operation is often presented as a trade-off between customer waiting time and system utilization. What is certainly important in making capacity decisions is being able to predict both of these factors for a given queuing system. The supplement to this chapter details some of the more simple mathematical approaches to understanding queue behaviour.

Variability in demand or supply

Variability reduces effective capacity

The variability, either in demand or capacity, as discussed above, will reduce the ability of an operation to process its inputs. That is, it will **reduce its effective capacity**. This effect was explained in Chapter 4 when the consequences of variability in individual processes were discussed. As a reminder, the greater the variability in arrival time or activity time at a process the more the process will suffer both high throughput times and reduced utilization. This principle holds true for whole operations, and because long throughput times mean that queues will build up in the operation, high variability also affects inventory levels. This is illustrated in Figure 11.17. The implication of this is that the greater the variability, the more extra capacity will need to be provided to compensate for the reduced utilization of available capacity. Therefore, operations with high levels of variability will tend to set their base level of capacity relatively high in order to provide this extra capacity.

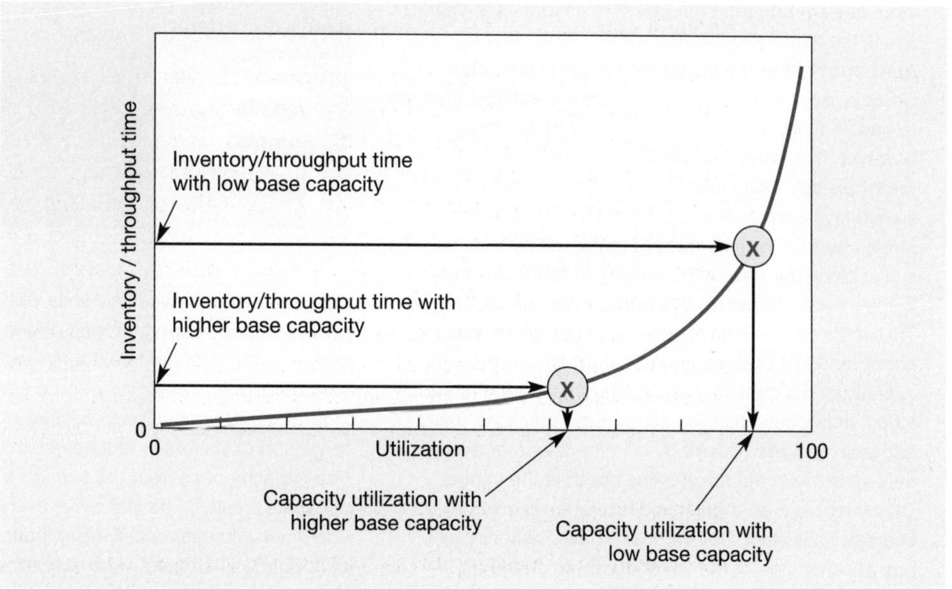

Figure 11.17 The effect of variability on the utilization of capacity

Customer perceptions of queuing

If the 'customers' waiting in a queue are real human customers, an important aspect of how they judge the service they receive from a queuing system is how they perceive the time spent queuing. It is well known that if you are told that you'll be waiting in a queue for twenty minutes and you are actually serviced in ten minutes, your perception of the queuing experience will be more positive than if you were told that you would be waiting ten minutes but the queue actually took twenty minutes. Because of this, the management of queuing systems usually involves attempting to manage customers' perceptions and expectations in some way (see the Short case on Madame Tussaud's for an example of this). One expert in queuing has come up with a number of principles that influence how customers perceive waiting times.[7]

- Time spent idle is perceived as longer than time spent occupied.
- The wait before a service starts is perceived as more tedious than a wait within the service process.
- Anxiety and/or uncertainty heightens the perception that time spent waiting is long.
- A wait of unknown duration is perceived as more tedious than a wait whose duration is known.
- An unexplained wait is perceived as more tedious than a wait that is explained.
- The higher the value of the service for the customer, the longer the wait that will be tolerated.
- Waiting on one's own is more tedious than waiting in a group (unless you really don't like the others in the group).

Short case
Managing queues at Madame Tussaud's, Amsterdam

Source: Madame Tussaud's

A short holiday in Amsterdam would not be complete without a visit to Madame Tussaud's, located on four upper floors of the city's most prominent department store in Dam Square. With 600,000 visitors each year, this is the third most popular tourist attraction in Amsterdam, after the flower market and canal trips. On busy days in the summer, the centre can just manage to handle 5,000 visitors. On a wet day in January, however, there may only be 300 visitors throughout the whole day. The centre is open for admission, seven days a week, from 10.00 am to 5.30 pm. In the streets outside, orderly queues of expectant tourists snake along the pavement, looking in at the displays in the store windows. In this public open space, Tussaud's can do little to entertain the visitors, but entrepreneurial buskers and street artists are quick to capitalize on a captive market. On reaching the entrance lobby, individuals, families and groups purchase their admission tickets. The lobby is in the shape of a large horseshoe, with the ticket sales booth in the centre. On winter days or at quiet spells, there will only be one sales assistant, but on busier days, visitors can pay at either side of the ticket booth, to speed up the process. Having paid, the visitors assemble in the lobby outside the two lifts. While waiting in this area, a photographer wanders around offering to take photos of the visitors standing next to life-sized wax figures of famous people. They may also be entertained by living look-alikes of famous personalities who act as guides to groups of visitors in batches of around 25 customers (the capacity of each of the two lifts which takes visitors up to the facility). The lifts arrive every four minutes and customers simultaneously disembark, forming one group of about 50 customers, who stay together throughout the session.

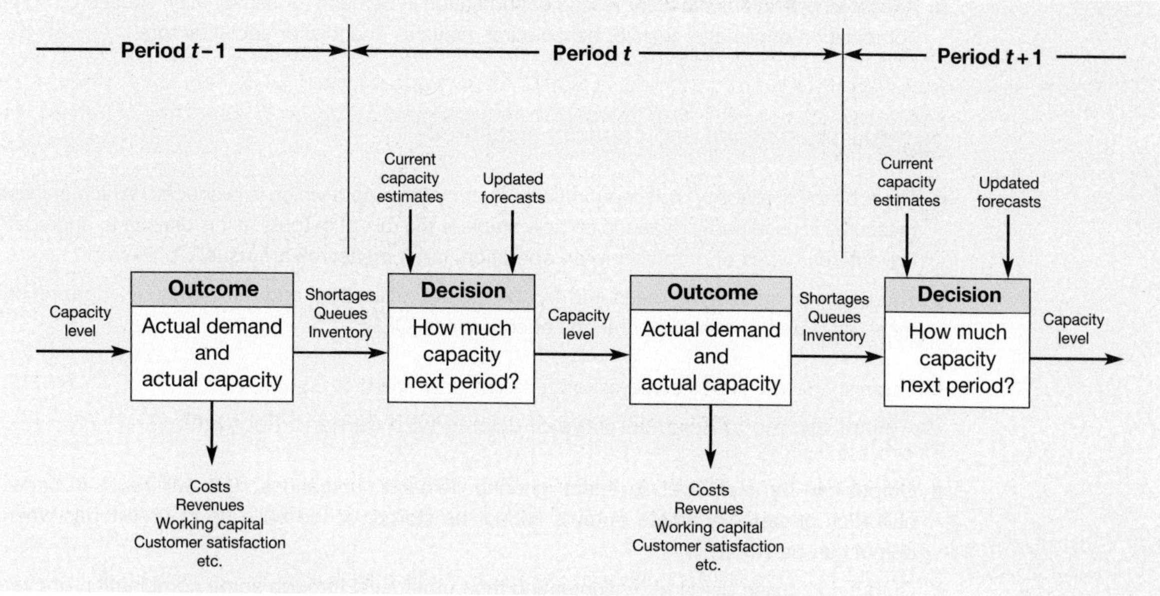

Figure 11.18 Capacity planning and control as a dynamic sequence of decisions

The dynamics of capacity planning and control

Our emphasis so far has been on the planning aspects of capacity management. In practice, the management of capacity is a far more dynamic process which involves controlling and reacting to *actual* demand and *actual* capacity as it occurs. The capacity control process can be seen as a sequence of partially reactive capacity decision processes as shown in Figure 11.18. At the beginning of each period, operations management considers its forecasts of demand, its understanding of current capacity and, if appropriate, how much inventory has been carried forward from the previous period. Based on all this information, it makes plans for the following period's capacity. During the next period, demand might or might not be as forecast and the actual capacity of the operation might or might not turn out as planned. But whatever the actual conditions during that period, at the beginning of the next period the same types of decisions must be made, in the light of the new circumstances.

Summary answers to key questions

Check and improve your understanding of this chapter using self assessment questions and a personalised study plan, audio and video downloads, and an eBook – all at ***www.myomlab.com****.*

➤ What is capacity planning and control?

- It is the way operations organize the level of value-added activity which they can achieve under normal operating conditions over a period of time.
- It is usual to distinguish between long-, medium- and short-term capacity decisions. Medium- and short-term capacity management where the capacity level of the organization is adjusted within the fixed physical limits which are set by long-term capacity decisions is sometimes called aggregate planning and control.

- Almost all operations have some kind of fluctuation in demand (or seasonality) caused by some combination of climatic, festive, behavioural, political, financial or social factors.

➤ How are demand and capacity measured?

- Either by the availability of its input resources or by the output which is produced. Which of these measures is used partly depends on how stable is the mix of outputs. If it is difficult to aggregate the different types of output from an operation, input measures are usually preferred.
- The usage of capacity is measured by the factors 'utilization' and 'efficiency'. A more recent measure is that of overall operations effectiveness (OEE).

➤ What are the alternative ways of coping with demand fluctuation?

- Output can be kept level, in effect ignoring demand fluctuations. This will result in under-utilization of capacity where outputs cannot be stored, or the build-up of inventories where output can be stored.
- Output can chase demand by fluctuating the output level through some combination of overtime, varying the size of the workforce, using part-time staff and subcontracting.
- Demand can be changed, either by influencing the market through such measures as advertising and promotion, or by developing alternative products with a counter-seasonal demand pattern.
- Most operations use a mix of all these three 'pure' strategies.

➤ How can operations plan and control their capacity level?

- Representing demand and output in the form of cumulative representations allows the feasibility of alternative capacity plans to be assessed.
- In many operations, especially service operations, a queuing approach can be used to explore capacity strategies.

➤ How can queuing theory be used to plan capacity?

- By considering the capacity decision as a dynamic decision which periodically updates the decisions and assumptions upon which decisions are based.

Case study
Holly farm

In 2003, Charles and Gillian Giles decided to open up their farm to the paying public, in response to diminishing profits from their milk and cereals activities. They invested all their savings into building a 40-space car park and an area with spaces for six 40-seater buses, a safe viewing area for the milking parlour, special trailers for passengers to be transported around the farm on guided tours, a permanent exhibition of equipment, a 'rare breeds' paddock, a children's adventure playground, a picnic area, a maize maze and a farm shop. Behind the farm shop they built a small 'factory' making real dairy ice cream, which also provided for public viewing. Ingredients for the ice cream, pasteurized cream and eggs, sugar, flavourings, etc., were bought out, although this was not obvious to the viewing public.

Source: Wistow Maze, Leicestershire

Source: Sue Williams

The maize maze at Holly Farm

Gillian took responsibility for all these new activities and Charles continued to run the commercial farming business. Through advertising, giving lectures to local schools and local organizations, the number of visitors to the farm increased steadily. By 2006 Gillian became so involved in running her business that she was unable to give so much time to these promotional activities, and the number of paying visitors levelled out at around 15,000 per year. Although the farm opened to the public at 11.00 am and closed at 7.00 pm after milking was finished, up to 90 per cent of visitors in cars or coaches would arrive later than 12.30 pm, picnic until around 2.00 pm, and tour the farm until about 4.00 pm. By that time, around 20 per cent would have visited the farm shop and left, but the remainder would wait to view the milking, then visit the shop to purchase ice cream and other produce, and then depart.

Gillian opened the farm to the public each year from April to October inclusive. Demand would be too low outside this period, the conditions were often unsuitable for regular tractor rides, and most of the animals had to be kept inside. Early experience had confirmed that mid-week demand was too low to justify opening, but Friday to Monday was commercially viable, with almost exactly twice as many visitors on Saturdays and Sundays as on Fridays or Mondays. Gillian summed up the situation. *'I have decided to attempt to increase the number of farm visitors in 2008 by 50 per cent. This would not only improve our return on "farm tours" assets, but also would help the farm shop to achieve its targets, and the extra sales of ice cream would help to keep the "factory" at full output. The real problem is whether to promote sales to coach firms or to intensify local advertising to attract more families in cars. We could also consider tie-ups with schools for educational visits, but I would not want to use my farm guide staff on any extra weekdays, as Charles needs them three days per week for "real" farming work. However, most of the farm workers are glad of this extra of work as if fits in well with their family life, and helps them to save up for the luxuries most farm workers cannot afford.'*

The milking parlour

With 150 cows to milk, Charles invested in a 'carousel' parlour where cows are milked on a slow-moving turntable. Milking usually lasts from 4.30 pm to 7.00 pm, during which time visitors can view from a purpose-built gallery which has space and explanatory tape recordings, via headphones, for twelve people. Gillian has found that on average spectators like to watch for ten minutes, including five minutes for the explanatory tape. *'We're sometimes a bit busy on Saturdays and Sundays and a queue often develops before 4.00 pm as some people want to see the milking and then go home. Unfortunately, neither Charles nor the cows are prepared to start earlier. However, most people are patient and everybody gets their turn to see this bit of high technology. In a busy period, up to 80 people per hour pass through the gallery.'*

The ice cream 'factory'

The factory is operated 48 weeks per year, four days per week, eight hours per day, throughout the year. The three employees, farm workers' wives, are expected to work in line with farm opening from April to October, but hours and days are by negotiation in other months. All output is in one-litre plastic boxes, of which 350 are made every day, which is the maximum mixing and fast-freezing capacity. Although extra mixing hours would create more unfrozen ice cream, the present equipment cannot safely and fully fast-freeze more than 350 litres over a 24-hour period. Ice cream that is not fully frozen cannot be transferred to the finished goods freezer, as slower freezing spoils the texture of the product. As it takes about one hour to clean out between flavours, only one of the four flavours is made on any day. The finished goods freezer holds a maximum of 10,000 litres, but to allow stock rotation, it cannot in practice be loaded to above 7,000 litres. Ideally no ice cream should be held more than six weeks at the factory, as the total recommended storage time is only twelve weeks prior to retail sale (there is no preservative used). Finished goods inventory at the end of December 2007 was 3,600 litres.

Gillian's most recent figures indicated that all flavours cost about £4.00 per litre to produce (variable cost of materials, packaging and labour). The factory layout is by process with material preparation and weighing sections, mixing area, packing equipment, and separate freezing equipment. It is operated as a batch process.

Ice cream sales

The majority of output is sold through regional speciality shops and food sections of department stores. These outlets are given a standard discount of 25 per cent to allow a 33 per cent mark-up to the normal retail price of £8.00 per litre. Minimum order quantity is 100 litres, and deliveries are made by Gillian in the van on Tuesdays. Also, having been shown around the farm and 'factory', a large proportion of visitors buy ice cream at the farm shop, and take it away in well-insulated containers that keep it from melting for up to two hours in the summer. Gillian commented *'These are virtually captive customers. We have analysed this demand and found that on average one out of two coach customers buys a one-litre box. On average, a car comes with four occupants, and two 1-litre boxes are purchased. The farm shop retail price is £2.00 per box, which gives us a much better margin than for our sales to shops.'*

In addition, a separate, fenced, road entrance allows local customers to purchase goods at a separate counter of the farm shop without payment for, or access to, the other farm facilities. *'This is a surprisingly regular source of sales. We believe this is because householders make very infrequent visits to stock up their freezers almost regardless of the time of year, or the weather. We also know that local hotels also buy a lot this way, and their use of ice cream is year-round, with a peak only at Christmas when there are a larger number of banquets.' All sales in this category are at the full retail price (£8.00). The finished product is sold to three categories of buyers*. See Table 11.3. (Note – (a) no separate record is kept of those sales to the paying farm visitors and those to the 'Farm Shop only', (b) the selling prices and discounts for 2008 will be as for 2007, (c) Gillian considered that 2007 was reasonably typical in terms of weather, although rainfall was a little higher than average during July and August.)

Table 11.3 Analysis of annual sales of ice cream (£000s) from 2003 to 2007, and forecast sales for 2008

	2003	*2004*	*2005*	*2006*	*2007*	*2008 forecast*
Retail shops	32	104	156	248	300	260
Farm shop total	40	64	80	100	108	160
Total	72	168	236	348	408	420

Table 11.4 gives details of visitors to the farm and ice cream sales in 2007. Gillian's concluding comments were *'We have a long way to go to make this enterprise meet our expectations. We will probably make only a small return on capital employed in 2007, so must do all we can to increase our profitability. Neither of us wants to put more capital into the business, as we would have to borrow at interest rates of up to 15 per cent. We must make our investment work better. As a first step, I have decided to increase the number of natural flavours of our ice cream to ten in 2008 (currently only four) to try and defend the delicatessen trade against a competitor's aggressive marketing campaign. I don't expect that to fully halt the decline in our sales to these outlets, and this is reflected in our sales forecast.'*

Questions

1 Evaluate Gillian's proposal to increase the number of farm visitors in 2008 by 50 per cent. (You may wish to consider: What are the main capacity constraints within these businesses? Should she promote coach company visits, even if this involves offering a discount on the admission charges? Should she pursue increasing visitors by car or school parties? In what other ways is Gillian able to manage capacity? What other information would help Gillian to take these decisions?)

2 What factors should Gillian consider when deciding to increase the number of flavours from four to ten?

(*Note*: For any calculations, assume that each month consists of four weeks. The effects of statutory holidays should be ignored for the purpose of this initial analysis.)

Table 11.4 Records of farm visitors and ice cream sales (in £000) in 2007

	Jan	*Feb*	*Mar*	*Apr*	*May*	*June*	*July*	*Aug*	*Sept*	*Oct*	*Nov*	*Dec*	*TOTAL*
Total number of paying farm visitors	0	0	0	1,200	1,800	2,800	3,200	3,400	1,800	600	0	0	14,800
Monthly ice cream sales	18	20.2	35	26.8	36	50.2	50.6	49.2	39	25.6	17.4	40	408.8

Problems and applications

These problems and applications will help to improve your analysis of operations. You can find more practice problems as well as worked examples and guided solutions on MyOMLab at ***www.myomlab.com.***

1. A local government office issues hunting licences. Demand for these licences is relatively slow in the first part of the year but then increases after the middle of the year before slowing down again towards the end of the year. The department works a 220-day year on a 5-days-a-week basis. Between working days 0 and 100, demand is 25 per cent of demand during the peak period which lasts between day 100 and day 150. After 150 demand reduces to about 12 per cent of the demand during the peak period. In total, the department processes 10,000 applications per year. The department has 2 permanent members of staff who are capable of processing 15 licence applications per day. If an untrained temporary member of staff can only process 10 licences per day, how many temporary staff should the department recruit between days 100 and 150?

2. In the example above, if a new computer system is installed that allows experienced staff to increase their work rate to 20 applications per day, and untrained staff to 15 applications per day, (a) does the department still need 2 permanent staff, and (b) how many temporary members of staff will be needed between days 100 and 150?

3. A field service organization repairs and maintains printing equipment for a large number of customers. It offers one level of service to all its customers and employs 30 staff. The operation's marketing vice-president has decided that in future the company will offer 3 standards of service, platinum, gold and silver. It is estimated that platinum-service customers will require 50 per cent more time from the company's field service engineers than the current service. The current service is to be called 'the gold service'. The silver service is likely to require about 80 per cent of the time of the gold service. If future demand is estimated to be 20 per cent platinum, 70 per cent gold and 10 per cent silver service, how many staff will be needed to fulfil demand?

4. Look again at the principles which govern customers' perceptions of the queuing experience. For the following operations, apply the principles to minimize the perceived negative effects of queuing.

   (a) A cinema
   (b) A doctor's surgery
   (c) Waiting to board an aircraft.

5. Consider how airlines cope with balancing capacity and demand. In particular, consider the role of yield management. Do this by visiting the web site of a low-cost airline, and for a number of flights price the fare that is being charged by the airline from tomorrow onwards. In other words, how much would it cost if you needed to fly tomorrow, how much if you needed to fly next week, how much if you needed to fly in 2 weeks, etc. Plot the results for different flights and debate the findings.

6. Calculate the overall equipment efficiency (OEE) of the following facilities by investigating their use.

   (a) A lecture theatre
   (b) A cinema
   (c) A coffee machine

   Discuss whether it is worth trying to increase the OEE of these facilities and, if it is, how you would go about it.

Selected further reading

Brandimarte, P. and Villa, A. (1999) *Modelling Manufacturing Systems: From Aggregate Planning to Real Time Control*, Springer, New York, NY. Very academic although it does contain some interesting pieces if you need to get 'under the skin' of the subject.

Hopp, W.J. and Spearman, M.L. (2000) *Factory Physics*, 2nd edn, McGraw-Hill, New York, NY. Very mathematical indeed, but includes some interesting maths on queuing theory.

Olhager, J., Rudberg, M. and Wikner, J. (2001) Long-term capacity management: linking the perspectives from manufacturing strategy and sales and operations planning, *International Journal of Production Economics*, vol. 69, issue 2, 215–25. Academic article, but interesting.

Vollmann, T., Berry, W., Whybark, D.C. and Jacobs, F.R. (2004) *Manufacturing Planning and Control Systems for Supply Chain Management: The Definitive Guide for Professionals*, McGraw-Hill Higher Education. The latest version of the 'bible' of manufacturing planning and control. It's exhaustive in its coverage of all aspects of planning and control including aggregate planning.

Useful web sites

www.dti.gov.uk/er/index Web site of the Employment Relations Directorate which has developed a framework for employers and employees which promotes a skilled and flexible labour market founded on principles of partnership.

www.worksmart.org.uk/index.php This site is from the Trades Union Congress. Its aim is 'to help today's working people get the best out of the world of work'.

www.opsman.org Lots of useful stuff.

www.eoc-law.org.uk/ This web site aims to provide a resource for legal advisers and representatives who are conducting claims on behalf of applicants in sex discrimination and equal pay cases in England and Wales. This site covers employment-related sex discrimination only.

www.dol.gov/index.htm US Department of Labor's site with information regarding using part-time employees.

www.downtimecentral.com/ Lots of information on operational equipment efficiency (OEE).

*Now that you have finished reading this chapter, why not visit MyOMLab at **www.myomlab.com** where you'll find more learning resources to help you make the most of your studies and get a better grade?*

Supplement to Chapter 11 Analytical queuing models

Introduction

In the main part of Chapter 11 we described how the queuing approach (in the United States it would be called the 'waiting line approach') can be useful in thinking about capacity, especially in service operations. It is useful because it deals with the issue of variability, both of the arrival of customers (or items) at a process and of how long each customer (or item) takes to process. And where variability is present in a process (as it is in most processes, but particularly in service processes) the capacity required by an operation cannot easily be based on averages but must include the effects of the variation. Unfortunately, many of the formulae that can be used to understand queuing are extremely complicated, especially for complex systems, and are beyond the scope of this book. In fact, computer programs are almost always now used to predict the behaviour of queuing systems. However, studying queuing formulae can illustrate some useful characteristics of the way queuing systems behave.

Notation

Unfortunately there are several different conventions for the notation used for different aspects of queuing system behaviour. It is always advisable to check the notation used by different authors before using their formulae. We shall use the following notation:

t_a = average time between arrival
r_a = arrival rate (items per unit time) $= 1/t_a$
c_a = coefficient of variation of arrival times
m = number of parallel servers at a station
t_e = mean processing time
r_e = processing rate (items per unit time) $= m/t_e$
c_e = coefficient of variation of process time
u = utilization of station $= r_a/r_e = (r_a\, t_e)/m$
WIP = average work-in-progress (number of items) in the queue
WIP_q = expected work-in-progress (number of times) in the queue
W_q = expected waiting time in the queue
W = expected waiting time in the system (queue time + processing time)

Some of these factors are explained later.

Variability

The concept of variability is central to understanding the behaviour of queues. If there were no variability there would be no need for queues to occur because the capacity of a process could be relatively easily adjusted to match demand. For example, suppose one member of staff (a server) serves at a bank counter customers who always arrive exactly every five minutes (i.e. 12 per hour). Also suppose that every customer takes exactly five minutes to be served, then because,

(a) the arrival rate is ≤ processing rate, and
(b) there is no variation

no customer need ever wait because the next customer will arrive when, or before, the previous customer. That is, $WIP_q = 0$.

Also, in this case, the server is working all the time, again because exactly as one customer leaves the next one is arriving. That is, $u = 1$.

Even with more than one server, the same may apply. For example, if the arrival time at the counter is five minutes (12 per hour) and the processing time for each customer is now always exactly 10 minutes, the counter would need two servers, and because,

(a) arrival rate is ≤ processing rate m, and
(b) there is no variation

again, $WIP_q = 0$, and $u = 1$.

Of course, it is convenient (but unusual) if arrival rate/processing rate = a whole number. When this is not the case (for this simple example with no variation),

Utilization = processing rate/(arrival rate multiplied by m)

For example, if arrival rate, $r_a = 5$ minutes
processing rate, $r_e = 8$ minutes
number of servers, $m = 2$
then, utilization, $u = 8 / (5 \times 2) = 0.8$ or 80%

Incorporating variability

The previous examples were not realistic because the assumption of no variation in arrival or processing times very rarely occurs. We can calculate the average or mean arrival and process times but we also need to take into account the variation around these means. To do that we need to use a probability distribution. Figure S11.1 contrasts two processes with different arrival distributions. The units arriving are shown as people, but they could be jobs arriving at a machine, trucks needing servicing, or any other uncertain event. The top example shows low variation in arrival time where customers arrive in a relatively predictable manner. The bottom example has the same average number of customer arriving but this time they arrive unpredictably with sometimes long gaps between arrivals and at other times two or three customers arriving close together. Of course, we could do a similar analysis to describe processing times. Again, some would have low variation, some higher variation and others be somewhere in between.

In Figure S11.1 high arrival variation has a distribution with a wider spread (called 'dispersion') than the distribution describing lower variability. Statistically the usual measure for indicating the spread of a distribution is its standard deviation, σ. But variation does not only depend on standard deviation. For example, a distribution of arrival times may have a standard deviation of 2 minutes. This could indicate very little variation when the average arrival time is 60 minutes. But it would mean a very high degree of variation when the

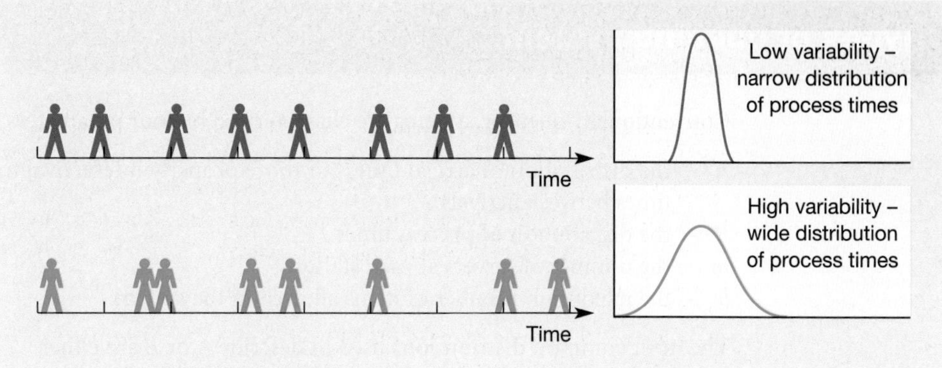

Figure S11.1 Low and high arrival variation

average arrival time is 3 minutes. Therefore to normalize standard deviation, it is divided by the mean of its distribution. This measure is called the coefficient of variation of the distribution. So,

$$c_a = \text{coefficient of variation of arrival times} = \sigma_a / t_a$$
$$c_e = \text{coefficient of variation of processing times} = \sigma_e / t_e$$

Incorporating Little's law

In Chapter 4 we discussed on of the fundamental laws of processes that describes the relationship between the cycle time of a process (how often something emerges from the process), the working in progress in the process and the throughput time of the process (the total time it takes for an item to move through the whole process including waiting time). It was called Little's law and it was denoted by the following simple relationship.

$$\text{Work-in-progress} = \text{cycle time} \times \text{throughput time}$$

Or,

$$\text{WIP} = C \times T$$

We can make use of Little's law to help understand queuing behaviour. Consider the queue in front of a station.

Work-in-progress in the queue = the arrival rate at the queue (equivalent to cycle time) × waiting time in the queue (equivalent to throughput time)

$$\text{WIP}_q = r_a \times W_q$$

and

Waiting time in the whole system = the waiting time in the queue + the average process time at the station

$$W = W_q + t_e$$

We will use this relationship later to investigate queuing behaviour.

Types of queuing system

Conventionally queuing systems are characterized by four parameters.

A – the distribution of arrival times (or more properly interarrival times, the elapsed times between arrivals)
B – the distribution of process times
m – the number of servers at each station
b – the maximum number of items allowed in the system.

The most common distributions used to describe *A* or *B* are either

(a) the exponential (or Markovian) distribution denoted by M; or
(b) the general (for example normal) distribution denoted by G.

So, for example, an M/G/1/5 queuing system would indicate a system with exponentially distributed arrivals, process times described by a general distribution such as a normal distribution, with one server and a maximum number of items allowed in the system of 5. This type of notation is called Kendall's notation.

Queuing theory can help us investigate any type of queuing system, but in order to simplify the mathematics, we shall here deal only with the two most common situations. Namely,

M/M/m queues

- M/M/*m* – the exponential arrival and processing times with *m* servers and no maximum limit to the queue.

G/G/m queues

- G/G/*m* – general arrival and processing distributions with *m* servers and no limit to the queue.

And first we will start by looking at the simple case when $m = 1$.

For M/M/1 queuing systems

The formulae for this type of system are as follows.

$$\text{WIP} = \frac{u}{1-u}$$

Using Little's law,

$$\text{WIP} = \text{cycle time} \times \text{throughput time}$$
$$\text{Throughput time} = \text{WIP} \,/\, \text{cycle time}$$

Then,

$$\text{Throughput time} = \frac{u}{1-u} \times \frac{1}{r_a} = \frac{t_e}{1-u}$$

and since, throughput time in the queue = total throughput time – average processing time,

$$W_q = W - t_e$$

$$= \frac{t_e}{1-u} - t_e$$

$$= \frac{t_e - t_e(1-u)}{1-u} = \frac{t_e - t_e - ut_e}{1-u}$$

$$= \frac{u}{(1-u)}t_e$$

again, using Little's law

$$\text{WIP}_q = r_a \times W_q = \frac{u}{(1-u)} t_e r_a$$

and since

$$u = \frac{r_a}{r_e} = r_a t_e$$

$$r_a = \frac{u}{t_e}$$

then,

$$\text{WIP}_q = \frac{u}{(1-u)} \times t_e \times \frac{u}{t_e}$$

$$= \frac{u^2}{(1-u)}$$

For M/M/*m* systems

When there are *m* servers at a station the formula for waiting time in the queue (and therefore all other formulae) needs to be modified. Again, we will not derive these formulae but just state them.

$$W_q = \frac{u^{\sqrt{2(m+1)}-1}}{m(1-u)} t_e$$

From which the other formulae can be derived as before.

For G/G/1 systems

The assumption of exponential arrival and processing times is convenient as far as the mathematical derivation of various formulae are concerned. However, in practice, process times in particular are rarely truly exponential. This is why it is important to have some idea of how a G/G/1 and G/G/*m* queue behaves. However, exact mathematical relationships are not possible with such distributions. Therefore some kind of approximation is needed. The one here is in common use, and although it is not always accurate, it is for practical purposes. For G/G/1 systems the formula for waiting time in the queue is as follows.

$$W_q = \left(\frac{c_a^2 + c_e^2}{2}\right)\left(\frac{u}{(1-u)}\right) t_e$$

VUT formula

There are two points to make about this equation. The first is that it is exactly the same as the equivalent equation for an M/M/1 system but with a factor to take account of the variability of the arrival and process times. The second is that this formula is sometimes known as the **VUT formula** because it describes the waiting time in a queue as a function of:

V – the variability in the queuing system
U – the utilization of the queuing system (that is demand versus capacity), and
T – the processing times at the station.

In other words, we can reach the intuitive conclusion that queuing time will increase as variability, utilization or processing time increases.

For G/G/*m* systems

The same modification applies to queuing systems using general equations and *m* servers. The formula for waiting time in the queue is now as follows.

$$W_q = \left(\frac{c_a^2 + c_e^2}{2}\right)\left(\frac{u^{\sqrt{2(m+1)}-1}}{m(1-u)}\right)t_e$$

Worked example 1

'I can't understand it. We have worked out our capacity figures and I am sure that one member of staff should be able to cope with the demand. We know that customers arrive at a rate of around 6 per hour and we also know that any trained member of staff can process them at a rate of 8 per hour. So why is the queue so large and the wait so long? Have at look at what is going on there please.'

Sarah knew that it was probably the variation, both in customers arriving and in how long it took each of them to be processed, that was causing the problem. Over a two-day period when she was told that demand was more or less normal, she timed the exact arrival times and processing times of every customer. Her results were as follows.

The coefficient of variation, c_a of customer arrivals = 1
The coefficient of variation, c_e of processing time = 3.5
The average arrival rate of customers, r_a = 6 per hour
therefore, the average inter-arrival time = 10 minutes
The average processing rate, r_e = 8 per hour
therefore, the average processing time = 7.5 minutes
Therefore the utilization of the single server, u = 6/8 = 0.75

Using the waiting time formula for a G/G/1 queuing system

$$W_q = \left(\frac{1 + 12.25}{2}\right)\left(\frac{0.75}{1 - 0.75}\right)7.5$$

$$= 6.625 \times 3 \times 7.5 = 149.06 \text{ mins}$$

$$= 2.48 \text{ hours}$$

Also because,

$$\text{WIP}_q = \text{cycle time} \times \text{throughput time}$$

$$\text{WIP}_q = 6 \times 2.48 = 14.68$$

So, Sarah had found out that the average wait that customers could expect was 2.48 hours and that there would be an average of 14.68 people in the queue.

'Ok, so I see that it's the very high variation in the processing time that is causing the queue to build up. How about investing in a new computer system that would standardize processing time to a greater degree? I have been talking with our technical people and they reckon that, if we invested in a new system, we could cut the coefficient of variation of processing time down to 1.5. What kind of a different would this make?'

Under these conditions with $c_e = 1.5$

$$W_q = \left(\frac{1 + 2.25}{2}\right)\left(\frac{0.75}{1 - 0.75}\right)7.5$$

$$= 1.625 \times 3 \times 7.5 = 36.56 \text{ mins}$$

$$= 0.61 \text{ hour}$$

Therefore,

$$\text{WIP}_q = 6 \times 0.61 = 3.66$$

In other words, reducing the variation of the process time has reduced average queuing time from 2.48 hours down to 0.61 hour and has reduced the expected number of people in the queue from 14.68 down to 3.66.

Worked example 2

A bank wishes to decide how many staff to schedule during its lunch period. During this period customers arrive at a rate of 9 per hour and the enquiries that customers have (such as opening new accounts, arranging loans, etc.) take on average 15 minutes to deal with. The bank manager feels that four staff should be on duty during this period but wants to make sure that the customers do not wait more than 3 minutes on average before they are served. The manager has been told by his small daughter that the distributions that describe both arrival and processing times are likely to be exponential. Therefore,

$r_a = 9$ per hour, therefore
$t_a = 6.67$ minutes
$r_e = 4$ per hour, therefore
$t_e = 15$ minutes

The proposed number of servers, $m = 4$

therefore, the utilization of the system, $u = 9/(4 \times 4) = 0.5625$.

From the formula for waiting time for a M/M/m system,

$$W_q = \frac{u^{\sqrt{2(m+1)}-1}}{m(1-u)} t_e$$

$$W_q = \frac{0.5625^{\sqrt{10}-1}}{4(1-0.5625)} \times 0.25$$

$$= \frac{0.5625^{2.162}}{1.75} \times 0.25$$

$$= 0.042 \text{ hour}$$

$$= 2.52 \text{ minutes}$$

Therefore the average waiting time with 4 servers would be 2.52 minutes, which is well within the manager's acceptable waiting tolerance.

Chapter 12

Inventory planning and control

Key questions

- What is inventory?
- Why is inventory necessary?
- What are the disadvantages of holding inventory?
- How much inventory should an operation hold?
- When should an operation replenish its inventory?
- How can inventory be controlled?

Introduction

Operations managers often have an ambivalent attitude towards inventories. On the one hand, they are costly, sometimes tying up considerable amounts of working capital. They are also risky because items held in stock could deteriorate, become obsolete or just get lost, and, furthermore, they take up valuable space in the operation. On the other hand, they provide some security in an uncertain environment that one can deliver items in stock, should customers demand them. This is the dilemma of inventory management: in spite of the cost and the other disadvantages associated with holding stocks, they do facilitate the smoothing of supply and demand. In fact they only exist because supply and demand are not exactly in harmony with each other (*see* Fig. 12.1).

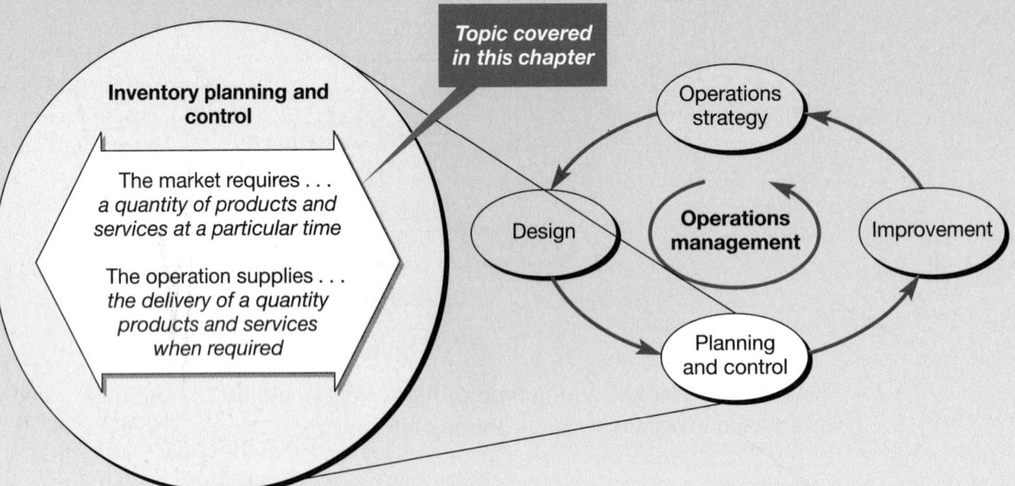

Figure 12.1 This chapter covers inventory planning and control

Check and improve your understanding of this chapter using self assessment questions and a personalised study plan, audio and video downloads, and an eBook – all at ***www.myomlab.com****.*

Operations in practice The UK's National Blood Service[1]

No inventory manager likes to run out of stock. But for blood services, such as the UK's National Blood Service (NBS) the consequences of running out of stock can be particularly serious. Many people owe their lives to transfusions that were made possible by the efficient management of blood, stocked in a supply network that stretches from donation centres through to hospital blood banks. The NBS supply chain has three main stages:

1 *Collection*, which involves recruiting and retaining blood donors, encouraging them to attend donor sessions (at mobile or fixed locations) and transporting the donated blood to their local blood centre.
2 *Processing*, which breaks blood down into its constituent parts (red cells, platelets and plasma) as well over twenty other blood-based 'products'.
3 *Distribution*, which transports blood from blood centres to hospitals in response to both routine and emergency requests. Of the Service's 200,000 deliveries a year, about 2,500 are emergency deliveries.

Inventory accumulates at all three stages, and in individual hospitals' blood banks. Within the supply chain, around 11.5 per cent of donated red blood cells donated are lost. Much of this is due to losses in processing, but around 5 per cent is not used because it has 'become unavailable', mainly because it has been stored for too long. Part of the Service's inventory control task is to keep this 'time-expired' loss to a minimum. In fact, only small losses occur within the NBS, most blood being lost when it is stored in hospital blood banks that are outside its direct control. However, it does attempt to provide advice and support to hospitals to enable them to use blood efficiently.

Blood components and products need to be stored under a variety of conditions, but will deteriorate over time. This varies depending on the component; platelets have a shelf life of only five days and demand can fluctuate significantly. This makes stock control particularly difficult. Even red blood cells that have a shelf life of 35 days may not be acceptable to hospitals if they are close to their 'use-by date'. Stock accuracy is crucial. Giving a patient the wrong type of blood can be fatal.

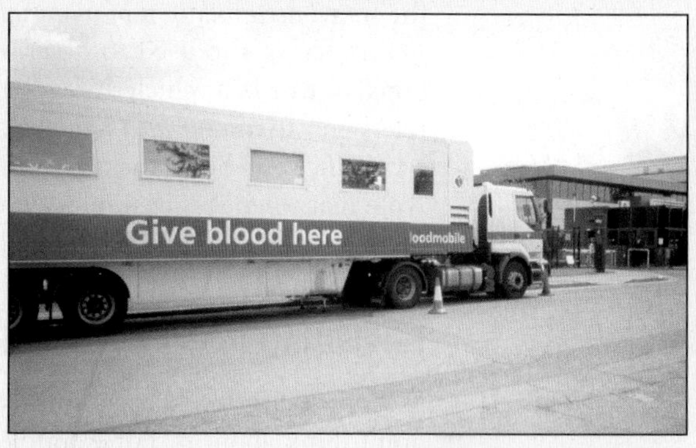

Source: Alamy/Van Hilversum

At a local level demand can be affected significantly by accidents. One serious accident involving a cyclist used 750 units of blood, which completely exhausted the available supply (miraculously, he survived). Large-scale accidents usually generate a surge of offers from donors wishing to make immediate donations. There is also a more predictable seasonality to the donating of blood, however, with a low period during the summer vacation. Yet there is always an unavoidable tension between maintaining sufficient stocks to provide a very high level of supply dependability to hospitals and minimizing wastage. Unless blood stocks are controlled carefully, they can easily go past the 'use-by date' and be wasted. But avoiding outdated blood products is not the only inventory objective at NBS. It also measures the percentage of requests that it was able to meet in full, the percentage emergency requests delivered within two hours, the percentage of units banked to donors bled, the number of new donors enrolled, and the number of donors waiting longer than 30 minutes before they are able to donate. The traceability of donated blood is also increasingly important. Should any problems with a blood product arise, its source can be traced back to the original donor.

What is inventory?

Inventory

Inventory, or 'stock' as it is more commonly called in some countries, is defined here as the *stored accumulation of material resources in a transformation system*. Sometimes the term 'inventory' is also used to describe any capital-transforming resource, such as rooms in a hotel, or cars in a vehicle-hire firm, but we will not use that definition here. Usually the term refers only to *transformed resources*. So a manufacturing company will hold stocks of materials, a tax office will hold stocks of information, and a theme park will hold stocks of customers. Note that when it is customers who are being processed we normally refer to the 'stocks' of them as 'queues'. This chapter will deal particularly with inventories of materials.

Revisiting operations objectives; the roles of inventory

Most of us are accustomed to keeping inventory for use in our personal lives, but often we don't think about it. For example, most families have some stocks of food and drinks, so that they don't have to go out to the shops before every meal. Holding a variety of food ingredients in stock in the kitchen cupboard or freezer gives us the ability to respond quickly (with *speed*) in preparing a meal whenever unexpected guests arrive. It also allows us the *flexibility* to choose a range of menu options without having to go to the time and trouble of purchasing further ingredients. We may purchase some items because we have found something of exceptional *quality*, but intend to save it for a special occasion. Many people buy multiple packs to achieve lower *costs* for a wide range of goods. In general, our inventory planning protects us from critical stock-outs; so this approach gives a level of *dependability* of supplies.

It is, however, entirely possible to manage our inventory planning differently. For example, some people (students?) are short of available cash and/or space, and so cannot 'invest' in large inventories of goods. They may shop locally for much smaller quantities. They forfeit the cost benefits of bulk-buying, but do not have to transport heavy or bulky supplies. They also reduce the risk of forgetting an item in the cupboard and letting it go out of date. Essentially, they purchase against specific known requirements (the next meal). However, they may find that the local shop is temporarily out of stock of a particular item, forcing them, for example, to drink coffee without their usual milk. How we control our own supplies is therefore a matter of choice which can affect their quality (e.g. freshness), availability or speed of response, dependability of supply, flexibility of choice, and cost. It is the same for most organizations. Significant levels of inventory can be held for a range of sensible and pragmatic reasons but it must also be tightly controlled for other equally good reasons.

Why is inventory necessary?

No matter what is being stored as inventory, or where it is positioned in the operation, it will be there because there is a difference in the timing or rate of supply and demand. If the supply of any item occurred exactly when it was demanded, the item would never be stored. A common analogy is the water tank shown in Figure 12.2. If, over time, the rate of supply of water to the tank differs from the rate at which it is demanded, a tank of water (inventory) will be needed if supply is to be maintained. When the rate of supply exceeds the rate of demand, inventory increases; when the rate of demand exceeds the rate of supply, inventory decreases. So if an operation can match supply and demand rates, it will also succeed in reducing its inventory levels.

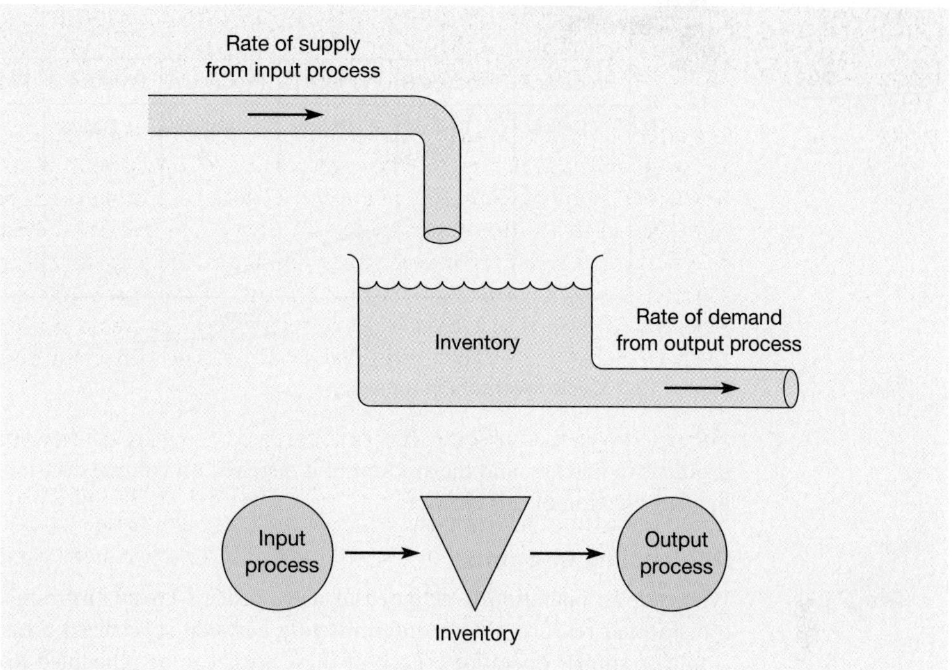

Figure 12.2 Inventory is created to compensate for the differences in timing between supply and demand

Types of inventory

The various reasons for an imbalance between the rates of supply and demand at different points in any operation lead to the different types of inventory. There are five of these: buffer inventory, cycle inventory, de-coupling inventory, anticipation inventory and pipeline inventory.

Buffer inventory

Buffer inventory
Safety inventory

Buffer inventory is also called **safety inventory**. Its purpose is to compensate for the unexpected fluctuations in supply and demand. For example, a retail operation can never forecast demand perfectly, even when it has a good idea of the most likely demand level. It will order goods from its suppliers such that there is always a certain amount of most items in stock. This minimum level of inventory is there to cover against the possibility that demand will be greater than expected during the time taken to deliver the goods. This is *buffer*, or *safety inventory*. It can also compensate for the uncertainties in the process of the supply of goods into the store, perhaps because of the unreliability of certain suppliers or transport firms.

Cycle inventory

Cycle inventory

Cycle inventory occurs because one or more stages in the process cannot supply all the items it produces simultaneously. For example, suppose a baker makes three types of bread, each of which is equally popular with its customers. Because of the nature of the mixing and baking process, only one kind of bread can be produced at any time. The baker would have to produce each type of bread in batches (batch processes were described in Chapter 4) as shown in Figure 12.3. The batches must be large enough to satisfy the demand for each kind of bread between the times when each batch is ready for sale. So even when demand is steady and predictable, there will always be some inventory to compensate for the intermittent supply of each type of bread. Cycle inventory only results from the need to produce

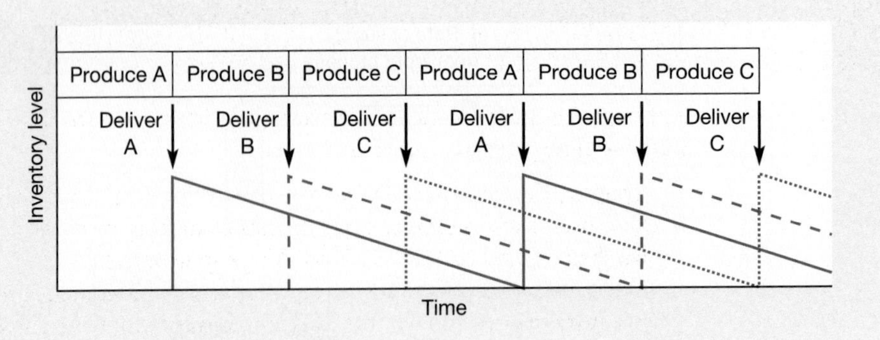

Figure 12.3 Cycle inventory in a bakery

products in batches, and the amount of it depends on volume decisions which are described in a later section of this chapter.

De-coupling Inventory

De-coupling inventory

Wherever an operation is designed to use a process layout (introduced in Chapter 7), the transformed resources move intermittently between specialized areas or departments that comprise similar operations. Each of these areas can be scheduled to work relatively independently in order to maximize the local utilization and efficiency of the equipment and staff. As a result, each batch of work-in-progress inventory joins a queue, awaiting its turn in the schedule for the next processing stage. This also allows each operation to be set to the optimum processing speed (cycle time), regardless of the speed of the steps before and after. Thus **de-coupling inventory** creates the opportunity for independent scheduling and processing speeds between process stages.

Anticipation inventory

Anticipation inventory

In Chapter 11 we saw how anticipation inventory can be used to cope with seasonal demand. Again, it was used to compensate for differences in the timing of supply and demand. Rather than trying to make the product (such as chocolate) only when it was needed, it was produced throughout the year ahead of demand and put into inventory until it was needed. **Anticipation inventory** is most commonly used when demand fluctuations are large but relatively predictable. It might also be used when supply variations are significant, such as in the canning or freezing of seasonal foods.

Pipeline inventory

Pipeline inventory

Pipeline inventory exists because material cannot be transported instantaneously between the point of supply and the point of demand. If a retail store orders a consignment of items from one of its suppliers, the supplier will allocate the stock to the retail store in its own warehouse, pack it, load it onto its truck, transport it to its destination, and unload it into the retailer's inventory. From the time that stock is allocated (and therefore it is unavailable to any other customer) to the time it becomes available for the retail store, it is pipeline inventory. Pipeline inventory also exists within processes where the layout is geographically spread out. For example, a large European manufacturer of specialized steel regularly moves cargoes of part-finished materials between its two mills in the UK and Scandinavia using a dedicated vessel that shuttles between the two countries every week. All the thousands of tonnes of material in transit are pipeline inventory.

Some disadvantages of holding inventory

Although inventory plays an important role in many operations performance, there are a number of negative aspects of inventory.

- Inventory ties up money, in the form of working capital, which is therefore unavailable for other uses, such as reducing borrowings or making investment in productive fixed assets (we shall expand on the idea of working capital later).
- Inventory incurs storage costs (leasing space, maintaining appropriate conditions, etc.).
- Inventory may become obsolete as alternatives become available.
- Inventory can be damaged, or deteriorate.
- Inventory could be lost, or be expensive to retrieve, as it gets hidden amongst other inventory.
- Inventory might be hazardous to store (for example flammable solvents, explosives, chemicals and drugs), requiring special facilities and systems for safe handling.
- Inventory uses space that could be used to add value.
- Inventory involves administrative and insurance costs.

The position of inventory

Not only are there several reasons for supply–demand imbalance, there could also be several points where such imbalance exists between different stages in the operation. Figure 12.4 illustrates different levels of complexity of inventory relationships within an operation. Perhaps the simplest level is the single-stage inventory system, such as a retail store, which will have only one stock of goods to manage. An automotive parts distribution operation will have a central depot and various local distribution points which contain inventories. In many manufacturers of standard items, there are three types of inventory. The **raw material** and **components inventories** (sometimes called input inventories) receive goods from the operation's suppliers; the raw materials and components work their way through the various stages of the production process but spend considerable amounts of time as **work-in-progress** (or work-in-process) (WIP) before finally reaching the **finished goods inventory**.

Raw materials inventory
Components inventory
Work-in-progress
Finished goods inventory
Multi-echelon inventory

A development of this last system is the **multi-echelon inventory** system. This maps the relationship of inventories between the various operations within a supply network (*see* Chapter 6). In Figure 12.4(d) there are five interconnected sets of inventory systems. The second-tier supplier's (yarn producer's) inventories will feed the first-tier supplier's (cloth producer's) inventories, who will in turn supply the main operation. The products are distributed to local warehouses from where they are shipped to the final customers. We will discuss the behaviour and management of such multi-echelon systems in the next chapter.

Day-to-day inventory decisions

At each point in the inventory system, operations managers need to manage the day-to-day tasks of running the system. Orders will be received from internal or external customers; these will be dispatched and demand will gradually deplete the inventory. Orders will need to be placed for replenishment of the stocks; deliveries will arrive and require storing. In managing the system, operations managers are involved in three major types of decision:

- *How much to order*. Every time a replenishment order is placed, how big should it be (sometimes called the *volume decision*)?
- *When to order*. At what point in time, or at what level of stock, should the replenishment order be placed (sometimes called the *timing decision*)?
- *How to control the system*. What procedures and routines should be installed to help make these decisions? Should different priorities be allocated to different stock items? How should stock information be stored?

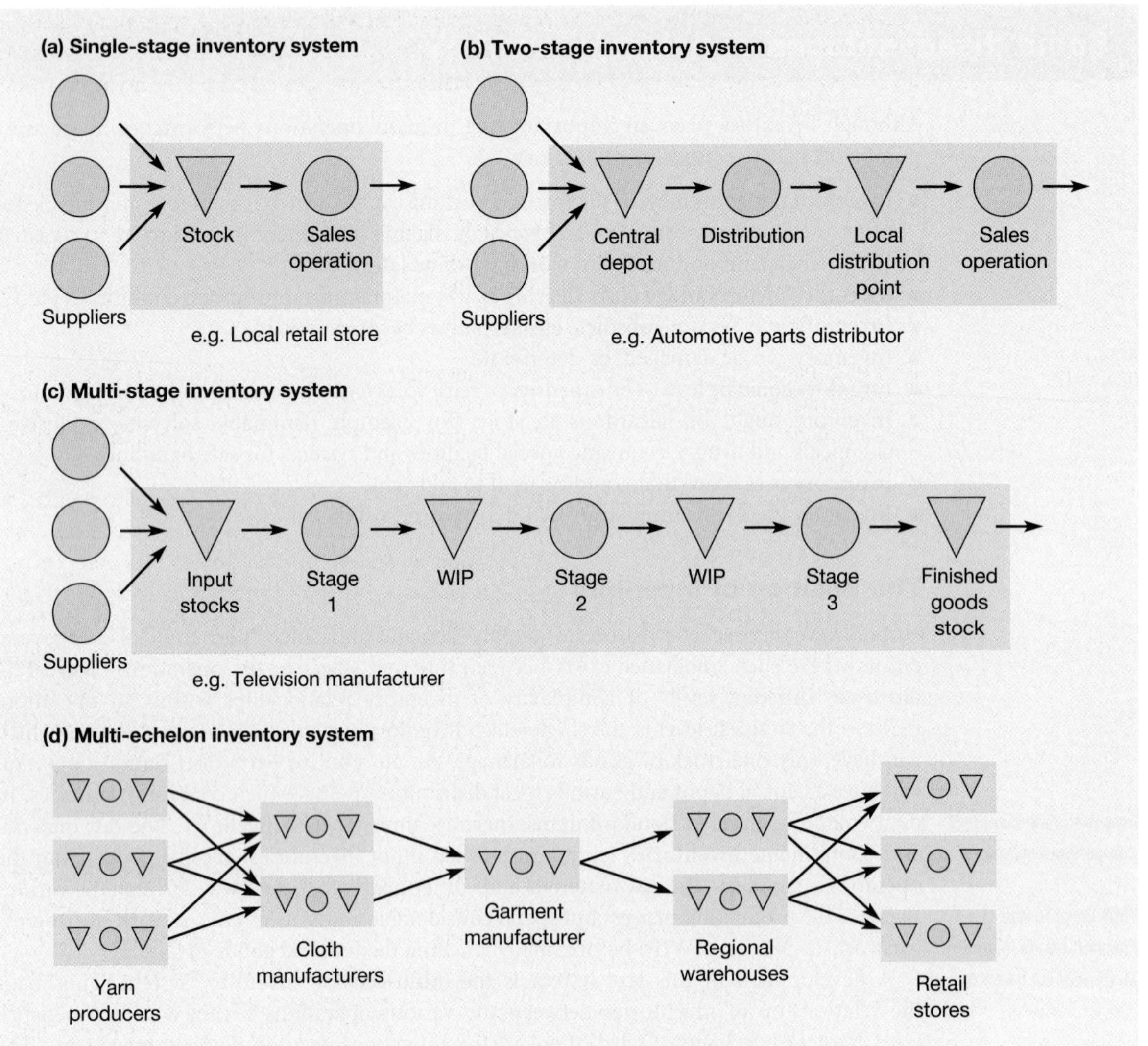

Figure 12.4 (a) Single-stage, (b) two-stage, (c) multi-stage and (d) multi-echelon inventory systems

The volume decision – how much to order

To illustrate this decision, consider again the example of the food and drinks we keep at our home. In managing this inventory we implicitly make decisions on *order quantity*, which is how much to purchase at one time. In making this decision we are balancing two sets of costs: the costs associated with going out to purchase the food items and the costs associated with holding the stocks. The option of holding very little or no inventory of food and purchasing each item only when it is needed has the advantage that it requires little money since purchases are made only when needed. However, it would involve purchasing provisions several times a day, which is inconvenient. At the very opposite extreme, making one journey to the local superstore every few months and purchasing all the provisions we would need until our next visit reduces the time and costs incurred in making the purchase but requires a very large amount of money each time the trip is made – money which could otherwise be in the bank and earning interest. We might also have to invest in extra cupboard units and a very large freezer. Somewhere between these extremes there will lie an ordering strategy which will minimize the total costs and effort involved in the purchase of food.

Inventory costs

The same principles apply in commercial order-quantity decisions as in the domestic situation. In making a decision on how much to purchase, operations managers must try to identify the costs which will be affected by their decision. Several types of costs are directly associated with order size.

1 *Cost of placing the order.* Every time that an order is placed to replenish stock, a number of transactions are needed which incur costs to the company. These include the clerical tasks of preparing the order and all the documentation associated with it, arranging for the delivery to be made, arranging to pay the supplier for the delivery, and the general costs of keeping all the information which allows us to do this. Also, if we are placing an 'internal order' on part of our own operation, there are still likely to be the same types of transaction concerned with internal administration. In addition, there could also be a 'changeover' cost incurred by the part of the operation which is to supply the items, caused by the need to change from producing one type of item to another.
2 *Price discount costs.* In many industries suppliers offer discounts on the normal purchase price for large quantities; alternatively they might impose extra costs for small orders.
3 *Stock-out costs.* If we misjudge the order-quantity decision and our inventory runs out of stock, there will be costs to us incurred by failing to supply our customers. If the customers are external, they may take their business elsewhere; if internal, stock-outs could lead to idle time at the next process, inefficiencies and, eventually, again, dissatisfied external customers.
4 *Working capital costs.* Soon after we receive a replenishment order, the supplier will demand payment for their goods. Eventually, when (or after) we supply our own customers, we in turn will receive payment. However, there will probably be a lag between paying our suppliers and receiving payment from our customers. During this time we will have to fund the costs of inventory. This is called the *working capital* of inventory. The costs associated with it are the interest we pay the bank for borrowing it, or the opportunity costs of not investing it elsewhere.
5 *Storage costs.* These are the costs associated with physically storing the goods. Renting, heating and lighting the warehouse, as well as insuring the inventory, can be expensive, especially when special conditions are required such as low temperature or high security.
6 *Obsolescence costs.* When we order large quantities, this usually results in stocked items spending a long time stored in inventory. Then there is a risk that the items might either become obsolete (in the case of a change in fashion, for example) or deteriorate with age (in the case of most foodstuffs, for example).
7 *Operating inefficiency costs.* According to lean synchronization philosophies, high inventory levels prevent us seeing the full extent of problems within the operation. This argument is fully explored in Chapter 15.

There are two points to be made about this list of costs. The first is that some of the costs will decrease as order size is increased; the first three costs are like this, whereas the other costs generally increase as order size is increased. The second point is that it may not be the same organization that incurs the costs. For example, sometimes suppliers agree to hold **consignment stock**. This means that they deliver large quantities of inventory to their customers to store but will only charge for the goods as and when they are used. In the meantime they remain the supplier's property so do not have to be financed by the customer, who does, however, provide storage facilities.

Consignment stock

Short case
Croft Port

Not all inventory is purely a source of cost. Some industries rely on it to add value. Oporto, a Portuguese city famous for port wine is awash with inventory. While wines in the style of port are produced around the world in several countries, including Australia and South Africa, only the product from Portugal may be labelled as port. One of the famous port brands is Croft Port which was founded in 1678. It owns one of the best wine-growing estates in the Douro valley, Quinta da Roêda. When the grapes have been picked they are crushed at the wineries (in the Douro valley). They used to be crushed by treading by foot with a row of people holding on to each other and walking back and forth across the granite 'baths' filled with the grapes. Now mechanical methods are used. As the grapes are squashed fermentation begins as the natural sugars in the juice are converted into alcohol by micro-organisms (yeast) in the grapes. The grape skins are retained during crushing to ensure their colour and tannins are released into the wine. After a while the skins are allowed to float to the surface and the fermenting juice is drawn from underneath. It is then mixed with a neutral grape spirit (fortification) to raise the strength of the wine and also stop fermentation in order to preserve some of the natural grape sugars in the finished product. The wine is then stored and aged in barrels in the cool dark caves (cellars) in Vila Nova de Gaia to allow the wine to mellow and develop its flavours before being bottled. There are essentially two styles of port, wood-aged and bottle-aged. Most port wines are wood-aged in oak vats or casks for five or six years for full-bodied wines or for 10–20 years for tawny ports. They are then bottled and ready to drink. The main type of bottle-aged port is vintage port, the best and rarest of all ports. This is made up of a selection of the very best grapes from the harvest of exceptional years. Although this port is only stored in the oak barrels for two years it is then allowed to mature and age in the bottles for many years, often decades.

Inventory profiles

An inventory profile is a visual representation of the inventory level over time. Figure 12.5 shows a simplified inventory profile for one particular stock item in a retail operation. Every time an order is placed, Q items are ordered. The replenishment order arrives in one batch instantaneously. Demand for the item is then steady and perfectly predictable at a rate of D units per month. When demand has depleted the stock of the items entirely, another order of Q items instantaneously arrives, and so on. Under these circumstances:

The average inventory $= \dfrac{Q}{2}$ (because the two shaded areas in Fig. 12.5 are equal)

The time interval between deliveries $= \dfrac{Q}{D}$

The frequency of deliveries = the reciprocal of the time interval $= \dfrac{D}{Q}$

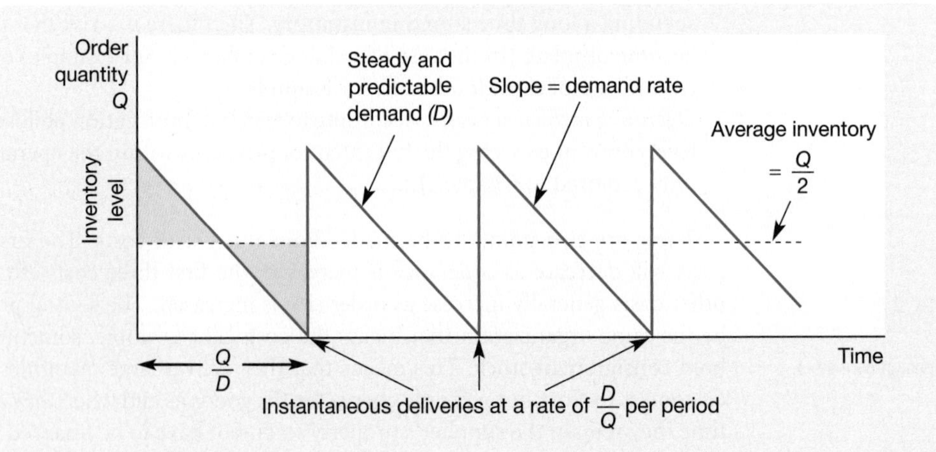

Figure 12.5 Inventory profiles chart the variation in inventory level

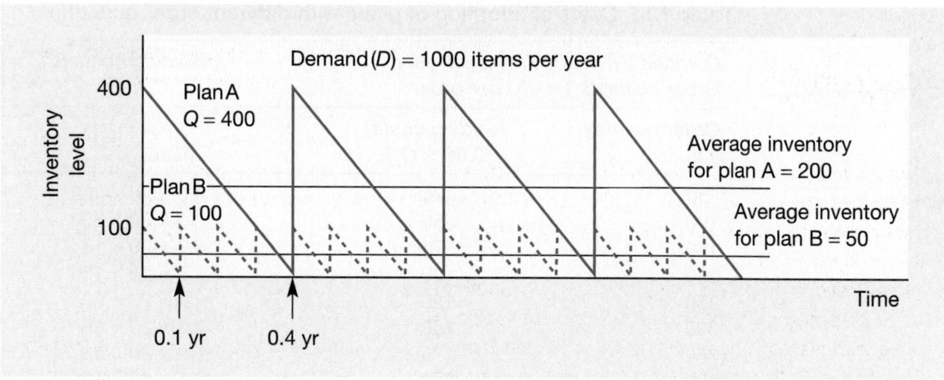

Figure 12.6 Two alternative inventory plans with different order quantities (Q)

The economic order quantity (EOQ) formula

Economic order quantity

The most common approach to deciding how much of any particular item to order when stock needs replenishing is called the **economic order quantity** (EOQ) approach. This approach attempts to find the best balance between the advantages and disadvantages of holding stock. For example, Figure 12.6 shows two alternative order-quantity policies for an item. Plan A, represented by the unbroken line, involves ordering in quantities of 400 at a time. Demand in this case is running at 1,000 units per year. Plan B, represented by the dotted line, uses smaller but more frequent replenishment orders. This time only 100 are ordered at a time, with orders being placed four times as often. However, the average inventory for plan B is one-quarter of that for plan A.

To find out whether either of these plans, or some other plan, minimizes the total cost of stocking the item, we need some further information, namely the total cost of holding one unit in stock for a period of time (C_h) and the total costs of placing an order (C_o). Generally, holding costs are taken into account by including:

- working capital costs
- storage costs
- obsolescence risk costs.

Order costs are calculated by taking into account:

- cost of placing the order (including transportation of items from suppliers if relevant);
- price discount costs.

In this case the cost of holding stocks is calculated at £1 per item per year and the cost of placing an order is calculated at £20 per order.

We can now calculate total holding costs and ordering costs for any particular ordering plan as follows:

$$\text{Holding costs} = \text{holding cost/unit} \times \text{average inventory}$$

$$= C_h \times \frac{Q}{2}$$

$$\text{Ordering costs} = \text{ordering cost} \times \text{number of orders per period}$$

$$= C_o \times \frac{D}{Q}$$

$$\text{So, total cost, } C_t = \frac{C_h Q}{2} + \frac{C_o D}{Q}$$

Table 12.1 Costs of adoption of plans with different order quantities

Demand (D) = 1,000 units per year *Order costs (C_o) = £20 per order*			*Holding costs (C_h) = £1 per item per year*		
Order quantity (Q)	*Holding costs ($0.5Q \times C_h$)*	+	*Order costs ($(D/Q) \times C_o$)*	=	*Total costs*
50	25		20 × 20 = 400		425
100	50		10 × 20 = 200		250
150	75		6.7 × 20 = 134		209
200	100		5 × 20 = 100		200*
250	125		4 × 20 = 80		205
300	150		3.3 × 20 = 66		216
350	175		2.9 × 20 = 58		233
400	200		2.5 × 20 = 50		250

*Minimum total cost.

We can now calculate the costs of adopting plans with different order quantities. These are illustrated in Table 12.1. As we would expect with low values of Q, holding costs are low but the costs of placing orders are high because orders have to be placed very frequently. As Q increases, the holding costs increase but the costs of placing orders decrease. Initially the decrease in ordering costs is greater than the increase in holding costs and the total cost falls. After a point, however, the decrease in ordering costs slows, whereas the increase in holding costs remains constant and the total cost starts to increase. In this case the order quantity, Q, which minimizes the sum of holding and order costs, is 200. This 'optimum' order quantity is called the *economic order quantity* (*EOQ*). This is illustrated graphically in Figure 12.7.

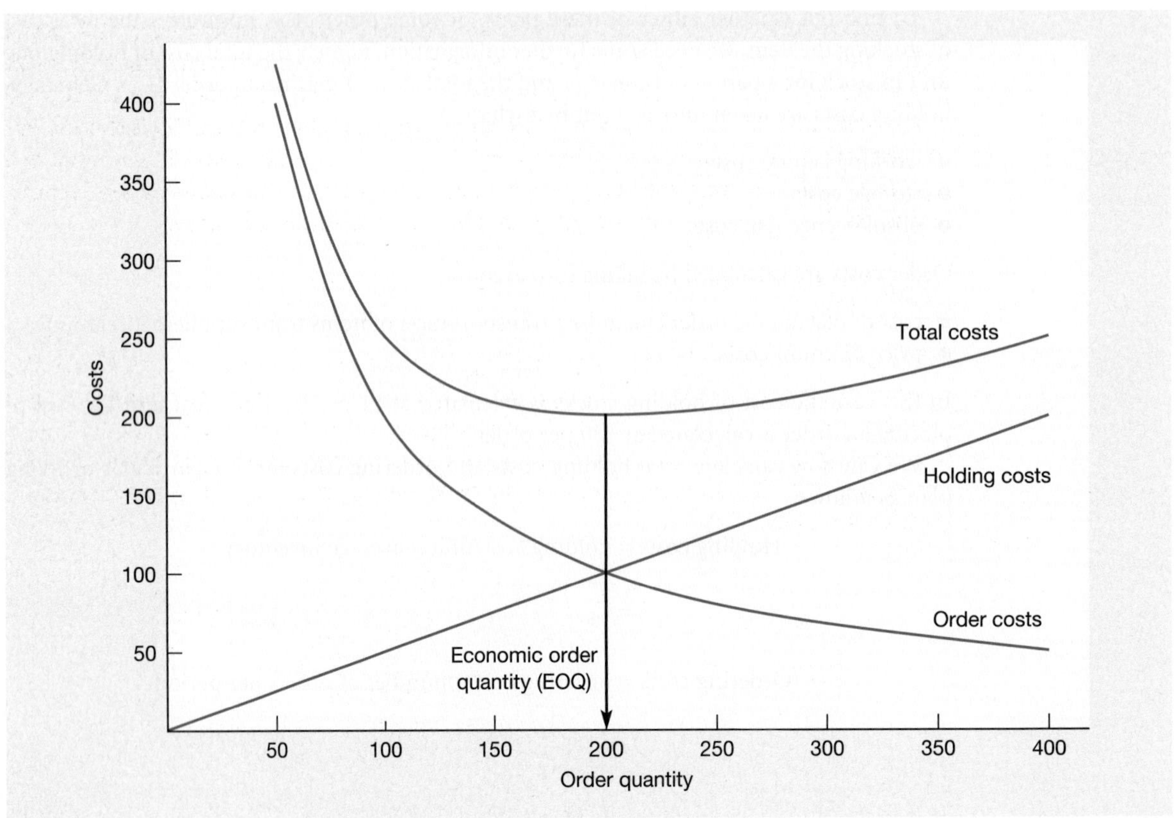

Figure 12.7 Graphical representation of the economic order quantity

A more elegant method of finding the EOQ is to derive its general expression. This can be done using simple differential calculus as follows. From before:

$$\text{Total cost} = \text{holding cost} + \text{order cost}$$

$$C_t = \frac{C_h Q}{2} + \frac{C_o D}{Q}$$

The rate of change of total cost is given by the first differential of C_t with respect to Q:

$$\frac{dC_t}{dQ} = \frac{C_h}{2} - \frac{C_o D}{Q^2}$$

The lowest cost will occur when $dC_t/dQ = 0$, that is:

$$0 = \frac{C_h}{2} - \frac{C_o D}{Q_o^{\,2}}$$

where Q_o = the EOQ. Rearranging this expression gives:

$$Q_o = \text{EOQ} = \sqrt{\frac{2C_o D}{C_h}}$$

When using the EOQ:

$$\text{Time between orders} = \frac{\text{EOQ}}{D}$$

$$\text{Order frequency} = \frac{D}{\text{EOQ}} \text{ per period}$$

Sensitivity of the EOQ

Examination of the graphical representation of the total cost curve in Figure 12.7 shows that, although there is a single value of Q which minimizes total costs, any relatively small deviation from the EOQ will not increase total costs significantly. In other words, costs will be near-optimum provided a value of Q which is reasonably close to the EOQ is chosen. Put another way, small errors in estimating either holding costs or order costs will not result in a significant deviation from the EOQ. This is a particularly convenient phenomenon because, in practice, both holding and order costs are not easy to estimate accurately.

Worked example

A building materials supplier obtains its bagged cement from a single supplier. Demand is reasonably constant throughout the year, and last year the company sold 2,000 tonnes of this product. It estimates the costs of placing an order at around £25 each time an order is placed, and calculates that the annual cost of holding inventory is 20 per cent of purchase cost. The company purchases the cement at £60 per tonne. How much should the company order at a time?

$$\text{EOQ for cement} = \sqrt{\frac{2C_o D}{C_h}}$$

$$= \sqrt{\frac{2 \times 25 \times 2{,}000}{0.2 \times 60}}$$

$$= \sqrt{\frac{100{,}000}{12}}$$

$$= 91.287 \text{ tonnes}$$

→

After calculating the EOQ the operations manager feels that placing an order for 91.287 tonnes *exactly* seems somewhat over-precise. Why not order a convenient 100 tonnes?

Total cost of ordering plan for Q = 91.287:

$$= \frac{C_h Q}{2} + \frac{C_o D}{Q}$$

$$= \frac{(0.2 \times 60) \times 91.287}{2} + \frac{25 \times 2{,}000}{91.287}$$

$$= £1{,}095.454$$

Total cost of ordering plan for Q = 100:

$$= \frac{(0.2 \times 60) \times 100}{2} + \frac{25 \times 2{,}000}{100}$$

$$= £1{,}100$$

The extra cost of ordering 100 tonnes at a time is £1,100 – £1,095.45 = £4.55. The operations manager therefore should feel confident in using the more convenient order quantity.

Gradual replacement – the economic batch quantity (EBQ) model

Although the simple inventory profile shown in Figure 12.5 made some simplifying assumptions, it is broadly applicable in most situations where each complete replacement order arrives at one point in time. In many cases, however, replenishment occurs over a time period rather than in one lot. A typical example of this is where an internal order is placed for a batch of parts to be produced on a machine. The machine will start to produce the parts and ship them in a more or less continuous stream into inventory, but at the same time demand is continuing to remove parts from the inventory. Provided the rate at which parts are being made and put into the inventory (P) is higher than the rate at which demand is depleting the inventory (D), then the size of the inventory will increase. After the batch has been completed the machine will be reset (to produce some other part), and demand will continue to deplete the inventory level until production of the next batch begins. The resulting profile is shown in Figure 12.8. Such a profile is typical for cycle inventories supplied by

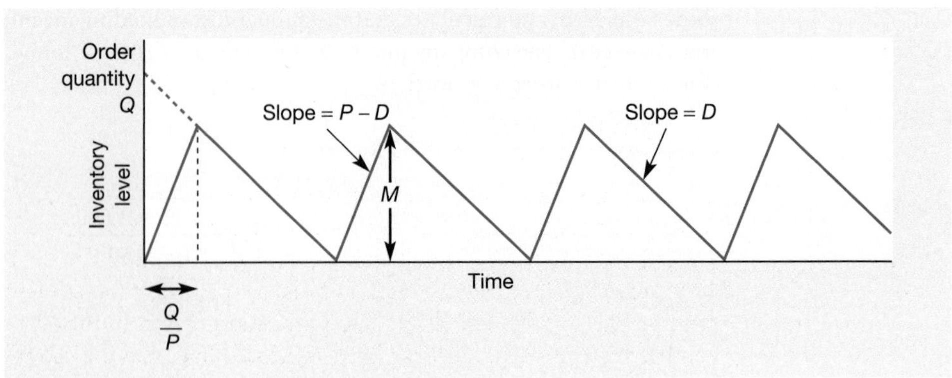

Figure 12.8 Inventory profile for gradual replacement of inventory

Economic batch quantity

batch processes, where items are produced internally and intermittently. For this reason the minimum-cost batch quantity for this profile is called the **economic batch quantity** (EBQ). It is also sometimes known as the economic manufacturing quantity (EMQ), or the production order quantity (POQ). It is derived as follows:

$$\text{Maximum stock level} = M$$

$$\text{Slope of inventory build-up} = P - D$$

Also, as is clear from Figure 12.8:

$$\text{Slope of inventory build-up} = M \div \frac{Q}{P}$$

$$= \frac{MP}{Q}$$

So,

$$\frac{MP}{Q} = P - D$$

$$M = \frac{Q(P - D)}{P}$$

$$\text{Average inventory level} = \frac{M}{2}$$

$$= \frac{Q(P - D)}{2P}$$

As before:

$$\text{Total cost} = \text{holding cost} + \text{order cost}$$

$$C_t = \frac{C_h Q(P - D)}{2P} + \frac{C_o D}{Q}$$

$$\frac{dC_t}{dQ} = \frac{C_h(P - D)}{2P} - \frac{C_o D}{Q^2}$$

Again, equating to zero and solving Q gives the minimum-cost order quantity EBQ:

$$\text{EBQ} = \sqrt{\frac{2C_o D}{C_h(1 - (D/P))}}$$

Worked example

The manager of a bottle-filling plant which bottles soft drinks needs to decide how long a 'run' of each type of drink to process. Demand for each type of drink is reasonably constant at 80,000 per month (a month has 160 production hours). The bottling lines fill at a rate of 3,000 bottles per hour, but take an hour to clean and reset between different drinks. The cost (of labour and lost production capacity) of each of these changeovers has been calculated at £100 per hour. Stock-holding costs are counted at £0.1 per bottle per month.

→

$$D = 80{,}000 \text{ per month}$$
$$= 500 \text{ per hour}$$
$$\text{EBQ} = \sqrt{\frac{2C_oD}{C_h(1 - (D/P))}}$$
$$= \sqrt{\frac{2 \times 100 \times 80{,}000}{0.1(1 - (500/3{,}000))}}$$
$$\text{EBQ} = 13{,}856$$

The staff who operate the lines have devised a method of reducing the changeover time from 1 hour to 30 minutes. How would that change the EBQ?

$$\text{New } C_o = £50$$
$$\text{New EBQ} = \sqrt{\frac{2 \times 50 \times 80{,}000}{0.1(1 - (500/3{,}000))}}$$
$$= 9{,}798$$

Critical commentary

The approach to determining order quantity which involves optimizing costs of holding stock against costs of ordering stock, typified by the EOQ and EBQ models, has always been subject to criticisms. Originally these concerned the validity of some of the assumptions of the model; more recently they have involved the underlying rationale of the approach itself. The criticisms fall into four broad categories, all of which we shall examine further:

- **The assumptions included in the EOQ models are simplistic.**
- **The real costs of stock in operations are not as assumed in EOQ models.**
- **The models are really descriptive, and should not be used as prescriptive devices.**
- **Cost minimization is not an appropriate objective for inventory management.**

Responding to the criticisms of EOQ

In order to keep EOQ-type models relatively straightforward, it was necessary to make assumptions. These concerned such things as the stability of demand, the existence of a fixed and identifiable ordering cost, that the cost of stock holding can be expressed by a linear function, shortage costs which were identifiable, and so on. While these assumptions are rarely strictly true, most of them can approximate to reality. Furthermore, the shape of the total cost curve has a relatively flat optimum point which means that small errors will not significantly affect the total cost of a near-optimum order quantity. However, at times the assumptions do pose severe limitations to the models. For example, the assumption of steady demand (or even demand which conforms to some known probability distribution) is untrue for a wide range of the operation's inventory problems. For example, a bookseller might be very happy to adopt an EOQ-type ordering policy for some of its most regular and stable products such as dictionaries and popular reference books. However, the demand patterns for many other books could be highly erratic, dependent on critics' reviews and word-of-mouth recommendations. In such circumstances it is simply inappropriate to use EOQ models.

Cost of stock

Other questions surround some of the assumptions made concerning the nature of stock-related costs. For example, placing an order with a supplier as part of a regular and multi-item order might be relatively inexpensive, whereas asking for a special one-off delivery of an item could prove far more costly. Similarly with stock-holding costs – although many companies make a standard percentage charge on the purchase price of stock items, this might not be appropriate over a wide range of stock-holding levels. The marginal costs of increasing stock-holding levels might be merely the cost of the working capital involved. On the other hand, it might necessitate the construction or lease of a whole new stock-holding facility such as a warehouse. Operations managers using an EOQ-type approach must check that the decisions implied by the use of the formulae do not exceed the boundaries within which the cost assumptions apply. In Chapter 15 we explore the just-in-time approach which sees inventory as being largely negative. However, it is useful at this stage to examine the effect on an EOQ approach of regarding inventory as being more costly than previously believed. Increasing the slope of the holding cost line increases the level of total costs of *any* order quantity, but more significantly, shifts the minimum cost point substantially to the left, in favour of a lower economic order quantity. In other words, the less willing an operation is to hold stock on the grounds of cost, the more it should move towards smaller, more frequent ordering.

Using EOQ models as prescriptions

Perhaps the most fundamental criticism of the EOQ approach again comes from the Japanese-inspired 'lean' and JIT philosophies. The EOQ tries to optimize order decisions. Implicitly the costs involved are taken as fixed, in the sense that the task of operations managers is to find out what are the true costs rather than to change them in any way. EOQ is essentially a reactive approach. Some critics would argue that it fails to ask the right question. Rather than asking the EOQ question of 'What is the optimum order quantity?', operations managers should really be asking, 'How can I change the operation in some way so as to reduce the overall level of inventory I need to hold?' The EOQ approach may be a reasonable description of stock-holding costs but should not necessarily be taken as a strict prescription over what decisions to take. For example, many organizations have made considerable efforts to reduce the effective cost of placing an order. Often they have done this by working to reduce changeover times on machines. This means that less time is taken changing over from one product to the other, and therefore less operating capacity is lost, which in turn reduces the cost of the changeover. Under these circumstances, the order cost curve in the EOQ formula reduces and, in turn, reduces the effective economic order quantity. Figure 12.9 shows the EOQ formula represented graphically with increased holding costs (*see* the previous discussion) and reduced order costs. The net effect of this is to significantly reduce the value of the EOQ.

Should the cost of inventory be minimized?

Many organizations (such as supermarkets and wholesalers) make most of their revenue and profits simply by holding and supplying inventory. Because their main investment is in the inventory it is critical that they make a good return on this capital, by ensuring that it has the highest possible 'stock turn' (defined later in this chapter) and/or gross profit margin. Alternatively, they may also be concerned to maximize the use of space by seeking to maximize the profit earned per square metre. The EOQ model does not address these objectives. Similarly for products that deteriorate or go out of fashion, the EOQ model can result in excess inventory of slower-moving items. In fact, the EOQ model is rarely used in such organizations, and there is more likely to be a system of periodic review (described later) for regular ordering of replenishment inventory. For example, a typical builders' supply merchant might carry around 50,000 different items of stock (SKUs – stock-keeping units). However, most of these cluster into larger families of items such as paints, sanitaryware or metal fixings. Single orders are placed at regular intervals for all the required replenishments in the supplier's range, and these are then delivered together at one time. For example, if such deliveries were made weekly, then on average, the individual item order quantities will be for only one week's usage. Less popular items, or ones with erratic demand patterns, can be individually ordered at the same time, or (when urgent) can be delivered the next day by carrier.

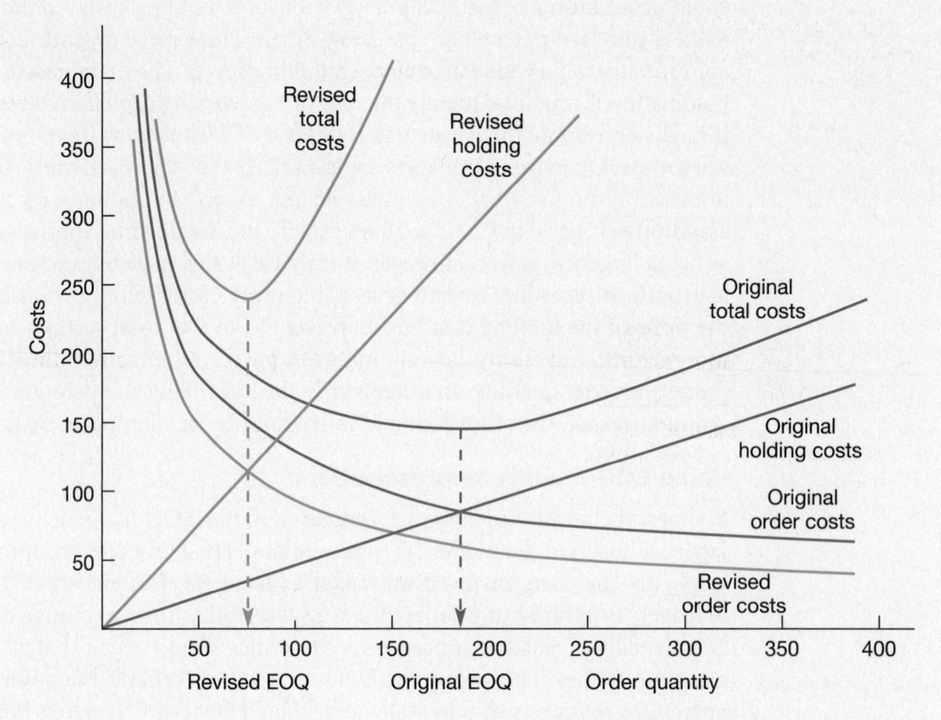

Figure 12.9 If the true costs of stock holding are taken into account, and if the cost of ordering (or changeover) is reduced, the economic order quantity (EOQ) is much smaller

Short case
Howard Smith Paper Group[2]

The Howard Smith Paper Group operates the most advanced warehousing operation within the European paper merchanting sector, delivering over 120,000 tonnes of paper annually. The function of a paper merchant is to provide the link between the paper mills and the printers or converters. This is illustrated in Figure 12.10. It is a sales- and service-driven business, so the role of the operation function is to deliver whatever the salesperson has promised to the customer. Usually, this means precisely the right product at the right time at the right place and in the right quantity. The company's operations are divided into two areas, 'logistics' which combines all warehousing and logistics tasks, and 'supply side' which includes inventory planning, purchasing and merchandizing decisions. Its main stocks are held at the national distribution centre, located in Northampton in the middle part of the UK. This location was chosen because it is at the centre of the company's main customer location and also because it has good access to motorways. The key to any efficient merchanting operation lies in its ability to do three things well. First, it must efficiently store the desired volume of required inventory. Second, it must have a 'goods inward' programme that sources the required volume of desired inventory. Third, it must be able to fulfil customer orders by 'picking' the desired goods fast and accurately from its warehouse. The warehouse is operational 24 hours per day, 5 days per week. A total of 52 staff are employed in the warehouse, including maintenance and cleaning staff. Skill sets are not an issue, since all pickers are trained for all tasks. This facilitates easier capacity management, since pickers can be deployed where most urgently needed. Contract labour is used on occasions, although this is less

Source: Howard Smith Paper Group

Dispatch activity at Howard Smith Paper Group

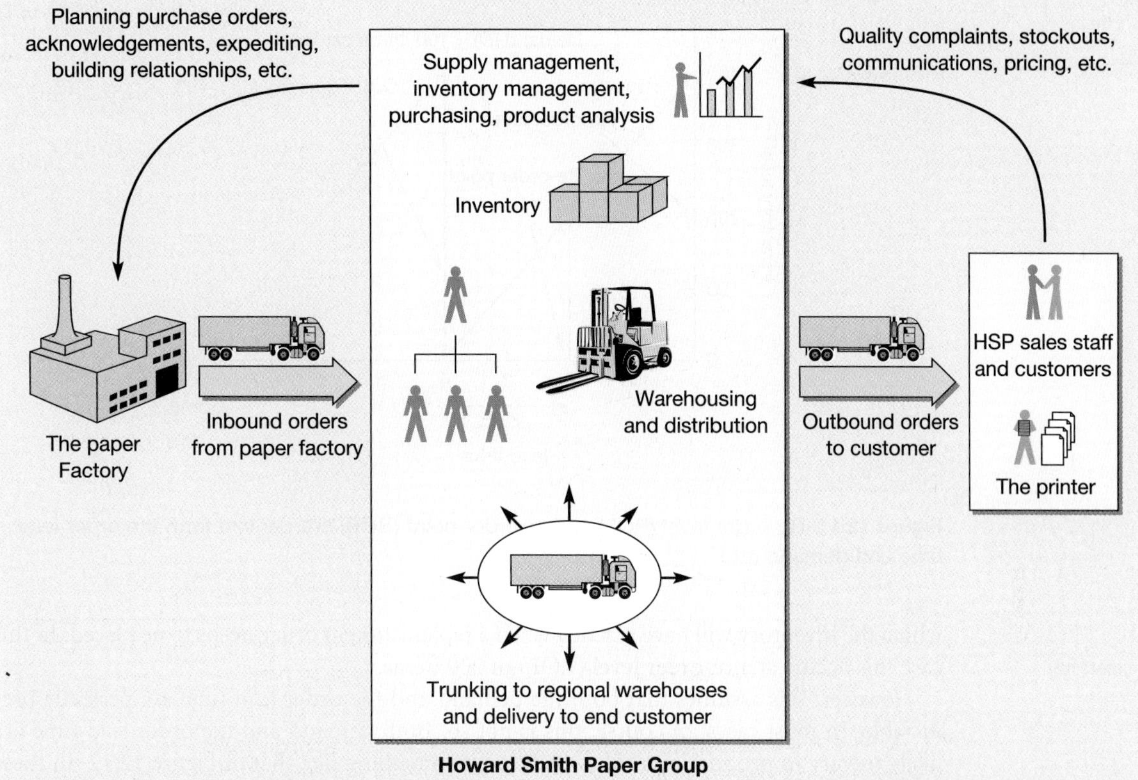

Figure 12.10 The role of the paper merchant

effective because the staff tend to be less motivated, and have to learn the job.

At the heart of the company's operations is a warehouse known as a 'dark warehouse'. All picking and movement within the dark warehouse is fully automatic and there is no need for any person to enter the high-bay stores and picking area. The important difference with this warehouse operation is that pallets are brought to the pickers. Conventional paper merchants send pickers with handling equipment into the warehouse aisles for stock. A warehouse computer system (WCS) controls the whole operation without the need for human input. It manages pallet location and retrieval, robotic crane missions, automatic conveyors, bar-code label production and scanning, and all picking routines and priorities. It also calculates operator activity and productivity measures, as well as issuing documentation and planning transportation schedules. The fact that all products are identified by a unique bar code means that accuracy is guaranteed. The unique user log-on ensures that any picking errors can be traced back to the name of the picker, to ensure further errors do not occur. The WCS is linked to the company's ERP system (we will deal with ERP in Chapter 14), such that once the order has been placed by a customer, computers manage the whole process from order placement to order dispatch.

The timing decision – when to place an order

When we assumed that orders arrived instantaneously and demand was steady and predictable, the decision on when to place a replenishment order was self-evident. An order would be placed as soon as the stock level reached zero. This would arrive instantaneously and prevent any stock-out occurring. If replenishment orders do not arrive instantaneously, but have a lag between the order being placed and it arriving in the inventory, we can calculate the timing of a replacement order as shown in Figure 12.11. The lead time for an order to arrive is in this case two weeks, so the **re-order point** (ROP) is the point at which stock will fall to zero minus the order lead time. Alternatively, we can define the point in terms of the level

Re-order point

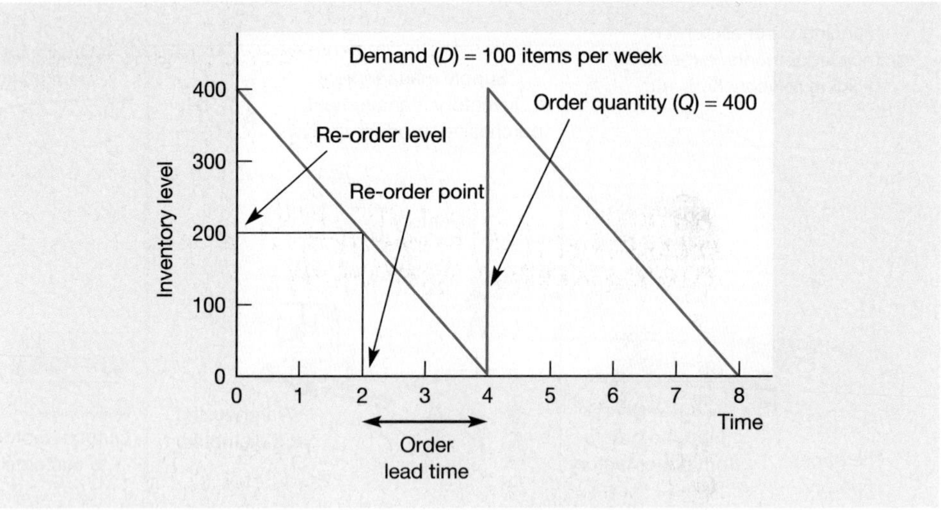

Figure 12.11 Re-order level (ROL) and re-order point (ROP) are derived from the order lead time and demand rate

which the inventory will have reached when a replenishment order needs to be placed. In this case this occurs at a **re-order level** (ROL) of 200 items.

Re-order level

However, this assumes that both the demand and the order lead time are perfectly predictable. In most cases, of course, this is not so. Both demand and the order lead time are likely to vary to produce a profile which looks something like that in Figure 12.12. In these circumstances it is necessary to make the replenishment order somewhat earlier than would be the case in a purely deterministic situation. This will result in, on average, some stock still being in the inventory when the replenishment order arrives. This is buffer (safety) stock. The earlier the replenishment order is placed, the higher will be the expected level of safety stock (s) when the replenishment order arrives. But because of the variability of both lead time (t) and demand rate (d), there will sometimes be a higher-than-average level of safety stock and sometimes lower. The main consideration in setting safety stock is not so much the average level of stock when a replenishment order arrives but rather the probability that the stock will not have run out before the replenishment order arrives.

The key statistic in calculating how much safety stock to allow is the probability distribution which shows the **lead-time usage**. The lead-time usage distribution is a combination of

Lead-time usage

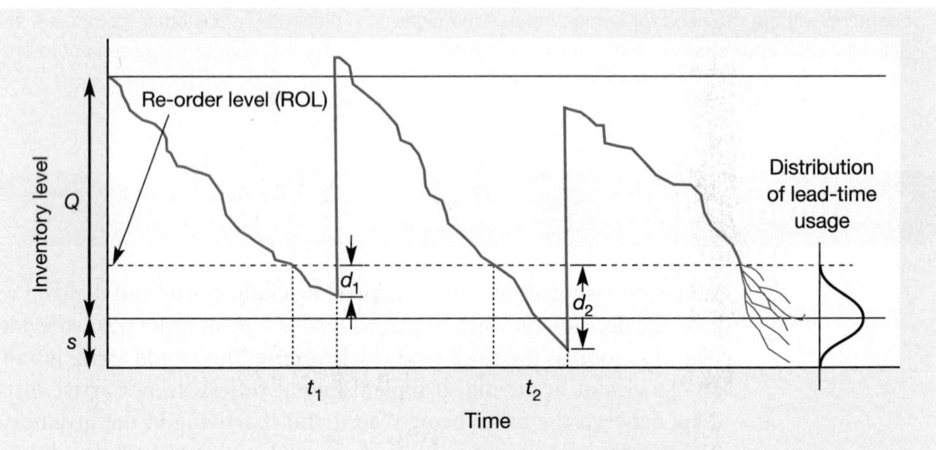

Figure 12.12 Safety stock (s) helps to avoid stock-outs when demand and/or order lead time are uncertain

the distributions which describe lead-time variation and the demand rate during the lead time. If safety stock is set below the lower limit of this distribution then there will be shortages every single replenishment cycle. If safety stock is set above the upper limit of the distribution, there is no chance of stock-outs occurring. Usually, safety stock is set to give a predetermined likelihood that stock-outs will not occur. Figure 12.12 shows that, in this case, the first replenishment order arrived after t_1, resulting in a lead-time usage of d_1. The second replenishment order took longer, t_2, and demand rate was also higher, resulting in a lead-time usage of d_2. The third order cycle shows several possible inventory profiles for different conditions of lead-time usage and demand rate.

Worked example

A company which imports running shoes for sale in its sports shops can never be certain of how long, after placing an order, the delivery will take. Examination of previous orders reveals that out of ten orders: one took one week, two took two weeks, four took three weeks, two took four weeks and one took five weeks. The rate of demand for the shoes also varies between 110 pairs per week and 140 pairs per week. There is a 0.2 probability of the demand rate being either 110 or 140 pairs per week, and a 0.3 chance of demand being either 120 or 130 pairs per week. The company needs to decide when it should place replenishment orders if the probability of a stock-out is to be less than 10 per cent.

Both lead time and the demand rate during the lead time will contribute to the lead-time usage. So the distributions which describe each will need to be combined. Figure 12.13 and Table 12.2 show how this can be done. Taking lead time to be one, two, three, four or five weeks, and demand rate to be 110, 120, 130 or 140 pairs per week, and also assuming the two variables to be independent, the distributions can be combined as shown in Table 12.2. Each element in the matrix shows a possible lead-time usage with the probability of its occurrence. So if the lead time is one week and the demand rate is 110 pairs per week, the actual lead-time usage will be $1 \times 110 = 110$ pairs. Since there is a 0.1 chance of the lead time being one week, and a 0.2 chance of demand rate being 110 pairs per week, the probability of both these events occurring is $0.1 \times 0.2 = 0.02$.

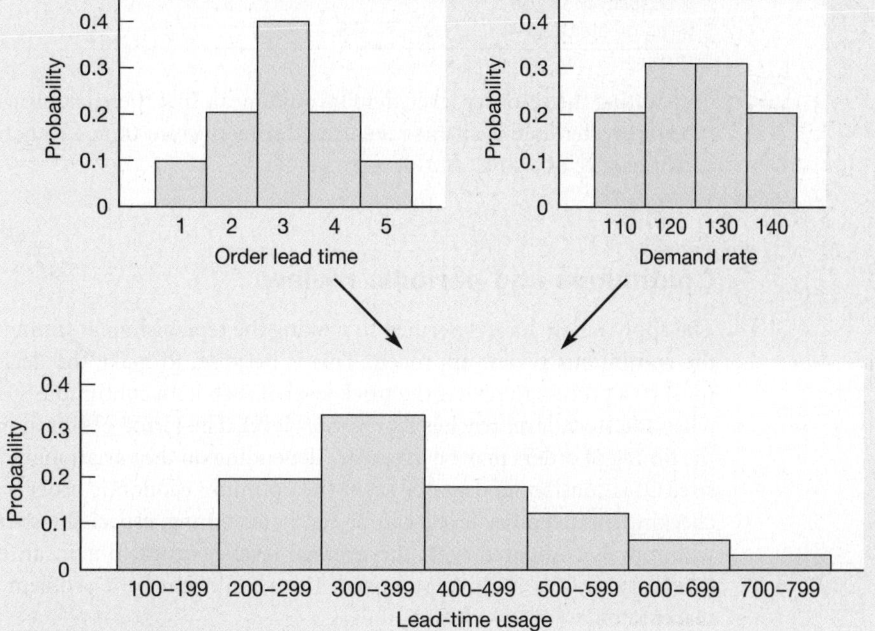

Figure 12.13 The probability distributions for order lead time and demand rate combine to give the lead-time usage distribution

→

Table 12.2 Matrix of lead-time and demand-rate probabilities

			Lead-time probabilities				
			1 0.1	2 0.2	3 0.4	4 0.2	5 0.1
Demand-rate probabilities	110	0.2	110 (0.02)	220 (0.04)	330 (0.08)	440 (0.04)	550 (0.02)
	120	0.3	120 (0.03)	240 (0.06)	360 (0.12)	480 (0.06)	600 (0.03)
	130	0.3	130 (0.03)	260 (0.06)	390 (0.12)	520 (0.06)	650 (0.03)
	140	0.2	140 (0.02)	280 (0.04)	420 (0.08)	560 (0.04)	700 (0.02)

We can now classify the possible lead-time usages into histogram form. For example, summing the probabilities of all the lead-time usages which fall within the range 100–199 (all the first column) gives a combined probability of 0.1. Repeating this for subsequent intervals results in Table 12.3.

Table 12.3 Combined probabilities

Lead-time usage	100–199	200–299	300–399	400–499	500–599	600–699	700–799
Probability	0.1	0.2	0.32	0.18	0.12	0.06	0.02

This shows the probability of each possible range of lead-time usage occurring, but it is the cumulative probabilities that are needed to predict the likelihood of stock-out (*see* Table 12.4).

Table 12.4 Combined probabilities

Lead-time usage X	100	200	300	400	500	600	700	800
Probability of usage being greater than X	1.0	0.9	0.7	0.38	0.2	0.08	0.02	0

Setting the re-order level at 600 would mean that there is only a 0.08 chance of usage being greater than available inventory during the lead time, i.e. there is a less than 10 per cent chance of a stock-out occurring.

Continuous and periodic review

Continuous review

The approach we have described to making the replenishment timing decision is often called the **continuous review** approach. This is because, to make the decision in this way, there must be a process to review the stock level of each item continuously and then place an order when the stock level reaches its re-order level. The virtue of this approach is that, although the timing of orders may be irregular (depending on the variation in demand rate), the order size (Q) is constant and can be set at the optimum economic order quantity. Such continual checking on inventory levels can be time-consuming, especially when there are many stock withdrawals compared with the average level of stock, but in an environment where all inventory records are computerized, this should not be a problem unless the records are inaccurate.

Periodic review

An alternative and far simpler approach, but one which sacrifices the use of a fixed (and therefore possibly optimum) order quantity, is called the **periodic review** approach. Here, rather than ordering at a predetermined re-order level, the periodic approach orders at a

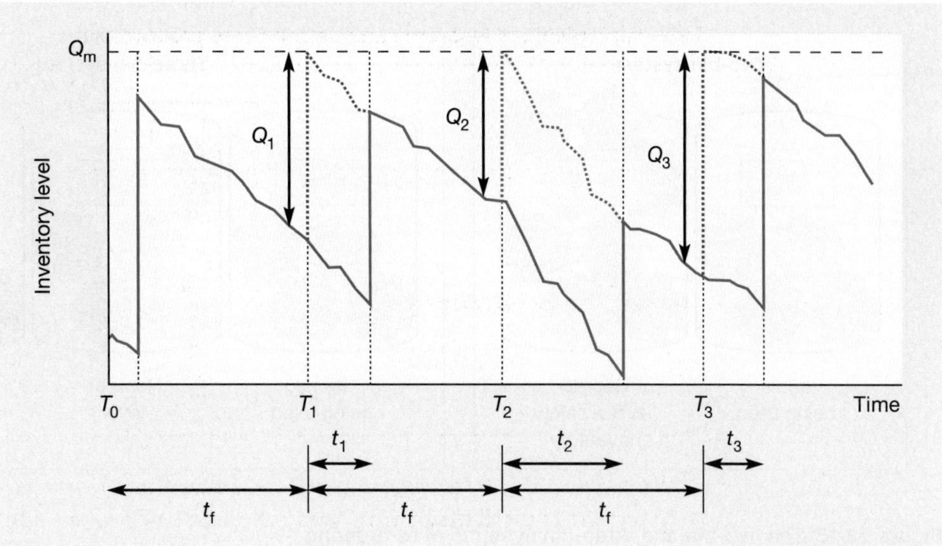

Figure 12.14 A periodic review approach to order timing with probabilistic demand and lead time

fixed and regular time interval. So the stock level of an item could be found, for example, at the end of every month and a replenishment order placed to bring the stock up to a pre-determined level. This level is calculated to cover demand between the replenishment order being placed and the following replenishment order arriving. Figure 12.14 illustrates the parameters for the periodic review approach.

At time T_1 in Figure 12.14 the inventory manager would examine the stock level and order sufficient to bring it up to some maximum, Q_m. However, that order of Q_1 items will not arrive until a further time of t_1 has passed, during which demand continues to deplete the stocks. Again, both demand and lead time are uncertain. The Q_1 items will arrive and bring the stock up to some level lower than Q_m (unless there has been no demand during t_1). Demand then continues until T_2, when again an order Q_2 is placed which is the difference between the current stock at T_2 and Q_m. This order arrives after t_2, by which time demand has depleted the stocks further. Thus the replenishment order placed at T_1 must be able to cover for the demand which occurs until T_2 and t_2. Safety stocks will need to be calculated, in a similar manner to before, based on the distribution of usage over this period.

The time interval

The interval between placing orders, t_1, is usually calculated on a deterministic basis, and derived from the EOQ. So, for example, if the demand for an item is 2,000 per year, the cost of placing an order £25, and the cost of holding stock £0.5 per item per year:

$$\text{EOQ} = \sqrt{\frac{2C_oD}{C_h}} = \sqrt{\frac{2 \times 2{,}000 \times 25}{0.5}} = 447$$

The optimum time interval between orders, t_f, is therefore:

$$t_f = \frac{\text{EOQ}}{D} = \frac{447}{2{,}000}\text{ years}$$

$$= 2.68 \text{ months}$$

It may seem paradoxical to calculate the time interval assuming constant demand when demand is, in fact, uncertain. However, uncertainties in both demand and lead time can be allowed for by setting Q_m to allow for the desired probability of stock-out based on usage during the period t_f + lead time.

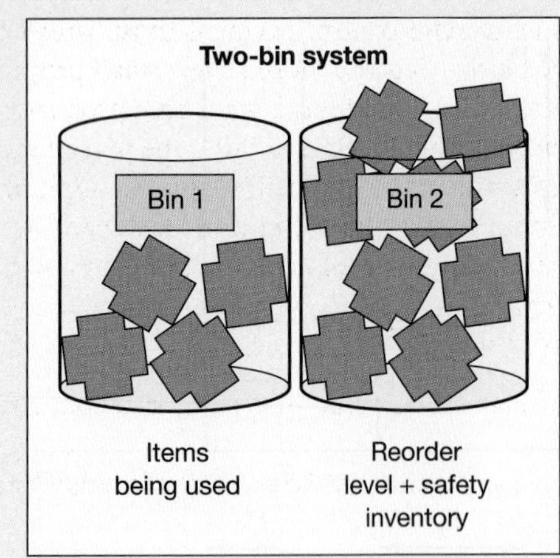

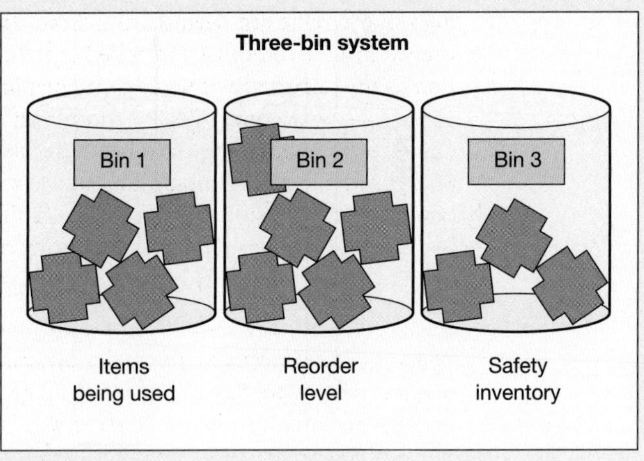

Figure 12.15 The two-bin and three-bin systems of re-ordering

Two-bin and three-bin systems

Two-bin system

Three-bin system

Keeping track of inventory levels is especially important in continuous review approaches to re-ordering. A simple and obvious method of indicating when the re-order point has been reached is necessary, especially if there are a large number of items to be monitored. The two- and three-bin systems illustrated in Figure 12.15 are such methods. The simple **two-bin system** involves storing the re-order point quantity plus the safety inventory quantity in the second bin and using parts from the first bin. When the first bin empties, that is the signal to order the next re-order quantity. Sometimes the safety inventory is stored in a third bin (the **three-bin system**), so it is clear when demand is exceeding that which was expected. Different 'bins' are not always necessary to operate this type of system. For example, a common practice in retail operations is to store the second 'bin' quantity upside-down behind or under the first 'bin' quantity. Orders are then placed when the upside-down items are reached.

Inventory analysis and control systems

The models we have described, even the ones which take a probabilistic view of demand and lead time, are still simplified compared with the complexity of real stock management. Coping with many thousands of stocked items, supplied by many hundreds of different suppliers, with possibly tens of thousands of individual customers, makes for a complex and dynamic operations task. In order to control such complexity, operations managers have to do two things. First, they have to discriminate between different stocked items, so that they can apply a degree of control to each item which is appropriate to its importance. Second, they need to invest in an information-processing system which can cope with their particular set of inventory control circumstances.

Inventory priorities – the ABC system

In any inventory which contains more than one stocked item, some items will be more important to the organization than others. Some, for example, might have a very high usage rate, so if they ran out many customers would be disappointed. Other items might be of particularly high value, so excessively high inventory levels would be particularly expensive. One common way of discriminating between different stock items is to rank them by the

Usage value

Pareto law

ABC inventory control

usage value (their usage rate multiplied by their individual value). Items with a particularly high usage value are deemed to warrant the most careful control, whereas those with low usage values need not be controlled quite so rigorously. Generally, a relatively small proportion of the total range of items contained in an inventory will account for a large proportion of the total usage value. This phenomenon is known as the **Pareto law** (after the person who described it), sometimes referred to as the 80/20 rule. It is called this because, typically, 80 per cent of an operation's sales are accounted for by only 20 per cent of all stocked item types. The relationship can be used to classify the different types of items kept in an inventory by their usage value. **ABC inventory control** allows inventory managers to concentrate their efforts on controlling the more significant items of stock.

- *Class A items* are those 20 per cent or so of high-usage-value items which account for around 80 per cent of the total usage value.
- *Class B items* are those of medium usage value, usually the next 30 per cent of items which often account for around 10 per cent of the total usage value.
- *Class C items* are those low-usage-value items which, although comprising around 50 per cent of the total types of items stocked, probably only account for around 10 per cent of the total usage value of the operation.

Worked example

Table 12.5 shows all the parts stored by an electrical wholesaler. The 20 different items stored vary in terms of both their usage per year and cost per item as shown. However, the wholesaler has ranked the stock items by their usage value per year. The total usage value per year is £5,569,000. From this it is possible to calculate the usage value per year of each item as a percentage of the total usage value, and from that a running cumulative total of the usage value as shown. The wholesaler can then plot the cumulative percentage of all stocked items against the cumulative percentage of their value. So, for example, the part with stock number A/703 is the highest-value part and accounts for 25.14 per cent

Table 12.5 Warehouse items ranked by usage value

Stock no.	*Usage (items/year)*	*Cost (£/item)*	*Usage value (£000/year)*	*% of total value*	*Cumulative % of total value*
A/703	700	20.00	1,400	25.14	25.14
D/012	450	2.75	1,238	22.23	47.37
A/135	1,000	0.90	900	16.16	63.53
C/732	95	8.50	808	14.51	78.04
C/375	520	0.54	281	5.05	83.09
A/500	73	2.30	168	3.02	86.11
D/111	520	0.22	114	2.05	88.16
D/231	170	0.65	111	1.99	90.15
E/781	250	0.34	85	1.53	91.68
A/138	250	0.30	75	1.34	93.02
D/175	400	0.14	56	1.01	94.03
E/001	80	0.63	50	0.89	94.92
C/150	230	0.21	48	0.86	95.78
F/030	400	0.12	48	0.86	96.64
D/703	500	0.09	45	0.81	97.45
D/535	50	0.88	44	0.79	98.24
C/541	70	0.57	40	0.71	98.95
A/260	50	0.64	32	0.57	99.52
B/141	50	0.32	16	0.28	99.80
D/021	20	0.50	10	0.20	100.00
Total			5,569	100.00	

of the total inventory value. As a part, however, it is only one-twentieth or 5 per cent of the total number of items stocked. This item together with the next highest value item (D/012) accounts for only 10 per cent of the total number of items stocked, yet accounts for 47.37 per cent of the value of the stock, and so on.

This is shown graphically in Figure 12.16. Here the wholesaler has classified the first four part numbers (20 per cent of the range) as Class A items and will monitor the usage and ordering of these items very closely and frequently. A few improvements in order quantities or safety stocks for these items could bring significant savings. The six next, part numbers C/375 through to A/138 (30 per cent of the range), are to be treated as Class B items with slightly less effort devoted to their control. All other items are classed as Class C items whose stocking policy is reviewed only occasionally.

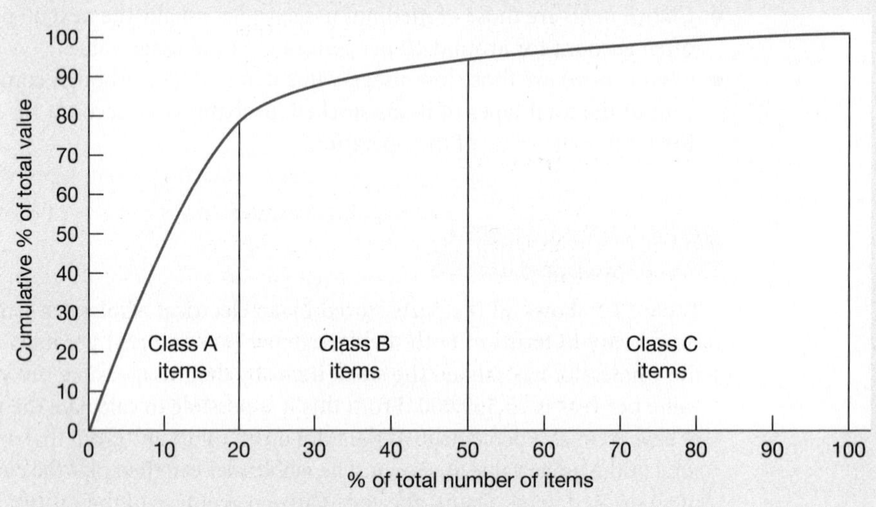

Figure 12.16 Pareto curve for items in a warehouse

Although annual usage and value are the two criteria most commonly used to determine a stock classification system, other criteria might also contribute towards the (higher) classification of an item:

- *Consequence of stock-out.* High priority might be given to those items which would seriously delay or disrupt other operations, or the customers, if they were not in stock.
- *Uncertainty of supply.* Some items, although of low value, might warrant more attention if their supply is erratic or uncertain.
- *High obsolescence or deterioration risk.* Items which could lose their value through obsolescence or deterioration might need extra attention and monitoring.

Some more complex stock classification systems might include these criteria by classifying on an A, B, C basis for each. For example, a part might be classed as A/B/A meaning it is an A category item by value, a class B item by consequence of stock-out and a class A item by obsolescence risk.

Critical commentary

This approach to inventory classification can sometimes be misleading. Many professional inventory managers point out that the Pareto law is often misquoted. It does not say that 80 per cent of the SKUs (stock-keeping units) account for only 20 per cent inventory value. It accounts for 80 per cent of inventory 'usage' or throughput value, in other words sales value. In fact it is the slow-moving items (the C category items) that often pose the greatest challenge in inventory management. Often these slow-moving items, although only accounting for 20 per cent of sales, require a large part (typically between one-half and two-thirds) of the total investment in stock. This is why slow-moving items are a real problem. Moreover, if errors in forecasting or ordering result in excess stock in 'A class' fast-moving items, it is relatively unimportant in the sense that excess stock can be sold quickly. However, excess stock in a slow-moving C item will be there a long time. According to some inventory managers, it is the A items that can be left to look after themselves, it is the B and even more the C items that need controlling.

Measuring inventory

In our example of ABC classifications we used the monetary value of the annual usage of each item as a measure of inventory usage. Monetary value can also be used to measure the absolute level of inventory at any point in time. This would involve taking the number of each item in stock, multiplying it by its value (usually the cost of purchasing the item) and summing the value of all the individual items stored. This is a useful measure of the investment that an operation has in its inventories but gives no indication of how large that investment is relative to the total throughput of the operation. To do this we must compare the total number of items in stock against their rate of usage. There are two ways of doing this. The first is to calculate the amount of time the inventory would last, subject to normal demand, if it were not replenished. This is sometimes called the number of weeks' (or days', months', years', etc.) *cover* of the stock. The second method is to calculate how often the stock is used up in a period, usually one year. This is called the **stock turn** or turnover of stock and is the reciprocal of the stock-cover figure mentioned earlier.

Stock turn

Worked example

A small specialist wine importer holds stocks of three types of wine, Chateau A, Chateau B and Chateau C. Current stock levels are 500 cases of Chateau A, 300 cases of Chateau B and 200 cases of Chateau C. Table 12.6 shows the number of each held in stock, their cost per item and the demand per year for each.

$$\begin{aligned}\text{The total value of stock} &= \Sigma(\text{average stock level} \times \text{cost per item})\\ &= (500 \times 3) + (300 \times 4) + (200 \times 5)\\ &= 3{,}700\end{aligned}$$

The amount of *stock cover* provided by each item stocked is as follows (assuming 50 sales weeks per year):

$$\text{Chateau A, stock cover} = \frac{\text{stock}}{\text{demand}} = \frac{500}{2{,}000} \times 50 = 12.5 \text{ weeks}$$

$$\text{Chateau B, stock cover} = \frac{\text{stock}}{\text{demand}} = \frac{300}{1{,}500} \times 50 = 10 \text{ weeks}$$

$$\text{Chateau C, stock cover} = \frac{\text{stock}}{\text{demand}} = \frac{200}{1{,}000} \times 50 = 10 \text{ weeks}$$

→

Table 12.6 Stock, cost and demand for three stocked items

Item	*Average number in stock*	*Cost per item (£)*	*Annual demand*
Chateau A	500	3.00	2,000
Chateau B	300	4.00	1,500
Chateau C	200	5.00	1,000

The *stock turn* for each item is calculated as follows:

$$\text{Chateau A, stock turn} = \frac{\text{demand}}{\text{stock}} = \frac{2{,}000}{500} = 4 \text{ times/year}$$

$$\text{Chateau B, stock turn} = \frac{\text{demand}}{\text{stock}} = \frac{1{,}500}{300} = 5 \text{ times/year}$$

$$\text{Chateau C, stock turn} = \frac{\text{demand}}{\text{stock}} = \frac{1{,}000}{200} = 5 \text{ times/year}$$

To find the average stock cover or stock turn for the total items in the inventory, the individual item measures can be weighted by their demand levels as a proportion of total demand (4,500). Thus:

$$\text{Average stock cover} = \left(12.5 \times \frac{2{,}000}{4{,}500}\right) + \left(10 \times \frac{1{,}500}{4{,}500}\right) + \left(10 \times \frac{1{,}000}{4{,}500}\right)$$

$$= 11.11$$

$$\text{Average stock turn} = \left(4 \times \frac{2{,}000}{4{,}500}\right) + \left(5 \times \frac{1{,}500}{4{,}500}\right) + \left(5 \times \frac{1{,}000}{4{,}500}\right)$$

$$= 4.56$$

Inventory information systems

Most inventories of any significant size are managed by computerized systems. The many relatively routine calculations involved in stock control lend themselves to computerized support. This is especially so since data capture has been made more convenient through the use of bar-code readers and the point-of-sale recording of sales transactions. Many commercial systems of stock control are available, although they tend to share certain common functions.

Updating stock records

Every time a transaction takes place (such as the sale of an item, the movement of an item from a warehouse into a truck, or the delivery of an item into a warehouse) the position, status and possibly value of the stock will have changed. This information must be recorded so that operations managers can determine their current inventory status at any time.

Generating orders

The two major decisions we have described previously, namely how much to order and when to order, can both be made by a computerized stock control system. The first decision, setting the value of how much to order (Q), is likely to be taken only at relatively infrequent intervals. Originally almost all computer systems automatically calculated order quantities by using the EOQ formulae covered earlier. Now more sophisticated algorithms are used, often using probabilistic data and based on examining the marginal return on investing in stock. The system will hold all the information which goes into the ordering algorithm but might periodically check to see if demand or order lead times, or any of the other parameters, have changed significantly and recalculate Q accordingly. The decision on when to order, on the other hand, is a far more routine affair which computer systems make according to whatever decision rules operations managers have chosen to adopt: either continuous review or periodic review. Furthermore, the systems can automatically generate whatever documentation is required, or even transmit the re-ordering information electronically through an electronic data interchange (EDI) system.

Generating inventory reports

Inventory control systems can generate regular reports of stock value for the different items stored, which can help management monitor its inventory control performance. Similarly, customer service performance, such as the number of stock-outs or the number of incomplete orders, can be regularly monitored. Some reports may be generated on an exception basis. That is, the report is only generated if some performance measure deviates from acceptable limits.

Forecasting

Inventory replenishment decisions should ideally be made with a clear understanding of forecast future demand. The inventory control system can compare actual demand against forecast and adjust the forecast in the light of actual levels of demand. Control systems of this type are treated in more detail in Chapter 14.

Common problems with inventory systems

Our description of inventory systems has been based on the assumption that operations (a) have a reasonably accurate idea of costs such as holding cost, or order cost, and (b) have accurate information that really does indicate the actual level of stock and sales. But data inaccuracy often poses one of the most significant problems for inventory managers. This is because most computer-based inventory management systems are based on what is called the **perpetual inventory principle**. This is the simple idea that stock records are (or should be) automatically updated every time that items are recorded as having been received into an inventory or taken out of the inventory. So,

Perpetual inventory principle

opening stock level + receipts in – dispatches out = new stock level.

Any errors in recording these transactions and/or in handling the physical inventory can lead to discrepancies between the recorded and actual inventory, and these errors are perpetuated until physical stock checks are made (usually quite infrequently). In practice there are many opportunities for errors to occur, if only because inventory transactions are numerous. This means that it is surprisingly common for the majority of inventory records to be in inaccurate. The underlying causes of errors include:

- keying errors: entering the wrong product code
- quantity errors: a mis-count of items put into or taken from stock
- damaged or deteriorated inventory not recorded as such, or not correctly deleted from the records when it is destroyed
- the wrong items being taken out of stock, but the records not being corrected when they are returned to stock
- delays between the transactions being made and the records being updated
- items stolen from inventory (common in retail environments, but also not unusual in industrial and commercial inventories).

Summary answers to key questions

*Check and improve your understanding of this chapter using self assessment questions and a personalised study plan, audio and video downloads, and an eBook – all at **www.myomlab.com.***

➤ What is inventory?

- Inventory, or stock, is the stored accumulation of the transformed resources in an operation. Sometimes the words 'stock' and 'inventory' are also used to describe transforming resources, but the terms *stock control* and *inventory control* are nearly always used in connection with transformed resources.
- Almost all operations keep some kind of inventory, most usually of materials but also of information and customers (customer inventories are normally called 'queues').

➤ Why is inventory necessary?

- Inventory occurs in operations because the timing of supply and the timing of demand do not always match. Inventories are needed, therefore, to smooth the differences between supply and demand.
- There are five main reasons for keeping inventory:
  - to cope with random or unexpected interruptions in supply or demand (buffer inventory);
  - to cope with an operation's inability to make all products simultaneously (cycle inventory);
  - to allow different stages of processing to operate at different speeds and with different schedules (de-coupling inventory);
  - to cope with planned fluctuations in supply or demand (anticipation inventory);
  - to cope with transportation delays in the supply network (pipeline inventory).

➤ What are the disadvantages of holding inventory?

- Inventory is often a major part of working capital, tying up money which could be used more productively elsewhere.
- If inventory is not used quickly, there is an increasing risk of damage, loss, deterioration, or obsolescence.
- Inventory invariably takes up space (for example, in a warehouse), and has to be managed, stored in appropriate conditions, insured and physically handled when transactions occur. It therefore contributes to overhead costs.

➤ How much inventory should an operation hold?

- This depends on balancing the costs associated with holding stocks against the costs associated with placing an order. The main stock-holding costs are usually related to working capital, whereas the main order costs are usually associated with the transactions necessary to generate the information to place an order.
- The best-known approach to determining the amount of inventory to order is the economic order quantity (EOQ) formula. The EOQ formula can be adapted to different types of inventory profile using different stock behaviour assumptions.
- The EOQ approach, however, has been subject to a number of criticisms regarding the true cost of holding stock, the real cost of placing an order, and the use of EOQ models as prescriptive devices.

➤ When should an operation replenish its inventory?

- Partly this depends on the uncertainty of demand. Orders are usually timed to leave a certain level of average safety stock when the order arrives. The level of safety stock is influenced by the variability of both demand and the lead time of supply. These two variables are usually combined into a lead-time usage distribution.
- Using re-order level as a trigger for placing replenishment orders necessitates the continual review of inventory levels. This can be time-consuming and expensive. An alternative approach is to make replenishment orders of varying size but at fixed time periods.

➤ How can inventory be controlled?

- The key issue here is how managers discriminate between the levels of control they apply to different stock items. The most common way of doing this is by what is known as the ABC classification of stock. This uses the Pareto principle to distinguish between the different values of, or significance placed on, types of stock.
- Inventory is usually managed through sophisticated computer-based information systems which have a number of functions: the updating of stock records, the generation of orders, the generation of inventory status reports and demand forecasts. These systems critically depend on maintaining accurate inventory records.

Case study
Trans-European Plastics

Trans-European Plastics (TEP) is one of Europe's largest manufacturers of plastic household items. Its French factory makes a range of over 500 products that are sold to wholesalers and large retailers throughout Europe. The company dispatches orders within 24 hours of receipt using an international carrier. All customers would expect to receive their requirements in full within one week. The manufacturing operation is based on batch production, employing 24 large injection-moulding machines. Weekly production schedules are prepared by the Planning and Control office, detailing the sequence of products (moulds and colours) to be used, the quantity required for each batch, and the anticipated timing of each production run. Mould changes ('set-ups') take on average three hours, at an estimated cost of €500 per set-up.

Source: Alamy/ArchivBerlin Fotoagentur GmbH

Concerned about the declining delivery reliability, increased levels of finished goods inventory and falling productivity (apparently resulting from 'split batches' where only part of a planned production batch is produced to overcome immediate shortages), the CEO, Francis Lamouche, employed consultants to undertake a complete review of operations. On 2 January, a full physical inventory check was taken. A representative sample of 20 products from the range is shown in Table 12.7.

Because of current high demand for many products, the backlog of work for planned stock replenishment currently averages two weeks, and so all factory orders must be planned at least that far in advance. The re-order quantities (*see* Table 12.7) had always been established by the Estimating Department at the time when each new product was designed and the manufacturing costs were established, based on Marketing's estimates of likely demand. Recently, however, to minimize the total cost of set-ups and to maximize capacity utilization, all products are planned for a *minimum* production run of 20 hours. The individual re-order levels have not been reviewed for several years, but were originally based on two weeks' average sales at that time. About 20 per cent of the →

Table 12.7 Details of a representative sample of 20 TEP products

*Product reference number**	*Description*	*Unit manuf'g variable cost (Euro)*	*Last 12 mths' sales (000s)*	*Physical inventory 2 Jan (000s)*	*Re-order quantity (000s)*	*Standard moulding rate** (items/hour))*
016GH	Storage bin large	2.40	10	0	5	240
033KN	Storage jar + lid	3.60	60	6	4	200
041GH	10 litre bucket	0.75	2,200	360	600	300
062GD	Grecian-style pot	4.50	40	15	20	180
080BR	Bathroom mirror	7.50	5	6	5	250
101KN	1 litre jug	0.90	100	22	20	600
126KN	Pack (10) bag clips	0.45	200	80	50	2,000
143BB	Baby bath	3.75	50	1	2	90
169BB	Baby potty	2.25	60	0	4	180
188BQ	Barbecue table	16.20	10	8	5	120
232GD	Garden bird bath	3.00	2	6	4	200
261GH	Broom head	1.20	60	22	20	400
288KN	Pack (10) clothes pegs	1.50	10	17	50	1,000
302BQ	Barbecue salad fork	0.30	5	12	8	400
351GH	Storage bin small	1.50	25	1	6	300
382KN	Round mixing bowl	0.75	800	25	80	650
421KN	Pasta jar	3.00	1	3	5	220
444GH	Wall hook	0.75	200	86	60	3,000
472GH	Dustbin + lid	9.00	300	3	10	180
506BR	Soap holder	1.20	10	9	20	400

*The reference number uses the following codes for ranges:

BB = Babycare BQ = Barbecue BR = Bathroom GD = Garden GH = General household KN = Kitchen

**Moulding rate is for the product as described (e.g. includes lids, or pack quantities).

products are very seasonal (e.g. Garden Range), with peak demand from April to August. Storage bins sell particularly well from October to December.

The European Marketing Manager summarized the current position, *'Our coverage of the market has never been so comprehensive; we are able to offer a full range of household plastics, which appeals to most European tastes. But we will not retain our newly developed markets unless we can give distributors confidence that we will supply all their orders within one week. Unfortunately, at the moment, many receive several deliveries for each order, spread over many weeks. This certainly increases their administrative and handling costs, and our haulage costs. And sometimes the shortfall is only some small, low-value items like clothes pegs.'*

The factory operates on three seven-hour shifts, Monday to Friday: 105 hours per week, for 50 weeks per year. Regular overtime, typically 15 hours on a Saturday, has been worked most of the last year. Sunday is never used for production, allowing access to machines for routine and major overhauls. Machines are laid out in groups so that each operator can be kept highly utilized, attending to at least four machines. Any product can be made on any machine.

Pierre Dumas, the production manager, was concerned about storage space: *'At the moment our warehouse is full, with products stacked on the floor in every available corner, which makes it vulnerable to damage from passing forklifts and from double-handling. We have finally agreed to approve an extension (costing over one million Euros) to be constructed in June–September this year, which will replace contract warehousing and associated transport which is costing us about 5 per cent of the manufacturing costs of the stored items. The return on investment for this project is well above our current 8 per cent cost of capital. There is no viable alternative, because if we run out of space, production will have to stop for a time. Some of our products occupy very large volumes of rack space. However, in the meantime we have decided to review all the re-order quantities. They seem either to result in excessive stock or too little stock to provide the service required. Large items such as the Baby Bath (Item 143BB) could be looked at first. This is a good starting point because the product has stable and non-seasonal demand. We estimate that it costs us around 20 per cent of the manufacturing variable costs to store such items for one year.'*

Questions

1 Why is TEP unable to deliver all its products reliably within the target of one week, and what effects might that have on the distributors?

2 Applying the EBQ model, what batch size would you recommend for this product? How long will each batch take to produce, and how many batches per year will be made? Should this model be applied to calculate the re-order quantity for all the products, and if not, why?

3 How would the EBQ change if the set-up costs were reduced by 50 per cent, and the holding costs were reassessed at 40 per cent, taking account of the opportunity costs of capital at TEP?

4 What internal problems result from the current planning and control policies? In particular, analyse stock turns and availability (e.g. high and low levels).

5 Using Pareto analysis, categorize the products into Classes A,B,C, based on usage value. Would this approach be useful for categorizing and controlling stock levels of all the products at TEP?

6 What overall recommendations would you make to Francis Lamouche about the proposed investment in the warehouse extension?

Problems and applications

These problems and applications will help to improve your analysis of operations. You can find more practice problems as well as worked examples and guided solutions on MyOMLab at ***www.myomlab.com****.*

1 An electronics circuit supplier buys microchips from a large manufacturer. Last year the company supplied 2,000 specialist D/35 chips to customers. The cost of placing an order is $50 and the annual holding cost is estimated to be $2.4 per chip per year. How much should the company order at a time, and what is the total cost of carrying inventory of this product?

2 Supermedicosupplies.com is an Internet supplier of medical equipment. One of its most profitable lines is the 'Thunderer' stethoscope. Demand for this product is 15,000 per year, the cost of holding the product is estimated to be €25 per year and the cost of placing an order €75. How many stethoscopes should the company order at a time?

3 Supermedicosupplies.com works a 44-week year. If the lead time between placing an order for stethoscopes and receiving them is two weeks, what is the re-order point for the Thunderer stethoscopes?

4 The Super Pea Canning Company produces canned peas. It uses 10,000 litres of green dye per month. Because of the hazardous nature of this product it needs special transport; therefore the cost of placing an order is €2,000. If the storage costs of holding the dye are €5 per litre per month, how much dye should be ordered at a time?

5 In the example above, if the storage costs of keeping the dye reduce to €3 per litre per month, how much will inventory costs reduce?

6 Obtain the last few years' Annual Report and Accounts (you can usually download these from the company's web site) for two materials-processing operations (as opposed to customer or information processing operations) within one industrial sector. Calculate each operation's stock–turnover ratio and the proportion of inventory to current assets over the last few years. Try to explain what you think are the reasons for any differences and trends you can identify and discuss the likely advantages and disadvantages for the organizations concerned.

Selected further reading

DeHoratius, N. and Raman, Ananth (2008) Inventory Record Inaccuracy: An Empirical Analysis, University of Chicago, http://faculty.chicagobooth.edu/nicole.dehoratius/research.

Viale, J.D. (1997) *The Basics of Inventory Management*, Crisp Publications, Menlo Park, Calif. Very much 'the basics', but that is exactly what most people need.

Waters, D. (2003) *Inventory Control and Management*, John Wiley and Sons Ltd, Chichester. Conventional but useful coverage of the topic.

Wild, T. (2002) *Best Practice in Inventory Management*, Butterworth-Heinemann. A straightforward and readable practice-based approach to the subject.

Useful web sites

www.inventoryops.com/dictionary.htm A great source for information on inventory management and warehouse operations.

www.mapnp.org/libary/ops mgnt/ops mgnt.htm General 'private' site on operations management, but with some good content.

www.apics.org Site of APICS: a US 'educational society for resource managers'.

www.inventorymanagement.com Site of the Centre for Inventory Management. Cases and links.

www.opsman.org Lots of useful stuff.

*Now that you have finished reading this chapter, why not visit MyOMLab at **www.myomlab.com** where you'll find more learning resources to help you make the most of your studies and get a better grade?*

Chapter 13 Supply chain planning and control

Key questions

- What is supply chain management?
- What are the activities of supply chain management?
- What are the types of relationship between operations in supply chains?
- How do supply chains behave in practice?
- How can supply chains be improved?

Introduction

Operations managers have to look beyond an internal view if they want to manage their operations effectively. As operations outsource many of their activities and buy more of their services and materials from outside specialists, the way they manage the supply of products and services to their operations becomes increasingly important, as does the integration of their distribution activities. Even beyond this immediate supply chain, there are benefits from managing the flow between customers' customers and suppliers' suppliers. This activity is now commonly termed *supply chain management*. In Chapter 6 we raised the strategic and structural issues of supply network management; this chapter considers the more 'infrastructural' issues of planning and controlling the individual chains in the supply network.

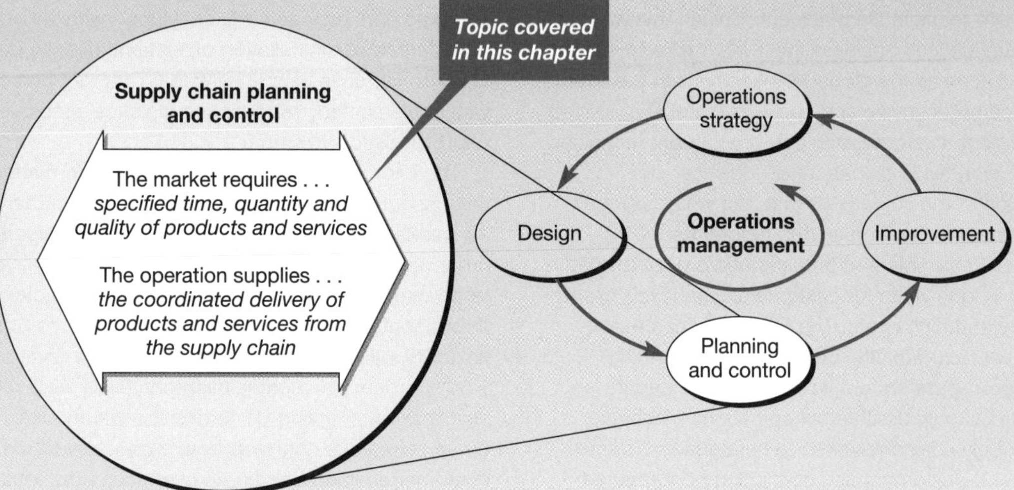

Figure 13.1 This chapter covers supply chain planning and control

Check and improve your understanding of this chapter using self assessment questions and a personalised study plan, audio and video downloads, and an eBook – all at ***www.myomlab.com****.*

Operations in practice Siemens 'SCOR' a success[1]

by Carsten Dittrich, University of Southern Denmark

Siemens AG, with over 450,000 people, sales of around €70 billion and operating in more than 190 countries, is one of the world's top five electrical engineering and electronics companies, producing products from mobile phones to power plants. For over a decade Siemens has used the Supply-Chain Operations Reference (SCOR) model to improve its supply chain efficiency and process performance. (The SCOR model is explained later in this chapter.) The implementation of the model was initially intended to support the company's move to a considerably stronger focus on e-business. Teams of more than 250 internal change agents were formed to start to review strategies, opportunities and challenges.

Source: Alamy Images

Siemens initially developed what they called their 'Generic Business Process' version of the SCOR model so that it could be applied in all their markets. However, Siemens soon realized that different kinds of business required different supply chain solutions. For example, Siemens used SCOR to streamline the Make-to-Order processes of its 'Siemens Medical Solutions' business whose computed tomography (CT) devices are made in Germany and China. This was a particularly difficult business involving 'make-to-order' functions such as the global management of customer orders, comprehensive and complex material management, customization and production, technical support, worldwide dispatch and logistics, and installation at the customer's site. Yet while Siemens was the clear innovation leader, before the SCOR initiative its inflexible and bureaucratic processes had resulted in long waits for customers, high levels of inventory and high costs. The CT supply chain was not connected, with little common understanding of how processes should work or what its supply objectives should be. Internal operations managers in the supply chain answered to headquarters rather than to end-customers and conflicting performance objectives led to fluctuating demands throughout the chain. It was the SCOR process that helped Siemens tackle these problems directly. Order management and planning and control processes moved from individual and fragmented order handling to the management of all worldwide customer orders; sourcing was simplified and integrated using 22 'A suppliers' rather than the 250 used previously, production of small quantities was organized according to customer specifications, strategic partnerships were developed with service providers, quick installation of systems directly delivered to customer sites using qualified CT factory personal was implemented, and 'reverse logistics' employed to refurbish used systems.

The improvements in supply chain performance were spectacular. Order to delivery time reduced from 22 weeks to 2 weeks, the simplified and transparent order on the factories allowed two production lines to do the work of the four used previously, factory throughput time was reduced from 13 days to 6 days, flexibility was increased tremendously to a level of ± 50% orders per month, inventory levels were reduced significantly, enabling CT to divest a warehouse, direct shipments non-stop from the factory to the customer enabled delivery to customer sites within 5 working days and also allowed customers to track shipments.

What is supply chain management?

A supply network is all the operations linked together to provide goods and services through to the end-customers

A supply chain is a strand of linked operations

Supply chain pipeline

Supply chain management is the management of the interconnection of organizations that relate to each other through upstream and downstream linkages between the processes that produce value to the ultimate consumer in the form of products and services. It is a holistic approach to managing across company boundaries. In Chapter 6 we used the term '**supply network**' to refer to all the operations that were linked together so as to provide goods and services through to the end-customers. In this chapter we deal with the 'ongoing' flow of goods and services through this network along individual channels or strands of that network. In large organizations there can be many hundreds of strands of linked operations passing through the operation. These strands are more commonly referred to as **supply chains**. An analogy often used to describe supply chains is that of the 'pipeline'. Just as liquids flow through a pipeline, so physical goods (and services, but the metaphor is more difficult to imagine) flow down a supply chain. Long pipelines will, of course, contain more liquid than short ones. So, the time taken for liquid to flow all the way through a long pipeline will be longer than if the pipeline were shorter. Stocks of inventory held in the supply chain can be thought of as analogous to storage tanks. On the journey through the **supply chain pipeline**, products are processed by different operations in the chain and also stored at different points.

Supply chain management objectives

All supply chain management shares one common, and central, objective – to satisfy the end-customer. All stages in a chain must eventually include consideration of the final customer, no matter how far an individual operation is from the end-customer. When a customer decides to make a purchase, he or she triggers action back along the whole chain. All the businesses in the supply chain pass on portions of that end-customer's money to each other, each retaining a margin for the value it has added. Each operation in the chain should be satisfying its own customer, but also making sure that eventually the end-customer is also satisfied.

For a demonstration of how end-customer perceptions of supply satisfaction can be very different from that of a single operation, examine the customer 'decision tree' in Figure 13.2. It charts the hypothetical progress of a hundred customers requiring service (or products) from a business (for example, a printer requiring paper from an industrial paper stockist). Supply performance, as seen by the core operation (the warehouse), is represented by the shaded part of the diagram. It has received 20 orders, 18 of which were 'produced' (shipped to customers) as promised (on time, and in full). However, originally 100 customers may have requested service, 20 of who found the business did not have appropriate products (did not stock the right paper), 10 of whom could not be served because the products were not available (out of stock), 50 of whom were not satisfied with the price and/or delivery (of whom 10 placed an order notwithstanding). Of the 20 orders received, 18 were produced as promised (shipped) but 2 were not received as promised (delayed or damaged in transport). So what seems a 90 per cent supply performance is in fact an 8 per cent performance from the customer's perspective. And this is just one operation. Include the cumulative effect of similar reductions in performance for all the operations in a chain, and the probability that the end-customer is adequately served could become remote. The point here is that the performance both of the supply chain as a whole, and its constituent operations, should be judged in terms of how all end-customer needs are satisfied.

Supply chain objectives

Meeting the requirements of end-customers requires the supply chain to achieve appropriate levels of the five operations performance objectives: quality, speed, dependability, flexibility and cost.

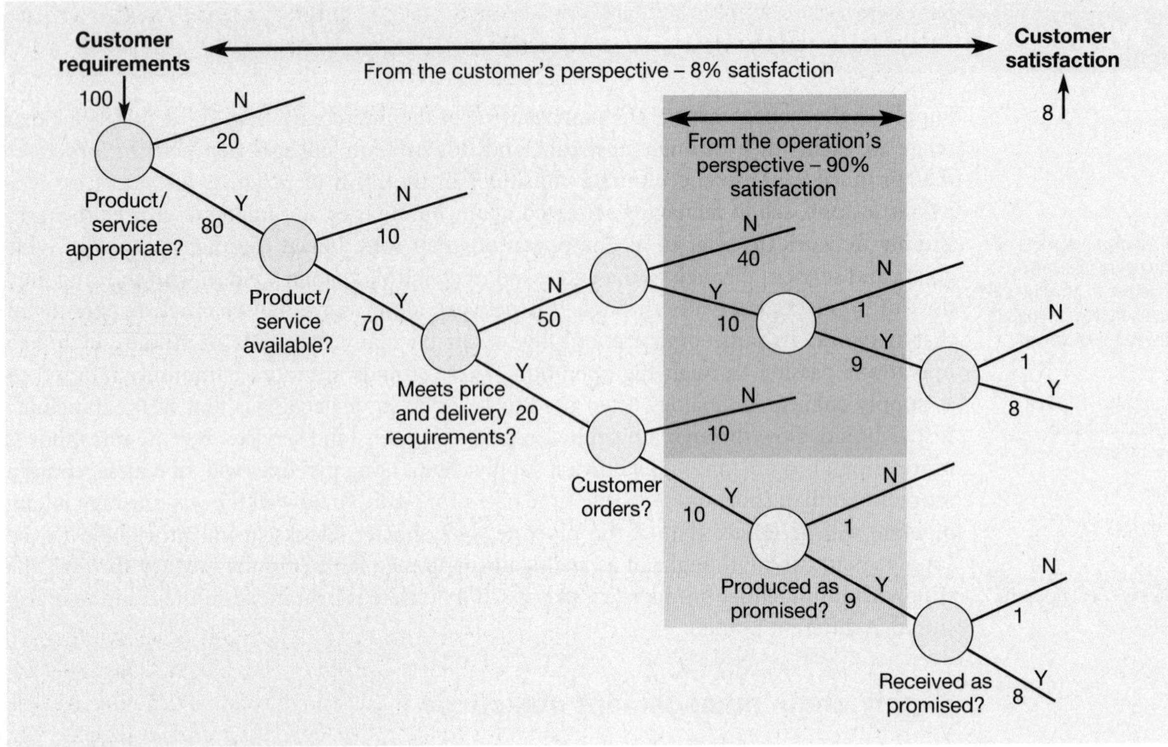

Figure 13.2 Taking a customer perspective of supply chain performance can lead to very different conclusions

Quality – the quality of a product or service when it reaches the customer is a function of the quality performance of every operation in the chain that supplied it. Errors in each stage of the chain can multiply in their effect on end-customer service, so if each of 7 stages in a supply chain has a 1 per cent error rate, only 93.2 per cent of products or services will be of good quality on reaching the end-customer (i.e. 0.99^1). This is why, only by every stage taking some responsibility for its own *and its suppliers'* performance, can a supply chain achieve high end-customer quality.

Speed has two meanings in a supply chain context. The first is how fast customers can be served, an important element in any business's ability to compete. However, fast customer response can be achieved simply by over-resourcing or over-stocking within the supply chain. For example, very large stocks in a retail operation can reduce the chances of stock-out to almost zero, so reducing customer waiting time virtually to zero. Similarly, an accounting firm may be able to respond quickly to customer demand by having a very large number of accountants on standby waiting for demand that may (or may not) occur. An alternative perspective on speed is the time taken for goods and services to move through the chain. So, for example, products that move quickly down a supply chain will spend little time as inventory because to achieve fast throughput time, material cannot dwell for significant periods as inventory. This in turn reduces inventory-related costs in the supply chain.

Dependability – like speed, one can almost guarantee 'on-time' delivery by keeping excessive resources, such as inventory, within the chain. However, dependability of throughput time is a much more desirable aim because it reduces uncertainty within the chain. If the individual operations in a chain do not deliver as promised on time, there will be a tendency for customers to over-order, or order early, in order to provide some kind of insurance against late delivery. This is why delivery dependability is often measured as 'on time, in full' in supply chains.

Flexibility – in a supply chain context is usually taken to mean the chain's ability to cope with changes and disturbances. Very often this is referred to as supply chain agility. The concept of agility includes previously discussed issues such as focusing on the end-customer and ensuring fast throughput and responsiveness to customer needs. But, in addition, agile supply chains are sufficiently flexible to cope with changes, either in the nature of customer demand or in the supply capabilities of operations within the chain.

Cost – in addition to the costs incurred within each operation, the supply chain as a whole incurs additional costs that derive from each operation in a chain doing business with each other. These may include such things as the costs of finding appropriate suppliers, setting up contractual agreements, monitoring supply performance, transporting products between operations, holding inventories, and so on. Many developments in supply chain management, such as partnership agreements or reducing the number of suppliers, are attempts to minimize transaction costs.

The activities of supply chain management

Some of the terms used in supply chain management are not universally applied. Furthermore, some of the concepts behind the terminology overlap in the sense that they refer to common parts of the total supply network. This is why it is useful first of all to distinguish between the different terms we shall use in this chapter. These are illustrated in Figure 13.3. *Supply chain management* coordinates all the operations on the supply side and the demand side. *Purchasing and supply management* deals with the operation's interface with its supply markets. *Physical distribution management* may mean supplying immediate customers, while *logistics* is an extension that often refers to materials and information flow down through a distribution channel, to the retail store or consumers (increasingly common because of the growth of internet-based retailing). The term *third-party logistics* (TPL) indicates outsourcing

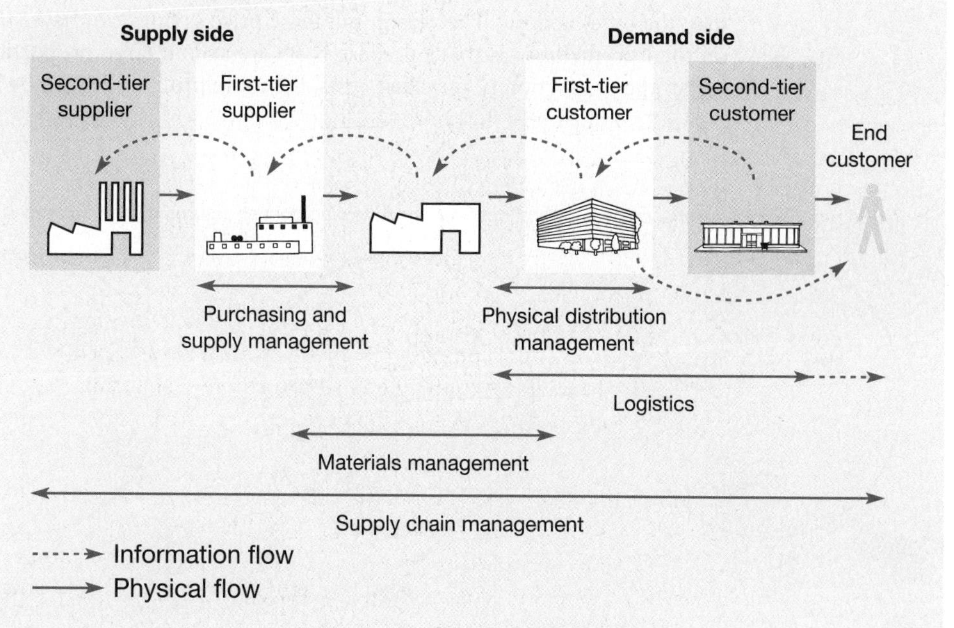

Figure 13.3 Some of the terms used to describe the management of different parts of the supply chain

to a specialist logistics company. *Materials management* is a more limited term and refers to the flow of materials and information only through the immediate supply chain.

Purchasing (procurement) and supply management

Purchasing

At the supply end of the business, **purchasing** (sometimes called '**procurement**') buys in materials and services from suppliers. Typically the volume and value of these purchases are increasing as organizations concentrate on their 'core tasks'. Purchasing managers provide a vital link between the operation itself and its suppliers. They must understand the requirements of all the processes within the operation and also the capabilities of the suppliers (sometimes thousands in number) who could potentially provide products and services for the operation. Purchasing can have a very significant impact on any operation's costs, and therefore profits. To illustrate the impact that price-conscious purchasing can have on profits, consider a simple manufacturing operation with the following financial details:

Total sales	£10,000,000
Purchased services and materials	£7,000,000
Salaries	£2,000,000
Overheads	£500,000

Therefore, profit = £500,000. Profits could be doubled to £1 million by any of the following:

- increase sales revenue by up to 100 per cent
- decrease salaries by 25 per cent
- decrease overheads by 100 per cent
- decrease purchase costs by 7.1 per cent.

A doubling of sales revenue does sometimes occur in very fast-growing markets, but this would be regarded by most sales and marketing managers as an exceedingly ambitious target. Decreasing the salaries bill by a quarter is likely to require substantial alternative investment – for example, in automation – or reflects a dramatic reduction in medium- to long-term sales. Similarly, a reduction in overheads by 100 per cent is unlikely to be possible over the short-to-medium term without compromising the business. However, reducing purchase costs by 7.1 per cent, although a challenging objective, is usually far more of a realistic option than the other actions. The reason purchase price savings can have such a dramatic impact on total profitability is that purchase costs are such a large proportion of total costs. The higher the proportion of purchase costs, the more profitability can be improved in this way. Figure 13.4 illustrates this.

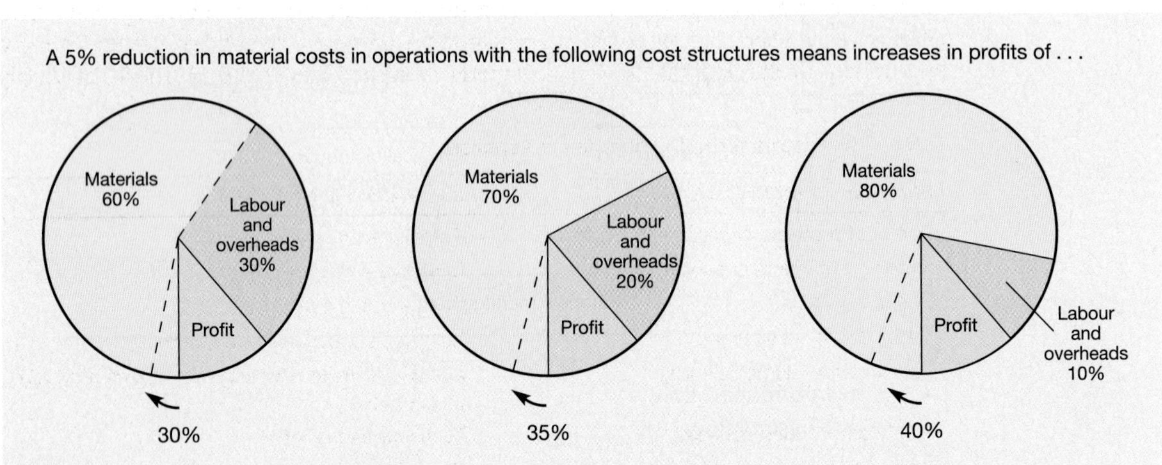

Figure 13.4 The larger the level of material costs as a proportion of total costs, the greater the effect on profitability of a reduction in material costs

Short case
Ford Motors' team value management[2]

Source: Getty Images/Getty Images News

Purchasing managers are a vital link between an operation and its suppliers. But they work best when teamed up with mainstream operations managers who know what the operation really needs, especially if, between them, they take a role that challenges previous assumptions. That is the basis behind Ford Motor Company's 'team value management' (TVM) approach. Reputedly, it all started when Ford's Head of Global Purchasing, David Thursfield, discovered that a roof rack designed for one of Ford's smaller cars was made of plastic-coated aluminium and capable of bearing a 100 kg load. This prompted the questions, *'Why is this rack covered in plastic? Why would anyone want to put 100 kg on the roof of a car that small?'* He found that no one had ever questioned the original specification. When Ford switched to using steel roof racks capable of bearing a smaller weight, they halved the cost. *'It is important'*, he says, *'to check whether the company is getting the best price for parts and raw material that provide the appropriate level of performance without being too expensive.'* The savings in a large company such as Ford can be huge. Often in multinationals, each part of the business makes sourcing and design decisions independently and does not exploit opportunities for cross-usage of components. The TVM approach is designed to bring together engineering and purchasing staff and identify where cost can be taken out of purchased parts and where there is opportunity for parts commonality (see Chapter 5) between different models. When a company's global purchasing budget is $75bn like Ford's, the potential for cost savings is significant.

Supplier selection

Choosing appropriate suppliers should involve trading off alternative attributes. Rarely are potential suppliers so clearly superior to their competitors that the decision is self-evident. Most businesses find it best to adopt some kind of supplier 'scoring' or assessment procedure. This should be capable of rating alternative suppliers in terms of factors such as those in Table 13.1.

Supplier selection

Choosing **suppliers** should involve evaluating the relative importance of all these factors. So, for example, a business might choose a supplier that, although more expensive than alternative suppliers, has an excellent reputation for on-time delivery, because that is more appropriate to the way the business competes itself, or because the high level of supply

Table 13.1 Factors for rating alternative suppliers

Short-term ability to supply	*Longer-term ability to supply*
Range of products or services provided	Potential for innovation
Quality of products or services	Ease of doing business
Responsiveness	Willingness to share risk
Dependability of supply	Long-term commitment to supply
Delivery and volume flexibility	Ability to transfer knowledge as well as products and services
Total cost of being supplied	Technical capability
Ability to supply in the required quantity	Operations capability Financial capability Managerial capability

dependability allows the business to hold lower stock levels, which may even save costs overall. Other trade-offs may be more difficult to calculate. For example, a potential supplier may have high levels of technical capability, but may be financially weak, with a small but finite risk of going out of business. Other suppliers may have little track record of supplying the products or services required, but show the managerial talent and energy for potential customers to view developing a supply relationship as an investment in future capability.

Worked example

A hotel chain has decided to change its supplier of cleaning supplies because its current supplier has become unreliable in its delivery performance. The two alternative suppliers that it is considering have been evaluated, on a 1–10 scale, against the criteria shown in Table 13.2. That also shows the relative importance of each criterion, also on a 1–10 scale. Based on this evaluation, Supplier B has the superior overall score.

Table 13.2 Weighted supplier selection criteria for the hotel chain

Factor	*Weight*	*Supplier A score*	*Supplier B score*
Cost performance	10	8 (8 × 10 = 80)	5 (5 × 10 = 50)
Quality record	10	7 (7 × 10 = 70)	9 (9 × 10 = 90)
Delivery speed promised	7	5 (5 × 7 = 35)	5 (5 × 7 = 35)
Delivery speed achieved	7	4 (4 × 7 = 28)	8 (8 × 7 = 56)
Dependability record	8	6 (6 × 8 = 48)	8 (8 × 8 = 64)
Range provided	5	8 (8 × 5 = 40)	5 (5 × 5 = 25)
Innovation capability	4	6 (6 × 4 = 24)	9 (9 × 4 = 36)
Total weighted score		325	356

Single- and multi-sourcing

Single-sourcing
Multi-sourcing

An important decision facing most purchasing managers is whether to source each individual product or service from one or more than one supplier, known, respectively, as **single-sourcing** and **multi-sourcing**. Some of the advantages and disadvantages of single- and multi-sourcing are shown in Table 13.3.

Table 13.3 Advantages and disadvantages of single- and multi-sourcing

	Single-sourcing	*Multi-sourcing*
Advantages	• Potentially better quality because more SQA possibilities • Strong relationships which are more durable • Greater dependency encourages more commitment and effort • Better communication • Easier to cooperate on new product/service development • More scale economies • Higher confidentiality	• Purchaser can drive price down by competitive tendering • Can switch sources in case of supply failure • Wide sources of knowledge and expertise to tap
Disadvantages	• More vulnerable to disruption if a failure to supply occurs • Individual supplier more affected by volume fluctuations • Supplier might exert upward pressure on prices if no alternative supplier is available	• Difficult to encourage commitment by supplier • Less easy to develop effective SQA • More effort needed to communicate • Suppliers less likely to invest in new processes • More difficult to obtain scale economies

It may seem as though companies that multi-source do so exclusively for their own short-term benefit. However, this is not always the case: multi-sourcing can bring benefits to both supplier and purchaser in the long term. For example, Robert Bosch GmbH, the German automotive components business, required that subcontractors do no more than 20 per cent of their total business with them. This was to prevent suppliers becoming too dependent and allow volumes to be fluctuated without pushing the supplier into bankruptcy. However, there has been a trend for purchasing functions to reduce the number of companies supplying any one part or service.

Purchasing, the Internet and e-procurement

For some years, electronic means have been used by businesses to confirm purchased orders and ensure payment to suppliers. The rapid development of the Internet, however, opened up the potential for far more fundamental changes in purchasing behaviour. Partly this was as the result of supplier information made available through the Internet. By making it easier to search for alternative suppliers, the Internet changed the economics of the search process and offers the potential for wider searches. It also changed the economics of scale in purchasing. For example, purchasers requiring relatively low volumes find it easier to group together in order to create orders of sufficient size to warrant lower prices. **E-procurement** is the generic term used to describe the use of electronic methods in every stage of the purchasing process from identification of requirement through to payment, and potentially to contract management.[3] Many of the large automotive, engineering and petrochemical companies, for example, have adopted such an approach. Typical of these companies' motives are those put forward by Shell Services International, part of the petrochemical giant:[4]

E-procurement

> *'Procurement is an obvious first step in e-commerce. First, buying through the web is so slick and cheap compared to doing it almost any other way. Second, it allows you to aggregate, spend and ask: Why am I spending this money, or shouldn't I be getting a bigger discount? Third, it encourages new services like credit, insurance and accreditation to be built around it.'*

Generally the benefits of e-procurement are taken to include the following.

- It promotes efficiency improvements (the way people work) in purchasing processes.
- It improves commercial relationships with suppliers.
- It reduces the transaction costs of doing business for suppliers.
- It opens up the marketplace to increased competition and therefore keeps prices competitive.
- It improves a business's ability to manage their supply chain more efficiently.

The benefits of e-procurement go beyond reducing costs

Note how lowering prices (purchase costs to the buyer) is only one of **the benefits of e-procurement**. The cost savings from purchased goods may be the most visible advantages of e-procurement, but some managers say that it is just the tip of the iceberg. It can also be far more efficient because purchasing staff are no longer chasing purchase orders and performing routine administrative tasks. Much of the advantage and time savings comes from the decreased need to re-enter information, from streamlining the interaction with suppliers and from having a central repository for data with everything contained in one system. Purchasing staff can negotiate with vendors faster and more effectively. Online auctions can compress negotiations from months to one or two hours, or even minutes.

Electronic marketplaces

E-procurement has grown largely because of the development over the last ten years of electronic marketplaces (also sometimes called infomediaries or cybermediaries). These operations which have emerged in business-to-business commerce offer services to both buyers and sellers. They have been defined as, 'an information system that allows buyers and sellers to exchange information about prices and product (and service) offerings, and the firm operating the electronic marketplace acts as in intermediary'.[5] They can be categorized as consortium, private or third party.

- A private e-marketplace is where buyers or sellers conduct business in the market only with their partners and suppliers by previous arrangement.
- The consortium e-marketplace is where several large businesses combine to create an e-marketplace controlled by the consortium.
- A third-party e-marketplace is where an independent party creates an unbiased, market-driven e-marketplace for buyers and sellers in an industry.

The scope of e-procurement

The influence of the Internet on purchasing behaviour is not confined to when the trade actually takes place over the Internet. It is also an important source of purchasing information, even if the purchase is actually made by using more traditional methods. Also, even though many businesses have gained advantages by using e-procurement, it does not mean that everything should be bought electronically. When businesses purchase very large amounts of strategically important products or services, it will negotiate multimillion-euro deals, which involve months of discussion, arranging for deliveries up to a year ahead. In such environments, e-procurement adds little value. Deciding whether to invest in e-procurement applications (which can be expensive), say some authorities, depends on what is being bought. For example, simple office supplies such as pens, paper clips and copier paper may be appropriate for e-procurement, but complex, made-to-order engineered components are not. Four questions seem to influence whether e-procurement will be appropriate:[6]

- *Is the value of the spend high or low?* High spending on purchased products and services gives more potential for savings from e-procurement.
- *Is the product or commodity highly substitutable or not?* When products and services are 'substitutable' (there are alternatives), e-procurement can identify and find lower-cost alternatives.
- *Is there a lot of competition or a little?* When several suppliers are competing, e-procurement can manage the process of choosing a preferred supplier more effectively and with more transparency.
- *How efficient are your internal processes?* When purchasing processes are relatively inefficient, e-procurement's potential to reduce processing costs can be realized.

Global sourcing

Global sourcing

One of the major supply chain developments of recent years has been the expansion in the proportion of products and (occasionally) services which businesses are willing to source from outside their home country; this is called **global sourcing.** It is the process of identifying, evaluating, negotiating and configuring supply across multiple geographies. Traditionally, even companies that exported their goods and services all over the world (that is, they were international on their demand side) still sourced the majority of their supplies locally (that is, they were not international on their supply side). This has changed – companies are now increasingly willing to look further afield for their supplies, and for very good reasons. Most companies report a 10 per cent to 35 per cent cost savings by sourcing from low-cost-country suppliers.[7] There are a number of other factors promoting global sourcing:

- The formation of trading blocs in different parts of the world has had the effect of lowering tariff barriers, at least within those blocs. For example, the single market developments within the European Union (EU), the North American Free Trade Agreement (NAFTA) and the South American Trade Group (MERCOSUR) have all made it easier to trade internationally within the regions.

- Transportation infrastructures are considerably more sophisticated and cheaper than they once were. Super-efficient port operations in Rotterdam and Singapore, for example, integrated road–rail systems, jointly developed autoroute systems, and cheaper air freight have all reduced some of the cost barriers to international trade.
- Perhaps most significantly, far tougher world competition has forced companies to look to reducing their total costs. Given that in many industries bought-in items are the largest single part of operations costs, an obvious strategy is to source from wherever is cheapest.

There are, of course, problems with global sourcing. The risks of increased complexity and increased distance need managing carefully. Suppliers that are a significant distance away need to transport their products across long distances. The risks of delays and hold-ups can be far greater than when sourcing locally. Also, negotiating with suppliers whose native language is different from one's own makes communication more difficult and can lead to misunderstandings over contract terms. Therefore global sourcing decisions require businesses to balance cost, performance, service and risk factors, not all of which are obvious. These factors are important in global sourcing because of non-price or 'hidden' cost factors such as cross-border freight and handling fees, complex inventory stocking and handling requirements, and even more complex administrative, documentation and regulatory requirements. The factors that must be understood and included in evaluating global sourcing opportunities are as follows.

- *Purchase price* – the total price, including transaction and other costs related to the actual product or service delivered
- *Transportation costs* – transportation and freight costs, including fuel surcharges and other costs of moving products or services from where they are produced to where they are required
- *Inventory carrying costs* – storage, handling, insurance, depreciation, obsolescence and other costs associated with maintaining inventories, including the opportunity costs of working capital (see Chapter 12)
- *Cross-border taxes, tariffs and duty costs* – sometimes called 'landed costs', which are the sum of duties, shipping, insurance and other fees and taxes for door-to-door delivery
- *Supply performance* – the cost of late or out-of-specification deliveries, which, if not managed properly, can offset any price gains attained by shifting to an offshore source
- *Supply and operational risks* – including geopolitical factors, such as changes in country leadership, trade policy changes, the instability caused by war and/or terrorism or natural disasters and disease, all of which may disrupt supply.

Global sourcing and social responsibility

Although the responsibility of operations to ensure that they only deal with ethical suppliers has always been important, the expansion of global sourcing has brought the issue into sharper focus. Local suppliers can (to some extent) be monitored relatively easily. However, when suppliers are located around the world, often in countries with different traditions and ethical standards, monitoring becomes more difficult. Not only that, but there may be genuinely different views of what is regarded as ethical practice. Social, cultural and religious differences can easily make for mutual incomprehension regarding each other's ethical perspective. This is why many companies are putting significant effort into articulating and clarifying their supplier selection policies. The short case on Levi Strauss's policy is typical of an enlightened organization's approach to global sourcing.

Short case
Extracts from Levi Strauss's global sourcing policy[8]

Source: Corbis/Jose Luis Pelaez

Our Global Sourcing and Operating Guidelines help us to select business partners who follow workplace standards and business practices that are consistent with our company's values. These requirements are applied to every contractor who manufactures or finishes products for Levi Strauss & Co. Trained inspectors closely audit and monitor compliance among approximately 600 cutting, sewing, and finishing contractors in more than 60 countries . . . The numerous countries where Levi Strauss & Co. has existing or future business interests present a variety of cultural, political, social and economic circumstances . . . The Country Assessment Guidelines help us assess any issue that might present concern in light of the ethical principles we have set for ourselves. Specifically, we assess . . . the . . . Health and Safety Conditions Human Rights Environment, the Legal System and the Political, Economic and Social Environment that would protect the company's commercial interests and brand/corporate image. The company's employment standards state that they will only do business with partners who adhere to the following guidelines:

- *Child Labor*: Use of child labor is not permissible. Workers can be no less than 15 years of age and not younger than the compulsory age to be in school. We will not utilize partners who use child labor in any of their facilities.
- *Prison Labor/Forced Labor*: We will not utilize prison or forced labor in contracting relationships in the manufacture and finishing of our products. We will not utilize or purchase materials from a business partner utilizing prison or forced labor.
- *Disciplinary Practices*: We will not utilize business partners who use corporal punishment or other forms of mental or physical coercion.
- *Working Hours*: While permitting flexibility in scheduling, we will identify local legal limits on work hours and seek business partners who do not exceed them except for appropriately compensated overtime. Employees should be allowed at least one day off in seven.
- *Wages and Benefits*: We will only do business with partners who provide wages and benefits that comply with any applicable law and match the prevailing local manufacturing or finishing industry practices.
- *Freedom of Association*: We respect workers' rights to form and join organizations of their choice and to bargain collectively. We expect our suppliers to respect the right to free association and the right to organize and bargain collectively without unlawful interference.
- *Discrimination*: While we recognize and respect cultural differences, we believe that workers should be employed on the basis of their ability to do the job, rather than on the basis of personal characteristics or beliefs. We will favor business partners who share this value.
- *Health and Safety*: We will only utilize business partners who provide workers with a safe and healthy work environment. Business partners who provide residential facilities for their workers must provide safe and healthy facilities.

Physical distribution management and the Internet

Physical distribution management
Logistics
Distribution

In supply chains dealing with tangible products, the products need to be transported to customers. This is called **physical distribution management**, but sometimes the term **logistics**, or simply **distribution**, is used. The potential offered by Internet communications in physical distribution management has had two major effects. The first is to make information available more readily along the distribution chain. This means that the transport companies, warehouses, suppliers and customers that make up the chain can share knowledge of where goods are in the chain. This allows the operations within the chain to coordinate their activities more readily, with potentially significant cost savings. For example, an important issue for

Back-loading

transportation companies is **back-loading.** When the company is contracted to transport goods from A to B, its vehicles may have to return from B to A empty. Back-loading means finding a potential customer that wants their goods transported from B to A in the right time frame. Companies which can fill their vehicles on both the outward and return journeys will have significantly lower costs per distance travelled than those whose vehicles are empty for half the total journey.

The second impact of the Internet has been in the 'business to consumer' (B2C, *see* the discussion on supply chain relationships later) part of the supply chain. While the last few years have seen an increase in the number of goods bought by consumers online, most goods still have to be physically transported to the customer. Often early e-retailers ran into major problems in the **order fulfilment** task of actually supplying their customers. Partly this was because many traditional warehouse and distribution operations were not designed for e-commerce fulfilment. Supplying a conventional retail operation requires relatively large vehicles to move relatively large quantities of goods from warehouses to shops. Distributing to individual customers requires a large number of smaller deliveries.

Order fulfilment

Short case
TDG serving the whole supply chain[9]

Source: TDG Logistics

TDG are specialists in providing *third-party* logistics services to the growing number of manufacturers and retailers that choose not to do their own distribution. Instead they outsource to companies like TDG, which have operations spread across 250 sites that cover the UK, Ireland, France, Spain, Poland and Holland, employ 8,000 employees and use 1,600 vehicles. They provided European logistics services through their own operations in the Netherlands and Ireland and, with the support of alliance partners, in several other European companies.

'There are a number of different types of company providing distribution services', says David Garman, Chief Executive Officer of TDG, *'each with different propositions for the market. At the simplest level, there are the "haulage" and "storage" businesses. These companies either move goods around or they store them in warehouses. Clients plan what has to be done and it is done to order. One level up from the haulage or storage operations are the physical distribution companies, who bring haulage and storage together. These companies collect clients' products, put them into storage facilities and deliver them to the end-customer as and when required. After that there are the companies who offer contract logistics. As a contract logistics service provider you are likely to be dealing with the more sophisticated clients who are looking for better quality facilities and management and the capability to deal with more complex operations. One level further up is the market for supply chain management services. To do this you have to be able to manage supply chains from end to end, or at least some significant part of the whole chain. Doing this requires a much greater degree of analytical and modelling capability, business process reengineering and consultancy skills.'*

TDG, along with other prominent logistics companies, describes itself as a 'lead logistics provider' or LLP, This means that they can provide the consultancy-led, analytical and strategic services integrated with a sound base of practical experience in running successful 'on-the-road' operations. *'In 1999 TDG was a UK distribution company'*, says David Garman, *'now we are a European contract logistics provider with a vision to becoming a full supply chain management company. Providing such services requires sophisticated operations capability, especially in terms of information technology and management dynamism. Because our sites are physically dispersed with our vehicles at any time spread around the motorways of Europe, IT is fundamental to this industry. It gives you visibility of your operation. We need the best operations managers, supported by the best IT.'*

Types of relationships in supply chains

One of the key issues within a supply chain is how relationships with immediate suppliers and customers should be managed. The behaviour of the supply chain as a whole is, after all, made up of the relationships which are formed between individual pairs of operations in the chain. It is important, therefore, to have some framework which helps us to understand the different ways in which supply chain relationships can be developed.

Business or consumer relationships?

The growth in e-commerce has established broad categorization of supply chain relationships. This happened because Internet companies have categorized market sectors defined by who is supplying whom. Figure 13.5 illustrates this categorization, and distinguishes between relationships that are the final link in the supply chain, involving the ultimate consumer, and those involving two commercial businesses. So, **business-to-business** (B2B) relationships are by far the most common in a supply chain context and include some of the e-procurement exchange networks discussed earlier. **Business-to-consumer** (B2C) relationships include both 'bricks and mortar' retailers and online retailers. **Consumer-to-business** (C2B) relationships involve consumers posting their needs on the web (sometimes stating the price they are willing to pay), companies then deciding whether to offer. **Customer-to-customer** (C2C) or peer-to-peer (P2P) relationships include the online exchange and auction services and file sharing services. In this chapter we deal almost exclusively with B2B relationships.

Business to business

Business to consumer

Consumer to business

Customer to customer

Types of business-to-business relationship

A convenient way of categorizing supply chain relationships is to examine the extent and nature of what a company chooses to buy in from suppliers. Two dimensions are particularly important – *what* the company chooses to outsource, and *who* it chooses to supply it. In terms of what is outsourced, key questions are, 'how many activities are outsourced (from doing everything in-house at one extreme, to outsourcing everything at the other extreme), and

Relationship – from . . .	Relationship – to . . . Business	Relationship – to . . . Consumer (Peer)
Business	**B2B** *Relationship* • Most common, all but the last link in the supply chain *E-commerce examples* • Electronic marketplaces • e.g. b2b Index	**B2C** *Relationship* • Retail operations • Comparison web sites *E-commerce examples* • Online retailers • e.g. Amazon.com
Consumer (Peer)	**C2B** *Relationship* • Consumers offer, business responds *E-commerce examples* • Usually focused on specialist area • e.g. Google Adsense	**C2C (P2P)** *Relationship* • Originally one of the driving forces behind the modern Internet (ARPANET) *E-commerce examples* • File sharing networks (legal and illegal) • e.g. Napster, Gnutella

Figure 13.5 The business–consumer relationship matrix

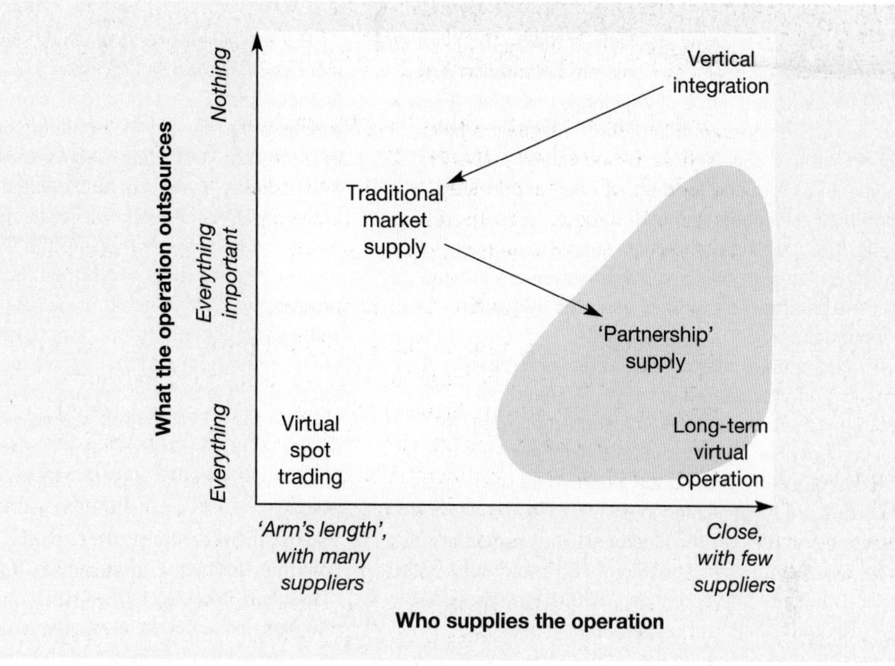

Figure 13.6 Types of supply chain relationship

'how important are the activities outsourced (from outsourcing only trivial activities at one extreme, to outsourcing even core activities at the other extreme)? In terms of who is chosen to supply products and services, again two questions are important, 'how many suppliers will be used by the operation (from using many suppliers to perform the same set of activities at one extreme, through to only one supplier for each activity at the other extreme), and 'how close are the relationships (from 'arm's length' relationships at one extreme, through to close and intimate relationships at the other extreme)? Figure 13.6 illustrates this way of characterizing relationships. It also identifies some of the more common types of relationship and shows some of the trends in how supply chain relationships have moved.

Short case
Northern Foods wins a slice of the in-flight meals business[10]

The companies that provide airline catering services are in a tough business. Meals must be of a quality that is appropriate for the class and type of flight, yet the airlines that are their customers are always looking to keep costs as low as possible, menus must change frequently (3-monthly) and the airlines must respond promptly to customer feedback. If this were not enough, forecasting passenger numbers is particularly difficult. Catering suppliers are advised of the likely numbers of passengers for each flight several days in advance, but the actual minimum number of passengers for each class is only fixed six hours before take-off (although numbers can still be increased after this, due to late sales). Also, flight arrivals are sometimes delayed, putting pressure on everyone to reduce the turnaround time, and upsetting work schedules. And even when a flight lands on time

Specialized companies have developed that prepare food in specialized factories, often for several airlines.

no more than 40 minutes are allowed before the flight is ready for take-off again, so complete preparation and a well-ordered sequence of working is essential. It is a specialized business, and in order to maintain a fast, responsive and agile service, airline caterers have traditionally produced food on, or near, airport sites using their own chefs and staff to cook and tray-set meals. The catering companies' suppliers are also usually airline specialists who themselves are located near the caterers so that they can offer very short response times.

The companies that provide catering services may also provide related services. For example, LSG Sky Chefs (a subsidiary of Deutsche Lufthansa AG) is a provider of tailor-made in-flight services for all types of airlines around the world. Their main areas of service are Airline Catering, In-flight Equipment and Logistics and In-flight Management. They are also large, employing 30,000 people at 200 customer service centres in 49 countries. In 2007 they produced 418 million meals for more than 300 airlines, representing more than 30 per cent of the global airline catering market.

But the airline sector has over recent years suffered a series of shocks including 9/11, oil price volatility, financial crises and world recession. This has meant that airlines are reviewing their catering supply solutions. In December 2008 Gate Gourmet, the world's largest independent provider of airline catering lost the contract to supply British Airways' short-haul flights out of Heathrow to new entrants into the airline catering market, a consortium of Northern Foods, a leading food producer, whose normal business is supplying retailers with own-label and branded food, and DHL, a subsidiary of Deutsche Post and the market-leading international express and logistics company. DHL is already a large supplier to 'airside' caterers at Heathrow and already has its own premises at the airport. Northern Foods will make the food at its existing factories and deliver it to DHL, which will assemble onto airline catering trays and transfer them onto aircraft. The new contract is the first time that Northern Foods, whose biggest customer is Marks and Spencer, the UK retail chain, has developed new business outside its normal supermarket customer base. It said it was 'delighted to have been chosen by BA based on the quality of our food'.

Traditional market supply relationships

Short-term transactional relationships

The very opposite of performing an operation in-house is to purchase goods and services from outside in a 'pure' market fashion, often seeking the 'best' supplier every time it is necessary to purchase. Each transaction effectively becomes a separate decision. The **relationship** between buyer and seller, therefore, can be very short-term. Once the goods or services are delivered and payment is made, there may be no further trading between the parties. The advantages of traditional market supplier relationships are usually seen as follows:

- They maintain competition between alternative suppliers. This promotes a constant drive between suppliers to provide best value.
- A supplier specializing in a small number of products or services (or perhaps just one), but supplying them to many customers, can gain natural economies of scale. This enables the supplier to offer the products and services at a lower price than would be obtained if customers performed the activities themselves on a smaller scale.
- There is inherent flexibility in outsourced supplies. If demand changes, customers can simply change the number and type of suppliers. This is a far faster and simpler alternative to having to redirect their internal activities.
- Innovations can be exploited no matter where they originate. Specialist suppliers are more likely to come up with innovative products and services which can be bought in faster and cheaper than would be the case if the company were itself trying to innovate.
- They help operations to concentrate on their core activities. One business cannot be good at everything. It is sensible therefore to concentrate on the important activities and outsource the rest.

There are, however, disadvantages in buying in a totally 'free market' manner:

- There may be supply uncertainties. Once an order has been placed, it is difficult to maintain control over how that order is fulfilled.
- Choosing who to buy from takes time and effort. Gathering sufficient information and making decisions continually are, in themselves, activities which need to be resourced.

- There are strategic risks in subcontracting activities to other businesses. An over-reliance on outsourcing can 'hollow out' the company, leaving it with no internal capabilities which it can exploit in its markets.

Short-term relationships may be used on a trial basis when new companies are being considered as more regular suppliers. Also, many purchases which are made by operations are one-off or very irregular. For example, the replacement of all the windows in a company's office block would typically involve this type of competitive-tendering market relationship. In some public-sector operations, purchasing is still based on short-term contracts. This is mainly because of the need to prove that public money is being spent as judiciously as possible. However, this short-term, price-oriented type of relationship can have a downside in terms of ongoing support and reliability. This may mean that a short-term 'least-cost' purchase decision will lead to long-term high cost.

Virtual operations

Virtual operation

An extreme form of outsourcing operational activities is that of the **virtual operation**. Virtual operations do relatively little themselves, but rely on a network of suppliers that can provide products and services on demand. A network may be formed for only one project and then disbanded once that project ends. For example, some software and Internet companies are virtual in the sense that they buy in all the services needed for a particular development. This may include not only the specific software development skills but also such things as project management, testing, applications prototyping, marketing, physical production, and so on. Much of the Hollywood film industry also operates in this way. A production company may buy and develop an idea for a movie, but it is created, edited and distributed by a loose network of agents, actors, technicians, studios and distribution companies. The advantage of virtual operations is their flexibility and the fact that the risks of investing in production facilities are far lower than in a conventional operation. However, without any solid base of resources, a company may find it difficult to hold onto and develop a unique core of technical expertise. The resources used by virtual companies will almost certainly be available to competitors. In effect, the core competence of a virtual operation can only lie in the way it is able to manage its supply network.

'Partnership' supply relationships

Partnership relationships

Partnership relationships in supply chains are sometimes seen as a compromise between vertical integration on the one hand (owning the resources which supply you) and pure market relationships on the other (having only a transactional relationship with those who supply you). Although to some extent this is true, partnership relationships are not only a simple mixture of vertical integration and market trading, although they do attempt to achieve some of the closeness and coordination efficiencies of vertical integration, but at the same time attempt to achieve a relationship that has a constant incentive to improve. Partnership relationships are defined as: *'relatively enduring inter-firm cooperative agreements, involving flows and linkages that use resources and/or governance structures from autonomous organizations, for the joint accomplishment of individual goals linked to the corporate mission of each sponsoring firm'.*[11] What this means is that suppliers and customers are expected to cooperate, even to the extent of sharing skills and resources, to achieve joint benefits beyond those they could have achieved by acting alone. At the heart of the concept of partnership lies the issue of the *closeness* of the relationship. Partnerships are close relationships, the degree of which is influenced by a number of factors, as follows:

- *Sharing success.* An attitude of shared success means that both partners work together in order to increase the total amount of joint benefit they receive, rather than manoeuvring to maximize their own individual contribution.

- *Long-term expectations.* Partnership relationships imply relatively long-term commitments, but not necessarily permanent ones.
- *Multiple points of contact.* Communication between partners is not only through formal channels, but may take place between many individuals in both organizations.
- *Joint learning.* Partners in a relationship are committed to learn from each other's experience and perceptions of the other operations in the chain.
- *Few relationships.* Although partnership relationships do not necessarily imply single sourcing by customers, they do imply a commitment on the part of both parties to limit the number of customers or suppliers with whom they do business. It is difficult to maintain close relationships with many different trading partners.
- *Joint coordination of activities.* Because there are fewer relationships, it becomes possible jointly to coordinate activities such as the flow of materials or service, payment, and so on.
- *Information transparency.* An open and efficient information exchange is seen as a key element in partnerships because it helps to build confidence between the partners.
- *Joint problem-solving.* Although partnerships do not always run smoothly, jointly approaching problems can increase closeness over time.
- *Trust.* This is probably the key element in partnership relationships. In this context, trust means the willingness of one party to relate to the other on the understanding that the relationship will be beneficial to both, even though that cannot be guaranteed. Trust is widely held to be both the key issue in successful partnerships, but also, by far, the most difficult element to develop and maintain.

Customer relationship management (CRM)

There is a story (which may or may not be true) that is often quoted to demonstrate the importance of using information technology to analyse customer information. It goes like this: Wal-Mart, the huge US-based supermarket chain, did an analysis of customers' buying habits and found a statistically significant correlation between purchases of beer and purchases of diapers (nappies), especially on Friday evenings. The reason? Fathers were going to the supermarket to buy nappies for their babies, and because fatherhood restricted their ability to go out for a drink as often, they would also buy beer. Supposedly this led the supermarket to start locating nappies next to the beer in their stores, resulting in increased sales of both.

Customer relationship management

Whether it is true or not, it does illustrate the potential of analysing data to understand customers. This is the basis of **customer relationship management** (CRM). It is a method of learning more about customers' needs and behaviours in order to develop stronger relationships with them. Although CRM usually depends on information technology, it is misleading to see it as a 'technology'. Rather it is a process that helps us to understand customers' needs and develop ways of meeting those needs while maximizing profitability. CRM brings together all the disparate information about customers so as to gain insight into their behaviour and their value to the business. It helps to sell products and services more effectively and increase revenues by:

- Providing services and products that are exactly what your customers want
- Retaining existing customers and discovering new ones
- Offering better customer service
- Cross-selling products more effectively.

CRM tries to help organizations understand who their customers are and what their value is over a lifetime. It does this by building a number of steps into its customer interface processes. First, the business must determine the needs of its customers and how best to meet those needs. For example, banks may keep track of its customers' age and lifestyle so that it can offer appropriate products like mortgages or pensions to them when they fit their needs. Second, the business must examine all the different ways and parts of the organization where customer-related information is collected, stored and used. Businesses may interact with customers in different ways and through different people. For example, sales people, call centres, technical staff, operations and distribution managers may all, at different times, have contact with customers. CRM systems should integrate these data. Third, all customer-related data must be analysed to obtain a holistic view of each customer and identify where service can be improved.

Critical commentary

Despite its name, some critics of CRM argue that the greatest shortcoming is that it is insufficiently concerned with directly helping customers. CRM systems are sold to executives as a way to increase efficiency, force standardized processes and gain better insight into the state of the business. But they rarely address the need to help organizations resolve customer problems, answer customer questions faster, or help them solve their own problems. This may explain the trend towards a shift in focus from automating internal front-office functions to streamlining processes such as online customer support.

Supply chain behaviour

A fundamental question in supply chain management is: 'How should supply chains be managed when operations compete in different ways in different markets?' One answer, proposed by Professor Marshall Fisher of Wharton Business School, is to organize the supply chains serving those individual markets in different ways.[12] He points out that many companies have seemingly similar products which, in fact, compete in different ways. Shoe manufacturers may produce classics which change little over the years, as well as fashions which last only one or two seasons. Chocolate manufacturers have stable lines which have been sold for 50 years, but also product 'specials' associated with an event or film release, maybe selling only for a few months. Demand for the former products will be relatively stable and predictable, but demand for the latter will be far more uncertain. Also, the profit margin commanded by the innovative product will probably be higher than that of the more functional product. However, the price (and therefore the margin) of the innovative product may drop rapidly once it has become unfashionable in the market.

Efficient supply chains

Responsive supply chains

The supply chain policies which are seen to be appropriate for functional products and innovative products are termed by Fisher **efficient supply chain** policies and **responsive supply chain** policies, respectively. Efficient supply chain policies include keeping inventories low, especially in the downstream parts of the network, so as to maintain fast throughput and reduce the amount of working capital tied up in the inventory. What inventory there is in the network is concentrated mainly in the manufacturing operation, where it can keep utilization high and therefore manufacturing costs low. Information must flow quickly up and down the chain from retail outlets back up to the manufacturer so that schedules can be given the maximum amount of time to adjust efficiently. The chain is then managed to make sure that products flow as quickly as possible down the chain to replenish what few stocks are kept downstream. By contrast, responsive supply chain policy stresses high service levels and responsive supply to the end-customer. The inventory in the network will be deployed as closely as possible to the customer. In this way, the chain can still supply even when dramatic changes occur in customer demand. Fast throughput from the upstream parts of the chain will still be needed to replenish downstream stocks. But those downstream stocks are needed to ensure high levels of availability to end-customers. Figure 13.7 illustrates how the different supply chain policies match the different market requirements implied by functional and innovative products.

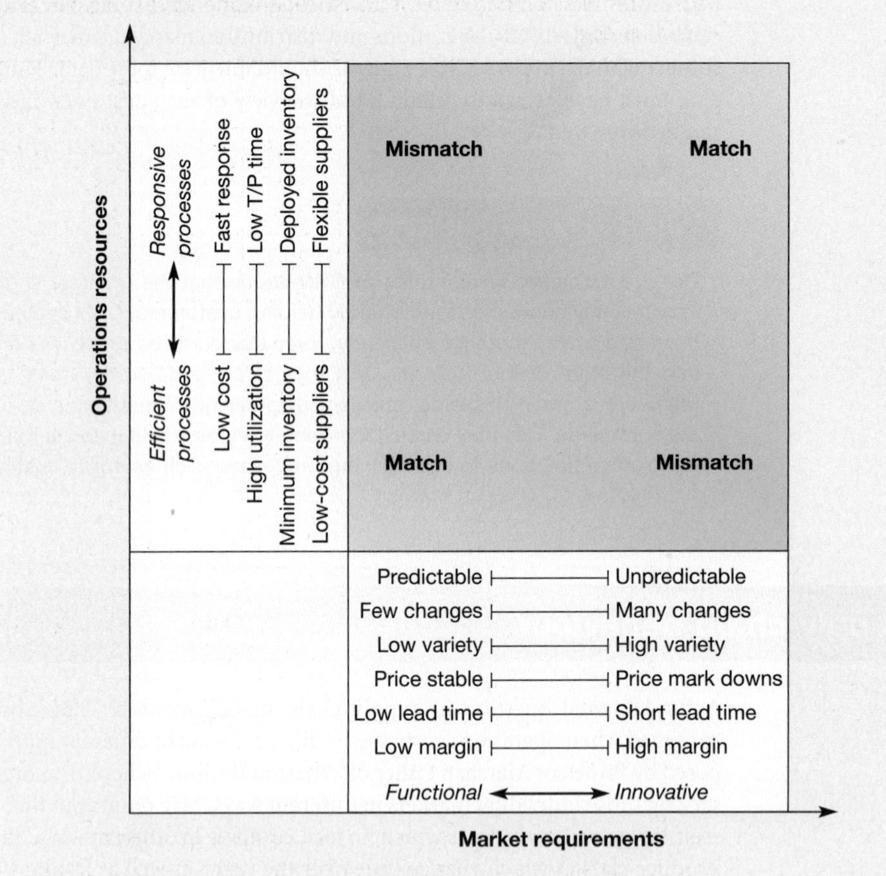

Figure 13.7 Matching the operations resources in the supply chain with market requirements

Source: Adapted from Fisher, M.C. (1997) What is the right supply chain for your product? *Harvard Business Review*, March–April, 105–16.

The bullwhip effect – supply chain dynamics

The bullwhip effect

The '**bullwhip effect**', is used to describe how a small disturbance at the downstream end of a supply chain causes increasingly large disturbances, errors, inaccuracies and volatility as it works its way upstream. Its main cause is an understandable desire by the different links in the supply chain to manage their production rates and inventory levels sensibly. To demonstrate this, examine the production rate and stock levels for the supply chain shown in Table 13.4. This is a four-stage supply chain where an original equipment manufacturer (OEM) is served by three tiers of suppliers. The demand from the OEM's market has been running at a rate of 100 items per period, but in period 2 demand reduces to 95 items. All stages in the supply chain work on the principle that they will keep in stock one period's demand (a simplification but not a gross one). The 'stock' column shows the starting stock at the beginning, and the finish stock at the end, of the period. At the beginning of period 2, the OEM has 100 units in stock. Demand in period 2 is 95 and the OEM must produce enough to finish up at the end of the period with 95 in stock (this being the new demand rate). To do this, it need only manufacture 90 items; these, together with 5 items taken out of the starting stock, will supply demand and leave a finished stock of 95 items and the OEM can operate at a steady rate of 95 items per period. Note, however, that a change in demand of only 5 items has produced a fluctuation of 10 items in the OEM's production rate.

Now carry this same logic through to the first-tier supplier. At the beginning of period 2, the second-tier supplier has 100 items in stock. The demand which it has to supply in period 2 is derived from the production rate of the OEM. This has dropped down to 90 in period 2. The

Table 13.4 Fluctuations of production levels along supply chain in response to small change in end-customer demand

Period	Third-tier supplier		Second-tier supplier		First-tier supplier		Original equipment mfr		Demand
	Prodn.	Stock	Prodn.	Stock	Prodn.	Stock	Prodn.	Stock	
1	100	100 100	100	100 100	100	100 100	100	100 100	100
2	20	100 60	60	100 80	80	100 90	90	100 95	95
3	180	60 120	120	80 100	100	90 95	95	95 95	95
4	60	120 90	90	100 95	95	95 95	95	95 95	95
5	100	90 95	95	95 95	95	95 95	95	95 95	95
6	95	95 95	95	95 95	95	95 95	95	95 95	95

(Note all operations keep one period's inventory.)

first-tier supplier therefore has to produce sufficient to supply the demand of 90 and leave one month's demand (now 90 items) as its finish stock. A production rate of 80 items per month will achieve this. It will therefore start period 3 with an opening stock of 90 items, but the demand from the OEM has now risen to 95 items. It therefore has to produce sufficient to fulfil this demand of 95 items and leave 95 items in stock. To do this, it must produce 100 items in period 3. This logic can be extended right back to the third-tier supplier. The further back up the supply chain an operation is placed, the more drastic are the fluctuations caused by the relatively small change in demand from the final customer. The decision of how much to produce each month was governed by the following relationship:

$$\text{Total available for sale in any period} = \text{Total required in the same period}$$
$$\text{Starting stock} + \text{Production rate} = \text{Demand} + \text{Closing stock}$$
$$\text{Starting stock} + \text{Production rate} = 2 \times \text{Demand (because closing stock must be equal to demand)}$$
$$\text{Production rate} = 2 \times \text{Demand} - \text{Starting stock}$$

This relatively simple exercise does not include any time lag between a demand occurring in one part of the supply chain and it being transmitted to its supplier. In practice there will be such a lag, and this will make the fluctuations even more marked.

Miscommunication in the supply chain

Whenever two operations in a supply chain arrange for one to provide products or services to the other, there is the potential for misunderstanding and miscommunication. This may be caused simply by not being sufficiently clear about what a customer expects or what a supplier is capable of delivering. There may also be more subtle reasons stemming from differences in perception of seemingly clear agreements. The effect is analogous to the children's game of 'Chinese whispers'. The first child whispers a message to the next child who, whether he or she has heard it clearly or not, whispers an interpretation to the next child, and so on. The more children the message passes between, the more distorted it tends to become. The last

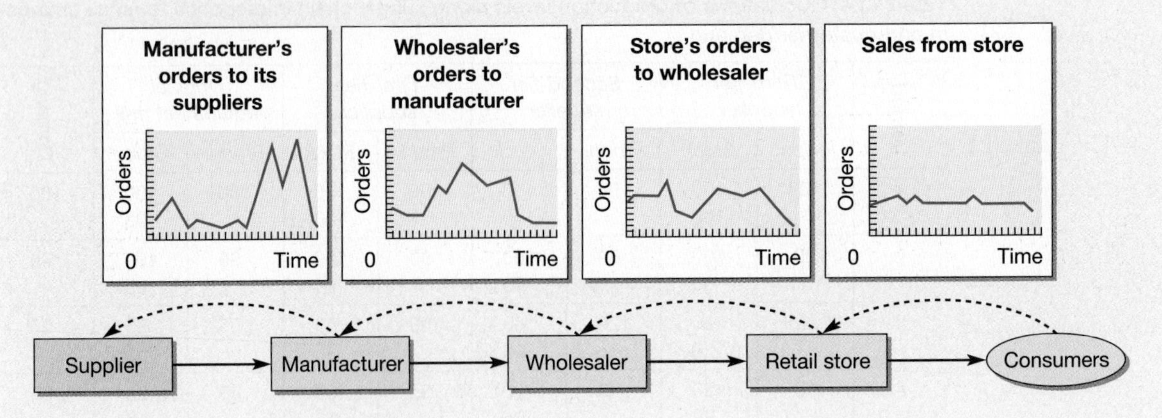

Figure 13.8 Typical supply chain dynamics

child says out loud what the message is, and the children are amused by the distortion of the original message. Figure 13.8 shows the bullwhip effect in a typical supply chain, with relatively small fluctuations in the market cause increasing volatility further back in the chain.

Supply chain improvement

Increasingly important in supply chain practice are attempts to improve supply chain performance. These are usually attempts to understand the complexity of supply chain processes; others focus on coordinating activities throughout the chain.

The SCOR model

The Supply Chain Operations Reference model (SCOR) is a broad, but highly structured and systematic, framework to supply chain improvement that has been developed by the Supply Chain Council (SCC), a global non-profit consortium. The framework uses a methodology, diagnostic and benchmarking tools that are increasingly widely accepted for evaluating and comparing supply chain activities and their performance. Just as important, the SCOR model allows its users to improve, and communicate supply chain management practices within and between all interested parties in their supply chain by using a standard language and a set of structured definitions. The SCC also provides a benchmarking database by which companies can compare their supply chain performance to others in their industries and training classes. Companies that have used the model include BP, AstraZeneca, Shell, SAP AG, Siemens AG and Bayer. The model uses three well-known individual techniques turned into an integrated approach. These are:

- Business process modelling
- Benchmarking performance
- Best practice analysis.

Business process modelling

SCOR does not represent organizations or functions, but rather processes. Each basic 'link' in the supply chain is made up of five types of process, each process being a 'supplier–customer' relationship, see Figure 13.9.

- 'Source' is the procurement, delivery, receipt and transfer of raw material items, subassemblies, products and/or services.

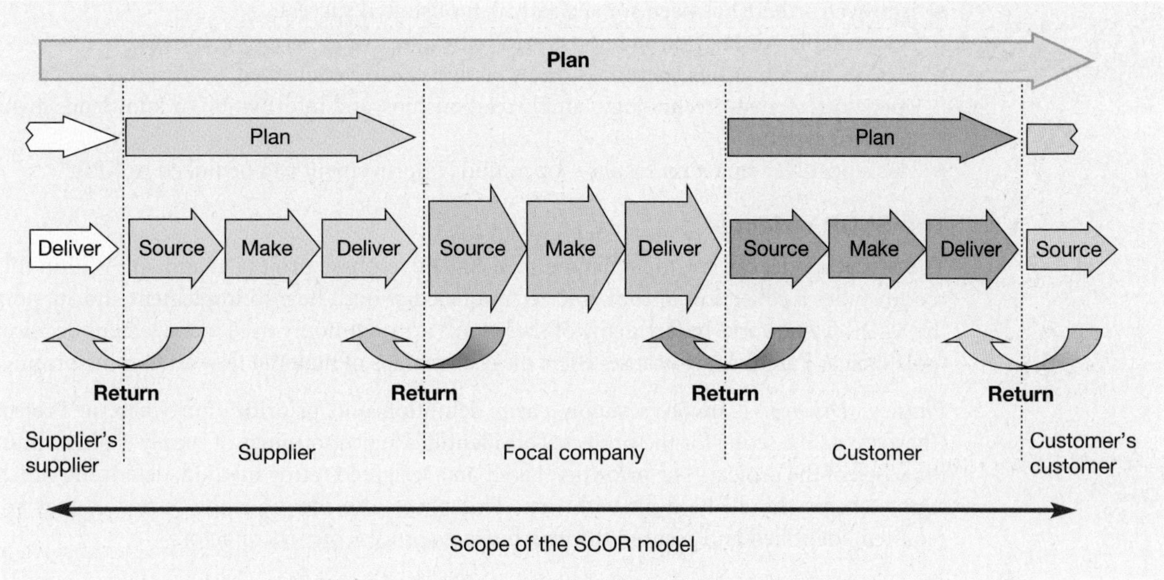

Figure 13.9 Matching the operations resources in the supply chain with market requirements

- 'Make' is the transformation process of adding value to products and services through mixing production operations processes.
- 'Deliver' processes perform all customer-facing order management and fulfilment activities including outbound logistics.
- 'Plan' processes manage each of these customer–supplier links and balance the activity of the supply chain. They are the supply and demand reconciliation process, which includes prioritization when needed.
- 'Return' processes look after the reverse logistics flow of moving material back from end-customers upstream in the supply chain because of product defects or post-delivery customer support.

All these processes are modelled at increasingly detailed levels from level 1 through to more detailed process modelling at level 3.

Benchmarking performance

Performance metrics in the SCOR model are also structured by level, as is process analysis. Level 1 metrics are the yardsticks by which an organization can measure how successful it is in achieving its desired positioning within the competitive environment, as measured by the performance of a particular supply chain. These level 1 metrics are the key performance indicators (KPIs) of the chain and are created from lower-level diagnostic metrics (called level 2 and level 3 metrics) which are calculated on the performance of lower-level processes. Some metrics do not 'roll up' to level 1, these are intended to diagnose variations in performance against plan.

Best practice analysis

Best practice analysis follows the benchmarking activity that should have measured the performance of the supply chain processes and identified the main performance gaps. Best practice analysis identifies the activities that need to be performed to close the gaps. SCC members have identified more than 400 'best practices' derived from their experience. The definition of a 'best practice' in the SCOR model is one that:

- Is current – neither untested (emerging) nor outdated.
- Is structured – it has clearly defined goals, scope and processes.

- Is proven – there has been some clearly demonstrated success.
- Is repeatable – it has been demonstrated to be effective in various contexts.
- Has an unambiguous method – the practice can be connected to business processes, operations strategy, technology, supply relationships, and information or knowledge management systems.
- Has a positive impact on results – operations improvement can be linked to KPIs.

The SCOR roadmap

The SCOR model can be implemented by using a five-phase project 'roadmap'. Within this roadmap lies a collection of tools and techniques that both help to implement and support the SCOR framework. In fact many of these tools are commonly used management decision tools such as Pareto charts, cause–effect diagrams, maps of material flow and brainstorming.

Phase 1: Discover – Involves supply-chain definition and prioritization where a 'Project Charter' sets the scope for the project. This identifies logic groupings of supply chains within the scope of the project. The priorities, based on a weighted rating method, determine which supply chains should be dealt with first. This phase also identifies the resources that are required, identified and secured through business process owners or actors.

Phase 2: Analyse – Using data from benchmarking and competitive analysis, the appropriate level of performance metrics are identified; that will define the strategic requirements of each supply chain.

Phase 3: Material flow design – In this phase the project teams have their first go at creating a common understanding of how processes can be developed. The current state of processes is identified and an initial analysis attempts to see where there are opportunities for improvement.

Phase 4: Work and information flow design – The project teams collect and analyse the work involved in all relevant processes (plan, source, make, deliver and return) and map the productivity and yield of all transactions.

Phase 5: Implementation planning – This is the final and preparation phase for communicating the findings of the project. Its purpose is to transfer the knowledge of the SCOR team(s) to individual implementation or deployment teams.

Benefits of the SCOR model

Claimed benefits from using the SCOR model include improved process understanding and performance, improved supply chain performance, increased customer satisfaction and retention, a decrease in required capital, better profitability and return on investment, and increased productivity. And, although most of these results could arguably be expected when any company starts focusing on business processes improvements, SCOR proponents argue that using the model gives an above average and supply focused improvement.

Critical commentary

Although the SCOR model is increasingly being adopted, it has been criticized for underemphasizing people issues. The SCOR model assumes, but does not explicitly address, the human resource base skill set, notwithstanding the model's heavy reliance on supply chain knowledge to understand the model and methodology properly. Often external expertise is needed to support the process. This, along with the nature of the SCC membership, also implies that the SCOR model may be appropriate only for relatively large companies that are more likely to have the necessary business capabilities to implement the model. Many small to medium-sized companies may find difficulty in handle full-scale model implementation. Some critics would also argue that the model lacks a link to the financial plans of a company, making it very difficult to highlight the benefits obtainable, as well as inhibiting senior management support.

The effects of e-business on supply chain management practice[13]

New information technology applications combined with internet-based e-business have transformed supply chain management practice. Largely, this is because they provide better and faster information to all stages in the supply chain. Information is the lifeblood of supply chain management. Without appropriate information, supply chain managers cannot make the decisions that coordinate activities and flows through the chain. Without appropriate information, each stage in the supply chain has relatively few cues to tell them what is happening elsewhere in the chain. To some extent, they are 'driving blind' and having to rely on the most obvious of mismatches between the activities of different stages in the chain (such as excess inventory) to inform their decisions. Conversely, with accurate and 'near real-time' information, the disparate elements in supply chains can integrate their efforts to the benefit of the whole chain and, eventually, the end-customer. Just as importantly, the collection, analysis and distribution of information using e-business technologies is far less expensive to arrange than previous, less automated methods. Table 13.5 summarizes some of the effects of e-business on three important aspects of supply chain management – business and market information flow, product and service flow, and the cash flow that comes as a result of product and service flow.

Table 13.5 Some effects of e-business on supply chain management practice

	Market/sales information flow	*Product/service flow*	*Cash flow*
Supply-chain-related activities	Understanding customers' needs Designing appropriate products / services Demand forecasting	Purchasing Inventory management Throughput / waiting times Distribution	Supplier payments Customer invoicing Customer receipts
Beneficial effects of e-business practices	Better customer relationship management Monitoring real-time demand On-line customization Ability to coordinate output with demand	Lower purchasing administration costs Better purchasing deals Reduced bullwhip effect Reduced inventory More efficient distribution	Faster movement of cash Automated cash movement Integration of financial information with sales and operations activities

Information-sharing

Information sharing helps improve supply chain performance

One of the reasons for the fluctuations in output described in the example earlier was that each operation in the chain reacted to the orders placed by its immediate customer. None of the operations had an overview of what was happening throughout the chain. If information had been available and **shared throughout the chain**, it is unlikely that such wild fluctuations would have occurred. It is sensible therefore to try to transmit information throughout the chain so that all the operations can monitor true demand, free of these distortions. An obvious improvement is to make information on end-customer demand available to upstream operations. Electronic point-of-sale (EPOS) systems used by many retailers attempt to do this. Sales data from checkouts or cash registers are consolidated and transmitted to the warehouses, transportation companies and supplier manufacturing operations that form their supply chain. Similarly, electronic data interchange (EDI) helps to share information (*see* the short case on Seven-Eleven Japan). EDI can also affect the economic order quantities shipped between operations in the supply chain.

Short case
Seven-Eleven Japan's agile supply chain[14]

Source: Getty Images

Seven-Eleven Japan (SEJ) is that country's largest and most successful retailer. The average amount of stock in an SEJ store is between 7 and 8.4 days of demand, a remarkably fast stock turnover for any retailer. Industry analysts see SEJ's agile supply chain management as being the driving force behind its success. It is an agility that is supported by a fully integrated information system that provides visibility of the whole supply chain and ensures fast replenishment of goods in its stores customized exactly to the needs of individual stores. As a customer comes to the checkout counter the assistant first keys in the customer's gender and approximate age and then scans the bar codes of the purchased goods. This sales data is transmitted to the Seven-Eleven headquarters through its own high-speed lines. Simultaneously, the store's own computer system records and analyzes the information so that store managers and headquarters have immediate point-of-sale information. This allows both store managers and headquarters to, hour by hour, analyze sales trends, any stock-outs, types of customer buying certain products, and so on. The headquarters computer aggregates all this data by region, product and time so that all parts of the supply chain, from suppliers through to the stores, have the information by the next morning. Every Monday, the company chairman and top executives review all performance information for the previous week and develop plans for the up-coming week. These plans are presented on Tuesday morning to SEJ's 'operations field counsellors' each of which is responsible for facilitating performance improvement in around eight stores. On Tuesday afternoon the field counsellors for each region meet to decide how they will implement the overall plans for their region. On Tuesday night the counsellors fly back to their regions and by next morning are visiting their stores to deliver the messages developed at headquarters which will help the stores implement their plans. SEJ's physical distribution is also organized on an agile basis. The distribution company maintains radio communications with all drivers and SEJ's headquarters keeps track of all delivery activities. Delivery times and routes are planned in great detail and published in the form of a delivery time-table. On average each delivery takes only one and half minutes at each store, and drivers are expected to make their deliveries within ten minutes of scheduled time. If a delivery is late by more than thirty minutes the distribution company has to pay the store a fine equivalent to the gross profit on the goods being delivered. The agility of the whole supply system also allows SEJ headquarters and the distribution company to respond to disruptions. For example, on the day of the Kobe earthquake, SEJ used 7 helicopters and 125 motor cycles to rush through a delivery of 64,000 rice balls to earthquake victims.

Channel alignment

Channel alignment helps improve supply chain performance

Vendor-managed inventory

Channel alignment means the adjustment of scheduling, material movements, stock levels, pricing and other sales strategies so as to bring all the operations in the chain into line with **each other**. This goes beyond the provision of information. It means that the systems and methods of planning and control decision-making are harmonized through the chain. For example, even when using the same information, differences in forecasting methods or purchasing practices can lead to fluctuations in orders between operations in the chain. One way of avoiding this is to allow an upstream supplier to manage the inventories of its downstream customer. This is known as **vendor-managed inventory** (VMI). So, for example, a packaging supplier could take responsibility for the stocks of packaging materials held by a food manufacturing customer. In turn, the food manufacturer takes responsibility for the stocks of its products which are held in its customer's, the supermarket's warehouses.

Operational efficiency

'Operational efficiency' means the efforts that each operation in the chain can make to reduce its own complexity, reduce the cost of doing business with other operations in the chain and increase throughput time. The cumulative effect of these individual activities is to simplify throughput in the whole **chain**. For example, imagine a chain of operations whose performance level is relatively poor: quality defects are frequent, the lead time to order products and services is long, and delivery is unreliable and so on. The behaviour of the chain would be a continual sequence of errors and effort wasted in replanning to compensate for the errors. Poor quality would mean extra and unplanned orders being placed, and unreliable delivery and slow delivery lead times would mean high safety stocks. Just as important, most operations managers' time would be spent coping with the inefficiency. By contrast, a chain whose operations had high levels of operations performance would be more predictable and have faster throughput, both of which would help to minimize supply chain fluctuations.

Operational efficiency helps improve supply chain performance

One of the most important approaches to improving the operational efficiency of supply chains is known as **time compression**. This means speeding up the flow of materials down the chain and the flow of information back up the chain. The supply chain dynamics effect we observed in Table 13.4 was due partly to the slowness of information moving back up the chain. Figure 13.10 illustrates the advantages of supply chain time compression in terms of its overall impact on profitability.[15]

Supply chain time compression

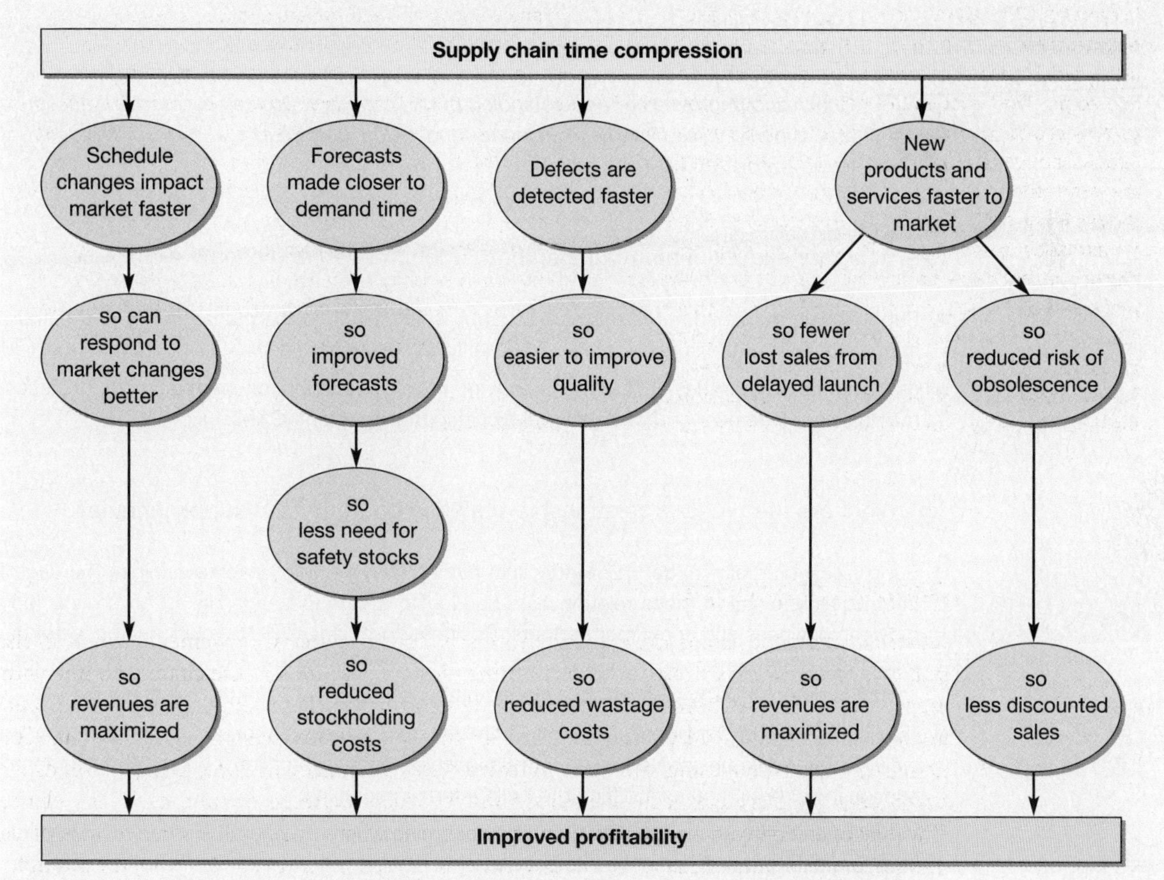

Figure 13.10 Supply chain time compression can both reduce costs and increase revenues

Source: Based on Towill

Supply chain vulnerability

Supply chain risk

One of the consequences of the agile supply chain concept has been to take more seriously the possibility of **supply chain risk** and disruption. The concept of agility includes consideration of how supply chains have to cope with common disruptions such as late deliveries, quality problems, incorrect information, and so on. Yet far more dramatic events can disrupt supply chains. Global sourcing means that parts are shipped around the world on their journey through the supply chain. Microchips manufactured in Taiwan could be assembled to printed circuit boards in Shanghai which are then finally assembled into a computer in Ireland. Perhaps most significantly, there tends to be far less inventory in supply chains that could buffer interruptions to supply. According to Professor Martin Christopher, an authority on supply chain management, '*Potentially the risk of disruption has increased dramatically as the result of a too-narrow focus on supply chain efficiency at the expense of effectiveness. Unless management recognizes the challenge and acts upon it, the implications for us all could be chilling.*'[16] These 'chilling' effects can arise as a result of disruptions such as natural disasters, terrorist incidents, industrial or direct action such as strikes and protests, accidents such as fire in a vital component supplier's plant, and so on. Of course, many of these disruptions have always been present in business. It is the increased vulnerability of supply chains that has made many companies place more emphasis on understanding supply chain risks.

Summary answers to key questions

*Check and improve your understanding of this chapter using self assessment questions and a personalised study plan, audio and video downloads, and an eBook – all at **www.myomlab.com**.*

➤ What are supply chain management and its related activities?

- Supply chain management is a broad concept which includes the management of the entire supply chain from the supplier of raw material to the end-customer.
- Its component activities include purchasing, physical distribution management, logistics, materials management and customer relationship management (CRM).

➤ What are the types of relationship between operations in supply chains?

- Supply networks are made up of individual pairs of buyer–supplier relationships. The use of Internet technology in these relationships has led to a categorization based on a distinction between business and consumer partners. Business-to-business (B2B) relationships are of the most interest in operations management terms. They can be characterized on two dimensions – what is outsourced to a supplier, and the number and closeness of the relationships.
- Traditional market supplier relationships are where a purchaser chooses suppliers on an individual periodic basis. No long-term relationship is usually implied by such 'transactional' relationships, but it makes it difficult to build internal capabilities.
- Virtual operations are an extreme form of outsourcing where an operation does relatively little itself and subcontracts almost all its activities.
- Partnership supplier relationships involve customers forming long-term relationships with suppliers. In return for the stability of demand, suppliers are expected to commit to high levels of service. True partnerships are difficult to sustain and rely heavily on the degree of trust which is allowed to build up between partners.

- Customer relationship management (CRM) is a method of learning more about customers' needs and behaviours in order to develop stronger relationships with them. It brings together all information about customers to gain insight into their behaviour and their value to the business.

➤ What is the 'natural' pattern of behaviour in supply chains?

- Marshall Fisher distinguishes between functional markets and innovative markets. He argues that functional markets, which are relatively predictable, require efficient supply chains, whereas innovative markets, which are less predictable, require 'responsive' supply chains.
- Supply chains exhibit a dynamic behaviour known as the 'bullwhip' effect. This shows how small changes at the demand end of a supply chain are progressively amplified for operations further back in the chain.

➤ How can supply chains be improved?

- The Supply Chain Operations Reference model (SCOR) is a highly structured framework for supply chain improvement that has been developed by the Supply Chain Council (SCC).
- The model uses three well-known individual techniques turned into an integrated approach. These are:
  - Business process modelling
  - Benchmarking performance
  - Best practice analysis.
- To reduce the 'bullwhip' effect, operations can adopt some mixture of three coordination strategies:
  - information-sharing: the efficient distribution of information throughout the chain can reduce demand fluctuations along the chain by linking all operations to the source of demand;
  - channel alignment: this means adopting the same or similar decision-making processes throughout the chain to coordinate how and when decisions are made;
  - operational efficiency: this means eliminating sources of inefficiency or ineffectiveness in the chain; of particular importance is 'time compression', which attempts to increase the throughput speed of the operations in the chain.
- Increasingly, supply risks are being managed as a countermeasure to their vulnerability.

Case study
Supplying fast fashion[17]

Garment retailing has changed. No longer is there a standard look that all retailers adhere to for a whole season. Fashion is fast, complex and furious. Different trends overlap and fashion ideas that are not even on a store's radar screen can become 'must haves' within six months. Many retail businesses with their own brands, such as H&M and Zara, sell up-to-the-minute fashionability at low prices, in stores that are clearly focused on one particular market. In the world of fast fashion catwalk designs speed their way into high-street stores at prices anyone can afford. The quality of the garment means that it may only last one season, but fast-fashion customers don't want yesterday's trends. As *Newsweek* puts it, *'being a "quicker picker-upper" is what made fashion retailers H&M and Zara successful. [They] thrive by practicing the new science of "fast fashion"; compressing product development cycles as much as six times.'*

Source: Press Association Images

But the retail operations that customers see are only the end part of the supply chain that feeds them. And these have also changed.

At its simplest level, the fast-fashion supply chain has four stages. First, the garments are designed, after which they are manufactured; they are then distributed to the retail outlets where they are displayed and sold in retail operations designed to reflect the businesses' brand values. In this short case we examine two fast-fashion operations, Hennes and Mauritz (known as H&M) and Zara, together with United Colors of Benetton (UCB), a similar chain, but with a different market positioning.

Benetton – almost fifty years ago Luciano Benetton took the world of fashion by storm by selling the bright, casual sweaters designed by his sister across Europe (and later the rest of the world), promoted by controversial advertising. By 2005 the Benetton Group was present in 120 countries throughout the world. Selling casual garments, mainly under its United Colors of Benetton (UCB) and its more fashion-oriented Sisley brands, it produces 110 million garments a year, over 90 per cent of them in Europe. Its retail network of over 5,000 stores produces revenue of around €2 billion. Benetton products are seen as less 'high fashion' but higher quality and durability, with higher prices, than H&M and Zara.

H&M – established in Sweden in 1947, now sells clothes and cosmetics in over 1,000 stores in 20 countries around the world. The business concept is 'fashion and quality at the best price'. With more than 40,000 employees, and revenues of around SEK 60,000 million, its biggest market is Germany, followed by Sweden and the UK. H&M are seen by many as the originator of the fast fashion concept. Certainly they have years of experience at driving down the price of up-to-the-minute fashions. *'We ensure the best price,'* they say, *'by having few middlemen, buying large volumes, having extensive experience of the clothing industry, having a great knowledge of which goods should be bought from which markets, having efficient distribution systems, and being cost-conscious at every stage'.*

Zara – the first store opened almost by accident in 1975 when Amancio Ortega Gaona, a women's pyjama manufacturer, was left with a large cancelled order. The shop he opened was intended only as an outlet for cancelled orders. Now, Inditex, the holding group that includes the Zara brand, has over 1,300 stores in 39 countries with sales of over €3 billion. The Zara brand accounts for over 75 per cent of the group's total retail sales, and is still based in northwest Spain. By 2003 it had become the world's fastest-growing volume garment retailer. The Inditex group also has several other branded chains including Pull and Bear, and Massimo Dutti. In total it employs almost 40,000 people in a business that is known for a high degree of vertical integration compared with most fast-fashion companies. The company believes that it is their integration along the supply chain that allows them to respond to customer demand fast and flexibly while keeping stock to a minimum.

Design

All three businesses emphasize the importance of design in this market. Although not *haute couture,* capturing design trends is vital to success. Even the boundary between high and fast fashion is starting to blur. In 2004 H&M recruited high-fashion designer Karl Lagerfeld, previously noted for his work with more exclusive brands. For H&M his designs were priced for value rather than exclusivity, *'Why do I work for H&M? Because I believe in inexpensive clothes, not "cheap" clothes'*, said Lagerfeld. Yet most of H&M's products come from over a hundred designers in Stockholm who work with a team of 50 pattern designers, around 100 buyers and a number of budget controllers. The department's task is to find the optimum balance between the three components making up H&M's business concept – fashion, price and quality. Buying volumes and delivery dates are then decided.

Zara's design functions are organized in a different way from most similar companies'. Conventionally, the design input comes from three *separate* functions: the designers themselves, market specialists, and buyers who place orders on to suppliers. At Zara the design stage is split into three product areas: women's, men's and children's garments.

In each area, designers, market specialists and buyers are co-located in design halls that also contain small workshops for trying out prototype designs. The market specialists in all three design halls are in regular contact with Zara retail stores, discussing customer reaction to new designs. In this way, the retail stores are not the end of the whole supply chain but the beginning of the design stage of the chain. Zara's around 300 designers, whose average age is 26, produce approximately 40,000 items per year of which about 10,000 go into production.

Benetton also has around 300 designers, who not only design for all their brands, but also are engaged in researching new materials and clothing concepts. Since 2000 the company has moved to standardize their range globally. At one time more than 20 per cent of its ranges were customized to the specific needs of each country, now only between 5 and 10 per cent of garments are customized. This reduced the number of individual designs offered globally by over 30 per cent, strengthening the global brand image and reducing production costs.

Both H&M and Zara have moved away from the traditional industry practice of offering two 'collections' a year, for Spring/Summer and Autumn/Winter. Their 'seasonless cycle' involves the continual introduction of new products on a rolling basis throughout the year. This allows designers to learn from customers' reactions to their new products and incorporate them quickly into more new products. The most extreme version of this idea is practised by Zara. A garment will be designed and a batch manufactured and 'pulsed' through the supply chain. Often the design is never repeated; it may be modified and another batch produced, but there are no 'continuing' designs as such. Even Benetton have increased the proportion of what they call 'flash' collections, small collections that are put into its stores during the season.

Manufacturing

At one time Benetton focused its production on its Italian plants. Then it significantly increased its production outside Italy to take advantage of lower labour costs. Non-Italian operations include factories in North Africa, Eastern Europe and Asia. Yet each location operates in a very similar manner. A central, Benetton-owned, operation performs some manufacturing operations (especially those requiring expensive technology) and coordinates the more labour-intensive production activities that are performed by a network of smaller contractors (often owned and managed by ex-Benetton employees). These contractors may in turn subcontract some of their activities. The company's central facility in Italy allocates production to each of the non-Italian networks, deciding what and how much each is to produce. There is some specialization, for example, jackets are made in Eastern Europe while T-shirts are made in Spain. Benetton also has a controlling share in its main supplier of raw materials, to ensure fast supply to its factories. Benetton are also known for the practice of dyeing garments after assembly rather than using dyed thread or fabric. This postpones decisions about colours until late in the supply process so that there is a greater chance of producing what is needed by the market.

H&M does not have any factories of its own, but instead works with around 750 suppliers. Around half of production takes place in Europe and the rest mainly in Asia. It has 21 production offices around the world that between them are responsible for coordinating the suppliers who produce over half a billion items a year for H&M. The relationship between production offices and suppliers is vital, because it allows fabrics to be bought in early. The actual dyeing and cutting of the garments can then be decided at a later stage in the production The later an order can be placed on suppliers, the less the risk of buying the wrong thing. Average supply lead times vary from three weeks up to six months, depending on the nature of the goods. However, *'The most important thing'*, they say, *'is to find the optimal time to order each item. Short lead times are not always best. With some high-volume fashion basics, it is to our advantage to place orders far in advance. Trendier garments require considerably shorter lead times.'*

Zara's lead times are said to be the fastest in the industry, with a 'catwalk to rack' time of as little of as 15 days. According to one analyst this is because they *'owned most of the manufacturing capability used to make their products, which they use as a means of exciting and stimulating customer demand'*. About half of Zara's products are produced in its network of 20 Spanish factories, which, like at Benetton, tended to concentrate on the more capital-intensive operations such as cutting and dyeing. Subcontractors are used for most labour-intensive operations like sewing. Zara buy around 40 per cent of its fabric from its own wholly owned subsidiary, most of which is in undyed form for dyeing after assembly. Most Zara factories and their subcontractors work on a single-shift system to retain some volume flexibility.

Distribution

Both Benetton and Zara have invested in highly automated warehouses, close to their main production centres that store, pack and assemble individual orders for their retail networks. These automated warehouses represent a major investment for both companies. In 2001, Zara caused some press comment by announcing that it would open a second automated warehouse even though, by its own calculations, it was only using about half its existing warehouse capacity. More recently, Benetton caused some controversy by announcing that it was exploring the use of RFID tags to track its garments.

At H&M, while the stock management is primarily handled internally, physical distribution is subcontracted. A large part of the flow of goods is routed from production site to the retail country via H&M's transit terminal in Hamburg. Upon arrival the goods are inspected and allocated to the stores or to the centralized store stockroom. The centralized

store stockroom, within H&M referred to as 'Call-Off warehouse' replenishes stores on item level according to what is selling.

Retail

All H&M stores (average size, 1,300 square metres) are owned and solely run by H&M. The aim is to '*create a comfortable and inspiring atmosphere in the store that makes it simple for customers to find what they want and to feel at home*'. This is similar to Zara stores, although they tend to be smaller (average size, 800 square metres). Perhaps the most remarkable characteristic of Zara stores is that garments rarely stay in the store for longer than 2 weeks. Because product designs are often not repeated and are produced in relatively small batches, the range of garments displayed in the store can change radically every two or three weeks. This encourages customers both to avoid delaying a purchase and to revisit the store frequently.

Since 2000 Benetton has been reshaping its retail operations. At one time the vast majority of Benetton retail outlets were small shops run by third parties. Now these small stores have been joined by several, Benetton-owned and -operated, larger stores (1,500 to 3,000 square metres). These mega-stores can display the whole range of Benetton products and reinforce the Benetton shopping experience.

Question

Compare and contrast the approaches taken by H&M, Benetton and Zara to managing their supply chains.

Problems and applications

These problems and applications will help to improve your analysis of operations. You can find more practice problems as well as worked examples and guided solutions on MyOMLab at ***www.myomlab.com****.*

1 'Look, why should we waste our time dealing with suppliers who can merely deliver good product, on time, and in full? There are any number of suppliers who can do that. What we are interested in is developing a set of suppliers who will be able to supply us with suitable components for the generation of products that comes after the next products we launch. It's the underlying capability of suppliers that we are really interested in.'

(a) Devise a set of criteria that this manager could use to evaluate alternative suppliers.
(b) Suggest ways in which she could determine how to weight each criterion.

2 Three managers are attending a seminar on 'Getting More Value from Your Purchasing Function'. One manager is from a large retail bank, one is from a general hospital and the third is from a printing company. At the seminar they were discussing their problems during coffee.

'This is really useful; I think that even a relatively small reduction in our bought-in supplies bill could have a major impact on the profitability of our printing company.'

'Yes, I agree the hospital will also benefit from an exercise that would reduce the bought-in supplies bill. At the moment it accounts for almost 30 per cent of all our expenditure.'

'Yes, at the bank we spend almost 20 per cent of our expenditure on bought-in supplies. Given that our profit is 20 per cent of our total revenue, any saving in bought-in supplies would be valuable.'

'I have to say that profits are not so high in the printing industry. Our profits are only 10 per cent of sales revenue. However, with bought-in supplies accounting for 70 per cent of our total costs, I am sure that any reduction in bought-in supplies costs will be useful.'

Which of these three managers would benefit most from a 5 per cent reduction in their bought-in supplies bill?

3 The example of the bullwhip effect shown in Table 13.4 shows how a simple 5 per cent reduction in demand at the end of supply chain causes fluctuations that increase in severity the further back an operation is placed in the chain.

(a) Using the same logic and the same rules (i.e. all operations keep one period's inventory), what would the effect on the chain be if demand fluctuated period by period between 100 and 95? That is, period 1 has a demand of 100, period 2 has a demand of 95, period 3 a demand of 100, period 4 a demand of 95, and so on?
(b) What happens if all operations in the supply chain decided to keep only half of the period's demand as inventory?

4 If you were the owner of a small local retail shop, what criteria would you use to select suppliers for the goods which you wish to stock in your shop? Visit three shops which are local to you and ask the owners how they select their suppliers. In what way were their answers different from what you thought they might be?

5 Visit a C2C auction site (for example eBay) and analyse the function of the site in terms of the way it facilitates transactions. What does such a site have to get right to be successful?

Selected further reading

Andersen, M. and Skjoett-Larsen, T. (2009) Corporate social responsibility in global supply chains, *Supply Chain Management: An International Journal*, vol. 14, issue 2, 75–86. A good review of the topic.

Christopher, M. (2004) *Logistics and Supply Chain Management: Creating Value-adding Networks*, Financial Times Prentice Hall, Harlow. Updated version of a classic that gives a comprehensive treatment on supply chain management from a distribution perspective by one of the gurus of supply chain management.

Fisher, M.L. (1997) What is the right supply chain for your product?, *Harvard Business Review*, vol. 75, no. 2. A particularly influential article that explores the issue of how supply chains are not all the same.

Green, K.W. Jr, Whitten, D. and Inman, R.A. (2008) The impact of logistics performance on organizational performance in a supply chain context, *Supply Chain Management: An International Journal*, vol. 13, issue 4, 317–27. What it says in the title.

Harrison, A. and van Hoek, R. (2002) *Logistics Management and Strategy*, Financial Times Prentice Hall, Harlow. A short but readable book that explains many of the modern ideas in supply chain management including lean supply chains and agile supply chains.

Useful web sites

www.cio.com/research/scm/edit/012202_scm Site of CIO's Supply Chain Management Research Center. Topics include procurement and fulfilment, with case studies.

www.stanford.edu/group/scforum/ Stanford University's supply chain forum. Interesting debate.

www.rfidc.com/ Site of the RFID Centre that contains RFID demonstrations and articles to download.

www.spychips.com/ Vehemently anti-RFID site. If you want to understand the nature of some activists' concern over RFID, this site provides the arguments.

www.cips.org/ The Chartered Institute of Purchasing and Supply (CIPS) is an international organization, serving the purchasing and supply profession and dedicated to promoting best practice. Some good links.

www.opsman.org Lots of useful stuff.

*Now that you have finished reading this chapter, why not visit MyOMLab at **www.myomlab.com** where you'll find more learning resources to help you make the most of your studies and get a better grade?*

Chapter 14

Enterprise resource planning (ERP)

Key questions

- ➤ What is ERP?
- ➤ How did ERP develop?
- ➤ How should ERP systems be implemented?

Introduction

One of the most important issues in planning and controlling operations is managing the sometimes vast amounts of information generated by the activity. It is not just the operations function that is the author and recipient of this information – almost every other function of a business will be involved. So, it is important that all relevant information that is spread throughout the organization is brought together. Then it can inform planning and control decisions such as when activities should take place, where they should happen, who should be doing them, how much capacity will be needed, and so on. This is what enterprise resource planning (ERP) does. It grew out of a set of calculations known as material requirements planning (MRP), which is described in the supplement to this chapter.

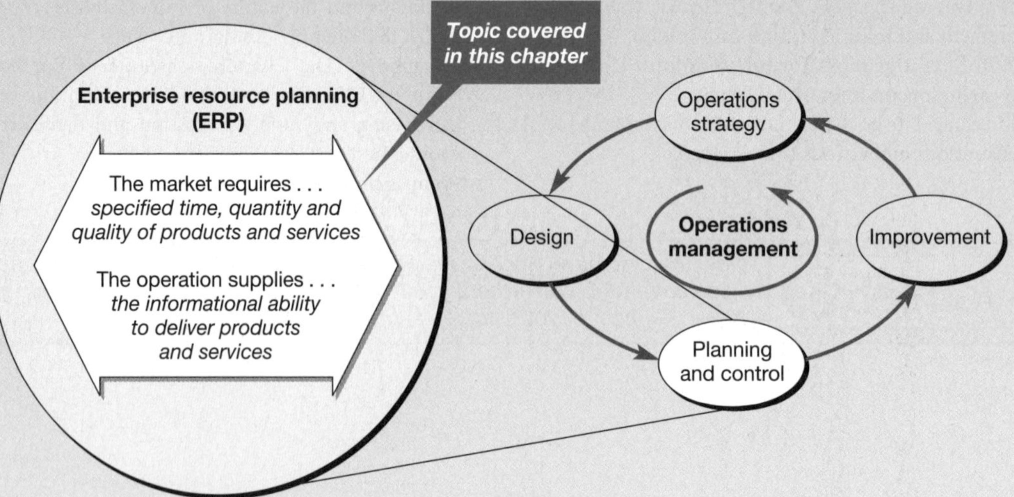

Figure 14.1 This chapter covers enterprise resource planning (ERP)

*Check and improve your understanding of this chapter using self assessment questions and a personalised study plan, audio and video downloads, and an eBook – all at **www.myomlab.com**.*

Operations in practice SAP at Rolls Royce[1]

Rolls-Royce is one of the world's largest manufacturers of the gas turbines that are used to propel civil aircraft, military aircraft and ships, and in power generation as well as many other uses. They are exceptionally complex products, typically with around 25,000 parts, and hundreds of assemblies and sub-assemblies, and their production is equally complex, with over 600 external suppliers and thousands of work centres in many different locations. This makes planning a complex task, which is why Rolls-Royce was one of the earliest users of computers to help with the task. Traditionally the company had developed its own software; however, this had become increasingly expensive compared with buying off-the-shelf systems. It was also risky because customized and complex software could be difficult to update and often could not exchange or share data. So, the company decided to implement a standard 'enterprise resource planning' (ERP) system from the market-leading German SAP company. Because it was a 'commercial' off-the-shelf system it would force the company to adopt a standardized approach. Also, it would fully integrate all the company's systems, and updates would be made available by SAP. Finally, the whole organization would be able to use a single database, reducing duplication and errors. The database modules included product information, resource information (plant assets, capacities of machines, all human resource data, etc.), inventory, external suppliers, order processing information and external sales.

Yet the company knew that many ERP implementations had been expensive disasters. *'We were determined to ensure that this did not happen in Rolls-Royce'*, said Julian Goulder, who led the implementation. *'The project was too important to us; it was the largest single element within our strategic investment plan. So, we had a core technical team that led the design of the systems, and a large implementation team that was spread around the businesses. We always made sure that we communicated the changes throughout the company and used extensive education, and training. We also phased the implementation to avoid any risky "big-bang" approach. There was an extensive data "clean-up" to ensure accuracy and integrity of existing information, and all existing processes were reviewed and standardized. In fact, this implementation forced us to re-examine all of our processes, to make sure that they fitted the SAP system. Within operations we have already seen a significant reduction in inventory, improved customer service, and substantially improved business information and controls.'*

Source: © Rolls-Royce plc

What is ERP?

Enterprise resource planning

An easy way of thinking about **enterprise resource planning** (ERP) is to imagine that you have decided to hold a party in two weeks' time and expect about 40 people to attend. As well as drinks, you decide to provide sandwiches and snacks. You will probably do some simple calculations, estimating guests' preferences and how much people are likely to drink and eat. You may already have some food and drink in the house which you will use, so you will take that into account when making your shopping list. If any of the food is to be cooked from a recipe, you may have to multiply up the ingredients to cater for 40 people. Also, you may also wish to take into account the fact that you will prepare some of the food the week before and freeze it, while you will leave the rest to either the day before or the day of the party. So, you will need to decide when each item is required so that you can shop in time. In fact, planning a party requires a series of interrelated decisions about the volume (quantity) and timing of the *materials* needed. This is the basis of the foundation concept for ERP called **materials requirement planning** (MRP). It is a process that helps companies make volume and timing calculations (similar to those in the party, but on a much larger scale, and with a greater degree of complexity). But your planning may extend beyond 'materials'. You may want to hire in a sound system from a local supplier – you will have to plan for this. The party also has financial implications. You may have to agree a temporary increase to your credit card limit. Again, this requires some forward planning and calculations of how much it is going to cost, and how much extra credit you require. Both the equipment and financial implications may vary if you increase the number of guests. But, if you postpone the party for a month, these arrangements will change. Also, there are also other implications of organizing the party. You will need to give friends, who are helping with the organization, an idea of when they should come and for how long. This will depend on the timing of the various tasks to be done (making sandwiches etc.).

Materials requirement planning

So, even for this relatively simple activity, the key to successful planning is how we generate, integrate and organize all the information on which planning and control depends. Of course, in business operations it is more complex than this. Companies usually sell many different products to many hundreds of customers who are likely to vary their demand for the products. This is a bit like organizing 200 parties one week, 250 the next and 225 the following week, all for different groups of guests with different requirements who keep changing their minds about what they want to eat and drink. This is what ERP does, it helps companies 'forward-plan' these types of decisions and understand all the implications of any changes to the plan.

How did ERP develop?

Enterprise resource planning is the latest, and the most significant, development of the original materials requirements planning (MRP) philosophy. The (now) large companies which have grown almost exclusively on the basis of providing ERP systems include SAP and Oracle. Yet to understand ERP, it is important to understand the various stages in its development, summarized in Figure 14.2. The original MRP became popular during the 1970s, although the planning and control logic that underlies it had, by then, been known for some time. What popularized MRP was the availability of computer power to drive the basic planning and control mathematics. We will deal with MRP in detail in the supplement to this chapter, it uses product information in the form of a **bill of material** (BOM) which is similar to the 'component structure' that was discussed in Chapter 5, together with demand information in the form of a **master production schedule** (MPS).

Bill of material

Master production schedule

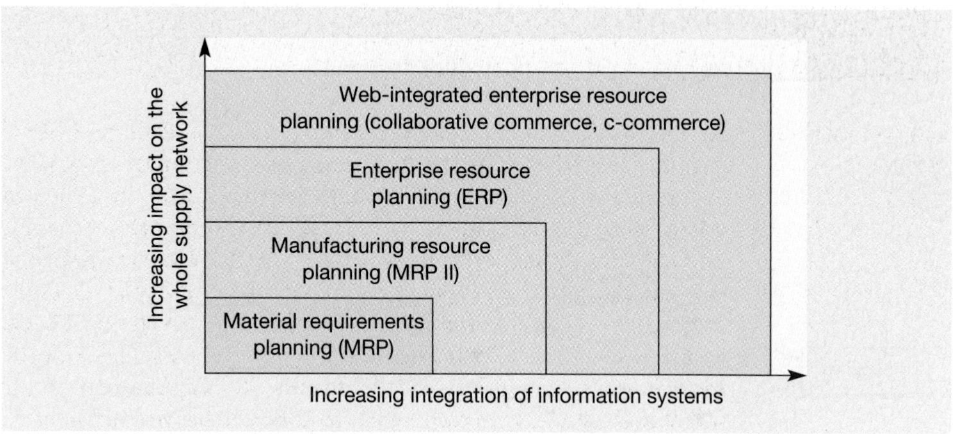

Figure 14.2 The development of ERP

Manufacturing Resource Planning

Manufacturing Resource Planning (MRP II) expanded out of MRP during the 1980s. Again, it was a technology innovation that allowed the development. Local-area networks (LANs, see Chapter 8), together with increasingly powerful desktop computers, allowed a much higher degree of processing power and communication between different parts of a business. Also MRP II's extra sophistication allowed the forward modelling of 'what-if' scenarios. The strength of MRP and MRP II lay always in the fact that it could explore the *consequences* of any changes to what an operation was required to do. So, if demand changed, the MRP system would calculate all the 'knock-on' effects and issue instructions accordingly. This same principle also applies to ERP, but on a much wider basis. **Enterprise resource planning** (ERP) has been defined as,

Enterprise resource planning

'*a complete enterprise wide business solution. The ERP system consists of software support modules such as: marketing and sales, field service, product design and development, production and inventory control, procurement, distribution, industrial facilities management, process design and development, manufacturing, quality, human resources, finance and accounting, and information services. Integration between the modules is stressed without the duplication of information.*'[2]

Some authorities caution against taking a naïve view of ERP. Look at this view:

'*Enterprise resource planning software, or ERP, doesn't live up to its acronym. Forget about planning – it doesn't do much of that – and forget about resource,* [it is] *a throwaway term. But remember the enterprise part. This is ERP's true ambition. It attempts to integrate all departments and functions across a company onto a single computer system that can serve all those different departments' particular needs.*'[3]

So, ERP systems allow decisions and databases from all parts of the organization to be integrated so that the consequences of decisions in one part of the organization are reflected in the planning and control systems of the rest of the organization (*see* Fig. 14.3). ERP is the equivalent of the organization's central nervous system, sensing information about the condition of different parts of the business and relaying the information to other parts of the business that need it. The information is updated in real time by those who use it and yet is always available to everyone connected to the ERP system.

Also, the potential of web-based communication has provided a further boost to ERP development. Many companies have suppliers, customers and other businesses with whom they collaborate who themselves have ERP-type systems. An obvious development is to allow these systems to communicate. However, the technical, as well as organizational and strategic consequences of this can be formidable. Nevertheless, many authorities believe that the true value of ERP systems is only fully exploited when such **web-integrated ERP** (known by some people as 'collaborative commerce', or c-commerce) becomes widely implemented.

Web-integrated ERP

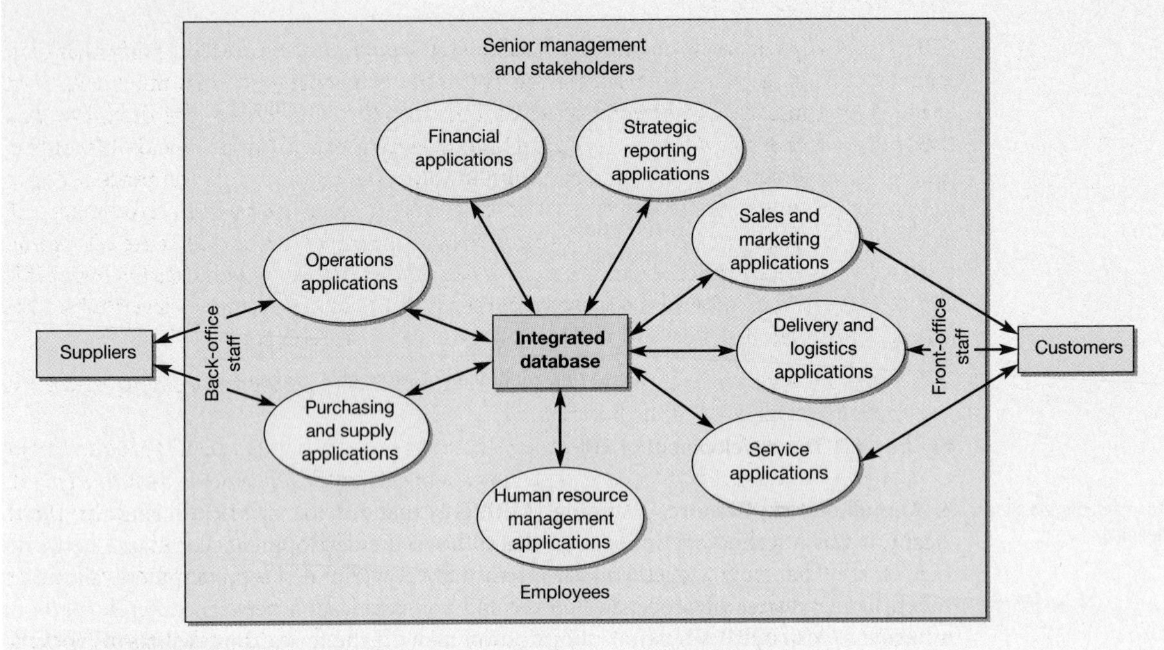

Figure 14.3 ERP integrates information from all parts of the organization

Short case
SAP and its partners[4]

The largest European software company, based in Walldorf, Germany, SAP's growth over the years has matched the popularity of the ERP systems which are still the foundation of its success. Founded by five former IBM engineers in 1972, SAP launched its ground-breaking SAP R/1 system one year later. This was followed by SAP R/2 in 1979 and R/3 in 1992. In 1999 SAP anticipated the influence of the Internet on network integration with its 'mySAP.com' product. Now customers in more than 120 countries run SAP 'business software' applications. These range, as the Company phrases it, from distinct solutions addressing the needs of small businesses and midsize companies to suite offerings for global organizations. SAP defines 'business software' as comprising enterprise resource planning and related applications such as supply chain management, customer relationship management, product life-cycle management, and supplier relationship management.

SAP is well known for developing a network of 'business partners' to develop new products, sell its 'solutions', implement them into customers' operations, provide service, educate end users, and several other activities. There are various categories of partnerships.

- *Global Alliances* – SAP global alliance partners are themselves global leaders and are therefore strategic partners with significant global presence. Membership is by invitation only.

Source: SAP

- *Original equipment manufacturers (OEM)* – This is for independent software vendors who integrate SAP technologies with their own products. OEM partners may add on, bundle, host, or embed SAP software.
- *Solution providers* – These partners offer customized solutions (a combination of business, technical, or application expertise) that include SAP software.
- *Complementary technology partners* – These partners provide complete, technically verified turnkey (out-of-the-box) software solutions that extend and add value to SAP solutions.
- *Volume resellers* – These partners resell all or part of the SAP software portfolio and derive their primary revenue from license sales.
- *Authorized education* – Partners are authorized by SAP to provide official training and education services to ensure that customers' employees gain optimal training.

The benefits of ERP

ERP is generally seen as having the potential to very significantly improve the performance of many companies in many different sectors. This is partly because of the very much enhanced visibility that information integration gives, but it is also a function of the discipline that ERP demands. Yet this discipline is itself a 'double-edged' sword. On one hand, it 'sharpens up' the management of every process within an organization, allowing best practice (or at least common practice) to be implemented uniformly through the business. No longer will individual idiosyncratic behaviour by one part of a company's operations cause disruption to all other processes. On the other hand, it is the rigidity of this discipline that is both difficult to achieve and (arguably) inappropriate for all parts of the business. Nevertheless, the generally accepted benefits of ERP are usually held to be the following.

- Because software communicates across all functions, there is absolute visibility of what is happening in all parts of the business.
- The discipline of forcing business-process-based changes (Chapters 1 and 18 look at business process) is an effective mechanism for making all parts of the business more efficient.
- There is better 'sense of control' of operations that will form the basis for continuous improvement (albeit within the confines of the common process structures).
- It enables far more sophisticated communication with customers, suppliers and other business partners, often giving more accurate and timely information.
- It is capable of integrating whole supply chains including suppliers' suppliers and customers' customers.

In fact, although the integration of several databases lies at the heart of ERP's power, it is nonetheless difficult to achieve in practice. This is why ERP installation can be particularly expensive. Attempting to get new systems and databases to talk to old (sometimes called *legacy*) systems can be very problematic. Not surprisingly, many companies choose to replace most, if not all, of their existing systems simultaneously. New common systems and relational databases help to ensure the smooth transfer of data between different parts of the organization. In addition to the integration of systems, ERP usually includes other features which make it a powerful planning and control tool:

- It is based on a client–server architecture; that is, access to the information systems is open to anyone whose computer is linked to central computers.
- It can include decision support facilities (*see* Chapter 8) which enable operations decision-makers to include the latest company information.
- It is often linked to external extranet systems, such as the electronic data interchange (EDI) systems, which are linked to the company's supply chain partners.
- It can be interfaced with standard applications programs which are in common use by most managers, such as spreadsheets etc.
- Often, ERP systems are able to operate on most common platforms such as Windows or UNIX, or Linux.

The life and times of a chicken salad sandwich – part two[5]

In Chapter 10 we looked at the schedule for the manufacture of a chicken salad sandwich. This concentrated on the lead times for the ordering of the ingredients and the manufacturing schedule for producing the sandwiches during the afternoon and night-time of each day for delivery during the evening and the night-time, and the morning of the following day. But that is only one half of the story, the half that is concerned with planning and controlling the timing of events. The other half concerns how the sandwich company manages the *quantity* of ingredients to order, the quantity of sandwiches to be made, and the whole chain of implications for the whole company. In fact, this sandwich company uses an ERP system that has at its core an MRP II package. This MRP II system has the two normal basic drivers of, first, a continually updated sales forecast, and, second, a product structure database. In this case the product structure and/or bill of materials is the 'recipe' for the sandwich, within the company this database is called the 'Recipe Management System'. The 'recipe' for

→

Table 14.1 Bill of Materials for a chicken salad sandwich

FUNCTION: MBIL *MULTI-LEVEL BILL INQUIRY*

PARENT: BTE80058 *DESC:* *HE CHICKEN SALAD TRAY*
RV: *UM:EA* *RUNLT:* *0* *FIXED LT:* *0*
PLNR: LOU *PLN POL: N* *DRWG: WA1882* *LA*

LEVEL 1 . . . 5 . . . 10	*PT USE*	*SEQN*	*COMPONENT*	*C T*	*PARTIAL DESCRIPTION*	*QTY*	*UM*
1	PACK	010	FTE80045	P	H.E. CHICKENS	9	EA
2	ASSY	010	MBR–0032	P	BREAD HARVESTE	2	SL
3	HRPR	010	RBR–0023	N	BREAD HARVESTE	.04545455	EA
2	ASSY	020	RDY–0001	N	SPREAD BUTTER	.006	KG
2	ASSY	030	RMA–0028	N	MAYONNAISE MYB	.01	KG
2	ASSY	040	MFP–0016	P	CHICKEN FRESH	.045	KG
3	HRPR	010	RFP–0008	N	CHICKEN FRESH	1	KG
	ASSY	050	MVF–0063	P	TOMATO SLICE 4	3	SL
3	ALTI	010	RVF–0026	P	TOMATOES PRE–S	.007	KG
4	HRPR	010	RVF–0018	N	TOMATOES	1	KG
2	ASSY	060	MVF–0059	P	CUCUMBER SLICE	2	SL
3	ALTI	010	RVF–0027	P	CUCUMBER SLICE	.004	KG
4	TRAN	010	RVF–0017	N	CUCUMBER	1	KG
2	ASSY	070	MVF–0073	P	LETTUCE COS SL	.02	KG
3	HRPR	010	RVF–0015	N	LETTUCE COS	1	KG
2	ASSY	080	RPA–0070	N	WEBB BASE GREY	.00744	KG
2	ASSY	090	RPA–0071	N	WEBB TOP WHITE	.0116	KG
2	ASSY	100	RLA–0194	N	LABEL SW H	1	EA
2	ASSY	110	RLA–0110	N	STICKER NE	1	EA
1	PACK	010	RPA–0259	N	SOT LABELL	1	EA
1	PACK	030	RPA–0170	N	TRAY GREEN	1	EA

the chicken sandwich (its bill of materials), is shown in Table 14.1.

Figure 14.4 shows the ERP system used by this sandwich company. Orders are received from customers electronically through the EDI system. These orders are then checked through what the company calls a Validation System that checks the order against current product codes and expected quantities to make sure that the customer has not made any mistakes, such as forgetting to order some products (this happens surprisingly often). After validation the orders are transferred through the central database to the MRP II system that performs the main requirements breakdown. Based on these requirements and forecasted requirements for the next few days, orders are placed to the company's suppliers for raw materials and packaging. Simultaneously, confirmation is sent to customers, accounts are updated, staffing schedules are finalized for the next two weeks (on a rolling basis), customers are invoiced, and all this information is made available both to the customer's own ERP systems and the transportation company's planning system.

Interestingly, the company, like many others, found it difficult to implement its ERP system. *'It was a far bigger job than we thought'*, according to the company's operations director, *'We had to change the way we organized our processes so that they would fit*

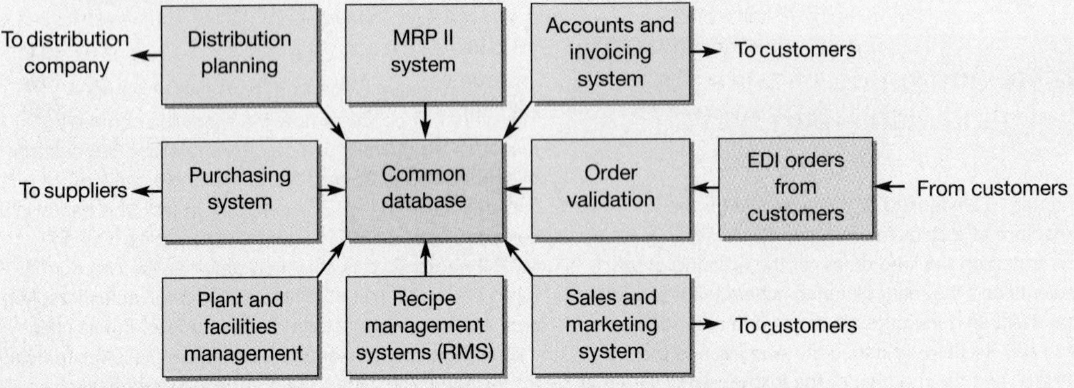

Figure 14.4 The ERP structure for the sandwich company

in with the ERP system that we bought. But that was relatively easy compared to making sure that the system integrated with our customers', suppliers' and distributors' systems. Because some of these companies were also implementing new systems at the time, it was like trying to hit a moving target'. However, three years after the start of implementation, the whole process was working relatively smoothly.

ERP changes the way companies do business

Arguably the most significant issue in many a company's decision to buy an off-the-shelf ERP system is that of its compatibility with the company's current business processes and practices. The advice that is emerging from the companies that have adopted ERP (either successfully or unsuccessfully) is that it is extremely important to make sure that their current way of doing business will fit (or can be changed to fit) with a standard ERP package. In fact, one of the most common reasons for companies to decide not to install ERP is that they cannot reconcile the assumptions in the software of the ERP system with their core business processes. If, as most businesses find, their current processes do not fit, they can do one of two things. They could change their processes to fit the ERP package. Alternatively, they could modify the software within the ERP package to fit their processes. Both of these options involve costs and risks. Changing business practices that are working well will involve reorganization costs as well as introducing the potential for errors to creep into the processes. Adapting the software will both slow down the project and introduce potentially dangerous software 'bugs' into the system. It would also make it difficult to upgrade the software later on.

Why did companies invest in ERP?

If one accepts only some of the criticisms of ERP outlined in the critical commentary box, it does pose the question as to why companies have invested such large amounts of money in it. Partly it was the attraction of turning the company's information systems into a 'smooth running and integrated machine'. The prospect of such organizational efficiency is attractive to most managers, even if it does presuppose a very simplistic model of how organizations work in practice. After a while, although organizations could now see the formidable problems in ERP implementation, the investments were justified on the basis that 'even if we gain no significant advantage by investing in ERP, we will be placed at a disadvantage by *not* investing in it because all our competitors are doing so'. There is probably some truth in this; sometimes businesses have to invest just to stand still.

Critical commentary

Far from being the magic ingredient which allows operations to fully integrate all their information, ERP is regarded by some as one of the most expensive ways of getting zero or even negative return on investment. For example, the American chemicals giants, Dow Chemical, spent almost half a billion dollars and seven years implementing an ERP system which became outdated almost as soon as it was implemented. One company, FoxMeyer Drug, claimed that the expense and problems which it encountered in implementing ERP eventually drove it into bankruptcy. One problem is that ERP implementation is expensive. This is partly because of the need to customize the system, understand its implications on the organization, and train staff to use it. Spending on what some call the *ERP ecosystem* (consulting, hardware, networking and complementary applications) has been estimated as being twice the spending on the software itself. But it is not only the expense which has disillusioned many companies, it is also the returns they have had for their investment. Some studies show that the vast majority of companies implementing ERP are disappointed with the effect it has had on their businesses. Certainly many companies find that they have to (sometimes fundamentally) change the way they organize their operations in order to fit in with ERP systems. This organizational impact of ERP (which has been described as the corporate equivalent of root-canal work) can have a significantly disruptive effect on the organization's operations.

Web-integrated ERP

Perhaps the most important justification for embarking on ERP is the potential it gives the organization to link up with the outside world. For example, it is much easier for an operation to move into internet-based trading if it can integrate its external Internet systems into its internal ERP systems. However, as has been pointed out by some critics of the ERP software companies, ERP vendors were not prepared for the impact of e-commerce and had not made sufficient allowance in their products for the need to interface with internet-based communication channels. The result of this has been that whereas the internal complexity of ERP systems was designed only to be intelligible to systems experts, the Internet has meant that customers and suppliers (who are non-experts) are demanding access to the same information. So, important pieces of information such as the status of orders, whether products are in stock, the progress of invoicing, etc., need to be available, via the ERP system, on a company's web site.

One problem is that different types of external company often need different types of information. Customers need to check the progress of their orders and invoicing, whereas suppliers and other partners want access to the details of operations planning and control. Not only that, but they want access all the time. The Internet is always there, but **web-integrated ERP** systems are often complex and need periodic maintenance. This can mean that every time the ERP system is taken offline for routine maintenance or other changes, the web site also goes offline. To combat this some companies configure their ERP and e-commerce links in such a way that they can be decoupled so that ERP can be periodically shut down without affecting the company's web presence.

Web-integrated ERP

Short case
SAP at Vijay Dairy & Farm Products[6]

The market-leading ERP systems supplier SAP, like many other similar companies, relies on independent consultants to sell and implement its products. Here is a typical example.

Satyam Computer Services Ltd., a global consulting and IT services provider, announced in 2009 that it had been awarded a contract to implement a SAP product (SAP Business All-in-One) for Vijay Dairy & Farm Products, one of the leading dairy processors in India. The dairy firm started in 1995. It produces milk and milk products, such as butter, ghee, curd, butter milk, and flavoured milk in bottles, by buying surplus cows' milk from farmers and using superior technology to process it. It has a processing capacity of 125,000 litres of cows' milk per day, and a distribution network covering the entire state of Tamil Nadu. With demanding hygiene requirements, perishable products and supply schedules that demand daily accuracy, managing the company's planning process is a complex task. That is why the company opted for an ERP system to help it keep control of its operations. The ERP solution should automate and integrate key business processes across the company, speeding workflow, improving quality, and lowering costs. *'Managing our supply – especially procurement and pricing – is a complex process that will now be greatly simplified. Stand-alone processes will be integrated for the first time, and we will be able to monitor product quality at multiple points during procurement and production, enabling us to deliver the freshest quality products to customers at lower costs'* (J. Madhan Mohan, Managing Director, Vijay Dairy & Farm Products).

Source: Alamy Images

But why did they choose Satyam to implement the new ERP system? *'Satyam understands the business challenges faced by Vijay Dairy & Farm Products, and will deliver a powerful, proven solution to transform their entire Procurement-to-Sales process'*, said Manish Mehta, Global Head, SAP and Managed Testing Practices at Satyam. *'Decision-makers at Vijay will have much faster access to more (and more accurate) information from across their enterprise, resulting in improved operational efficiency and effectiveness', he added.* Satyam is also an Indian company, although it has operations world-wide, so it fully understands the operating and implementation environment. At the same time it is a global information technology company, with experience of ERP and other systems implementations in many industries. *'We selected Satyam for their unrivaled SAP credentials, their strong domain knowledge, and their ability to deliver a cost-effective solution in less time. Satyam also demonstrated excellent partnership abilities* [it] *means lower risk and faster deployment'* (Manish Mehta).

Supply chain ERP

The step beyond integrating internal ERP systems with immediate customers and suppliers is to integrate all the ERP and similar systems along a supply chain. Of course, this can never be straightforward and is often exceptionally complicated. Not only do different ERP systems have to communicate together, they have to integrate with other types of system. For example, sales and marketing functions often use systems such as customer relationship management (CRM, see Chapter 13) that manage the complexities of customer requirements, promises and transactions. Getting ERP and CRM systems to work together is itself often difficult. Sometimes the information from ERP systems has to be translated into a form that CRM and other e-commerce applications are able to understand. Nevertheless, such web-integrated ERP or c-commerce (collaborative commerce) applications are emerging and starting to make an impact on the way companies do business. Although a formidable task, the benefits are potentially great. The costs of communicating between supply chain partners could be dramatically reduced and the potential for avoiding errors as information and products move between partners in the supply chain are significant. Yet, as a final warning note, it is well to remember that although integration can bring all the benefits of increased transparency in a supply chain, it may also transmit systems failure. If the ERP system of one operation within a supply chain fails for some reason, it may block the effective operation of the whole integrated information system throughout the chain.

Implementation of ERP systems

By their nature, ERP systems are designed to address problems of information fragmentation. Therefore any ERP system will be complex and difficult to get right. Implementing this type of system will necessarily involve crossing organizational boundaries and integrating internal processes that cover many, if not all, functional areas of a business. Building a single system that simultaneously satisfies the requirements of operations managers, marketing and sales managers, finance managers and everyone else in the organization is never going to be easy. It is likely that each function will have its own set of processes and a well-understood system that has been designed for its specific needs. Moving everyone onto a single, integrated system that runs off a single database is going to be potentially very unpopular. Furthermore, few people like to change, and ERP asks almost everyone to change how they do their jobs. If ERP implementation were not difficult there would not be so many reports of the failure of ERP implementations, or even the complete abandonment of systems.

One of the key issues in ERP implementation is what critical success factors (CSFs) should be managed to increase the chances of a successful implementation. In this case, CSFs are those things that the organization must 'get right' in order for the ERP system to work effectively. Much of the research in this area has been summarized by Finney and Corbett[7] who distinguish between the broad, organization-wide or strategic factors, and the more project specific, or tactical, factors. These are shown in Table 14.2.

Table 14.2 Strategic and tactical critical success factors (CSF) related to successful ERP implementation

Strategic critical success factors	*Tactical critical success factors*
• Top management commitment and support – strong and committed leadership at the top management level is essential to the success of an ERP implementation • Visioning and planning – articulating a business vision to the organization, identifying clear goals and objectives, and providing a clear link between business goals and systems strategy • Project champion – the individual should possess strong leadership skills as well as business, technical and personal managerial competencies • Implementation strategy and time frame – implement the ERP under a time-phased approach • Project management – the ongoing management of the implementation plan • Change management – this concept refers to the need for the implementation team to formally prepare a change management programme and be conscious of the need to consider the implications of such a project. One key task is to build user acceptance of the project and a positive employee attitude. This might be accomplished through education about the benefits and need for an ERP system. Part of this building of user acceptance should also involve securing the support of opinion leaders throughout the organization. There is also a need for the team leader to effectively negotiate between various political turfs. Some authorities also stress that in planning the ERP project, it must be looked upon as a change management initiative not an IT initiative	• Balanced team – the need for an implementation team that spans the organization, as well as one that possesses a balance of business and IT skills • Project team – there is a critical need to put in place a solid, core implementation team that is composed of the organization's 'best and brightest' individuals. These individuals should have a proven reputation and there should be a commitment to 'release' these individuals to the project on a full-time basis • Communication plan – planned communication among various functions and organizational levels (specifically between business and IT personnel) is important to ensure that open communication occurs within the entire organization, as well as with suppliers and customers • Project cost planning and management – it is important to know upfront exactly what the implementation costs will be and dedicate the necessary budget • IT infrastructure – it is critical to assess the IT readiness of the organization, including the architecture and skills. If necessary, infrastructure might need to be upgraded or revamped • Selection of ERP – the selection of an appropriate ERP package that matches the business's processes • Consultant selection and relationship – some authorities advocate the need to include an ERP consultant as part of the implementation team • Training and job redesign – training is a critical aspect of an implementation. It is also necessary to consider the impact of the change on the nature of work and the specific job descriptions • Troubleshooting/crisis management – it is important to be flexible in ERP implementations and to learn from unforeseen circumstances, as well as be prepared to handle unexpected crisis situations. The need for troubleshooting skills will be an ongoing requirement of the implementation process

Based on Sherry Finney and Martin Corbett (2007) ERP implementation: a compilation and analysis of critical success factors, *Business Process Management Journal*, vol. 13, no. 3, 329–47.

Of course, some of these CSFs could be appropriate for any kind of complex implementation, whether of an ERP system or some other major change to an operation. But that is the point. ERP implementation certainly has some specific technical requirements, but good ERP implementation practice is very similar to other complicated and sensitive implementations. Again, what is different about ERP is that it is enterprise-wide, so implementation should always be considered on an enterprise-wide level. Therefore there will at all times be many different stakeholders to consider, each with their own concerns. That is why implementing an ERP system is always going to be an exercise in change management. Only if the anxieties of all relevant groups are addressed effectively will the prospect of achieving superior system performance be high.

Short case
What a waste![8]

Source: Alamy Images

Not only can ERP implementation go wrong, even when undertaken by experienced professionals, sometimes it can end up in the law courts. Waste Management, Inc. is the leading provider of waste and environmental services in North America. In 2008 it announced that it was suing SAP (see earlier short case) over the failure of an ERP implementation. Waste Management said that it was seeking the recovery of more than $100 million in project expenses as well as 'the savings and benefits that the SAP software was promised to deliver to Waste Management'. It said that SAP promised that the software could be fully implemented throughout all of Waste Management within 18 months, and that its software was an 'out-of-the-box' solution that would meet Waste Management's needs without any customization or enhancements.

Waste Management signed a sales pact with SAP in October 2005, but according to Waste Management, 'Almost immediately following execution of the agreements, the SAP implementation team discovered significant "gaps" between the software's functionality and Waste Management's business requirements. Waste Management has discovered that these gaps were already known to the product development team in Germany even before the SLA (service level agreement) was signed.' But members of SAP's implementation team had reportedly blamed Waste Management for the functional gaps and had submitted change orders requiring that Waste Management pay for fixing them.

At a purely practical level, many consultants who have had to live through the difficulties of implementing ERP have summarized their experiences. The following list of likely problems with an ERP implementation is typical (and really does reflect reality).

- The total cost is likely to be underestimated.
- The time and effort to implement it is likely to be underestimated.
- The resourcing from both the business and the IT function is likely to be higher than anticipated.
- The level of outside expertise required will be more than anticipated.
- The changes required to business processes will be greater than expected.
- Controlling the scope of the project will be more difficult than expected.
- There will never be enough training.
- The need for change management is not likely to be recognized until it is too late, and the changes required to corporate culture are likely to be grossly underestimated. (This is the single biggest failure point for ERP implementations.)

Summary answers to key questions

Check and improve your understanding of this chapter using self assessment questions and a personalised study plan, audio and video downloads, and an eBook – all at ***www.myomlab.com.***

➤ What is ERP?

- ERP is an enterprise-wise information system that integrates all the information from many functions, that is needed for planning and controlling operations activities. This integration around a common database allows for transparency.

- It often requires very considerable investment in the software itself, as well as its implementation. More significantly, it often requires a company's processes to be changed to bring them in line with the assumptions built into the ERP software.

➤ How did ERP develop?

- ERP can be seen as the latest development from the original planning and control approach known as materials requirements planning (MRP).
- Although ERP is becoming increasingly competent at the integration of internal systems and databases, there is the even more significant potential of integration with other organizations' ERP (and equivalent) systems.
- In particular, the use of internet-based communication between customers, suppliers and other partners in the supply chain has opened up the possibility of web-based integration.

➤ How should ERP systems be implemented?

- Because ERP systems are designed to address problems of information fragmentation implementation will be complex and cross organizational boundaries.
- There are a number of critical success factors (CSFs) that the organization must 'get right' in order for the ERP system to work effectively. Some of these are broad, organization-wide, or strategic, factors. Others are more project-specific, or tactical, factors.

Case study
Psycho Sports Ltd

Peter Townsend knew that he would have to make some decisions pretty soon. His sports goods manufacturing business, Psycho Sports, had grown so rapidly over the last two years that he would soon have to install some systematic procedures and routines to manage the business. His biggest problem was in manufacturing control. He had started making specialist high-quality table tennis bats but now made a wide range of sports products, including tennis balls, darts and protective equipment for various games. Furthermore, his customers, once limited to specialist sports shops, now included some of the major sports retail chains.

'We really do have to get control of our manufacturing. I keep getting told that we need what seems to be called an MRP system. I wasn't sure what this meant and so I have bought a specialist production control book from our local bookshop and read all about MRP principles. I must admit, these academics seem to delight in making simple things complicated. And there is so much jargon associated with the technique, I feel more confused now than I did before.

Perhaps the best way forward is for me to take a very simple example from my own production unit and see

Source: Corbis/Mark Cooper

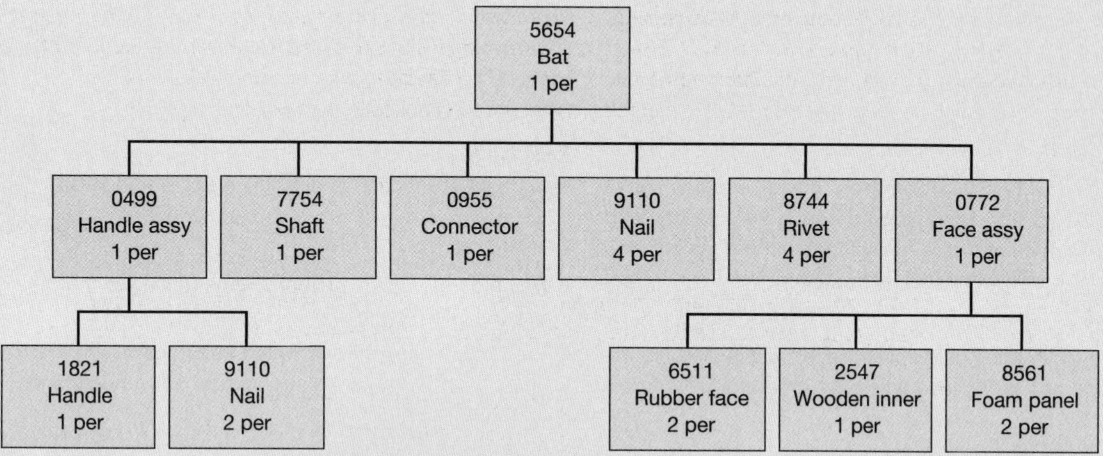

Figure 14.5 Product structure for bat 5654

whether I can work things out manually. If I can follow the process through on paper then I will be far better equipped to decide what kind of computer-based system we should get, if any!'

Peter decided to take as his example one of his new products: a table tennis bat marketed under the name of 'the high-resolution' bat, but known within the manufacturing unit more prosaically as Part Number 5654. Figure 14.5 shows the product structure for this table tennis bat, showing the table tennis bat made up of two main assemblies: a handle assembly and a face assembly. In order to bring the two main assemblies together to form the finished bat, various fixings are required, such as nails, connectors, etc.

The gross requirements for this particular bat are shown below. The bat is not due to be launched until Week 13 (it is now Week 1), and sales forecasts have been made for the first 23 weeks of sales:

Weeks 13–21 inclusive, 100 per week
Weeks 22–29 inclusive, 150 per week
Weeks 30–35 inclusive, 200 per week.

Peter also managed to obtain information on the current inventory levels of each of the parts which made up the finished bat, together with cost data and lead times. He was surprised, however, how long it took him to obtain this information. *'It has taken me nearly two days to get hold of all the information I need. Different people held it, nowhere was it conveniently put together, and sometimes it was not even written down. To get the inventory data, I actually had to go down to the stores and count how many parts were in the boxes.'*

The data Peter collected were as shown in Table 14.3.

Peter set himself six exercises which he knew he would have to master if he was to understand fully the basics of MRP.

Exercise 1

Draw up:

(a) the single-level bill of materials for each level of assembly;

(b) a complete indented bill of materials for all levels of assembly.

Exercise 2

(a) Create the materials requirements planning records for each part and sub-assembly in the bat.

Table 14.3 Inventory, cost and lead-time information for parts

Part no.	*Description*	*Inventory*	*EQ*	*LT*	*Std cost*
5645	Bat	0	500	2	12.00
0499	Handle assy	0	400	3	4.00
7754	Shaft	15	1,000	5	1.00
0955	Connector	350	5,000	4	0.02
9110	Nail	120	5,000	4	0.01
8744	Rivet	3,540	5,000	4	0.01
0772	Face assy	0	250	4	5.00
1821	Handle	0	500	4	2.00
6511	Rubber face	0	2,000	10	0.50
2547	Wooden inner	10	300	7	1.50
8561	Foam panel	0	1,000	8	0.50

LT = lead time for ordering (in weeks); EQ = economic quantity for ordering; Std cost = standard cost in £.

→

(b) List any problems that the completed MRP records identify.

(c) What alternatives are there that the company could take to solve any problems? What are their relative merits?

Exercise 3

Based on the first two exercises, create another set of MRP records, this time allowing one week's safety lead time for each item: that is, ensuring the items are in stock the week prior to when they are required.

Exercise 4

Over the time period of the exercise, what effect would the imposition of a safety lead time have on average inventory value?

Exercise 5

If we decided that our first task was to reduce inventory costs by 15 per cent, what action would we recommend? What are the implications of our action?

Exercise 6

How might production in our business be smoothed?

Questions

1 Why did Peter have such problems getting to the relevant information?

2 Perform all the exercises which Peter set for himself. Do you think he should now fully understand MRP?

Problems and applications

These problems and applications will help to improve your analysis of operations. You can find more practice problems as well as worked examples and guided solutions on MyOMLab at ***www.myomlab.com****.*

1 Your company has developed a simple, but amazingly effective, mango peeler. It is constructed from a blade and a supergrip handle that has a top piece and a bottom piece. The assembled mango peeler is packed in a simple recycled card pack. All the parts simply clip together and are bought in from suppliers, who can deliver the parts within one week of orders being placed. Given enough parts, your company can produce products within a day of firm orders being placed. Initial forecasts indicate that demand will be around 500 items per week. (Read the supplement to this chapter before attempting this and the following question.)

(a) Draw a component structure and Bill of Materials for the mango peeler.

(b) Develop a Master Production Schedule for the product.

(c) Develop a schedule indicating when and how many of each component should be ordered (your scheduler tells you that the economic order quantity, EOQ, for all parts is 2,500).

2 The mango peeler described above was a huge success. Demand is now level at 800 items per week. You now have also developed two further products, a melon baller and a passion fruit pulper. Both new products use the same handle, but have their own specially designed handle and pack. Demand for the new products is expected to be 400 items per week. Also your suppliers have indicated that, because of the extra demand, they will need two weeks to deliver orders. Similarly, your own assembly department is now taking a week to assemble the products.

(a) Draw new component structures and Bills of Material for the new products.

(b) Develop a Master Production Schedule for all the products.

(c) Develop a schedule indicating when and how many of each component should be ordered.

3 Using a cookery book, choose three similar, fairly complex, recipe items such as layered and decorated gateaux (cakes) or desserts. For each, construct the indented bill of materials and identify all the different materials, sub-assemblies and final products with one set of part numbers (i.e. no duplication). Using the times given in the recipes (or your own estimates), construct a table of lead times (e.g. in minutes or hours) for each stage of production and for procurement of the ingredients. Using these examples (and a bit of your own imagination!), show how this information could be used with an MRP system to plan and control the batch production processes within a small cake or dessert factory making thousands of each product every week. Show part of the MRP records and calculations that would be involved.

4 **(Advanced)** Working in a small study group, construct a model of the information systems that you think would be needed to plan and control the most important day-to-day operations and finances of a large university or college. In particular, identify and include at least three processes that cross departmental and functional boundaries, and show how ERP might be used to improve the quality, speed, dependability, flexibility and/or costs of such processes. Then discuss:

(a) If ERP is not already in use at your chosen organization, should it be introduced, and if so why? What would the difficulties be in doing this, and how could they be overcome?

(b) If ERP is already in use, what advantages and disadvantages are already apparent to the staff (e.g. ask a lecturer, an administrator, and a support services manager, such as someone who runs cleaning or catering services)?

Selected further reading

Davenport, T.H. (1998) Putting the enterprise into the enterprise system, *Harvard Business Review*, July–August. Covers some of the more managerial and strategic aspects of ERP.

Finney, S. and Corbett, M. (2007) ERP implementation: a compilation and analysis of critical success factors, *Business Process Management Journal*, vol. 13, no. 3, 329–47. Both interesting and practical.

Koch, C. and Wailgum, T. (2007) ERP definition and solutions, www.cio.com. CIO.com has some really useful articles and this is one of the most thought-provoking.

Turbit, N. (2005) ERP Implementation – The Traps, The Project Perfect White Paper Collection, www.projectperfect.com.au. Practical (and true).

Vollmann, T., Berry, W., Whybark, D.C. and Jacobs, F.R. (2004) *Manufacturing Planning and Control Systems for Supply Chain Management: The Definitive Guide for Professionals*, McGraw-Hill Higher Education. The latest version of the 'bible' of manufacturing planning and control. Explains the 'workings' of MRP and ERP in detail.

Wallace, T.F. and Krezmar, M.K. (2001) *ERP: Making it Happen*, Wiley. Another practitioner guide but with useful hints on the interior mechanisms of MRP.

Useful web sites

www.bpic.co.uk/ Some useful information on general planning and control topics.

www.cio.com/research/erp/edit/erpbasics.html Several descriptions and useful information on ERP-related topics.

www.erpfans.com/ Yes, even ERP has its own fan club! Debates and links for the enthusiast.

www.sap.com/index.epx *'Helping to build better businesses for more than three decades'*, SAP has been the leading worldwide supplier of ERP systems for ages. They should know how to do it by now!

www.sapfans.com/ Another fan club – this one is for SAP enthusiasts.

www.apics.org. The American professional and education body that has its roots in planning and control activities.

www.opsman.org Lots of useful stuff.

*Now that you have finished reading this chapter, why not visit MyOMLab at **www.myomlab.com** where you'll find more learning resources to help you make the most of your studies and get a better grade?*

Supplement to Chapter 14 Materials requirements planning (MRP)

Introduction

Materials requirements planning (MRP) is an approach to calculating how many parts or materials of particular types are required and what times they are required. This requires data files which, when the MRP program is run, can be checked and updated. Figure S14.1 shows how these files relate to each other. The first inputs to materials requirements planning are customer orders and forecast demand. MRP performs its calculations based on the combination of these two parts of future demand. All other requirements are derived from, and dependent on, this demand information.

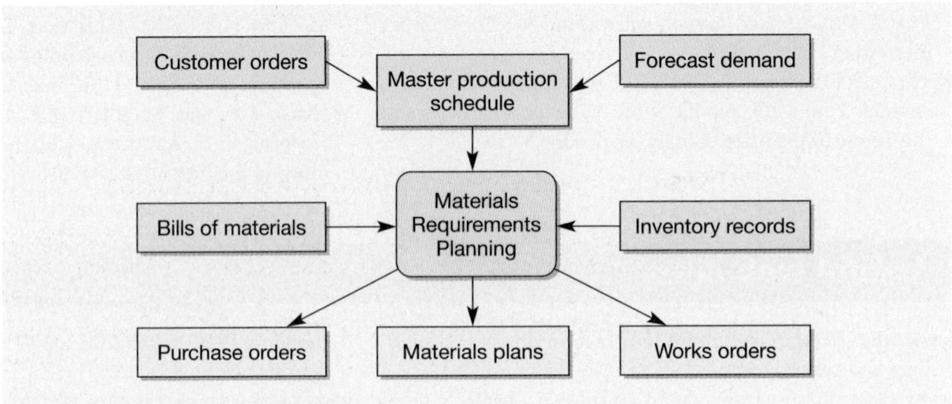

Figure S14.1 Materials requirements planning (MRP) schematic

Master production schedule

The master production schedule (MPS) forms the main input to materials requirements planning and contains a statement of the volume and timing of the end-products to be made. It drives all the production and supply activities that eventually will come together to form the end-products. It is the basis for the planning and utilization of labour and equipment, and it determines the provisioning of materials and cash. The MPS should include all sources of demand, such as spare parts, internal production promises, etc. For example, if a manufacturer of earth excavators plans an exhibition of its products and allows a project team to raid the stores so that it can build two pristine examples to be exhibited, this is likely to leave the factory short of parts. MPS can also be used in service organizations. For example, in a hospital theatre there is a master schedule that contains a statement of which operations are planned and when. This can be used to provision materials for the operations, such as the sterile instruments, blood and dressings. It may also govern the scheduling of staff for operations.

The master production schedule record

Master production schedules are time-phased records of each end-product, which contain a statement of demand and currently available stock of each finished item. Using this information, the available inventory is projected ahead in time. When there is insufficient inventory to satisfy forward demand, order quantities are entered on the master schedule line. Table S14.1 is a simplified example of part of a master production schedule for one item. In the first row the known sales orders and any forecast are combined to form 'Demand'. The second row, 'Available', shows how much inventory of this item is expected to be in stock at the end of each weekly period. The opening inventory balance, 'On hand', is shown separately at the bottom of the record. The third row is the master production schedule, or MPS; this shows how many finished items need to be completed and available in each week to satisfy demand.

Table S14.1 Example of a master production schedule

	Week number								
	1	*2*	*3*	*4*	*5*	*6*	*7*	*8*	*9*
Demand	10	10	10	10	15	15	15	20	20
Available	20	10	0	0	0	0	0	0	0
MPS	0	0	10	10	15	15	15	20	20
On hand	30								

Chase or level master production schedules

In the example in Table S14.1, the MPS increases as demand increases and aims to keep available inventory at 0. The master production schedule is 'chasing' demand (see Chapter 11) and so adjusting the provision of resources. An alternative 'levelled' MPS for this situation is shown in Table S14.2. Level scheduling involves averaging the amount required to be completed to smooth out peaks and troughs; it generates more inventory than the previous MPS.

Table S14.2 Example of a 'level' master production schedule

	Week number								
	1	*2*	*3*	*4*	*5*	*6*	*7*	*8*	*9*
Demand	10	10	10	10	15	15	15	20	20
Available	31	32	33	34	30	26	22	13	4
MPS	11	11	11	11	11	11	11	11	11
On hand	30								

Available to promise (ATP)

The master production schedule provides the information to the sales function on what can be promised to customers and when delivery can be promised. The sales function can load known sales orders against the master production schedule and keep track of what is available to promise (ATP) (*see* Table S14.3). The ATP line in the master production schedule shows the maximum that is still available in any one week, against which sales orders can be loaded.

Table S14.3 Example of a level master production schedule including available to promise

	Week number								
	1	*2*	*3*	*4*	*5*	*6*	*7*	*8*	*9*
Demand	10	10	10	10	15	15	15	20	20
Sales orders	10	10	10	8	4				
Available	31	32	33	34	30	26	22	13	4
ATP	31	1	1	3	7	11	11	11	11
MPS	11	11	11	11	11	11	11	11	11
On hand	30								

The bill of materials (BOM)

From the master schedule, MRP calculates the required volume and timing of assemblies, sub-assemblies and materials. To do this it needs information on what parts are required for each product. This is called the 'bill of materials'. Initially it is simplest to think about these as a product structure. The product structure in Figure S14.2 is a simplified structure showing the parts required to make a simple board game. Different 'levels of assembly' are shown with the finished product (the boxed game) at level 0, the parts and sub-assemblies that go into the boxed game at level 1, the parts that go into the sub-assemblies at level 2, and so on.

A more convenient form of the product structure is the 'indented bill of materials'. Table S14.4 shows the whole indented bill of materials for the board game. The term 'indented' refers to the indentation of the level of assembly, shown in the left-hand column. Multiples of some parts are required; this means that MRP has to know the required number of each part to be able to multiply up the requirements. Also, the same part (for example, the TV label, part number 10062) may be used in different parts of the product structure. This means that MRP has to cope with this commonality of parts and, at some stage, aggregate the requirements to check how many labels in total are required.

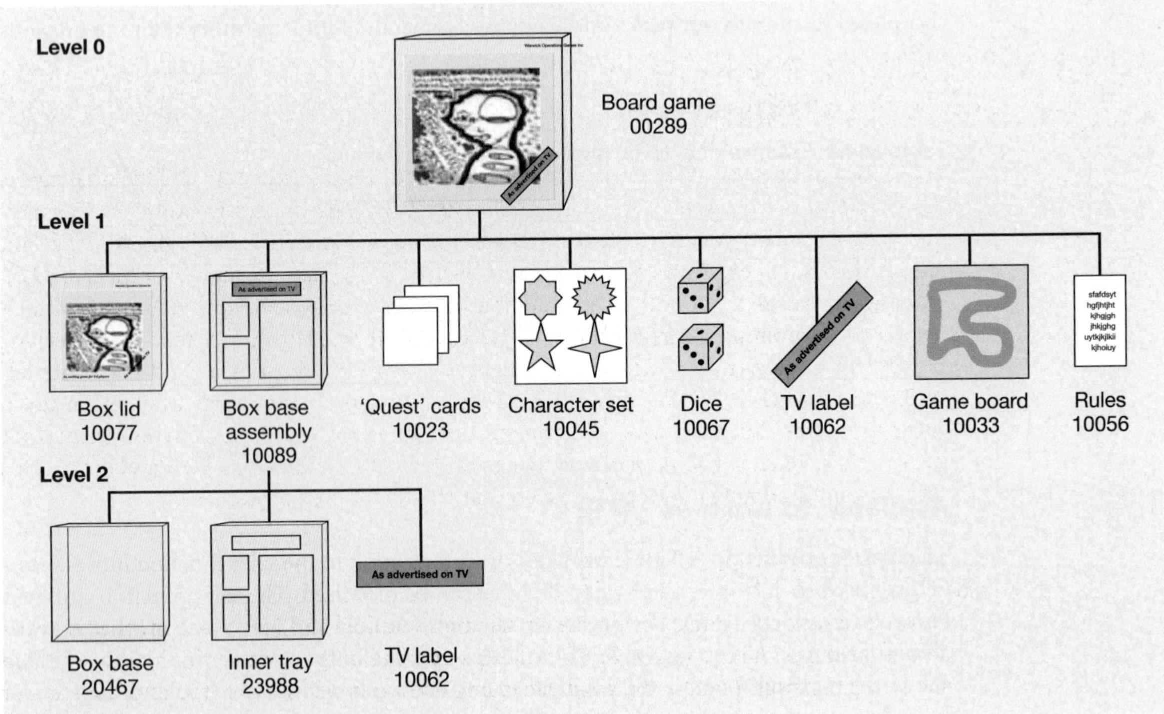

Figure S14.2 Product structure for the Treasure Hunt game

Table S14.4 Indented bill of materials for board game

Part number: 00289
Description: Board game
Level: 0

Level	*Part number*	*Description*	*Quantity*
0	00289	Board game	1
. 1	10077	Box lid	1
. 1	10089	Box base assy	1
. . 2	20467	Box base	1
. . 2	10062	TV label	1
. . 2	23988	Inner tray	1
. 1	10023	Quest cards set	1
. 1	10045	Character set	1
. 1	10067	Die	2
. 1	10062	TV label	2
. 1	10033	Game board	1
. 1	10056	Rules booklet	1

Inventory records

MRP calculations need to recognize that some required items may already be in stock. So, it is necessary, starting at level 0 of each bill, to check how much inventory is available of each finished product, sub-assembly and component, and then to calculate what is termed the 'net' requirements, that is the extra requirements needed to supplement the inventory so that demand can be met. This requires that three main inventory records are kept: the item master file, which contains the unique standard identification code for each part or component, the transaction file, which keeps a record of receipts into stock, issues from stock and a running balance, and the location file, which identifies where inventory is located.

The MRP netting process

The information needs of MRP are important, but it is not the 'heart' of the MRP procedure. At its core, MRP is a systematic process of taking this planning information and calculating the volume and timing requirements which will satisfy demand. The most important element of this is the MRP netting process. Figure S14.3 illustrates the process that MRP performs to calculate the volumes of materials required. The master production schedule is 'exploded', examining the implications of the schedule through the bill of materials, checking how many sub-assemblies and parts are required. Before moving down the bill of materials to the next level, MRP checks how many of the required parts are already available in stock. It then generates 'works orders', or requests, for the net requirements of items. These form the schedule which is again exploded through the bill of materials at the next level down. This process continues until the bottom level of the bill of materials is reached.

Back-scheduling

In addition to calculating the volume of materials required, MRP also considers when each of these parts is required, that is, the timing and scheduling of materials. It does this by a process called back-scheduling which takes into account the lead time (the time allowed for completion of each stage of the process) at every level of assembly. Again using the example of the board game, assume that 10 board games are required to be finished by a notional

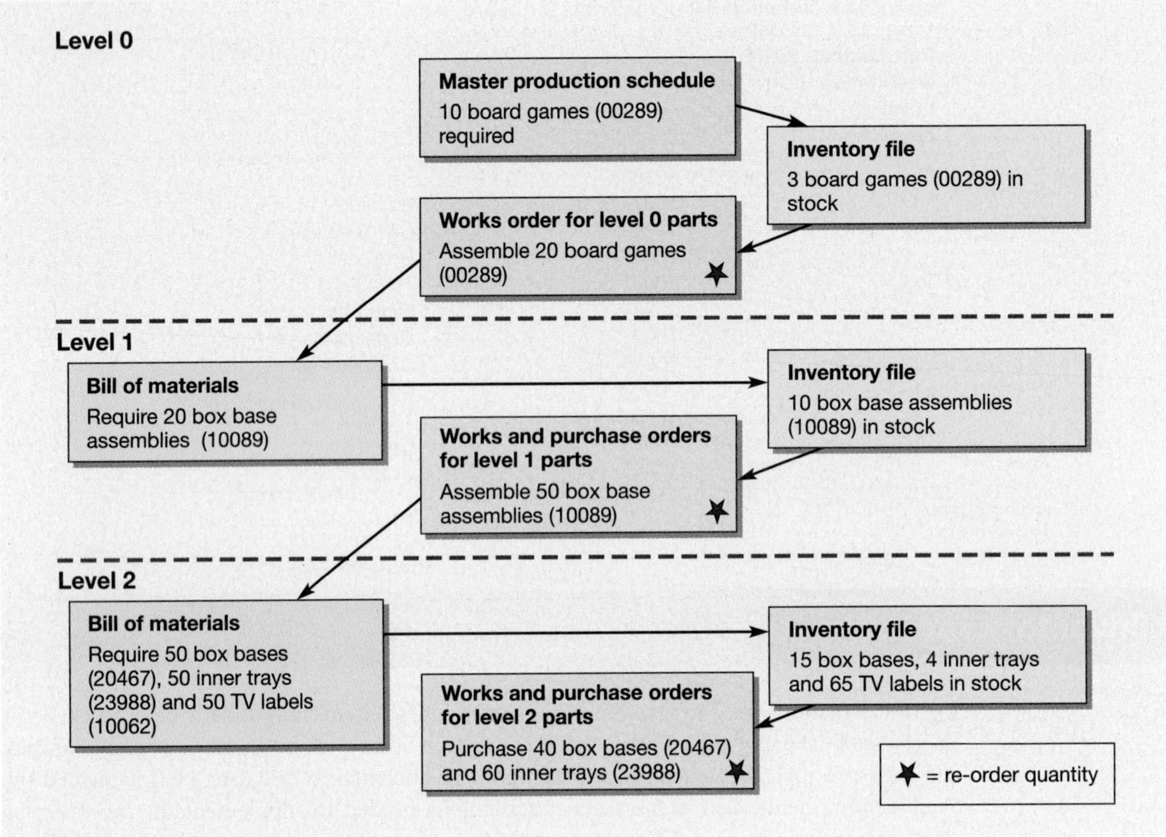

Figure S14.3 Example of the MRP netting process for the board game

planning day which we will term day 20. To determine when we need to start work on all the parts that make up the game, we need to know all the lead times that are stored in MRP files for each part (*see* Table S14.5).

Using the lead-time information, the programme is worked backwards to determine the tasks that have to be performed and the purchase orders that have to be placed. Given the lead times and inventory levels shown in Table S14.5, the MRP records shown in Figure S14.4 can be derived.

Table S14.5 Back-scheduling of requirements in MRP

Part no.	*Description*	*Inventory on-hand day 0*	*Lead time (days)*	*Re-order quantity*
00289	Board game	3	2	20
10077	Box lid	4	8	25
10089	Box base assy	10	4	50
20467	Box base	15	12	40
23988	Inner tray	4	14	60
10062	TV label	65	8	100
10023	Quest cards set	4	3	50
10045	Character set	46	3	50
10067	Die	22	5	80
10033	Game board	8	15	50
10056	Rules booklet	0	3	80

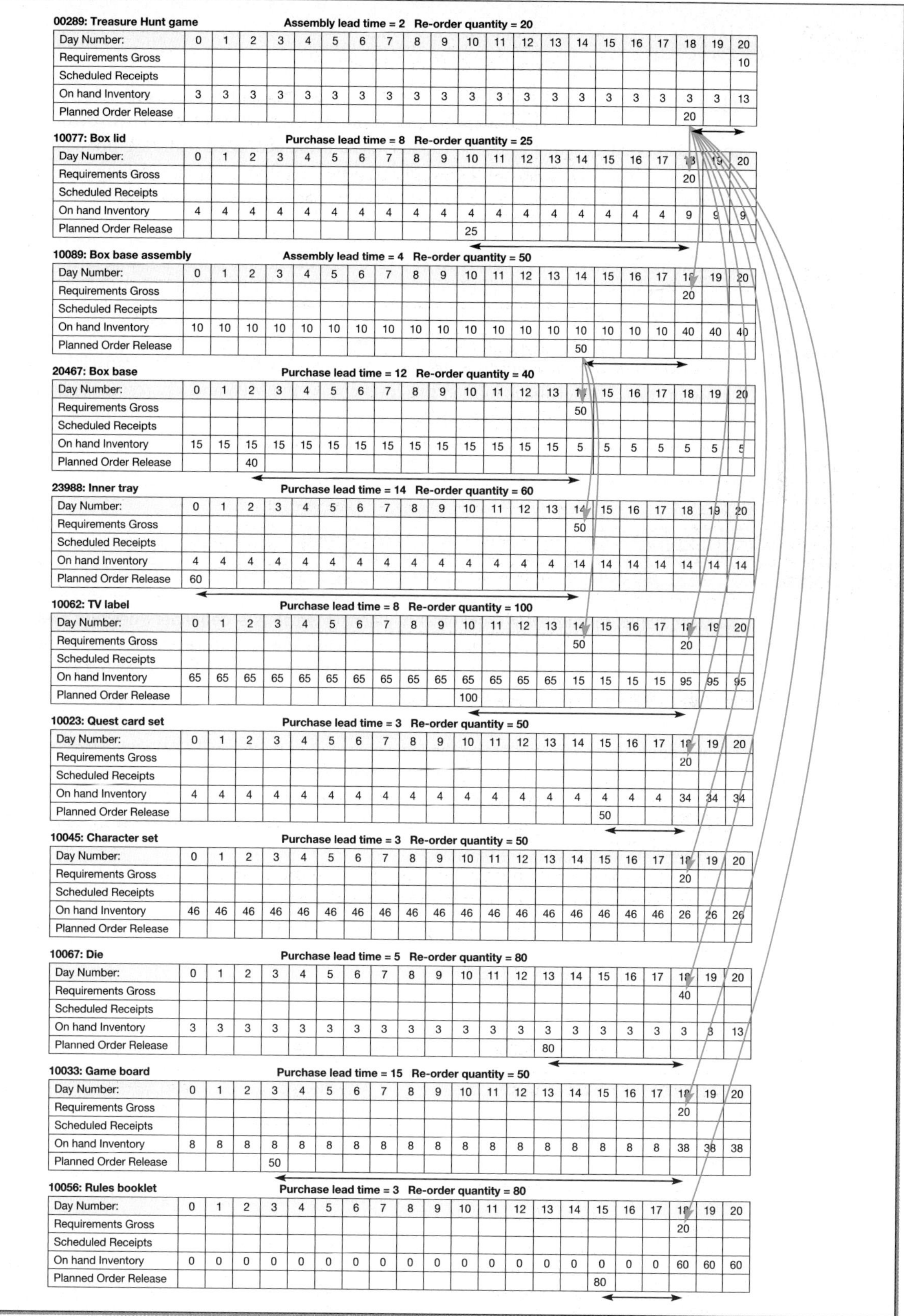

00289: Treasure Hunt game — Assembly lead time = 2 Re-order quantity = 20

Day Number:	0	1	2	3	4	5	6	7	8	9	10	11	12	13	14	15	16	17	18	19	20
Requirements Gross																					10
Scheduled Receipts																					
On hand Inventory	3	3	3	3	3	3	3	3	3	3	3	3	3	3	3	3	3	3	3	3	13
Planned Order Release																			20		

10077: Box lid — Purchase lead time = 8 Re-order quantity = 25

Day Number:	0	1	2	3	4	5	6	7	8	9	10	11	12	13	14	15	16	17	18	19	20
Requirements Gross																			20		
Scheduled Receipts																					
On hand Inventory	4	4	4	4	4	4	4	4	4	4	4	4	4	4	4	4	4	4	9	9	9
Planned Order Release											25										

10089: Box base assembly — Assembly lead time = 4 Re-order quantity = 50

Day Number:	0	1	2	3	4	5	6	7	8	9	10	11	12	13	14	15	16	17	18	19	20
Requirements Gross																			20		
Scheduled Receipts																					
On hand Inventory	10	10	10	10	10	10	10	10	10	10	10	10	10	10	10	10	10	10	40	40	40
Planned Order Release															50						

20467: Box base — Purchase lead time = 12 Re-order quantity = 40

Day Number:	0	1	2	3	4	5	6	7	8	9	10	11	12	13	14	15	16	17	18	19	20
Requirements Gross															50						
Scheduled Receipts																					
On hand Inventory	15	15	15	15	15	15	15	15	15	15	15	15	15	15	5	5	5	5	5	5	5
Planned Order Release			40																		

23988: Inner tray — Purchase lead time = 14 Re-order quantity = 60

Day Number:	0	1	2	3	4	5	6	7	8	9	10	11	12	13	14	15	16	17	18	19	20
Requirements Gross															50						
Scheduled Receipts																					
On hand Inventory	4	4	4	4	4	4	4	4	4	4	4	4	4	4	14	14	14	14	14	14	14
Planned Order Release	60																				

10062: TV label — Purchase lead time = 8 Re-order quantity = 100

Day Number:	0	1	2	3	4	5	6	7	8	9	10	11	12	13	14	15	16	17	18	19	20
Requirements Gross															50				20		
Scheduled Receipts																					
On hand Inventory	65	65	65	65	65	65	65	65	65	65	65	65	65	65	15	15	15	15	95	95	95
Planned Order Release											100										

10023: Quest card set — Purchase lead time = 3 Re-order quantity = 50

Day Number:	0	1	2	3	4	5	6	7	8	9	10	11	12	13	14	15	16	17	18	19	20
Requirements Gross																			20		
Scheduled Receipts																					
On hand Inventory	4	4	4	4	4	4	4	4	4	4	4	4	4	4	4	4	4	4	34	34	34
Planned Order Release																50					

10045: Character set — Purchase lead time = 3 Re-order quantity = 50

Day Number:	0	1	2	3	4	5	6	7	8	9	10	11	12	13	14	15	16	17	18	19	20
Requirements Gross																			20		
Scheduled Receipts																					
On hand Inventory	46	46	46	46	46	46	46	46	46	46	46	46	46	46	46	46	46	46	26	26	26
Planned Order Release																					

10067: Die — Purchase lead time = 5 Re-order quantity = 80

Day Number:	0	1	2	3	4	5	6	7	8	9	10	11	12	13	14	15	16	17	18	19	20
Requirements Gross																			40		
Scheduled Receipts																					
On hand Inventory	3	3	3	3	3	3	3	3	3	3	3	3	3	3	3	3	3	3	3	3	13
Planned Order Release														80							

10033: Game board — Purchase lead time = 15 Re-order quantity = 50

Day Number:	0	1	2	3	4	5	6	7	8	9	10	11	12	13	14	15	16	17	18	19	20
Requirements Gross																			20		
Scheduled Receipts																					
On hand Inventory	8	8	8	8	8	8	8	8	8	8	8	8	8	8	8	8	8	8	38	38	38
Planned Order Release				50																	

10056: Rules booklet — Purchase lead time = 3 Re-order quantity = 80

Day Number:	0	1	2	3	4	5	6	7	8	9	10	11	12	13	14	15	16	17	18	19	20
Requirements Gross																			20		
Scheduled Receipts																					
On hand Inventory	0	0	0	0	0	0	0	0	0	0	0	0	0	0	0	0	0	0	60	60	60
Planned Order Release																80					

Figure S14.4 Extract of the MRP records for the board game

MRP capacity checks

The MRP process needs a feedback loop to check whether a plan was achievable and whether it has actually been achieved. Closing this planning loop in MRP systems involves checking production plans against available capacity and, if the proposed plans are not achievable at any level, revising them All but the simplest MRP systems are now closed-loop systems. They use three planning routines to check production plans against the operation's resources at three levels.

- Resource requirements plans (RRPs) – involve looking forward in the long term to predict the requirements for large structural parts of the operation, such as the numbers, locations and sizes of new plants.
- Rough-cut capacity plans (RCCPs) – are used in the medium-to-short term, to check the master production schedules against known capacity bottlenecks, in case capacity constraints are broken. The feedback loop at this level checks the MPS and key resources only.
- Capacity requirements plans (CRPs) – look at the day-to-day effect of the works orders issued from the MRP on the loading individual process stages.

Summary

- MRP stands for materials requirements planning which is a dependent demand system that calculates materials requirements and production plans to satisfy known and forecast sales orders. It helps to make volume and timing calculations based on an idea of what will be necessary to supply demand in the future.
- MRP works from a master production schedule which summarizes the volume and timing of end products or services. Using the logic of the bill of materials (BOM) and inventory records, the production schedule is 'exploded' (called 'the MRP netting process') to determine how many sub-assemblies and parts are required, and when they are required.
- Closed-loop MRP systems contain feedback loops which ensure that checks are made against capacity to see if plans are feasible.
- MRP II systems are a development of MRP. They integrate many processes that are related to MRP, but which are located outside the operation's function.

Chapter 15

Lean synchronization

Key questions

- What is lean synchronization?
- How does lean synchronization eliminate waste?
- How does lean synchronization apply throughout the supply network?
- How does lean synchronization compare with other approaches?

Introduction

This chapter examines an approach that we call 'lean synchronization' or just 'lean'. It was originally called 'just-in-time' (JIT) when it started to be adopted outside its birthplace, Japan. It is both a philosophy and a method of operations planning and control. Lean synchronization aims to meet demand instantaneously, with perfect quality and no waste. This involves supplying products and services in perfect synchronization with the demand for them. These principles were once a radical departure from traditional operations practice, but have now become orthodox in promoting the synchronization of flow through processes, operations and supply networks. Although we will focus on planning and control issues, in practice the 'lean' concept has much wider implications for improving operations performance. Figure 15.1 places lean synchronization in the overall model of operations management.

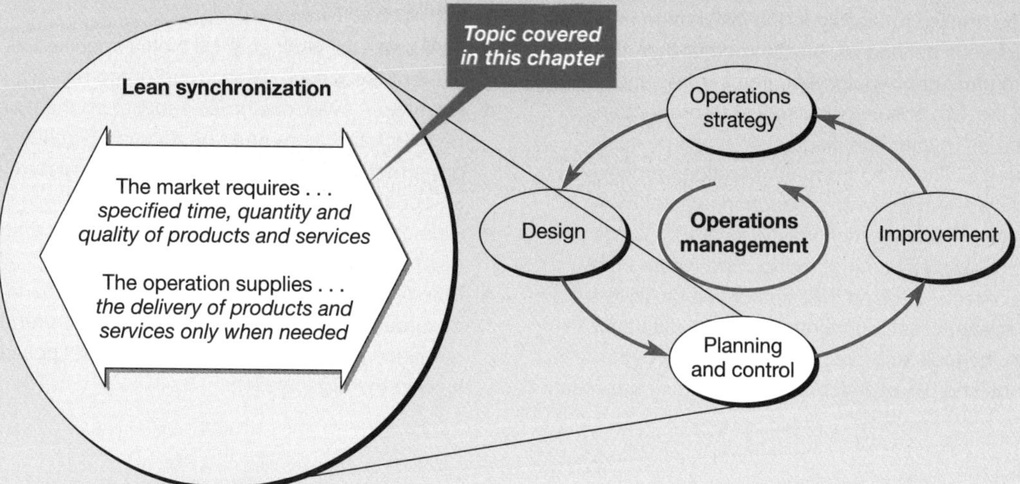

Figure 15.1 This chapter covers lean synchronization

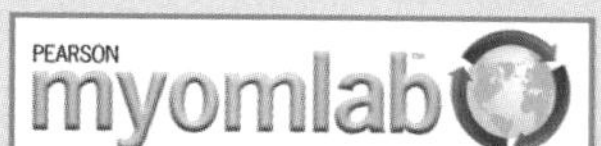

*Check and improve your understanding of this chapter using self assessment questions and a personalised study plan, audio and video downloads, and an eBook – all at **www.myomlab.com**.*

Operations in practice Toyota

Seen as the leading practitioner and the main originator of the lean approach, the Toyota Motor Company has progressively synchronized all its processes simultaneously to give high-quality, fast throughput and exceptional productivity. It has done this by developing a set of practices that has largely shaped what we now call 'lean' or 'just-in-time' but which Toyota calls the Toyota Production System (TPS). The TPS has two themes, 'just-in-time' and 'jidoka'. Just-in-time is defined as the rapid and coordinated movement of parts throughout the production system and supply network to meet customer demand. It is operationalized by means of *heijunka* (levelling and smoothing the flow of items), *kanban* (signalling to the preceding process that more parts are needed) and *nagare* (laying out processes to achieve smoother flow of parts throughout the production process). *Jidoka* is described as 'humanizing the interface between operator and machine'. Toyota's philosophy is that the machine is there to serve the operator's purpose. The operator should be left free to exercise his or her judgement. Jidoka is operationalized by means of fail-safeing (or machine jidoka), line-stop authority (or human jidoka) and visual control (at-a-glance status of production processes and visibility of process standards).

Toyota believes that both just-in-time and jidoka should be applied ruthlessly to the elimination of waste, where waste is defined as 'anything other than the minimum amount of equipment, items, parts and workers that are absolutely essential to production'. Fujio Cho of Toyota identified seven types of waste that must be eliminated from all operations processes. They are: waste from over-production, waste from waiting time, transportation waste, inventory waste, processing waste, waste of motion and waste from product defects. Beyond this, authorities on Toyota claim that its strength lies in understanding the differences between the tools and practices used with Toyota operations and the overall philosophy of their approach

Source: Corbis/Denis Balihouse

to lean synchronization. This is what some have called the apparent paradox of the Toyota production system: 'namely, that activities, connections and production flows in a Toyota factory are rigidly scripted, yet at the same time Toyota's operations are enormously flexible and adaptable. Activities and processes are constantly being challenged and pushed to a higher level of performance, enabling the company to continually innovate and improve.'

One influential study of Toyota identified four rules that guide the design, delivery, and development activities within the company.[1]

- *Rule one* – all work shall be highly specified as to content, sequence, timing, and outcome.
- *Rule two* – every customer–supplier connection must be direct and there must be an unambiguous yes or no method of sending requests and receiving responses.
- *Rule three* – the route for every product and service must be simple and direct.
- *Rule four* – any improvement must be made in accordance with the scientific method, under the guidance of a teacher, and at the lowest possible level in the organization.

What is lean synchronization?

Synchronization means that the flow of products and services always delivers exactly what customers want (perfect quality), in exact quantities (neither too much nor too little), exactly when needed (not too early or too late), and exactly where required (not to the wrong location). *Lean* synchronization is to do all this at the lowest possible cost. It results in items flowing rapidly and smoothly through processes, operations and supply networks.

The benefits of synchronized flow

When first introduced, the lean synchronization (or 'lean' or 'just-in-time') approach was relatively radical, even for large and sophisticated companies. Now the lean, just-in-time approach is being adopted outside its traditional automotive, high-volume and manufacturing roots. But wherever it is applied, the principles remain the same. The best way to understand how lean synchronization differs from more traditional approaches to managing flow is to contrast the two simple processes in Figure 15.2. The traditional approach assumes that each stage in the process will place its output in an inventory that 'buffers' that stage from the next one downstream in the process. The next stage down will then (eventually) take outputs from the inventory, process them, and pass them through to the next buffer inventory. These buffers are there to insulate each stage from its neighbours, making each stage relatively independent so that if, for example, stage A stops operating for some reason, stage B can continue, at least for a time. The larger the buffer inventory, the greater the degree of insulation between the stages. This insulation has to be paid for in terms of inventory and slow throughput times because items will spend time waiting in the buffer inventories.

But, the main argument against this traditional approach lies in the very conditions it seeks to promote, namely the insulation of the stages from one another. When a problem occurs at one stage, the problem will not immediately be apparent elsewhere in the system. The responsibility for solving the problem will be centred largely on the people within that stage, and the consequences of the problem will be prevented from spreading to the whole system. However, contrast this with the pure lean synchronized process illustrated in Figure 15.2.

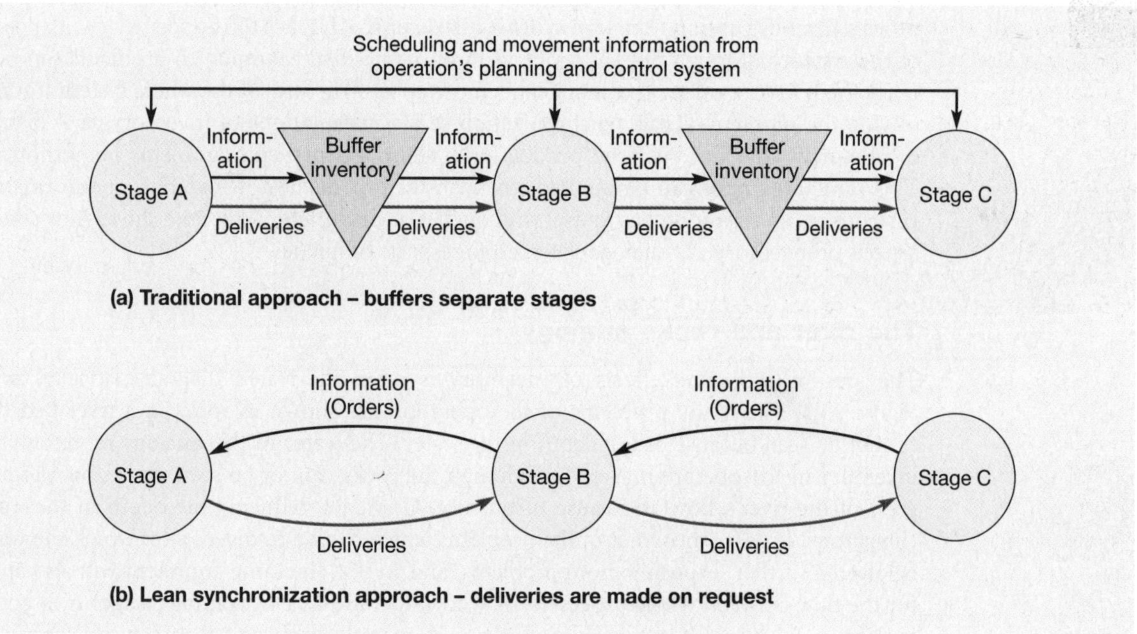

Figure 15.2 (a) Traditional and (b) lean synchronized flow between stages

Table 15.1 Inventories of materials, information or customers have similar characteristics

	Inventory		
	Of material (queue of material)	*Of information (queue of information)*	*Of customers (queue of people)*
Cost	Ties up working capital	Less current information and so worth less	Wastes customers' time
Space	Needs storage space	Needs memory capacity	Needs waiting area
Quality	Defects hidden, possible damage	Defects hidden, possible data corruption	Gives negative perception
De-coupling	Makes stages independent	Makes stages independent	Promotes job specialization / fragmentation
Utilization	Stages kept busy by work-in-progress	Stages kept busy by work in data queues	Servers kept busy by waiting customers
Coordination	Avoids need for synchronization	Avoids need for straight-through processing	Avoids having to match supply and demand

Source: Adapted from Fitzsimmons, J.A. (1990) Making continual improvement: a competitive strategy for service firms, *in* Bowen, D.E., Chase, R.B., Cummings, T.G. and Associates (eds) *Service Management Effectiveness*, Jossey-Bass.

Here items are processed and then passed directly to the next stage 'just-in-time' for them to be processed further. Problems at any stage have a very different effect in such a system. Now if stage A stops processing, stage B will notice immediately and stage C very soon after. Stage A's problem is now quickly exposed to the whole process, which is immediately affected by the problem. This means that the responsibility for solving the problem is no longer confined to the staff at stage A. It is now shared by everyone, considerably improving the chances of the problem being solved, if only because it is now too important to be ignored. In other words, by preventing items accumulating between stages, the operation has increased the chances of the intrinsic efficiency of the plant being improved.

Non-synchronized approaches seek to encourage efficiency by protecting each part of the process from disruption. The lean synchronized approach takes the opposite view. Exposure of the system (although not suddenly, as in our simplified example) to problems can both make them more evident and change the 'motivation structure' of the whole system towards solving the problems. Lean synchronization sees accumulations of inventory as a 'blanket of obscurity' that lies over the production system and prevents problems being noticed. This same argument can be applied when, instead of queues of material, or information (inventory), an operation has to deal with queues of customers. Table 15.1 shows how certain aspects of inventory are analogous to certain aspects of queues.

The river and rocks analogy

The idea of obscuring effects of inventory is often illustrated diagrammatically, as in Figure 15.3. The many problems of the operation are shown as rocks in a river bed that cannot be seen because of the depth of the water. The water in this analogy represents the inventory in the operation. Yet, even though the rocks cannot be seen, they slow the progress of the river's flow and cause turbulence. Gradually reducing the depth of the water (inventory) exposes the worst of the problems which can be resolved, after which the water is lowered further, exposing more problems, and so on. The same argument will also apply for the flow between whole processes, or whole operations. For example, stages A, B and C in Figure 15.2 could be a supplier operation, a manufacturer and a customer's operation, respectively.

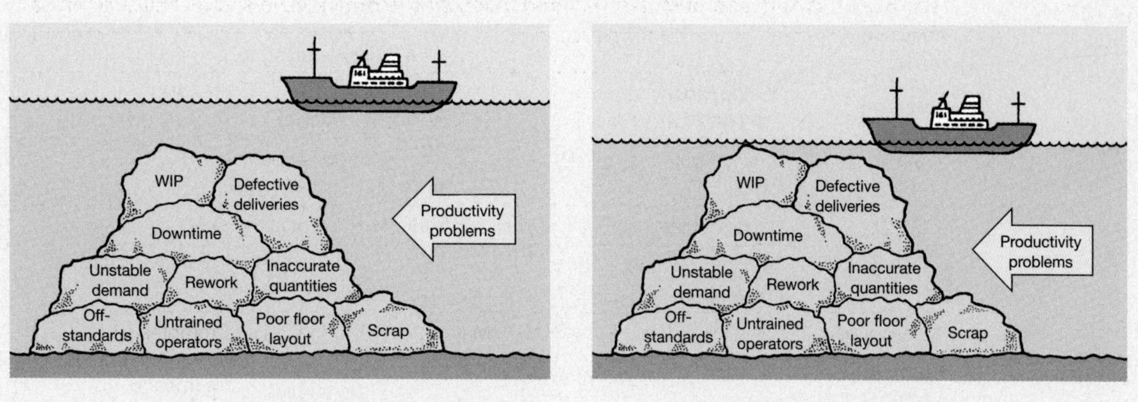

Figure 15.3 Reducing the level of inventory (water) allows operations management (the ship) to see the problems in the operation (the rocks) and work to reduce them

Synchronization, 'lean' and 'just-in-time'

Different terms are used to describe what here we call 'lean synchronization'. Our definition – '*lean synchronization aims to meet demand instantaneously, with perfect quality and no waste*' – could also be used to describe the general concept of 'lean', or 'just-in-time' (JIT). The concept of 'lean' stresses the elimination of waste, while 'just-in-time' emphasizes the idea of producing items only when they are needed. But all three concepts overlap to a large degree, and no definition fully conveys the full implications for operations practice. Here we use the term 'lean synchronization' because it best describes the impact of these ideas on flow and delivery.

Lean synchronization and capacity utilization

Lean synchronization has many benefits but these come at the cost of capacity utilization. Return to the process shown in Figure 15.2. When stoppages occur in the traditional system, the buffers allow each stage to continue working and thus achieve high-capacity utilization. The high utilization does not necessarily make the process as a whole produce more. Often extra 'production' goes into buffer inventories. In a lean process, any stoppage will affect the whole process. This will necessarily lead to lower-capacity utilization, at least in the short term. However, there is no point in producing output just for its own sake. Unless the output is useful and causes the operation as a whole to produce saleable products, there is no point in producing it anyway. In fact, producing just to keep utilization high is not only pointless, it is counter-productive, because the extra inventory produced merely serves to make improvements less likely. Figure 15.4 illustrates the two approaches to capacity utilization.

The lean philosophy

Terminology in this area is sometimes a little confusing and has evolved over time, as mentioned previously. To make things more complicated, lean synchronization can be viewed as a broad philosophy of operations management, a set of useful prescriptions of how to manage day-to-day operations, and a collection of tools and techniques for improving operations performance. Some of these tools and techniques are well known outside the lean sphere and relate to activities covered in other chapters of this book. As a philosophy, lean synchronization is founded on smoothing flow through processes by doing all the simple things well, on gradually doing them better and (above all) on squeezing out waste every step of the way. Three key issues define the lean philosophy, the involvement of staff in the operation, the drive for continuous improvement, and the elimination of waste.[2] We will look at the first two issues briefly, but devote a whole section to the central idea of the elimination of waste.

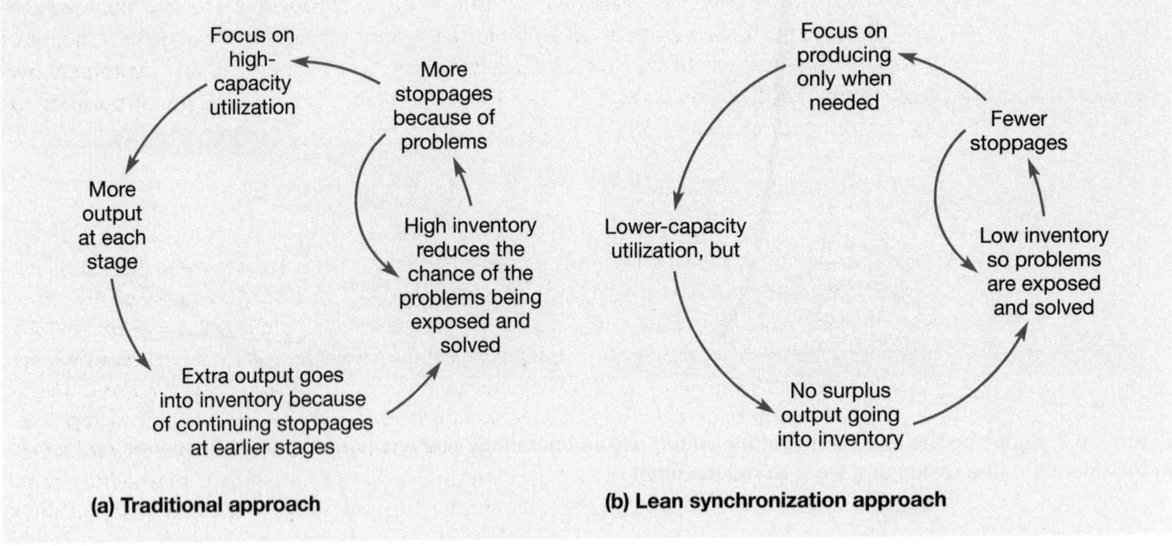

Figure 15.4 The different views of capacity utilization in (a) traditional and (b) JIT approaches to operations

The involvement of everyone

Lean philosophy is often put forward as a 'total' system. Its aim is to provide guidelines which embrace everyone and every process in the organization. An organization's culture is seen as being important in supporting these objectives through an emphasis on involving all of the organization's staff. This new culture is sometimes seen as synonymous with 'total quality' and is discussed in detail in Chapter 17. The lean approach to people management has also been called the **respect-for-humans** system. It encourages (and often requires) team-based problem-solving, job enrichment (by including maintenance and set-up tasks in operators' jobs), job rotation and multi-skilling. The intention is to encourage a high degree of personal responsibility, engagement and 'ownership' of the job.

Respect for humans

What are called **basic working practices** are sometimes used to implement the 'involvement of everyone' principle. They include the following:

Basic working practices

- *Discipline*. Work standards which are critical for the safety of company members and the environment, and for the quality of the product, must be followed by everyone all the time.
- *Flexibility*. It should be possible to expand responsibilities to the extent of people's capabilities. This applies as equally to managers as it does to shop-floor personnel. Barriers to flexibility, such as grading structures and restrictive practices, should be removed.
- *Equality*. Unfair and divisive personnel policies should be discarded. Many companies implement the egalitarian message through to company uniforms, consistent pay structures which do not differentiate between full-time staff and hourly rated staff, and open-plan offices.
- *Autonomy*. Delegate increasing responsibility to people involved in direct activities of the business, so that management's task becomes one of supporting the shop floor. Delegation means such things as giving direct-line staff the responsibility for stopping processes in the event of problems, scheduling work and materials arrival, gathering performance monitoring data, and general problem-solving.
- *Development of personnel*. Over time, the aim is to create more company members who can support the rigours of being competitive.
- *Quality of working life (QWL)*. This may include, for example, involvement in decision-making, security of employment, enjoyment and working area facilities.
- *Creativity*. This is one of the indispensable elements of motivation. Most of us enjoy not just doing the job successfully, but also improving it for the next time.

- *Total people involvement.* Staff take on much more responsibility to use their abilities to the benefit of the company as a whole. They are expected to participate in activities such as the selection of new recruits, dealing directly with suppliers and customers over schedules, quality issues and delivery information, spending improvement budgets and planning and reviewing work done each day through communication meetings.

Critical commentary

Not all commentators see JIT-influenced people-management practices as entirely positive. The JIT approach to people management can be viewed as patronizing. It may be, to some extent, less autocratic than some Japanese management practice dating from earlier times. However, it is certainly not in line with some of the job design philosophies which place a high emphasis on contribution and commitment, described in Chapter 9. Even in Japan the approach of JIT is not without its critics. Kamata wrote an autobiographical description of life as an employee at a Toyota plant called *Japan in the Passing Lane*.[3] His account speaks of 'the inhumanity and the unquestioning adherence' of working under such a system. Similar criticisms have been voiced by some trade union representatives.

Continuous improvement

Kaizen

Lean objectives are often expressed as ideals, such as our definition: 'to meet demand instantaneously with perfect quality and no waste'. While any operation's current performance may be far removed from such ideals, a fundamental lean belief is that it is possible to get closer to them over time. Without such beliefs to drive progress, lean proponents claim improvement is more likely to be transitory than continuous. This is why the concept of continuous improvement is such an important part of the lean philosophy. If its aims are set in terms of ideals which individual organizations may never fully achieve, then the emphasis must be on the way in which an organization moves closer to the ideal state. The Japanese word for continuous improvement is **kaizen**, and it is a key part of the lean philosophy. It is explained fully in Chapters 18 and 20.

Eliminate waste

The elimination of waste is central to lean approaches

Arguably the most significant part of the lean philosophy is its focus on the **elimination of all forms of waste.** Waste can be defined as any activity that does not add value. For example, studies often show that as little as 5 per cent of total throughput time is actually spent directly adding value. This means that for 95 per cent of its time, an operation is adding cost to the product or service, not adding value. Such calculations can alert even relatively efficient operations to the enormous waste which is dormant within all operations. This same phenomenon applies as much to service processes as it does to manufacturing ones. Relatively simple requests, such as applying for a driving licence, may only take a few minutes to actually process, yet take days (or weeks) to be returned.

The seven types of waste

The seven types of waste

Identifying waste is the first step towards eliminating it. Toyota have identified **seven types of waste**, which have been found to apply in many different types of operations – both service and production – and which form the core of lean philosophy:

1 *Over-production.* Producing more than is immediately needed by the next process in the operation is the greatest source of waste according to Toyota.

2 *Waiting time.* Equipment efficiency and labour efficiency are two popular measures which are widely used to measure equipment and labour waiting time, respectively. Less obvious is the amount of waiting time of items, disguised by operators who are kept busy producing WIP which is not needed at the time.
3 *Transport.* Moving items around the operation, together with the double and triple handling of WIP, does not add value. Layout changes which bring processes closer together, improvements in transport methods and workplace organization can all reduce waste.
4 *Process.* The process itself may be a source of waste. Some operations may only exist because of poor component design, or poor maintenance, and so could be eliminated.
5 *Inventory.* All inventory should become a target for elimination. However, it is only by tackling the causes of inventory that it can be reduced.
6 *Motion.* An operator may look busy but sometimes no value is being added by the work. Simplification of work is a rich source of reduction in the waste of motion.
7 *Defectives.* Quality waste is often very significant in operations. Total costs of quality are much greater than has traditionally been considered, and it is therefore more important to attack the causes of such costs. This is discussed further in Chapter 17.

Between them, these seven types of waste contribute to four barriers to any operation achieving lean synchronization. They are: waste from irregular (non-streamlined) flow, waste from inexact supply, waste from inflexible response, and waste from variability. We will examine each of these barriers to achieving lean synchronization.

Eliminate waste through streamlined flow

The smooth flow of materials, information and people in the operation is a central idea of lean synchronization. Long process routes provide opportunities for delay and inventory build-up, add no value, and slow down throughput time. So, the first contribution any operation can make to streamlining flow is to reconsider the basic layout of its processes. Primarily, reconfiguring the layout of a process to aid lean synchronization involves moving it down the 'natural diagonal' of process design that was discussed in Chapter 4. Broadly speaking, this means moving from functional layouts towards cell-based layouts, or from cell-based layouts towards product layouts. Either way, it is necessary to move towards a layout that brings more systematization and control to the process flow. At a more detailed level, typical layout techniques include: placing workstations close together so that inventory physically just cannot build up because there is no space for it to do so, and arranging workstations in such a way that all those who contribute to a common activity are in sight of each other and can provide mutual help, for example by facilitating movement between workstations to balance capacity.

Examine all elements of throughput time

Throughput time is often taken as a surrogate measure for waste in a process. The longer that items being processed are held in inventory, moved, checked, or subject to anything else that does not add value, the longer they take to progress through the process. So, looking at exactly what happens to items within a process is an excellent method of identifying sources of waste.

Value stream mapping

Value stream mapping (also known as 'end-to-end' system mapping) is a simple but effective approach to understanding the flow of material and information as a product or service has value added as it progresses through a process, operation, or supply chain. It visually maps a product or services 'production' path from start to finish. In doing so it records, not only the direct activities of creating products and services, but also the 'indirect' information systems that support the direct process. It is called 'value stream' mapping because it focuses on value-adding activities and distinguishes between value-adding and non-value-adding activities. It is similar to process mapping (see Chapter 4) but different in four ways:

- It uses a broader range of information than most process maps.
- It is usually at a higher level (5–10 activities) than most process maps.
- It often has a wider scope, frequently spanning the whole supply chain.
- It can be used to identify where to focus future improvement activities.

A value stream perspective involves working on (and improving) the 'big picture', rather than just optimizing individual processes. Value stream mapping is seen by many practitioners as a starting point to help recognize waste and identify its causes. It is a four-step technique that identifies waste and suggests ways in which activities can be streamlined. First, it involves identifying the value stream (the process, operation or supply chain) to map. Second, it involves physically mapping a process, then above it mapping the information flow that enables the process to occur. This is the so-called 'current state' map. Third, problems are diagnosed and changes suggested, making a future state map that represents the improved process, operation or supply chain. Finally, the changes are implemented. Figure 15.5 shows a value stream map for an industrial air conditioning installation service. The service process itself is broken down into five relatively large stages and various items of data for each stage are marked on the chart. The type of data collected here does vary, but all types of value stream map compare the total throughput time with the amount of value-added time within the larger process. In this case, only 8 of the 258 hours of the process is value-adding.

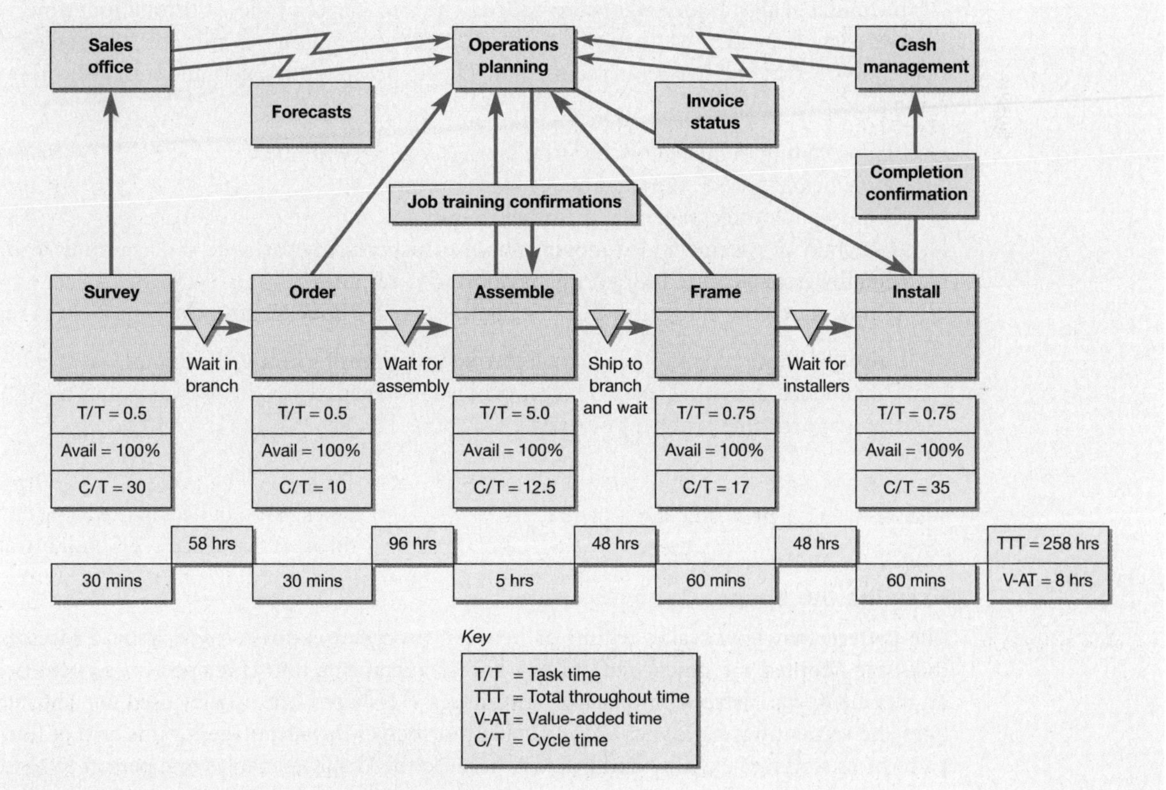

Figure 15.5 Value stream map for an industrial air conditioning installation service

Worked example[4]

An ordinary flight, just a trip to Amsterdam for two or three days. Breakfast was a little rushed but left the house at 6.15. Had to return a few minutes later, forgot my passport. Managed to find it and leave (again) by 6.30. Arrived at the airport 7.00, dropped Angela off with bags at terminal and went to the long-term car park. Eventually found a parking space after 10 minutes. Waited 8 minutes for the courtesy bus. Six minute journey back to the terminal, we start queuing at the check-in counters by 7.24. Twenty minute wait. Eventually get to check-in and find that we have been allocated seats at different ends of the plane. Staff helpful but takes 8 minutes to sort it out. Wait in queue for security checks for 10 minutes. Security decide I look suspicious and search bags for 3 minutes. Waiting in lounge by 8.05. Spend 1 hour and 5 minutes in lounge reading computer magazine and looking at small plastic souvenirs. Hurrah, flight is called 9.10, takes 2 minutes to rush to the gate and queue for further 5 minutes at gate. Through the gate and on to air bridge which is continuous queue going onto plane, takes 4 minutes but finally in seats by 9.21. Wait for plane to fill up with other passengers for 14 minutes. Plane starts to taxi to runway at 9.35. Plane queues to take-off for 10 minutes. Plan takes off 9.45. Smooth flight to Amsterdam, 55 minutes. Stacked in queue of planes waiting to land for 10 minutes. Touch down at Schipol Airport 10.50. Taxi to terminal and wait 15 minutes to disembark. Disembark at 11.05 and walk to luggage collection (calling at lavatory on way), arrive luggage collection 11.15. Wait for luggage 8 minutes. Through customs (not searched by Netherlands security who decide I look trustworthy) and to taxi rank by 11.26. Wait for taxi 4 minutes. In to taxi by 11.30, 30 minutes ride into Amsterdam. Arrive hotel 12.00.

Analysis

How much of all this time was value-added? The total elapsed time, or throughput time, for the whole process was between 6.15 and 12.00, i.e. 5 hours 45 minutes. A detailed analysis of what was happening to the items being processed (Angela and me) indicates the following breakdown.

Time waiting in queue for check-in, luggage, etc. = 59 minutes
Time being 'served' at end of queue = 11 minutes
Waiting in lounge/plane etc. = 1 hour 55 minutes
Generally non-value-added moving about in airports, car parks etc. = 31 minutes
Quality error because I forgot my passport = 15 minutes
Value-added travelling time in car + plane + taxi = 1 hour 55 minutes.

So, only 1 hour 55 minutes of a total throughput time of 5 hours 45 minutes was spent in value-added activity. That is, 33.3 per cent value-added. Note, this was a smooth flight with no appreciable problems or delays.

Examine the shape of process flow

The pattern that flow makes within or between processes is not a trivial issue. Processes that have adopted the practice of curving line arrangements into U-shaped or 'serpentine' arrangements can have a number of advantages (U shapes are usually used for shorter lines and serpentines for longer lines). One authority sees the advantages of this type of flow patterns as staffing flexibility and balance, because the U shape enables one person to tend several pieces of work, rework, because it is easy to return faulty work to an earlier station, free flow, because long straight lines interfere with cross-travel in the rest of the operation, and teamwork, because the shape encourages a team feeling.

Ensure visibility

Appropriate layout also includes the extent to which all movement is transparent to everyone within the process. High visibility of flow makes it easier to recognize potential improvements to flow. It also promotes quality within a process because the more transparent the operation or process, the easier it is for all staff to share in its management and improvement. Problems are more easily detectable and information becomes simple, fast and visual. Visibility measures include the following.

- Clearly indicated process routes using signage.
- Performance measures clearly displayed in the workplace.
- Coloured lights used to indicate stoppages.
- An area is devoted to displaying samples of one's own and competitors' process outputs, together with samples of good and defective output.
- Visual control systems (e.g. kanbans, discussed later).

An important technique used to ensure flow visibility is the use of simple, but highly visual signals to indicate that a problem has occurred, together with operational authority to stop the process. For example, on an assembly line, if an employee detects some kind of quality problem, he or she could activate a signal that illuminates a light (called an 'andon' light) above the workstation and stops the line. Although this may seem to reduce the efficiency of the line, the idea is that this loss of efficiency in the short term is less than the accumulated losses of allowing defects to continue on in the process. Unless problems are tackled immediately, they may never be corrected.

Use small-scale simple process technology

There may also be possibilities to encourage smooth streamlined flow through the use of small-scale technologies. That is, using several small units of process technology (for example, machines), rather than one large unit. Small machines have several advantages over large ones. First, they can process different products and services simultaneously. For example, in Figure 15.6 one large machine produces a batch of A, followed by a batch of B, and followed by a batch of C. However, if three smaller machines are used they can each producc A, B or C simultaneously. The system is also more robust. If one large machine breaks down, the whole system ceases to operate. If one of the three smaller machines breaks down, it is still operating at two-thirds effectiveness. Small machines are also easily moved, so that layout flexibility is enhanced, and the risks of making errors in investment decisions are reduced. However, investment in capacity may increase in total because parallel facilities are needed, so utilization may be lower (see the earlier arguments).

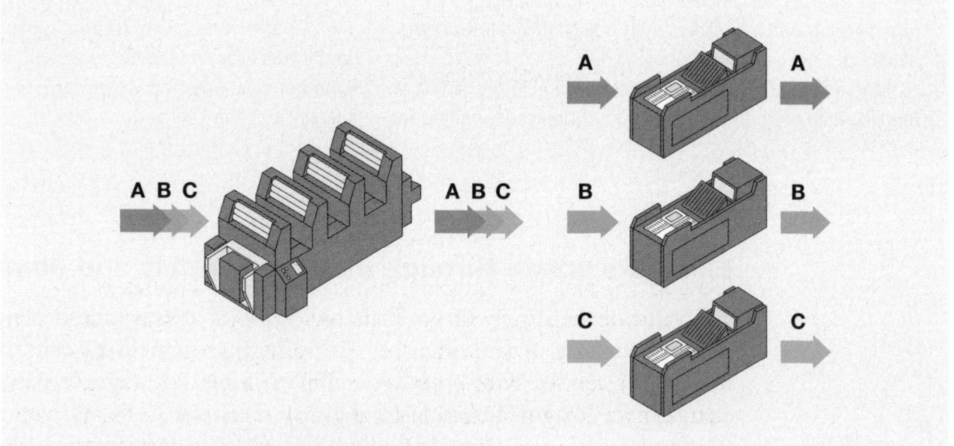

Figure 15.6 Using several small machines rather than one large one, allows simultaneous processing, is more robust, and is more flexible

Short case
Lean hospitals[5]

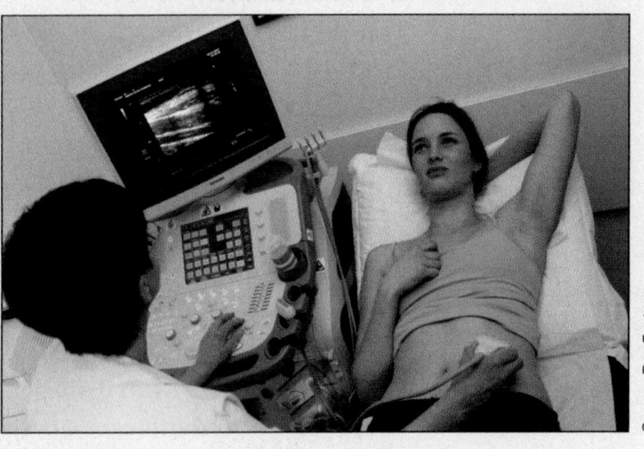
Source: Rex Features

One of the increasing number of health-care services to adopt lean principles, the Bolton Hospitals National Health Service Trust in the north of England, has reduced its hospitals' mortality rate in one injury by more than a third. David Fillingham, chief executive of Bolton Hospitals NHS Trust said, '*We had far more people dying from fractured hips than should have been dying.*' Then the trust greatly reduced its mortality rate for fractured neck of femur by redesigning the patient's stay in hospital to reduce or remove the waits between 'useful activity'. The mortality rate fell from 22.9% to 14.6%, which is the equivalent of 14 more patients surviving every six months. At the same time, average length of stay fell by a third from 34.6 days to 23.5 days. The trust held five 'rapid improvement events', involving employees from across the organization who spent several days examining processes and identifying alternative ways how to improve them. Some management consultants were also used but strictly in an advisory role. In addition third-party experts were brought in. These included staff from the Royal Air Force, who had been applying lean principles to running aircraft carriers. The value of these outsiders was not only their expertise, '*They asked all sorts of innocent, naïve questions*', said Mr Fillingham, '*to which, often, no member of staff has an answer.*' Other lean-based improvement initiatives included examining the patient's whole experience from start to finish so that delays (some of which could prove fatal) could be removed on their journey to the operating theatre, radiology process were speeded up and unnecessary paperwork was eliminated. Cutting the length of stay and reducing process complications should also start to reduce costs, although Mr Fillingham says that it could take several years for the savings to become substantial. Not only that, but staff are also said to be helped by the changes because they can spend more time helping patients rather than doing non-value-added activities.

Meanwhile at Salisbury district hospital in the south of the UK, lean principles have reduced delays in waiting for the results of tests from the ultrasound department. Waiting lists have been reduced from 12 weeks to between 2 weeks and zero after an investigation showed that 67% of demand was coming from just 5% of possible ultrasound tests: abdominal, gynaecological and urological. So all work was streamed into routine 'green' streams and complex 'red' ones. This is like having different traffic lanes on a motorway dedicated to different types of traffic with fast cars in one lane and slow trucks in another. Mixing both types of work is like mixing fast cars and slow-moving trucks in all lanes. The department then concentrated on doing the routine 'green' work more efficiently. For example, the initial date scan used to check the age of a foetus took only two minutes, so a series of five-minute slots were allocated just for these. '*The secret is to get the steady stream of high-volume, low-variety chugging down the ultrasound motorway*', says Kate Hobson, who runs the department. Streaming routine work in this way has left more time to deal with the more complex jobs, yet staff are not overloaded. They are more likely to leave work on time and also believe that the department is doing a better job, all of which has improved morale says Kate Hobson, '*I think people feel their day is more structured now. It's not that madness, opening the doors and people coming at you.*' Nor has this more disciplined approach impaired the department's ability to treat really urgent jobs. In fact it has stopped leaving space in its schedule for emergencies – the, now standard, short waiting time is usually sufficient for urgent jobs.

Eliminate waste through matching supply and demand exactly

The value of the supply of products or services is always time-dependent. Something that is delivered early or late often has less value than something delivered exactly when it is needed. We can see many everyday examples of this. For example, parcel delivery companies charge more for guaranteed faster delivery. This is because our real need for the delivery is often for it to be as fast as possible. The closer to instantaneous delivery we can get the more value the delivery has for us and the more we are willing to pay for it. In fact delivery of information earlier than it is required can be even more harmful than late delivery because it results in information inventories that serve to confuse flow through the process. For example, an Australian tax office used to receive applications by mail, open the mail and send it through to the relevant department which, after processing it, sent it to the next department. This led to piles of unprocessed applications building up within its processes, causing problems in tracing applications, and losing them, sorting through and prioritizing applications, and worst of all, long throughput times. Now they only open mail when the stages in front can process it. Each department requests more work only when they have processed previous work.

Pull control

The exact matching of supply and demand is often best served by using 'pull control' wherever possible (discussed in Chapter 10). At its simplest, consider how some fast-food restaurants cook and assemble food and place it in the warm area only when the customer-facing server has sold an item. Production is being triggered only by real customer demand. Similarly supermarkets usually replenish their shelves only when customers have taken sufficient products off the shelf. The movement of goods from the 'back-office' store to the shelf is triggered only by the 'empty-shelf' demand signal. Some construction companies make it a rule to call for material deliveries to their sites, only the day before those items are actually needed. This not only reduces clutter and the chances of theft, it speeds up throughput time and reduces confusion and inventories. The essence of pull control is to let the downstream stage in a process, operation, or supply network, pull items through the system rather than have them 'pushed' to them by the supplying stage. As Richard Hall, an authority on lean operations put it, '*Don't send nothing nowhere, make 'em come and get it.*'[6]

Kanbans

The use of kanbans is one method of operationalizing pull control. Kanban is the Japanese for card or signal. It is sometimes called the 'invisible conveyor' that controls the transfer of items between the stages of an operation. In its simplest form, it is a card used by a customer stage to instruct its supplier stage to send more items. Kanbans can also take other forms. In some Japanese companies, they are solid plastic markers or even coloured ping-pong balls. Whichever kind of kanban is being used, the principle is always the same: the receipt of a kanban triggers the movement, production or supply of one unit or a standard container of units. If two kanbans are received, this triggers the movement, production or supply of two units or standard containers of units, and so on. Kanbans are the only means by which movement, production or supply can be authorized. Some companies use 'kanban squares'. These are marked spaces on the shop floor or bench that are drawn to fit one or more work pieces or containers. Only the existence of an empty square triggers production at the stage that supplies the square. As one would expect, at Toyota the key control tool is its kanban system. The kanban is seen as serving three purposes:

- It is an instruction for the preceding process to send more.
- It is a visual control tool to show up areas of over-production and lack of synchronization.
- It is a tool for kaizen (continuous improvement). Toyota's rules state that 'the number of kanbans should be reduced over time'.

The single-card system

There are a number of methods of using kanbans, of which the 'single-card system' is most often used because it is by far the simplest system to operate. Figure 15.7 shows the operation of a single-card kanban system. At each stage (only two stages are shown, A and B) there is a work centre and an area for holding inventory. All production and inventory are contained in standard containers, all of which contain exactly the same number of parts. When stage B requires some more parts to work on, it withdraws a standard container from the output stock point of stage A. After work centre B has used the parts in the container, it places the move kanban in a holding area and sends the empty container to the work centre at stage A.

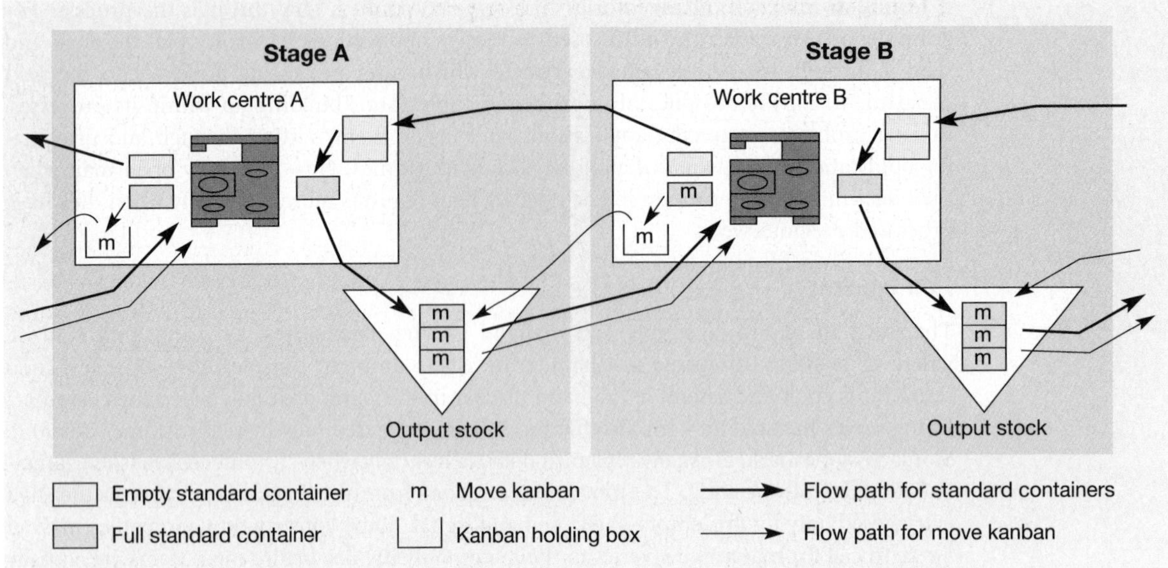

Figure 15.7 The operation of the single-card kanban system of pull control

The arrival of the empty containers at stage A's work centre is the signal for production to take place at work centre A. The move kanban is taken from the holding box back to the output stock point of stage A. This acts as authorization for the collection of a further full container to be moved from the output stock of stage A through to the work centre at stage B. Two closed loops effectively control the flow of materials between the stages. The move kanban loop (illustrated by the thin arrows) keeps materials circulating between the stages, and the container loop (illustrated by the thicker arrows) connects the work centres with the stock point between them and circulates the containers, full from A to B and empty back from B to A. This sequence of actions and the flow of kanbans may at first seem complicated. However, in practice their use provides a straightforward and transparent method of calling for material only when it is needed and limiting the inventory which accumulates between stages. The number of kanbans put into the loops between the stages or between the stock points and the work centres is equal to the number of containers in the system and therefore the inventory which can accumulate. Taking a kanban out of the loop has the effect of reducing the inventory.

Critical commentary

Just-in-time principles can be taken to an extreme. When just-in-time ideas first started to have an impact on operations practice in the West, some authorities advocated the reduction of between-process inventories to zero. While in the long term this provides the ultimate in motivation for operations managers to ensure the efficiency and reliability of each process stage, it does not admit the possibility of some processes always being intrinsically less than totally reliable. An alternative view is to allow inventories (albeit small ones) around process stages with higher than average uncertainty. This at least allows some protection for the rest of the system. The same ideas apply to just-in-time delivery between factories. The Toyota Motor Corp., often seen as the epitome of modern JIT, has suffered from its low inter-plant inventory policies. Both the Kobe earthquake and fires in supplier plants have caused production at Toyota's main factories to close down for several days because of a shortage of key parts. Even in the best-regulated networks, one cannot always account for such events.

Eliminate waste through flexible processes

Responding exactly and instantaneously to customer demand implies that operations resources need to be sufficiently flexible to change both what they do and how much they do of it without incurring high cost or long delays. In fact, flexible processes (often with flexible technologies) can significantly enhance smooth and synchronized flow. For example, new publishing technologies allow professors to assemble printed and e-learning course material customized to the needs of individual courses or even individual students. In this case flexibility is allowing customized, small batches to be delivered 'to order'. In another example, a firm of lawyers used to take ten days to prepare its bills for customers. This meant that customers were not asked to pay until ten days after the work had been done. Now they use a system that, every day, updates each customer's account. So, when a bill is sent it includes all work up to the day before the billing date. The principle here is that process inflexibility also delays cash flow.

Reduce set-up times

For many technologies, increasing process flexibility, means reducing set-up times; defined as the time taken to change over the process from one activity to the next. Compare the time it takes you to change the tyre on your car with the time taken by a Formula 1 team. Set-up reduction can be achieved by a variety of methods such as cutting out time taken to search for tools and equipment, the pre-preparation of tasks which delay changeovers, and the constant practice of set-up routines. Set-up time reduction is also called single-minute exchange of dies (SMED), because this was the objective in some manufacturing operations. The other common approach to set up time reduction is to convert work which was previously performed while the machine was stopped (called internal work) to work that is performed while the machine is running (called external work). There are three major methods of achieving the transfer of internal set-up work to external work:[7]

- Pre-prepare equipment instead of having to do it while the process is stopped. Preferably, all adjustment should be carried out externally.
- Make equipment capable of performing all required tasks so that changeovers become a simple adjustment.
- Facilitate the change of equipment, for example by using simple devices such as roller conveyors.

Fast changeovers are particularly important for airlines because they can't make money from aircraft that are sitting idle on the ground. It is called 'running the aircraft hot' in the industry. For many smaller airlines, the biggest barrier to running hot is that their markets are not large enough to justify passenger flights during the day and night. So, in order to avoid aircraft being idle over night, they must be used in some other way. That was the motive behind Boeing's 737 'Quick Change' (QC) aircraft. With it, airlines have the flexibility to use it for passenger flights during the day and, with less than a one-hour changeover (set-up) time, use it as a cargo aircraft throughout the night. Boeing engineers designed frames that hold entire rows of seats that could smoothly glide on and off the aircraft, allowing twelve seats to be rolled into place at once. When used for cargo, the seats are simply rolled out and replaced by special cargo containers designed to fit the curve of the fuselage and prevent damage to the interior. Before reinstalling the seats the sidewalls are thoroughly cleaned so that, once the seats are in place, passengers cannot tell the difference between a QC aircraft and a normal 737. Some airlines particularly value the aircraft's flexibility. It allows them to provide frequent reliable services in both passenger and cargo markets. So the aircraft that has been carrying passengers during the day can be used to ship freight during the night.

Eliminate waste through minimizing variability

One of the biggest causes of the variability that will disrupt flow and prevent lean synchronization is variation in the quality of items. This is why a discussion of lean synchronization should always include an evaluation of how quality conformance is ensured within processes.

In particular, the principles of statistical process control (SPC) can be used to understand quality variability. Chapter 17 and its supplement on SPC examine this subject, so in this section we shall focus on other causes of variability. The first of these is variability in the mix of products and services moving through processes, operations, or supply networks.

Level schedules as much as possible

Levelled scheduling (or heijunka) means keeping the mix and volume of flow between stages even over time. For example, instead of producing 500 parts in one batch, which would cover the needs for the next three months, levelled scheduling would require the process to make only one piece per hour regularly. Thus, the principle of levelled scheduling is very straightforward; however, the requirements to put it into practice are quite severe, although the benefits resulting from it can be substantial. The move from conventional to levelled scheduling is illustrated in Figure 15.8. Conventionally, if a mix of products were required in a time period (usually a month), a batch size would be calculated for each product and the batches produced in some sequence. Figure 15.8(a) shows three products that are produced in a 20-day time period in a production unit.

Quantity of product A required = 3,000
Quantity of product B required = 1,000
Quantity of product C required = 1,000

Batch size of product A = 600
Batch size of product B = 200
Batch size of product C = 200

Starting at day 1, the unit commences producing product A. During day 3, the batch of 600 As is finished and dispatched to the next stage. The batch of Bs is started but is not finished until day 4. The remainder of day 4 is spent making the batch of Cs and both batches are

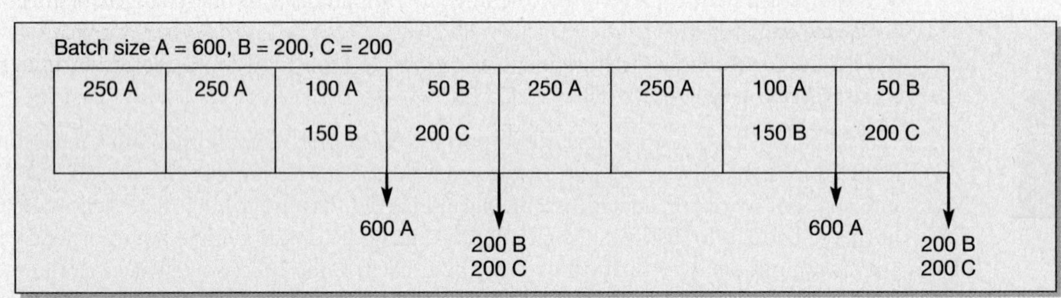

(a) Scheduling in large batches

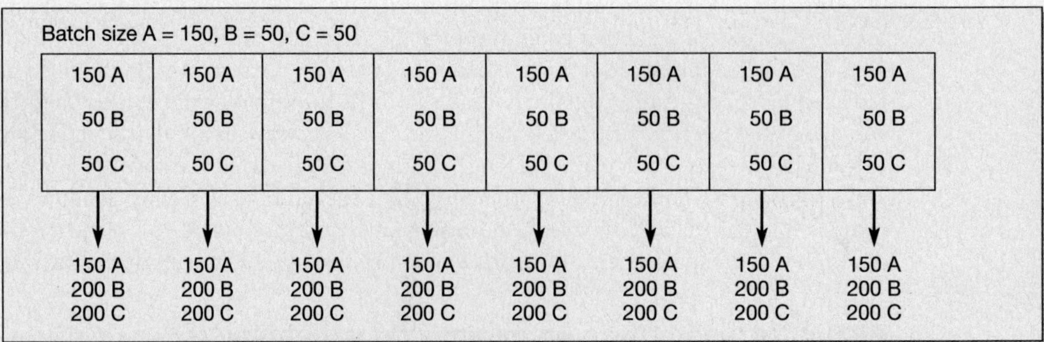

(b) Levelled scheduling

Figure 15.8 Levelled scheduling equalizes the mix of products made each day

dispatched at the end of that day. The cycle then repeats itself. The consequence of using large batches is, first, that relatively large amounts of inventory accumulate within and between the units, and second, that most days are different from one another in terms of what they are expected to produce (in more complex circumstances, no two days would be the same).

Now suppose that the flexibility of the unit could be increased to the point where the batch sizes for the products were reduced to a quarter of their previous levels without loss of capacity (see Fig. 15.8(b)):

Batch size of product A = 150
Batch size of product B = 50
Batch size of product C = 50

A batch of each product can now be completed in a single day, at the end of which the three batches are dispatched to their next stage. Smaller batches of inventory are moving between each stage, which will reduce the overall level of work-in-progress in the operation. Just as significant, however, is the effect on the regularity and rhythm of production at the unit. Now every day in the month is the same in terms of what needs to be produced. This makes planning and control of each stage in the operation much easier. For example, if on day 1 of the month the daily batch of As was finished by 11.00 am, and all the batches were successfully completed in the day, then the following day the unit will know that, if it again completes all the As by 11.00 am, it is on schedule. When every day is different, the simple question 'Are we on schedule to complete our production today?' requires some investigation before it can be answered. However, when every day is the same, everyone in the unit can tell whether production is on target by looking at the clock. Control becomes visible and transparent to all, and the advantages of regular, daily schedules can be passed to upstream suppliers.

Level delivery schedules

A similar concept to levelled scheduling can be applied to many transportation processes. For example, a chain of convenience stores may need to make deliveries of all the different types of products it sells every week. Traditionally it may have dispatched a truck loaded with one particular product around all its stores so that each store received the appropriate amount of the product that would last them for one week. This is equivalent to the large batches discussed in the previous example. An alternative would be to dispatch smaller quantities of all products in a single truck more frequently. Then, each store would receive smaller deliveries more frequently, inventory levels would be lower and the system could respond to trends in demand more readily because more deliveries means more opportunity to change the quantity delivered to a store. This is illustrated in Figure 15.9.

Adopt mixed modelling where possible

The principle of levelled scheduling can be taken further to give mixed modelling; that is, a repeated mix of outputs. Suppose that the machines in the production unit can be made so flexible that they achieve the JIT ideal of a batch size of one. The sequence of

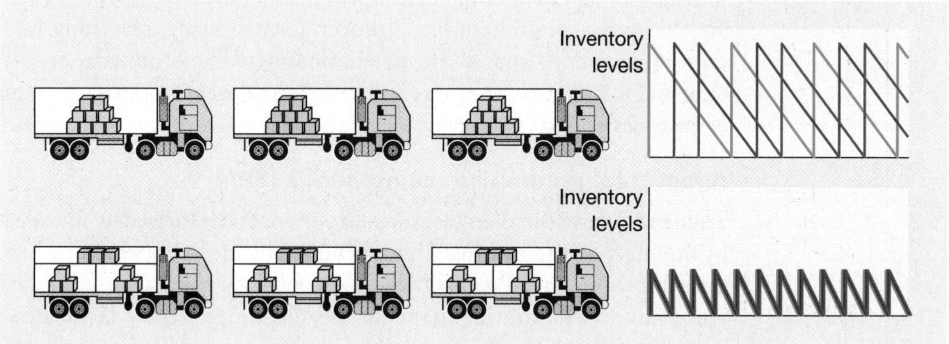

Figure 15.9 Delivering smaller quantities more often can reduce inventory levels

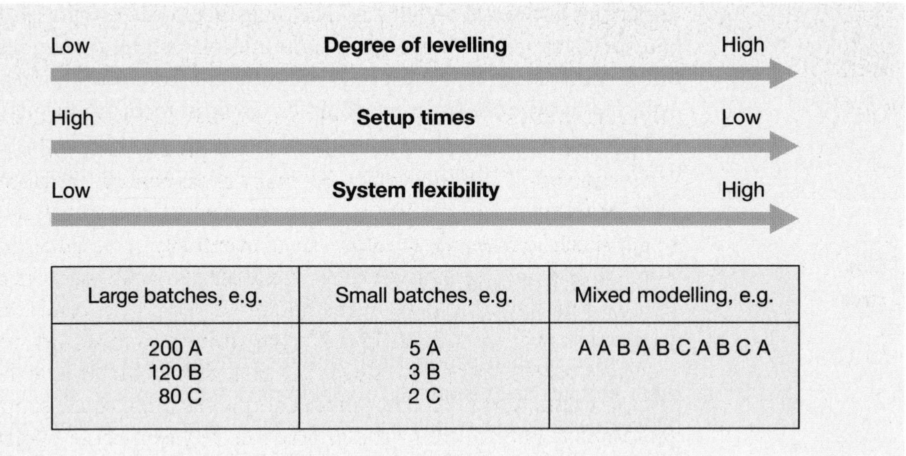

Large batches, e.g.	Small batches, e.g.	Mixed modelling, e.g.
200 A 120 B 80 C	5 A 3 B 2 C	A A B A B C A B C A

Figure 15.10 Levelled scheduling and mixed modelling: mixed modelling becomes possible as the batch size approaches one

individual products emerging from the unit could be reduced progressively as illustrated in Figure 15.10. This would produce a steady stream of each product flowing continuously from the unit. However, the sequence of products does not always fall as conveniently as in Figure 15.10. The unit production times for each product are not usually identical and the ratios of required volumes are less convenient. For example, if a process is required to produce products A, B and C in the ratio 8:5:4, it could produce 800 of A, followed by 500 of B, followed by 400 of A, or 80A, 50B, and 40C. But ideally, sequencing the products as smoothly as possible, it would produce in the order . . . BACABACABACABACAB . . . repeated . . . repeated . . . etc. Doing this achieves relatively smooth flow (but does rely on significant process flexibility).

Keep things simple – the 5 Ss

The 5 Ss

The **5-S terminology** came originally from Japan, and although the translation into English is approximate, they are generally taken to represent the following.

1 **Sort** (*Seiri*) – eliminate what is not needed and keep what is needed.
2 **Straighten** (*Seiton*) – position things in such a way that they can be easily reached whenever they are needed.
3 **Shine** (*Seiso*) – keep things clean and tidy; no refuse or dirt in the work area.
4 **Standardize** (*Seiketsu*) – maintain cleanliness and order – perpetual neatness.
5 **Sustain** (*Shitsuke*) – develop a commitment and pride in keeping to standards.

The 5 Ss can be thought of as a simple housekeeping methodology to organize work areas that focuses on visual order, organization, cleanliness and standardization. It helps to eliminate all types of waste relating to uncertainty, waiting, searching for relevant information, creating variation, and so on. By eliminating what is unnecessary, and making everything clear and predictable, clutter is reduced, needed items are always in the same place and work is made easier and faster.

Adopt total productive maintenance (TPM)

Total productive maintenance aims to eliminate the variability in operations processes caused by the effect of breakdowns. This is achieved by involving everyone in the search for maintenance improvements. Process owners are encouraged to assume ownership of their machines and to undertake routine maintenance and simple repair tasks. By so doing, maintenance specialists can then be freed to develop higher-order skills for improved maintenance systems. TPM is treated in more detail in Chapter 19.

Lean synchronization applied throughout the supply network

Although most of the concepts and techniques discussed in this chapter are devoted to the management of stages *within* processes and processes *within* an operation, the same principles can apply to the whole supply chain. In this context, the stages in a process are the whole businesses, operations or processes between which products flow. And as any business starts to approach lean synchronization it will eventually come up against the constraints imposed by the lack of lean synchronization of the other operations in its supply chain. So, achieving further gains must involve trying to spread lean synchronization practice outward to its partners in the chain. Ensuring lean synchronization throughout an entire supply network is clearly a far more demanding task than doing the same within a single process. It is a complex task. And it becomes more complex as more of the supply chain embraces the lean philosophy. The nature of the interaction between whole operations is far more complex than between individual stages within a process. A far more complex mix of products and services is likely to be being provided and the whole network is likely to be subject to a less predictable set of potentially disruptive events. To make a supply chain lean means more than making each operation in the chain lean. A collection of localized lean operations rarely leads to an overall lean chain. Rather one needs to apply the lean synchronization philosophy to the supply chain as a whole. Yet the advantages from truly lean chains can be significant.

And essentially the principles of lean synchronization are the same for a supply chain as they are for a process. Fast throughput throughout the whole supply network is still valuable and will save cost throughout the supply network. Lower levels of inventory will still make it easier to achieve lean synchronization. Waste is just as evident (and even larger) at the level of the supply network and reducing waste is still a worthwhile task. Streamline flow, exact matching of supply and demand, enhanced flexibility, and minimizing variability are all still tasks that will benefit the whole network. The principles of pull control can work between whole operations in the same way as they can between stages within a single process. In fact, the principles and the techniques of lean synchronization are essentially the same no matter what level of analysis is being used. And because lean synchronization is being implemented on a larger scale, the benefits will also be proportionally greater.

One of the weaknesses of lean synchronization principles is that it is difficult to achieve when conditions are subject to unexpected disturbance. This is especially a problem with applying lean synchronization principles in the context of the whole supply network. Whereas unexpected fluctuations and disturbances do occur within operations, local management has a reasonable degree of control that it can exert in order to reduce them. Outside the operation, within the supply network, it is far more difficult. Nevertheless, it is generally held that, although the task is more difficult and although it may take longer to achieve, the aim of lean synchronization is just as valuable for the supply network as a whole as it is for an individual operation.

Lean supply chains are like air traffic control systems[8]

The concept of the lean supply chain has been likened to an air traffic control system, in that it attempts to provide continuous, 'real-time visibility and control' to all elements in the chain. This is the secret of how the world's busiest airports handle thousands of departures and arrivals daily. All aircraft are given an identification number that shows up on a radar map. Aircraft approaching an airport are detected by the radar and contacted using radio. The control tower precisely positions the aircraft in an approach pattern which it coordinates. The radar detects any small adjustments that are necessary, which are communicated to the aircraft. This real-time visibility and control can optimize airport throughput while maintaining extremely high safety and reliability.

Contrast this to how most supply chains are coordinated. Information is captured only periodically, probably once a day, and any adjustments to logistics, output levels at the various operations in the supply chain are adjusted, and plans rearranged. But imagine what would happen if this was how the airport operated, with only a 'radar snapshot' once a day

Coordinating aircraft with sufficient tolerance to arrange take-offs and landings every two minutes would be out of the question. Aircraft would be jeopardized, or alternatively, if aircraft were spaced further apart to maintain safety, throughput would be drastically reduced. Yet this is how most supply chains have traditionally operated. They use a daily 'snapshot' from their ERP systems (see Chapter 14 for an explanation of ERP). This limited visibility means operations must either space their work out to avoid 'collisions' (i.e. missed customer orders) thereby reducing output, or they must 'fly blind' thereby jeopardizing reliability.

Lean service

Any attempt to consider how lean ideas apply throughout a whole supply chain must also confront the fact that these chains include service operations, often dealing in intangibles. So how can lean principles be applied in these parts of the chain? The idea of lean factory operations is relatively easy to understand. Waste is evident in over-stocked inventories, excess scrap, badly sited machines and so on. In services it is less obvious, inefficiencies are more difficult to see. Yet most of the principles and techniques of lean synchronization, although often described in the context of manufacturing operations, are also applicable to service settings. In fact, some of the philosophical underpinning to lean synchronization can also be seen as having its equivalent in the service sector. Take, for example, the role of inventory. The comparison between manufacturing systems that hold large stocks of inventory between stages and those that did not centred on the effect which inventory had on improvement and problem-solving. Exactly the same argument can be applied when, instead of queues of material (inventory), an operation has to deal with queues of information, or even customers. With its customer focus, standardization, continuous quality improvement, smooth flow and efficiency, lean thinking have direct application in all operations, manufacturing or service. Bradley Staats and David Upton of Harvard Business School[9] have studied how lean ideas can be applied in service operations. They make three main points:

1 In terms of operations and improvements, the service industries in general are a long way behind manufacturing.
2 Not all lean manufacturing ideas translate from factory floor to office cubicle. For example, tools such as empowering manufacturing workers to 'stop the line' when they encounter a problem is not directly replicable when there is no line to stop.
3 Adopting lean operations principles alters the way a company learns through changes in problem solving, coordination through connections, and pathways and standardization.

Examples of lean service (a summary)

Many of the examples of lean philosophy and lean techniques in service industries are directly analogous to those found in manufacturing industries because physical items are being moved or processed in some way. Consider the following examples.

- Supermarkets usually replenish their shelves only when customers have taken sufficient products off the shelf. The movement of goods from the 'back-office' store to the shelf is triggered only by the 'empty-shelf' demand signal. ***Principle:*** *pull control.*
- An Australian tax office used to receive applications by mail, open the mail and send it through to the relevant department which, after processing it, sent it to the next department. Now they only open mail when the stages in front can process it. Each department requests more work only when they have processed previous work. ***Principle:*** *don't let inventories build up, use pull control.*
- One construction company makes a rule of only calling for material deliveries to its sites the day before materials are needed. This reduces clutter and the chances of theft. ***Principle:*** *pull control reduces confusion.*
- Many fast-food restaurants cook and assemble food and place it in the warm area only when the customer-facing server has sold an item. ***Principle:*** *pull control reduces throughput time.*

Other examples of lean concepts and methods apply even when most of the service elements are intangible.

- Some web sites allow customers to register for a reminder service that automatically e-mails reminders for action to be taken, for example, the day before a partner's birthday, in time to prepare for a meeting, etc. ***Principle:*** *the value of delivered information, like delivered items, can be time-dependent; too early and it deteriorates (you forget it), too late and it's useless (because it's too late).*
- A firm of lawyers used to take ten days to prepare its bills for customers. This meant that customers were not asked to pay until ten days after the work had been done. Now they use a system that, every day, updates each customer's account. So, when a bill is sent it includes all work up to the day before the billing date. ***Principle:*** *process delays also delay cash flow, fast throughput improves cash flow.*
- New publishing technologies allow professors to assemble printed and e-learning course material customized to the needs of individual courses or even individual students. ***Principle:*** *flexibility allows customization and small batch sizes delivered 'to order'.*

Lean synchronization and other approaches

Either as a broad philosophy or a practical method of operations planning and control, lean synchronization is not the only approach that is used in practice. There are other approaches that can be used to underpin operations improvement and operations planning and control. We will describe how lean compares with other improvement approaches in Chapter 18. In this chapter we look briefly at two alternatives to lean synchronization as a planning and control method: the theory of constraints (TOC), and material requirements planning (MRP) which we examined in the supplement to Chapter 14.

Lean synchronization and the theory of constraints

A central idea of lean synchronization is the smooth flow of items through processes, operations and supply networks. Any bottleneck will disrupt this smooth progress. Therefore, it is important to recognize the significance of capacity constraints to the planning and control process. This is the idea behind the theory of constraints (TOC) which has been developed to focus attention on the capacity constraints or bottleneck parts of the operation. By identifying the location of constraints, working to remove them, then looking for the next constraint, an operation is always focusing on the part that critically determines the pace of output. The approach which uses this idea is called optimized production technology (OPT). Its development and the marketing of it as a proprietary software product were originated by Eliyahu Goldratt.[10] OPT is a computer-based technique and tool which helps to schedule production systems to the pace dictated by the most heavily loaded resources, that is, bottlenecks. If the rate of activity in any part of the system exceeds that of the bottleneck, then items are being produced that cannot be used. If the rate of working falls below the pace at the bottleneck, then the entire system is under-utilized. There are principles underlying OPT which demonstrate this focus on bottlenecks:

1. Balance flow, not capacity. It is more important to reduce throughput time rather than achieving a notional capacity balance between stages or processes.
2. The level of utilization of a non-bottleneck is determined by some other constraint in the system, not by its own capacity. This applies to stages in a process, processes in an operation, and operations in a supply network.
3. Utilization and activation of a resource are not the same. According to the TOC a resource is being utilized only if it contributes to the entire process or operation creating more

output. A process or stage can be activated in the sense that it is working, but it may only be creating stock or performing other non-value-added activity.

4 An hour lost (not used) at a bottleneck is an hour lost for ever out of the entire system. The bottleneck limits the output from the entire process or operation, therefore the under-utilization of a bottleneck affects the entire process or operation.
5 An hour saved at a non-bottleneck is a mirage. Non-bottlenecks have spare capacity anyway. Why bother making them even less utilized?
6 Bottlenecks govern both throughput and inventory in the system. If bottlenecks govern flow, then they govern throughput time, which in turn governs inventory.
7 You do not have to transfer batches in the same quantities as you produce them. Flow will probably be improved by dividing large production batches into smaller ones for moving through a process.
8 The size of the process batch should be variable, not fixed. Again, from the EBQ model, the circumstances that control batch size may vary between different products.
9 Fluctuations in connected and sequence-dependent processes add to each other rather than averaging out. So, if two parallel processes or stages are capable of a particular average output rate, in parallel, they will never be able to achieve the same average output rate.
10 Schedules should be established by looking at all constraints simultaneously. Because of bottlenecks and constraints within complex systems, it is difficult to work out schedules according to a simple system of rules. Rather, all constraints need to be considered together.

OPT uses the terminology of 'drum, buffer, rope' to explain its planning and control approach. We explained this idea in Chapter 10. The bottleneck work centre becomes a 'drum', beating the pace for the rest of the factory. This 'drum beat' determines the schedules in non-bottleneck areas, pulling through work (the rope) in line with the bottleneck capacity, not the capacity of the work centre. A bottleneck should never be allowed to be working at less than full capacity; therefore, inventory buffers should be placed before it to ensure that it never runs out of work.

The five steps of the theory of constraints

As a practical method of synchronizing flow, TOC emphasizes the following five steps.[11]

1 *Identify the system constraint* – the part of a system that constitutes its weakest link; it could be a physical constraint or even a decision-making or policy constraint.
2 *Decide how to exploit the constraint* – obtain as much capability as possible from the constraint, preferably without expensive changes. For example, reduce or eliminate any non-productive time at the bottleneck.
3 *Subordinate everything to the constraint* – the non-constraint elements of the process are adjusted to a level so that the constraint can operate at maximum effectiveness. After this, the overall process is evaluated to determine if the constraint has shifted elsewhere in the process. If the constraint has been eliminated, go to step 5.
4 *Elevate the constraint* – 'elevating' the constraint means eliminating it. This step is only considered if steps 2 and 3 have not been successful. Major changes to the existing system are considered at this step.
5 *Start again from step 1.*

Table 15.2 shows some of the differences between the theory of constraints and lean synchronization. Arguably, the main contribution of TOC to smooth, synchronized flow is its inclusion of the idea that the effects of bottleneck constraints (a) must be prioritized, and (b) can 'excuse' inventory, if it means maximizing the utilization of the bottleneck. Nor (unlike ERP / MRP, for example) does it necessarily require large investment in new information technology. Further, because it attempts to improve the flow of items through a process, it can release inventory that in turn releases invested capital. Claims of the financial payback from OPT are often based on this release of capital and fast throughput.

Table 15.2 Theory of constraints compared with lean synchronization[12]

	Theory of constraints	*Lean synchronization*
Overall objectives	To increase profit by increasing the throughput of a process or operation	To increase profit by adding value from the customers' perspective
Measures of effectiveness	• Throughput • Inventory • Operating expense	• Cost • Throughput time • Value-added efficiency
Achieve improvement by . . .	Focusing on the constraints (the 'weakest links') in the process	Eliminating waste and adding value by considering the entire process, operation or supply network
How to implement	A five-step, continuous process (see above) emphasizing acting locally	Continuous improvement emphasizing the whole supply network

Lean synchronization and MRP

The operating philosophies of lean synchronization and MRP do seem to be fundamentally opposed. Lean synchronization encourages a 'pull' system of planning and control, whereas MRP is a 'push' system. Lean synchronization has aims which are wider than the operations planning and control activity, whereas MRP is essentially a planning and control 'calculation mechanism'. Yet the two approaches can reinforce each other in the same operation, provided their respective advantages are preserved. The irony is that lean synchronization and MRP have similar objectives. JIT scheduling aims to connect the new network of internal and external supply processes by means of invisible conveyors so that parts only move in response to coordinated and synchronized signals derived from end-customer demand. MRP seeks to meet projected customer demand by directing that items are only produced as needed to meet that demand. However, there are differences. MRP is driven by the master production schedule, which identifies future end-item demand. It models a fixed lead-time environment, using the power of the computer to calculate how many of, and when, each part should be made. Its output is in the form of time-phased requirements plans that are centrally calculated and coordinated. Parts are made in response to central instructions. Day-to-day disturbances, such as inaccurate stock records, undermine MRP authority and can make the plans unworkable. While MRP is excellent at planning, it is weak at control. On the other hand, lean synchronization scheduling aims to meet demand instantaneously through simple control systems based on kanban. If the total throughput time (P) is less than the demand lead time (D), then lean synchronization systems should be capable of meeting that demand. But if the P:D ratio is greater than 1, some speculative production will be needed. And if demand is suddenly far greater than expected for certain products, the JIT system may be unable to cope. Pull scheduling is a reactive concept that works best when independent demand has been levelled and dependent demand synchronized. While lean synchronization may be good at control, it is weak on planning.

MRP is also better at dealing with complexity, as measured by numbers of items being processed. It can handle detailed requirements even for 'strangers'. Lean synchronization pull scheduling is less capable of responding instantaneously to changes in demand as the part count, options and colours increase. Therefore, lean synchronization production systems favour designs based on simpler product structures with high parts commonality. Such disciplines challenge needless complexity, so that more parts may be brought under pull-scheduling control.

When to use lean synchronization, MRP and combined systems

Figure 15.11 distinguishes between the complexity of product structures and the complexity of the flow-path routeings through which they must pass.[13] Simple product structures which have routeings with high repeatability are prime candidates for pull control. Lean

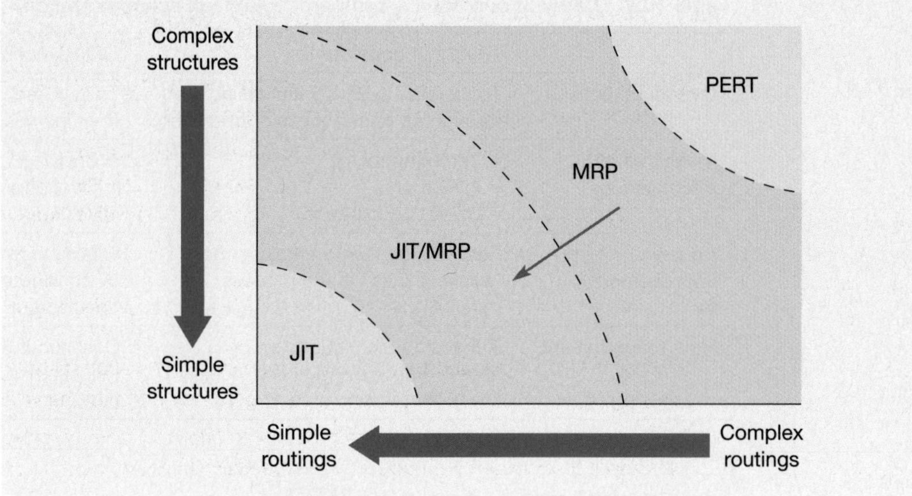

Figure 15.11 Complexity as a determinant of an appropriate planning and control system

Source: From Voss, C.A. and Harrison, A. (1987) 'Strategies for implementing JIT' in Voss, C.A. (ed.) *Just-in-Time Manufacture*, IFS/Springer-Verlag. Copyright © 1987 Springer, reproduced with permission.

synchronization can easily cope with their relatively straightforward requirements. As structures and routeings become more complex, so the power of the computer is needed in order to break down product structures and so assign orders to suppliers. In many environments, it is possible to use pull scheduling for the control of most internal materials. Again, prime candidates for pull control are materials which are used regularly each week or each month. Their number can be increased by design standardization, as indicated by the direction of the arrow in Figure 15.11. As structures and routings become even more complex, and parts usages become more irregular, so the opportunities for using pull scheduling decrease. Very complex structures require networking methods like PERT (program evaluation and review technique – *see* Chapter 16) for planning and control.

Summary answers to key questions

Check and improve your understanding of this chapter using self assessment questions and a personalised study plan, audio and video downloads, and an eBook – all at ***www.myomlab.com.***

➤ What is lean synchronization?

- Lean synchronization is an approach to operations which tries to meet demand instantaneously with perfect quality and no waste. It is an approach which differs from traditional operations practices insomuch as it stresses waste elimination and fast throughput, both of which contribute to low inventories.
- The ability to deliver just-in-time not only saves working capital (through reducing inventory levels) but also has a significant impact on the ability of an operation to improve its intrinsic efficiency.
- The lean synchronization philosophy can be summarized as concerning three overlapping elements, (a) the elimination of waste in all its forms, (b) the inclusion of all staff of the operation in its improvement, and (c) the idea that all improvement should be on a continuous basis.

➤ How does lean synchronization eliminate waste?

- The most significant part of the lean philosophy is its focus on the elimination of all forms of waste, defined as any activity that does not add value.
- Lean synchronization identifies seven types of waste that, together, form four barriers to achieving lean synchronization. They are: waste from irregular (non-streamlined) flow, waste from inexact supply, waste from inflexible response, and waste from variability.

➤ How does lean synchronization apply throughout the supply network?

- Most of the concepts and techniques of lean synchronization, although usually described as applying to individual processes and operations, also apply to the whole supply networks.
- The concept of the lean supply chain has been likened to an air traffic control system, in that it attempts to provide continuous, 'real-time visibility and control' to all elements in the chain.
- Most of the ideas of lean synchronization are directly applicable to all the service operations in the supply network.

➤ How does lean synchronization compare with other approaches?

- There are other approaches that attempt to perform the same function as lean synchronization. Two alternatives to lean synchronization as a planning and control method are the theory of constraints (TOC), and material requirements planning (MRP).
- Although both TOC and MRP may seem to be different approaches, they can be combined.
- The way in which they can be combined depends on the complexity of product structures, the complexity of product routeing, the volume–variety characteristics of the operation and the level of control required.

Case study
Boys and Boden (B&B)

'There ***must*** *be a better way of running this place!'*, said Dean Hammond, recently recruited General Manager of B&B, as he finished a somewhat stressful conversation with a complaining customer, a large and loyal local building contractor. *'We had six weeks to make their special staircase, and we are still late. I'll have to persuade one of the joiners to work overtime this weekend to get everything ready for Monday. We never seem to get complaints about quality . . . our men always do an excellent job, but there is usually a big backlog of work, so how can we set priorities? We could do the most profitable work first, or the work for our biggest customers, or the jobs which are most behind. In practice, we try to satisfy everyone as best we can, but inevitably someone's order will be late. On paper, each job should be quite profitable, since we build in a big allowance for waste, and for timber defects. And we know the work content of almost any task we would have to do, and this is the basis of our estimating system. But, overall, the department isn't very profitable in comparison to our other operations, and most problems seem to end up with higher-than-anticipated costs and late deliveries!'*

Boys and Boden was a small, successful, privately owned timber and building materials merchant based in a small town. Over the years it had established its large Joinery Department, which made doors, windows, staircases and other timber products, all to the exact special requirements of the customers, comprising numerous local and regional builders. In addition, the joiners would cut and prepare special orders of timber, such as non-standard sections, and special profiles including old designs of skirting board, sometimes at very short notice while the customers waited. Typically, for joinery items, the customer provided simple dimensioned sketches of the required products. These were then passed to the central Estimating/Quotations

Department which, in conjunction with the Joinery Manager, calculated costs and prepared a written quotation which was faxed to the customer. This first stage was normally completed within two or three days, but on occasions could take a week or more. On receipt of an order, the original sketches and estimating details were passed back to the Joinery Manager across the yard, who roughly scheduled them into his plan, allocating them to individual craftsmen as they became available. Most of the joiners were capable of making any product, and enjoyed the wide variety of challenging work.

The Joinery Department appeared congested and somewhat untidy, but everyone believed that this was acceptable and normal for job shops, since there was no single flow route for materials. Whatever the design of the item being made, or the quantity, it was normal for the joiner to select the required timber from the storage building across the yard. The timber was then prepared using a planer/thicknesser. After that, the joiner would use a variety of processes, depending on the product. The timber could be machined into different cross-sectional shapes, cut into component lengths using a radial arm saw, joints formed by hand tools, or using a mortise/tenon machine, and so on. Finally the products would be glued and assembled, sanded smooth by hand or machine, and treated with preservatives, stains or varnishes if required. All the large and more expensive machines were grouped together by type (for example, saws) or were single pieces of equipment shared by all 10 or so joiners.

Dean described what one might observe on a random visit to the Joinery Department: *'One or two long staircases partly assembled, and crossing several work areas; large door frames on trestles being assembled; stacks of window components for a large contract being prepared and jointed, and so on. Off-cuts and wood shavings are scattered around the work area, but are cleared periodically when they get in the way or form a hazard. The joiners try to fit in with each other over the use of machinery, so are often working on several, part-finished items at once. Varnishing or staining has to be done when it's quiet – for example, evenings or weekends – or outside, to avoid dust contamination. Long off-cuts are stacked around the workshop, to be used up on any future occasion when these lengths or sections are required. However, it is often easier to take a new length of timber for each job, so the off-cuts do tend to build up over time. Unfortunately, everything I have described is getting worse as we get busier . . . our sales are increasing so the system is getting more congested. The joiners are almost climbing over each other to do their work. Unfortunately, despite having more orders, the department has remained stubbornly unprofitable!*

Whilst analysing in detail the lack of profit, we were horrified to find that, for the majority of orders, the actual times booked by the joiners exceeded the estimated times by up to 50 per cent. Sometimes this was attributable to new, inexperienced joiners. Although fully trained and qualified, they might lack the experience needed to complete a complex job in the time an estimator would expect, but there had been no feedback of this to the individual. We put one of these men on doors only; having overcome his initial reluctance, he has become our enthusiastic "door expert", and gets closely involved in quotations too, so he always does his work within the time estimates! However, the main time losses were found to be the result of general delays caused by congestion, interference, double handling and rework to rectify in-process damage. Moreover, we found that a joiner walked an average of nearly 5 km a day, usually carrying around bits of wood.

When I did my operations management course on my MBA, the professor described the application of cellular manufacturing and JIT. From what I can remember, the idea seemed to be to get better flow, reducing the times and distances in the process, and thus achieving quicker throughput times. That is just what we need, but these concepts were explained in the context of high-volume, repetitive production of bicycles, whereas everything we make is "one-offs". However, although we do make a lot of different staircases, they all use roughly the same process steps:

1 *Cutting timber to width and length*
2 *Sanding*
3 *Machining*
4 *Tenoning*
5 *Manual assembly (glue and wedges).*

We have a lot of unused factory floor-space, so it would be relatively easy to set up a self-contained staircase cell. There is huge demand for special stairs in this region, but also a lot of competing small joinery businesses which can beat us on price and lead time. So we go to a lot of trouble quoting for stairs, but only win about 20 per cent of the business. If we got the cell idea to work, we could be more competitive on price and delivery, hence winning more orders. I know we will need a lot more volume to justify establishing the cell, so it's really a case of "chicken and egg"!'

Questions

1 To what extent could (or should) Dean expect to apply the philosophies and techniques of JIT described in this chapter to the running of a staircase cell?

2 What are likely to be the main categories of costs and benefits in establishing the cell? Are there any non-financial benefits which should be taken into account?

3 At what stage, and how, should Dean sell his idea to the Joinery Manager and the workers?

4 How different would the cell work be to that in the main Joinery Department?

5 Should Dean differentiate the working environment by providing distinctive work-wear such as T-shirts and distinctively painted machines, in order to reinforce a cultural change?

6 What risks are associated with Dean's proposal?

Problems and applications

These problems and applications will help to improve your analysis of operations. You can find more practice problems as well as worked examples and guided solutions on MyOMLab at ***www.myomlab.com****.*

1 Revisit the worked example earlier in the chapter that analysed a journey in terms of value-added time (actually going somewhere) and non-value-added time (the time spent queuing etc.). Calculate the value-added time for a recent journey that you have taken.

2 A simple process has four stages: A, B, C and D. The average amount of work needed to process items passing through these stages is as follows: Stage A = 68 minutes, Stage B = 55 minutes, Stage C = 72 minutes and Stage D = 60 minutes. A spot check on the work-in-progress between each stage reveals the following: between Stages A and B there are 82 items, between Stages B and C there are 190 items, and between Stages C and D there are 89 items.

(a) Using Little's law (see Chapter 4) calculate the throughput time of the process.
(b) What is the throughput efficiency of the process?

3 In the example above, the operations manager in charge of the process reallocates the work at each stage to improve the 'balance' of the process. Now each stage has an average of 64 minutes of work. Also, the work-in-progress in front of Stages B, C and D is 75, 80 and 82 units respectively. How has this changed the throughput efficiency of the process?

4 A production process is required to produce 1,400 of product X, 840 of product Y and 420 of product Z in a 4-week period. If the process works 7 hours per day and 5 days per week, devise a mixed model schedule in terms of the number of each products required to be produced every hour, that would satisfy demand.

5 Revisit the 'Operations in action' at the beginning of this chapter, and (a) list all the different techniques and practices which Toyota adopts. (b) How are operations objectives (quality, speed, dependability, flexibility, cost) influenced by the practices which Toyota adopts?

6 Consider how set-up reduction principles can be used on the following.

(a) changing a tyre at the side of the road (following a puncture);
(b) cleaning out an aircraft and preparing it for the next flight between an aircraft on its inbound flight landing and disembarking its passengers, and the same aircraft being ready to take-off on its outbound flight;
(c) the time between the finish of one surgical procedure in a hospital's operating theatre, and the start of the next one;
(d) the 'pitstop' activities during a Formula One race (how does this compare to (a) above?).

Selected further reading

Ahlsrom, P. (2004) Lean service operations: translating lean production principles to service operations, *International Journal of Services, Technology and Management*, vol. 5, nos 5/6. Explains how lean can be used in services.

Bicheno, J. and Holweg, M. (2009) *The Lean Toolbox: The Essential Guide to Lean Transformation*, 4th edn, Piscie Press, Buckingham. A manual of lean techniques, very much a 'how to do it' book, and none the worse for it.

Holweg, M. (2007) The genealogy of lean production, *Journal of Operations Management*, vol. 25, 420–37. An excellent overview of how lean ideas developed.

Liker, J. (2004) *The Toyota Way: 14 Management Principles from the World's Greatest Manufacturer*, McGraw-Hill Education.

Schonberger, R.J. (1996) *World Class Manufacturing: The Next Decade*, The Free Press. As above (and above that) but more speculative.

Spear, S. and Bowen, H.K. (1999) Decoding the DNA of the Toyota Production System, *Harvard Business Review*, September–October. Revisits the leading company as regards JIT practice and re-evaluates the underlying philosophy behind the way it manages its operations. Recommended.

Womack, J.P. and Jones, D.T. (1996) *Lean Thinking: Banish Waste and Create Wealth in Your Corporation*, Simon and Schuster, New York. Some of the lessons from *The Machine that Changed the World* but applied in a broader context.

Womack, J.P., Jones, D.T. and Roos, D. (1990) *The Machine that Changed the World*, Rawson Associates, New York. Arguably the most influential book on operations management practice of the last fifty years. Firmly rooted in the automotive sector but did much to establish lean.

Useful web sites

www.lean.org/ Site of the lean enterprise unit, set up by one of the founders of the lean thinking movement.

www.iee.org/index.cfm The site of the Institution Electrical Engineers (which includes manufacturing engineers surprisingly) has material on this and related topics as well as other issues covered in this book.

www.mfgeng.com The manufacturing engineering site.

www.opsman.org Lots of useful stuff.

Now that you have finished reading this chapter, why not visit MyOMLab at ***www.myomlab.com*** *where you'll find more learning resources to help you make the most of your studies and get a better grade?*

Chapter 16 Project planning and control

Key questions

- ➤ What is a project?
- ➤ What makes project management successful?
- ➤ How are projects planned and controlled?
- ➤ What is project planning and why is it important?
- ➤ How can the techniques of network planning help project management?

Introduction

This chapter is concerned with the planning and control of operations that occupy the low-volume–high-variety end of the continuum which we introduced in Chapter 4. These 'project' operations are engaged in complex, often large-scale, activities with a defined beginning and end. The pioneers of planning and controlling project operations were the engineers and planners who worked on complex defence and construction projects. Now their methods are used on projects as diverse as new product launches, education projects and movie making. Project planning and control is important because all managers will, at some point, get involved with managing projects. (*See* Figure 16.1.)

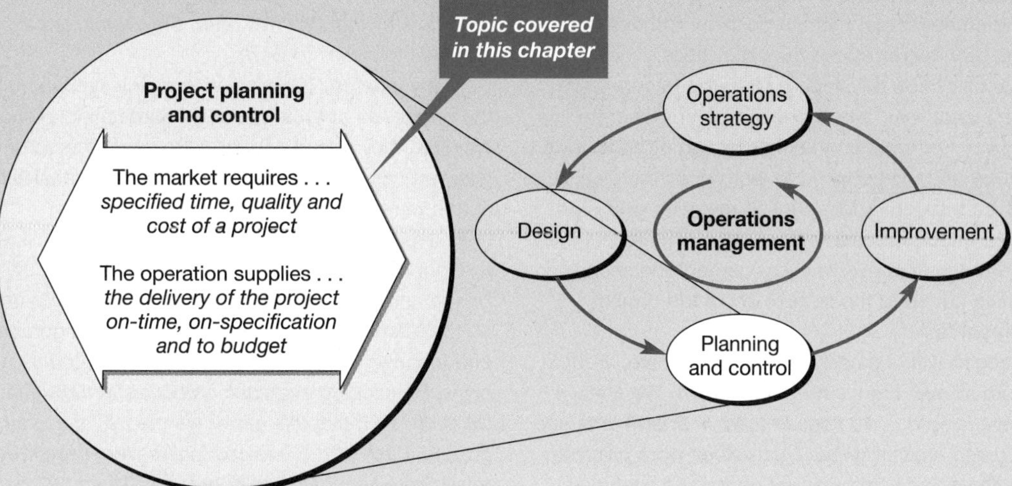

Figure 16.1 This chapter covers project planning and control

*Check and improve your understanding of this chapter using self assessment questions and a personalised study plan, audio and video downloads, and an eBook – all at **www.myomlab.com**.*

Operations in practice The Millau bridge[1]

Source: Jean-Philippe Arles/Reuters/Corbis

For decades French motorists called the little bridge at Millau 'the Millau cork'. It held up all the traffic on what should have been one of the busiest north–south routes through France. No longer. In place of the little bridge is one of the most impressive and beautiful civil engineering successes of the last century. Lord Foster, the bridge's architect, described it as having the 'delicacy of a butterfly', with the environment dominating the scene rather than the bridge. And although the bridge appears to float on the clouds, it is also a remarkable technical achievement. At 300 metres it is the highest road bridge in the world, weighing 36,000 tonnes. The central pillar is higher than the Eiffel Tower, and took only three years to complete, notwithstanding the new engineering techniques that were needed.

Outline plans for the bridge were produced back in 1987, but construction did not begin until December 2001. It was completed in December 2004, on time and budget, having proved the effectiveness of its new construction technique. The traditional method of building this type of bridge (called a 'cable stay bridge') involves building sections of the roadway on the ground and using cranes to put them in position. Because of its height, 300 metres above the valley floor, a new technique had to be developed. First, the towers were built in the usual way, with steel-reinforced concrete. The roadway was built on the high ground at either side of the valley and then pushed forward into space as further sections were added, until it met with precision (to the nearest centimetre) in the centre. This technique had never been tried before and it carried engineering risks, which added to the complexity of the project management task.

It all began with a massive recruitment drive. *'People came from all over France for employment. We knew it would be a long job. We housed them in apartments and houses in and around Millau. Guarantees were given to all the tenants and a unit was set up to help everyone with the paperwork involved in this. It was not unusual for a worker to be recruited in the morning and have his apartment available the same evening with electricity and a telephone available'* (Jean-Pierre Martin, Chief Engineer of Groupe Eiffage and director of building). Over 3,000 workers contributed to the project, with 500 of them on the project site, working in all weathers to complete the project on time. *'Every day I would ask myself what was the intense force that united these men'*, said Jean-Pierre Martin. *'They had a very strong sense of pride and they belonged to a community that was to build the most beautiful construction in the world. It was never necessary to shout at them to get them to work. Life on a construction site has many ups and downs. Some days we were frozen. Other days we were subjected to a heat wave. But even on days of bad weather, one had to force them to stay indoors. Yet often they would leave their lodgings to return to work.'*

Many different businesses were involved in building the bridge. All of them needed coordinating in such a way that they would cooperate towards the common goal, but yet avoid any loss of overall responsibility. Jean-Pierre Martin came up with the idea of 9 autonomous work groups. One group was placed at the foot of each of the 7 piles that would support the bridge and two others at either end. The motto adopted by the teams was 'rigueur et convivialité', rigorous quality and friendly cooperation. *'The difficulty with this type of project is keeping everyone enthusiastic throughout its duration. To make this easier we created these small groups. Each of the 9 teams' shifts were organized in relays between 7 and 14 hours, and 14 and 21 hours.'* So, to maintain the good atmosphere, no expense was spared to celebrate important events in the construction of the viaduct, for example, a pile or another piece of road completed. Sometimes, to boost the morale of the teams, and to celebrate these important events Jean-Pierre would organize a *'méchouis'* – a spit roast of lamb, especially popular with the many workers who were of North African origin.

What is a project?

A project is a set of activities with a defined start point and a defined end state

A **project** is a set of activities with a defined start point and a defined end state, which pursues a defined goal and uses a defined set of resources. Technically many small-scale operations management endeavours, taking minutes or hours, conform to this definition of a project. However, in this chapter we will be examining the management of larger-scale projects taking days, months or years. Large-scale (and therefore complex) undertakings consume a relatively large amount of resources, take a long time to complete and typically involve interactions between different parts of an organization. Projects come in many and various forms, including the following:

- organizing emergency aid to earthquake victims
- producing a television programme
- constructing the Channel Tunnel
- designing an aircraft
- running a one-week course in project management
- relocating a factory
- refurbishing an hotel
- installing a new information system.

What do projects have in common?

To a greater or lesser extent, all the projects listed above have some elements in common. They all have *an objective*, a definable end result or output that is typically defined in terms of cost, quality and timing. They are all *unique*. A project is usually a 'one-off', not a repetitive undertaking. Even 'repeat' projects, such as the construction of another chemical plant to the same specification, will have distinctive differences in terms of resources used and the actual environment in which the project takes place. They are all of a *temporary nature*. Projects have a defined beginning and end, so a temporary concentration of resources is needed to carry out the undertaking. Once their contribution to the project objectives has been completed, the resources are usually redeployed. They will all have some degree of *complexity*. Many different tasks are required to be undertaken to achieve a project's objectives. The relationship between all these tasks can be complex, especially when the number of separate tasks in the project is large. Finally, all projects have to cope with some *uncertainty*. All projects are planned before they are executed and therefore carry an element of risk. A 'blue sky' research project carries the risk that expensive, high-technology resources will be committed with no worthwhile outcome.

Programme has no defined end point

At this point it is worth pointing out the distinction between 'projects' and 'programmes'. A **programme**, such as a continuous improvement programme, has no defined end point. Rather it is an ongoing process of change. Individual projects, such as the development of training processes, may be individual sub-sections of an overall programme, such as an integrated skills development programme. Programme management will overlay and integrate the individual projects. Generally, it is a more difficult task in the sense that it requires resource coordination, particularly when multiple projects share common resources, as emphasized in the following quotation.

> *'Managing projects is, it is said, like juggling three balls – cost, quality, and time. Programme management . . . is like organizing a troupe of jugglers all juggling three balls and swapping balls from time to time.'*[2]

A typology of projects

Projects can be defined in terms of their complexity and their uncertainty

Figure 16.2 illustrates a typology for projects according to their *complexity* – in terms of size, value and the number of people involved in the project – and their ***uncertainty*** of achieving the project objectives of cost, time and quality.

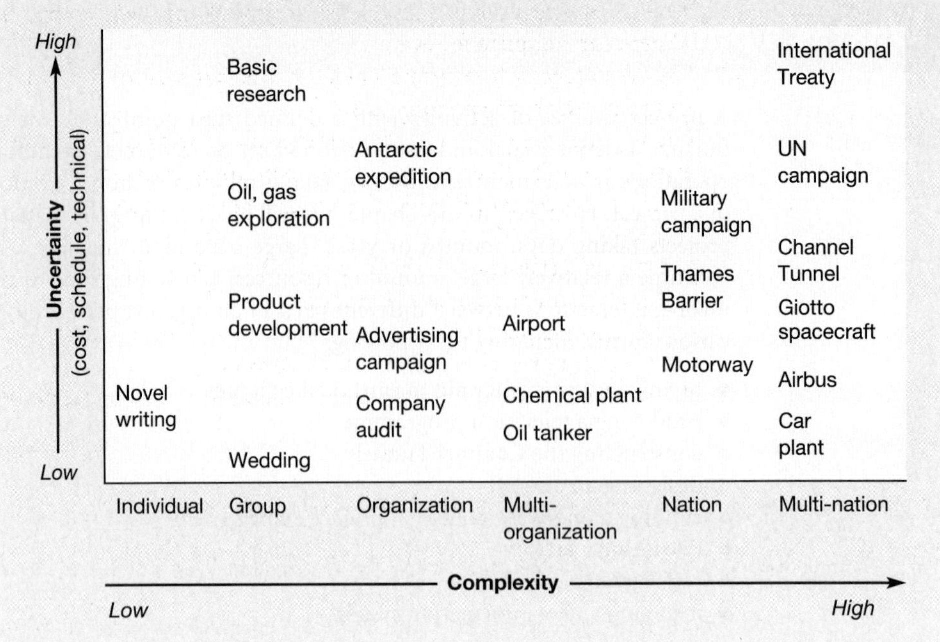

Figure 16.2 A typology of projects

Source: Adapted from Nicholas, J.M. (1990) *Managing Business and Engineering Projects: Concepts and Implementations*, Prentice Hall.

The typology helps to give a rational presentation of the vast range of undertakings where project management principles can be applied. It also gives a clue to the nature of the projects and the difficulties of managing them. Uncertainty particularly affects project planning, and complexity particularly affects project control.

Projects with *high uncertainty* are likely to be especially difficult to define and set realistic objectives for. If the exact details of a project are subject to change during the course of its execution, the planning process is particularly difficult. Resources may be committed, times may be agreed, but if the objectives of the project change or the environmental conditions change, or if some activity is delayed, then all the plans which were made prior to the changes will need to be redrawn. When uncertainty is high, the whole project planning process needs to be sufficiently flexible to cope with the consequences of change. For example, the implementation of a political treaty in the European Union is subject to the ratification of all the member governments. Politics being an uncertain business, any of the member countries might either fail to ratify the treaty or attempt to renegotiate it. The central planners at EU headquarters must therefore have contingency plans in place which indicate how they might have to change the 'project' to cope with any political changes.

Projects with *high levels of complexity* need not necessarily be difficult to plan, although they might involve considerable effort; controlling them can be problematic, however. As projects become more detailed with many separate activities, resources and groups of people involved, the scope for things to go wrong increases. Furthermore, as the number of separate activities in a project increases, the ways in which they can impact on each other increases exponentially. This increases the effort involved in monitoring each activity. It also increases the chances of overlooking some part of the project which is deviating from the plan. Most significantly, it increases the 'knock-on' effect of any problem.

The (only partly joking) 'laws of project management' which were issued by the American Production and Inventory Control Society give a flavour of uncertain and complex projects:

1 No major project is ever installed on time, within budget, or with the same staff that started it. Yours will not be the first.

2 Projects progress quickly until they become 90 per cent complete, then they remain at 90 per cent complete for ever.
3 One advantage of fuzzy project objectives is that they let you avoid the embarrassment of estimating the corresponding costs.
4 When things are going well, something will go wrong. When things just cannot get any worse, they will. When things appear to be going better, you have overlooked something.
5 If the project content is allowed to change freely, the rate of change will exceed the rate of progress.
6 No system is ever completely debugged. Attempts to debug a system inevitably introduce new bugs that are even harder to find.
7 A carelessly planned project will take three times longer to complete than expected; a carefully planned project will take only twice as long.
8 Project teams detest progress reporting because it vividly manifests their lack of progress.

Successful project management

There are some points of commonality in project success and failure, which allow us to identify some general points which seem to minimize the chances of a project failing to meet its objectives. The following factors are particularly important:[3]

- *Clearly defined goals*: including the general project philosophy or general mission of the project, and a commitment to those goals on the part of the project team members.
- *Competent project manager*: a skilled project leader who has the necessary interpersonal, technical and administrative skills.
- *Top-management support*: top-management commitment for the project that has been communicated to all concerned parties.
- *Competent project team members*: the selection and training of project team members, who between them have the skills necessary to support the project.
- *Sufficient resource allocation*: resources, in the form of money, personnel, logistics, etc., which are available for the project in the required quantity.
- *Adequate communications channels*: sufficient information is available on project objectives, status, changes, organizational conditions and client's needs.
- *Control mechanisms*: the mechanisms which are in place to monitor actual events and recognize deviations from plan.
- *Feedback capabilities*: all parties concerned with the project are able to review the project's status and make suggestions and corrections.
- *Responsiveness to clients*: all potential users of the project are concerned with and are kept up to date on the project's status.
- *Troubleshooting mechanisms*: a system or set of procedures which can tackle problems when they arise, trace them back to their root cause and resolve them.
- *Project staff continuity*: the continued involvement of key project personnel through its life. Frequent turnover of staff can dissipate the team's acquired learning.

Project managers

Competent project managers are vital for project success

In order to coordinate the efforts of many people in different parts of the organization (and often outside it as well), all projects need a **project manager**. Many of a project manager's activities are concerned with managing human resources. The people working in the project team need a clear understanding of their roles in the (usually temporary) organization. Controlling an uncertain project environment requires the rapid exchange of relevant information with the project stakeholders, both within and outside the organization. People, equipment and other resources must be identified and allocated to the various tasks. Undertaking these tasks successfully makes the management of a project a particularly challenging operations activity. Five characteristics in particular are seen as important in an effective project manager:[4]

- background and experience which are consistent with the needs of the project;
- leadership and strategic expertise, in order to maintain an understanding of the overall project and its environment, while at the same time working on the details of the project;
- technical expertise in the area of the project in order to make sound technical decisions;
- interpersonal competence and the people skills to take on such roles as project champion, motivator, communicator, facilitator and politician;
- proven managerial ability in terms of a track record of getting things done.

The project planning and control process

Figure 16.3 shows the stages in project management, four of which are relevant to project planning and control:

Stage 1 Understanding the project environment – internal and external factors which may influence the project.
Stage 2 Defining the project – setting the objectives, scope and strategy for the project.
Stage 3 Project planning – deciding how the project will be executed.
Stage 4 Technical execution – performing the technical aspects of the project.
Stage 5 Project control – ensuring that the project is carried out according to plan.

We shall examine project planning and control under the headings of stages 1, 2, 3 and 5 (stage 4, the technical execution of the project, is determined by the specific technicalities of individual projects). However, it is important to understand that the stages are not a simple

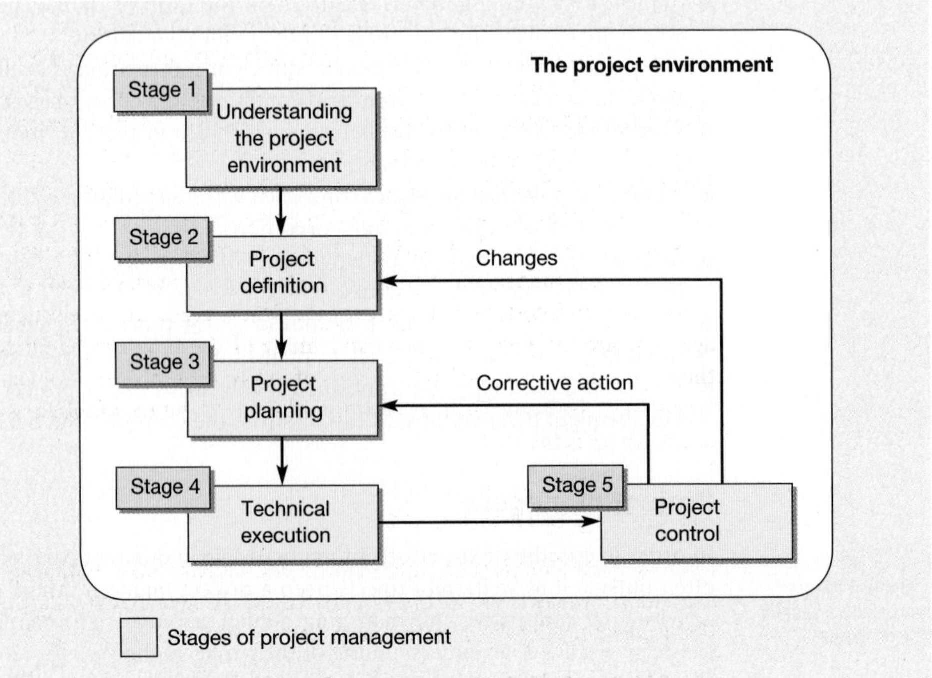

Figure 16.3 The project management model

sequential chain of steps. Project management is essentially an *iterative* process. Problems or changes which become evident in the control stage may require replanning and may even cause modifications to the original project definition.

Stage 1 – Understanding the project environment

Project environment

The **project environment** comprises all the factors which may affect the project during its life. It is the context and circumstances in which the project takes place. Understanding the project environment is important because the environment affects the way in which a project will need to be managed and (just as important) the possible dangers that may cause the project to fail. Environmental factors can be considered under the following four headings.

- *Geo-social environment* – geographical, climatic and cultural factors that may affect the project.
- *Econo-political environment* – the economic, governmental and regulatory factors in which the project takes place.
- *Business environment* – industrial, competitive, supply network and customer expectation factors that shape the likely objectives of the project.
- *Internal environment* – the individual company's strategy and culture, the resources available and the interaction with other projects that will influence the project.

Stakeholders

Stakeholders

One way of operationalizing the importance of understanding a project's environment is to consider the various 'stakeholders' who have some kind of interest in the project. The **stakeholders** in any project are the individuals and groups who have an interest in the project process or outcome. All projects will have stakeholders, complex projects will have many. They are likely to have different views on a project's objectives that may conflict with other stakeholders'. At the very least, different stakeholders are likely to stress different aspects of a project. So, as well as an ethical imperative to include as many people as possible in a project from an early stage, it is often useful in preventing objections and problems later in the project. Moreover, there can be significant direct benefits from using a stakeholder-based approach. Project managers can use the opinions of powerful stakeholders to shape the project at an early stage. This makes it more likely that they will support the project, and also can improve its quality. Communicating with stakeholders early and frequently can ensure that they fully understand the project and understand potential benefits. Stakeholder support may even help to win more resources, making it more likely that projects will be successful. Perhaps most important, one can anticipate stakeholder reaction to various aspects of the project, and plan the actions that could prevent opposition, or build support.

Some (even relatively experienced) project managers are reluctant to include stakeholders in the project management process, preferring to 'manage them at a distance' rather than allow them to interfere with the project. Others argue that the benefits of stakeholder management are too great to ignore and many of the risks can be moderated by emphasizing the responsibilities as well as the rights of project stakeholders. For example, one information technology company formally identifies the rights and responsibilities of project stakeholders as shown in Table 16.1.

Managing stakeholders

Managing stakeholders can be a subtle and delicate task, requiring significant social and, sometimes, political skills. But it is based on three basic activities, identifying, prioritizing and understanding the stakeholder group.

Identify stakeholders – Think of all the people who are affected by your work, who have influence or power over it, or have an interest in its successful or unsuccessful conclusion.

Table 16.1 The rights and responsibilities of stakeholders in one IT company

The rights of stakeholders	*The responsibilities of project stakeholders*
1 To expect developers to learn and speak their language 2 To expect developers to identify and understand their requirements 3 To receive explanations of artefacts that developers use as part of working with project stakeholders, such as models they create with them (e.g. user stories or essential UI prototypes), or artefacts that they present to them (e.g. UML deployment diagrams) 4 To expect developers to treat them with respect 5 To hear ideas and alternatives for requirements 6 To describe characteristics that make the product easy to use 7 To be presented with opportunities to adjust requirements to permit reuse, reduce development time, or to reduce development costs 8 To be given good-faith estimates 9 To receive a system that meets their functional and quality needs	1 Provide resources (time, money, . . .) to the project team 2 Educate developers about their business 3 Spend the time to provide and clarify requirements 4 Be specific and precise about requirements 5 Make timely decisions 6 Respect a developer's assessment of cost and feasibility 7 Set requirement priorities 8 Review and provide timely feedback regarding relevant work artefacts of developers 9 Promptly communicate changes to requirements 10 Own your organization's software processes: to both follow them and actively help to fix them when needed

Although stakeholders may be both organizations and people, ultimately you must communicate with people. Make sure that you identify the correct individual stakeholders within a stakeholder organization.

Prioritize stakeholders – Many people and organizations will be affected by a project. Some of these may have the power either to block or advance the project. Some may be interested in what you are doing, others may not care. Map out stakeholders using the power–interest grid (see below), and classify them by their power and by their interest in the project.

Understand key stakeholders – It is important to know about key stakeholders. One needs to know how they are likely to feel about and react to the project. One also needs to know how best to engage them in the project and how best to communicate with them.

The power–interest grid

The power–interest grid distinguishes between stakeholders' power to influence the project and their interest in doing so

One approach to discriminating between different stakeholders, and more important, how they should be managed, is to distinguish between their power to influence the project and their interest **in doing so**. Stakeholders who have the power to exercise a major influence over the project should not ever be ignored. At the very least, the nature of their interest, and their motivation, should be well understood. But not all stakeholders who have the power to exercise influence over a project will be interested in doing so, and not everyone who is interested in the project has the power to influence it. The power–interest grid, shown in Figure 16.4, classifies stakeholders simply in terms of these two dimensions. Although there will be graduations between them, the two dimensions are useful in providing an indication of how stakeholders can be managed in terms of four categories.

Stakeholders' positions on the grid gives an indication of how they might be managed. High-power, interested groups must be fully engaged, with the greatest efforts made to satisfy them. High-power, less-interested groups require enough effort to keep them satisfied, but not so much that they become bored or irritated with the message. Low-power, interested groups need to be kept adequately informed, with checks to ensure that no major issues are arising. These groups may be very helpful with the detail of the project. Low-power, less-interested groups need monitoring, but without excessive communication. Some key questions that can help to understand high-priority stakeholders include the following.

- What financial or emotional interest do they have in the outcome of the project? Is it positive or negative?

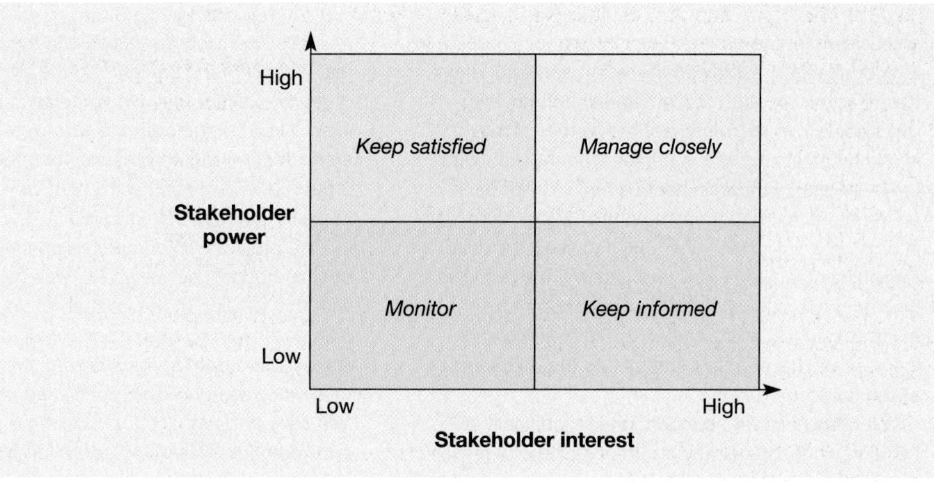

Figure 16.4 The stakeholder power–interest grid

- What motivates them most of all?
- What information do they need?
- What is the best way of communicating with them?
- What is their current opinion of the project?
- Who influences their opinions? Do some of these influencers therefore become important stakeholders in their own right?
- If they are not likely to be positive, what will win them around to support the project?
- If you don't think you will be able to win them round, how will you manage their opposition?

Short case
The Workhouse at The National Trust[5]

'Our projects can be funded by a variety of sources, involve the sensitive restoration of literally irreplaceable buildings, need a clear vision of how to reconcile historical integrity with commercial viability, and rely on the support of volunteers, our members and the community. It isn't surprising that we need to involve all stakeholders all the way through the project' (Leigh Rix, Project Manager, The Workhouse).

The National Trust of England, Wales and Northern Ireland was formed in 1895 with the objective of preserving places of historic interest or natural beauty permanently for the nations to enjoy. 'The Workhouse' was one of its more intriguing projects. Originally built in 1824, for over 150 years it housed the local poor. But by 1997 this nationally important protected building was under threat of being turned into residential apartments. In order to aid the understanding of poverty for this, and future generations, the National Trust purchased The Workhouse with the intention of bringing this important part of social history to a modern generation.

Source: Alamy Images

'Our vision for the Workhouse was to take a building that originally nobody wanted to enter and create a heritage facility that anyone would want to visit and where everyone is welcome.'

Leigh Rix and his project team understood from their previous experience that careful and sensitive stakeholder management was often key to the success of this type of project. The team drew up a list of stakeholders and set out to win them over with their

→

enthusiasm for the project. They invited local people to attend meetings, explained the vision and took them to look round the site. Out of these meetings they met people with knowledge of the history of the site and sometimes with a personal connection with the building. A woman in her 90s had worked as an assistant matron, aged 14, in the 1920s. More surprisingly, a woman in her 30s had lived there as recently as the 1970s when her family were homeless. Finding these links allowed the project team to re-examine their interpretation of the building and incorporate real people's stories into the presentation of the building's history.

With the need for so much, often technically difficult, building work another key group of stakeholders was the builders. Before work started the curator took all the building staff on the same tour of the site as they had taken the various groups of VIPs who provided the funding. *'Involving the builders in the project sparked a real interest in the project and the archaeological history of the site. Often they would come across something interesting, tell the foreman who would involve an archaeologist and so preserve an artefact that might otherwise have been destroyed. They took a real interest in their work, they felt involved.'*

The project was completed on time and within the original budget, but Leigh Rix was particularly pleased with the 'quality' of the finished project, *'It may seem like a time-consuming and expensive activity to involve all stakeholders right at the start of a project, particularly when they seem to have conflicting needs and interests. Yet, as with many of our projects it is worth the effort. Looking back, identifying and involving the stakeholders not only allowed the project to be completed on time and within budget, it improved the eventual quality in ways we could not have anticipated.'*

Stage 2 – Project definition

Before starting the complex task of planning and executing a project, it is necessary to be clear about exactly what the project is – its definition. This is not always straightforward, especially in projects with many stakeholders. Three different elements define a project:

- its objectives: the end state that project management is trying to achieve;
- its scope: the exact range of the responsibilities taken on by project management;
- its strategy: how project management is going to meet its objectives.

Project objectives

Objectives help to provide a definition of the end point which can be used to monitor progress and identify when success has been achieved. They can be judged in terms of the five performance objectives – quality, speed, dependability, flexibility and cost. However, flexibility is regarded as a 'given' in most projects which, by definition, are to some extent one-offs, and speed and dependability are compressed to one composite objective – 'time'. This results in what are known as the 'three objectives of project management' – cost, time and quality. Figure 16.5 shows the 'project objectives triangle' with these three types of project marked.[6]

The relative importance of each objective will differ for different projects. Some aerospace projects, such as the development of a new aircraft, which impact on passenger safety, will place a very high emphasis on quality objectives. With other projects, for example a research project that is being funded by a fixed government grant, cost might predominate. Other

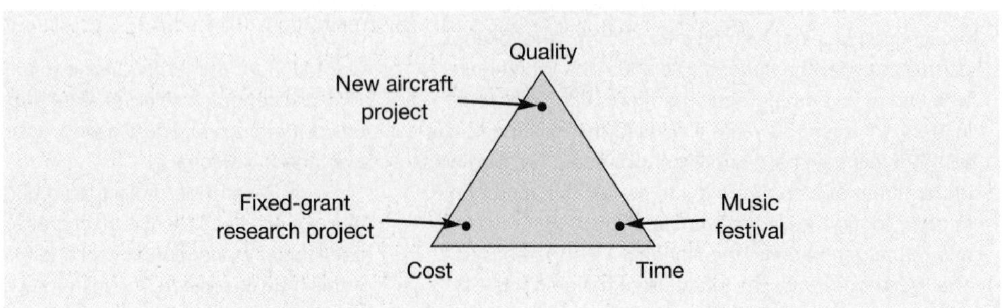

Figure 16.5 The project objectives triangle

projects emphasize time: for example, the organization of an open-air music festival has to happen on a particular date if the project is to meet its objectives. In each of these projects, although one objective might be particularly important, the other objectives can never be totally forgotten. Good objectives are those which are clear, measurable and, preferably, quantifiable. Clarifying objectives involves breaking down project objectives into three categories – the purpose, the end results and the success criteria. For example, a project that is expressed in general terms as 'improve the budgeting process' could be broken down into:

- *Purpose* – to allow budgets to be agreed and confirmed prior to the annual financial meeting.
- *End result* – a report that identifies the causes of budget delay, and which recommends new budgeting processes and systems.
- *Success criteria* – the report should be completed by 30 June, meet all departments' needs and enable integrated and dependable delivery of agreed budget statements. Cost of the recommendations should not exceed $200,000.

Project scope

The scope of a project identifies its work content and its products or outcomes. It is a boundary-setting exercise which attempts to define the dividing line between what each part of the project will do and what it won't do. Defining scope is particularly important when part of a project is being outsourced. A supplier's scope of supply will identify the legal boundaries within which the work must be done. Sometimes the scope of the project is articulated in a formal 'project specification'. This is the written, pictorial and graphical information used to define the output, and the accompanying terms and conditions.

Project strategy

The third part of a project's definition is the project strategy, which defines, in a general rather than a specific way, how the project is going to meets its objectives. It does this in two ways; by defining the phases of the project, and by setting milestones and/or 'stagegates'. Milestones are important events during the project's life. Stagegates are the decision points that allow the project to move onto its next phase. A stagegate often launches further activities and therefore commits the project to additional costs etc. Milestone is a more passive term, which may herald the review of a part-complete project or mark the completion of a stage, but does not necessarily have more significance than a measure of achievement or completeness. At this stage the actual dates for each milestone are not necessarily determined. It is useful, however, to at least identify the significant milestones and stagegates, either to define the boundary between phases or to help in discussions with the project's customer.

Stage 3 – Project planning

The planning process fulfils four distinct purposes:

- It determines the cost and duration of the project. This enables major decisions to be made – such as the decision whether to go ahead with the project at the start.
- It determines the level of resources which will be needed.
- It helps to allocate work and to monitor progress. Planning must include the identification of who is responsible for what.
- It helps to assess the impact of any changes to the project.

Planning is not a one-off process. It may be repeated several times during the project's life as circumstances change. Nor is replanning a sign of project failure or mismanagement. In uncertain projects, in particular, it is a normal occurrence. In fact, later-stage plans typically mean that more information is available, and that the project is becoming less uncertain. The process of project planning involves five steps (*see* Fig. 16.6).

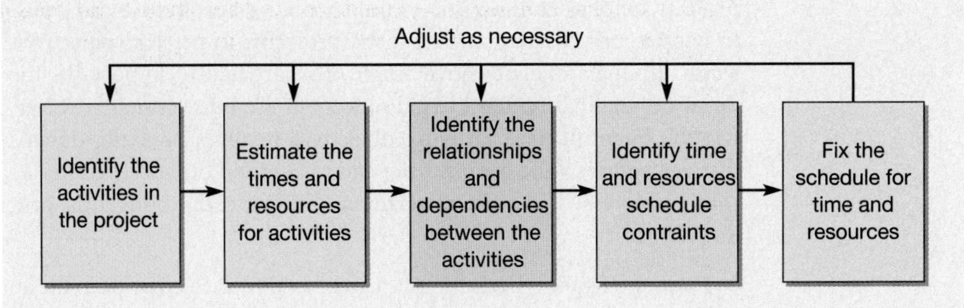

Figure 16.6 Stages in the planning process

Identify activities – the work breakdown structure

Work breakdown structure

Most projects are too complex to be planned and controlled effectively unless they are first broken down into manageable portions. This is achieved by structuring the project into a 'family tree', along similar lines to the component structure (Chapter 5), but which specifies major tasks or sub-projects. These in turn are divided up into smaller tasks until a defined, manageable series of tasks, called a *work package*, is arrived at. Each work package can be allocated its own objectives in terms of time, cost and quality. The output from this is called the **work breakdown structure** (WBS). The WBS brings clarity and definition to the project planning process. It shows 'how the jigsaw fits together'.[7] It also provides a framework for building up information for reporting purposes.

Example project

As a simple example to illustrate the application of each stage of the planning process, let us examine the following domestic project. The project definition is:

- *purpose:* to make breakfast in bed;
- *end result:* breakfast in bed of boiled egg, toast and orange juice;
- *success criteria:* plan uses minimum staff resources and time, and product is high-quality (egg freshly boiled, warm toast, etc.);
- *scope:* project starts in kitchen at 6.00 am, and finishes in bedroom; needs one operator and normal kitchen equipment.

The work breakdown structure is based on the above definition and can be constructed as shown in Figure 16.7.

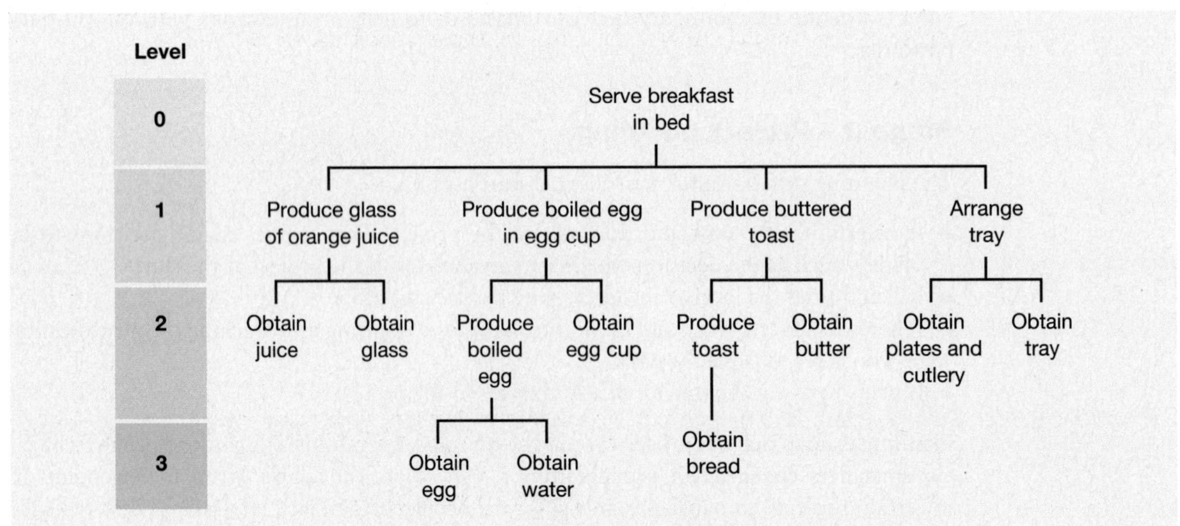

Figure 16.7 A work breakdown structure for a simple domestic project

Table 16.2 Time and resources estimates for a 'breakfast-in-bed' project

Activity	*Effort (person-min)*	*Duration (min)*
Butter toast	1	1
Pour orange juice	1	1
Boil egg	0	4
Slice bread	1	1
Fill pan with water	1	1
Bring water to boil	0	3
Toast bread	0	2
Take loaded tray to bedroom	1	1
Fetch tray, plates, cutlery	1	1

Estimate times and resources

The next stage in planning is to identify the time and resource requirements of the work packages. Without some idea of how long each part of a project will take and how many resources it will need, it is impossible to define what should be happening at any time during the execution of the project. Estimates are just that, however – a systematic best guess, not a perfect forecast of reality. Estimates may never be perfect but they can be made with some idea of how accurate they might be.

Example project

Returning to our very simple example 'breakfast-in-bed' project, the activities were identified and times estimated as in Table 16.2. While some of the estimates may appear generous, they take into account the time of day and the state of the operator.

Probabilistic estimates

The amount of uncertainty in a project has a major bearing on the level of confidence which can be placed on an estimate. The impact of uncertainty on estimating times leads some project managers to use a probability curve to describe the estimate. In practice, this is usually a positively skewed distribution, as in Figure 16.8. The greater the risk, the greater the range of the distribution. The natural tendency of some people is to produce *optimistic* estimates, but these will have a relatively low probability of being correct because they represent the time which would be taken if *everything* went well. *Most likely* estimates have the highest probability of proving correct. Finally, *pessimistic* estimates assume that almost everything which could go wrong does go wrong. Because of the skewed nature of the distribution, the expected time for the activity will not be the same as the most likely time.

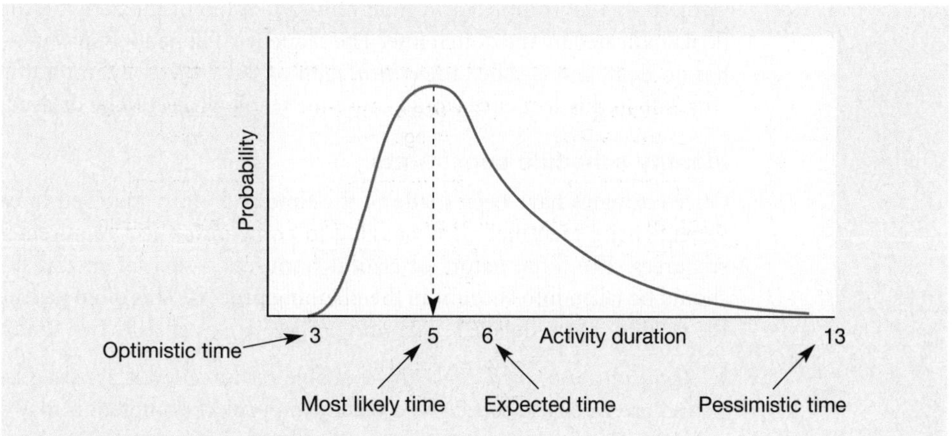

Figure 16.8 Probability distribution of time estimates

Critical commentary

When project managers talk of 'time estimates', they are really talking about guessing. By definition, planning a project happens in advance of the project itself. Therefore, no one really knows how long each activity will take. Of course, some kind of guess is needed for planning purposes. However, some project managers believe that too much faith is put in time estimates. The really important question, they claim, is not how long *will* something take, but how long *could* something take without delaying the whole project. (We deal with this issue partially when we discuss the concept of float later in the chapter.) Also, if a single most likely time estimate is difficult to estimate, then using three, as one does for probabilistic estimates, is merely over-analysing what are highly dubious data in the first place.

Identify relationships and dependencies

All the activities which are identified as composing a project will have some relationship with one another that will depend on the logic of the project. Some activities will, by necessity, need to be executed in a particular order. For example, in the construction of a house, the foundations must be prepared before the walls are built, which in turn must be completed before the roof is put in place. These activities have a *dependent* or *series* relationship. Other activities do not have any such dependence on each other. The rear garden of the house could probably be prepared totally independently of the garage being built. These two activities have an *independent* or *parallel* relationship.

Example project

Table 16.2 identified the activities for the breakfast preparation project. The list shows that some of the activities must necessarily follow others. For example, 'boil egg' cannot be carried out until 'fill pan with water' and 'bring water to boil' have been completed. Further logical analysis of the activities in the list shows that there are two major 'chains', where activities must be carried out in a definite sequence:

Slice bread – Toast bread – Butter toast
Fill pan with water – Bring water to boil – Boil egg

Both of these sequences must be completed before the activity 'take loaded tray to bedroom'. The remaining activities ('pour orange juice' and 'fetch tray, plates, cutlery') can be done at any time provided that they are completed before 'take loaded tray to bedroom'. An initial project plan might be as shown in Figure 16.9. Here, the activities have been represented as blocks of time in proportion to their estimated durations. From this, we can see that the 'project' can be completed in nine minutes. Some of the activities have spare time (called float) indicated by the dotted line. The sequence 'Fill pan – Boil water – Boil egg – Bedroom' has no float, and is called the *critical path* of the project. By implication, any activity which runs late in this sequence would cause the whole project to be delayed accordingly.

Identify schedule constraints

Once estimates have been made of the time and effort involved in each activity, and their dependencies identified, it is possible to compare project requirements with the available resources. The finite nature of critical resources – such as special skills – means that they should be taken into account in the planning process. This often has the effect of highlighting the need for more detailed replanning. There are essentially two fundamental approaches:[8]

- *Resource-constrained.* Only the available resource levels are used in resource scheduling, and are never exceeded. As a result, the project completion may slip. Resource-limited scheduling is used, for example, when a project company has its own highly specialized assembly and test facilities.

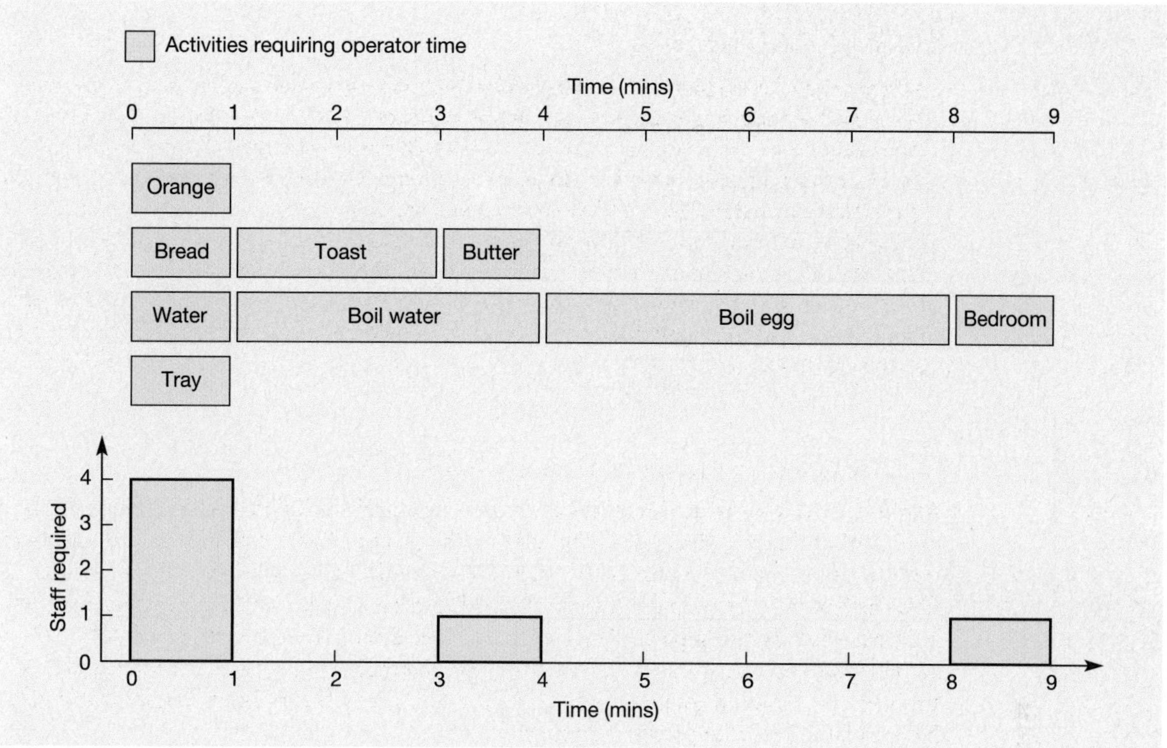

Figure 16.9 Initial project plan for a simple project, with resources

- *Time-constrained.* The overriding priority is to complete the project within a given time. Once normally available resources have been used up, alternative ('threshold') resources are scheduled.

Example project

Returning to the breakfast-in-bed project, we can now consider the resource implications of the plan in Figure 16.9. Each of the four activities scheduled at the start (pour orange, cut bread, fill pan, fetch tray) consumes staff resources. There is clearly a resource-loading problem, because the project definition states that only one person is available. This is not an insuperable difficulty, however, because there is sufficient float to move some of the activities. A plan with levelled resources can be produced, as shown in Figure 16.10. All that has been necessary is to delay the toast preparation by one minute, and to use the elapsed time during the toasting and water-boiling processes to pour orange and fetch the tray.

Fix the schedule

Project planners should ideally have a number of alternatives to choose from. The one which best fits project objectives can then be chosen or developed. For example, it may be appropriate to examine both resource-limited and time-limited options. However, it is not always possible to examine several alternative schedules, especially in very large or very uncertain projects, as the computation could be prohibitive. However, modern computer-based project management software is making the search for the best schedule more feasible.

Example project

A further improvement to the plan can be made. Looking again at the project definition, the success criteria state that the product should be 'high-quality'. In the plan shown in Figure 16.10, although the egg is freshly boiled, the toast might be cold. An 'optimized' plan which would provide hot toast would be to prepare the toast during the 'boil egg' activity. This plan is shown in Figure 16.11.

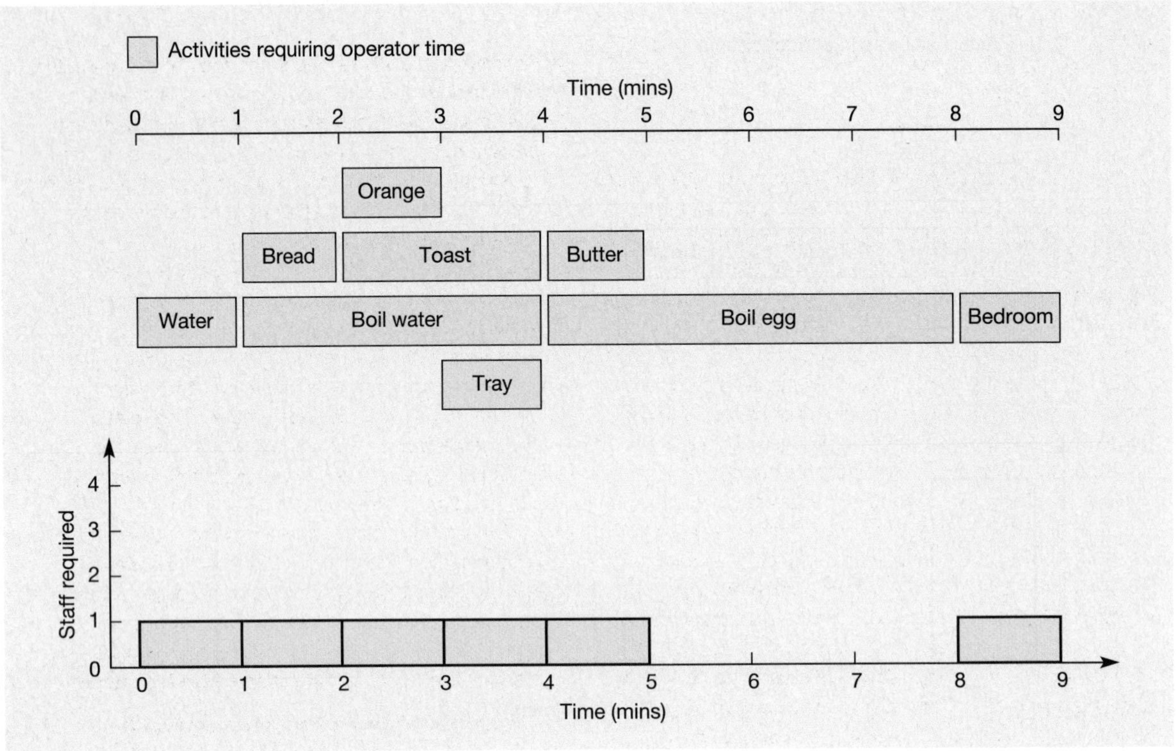

Figure 16.10 Revised plan with levelled resources

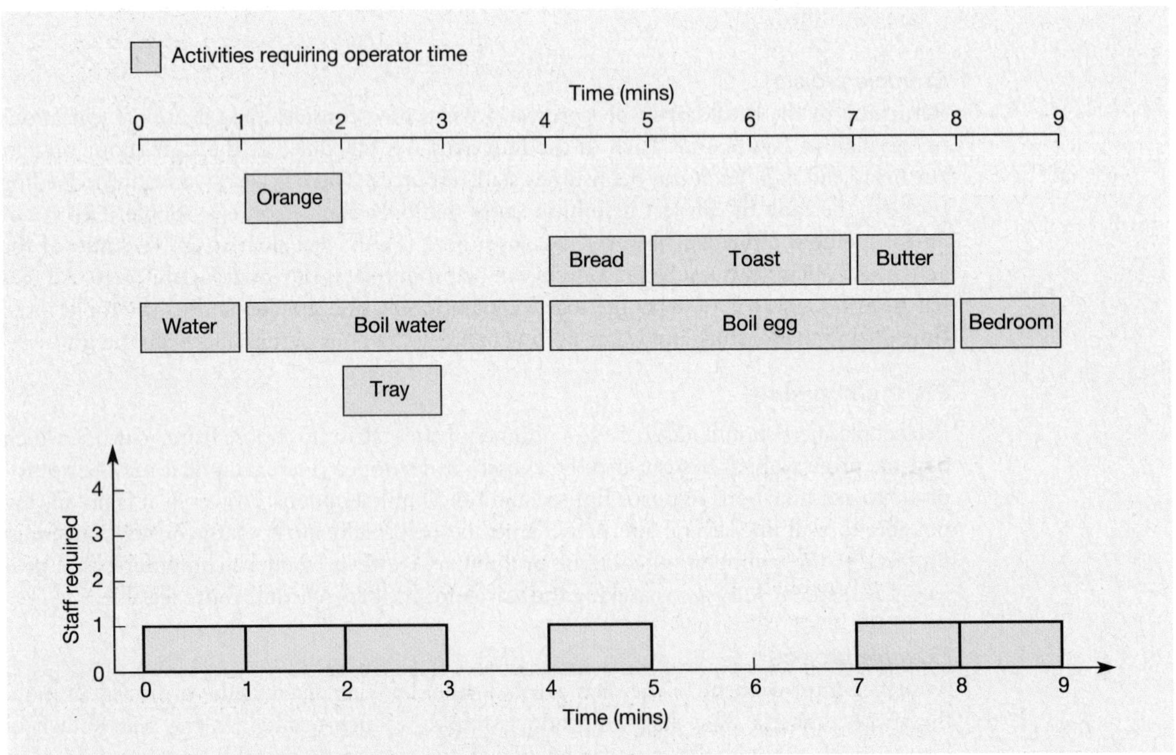

Figure 16.11 Revised plan with levelled resources and warm toast

Short case
Access HK[9]

Access HK is an independent non-profit organization that works to fight inequality and to provide underprivileged children with educational opportunities that are otherwise unaffordable by them. Every summer, Access HK's volunteers, mostly students studying at overseas universities, return to Hong Kong to give a free summer school to children in need. It was set up in the summer of 2001 by a group of Hong Kong students at leading UK and US universities. Since then it has organized several large-scale events to help underprivileged children, including free 4-week summer schools during which children are taught in interactive formats on subjects such as the English language, current affairs, speech and drama. Oxford student Ng Kwan-hung, Access HK's external secretary, said: *'We share a common belief that what distinguishes one child from another is not ability but access – access to opportunities, access to education, access to love. All of us realize the importance of a good learning environment for a child's development.'* Chung Tin-Wong, a law student at Oxford and sub-committee member, added: *'We are all dedicated to providing the best education for underprivileged children.'*

Project-managing the summer schools is particularly important to Access HK because their opportunities to make a difference to the underprivileged are limited largely to the vacation periods when their student volunteers are available. Project failure would mean waiting until the next year to get another chance. Also, like many charities, the budget is limited with every dollar having to count. Because of this, the student volunteers soon learn some of the arts of the project management, including how to break the project down into four phases for ease of planning and control.

- *Conceptual phase* – during which the Access HK central committee agrees with the Summer School Committee, its direction, aim and goal.
- *Planning phase* – when the Summer School Committee sets the time and cost parameters for the project. The time frame for the summer school is always tight. Students volunteers only become available after they have completed their summer exams, and the summer school must be ready to run when the primary school students have their summer break.
- *Definition and design phase* – when the detailed implementation plans for the summer school are finalized. Communication within the team of volunteers is particularly important to ensure contributed smooth implementation later. Many of them, although enthusiastic, have little project management experience, and therefore need the support of detailed instructions as to how to carry out their part of the project.
- *Implementation phase* – again, it is the relative inexperience of the volunteer force that dictates how the summer school project is implemented. It is important to ensure that control mechanisms are in place that can detect any problems or deviations from the plan quickly, and help to bring it back on target.

'The success of these summer school projects depends very much on including all our stakeholders in the process', says one summer school coordinator. *'All our stakeholders are important but they have different interests. The students on the summer schools, even if they don't articulate their objectives, need to feel they are benefiting from the experience. Our volunteers are all bright and enthusiastic and are interested in helping to manage the process as well as taking part in it. Access HK wants to be sure that we are doing our best to fulfil their objectives and uphold their reputation. The Hong Kong government has an obvious interest in the success and integrity of the summer schools, and the sponsors need to be assured that their donations are being used wisely. In addition the schools who lend us their buildings and many other interested parties all need to be included, in different ways and to different extents, in our project management process.'*

Stage 5 – Project control

The stages in project planning and control have so far all taken place before the actual project takes place. This stage deals with the management activities which take place during the execution of the project. Project control is the essential link between planning and doing. It involves three sets of decisions:

- how to *monitor* the project in order to check on its progress;
- how to *assess the performance* of the project by comparing monitored observations of the project with the project plan;
- how to *intervene* in the project in order to make the changes that will bring it back to plan.

Project monitoring

Project managers have first to decide what they should be looking for as the project progresses. Usually a variety of measures are monitored. To some extent, the measures used will depend on the nature of the project. However, common measures include current expenditure to date, supplier price changes, amount of overtime authorized, technical changes to project, inspection failures, number and length of delays, activities not started on time, missed milestones, etc. Some of these monitored measures affect mainly cost, some mainly time. However, when something affects the quality of the project, there are also time and cost implications. This is because quality problems in project planning and control usually have to be solved in a limited amount of time.

Assessing project performance

The monitored measures of project performance at any point in time need to be assessed so that project management can make a judgement concerning overall performance. A typical planned cost profile of a project through its life is shown in Figure 16.12. At the beginning of a project some activities can be started, but most activities will be dependent on finishing. Eventually, only a few activities will remain to be completed. This pattern of a slow start followed by a faster pace with an eventual tail-off of activity holds true for almost all projects, which is why the rate of total expenditure follows an S-shaped pattern as shown in Figure 16.13, even when the cost curves for the individual activities are linear. It is against this curve that actual costs can be compared in order to check whether the project's costs are being incurred to plan. Figure 16.14 shows the planned and actual cost figures compared in this way. It shows that the project is incurring costs, on a cumulative basis, ahead of what was planned.

Intervening to change the project

If the project is obviously out of control in the sense that its costs, quality levels or times are significantly different from those planned, then some kind of intervention is almost certainly likely to be required. The exact nature of the intervention will depend on the technical characteristics of the project, but it is likely to need the advice of all the people who would be affected. Given the interconnected nature of projects – a change to one part of the project will have knock-on effects elsewhere – this means that interventions often require wide consultation. Sometimes intervention is needed even if the project looks to be proceeding according

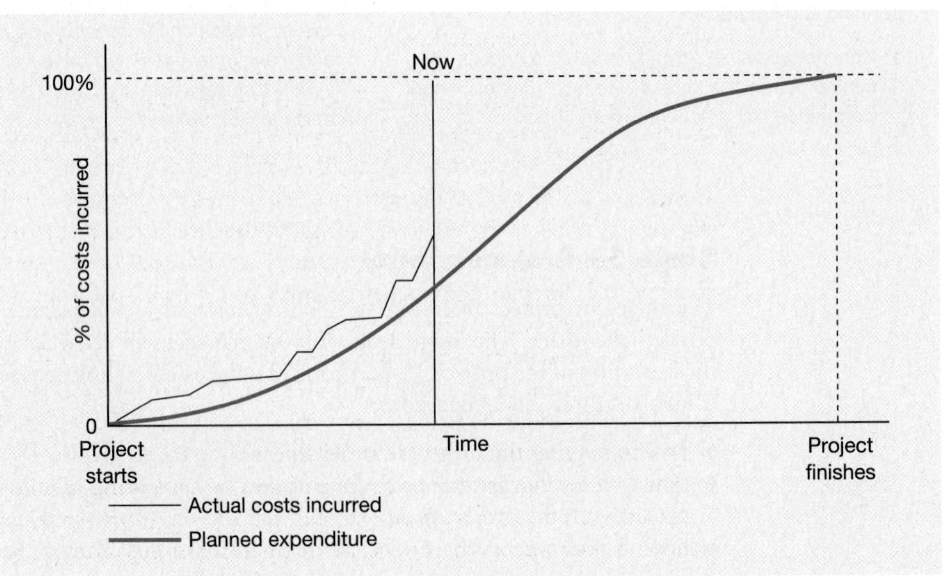

Figure 16.12 Comparing planned and actual expenditure

to plan. For example, the schedule and cost for a project may seem to be 'to plan', but when the project managers project activities and cost into the future, they see that problems are very likely to arise. In this case it is the *trend* of performance which is being used to trigger intervention.

Network planning

The process of project planning and control is greatly aided by the use of techniques which help project managers to handle its complexity and time-based nature. The simplest of these techniques is the Gantt chart (or bar chart) which we introduced in Chapter 10. Gantt charts are the simplest way to exhibit an overall project plan, because they have excellent visual impact and are easy to understand. They are also useful for communicating project plans and status to senior managers as well as for day-to-day project control. Later techniques, most of which go under the collective name of **network analysis** are now used, almost universally, to help plan and control all significant projects, but can also prove helpful in smaller ventures. The two network analysis methods we will examine are the **critical path method** (CPM) or analysis (CPA) and **programme evaluation and review technique** (PERT).

CADCENTRE's visuality group Reality Center visualization system enables project teams to check out and validate proposals using interactive computer models

Network analysis

Critical path method

Programme evaluation and review technique

Critical path method (CPM)

As project complexity increases, so it becomes necessary to identify the relationships between activities. It becomes increasingly important to show the logical sequence in which activities must take place. The critical path method (CPM) models the project by clarifying the relationships between activities diagrammatically. The first way we can illustrate this is by using arrows to represent each **activity** in a project. For example, examine the simple project in Figure 16.13 which involves the decoration of an apartment. Six activities are identified together with their relationships. The first, activity a, 'remove furniture', does not require any of the other activities to be completed before it can be started. However, activity b, 'prepare bedroom', cannot be started until activity a has been completed. The same applies to activity d, 'prepare the kitchen'. Similarly activity c, 'paint bedroom', cannot be started until activity b has been completed. Nor can activity e, 'paint the kitchen', be started until the kitchen has been prepared. Only when both the bedroom and the kitchen have been painted can the apartment be furnished again. The logic of these relationships is shown as an arrow diagram, where each activity is represented by an arrow (the length of the arrows is not proportional to the duration of the activities).

Activity

This arrow diagram can be developed into a network diagram as shown in Figure 16.14. At the tail (start) and head (finish) of each *activity* (represented by an arrow) is a circle which represents an **event**. Events are moments in time which occur at the start or finish of an activity. They have no duration and are of a definite recognizable nature. Networks of this type are composed only of activities and events.

Event

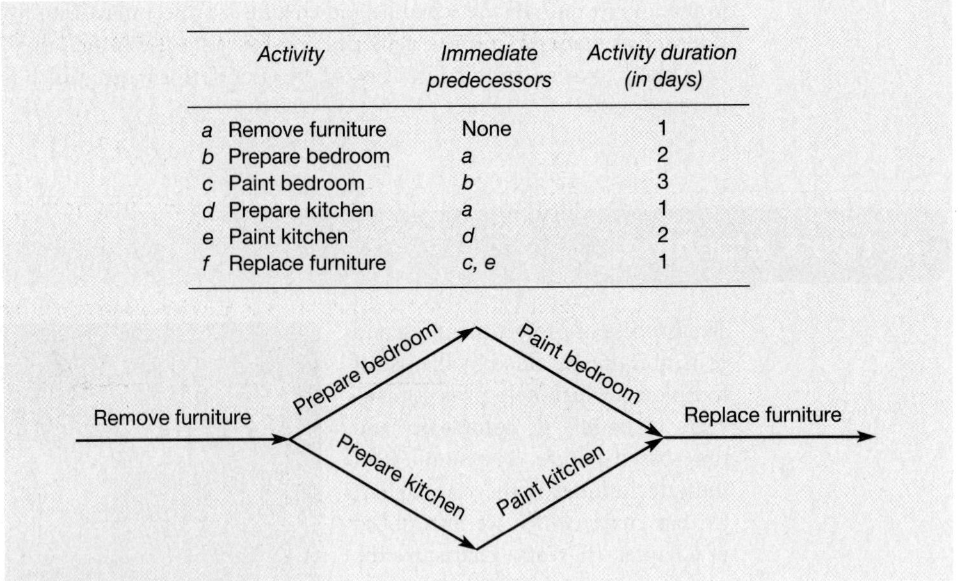

Activity	Immediate predecessors	Activity duration (in days)
a Remove furniture	None	1
b Prepare bedroom	*a*	2
c Paint bedroom	*b*	3
d Prepare kitchen	*a*	1
e Paint kitchen	*d*	2
f Replace furniture	*c, e*	1

Figure 16.13 The activities, relationships, durations and arrow diagram for the project 'decorate apartment'

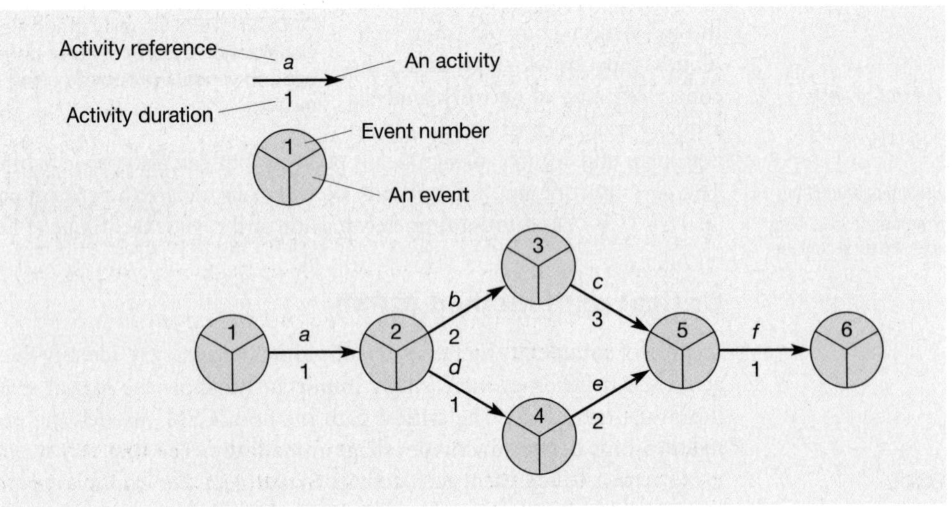

Figure 16.14 A network diagram for the project 'decorate apartment'

The rules for drawing this type of network diagram are fairly straightforward:

Rule 1 An event cannot be reached until all activities leading to it are complete. Event 5 in Figure 16.14 is not reached until activities c and e are complete.

Rule 2 No activity can start until its tail event is reached. In Figure 16.14 activity f cannot start until event 5 is reached.

Dummy activity

Rule 3 No two activities can have the same head and tail events. In Figure 16.15 activities x and y cannot be drawn as first shown; they must be drawn using a **dummy activity**. These have no duration and are usually shown as a dotted-line arrow. They are used either for clarity of drawing or to keep the logic of the diagram consistent with that of the project.

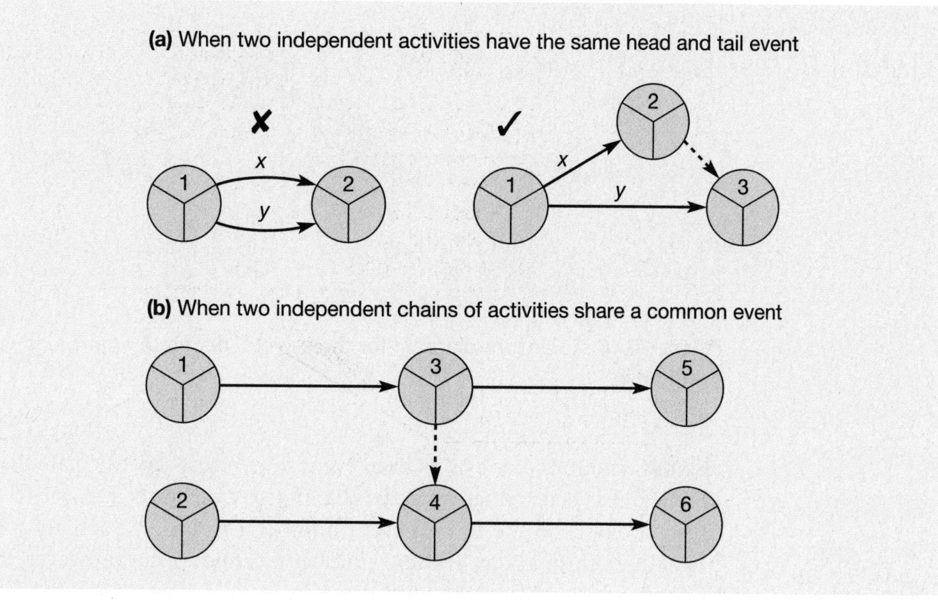

Figure 16.15 When dummy activities are necessary

The critical path

In all network diagrams where the activities have some parallel relationships, there will be more than one sequence of activities which will lead from the start to the end of the project. These sequences of activities are called *paths* through the network. Each path will have a total duration which is the sum of all its activities. The path which has the longest sequence of activities is called the **critical path** of the network (note that it is possible to have more than one critical path if they share the same joint longest time). It is called the critical path because any delay in any of the activities on this path will delay the whole project. In Figure 16.14, therefore, the critical path through the network is a, b, c, f, which is seven days long. This is the minimum duration of the whole project. By drawing the network diagram we can:

Critical path

- identify which are the particularly important activities;
- calculate the duration of the whole project.

Calculating float

Float

Earlier in the chapter we described the flexibility to change the timings of activities, which is inherent in various parts of a project, as **float**. We can use the network diagram to calculate this for each activity. The procedure is relatively simple:

Earliest event time

Latest event time

1 Calculate the earliest and latest event times for each event. The **earliest event time** (EET) is the very earliest the event could possibly occur if all preceding activities are completed as early as possible. The **latest event time** (LET) is the latest time that the event could possibly take place without delaying the whole project.
2 Calculate the 'time window' within which an activity must take place. This is the time between the EET of its tail event and the LET of its head event.
3 Compare the actual duration of the activity with the time window within which it must take place. The difference between them is the float of the activity.

Consider again the simple network example. The critical path is the sequence of activities a, b, c, f. We can calculate the EET and LET for each event as shown in Figure 16.16. If activity a starts at time 0, the earliest it can finish is 1 because it is a one-day activity. If activity b is started immediately, it will finish at day 3 (EET of tail event + duration, 1 + 2). Activity c can then start at day 3 and because it is of three days' duration it will finish at day 6. Activity e

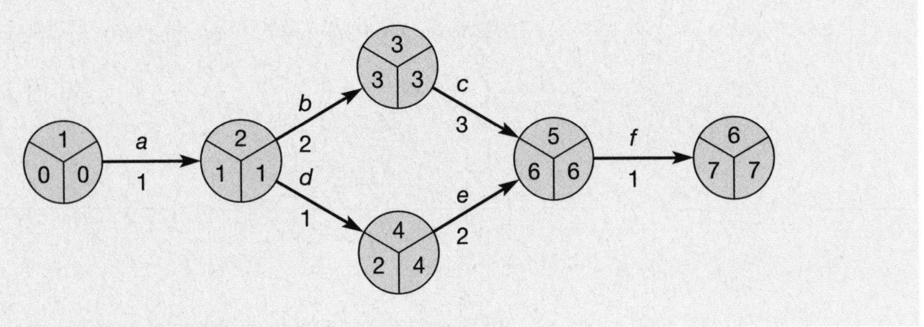

Figure 16.16 A network diagram for the project 'decorate apartment' with earliest and latest event times

also has event number 5 as its head event so we must also calculate the EET of activity e's tail event. This is determined by activity d. If activity d starts at day 1 (the earliest it can) it will finish at day 2. So the EET of event number 4 is day 2. If activity e is started immediately, it will then finish at day 4. Event number 5 cannot occur, however, until both e and c have finished, which will not be until day 6 (*see* rule 1 above). Activity f can then start and will finish at day 7.

The LETs can be calculated by using the reverse logic. If event number 6 *must* occur no later than day 7, the LET for event number 5 is day 6. Any later than this and the whole project will be delayed. Working back, if activity c must finish by day 6 it cannot start later than day 3, and if activity b must finish by day 3 it must start by day 1. Similarly, if activity e is to finish by day 6 it must start no later than day 4, and if activity d is to finish by day 4 it must start no later than day 3. Now we have two activities with event number 2 as their tail event, one of which needs to start by day 1 at the latest, the other by day 3 at the latest. The LET for event number 2, therefore, must be the smaller of the two. If it were delayed past this point, activity b, and therefore the whole project, would be delayed.

Worked example

The chief surveyor of a firm that moves earth in preparation for the construction of roads has identified the activities and their durations for each stage of an operation to prepare a difficult stretch of motorway (*see* Table 16.3). The surveyor needs to know how long the project will take and which are the critical activities.

Table 16.3 Road construction activities

Activity	*Duration (days)*	*Preceding activities*
A	5	–
B	10	–
C	1	–
D	8	B
E	10	B
F	9	B
G	3	A, D
H	7	A, D
I	4	F
J	3	F
K	5	C, J
L	8	H, E, I, K
M	4	C, J

Figure 16.17 shows the network diagram for the project. Drawing these diagrams from the type of information in Table 16.3 is a matter of sketching the logic of the relationships between the activities on a piece of paper until it conforms to the relationships as stated, and then drawing the diagram again in a neater fashion. So, for example, A, B and C have no predecessors and therefore are the activities that can be commenced at the beginning of the project. Activities D, E and F all can start after the completion of activity B, and so on. The diagram also shows the latest and earliest event times for the activities. It shows that the critical path for the project is the sequence of activities B, F, J, K, L. The total length of the project is 35 days, this being the length of the critical path sequence of activities.

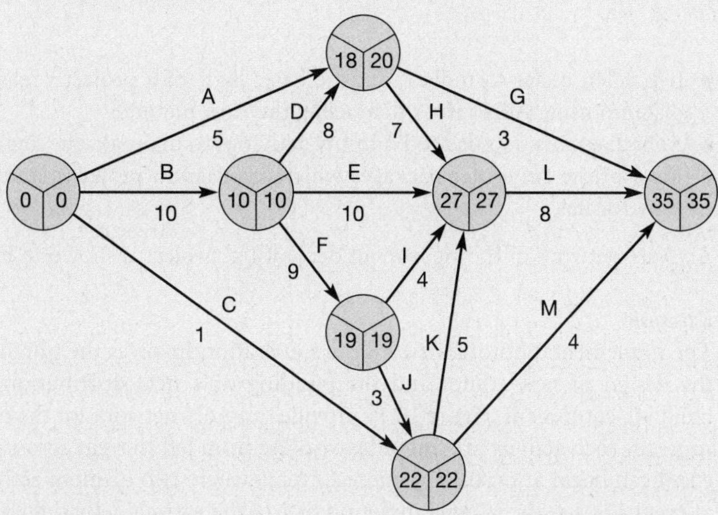

Figure 16.17 Network diagram for the motorway project

Critical commentary

The idea that all project activities can be identified as entities with a clear beginning and a clear end point and that these entities can be described in terms of their relationship with each other is an obvious simplification. Some activities are more or less continuous and evolve over time. For example, take a simple project such as digging a trench and laying a communications cable in it. The activity 'dig trench' does not have to be completed before the activity 'lay cable' is started. Only two or three metres of the trench needs to be dug before cable laying can commence. A simple relationship, but one that is difficult to illustrate on a network diagram. Also, if the trench is being dug in difficult terrain, the time taken to complete the activity, or even the activity itself may change, to include rock drilling activities for example. However, if the trench cannot be dug because of rock formations, it may be possible to dig more of the trench elsewhere, a contingency not allowed for in the original plan. So, even for this simple project, the original network diagram may reflect neither what *will* happen nor what *could* happen.

Activity on node networks

Activity on arrow
Activity on node

The network we have described so far uses arrows to represent activities and circles at the junctions or nodes of the arrows to represent events. This method is called the **activity on arrow** (AoA) method. An alternative method of drawing networks is the **activity on node** (AoN) method. In the AoN representation, activities are drawn as boxes, and arrows are used to define the relationships between them. There are three advantages to the AoN method:

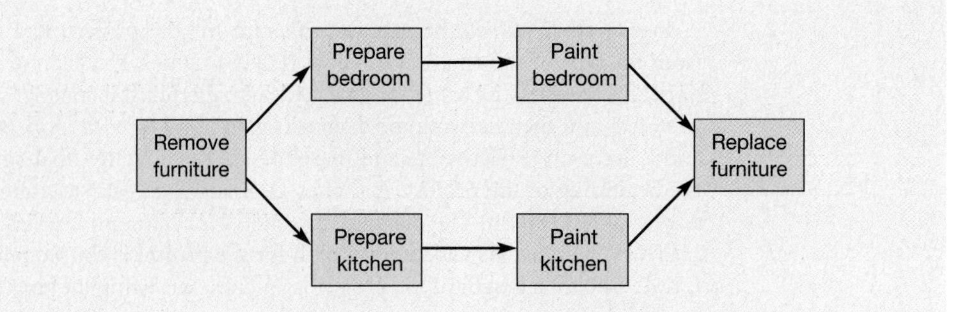

Figure 16.18 Activity on node network diagram for project 'decorate apartment'

- It is often easier to move from the basic logic of a project's relationships to a network diagram using AoN rather than using the AoA method.
- AoN diagrams do not need dummy activities to maintain the logic of relationships.
- Most of the computer packages which are used in project planning and control use an AoN format.

An AoN network of the 'apartment decorating' project is shown in Figure 16.18.

Example

The implementation of a new logistics operation involves the purchase of a fleet of trucks, the design of new routes and the building of a new distribution centre and associated handling equipment. Figure 16.19 provides an AoN network for the project. The *earliest start times* for each activity are found by working from left to right across the network. Each start event can begin at $t = 0$. At a 'merge' event (where two or more activities come together, as at event 12), use the latest completion date of the various activities which lead into it. Earliest finish times of a 'burst' activity (such as activity 6, where five succeeding activities literally 'burst' out) are carried forward to form the earliest start dates of the succeeding activities (7 through 11). The *latest start times* for each activity are found by working back from right to left across the network. The earliest start time for the final event on the network is often used as the latest start time for that event as well. At a 'merge' event (such as event 6), use the earliest completion date of the various activities.

First, we carry out a *forward pass* of the network (i.e. proceed from left to right). Activity 1 is given a start date of week 0. The earliest finish is then week 17, because the duration is 17 weeks. The earliest start date for activity 2 must then also be week 17. Activity 5 starts at 17 + 34, the duration for activity 2. Activity 4 is in parallel with activity 2, and can start at the same time. The rest of the forward pass is straight-forward until we reach activity 12. Here, seven activities merge, so we must use the highest earliest finish of the activities which lead into it as the earliest start time for activity 12. This is 91 (the earliest finish time for activity 4). Since the duration of activity 12 is two weeks, the earliest finish time for the whole network is 93 weeks.

Now we can carry out a *backward pass* by assuming that the latest finish time is also 93 weeks (the bottom right-hand box on activity 12). This means that there is no 'float', i.e. the difference between the earliest and latest start dates for this activity is zero. Hence, the latest start time is also week 91. This gets down-dated into activities 7 through 11, which have week 91 as the latest finish time. The difference between week 91 and the various earliest finish times for these activities means that there is float on each one. That is, that they can start much later than indicated by the earliest start dates. On the backward pass, activity 6 forms a merge event for activities 7 through 11. Take the lowest latest start time from these activities, i.e. week 67, as the latest finish time for activity 6. If all goes well, and the analysis is correct, there should also be zero float for activity 1. The *critical path* for the network is then the line which joins the activities with minimum float, i.e. activities 1, 4 and 12.

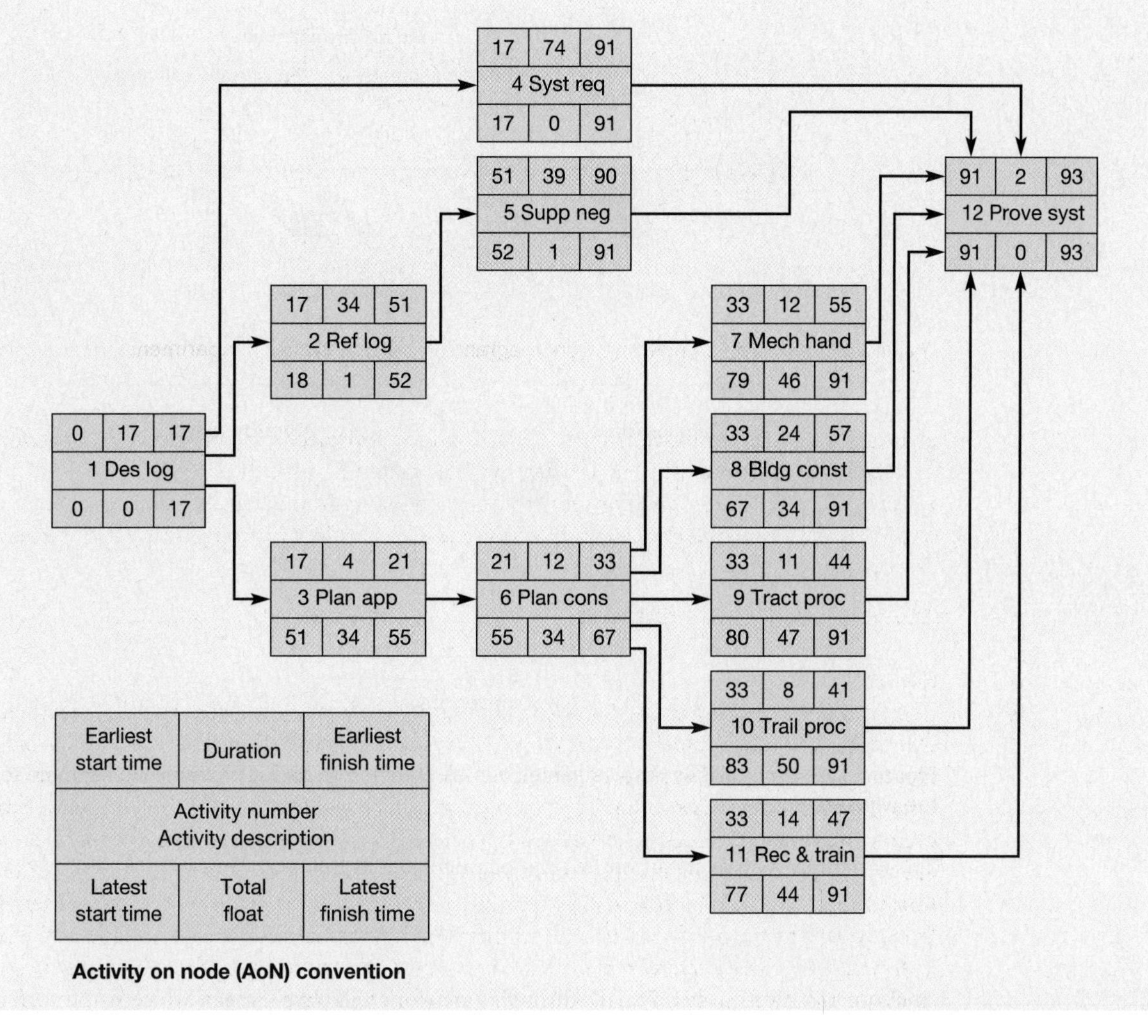

Figure 16.19 New logistics operation: precedence network

Programme evaluation and review technique (PERT)

The programme evaluation and review technique, or PERT as it is universally known, had its origins in planning and controlling major defence projects in the US Navy. PERT had its most spectacular gains in the highly uncertain environment of space and defence projects. The technique recognizes that activity durations and costs in project management are not deterministic (fixed), and that probability theory can be applied to estimates, as was mentioned earlier. In this type of network each activity duration is estimated on an optimistic, a most likely and a pessimistic basis, as shown in Figure 16.20. If it is assumed that these time estimates are consistent with a beta probability distribution, the mean and variance of the distribution can be estimated as follows:

$$t_e = \frac{t_o + 4t_l + t_p}{6}$$

where

t_e = the expected time for the activity
t_o = the optimistic time for the activity
t_l = the most likely time for the activity
t_p = the pessimistic time for the activity.

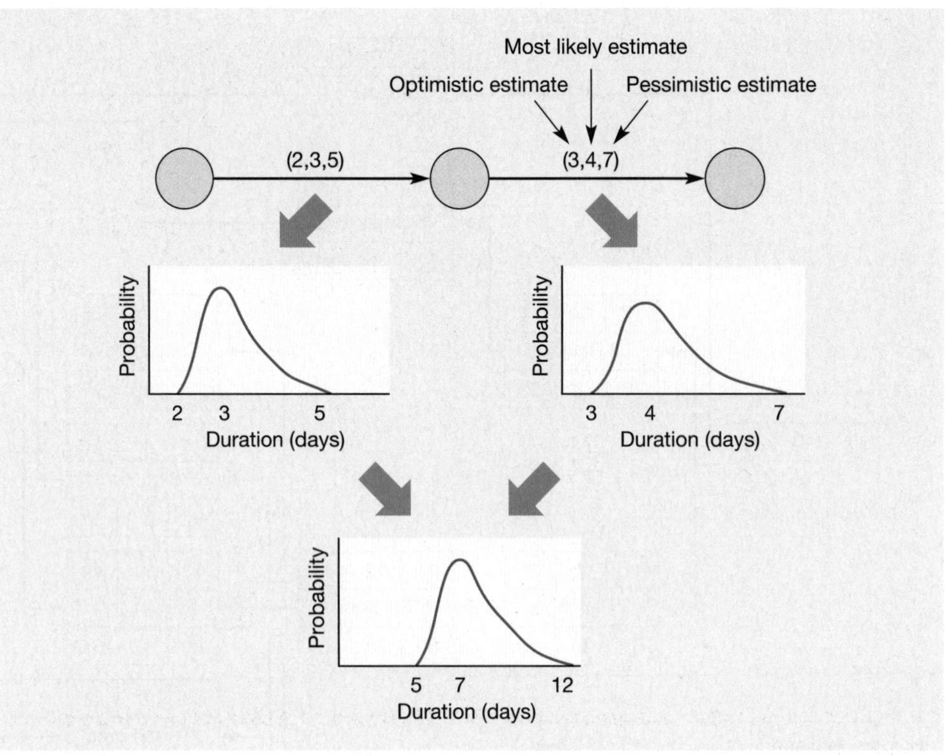

Figure 16.20 Probabilistic time estimates can be summed to give a probabilistic estimate for the whole project

The variance of the distribution (V) can be calculated as follows:

$$V = \frac{(t_p - t_o)^2}{6^2} = \frac{(t_p - t_o)^2}{36}$$

The time distribution of any path through a network will have a mean which is the sum of the means of the activities that make up the path, and a variance which is a sum of their variances. In Figure 16.21:

$$\text{The mean of the first activity} = \frac{2 + (4 \times 3) + 5}{6} = 3.17$$

$$\text{The variance of the first activity} = \frac{(5 - 2)^2}{36} = 0.25$$

$$\text{The mean of the second activity} = \frac{3 + (4 \times 4) + 7}{6} = 4.33$$

$$\text{The variance of the second activity} = \frac{(7 - 3)^2}{36} = 0.44$$

$$\text{The mean of the network distribution} = 3.17 + 4.33 = 7.5$$

$$\text{The variance of the network distribution} = 0.25 + 0.44 = 0.69$$

It is generally assumed that the whole path will be normally distributed.

The advantage of this extra information is that we can examine the 'riskiness' of each path through a network as well as its duration. For example, Figure 16.21 shows a simple two-path network. The top path is the critical one; the distribution of its duration is 10.5 with a variance of 0.06 (therefore a standard deviation of 0.245). The distribution of the non-critical path has a mean of 9.67 and a variance of 0.66 (therefore a standard deviation of 0.812). The

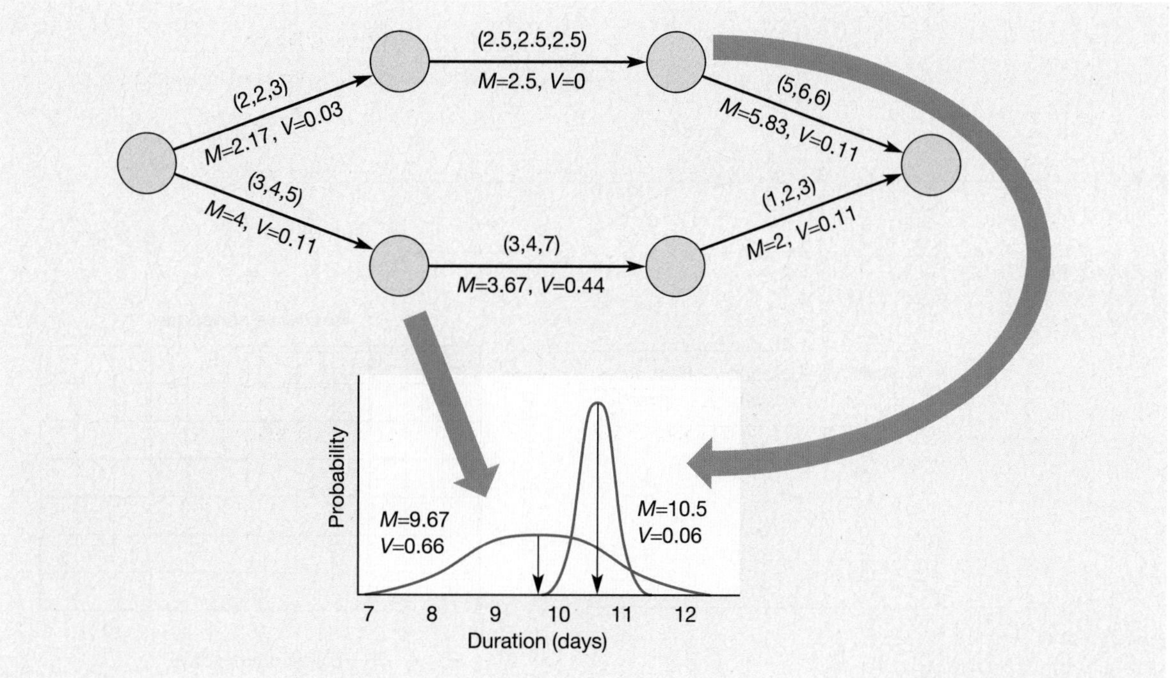

Figure 16.21 One path in the network can have the longest expected duration while another path has the greater variance

implication of this is that there is a chance that the non-critical path could in reality be critical. Although we will not discuss the probability calculations here, it is possible to determine the probability of any sub-critical path turning out to be critical when the project actually takes place. However, on a practical level, even if the probability calculations are judged not to be worth the effort involved, it is useful to be able to make an approximate assessment of the riskiness of each part of a network.

Introducing resource constraints

The logic which governs network relationships is primarily derived from the technical details of the project as we have described. However, the availability of resources may impose its own constraints, which can materially affect the relationships between activities. Figure 16.22 shows a simple two-path network with details of both the duration of each activity and the number of staff required to perform each activity. The total resource schedule is also shown. The three activities on the critical path, a, c and e, have been programmed into the resource schedule first. The remaining activities all have some float and therefore have flexibility as to when they are performed.

The resource schedule in Figure 16.22 has the non-critical activities starting as soon as is possible. This results in a resource profile which varies from seven staff down to three. Even if seven staff are available, the project manager might want to even out the loading for organizational convenience. If the total number of staff available is less than seven, however, the project will need rescheduling. Suppose only five staff are available. It is still possible to complete the project in the same time, as shown in Figure 16.23. Activity b has been delayed until after activity a has finished. This results in a resource profile which varies only between four and five staff and is within the resourcing limit of five staff.

However, in order to achieve this it is necessary to *require* activity b to start only when activity a is completed. This is a logic constraint which, if it were included in the network, would change it as shown in Figure 16.23. In this network all activities are critical, as indeed one can see from the resource schedule.

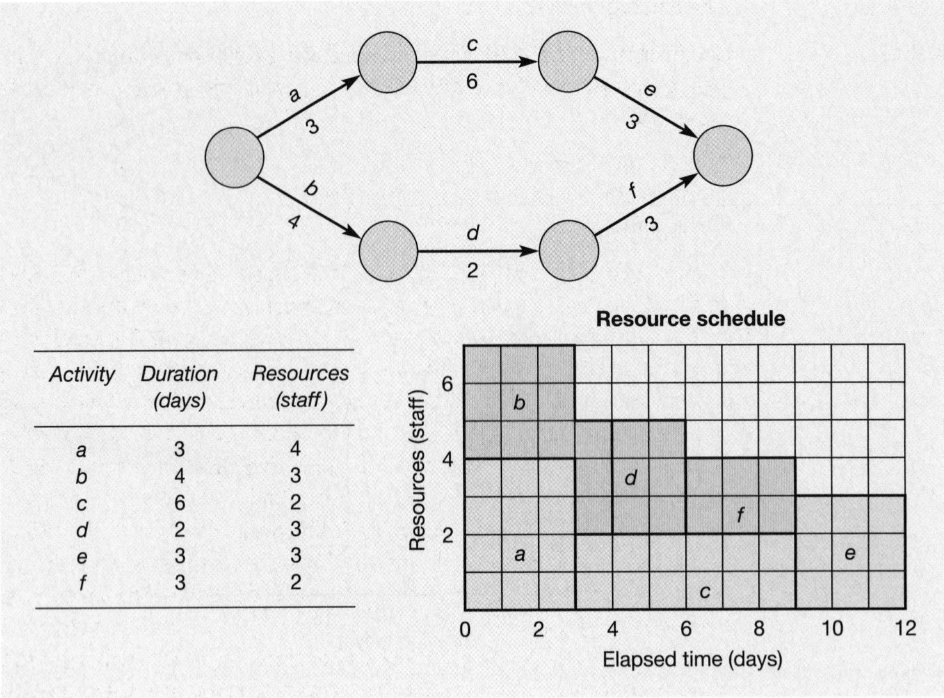

Activity	Duration (days)	Resources (staff)
a	3	4
b	4	3
c	6	2
d	2	3
e	3	3
f	3	2

Figure 16.22 Resource profile of a network assuming that all activities are started as soon as possible

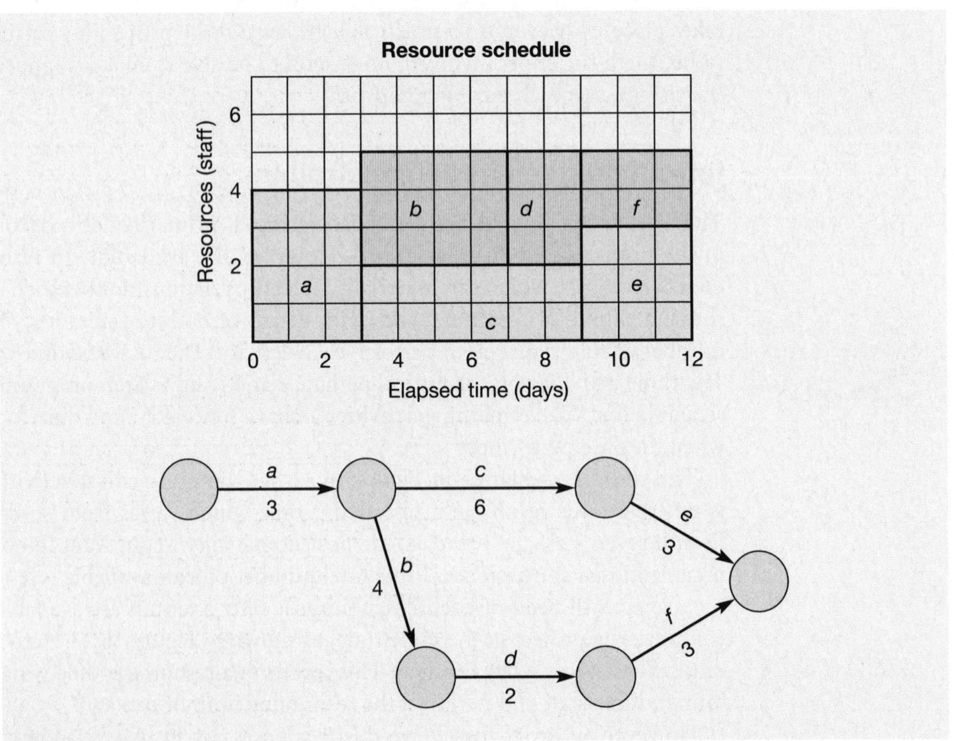

Figure 16.23 Resource profile of a network with non-critical activities delayed to fit resource constraints; in this case this effectively changes the network logic to make all activities critical

Crashing networks

Crashing

Crashing networks is the process of reducing time spans on critical path activities so that the project is completed in less time. Usually, crashing activities incurs extra cost. This can be as a result of:

- overtime working;
- additional resources, such as manpower;
- subcontracting.

Figure 16.24 shows an example of crashing a simple network. For each activity the duration and normal cost are specified, together with the (reduced) duration and (increased) cost of crashing them. Not all activities are capable of being crashed; here activity e cannot be crashed. The critical path is the sequence of activities a, b, c, e. If the total project time is to be reduced, one of the activities on the critical path must be crashed. In order to decide which activity to crash, the 'cost slope' of each is calculated. This is the cost per time period of reducing durations. The most cost-effective way of shortening the whole project then is to crash the activity on the critical path which has the lowest cost slope. This is activity a, the crashing of which will cost an extra £2,000 and will shorten the project by one week. After this, activity c can be crashed, saving a further two weeks and costing an extra £5,000. At this point all the activities have become critical and further time savings can only be achieved by crashing two activities in parallel. The shape of the time–cost curve in Figure 16.24 is entirely typical. Initial savings come relatively inexpensively if the activities with the lowest cost slope are chosen. Later in the crashing sequence the more expensive activities need to be crashed and eventually two or more paths become jointly critical. Inevitably by that point, savings in time can only come from crashing two or more activities on parallel paths.

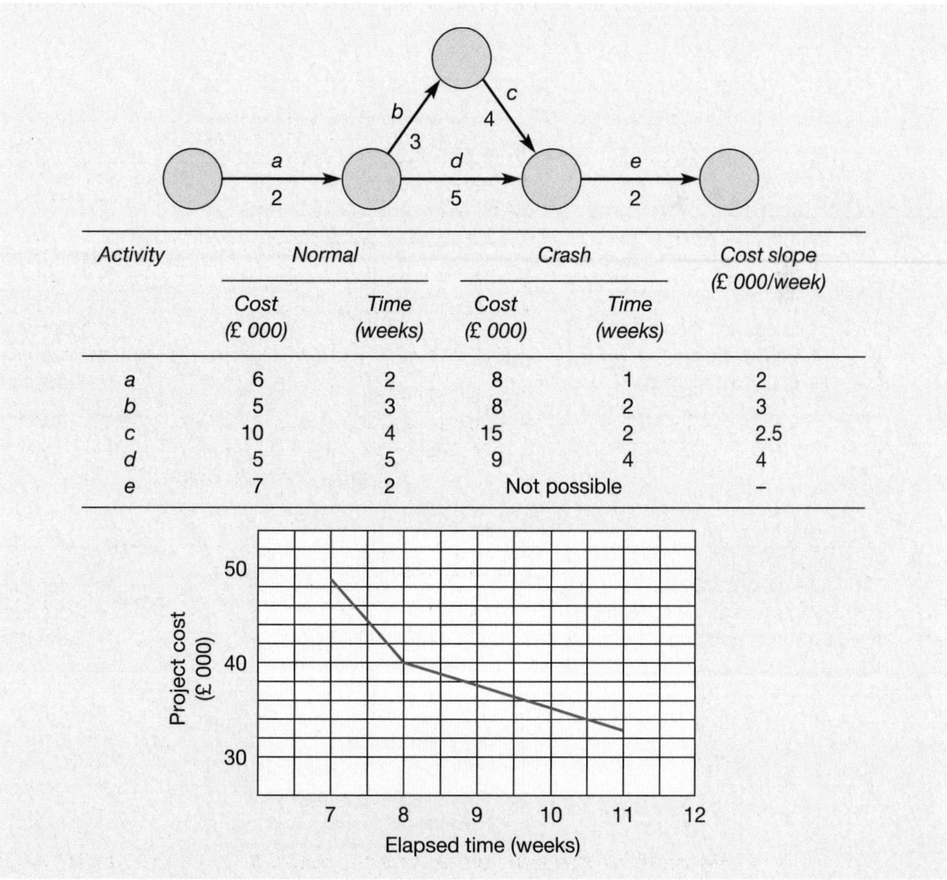

Activity	Normal Cost (£ 000)	Normal Time (weeks)	Crash Cost (£ 000)	Crash Time (weeks)	Cost slope (£ 000/week)
a	6	2	8	1	2
b	5	3	8	2	3
c	10	4	15	2	2.5
d	5	5	9	4	4
e	7	2	Not possible		–

Figure 16.24 Crashing activities to shorten project time becomes progressively more expensive

Computer-assisted project management

For many years, since the emergence of computer-based modelling, increasingly sophisticated software for project planning and control has become available. The rather tedious computation necessary in network planning can relatively easily be performed by project planning models. All they need are the basic relationships between activities together with timing and resource requirements for each activity. Earliest and latest event times, float and other characteristics of a network can be presented, often in the form of a Gantt chart. More significantly, the speed of computation allows for frequent updates to project plans. Similarly, if updated information is both accurate and frequent, such a computer-based system can also provide effective project control data. More recently, the potential for using computer-based project management systems for communication within large and complex projects has been developed in so-called **Enterprise Project Management** (EPM) systems.

Enterprise Project Management

Figure 16.25 illustrates just some of the elements that are integrated within EPM systems. Most of these activities have been treated in this chapter. Project planning involves critical path analysis and scheduling, an understanding of float, and the sending of instructions on when to start activities. Resource scheduling looks at the resource implications of planning decisions and the way a project may have to be changed to accommodate resource constraints. Project control includes simple budgeting and cost management together with more sophisticated earned value control. However, EPM also includes other elements. Project modelling involves the use of project planning methods to explore alternative approaches to a project, identifying where failure might occur and exploring the changes to the project which may have to be made under alternative future scenarios. Project portfolio analysis acknowledges that, for many organizations, several projects have to be managed simultaneously. Usually these share common resources. Therefore, not only delays in one activity within a project affect other activities in that project, they may also have an impact on completely different projects

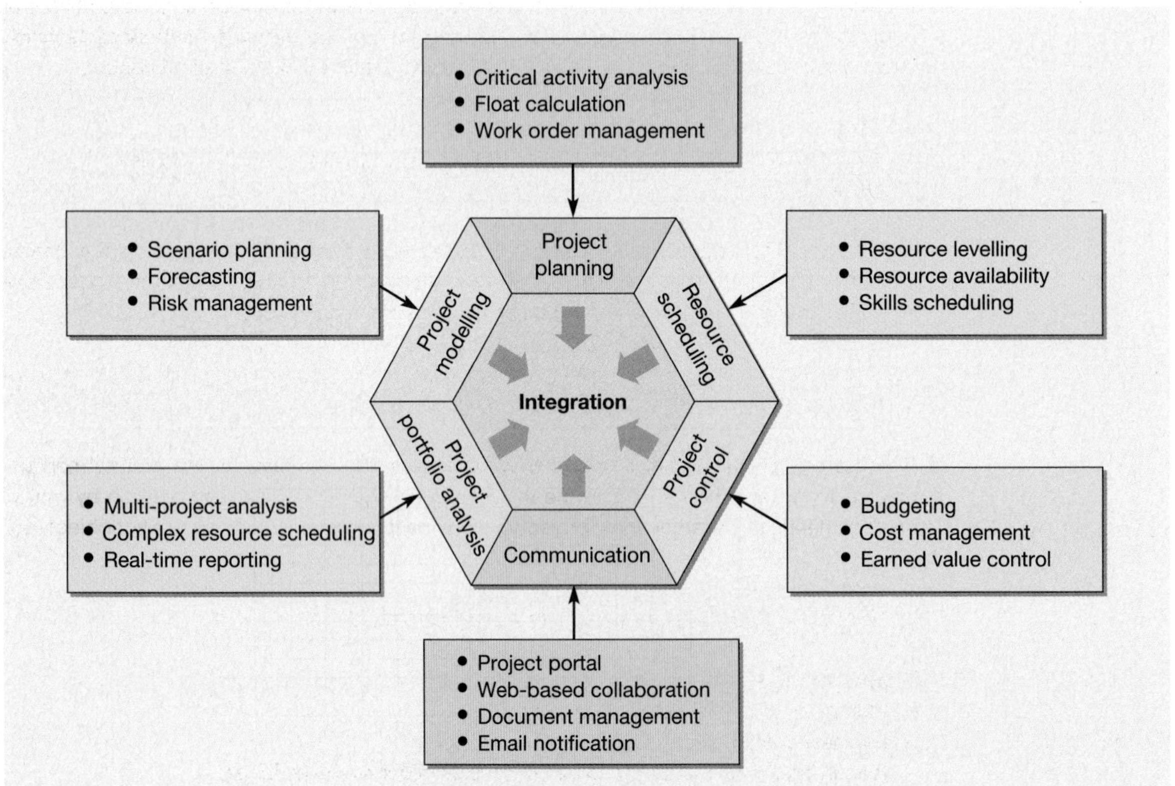

Figure 16.25 Some of the elements integrated in enterprise project management systems

which are relying on the same resource. Finally, integrated EPM systems can help to communicate, both within a project and to outside organizations which may be contributing to the project. Much of this communication facility is web-based. Project portals can allow all stakeholders to transact activities and gain a clear view of the current status of a project. Automatic notification of significant milestones can be made by e-mail. At a very basic level, the various documents that specify parts of the project can be stored in an online library. Some people argue that it is this last element of communication capabilities that is the most useful part of EPM systems.

Summary answers to key questions

Check and improve your understanding of this chapter using self assessment questions and a personalised study plan, audio and video downloads, and an eBook – all at ***www.myomlab.com.***

➤ What is a project?

- A project is a set of activities with a defined start point and a defined end state, which pursues a defined goal and uses a defined set of resources.
- All projects can be characterized by their degree of complexity and the inherent uncertainty in the project.
- Project management has five stages, four of which are relevant to project planning and control: understanding the project environments, defining the project, planning the project, technical execution of the project (not part of project planning and control) and project control.

➤ Why is it important to understand the environment in which a project takes place?

- It is important for two reasons. First, the environment influences the way a project is carried out, often through stakeholder activity. Second, the nature of the environment in which a project takes place is the main determinant of the uncertainty surrounding it.

➤ How are projects planned and controlled?

- Projects can be defined in terms of their objectives (the end state which project management is trying to achieve), scope (the exact range of the responsibilities taken on by project management), and strategy (how project management is going to meet the project objectives).

➤ What is project planning and why is it important?

- Project planning involves five stages.
  - Identifying the activities within a project;
  - Estimating times and resources for the activities;
  - Identifying the relationship and dependencies between the activities;
  - Identifying the schedule constraints;
  - Fixing the schedule.

➔

- Project planning is particularly important where complexity of the project is high. The interrelationship between activities, resources and times in most projects, especially complex ones, is such that unless they are carefully planned, resources can become seriously overloaded at times during the project.

➤ What techniques can be used for project planning?

- Network planning and Gantt charts are the most common techniques. The former (using either the activity-on-arrow or activity-on-node format) is particularly useful for assessing the total duration of a project and the degree of flexibility or float of the individual activities within the project. The most common method of network planning is called the critical path method (CPM).
- The logic inherent in a network diagram can be changed by resource constraints.
- Network planning models can also be used to assess the total cost of shortening a project where individual activities are shortened.

➤ What is project control and how is it done?

- The process of project control involves three sets of decisions: how to monitor the project in order to check its progress, how to assess the performance of the project by comparing monitored observations to the project plan, and how to intervene in the project in order to make the changes which will bring it back to plan.
- Enterprise Project Management systems can be used to integrate all the information needed to plan and control projects.

Case study
United Photonics Malaysia Sdn Bhd

Introduction

Anuar Kamaruddin, COO of United Photonics Malaysia (EPM), was conscious that the project in front of him was one of the most important he had handled for many years. The number and variety of the development projects under way within the company had risen sharply in the last few years, and although they had all seemed important at the time, this one – the 'Laz-skan' project – clearly justified the description given it by the President of United Photonics Corporation, the US parent of UPM, *'the make or break opportunity to ensure the division's long term position in the global instrumentation industry'*.

Source: Corbis/Eric K K Yu

The United Photonics Group

United Photonics Corporation had been founded in the 1920s (as the Detroit Gauge Company), a general instrument and gauge manufacturer for the engineering industry. By expanding its range into optical instruments in the early 1930s, it eventually moved also into the manufacture of high-precision and speciality lenses, mainly for the photographic industry. Its reputation as a specialist lens manufacturer led to such a growth in sales that by 1969 the optical side of the company accounted for about 60 per cent of total business and it ranked as one of the top two or three optics companies of its type in the world. Although its reputation for skilled lens-making had not diminished since then, the instrument side of the company had come to dominate sales once again in the 1980s and 1990s.

UPM product range

UPM's product range on the optical side included lenses for inspection systems which were used mainly in the manufacture of microchips. These lenses were sold both to the inspection system manufacturers and to the chip manufacturers themselves. They were very high-precision lenses; however, most of the company's optical products were specialist photographic and cinema lenses. In addition about 15 per cent of the company's optical work was concerned with the development and manufacture of 'one or two off' extremely high-precision lenses for defence contracts, specialist scientific instrumentation, and other optical companies. The Group's instrument product range consisted largely of electromechanical assemblies with an increasing emphasis on software-based recording, display and diagnostic abilities. This move towards more software-based products had led the instrument side of the business towards accepting some customized orders. The growth of this part of the instrumentation had resulted in a special development unit being set up: the Customer Services Unit (CSU) which modified, customized or adapted products for those customers who required an unusual application. Often CSU's work involved incorporating the company's products into larger systems for a customer.

In 1995 United Photonics Corporation had set up its first non-North American facility just outside Kuala Lumpur in Malaysia. United Photonics Malaysia Sdn Bhd (UPM) had started by manufacturing subassemblies for Photonics instrumentation products, but soon had developed into a laboratory for the modification of United Photonics products for customers throughout the Asian region. This part of the Malaysian business was headed by T.S. Lim, a Malaysian engineer who had taken his postgraduate qualifications at Stanford and three years ago moved back to his native KL to head up the Malaysian outpost of the CSU, reporting directly to Bob Brierly, the Vice-President of Development, who ran the main CSU in Detroit. Over the last three years, T.S. Lim and his small team of engineers had gained quite a reputation for innovative development. Bob Brierly was delighted with their enthusiasm. *'Those guys really do know how to make things happen. They are giving us all a run for our money.'*

The Laz-skan project

The idea for Laz-skan had come out of a project which T.S. Lim's CSU had been involved with in 2004. At that time the CSU had successfully installed a high-precision Photonics lens into a character recognition system for a large clearing bank. The enhanced capability which the lens and software modifications had given had enabled the bank to scan documents even when they were not correctly aligned. This had led to CSU proposing the development of a 'vision metrology' device that could optically scan a product at some point in the manufacturing process, and check the accuracy of up to twenty individual dimensions. The geometry of the product to be scanned, the dimensions to be gauged, and the tolerances to be allowed, could all be programmed into the control logic of the device. The T.S. Lim team were convinced that the idea could have considerable potential. The proposal, which the CSU team had called the Laz-skan project, was put forward to Bob Brierly in August 2004. Brierly both saw the potential value of the idea and was again impressed by the CSU team's enthusiasm. *'To be frank, it was their evident enthusiasm that influenced me as much as anything. Remember that the Malaysian CSU had only been in existence for two years at this time – they were a group of keen but relatively young engineers. Yet their proposal was well thought out and, on reflection, seemed to have considerable potential.'*

In November 2004 Lim and his team were allocated funds (outside the normal budget cycle) to investigate the feasibility of the Laz-skan idea. Lim was given one further engineer and a technician, and a three-month deadline to report to the board. In this time he was expected to overcome any fundamental technical problems, assess the feasibility of successfully developing the concept into a working prototype, and plan the development task that would lead to the prototype stage.

The Lim investigation

T.S. Lim, even at the start of his investigation, had some firm views as to the appropriate 'architecture' for the Laz-skan project. By 'architecture' he meant the major elements of the system, their functions, and how they related to each other. The Laz-skan system architecture would consider five major subsystems: the lens and lens mounting, the vision support system, the display system, the control logic software, and the documentation.

T.S. Lim's first task, once the system's overall architecture was set, was to decide whether the various components in the major subsystems would be developed in-house, developed by outside specialist companies from UPM's specifications, or bought in as standard units and if necessary modified in-house. Lim and his colleagues made these decisions themselves, while recognizing that a more consultative process might have been preferable. *'I am fully aware that ideally we should have made more use of the expertise within the company to decide how units were to be developed. But within the time available we just did not have the time to explain the product concept, explain the choices, and wait for already busy people to come up with a recommendation. Also there was the security*

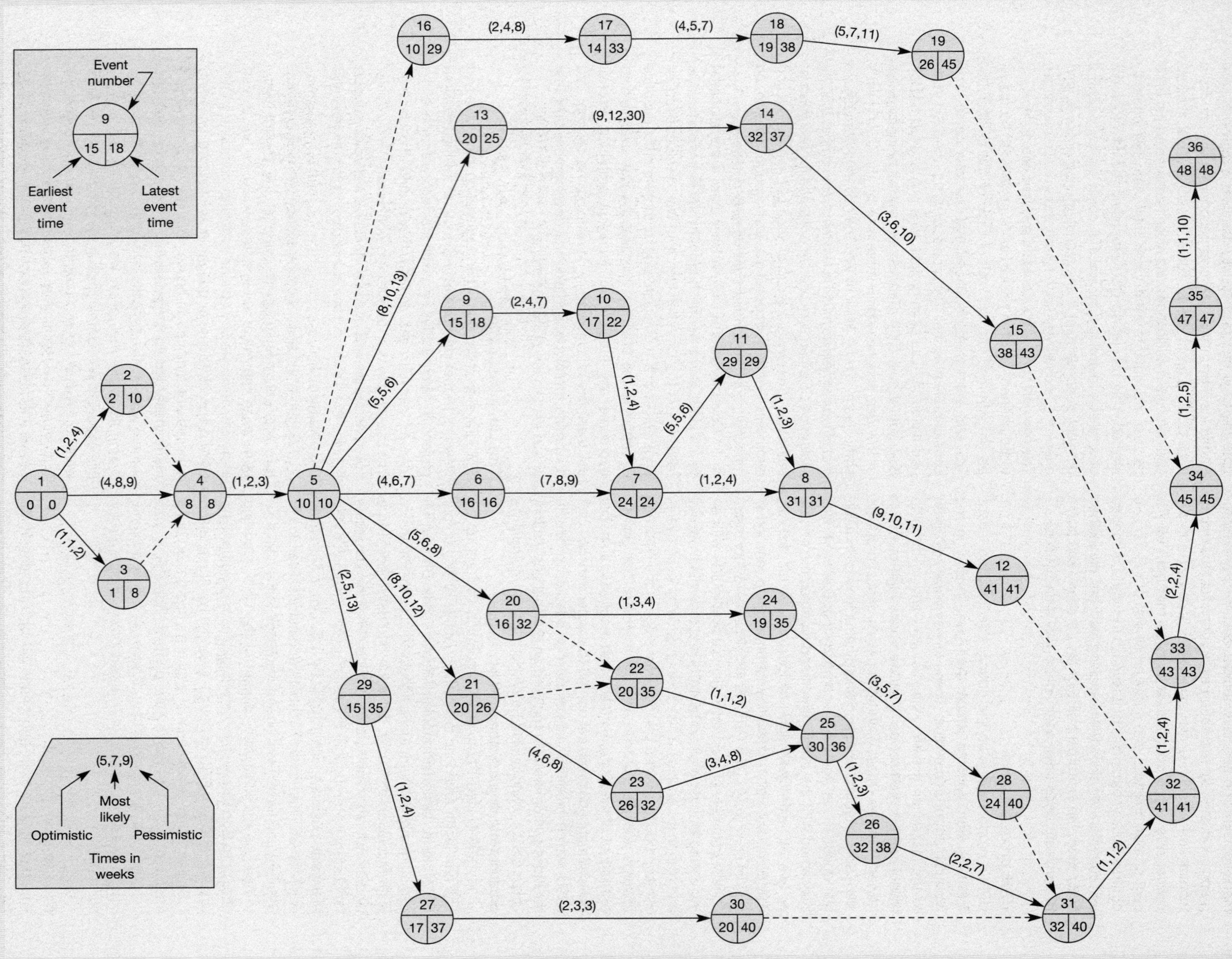
Event number
Earliest event time
Latest event time
(5,7,9)
Optimistic
Most likely
Pessimistic
Times in weeks

aspect to think of. I'm sure our employees are to be trusted but the more people who know about the project, the more chance there is for leaks. Anyway, we did not see our decisions as final. For example, if we decided that a component was to be bought in and modified for the prototype building stage it does not mean that we can't change our minds and develop a better component in-house at a later stage.'

By February 2005, TS's small team had satisfied themselves that the system could be built to achieve their original technical performance targets. Their final task before reporting to Brierly would be to devise a feasible development plan.

Planning the Laz-skan development

As a planning aid the team drew up a network diagram for all the major activities within the project from its start through to completion, when the project would be handed over to Manufacturing Operations. This is shown in Figure 16.26 and the complete list of all events in the diagram is shown in Table 16.4. The duration of all the activities in the project were estimated either by T.S. Lim or (more often) by him consulting a more experienced engineer back in Detroit. While he was reasonably confident in the estimates, he was keen to stress that they were just that – estimates.

Two draughting conventions on these networks need explanation. The three figures in brackets by each activity arrow represent the 'optimistic', 'most likely' and 'pessimistic' times (in weeks) respectively. The left-side figure in the event circles indicates the earliest time the event could take place and the figure in the right side of the circles indicates the latest time the event could take place without delaying the whole project. Dotted lines represent 'dummy' activities. These are nominal activities which have no time associated with them and are there either to maintain the logic of the network or for draughting convenience.

1 The lens (events 5-13-14-15)

The lens was particularly critical since the shape was complex and precision was vital if the system was to perform up to its intended design specification. T.S. Lim was relying heavily upon the skill of the Group's expert optics group in Pittsburg to produce the lens to the required high tolerance. Since what in effect was a trial and error approach was involved in their manufacture, the exact time to manufacture would be uncertain. T.S. Lim realized this.

> *'The lens is going to be a real problem. We just don't know how easy it will be to make the particular geometry and precision we need. The optics people won't commit themselves even though they are regarded as some of the best optics technicians in the world. It is a relief that lens development is not amongst the "critical path" activities.'*

2 Vision support system (events 6-7-8-12, 9-5, 11)

The vision support system included many components which were commercially available, but considerable engineering effort would be required to modify them. Although the development design and resting of the vision support system was complicated, there was no great uncertainty in the individual activities, or therefore the schedule of completion. If more funds were allocated to their development, some tasks might even be completed ahead of time.

Table 16.4 Event listing for the Laz-skan project

Event number	*Event description*
1	Start systems engineering
2	Complete interface transient tests
3	Complete compatibility testing
4	Complete overall architecture block and simulation
5	Complete costing and purchasing tender planning
6	End alignment system design
7	Receive S/T/G, start synch mods
8	Receive Triscan/G, start synch mods
9	Complete B/A mods
10	Complete S/T/G mods
11	Complete Triscan/G mods
12	Start laser subsystem compatibility tests
13	Complete optic design and specification, start lens manufacture
14	Complete lens manufacture, start lens housing S/A
15	Lens S/A complete, start tests
16	Start technical specifications
17	Start help routine design
18	Update engineering mods
19	Complete doc sequence
20	Start vision routines
21	Start interface (tmsic) tests
22	Start system integration compatibility routines
23	Coordinate trinsic tests
24	End interface development
25	Complete alignment integration routine
26	Final alignment integration data consolidation
27	Start interface (tmnsic) programming
28	Complete alignment system routines
29	Start tmnsic comparator routines
30	Complete (interface) trinsic coding
31	Begin all logic system tests
32	Start cycle tests
33	Lens S/A complete
34	Start assembly of total system
35	Complete total system assembly
36	Complete final tests and dispatch

3 The control software (events 20 to 26, 28)

The control software represented the most complex task, and the most difficult to plan and estimate. In fact, the software development unit had little experience of this type of work but (partly in anticipation of this type of development) had recently recruited a young software engineer with some experience of the type of work which would be needed for Laz-skan. He was confident that any technical problems could be solved even though the system needs were novel, but completion times would be difficult to predict with confidence.

4 Documentation (events 5-16-17-18-19)

A relatively simple subsystem, 'documentation' included specifying and writing the technical manuals, maintenance routines, online diagnostics, and 'help desk' information. It was a relatively predictable activity, part of which was subcontracted to technical writers and translation companies in Kuala Lumpur.

5 Display system (events 29-27-30)

The simplest of the subsystems to plan, the display system, would need to be manufactured entirely out of the company and tested and calibrated on receipt.

Market prospects

In parallel with T.S. Lim's technical investigation, Sales and Marketing had been asked to estimate the market potential of Laz-skan. In a very short time, the Laz-skan project had aroused considerable enthusiasm within the function, to the extent that Halim Ramli, the Asian Marketing Vice President, had taken personal charge of the market study. The major conclusions from this investigation were:

(a) The global market for Laz-skan type systems was unlikely to be less than 50 systems per year in 2008, climbing to more than 200 per year by 2012.
(b) The volume of the market in financial terms was more difficult to predict, but each system sold was likely to represent around US$300,000 of turnover.
(c) Some customization of the system would be needed for most customers. This would mean greater emphasis on commissioning and post-installation service than was necessary for UPM's existing products.
(d) Timing the launch of Laz-skan would be important. Two 'windows of opportunity' were critical. The first and most important was the major world trade show in Geneva in April 2006. This show, held every two years, was the most prominent show-case for new products such as Laz-skan. The second related to the development cycles of the original equipment manufacturers who would be the major customers for Laz-skan. Critical decisions would be taken in the fall of 2006. If Laz-skan was to be incorporated into these companies' products it would have to be available from October 2006.

The Laz-skan go ahead

At the end of February 2005 UPM considered both the Lim and Ramli reports. In addition estimates of Laz-skan's manufacturing costs had been sought from George Hudson, the head of Instrument Development. His estimates indicated that Laz-skan's operating contribution would be far higher than the company's existing products. The board approved the immediate commencement of the Laz-skan development through to prototype stage, with an initial development budget of US$4.5 m. The objective of the project was to, *'build three prototype Laz-skan systems to be "up and running" for April 2006'.*

The decision to go ahead was unanimous. Exactly how the project was to be managed provoked far more discussion. The Laz-skan project posed several problems. First, engineers had little experience of working on such a major project. Second, the crucial deadline for the first batch of prototypes meant that some activities might have to be been accelerated, an expensive process that would need careful judgement. A very brief investigation into which activities could be accelerated had identified those where acceleration definitely would be possible and the likely cost of acceleration (Table 16.5). Finally, no one could agree either whether there should be a single project leader, which function he or she should come from, or how senior the project leader should be. Anuar Kamaruddin knew that these decisions could affect the success of the project, and possibly the company, for years to come.

Table 16.5 Acceleration opportunities for Laz-skan

Activity	*Acceleration cost (US$/week)*	*Likely maximum activity time, with acceleration (weeks)*	*Normal most likely time (weeks)*
5–6	23,400	3	6
5–9	10,500	2	5
5–13	25,000	8	10
20–24	5,000	2	3
24–28	11,700	3	5
33–34	19,500	1	2

Questions

1 Who do you think should manage the Laz-skan Development Project?

2 What are the major dangers and difficulties that will be faced by the development team as they manage the project towards its completion?

3 What can they do about these dangers and difficulties?

Problems and applications

These problems and applications will help to improve your analysis of operations. You can find more practice problems as well as worked examples and guided solutions on MyOMLab at ***www.myomlab.com****.*

1 The activities, their durations and precedences for designing, writing and installing a bespoke computer database are shown in Table 16.6. Draw a Gantt chart and a network diagram for the project and calculate the fastest time in which the operation might be completed.

Table 16.6 Bespoke computer database activities

Activity		*Duration (weeks)*	*Activities that must be completed before it can start*
1	Contract negotiation	1	–
2	Discussions with main users	2	1
3	Review of current documentation	5	1
4	Review of current systems	6	2
5	Systems analysis (a)	4	3, 4
6	Systems analysis (b)	7	5
7	Programming	12	5
8	Testing (prelim)	2	7
9	Existing system review report	1	3, 4
10	System proposal report	2	5, 9
11	Documentation preparation	19	5, 8
12	Implementation	7	7, 11
13	System test	3	12
14	Debugging	4	12
15	Manual preparation	5	11

2 A business is launching a new product. The launch will require a number of related activities as follows – hire a sales manager (5 weeks), require the sales manager to recruit sales people (4 weeks), train the sales people (7 weeks), select an advertising agency (2 weeks), plan an advertising campaign with the agency (4 weeks), conduct the advertising campaign (10 weeks), design the packaging of the product (4 weeks), set up packing operation (12 weeks), pack enough products for the launch stock (8 weeks), order the launch quantity of products from the manufacturer (13 weeks), select distributors for the product (9 weeks), take initial orders from the distributors (3 weeks), dispatch the initial orders to the distributors (2 weeks). (a) What is the earliest time that the new product can be introduced to the market? (b) If the company hire trained salesmen who do not need further training, could the product be introduced 7 weeks earlier? (c) How long could one delay selecting the advertising agency?

3 In the example above, if the sales manager cannot be hired for 3 weeks, how will that affect the total project?

4 In the previous example, if the whole project launch operation is to be completed as rapidly as possible, what activities must have been completed by the end of week 16?

5 Identify a project of which you have been part (for example moving apartments, a holiday, dramatic production, revision for an examination, etc.). (a) Who were the stakeholders in this project? (b) What was the overall project objective (especially in terms of the relative importance of cost, quality and time)? (c) Were there any resource constraints? (d) Looking back, how could you have managed the project better?

6 Identify your favourite sporting team (Manchester United, the Toulon rugby team, or if you are not a sporting person, choose any team you have heard of). What kind of projects do you think they need to manage? For example, merchandising, sponsorship, etc. What do you think are the key issues in making a success of managing each of these different types of project?

Selected further reading

There are hundreds of books on project management. They range from the introductory to the very detailed and from the managerial to the highly mathematical. Here are two general (as opposed to mathematical) books which are worth looking at.

Maylor, H. (2003) *Project Management*, 3rd edn, Financial Times Prentice Hall, Harlow.

Newton, R. (2005) *Project Manager: Mastering the Art of Delivery in Project Management*, Financial Times Prentice Hall, Harlow.

Useful web sites

http://apm.org.uk The UK Association for Project Management. Contains a description of what professionals consider to be the body of knowledge of project management.

http://pmi.org The Project Management Institute's home page. An American association for professionals. Insights into professional practice.

http://ipma.ch The International Project Management Association, based in Zurich. Some definitions and links.

www.comp.glam.ac.uk/pages/staff/dwfarth/projman.htm#automated A great site with lots of interesting stuff on software, project management and related issues, but also very good for general project management.

Now that you have finished reading this chapter, why not visit MyOMLab at ***www.myomlab.com*** *where you'll find more learning resources to help you make the most of your studies and get a better grade?*

Chapter 17

Quality management

Key questions

- ➤ What is quality and why is it so important?
- ➤ How can quality problems be diagnosed?
- ➤ What steps lead towards conformance to specification?
- ➤ What is total quality management (TQM)?

Introduction

Quality is the only one of the five 'operations performance criteria' to have its own dedicated chapter in this book. There are two reasons for this. First, in some organizations a separate function is devoted exclusively to the management of quality. Second, quality is a key concern of almost all organizations. High-quality goods and services can give an organization a considerable competitive edge. Good quality reduces the costs of rework, waste, complaints and returns and, most importantly, generates satisfied customers. Some operations managers believe that, in the long run, quality is the most important single factor affecting an organization's performance relative to its competitors.

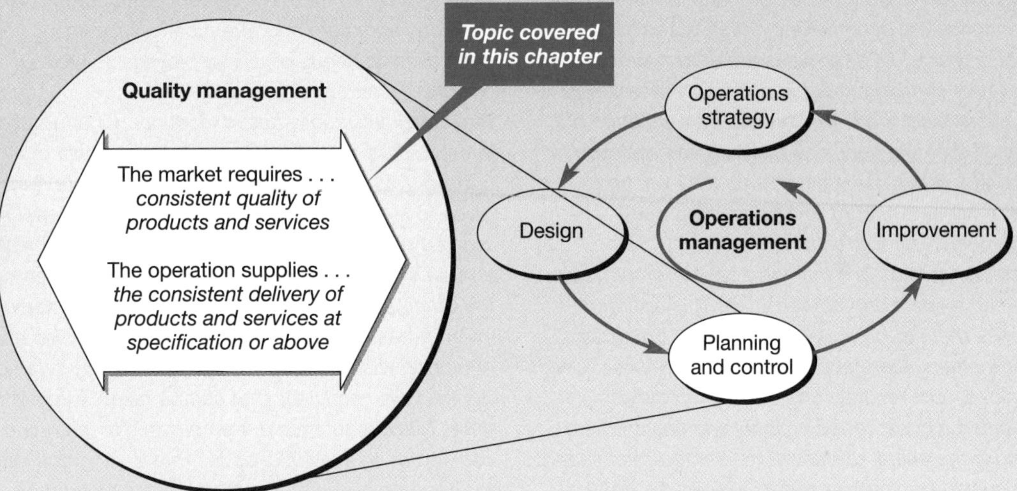

Figure 17.1 This chapter covers quality management

*Check and improve your understanding of this chapter using self assessment questions and a personalised study plan, audio and video downloads, and an eBook – all at **www.myomlab.com**.*

Operations in practice Quality at the Four Seasons Canary Wharf[1]

Source: Four Seasons Hotels, Photographer Robert Miller

The first Four Seasons Hotel opened over 45 years ago. Since then the company has grown to 81 properties in 34 countries. Famed for its quality of service, the hotel group has won countless awards including the prestigious Zagat survey and numerous AAA Five Diamond Awards, and it is also one of only 14 organizations that have been on the *Fortune* magazine's list of '100 Best Companies to Work For' every year since it launched in 1998, thus ranking as 'top hotel chain' internationally. From its inception the group has had the same guiding principle, 'to make the quality of our service our competitive advantage'. The company has what it calls its Golden Rule: 'Do to others (guests and staff) as you would wish others to do to you.' It is a simple rule, but it guides the whole organization's approach to quality.

'Quality service is our distinguishing edge and the company continues to evolve in that direction. We are always looking for better, more creative and innovative ways of serving our guests', says Michael Purtill, the General Manager of the Four Seasons Hotel Canary Wharf in London. *'We have recently refined all of our operating standards across the company, enabling us to further enhance the personalized, intuitive service that all our guests receive. All employees are empowered to use their creativity and judgement in delivering exceptional service and making their own decisions to enhance our guests' stay. For example, one morning an employee noticed that a guest had a flat tyre on their car and decided of his own accord to change it for them, which was very much appreciated by the guest.*

The golden rule means that we treat our employees with dignity, respect and appreciation. This approach encourages them to be equally sensitive to our guests' needs and offer sincere and genuine service that exceeds expectations. Just recently one of our employees accompanied a guest to the hospital and stayed there with him for the entire afternoon. He wanted to ensure that the guest wasn't alone and was given the medical attention he needed. The following day that same employee took the initiative to return to the hospital (even though it was his day off) to visit and made sure that that guest's family in America was kept informed about his progress. We ensure that we have an ongoing focus on recognizing these successes and publicly praise and celebrate all individuals who deliver these warm, spontaneous, thoughtful touches.

At Four Seasons we believe that our greatest asset and strength is our people. We pay a great deal of attention to selecting the right people with an attitude that takes great pride in delivering exceptional service. We know that motivated and happy employees are essential to our service culture and are committed to developing our employees to their highest potential. Our extensive training programmes and career development plans are designed with care and attention to support the individual needs of our employees as well as operational and business demands. In conjunction with traditional classroom-based learning, we offer tailor-made internet-based learning featuring exceptional quality courses for all levels of employee. Such importance is given to learning and development that the hotel has created two specialized rooms, designated for learning and development. One is intended for group learning and the other is equipped with private computer stations for internet-based individual learning. There is also a library equipped with a broad variety of hospitality-related books, CDs and DVDs that can be taken home at any time. This encourages our employees to learn and develop at an individual pace. This is very motivating for our employees and in the same instance their development is invaluable to the growth of our company. Career-wise, the sky is the limit and our goal is to build lifelong, international careers with Four Seasons.

Our objective is to exceed guest expectations and feedback from our guests and our employees is an invaluable barometer of our performance. We have created an in-house database that is used to record all guest feedback (whether positive or negative). We also use an online guest survey and guest comment cards which are all personally responded to and analysed to identify any potential service gaps. We continue to focus on delivering individual personalized experiences and our Guest History database remains vital in helping us to achieve this. All preferences and specific comments about service experience are logged on the database. Every comment and every preference is discussed and planned for, for every guest, for every visit. It is our culture that sets Four Seasons apart: the drive to deliver the best service in the industry that keeps our guests returning again and again.'

What is quality and why is it so important?

It is worth revisiting some of the arguments which were presented in Chapter 2 regarding the benefits of high quality. This will explain why quality is seen as being so important by most operations. Figure 17.2 illustrates the various ways in which quality improvements can affect other aspects of operations performance. Revenues can be increased by better sales and enhanced prices in the market. At the same time, costs can be brought down by improved efficiencies, productivity and the use of capital. So, a key task of the operations function must be to ensure that it provides quality goods and services, to both its internal and external customers.

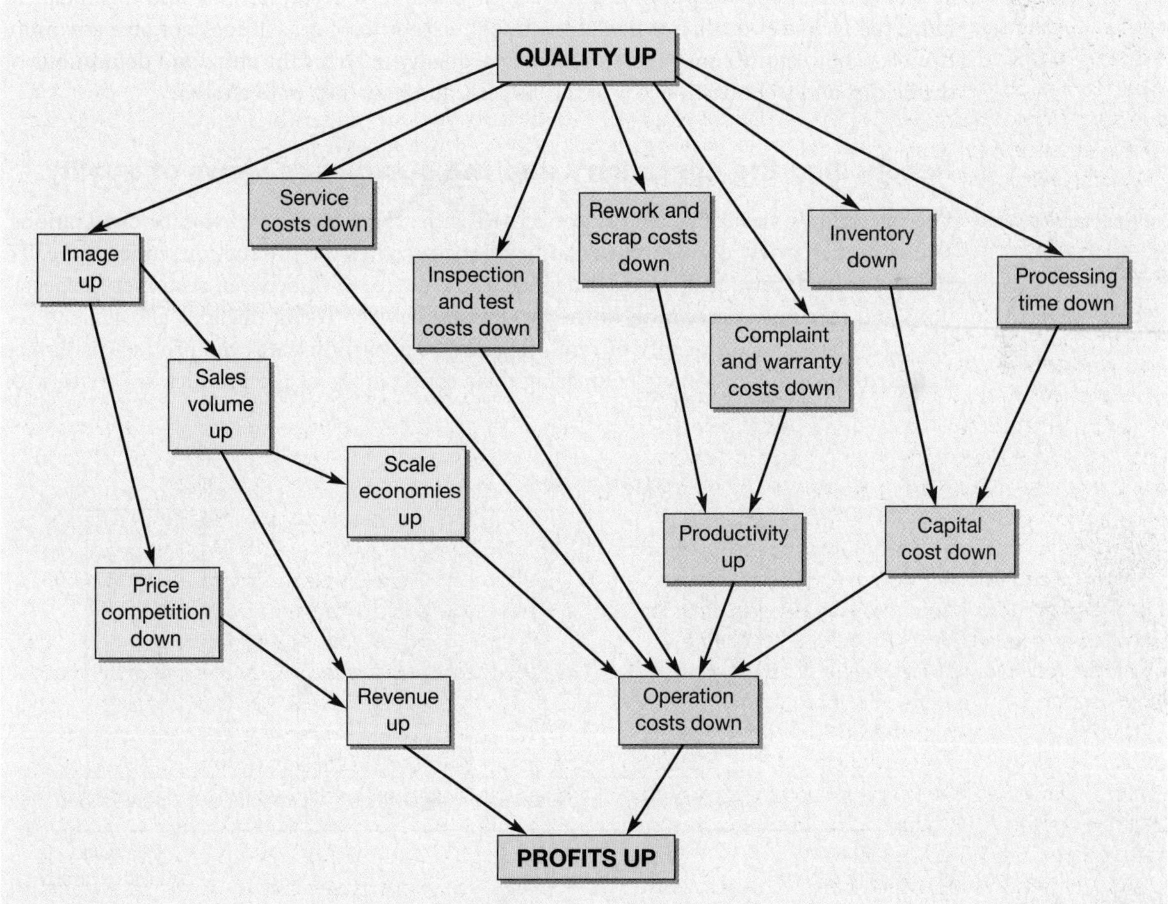

Figure 17.2 Higher quality has a beneficial effect on both revenues and costs

Source: Based on Gummerson, E. (1993)[2]

The operation's view of quality

There are many definitions of quality

There are many definitions of **quality**; here we define it as *'consistent conformance to customers' expectations'*.

The use of the word 'conformance' implies that there is a need to meet a clear specification. Ensuring a product or service conforms to specification is a key operations task. 'Consistent' implies that conformance to specification is not an *ad hoc* event but that the product or service meets the specification because quality requirements are used to design and run the processes that produce products and services. The use of 'customers' expectations' recognizes that the product or service must take the views of customers into account, which may be influenced by price. Also note the use of the word 'expectations' in this definition, rather than 'needs' or 'wants'.

Customers' view of quality

Past experiences, individual knowledge and history will all shape customers' expectations. Furthermore, customers may each *perceive* a product or service in different ways. One person may perceive a long-haul flight as an exciting part of a holiday; the person on the next seat may see it as a necessary chore to get to a business meeting. So quality needs to be understood from a customer's point of view because, to the customer, the quality of a particular product or service is whatever he or she perceives it to be. If the passengers on a skiing charter flight perceive it to be of good quality, despite long queues at check-in or cramped seating and poor meals, then the flight really is of good perceived quality.[3] Also customers may be unable to judge the 'technical' specification of the service or product and so use surrogate measures as a basis for their perception of quality.[4] For example, a customer may find it difficult to judge the technical quality of dental treatment, except insofar as it does not give any more trouble. The customer may therefore perceive quality in terms the attire and demeanour of the dentist and technician, décor of the surgery, and how they were treated.

Reconciling the operation's and the customer's views of quality

Customer expectations

Customer perception

The operation's view of quality is concerned with trying to meet **customer expectations**. The customer's view of quality is what he or she *perceives* the product or service to be. To create a unified view, quality can be defined as the degree of fit between customers' expectations and **customer perception** of the product or service.[5] Using this idea allows us to see the customers' view of quality of (and, therefore, satisfaction with) the product or service as the result of the customers comparing their expectations of the product or service with

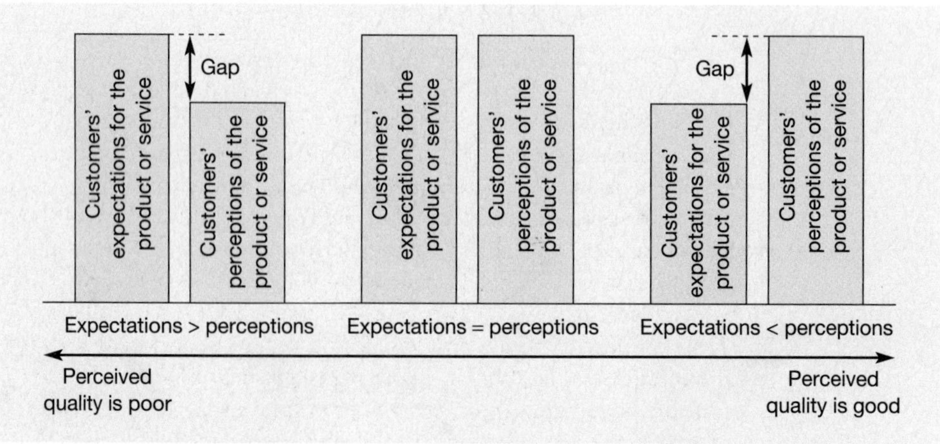

Figure 17.3 Perceived quality is governed by the magnitude and direction of the gap between customers' expectations and their perceptions of the product or service

their perception of how it performs. This is not always straightforward; see the short case 'Tea and Sympathy'. Also, if the product or service experience was better than expected then the customer is satisfied and quality is perceived to be high. If the product or service was less than his or her expectations then quality is low and the customer may be dissatisfied. If the product or service matches expectations then the perceived quality of the product or service is seen to be **acceptable.** These relationships are summarized in Figure 17.3.

A customer's view of quality is shaped by the gap between perception and expectation

Short case
Tea and Sympathy[6]

Source: Corbis

Defining quality in terms of perception and expectation can sometimes reveal some surprising results. For example, Tea and Sympathy is a British restaurant and café in the heart of New York's West Village. Over the last ten years it has become a fashionable landmark in a city with one of the broadest range of restaurants in the world. Yet it is tiny, around a dozen tables packed into an area little bigger than the average British sitting room. Not only expatriate Brits but also native New Yorkers and celebrities queue to get in. As the only British restaurant in New York, it has a novelty factor, but also it has become famous for the unusual nature of its service. *'Everyone is treated in the same way',* says Nicky Perry, one of the two ex-Londoners who run it, *'We have a firm policy that we don't take any shit.'* This robust attitude to the treatment of customers is reinforced by 'Nicky's Rules' which are printed on the menu.

1 Be pleasant to the waitresses – remember Tea and Sympathy girls are always right.
2 You will have to wait outside the restaurant until your entire party is present – no exceptions.
3 Occasionally, you may be asked to change tables so that we can accommodate all of you.
4 If we don't need the table you may stay all day, but if people are waiting it's time to naff off.
5 These rules are strictly enforced. Any argument will incur Nicky's wrath. You have been warned.

Most of the waitresses are also British and enforce Nicky's Rules strictly. If customers object they are thrown out. Nicky says that she has had to train 'her girls' to toughen up. *'I've taught them that when people cross the line they can tear their throats out as far as I'm concerned. What we've discovered over the years is that if you are really sweet, people see it as a weakness. People get thrown out of the restaurant about twice a week and yet customers still queue for the genuine shepherd's pie, a real cup of tea, and of course the service.'*

Both customers' expectations and perceptions are influenced by a number of factors, some of which cannot be controlled by the operation and some of which, to a certain extent, can be managed. Figure 17.4 shows some of the factors that will influence the gap between expectations and perceptions. This model of customer-perceived quality can help us understand how operations can manage quality and identifies some of the problems in so doing. The bottom part of the diagram represents the operation's 'domain' of quality and the top part the customer's 'domain'. These two domains meet in the actual product or service, which is provided by the organization and experienced by the customer. Within the operation's domain, management is responsible for designing the product or service and providing a specification of the quality to which the product or service has to be created. Within the customer's domain, his or her expectations are shaped by such factors as previous experiences with the particular product or service, the marketing image provided by the organization and word-of-mouth information from other users. These expectations are internalized as a set of quality characteristics.

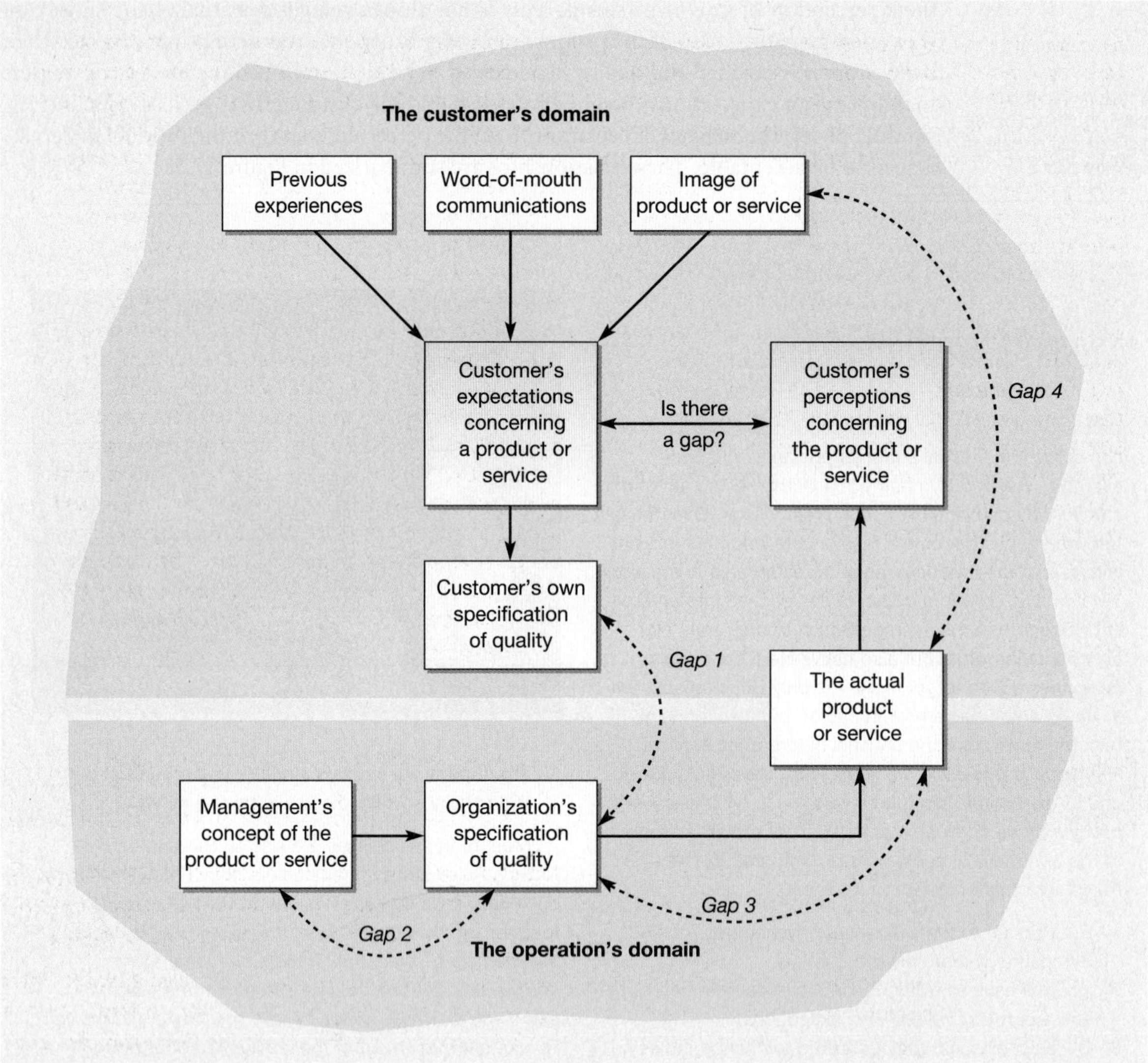

The customer's domain

Previous experiences

Word-of-mouth communications

Image of product or service

Customer's expectations concerning a product or service

Is there a gap?

Customer's perceptions concerning the product or service

Gap 4

Customer's own specification of quality

Gap 1

The actual product or service

Management's concept of the product or service

Organization's specification of quality

Gap 3

Gap 2

The operation's domain

Figure 17.4 The customer's domain and the operations domain in determining the perceived quality, showing how the gap between customers' expectations and their perception of a product or service could be explained by one or more gaps elsewhere in the model

Source: Adapted from Parasuraman, A. *et al.* (1985) A conceptual model of service quality and implications for future research, *Journal of Marketing*, vol. 49, Fall, pp. 41–50. Reproduced with permission from the American Marketing Association.

Short case
Quality at Magic Moments

Source: Alamy Images

Magic Moments is a small, but successful wedding photography business. Its owner, Richard Webber, has seen plenty of changes over the last twenty years. *'In the past, my job involved taking a few photos during the wedding ceremony and then formal group shots outside. I was rarely at a wedding for more than two hours. Clients would select around 30 photos to go in a standard wedding album. It was important to get the photos right, because that was really the only thing I was judged on. Now it's different. I usually spend all day at a wedding, and sometimes late into the evening as well. This creates a very different dynamic with the wedding party, as you're almost like another guest. Whilst the bride and groom are still my primary concern, other guests at the wedding are also important. The challenge is to find the right balance between getting the best photos possible whilst being as discreet as possible. I could spend hours getting the perfect picture, but annoy everyone in the process. It's difficult, because clients judge you on both the technical quality of your work and the way you interact with everyone on the day. The product has changed too. Clients receive a CD or memory stick with around 500 photos taken during the day. Also I can give them a choice of 10 albums in different sizes, ranging from 30 to 100 photos. This year, I have started offering photo books which allow a much greater level of customization and have proved popular for younger couples. For the future, I'm considering offering albums with wedding items such as invitations, confetti and menus, and individual paintings created from photographs. Obviously I would have to outsource the paintings. I'm also going to upgrade our web site, so wedding guests can order photos and related products online. This will generate revenue and act as a good marketing tool. My anxiety is that advertising this additional service at the wedding will be seen as being too commercial, even if it's actually of benefit to guests.*

One of the biggest problems for the business is the high level of demand in the summer months. Weekends in June, July and August are often booked up two years in advance. One option is to take on additional photographers during busy periods. However, the best ones are busy themselves. The concern is that the quality of the service I offer would deteriorate. A large part of the business is about how one relates to clients and that's hard to replicate. Having been to so many weddings, I often offer clients advice on various aspects of their wedding, such as locations, bands, caterers and florists. However, with development, wedding planning is clearly an area that could be profitable to the business. Of course, another option is to move beyond weddings into other areas, such as school photos, birthdays, celebrations, or studio work.'

Diagnosing quality problems[7]

Figure 17.4 shows how quality problems can be diagnosed. If the perceived quality gap is such that customers' perceptions of the product or service fail to match their expectations of it, then the reason (or reasons) must lie in other gaps elsewhere in the model as follows.

Gap 1: The customer's specification–operation's specification gap. Perceived quality could be poor because there may be a mismatch between the organization's own internal quality specification and the specification which is expected by the customer. For example, a car may be designed to need servicing every 10,000 kilometres but the customer may expect 15,000-kilometre service intervals.

Gap 2: The concept–specification gap. Perceived quality could be poor because there is a mismatch between the product or service concept (see Chapter 5) and the way the organization has specified quality internally. For example, the concept of a car might have been for an inexpensive, energy-efficient means of transportation, but the inclusion of a climate control system may have both added to its cost and made it less energy-efficient.

Gap 3: The quality-specification–actual-quality gap. Perceived quality could be poor because there is a mismatch between actual quality and the internal quality specification (often called 'conformance to specification'). For example, the internal quality specification for a car may be that the gap between its doors and body, when closed, must not exceed 7 mm. However, because of inadequate equipment, the gap in reality is 9 mm.

Gap 4: The actual-quality–communicated-image gap. Perceived quality could be poor because there is a gap between the organization's external communications or market image and the actual quality delivered to the customer. This may be because the marketing function has set unachievable expectations or operations is not capable of the level of quality expected by the customer. For example, an advertising campaign for an airline might show a cabin attendant offering to replace a customer's shirt on which food or drink has been spilt, whereas such a service may not in fact be available should this happen.

Conformance to specification

Conformance to specification means producing a product or providing a service to its design specification. It is usually seen as the most important contribution that operations management can make to the customer's perception of quality. We shall examine how it can be achieved in the remainder of this chapter by describing quality management as six sequential steps. This chapter, and Chapters 18, 19 and 20, will deal with these steps.

Step 1 Define the quality characteristics of the product or service.
Step 2 Decide how to measure each quality characteristic.
Step 3 Set quality standards for each quality characteristic.
Step 4 Control quality against those standards.
Step 5 Find and correct causes of poor quality.
Step 6 Continue to make improvements.

Step 1 – Define the quality characteristics

Much of the 'quality' of a product or service will have been specified in its design. But not all the design details are useful in controlling quality. For example, the design of a television may specify that its outer cabinet is made with a particular veneer. Each television is not checked, however, to make sure that the cabinet is indeed made from that particular veneer. Rather it is the *consequences* of the design specification which are examined – the appearance of the cabinet, for example. These consequences for quality planning and control of the design are called the **quality characteristics** of the product or service. Table 17.1 shows a list of the quality characteristics which are generally useful.

Quality characteristics

Table 17.1 Quality characteristics for a car, a bank loan and an air journey

Quality characteristic	*Car (material transformation process)*	*Bank loan (information transformation process)*	*Air journey (customer transformation process)*
Functionality – how well the product or service does its job	Speed, acceleration, fuel consumption, ride quality, road-holding, etc.	Interest rate, terms and conditions	Safety and duration of journey, onboard meals and drinks, car and hotel booking services
Appearance – the sensory characteristics of the product or service: its aesthetic appeal, look, feel, etc.	Aesthetics, shape, finish, door gaps, etc.	Aesthetics of information, web site, etc.	Décor and cleanliness of aircraft, lounges and crew
Reliability – the consistency of the product's or service's performance over time	Mean time to failure	Keeping promises (implicit and explicit)	Keeping to the published flight times
Durability – the total useful life of the product or service	Useful life (with repair)	Stability of terms and conditions	Keeping up with trends in the industry
Recovery – the ease with which problems with the product or service can be resolved	Ease of repair	Resolution of service failures	Resolution of service failures
Contact – the nature of the person-to-person contact which might take place	Knowledge and courtesy of sales staff	Knowledge and courtesy of branch and call centre staff	Knowledge, courtesy and sensitivity of airline staff

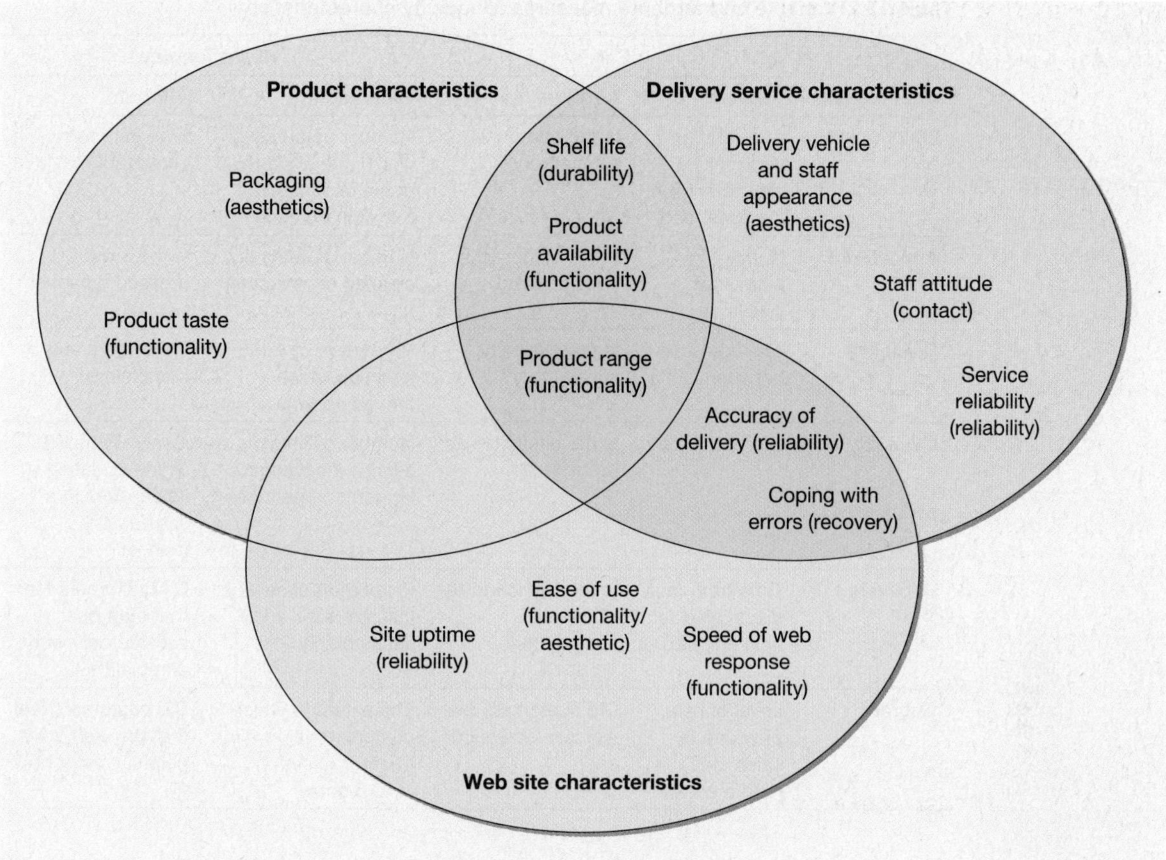

Figure 17.5 Some quality characteristics for an online grocery shopping service

Quality characteristics of the total package

Many services are a whole package of several elements, each of which will have its own quality characteristics. Some aspects of quality may be influenced by two or more elements within the total package. To understand the quality characteristics of the whole package therefore it is necessary to understand the individual characteristics within and between each element of the package. For example, Figure 17.5 shows some of the quality characteristics for a web-based online grocery shopping service. To judge this service it is necessary to consider the web site through which information is transmitted and orders are placed, the products that are sold through the site and the delivery service that transports purchases to the customer. Identifying where each characteristic of quality lies is useful because it is the first step towards understanding which part of the total service should be given responsibility for maintaining each aspect of quality.

Step 2 – Decide how to measure each characteristic

These characteristics must be defined in such a way as to enable them to be measured and then controlled. This involves taking a very general quality characteristic such as 'appearance' and breaking it down, as far as one can, into its constituent elements. 'Appearance' is difficult to measure as such, but 'colour match', 'surface finish' and 'number of visible scratches' are all capable of being described in a more objective manner. They may even be quantifiable. Other quality characteristics pose more difficulty. The 'courtesy' of airline staff, for example,

Table 17.2 Variable and attribute measures for quality characteristics

Quality characteristic	*Car*		*Airline journey*	
	Variable	*Attribute*	*Variable*	*Attribute*
Functionality	Acceleration and braking characteristics from test bed	Is the ride quality satisfactory?	Number of journeys which actually arrived at the destination (i.e. didn't crash!)	Was the food acceptable?
Appearance	Number of blemishes visible on car	Is the colour to specification?	Number of seats not cleaned satisfactorily	Is the crew dressed smartly?
Reliability	Average time between faults	Is the reliability satisfactory?	Proportion of journeys which arrived on time	Were there any complaints?
Durability	Life of the car	Is the useful life as predicted?	Number of times service innovations lagged competitors	Generally, is the airline updating its services in a satisfactory manner?
Recovery	Time from fault discovered to fault repaired	Is the serviceability of the car acceptable?	Proportion of service failures resolved satisfactorily	Do customers feel that staff deal satisfactorily with complaints?
Contact	Level of help provided by sales staff (1 to 5 scale)	Did customers feel well served (yes or no)?	The extent to which customers feel well treated by staff (1 to 5 scale)	Did customers feel that the staff were helpful (yes or no)?

has no objective quantified measure. Yet operations with high customer contact, such as airlines, place a great deal of importance on the need to ensure courtesy in their staff. In cases like this, the operation will have to attempt to measure customer *perceptions* of courtesy.

Variables and attributes

Variables

Attributes

The measures used by operations to describe quality characteristics are of two types: **variables** and **attributes**. Variable measures are those that can be measured on a continuously variable scale (for example, length, diameter, weight or time). Attributes are those which are assessed by judgement and are dichotomous, i.e. have two states (for example, right or wrong, works or does not work, looks OK or not OK). Table 17.2 categorizes some of the measures which might be used for the quality characteristics of the car and the airline journey.

Step 3 – Set quality standards

When operations managers have identified how any quality characteristic can be measured, they need a quality standard against which it can be checked; otherwise they will not know whether it indicates good or bad performance. The quality standard is that level of quality which defines the boundary between acceptable and unacceptable. Such standards may well be constrained by operational factors such as the state of technology in the factory, and the cost limits of making the product. At the same time, however, they need to be appropriate to the expectations of customers. But quality judgements can be difficult. If one airline passenger out of every 10,000 complains about the food, is that good because 9,999 passengers out of 10,000 are satisfied? Or is it bad because, if one passenger complains, there must be others who, although dissatisfied, did not bother to complain? And if that level of complaint is similar for other airlines, should it regard its quality as satisfactory?

Short case

Quality is vital at Vitacress[8]

Source: Alamy Images

Starting with less than half a hectare of watercress beds, Vitacress now has more than 300,000 sq m of growing beds and employs over 1,000 full-time staff, with farms in the south of the UK and in Portugal. The group is the world's leading watercress producer. Now owned by RAR Group, a private Portuguese company, it supplies baby leaf salads in the UK and is a major European grower and packer of salads and speciality vegetables for major supermarkets' own-label products. Since 2003 it has also sold premium products under its own 'Vitacress' brand.

The market for pre-packed baby leaves is growing. It is worth more than £500 million per year in the UK alone and is forecast to continue expanding as the trend for convenient and healthy foods continues. Consumers are increasingly shunning the purchase of a single whole-head lettuce and are instead buying a bag of mixed baby leaves with a combination of different colours and flavours. But the fresh salad market is a competitive one with customers demanding the very highest quality, and the quality control task is not straightforward with leaves grown and harvested from locations across the world to provide the supermarkets with fresh, bagged, salad 365 days of the year. So what does 'quality' mean for Vitacress, and how does it go about delivering it?

Both taste and appearance are important to consumers, as they are to Vitacress's retail customers, who also want the product to maintain its nutrient levels and healthy leaf appearance throughout its shelf life. The challenge facing Vitacress is that baby salad leaves are a highly delicate and perishable commodity, with damage to the leaves giving rise to an increased rate of breakdown and a reduced shelf life of the product. The leaves are subjected to potential damage at all stages in the processing chain from field to supermarket shelf, including washing, drying and packing. Understanding the science that underlies the growing, harvesting, packing, transportation and storage of their products is fundamental to maintaining quality levels. This is why Vitacress cooperates in university-based research projects that could impact final quality levels. For example, in one study supported by Vitacress, it was found that baby salad leaves had an increased post-harvest shelf life of from 1 to 6 days (depending on the variety), when harvested at the end of the day compared with leaves harvested at the start of the day. In another project, the effect of environmental legislation that reduced residual pesticide levels in fresh food posed a potential problem if insects or foreign bodies found their way into the final product. Mike Rushworth, Operations Director at Vitacress, contacted the University of Bath's Faculty of Engineering Design for advice on improving their washing and inspection process. A new inspection system was designed that included devices to separate leaves without manual handling. The project also evaluated the leaf washing system, by introducing artificial 'bugs' to provide a continual check on the effectiveness of this system. The bugs contained transponders to transmit signals if they make it through the washing and inspection without being extracted.

Yet any natural food product will deteriorate over time, and no matter how inventive Vitacress are in processing their leaves, unless the product reaches the supermarket shelves soon after harvesting its effective 'quality life' will be truncated. This is why Vitacress takes only 24 hours to get salad goods from the field to the supermarket, chilling the crops within 60 minutes of harvesting to ensure maximum freshness. The company uses vacuum coolers on all its farms and speedy supply chains so products reach customers as fast as possible, an achievement recognized when Vitacress picked up the Zurich Best Factory of the Year award for good manufacturing practices at its Andover, UK plant.

Step 4 – Control quality against those standards

After setting up appropriate standards the operation will then need to check that the products or services conform to those standards: doing things right, first time, every time. This involves three decisions:

1 Where in the operation should they check that it is conforming to standards?
2 Should they check every product or service or take a sample?
3 How should the checks be performed?

Where should the checks take place?

At the start of the process incoming resources may be inspected to make sure that they are to the correct specification. For example, a car manufacturer will check that components are of the right specification. A university will screen applicants to try to ensure that they have a high chance of getting through the programme. During the process checks may take place before a particularly costly process, prior to 'difficult to check', immediately after a process with a high defective rate, before potential damage or distress might be caused, and so on. Checks may also take place after the process itself to ensure that customers do not experience non-conformance.

Check every product and service or take a sample?

Quality sampling

While it might seem ideal to check every single product or service, a **sample** may be more practical for a number of reasons.

- It might be dangerous to inspect everything. A doctor, for example, checks just a small sample of blood rather than taking all of a patient's blood! The characteristics of this sample are taken to represent those of the rest of the patient's blood.
- Checking everything might destroy the product or interfere with the service. Not every light bulb is checked for how long it lasts – it would destroy every bulb. Waiters do not check that customers are enjoying the meal every 30 seconds.
- Checking everything can be time-consuming and costly. It may not be feasible to check all output from a high-volume machine or to check the feelings of every bus commuter every day.

Also 100 per cent checking may not guarantee that all defects will be identified. Sometimes it is intrinsically difficult. For example, although a physician may undertake the correct testing procedure, he or she may not necessarily diagnose a (real) disease. Nor is it easy to notice everything. For example, try counting the number of 'e's on this page. Count them again and see if you get the same score.

Type I and type II errors

Although it reduces checking time, using a sample to make a decision about quality does have its own inherent problems. Like any decision activity, we may get the decision wrong. Take the example of a pedestrian waiting to cross a street. He or she has two main decisions: whether to continue waiting or to cross. If there is a satisfactory break in the traffic and the pedestrian crosses then a correct decision has been made. Similarly, if that person continues to wait because the traffic is too dense then he or she has again made a correct decision. There are two types of incorrect decisions or errors, however. One incorrect decision would be if he or she decides to cross when there is not an adequate break in the traffic, resulting in an accident – this is referred to as a type I error. Another incorrect decision would occur if he or she decides not to cross even though there was an adequate gap in the traffic – this is called a type II error. In crossing the road, therefore, there are four outcomes, which are summarized in Table 17.3.

Type I errors are those which occur when a decision was made to do something and the situation did not warrant it. Type II errors are those which occur when nothing was done, yet a decision to do something should have been taken as the situation did indeed warrant it. For example, if a school's inspector checks the work of a sample of 20 out of 1,000 pupils and

Table 17.3 Type I and type II errors for a pedestrian crossing the road

	Road conditions	
Decision	*Unsafe*	*Safe*
Cross	Type I error	Correct decision
Wait	Correct decision	Type II error

all 20 of the pupils in the sample have failed, the inspector might draw the conclusion that all the pupils have failed. In fact, the sample just happened to contain 20 out of the 50 students who had failed the course. The inspector, by assuming a high fail rate would be making a type I error. Alternatively, if the inspector checked 20 pieces of work all of which were of a high standard, he or she might conclude that all the pupils' work was good despite having been given, or having chosen, the only pieces of good work in the whole school. This would be a type II error. Although these situations are not likely, they are possible. Therefore any sampling procedure has to be aware of these risks (see the short case on, 'Surgical statistics').

How should the checks be performed?

In practice most operations will use some form of sampling to check the quality of their products or services. The decision then is what kind of sample procedure to adopt. There are two different methods in common use for checking the quality of a sample product or service so as to make inferences about all the output from an operation. Both methods take into account the statistical risks involved in sampling. The first, and by far the best known, is the procedure called **statistical process control** (SPC). SPC is concerned with sampling the process during the production of the goods or the delivery of service. Based on this sample, decisions are made as to whether the process is 'in control', that is, operating as it should be. The second method is called **acceptance sampling** and is more concerned with whether to regard an incoming or outgoing batch of materials or customers as acceptable or not. Both of these approaches are explained in the supplement to this chapter.

Statistical process control

Acceptance sampling

Short case
Surgical statistics[9]

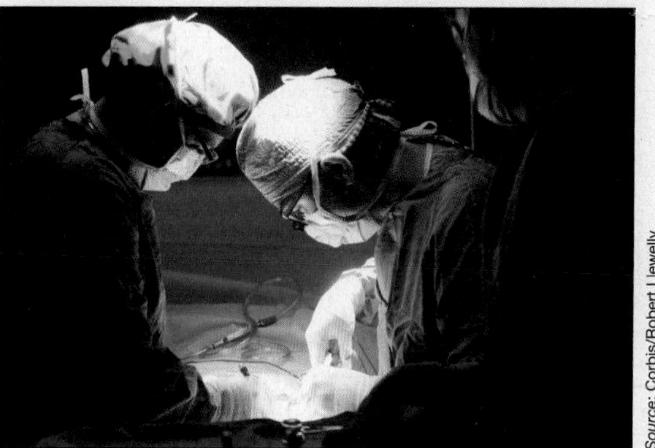
Source: Corbis/Robert Llewelly

Understanding the nature of type I and type II errors is an essential part of any surgeon's quality planning. Take the well-known appendectomy operation, for example. This is the removal of the appendix when it becomes infected or inflamed. Removal is necessary because of the risk of the appendix bursting and causing peritonitis, a potentially fatal poisoning of the blood. The surgical procedure itself is a relatively simple operation with expected good results but there is always a small risk associated with any invasive surgery needing a general anaesthetic. In addition, like any surgical procedure, it is expensive. The cost of the USA's approximately quarter-of-a-million appendectomies averages out to around $4,500 per operation. Unfortunately, appendicitis is difficult to diagnose accurately. Using standard X-ray procedures a definite diagnosis can only be obtained about 10 per cent of the time. But now a new technique, developed in the Massachusetts General Hospital in Boston, claims to be able to identify 100 per cent of true appendicitis cases before surgery is carried out. The new technique (Focused Appendix Computed Tomography) uses spiral X-ray images together with a special dye. It scans only the relevant part of the body, so exposure to radiation is not as major an issue as with conventional X-ray techniques. The technique can also help in providing an alternative diagnosis when an appendectomy is not needed. Most significantly, the potential cost savings are very great. The test itself costs less than $250, which means that one single avoided surgery pays for around 20 tests.

Steps 5 and 6 – Find and correct causes of poor quality and continue to make improvements

The final two steps in our list of quality management activities are, in some ways, the most important yet also the most difficult. They also blend into the general area of operations improvement. The material covered in Chapters 18, 19 and 20 all has contributions to make to these two steps. Nevertheless, there is an aspect of quality management that has been particularly important in shaping how quality is improved and the improvement activity made self-sustaining. This is total quality management (TQM). The remainder of the main body of this chapter is devoted to TQM.

Total quality management (TQM)

Total quality management

Total quality management (TQM) was one of the earliest of the current wave of management 'fashions'. Its peak of popularity was in the late 1980s and early 1990s. As such it has suffered from something of a backlash in recent years and there is little doubt that many companies adopted TQM in the simplistic belief that it would transform their operations performance overnight. Yet the general precepts and principles that constitute TQM are still the dominant mode of organizing operations improvement. The approach we take here is to stress the importance of the 'total' in total quality management and how it can guide the agenda for improvement.

TQM as an extension of previous practice

TQM can be viewed as a logical extension of the way in which quality-related practice has progressed (*see* Fig. 17.6). Originally quality was achieved by inspection – screening out defects before they were noticed by customers. The quality control (QC) concept developed a more systematic approach to not only detecting, but also treating quality problems. Quality assurance (QA) widened the responsibility for quality to include functions other than direct operations. It also made increasing use of more sophisticated statistical quality techniques. TQM included much of what went before but developed its own distinctive themes. We will use some of these themes to describe how TQM represents a clear shift from traditional approaches to quality.

What is TQM?

TQM is a philosophy of how to approach the organization of quality improvement

TQM is 'an effective system for integrating the quality development, quality maintenance and quality improvement efforts of the various groups in an organization so as to enable production and service at the most economical levels which allow for full customer satisfaction'.[10] However, it was the Japanese who first made the concept work on a wide scale and subsequently popularized the approach and the term 'TQM'. It was then developed further by several, so-called, 'quality gurus'. Each 'guru' stressed a different set of issues, from which emerged the TQM approach. It is best thought of as a philosophy of how to approach quality improvement. This philosophy, above everything, stresses the 'total' of TQM. It is an approach that puts quality at the heart of everything that is done by an operation and including all activities within an operation. This totality can be summarized by the way TQM lays particular stress on the following:

- meeting the needs and expectations of customers;
- covering all parts of the organization;
- including every person in the organization;
- examining all costs which are related to quality, especially failure costs and getting things 'right first time';
- developing the systems and procedures which support quality and improvement;
- developing a continuous process of improvement (this will be treated in the broader context of improvement, in Chapter 18).

TQM means meeting the needs and expectations of customers

Earlier in this chapter we defined quality as 'consistent conformance to customers' expectations'. Therefore any approach to quality management must necessarily include the customer perspective. In TQM this customer perspective is particularly important. It may be referred

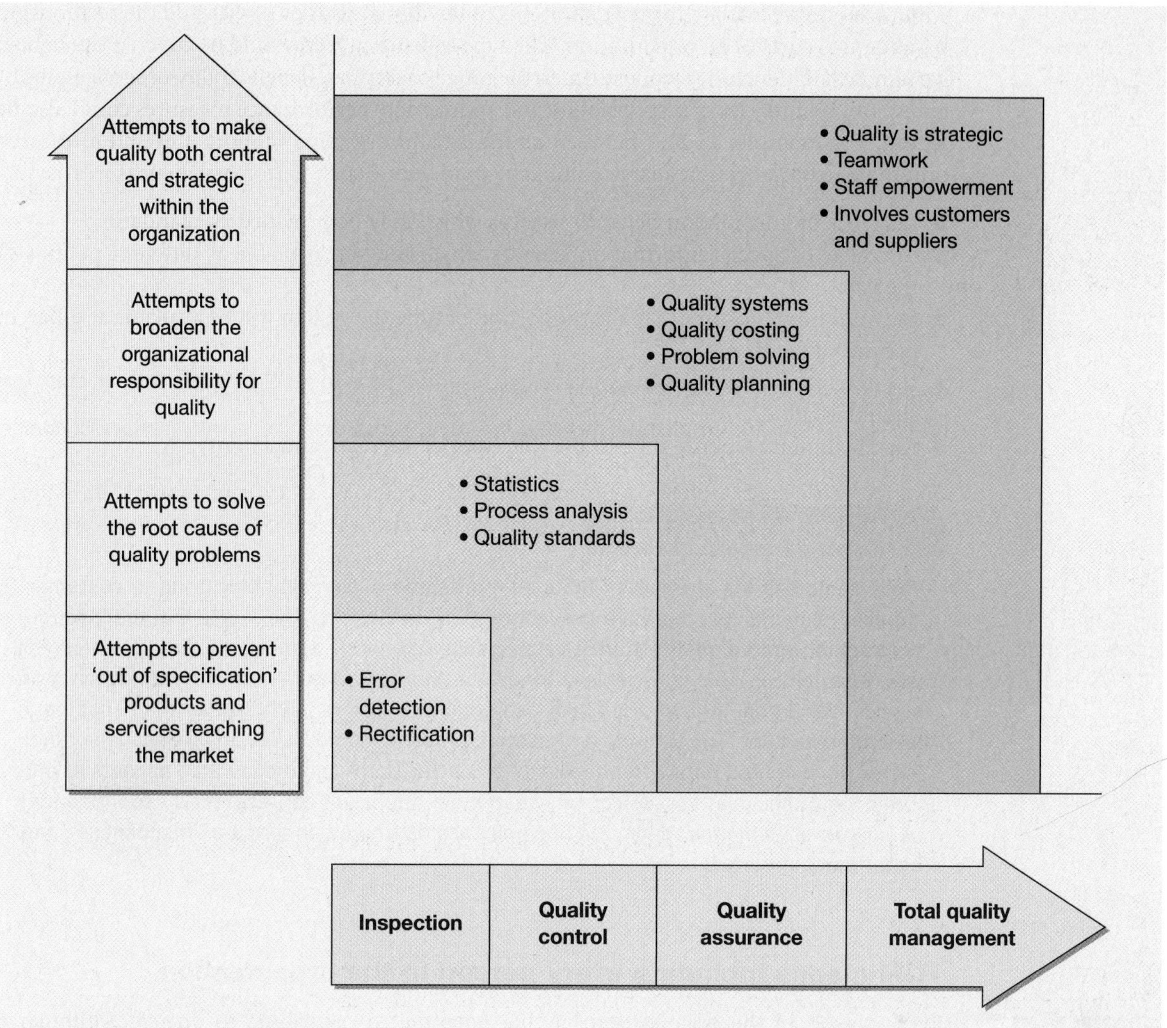

Figure 17.6 TQM as an extension

to as 'customer-centricity' (discussed briefly in Chapter 18) or the 'voice of the customer'. However it is called, TQM stresses the importance of starting with an insight into customer needs, wants, perceptions and preferences. This can then be translated into quality objectives and used to drive quality improvement.

TQM means covering all parts of the organization

For an organization to be truly effective, every single part of it, each department, each activity, and each person and each level, must work properly together, because every person and every activity affects and in turn is affected by others. One of the most powerful concepts that has emerged from various improvement approaches is the concept of the **internal customer or supplier**. This is recognition that everyone is a customer within the organization and consumes goods or services provided by other internal suppliers, and everyone is also an internal supplier of goods and services for other internal customers. The implication of this is that errors in the service provided within an organization will eventually affect the product or service which reaches the external customer.

Internal customer or supplier

Service-level agreements

Some organizations bring a degree of formality to the internal customer concept by encouraging (or requiring) different parts of the operation to agree **service-level agreements** (SLAs)

Service-level agreements

with each other. SLAs are formal definitions of the dimensions of service and the relationship between two parts of an organization. The type of issues which would be covered by such an agreement could include response times, the range of services, dependability of service supply, and so on. Boundaries of responsibility and appropriate performance measures could also be agreed. For example, an SLA between an information systems support unit and a research unit in the laboratories of a large company could define such performance measures as:

- the types of information network services which may be provided as 'standard';
- the range of special information services which may be available at different periods of the day;
- the minimum 'up-time', i.e. the proportion of time the system will be available at different periods of the day;
- the maximum response time and average response time to get the system fully operational should it fail;
- the maximum response time to provide 'special' services, and so on.

Critical commentary

While some see the strength of SLAs as the degree of formality they bring to customer–supplier relationships, there are also some clear drawbacks. The first is that the 'pseudo-contractual' nature of the formal relationship can work against building partnerships (*see* Chapter 13). This is especially true if the SLA includes penalties for deviation from service standards. Indeed, the effect can sometimes be to inhibit rather than encourage joint improvement. The second, and related, problem is that SLAs, again because of their formal documented nature, tend to emphasize the 'hard' and measurable aspects of performance rather than the 'softer' but often more important aspects. So a telephone may be answered within four rings, but how the caller is treated, in terms of 'friendliness', may be far more important.

TQM means including every person in the organization

Every person in the organization has the potential to contribute to quality. Although it may be necessary to develop some specialists to assist with maintaining quality levels, TQM was amongst the first approaches to stress the centrality of harnessing everyone's impact on quality and therefore their potential contribution to quality. There is scope for creativity and innovation even in relatively routine activities, claim TQM proponents. The shift in attitude which is needed to view employees as the most valuable intellectual and creative resource which the organization possesses can still prove difficult for some organizations. When TQM practices first began to migrate from Japan in the late 1970s, the ideas seemed even more radical. Some Japanese industrialists even thought (mistakenly) that companies in Western economies would never manage to change. Take, for example, a statement by Konosuke Matsushito which attracted considerable publicity:

> *'We are going to win and the industrial West is going to lose out – there is nothing much you can do about it, because the reasons for your failure are within yourselves. For you, the essence of management is getting the ideas out of the heads of bosses into the hands of labour. For us, the core of management is precisely the art of mobilizing and pulling together the intellectual resources of all employees in the service of the firm. Only by drawing on the combined brainpower of all its employees can a firm face up to the turbulence and constraints of today's environment. That is why our large companies give their employees three to four times more training than yours. This is why they foster within the firm such intensive exchange and communication. This is why they seek constantly everybody's suggestions and why they demand from the educational system increasing numbers of graduates as well as bright and well-educated generalists, because these people are the lifeblood of industry.'*[11]

TQM means all costs of quality are considered

The costs of controlling quality may not be small, whether the responsibility lies with each individual or a dedicated quality control department. It is therefore necessary to examine all the costs and benefits associated with quality (in fact 'cost of quality' is usually taken to refer to both costs and benefits of quality). These costs of quality are usually categorized as *prevention costs, appraisal costs, internal failure costs* and *external failure costs.*

Prevention costs

Prevention costs are those costs incurred in trying to prevent problems, failures and errors from occurring in the first place. They include such things as:

- identifying potential problems and putting the process right before poor quality occurs;
- designing and improving the design of products and services and processes to reduce quality problems;
- training and development of personnel in the best way to perform their jobs;
- process control through SPC.

Appraisal costs

Appraisal costs are those costs associated with controlling quality to check to see if problems or errors have occurred during and after the creation of the product or service. They might include such things as:

- the setting up of statistical acceptance sampling plans;
- the time and effort required to inspect inputs, processes and outputs;
- obtaining processing inspection and test data;
- investigating quality problems and providing quality reports;
- conducting customer surveys and quality audits.

Internal failure costs

Internal failure costs are failure costs associated with errors which are dealt with inside the operation. These costs might include such things as:

- the cost of scrapped parts and material;
- reworked parts and materials;
- the lost production time as a result of coping with errors;
- lack of concentration due to time spent troubleshooting rather than improvement.

External failure costs

External failure costs are those which are associated with an error going out of the operation to a customer. These costs include such things as:

- loss of customer goodwill affecting future business;
- aggrieved customers who may take up time;
- litigation (or payments to avoid litigation);
- guarantee and warranty costs;
- the cost to the company of providing excessive capability (too much coffee in the pack or too much information to a client).

The relationship between quality costs

In traditional quality management it was assumed that failure costs reduce as the money spent on appraisal and prevention increases. Furthermore, it was assumed that there is an *optimum* amount of quality effort to be applied in any situation, which minimizes the total costs of quality. The argument is that there must be a point beyond which diminishing returns set in – that is, the cost of improving quality gets larger than the benefits which it brings. Figure 17.7(a) sums up this idea. As quality effort is increased, the costs of providing the effort – through extra quality controllers, inspection procedures, and so on – increases proportionally. At the same time, however, the cost of errors, faulty products, and so on, decreases because there are fewer of them. However, TQM proponents believe that this logic is flawed. First, it implies that failure and poor quality are acceptable. Why, TQM proponents argue, should any operation accept the *inevitability* of errors? Some occupations seem to be able to accept a zero-defect standard. No one accepts that pilots are allowed to crash a certain proportion of their aircraft, or that nurses will drop a certain proportion of the babies

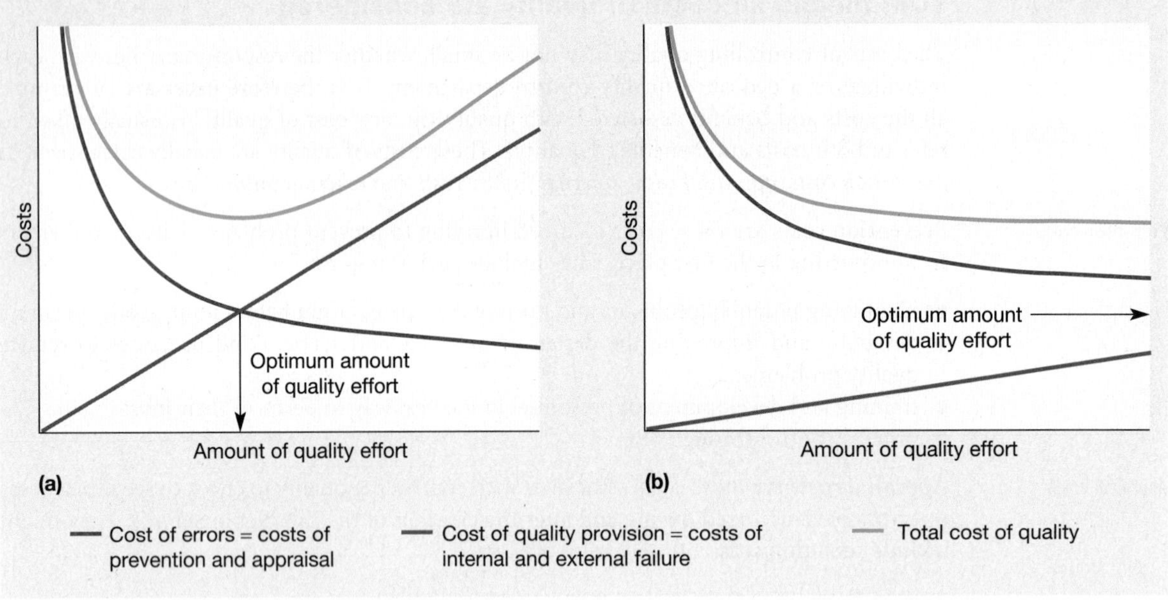

Figure 17.7 (a) The traditional cost of quality model, and (b) the traditional cost of quality model with adjustments to reflect TQM criticisms

they deliver. Second, it assumes that costs are known and measurable. In fact putting realistic figures to the cost of quality is not a straightforward matter. Third, it is argued that failure costs in the traditional model are greatly underestimated. In particular, all the management time wasted by failures and the loss of concentration it causes are rarely accounted for. Fourth, it implies that prevention costs are inevitably high because it involves expensive inspection. But why should not quality be an integral part of everyone's work rather than employing extra people to inspect. Finally, the 'optimum-quality level' approach, by accepting compromise, does little to challenge operations managers and staff to find ways of improving quality. Put these corrections into the optimum-quality effort calculation and the picture looks very different (*see* Fig. 17.7b). If there is an 'optimum', it is a lot further to the right, in the direction of putting more effort (but not necessarily cost) into quality.

Short case
Deliberate defectives

A story which illustrates the difference in attitude between a TQM and a non-TQM company has become almost a legend among TQM proponents. It concerns a plant in Ontario, Canada, of IBM, the computer company. It ordered a batch of components from a Japanese manufacturer and specified that the batch should have an acceptable quality level (AQL) of three defective parts per thousand. When the parts arrived in Ontario they were accompanied by a letter which expressed the supplier's bewilderment at being asked to supply defective parts as well as good ones. The letter also explained that they had found it difficult to make parts which were defective, but had indeed managed it. These three defective parts per thousand had been included and were wrapped separately for the convenience of the customer.

The TQM quality cost model

TQM rejects the optimum-quality level concept and strives to reduce all known and unknown failure costs by preventing errors and failure taking place. Rather than looking for 'optimum' levels of quality effort, TQM stresses the relative balance between different types of quality cost. Of the four cost categories, two (costs of prevention and costs of appraisal) are open to managerial influence, while the other two (internal costs of failure and external costs of

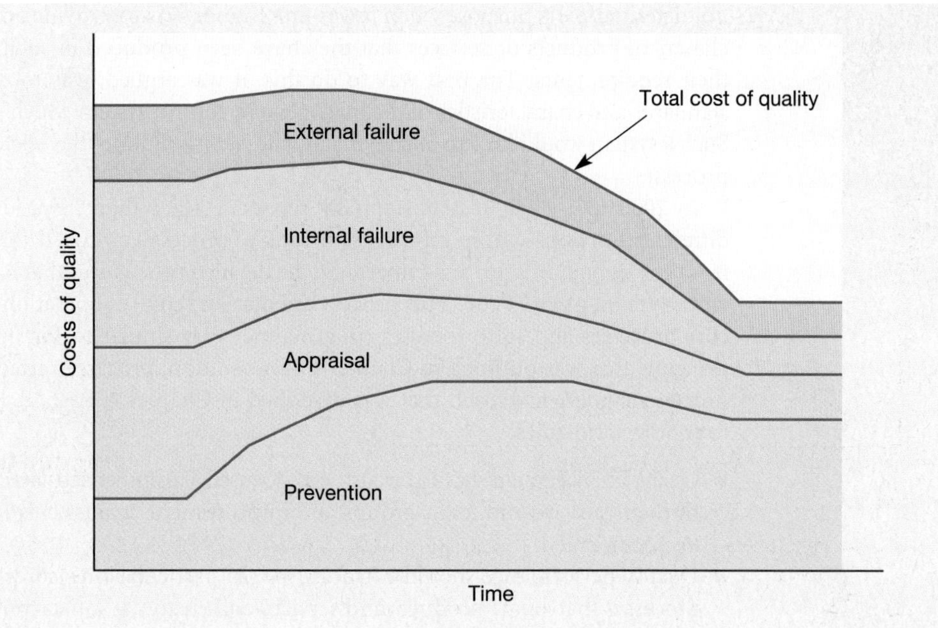

Figure 17.8 Increasing the effort spent on preventing errors occurring in the first place brings a more than equivalent reduction in other cost categories

failure) show the consequences of changes in the first two. So, rather than placing most emphasis on appraisal (so that 'bad products and service don't get through to the customer') TQM emphasizes prevention (to stop errors happening in the first place). That is because the more effort that is put into error prevention, the more internal and external failure costs are reduced. Then, once confidence has been firmly established, appraisal costs can be reduced. Eventually even prevention costs can be stepped down in absolute terms, though prevention remains a significant cost in relative terms. Figure 17.8 illustrates this idea. Initially total quality costs may rise as investment in some aspects of prevention – mainly training – is increased. However, a reduction in total costs can quickly follow.

Getting things 'right first time'

Accepting the relationships between categories of quality cost as illustrated in Figure 17.8 has a particularly important implication for how quality is managed. It shifts the emphasis from *reactive* (waiting for something to happen) to *proactive* (doing something before anything happens). This change in the view of quality costs has come about with a movement from an inspect-in (appraisal-driven) approach to a design-in (**getting it right first time**) approach.

Getting it right first time

Developing the systems and procedures which support quality and improvement

The emphasis on highly formalized systems and procedures to support TQM has declined in recent years, yet one aspect is still active for many companies. This is the adoption of the ISO 9000 standard. And although ISO 9000 can be regarded as a stand-alone issue, it is very closely associated with TQM.

The ISO 9000 approach

ISO 9000

The **ISO 9000** series is a set of worldwide standards that establishes requirements for companies' quality management systems. ISO 9000 is being used worldwide to provide a framework for quality assurance. Registration requires a third-party assessment of a company's quality standards and procedures and regular audits are made to ensure that the systems do not deteriorate. Its purpose when it was first framed was to provide an assurance to the purchasers of products or services that they have been produced in such a way that they meet their requirements. The best way to do this, it was argued, was to define the procedures, standards and characteristics of the management control system which governs the operation. Such a system would help to ensure that quality was 'built into' the operation's transformation processes.

In 2000 ISO 9000 was substantially revised. Rather than using different standards for different functions within a business it took a 'process' approach that focused on outputs from any operation's process rather than the detailed procedures that had dominated the previous version of ISO 9000. This process orientation requires operations to define and record core processes and sub-processes (in a manner very similar to the 'hierarchy of processes' principle that was outlined in Chapter 1). In addition, processes are documented using the process mapping approach that was described in Chapter 4. Also, ISO 9000 (2000) stresses four other principles.

- Quality management should be customer-focused. Customer satisfaction should be measured through surveys and focus groups and improvement against customer standards should be documented.
- Quality performance should be measured. In particular, measures should relate both to processes that create products and services and customer satisfaction with those products and services. Furthermore, measured data should be analysed in order to understand processes.
- Quality management should be improvement-driven. Improvement must be demonstrated in both process performance and customer satisfaction.
- Top management must demonstrate their commitment to maintaining and continually improving management systems. This commitment should include communicating the importance of meeting customer and other requirements, establishing a quality policy and quality objectives, conducting management reviews to ensure the adherence to quality policies, and ensuring the availability of the necessary resources to maintain quality systems.

ISO 9000 is seen as providing benefits both to the organizations adopting it (because it gives them detailed guidance on how to design their control procedures) and especially to customers (who have the assurance of knowing that the products and services they purchase are produced by an operation working to a defined standard). It may also provide a useful discipline to stick to 'sensible' process-oriented procedures which lead to error reduction, reduced customer complaints and reduced costs of quality, and may even identify existing procedures which are not necessary and can be eliminated. Moreover, gaining the certificate demonstrates that the company takes quality seriously; it therefore has a marketing benefit.

Critical commentary

Notwithstanding its widespread adoption (and its revision to take into account some of its perceived failings), ISO 9000 is not seen as beneficial by all authorities, and is still subject to some specific criticisms. These include the following:

- **The continued use of standards and procedures encourages 'management by manual' and over-systematized decision-making.**
- **The whole process of documenting processes, writing procedures, training staff and conducting internal audits is expensive and time-consuming.**
- **Similarly, the time and cost of achieving and maintaining ISO 9000 registration are excessive.**
- **It is too formulaic. It encourages operations to substitute a 'recipe' for a more customized and creative approach to managing operations improvement.**

Summary answers to key questions

*Check and improve your understanding of this chapter using self assessment questions and a personalised study plan, audio and video downloads, and an eBook – all at **www.myomlab.com**.*

➤ What is quality and why is it so important?

- The definition of quality used in this book defines quality as 'consistent conformance to customers' expectations'.

➤ How can quality problems be diagnosed?

- At a broad level, quality is best modelled as the gap between customers' expectations concerning the product or service and their perceptions concerning the product or service.
- Modelling quality this way will allow the development of a diagnostic tool which is based around the perception–expectation gap. Such a gap may be explained by four other gaps:
  - the gap between a customer's specification and the operation's specification;
  - the gap between the product or service concept and the way the organization has specified it;
  - the gap between the way quality has been specified and the actual delivered quality;
  - the gap between the actual delivered quality and the way the product or service has been described to the customer.

➤ What steps lead towards conformance to specification?

- There are six steps:
  - define quality characteristics;
  - decide how to measure each of the quality characteristics;
  - set quality standards for each characteristic;
  - control quality against these standards;
  - find and correct the causes of poor quality;
  - continue to make improvements.
- Most quality planning and control involves sampling the operations performance in some way. Sampling can give rise to erroneous judgements which are classed as either type I or type II errors. Type I errors involve making corrections where none are needed. Type II errors involve not making corrections where they are in fact needed.

➤ What is total quality management (TQM)?

- TQM is 'an effective system for integrating the quality development, quality maintenance and quality improvement efforts of the various groups in an organization so as to enable production and service at the most economical levels which allow for full customer satisfaction'.
- It is best thought of as a philosophy that stresses the 'total' of TQM and puts quality at the heart of everything that is done by an operation.
- 'Total' in TQM means the following:
  - meeting the needs and expectations of customers;
  - covering all parts of the organization;
  - including every person in the organization;
  - examining all costs which are related to quality, and getting things 'right first time';
  - developing the systems and procedures which support quality and improvement;
  - developing a continuous process of improvement.

Case study
Turnround at the Preston plant

Source: Getty Images/Digital Vision

*'Before the crisis the quality department was just for looks, we certainly weren't used much for problem solving, the most we did was inspection. Data from the quality department was brought to the production meeting and they would all look at it, but no one was looking **behind** it'* (Quality Manager, Preston Plant).

The Preston plant of Rendall Graphics was located in Preston, Vancouver, across the continent from their headquarters in Massachusetts. The plant had been bought from the Georgetown Corporation by Rendall in March 2000. Precision coated papers for ink-jet printers accounted for the majority of the plant's output, especially paper for specialist uses. The plant used coating machines that allowed precise coatings to be applied. After coating, the conversion department cut the coated rolls to the final size and packed the sheets in small cartons.

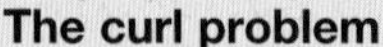

The curl problem

In late 1998 Hewlett-Packard (HP), the plant's main customer for ink-jet paper, informed the plant of some problems it had encountered with paper curling under conditions of low humidity. There had been no customer complaints to HP, but their own personnel had noticed the problem, and they wanted it fixed. Over the next seven or eight months a team at the plant tried to solve the problem. Finally, in October of 1999 the team made recommendations for a revised and considerably improved coating formulation. By January 2000 the process was producing acceptably. However, 1999 had not been a good year for the plant. Although sales were reasonably buoyant the plant was making a loss of around $2 million for the year. In October 1999, Tom Branton, previously accountant for the business, was appointed as Managing Director.

Slipping out of control

In the spring of 2000, productivity, scrap and re-work levels continued to be poor. In response to this the operations management team increased the speed of the line and made a number of changes to operating practice in order to raise productivity.

*'Looking back, changes were made without any proper discipline, and there was no real concept of control. We were always meeting specification, yet we didn't fully understand how close we really were to not being able to make it. The culture here said, "If it's within specification then it's OK" and we were very diligent in making sure that the product which was shipped **was** in specification. However, Hewlett-Packard gets "process charts" that enable them to see more or less exactly what is happening right inside your operation. We were also getting all the reports but none of them were being internalized, we were using them just to satisfy the customer. By contrast, HP have a statistically-based analytical mentality that says to itself, "You might be capable of making this product but we are thinking two or three product generations forward and asking ourselves, will you have the capability then, and do we want to invest in this relationship for the future?"'* (Tom Branton)

The spring of 2000 also saw two significant events. First, Hewlett-Packard asked the plant to bid for the contract to supply a new ink-jet platform, known as the Vector project, a contract that would secure healthy orders for several years. The second event was that the plant was acquired by Rendall.

'What did Rendall see when they bought us? They saw a small plant on the Pacific coast losing lots of money.' (Finance Manager, Preston Plant)

Rendall were not impressed by what they found at the Preston plant. It was making a loss and had only just escaped from incurring a major customer's disapproval over the curl issue. If the plant did not get the Vector contract, its future looked bleak. Meanwhile the chief concern continued to be productivity. But also, once again, there were occasional complaints about quality levels. However HP's attitude caused some bewilderment to the operations management team.

'When HP asked questions about our process the operations guys would say, "Look we're making roll after roll of paper, it's within specification. What's the problem?"' (Quality Manager, Preston Plant)

But it was not until summer that the full extent of HP's disquiet was made. *'I will never forget June of 2000. I was at a meeting with HP in Chicago. It was not even about quality. But during the meeting one of their engineers handed me a control chart, one that we supplied with every batch of product. He said "Here's your latest control chart. We think you're out of control and you don't know that you're out of control and we think that we are looking at this data more than you are." He was absolutely right, and I fully understood how serious the position was. We had our most important customer telling us we couldn't run our processes just at the time we were trying to persuade them to give us the Vector contract.'* (Tom Branton)

The crisis

Tom immediately set about the task of bringing the plant back under control. They first of all decided to go back to the conditions which prevailed in the January, when the curl team's recommendations had been implemented. This was the state before productivity pressures had caused the process to be adjusted. At the same time the team worked on ways of implementing unambiguous 'shut-down rules' that would allow operators to decide under what conditions a line should be halted if they were in doubt about the quality of the product they were making.

'At one point in May of 2000 we had to throw away 64 jumbo rolls of out-of-specification product. That's over $100,000 of product scrapped in one run. Basically that was because they had been afraid to shut the line down. Either that or they had tried to tweak the line while it was running to get rid of the defect. The shut-down guidelines in effect say, "We are not going to operate when we are not in a state of control". Until then our operators just couldn't win. If they failed to keep the machines running we would say, "You've got to keep productivity up". If they kept the machines running but had quality problems as a result, we criticized them for making garbage. Now you get into far more trouble for violating process procedures than you do for not meeting productivity targets.' (Engineer, Preston Plant)

This new approach needed to be matched by changes in the way the communications were managed in the plant.

'We did two things that we had never done before. First, each production team started holding daily reviews of control chart data. Second, one day a month we took people away from production and debated the control chart data. Several people got nervous because we were not producing anything. But it was necessary. For the first time you got operators from the three shifts meeting together and talking about the control chart data and other quality issues. Just as significantly we invited HP up to attend these meetings. Remember these weren't staged meetings, it was the first time these guys had met together and there was plenty of heated discussion, all of which the Hewlett-Packard representatives witnessed.' (Engineer, Preston Plant)

At last something positive was happening in the plant and morale on the shop floor was buoyant. By September 2000 the results of the plant's teams efforts were starting to show results. Process were coming under control, quality levels were improving and, most importantly, personnel both on the shop floor and in the management team were beginning to get into the 'quality mode' of thinking. Paradoxically, in spite of stopping the line periodically, the efficiency of the plant was also improving.

Yet the Preston team did not have time to enjoy their emerging success. In September of 2000 the plant learned that it would not get the Vector project because of their recent quality problems. Then Rendall decided to close the plant. *'We were losing millions, we had lost the Vector project, and it was really no surprise. I told the senior management team and said that we would announce it probably in April of 2001. The real irony was that we knew that we had actually already turned the corner.'* (Tom Branton)

Notwithstanding the closure decision, the management team in Preston set about the task of convincing Rendall that the plant could be viable. They figured it would take three things. First, it was vital that they continue to improve quality. Progressing with their quality initiative involved establishing full statistical process control (SPC).

Second, costs had to be brought down. Working on cost reduction was inevitably going to be painful. The first task was to get an understanding of what should be an appropriate level of operating costs. *'We went through a zero-based assessment to decide what an ideal plant would look like, and the minimum number of people needed to run it'* (Tom Branton).

By December of 2000 there were 40 per cent fewer people in the plant than two months earlier. All departments were affected. The quality department shrank more than most, moving from 22 people down to 6. *'When the plant was considering down-sizing they asked me, "How can we run a lab with six technicians?" I said, "Easy. We just make good paper in the first place, and then we don't have to inspect all the garbage. That alone would save an immense amount of time."* (Quality Manager, Preston Plant)

Third, the plant had to create a portfolio of new product ideas which could establish a greater confidence in future sales. Several new ideas were under active investigation. The most important of these was 'Protowrap', a wrap for newsprint that could be repulped. It was a product that was technically difficult. However, the plant's newly acquired capabilities allowed the product to be made economically.

Out of the crisis

In spite of their trauma, the plant's management team faced Christmas of 2000 with increasing optimism. They had just made a profit for the first time for over two years. By spring of 2001 even HP, at a corporate level, was starting to take notice. It was becoming obvious that the Preston plant really had made a major change. More significantly, HP had asked the plant to bid for a new product. April 2001 was a good month for the plant. It had chalked up three months of profitability and HP formally gave the new 

contract to Preston. Also in April, Rendall reversed their decision to close the plant.

Questions

1 What are the most significant events in the story of how the plant survived because of its adoption of quality-based principles?

2 The plant's processes eventually were brought under control. What were the main benefits of this?

3 SPC is an operational level technique of ensuring quality conformance. How many of the benefits of bringing the plant under control would you class as strategic?

Problems and applications

These problems and applications will help to improve your analysis of operations. You can find more practice problems as well as worked examples and guided solutions on MyOMLab at ***www.myomlab.com****.*

(Read the supplement on statistical process control, before attempting these problems.)

1 A call centre for a bank answers customers' queries about their loan arrangements. All calls are automatically timed by the call centre's information system and the mean and standard deviation of call lengths is monitored periodically. The bank has decided that only on very rare occasions should calls be less than 0.5 minute because customers would think this was impolite even if the query was so simple that it could be answered in this time. Also, the bank reckoned that it was unlikely that any query should ever take more than 7 minutes to answer satisfactorily. The figures for last week's calls show that the mean of all call lengths was 3.02 minutes and the standard deviation was 1.58 minutes. Calculate the C_p and the C_{pk} for the call centre process.

2 In the above call centre, if the mean call length changes to 3.2 minutes and the standard deviation is 0.9 minute, how does this affect the C_p and C_{pk}? Do you think this is an appropriate way for the bank to monitor its call centre performance?

3 A vaccine production company has invested in an automatic tester to monitor the impurity levels in its vaccines. Previously all testing was done by hand on a sample of batches of serum. According to the company's specifications, all vaccine must have impurity levels of less than 0.03 milligram per 1,000 litres. In order to test the effectiveness of its new automatic sampling equipment, the company runs a number of batches through the process with known levels of impurity. The table below shows the level of impurity of each batch and whether the new process accepted or rejected the batch. From these data, estimate the Type I and Type II error levels for the process.

0.035 (rejected)	0.028 (accepted)	0.031 (accepted)	0.029 (accepted)	0.028 (accepted)	0.034 (accepted)	0.031 (accepted)
0.040 (rejected)	0.011 (accepted)	0.028 (rejected)	0.025 (accepted)	0.019 (accepted)	0.018 (accepted)	0.033 (rejected)
0.022 (accepted)	0.029 (rejected)	0.012 (accepted)	0.034 (accepted)	0.027 (accepted)	0.017 (accepted)	0.021 (accepted)
0.031 (rejected)	0.015 (accepted)	0.037 (rejected)	0.030 (accepted)	0.025 (accepted)	0.034 (rejected)	0.020 (accepted)

4 A utility has a department that does nothing but change the addresses of customers on the company's information systems when customers move house. The process is deemed to be in control at the moment and a random sample of 2,000 transactions shows that 2.5 per cent of these transactions had some type of error. If the company is to use statistical process control to monitor error levels, calculate the mean, upper control level (UCL) and lower control level (LCL) for their SPC chart.

5 Find two products, one a manufactured food item (for example, a pack of breakfast cereals, packet of biscuits, etc.) and the other a domestic electrical item (for example, electric toaster, coffee maker, etc.).

(a) Identify the important quality characteristics for these two products.
(b) How could each of these quality characteristics be specified?
(c) How could each of these quality characteristics be measured?

6 Many organizations check up on their own level of quality by using 'mystery shoppers'. This involves an employee of the company acting the role of a customer and recording how they are treated by the operation. Choose two or three high-visibility operations (for example, a cinema, a department store, the branch of a retail bank, etc.) and discuss how you would put together a mystery shopper approach to testing their quality. This may involve you determining the types of characteristics you would wish to observe, the way in which you would measure these characteristics, an appropriate sampling rate, and so on. Try out your mystery shopper plan by visiting these operations.

Selected further reading

Dale, B.G. (ed.) (2003) *Managing Quality*, Blackwell, Oxford. This latest version of a long-established, comprehensive and authoritative text.

Garvin, D.A. (1988) *Managing Quality*, The Free Press, New York. Somewhat dated now but relates to our discussion at the beginning of this chapter.

George, M.L., Rowlands, D. and Kastle, B. (2003) *What Is Lean Six Sigma?* McGraw-Hill. Very much a quick introduction on what Lean Six Sigma is and how to use it.

Pande, P.S., Neuman, R.P. and Kavanagh, R.R. (2000) *The Six Sigma Way*, McGraw-Hill, New York. There are many books written by consultants for practising managers on the now fashionable Six Sigma Approach. This is as readable as any.

Useful web sites

www.quality-foundation.co.uk/ The British Quality Foundation is a not-for-profit organization promoting business excellence.

www.juran.com The Juran Institute's mission statement is to provide clients with the concepts, methods and guidance for attaining leadership in quality.

www.asq.org/ The American Society for Quality site. Good professional insights.

www.opsman.org Lots of useful stuff.

www.quality.nist.gov/ American Quality Assurance Institute. Well-established institution for all types of business quality assurance.

www.gslis.utexas.edu/~rpollock/tqm.html Non-commercial site on total quality management with some good links.

www.iso.org/iso/en/ISOOnline.frontpage Site of the International Standards Organization that runs the ISO 9000 and ISO 14000 families of standards. ISO 9000 has become an international reference for quality management requirements.

Now that you have finished reading this chapter, why not visit MyOMLab at ***www.myomlab.com*** *where you'll find more learning resources to help you make the most of your studies and get a better grade?*

Supplement to Chapter 17 Statistical process control (SPC)

Introduction

Statistical process control (SPC) is concerned with checking a product or service during its creation. If there is reason to believe that there is a problem with the process, then it can be stopped and the problem can be identified and rectified. For example, an international airport may regularly ask a sample of customers if the cleanliness of its restaurants is satisfactory. If an unacceptable number of customers in one sample are found to be unhappy, airport managers may have to consider improving their procedures. Similarly, a car manufacturer periodically will check whether a sample of door panels conforms to its standards so it knows whether the machinery which produces them is performing correctly.

Control charts

Control charts

The value of SPC is not just to make checks of a single sample but to monitor the quality over a period of time. It does this by using **control charts** to see if the process seems to be performing as it should, or alternatively if it is 'out of control'. If the process does seem to be going out of control, then steps can be taken *before* there is a problem. Actually, most operations chart their quality performance in some way. Figure S17.1, or something like it,

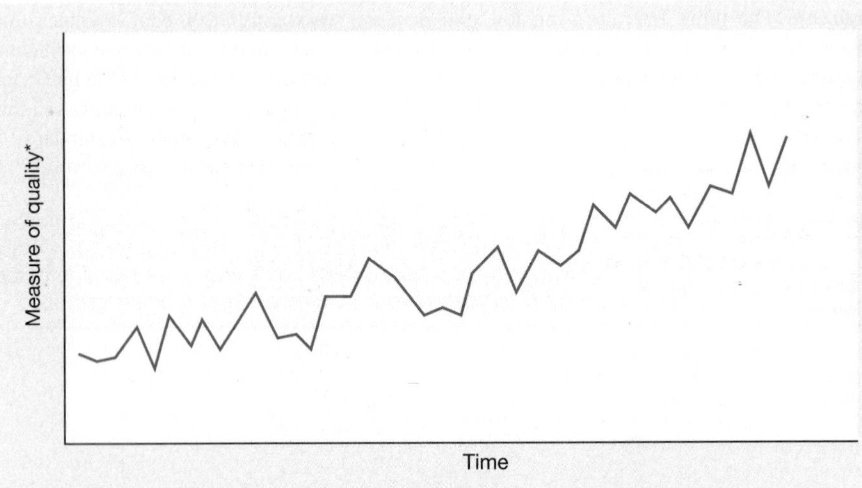

Figure S17.1 Charting trends in quality measures

could be found in almost any operation. The chart could, for example, represent the percentage of customers in a sample of 1,000 who, each month, were dissatisfied with the restaurant's cleanliness. While the amount of dissatisfaction may be acceptably small, management should be concerned that it has been steadily increasing over time and may wish to investigate why this is so. In this case, the control chart is plotting an attribute measure of quality (satisfied or not). Looking for trends is an important use of control charts. If the trend suggests the process is getting steadily worse, then it will be worth investigating the process. If the trend is steadily improving, it may still be worthy of investigation to try to identify what is happening that is making the process better. This information might then be shared with other parts of the organization, or, on the other hand, the process might be stopped as the cause could be adding unnecessary expense to the operation.

Variation in process quality

Common causes

The processes charted in Figure S17.1 showed an upwards trend. But the trend was neither steady nor smooth: it varied, sometimes up, sometimes down. All processes vary to some extent. No machine will give precisely the same result each time it is used. People perform tasks slightly differently each time. Given this, it is not surprising that the measure of quality will also vary. Variations which derive from these *common causes* can never be entirely eliminated (although they can be reduced). For example, if a machine is filling boxes with rice, it will not place *exactly* the same weight of rice in every box it fills. When the filling machine is in a stable condition (that is, no exceptional factors are influencing its behaviour) each box could be weighed and a histogram of the weights could be built up. Figure S17.2 shows how the histogram might develop. The first boxes weighed could lie anywhere within the natural variation of the process but are more likely to be close to the average weight

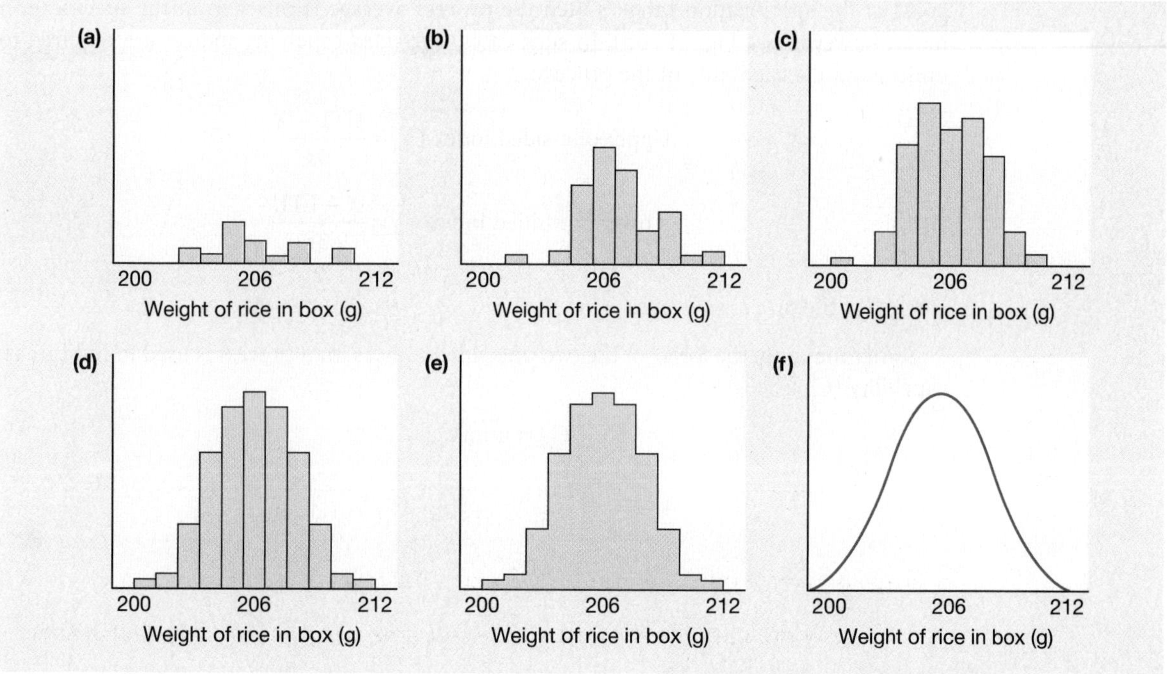

Figure S17.2 The natural variation in the filling process can be described by a normal distribution

(*see* Fig. S17.2a). As more boxes are weighed they clearly show the tendency to be close to the process average (*see* Fig. S17.2b and c). After many boxes have been weighed they form a smoother distribution (Fig. S17.2d), which can be drawn as a histogram (Fig. S17.2e), which will approximate to the underlying process variation distribution (Fig. S17.2f).

Usually this type of variation can be described by a normal distribution with 99.7 per cent of the variation lying within ±3 standard deviations. In this case the weight of rice in the boxes is described by a distribution with a mean of 206 grams and a standard deviation of 2 grams. The obvious question for any operations manager would be: 'Is this variation in the process performance acceptable?' The answer will depend on the acceptable range of weights which can be tolerated by the operation. This range is called the **specification range.** If the weight of rice in the box is too small then the organization might infringe labelling regulations; if it is too large, the organization is 'giving away' too much of its product for free.

Specification range

Process capability

Process capability

Process capability is a measure of the acceptability of the variation of the process. The simplest measure of capability (C_p) is given by the ratio of the specification range to the 'natural' variation of the process (i.e. ±3 standard deviations):

$$C_p = \frac{\text{UTL} - \text{LTL}}{6s}$$

where

UTL = the upper tolerance limit
LTL = the lower tolerance limit
s = the standard deviation of the process variability.

Generally, if the C_p of a process is greater than 1, it is taken to indicate that the process is 'capable', and a C_p of less than 1 indicates that the process is not 'capable', assuming that the distribution is normal (*see* Fig. S17.3a, b and c).

The simple C_p measure assumes that the average of the process variation is at the mid-point of the specification range. Often the process average is offset from the specification range, however (*see* Fig. S17.3d). In such cases, *one-sided* capability indices are required to understand the capability of the process:

$$\text{Upper one-sided index } C_{pu} = \frac{\text{UTL} - X}{3s}$$

$$\text{Lower one-sided index } C_{pl} = \frac{X - \text{LTL}}{3s}$$

where X = the process average.

Sometimes only the lower of the two one-sided indices for a process is used to indicate its capability (C_{pk}):

$$C_{pk} = \min(C_{pu}, C_{pl})$$

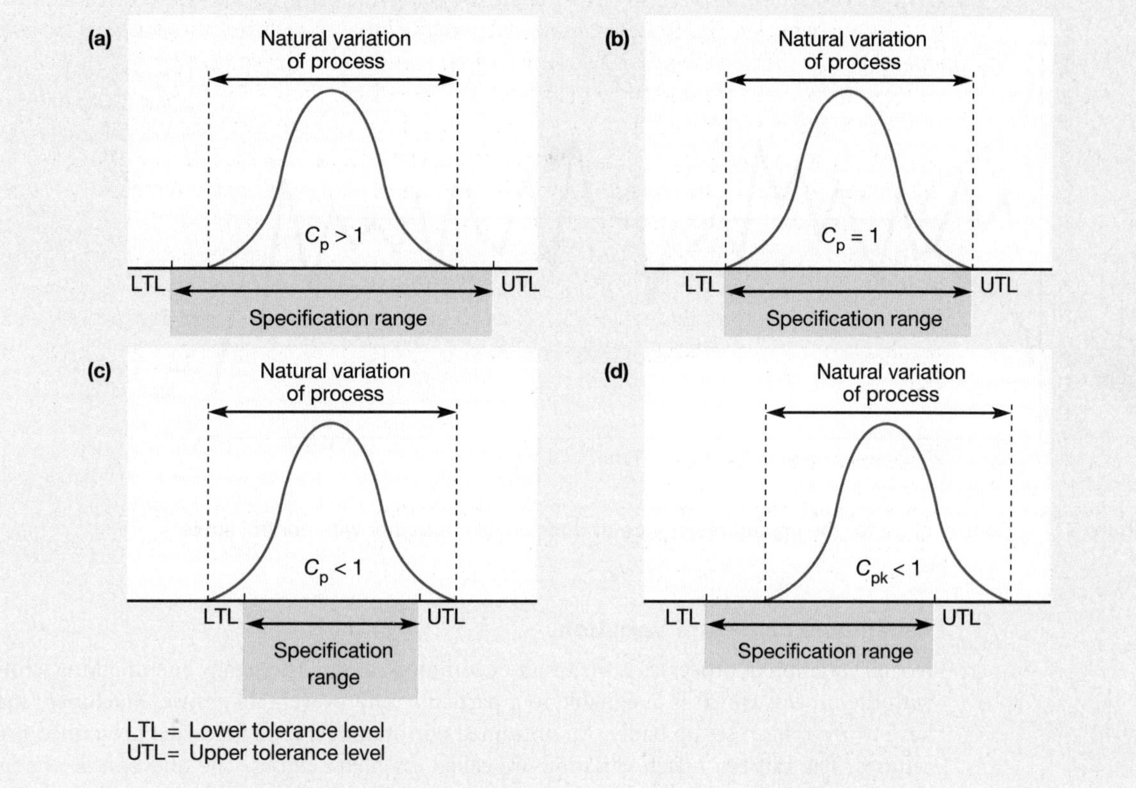

Figure S17.3 Process capability compares the natural variation of the process with the specification range which is required

Worked example

In the case of the process filling boxes of rice, described previously, process capability can be calculated as follows:

$$
\begin{aligned}
\text{Specification range} &= 214 - 198 = 16 \text{ g} \\
\text{Natural variation of process} &= 6 \times \text{standard deviation} \\
&= 6 \times 2 = 12 \text{ g} \\
C_p &= \text{process capability} \\
&= \frac{\text{UTL} - \text{LTL}}{6s} \\
&= \frac{214 - 198}{6 \times 2} = \frac{16}{12} \\
&= 1.333
\end{aligned}
$$

If the natural variation of the filling process changed to have a process average of 210 grams but the standard deviation of the process remained at 2 grams:

$$C_{pu} = \frac{214 - 210}{3 \times 2} = \frac{4}{6} = 0.666$$

$$C_{pl} = \frac{210 - 198}{3 \times 2} = \frac{12}{6} = 2.0$$

$$
\begin{aligned}
C_{pk} &= \min(0.666, 2.0) \\
&= 0.666
\end{aligned}
$$

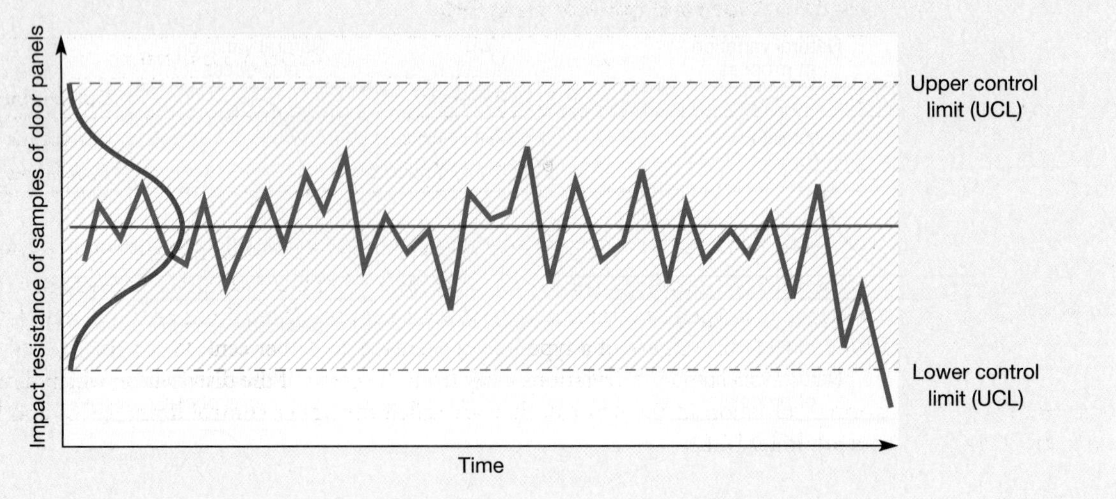

Figure S17.4 Control chart for the impact resistance of door panels, together with control limits

Assignable causes of variation

Not all variation in processes is the result of common causes. There may be something wrong with the process which is assignable to a particular and preventable cause. Machinery may have worn or been set up badly. An untrained person may not be following prescribed procedures. The causes of such variation are called *assignable causes*. The question is whether the results from any particular sample, when plotted on the control chart, simply represent the variation due to common causes or due to some specific and correctable *assignable* cause. Figure S17.4, for example, shows the control chart for the average impact resistance of samples of door panels taken over time. Like any process the results vary, but the last three points seem to be lower than usual. So, is this natural (common cause) variation, or the symptom of some more serious (assignable) cause?

Control limits

To help make this decision, **control limits** can be added to the control chart (the red dashed lines) which indicates the expected extent of 'common-cause' variation. If any points lie outside these control limits (the shaded zone) then the process can be deemed out of control in the sense that variation is likely to be due to assignable causes. These control limits could be set intuitively by examining past variation during a period when the process was thought to be free of any variation which could be due to assignable causes. But control limits can also be set in a more statistically revealing manner. For example, if the process which tests door panels had been measured to determine the normal distribution which represents its common-cause variation, then control limits can be based on this distribution. Figure S17.4 also shows how control limits can be added; here they are put at ±3 standard deviations (of the population of sample means) away from the mean of sample averages. It shows that the probability of the final point on the chart being influenced by an assignable cause is very high indeed. When the process is exhibiting behaviour which is outside its normal 'common-cause' range, it is said to be 'out of control'. Yet there is a small but finite chance that the (seemingly out of limits) point is just one of the rare but natural results at the tail of the distribution which describes perfectly normal behaviour. Stopping the process under these circumstances would represent a type I error because the process is actually in control. Alternatively, ignoring a result which in reality is due to an assignable cause is a type II error (*see* Table S17.1).

Control limits are usually set at three standard deviations either side of the population mean. This would mean that there is only a 0.3 per cent chance of any sample mean falling outside these limits by chance causes (that is, a chance of a type I error of 0.3 per cent). The control limits may be set at any distance from the population mean, but the closer the limits

Table S17.1 Type I and type II errors in SPC

	Actual process state	
Decision	*In control*	*Out of control*
Stop process	Type I error	Correct decision
Leave alone	Correct decision	Type II error

are to the population mean, the higher the likelihood of investigating and trying to rectify a process which is actually problem-free. If the control limits are set at two standard deviations, the chance of a type I error increases to about 5 per cent. If the limits are set at one standard deviation then the chance of a type I error increases to 32 per cent. When the control limits are placed at ±3 standard deviations away from the mean of the distribution which describes 'normal' variation in the process, they are called the **upper control limit** (UCL) and **lower control limit** (LCL).

Upper control limit
Lower control limit

Critical commentary

When its originators first described SPC more than half a century ago, the key issue was only to decide whether a process was 'in control' or not. Now, we expect SPC to reflect common sense as well as statistical elegance and promote continuous operations improvement. This is why two (related) criticisms have been levelled at the traditional approach to SPC. The first is that SPC seems to assume that any values of process performance which lie within the control limits are equally acceptable, while any values outside the limits are not. However, surely a value close to the process average or 'target' value will be more acceptable than one only just within the control limits. For example, a service engineer arriving only 1 minute late is a far better 'performance' than one arriving 59 minutes late, even if the control limits are 'quoted time ± one hour'. Also, arriving 59 minutes late would be almost as bad as 61 minutes late! Second, a process always within its control limits may not be deteriorating, but is it improving. So rather than seeing control limits as fixed, it would be better to view them as a reflection of how the process is being improved. We should expect any improving process to have progressively narrowing control limits.

The Taguchi loss function

Genichi Taguchi proposed a resolution of both the criticisms of SPC described in the critical commentary box.[12] He suggested that the central issue was the first problem – namely that the consequences of being 'off-target' (that is, deviating from the required process average performance) were inadequately described by simple control limits. Instead, he proposed a **quality loss function** (QLF) – a mathematical function which includes all the costs of poor quality. These include wastage, repair, inspection, service, warranty and generally, what he termed, 'loss to society' costs. This loss function is expressed as follows:

Quality loss function

$$L = D^2C$$

where

L = total loss to society costs
D = deviation from target performance
C = a constant.

Figure S17.5 illustrates the difference between the conventional and Taguchi approaches to interpreting process variability. The more graduated approach of the QLF also answers the second problem raised in the critical commentary box. With losses increasing quadratically as performance deviates from target, there is a natural tendency to progressively reduce process variability. This is sometimes called a **target-oriented quality** philosophy.

Target-oriented quality

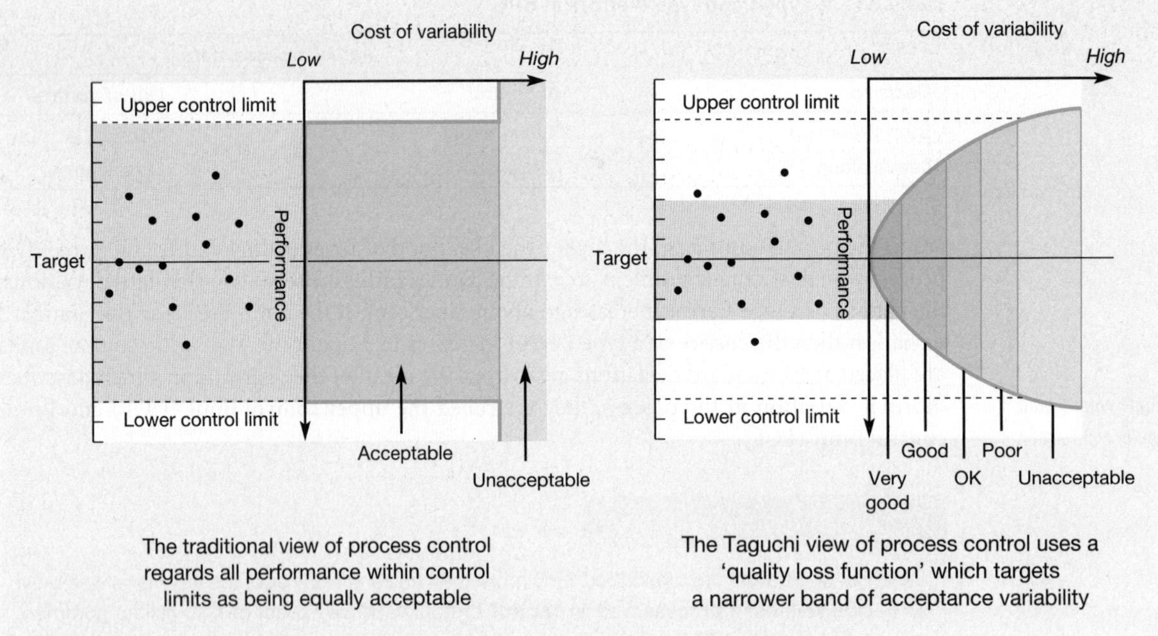

Figure S17.5 The conventional and Taguchi views of the cost of variability

Why variability is a bad thing

Assignable variation is a signal that something has changed in the process which therefore must be investigated. But normal variation is itself a problem because it masks any changes in process behaviour. Figure S17.6 shows the performance of two processes both of which are subjected to a change in their process behaviour at the same time. The process on the left has such a wide natural variation that it is not immediately apparent that any change has taken place. Eventually it will become apparent because the likelihood of process performance violating the lower (in this case) control limit has increased, but this may take some time. By contrast, the process on the right has a far narrower band of natural variation. Because of this, the same change in average performance is more easily noticed (both visually and statistically). So, the narrower the natural variation of a process, the more obvious are changes in the behaviour of that process. And the more obvious are process changes, the easier it is to understand how and why the process is behaving in a particular way. Accepting any variation in any process is, to some degree, admitting to ignorance of how that process works.

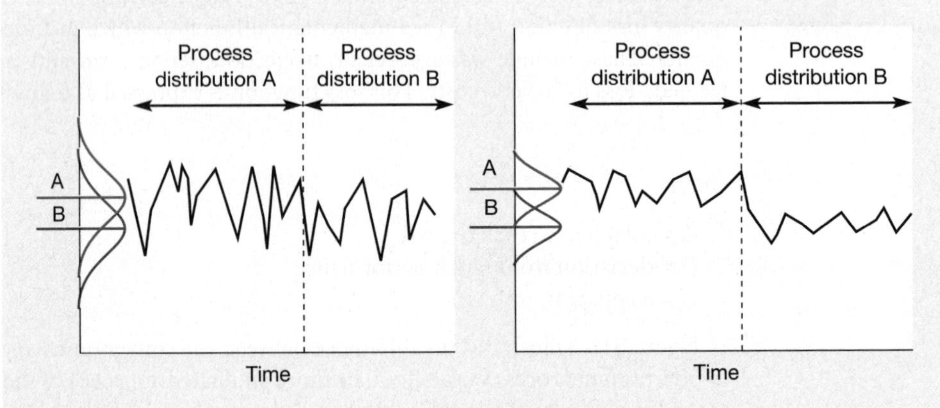

Figure S17.6 Low process variation allows changes in process performance to be readily detected

Control charts for attributes

Attributes have only two states – 'right' and 'wrong', for example – so the statistic calculated is the proportion of wrongs (p) in a sample. (This statistic follows a binomial distribution.) Control charts using p are called 'p-charts'. In calculating the limits, the population mean ($\bar{p}$) – the actual, normal or expected proportion of 'defectives' or wrongs to rights – may not be known. Who knows, for example, the actual number of city commuters who are dissatisfied with their journey time? In such cases the population mean can be estimated from the average of the proportion of 'defectives' ($\bar{p}$), from m samples each of n items, where m should be at least 30 and n should be at least 100:

$$\bar{p} = \frac{p^1 + p^2 + p^3 + \ldots + p^n}{m}$$

One standard deviation can then be estimated from:

$$\sqrt{\frac{\bar{p}(1 - \bar{p})}{n}}$$

The upper and lower control limits can then be set as:

$$\text{UCL} = \bar{p} + 3 \text{ standard deviations}$$
$$\text{LCL} = \bar{p} - 3 \text{ standard deviations.}$$

Of course, the LCL cannot be negative, so when it is calculated to be so it should be rounded up to zero.

Worked example

A credit card company deals with many hundreds of thousands of transactions every week. One of its measures of the quality of service it gives its customers is the dependability with which it mails customers' monthly accounts. The quality standard it sets itself is that accounts should be mailed within two days of the 'nominal post date' which is specified to the customer. Every week the company samples 1,000 customer accounts and records the percentage which was not mailed within the standard time. When the process is working normally, only 2 per cent of accounts are mailed outside the specified period, that is, 2 per cent are 'defective'.

Control limits for the process can be calculated as follows:

$$\text{Mean proportion defective, } \bar{p} = 0.02$$
$$\text{Sample size } n = 1{,}000$$
$$\text{Standard deviation } s = \sqrt{\frac{\bar{p}(1 - \bar{p})}{n}}$$
$$= \sqrt{\frac{0.02(0.98)}{1{,}000}}$$
$$= 0.0044$$

With the control limits at $\bar{p} \pm 3s$:

$$\text{Upper control limit (UCL)} = 0.02 + 3(0.0044) = 0.0332$$
$$= 3.32\%$$

and

$$\text{lower control limit (LCL)} = 0.02 - 3(0.0044) = 0.0068$$
$$= 0.68\%$$

→

Figure S17.7 shows the company's control chart for this measure of quality over the last few weeks, together with the calculated control limits. It also shows that the process is in control. Sometimes it is more convenient to plot the actual number of defects (c) rather than the proportion (or percentage) of defectives, on what is known as a *c*-chart. This is very similar to the *p*-chart but the sample size must be constant and the process mean and control limits are calculated using the following formulae:

$$\text{Process mean } \bar{c} = \frac{c_1 + c_2 + c_3 + \ldots + c_m}{m}$$

$$\text{Control limits} = \bar{c} \pm 3\sqrt{c}$$

where

$$c = \text{number of defects}$$
$$m = \text{number of samples}$$

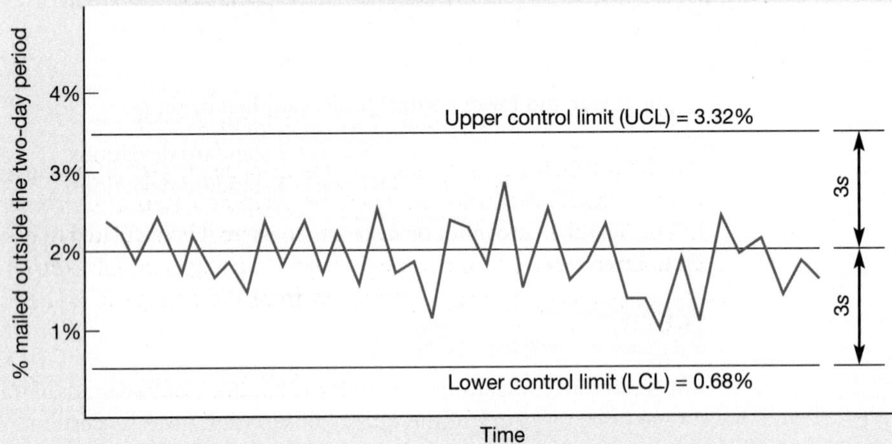

Figure S17.7 Control chart for the percentage of customer accounts which are mailed outside their two-day period

Control chart for variables

The most commonly used type of control chart employed to control variables is the $\bar{X} - R$ *chart*. In fact this is really two charts in one. One chart is used to control the sample average or mean ($\bar{X}$). The other is used to control the variation within the sample by measuring the range (R). The range is used because it is simpler to calculate than the standard deviation of the sample.

The means ($\bar{X}$) chart can pick up changes in the average output from the process being charted. Changes in the means chart would suggest that the process is drifting generally away from its supposed process average, although the variability inherent in the process may not have changed (*see* Fig. S17.8).

The range (R) chart plots the range of each sample, that is the difference between the largest and the smallest measurement in the samples. Monitoring sample range gives an indication of whether the variability of the process is changing, even when the process average remains constant (*see* Fig. S17.8).

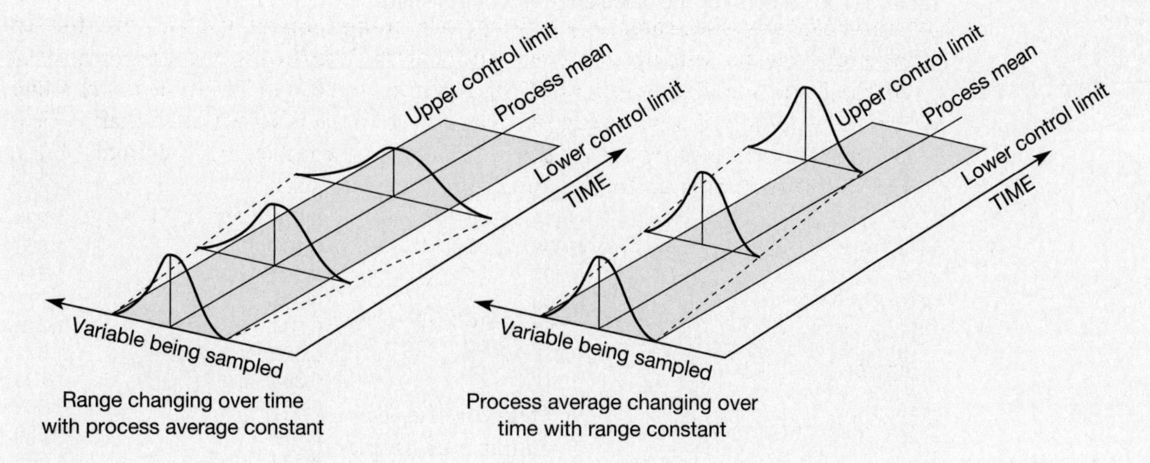

Figure S17.8 The process mean or the process range (or both) can change over time

Control limits for variables control chart

As with attributes control charts, a statistical description of how the process operates under normal conditions (when there are no assignable causes) can be used to calculate control limits. The first task in calculating the control limits is to estimate the grand average or population mean ($\bar{\bar{X}}$) and average range ($\bar{R}$) using m samples each of sample size n.

The population mean is estimated from the average of a large number (m) of sample means:

$$\bar{\bar{X}} = \frac{\bar{X}_1 + \bar{X}_2 + \ldots + \bar{X}_m}{m}$$

The average range is estimated from the ranges of the large number of samples:

$$\bar{R} = \frac{R_1 + R_2 + \ldots + R_m}{m}$$

The control limits for the sample means chart are:

$$\text{Upper control limit (UCL)} = \bar{\bar{X}} + A_2\bar{R}$$
$$\text{Lower control limit (LCL)} = \bar{\bar{X}} - A_2\bar{R}$$

The control limits for the range charts are:

$$\text{Upper control limit (UCL)} = D_4\bar{R}$$
$$\text{Lower control limit (LCL)} = D_3\bar{R}$$

The factors A_2, D_3 and D_4 vary with sample size and are shown in Table S17.2.

The LCL for the means chart may be negative (for example, temperature or profit may be less than zero) but it may not be negative for a range chart (or the smallest measurement in the sample would be larger than the largest). If the calculation indicates a negative LCL for a range chart then the LCL should be set to zero.

Table S17.2 Factors for the calculation of control limits

Sample size n	A_2	D_3	D_4
2	1.880	0	3.267
3	1.023	0	2.575
4	0.729	0	2.282
5	0.577	0	2.115
6	0.483	0	2.004
7	0.419	0.076	1.924
8	0.373	0.136	1.864
9	0.337	0.184	1.816
10	0.308	0.223	1.777
12	0.266	0.284	1.716
14	0.235	0.329	1.671
16	0.212	0.364	1.636
18	0.194	0.392	1.608
20	0.180	0.414	1.586
22	0.167	0.434	1.566
24	0.157	0.452	1.548

Worked example

GAM (Groupe As Maquillage) is a contract cosmetics company, based in France but with plants around Europe, which manufactures and packs cosmetics and perfumes for other companies. One of its plants, in Ireland, operates a filling line which automatically fills plastic bottles with skin cream and seals the bottles with a screw-top cap. The tightness with which the screw-top cap is fixed is an important part of the quality of the filling line process. If the cap is screwed on too tightly, there is a danger that it will crack; if screwed on too loosely it might come loose when packed. Either outcome could cause leakage of the product during its journey between the factory and the customer. The Irish plant had received some complaints of product leakage which it suspected was caused by inconsistent fixing of the screw-top caps on its filling line. The 'tightness' of the screw tops could be measured by a simple test device which recorded the amount of turning force (torque) that was required to unfasten the tops. The company decided to take samples of the bottles coming out of the filling-line process, test them for their unfastening torque and plot the results on a control chart. Several samples of four bottles were taken during a period when the process was regarded as being in control. The following data were calculated from this exercise:

$$\text{The grand average of all samples } \bar{\bar{X}} = 812 \text{ g/cm}^3$$
$$\text{The average range of the sample } \bar{R} = 6 \text{ g/cm}^3$$

Control limits for the means ($\bar{X}$) chart were calculated as follows:

$$\begin{aligned} \text{UCL} &= \bar{\bar{X}} + A_2\bar{R} \\ &= 812 + (A_2 \times 6) \end{aligned}$$

From Table 17.6, we know, for a sample size of four, $A_2 = 0.729$. Thus:

$$\begin{aligned} \text{UCL} &= 812 + (0.729 \times 6) \\ &= 816.37 \end{aligned}$$

$$\begin{aligned} \text{LCL} &= \bar{\bar{X}} - (A_2\bar{R}) \\ &= 812 - (0.729 \times 6) \\ &= 807.63 \end{aligned}$$

Control limits for the range chart (R) were calculated as follows:

$$\begin{aligned} UCL &= D_4 \times \bar{R} \\ &= 2.282 \times 6 \\ &= 13.69 \end{aligned}$$

$$\begin{aligned} LCL &= D_3 \bar{R} \\ &= 0 \times 6 \\ &= 0 \end{aligned}$$

After calculating these averages and limits for the control chart, the company regularly took samples of four bottles during production, recorded the measurements and plotted them as shown in Figure S17.9. The control chart revealed that only with difficulty could the process average be kept in control. Occasional operator interventions were required. Also the process range was moving towards (and once breaking) the upper control limit. The process seemed to be becoming more variable. After investigation it was discovered that, because of faulty maintenance of the line, skin cream was occasionally contaminating the torque head (the part of the line which fitted the cap). This resulted in erratic tightening of the caps.

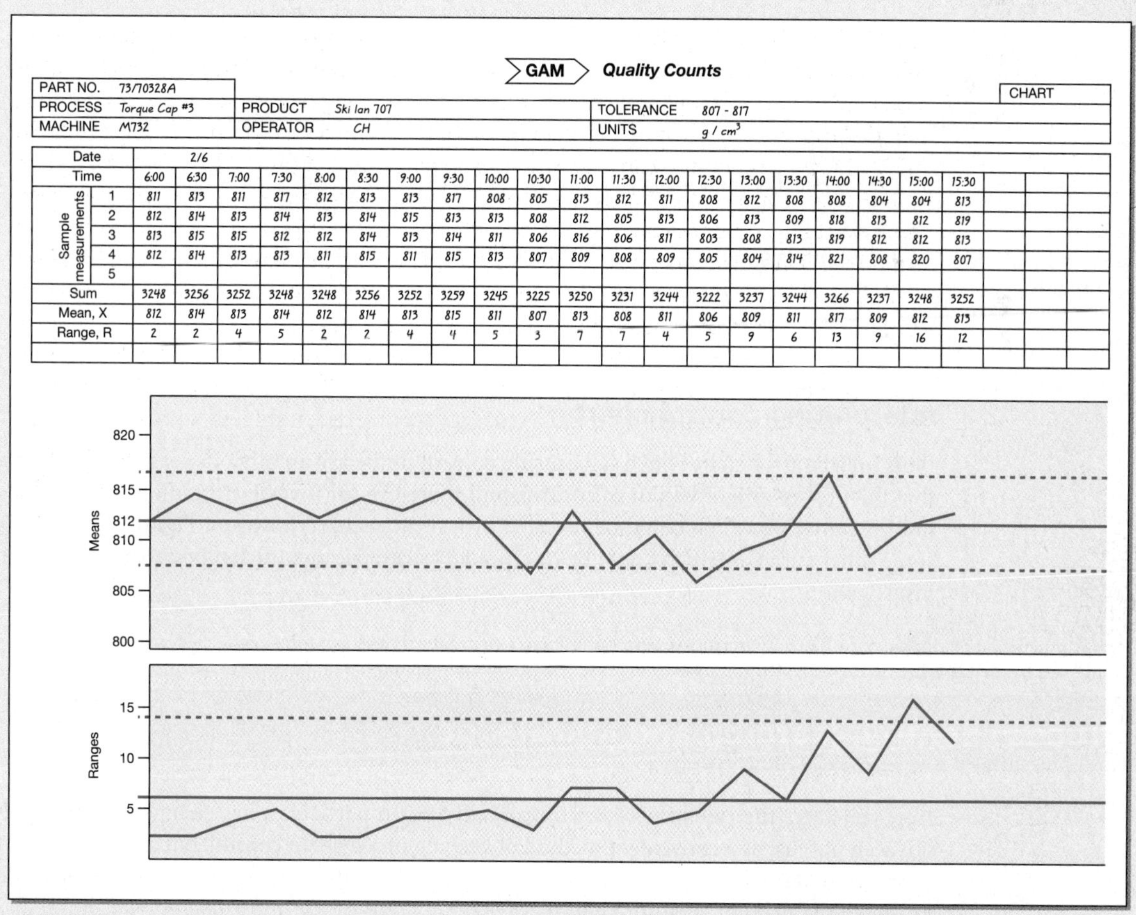

GAM Quality Counts

CHART

PART NO.	73/70328A				
PROCESS	Torque Cap #3	PRODUCT	Ski lan 707	TOLERANCE	807 - 817
MACHINE	M732	OPERATOR	CH	UNITS	g / cm³

Date		2/6																			
Time		6:00	6:30	7:00	7:30	8:00	8:30	9:00	9:30	10:00	10:30	11:00	11:30	12:00	12:30	13:00	13:30	14:00	14:30	15:00	15:30
Sample measurements	1	811	813	811	817	812	813	813	817	808	805	813	812	811	808	812	808	808	804	804	813
	2	812	814	813	814	813	814	815	813	813	808	812	805	813	806	813	809	818	813	812	819
	3	813	815	815	812	812	814	813	814	811	806	816	806	811	803	808	813	819	812	812	813
	4	812	814	813	813	811	815	811	815	813	807	809	808	809	805	804	814	821	808	820	807
	5																				
Sum		3248	3256	3252	3248	3248	3256	3252	3259	3245	3225	3250	3231	3244	3222	3237	3244	3266	3237	3248	3252
Mean, X		812	814	813	814	812	814	813	815	811	807	813	808	811	806	809	811	817	809	812	813
Range, R		2	2	4	5	2	2	4	4	5	3	7	7	4	5	9	6	13	9	16	12

Figure S17.9 The completed control form for GAM's torque machine showing the mean ($\bar{X}$) and range ($\bar{R}$) charts

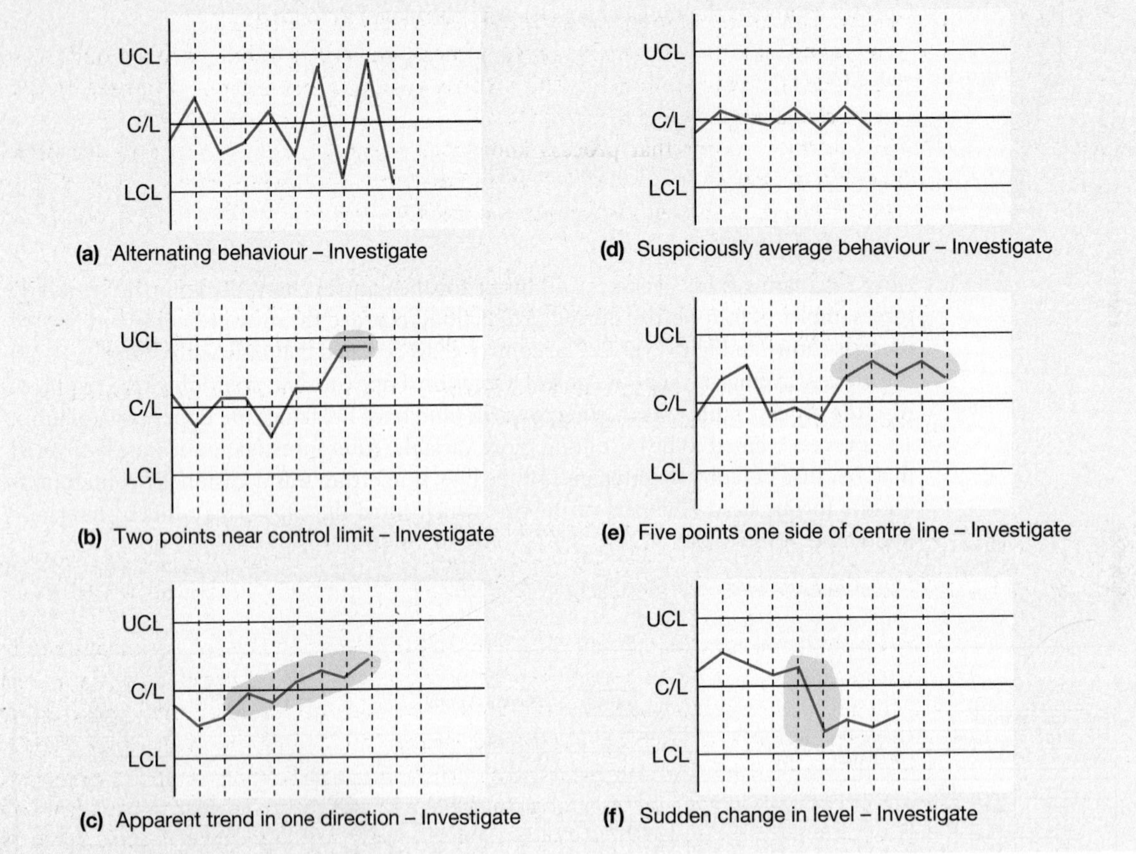

Figure S17.10 In addition to points falling outside the control limits, other unlikely sequences of points should be investigated

Interpreting control charts

Plots on a control chart which fall outside control limits are an obvious reason for believing that the process might be out of control, and therefore for investigating the process. This is not the only clue which could be revealed by a control chart, however. Figure S17.10 shows some other patterns which could be interpreted as behaviour sufficiently unusual to warrant investigation.

Process control, learning and knowledge

In recent years the role of process control and SPC in particular, has changed. Increasingly, it is seen not just as a convenient method of keeping processes in control, but also as an activity which is fundamental to the acquisition of competitive advantage. This is a remarkable shift in the status of SPC. Traditionally it was seen as one of the most *operational*, immediate and 'hands-on' operations management techniques. Yet it is now being connected with an operation's *strategic* capabilities. This is how the logic of the argument goes:

1 SPC is based on the idea that process variability indicates whether a process is in control or not.

2 Processes are brought into *control* and improved by progressively reducing process variability. This involves eliminating the assignable causes of variation.
3 One cannot eliminate assignable causes of variation without gaining a better understanding of how the process operates. This involves *learning* about the process, where its nature is revealed at an increasingly detailed level.

Process knowledge

4 This learning means that **process knowledge** is enhanced, which in turn means that operations managers are able to predict how the process will perform under different circumstances. It also means that the process has a greater capability to carry out its tasks at a higher level of performance.
5 This increased *process capability* is particularly difficult for competitors to copy. It cannot be bought 'off-the-shelf'. It only comes from time and effort being invested in controlling operations processes. Therefore, process capability leads to strategic advantage.

In this way, process control leads to learning which enhances process knowledge and builds difficult-to-imitate process capability.

Acceptance sampling

Process control is usually the preferred method of controlling quality because quality is being 'built in' to the process rather than being inspected afterwards. However, sometimes it may be necessary to inspect batches of products or services either before or after a process. The purpose of acceptance sampling is to decide whether, on the basis of a sample, to accept or reject the whole batch, for example a batch of component parts from a supplier. Acceptance sampling uses the proportion of wrongs to rights (or defectives to acceptable) and is usually carried out on attributes rather than variables. Again, it is important to understand the risks inherent in using a sample to make a judgement about a far larger batch. Table S17.3 illustrates the risks of acceptance sampling in the form of type I and type II errors. In acceptance sampling the type I risk is often referred to as the producer's risk because it is the risk that the operation rejects a batch that is actually of good quality. The type II risk is usually called the consumer's risk because it is the risk of accepting a batch that is actually poor and sending it to the consumer of the product or service.

Table S17.3 The risks inherent in acceptance sampling

Decision	*The batch actually is*	
	OK	*Not OK*
Reject batch	Type I error	Correct decision
Accept batch	Correct decision	Type II error

Sampling plans

Sampling plan

Acceptance sampling involves a sample being taken from a batch and a decision to accept or reject the batch being made by comparing the number of 'defects' found in the sample to a predetermined acceptable number. The **sampling plan** which describes this procedure is defined by two factors, n and c, where:

n = the sample size
c = the acceptance number of defects in the sample.

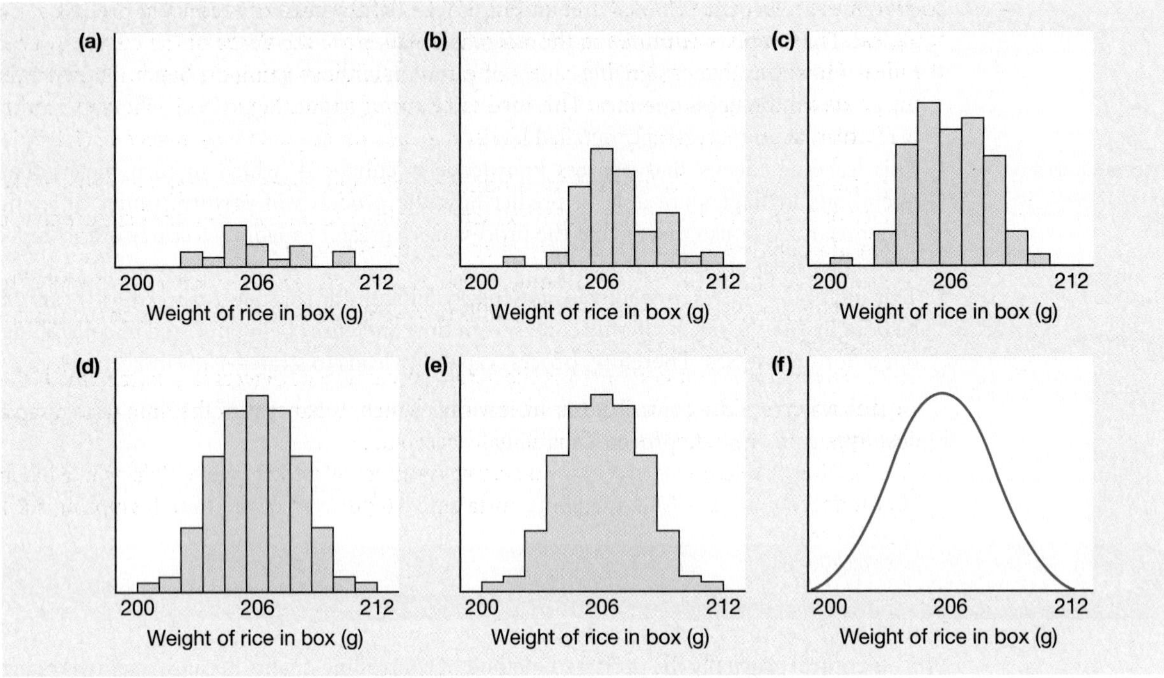

Figure S17.11 Ideal and real operating characteristics showing acceptable quality level (AQL), lot tolerance percentage defective (LTPD), producer's risk and consumer's risk

If x = number of defects actually found in the sample, a decision is made based on the following simple decision rule:

If $x \leq c$ then accept the whole batch.
If $x > c$ then reject the whole batch.

A set of tables called the Dodge–Romig Sampling Inspection Tables provides values for n and c for a given set of risks (using these tables is beyond the scope of this book). The ability of this plan to discriminate between good batches and bad ones is based upon the binomial distribution and is described by an operating characteristic (OC) curve. The OC curve for a sampling plan shows the probability of accepting a batch as the actual percentage of defects varies. An ideal OC curve would look like the blue line in Figure S17.11.

In this example the level of defects which is regarded as acceptable is 0.4 per cent and the sampling plan is perfect at discriminating between acceptable and unacceptable batches. The probability of accepting a batch whose actual level of defects is less than 0.4 per cent is 100 per cent and there is no chance of ever accepting a batch whose actual level of defects is more than 0.4 per cent. However, in practice, no procedure based on sampling, and therefore carrying risk, could ever deliver such an ideal curve. Only 100 per cent inspection using a perfect inspector could do so. Any use of sampling will have to accept the existence of type I and type II errors. Figure S17.11 also shows the blue line which represents a sampling plan for sampling 250 items ($n = 250$) and rejecting the batch if there is more than one defect ($c = 1$) in the sample. A batch is acceptable if it contains 0.4 per cent or fewer defects ($1/250 = 0.04$ per cent).

What is not known is the actual percentage of defective items in any one batch, and because the procedure relies on a sample, there will always be a probability of rejecting a good batch because the number of defects in the sample is two or more despite the batch in fact being acceptable (type I risk shown by the top shaded area). There is also a probability that in spite of accepting a batch (because the number of defects it contains is zero or one) the actual number of defects in the whole batch might be greater than 0.04 per cent (type II risk shown in the lower blue shaded area of Fig. S17.11). If the sizes of these risks are felt to be too great, the sample size can be increased, which will move the shape of the curve towards the ideal. However, this implies increased time and cost in inspecting the batch. To create an appropriate sampling plan four factors need to be specified (see Figure S17.11): type I error, type II error, acceptable quality level (AQL) and lot tolerance percentage defective (LTPD):

- *Type I error*. The usual value used for producer's risk (type I error) is often set with a probability of 0.05. This means that management is willing to take a 5 per cent chance that a batch of good quality will be rejected when it is actually acceptable.
- *Type II error*. The value for the consumer's risk (type II error) is often set with a probability of 0.1. This means that management is willing to risk at most a 10 per cent chance that a poor-quality batch will be accepted.
- *AQL*. The acceptable quality level is the actual percentage of defects in a batch which the organization is willing to reject mistakenly (by chance) 5 per cent of the time (assuming a 0.05 type I error) when the batch is actually acceptable.
- *LTPD*. The lot tolerance percentage defective is the actual percentage of defects in a batch that management is willing to accept mistakenly 10 per cent of the time (assuming a 0.1 type II error).

Critical commentary

A frequently made criticism of acceptance sampling is that it assumes that some amount of defects and failure is acceptable to the organization or its customers. By accepting the inevitability of failure and poor quality, it is argued, the operation will become 'lazy' at trying to eliminate the causes of bad quality. Rather than see quality as primarily something to be improved, acceptance sampling views it as being almost 'predetermined' by the characteristics of the process. The main task is to measure output and understand the risks involved, not to get to the root causes of poor quality. More recent approaches to quality management (such as TQM) suggest that 'right first time every time' is the only acceptable approach and that organizations should strive to produce zero defective items rather than some 'acceptable quality level'.

Summary

- Statistical process control (SPC) involves using control charts to track the performance of one or more quality characteristics in the operation. The power of control charting lies in its ability to set control limits derived from the statistics of the natural variation of processes. These control limits are often set at ± 3 standard deviations of the natural variation of the process samples.
- Control charts can be used for either attributes or variables. An attribute is a quality characteristic which has two states (for example, right or wrong). A variable is one which can be measured on a continuously variable scale.
- Process control charts allow operations managers to distinguish between the 'normal' variation inherent in any process and the variations which could be caused by the process going out of control.
- Acceptance sampling helps managers to understand the risks they are taking when they make decisions about a whole batch of products on the basis of a sample taken from that batch. The risks of any particular sampling plan are shown on its operating characteristic (OC) curve. However, some of its assumptions make acceptance sampling controversial.

Selected further reading

Woodall, W.H. (2000) Controversies and contradictions in statistical process control. Paper presented at the Journal of Quality Technology Session at the 44th Annual Fall Technical Conference of the Chemical and Process Industries Division and Statistics Division of the American Society for Quality and the Section on Physical & Engineering Sciences of the American Statistical Association in Minneapolis, Minnesota, October 12–13, 2000. Academic but interesting.

Useful web sites

www.asq.org/ The American Society for Quality site. Good professional insights.

Key operations questions

Chapter 18 **Operations improvement**

- Why is improvement so important in operations management?
- What are the key elements of operations improvement?
- What are the broad approaches to managing improvement?
- What techniques can be used for improvement?

Chapter 19 **Risk management**

- What is risk management?
- How can operations assess the potential causes of, and risks from failure?
- How can failures be prevented?
- How can operations mitigate the effects of failure?
- How can operations recover from the effects of failure?

Chapter 20 **Organizing improvement**

- Why does improvement need organizing?
- How should the improvement effort be linked to strategy?
- What information is needed for improvement?
- What should be improvement priorities?
- How can organizational culture affect improvement?
- What are the key implementation issues?

Even the best operation will need to improve because the operation's competitors will also be improving. This part of the book looks at how managers can make their operation perform better, how they can stop it failing, and how they can bring their improvement activities together.

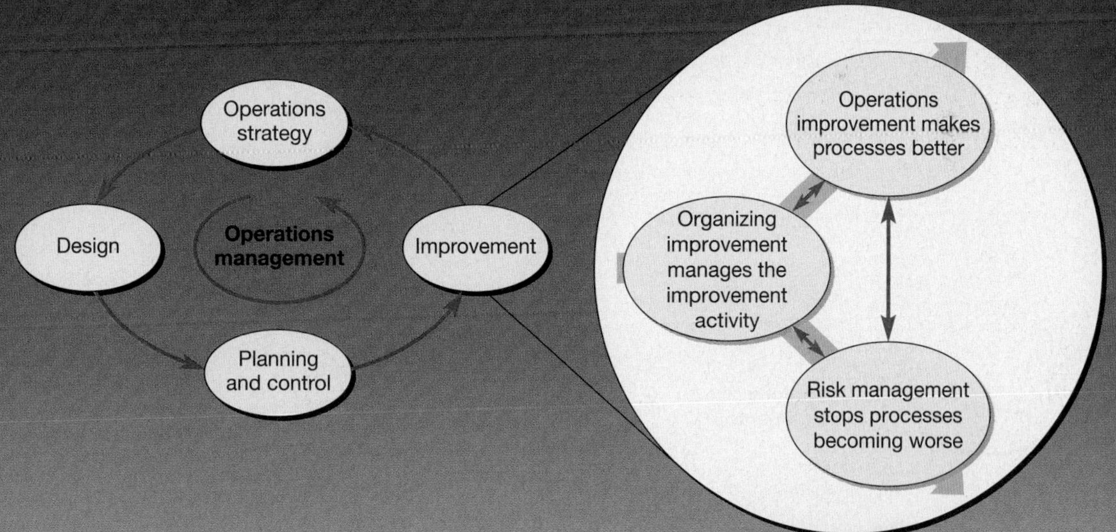

Chapter 18

Operations improvement

Key questions

- ➤ Why is improvement so important in operations management?
- ➤ What are the key elements of operations improvement?
- ➤ What are the broad approaches to managing improvement?
- ➤ What techniques can be used for improvement?

Introduction

Even when an operation is designed and its activities planned and controlled, the operations manager's task is not finished. All operations, no matter how well managed, are capable of improvement. In fact, in recent years the emphasis has shifted markedly towards making improvement one of the main responsibilities of operations managers. We treat improvement activities in three stages. This chapter looks at the elements commonly found in various improvement approaches, examines four of the more widely used approaches, then illustrates some of the techniques which can be adopted to improve the operation. Chapter 19 looks at improvement from another perspective, that is, how operations can improve by managing risks. Finally, Chapter 20, looks at how improvement activities can be organized, supported and implemented. These three stages are interrelated as shown in Figure 18.1.

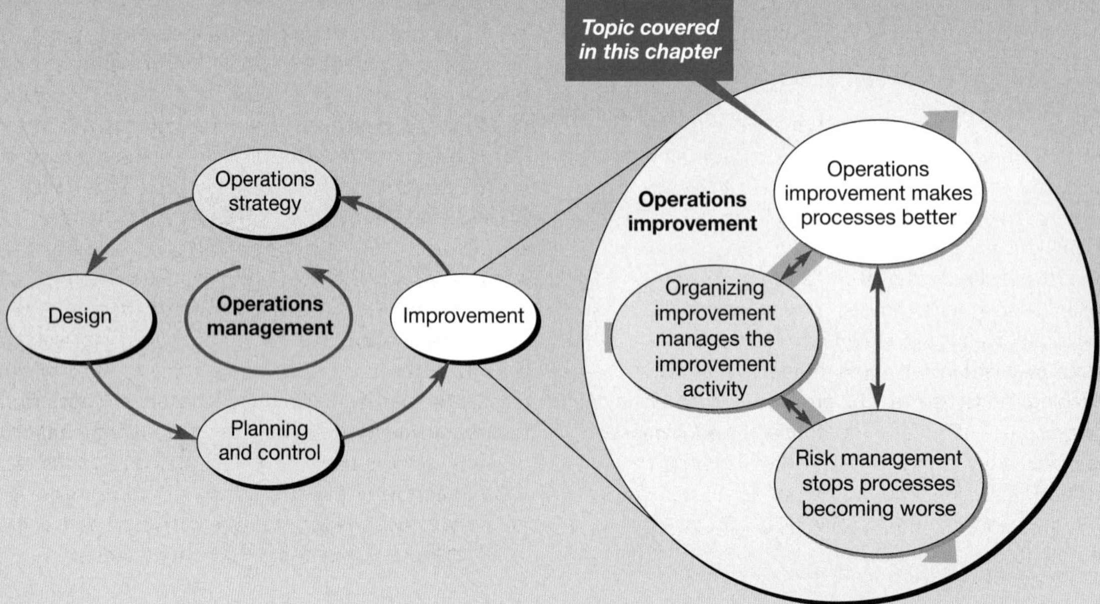

Figure 18.1 This chapter covers operations improvement

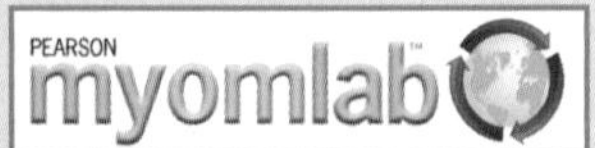

*Check and improve your understanding of this chapter using self assessment questions and a personalised study plan, audio and video downloads, and an eBook – all at **www.myomlab.com**.*

Operations in practice **Improvement at Heineken[1]**

Heineken International brews beer that is sold around the world. Operating in over 170 countries, it has succeeded in growing sales, especially in its Heineken and Amstel brands. However, sales growth can put pressure on any company's operations. For example, Heineken's Zoeterwoude facility, a packaging plant that fills bottles and cans in The Netherlands has had to increase its volume by between 8 and 10 per cent per year on a regular basis. In a competitive market, the company faced two challenges. First, it needed to improve its operations processes to reduce its costs. Second, because it would have taken a year to build a new packaging line, it needed to improve the efficiency of its existing lines in order to increase its capacity. Improving line efficiency therefore was vital if the plant was to cut its costs and create the extra capacity it needed to delay investment in a new packaging line.

The objective of the improvement project was to improve the plant's operating equipment efficiency (OEE) (see Chapter 11 for a discussion of OEE) by 20 per cent. Setting a target of 20 per cent was seen as important because it was challenging yet achievable as well as meeting the cost and capacity objectives of the project. It was also decided to focus the improvement project around two themes: (a) obtaining accurate operational data that could be converted into useful business information on which improvement decisions could be based, and (b) changing the culture of the operation to promote fast and effective decision-making. This would help people at all levels in the plant to have access to accurate and up-to-date information as well as encouraging staff to focus on the improvement of how they do their job rather than just 'doing the job'. Before the improvement, project staff at the Zoeterwoude plant had approached problem-solving as an *ad hoc* activity, only to be done when circumstances made it unavoidable. By contrast, the improvement initiative taught the staff on each packaging line to use various problem-solving techniques such as cause–effect and Pareto diagrams (discussed later in this chapter). Other techniques included the analysis of improved equipment maintenance and failure mode and effective analysis (FMEA) (both discussed in Chapter 19).

Source: Getty Images

'Until we started using these techniques', says Wilbert Raaijmakers, Heineken Netherlands Brewery Director, *'there was little consent regarding what was causing any problems. There was poor communication between the various departments and job grades. For example, maintenance staff believed that production stops were caused by operating errors, while operators were of the opinion that poor maintenance was the cause.'* The use of better information, analysis and improvement techniques helped the staff to identify and treat the root causes of problems. With many potential improvements to make, staff teams were encouraged to set priorities that would reflect the overall improvement target. There was also widespread use of benchmarking performance against targets periodically so that progress could be reviewed.

At the end of twelve months the improvement project had achieved its objectives of a 20 per cent improvement in OEE, not just for one packaging line but for all nine. This allowed the plant to increase the volume of its exports and cut its costs significantly. Not only that, but other aspects of the plant's performance improved. Up to that point, the plant had gained a reputation for poor delivery dependability. After the project it was seen by the other operations in its supply chain as a much more reliable partner. Yet Wilbert Raaijmakers still sees room for improvement, *'The optimization of an organization is a never-ending process. If you sit back and do the same thing tomorrow as you did today, you'll never make it. We must remain alert to the latest developments and stress the resulting information to its full potential.'*

Why improvement is so important

Operations management involves four areas of activity, as we explained in Chapter 1. These are: devising a strategy for the operations function, designing operations processes and the products and services they produce, planning and controlling; that is, running operations over time, and improving operations processes. At one time the focus of most operations management was seen as the planning and control activity. Operations managers were expected to get on with running the operation on a day-by-day and month-by-month basis (but rarely thinking in the longer term). Design activities such as process design, layout, etc. were often the domain of specialists, and changes in process design would happen relatively infrequently. Similarly, improvement was organized separately from mainstream operations management and again was often the province of specialists. Operations strategy was rarely considered at all. This has changed radically. Two things have happened. First, all four activities (strategy, design, planning and control, and improvement) are seen as interrelated and interdependent. Second, the locus of the operations management job has moved from planning and control (important though this still is) to improvement. Operations managers are judged not only on how they meet their ongoing responsibilities of producing products and services to acceptable levels of quality, speed, dependability, flexibility and cost, but also on how they improve the performance of the operations function overall.

The Red Queen effect

The scientist Leigh Van Valen was looking to describe a discovery that he had made while studying marine fossils. He had established that, no matter how long a family of animals had already existed, the probability that the family will become extinct is unaffected. In other words, the struggle for survival never gets easier. However well a species fits with its environment it can never relax. The analogy that Van Valen drew came from *Alice's Adventures through the Looking Glass*, by Lewis Carroll. In the book, Alice had encountered living chess pieces and, in particular, the Red Queen.

'Well, in our country', said Alice, still panting a little, 'you'd generally get to somewhere else – if you ran very fast for a long time, as we've been doing.' 'A slow sort of country!' said the Queen. 'Now, here, you see, it takes all the running you can do, to keep in the same place. If you want to get somewhere else, you must run at least twice as fast as that!'[2]

In many respects this is like business. Improvements and innovations may be imitated or countered by competitors. For example, in the automotive sector, the quality of most firms' products is very significantly better than it was two decades ago. This reflects the improvement in those firms' operations processes. Yet their relative competitive position has in many cases not changed. Those firms that have improved their competitive position have improved their operations performance *more than* competitors. Where improvement has simply matched competitors, survival has been the main benefit. The implications for operations improvement are clear. It is even more important, especially when competitors are actively improving their operations.

Elements of improvement

There are many approaches to improvement. Some have been used for over a century (for example some work study techniques come from the 'scientific management' movement of the early 20th century, see Chapter 9), others are relatively recent (for example, Six Sigma, explained later). But do not think that these approaches to improvement are different in all respects. There are many elements that are common to several approaches. Think of these 'elements' as the building blocks of the various improvement approaches. Furthermore, as these approaches develop over time, they may acquire elements from elsewhere. So the Six Sigma approach has developed beyond its process control roots to encompass many other elements. This section explains some of these elements. The following section (Improvement approaches) will then show how these elements are combined to form different improvement approaches.

Radical or breakthrough change

Breakthrough improvement

Radical **breakthrough improvement** (or 'innovation'-based improvement as it is sometimes called) is a philosophy that assumes that the main vehicle of improvement is major and dramatic change in the way the operation works. The introduction of a new, more efficient machine in a factory, the total redesign of a computer-based hotel reservation system, and the introduction of an improved degree programme at a university are all examples of breakthrough improvement. The impact of these improvements is relatively sudden and represents a step change in practice (and hopefully performance). Such improvements are rarely inexpensive, usually calling for high investment of capital, often disrupting the ongoing workings of the operation, and frequently involving changes in the product/service or process technology. The bold line in Figure 18.2(a) illustrates the pattern of performance with several breakthrough improvements. The improvement pattern illustrated by the dashed line in Figure 18.2(a) is regarded by some as being more representative of what really occurs when operations rely on pure breakthrough improvement. Breakthrough improvement places a high value on creative solutions. It encourages free thinking and individualism. It is a radical philosophy insomuch as it fosters an approach to improvement which does not accept many constraints on what is possible. 'Starting with a clean sheet of paper', 'going back to first principles' and 'completely rethinking the system' are all typical breakthrough improvement principles.

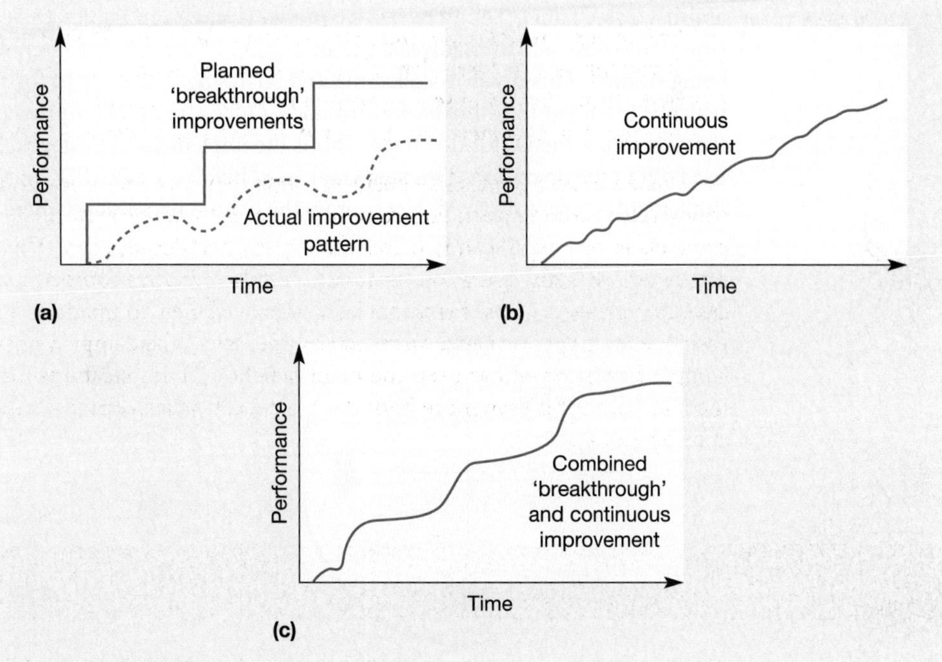

Figure 18.2 (a) 'Breakthrough' improvement, (b) 'continuous' improvement and (c) combined improvement patterns

Continuous improvement

Continuous improvement

Continuous improvement, as the name implies, adopts an approach to improving performance which assumes many small incremental improvement steps. For example, modifying the way a product is fixed to a machine to reduce changeover time, simplifying the question sequence when taking a hotel reservation, and rescheduling the assignment completion dates on a university course so as to smooth the students' workload are all examples of incremental improvements. While there is no guarantee that such small steps towards better performance will be followed by other steps, the whole philosophy of continuous improvement attempts to ensure that they will be. Continuous improvement is not concerned with promoting small improvements *per se*. It does see small improvements, however, as having one significant advantage over large ones – they can be followed relatively painlessly by other small improvements (*see* Fig. 18.2(b)). Continuous improvement is also known as **kaizen**. Kaizen is a Japanese word, the definition of which is given by Masaaki Imai[3] (who has been one of the main proponents of continuous improvement) as follows. '*Kaizen means improvement. Moreover, it means improvement in personal life, home life, social life and work life. When applied to the workplace, kaizen means continuing improvement involving everyone – managers and workers alike.*'

Kaizen

In continuous improvement it is not the *rate* of improvement which is important; it is the *momentum* of improvement. It does not matter if successive improvements are small; what does matter is that every month (or week, or quarter, or whatever period is appropriate) some kind of improvement has actually taken place.

Improvement cycles

An important element within some improvement approaches is the use of a literally never-ending process of repeatedly questioning and re-questioning the detailed working of a process or activity. This repeated and cyclical questioning is usually summarized by the idea of the **improvement cycle**, of which there are many, but two are widely used models – the PDCA cycle (sometimes called the Deming cycle, named after the famous quality 'guru', W.E. Deming) and the DMAIC (pronounced de-make) cycle, made popular by the Six Sigma approach (see later). The **PDCA cycle** model is shown in Figure 18.3(a). It starts with the P (for plan) stage, which involves an examination of the current method or the problem area being studied. This involves collecting and analysing data so as to formulate a plan of action which is intended to improve performance. Once a plan for improvement has been agreed, the next step is the D (for do) stage. This is the implementation stage during which the plan is tried out in the operation. This stage may itself involve a mini-PDCA cycle as the problems of implementation are resolved. Next comes the C (for check) stage where the new implemented

Improvement cycle

PDCA cycle

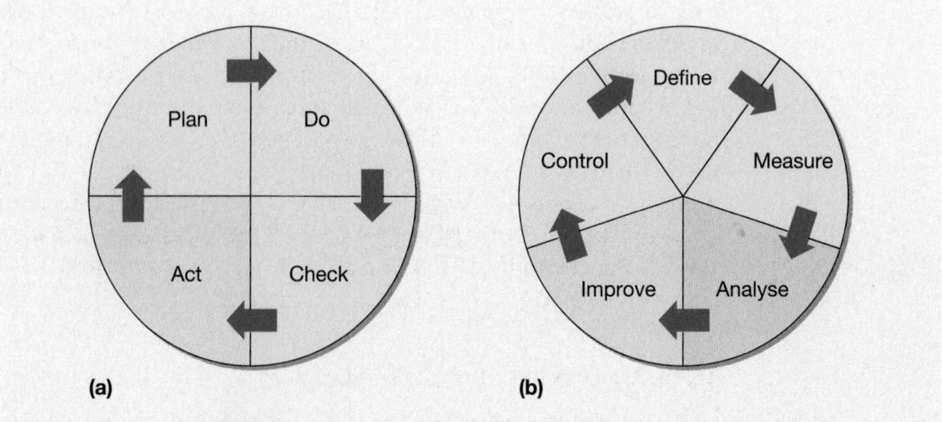

Figure 18.3 (a) The plan–do–check–act, or Deming improvement cycle, and (b) the define–measure–analyse–improve–control, or DMAIC Six Sigma improvement cycle

solution is evaluated to see whether it has resulted in the expected performance improvement. Finally, at least for this cycle, comes the A (for act) stage. During this stage the change is consolidated or standardized if it has been successful. Alternatively, if the change has not been successful, the lessons learned from the 'trial' are formalized before the cycle starts again.

DMAIC cycle

The DMAIC cycle is in some ways more intuitively obvious than the PDCA cycle insomuch as it follows a more 'experimental' approach. The **DMAIC cycle** starts with defining the problem or problems, partly to understand the scope of what needs to be done and partly to define exactly the requirements of the process improvement. Often at this stage a formal goal or target for the improvement is set. After definition comes the measurement stage. This stage involves validating the problem to make sure that it really is a problem worth solving, using data to refine the problem and measuring exactly what is happening. Once these measurements have been established, they can be analysed. The analysis stage is sometimes seen as an opportunity to develop hypotheses as to what the root causes of the problem really are. Such hypotheses are validated (or not) by the analysis and the main root causes of the problem identified. Once the causes of the problem are identified, work can begin on improving the process. Ideas are developed to remove the root causes of problems, solutions are tested and those solutions that seem to work are implemented and formalized and results measured. The improved process needs then to be continually monitored and controlled to check that the improved level of performance is sustaining. After this point the cycle starts again and defines the problems which are preventing further improvement. Remember though, it is the last point about both cycles that is the most important – the cycle starts again. It is only by accepting that in a continuous improvement philosophy these cycles quite literally never stop that improvement becomes part of every person's job.

A process perspective

Even if some improvement approaches do not explicitly or formally include the idea that taking a process perspective should be central to operations improvement, almost all do so implicitly. This has two major advantages. First, it means that improvement can be focused on what actually happens rather than on which part of the organization has responsibility for what happens. In other words, if improvement is not reflected in the process of creating products and services, then it is not really improvement as such. Second, as we have mentioned before, all parts of the business manage processes. This is what we call operations as activity rather than operations as a function. So, if improvement is described in terms of how processes can be made more effective, those messages will have relevance for all the other functions of the business in addition to the operations function.

End-to-end processes

Some improvement approaches take the process perspective further and prescribe exactly how processes should be organized. One of the more radical prescriptions of business process re-engineering (BPR, see later), for example, is the idea that operations should be organized around the total process which adds value for customers, rather than the functions or activities which perform the various stages of the value-adding activity. We have already pointed out the difference between conventional processes within a specialist function, and an end-to-end business process in Chapter 1. Identified customer needs are entirely fulfilled by an 'end-to-end' business process. In fact the processes are designed specifically to do this, which is why they will often cut across conventional organizational boundaries. Figure 18.4 illustrates this idea.

Evidence-based problem-solving

In recent years there has been a resurgence of the use of quantitative techniques in improvement approaches. Six Sigma (see later) in particular promotes systematic use of (preferably quantitative) evidence. Yet Six Sigma is not the first of the improvement approaches to

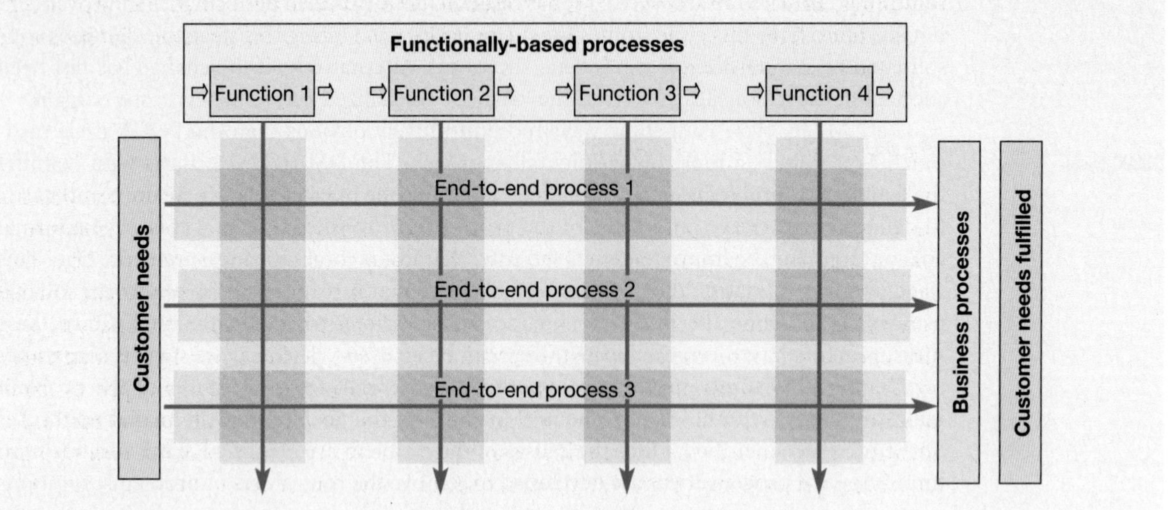

Figure 18.4 BPR advocates reorganizing (re-engineering) micro-operations to reflect the natural customer-focused business processes

use quantitative methods (some of the TQM gurus promoted statistical process control for example) although it has done a lot to emphasize the use of quantitative evidence. In fact, much of the considerable training required by Six Sigma consultants is devoted to mastering quantitative analytical techniques. However, the statistical methods used in improvement activities do not always reflect conventional academic statistical knowledge as such. They emphasize observational methods of collecting data and the use of experimentation to examine hypotheses. Techniques include graphical methods, analysis of variance, and two-level factorial experiment design. Underlying the use of these techniques is an emphasis on the scientific method, responding only to hard evidence, and using statistical software to facilitate analysis.

Customer-centricity

There is little point in improvement unless it meets the requirements of the customers. However, in most improvement approaches, meeting the expectations of customers means more than this. It involves the whole organization in understanding the central importance of customers to its success and even to its survival. Customers are seen not as being external to the organization but as the most important part of it. However, the idea of being customer-centric does not mean that customers must be provided with everything that they want. Although 'What's good for customers' may frequently be the same as 'What's good for the business', it is not always. Operations managers are always having to strike a balance between what customers would like and what the operation can afford (or wants) to do.

Systems and procedures

Improvement is not something that happens simply by getting everyone to 'think improvement'. Some type of system that supports the improvement effort may be needed. An improvement system (sometimes called a 'quality system') is defined as:

> *'the organizational structure, responsibilities, procedures, processes and resources for implementing quality management'.*[4]

It should

> *'define and cover all facets of an organization's operation, from identifying and meeting the needs and requirements of customers, design, planning, purchasing, manufacturing, packaging,*

storage, delivery and service, together with all relevant activities carried out within these functions. It deals with organization, responsibilities, procedures and processes. Put simply [it] *is good management practice.*'[5]

Reduce process variation

Processes change over time, as does their performance. Some aspect of process performance (usually an important one) is measured periodically (either as a single measurement or as a small sample of measurements). These are then plotted on a simple timescale. This has a number of advantages. The first is to check that the performance of the process is, in itself, acceptable (capable). They can also be used to check if process performance is changing over time, and to check on the extent of the variation in process performance. In the supplement to Chapter 17 we illustrated how random variation in the performance of any process could obscure what was really happening within the process. So a potentially useful method of identifying improvement opportunities is to try and identify the sources of random variation in process performance. Statistical process control is one way of doing this.

Synchronized flow

This is another idea that we have seen before – in Chapter 15, as part of the lean philosophy. Synchronized flow means that items in a process, operation or supply network flow smoothly and with even velocity from start to finish. This is a function of how inventory accumulates within the operation. Whether inventory is accumulated in order to smooth differences between demand and supply, or as a contingency against unexpected delays, or simply to batch for purposes of processing or movement, it all means that flow becomes asynchronous. It waits as inventory rather than progressing smoothly on. Once this state of perfect synchronization of flow has been achieved, it becomes easier to expose any irregularities of flow which may be the symptoms of more deep-rooted underlying problems.

Emphasize education and training

Several improvement approaches stress the idea that structured training and organization of improvement should be central to improvement. Not only should the techniques of improvement be fully understood by everyone engaged in the improvement process, the business and organizational context of improvement should also be understood. After all, how can one improve without knowing what kind of improvement would best benefit the organization and its customers? Furthermore, education and training have an important part to play in motivating all staff towards seeing improvement as a worthwhile activity. Some improvement approaches in particular place great emphasis on formal education. Six Sigma for example (see later) and its proponents often mandate a minimum level of training (measured in hours) that they deem necessary before improvement projects should be undertaken.

Perfection is the goal

Almost all organization-wide improvement programmes will have some kind of goal or target that the improvement effort should achieve. And while targets can be set in many different ways, some improvement authorities hold that measuring process performance against some kind of absolute target does most for encouraging improvement. By an 'absolute target' one literally means the theoretical level of perfection, for example, zero errors, instant delivery, delivery absolutely when promised, infinite flexibility, zero waste, etc. Of course, in reality such perfection may never be achievable. That is not the point. What is important is that current performance can be calibrated against this target of perfection in order to indicate how much more improvement is possible. Improving (for example) delivery accuracy by five per cent may seem good until it is realized that only an improvement of thirty per cent would eliminate all late deliveries.

Waste identification

All improvement approaches aspire to eliminate waste. In fact, any improvement implies that some waste has been eliminated, where waste is any activity that does not add value. But the identification and elimination of waste is sometimes a central feature. For example, as we discussed in Chapter 15, it is arguably the most significant part of the lean philosophy.

Include everybody

Harnessing the skills and enthusiasm of every person and all parts of the organization seems an obvious principle of improvement. The phrase 'quality at source' is sometimes used, stressing the impact that each individual has on improvement. The contribution of all individuals in the organization may go beyond understanding their contribution to 'not make mistakes'. Individuals are expected to bring something positive to improving the way they perform their jobs. The principles of 'empowerment' are frequently cited as supporting this aspect of improvement. When Japanese improvement practices first began to migrate in the late 1970s, this idea seemed even more radical. Yet now it is generally accepted that individual creativity and effort from all staff represents a valuable source of development. However, not all improvement approaches have adopted this idea. Some authorities believe that a small number of internal improvement consultants or specialists offer a better method of organizing improvement. However, these two ideas are not incompatible. Even with improvement specialists used to lead improvement efforts, the staff who actually operate the process can still be used as a valuable source of information and improvement ideas.

Develop internal customer–supplier relationships

One of the best ways to ensure that external customers are satisfied is to establish the idea that every part of the organization contributes to external customer satisfaction by satisfying its own internal customers. This idea was introduced in Chapter 17, as was the related concept of service-level agreements (SLAs). It means stressing that each process in an operation has a responsibility to manage these internal customer–supplier relationships. They do this primarily by defining as clearly as possible what their own and their customers' *requirements* are. In effect this means defining what constitutes 'error-free' service – the quality, speed, dependability and flexibility required by internal customers.

Short case
Erdington embraces the spirit of improvement[6]

Source: Rex Features

The Erdington Group is a major private group in the Scotch whisky industry with a number of specialist operations covering every facet of Scotch whisky distilling, blending and bottling. With a history that goes back to the 1850s, the Group is owned by The Robertson Trust, which gives more than £7m of dividend income to charitable causes in Scotland each year, and its employees, more than 90% of whom are shareholders. Erdington's brands are well known: The Famous Grouse,

Cutty Sark, and a malt, The Macallan, which is matured in selected ex-sherry oak casks. Another, Highland Park, was recently named 'best spirit in the world' by *The Spirit Journal*, USA. The Group's Glasgow site has been commended in a 'Best Factory' award scheme for its use of improvement approaches in achieving excellence in quality, productivity and flexibility. This is a real achievement given the constraints of whisky production, bottling and distribution. Some whisky can take 30 years to mature and with malts, there is a limited number of available ex-sherry casks. Production planning must look forward to what may be needed in 10, 18 or even 30 years' time, and having the right malts in stock is crucial. After the whisky has been blended in vats, it is decanted into casks again for the 'marrying' process. The whisky stays in these casks for three months. After this, it is ready for bottling. The main bottling line runs at 600 bottles per minute, which is fast, so dealing with problems in the plant is important. Production must be efficient and reliable, with changeovers as fast as possible.

This is where the company's improvement efforts have paid dividends. It has used several improvement approaches to help it maintain its operations performance. *'We did TQM, then CIP and six sigma (there are 10 black belts on site and 30 green belts) and now lean, which is an evolution for us'* explains Stan Marshall, director of operational excellence. *'Lean has helped the line and has helped us'*, says Roseann McAlindon, a line operator on line 8, the lean pilot line, who has worked in the site for 17 years. *'On changeovers, parts were reviewed for ease of fitment, made lighter and easier to handle, and procedures written down.'*

Approaches to improvement

Many of the elements described above are present in one or more of the commonly used approaches to improvement. Some of these approaches have already been described. For example, both lean (Chapter 15) and TQM (Chapter 17) have been discussed in some detail. In this section we will briefly re-examine TQM and lean, specifically from an improvement perspective and also add two further approaches – business process re-engineering (BPR) and Six Sigma.

Total quality management as an improvement approach

Total quality management was one of the earliest management 'fashions'. Its peak of popularity was in the late 1980s and early 1990s. As such it has suffered from something of a backlash in recent years. Yet the general precepts and principles that constitute TQM are still hugely influential. Few, if any, managers have not heard of TQM and its impact on improvement. Indeed, TQM has come to be seen as an approach to the way operations and processes should be managed and improved, generally. It is best thought of as a philosophy of how to approach improvement. This philosophy, above everything, stresses the 'total' of TQM. It is an approach that puts quality (and indeed improvement generally) at the heart of everything that is done by an operation. As a reminder, this totality can be summarized by the way TQM lays particular stress on the following elements (see Chapter 17):

- Meeting the needs and expectations of customers;
- Improvement covers all parts of the organization (and should be group-based);
- Improvement includes every person in the organization (and success is recognized);
- Including all costs of quality;
- Getting things 'right first time', i.e. designing-in quality rather than inspecting it in;
- Developing the systems and procedures which support improvement.

Even if TQM is not the label given to an improvement initiative, many of its elements will almost certainly have become routine. The fundamentals of TQM have entered the vernacular of operations improvement. Elements such as the internal customer concept, the idea of internal and external failure-related costs, and many aspects of individual staff empowerment, have all become widespread.

Lean as an improvement approach

The idea of lean (also known as just-in-time, lean synchronization, continuous flow operations, and so on) spread beyond its Japanese roots and became fashionable in the West at about the same time as TQM. And although its popularity has not declined to the same extent as TQM's, over 25 years of experience (at least in manufacturing), have diminished the excitement once associated with the approach. But, unlike TQM, it was seen initially as an approach to be used exclusively in manufacturing. Now, lean has become newly fashionable as an approach that can be applied in service operations. As a reminder (see Chapter 15) the lean approach aims to meet demand instantaneously, with perfect quality and no waste. Put another way, it means that the flow of products and services always delivers exactly what customers want (perfect quality), in exact quantities (neither too much nor too little), exactly when needed (not too early or too late), exactly where required (not to the wrong location), and at the lowest possible cost. It results in items flowing rapidly and smoothly through processes, operations and supply networks. The key elements of the lean when used as an improvement approach are as follows.

- Customer-centricity
- Internal customer–supplier relationships
- Perfection is the goal
- Synchronized flow
- Reduce variation
- Include all people
- Waste elimination.

Some organizations, especially now that lean is being applied more widely in service operations, view waste elimination as the most important of all the elements of the lean approach. In fact, they sometimes see the lean approach as consisting almost exclusively of waste elimination. What they fail to realize is that effective waste elimination is best achieved through changes in behaviour. It is the behavioural change brought about through synchronized flow and customer triggering that provides the window onto exposing and eliminating waste.

It is easy to forget just how radical, and more importantly, counter-intuitive lean once seemed. Although ideas of continuous improvement were starting to be accepted, the idea that inventories were generally a bad thing, and that throughput time was more important than capacity utilization seemed to border on the insane to the more traditionally minded. So, as lean ideas have been gradually accepted, we have likewise come to be far more tolerant of ideas that are radical and/or counter-intuitive. This is an important legacy because it opened up the debate on operations practice and broadened the scope of what are regarded as acceptable approaches. It is also worth remembering that when Taiichi Ohno wrote his seminal book[7] on lean (after retiring from Toyota in 1978) he was able to portray Toyota's manufacturing plants as embodying a coherent production approach. However, this encouraged observers to focus in on the specific techniques of lean production and de-emphasized the importance of 30 years of 'trial and error'. Maybe the real achievement of Toyota was not so much what they did but how long they stuck at it.

Business process re-engineering (BPR)

The idea of business process re-engineering originated in the early 1990s when Michael Hammer proposed that rather than using technology to automate work, it would be better applied to doing away with the need for the work in the first place ('don't automate, obliterate'). In doing this he was warning against establishing non-value-added work within an information technology system where it would be even more difficult to identify and eliminate. All work, he said, should be examined for whether it adds value for the customer and if not processes should be redesigned to eliminate it. In doing this BPR was echoing similar objectives in both scientific management and more recently lean approaches. But BPR, unlike those two earlier approaches, advocated radical changes rather than incremental changes to processes. Shortly after Hammer's article, other authors developed the ideas, again the majority of them stressing the importance of a radical approach to elimination of non-value-added work. This radicalism was summarized by Davenport who, when discussing the difference between BPR and continuous improvement, held that 'Today's firms must seek not fractional, but multiplicative levels of improvement – ten times rather than ten per cent'.

BPR has been defined[8] as

> *'the fundamental rethinking and radical redesign of business processes to achieve dramatic improvements in critical, contemporary measures of performance, such as cost, quality, service and speed'.*

But there is far more to it than that. In fact, BPR was a blend of a number of ideas which had been current in operations management for some time. Lean concepts, process flow charting, critical examination in method study, operations network management and customer-focused operations all contribute to the BPR concept. It was the potential of information technologies to enable the fundamental redesign of processes, however, which acted as the catalyst in bringing these ideas together. It was the information technology that allowed radical process redesign even if many of the methods used to achieve the redesign had been explored before. For example, '*Business Process Reengineering, although a close relative, seeks radical rather than merely continuous improvement. It escalates the effort of* . . . [lean] . . . *and TQM to make process orientation a strategic tool and a core competence of the organization. BPR concentrates on core business processes, and uses the specific techniques within the* . . . [lean] . . . *and TQM tool boxes as enablers, while broadening the process vision.*'[9]

The main principles of BPR can be summarized in the following points.

- Rethink business processes in a cross-functional manner which organizes work around the natural flow of information (or materials or customers).
- Strive for dramatic improvements in performance by radically rethinking and redesigning the process.
- Have those who use the output from a process, perform the process. Check to see if all internal customers can be their own supplier rather than depending on another function in the business to supply them (which takes longer and separates out the stages in the process).
- Put decision points where the work is performed. Do not separate those who do the work from those who control and manage the work.

Example[10]

We can illustrate this idea of reorganizing (or re-engineering) around business processes through the following simple example. Figure 18.5(a) shows the traditional organization of a trading company which purchases consumer goods from several suppliers, stores them, and sells them on to retail outlets. At the heart of the operation is the warehouse which receives the goods, stores them, and packs and dispatches them when they are required by customers. Orders for more stock are placed by Purchasing which also takes charge of materials planning and stock control. Purchasing buys the goods based on a forecast which is prepared by Marketing, which takes advice from the Sales department which is processing customers' orders. When a customer does place an order, it is the Sales department's job to instruct the warehouse to pack and dispatch the order and tell the Finance department to invoice the customer for the goods. So, traditionally, five departments (each a micro-operation) have between them organized the flow of materials and information within the total operation. But at each interface between the departments there is the possibility of errors and miscommunication arising. Furthermore, *who is responsible for looking after the customer's needs?* Currently, three separate departments all have dealings with the customer. Similarly, *who is responsible for liaising with suppliers?* This time two departments have contact with suppliers.

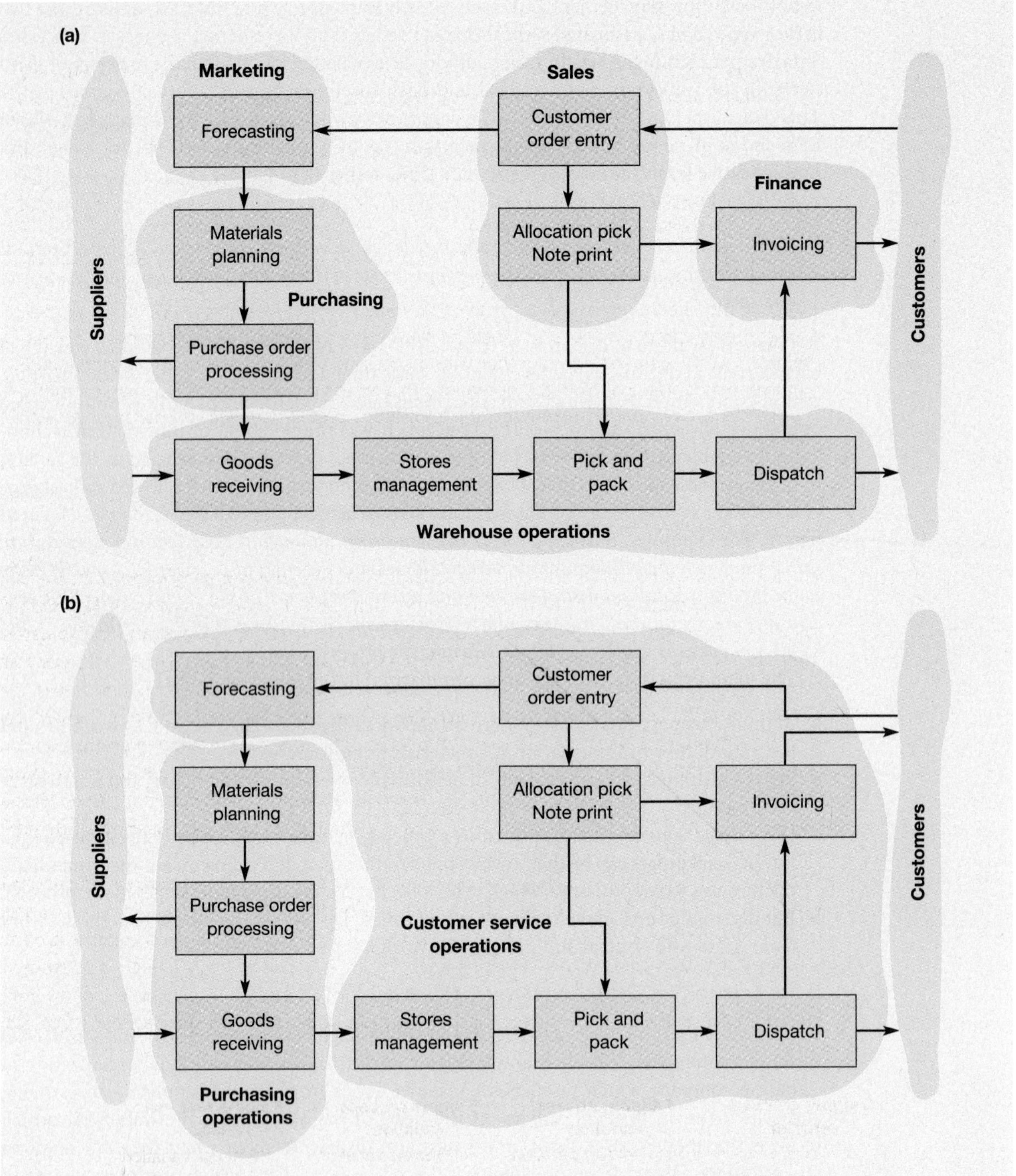

Figure 18.5 **(a) Before and (b) after re-engineering a consumer goods trading company**

Eventually the company reorganized around two essential business processes. The first process (called purchasing operations) dealt with everything concerning relationships with suppliers. It was this process's focused and unambiguous responsibility to develop good working relationships with suppliers. The other business process (called customer service operations) had total responsibility for satisfying customers' needs. This included speaking 'with one voice' to the customer.

Critical commentary

BPR has aroused considerable controversy, mainly because BPR sometimes looks only at work activities rather than at the people who perform the work. Because of this, people become 'cogs in a machine'. Many of these critics equate BPR with the much earlier principles of scientific management, pejoratively known as 'Taylorism'. Generally these critics mean that BPR is overly harsh in the way it views human resources. Certainly there is evidence that BPR is often accompanied by a significant reduction in staff. Studies at the time when BPR was at its peak often revealed that the majority of BPR projects could reduce staff levels by over 20 per cent.[11] Often BPR was viewed as merely an excuse for getting rid of staff. Companies that wished to 'downsize' were using BPR as the pretext, putting the short-term interests of the shareholders of the company above either their longer-term interests or the interests of the company's employees. Moreover, a combination of radical redesign together with downsizing could mean that the essential core of experience was lost from the operation. This leaves it vulnerable to any marked turbulence since it no longer possessed the knowledge and experience of how to cope with unexpected changes.

Six Sigma

The Six Sigma approach was first popularized by Motorola, the electronics and communications systems company. When it set its quality objective as 'total customer satisfaction' in the 1980s, it started to explore what the slogan would mean to its operations processes. They decided that true customer satisfaction would only be achieved when its products were delivered when promised, with no defects, with no early-life failures and when the product did not fail excessively in service. To achieve this, Motorola initially focused on removing manufacturing defects. However, it soon came to realize that many problems were caused by latent defects, hidden within the design of its products. These may not show initially but eventually could cause failure in the field. The only way to eliminate these defects was to make sure that design specifications were tight (i.e. narrow tolerances) and its processes very capable.

Motorola's Six Sigma quality concept was so named because it required the natural variation of processes (± 3 standard deviations) should be half their specification range. In other words, the specification range of any part of a product or service should be ± 6 the standard deviation of the process (see Chapter 17). The Greek letter sigma (σ) is often used to indicate the standard deviation of a process, hence the Six Sigma label. Figure 18.6 illustrates the effect of progressively narrowing process variation on the number of defects

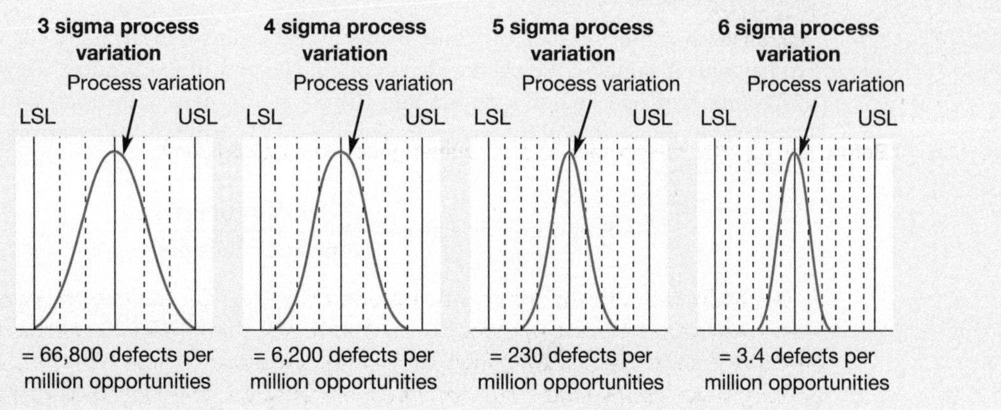

Figure 18.6 Process variation and its impact on process defects per million

Defects per million
Zero defect

produced by the process, in terms of **defects per million**. The defects per million measure is used within the Six Sigma approach to emphasize the drive towards a virtually **zero defect** objective. Now the definition of Six Sigma has widened to well beyond this rather narrow statistical perspective. General Electric (GE), who were probably the best known of the early adopters of Six Sigma, defined it as, 'A disciplined methodology of defining, measuring, analysing, improving, and controlling the quality in every one of the company's products, processes, and transactions – with the ultimate goal of virtually eliminating all defects'. So, now Six Sigma should be seen as a broad improvement concept rather than a simple examination of process variation, even though this is still an important part of process control, learning and improvement.

Measuring performance

The Six Sigma approach uses a number of related measures to assess the performance of operations processes.

- *A defect* is a failure to meet customer-required performance (defining performance measures from a customer's perspective is an important part of the Six Sigma approach).
- *A defect unit or item* is any unit of output that contains a defect (i.e. only units of output with no defects are not defective, defective units will have one or more than one defect).
- *A defect opportunity* is the number of different ways a unit of output can fail to meet customer requirements (simple products or services will have few defect opportunities, but very complex products or services may have hundreds of different ways of being defective).
- *Proportion defective* is the percentage or fraction of units that have one or more defect.
- *Process yield* is the percentage or fraction of total units produced by a process that are defect-free (i.e. 1 – proportion defective).
- *Defect per unit (DPU)* is the average number of defects on a unit of output (the number of defects divided by the number of items produced).
- *Defects per opportunity* is the proportion or percentage of defects divided by the total number of defect opportunities (the number of defects divided by (the number items produced × the number of opportunities per item)).
- *Defects per million opportunities (DPMO)* is exactly what it says, the number of defects which the process will produce if there were one million opportunities to do so.
- *The Sigma measurement* is derived from the DPMO and is the number of standard deviations of the process variability that will fit within the customer specification limits.

Worked example

An insurance process checks details of insurance claims and arranges for customers to be paid. It samples 300 claims at random at the end of the process. They find that 51 claims had one or more defects and there were 74 defects in total. Four types of error were observed, coding errors, policy conditions errors, liability errors and notification errors.

$$\text{Proportion defective} = \frac{\text{Number of defects}}{\text{Number of units processed}}$$

$$= \frac{51}{300} = 0.17 \text{ (17\% defective)}$$

$$\text{Yield} = 1 - \text{Proportion of defectives}$$

$$= 1 - 0.17 = 0.83 \text{ or (83\% yield)}$$

$$\text{Defects per unit} = \frac{\text{Number of defects}}{\text{Number of units processed}}$$

$$= \frac{74}{300} = 0.247 \text{ (or 24.7) DPU}$$

$$\text{Defects per opportunity} = \frac{\text{Number of defects}}{\text{Number of units produced} \times \text{Number of opportunities}}$$

$$= \frac{74}{300 \times 4} = 0.062 \text{ DPO}$$

$$\text{Defects per million opportunities} = \text{DPO} \times 10^6$$

$$= 62{,}000 \text{ DPMO}$$

Although the scope of Six Sigma is disputed, among elements frequently associated with Six Sigma include the following:

- *Customer-driven objectives* – Six Sigma is sometimes defined as 'the process of comparing process outputs against customer requirements'. It uses a number of measures to assess the performance of operations processes. In particular it expresses performance in terms of defects per million opportunities (DPMO). This is exactly what it says, the number of defects which the process will produce if there were one million opportunities to do so. This is then related to the 'Sigma measurement' of a process and is the number of standard deviations of the process variability that will fit within the customer specification limits.
- *Use of evidence* – Although Six Sigma is not the first of the new approaches to operations to use statistical methods it has done a lot to emphasize the use of quantitative evidence. In fact much of the considerable training required by Six Sigma consultants is devoted to mastering quantitative analytical techniques.
- *Structured improvement cycle* – The structured improvement cycle used in Six Sigma is the DMAIC cycle.
- *Process capability and control* – Not surprisingly, given its origins, process capability and control is important within the Six Sigma approach.
- *Process design* – Latterly Six Sigma proponents also include process design into the collection of elements that define the Six Sigma approach.
- *Structured training and organization of improvement* – The Six Sigma approach holds that improvement initiatives can only be successful if significant resources and training are devoted to their management. It recommends a specially trained cadre of practitioners and internal consultants named after 'martial arts' grades, see below.

The 'martial arts' analogy

The terms that have become associated with Six Sigma experts (and denote their level of expertise) are, Master Black Belt, Black Belt and Green Belt. Master Black Belts are experts in the use of Six Sigma tools and techniques as well as how such techniques can be used and implemented. Primarily Master Black Belts are seen as teachers who can not only guide improvement projects, but also coach and mentor Black Belts and Green Belts who are closer to the day-to-day improvement activity. They are expected to have the quantitative analytical skills to help with Six Sigma techniques and also the organizational and interpersonal skills to teach and mentor. Given their responsibilities, it is expected that Master Black Belts are employed full-time on their improvement activities. Black Belts can take a direct hand in organizing improvement teams. Like Master Black Belts, Black Belts are expected to develop their quantitative analytical skills and also act as coaches for Green Belt. Black Belts are dedicated full-time to improvement, and although opinions vary on how many Black Belts should be employed in an operation, some organizations recommend one Black Belt for every hundred employees. Green Belts work within improvement teams, possibly as team leaders. They have significant amounts of training, although less than Black Belts. Green Belts are not full-time positions; they have normal day-to-day process responsibilities but are expected to spend at least twenty per cent of their time on improvement projects.

Short case
Six Sigma at Xchanging[12]

'I think Six Sigma is powerful because of its definition; it is the process of comparing process outputs against customer requirements. Processes operating at less than 3.4 defects per million opportunities means that you must strive to get closer to perfection and it is the customer that defines the goal. Measuring defects per opportunity means that you can actually compare the process of, say, a human resources process with a billing and collection process.' Paul Ruggier head of Process at Xchanging is a powerful advocate of Six Sigma, and credits the success of the company, at least partly, to the approach.

Xchanging, created in 1998, is one of a new breed of companies, operating as an outsourcing business for 'back-office' functions for a range of companies, such as Lloyds of London, the insurance centre. Xchanging's business proposition is for the client company to transfer the running of the whole or part of their back office to Xchanging, either for a fixed price or one determined by cost savings achieved. The challenge Xchanging faces is to run that back office in a more effective and efficient manner than the client company had managed in the past. So, the more effective Xchanging is at running the processes, the greater its profit. To achieve these efficiencies Xchanging offers larger scale, a higher level of process expertise, focus and investment in technology. But above all, they offer, a Six Sigma approach. *'Everything we do can be broken down into a process'*, says Paul Ruggier. *'It may be more straightforward in a manufacturing business, frankly they've been using a lot of Six Sigma tools and techniques for decades. But the concept of process improvement is relatively new in many service companies. Yet the concept is powerful. Through the implementation of this approach we have achieved 30% productivity improvements in 6 months.'*

The company also adopts the Six Sigma terminology for its improvement practitioners – Master Black Belts, Black Belts and Green Belts. Attaining the status of Black Belt is very much sought after as well as being fulfilling, says Rebecca Whittaker who is a Master Black Belt at Xchanging. *'At the end of a project it is about having a process which is redesigned to such an extent, that is simplified and consolidated and people come back and say, "It's so much better than it used to be". It makes their lives better and it makes the business results better and those are the things that make being a Black Belt worthwhile.'*

Rebecca was recruited by Xchanging along with a number of other Master Black Belts as part of a strategic decision to kick-start Six Sigma in the company. It is seen as a particularly responsible position by the company and Master Black Belts are expected to be well versed in the Six Sigma techniques and be able to provide the training and knowhow to develop other staff within the company. In Rebecca's case she has been working as a Six Sigma facilitator for five years, initially as a Green Belt, then as a Black Belt.

Source: Rex Features

Typically a person identified as having the right analytical and interpersonal skills will be taken off their job for at least a year, training and immersed in the concepts of improvement and then sent to work with line staff as project manager/facilitator. Their role as Black Belt will be to guide the line staff to make improvements in the way they do the job. One of the new Black Belts at Xchanging, Sarah Frost, is keen to stress the responsibility she owes to the people who will have to work in the improvement process. *'Being a Black Belt is about being a project manager. It is about working with the staff and combining our skills in facilitation and our knowledge of the Six Sigma process with their knowledge of the business. You always have to remember that you will go onto another project but they [process staff] will have to live with the new process. It is about building solutions that they can believe in.'*

Critical commentary

One common criticism of Six Sigma is that it does not offer anything that was not available before. Its emphasis on improvement cycles comes from TQM, its emphasis on reducing variability comes from statistical process control, its use of experimentation and data analysis is simply good quantitative analysis. The only contribution that Six Sigma has made, argue its critics, is using the rather gimmicky martial arts analogy of Black Belt etc. to indicate a level of expertise in Six Sigma methods. All Six Sigma has done is package pre-existing elements together in order for consultants to be able to sell them to gullible chief executives. In fact it's difficult to deny some of these points. Maybe the real issue is whether it is really a criticism. If bringing these elements together really does form an effective problem-solving approach, why is this is a problem? Six Sigma is also accused of being too hierarchical in the way it structures its various levels of involvement in the improvement activity (as well as the dubious use of martial-arts-derived names such as Black Belt). It is also expensive. Devoting such large amount of training and time to improvement is a significant investment, especially for small companies. Nevertheless, Six Sigma proponents argue that the improvement activity is generally neglected in most operations and if it is to be taken seriously, it deserves the significant investment implied by the Six Sigma approach. Furthermore, they argue, if operated well, Six Sigma improvement projects run by experienced practitioners can save far more than their cost. There are also technical criticisms of Six Sigma. Most notably that in purely statistical terms the normal distribution which is used extensively in Six Sigma analysis does not actually represent most process behaviour. Other technical criticisms (that are not really the subject of this book) imply that aiming for the very low levels of defects per million opportunities, as recommended by Six Sigma proponents, is far too onerous.

Differences and similarities

In this chapter we have chosen to very briefly explain four improvement approaches. It could have been more. Enterprise resource planning (ERP, see Chapter 14), total preventive maintenance (TPM, see Chapter 19), lean Sigma (a combination of lean and Six Sigma), and others could have been added. But these four constitute a representative sample of the most commonly used approaches. Nor do we have the space to describe them fully. Each of the approaches is the subject of several books that describe them in great detail. There is no shortage of advice from consultants and academics as to how they should be used. And there are clearly some common elements between some of these approaches that we have described. Yet there are also differences between them in that each approach includes a different set of elements and therefore a different emphasis and these differences need to be understood. For example, one important difference relates to whether the approaches emphasize a gradual, continuous approach to change, or whether they recommend a more radical 'breakthrough' change. Another difference concerns the aim of the approach. What is the balance between whether the approach emphasizes *what* changes should be made or *how* changes should be made? Some approaches have a firm view of what is the best way to organize the operation's processes and resources. Other approaches hold no particular view on what an operation should do but rather concentrate on how the management of an operation should decide what to do. Indeed we can position each of the elements and the approaches that include them. This is illustrated in Figure 18.7. The approaches differ in the extent that they prescribe appropriate operations practice. BPR for example is very clear in what it is recommending. Namely, that all processes should be organized on an end-to-end basis. Its focus is *what* should happen rather than *how* it should happen. To a slightly lesser extent lean is the same. It has a definite list of things that processes should or should not be – waste should be eliminated, inventory should be reduced, technology should be flexible, and so on. Contrast this with both Six Sigma and TQM which focus to a far greater extent

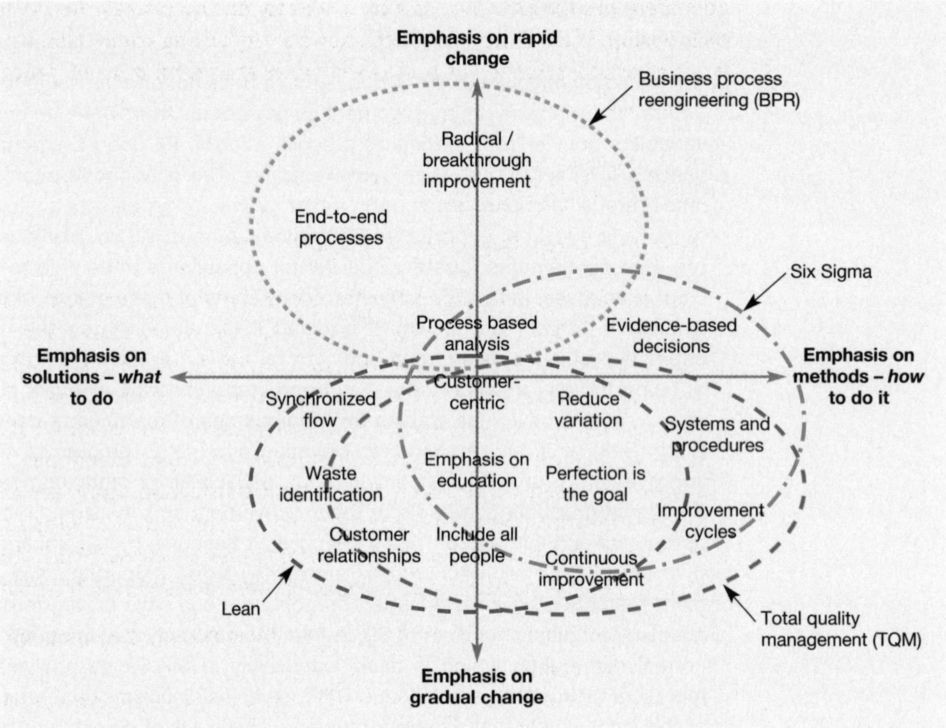

Figure 18.7 The four approaches on the two dimensions of improvement

on *how* operations should be improved. Six Sigma in particular has relatively little to say about what is good or bad in the way operations resources are organized (with the possible exception of its emphasizing the negative effects of process variation). Its concern is largely the way improvements should be made: using evidence, using quantitative analysis, using the DMAIC cycle, and so on. They also differ in terms of whether they emphasize gradual or rapid change. BPR is explicit in its radical nature. By contrast TQM and lean both incorporate ideas of continuous improvement. Six Sigma is relatively neutral on this issue and can be used for small or very large changes.

Improvement techniques

All the techniques described in this book and its supplements can be regarded as 'improvement' techniques. However, some techniques are particularly useful for improving operations and processes generally. Here we select some techniques which either have not been described elsewhere or need to be reintroduced in their role of helping operations improvement particularly.

Scatter diagrams

Scatter diagrams

Scatter diagrams provide a quick and simple method of identifying whether there is evidence of a connection between two sets of data: for example, the time at which you set off for work every morning and how long the journey to work takes. Plotting each journey on a graph which has departure time on one axis and journey time on the other could give an indication of whether departure time and journey time are related, and if so, how. Scatter diagrams can be treated in a far more sophisticated manner by quantifying how strong is the relationship between the sets of data. But, however sophisticated the approach, this type of graph only identifies the existence of a relationship, not necessarily the existence of a cause–effect relationship. If the scatter diagram shows a very strong connection between the sets of data, it is important evidence of a cause–effect relationship, but not proof positive. It could be coincidence!

Worked example

Kaston Pyral Services Ltd (A)

Kaston Pyral Services Ltd (KPS) installs and maintains environmental control, heating and air conditioning systems. It has set up an improvement team to suggest ways in which it might improve its levels of customer service. The improvement team has completed its first customer satisfaction survey. The survey asked customers to score the service they received from KPS in several ways. For example, it asked customers to score services on a scale of one to ten on promptness, friendliness, level of advice, etc. Scores were then summed to give a 'total satisfaction score' for each customer – the higher the score, the greater the satisfaction. The spread of satisfaction scores puzzled the team and they considered what factors might be causing such differences in the way their customers viewed them. Two factors were put forward to explain the differences.

(a) the number of times in the past year the customer had received a preventive maintenance visit;

(b) the number of times the customer had called for emergency service.

All these data were collected and plotted on scatter diagrams as shown in Figure 18.8(a). It shows that there seems to be a clear relationship between a customer's satisfaction score and the number of times the customer was visited for regular servicing. The scatter diagram in Figure 18.8(b) is less clear. Although all customers who had very high satisfaction scores had made very few emergency calls, so had some customers with low satisfaction scores. As a result of this analysis, the team decided to survey customers' views on its emergency service.

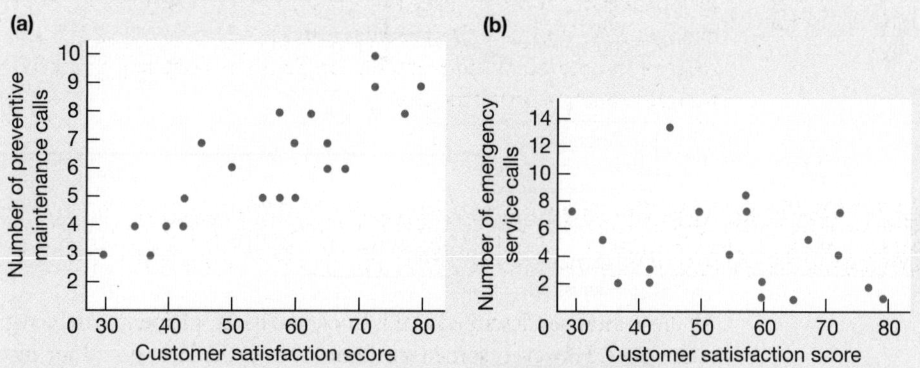

Figure 18.8 Scatter diagrams for customer satisfaction versus (a) number of preventive maintenance calls and (b) number of emergency service calls

Process maps (flow charts)

Process maps

Process maps (sometimes called 'flow charts' in this context) can be used to give a detailed understanding prior to improvement. They were described in Chapter 4 and are widely used in improvement activities. The act of recording each stage in the process quickly shows up poorly organized flows. Process maps can also clarify improvement opportunities and shed further light on the internal mechanics or workings of an operation. Finally, and probably most importantly, they highlight problem areas where no procedure exists to cope with a particular set of circumstances.

Worked example

Kaston Pyral Services Ltd (B)

As part of its improvement programme the team at KPS is concerned that customers are not being served well when they phone in with minor queries over the operation of their heating systems. These queries are not usually concerned with serious problems, but often concern minor irritations which can be equally damaging to the customers' perception of KPS's service. Figure 18.9 shows the process map for this type of customer query. The team found the map illuminating. The procedure had never been formally laid out in this way before, and it showed up three areas where information was not being recorded. These are the three points marked with question marks on the process map in Figure 18.9. As a result of this investigation, it was decided to log all customer queries so that analysis could reveal further information on the nature of customer problems.

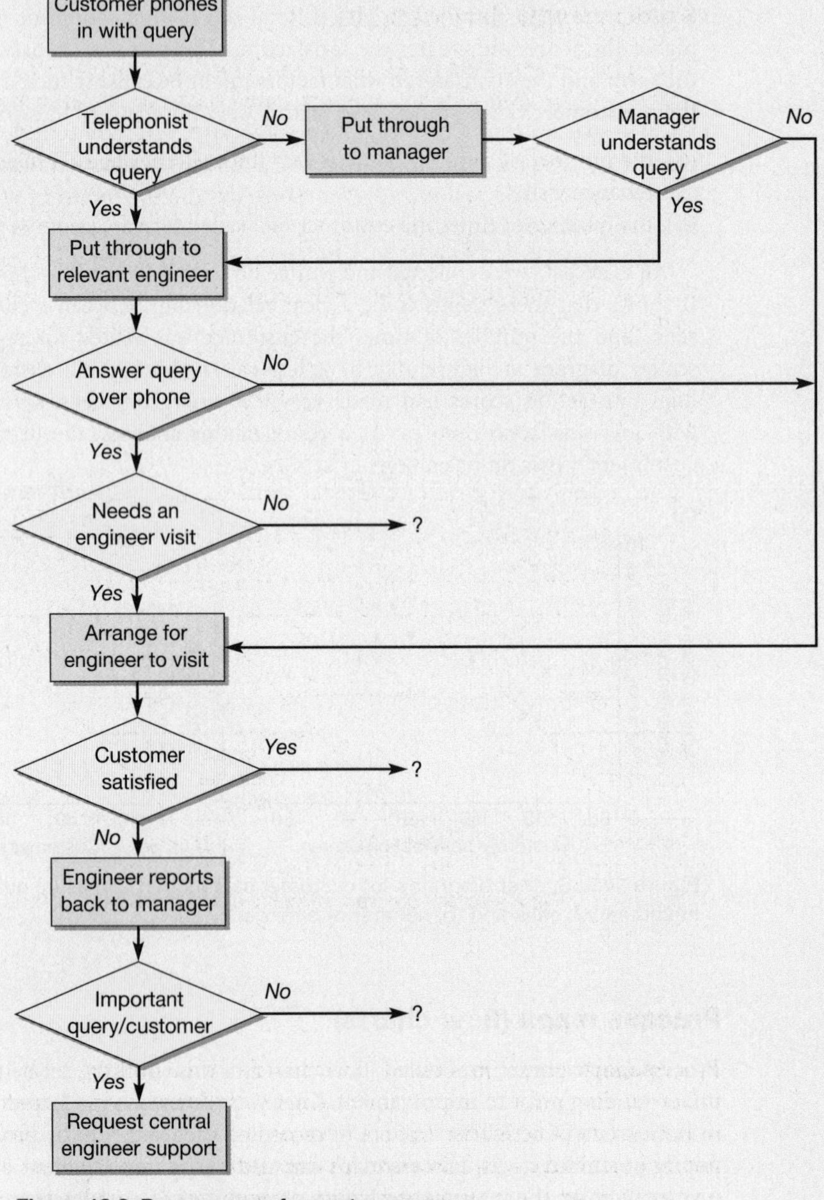

Figure 18.9 Process map for customer query

Cause–effect diagrams

Cause–effect diagrams

Cause–effect diagrams are a particularly effective method of helping to search for the root causes of problems. They do this by asking what, when, where, how and why questions, but also add some possible 'answers' in an explicit way. They can also be used to identify areas where further data are needed. Cause–effect diagrams (which are also known as 'Ishikawa diagrams') have become extensively used in improvement programmes. This is because they provide a way of structuring group brainstorming sessions. Often the structure involves identifying possible causes under the (rather old-fashioned) headings of: machinery, manpower, materials, methods and money. Yet in practice, any categorization that comprehensively covers all relevant possible causes could be used.

Worked example

Kaston Pyral Services Ltd (C)

The improvement team at KPS was working on a particular area which was proving a problem. Whenever service engineers were called out to perform emergency servicing for a customer, they took with them the spares and equipment which they thought would be necessary to repair the system. Although engineers could never be sure exactly what materials and equipment they would need for a job, they could guess what was likely to be needed and take a range of spares and equipment which would cover most eventualities. Too often, however, the engineers would find that they needed a spare that they had not brought with them. The cause–effect diagram for this particular problem, as drawn by the team, is shown in Figure 18.10.

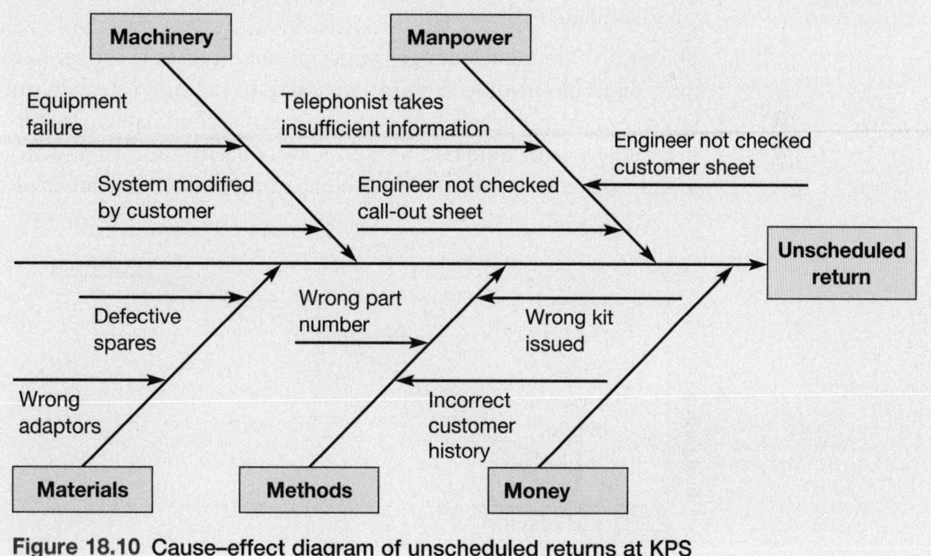

Figure 18.10 Cause–effect diagram of unscheduled returns at KPS

Pareto diagrams

In any improvement process, it is worthwhile distinguishing what is important and what is less so. The purpose of the Pareto diagram (which was first introduced in Chapter 12) is to distinguish between the 'vital few' issues and the 'trivial many'. It is a relatively straightforward technique which involves arranging items of information on the types of problem or causes of problem into their order of importance (usually measured by 'frequency of occurrence'). This can be used to highlight areas where further decision-making will be

Pareto analysis

useful. **Pareto analysis** is based on the phenomenon of relatively few causes explaining the majority of effects. For example, most revenue for any company is likely to come from relatively few of the company's customers. Similarly, relatively few of a doctor's patients will probably occupy most of his or her time.

Worked example

Kaston Pyral Services Ltd (D)

The KPS improvement team which was investigating unscheduled returns from emergency servicing (the issue which was described in the cause–effect diagram in Fig. 18.11) examined all occasions over the previous 12 months on which an unscheduled return had been made. They categorized the reasons for unscheduled returns as follows:

1 The wrong part had been taken to a job because, although the information which the engineer received was sound, he or she had incorrectly predicted the nature of the fault.
2 The wrong part had been taken to the job because there was insufficient information given when the call was taken.
3 The wrong part had been taken to the job because the system had been modified in some way not recorded on KPS's records.
4 The wrong part had been taken to the job because the part had been incorrectly issued to the engineer by stores.
5 No part had been taken because the relevant part was out of stock.
6 The wrong equipment had been taken for whatever reason.
7 Any other reason.

The relative frequency of occurrence of these causes is shown in Figure 18.11. About a third of all unscheduled returns were due to the first category, and more than half the returns were accounted for by the first and second categories together. It was decided that the problem could best be tackled by concentrating on how to get more information to the engineers which would enable them to predict the causes of failure accurately.

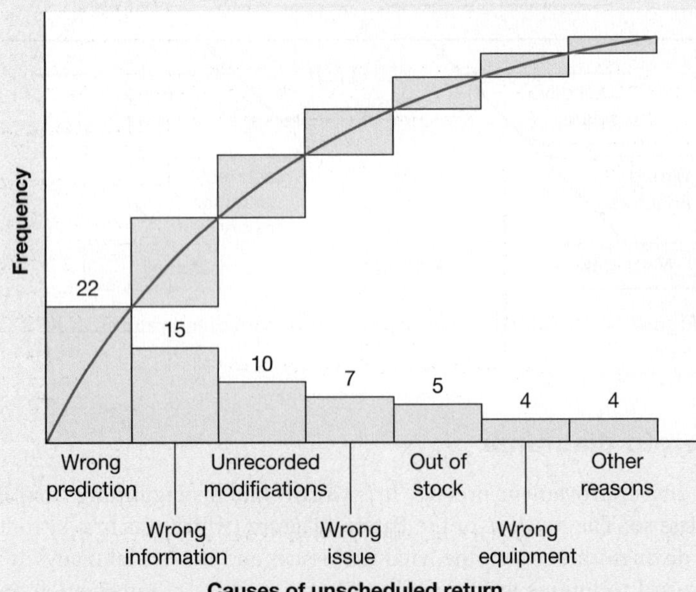

Figure 18.11 Pareto diagram for causes of unscheduled returns

Why–why analysis

Why–why analysis

Why–why analysis starts by stating the problem and asking *why* that problem has occurred. Once the reasons for the problem occurring have been identified, each of the reasons is taken in turn and again the question is asked *why* those reasons have occurred, and so on. This procedure is continued until either a cause seems sufficiently self-contained to be addressed by itself or no more answers to the question 'Why?' can be generated.

Worked example

Kaston Pyral Services Ltd (E)

The major cause of unscheduled returns at KPS was the incorrect prediction of reasons for the customer's system failure. This is stated as the 'problem' in the why–why analysis in Figure 18.12. The question is then asked, why was the failure wrongly predicted? Three answers are proposed: first, that the engineers were not trained correctly; second, that they had insufficient knowledge of the particular product installed in the customer's location; and third, that they had insufficient knowledge of the customer's particular system with its modifications. Each of these three reasons is taken in turn, and the questions are asked, why is there a lack of training, why is there a lack of product knowledge, and why is there a lack of customer knowledge? And so on.

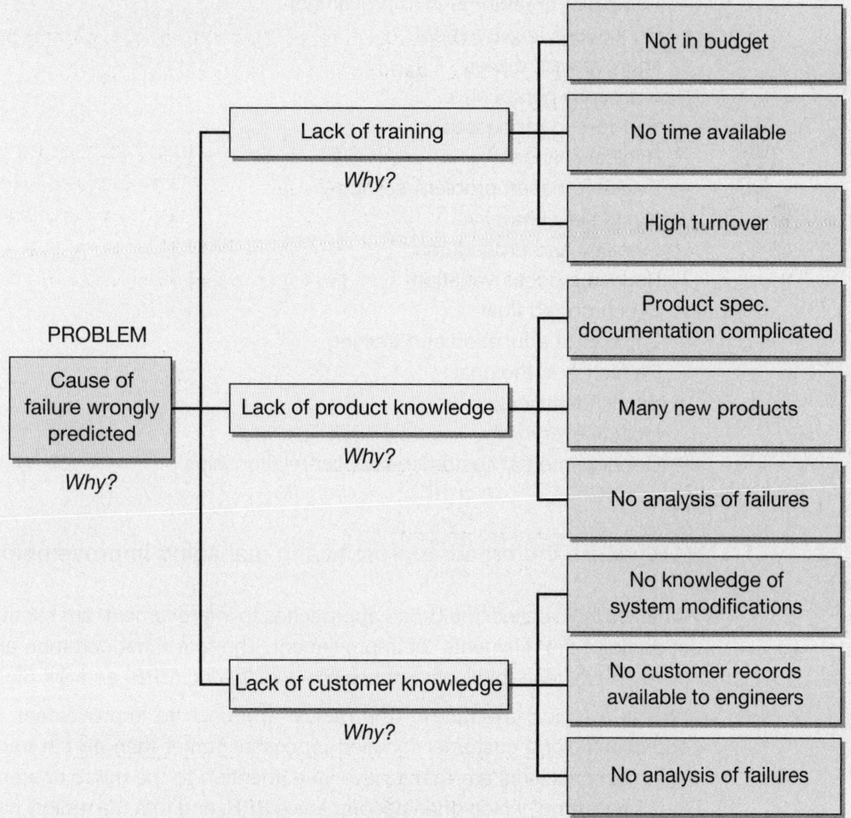

Figure 18.12 Why–why analysis for 'failure wrongly predicted'

Summary answers to key questions

Check and improve your understanding of this chapter using self assessment questions and a personalised study plan, audio and video downloads, and an eBook – all at ***www.myomlab.com.***

➤ Why is improvement so important in operations management?

- Improvement is now seen as the prime responsibility of operations management. Of the four areas of operations management activity (operations strategy, design, planning and control, and improvement) the focus of most operations managers has shifted from planning and control to improvement. Furthermore all operations management activities are really concerned with improvement in the long term. And all four activities are really interrelated and interdependent. Also, companies in many industries are having to improve simply to retain their position relative to their competitors. This is sometimes called the 'Red Queen' effect.

➤ What are the key elements of operations improvement?

- There are many 'elements' that are the building blocks of improvement approaches. The ones described in this chapter are:
  - Radical or breakthrough improvement
  - Continuous improvement
  - Improvement cycles
  - A process perspective
  - End-to-end processes
  - Radical change
  - Evidence-based problem-solving
  - Customer-centricity
  - Systems and procedures
  - Reduce process variation
  - Synchronized flow
  - Emphasize education and training
  - Perfection is the goal
  - Waste identification
  - Include everybody
  - Develop internal customer–supplier relationships.

➤ What are the broad approaches to managing improvement?

- What we have called 'the broad approaches to improvement' are relatively coherent collections of some of the 'elements' of improvement. The four most common are total quality management (TQM), lean, business process re-engineering (BPR) and Six Sigma.
- BPR is a typical example of the radical approach to improvement. It attempts to redesign operations along customer-focused processes rather than on the traditional functional basis. The main criticisms are that it pays little attention to the rights of staff who are the victims of the 'downsizing' which often accompanies BPR, and that the radical nature of the changes can strip out valuable experience from the operation.
- Total quality management was one of the earliest management 'fashions' and has suffered from a backlash, but the general precepts and principles of TQM are still influential. It is an approach that puts quality (and indeed improvement generally) at the heart of everything that is done by an operation.

- Lean was seen initially as an approach to be used exclusively in manufacturing, but has become seen as an approach that can be applied in service operations. Also lean, when first introduced was radical, and counter-intuitive. The idea that inventories had a negative effect, and that throughput time was more important than capacity utilization was difficult to accept by the more traditionally minded. So, as lean ideas have been gradually accepted, we have likewise come to be far more tolerant of ideas that are radical and/or counter-intuitive.
- Six Sigma is 'A disciplined methodology of defining, measuring, analysing, improving, and controlling the quality in every one of the company's products, processes, and transactions – with the ultimate goal of virtually eliminating all defects'. First popularized by Motorola, it was so named because it required that natural variation of processes (± 3 standard deviations) should be half their specification range. In other words, the specification range of any part of a product or service should be ± 6 times the standard deviation of the process. Now the definition of Six Sigma has widened beyond its statistical origins. It should be seen as a broad improvement concept rather than a simple examination of process variation, even though this is still an important part of process control, learning and improvement.
- There are differences between these improvement approaches. Each includes a different set of elements and therefore a different emphasis. They can be positioned on two dimensions. The first is whether the approaches emphasize a gradual, continuous approach to change or a more radical 'breakthrough' change. The second is whether the approach emphasizes *what* changes should be made or *how* changes should be made.

➤ What techniques can be used for improvement?

- Many of the techniques described throughout this book could be considered improvement techniques, for example statistical process control (SPC).
- Techniques often seen as 'improvement techniques' are:
  - scatter diagrams, which attempt to identify relationships and influences within processes;
  - flow charts, which attempt to describe the nature of information flow and decision-making within operations;
  - cause–effect diagrams, which structure the brainstorming that can help to reveal the root causes of problems;
  - Pareto diagrams, which attempt to sort out the 'important few' causes from the 'trivial many' causes;
  - Why–why analysis that pursues a formal questioning to find root causes of problems.

Case study
Geneva Construction and Risk

'This is not going to be like last time. Then, we were adopting an improvement programme because we were told to. This time it's our idea and, if it's successful, it will be us that are telling the rest of the group how to do it.' (Tyko Mattson, Six Sigma Champion, GCR)

Tyko Mattson was speaking as the newly appointed 'Champion' at Geneva Construction and Risk Insurance, which had been charged with 'steering the Six Sigma programme until it is firmly established as part of our ongoing practice'. The previous improvement initiative that he was referring to dated back many years to when GCR's parent company, Wichita Mutual Insurance, had insisted on the adoption of total quality management (TQM) in all its businesses. The TQM initiative had never been pronounced a failure and had managed to make some improvements, especially in customers' perception of the company's levels of service. However, the initiative had 'faded out' during the 1990s and, even though all departments still had to formally report on their improvement projects, their number and impact was now relatively minor.

Source: © Getty Images/Digital Vision

History

The Geneva Construction Insurance Company was founded in 1922 to provide insurance for building contractors and construction companies, initially in German-speaking Europe and then, because of the emigration of some family members to the USA, in North America. The company had remained relatively small and had specialized in housing construction projects until the early 1950s when it had started to grow, partly because of geographical expansion and partly because it has moved into larger (sometimes very large) construction insurance in the industrial, oil, petrochemical, and power plant construction areas. In 1983 it had been bought by the Wichita Mutual Group and had absorbed the group's existing construction insurance businesses.

By 2000 it had established itself as one of the leading providers of insurance for construction projects, especially complex, high-risk projects, where contractual and other legal issues, physical exposures and design uncertainty needed 'customized' insurance responses. Providing such insurance needed particular knowledge and skills from specialists including construction underwriters, loss adjusters, engineers, international lawyers and specialist risk consultants. Typically, the company would insure losses resulting from contractor failure, related public liability issues, delays in project completion, associated litigation, other litigation (such as ongoing asbestos risks), and negligence issues.

The company's headquarters were in Geneva and housed all major departments, including sales and marketing, underwriting, risk analysis, claims and settlement, financial control, general admin, specialist and general legal advice, and business research. There were also 37 local offices around the world, organized into four regional areas: North America, South America, Europe Middle East and Africa, and Asia. These regional offices provided localized help and advice directly to clients and also to the 890 agents that GCR used worldwide.

The previous improvement initiative

When Wichita Mutual had insisted that CGR adopt a TQM initiative, it had gone as far as to specify exactly how it should do it and which consultants should be used to help establish the programme. Tyko Mattson shakes his head as he describes it. *'I was not with the company at that time but, looking back; it's amazing that it ever managed to do any good. You can't impose the structure of an improvement initiative from the top. It has to, at least partially, be shaped by the people who are going to be involved in it. But everything had to be done according to the handbook. The cost of quality was measured for different departments according to the handbook. Everyone had to learn the improvement techniques that were described in the handbook. Everyone had to be part of a quality circle that was organized according to the handbook. We even had to have annual award ceremonies where we gave out special "certificates of merit" to those quality circles that had achieved the type of improvement that the handbook said they should.'* The TQM initiative had been run by the 'Quality Committee', a group of eight people with representatives from all the major departments at head office. Initially, it had spent much of its time setting up the improvement groups and organizing training in quality techniques. However, soon it had become swamped by the work needed to evaluate which improvement suggestions should be implemented. Soon the work load associated with assessing improvement ideas had become so great that the company decided to allocate small improvement budgets to each department on a quarterly basis that they could spend without reference to the Quality Committee. Projects requiring larger investment or that had a significant impact on other parts of the business still needed to be approved by the committee before they were implemented.

Department improvement budgets were still used within the business and improvement plans were still required from each department on an annual basis. However, the quality committee had stopped meeting by 1994 and the annual award ceremony had become a general communications meeting for all staff at the headquarters. *'Looking back'*, said Tyko, *'the TQM initiative faded away for three reasons. First, people just got tired of it. It was always seen as something extra rather than part of normal business life, so it was always seen as taking time away from doing your normal job. Second, many of the supervisory and middle management levels never really bought into it, I guess because they felt threatened. Third, only a very few of the local offices around the world ever adopted the TQM philosophy. Sometimes this was because they did not want the extra effort. Sometimes, however, they would argue that improvement initiatives of this type may be OK for head office processes, but not for the more dynamic world of supporting clients in the field.'*

The Six Sigma initiative

Early in 2005 Tyko Mattson, who for the last two years had been overseeing the outsourcing of some of GCR's claims processing to India, had attended a conference on 'Operations Excellence in Financial Services', and had heard several speakers detail the success they had achieved through using a Six Sigma approach to operations improvement. He had persuaded his immediate boss, Marie-Dominique Tomas, the head of claims for the company, to allow him to investigate its applicability to GCR. He had interviewed a number of other financial services that had implemented Six Sigma as well as a number of consultants and in September 2005 had submitted a report entitled '*What is Six Sigma and how might it be applied in GRC?*' Extracts from this are included in Appendix 1. Marie-Dominique Tomas was particularly concerned that they should avoid the mistakes of the TQM initiative.

'Looking back, it is almost embarrassing to see how naïve we were. We really did think that it would change the whole way that we did business. And although it did produce some benefits, it absorbed a large amount of time at all levels in the organization. This time we want something that will deliver results without costing too much or distracting us from focusing on business performance. That is why I like Six Sigma. It starts with clarifying business objectives and works from there.'

By late 2005 Tyko's report had been approved both by GCR and by Wichita Mutual's main board. Tyko had been given the challenge of carrying out the recommendations in his report, reporting directly to GCR's executive board. Marie-Dominique Tomas, was cautiously optimistic, *'It is quite a challenge for Tyko. Most of us on the executive board remember the TQM initiative and some are still sceptical concerning the value of such initiatives. However, Tyko's gradualist approach and his emphasis on the "three pronged" attack on revenue, costs, and risk, impressed the board. We now have to see whether he can make it work.'*

Appendix
Extract from '*What is Six Sigma and how might it be applied in GCR?*'

Six Sigma – pitfalls and benefits

Some pitfalls of Six Sigma

It is not simple to implement, and is resource hungry. The focus on measurement implies that the process data is available and reasonably robust. If this is not the case it is possible to waste a lot of effort in obtaining process performance data. It may also over-complicate things if advanced techniques are used on simple problems.

It is easier to apply Six Sigma to repetitive processes – characterized by high volume, low variety and low visibility to customers. It is more difficult to apply Six Sigma to low volume, higher variety and high visibility processes where standardization is harder to achieve and the focus is on managing the variety.

Six Sigma is not a 'quick fix'. Companies that have implemented Six Sigma effectively have not treated it as just another new initiative but as an approach that requires the long term systematic reduction of waste. Equally, it is not a panacea and should not be implemented as one.

Some benefits of Six Sigma

Companies have achieved significant benefits in reducing cost and improving customer service through implementing Six Sigma.

Six Sigma can reduce process variation, which will have a significant impact on operational risk. It is a tried and tested methodology, which combines the strongest parts of existing improvement methodologies. It lends itself to being customized to fit individual companies' circumstances. For example, Mestech Assurance has extended their Six Sigma initiative to examine operational risk processes.

Six Sigma could leverage a number of current initiatives. The risk self assessment methodology, Sarbanes Oxley, the process library, and our performance metrics work are all laying the foundations for better knowledge and measurement of process data.

Six Sigma – key conclusions for GCR

Six Sigma is a powerful improvement methodology. It is not all new but what it does do successfully is to combine some of the best parts of existing improvement methodologies, tools and techniques. Six Sigma has helped many companies achieve significant benefits.

Six Sigma could help GCR significantly improve risk management because it focuses on driving errors and exceptions out of processes.

Six Sigma has significant advantages over other process improvement methodologies.

- It engages senior management actively by establishing process ownership and linkage to strategic objectives. This is seen as integral to successful implementation in the literature and by all companies interviewed who had implemented it.
- It forces a rigorous approach to driving out variance in processes by analyzing the root cause of defects and errors and measuring improvement.
- It is an 'umbrella' approach, combining all the best parts of other improvement approaches.

Implementing Six Sigma across GCR is not the right approach

Companies who are widely quoted as having achieved the most significant headline benefits from Six Sigma were already relatively mature in terms of process management. Those companies, who understood their process capability, typically had achieved a degree of process standardization and had an established process improvement culture.

Six Sigma requires significant investment in performance metrics and process knowledge. GCR is probably not yet sufficiently advanced. However, we are working towards a position where key process data are measured and known and this will provide a foundation for Six Sigma.

A targeted implementation is recommended because:

Full implementation is resource hungry. Dedicated resource and budget for implementation of improvements is required. Even if the approach is modified, resource and budget will still be needed, just to a lesser extent. However, the evidence is that the investment is well worth it and pays back relatively quickly.

There was strong evidence from companies interviewed that the best implementation approach was to pilot Six Sigma, and select failing processes for the pilot. In addition, previous internal piloting of implementations has been successful in GCR – we know this approach works within our culture.

Six Sigma would provide a platform for GSR to build on and evolve over time. It is a way of leveraging the on-going work on processes, and the risk methodology (being developed by the Operational Risk Group). This diagnostic tool could be blended into Six Sigma, giving GCR a powerful model to drive reduction in process variation and improved operational risk management.

Recommendations

It is recommended that GCR management implement a Six Sigma pilot. The characteristics of the pilot would be as follows:

- A tailored approach to Six Sigma that would fit GCR's objectives and operating environment. Implementing Six Sigma in its entirety would not be appropriate.
- The use of an external partner: GCR does not have sufficient internal Six Sigma, and external experience will be critical to tailoring the approach, and providing training.
- Establishing where GCR's sigma performance is now. Different tools and approaches will be required to advance from 2 to 3 Sigma than those required to move from 3 to 4 Sigma.
- Quantifying the potential benefits. Is the investment worth making? What would a 1 Sigma increase in performance vs. risk be worth to us?
- Keeping the methods simple, if simple will achieve our objectives. As a minimum for us that means Team Based Problem Solving and basic statistical techniques.

Next steps

1. Decide priority and confirm budget and resourcing for initial analysis to develop a Six Sigma risk improvement programme in 2006.
2. Select external partner experienced in improvement and Six Sigma methodologies.
3. Assess GCR current state to confirm where to start in implementing Six Sigma.
4. Establish how much GCR is prepared to invest in Six Sigma and quantify the potential benefits.
5. Tailor Six Sigma to focus on risk management.
6. Identify potential pilot area (s) and criteria for assessing its suitability.
7. Develop a Six Sigma pilot plan.
8. Conduct and review the pilot programme.

Questions

1. How does the Six Sigma approach seem to differ from the TQM approach adopted by the company almost twenty years ago?
2. Is Six Sigma a better approach for this type of company?
3. Do you think Tyko can avoid the Six Sigma initiative suffering the same fate as the TQM initiative?

Problems and applications

*These problems and applications will help to improve your analysis of operations. You can find more practice problems as well as worked examples and guided solutions on MyOMLab at **www.myomlab.com**.*

1 Sophie was sick of her daily commute. 'Why', she thought 'should I have to spend so much time in a morning stuck in traffic listening to some babbling half-wit on the radio? We can work flexi-time after all. Perhaps I should leave the apartment at some other time? So resolved, Sophie deliberately varied her time of departure from her usual 8.30. Also, being an organized soul, she recorded her time of departure each day and her journey time. Her records are shown in Table 18.1.

(a) Draw a scatter diagram that will help Sophie decide on the best time to leave her apartment.
(b) How much time per (5-day) week should she expect to be saved from having to listen to a babbling half-wit?

Table 18.1 Sophie's journey times (in minutes)

Day	*Leaving time*	*Journey time*	*Day*	*Leaving time*	*Journey time*	*Day*	*Leaving time*	*Journey time*
1	7.15	19	6	8.45	40	11	8.35	46
2	8.15	40	7	8.55	32	12	8.40	45
3	7.30	25	8	7.55	31	13	8.20	47
4	7.20	19	9	7.40	22	14	8.00	34
5	8.40	46	10	8.30	49	15	7.45	27

2 The Printospeed Laser printer company was proud of its reputation for high-quality products and services. Because of this it was especially concerned with the problems that it was having with its customers returning defective toner cartridges. About 2,000 of these were being returned every month. Its European service team suspected that not all the returns were actually the result of a faulty product, which is why the team decided to investigate the problem. Three major problems were identified. First, some users were not as familiar as they should have been with the correct method of loading the cartridge into the printer, or in being able to solve their own minor printing problems. Second, some of the dealers were also unaware of how to sort out minor problems. Third, there was clearly some abuse of Hewlett-Packard's 'no-questions-asked' returns policy. Empty toner cartridges were being sent to unauthorized refilling companies who would sell the refilled cartridges at reduced prices. Some cartridges were being refilled up to five times and were understandably wearing out. Furthermore, the toner in the refilled cartridges was often not up to Printospeed's high quality standards.

(a) Draw a cause–effect diagram that includes both the possible causes mentioned, and any other possible causes that you think worth investigating.
(b) What is your opinion of the alleged abuse of the 'no-questions-asked' returns policy adopted by Printospeed?

3 Think back to the last product or service failure that caused you some degree of inconvenience. Draw a cause–effect diagram that identifies all the main causes of why the failure could have occurred. Try and identify the frequency with which such causes happen. This could be done by talking with the staff of the operation that provided the service. Draw a Pareto diagram that indicates the relatively frequency of each cause of failure. Suggest ways in which the operation could reduce the chances of failure.

Selected further reading

Goldratt, E.M. and Cox, J. (2004) *The Goal: A Process of Ongoing Improvement*, Gower, Aldershot. Updated version of a classic.

Hendry, L. and Nonthaleerak, P. (2004) Six sigma: Literature review and key future research areas, Lancaster University Management School, Working Paper, 2005/044 www.lums.lancs.ac.uk/publications/. Good overview of the literature on Six Sigma.

Hindo, B., At 3M, a struggle between efficiency and creativity: how CEO George Buckley is managing the yin and yang of discipline and imagination, *Business Week*, 11 June 2007. Readable article from the popular business press.

Pande, P.S., Neuman, R.P. and Cavanagh, R. (2002) *Six Sigma Way Team Field Book: An Implementation Guide for Project Improvement teams*, McGraw-Hill, New York. Obviously based on the Six Sigma principle and related to the book by the same author team recommended in Chapter 17, this is an unashamedly practical guide to the Six Sigma approach.

Paper, D.J., Rodger, J.A. and Pendharkar, P.C. (2001) A BPR case study at Honeywell, *Business Process Management Journal*, vol. 7, no. 2, 85–99. Interesting, if somewhat academic, case study.

Xingxing Zu, Fredendall L.D. and Douglas, T.J. (2008) the evolving theory of quality management: the role of Six Sigma, *Journal of Operations Management*, vol. 26, 630–50. As it says . . .

Useful web sites

www.processimprovement.com/ Commercial site but some content that could be useful.

www.kaizen-institute.com/ Professional institute for kaizen. Gives some insight into practitioner views.

www.imeche.org.uk/mx/index.asp The Manufacturing Excellence Awards site. Dedicated to rewarding excellence and best practice in UK manufacturing. Obviously manufacturing biased, but some good examples.

www.ebenchmarking.com Benchmarking information.

www.quality.nist.gov/ American Quality Assurance Institute. Well-established institution for all types of business quality assurance.

www.balancedscorecard.org/ Site of an American organization with plenty of useful links.

www.opsman.org Lots of useful stuff.

*Now that you have finished reading this chapter, why not visit MyOMLab at **www.myomlab.com** where you'll find more learning resources to help you make the most of your studies and get a better grade?*

Chapter 19

Risk management

Key questions

- ➤ What is risk management?
- ➤ How can operations assess the potential causes of, and risks from failure?
- ➤ How can failures be prevented?
- ➤ How can operations mitigate the effects of failure?
- ➤ How can operations recover from the effects of failure?

Introduction

No matter how much effort is put into improving operations, there is always a risk that something unexpected or unusual will happen that could reverse much, if not all, of the improvement effort. So, one obvious way of improving operations performance is by reducing the risk of failure (or of failure causing disruption) within the operation. Understanding and managing risk in operations can be seen as an improvement activity, even if it is in an 'avoiding the negative effects of failure' sense. But there is also a more conspicuous reason why risk management is increasingly a concern of operations managers. The sources of risk and the consequences of risk are becoming more difficult to handle. From sudden changes in demand to the bankruptcy of a key supplier, from terrorist attacks to cybercrime, the threats to normal smooth running of operations are not getting fewer. Nor are the consequences of such events becoming less serious. Sharper cost-cutting, lower inventories, higher levels of capacity utilization, increasingly effective regulation, and attentive media, can all serve to make the costs of operational failure greater. So for most operations managing risks is not just desirable, it is essential. But the risks to the smooth running of operations are not confined to major events. Even in less critical situations, having dependable processes can give a competitive advantage. And in this chapter we examine both the dramatic and more routine risks that can prevent operations working as they should. Figure 19.1 shows how this chapter fits into the operation's improvement activities.

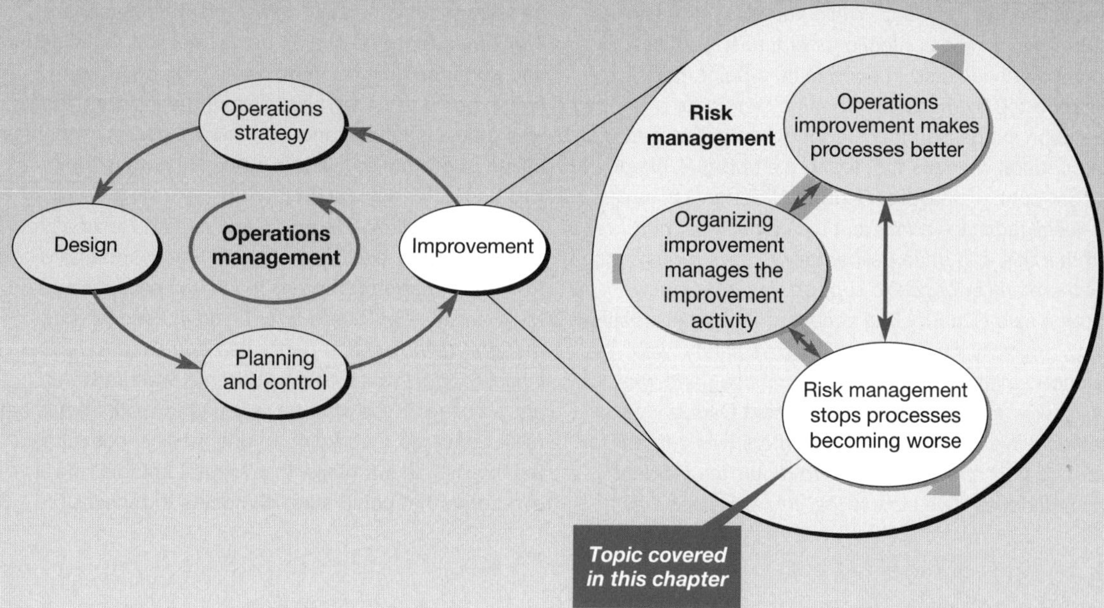

Figure 19.1 This chapter covers risk management

*Check and improve your understanding of this chapter using self assessment questions and a personalised study plan, audio and video downloads, and an eBook – all at **www.myomlab.com**.*

Operations in practice Cadbury's salmonella outbreak[1]

In June 2007, Cadbury, founded by a Quaker family in 1824, and now part of Cadbury Schweppes, one of the world's biggest confectionery companies, was fined £1 million plus costs of £152,000 for breaching food safety laws in a national salmonella outbreak that infected 42 people, including children aged under 10, who became ill with a rare strain of Salmonella montevideo. *'I regard this as a serious case of negligence'*, the judge said. *'It therefore needs to be marked as such to emphasise the responsibility and care which the law requires of a company in Cadbury's position.'* One prominant lawyer announced that *'Despite Cadbury's attempts to play down this significant fine, make no mistake it was intended to hurt and is one of the largest of its kind to date. This reflects no doubt the company's high profile and the length of time over which the admitted breach took place, but will also send out a blunt warning to smaller businesses of the government's intentions regarding enforcement of food safety laws.'*

Before the hearing, the company had, in fact, apologized, offering its 'sincere regrets' to those affected, and pleaded guilty to nine food safety offences. But at the beginning of the incident it had not been so open: one of the charges faced by Cadbury, which said it had cooperated fully with the investigation, admitted that it failed to notify the authorities of positive tests for salmonella as soon as they were known within the company. While admitting its mistakes, a spokesman for the confectioner emphasized that the company had acted in good faith, a point that was supported by the judge when he dismissed a prosecution suggestion that Cadbury had introduced the procedural changes that led to the outbreak simply as a cost-cutting measure. Cadbury, through its lawyers, said: *'Negligence we admit, but we certainly do not admit that this was done deliberately to save money and nor is there any evidence to support that conclusion.'* The judge said Cadbury had accepted that a new testing system, originally introduced to improve safety, was a *'distinct departure from previous practice'*, and was *'badly flawed and wrong'*. In a statement Cadbury said: *'Mistakenly, we did not believe that there was a threat to health and thus any requirement to report the incident to the authorities – we accept that this approach was incorrect. The processes that led to this failure ceased from June last year and will never be reinstated.'*

Source: Science Photo Library Ltd

The company was not only hit by the fine and court costs, it had to bear the costs of recalling one million bars that may have been contaminated, and face private litigation claims brought by its consumers who were affected. Cadbury said it lost around £30 million because of the recall and subsequent safety modifications, not including any private litigation claims. The London *Times* reported on the case of Shaun Garratty, one of the people affected. A senior staff nurse, from Rotherham, he spent seven weeks in hospital critically ill and now he fears that his nursing career might be in jeopardy. *The Times* reported him as being 'pleased that Cadbury's had admitted guilt but now wants to know what the firm is going to do for him'. Before the incident, it said, he was a fitness fanatic and went hiking, cycling, mountain biking or swimming twice a week. He always took two bars of chocolate on the trips, usually a Cadbury's Dairy Milk and a Cadbury's Caramel bar. He also ate one as a snack each day at work. *'My gastroenterologist told me if I had not been so fit I would have died'*, said Mr. Garratty. *'Six weeks after being in hospital they thought my bowel had perforated and I had to have a laparoscopy. I was told my intestines were inflamed and swollen.'* Even after he returned to work he has not fully recovered. According to one medical consultant, the illness had left him with a form of irritable bowel syndrome that could take 18 months to recover.

What is risk management?

Risk management is about things going wrong and what operations can do to stop things going wrong. It is important because there is always a chance that things might go wrong. But recognizing that things will sometimes go wrong is not the same as ignoring, or accepting it as inevitable. Generally operations managers try and prevent things going wrong. The Institute of Risk Management defines risk management as, *'the process which aims to help organisations understand, evaluate and take action on all their risks with a view to increasing the probability of their success and reducing the likelihood of failure'*.[2] They see risk management as being relevant to all organizations whether they are in the public or the private sector, or whether they are large or small, and is something that should form part of the culture of the organization.

Potential risks
Failure prevention
Risk mitigation
Failure recovery

From an operations perspective, risk is caused by some type of failure, and there are many different sources of failure in any operation. But dealing with failures, and therefore managing risk, generally involves four sets of activities. The first is concerned with understanding **what failures could potentially occur** in the operation and assessing their seriousness. The second task is to examine ways of **preventing failures** occurring. The third is to minimize the negative consequences of failure (called failure or **risk 'mitigation'**). The final task is to devise plans and procedures that will help the operation **to recover** from failures when they do occur. The remainder of this chapter deals with these four tasks, see Figure 19.2.

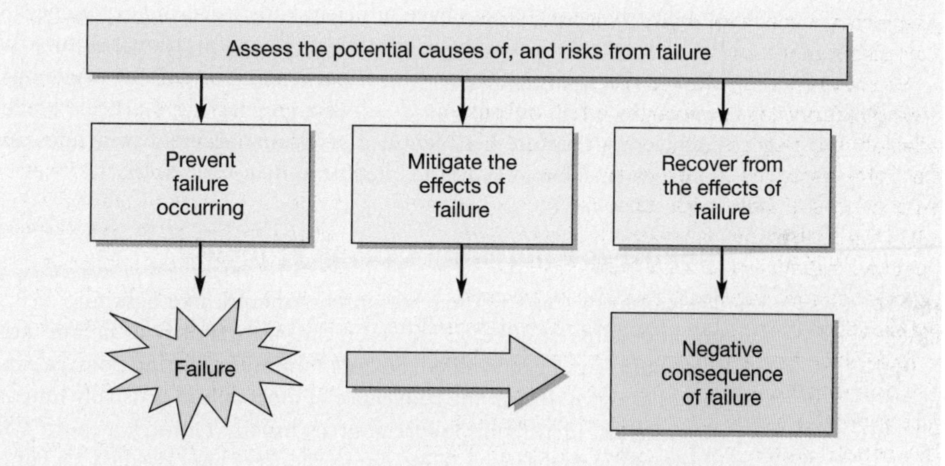

Figure 19.2 Risk management involves failure prevention, mitigating the negative consequences of failure, and failure recovery

Assess the potential causes of and risks from failure

The first aspect of risk management is to understand the potential sources of risk. This means assessing where failure might occur and what the consequences of failure might be. Often it is a 'failure to understand failure' that results in unacceptable risk. Each potential cause of failure needs to be assessed in terms of how likely it is to occur and the impact it may have. Only then can measures be taken to prevent or minimize the effect of the more important potential failures. The classic approach to assessing potential failures is to inspect and audit operations activities. Unfortunately, inspection and audit cannot, on their own, provide complete assurance that undesirable events will be avoided. The content of any audit has to be appropriate, the checking process has to be sufficiently frequent and comprehensive

Table 19.1 The seven management principles essential to effective risk management

Corporate perspective	• Viewing developments within the context of strategic goals • Recognizing both the potential value of opportunity and the potential impact of adverse effects
Forward-looking view	• Thinking toward tomorrow, identifying uncertainties, managing project resources and activities while anticipating uncertainties
Open communication	• Encouraging free-flowing information at and between all levels • Enabling formal, informal and impromptu communication • Using processes that value the individual voice (bringing unique knowledge and insight to identifying and managing risk)
Integrated management	• Making risk management an integral and vital part of operations • Adapting risk management methods and tools to a project's infrastructure and culture
Continuous process	• Sustaining constant vigilance • Identifying and managing risks routinely through all phases of change
Shared vision	• Mutual vision based on common purpose, shared ownership and collective communication • Focusing on results
Teamwork	• Working cooperatively to achieve common goals • Pooling talent, skills and knowledge

and the inspectors have to have sufficient knowledge and experience. But whatever approach to risk is taken, it can only be effective if the organizational culture that it is set in fully supports a 'risk-aware' attitude. This is particularly important where operations are producing new or uncertain outputs, as in software engineering. Carnegie Mellon University Software Engineering Institute has identified seven management principles essential to effective risk management.[3] Table 19.1 is adapted from those principles.

Identify the potential causes of failure

The causes of some failures are purely random, like lightning strikes, and are difficult, if not impossible, to predict. However, the vast majority of failures are caused by something that could have been avoided. So, as a minimum starting point, a simple checklist of failure causes is useful. In fact the root cause of most failure is usually human failure of some type; nevertheless, identifying failure sources usually requires a more evident set, such as that illustrated in Figure 19.3. Here, failure sources are classified as: failures of supply, internal failures such as those deriving from human organizational and technological sources, failures deriving from the design of products and services, failures deriving from customer failures, and general environmental failures.

Supply failure

Supply failure means any failure in the timing or quality of goods and services delivered into an operation. For example, suppliers delivering the wrong or faulty components, outsourced call centres suffering a telecoms failure, disruption to power supplies, and so on. It can be an important source of failure because of increasing dependence on outsourced activities in most industries. Also, global sourcing usually means that parts are shipped around the world on their journey through the supply chain. Microchips manufactured in Taiwan could be assembled to printed circuit boards in Shanghai which are then finally assembled into a computer in Ireland. At the same time, many industries are suffering increased volatility in demand. Perhaps most significantly there tends to be far less inventory in supply chains that could buffer interruptions to supply. According to one authority on supply chain management, '*Potentially the risk of disruption has increased dramatically as the result of a too-narrow focus on supply chain efficiency at the expense of effectiveness.*'[4]

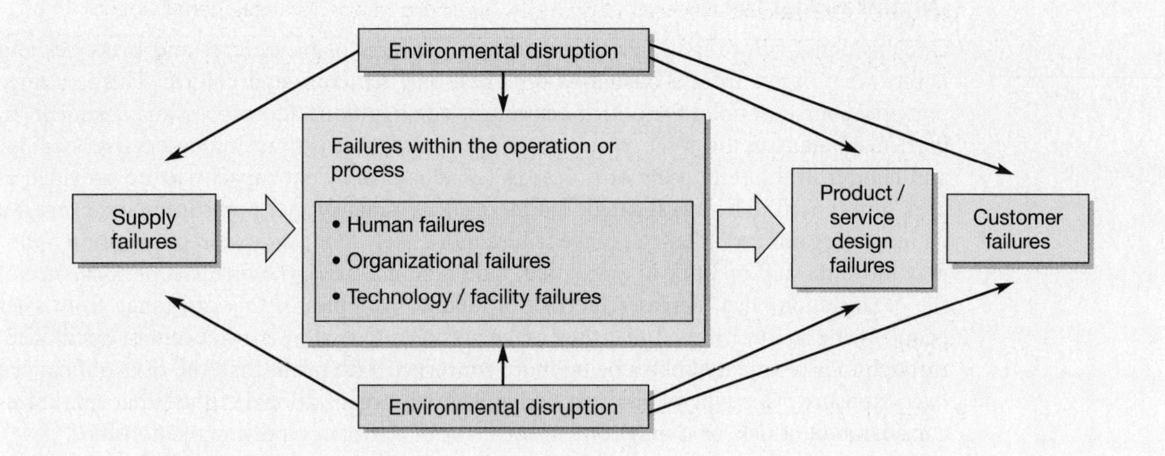

Figure 19.3 The sources of potential failure in operations

Human failures

There are two broad types of human failure. The first is where key personnel leave, become ill, die, or in some way cannot fulfil their role. The second is where people are doing their job but are making mistakes. Understanding risk in the first type of failure involves identifying the key people without whom operations would struggle to operate effectively. These are not always the most senior individuals, but rather those fulfilling crucial roles that require special skills or tacit knowledge. Human failure through 'mistakes' also comes in two types: errors and violations. '**Errors**' are mistakes in judgement, where a person should have done something different. For example, if the manager of a sports stadium fails to anticipate dangerous crowding during a championship event. '**Violations**' are acts which are clearly contrary to defined operating procedure. For example, if a maintenance engineer fails to clean a filter in the prescribed manner, it is eventually likely to cause failure. Catastrophic failures are often caused by a combination of errors and violations. For example, one kind of accident, where an aircraft appears to be under control and yet still flies into the ground, is very rare (once in two million flights). For this type of failure to occur, first, the pilot has to be flying at the wrong altitude (error). Second, the co-pilot would have to fail to cross-check the altitude (violation). Third, air traffic controllers would have to miss the fact that the plane was at the wrong altitude (error). Finally, the pilot would have to ignore the ground proximity warning alarm in the aircraft, which can be prone to give false alarms (violation).

Errors

Violations

Short case
Not what you want to hear[5]

The passengers never knew, and to be fair to the airline the pilot in question was intercepted before he could fly the aircraft, but it is unsettling to think about being flown by a pilot who has been drinking. So, if you are an anxious flyer, or of a nervous disposition, stop reading now.

It was a dramatic example of human failure increasing operational risk. The headline ran – 'Pilot arrested over alcohol fears!' Why? A pilot had been arrested after he had boarded a plane at Heathrow Airport on suspicion of being drunk. After giving a breath test to police, the 44-year-old pilot, who worked for the US carrier United Airlines, was arrested and held on suspicion of 'performing an aviation function whilst exceeding the alcohol limit'. Responding to the incident, United Airlines issued a statement saying that 'Safety is our number one priority' and confirming that the pilot had been 'removed from duty while we are co-operating with the authorities and conducting a full investigation'. A statement released by United Airlines said the company's alcohol policy was 'among the strictest in the industry. We have no tolerance for abuse or violations of this well-established policy', it said.

Organizational failure

Organizational failure is usually taken to mean failures of procedures and processes and failures that derive from a business's organizational structure and culture. This is a huge potential source of failure and includes almost all operations and process management. In particular, failure in the design of processes (such as bottlenecks causing system overloading) and failures in the resourcing of processes (such as insufficient capacity being provided at peak times) need to be investigated. But there are also many other procedures and processes within an organization that can make failure more likely. For example, remuneration policy may motivate staff to work in a way that, although increasing the financial performance of the organization, also increases the risk of failure. Examples of this can range from sales people being so incentivized that they make promises to customers that cannot be fulfilled, through to investment bankers being more concerned with profit than the risks of financial over-exposure. This type of risk can derive from an organizational culture that minimizes consideration of risk, or it may come from a lack of clarity in reporting relationships.

Technology and facilities failures

By 'technology and facilities' we mean all the IT systems, machines, equipment and buildings of an operation. All are liable to failure, or breakdown. The failure may be only partial, for example a machine that has an intermittent fault. Alternatively, it can be what we normally regard as a breakdown – a total and sudden cessation of operation. Either way, its effects could bring a large part of the operation to a halt. For example, a computer failure in a supermarket chain could paralyse several large stores until it is fixed.

Product / service design failures

In its design stage, a product or service might look fine on paper; only when it has to cope with real circumstances might inadequacies become evident. Of course, during the design process, potential risk of failure should have been identified and 'designed out'. But one only has to look at the number of 'product recalls' or service failures to understand that design failures are far from uncommon. Sometimes this is the result of a trade-off between fast time-to-market performance and the risk of the product or service failing in operation. And, while no reputable business would deliberately market flawed products or services, equally most businesses cannot delay a product or service launch indefinitely to eliminate every single small risk of failure.

Customer failures

Not all failures are (directly) caused by the operation or its suppliers. Customers may 'fail' in that they misuse products and services. For example, an IT system might have been well designed, yet the user could treat it in a way that causes it to fail. Customers are not 'always right'; they can be inattentive and incompetent. However, merely complaining about customers is unlikely to reduce the chances of this type of failure occurring. Most organizations will accept that they have a responsibility to educate and train customers, and to design their products and services so as to minimize the chances of failure.

Environmental disruption

Environmental disruption includes all the causes of failure that lie outside of an operation's direct influence. This source of potential failure has risen to near the top of many firms' agenda since 11 September 2001 and the global 'credit crunch' of 2008. As operations become increasingly integrated (and increasingly dependent on integrated technologies such as information technologies), businesses are more aware of the critical events and malfunctions that have the potential to interrupt normal business activity and even stop the entire company. Risks in this category include everything from cybercrime to hurricanes, from terrorism to political change.

Short case
Viruses, threats and 30 years of spam[6]

Happy birthday! 1 May 2008 saw the 30th anniversary of junk electronic mail, or spam as it has become known. It was in 1978 that Gary Thuerk, a Marketing Executive at the Digital Equipment Corporation (DEC), a US mini-computer manufacturer, decided it would be a great sales ploy to let Arpanet (the direct ancestor of the Internet) researchers on the west coast of the USA know that DEC had incorporated the network's protocols directly into one of its operating systems. So Thuerk's secretary typed in all the researchers' addresses and dispatched the message using the e-mail program, which at the time was very primitive. But not all the recipients were happy. Arpanet's rules said that the network could not be used for commercial purposes and not everyone wanted to know about the content of the message; it just seemed intrusive.

Since then unwanted Internet-distributed information has gone on to irritate, infuriate and threaten the whole Internet. For example, on 25 January 2003 the 'SQL Slammer' worm, a rogue program, spread at frightening speed throughout the Internet. It disrupted computers around the world and, at the height of the attack, its effect was such that half the traffic over the Internet was being lost (see Figure 19.4). Thousands of cash dispensers in North America ceased operating and one police force was driven back to using pencils and paper when its dispatching system crashed. Yet security experts believe that the SQL Slammer did more good than harm because it highlighted weaknesses in Internet security processes. Like most rogue software, it exploited a flaw in a commonly used piece of software. Much commonly used software has security flaws that can be exploited in this way. Software producers issue 'patch' software to fix flaws but this can actually direct Internet terrorists to vulnerable areas in the software, and not all systems managers get around to implementing all patches. Nevertheless, every rogue program that penetrates Internet security systems teaches a valuable lesson to those working to prevent security failures.

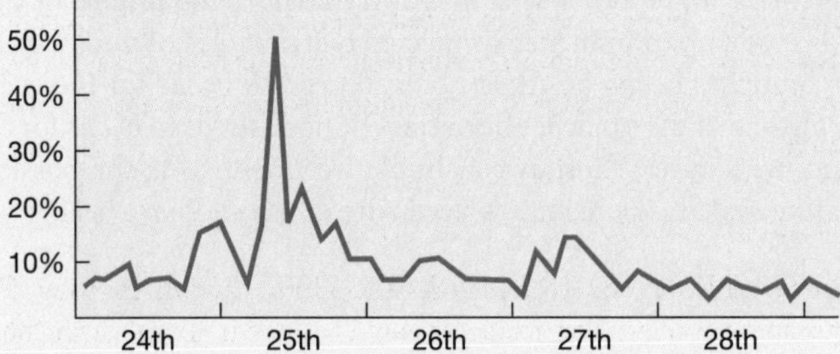

Figure 19.4 Internet traffic percentage loss January 2003

E-security[7]

Any advance in processes or technology creates risks. No real advance comes without threats and even danger. This applies particularly to e-business. In almost all businesses information has become critical. So, information security management has become a particularly high priority. But herein lies the problem. The Internet, which is the primary medium for conducting e-business, is by design an open non-secure medium. Since the original purpose of the Internet was not for commercial purposes, it is not designed to handle secure transactions. There is a trade-off between providing wider access through the Internet, and the security concerns it generates. Three developments have amplified e-security concerns. First, increased connectivity (who does not rely on internet-based systems?) means that everyone has at least the potential to 'see' everyone else. Organizations want to make enterprise systems and information more available to internal employees, business partners and customers (see Chapter 14 on ERP). Second, there has been a loss of 'perimeter' security as more people work from home or through mobile communications. For example, some banks have been targeted by criminals seeking to exploit home working, as a hitherto overlooked flaw in corporate security firewalls. Hackers had hoped to exploit lower levels of security in home computers to burrow into corporate networks. Third, for some new, sometimes unregulated, technologies, such as some mobile networks, it takes time to discover all possible sources of risk. The Internet, after all, is an open system and the rapid rate of development of new software and systems often means that users do not have an adequate knowledge about software and systems architecture. This makes users oblivious to potential vulnerabilities that can lead to serious security breaches.

Yet there is an increasing customer awareness of data security and data confidentiality which means that companies are viewing e-business security as a potential marketing advantage. One specialist in this area, Forrester Research, reported that 74 per cent of online consumers said that online security is an important consideration in choosing a financial service provider.

Post-failure analysis

One of the critical activities of operations and process resilience is to understand why a failure has occurred. This activity is called 'post-failure analysis'. It is used to uncover the root cause of failures. This includes such activities as the following.

- Accident investigation, where large-scale national disasters like oil tanker spillages and aeroplane accidents are investigated using specifically trained staff.
- Failure traceability, where procedures ensure that failures can be traced back to where they originated.
- Complaint analysis, where complaints (and compliments) are used as a valuable source for detecting the root causes of failures of customer service.
- Fault tree analysis, where a logical procedure starts with a failure or a potential failure and works backwards to identify all the possible causes and therefore the origins of that failure. Fault tree analysis is made up of branches connected by two types of nodes: AND nodes and OR nodes. The branches below an AND node all need to occur for the event above the node to occur. Only one of the branches below an OR node needs to occur for the event above the node to occur. Figure 19.5 shows a simple tree identifying the possible reasons for a filter in a heating system not being replaced when it should have been.

Likelihood of failure

The difficulty of estimating the chance of a failure occurring varies greatly. Some failures are well understood through a combination of rational causal analysis and historical performance. For example a mechanical component may fail between 10 and 17 months of its installation in 99 per cent of cases. Other types of failure are far more difficult to predict. The chances of a fire in a supplier's plant are (hopefully) low, but how low? There will be some data concerning fire hazards in this type of plant, but the estimated probability of failure will be subjective.

'Objective' estimates

Estimates of failure based on historical performance can be measured in three main ways: failure rates – how often a failure occurs; reliability – the chances of a failure occurring; and availability – the amount of available useful operating time. 'Failure rate' and 'reliability' are different ways of measuring the same thing – the propensity of an operation, or part of an operation, to fail. Availability is one measure of the consequences of failure in the operation.

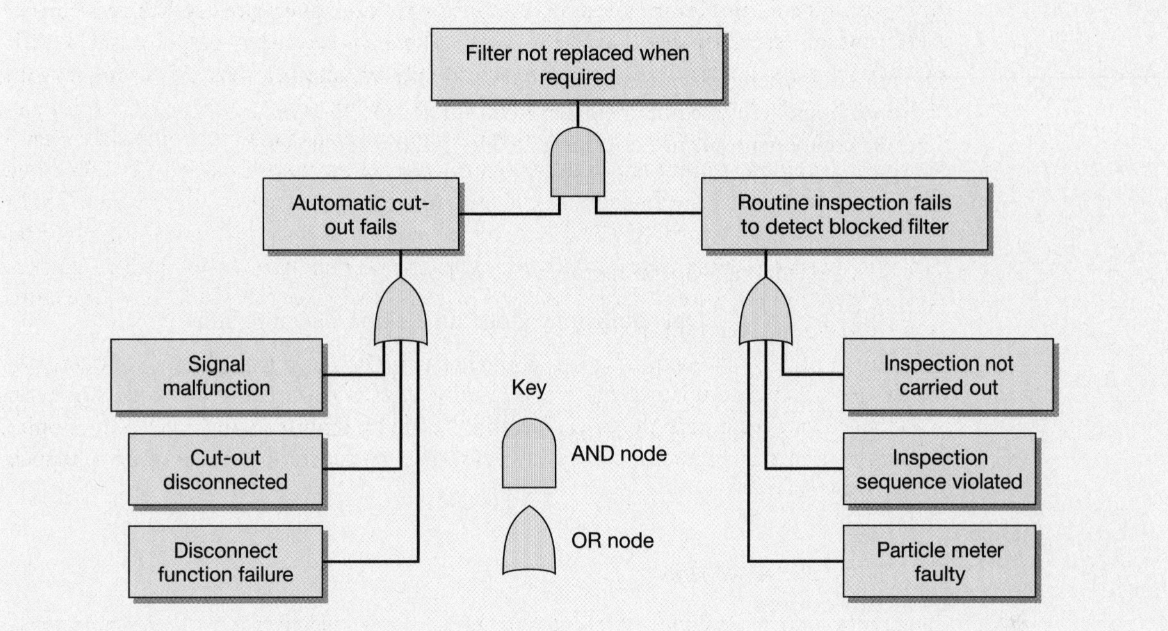

Figure 19.5 Fault tree analysis for failure to replace filter when required

Failure rate

Failure rate

Failure rate (FR) is calculated as the number of failures over a period of time. For example, the security of an airport can be measured by the number of security breaches per year, and the failure rate of an engine can be measured in terms of the number of failures divided by its operating time. It can be measured either as a percentage of the total number of products tested or as the number of failures over time:

$$FR = \frac{\text{number of failures}}{\text{total number of products tested}} \times 100$$

or

$$FR = \frac{\text{number of failures}}{\text{operating time}}$$

Worked example

A batch of 50 electronic components is tested for 2,000 hours. Four of the components fail during the test as follows:

Failure 1 occurred at 1,200 hours
Failure 2 occurred at 1,450 hours
Failure 3 occurred at 1,720 hours
Failure 4 occurred at 1,905 hours

$$\text{Failure rate (as a percentage)} = \frac{\text{number of failures}}{\text{number tested}} \times 100 = \frac{4}{50} \times 10 = 8\%$$

The total time of the test = 50 × 2,000 = 100,000 component hours

→

But:

one component was not operating 2,000 – 1,200 = 800 hours
one component was not operating 2,000 – 1,450 = 550 hours
one component was not operating 2,000 – 1,720 = 280 hours
one component was not operating 2,000 – 1,905 = 95 hours

Thus:

$$\text{Total non-operating time} = 1{,}725 \text{ hours}$$

$$\text{Operating time} = \text{total time} - \text{non-operating time}$$
$$= 100{,}000 - 1{,}725 = 98{,}275 \text{ hours}$$

$$\text{Failure rate (in time)} = \frac{\text{number of failures}}{\text{operating time}} = \frac{4}{98{,}275}$$
$$= 0.000041$$

Bath-tub curves

Sometimes failure is a function of time. For example, the probability of an electric lamp failing is relatively high when it is first used, but if it survives this initial stage, it could still fail at any point, and the longer it survives, the more likely its failure becomes. The curve which describes failure probability of this type is called the bath-tub curve. It comprises three distinct stages: the 'infant-mortality' or '**early-life**' stage where early failures occur caused by defective parts or improper use; the '**normal-life**' stage when the failure rate is usually low and reasonably constant, and caused by normal random factors; the '**wear-out**' stage when the failure rate increases as the part approaches the end of its working life and failure is caused by the ageing and deterioration of parts. Figure 19.6 illustrates three bath-tub curves with slightly different characteristics. Curve A shows a part of the operation which has a high initial infant-mortality failure but then a long, low-failure, normal life followed by the gradually increasing likelihood of failure as it approaches wear-out. Curve B is far less predictable. The

Early life failure
Normal life failure
Wear-out failure

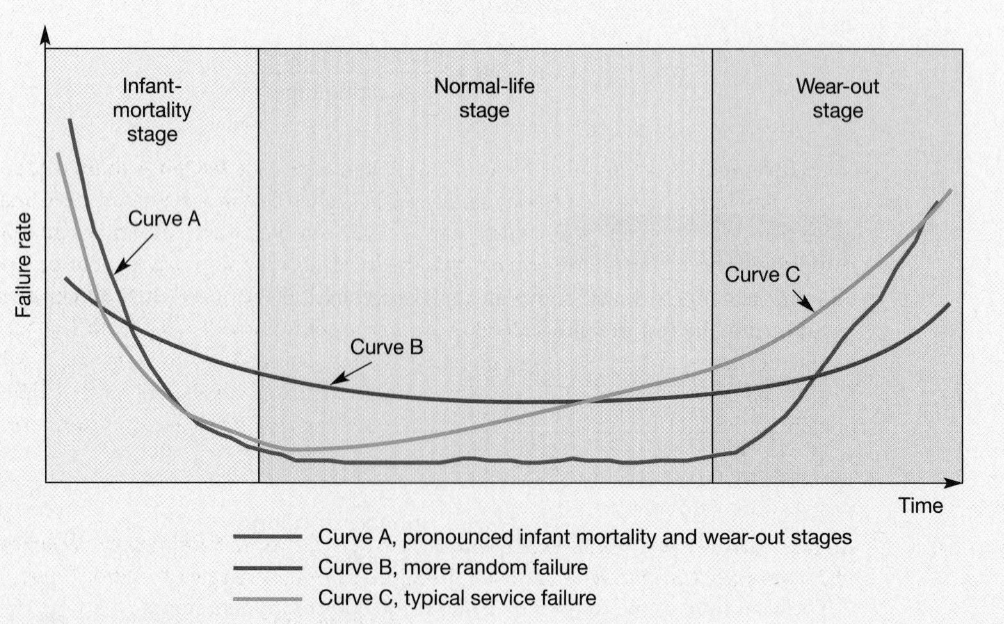

Figure 19.6 Bath-tub curves for three types of process

distinction between the three stages is less clear, with infant-mortality failure subsiding only slowly and a gradually increasing chance of wear-out failure. Failure of the type shown in curve B is far more difficult to manage in a planned manner. The failure of operations which rely more on human resources than on technology, such as some services, can be closer to curve C. They may be less susceptible to component wear-out but more so to staff complacency as the service becomes tedious and repetitive.

Reliability

Reliability

Reliability measures the ability to perform as expected over time. Usually the importance of any particular failure is determined partly by how interdependent the other parts of the system are. With interdependence, a failure in one component will cause the whole system to fail. So, if an interdependent system has n components each with their own reliability, R_1, R_2, . . . , R_n, the reliability of the whole system, R_s, is given by:

$$R_s = R_1 \times R_2 \times R_2 \times \ldots \times R_n$$

where

R_1 = reliability of component 1
R_2 = reliability of component 2

etc.

Worked example

An automated pizza-making machine in a food manufacturer's factory has five major components, with individual reliabilities (the probability of the component not failing) as follows:

Dough mixer	Reliability = 0.95
Dough roller and cutter	Reliability = 0.99
Tomato paste applicator	Reliability = 0.97
Cheese applicator	Reliability = 0.90
Oven	Reliability = 0.98

If one of these parts of the production system fails, the whole system will stop working. Thus the reliability of the whole system is:

$$R_s = 0.95 \times 0.99 \times 0.97 \times 0.90 \times 0.98$$
$$= 0.805$$

The number of components

In the example, the reliability of the whole system was only 0.8, even though the reliability of the individual components was significantly higher. If the system had been made up of more components, then its reliability would have been even lower. The more interdependent components an operation or process has, the lower its reliability will be. For one composed of components which each have an individual reliability of 0.99, with 10 components the system reliability will shrink to 0.9, with 50 components it is below 0.8, with 100 components it is below 0.4, and with 400 components it is down below 0.05. In other words, with a process of 400 components (not unusual in a large automated operation), even if the reliability of each individual component is 99 per cent, the whole system will be working for less than 5 per cent of its time.

Mean time between failures

Mean time between failures

An alternative (and common) measure of failure is the **mean time between failures** (MTBF) of a component or system. MTBF is the reciprocal of failure rate (in time). Thus:

$$\text{MTBF} = \frac{\text{operating hours}}{\text{number of failures}}$$

Worked example

In the previous worked example which was concerned with electronic components, the failure rate (in time) of the electronic components was 0.000041. For that component:

$$\text{MTBF} = \frac{1}{0.000041} = 24{,}390.24 \text{ hours}$$

That is, a failure can be expected once every 24,390.24 hours on average.

Availability

Availability

Availability is the degree to which the operation is ready to work. An operation is not available if it has either failed or is being repaired following failure. There are several different ways of measuring it depending on how many of the reasons for not operating are included. Lack of availability because of planned maintenance or changeovers could be included, for example. However, when 'availability' is being used to indicate the operating time excluding the consequence of failure, it is calculated as follows:

$$\text{Availability } (A) = \frac{\text{MTBF}}{\text{MTBF} + \text{MTTR}}$$

where

MTBF = the mean time between failures of the operation
MTTR = the mean time to repair, which is the average time taken to repair the operation, from the time it fails to the time it is operational again.

Worked example

A company which designs and produces display posters for exhibitions and sales promotion events competes largely on the basis of its speedy delivery. One particular piece of equipment which the company uses is causing some problems. This is its large platform colour laser printer. Currently, the mean time between failures of the printer is 70 hours and its mean time to repair is 6 hours. Thus:

$$\text{Availability} = \frac{70}{70 + 6} = 0.92$$

The company has discussed its problem with the supplier of the printer who has offered two alternative service deals. One option would be to buy some preventive maintenance (*see* later for a full description of preventive maintenance) which would be carried out each weekend. This would raise the MTBF of the printer to 90 hours. The other option would be to subscribe to a faster repair service which would reduce the MTTR to 4 hours. Both options would cost the same amount. Which would give the company the higher availability?

With MTBF increased to 90 hours:

$$\text{Availability} = \frac{90}{90 + 6} = 0.938$$

With MTTR reduced to 4 hours:

$$\text{Availability} = \frac{70}{70 + 4} = 0.946$$

Availability would be greater if the company took the deal which offered the faster repair time.

'Subjective' estimates

Failure assessment, even for subjective risks, is increasingly a formal exercise that is carried out using standard frameworks, often prompted by health and safety, environmental, or other regulatory reasons. These frameworks are similar to the formal quality inspection methods associated with quality standards like ISO 9000 that often implicitly assume unbiased objectivity. However, individual attitudes to risk are complex and subject to a wide variety of influences. In fact many studies have demonstrated that people are generally very poor at making risk-related judgements. Consider the success of state and national lotteries. The chances of winning, in nearly every case, are so low as to make the financial value of the investment entirely negative. If a player has to drive their car in order to purchase a ticket, they may be more likely to be killed or seriously injured than they are to win the top prize. But, although people do not always make rational decisions concerning the chances of failure, this does not mean abandoning the attempt. But it does mean that one must understand the limits to overly rational approaches to failure estimation, for example, how people tend to pay too much attention to dramatic low-probability events and overlook routine events.

Even when 'objective' evaluations of risks are used, they may still cause negative consequences. For example, when the oil giant Royal-Dutch Shell took the decision to employ deep-water disposal in the North Sea for their Brent Spar oil platform, they felt that they were making a rational operational decision based upon the best available scientific evidence concerning environmental risk. Unfortunately Greenpeace disagreed and put forward an alternative 'objective analysis' showing significant risk from deep-water disposal. Eventually Greenpeace admitted their evidence was flawed but by that time Shell had lost the public relations battle and had altered their plans.

Critical commentary

The idea that failure can be detected through in-process inspection is increasingly seen as only partially true. Although inspecting for failures is an obvious first step in detecting them, it is not even close to being 100 per cent reliable. Accumulated evidence from research and practical examples consistently indicates that people, even when assisted by technology, are not good at detecting failure and errors. This applies even when special attention is being given to inspection. For example, airport security was significantly strengthened after 11 September 2001, yet one in ten lethal weapons that were entered into airports' security systems (in order to test them) were not detected.[8] *'There is no such thing as one hundred per cent security, we are all human beings'*, says Ian Hutcheson, the Director of Security at Airport Operator BAA. No one is advocating abandoning inspection as a failure detection mechanism. Rather it is seen as one of a range of methods of preventing failure.

Failure mode and effect analysis

One of the best-known approaches to assessing the relative significance of failure is failure mode and effect analysis (FMEA). Its objective is to identify the factors that are critical to various types of failure as a means of identifying failures before they happen. It does this by providing a 'checklist' procedure built around three key questions for each possible cause of failure:

- What is the likelihood that failure will occur?
- What would the consequence of the failure be?
- How likely is such a failure to be detected before it affects the customer?

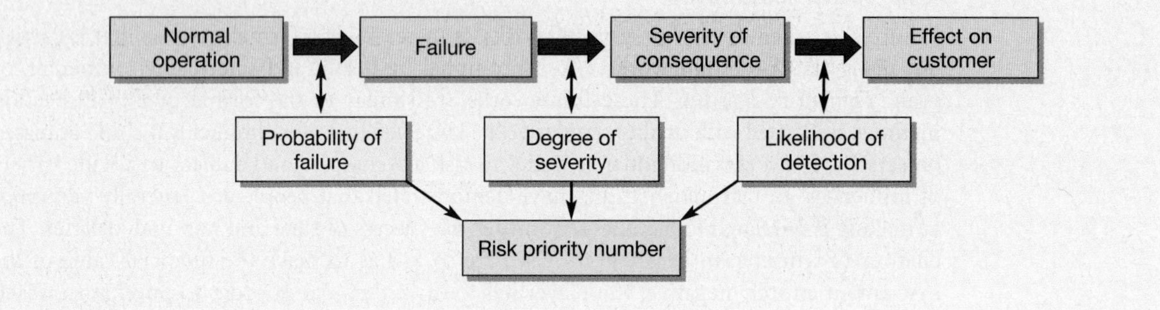

Figure 19.7 Procedure for failure mode and effect analysis (FMEA)

Based on a quantitative evaluation of these three questions, a risk priority number (RPN) is calculated for each potential cause of failure. Corrective actions, aimed at preventing failure, are then applied to those causes whose RPN indicates that they warrant priority, see Figure 19.7.

Worked example

Part of an FMEA exercise at a transportation company has identified three failure modes associated with the failure of 'goods arriving damaged' at the point of delivery:

Goods not secured (failure mode 1)
Goods incorrectly secured (failure mode 2)
Goods incorrectly loaded (failure mode 3).

The improvement group which is investigating the failures allocates scores for the probability of the failure mode occurring, the severity of each failure mode, and the likelihood that they will be detected using the rating scales shown in Table 19.2, as follows:

Probability of occurrence
Failure mode 1 5
Failure mode 2 8
Failure mode 3 7

Severity of failure
Failure mode 1 6
Failure mode 2 4
Failure mode 3 4

Probability of detection
Failure mode 1 2
Failure mode 2 6
Failure mode 3 7

The RPN of each failure mode is calculated:

Failure mode 1 (goods not secured) $5 \times 6 \times 2 = 60$
Failure mode 2 (goods incorrectly secured) $8 \times 4 \times 5 = 160$
Failure mode 3 (goods incorrectly loaded) $7 \times 4 \times 7 = 196$

Priority is therefore given to failure mode 3 (goods incorrectly loaded) when attempting to eliminate the failure.

Table 19.2 Rating scales for FMEA

A. Occurrence of failure

Description	*Rating*	*Possible failure occurrence*
Remote probability of occurrence	1	0
It would be unreasonable to expect failure to occur		
Low probability of occurrence	2	1:20,000
Generally associated with activities similar to		
previous ones with a relatively low number of failures	3	1:10,000
Moderate probability of occurrence	4	1:2,000
Generally associated with activities similar to previous	5	1:1,000
ones which have resulted in occasional failures	6	1:200
High probability of occurrence	7	1:100
Generally associated with activities similar		
to ones which have traditionally caused problems	8	1:20
Very high probability of occurrence	9	1:10
Near certainty that major failures will occur	10	1:2

B. Severity of failure

Description	*Rating*
Minor severity	1
A very minor failure which would have no noticeable effect on system performance	
Low severity	2
A minor failure causing only slight customer annoyance	3
Moderate severity	4
A failure which would cause some customer dissatisfaction,	5
discomfort or annoyance, or would cause noticeable	6
deterioration in performance	
High severity	7
A failure which would engender a high degree of	8
customer dissatisfaction	
Very high severity	9
A failure which would affect safety	
Catastrophic	10
A failure which may cause damage to property, serious injury or death	

C. Detection of failure

Description	*Rating*	*Probability of detection*
Remote probability that the defect will reach the customer	1	0 to 15%
(It is unlikely that such a defect would pass through inspection, test or assembly)		
Low probability that the defect will reach	2	6 to 15%
the customer	3	16 to 25%
Moderate probability that the defect will	4	26 to 35%
reach the customer	5	36 to 45%
	6	46 to 55%
High probability that the defect will reach	7	56 to 65%
the customer	8	66 to 75%
Very high probability that the defect will	9	76 to 85%
reach the customer	10	86 to 100%

Preventing failure occurring

Once a thorough understanding of the causes and effects of failure has been established, the next responsibility of operations managers is to try to prevent the failures occurring in the first place. The obvious way to do this is to systematically examine any processes involved and 'design out' any failure points. Many of the approaches used in Chapters 4 and 5 on process and product/service design and Chapter 17 on quality management can be used to do this. In this section we will look at three further approaches to reducing risk by trying to prevent failure: building redundancy into a process, 'fail-safeing' some of the activities in the process, and maintaining the physical facilities in the process.

Redundancy

Redundancy

Building in **redundancy** to an operation means having back-up systems or components in case of failure. It can be expensive and is generally used when the breakdown could have a critical impact. It means doubling or even tripling some parts of a process or system in case one component fails. Nuclear power stations, spacecraft and hospitals all have auxiliary systems in case of an emergency. Some organizations also have 'back-up' staff held in reserve in case someone does not turn up for work. Rear-brake lighting sets in buses and trucks contain two bulbs to reduce the likelihood of not showing a red light. Human bodies contain two of some organs – kidneys and eyes, for example – both of which are used in 'normal operation' but the body can cope with a failure in one of them. The reliability of a component together with its back-up is given by the sum of the reliability of the original component and the likelihood that the back-up component will both be needed *and* be working.

$$R_{a+b} = R_a + (R_b \times P\ (\text{failure}))$$

where

R_{a+b} = reliability of component a with its back-up component b
R_a = reliability of a alone
R_b = reliability of back-up component b
P (failure) = the probability that component a will fail and therefore component b will be needed.

Worked example

The food manufacturer in the earlier worked example has decided that the cheese depositor in the pizza-making machine is so unreliable that it needs a second cheese depositor to be fitted to the machine which will come into action if the first cheese depositor fails.

The two cheese depositors (each with reliability = 0.9) working together will have a reliability of:

$$0.9 + [0.9 \times (1 - 0.9)] = 0.99$$

The reliability of the whole machine is now:

$$0.95 \times 0.99 \times 0.97 \times 0.99 \times 0.98 = 0.885$$

Redundancy is often used for servers, where system availability is particularly important. In this context, the industry used three main types of redundancy.

- *Hot standby* – where both primary and secondary (backup) systems run simultaneously. The data are copied to the secondary server in real time so that both systems contain identical information.
- *Warm standby* – where the secondary system runs in the background to the primary system. Data are copied to the secondary server at regular intervals, so there are times when both servers do not contain exactly the same data.
- *Cold standby* – where the secondary system is only called upon when the primary system fails. The secondary system receives scheduled data backups, but less frequently than in a warm standby, so cold standby is mainly used for non-critical applications.

Fail-safeing

Fail-safeing
Poka-yoke

The concept of **fail-safeing** has emerged since the introduction of Japanese methods of operations improvement. Called **poka-yoke** in Japan (from *yokeru* (to prevent) and *poka* (inadvertent errors)), the idea is based on the principle that human mistakes are to some extent inevitable. What is important is to prevent them becoming defects. Poka-yokes are simple (preferably inexpensive) devices or systems which are incorporated into a process to prevent inadvertent operator mistakes resulting in a defect. Typical poka-yokes are such devices as:

- limit switches on machines which allow the machine to operate only if the part is positioned correctly;
- gauges placed on machines through which a part has to pass in order to be loaded onto, or taken off, the machine – an incorrect size or orientation stops the process;
- digital counters on machines to ensure that the correct number of cuts, passes or holes have been machined;
- checklists which have to be filled in, either in preparation for, or on completion of, an activity;
- light beams which activate an alarm if a part is positioned incorrectly.

More recently, the principle of fail-safeing has been applied to service operations. Service poka-yokes can be classified as those which 'fail-safe the server' (the creator of the service) and those which 'fail-safe the customer' (the receiver of the service). Examples of fail-safeing the server include:

- colour-coding cash register keys to prevent incorrect entry in retail operations;
- the McDonald's french-fry scoop which picks up the right quantity of fries in the right orientation to be placed in the pack;
- trays used in hospitals with indentations shaped to each item needed for a surgical procedure – any item not back in place at the end of the procedure might have been left in the patient;
- the paper strips placed round clean towels in hotels, the removal of which helps housekeepers to tell whether a towel has been used and therefore needs replacing.

Examples of fail-safeing the customer include:

- the locks on aircraft lavatory doors, which must be turned to switch the light on;
- beepers on ATMs to ensure that customers remove their cards;
- height bars on amusement rides to ensure that customers do not exceed size limitations;
- outlines drawn on the walls of a childcare centre to indicate where toys should be replaced at the end of the play period;
- tray stands strategically placed in fast-food restaurants to remind customers to clear their tables.

Critical commentary

Much of the previous discussion surrounding the prevention of failure has assumed a 'rational' approach. In other words, it is assumed that operations managers and customers alike will put more effort into preventing failures that are either more likely to occur or more serious in their consequences. Yet this assumption is based on a rational response to risk. In fact, being human, managers often respond to the perception of risk rather than its reality. For example, Table 19.3 shows the cost of each life saved by investment in various road and rail transportation safety (in other words, failure prevention) investments. The table shows that investing in improving road safety is very much more effective than investing in rail safety. And while no one is arguing for abandoning efforts on rail safety, it is noted by some transportation authorities that actual investment reflects more the public perception of rail deaths (low) compared with road deaths (very high).

Table 19.3 The cost per life saved of various safety (failure prevention) investments

Safety investment	*Cost per life (€M)*
Advanced train protection system	30
Train protection warning systems	7.5
Implementing recommended guidelines on rail safety	4.7
Implementing recommended guidelines on road safety	1.6
Local authority spending on road safety	0.15

Maintenance

Maintenance

Maintenance is how organizations try to avoid failure by taking care of their physical facilities. It is an important part of most operations' activities particularly in operations dominated by their physical facilities such as power stations, hotels, airlines and petrochemical refineries. The benefits of effective maintenance include enhanced safety, increased reliability, higher quality (badly maintained equipment is more likely to cause errors), lower operating costs (because regularly serviced process technology is more efficient), a longer lifespan for process technology, and higher 'end value' (because well-maintained facilities are generally easier to dispose of into the second-hand market).

The three basic approaches to maintenance

In practice an organization's maintenance activities will consist of some combination of the three basic approaches to the care of its physical facilities. These are run to breakdown (RTB), preventive maintenance (PM) and condition-based maintenance (CBM).

Run-to-breakdown maintenance

Run-to-breakdown maintenance – as its name implies involves allowing the facilities to continue operating until they fail. Maintenance work is performed only after failure has taken place. For example, the televisions, bathroom equipment and telephones in a hotel's guest rooms will probably only be repaired when they fail. The hotel will keep some spare parts and the staff available to make any repairs when needed. Failure in these circumstances is neither catastrophic (although perhaps irritating to the guest) nor so frequent as to make regular checking of the facilities appropriate.

Preventive maintenance

Preventive maintenance attempts to eliminate or reduce the chances of failure by servicing (cleaning, lubricating, replacing and checking) the facilities at pre-planned intervals. For example, the engines of passenger aircraft are checked, cleaned and calibrated according to a regular schedule after a set number of flying hours. Taking aircraft away from their regular duties for preventive maintenance is clearly an expensive option for any airline. The consequences of failure while in service are considerably more serious, however. The principle is also applied to facilities with less catastrophic consequences of failure. The regular cleaning and lubricating of machines, even the periodic painting of a building, could be considered preventive maintenance.

Condition-based maintenance

Condition-based maintenance attempts to perform maintenance only when the facilities require it. For example, continuous process equipment, such as that used in coating photographic paper, is run for long periods in order to achieve the high utilization necessary for cost-effective production. Stopping the machine to change, say, a bearing when it is not strictly necessary to do so would take it out of action for long periods and reduce its utilization. Here condition-based maintenance might involve continuously monitoring the vibrations, for example, or some other characteristic of the line. The results of this monitoring would then be used to decide whether the line should be stopped and the bearings replaced.

Mixed maintenance strategies

Each approach to maintaining facilities is appropriate for different circumstances. RTB is often used where repair is relatively straightforward (so the consequence of failure is small), where regular maintenance is very costly, or where failure is not at all predictable (failure is just as likely to occur after repair as before). PM is used where the cost of unplanned failure is high and where failure is not totally random. CBM is used where the maintenance activity is expensive, either because of the cost of providing the maintenance itself, or because of the disruption which the maintenance activity causes to the operation. Most operations adopt a mixture of these approaches. Even an automobile uses all three approaches (*see* Fig. 19.8). Light bulbs and fuses are normally replaced only when they fail. Engine oil is subject to preventive maintenance at a regular service. Finally, most drivers also monitor the condition of the auto, for example by measuring the amount of tread on the tyre.

Breakdown *versus* preventive maintenance

The balance between preventive and breakdown maintenance is usually set to minimize the total cost of breakdown. Infrequent preventive maintenance will cost little to provide but will result in a high likelihood (and therefore cost) of breakdown maintenance. Conversely, very frequent preventive maintenance will be expensive to provide but will reduce the cost of having to provide breakdown maintenance (*see* Fig. 19.9a). The total cost of maintenance appears to minimize at an 'optimum' level of preventive maintenance. However, the cost of providing preventive maintenance may not increase quite so steeply as indicated in Figure 19.9(a). The curve assumes that it is carried out by a separate set of people (skilled maintenance staff) from the 'operators' of the facilities. Furthermore, every time preventive maintenance takes place, the facilities cannot be used productively. This is why the slope of the curve increases, because the maintenance episodes start to interfere with the normal working of the operation. But in many operations some preventive maintenance can be performed by the operators themselves (which reduces the cost of providing it) and at times

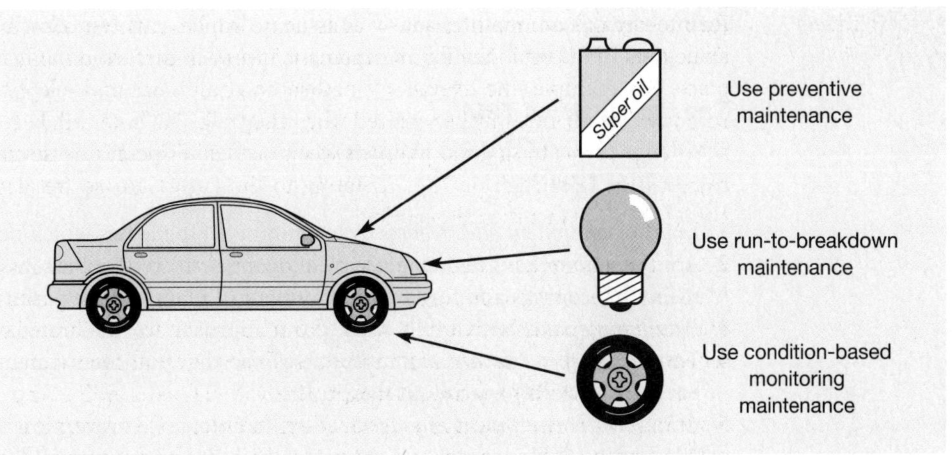

Figure 19.8 A mixture of maintenance approaches is often used – in a car, for example

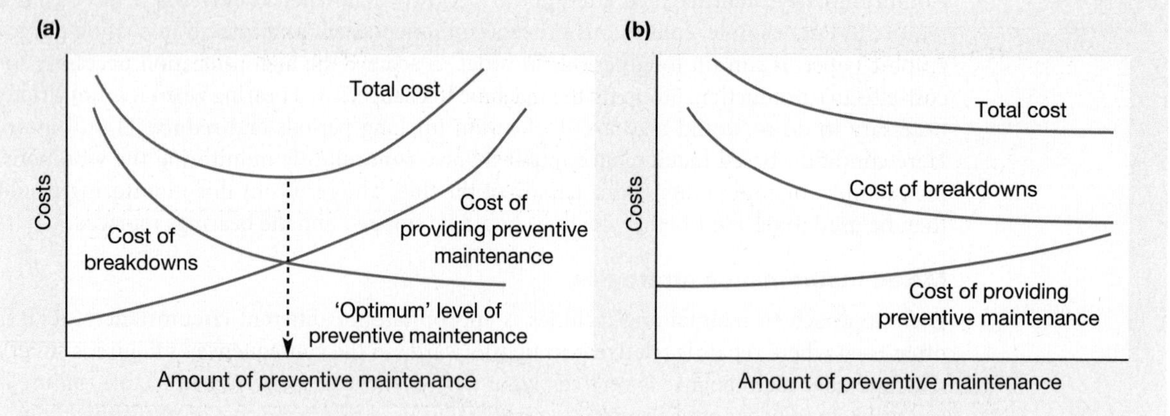

Figure 19.9 Two views of maintenance costs. (a) One model of the costs associated with preventive maintenance shows an optimum level of maintenance effort. (b) If routine preventive maintenance tasks are carried out by operators and if the real cost of breakdowns is considered, the 'optimum' level of preventive maintenance shifts toward higher levels

which are convenient for the operation (which minimizes the disruption to the operation). The cost of breakdowns could also be higher than is indicated in Figure 19.9(a). Unplanned breakdowns may do more than necessitate a repair and stop the operation; they can take away stability from the operation which prevents it being able to improve itself. Put these two ideas together and the minimizing total curve and maintenance cost curve look more like Figure 19.9(b). The emphasis is shifted more towards the use of preventive maintenance than run-to-breakdown maintenance.

Total productive maintenance

Total productive maintenance

Total productive maintenance (TPM) is 'the productive maintenance carried out by all employees through small group activities', where productive maintenance is 'maintenance management which recognizes the importance of reliability, maintenance and economic efficiency in plant design'.[9] In Japan, where TPM originated, it is seen as a natural extension in the evolution from run-to-breakdown to preventive maintenance. TPM adopts some of the team-working and empowerment principles discussed in Chapter 9, as well as a continuous improvement approach to failure prevention as discussed in Chapter 18. It also sees maintenance as an organization-wide issue, to which staff can contribute in some way. It is analogous to the total quality management approach discussed in Chapter 17.

The five goals of TPM

TPM aims to establish good maintenance practice in operations through the pursuit of 'the five goals of TPM':[9]

1 *Improve equipment effectiveness* by examining all the losses which occur.
2 *Achieve autonomous maintenance* by allowing staff to take responsibility for some of the maintenance tasks and for the improvement of maintenance performance.
3 *Plan maintenance* with a fully worked out approach to all maintenance activities.
4 *Train all staff in relevant maintenance skills* so that both maintenance and operating staff have all the skills to carry out their roles.
5 *Achieve early equipment management* by 'maintenance prevention' (MP), which involves considering failure causes and the maintainability of equipment during its design, manufacture, installation and commissioning.

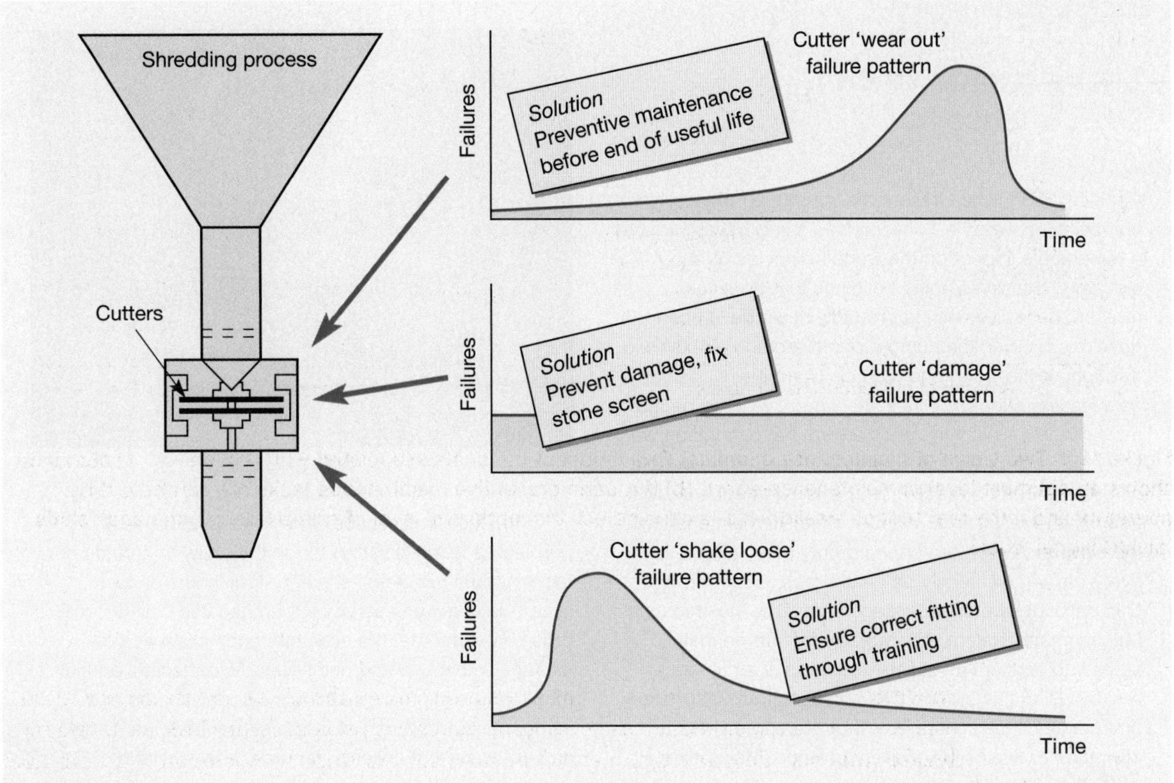

Figure 19.10 One part in one process can have several different failure modes, each of which requires a different approach

Reliability-centred maintenance

Reliability-centred maintenance

Reliability-centred maintenance (RCM) uses the pattern of failure for each type of failure mode of a part of a system to dictate the approach to its maintenance. For example, take the process illustrated in Figure 19.10. This is a simple shredding process which prepares vegetables prior to freezing. The most significant part of the process, which requires the most maintenance attention, is the cutter sub-assembly. However, there are several modes of failure which could lead to the cutters requiring attention. Sometimes they require changing simply because they have worn out through usage, sometimes they have been damaged by small stones entering the process, sometimes they have shaken loose because they were not fitted correctly. The failure patterns for these three failure modes are very different, as illustrated in Figure 19.10. Certainly, 'wear-out' can be managed by timing preventive maintenance intervals just prior to the increased likelihood of failure. But this approach would not help prevent stone damage which could happen at any time with equal likelihood. The approach here would be to prevent stones getting to the cutters in the first place, perhaps through fixing a screen. The failure pattern for the cutters shaking loose is different again. If the cutters have been incorrectly fitted, it would become evident soon after the fitting. Again, preventive maintenance is unlikely to help here; rather effort should be put into ensuring that the cutters are always correctly fitted, perhaps by organizing more appropriate training of staff. The approach of RCM is sometimes summarized as 'If we cannot stop it from happening, we had better stop it from mattering'. In other words, if maintenance cannot either predict or even prevent failure, and the failure has important consequences, then efforts need to be directed at reducing the impact of the failure.

Short case
Lifting maintenance performance[10]

Source: Alamy Images

Back in 1853 Elisha Graves Otis introduced the world's first safety elevator in Yonkers, New York. It was to have a remarkable impact on the world's skylines. Without elevators, the skyscraping buildings that dominate most modern cities would probably never have been developed. Given the number of elevators in regular use throughout the world and the Otis Company's position as a leading supplier, Otis is the world's leading people mover. And Otis is very much aware that every time we enter an elevator we are trusting our lives to the people who designed and made it, and, more immediately, the people who maintain it. Without effective maintenance the elevators which are often on duty every minute of every day would literally be death traps. Central to the Otis philosophy of maintenance is its 'Otis Maintenance Management System' (OMMS), a programme that takes into account its clients' elevators' maintenance needs. Using this system Otis can customize inspection and maintenance schedules for up to twelve years of operation or five million trips in advance. Maintenance procedures are determined by each elevator's individual pattern of use. Frequency of trips, the loads carried by the elevator and conditions of use, are all incorporated to determine the frequency and nature of maintenance activities. Because no component part of any equipment is perfect, Otis also monitors the life cycle characteristics of all its elevators' components. This information on wear and failure is made available to its customers via its twenty-four communications centre and web site. This ongoing understanding of component life also is used to update maintenance schedules.

With Otis's call service, when an elevator has a problem, a technician can be on their way to a customer's facility within minutes. Its twenty-four-hours-a-day, seven-days-a-week service which handles over 1.2 million calls a year can get the elevators back in service on average within two and half hours. Also the Otis on-site monitoring equipment system is a sophisticated and interconnected system of sensors, monitors, hardware and software that collects, records, analyses and communicates hundreds of different system functions. If the system detects a problem it automatically makes a service call, calling out a technician who has been provided with the information collected by the system and that will be used to help identify the component causing the problem. *'Around-the-clock response is important'*, says Otis, *'because problems don't keep office hours* . . . [the remote sensing] . . . *system detects deteriorating components, identifies intermittent anomalies, notes the small nuisances that . . . would have gone undetected. . . . It identifies most potential problems before they occur.'*

Mitigating the effects of failure

Risk, or failure, mitigation means isolating a failure from its negative consequences. It is an admission that not all failures can be avoided. However, in some areas of operations management relying on mitigation, rather than prevention, is unfashionable. For example, 'inspection' practices in quality management were based on the assumption that failures were inevitable and needed to be detected before they could cause harm. Modern total quality management places much more emphasis on prevention. Yet, in operations and process resilience, mitigation can be vital when used in conjunction with prevention in reducing overall risk.

Risk mitigation actions

The nature of the action taken to mitigate failure will obviously depend on the nature of the risk. In most industries technical experts have established a classification of risk mitigation actions that are appropriate for the types of risk likely to be suffered. So, for example, in agriculture, government agencies and industry bodies have published mitigation strategies for such risks as the outbreak of crop disease, contagious animal infections, and so on. Such documents will outline the various mitigation actions that can be taken under different circumstances and detail exactly who are responsible for each action. Although these classifications tend to be industry-specific, the following generic categorization gives a flavour of the types of mitigation actions that may be generally applicable.

Mitigation planning is the activity of ensuring that all possible failure circumstances have been identified and the appropriate mitigation actions identified. It is the overarching activity that encompasses all subsequent mitigation actions, and may be described in the form of a decision tree or guide rules.

Economic mitigation includes actions such as insurance against losses from failure, spreading the financial consequences of failure, and 'hedging' against failure. Insurance is the best known of these actions and is widely adopted, although ensuring appropriate insurance and effective claims management is a specialized skill in itself. Hedging often takes the form of financial instruments, for example, a business may purchase a financial 'hedge' against the price risk of a vital raw material deviating significantly from a set price.

Containment (spatial) means stopping the failure physically spreading to affect other parts of an internal or external supply network. Preventing contaminated food from spreading through the supply chain, for example, will depend on real-time information systems that provide traceability data.

Containment (temporal) means containing the spread of a failure over time. It particularly applies when information about a failure or potential failure needs to be transmitted without undue delay. For example, systems that give advanced warning of hazardous weather such as snow storms must transmit such information to local agencies such as the police and road clearing organizations in time for them to stop the problem causing excessive disruption.

Loss reduction covers any action that reduces the catastrophic consequences of failure by removing the resources that are likely to suffer those consequences. For example, the road signs that indicate evacuation routes in the event of severe weather, or the fire drills that train employees in how to escape in the event of an emergency, may not reduce all the consequences of failure, but can help in reducing loss of life or injury.

Substitution means compensating for failure by providing other resources that can substitute for those rendered less effective by the failure. It is a little like the concept of redundancy that was described earlier, but does not always imply excess resources if a failure has not occurred. For example, in a construction project, the risk of encountering unexpected geological problems may be mitigated by the existence of a separate work plan and that is invoked only if such problems are found.

Recovering from the effects of failure

Failure recovery

In parallel with considering how to prevent failures occurring, operations managers need to decide what they will do when failures do occur. This activity is called **failure recovery**. All types of operation can benefit from well-planned recovery. For example, a construction company whose mechanical digger breaks down can have plans in place to arrange a replacement from a hire company. The breakdown might be disruptive, but not as much as it might have been if the operations manager had not worked out what to do. Recovery procedures will also shape customers' perceptions of failure. Even where the customer sees a failure, it may not necessarily lead to dissatisfaction. Indeed, in many situations, customers may well accept that things do go wrong. If there is a metre of snow on the train lines, or if the restaurant is particularly popular, we may accept that the product or service does not work. It is not necessarily the failure itself that leads to dissatisfaction but often the organization's response to the breakdown. While mistakes may be inevitable, dissatisfied customers are not. A failure may even be turned into a positive experience. A good recovery can turn angry, frustrated customers into loyal ones. One research project used four service scenarios and examined the willingness of customers to use an organization's services again.[11] The four scenarios were:

1 The service is delivered to meet the customers' expectations and there is full satisfaction.
2 There are faults in the service delivery but the customer does not complain about them.
3 There are faults in the service delivery and the customer complains but he/she has been fobbed off or mollified. There is no real satisfaction with the service provider.
4 There are faults in the service delivery and the customer complains and feels fully satisfied with the resulting action taken by the service providers.

Customers who are fully satisfied and do not experience any problems (1) are the most loyal, followed by complaining customers whose complaints are resolved successfully (4). Customers who experience problems but don't complain (2) are in third place and last of all come customers who do complain but are left with their problems unresolved and feelings of dissatisfaction (3).

Recovery in high-visibility services

The idea of failure recovery has been developed particularly in service operations. As one specialist put it, '*If something goes wrong, as it often does, will anybody make special efforts to get it right? Will somebody go out of his or her way to make amends to the customer? Does anyone make an effort to offset the negative impact of a screw-up?*'[12] It has also been suggested that service recovery does not just mean 'return to a normal state' but to a state of enhanced perception. *All breakdowns require the deliverer to jump through a few hoops to get the customer back to neutral. More hoops are required for victims to recover.* Operations managers need to recognize that all customers have recovery expectations that they want organizations to meet. Recovery needs to be a planned process. Organizations therefore need to design appropriate responses to failure, linked to the cost and the inconvenience caused by the failure to the customer, which will meet the needs and expectations of the customer. Such recovery processes need to be carried out either by empowered front-line staff or by trained personnel who are available to deal with recovery in a way which does not interfere with day-to-day service activities.

Failure planning

Identifying how organizations can recover from failure is of particular interest to service operations because they can turn failures around to minimize the effect on customers or even to turn failure into a positive experience. It is also of interest to other industries, however, especially those where the consequences of failure are particularly severe. Bulk chemical manufacturers and nuclear processors, for example, spend considerable resources in deciding how they will cope with failures. The activity of devising the procedures which allow the operation to recover from failure is called **failure planning**. It is often represented by stage models, one of which is represented in Figure 19.11. We shall follow it through from the point where failure is recognized.

Failure planning

Discover. The first thing any manager needs to do when faced with a failure is to discover its exact nature. Three important pieces of information are needed: first of all, what exactly has happened; second, who will be affected by the failure; and, third, why did the failure occur? This last point is not intended to be a detailed inquest into the causes of failure (that comes

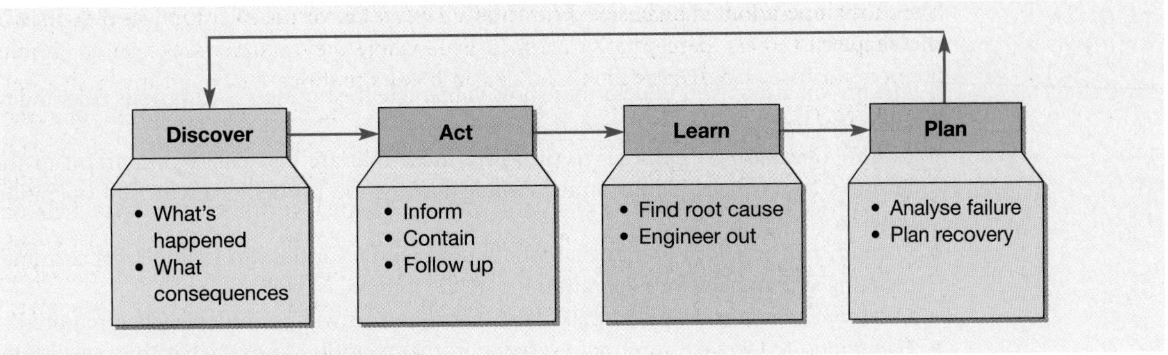

Figure 19.11 The stages in failure planning

later) but it is often necessary to know something of the causes of failure in case it is necessary to determine what action to take.

Act. The discover stage could only take minutes or even seconds, depending on the severity of the failure. If the failure is a severe one with important consequences, we need to move on to doing something about it quickly. This means carrying out three actions, the first two of which could be carried out in reverse order, depending on the urgency of the situation. First, tell the significant people involved what you are proposing to do about the failure. In service operations this is especially important where the customers need to be kept informed, both for their peace of mind and to demonstrate that something is being done. In all operations, however, it is important to communicate what action is going to happen so that everyone can set their own recovery plans in motion. Second, the effects of the failure need to be contained in order to stop the consequences spreading and causing further failures. The precise containment actions will depend on the nature of the failure. Third, there needs to be some kind of follow-up to make sure that the containment actions really have contained the failure.

Learn. As discussed earlier in this chapter, the benefits of failure in providing learning opportunities should not be underestimated. In failure planning, learning involves revisiting the failure to find out its root cause and then engineering out the causes of the failure so that it will not happen again. This is the key stage for much failure planning.

Plan. Learning the lessons from a failure is not the end of the procedure. Operations managers need formally to incorporate the lessons into their future reactions to failures. This is often done by working through 'in theory' how they would react to failures in the future. Specifically, this involves first identifying all the possible failures which might occur (in a similar way to the FMEA approach). Second, it means formally defining the procedures which the organization should follow in the case of each type of identified failure.

Business continuity

Business continuity

Many of the ideas behind failure, failure prevention and recovery are incorporated in the growing field of **business continuity**. This aims to help operations avoid and recover from disasters while keeping the business going, an issue that has risen to near the top of many firms' agenda since 11 September 2001. As operations become increasingly integrated (and increasingly dependent on integrated technologies such as information technologies), critical failures can result from a series of related and unrelated events and combine to disrupt totally a company's business. These events are the critical malfunctions which have the potential to interrupt normal business activity and even stop the entire company, such as natural disasters, fire, power or telecommunications failure, corporate crime, theft, fraud, sabotage, computer system failure, bomb blast, scare or other security alert, key personnel leaving, becoming ill or dying, key suppliers ceasing trading, contamination of product or processes, and so on.

The procedures adopted by business continuity experts are very similar to those described in this chapter:

- *Identify and assess risks* to determine how vulnerable the business is to various risks and to take steps to minimize or eliminate them.
- *Identify core business processes* to prioritize those that are particularly important to the business and which, if interrupted, would have to be brought back to full operation quickly.
- *Quantify recovery times* to make sure staff understand priorities (for example, get customer ordering system back into operation before the internal e-mail).
- *Determine resources needed* to make sure that resources will be available when required.
- *Communicate* to make sure that everyone in the operation knows what to do if disaster strikes.

One response to the threat of such large-scale failures has been a rise in the number of companies offering 'replacement office' operations. These are fully equipped offices, often with access to a company's current management information and with normal Internet and telephone communications links. They are fully working offices but with no people. Should a customer's main operation be affected by a disaster, business can continue in the replacement facility within days or even hours. The provision of this type of replacement office is, in effect, a variation of the 'redundancy' approach to reducing the impact of failure that was discussed earlier in this chapter.

Summary answers to key questions

Check and improve your understanding of this chapter using self assessment questions and a personalised study plan, audio and video downloads, and an eBook – all at ***www.myomlab.com.***

➤ What is risk management?

- Risk management is about things going wrong and what operations can do to stop things going wrong. Or, more formally, 'the process which aims to help organizations understand, evaluate and take action on all their risks with a view to increasing the probability of their success and reducing the likelihood of failure'.
- It consists of four broad activities:
  - Understanding what failures could occur.
  - Preventing failures occurring.
  - Minimizing the negative consequences of failure (called risk 'mitigation').
  - Recovering from failures when they do occur.

➤ How can operations assess the potential causes of, and risks from failure?

- There are several causes of operations failure including design failures, facilities failure, staff failure, supplier failure, customer failure and environmental disruption.
- There are three ways of measuring failure. 'Failure rates' indicate how often a failure is likely to occur. 'Reliability' measures the chances of a failure occurring. 'Availability' is the amount of available and useful operating time left after taking account of failures.

- Failure over time is often represented as a failure curve. The most common form of this is the so-called 'bath-tub curve' which shows the chances of failure being greater at the beginning and end of the life of a system or part of a system.
- Failure analysis mechanisms include accident investigation, product liability, complaint analysis, critical incident analysis, and failure mode and effect analysis (FMEA).

➤ How can failures be prevented?

- There are four major methods of improving reliability: designing out the fail points in the operation, building redundancy into the operation, 'fail-safeing' some of the activities of the operation, and maintenance of the physical facilities in the operation.
- Maintenance is the most common way operations attempt to improve their reliability, with three broad approaches. The first is running all facilities until they break down and then repairing them, the second is regularly maintaining the facilities even if they have not broken down, and the third is to monitor facilities closely to try to predict when breakdown might occur.
- Two specific approaches to maintenance have been particularly influential: total productive maintenance (TPM) and reliability-centred maintenance (RCM).

➤ How can operations mitigate the effects of failure?

- Risk, or failure, mitigation means isolating a failure from its negative consequences.
- Risk mitigation actions include:
  - Mitigation planning.
  - Economic mitigation.
  - Containment (spatial and temporal).
  - Loss reduction.
  - Substitution.

➤ How can operations recover from the effects of failure?

- Recovery can be enhanced by a systematic approach to discovering what has happened to cause failure, acting to inform, contain and follow up the consequences of failure, learning to find the root cause of the failure and preventing it taking place again, and planning to avoid the failure occurring in the future.
- The idea of 'business continuity' planning is a common form of recovery planning.

Case study
The Chernobyl failure[13]

At 1.24 in the early hours of Saturday morning on 26 April 1986, the worst accident in the history of commercial nuclear power generation occurred. Two explosions in quick succession blew off the 1,000-tonne concrete sealing cap of the Chernobyl-4 nuclear reactor. Molten core fragments showered down on the immediate area and fission products were released into the atmosphere. The accident cost probably hundreds of lives and contaminated vast areas of land in Ukraine.

Many reasons probably contributed to the disaster. Certainly the design of the reactor was not new – around 30 years old at the time of the accident – and had been

Source: © Vladimir Repik/Reuters/Corbis

conceived before the days of sophisticated computer-controlled safety systems. Because of this, the reactor's emergency-handling procedures relied heavily on the skill of the operators. This type of reactor also had a tendency to run 'out of control' when operated at low power. For this reason, the operating procedures for the reactor strictly prohibited it being operated below 20 per cent of its maximum power. It was mainly a combination of circumstance and human error which caused the failure, however. Ironically, the events which led up to the disaster were designed to make the reactor safer. Tests, devised by a specialist team of engineers, were being carried out to evaluate whether the emergency core cooling system (ECCS) could be operated during the 'free-wheeling' run-down of the turbine generator, should an off-site power failure occur. Although this safety device had been tested before, it had not worked satisfactorily and new tests of the modified device were to be carried out with the reactor operating at reduced power throughout the test period. The tests were scheduled for the afternoon of Friday, 25 April 1986 and the plant power reduction began at 1.00 pm. However, just after 2.00 pm, when the reactor was operating at about half its full power, the Kiev controller requested that the reactor should continue supplying the grid with electricity. In fact it was not released from the grid until 11.10 that night. The reactor was due to be shut down for its annual maintenance on the following Tuesday and the Kiev controller's request had in effect shrunk the 'window of opportunity' available for the tests.

The following is a chronological account of the hours up to the disaster, together with an analysis by James Reason, which was published in the *Bulletin of the British Psychological Society* the following year. Significant operator actions are italicized. These are of two kinds: *errors* (indicated by an '*E*') and *procedural violations* (marked with a '*V*').

25 April 1986

1.00 pm Power reduction started with the intention of achieving 25 per cent power for test conditions.

2.00 pm ECCS disconnected from primary circuit. (This was part of the test plan.)

2.05 pm Kiev controller asked the unit to continue supplying grid. *The ECCS was not reconnected (V)*. (This particular violation is not thought to have contributed materially to the disaster, but it is indicative of a lax attitude on the part of the operators toward the observance of safety procedures.)

11.10 pm The unit was released from the grid and continued power reduction to achieve the 25 per cent power level planned for the test programme.

26 April 1986

12.28 am *Operator seriously undershot the intended power setting (E)*. The power dipped to a dangerous one per cent. (The operator had switched off the 'auto-pilot' and had tried to achieve the desired level by manual control.)

1.00 am After a long struggle, the reactor power was finally stabilized at 7 per cent – well below the intended level and well into the low-power danger zone. *At this point, the experiment should have been abandoned, but it was not (E). This was the most serious mistake (as opposed to violation)*: it meant that all subsequent activity would be conducted within the reactor's zone of maximum instability. This was apparently not appreciated by the operators.

1.03 am *All eight pumps were started (V)*. The safety regulations limited the maximum number of pumps in use at any one time to six. This showed a profound misunderstanding of the physics of the reactor. The consequence was that the increased water flow (and reduced steam fraction) absorbed more neutrons, causing more control rods to be withdrawn to sustain even this low level of power.

1.19 am *The feedwater flow was increased threefold (V)*. The operators appear to have been attempting to cope with a falling steam-drum pressure and water level. The result of their actions, however, was to further reduce the amount of steam passing through the core, causing yet more control rods to be withdrawn. *They also overrode the steam-drum automatic shut-down (V)*. The effect of this was to strip the reactor of one of its automatic safety systems.

1.22 am The shift supervisor requested printout to establish how many control rods were actually in the core. The printout indicated only six to eight rods remaining. It was strictly forbidden to operate the reactor with fewer than twelve rods. *Yet the shift supervisor decided to continue with the tests (V)*. This was a fatal decision: the reactor was thereafter without 'brakes'.

1.23 am *The steam line valves to No 8 turbine generator were closed (V)*. The purpose of this was to establish the conditions necessary for repeated testing, but its consequence was to disconnect the automatic safety trips. This was perhaps the most serious violation of all.

1.24 am An attempt was made to 'scram' the reactor by driving in the emergency shut-off rods, but they jammed within the now-warped tubes.

1.24 am Two explosions occurred in quick succession. The reactor roof was blown off and 30 fires started in the vicinity.

1.30 am Duty firemen were called out. Other units were summoned from Pripyat and Chernobyl.

5.00 am Exterior fires had been extinguished, but the graphite fire in the core continued for several days.

The subsequent investigation into the disaster highlighted a number of significant points which contributed to it:

- The test programme was poorly worked out and the section on safety measures was inadequate. Because the ECCS was shut off during the test period, the safety of the reactor was in effect substantially reduced.
- The test plan was put into effect before being approved by the design group who were responsible for the reactor.
- The operators and the technicians who were running the experiment had different and non-overlapping skills.
- The operators, although highly skilled, had probably been told that getting the test completed before the shut-down would enhance their reputation. They were proud of their ability to handle the reactor even in unusual conditions and were aware of the rapidly reducing window of opportunity within which they had to complete the test. They had also probably 'lost any feeling for the hazards involved' in operating the reactor.
- The technicians who had designed the test were electrical engineers from Moscow. Their objective was to solve a complex technical problem. In spite of having designed the test procedures, they probably would not know much about the operation of the nuclear power station itself.

Again, in the words of James Reason: *'Together, they made a dangerous mixture: a group of single-minded but non-nuclear engineers directing a team of dedicated but over-confident operators. Each group probably assumed that the other knew what it was doing. And both parties had little or no understanding of the dangers they were courting, or of the system they were abusing.'*

Questions

1 What were the root causes which contributed to the ultimate failure?

2 How could failure planning have helped prevent the disaster?

Problems and applications

These problems and applications will help to improve your analysis of operations. You can find more practice problems as well as worked examples and guided solutions on MyOMLab at ***www.myomlab.com.***

1 *'We have a test bank where we test batches of 100 of our products continuously for 7 days and nights. This week only 3 failed, the first after 10 hours, the second after 72 hours, and the third after 1,020 hours.'*

What is the failure rate in percentage terms and in time terms for this product?

2 An automatic testing process takes samples of ore from mining companies and subjects them to four sequential tests. The reliability of the four different test machines that perform the tasks is different. The first test machine has a reliability of 0.99, the second has a reliability of 0.92, the third has a reliability of 0.98, and the fourth a reliability of 0.95. If one of the machines stops working, the total process will stop. What is the reliability of the total process?

3 For the product testing example in Problem 1, what is the mean time between failures (MTBF) for the products?

4 Conduct a survey amongst colleagues, friends and acquaintances of how they cope with the possibility that their computers might 'fail', either in terms of ceasing to operate effectively, or in losing data. Discuss how the concept of redundancy applies in such failure.

5 In terms of its effectiveness at managing the learning process, how does a university detect failures? What could it do to improve its failure detection processes?

Selected further reading

Dhillon, B.S. (2002) *Engineering Maintenance: A Modern Approach*, CRC Press, Boca Raton, Fla. A comprehensive book for the enthusiastic that stresses the 'cradle-to-grave' aspects of maintenance.

Li, Jun | Yu, Kui-Long | Wang, Liang-Xi | Song, Hai-Jun Zhuangjiabing Gongcheng Xueyuan Xuebao (2007) Research on operational risk management for equipment, *Journal of Academy of Armored Force Engineering*, vol. 21, no. 2, 8–11. Not as dull as it sounds. Deals with risks in military operations including complex equipment systems.

Regester, M. and Larkin, J. (2005) *Risk Issues and Crisis Management: A Casebook of Best Practice*, Kogan Page. Aimed at practising managers with lots of advice. Good for getting the flavour of how it is in practice.

Smith, D.J. (2000) *Reliability, Maintainability and Risk*, Butterworth-Heinemann. A comprehensive and excellent guide to all aspects of maintenance and reliability.

Useful web sites

www.smrp.org/ Site of the Society for Maintenance and Reliability Professionals. Gives an insight into practical issues.

www.sre.org/ American Society of Reliability Engineers. The newsletters give insights into reliability practice.

http://csob.berry.edu/faculty/jgrout/pokayoke.shtml The poka-yoke page of John Grout. Some great examples, tutorials, etc.

www.rspa.com/spi/SQA.html Lots of resources, involving reliability and poka-yoke.

http://sra.org/ Site of the Society for Risk Analysis. Very wide scope, but interesting.

www.hse.gov.uk/risk Health and Safety Executive of the UK government.

www.theirm.org The home page of the Institute of Risk Management.

www.opsman.org Lots of useful stuff.

Now that you have finished reading this chapter, why not visit MyOMLab at ***www.myomlab.com*** *where you'll find more learning resources to help you make the most of your studies and get a better grade?*

Chapter 20

Organizing for improvement

Key questions

- ➤ Why does improvement need organizing?
- ➤ How should the improvement effort be linked to strategy?
- ➤ What information is needed for improvement?
- ➤ What should be improvement priorities?
- ➤ How can organizational culture affect improvement?
- ➤ What are the key implementation issues?

Introduction

This is the third, and final, chapter devoted to operations improvement. It examines some of the managerial issues associated with improvement can be organized. There are no techniques as such in this chapter. Nor are all the issues dealt with easily defined. Rather it covers the 'soft' side of improvement. But do not dismiss this as in any way less important. In practice it is often the 'soft' stuff that determines the success or failure of improvement efforts. Moreover, the 'soft' stuff can be more difficult to get right than the 'hard', more technique-based, aspects of improvement. The 'hard' stuff is hard, but the 'soft' stuff is harder!

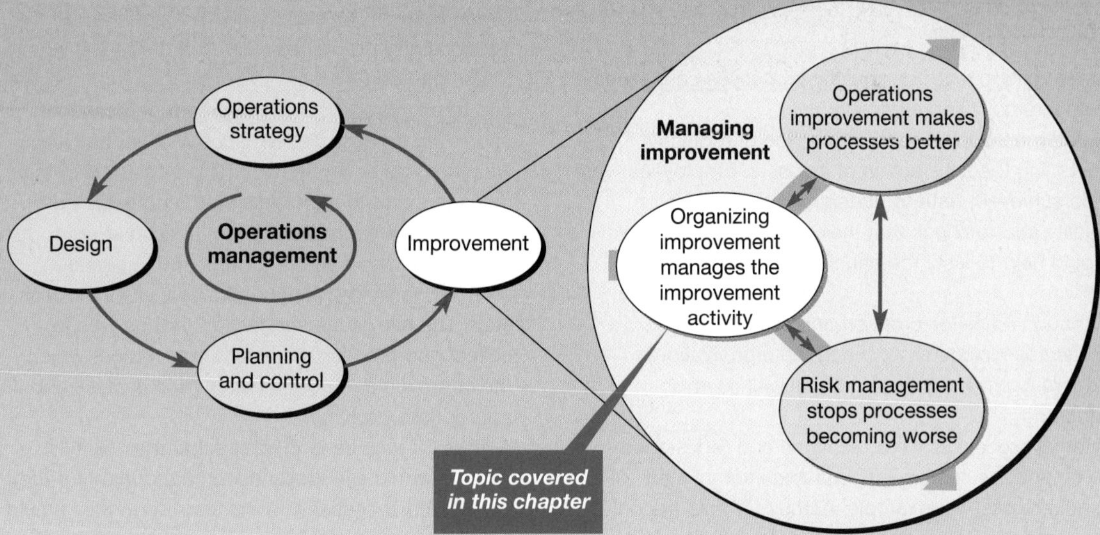

Figure 20.1 This chapter covers organizing of improvement

*Check and improve your understanding of this chapter using self assessment questions and a personalised study plan, audio and video downloads, and an eBook – all at **www.myomlab.com**.*

Operations in practice **Taxing quality**[1]

Operations effectiveness is just as important an issue in public-sector operations as it is for commercial companies. People have the right to expect that their taxes are not wasted on inefficient or inappropriate public processes. This is especially true of the tax collecting system itself. It is never a popular organization in any country, and taxpayers can be especially critical when the tax collection process is not well managed. This was very much on the minds of the Aarhus Region Customs and Tax unit (Aarhus CT) when they developed their award-winning quality initiative. The Aarhus Region is the largest of Denmark's twenty-nine local customs and tax offices. It acts as an agent for central government in collecting taxes in a professional and efficient manner while being able to respond to taxpayers' queries. Aarhus CT must, *'keep the user (customer) in focus'*, they say, *'Users must pay what is due – no more, no less and on time. But users are entitled to fair control and collection, fast and efficient case work, service and guidance, flexible employees, polite behaviour and a professional telephone service.'* The Aarhus CT approach to managing its quality initiative was built around a number of key points.

- A recognition that poor-quality processes cause waste both internally and externally.
- A determination to adopt a practice of regularly surveying the satisfaction of its users. Employees were also surveyed, both to understand their views on quality and to check that their working environment would help to instil the principles of high-quality service.
- Although a not-for-profit organization, quality measures included measuring the organization's adherence to financial targets as well as error reporting.
- Internal processes were redefined and redesigned to emphasize customer needs and internal staff requirements. For example, Aarhus CT was the only tax region in Denmark to develop an independent information process that was used to analyse customers' needs and 'prevent misunderstanding in users' perception of legislation'.

Source: Rex Features

- Internal processes were designed to allow staff the time and opportunity to develop their own skills, exchange ideas with colleagues and take on greater responsibility for management of their own work processes.
- The organization set up what it called its 'Quality Organization' (QO) structure which spanned all divisions and processes. The idea of the QO was to foster staff commitment to continuous improvement and to encourage the development of ideas for improving process performance. Within the QO was the Quality Group (QG). This consisted of four managers and four process staff, and reported directly to senior management. It also set up a number of improvement groups and suggestion groups consisting of managers as well as process staff. The role of the suggestion groups was to collect and process ideas for improvement which the improvement groups would then analyse and if appropriate implement.
- Aarhus CT was keen to stress that their Quality Groups would eventually become redundant if they were to be successful. In the short term they would maintain a stream of improvement ideas, but in the long term they should have fully integrated the idea of quality improvement into the day-to-day activities of all staff.

Why the improvement effort needs organizing

Improvement does not just happen. It needs organizing and it needs implementing. It also needs a purpose that is well thought through and clearly articulated. Although much operations improvement will take place at an operational level, and especially if one is following a continuous improvement philosophy (see previous chapter), it will be small-scale and incremental. Nevertheless, it must be placed in some kind of context. That is, it should be clear *why* improvement is happening as well as what it consists of. This means linking the improvement to the overall strategic objectives of the organization. This is why we start this chapter by thinking about improvement in a strategic context. Improvement must also be based on sound information. If the performance of operations and the processes within them are to be improved, one must first be able to define and measure exactly what we mean by 'performance'. Furthermore, benchmarking one's own activities and performance against other organizations' activities and performance can lead to valuable insights and help to quantify progress. It also helps to answer some basic improvement questions such as who should be in charge of it, when should it take place, and how one should go about ensuring that improvement really does impact the performance of the organization. This is why in this chapter we will deal with such issues as measuring performance, benchmarking, prioritization, learning and culture, and the role of systems of procedures in the implementation process.

Remember also that the issue of how improvement should be organized is not a new concern. It has been a concern of management writers for decades. For example, **W.E. Deming** (considered in Japan to be the father of quality control) asserted that quality starts with top management and is a strategic activity.[2] It is claimed that much of the success in terms of quality in Japanese industry was the result of his lectures to Japanese companies in the 1950s.[3] Deming's basic philosophy is that quality and productivity increase as 'process variability' (the unpredictability of the process) decreases. In his *14 points for quality improvement*, he emphasizes the need for statistical control methods, participation, education, openness and purposeful improvement:

1. Create constancy of purpose.
2. Adopt new philosophy.
3. Cease dependence on inspection.
4. End awarding business on price.
5. Improve constantly the system of production and service.
6. Institute training on the job.
7. Institute leadership.
8. Drive out fear.
9. Break down barriers between departments.
10. Eliminate slogans and exhortations.
11. Eliminate quotas or work standards.
12. Give people pride in their job.
13. Institute education and a self-improvement programme.
14. Put everyone to work to accomplish it.

Linking improvement to strategy

At one level, the objective of any improvement is obvious – it tries to make things better! But, does this mean better in every way or better in some specific manner? And how much better does better mean? This is why we need some more general framework to put any

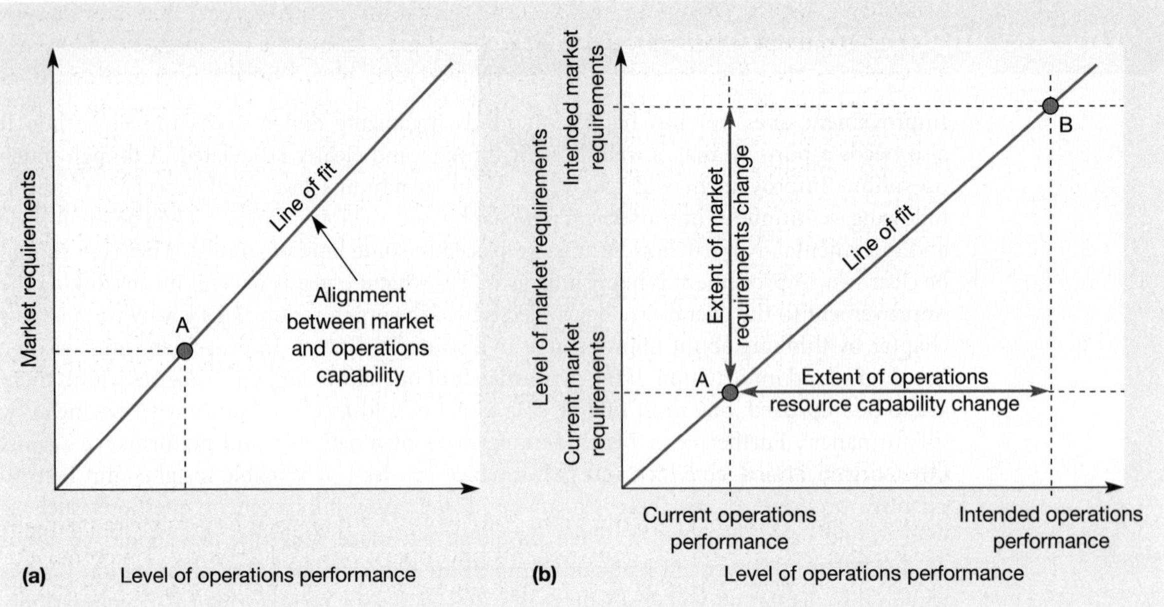

Figure 20.2 In operations improvement should achieve 'fit' between market requirements and operations performance

organization's improvement efforts into a broader context, preferably one that brings together an overall operation's performance with its market objectives. After all, at a strategic level, the whole purpose of operations improvement is to make operations performance better serve its markets. Figure 20.2(a) illustrates this idea by showing diagrammatically the approximate alignment or 'fit' between an operation's performance and the requirements of its markets.

The vertical dimension represents the level of market requirements either because they reflect the intrinsic needs of customers or because their expectations have been shaped by the firm's marketing activity. This includes such factors as the strength of brand and reputation, the degree of market differentiation and the extent of plausible market promises. Moving along this dimension indicates a broadly enhanced level of market performance. The horizontal scale represents the level of the organization's operations performance. This includes such things as its ability to achieve its competitive objectives and the efficiency with which it uses its resources. Again, moving along the dimension indicates a broadly enhanced level of operations performance and therefore operations capabilities. Be careful, however, in using this diagrammatic representation. It is a conceptual model rather than a practical tool. We have deliberately been vague in calibrating or even defining precisely the two axes in the figure. The model is intended merely to illustrate some ideas around the concept of strategic improvement.

In terms of the framework illustrated in Figure 20.2(a), improvement means three things.

1 *Achieving 'alignment'* – This means achieving an approximate balance between 'required market performance' and 'actual operations performance'. So when alignment is achieved a firm's customers do not need, or expect, levels of operations performance which it is unable to supply. Nor does the firm have operations strengths which are either inappropriate for market needs or remain unexploited in the market. The diagonal line in Figure 20.2(a) therefore represents a **'line of fit'** with market and operations in balance.

Line of fit

2 *Achieving 'sustainable' alignment* – It is not enough to achieve some degree of alignment to a single point in time. It also has to be sustained over time. So, asking the question 'how good are our operations at delivering the performance which our market requires?' is necessary but not sufficient over the long term. Equally important questions are 'how

could the market change and make current performance inadequate?' and 'how can we develop our operations processes so that they could adapt to the new market conditions?'

3 *Improving overall performance* – If the requirements placed on the organization by its markets are relatively undemanding, then the corresponding level of operations performance will not need to be particularly high. While the more demanding the level of market requirements, the greater will have to be the level of operations performance. But most firms would see their overall strategic objectives as achieving alignment at a level that implies some degree of long-term competitive success. In Figure 20.2(b) point A represents alignment at a low level, while point B represents alignment at a higher level. The assumption in most firms' operations strategies is that point B is a more desirable position than point A because it is more likely to represent a financially successful position. High levels of market performance, achieved as a result of high levels of operations performance being generally more difficult for competitors to match.

Deviating from the line of fit

During the improvement path from A to B in Figure 20.2 it may not be possible to maintain the balance between market requirements and operations performance. Sometimes the market may expect something that the operation cannot (temporarily) deliver. Sometimes operations may have capabilities that cannot be exploited in the market. At a strategic level, there are risks deriving from any deviation from the 'line of fit'. For example, delays in the improvement to a new web site could mean that customers do not receive the level of service they were promised. This is shown as position X in Figure 20.3. Under these circumstances, the risk to the organization is that its reputation (or brand) will suffer because market expectations exceed the operation's capability to perform at the appropriate level. At other times, the operation may make improvements before they could be fully exploited in the market. For example, the same online retailer may have improved its web site so that it can offer extra services, such as the ability to customize products, before those products have been stocked in its distribution centre. This means that, although an improvement to its ordering processes has been made, problems elsewhere in the company prevent the improvement from giving value to the company. This is represented by point Y on Figure 20.3. In both instances, improvement activity needs to move the operation back to the line of fit.

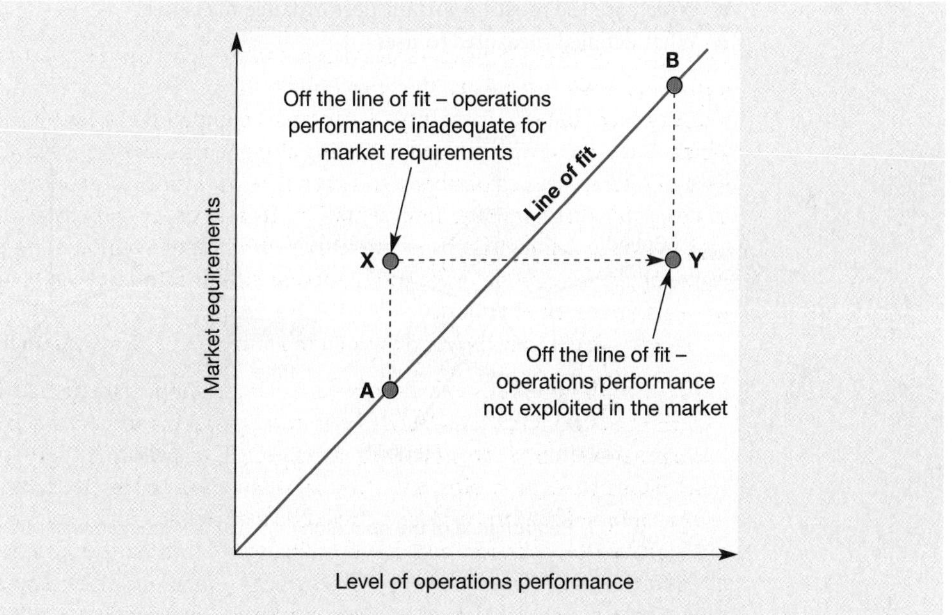

Figure 20.3 Deviation from the 'line of fit' between market requirements and operations performance can expose the operation to risk

Information for improvement

Performance measurement

Before operations managers can devise their approach to the improvement of their operations, they need to know how good they are already. The urgency, direction and priorities of improvement will be determined partly by whether the current performance of an operation is judged to be good, bad or indifferent. Therefore all operations need some kind of **performance measurement** as a prerequisite for improvement.

Performance measurement

Polar diagram

Performance measurement is the process of *quantifying action*, where measurement means the process of quantification and the performance of the operation is assumed to derive from actions taken by its management.[4] Performance here is defined as the degree to which an operation fulfils the five performance objectives at any point in time, in order to satisfy its customers. Some kind of *performance measurement* is a prerequisite for judging whether an operation is good, bad or indifferent. Without performance measurement, it would be impossible to exert any control over an operation on an ongoing basis. A performance measurement system that gives no help to ongoing improvement is only partially effective. The **polar diagrams** (which we introduced in Chapter 2) in Figure 20.4 illustrate this concept. The five performance objectives which we have used throughout this book can be regarded as the dimensions of overall performance that satisfy customers. The market's needs and expectations of each performance objective will vary. The extent to which an operation meets market requirements will also vary. In addition, market requirements and the operation's performance could change over time. In Figure 20.4 the operation is originally almost meeting the requirements of the market as far as quality and flexibility are concerned, but is under-performing on its speed, dependability and cost. Sometime later the operation has improved its speed and cost to match market requirements but its flexibility no longer matches market requirements, not because it has deteriorated in an absolute sense but because the requirements of the market have changed.

Performance measurement, as we are treating it here, concerns three generic issues.

- What factors to include as performance measures?
- Which are the most important performance measures?
- What detailed measures to use?

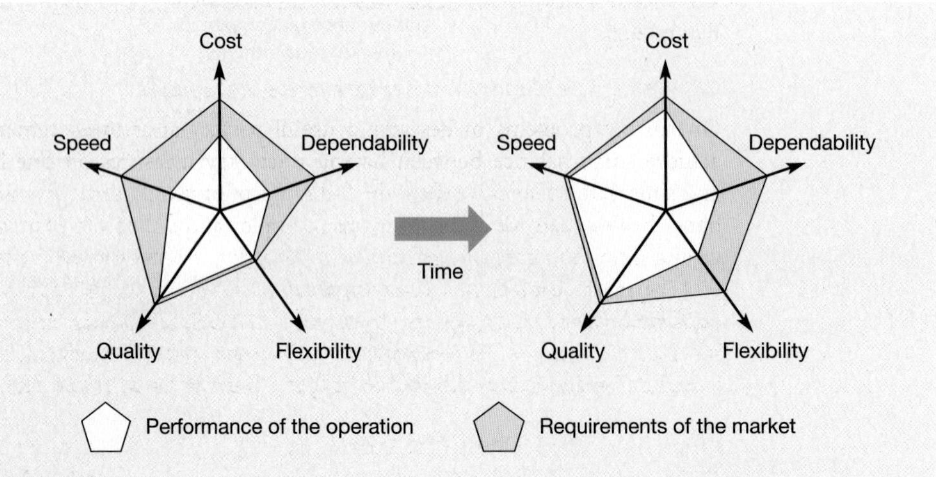

Figure 20.4 Customers' needs and the operation's performance might both change over time

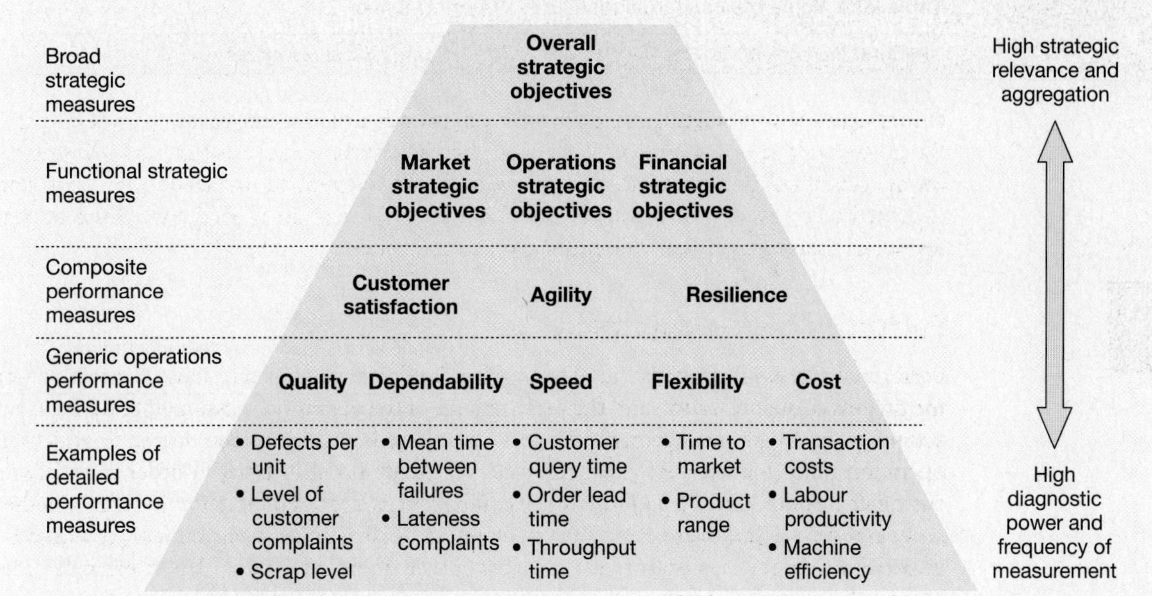

Figure 20.5 Performance measures can involve different levels of aggregation

What factors to include as performance measures?

The five generic performance objectives, quality, speed, dependability, flexibility and cost, can be broken down into more detailed measures, or they can be aggregated into 'composite' measures, such as 'customer satisfaction', 'overall service level', or 'operations agility'. These composite measures may be further aggregated by using measures such as 'achieve market objectives', 'achieve financial objectives', 'achieve operations objectives' or even 'achieve overall strategic objectives'. The more aggregated performance measures have greater strategic relevance insomuch as they help to draw a picture of the overall performance of the business, although by doing so they necessarily include many influences outside those that operations performance improvement would normally address. The more detailed performance measures are usually monitored more closely and more often, and although they provide a limited view of an operation's performance, they do provide a more descriptive and complete picture of what should be and what is happening within the operation. In practice, most organizations will choose to use performance targets from throughout the range. This idea is illustrated in Figure 20.5.

Choosing the important performance measures

Key performance indicators

One of the problems of devising a useful performance measurement system is trying to achieve some balance between having a few key measures on one hand (straightforward and simple, but may not reflect the full range of organizational objectives), and, on the other hand, having many detailed measures (complex and difficult to manage, but capable of conveying many nuances of performance). Broadly, a compromise is reached by making sure that there is a clear link between the operation's overall strategy, the most important (or '**key**') **performance indicators** (KPIs) that reflect strategic objectives, and the bundle of detailed measures that are used to 'flesh out' each key performance indicator. Obviously, unless strategy is well defined then it is difficult to 'target' a narrow range of key performance indicators.

What detailed measures to use?

The five performance objectives – quality, speed, dependability, flexibility and cost – are really composites of many smaller measures. For example, an operation's cost is derived from many factors which could include the purchasing efficiency of the operation, the efficiency

Table 20.1 Some typical partial measures of performance

Performance objective	*Some typical measures*
Quality	Number of defects per unit Level of customer complaints Scrap level Warranty claims Mean time between failures Customer satisfaction score
Speed	Customer query time Order lead time Frequency of delivery Actual *versus* theoretical throughput time Cycle time
Dependability	Percentage of orders delivered late Average lateness of orders Proportion of products in stock Mean deviation from promised arrival Schedule adherence
Flexibility	Time needed to develop new products/services Range of products/services Machine changeover time Average batch size Time to increase activity rate Average capacity/maximum capacity Time to change schedules
Cost	Minimum delivery time/average delivery time Variance against budget Utilization of resources Labour productivity Added value Efficiency Cost per operation hour

with which it converts materials, the productivity of its staff, the ratio of direct to indirect staff, and so on. All of these measures individually give a partial view of the operation's cost performance, and many of them overlap in terms of the information they include. However, each of them does give a perspective on the cost performance of an operation that could be useful either to identify areas for improvement or to monitor the extent of improvement. If an organization regards its 'cost' performance as unsatisfactory, disaggregating it into 'purchasing efficiency', 'operations efficiency', 'staff productivity', etc. might explain the root cause of the poor performance. Table 20.1 shows some of the partial measures which can be used to judge an operation's performance.

The balanced scorecard approach

Generally operations performance measures have been broadening in their scope. It is now generally accepted that the scope of measurement should, at some level, include external as well as internal, long-term as well as short-term, and 'soft' as well as 'hard' measures. The best-known manifestation of this trend is the '**balanced scorecard**' approach taken by Kaplan and Norton.

The balanced scorecard approach brings together the elements that reflect a business's strategic position

> *'The balanced scorecard retains traditional financial measures. But financial measures tell the story of past events, an adequate story for industrial age companies for which investments in long-term capabilities are customer relationships were not critical for success. These financial measures are inadequate, however, for guiding and evaluating the journey that information age companies must make to create future value through investment in customers, suppliers, employees, processes, technology, and innovation.'*[5]

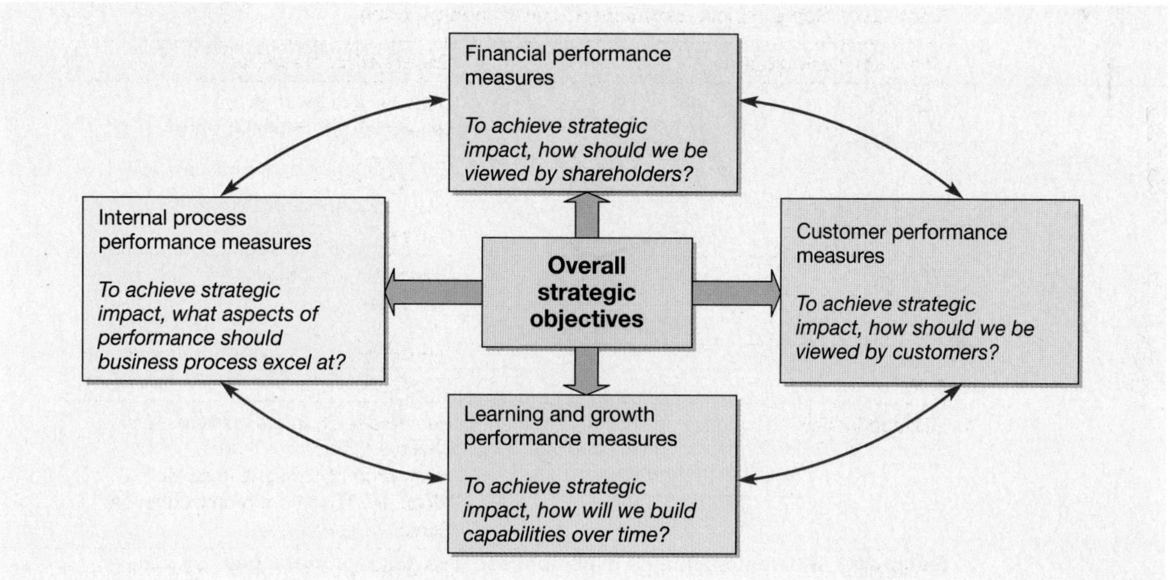

Figure 20.6 The measures used in the balanced scorecard

As well as including financial measures of performance, in the same way as traditional performance measurement systems, the balanced scorecard approach, also attempts to provide the important information that is required to allow the overall strategy of an organization to be reflected adequately in specific performance measures. In addition to financial measures of performance, it also includes more operational measures of customer satisfaction, internal processes, innovation and other improvement activities. In doing so it measures the factors behind financial performance which are seen as the key drivers of future financial success. In particular, it is argued that a balanced range of measures enables managers to address the following questions (see Figure 20.6).

- How do we look to our shareholders (financial perspective)?
- What must we excel at (internal process perspective)?
- How do our customers see us (the customer perspective)?
- How can we continue to improve and build capabilities (the learning and growth perspective)?

The balanced scorecard attempts to bring together the elements that reflect a business's strategic position, including product or service quality measures, product and service development times, customer complaints, labour productivity, and so on. At the same time it attempts to avoid performance reporting becoming unwieldy by restricting the number of measures and focusing especially on those seen to be essential. The advantages of the approach are that it presents an overall picture of the organization's performance in a single report, and by being comprehensive in the measures of performance it uses, encourages companies to take decisions in the interests of the whole organization rather than sub-optimizing around narrow measures. Developing a balanced scorecard is a complex process and is now the subject of considerable debate. One of the key questions that have to be considered is how specific measures of performance should be designed. Inadequately designed performance measures can result in dysfunctional behaviour, so teams of managers are often used to develop a scorecard which reflects their organization's specific needs.

Setting target performance

A performance measure means relatively little until it is compared against some kind of target. Knowing that only one document in five hundred is sent out to customers containing an error, tells us relatively little unless we know whether this is better or worse than we were

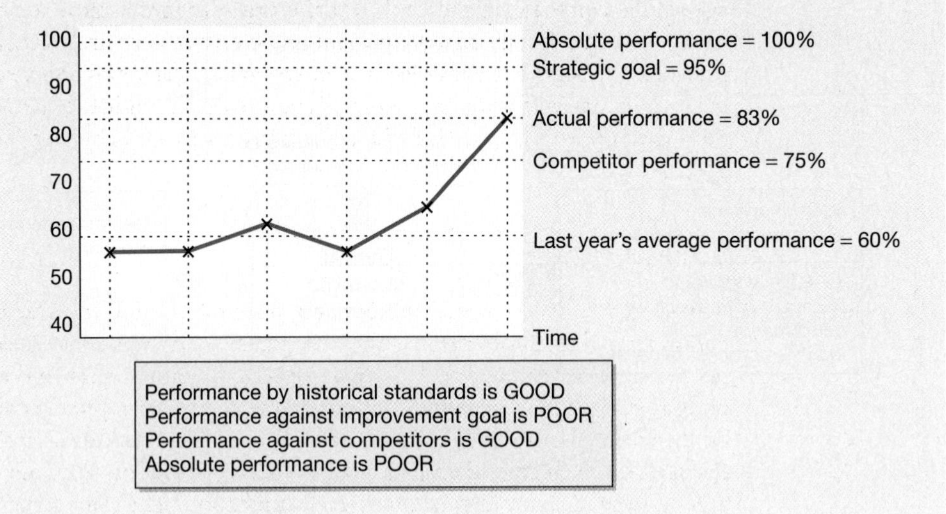

Figure 20.7 Different standards of comparison give different messages

achieving previously, and whether it is better or worse than other similar operations (especially competitors) are achieving. Setting performance targets transforms performance measures into performance 'judgements'. Several approaches to setting targets can be used, including the following.

- *Historically based targets* – targets that compare current against previous performance.
- *Strategic targets* – targets set to reflect the level of performance that is regarded as appropriate to achieve strategic objectives.
- *External performance-based targets* – targets set to reflect the performance that is achieved by similar, or competitor, external operations.
- *Absolute performance targets* – targets based on the theoretical upper limit of performance.

One of the problems in setting targets is that different targets can give very different messages regarding the improvement being achieved. So, for example, in Figure 20.7, one of an operation's performance measures is 'delivery' (in this case defined as the proportion of orders delivered on-time). The performance for one month has been measured at 83 per cent, but any judgement regarding performance will be dependent on the performance targets. Using a *historical* target, when compared to last year's performance of 60 per cent, this month's performance of 83 per cent is good. But, if the operation's *strategy* calls for a 95 per cent delivery performance, the actual performance of 83 per cent looks decidedly poor. The company may also be concerned with how they perform against *competitors*' performance. If competitors are currently averaging delivery performances of around 80 per cent the company's performance looks rather good. Finally, the more ambitious managers within the company may wish to at least try and seek perfection. Why not, they argue, use an *absolute* performance standard of 100 per cent delivery on time? Against this standard the company's actual 83 per cent again looks disappointing.

Performance measurement and performance management

It is worth noting the difference between performance *measurement*, which we describe here, and performance *management*. They are closely related (and sometimes are confused with each other). Performance management is broader than performance measurement. It is the 'process of assessing progress toward achieving predetermined goals. It involves building on that process, adding the relevant communication and action on the progress achieved against these predetermined goals. It helps organizations achieve their strategic goals'.[6] The objectives of performance management are to ensure coordination and coherence between individual, process or team objectives and overall strategic and organizational objectives. But more than that, performance management attempts to influence decisions, behaviours and skills development so that individuals and processes are better equipped to meet strategic objectives.

Benchmarking

Benchmarking, is 'the process of learning from others' and involves comparing one's own performance or methods against other comparable operations. It is a broader issue than setting performance targets, and includes investigating other organizations' operations practice in order to derive ideas that could contribute to performance improvement. Its rationale is based on the idea that (a) problems in managing processes are almost certainly shared by processes elsewhere, and (b) that there is probably another operation somewhere that has developed a better way of doing things. For example, a bank might learn some things from a supermarket about how it could cope with demand fluctuations during the day. **Benchmarking** is essentially about stimulating creativity in improvement practice.

Benchmarking is the process of learning from others

Types of benchmarking

There are many different types of benchmarking (which are not necessarily mutually exclusive), some of which are listed below:

- *Internal benchmarking* is a comparison between operations or parts of operations which are within the same total organization. For example, a large motor vehicle manufacturer with several factories might choose to benchmark each factory against the others.
- *External benchmarking* is a comparison between an operation and other operations which are part of a different organization.
- *Non-competitive benchmarking* is benchmarking against external organizations which do not compete directly in the same markets.
- *Competitive benchmarking* is a comparison directly between competitors in the same, or similar, markets.
- *Performance benchmarking* is a comparison between the levels of achieved performance in different operations. For example, an operation might compare its own performance in terms of some or all of our performance objectives – quality, speed, dependability, flexibility and cost – against other organizations' performance in the same dimensions.
- *Practice benchmarking* is a comparison between an organization's operations practices, or way of doing things, and those adopted by another operation. For example, a large retail store might compare its systems and procedures for controlling stock levels with those used by another department store.

Benchmarking as an improvement tool

Although benchmarking has become popular, some businesses have failed to derive maximum benefit from it. Partly this may be because there are some misunderstandings as to what benchmarking actually entails. First, it is not a 'one-off' project. It is best practised as a continuous process of comparison. Second, it does not provide 'solutions'. Rather, it provides ideas and information that can lead to solutions. Third, it does not involve simply copying or imitating other operations. It is a process of learning and adapting in a pragmatic manner. Fourth, it means devoting resources to the activity. Benchmarking cannot be done without some investment, but this does not necessarily mean allocating exclusive responsibility to a set of highly paid managers. In fact, there can be advantages in organizing staff at all levels to investigate and collate information from benchmarking targets.

Critical commentary

It can be argued that there is a fundamental flaw in the whole concept of benchmarking. Operations that rely on others to stimulate their creativity, especially those that are in search of 'best practice', are always limiting themselves to currently accepted methods of operating or currently accepted limits to performance. In other words, benchmarking leads companies only as far as others have gone. 'Best practice' is not 'best' in the sense that it cannot be bettered, it is only 'best' in the sense that it is the best one can currently find. Indeed accepting what is currently defined as 'best' may prevent operations from ever making the radical breakthrough or improvement that takes the concept of 'best' to a new and fundamentally improved level. This argument is closely related to the concept of breakthrough improvement discussed later in this chapter. Furthermore, methods or performance levels that are appropriate in one operation may not be in another. Because one operation has a set of successful practices in the way it manages its process does not mean that adopting those same practices in another context will prove equally successful. It is possible that subtle differences in the resources within a process (such as staff skills or technical capabilities) or the strategic context of an operation (for example, the relative priorities of performance objectives) will be sufficiently different to make the adoption of seemingly successful practices inappropriate.

Improvement priorities – what to start on?[7]

Improvement priorities

In Chapter 3, when discussing the 'market requirements' perspective, we identified two major influences on the way in which operations decide on their **improvement priorities**:

- the needs and preferences of customers;
- the performance and activities of competitors.

The consideration of customers' needs has particular significance in shaping the objectives of all operations. The fundamental purpose of operations is to create goods and services in such a way as to meet the needs of their customers. What customers find important, therefore, the operation should also regard as important. If customers for a particular product or service prefer low prices to wide range, then the operation should devote more energy to reducing its costs than to increasing the flexibility which enables it to provide a range of products or services. The needs and preferences of customers shape the *importance* of operations objectives within the operation.

The role of competitors is different from that of customers. Competitors are the points of comparison against which the operation can judge its performance. From a competitive viewpoint, as operations improve their performance, the improvement which matters most is that which takes the operation past the performance levels achieved by its competitors. The role of competitors then is in determining achieved *performance*.

Both importance and performance have to be brought together before any judgement can be made as to the relative priorities for improvement. Just because something is particularly important to its customers does not mean that an operation should necessarily give it immediate priority for improvement. It may be that the operation is already considerably better than its competitors at serving customers in this respect. Similarly, just because an operation is not very good at something when compared with its competitors' performance, it does not necessarily mean that it should be immediately improved. Customers may not particularly value this aspect of performance. Both importance and performance need to be viewed together to judge the prioritization of objectives.

(a) Importance scale for competitive factors	
Rating	**Description**
1	Provides a crucial advantage
2	Provides an important advantage
3	Provides a useful advantage
4	Needs to be up to good industry standards
5	Needs to be up to median industry standards
6	Needs to be within close range of rest of industry
7	Not usually important but could become so
8	Very rarely considered by customers
9	Never considered by customers

(b) Performance scale for competitive factors	
Rating	**Description**
1	Considerably better than competitors
2	Clearly better than competitors
3	Marginally better than competitors
4	Sometimes marginally better than competitors
5	About the same as most competitors
6	Slightly worse than the average of most competitors
7	Usually marginally worse than most competitors
8	Generally worse than most competitors
9	Consistently worse than competitors

Figure 20.8 Nine-point scales for judging importance and performance

Judging importance to customers

Order winners
Qualifiers
Less important

In Chapter 3 we introduced the idea of **order-winning, qualifying** and **less important** competitive factors. *Order-winning competitive factors* are those which directly win business for the operation. *Qualifying competitive factors* are those which may not win extra business if the operation improves its performance, but can certainly lose business if performance falls below a particular point, known as the qualifying level. *Less important competitive factors*, as their name implies, are those which are relatively unimportant compared with the others. In fact, to judge the relative importance of its competitive factors, an operation will usually need to use a slightly more discriminating scale. One way to do this is to take our three broad categories of competitive factors – order-winning, qualifying and less important – and to divide each category into three further points representing strong, medium and weak positions. Figure 20.8(a) illustrates such a scale.

Judging performance against competitors

At its simplest, a competitive performance standard would consist merely of judging whether the achieved performance of an operation is better than, the same, or worse than that of its competitors. However, in much the same way as the nine-point importance scale was derived, we can derive a more discriminating nine-point performance scale, as shown in Figure 20.8(b).

The importance–performance matrix

Importance–performance matrix

The priority for improvement which each competitive factor should be given can be assessed from a comparison of their importance and performance. This can be shown on an **importance–performance matrix** which, as its name implies, positions each competitive

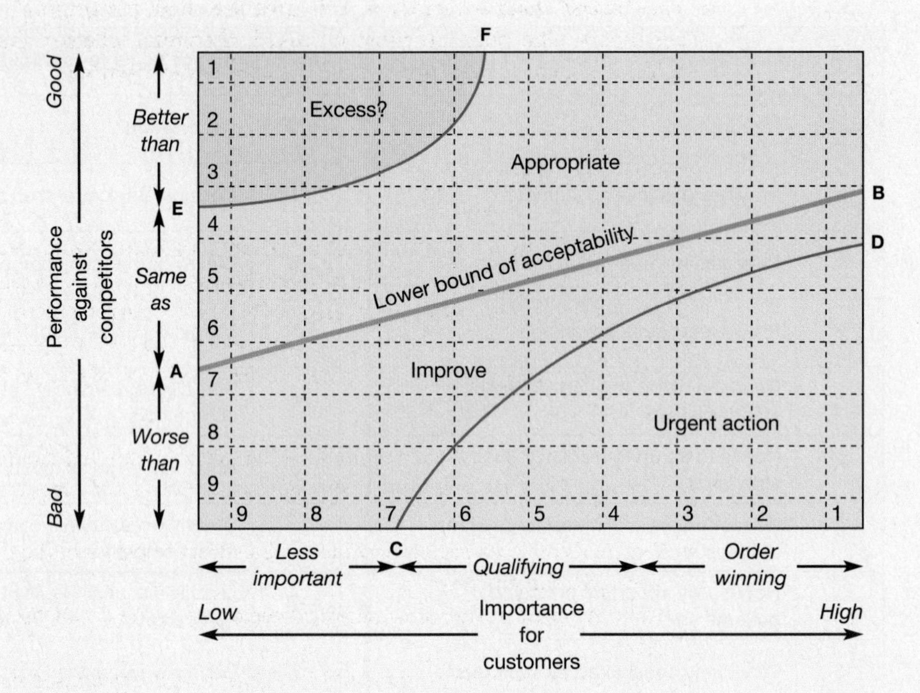

Figure 20.9 Priority zones in the importance–performance matrix

factor according to its scores or ratings on these criteria. Figure 20.9 shows an importance–performance matrix divided into zones of improvement priority. The first zone boundary is the 'lower bound of acceptability' shown as line AB in Figure 20.9. This is the boundary between acceptable and unacceptable performance. When a competitive factor is rated as relatively unimportant (8 or 9 on the importance scale), this boundary will in practice be low. Most operations are prepared to tolerate performance levels which are 'in the same ballpark' as their competitors (even at the bottom end of the rating) for unimportant competitive factors. They only become concerned when performance levels are clearly below those of their competitors. Conversely, when judging competitive factors which are rated highly (1 or 2 on the importance scale) they will be markedly less sanguine at poor or mediocre levels of performance. Minimum levels of acceptability for these competitive factors will usually be at the lower end of the 'better than competitors' class. Below this minimum bound of acceptability (AB) there is clearly a need for improvement; above this line there is no immediate urgency for any improvement. However, not all competitive factors falling below the minimum line will be seen as having the same degree of improvement priority. A boundary approximately represented by line CD represents a distinction between an urgent priority zone and a less urgent improvement zone. Similarly, above the line AB, not all competitive factors are regarded as having the same priority. The line EF can be seen as the approximate boundary between performance levels which are regarded as 'good' or 'appropriate' on one hand and those regarded as 'too good' or 'excess' on the other. Segregating the matrix in this way results in four zones which imply very different priorities:

- *The 'appropriate' zone* – competitive factors in this area lie above the lower bound of acceptability and so should be considered satisfactory.
- *The 'improve' zone* – lying below the lower bound of acceptability, any factors in this zone must be candidates for improvement.
- *The 'urgent-action' zone* – these factors are important to customers but performance is below that of competitors. They must be considered as candidates for immediate improvement.

- *The 'excess?' zone* – factors in this area are 'high-performing', but not important to customers. The question must be asked, therefore, whether the resources devoted to achieving such a performance could be used better elsewhere.

Worked example

EXL Laboratories is a subsidiary of an electronics company. It carries out research and development as well as technical problem-solving work for a wide range of companies, including companies in its own group. It is particularly keen to improve the level of service which it gives to its customers. However, it needs to decide which aspect of its performance to improve first. It has devised a list of the most important aspects of its service:

- *The quality of its technical solutions* – the perceived appropriateness by customers.
- *The quality of its communications with customers* – the frequency and usefulness of information.
- *The quality of post-project documentation* – the usefulness of the documentation which goes with the final report.
- *Delivery speed* – the time between customer request and the delivery of the final report.
- *Delivery dependability* – the ability to deliver on the promised date.
- *Delivery flexibility* – the ability to deliver the report on a revised date.
- *Specification flexibility* – the ability to change the nature of the investigation.
- *Price* – the total charge to the customer.

EXL assigns a score to each of these factors using the 1–9 scale described in Figure 20.8. After this, EXL turned their attention to judging the laboratory's performance against competitor organizations. Although they have benchmarked information for some aspects of performance, they have to make estimates for the others. Both these scores are shown in Figure 20.10.

EXL Laboratories plotted the importance and performance ratings it had given to each of its competitive factors on an importance–performance matrix. This is shown in Figure 20.11. It shows that the most important aspect of competitiveness – the ability to deliver sound technical solutions to its customers – falls comfortably within the appropriate zone. Specification flexibility and delivery flexibility are also in the appropriate zone, although only just. Both delivery speed and delivery dependability seem to be in

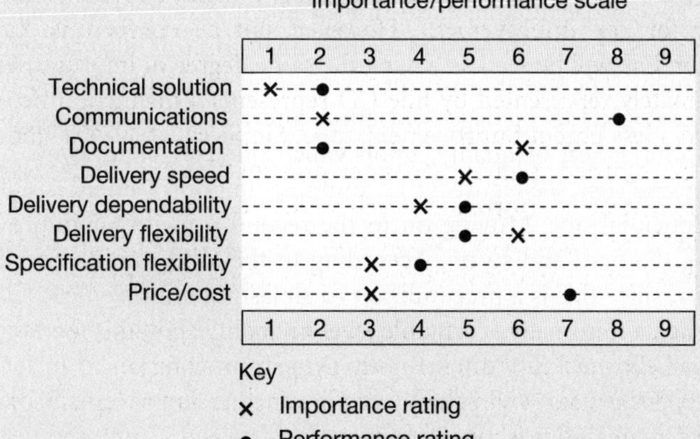

Figure 20.10 Rating 'importance to customers' and 'performance against competitors' on the nine-point scales for EXL Laboratories

→

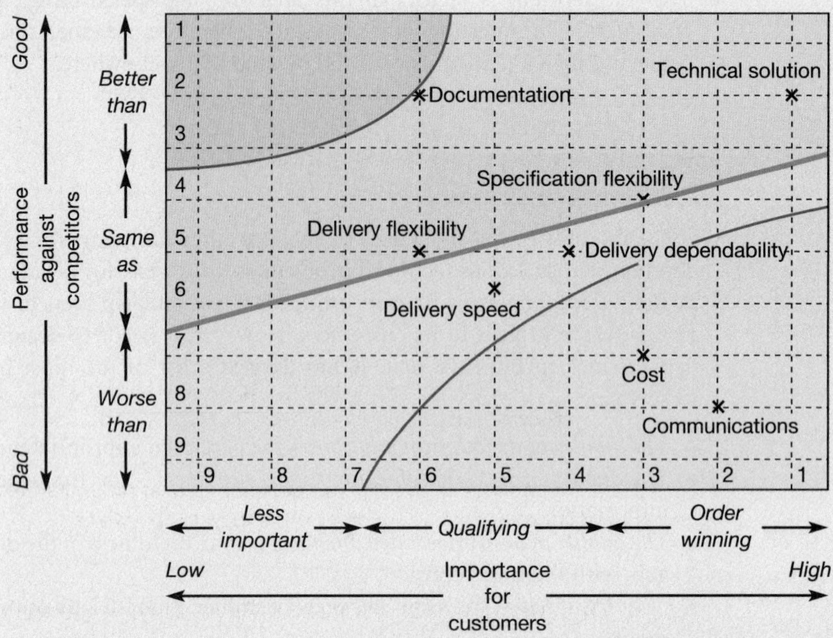

Figure 20.11 The importance–performance matrix for EXL Laboratories

need of improvement as each is below the minimum level of acceptability for their respective importance positions. However, two competitive factors, communications and cost/price, are clearly in need of immediate improvement. These two factors should therefore be assigned the most urgent priority for improvement. The matrix also indicates that the company's documentation could almost be regarded as 'too good'.

The matrix may not reveal any total surprises. The competitive factors in the 'urgent-action' zone may be known to be in need of improvement already. However, the exercise is useful for two reasons:

- It helps to discriminate between many factors which may be in need of improvement.
- The exercise gives purpose and structure to the debate on improvement priorities.

The sandcone theory

The sandcone theory holds that objectives should be prioritized in a particular order

As well as approaches that base improvement priority given on an operation's specific circumstances, some authorities believe that there is also a generic 'best' sequence of improvement. The best-known theory is called *the sandcone theory*,[8] so called because the sand is analogous to management effort and resources. Building a stable **sandcone** needs a stable foundation of quality, upon which one can build layers of dependability, speed, flexibility and cost, see Figure 20.12. Building up improvement is thus a cumulative process, not a sequential one. Moving on to the second priority for improvement does not mean dropping the first, and so on. According to the sandcone theory: the first priority should be *quality*, since this is a precondition to all lasting improvement. Only when the operation has reached a minimally acceptable level in quality should it then tackle the next issue, that of internal *dependability*. Importantly though, moving on to include dependability in the improvement process will actually require further improvement in quality. Once a critical level of dependability is reached, enough to provide some stability to the operation, the next stage is to improve the *speed* of internal throughput. But again only while continuing to improve quality and dependability further. Soon it will become evident that the most effective way to improve speed is through improvements in response *flexibility*, that is,

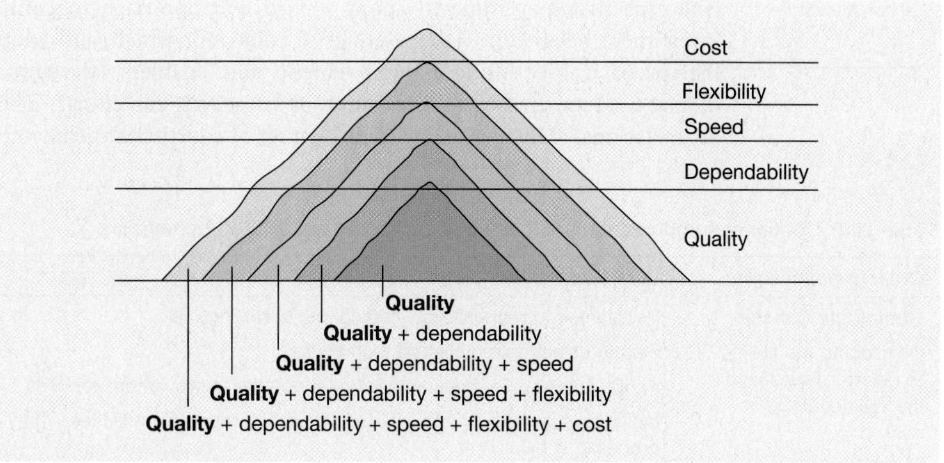

Figure 20.12 The sandcone model of improvement: cost reduction relies on a cumulative foundation of improvement in the other performance objectives

changing things within the operation faster. Again, including flexibility in the improvement process should not divert attention from continuing to work further on quality, dependability and speed. Only now, according to the sandcone theory, should *cost* be tackled head-on.

Improvement culture

Culture is the pattern of shared assumption

It is generally held by most organizational theorists that an organization's ability to improve its operations performance depends to a large extent on its '**culture**'. By 'organizational culture' we here mean '*the pattern of shared basic assumptions . . . that have worked well enough to be considered valid*',[9] or as some put it, '*the way we do things around here*'. Professor Gerry Johnson[10] is more specific, describing the elements of organizational culture as follows.

- The organization's mission and values
- Its control systems
- Its organizational structures, hierarchies, and processes
- Its power structures
- Its symbols, logos and designs including its symbols of power
- Its rituals, meetings and routines
- Its stories and myths that develop about people and events.

So, organizational culture and improvement are clearly related. A receptive organizational culture that encourages a constant search for improved ways to do things nurtures improvement. At the same time the organization's view of improvement is an important indication of its culture. But what is meant by 'an improvement culture'? Here we look at two aspects, first are the various elements that make up an improvement culture, second is the recurring theme of 'learning' as a key element of improvement culture.

Building an improvement capability

The ability to improve, especially on a continuous basis, is not something which always comes naturally to operations managers and staff. There are specific abilities, behaviours and actions which need to be consciously developed if improvement is to be sustained over the long term. Bessant and Caffyn[11] distinguish between what they call 'organizational abilities' (the capacity or aptitude to adopt a particular approach to continuous improvement), 'constituent behaviours' (the routines of behaviour which staff adopt and which reinforce the approach to continuous improvement) and 'enablers' (the procedural devices or techniques used to progress the continuous improvement effort). They identify six generic organizational abilities, each with its own set of constituent behaviours. These are identified

Table 20.2 Continuous improvement (CI) abilities and some associated behaviours

Organizational ability	*Constituent behaviours*
Getting the CI habit Developing the ability to generate sustained involvement in CI	People use formal problem-finding and solving cycle People use simple tools and techniques People use simple measurement to shape the improvement process Individuals and/or groups initiate and carry through CI activities – they participate in the process Ideas are responded to in a timely fashion – either implemented or otherwise dealt with Managers support the CI process through allocation of resources Managers recognize in formal ways the contribution of employees to CI Managers lead by example, becoming actively involved in design and implementation of CI Managers support experiment by not punishing mistakes, but instead encouraging learning from them
Focusing on CI Generating and sustaining the ability to link CI activities to the strategic goals of the company	Individuals and groups use the organization's strategic objectives to prioritize improvements Everyone is able to explain what the operation's strategy and objectives are Individuals and groups assess their proposed changes against the operation's objectives Individuals and groups monitor/measure the results of their improvement activity CI activities are an integral part of the individual's or group's work, not a parallel activity
Spreading the word Generating the ability to move CI activity across organizational boundaries	People cooperate in cross-functional groups People understand and share a holistic view (process understanding and ownership) People are oriented towards internal and external customers in their CI activity Specific CI projects with outside agencies (customers, suppliers, etc.) take place Relevant CI activities involve representatives from different organizational levels
CI on the CI system Generating the ability to manage strategically the development of CI	The CI system is continually monitored and developed There is a cyclical planning process whereby the CI system is regularly reviewed and amended There is periodic review of the CI system in relation to the organization as a whole Senior management make available sufficient resources (time, money, personnel) to support the continuing development of the CI system The CI system itself is designed to fit within the current structure and infrastructure When a major organizational change is planned, its potential impact on the CI system is assessed
Walking the talk Generating the ability to articulate and demonstrate CI's values	The 'management style' reflects commitment to CI values When something goes wrong, people at all levels look for reasons why, rather than blame individuals People at all levels demonstrate a shared belief in the value of small steps and that everyone can contribute, by themselves being actively involved in making and recognizing incremental improvements
Building the learning organization Generating the ability to learn through CI activity	Everyone learns from their experiences, both good and bad Individuals seeks out opportunities for learning/personal development Individuals and groups at all levels share their learning The organization captures and shares the learning of individuals and groups Managers accept and act on all the learning that takes place Organizational mechanisms are used to deploy what has been learned across the organization

in Table 20.2. Examples of enablers are the improvement techniques that were described in Chapter 18.

Improvement as learning

Note that many of the abilities and behaviours describes in Table 20.2 are directly or indirectly related to learning in some way. This is not surprising given that operations improvement implies some kind of intervention or change to the operation, and change will be evaluated in terms of whatever improvement occurs. This evaluation adds to our knowledge of how the operation really works, which in turn increases the chances that future interventions will also result in improvement. This idea of an improvement cycle was discussed in Chapter 18. What is important is to realize that it is a learning process, and it is crucial that improvement is organized so that it encourages, facilitates and exploits the learning that occurs during improvement. This requires us to recognize that there is a distinction between single- and double-loop learning.[12]

Single- and double-loop learning

Single-loop learning

Single-loop learning occurs when there is a repetitive and predictable link between cause and effect. Statistical process control (see Chapter 17), for example, measures output characteristics from a process, such as product weight, telephone response time, etc. These can then be used to alter input conditions, such as supplier quality, manufacturing consistency, staff training, with the intention of 'improving' the output. Every time an operational error or problem is detected, it is corrected or solved, and more is learned about the process. However, this happens without questioning or altering the underlying values and objectives of the process, which may, over time, create an unquestioning inertia that prevents it adapting to a changing environment. **Double-loop learning**, by contrast, questions the fundamental objectives or service or even the underlying culture of the operation. This kind of learning implies an ability to challenge existing operating assumptions in a fundamental way. It seeks to re-frame competitive assumptions and remain open to any changes in the competitive environment. But being receptive to new opportunities sometimes requires abandoning existing operating routines which may be difficult to achieve in practice, especially as many operations reward experience and past achievement (rather than potential) at both an individual and a group level. Figure 20.13 illustrates single and double-loop learning.

Double-loop learning

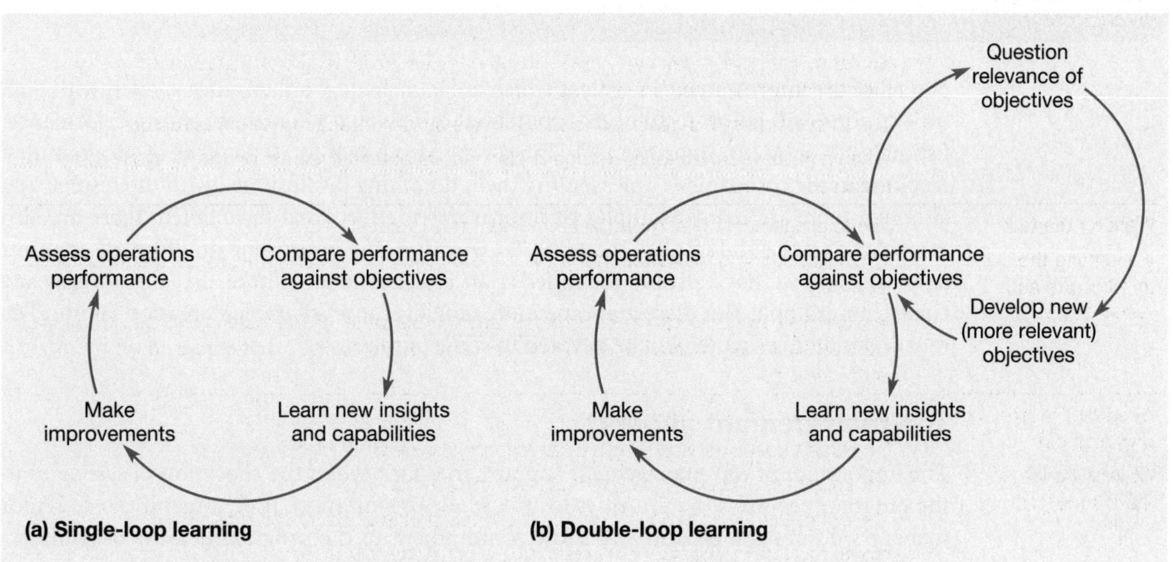

Figure 20.13 Single- and double-loop learning

Short case

Improvement at Heineken – Part II[13]

The improvement approach of Heineken's Zoeterwoude facility was described in Chapter 18. Although this description emphasized issues such as target setting and the use of techniques, of equal or more importance in making a success of the initiative was the way improvement teams were empowered, organized and motivated. In fact, before this improvement initiative, the company had started a 'cultural change' programme. *'Its aim'*, according to Wilbert Raaijmakers, the Brewery Director, *'was to move away from a command-and-control situation and evolve towards a more team-oriented organization.'* Fundamental to this was a programme to improve the skills and knowledge of individual operators through special training programmes. Nevertheless, the improvement initiative exposed a number of challenges. For example, the improvement team discovered that it was easier to motivate people to work on improvements when the demand on the plant clearly exceeded its capacity. What was more difficult was to keep them focused when the pressures of keeping up production levels were lower, such as during the winter season. In an attempt to overcome this, communication was improved so that staff were kept fully informed of future production levels and the upcoming schedule of training and maintenance activities that were planned during slumps in demand. The lesson that the improvement team learnt was that it is difficult to convince people of the necessity for change if they are not aware of the underlying reason for it. Notwithstanding these efforts it soon became evident that some groups were more ready to make changes than others. Some staff much preferred to stick with their traditional methods rather than explore how these could be improved. Similarly, some team leaders were more skilled at encouraging change than others. Many staff needed coaching and reassurance as well as more formal training on how to take ownership of problems and focus on achieving results in line with targets. Also, it was found that setting improvement targets in a step-by-step series of milestones could help to maintain the momentum of motivation.

During the improvement initiative, Heineken staff worked closely with a group of consultants (Celerant Consulting). Towards the end of the initiative, as is common in such improvement projects, the consultants gradually reduced their involvement to allow Heineken staff to take over control of the initiative. At this point there was a dip in the momentum of the improvement project. It needed the appointment of a special coordinator within the company to 'monitor, secure and audit' the various activities included in the project before it regained its momentum. Yet it did regain its momentum and, looking back over the experience, Heineken see one of the most significant outcomes from the initiative as its success in bringing home to every person in the company the realization that improvement is an ongoing process.

Implementing improvement

Not all of the improvement initiatives which are launched by organizations, often with high expectations, will go on to fulfil their potential of having a major impact on performance. Estimates of failure in improvement efforts range from half to 80 per cent of programmes, resulting in the companies implementing them becoming disillusioned with the results. Yet, although there are many examples of improvement efforts that have failed, there are also examples of successful implementations. So why do some improvement efforts disappoint? Some reasons we have already identified – an organizational culture that discourages any change for example. But there are some more tangible causes of implementation failure. The remainder of this chapter will be devoted to some of these.

Top-management support

Top-management support

The importance of **top-management support** goes far beyond the allocation of resources to the programme; it sets the priorities for the whole organization. If the organization's senior managers do not understand and show commitment to the programme, it is only understandable that others will ask why they should do so. Usually this is taken to mean that top management must:

- understand and believe in the benefits of the improvement approach
- communicate the principles and techniques of improvement
- participate in the improvement process
- formulate and maintain a clear 'improvement strategy'.

This last point is particularly important. Without thinking through the overall purpose and long-term goals of improvement it is difficult for any organization to know where it is going. An improvement strategy is necessary to provide the goals and guidelines which help to keep improvement efforts in line with strategic aims. Specifically, the improvement strategy should have something to say about the competitive priorities of the organization, the roles and improvement responsibilities of all parts of the organization, the resources available for improvement, and its overall improvement philosophy.

Senior managers may not fully understand the improvement approach

In Chapter 18, we described how there were several (related) improvement approaches. Each of these approaches is the subject of several books that describe them in great detail. There is no shortage of advice from consultants and academics as to how they should be used. Yet it is not difficult to find examples of where senior management have used one or more of these approaches without fully understanding them. The details of Six Sigma or lean, for example, are not simply technical matters. They are fundamental to how appropriate the approach could be in different contexts. Not every approach fits every set of circumstances. So understanding in detail what each approach means must be the first step in deciding whether it is appropriate.

Avoid excessive 'hype'

Operations improvement has, to some extent, become a fashion industry with new ideas and concepts continually being introduced as offering a novel way to improve business performance. There is nothing intrinsically wrong with this. Fashion stimulates and refreshes, through introducing novel ideas. Without it, things would stagnate. The problem lies not with new improvement ideas, but rather with some managers becoming victims of the process, where some new idea will entirely displace whatever went before. Most new ideas have something to say, but jumping from one fad to another will not only generate a backlash against any new idea, but also destroy the ability to accumulate the experience that comes from experimenting with each one. Avoiding becoming an improvement fashion victim is not easy. It requires that those directing the strategy process take responsibility for a number of issues.

(a) They must take responsibility for improvement as an ongoing activity, rather than becoming champions for only one specific improvement initiative.
(b) They must take responsibility for understanding the underlying ideas behind each new concept. Improvement is not 'following a recipe' or 'painting by numbers'. Unless one understands *why* improvement ideas are supposed to work, it is difficult to understand *how* they can be made to work properly.
(c) They must take responsibility for understanding the antecedents to a 'new' improvement idea, because it helps to understand it better and to judge how appropriate it may be for one's own operation.
(d) They must be prepared to adapt new ideas so that they make sense within the context of their own operation. 'One size' rarely fits all.
(e) They must take responsibility for the (often significant) education and learning effort that will be needed if new ideas are to be intelligently exploited.
(f) Above all they must avoid the over-exaggeration and hype that many new ideas attract. Although it is sometimes tempting to exploit the motivational 'pull' of new ideas

through slogans, posters and exhortations, carefully thought-out plans will always be superior in the long run, and will help avoid the inevitable backlash that follows 'over-selling' a single approach.

Short case
Work-Out at GE[14]

Source: Getty Images

The idea of including all staff in the process of improvement has formed the core of many improvement approaches. One of the best-known ways of this is the 'Work-Out' approach that originated in the US conglomerate GE. Jack Welch, the then boss of GE, reputedly developed the approach to recognize that employees were an important source of brainpower for new and creative ideas, and as a mechanism for *'creating an environment that pushes towards a relentless, endless companywide search for a better way to do everything we do'*. The Work-Out programme was seen as a way to reduce the bureaucracy often associated with improvement and *'giving every employee, from managers to factory workers, an opportunity to influence and improve GE's day-to-day operations'*. According to Welch, Work-Out was meant to help people stop *'wrestling with the boundaries, the absurdities that grow in large organizations. We're all familiar with those absurdities: too many approvals, duplication, pomposity, waste. Work-Out in essence turned the company upside down, so that the workers told the bosses what to do. That forever changed the way people behaved at the company. Work-Out is also designed to reduce, and ultimately eliminate all of the waste hours and energy that organizations like GE typically expend in performing day-to-day operations.'* GE also used what it called 'town meetings' of employees. And although proponents of Work-Out emphasize the need to modify the specifics of the approach to fit the context in which it is applied, there is a broad sequence of activities implied within the approach:

- Staff, other key stakeholders and their manager hold a meeting away from the operation (a so-called 'off-siter').
- At this meeting the manager gives the group the responsibility to solve a problem or set of problems shared by the group but which are ultimately the manager's responsibility.
- The manager then leaves and the group spend time (maybe two or three days) working on developing solutions to the problems, sometimes using outside facilitators.
- At the end of the meeting, the responsible manager (and sometimes the manager's boss) rejoins the group to be presented with its recommendations.
- The manager can respond in three ways to each recommendation; 'yes', 'no' or 'I have to consider it more'. If it is the last response the manager must clarify what further issues must be considered and how and when the decision will be made.

Work-Out programmes are expensive; outside facilitators, off-site facilities and the payroll costs of a sizeable group of people meeting away from work can be substantial, even without considering the potential disruption to everyday activities. But arguably the most important implications of adopting Work-Out are cultural. In its purest form Work-Out reinforces an underlying culture of fast (and some would claim, superficial) problem-solving. It also relies on full and near universal employee involvement and empowerment together with direct dialogue between managers and their subordinates. What distinguishes the Work-Out approach from the many other types of group-based problem-solving is fast decision-making and the idea that managers must respond immediately and decisively to team suggestions. But some claim that it is intolerant of staff and managers who are not committed to its values. In fact, it is acknowledged in GE that resistance to the process or outcome is not tolerated and that obstructing the efforts of the Work-Out process is 'a career-limiting move'.

Improvement or quality awards

Deming Prize

Malcolm Baldrige National Quality Award

European Quality Award

Various bodies have sought to stimulate improvement through establishing improvement (sometimes called 'quality') awards. The three best-known awards are the **Deming Prize**, the **Malcolm Baldrige National Quality Award** and the **European Quality Award.**

The Deming Prize

The Deming Prize was instituted by the Union of Japanese Scientists and Engineers in 1951 and is awarded to those companies, initially in Japan, but more recently opened to overseas companies, which have successfully applied 'company-wide quality control' based upon statistical quality control. There are 10 major assessment categories: policy and objectives, organization and its operation, education and its extension, assembling and disseminating of information, analysis, standardization, control, quality assurance, effects and future plans. The applicants are required to submit a detailed description of quality practices. This is a significant activity in itself and some companies claim a great deal of benefit from having done so.

The Malcolm Baldrige National Quality Award

In the early 1980s the American Productivity and Quality Center recommended that an annual prize, similar to the Deming Prize, should be awarded in America. The purpose of the awards was to stimulate American companies to improve quality and productivity, to recognize achievements, to establish criteria for a wider quality effort and to provide guidance on quality improvement. The main examination categories are: leadership, information and analysis, strategic quality planning, human resource utilization, quality assurance of products and services, quality results and customer satisfaction. The process, like that of the Deming Prize, includes a detailed application and site visits.

The EFQM Excellence Model

In 1988, 14 leading Western European companies formed the European Foundation for Quality Management (EFQM). An important objective of the EFQM is to recognize quality achievement. Because of this, it launched the European Quality Award (EQA), awarded to the most successful exponent of total quality management in Europe each year. To receive a prize, companies must demonstrate that their approach to total quality management has contributed significantly to satisfying the expectations of customers, employees and others with an interest in the company for the past few years. In 1999, the model on which the European Quality Award was based was modified and renamed **The EFQM Excellence Model or Business Excellence Model**. The changes made were not fundamental but did attempt to reflect some new areas of management and quality thinking (for example, partnerships and innovation) and placed more emphasis on customer and market focus. It is based on the idea that the outcomes of quality management in terms of what it calls 'people results', 'customer results', 'society results' and 'key performance results' are achieved through a number of 'enablers'. These enablers are leadership and constancy of purpose, policy and strategy, how the organization develops its people, partnerships and resources, and the way it organizes its processes. These ideas are incorporated in the EFQM Excellence Model as shown in Figure 20.14. The five enablers are concerned with how results are being achieved, while the four 'results' are concerned with what the company has achieved and is achieving.

The EFQM Excellence Model, or Business Excellence Model

Self-assessment

Self-assessment

The European Foundation for Quality Management (EFQM) defines **self-assessment** as *'a comprehensive, systematic, and regular review of an organization's activities and results referenced against a model of business excellence'*, in its case the model shown in Figure 20.14. The main advantage of using such models for self-assessment seems to be that companies find it easier to understand some of the more philosophical concepts of TQM when they are translated into specific areas, questions and percentages. Self-assessment also allows organizations to measure their progress in changing their organization and in achieving the benefits of TQM. An important aspect of self-assessment is an organization's ability to judge the relative importance of the assessment categories to its own circumstances. The EFQM Excellence Model originally placed emphasis on a generic set of weighting for each of its nine categories. With the increasing importance of self-assessment, the EFQM moved to encourage organizations using its model to allocate their own weightings in a rational and systematic manner.

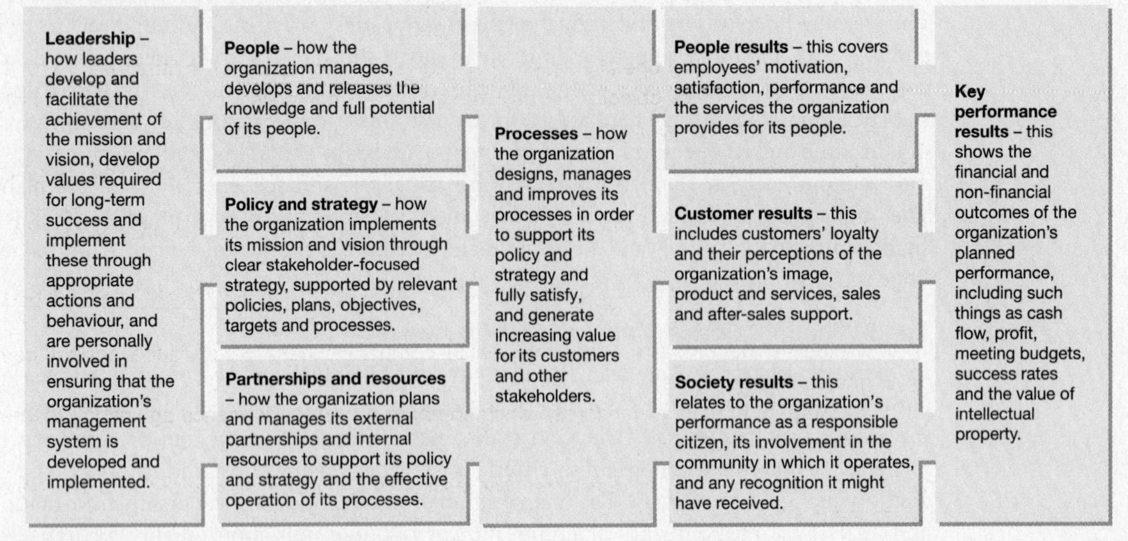

Figure 20.14 The EFQM Excellence Model

Summary answers to key questions

Check and improve your understanding of this chapter using self assessment questions and a personalised study plan, audio and video downloads, and an eBook – all at ***www.myomlab.com.***

➤ Why does improvement need organizing?

- Improvement does not just happen by itself. It needs organizing, information must be gathered so that improvement is treating the most appropriate issues, responsibility for looking after the improvement effort must be allocated, and resources must be allocated. It must also be linked to the organization's overall strategy. Without these decisions, it is unlikely that real improvement will take place.

➤ How should the improvement effort be linked to strategy?

- At a strategic level, the whole purpose of operations improvement is to make operations performance better serve its markets. Therefore there should be approximate alignment or 'fit' between an operation's performance and the requirements of its markets. In fact, improvement should do three things to achieve this:

  1. It should achieve an approximate balance between 'required market performance' and 'actual operations performance'.
  2. It should make this alignment 'sustainable' over time.
  3. It should 'move up' the line of fit, the assumption being that high levels of market performance, achieved as a result of high levels of operations performance are difficult for competitors to match.

➤ What information is needed for improvement?

- It is unlikely that for any operation a single measure of performance will adequately reflect the whole of a performance objective. Usually operations have to collect a whole bundle of partial measures of performance.
- Each partial measure then has to be compared against some performance standard. There are four types of performance standard commonly used:
  - historical standards, which compare performance now against performance sometime in the past;
  - target performance standards, which compare current performance against some desired level of performance;
  - competitor performance standards, which compare current performance against competitors' performance;
  - absolute performance standards, which compare current performance against its theoretically perfect state.
- The process of benchmarking is often used as a means of obtaining competitor performance standards.

➤ What should be improvement priorities?

- Improvement priorities can be determined by bringing together the relative importance of each performance objective or competitive factor as judged by customers, with the performance which the operation achieves as compared with its competition. This idea can be consolidated on an 'importance–performance matrix'.
- The 'sandcone model' provides an alternative approach to prioritization. It recommends that improvement should cumulatively emphasize quality, dependability, speed, flexibility, and then cost.

➤ How can organizational culture affect improvement?

- An organization's ability to improve its operations performance depends to a large extent on its 'culture', that is '*the pattern of shared basic assumptions . . . that have worked well enough to be considered valid*'. A receptive organizational culture that encourages a constant search for improved ways to do things can encourage improvement.
- According to Bessant and Caffyn there are specific abilities, behaviours and actions which need to be consciously developed if improvement is to sustain over the long term.
- Many of the abilities and behaviours related to an improvement culture relate to learning in some way. The learning process is important because it encourages, facilitates and exploits the learning that occurs during improvement. This involves two types of learning, single- and double-loop learning.
  - Single-loop learning occurs when there is repetitive and predictable link between cause and effect.
  - Double-loop learning questions the fundamental objectives, service or even the underlying culture of the operation.

➤ What are the key implementation issues?

- Improvement efforts often fail (estimates range from half to 80 per cent of programmes failing). Included in the reasons for this are the following.
  - Top-management support may be lacking
  - Senior managers may not fully understand the improvement approach
  - The improvement may be 'hyped up' excessively, leading to unrealistic (and therefore unrealized) expectations
  - Implementation problems may not be anticipated.
- ISO 9000 and its associated family of standards may be used to provide a structure around improvement implementation. They are concerned with the processes and procedures that support quality.
- So-called 'quality awards' and models may contribute towards implementation of improvement by providing a focused structure for organizations to assess their improvement efforts. The best known of these is probably the EFQM (Business Excellence Model). This is based on a nine-point model which distinguishes between the 'enablers' of quality and the 'results' of quality. It is often now used as a self-certification model.

Case study
Re-inventing Singapore's libraries[15]

By Professors Robert Johnston, Warwick Business School, Chai Kah Hin and Jochen Wirtz, National University of Singapore, and Christopher Lovelock, Yale University.

Source: National Library Board Singapore

The National Library Board (NLB) in Singapore oversees the management of the national, reference, regional, community and children's libraries, as well as over 30 libraries belonging to government agencies, schools and private institutions. Over the last 15 years the NLB has completely changed the nature of libraries in Singapore and its work has been used as a blueprint for many other libraries across the world. Yet it was not always like this. In 1995 libraries in Singapore were traditional, quiet places full of old books where you went to study or borrow books if you could not afford to buy them. There were long queues to have books stamped or returned and the staff seemed unhelpful and unfriendly. But today, things are very different. There are cafés in libraries to encourage people to come in, browse and sit down with a book, and libraries in community centres (putting libraries where the people are). The NLB has developed specialist libraries aimed at children, libraries in shopping malls aimed at attracting busy 18–35-year-olds into the library while they are shopping. There are libraries dedicated to teenagers, one of the most difficult groups to entice into the library. These have even been designed by the teenagers themselves so they include drinks machines, cushions and music systems. The library also hosts a wide range of events from mother and baby reading sessions to rock concerts to encourage a wide range of people into the library.

'We started this journey back in 1995 when Dr Christopher Chia was appointed as Chief Executive. Looking back, we were a very traditional public service. Our customers used words like "cold" and "unfriendly", though, in fairness, our staff were working under great

pressure to deal with the long queues for books and to answer enquiries on library materials posed by our customers. Christopher Chia and his team made a study of the problems, undertook surveys and ran focus groups. They then began to address the challenges with vision and imagination through the application of the project management methodology and the innovative use of technology. Staff involvement and contribution was key to the success of the transformation. We knew where we wanted to go, and were committed to the cause.' (Ms Ngian Lek Choh, the Deputy Chief Executive and Director of the National Library)

Underpinning many of the changes was the NLB's innovative use of technology. It was the first public library in the world to prototype radio-frequency identification (RFID) to create its Electronic Library Management System (ELiMS). RFID is an electronic system for automatically identifying items. It uses RFID tags, or transponders, which are contained in smart labels consisting of a silicon chip and coiled antenna. They receive and respond to radio-frequency queries from an RFID transceiver, which enables the remote and automatic retrieval, storing and sharing of information (see Chapter 8). RFID tags are installed in its 10 million books making it one of the largest users of the technology in the world. Customers spend very little time queuing, with book issuing and returns automated. Indeed books can be returned to any of the NLB's 24-hour book drops (which look a bit like ATM machines) where RFID enables not only fast and easy returns but also fast and easy sorting. The NLB has also launched a mobile service via SMS (text messaging). This allows users to manage their library accounts anytime and anywhere through their mobile phones. They can check their loan records, renew their books, pay library payments, and get reminder alerts to return library items before the due-date.

Improving its services meant fully understanding the Library's customers. Customers were studied using surveys and focus groups to understand how the library added value for customers, how customers could be segmented, the main learning and reading motivators, and people's general reading habits. And feedback from customers, both formal and informal, is an important source of design innovation – as are ideas from staff. Everyone in NLB, from the chief executive to the library assistant is expected to contribute to work improvement and innovations. So much so that innovation has become an integral part of NLB's culture, leading to a steady stream of both large and small innovations. In order to facilitate this, the chief executive holds '*express-o*' sessions discussions with staff. He also has a strategy called 'ask stupid questions' (ASQ) which encourages staff to challenge what is normally accepted. Dr Varaprasad, the chief executive commented, *'In my view there are no stupid questions there are only stupid answers! What we try to do is engage the staff by letting them feel they can ask stupid questions and that they are entitled to an answer.'*

The NLB also makes use of small improvement teams to brainstorm ideas and test them out with colleagues from other libraries across the island. Good ideas attract financial rewards from S$5 to $1,000. One such idea was using a simple system of coloured bands on the spines of books (representing the identification number of each book) which make it much easier to shelve the books in the right places and also spot books that have been misplaced by customers. Staff are also encouraged to travel overseas to visit other libraries to learn about how they use their space, their programmes and collections, attend and speak at conventions and also visit very different organizations to get new ideas. The automatic book return for example was an idea borrowed and modified from the Mass Rapid Transport stations in Hong Kong where, with the flash of a card, the user is identified and given access across the system. NLB applied a similar line of thought for seamless check-in and check-out of books and a return anywhere concept. NLB harvests ideas from many different industries including logistics, manufacturing, IT and supermarkets. However, some elements of NLB's improvement process have changed. In the early days their approach to implementing ideas was informal and intuitive. It is now much more structured. Now, each good idea that comes forward is managed as a project, starting with a 'proof of concept' stage which involves selling the idea to management and checking with a range of people that the idea seems feasible. Then the services or processes are re-engineered, often involving customers or users. The new concepts are then prototyped and piloted allowing managers to gather customer feedback to enable them to assess, refine and, if appropriate, develop them for other sites.

Questions

1. How would the culture of NLB have changed in order for it to make such improvements?
2. Where did the ideas for improvement originate? And how did NLB encourage improvement ideas?
3. Why, do you think, has the improvement process become more systematic over the years?
4. What could be the biggest challenges to NLB's improvement activities in the future?

Problems and applications

*These problems and applications will help to improve your analysis of operations. You can find more practice problems as well as worked examples and guided solutions on MyOMLab at **www.myomlab.com**.*

1 Reread the 'Operations in action' piece at the beginning of the chapter on 'Taxing quality' which describes the improvement initiative carried out by the Aarhus region customs and tax unit.

(a) How does the idea of a customer-focused approach to improvement need to be adapted for a customs and tax unit.

(b) Generally, how might the ideas of improvement organization outlined in this chapter need to be adapted for public-sector operations such as this one?

2 What are the differences and similarities between the approach taken by the Aarhus customs and tax unit and the example described in the short case on 'Improvement at Heineken'?

3 Compare and contrast the approaches taken by GE in their Work-Out approach described in a short case and that taken by Heineken, also described in a short case.

4 Ruggo Carpets encourages continuous improvement based around the 'drive for customer focus'. The company's total quality process has graduated from 'total customer satisfaction' to 'total customer delight', to its present form – 'bridging the gap', which is effectively a 'where we are' and 'where we should be' yardstick for the company. Developments in the warehouse are typical. The supervisor has been replaced by a group leader who acts as a 'facilitator', working within the team. They are also trained to carry out their own job plus five others. Fixed hours are a thing of the past, as is overtime. At peak times the team works the required hours to dispatch orders, and at off-peak times, when work is completed the team can leave. Dispatch labels and address labels are computer-generated and the carpets are bar-coded to reduce human error. Each process within the warehouse has been analysed and re-engineered.

(a) What is implied by the progression of the company's three initiatives from 'total customer satisfaction' to 'total customer delight' to 'bridging the gap'?

(b) Evaluate this example against the criteria included in the Business Excellence Model.

5 Look through the financial or business pages of a (serious) newspaper and find examples of businesses that have 'deviated from the line of fit', as described in the early part of this chapter.

6 Devise a performance measurement scheme for the performance of the course you are following.

Selected further reading

Deming, W.E. (1986) *Out of the Crisis*, MIT Press, Cambridge, Mass. One of the gurus. It had a huge impact in its day. Read it if you want to know what all the fuss was about.

George, M.L., Rowlands, D. and Kastle, B. (2003) *What Is Lean Six Sigma?* McGraw-Hill Publishing Co. Very much a quick introduction on what Lean Six Sigma is and how to use it.

Kaplan, R.S. and Norton, D.P. (2001) *The Strategy Focused Organisation*, Harvard Business School Press, Boston, MA.

Neely, A.D. and Adams, C. (2001) The performance prism perspective, *Journal of Cost Management*, vol. 25, no. 1, 7–15.

Schein, E.H. (2004) *Organizational Culture and Leadership*, 3rd edn, Jossey-Bass. A classic.

Useful web sites

www.quality-foundation.co.uk/ The British Quality Foundation is a not-for-profit organization promoting business excellence.

www.juran.com The Juran Institute's mission statement is to provide clients with the concepts, methods and guidance for attaining leadership in quality.

www.asq.org/ The American Society for Quality site. Good professional insights.

www.quality.nist.gov/ American Quality Assurance Institute. Well-established institution for all types of business quality assurance.

www.gslis.utexas.edu/~rpollock/tqm.html Non-commercial site on total quality management with some good links.

www.iso.org/iso/en/ISOOnline.frontpage Site of the International Standards Organisation that runs the ISO 9000 and ISO 14000 families of standards. ISO 9000 has become an international reference for quality management requirements.

www.opsman.org Lots of useful stuff.

Now that you have finished reading this chapter, why not visit MyOMLab at ***www.myomlab.com*** *where you'll find more learning resources to help you make the most of your studies and get a better grade?*

Key operations questions

Chapter 21

Operations and corporate social responsibility (CSR)

- ➤ What is corporate social responsibility?
- ➤ How does the wider view of corporate social responsibility influence operations management?
- ➤ How can operations managers analyse CSR issues?

Part Five

CORPORATE SOCIAL RESPONSIBILITY

The ultimate test for any operations manager is whether he or she can develop an operation which meets the challenges and decisions that lie ahead for the organization. In the preceding 20 chapters, we have outlined many of these challenges and decisions, and placed them in the context of the nature and purpose of operations management. In this final part of the book we examine an issue that is far wider than operations management, but with which operations management is intimately connected – corporate social responsibility (CSR). It is important to operations management because, of all the functions of any organization, it is operations management which can have the most practical impact on its CSR performance.

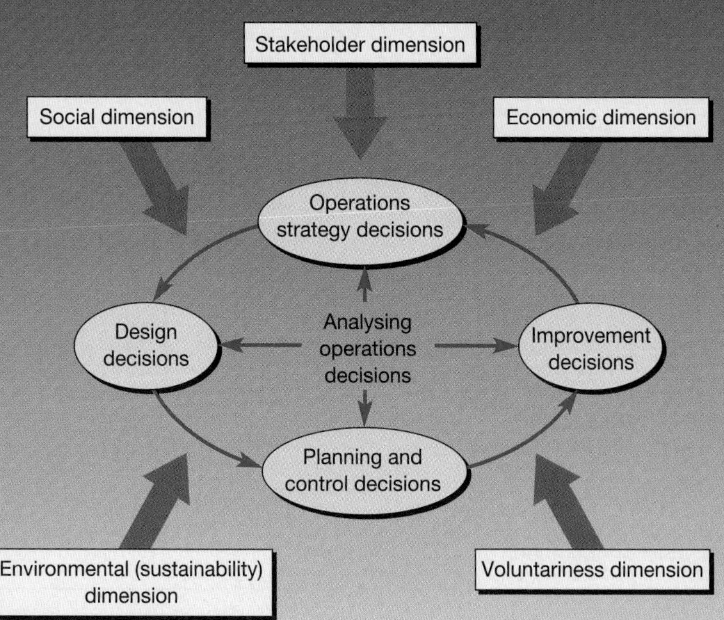

Chapter 21 Operations and corporate social responsibility (CSR)

Key questions

- ➤ What is corporate social responsibility?
- ➤ How does the wider view of corporate social responsibility influence operations management?
- ➤ How can operations managers analyse CSR issues?

Introduction

Operations managers make many decisions, some seemingly trivial, others more long-term and strategic. They also face many new challenges as the economic, social, political and technological environment changes. Many of these decisions and challenges seem largely economic in nature. What will be the impact on our costs of adding a new product or service feature? Can we generate an acceptable return if we invest in new technology? Other decisions have more of a 'social' aspect. How do we make sure that all our suppliers treat their staff fairly? Are we doing enough to reduce our carbon footprint? Yet the 'economic' decisions also have a 'social' aspect to them. Will a new product feature make end-of-life recycling more difficult? Will the new technology increase pollution? Similarly the 'social' decisions must be made in the context of their economic consequences. Sure, we want suppliers to treat staff well and, OK, we want to reduce our environmental impact, but we also need to make a profit. And this is the great dilemma of CSR. How do operations managers try to be, simultaneously, economically viable and socially responsible? It is a huge and, arguably, unsolvable issue, and in this chapter we can only skim some of the issues. Yet it is an important (some would say the most important) issue, and no treatment of operations management should ignore it. Figure 21.1 illustrates the CSR issues covered in this chapter.

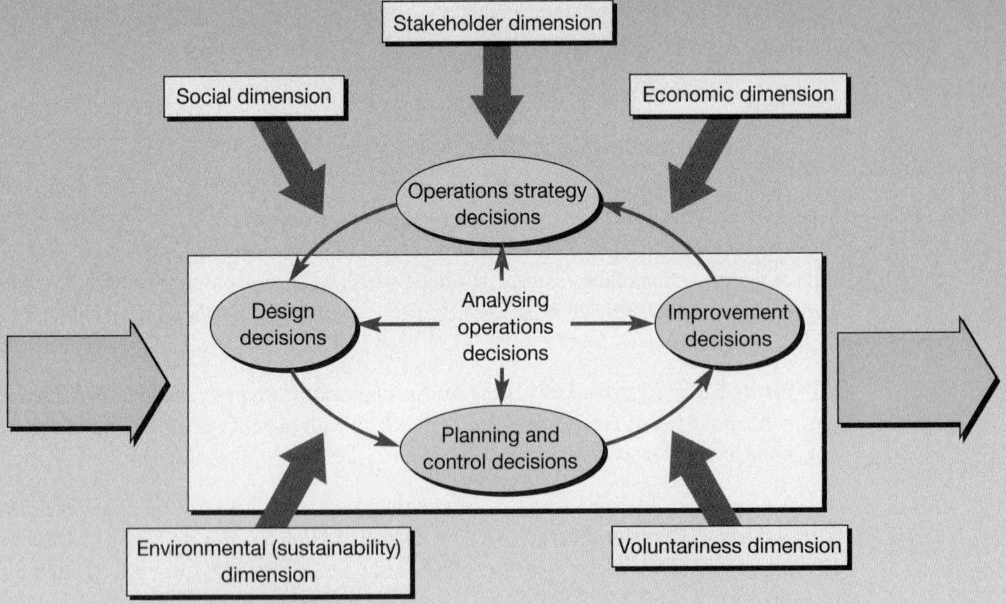

Figure 21.1 The five 'dimensions' of CSR for operations managers

*Check and improve your understanding of this chapter using self assessment questions and a personalised study plan, audio and video downloads, and an eBook – all at **www.myomlab.com**.*

What is corporate social responsibility?

Source: Rex Features

Although operations management is seen by some as being concerned largely with the routine aspects of business, it is in fact at the very forefront of almost all the new challenges to business practice. This is because whether it is new technologies, new approaches to organizing resources, changing market and environmental circumstances, changing regulatory frameworks, or shifts in how society views business practices, operations will have to understand the consequences of these changes and respond to them. That is why it is useful to reflect on current and future trends and how they will impact on operations management in practice. Of course, we could pick any number of issues that may become more important in the future and examine how operations management will have to respond. By definition, the future is unknown, so who knows what will be important in the future? However, one issue in particular has risen to the top of the list of things that concern many, if not most, businesses, regulatory authorities, governments and citizens generally. That issue is 'how should the relationship between business and wider society be viewed, assessed and (if possible) managed?' This issue is generally referred to as **corporate social responsibility** or simply CSR.

Corporate social responsibility

Defining CSR

Surprisingly, for such an important topic, there is no universally accepted definition of CSR. Here are just some that give a flavour of how CSR is seen.

> *'CSR is the business contribution to our sustainable development goals. Essentially it is about how business takes account of its economic, social and environmental impacts in the way it operates – maximizing the benefits and minimizing the downsides. Specifically, we see CSR as the voluntary actions that business can take, over and above compliance with minimum legal requirements, to address both its own competitive interests and the interests of wider society.'* (UK Government)

> *'Corporate Social Responsibility is the continuing commitment by business to behave ethically and contribute to economic development while improving the quality of life of the workforce and their families as well as of the local community and society at large.'*[1]

> *'Corporate Social Responsibility . . . is listening and responding to the needs of a company's stakeholders. This includes the requirements of sustainable development. We believe that building good relationships with employees, suppliers and wider society is the best guarantee of long-term success. This is the backbone of our approach to CSR.'*[2]

> *'CSR is a company's commitment to operating in an economically, socially and environmentally sustainable manner whilst balancing the interests of diverse stakeholders.'*[3]

> *'[Our vision is to] . . . enable the profitable and responsible growth of our airports. One of our six strategies to achieve that purpose is to earn the trust of our stakeholders. Corporate*

Table 21.1 The five dimensions and example phrases

The 'dimensions' of CSR	*What the definition refers to*	*Typical phrases used in the definition*
The environmental dimension	The natural environment and 'sustainability' of business practice	'a cleaner environment' 'environmental stewardship' 'environmental concerns in business operations'
The social dimension	The relationship between business and society in general	'contribute to a better society' 'integrate social concerns in their business operations' 'consider the full scope of their impact on communities'
The economic dimension	Socio-economic or financial aspects, including describing CSR in terms of its impact on the business operation	'preserving the profitability' 'contribute to economic development'
The stakeholder dimension	Considering all stakeholders or stakeholder groups	'interaction with their stakeholders' 'how organizations interact with their employees, suppliers, customers and communities' 'treating the stakeholders of the firm'
The voluntariness dimension	Actions not prescribed by law. Doing more that you have to.	'based on ethical values' 'beyond legal obligations' 'voluntary'

responsibility is about how we manage our social and environmental impacts as part of our day to day business, in order to earn that trust.'[4]

'CSR is about how companies manage the business processes to produce an overall positive impact on society.'[5]

'Corporate social responsibility is the commitment of businesses to contribute to sustainable economic development by working with employees, their families, the local community and society at large to improve their lives in ways that are good for business and for development.'[6]

'CSR is a concept whereby companies integrate social and environmental concerns in their business operations and in their interaction with their stakeholders on a voluntary basis.'[7]

Although there are so many definitions, according to Alexander Dahlsrud of the Norwegian University of Science and Technology[8] almost all of them involve five 'dimensions' of CSR, as shown in Table 21.1. We will use these dimensions, first to explore CSR in general and, second, to explore the role of operations management specifically in CSR.

The whole topic of CSR is also rising up the corporate agenda. Figure 21.2 shows how one survey of executives saw the progressive prioritization of CSR issues.

The environmental (sustainability) dimension of CSR

Environmental sustainability (according to the World Bank) means 'ensuring that the overall productivity of accumulated human and physical capital resulting from development actions more than compensates for the direct or indirect loss or degradation of the environment', or (according to the Brundtland Report from the United Nations) it is 'meeting the needs of the present without compromising the ability of future generations to meet their own needs'. Put more directly, it is generally taken to mean the extent to which business activity negatively impacts on the natural environment. It is clearly an important issue, not only because of the obvious impact on the immediate environment of hazardous waste, air and even noise pollution, but also because of the less obvious, but potentially far more damaging issues around global warming.

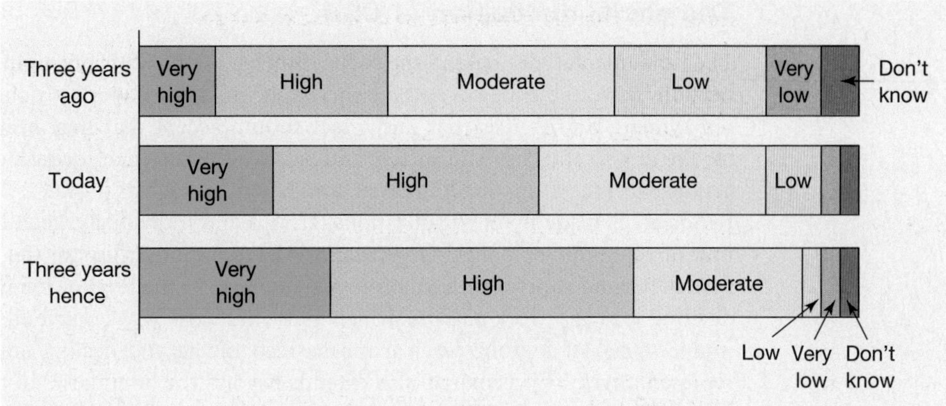

Figure 21.2 How executives view the importance (degree of priority) of corporate responsibility
Data from the Economist Intelligence Unit, Global Business Barometer, Nov–Dec 2007

From the perspective of individual organizations, the challenging issues of dealing with sustainability are connected with the scale of the problem and the general perception of 'green' issues. First, the scale issue is that cause and effect in the environmental sustainability area are judged at different levels. The effects of, and arguments for, environmentally sustainable activities are felt at a global level, while those activities themselves are essentially local. It has been argued that it is difficult to use the concept at a corporate or even at the regional level. Second, there is a paradox with sustainability-based decisions. It is that the more the public becomes sensitized to the benefits of firms acting in an environmentally sensitive way, the more those firms are tempted to exaggerate their environmental credentials, the so-called 'greenwashing' effect.

One way of demonstrating that operations, in a fundamental way, is at the heart of environmental management is to consider the total environmental burden (EB) created by the totality of operations activities:[9]

$$\text{EB} = P \times A \times T$$

where

P = the size of the population
A = the affluence of the population (a proxy measure for consumption)
T = technology (in its broadest sense, the way products and services are made and delivered, in other words operations management)

Achieving sustainability means reducing, or at least stabilizing, the environmental burden. Considering the above formula, this can only be done by decreasing the human population, lowering the level of affluence and therefore consumption, or changing the technology used to create products and services. Decreasing population is not feasible. Decreasing the level of affluence would not only be somewhat unpopular, but would also make the problem worse because low levels of affluence are correlated with high levels of birth rate. The only option left is to change the way goods and services are created.

Short case
Ecological footprints[10]

To supply the average person's basic needs in the United States, it takes 12.2 acres of land. In the Netherlands it takes 8 acres, and in India it takes 1 acre. Calculated this way, the Dutch ecological footprint covers 15 times the area of the Netherlands. India's ecological footprint is 1.35 of its area. Most dramatically, if the entire world lived like North Americans, it would take three planet earths to support the present world population.

The social dimension of CSR

The fundamental idea behind the social dimension of CSR is not simply that there is a connection between businesses and the society in which they operate (defined broadly) – that is self-evident. Rather it is that businesses should accept that they bear some responsibility for the impact they have on society and balance the external 'societal' consequences of their actions with the more direct internal consequences, such as profit.

Society is made up of organizations, groups and individuals. Each is more than a simple unit of economic exchange. Organizations have responsibility for the general well-being of society beyond short-term economic self-interest. At the level of the individual, this means devising jobs and work patterns which allow individuals to contribute their talents without undue stress. At a group level, it means recognizing and dealing honestly with employee representatives. This principle also extends beyond the boundaries of the organization. Any business has a responsibility to ensure that it does not knowingly disadvantage individuals in its suppliers or trading partners. Businesses are also a part of the larger community, often integrated into the economic and social fabric of an area. Increasingly, organizations are recognizing their responsibility to local communities by helping to promote their economic and social well-being. And of the many issues that affect society at large, arguably the one that has had the most profound effect on the way business has developed over the last few decades has been the globalization of business activity.

Globalization

The International Monetary Fund defines globalization as 'the growing economic interdependence of countries worldwide through increasing volume and variety of cross-border transactions in goods and services, free international capital flows, and more rapid and widespread diffusion of technology'. It reflects the idea that the world is a smaller place to do business in. Even many medium-sized companies are sourcing and selling their products and services on a global basis. Considerable opportunities have emerged for operations managers to develop both supplier and customer relationships in new parts of the world. All of this is exciting but it also poses many problems. **Globalization** of trade is considered by some to be the root cause of exploitation and corruption in many developing countries. Others see it as the only way of spreading the levels of prosperity enjoyed by developed countries throughout the world.

Globalization

The ethical globalization movement seeks to reconcile the globalization trend with how it can impact on societies. Typical aims include the following:

- Acknowledging shared responsibilities for addressing global challenges and affirming that our common humanity doesn't stop at national borders.
- Recognizing that all individuals are equal in dignity and have the right to certain entitlements, rather than viewing them as objects of benevolence or charity.
- Embracing the importance of gender and the need for attention to the often different impacts of economic and social policies on women and men.
- Affirming that a world connected by technology and trade must also be connected by shared values, norms of behaviour and systems of accountability.

The economic dimension of CSR

If business could easily adopt a more CSR-friendly position without any economic consequences, there would be no debate. But there are economic consequences to taking socially responsible decisions. Some of these will be positive, even in the short term. Others will be negative in the sense that managers believe that there is a real cost in the short term (to their companies specifically). Investment in CSR is a short-term issue, whereas payback from the investment may (possibly) be well into the future, although this is no different from other business investment, except for the uncertain payback and timescale. But also, investment is made largely by the individual business, whereas benefits are enjoyed by everyone (including competitors). Yet the direct business benefits of adopting a CSR philosophy are becoming more obvious as public opinion is more sensitized to business's CSR behaviour. Similarly, stock market investors are starting to pay more attention. According to Geoffrey Heal of Columbia Business School, some stock market analysts, who research the investment potential of companies' shares, have started to include environmental, social and governance issues into their stock valuations. Further, $1 out of every $9 under professional management in America now involves an element of '**socially responsible investment**'.[11]

Socially responsible investment

The stakeholder dimension of CSR

In Chapter 2 we looked at the various stakeholder groups from whose perspective operations performance could be judged. The groups included shareholders, directors and top management, staff, staff representative bodies (e.g. trade unions), suppliers (of materials, services, equipment, etc.), regulators (e.g. financial regulators), government (local, national, regional), lobby groups (e.g. environmental lobby groups), and society in general. In Chapter 16 we took this idea further in the context of project management (although the ideas work throughout operations management) and examined how different stakeholders could be managed in different ways. However, two further points should be made here. The first is that a basic tenet of CSR is that a broad range of stakeholders should be considered when making business decisions. In effect, this means that purely economic criteria are insufficient for a socially acceptable outcome. The second is that such judgements are not straightforward. While the various stakeholder groups will obviously take different perspectives on decisions, their perspective is a function not only of their stakeholder classification, but also of their cultural background. What might be unremarkable in one country's or company's ethical framework could be regarded as highly dubious in another's. Nevertheless, there is an emerging agenda of ethical issues to which, at the very least, all managers should be sensitive.

The voluntary dimension of CSR

In most of the world's economies, regulation requires organizations to conform to CSR standards. So, should simply conforming to regulatory requirements be regarded as CSR? Or should social responsibility go beyond merely complying with legally established regulations? In fact most authorities on CSR emphasize its voluntary nature. But this idea is not uncontested. Certainly some do not view CSR as *only* a voluntary activity. They stress the need for a mixture of voluntary and regulatory approaches. Globally, companies, they say, have, in practice, significant power and influence, yet 'their socially responsible behaviour does not reflect the accountability they have as a result of their size. Fifty-one of the largest 100 global economies are corporations . . . so . . . corporate power is significantly greater than those of most national governments and plays a dominant role in sectors that are of significance for national economies, especially of developing countries, which may be dependent on a few key sectors.'[12]

How does the wider view of corporate social responsibility influence operations management?

The concept of corporate social responsibility permeates operations management. Almost every decision taken by operations managers and every issue discussed in this book influences, and is influenced by, the various dimensions of CSR. In this section we identify and illustrate just some of the operations topics that have a significant relationship with CSR. We shall again use the five 'dimensions' of CSR.

Operations and the environmental dimension of CSR

Environmental protection

Operations managers cannot avoid responsibility for **environmental protection** generally, or their organization's environmental performance more specifically. It is often operational failures which are at the root of pollution disasters and operations decisions (such as product design) which impact on longer-term environmental issues. The pollution-causing disasters which make the headlines seem to be the result of a whole variety of causes – oil tankers run aground, nuclear waste is misclassified, chemicals leak into a river, or gas clouds drift over industrial towns. But in fact they all have something in common. They were all the result of an operational failure. Somehow operations procedures were inadequate. Less dramatic in the short term, but perhaps more important in the long term, is the environmental impact of products which cannot be recycled and processes which consume large amounts of energy – again, both issues which are part of the operations management's broader responsibilities.

Short case
HP's recycling program[13]

HP (Hewlett-Packard) provides technology solutions to consumers and businesses all over the world. Its recycling program seeks to reduce the environmental impact of its products, minimize waste going to landfills by helping customers discard products conveniently in an environmentally sound manner. Recovered materials, after recycling, have been used to make products, including auto body parts, clothes hangers, plastic toys, fence posts, and roof tiles. In 2005 it proudly announced that it had boosted its recycling rate by 17% in 2005, to a total of 63.5 million kilograms globally, the equivalent weight of 280 jumbo airliners. *'HP's commitment to environmental responsibility includes our efforts to limit the environmental impact of products throughout their life cycles'*, said David Lear, vice president, Corporate, Social and Environmental Responsibility, HP. *'One way we achieve this is through developing and investing in product return and recycling programs and technologies globally, giving our customers choices and control over how their products are managed at end of life.'*

But HP's interest in environmental issues goes back some way. It opened its first recycling facility in Roseville, California, in 1997, when it was the only major computer manufacturer to operate its own recycling facility. Now the company's recycling program goal is to expand its product return and recycling program and create new ways for customers to return and recycle their electronic equipment and print cartridges. As well as being environmentally responsible, all initiatives have to be convenient for customers if they are to be effective. For example, HP began a free hardware recycling service for commercial customers in EU countries who purchase replacement HP products, in advance. Partly, this reflects the EU Waste Electrical and Electronic Equipment Directive. A similar offer exists for HP commercial customers in the Asia Pacific region. In some parts of the world, HP has developed partnerships with retailers to offer free recycling at drop-off events.

Source: Awe Inspiring Images/Photographers Direct

Again, it is important to understand that broad issues such as environmental responsibility are intimately connected with the day-to-day decisions of operations managers. Many of these are concerned with waste. Operations management decisions in product and service design significantly affect the utilization of materials both in the short term and in long-term recyclability. Process design influences the proportion of energy and labour that is wasted as well as materials wastage. Planning and control may affect material wastage (packaging being wasted by mistakes in purchasing, for example), but also affects energy and labour wastage. Improvement, of course, is dedicated largely to reducing wastage. Here environmental responsibility and the conventional concerns of operations management coincide. Reducing waste, in all it forms, may be environmentally sound but it also saves cost for the organization.

At other times, decisions can be more difficult. Process technologies may be efficient from the operations point of view but may cause pollution, the economic and social consequences of which are borne by society at large. Such conflicts are usually resolved through regulation and legislation. Not that such mechanisms are always effective – there is evidence that just-in-time principles applied in Japan may have produced significant economic gains for the companies which adopted them, but at the price of an overcrowded and polluted road system. Table 21.2 identifies some of the issues concerned with environmental responsibility in each of the operations management decision areas. Figure 21.3 illustrates how one set of operations managers studied the reduction in the wastage of materials and energy, as well as the external environmental impact of their packaging policies.

Table 21.2 Some environmental considerations of operations management decisions

Decision area	*Some environmental issues*
Product/service design	Recyclability of materials Energy consumption Waste material generation
Network design	Environmental impact of location Development of suppliers in environmental practice Reducing transport-related energy
Layout of facilities	Energy efficiency
Process technology	Waste and product disposal Noise pollution Fume and emission pollution Energy efficiency
Job design	Transportation of staff to/from work Development in environmental education
Planning and control (including MRP, JIT and project planning and control)	Material utilization and wastage Environmental impact of project management Transport pollution of frequent JIT supply
Capacity planning and control	Over-production waste of poor planning Local impact of extended operating hours
Inventory planning and control	Energy management of replenishment transportation Obsolescence and wastage
Supply chain planning and control	Minimizing energy consumption in distribution Recyclability of transportation consumables
Quality planning and control and TQM	Scrap and wastage of materials Waste in energy consumption
Failure prevention and recovery	Environmental impact of process failures Recovery to minimize impact of failures

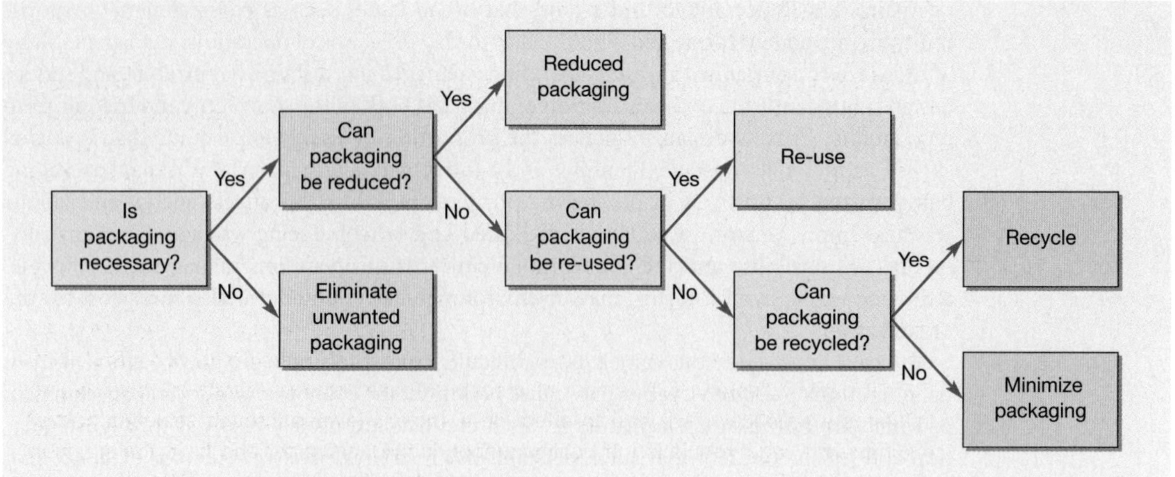

Figure 21.3 Identifying waste minimization in packaging

Green reporting[14]

Environmental reporting

Until recently, relatively few companies around the world provided information on their environmental practices and performance. Now **environmental reporting** is increasingly common. One estimate is that around 35 per cent of the world's largest corporations publish reports on their environmental policies and performance. Partly, this may be motivated by an altruistic desire to cause less damage to the planet. However, what is also becoming accepted is that green reporting makes good business sense.

ISO 14000

ISO 14000

Another emerging issue in recent years has been the introduction of the **ISO 14000** standard. It has a three-section environmental management system which covers initial planning, implementation and objective assessment. Although it has had some impact, it is largely limited to Europe.

ISO 14000 makes a number of specific requirements, including the following:

- a commitment by top-level management to environmental management;
- the development and communication of an environmental policy;
- the establishment of relevant and legal and regulatory requirements;
- the setting of environmental objectives and targets;
- the establishment and updating of a specific environmental programme, or programmes, geared to achieving the objectives and targets;
- the implementation of supporting systems such as training, operational control and emergency planning;
- regular monitoring and measurement of all operational activities;
- a full audit procedure to review the working and suitability of the system.

The ISO 14000 group of standards covers the following areas:

- Environmental Management Systems (14001, 14002, 14004)
- Environmental Auditing (14010, 14011, 14012)
- Evaluation of Environmental Performance (14031)
- Environmental Labelling (14020, 14021, 14022, 14023, 14024, 14025)
- Life-cycle Assessment (14040, 14041, 14042, 14043).

Critical commentary

The similarity of ISO 14000 to the quality procedures of ISO 9000 is a bit of a giveaway. ISO 14000 can contain all the problems of ISO 9000 (management by manual, obsession with procedures rather than results, a major expense to implement it, and, at its worst, the formalization of what was bad practice in the first place). But ISO 14000 also has some further problems. The main one is that it can become a 'badge for the smug'. It can be seen as 'all there is to do to be a good environmentally sensitive company'. At least with quality standards like ISO 9000 there are real customers continually reminding the business that quality does matter. Pressures to improve environmental standards are far more diffuse. Customers are not likely to be as energetic in forcing good environmental standards on suppliers as they are in forcing the good-quality standards from which they benefit directly. Instead of this type of procedure-based system, surely the only way to influence a practice which has an effect on a societal level is through society's normal mechanism – legal regulation. If quality suffers, individuals suffer and have the sanction of not purchasing goods and services again from the offending company. With bad environmental management, we all suffer. Because of this, the only workable way to ensure environmentally sensitive business policies is by insisting that our governments protect us. Legislation, therefore, is the only safe way forward.

Operations and the social dimension of CSR

The way in which an operation is managed has a significant impact on its customers, the individuals who work for it, the individuals who work for its suppliers and the local community in which the operation is located. The dilemma is how can operations be managed to be profitable, responsible employers and be good neighbours? As in the previous section we will look particularly at globalization, primarily because the world is a smaller place: very few operations do not either source from or sell to foreign markets. So, how do operations managers cope with this expanded set of opportunities?

Globalization and operations decisions

Most of the decision areas we have covered in this book have an international dimension to them. Often this is simply because different parts of the world with different cultures have different views on the nature of work. So, for example, highly repetitive work on an assembly line may be unpopular in parts of Europe, but it is welcome as a source of employment in other parts of the world. Does this mean that operations should be designed to accommodate the cultural reactions of people in different parts of the world? Probably. Does this mean that we are imposing lower standards on less wealthy parts of the world? Well, it depends on your point of view. The issue, however, is that cultural and economic differences do impact on the day-to-day activities of operations management decision-making.

Ethical globalization

If all this seems at too high a level for a humble subject like operations management, look at Table 21.3 and consider how many of these issues have an impact on day-to-day decision-making. If a company decides to import some of its components from a Third World country, where wages are substantially cheaper, is this a good or a bad thing? Local trade unions might oppose the 'export of jobs'. Shareholders would, presumably, like the higher profits. Environmentalists would want to ensure that natural resources were not harmed. Everyone with a social conscience would want to ensure that workers from a Third World country were not exploited (although one person's exploitation is another's very welcome employment opportunity). Such decisions are made every day by operations managers throughout the world. Table 21.3 identifies just some of the social responsibility issues for each of the major decision areas covered in this book.

Table 21.3 Some social considerations of operations management decisions

Decision area	*Some social issues*
Product/service design	Customer safety Social impact of product
Network design	Employment implications of location Employment implications of plant closure Employment implications of vertical integration
Layout of facilities	Staff safety Disabled access
Process technology	Staff safety Noise damage Repetitive/alienating work
Job design	Staff safety Workplace stress Repetitive/alienating work Unsocial working hours Customer safety (in high-contact operations)
Planning and control (including MRP, lean and project planning and control)	What priority to give customers waiting to be served Unsocial staff working hours Workplace stress Restrictive organizational cultures
Capacity planning and control	'Hire and fire' employment policies Working hours fluctuations Unsocial working hours Service cover in emergencies Relationships with subcontractors 'Dumping' of products below cost
Inventory planning and control	Price manipulation in restricted markets Warehouse safety
Supply chain planning and control	Honesty in supplier relationships Transparency of cost data Non-exploitation of developing-country suppliers Prompt payment to suppliers
Quality planning and control and TQM	Customer safety Staff safety Workplace stress
Failure prevention and recovery	Customer safety Staff safety

Short case
The Gap between perception, reality and intention[15]

Source: Alamy Images

It is expensive to manufacture garments in developed countries where wages, transport and infrastructure costs are high. It is also a competitive market. As customers, most of us look to secure a good deal when we shop. This is why most garments sold in developed countries are actually made in less developed countries. Large retail chains such as Gap select suppliers that can deliver acceptable quality at a cost that allows both them and the chain to make a profit. But what if the supplier achieves this by adopting practices that, while not unusual in the supplier's country are unacceptable to consumers? Then, in addition to any harm to the victims of the practice, the danger to the retail chain is one of 'reputational risk'. This is what happened to the garment retailer Gap when a British newspaper ran a story under the headline, *'Gap Child Labour Shame'*. The story went on, *'An Observer investigation into children making clothes has shocked the retail giant and may cause it to withdraw apparel ordered for Christmas. Amitosh concentrates as he pulls the loops of thread through tiny plastic beads and sequins on the toddler's blouse he is making. Dripping with sweat, his hair is thinly coated in dust. In Hindi his name means 'happiness'. The hand-embroidered garment on which his tiny needle is working bears the distinctive logo of international fashion chain Gap. Amitosh is 10.*

Within two days Gap responded as follows. *'Earlier this week . . . an allegation of child labor at a facility in India. An investigation was immediately launched. . . . a very small portion of one order . . . was apparently subcontracted to an unauthorized subcontractor without the company's knowledge . . . in direct violation of [our] agreement under [our] Code of Vendor Conduct. 'We strictly prohibit the use of child labor. This is a non-negotiable for us – and we are deeply concerned and upset by this allegation. As we've demonstrated in the past, Gap has a history of addressing challenges like this head-on. In 2006, Gap Inc. ceased business with 23 factories due to code violations. We have 90 people located around the world whose job is to ensure compliance with our Code of Vendor Conduct.'*

Operations and the economic dimension of CSR

Operations managers are at the forefront of trying to balance any costs of CSR with any benefits. In a practical sense this means attempting to understand where extra expenditure will be necessary in order to adopt socially responsible practices against the savings and/or benefits that will accrue from these same practices. Here it is useful to divide operations-related costs into input, transformation (or processing) and output costs.

Input costs – CSR-related costs are often associated with the nature of the relationship between an operation and its suppliers. As in the example of Gap above, socially responsible behaviour involves careful monitoring of all suppliers so as to ensure that their practices conform with what is generally accepted as good practice (although this does vary in different parts of the world) and does not involve dealing with ethically questionable sources. All this requires extra costs of monitoring, setting up audit procedures, and so on. The benefits of doing this are related to the avoidance of reputational risk. Good audit procedures allow firms to take advantage of lower input costs while avoiding the promotion of exploitative practices. In addition, from an ethical viewpoint, one could also argue that it provides employment and promotes good practice in developing parts of the world.

Transformation (processing) costs – Many operations' processes are significant consumers of energy and produce (potentially) significant amounts of waste. It is these two aspects of processing that may require investment, for example, in new energy-saving processes, but will generate a return, in the form of lower costs, in the longer term. Also in this category could be included staff-related costs such as those that promote staff well-being, work–life balance, diversity, etc. Again, although promoting these staff-related issues may have a cost, it will also generate economic benefits associated with committed staff and the multi-perspective benefits associated with diversity. In addition, of course, there are ethical benefits of reducing energy consumption, promoting social equality, and so on.

End-of-life responsibility

Output costs – Two issues are interesting here. First is that of **'end-of-life' responsibility**. Either through legislation or consumer pressure, businesses are having to invest in processes that recycle or reuse their products after disposal. Second, there is a broader issue of businesses being expected to try and substitute services in place of products. A service that hires or leases equipment for example, is deemed to be a more efficient user of resources than one that produces and sells the same equipment, leaving it to customers to use the equipment efficiently. This issue is close to that of servitization mentioned in Chapter 1. While both of these trends involve costs to the operation, they can also generate revenue. Taking responsibility for end-of-life collection and disposal allows companies to better understand how their products have been used. Substituting services for products can be more problematic, but offers the possibility of generating revenue through the services themselves. In addition, ethically, both these trends could result in a more effective and efficient use of global resources.

Operations and the stakeholder dimension of CSR

As we discussed in Chapter 2, almost all stakeholder groups will, in some way or other, be affected by operations decisions. Here we summarize just some of these effects.

Customers' welfare is directly affected by many operations decisions. The most obvious is that their safety might be compromised. If a product is badly assembled or if the equipment used in a service (such as a rail transport system) is not maintained, customers can come to harm. But customer safety is influenced by more than good manufacturing or maintenance practice; it could also be affected by the degree to which an operation discloses the details of its activities. When should an airline admit that it has received bomb threats? At a less serious level, the ethical framework of operations decisions can affect the fairness with which customers are treated. For example, should a bank discriminate between different customers in order to give priority to those from whom they can make more profit?

Staff are constantly exposed to the ethical framework of the organization throughout their working lives. Organizations have a duty to their staff to prevent their exposure to hazards at work. This means more than preventing catastrophic physical injuries; it means that organizations must take into account the longer-term threat to staff health from, say, repetitive strain injury (RSI) due to short-cycle, repetitive work motions. A more subtle ethical duty to staff is the operation's responsibility to avoid undue workplace stress. Stress could be caused through not providing employees with the information which allows them to understand the rationale and consequences of operations decisions, or expecting staff to take decisions for which they are not equipped. Again, many staff-related ethical decisions are not straightforward. Should an operation be totally honest with its staff regarding future employment changes when doing so might provoke a labour dispute, or signal the company's intentions to its competitors?

Suppliers are always a source of ethical dilemma for the operation. Is it legitimate to put suppliers under pressure not to trade with other organizations, either to ensure that you get focused service from them or to deny competitors this source of supply? Also, do you have any right to impose your own ethical standards on your suppliers, for example, because you would not wish to exploit workers in developing countries? How much effort should you put into making sure that your suppliers are operating as you would? More significantly, would you be prepared to pay a higher price for their product or service if it meant them abandoning what you regard as unethical practice?

The community also has a right to expect its organizations to adopt a responsible attitude. Yet there are often difficult trade-offs between commercial and societal objectives. However, businesses could claim that prospering commercially is also a very valuable contribution to society, as is stated by Rolls-Royce in this extract from their CSR policy. 'The most significant contribution Rolls-Royce makes in the field of Corporate Social Responsibility comes from the wealth created by maintaining the 35,000 highly-skilled jobs which arise from our business activities, mainly in the UK, North America, Germany and the Nordic Countries. In 2004 our global wage bill was £1.5 billion. In addition, the company's activities support thousands of jobs throughout our global supply chain.'

Operations and the voluntary dimension of CSR

Some critics of corporate behaviour claim that CSR is meaningless if it involves nothing more than what is required by legislation, or even simple good management. Unless it hurts, they seem to be saying, it does not count as true CSR. So, how should operations managers view

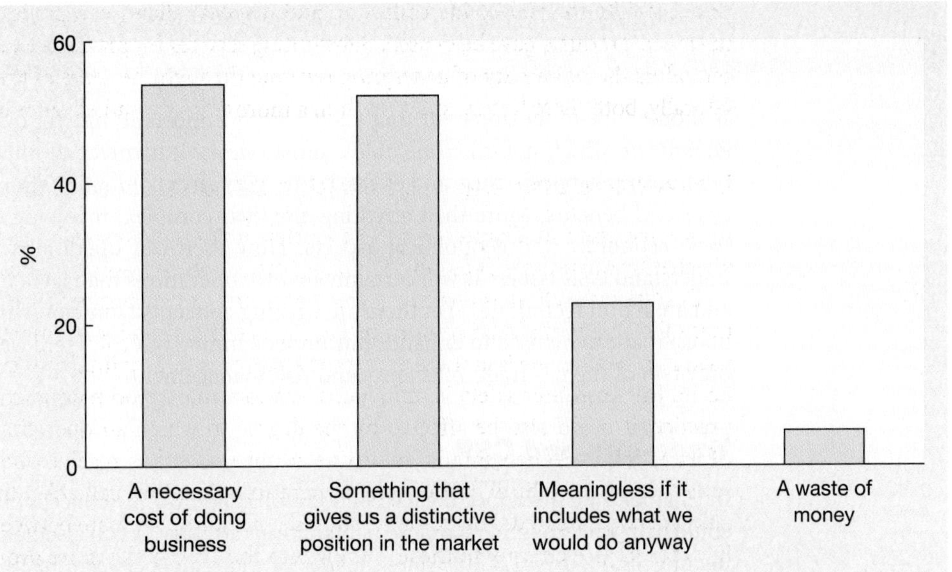

Figure 21.4 Survey results. Which of the following do you agree with? Corporate responsibility is . . .

Data from Economist Intelligence Unit, January 2008.

CSR? Figure 21.4 shows the result of one survey. The most popular response was that CSR was 'A necessary cost of doing business'. In other words, operations managers see it as something that has to be done because it is required either by legislation or through company policy. There is very little element of voluntariness in this response. Certainly there is no evidence that respondents who think this way see any advantage in going beyond what is strictly required. However, the second most popular response (running the first one very close) is that CSR gives the company something of a distinctive position in the market. In other words, there are market-based advantages in adopting CSR. While this is positive it is somewhat self-serving. CSR is seen simply as something that enhances a brand's position rather than something that tackles serious problems from a largely ethical perspective. After that, with less than half the scores of the first two categories of response, is that of CSR being meaningless if it includes what we would do anyway. This is true voluntarism. Perhaps CSR proponents will take comfort from the fact that a very small percentage of respondents thought that CSR was 'A waste of money'.

What does not come out in the survey, but is well worth considering, is that CSR activities can provide some genuine operations-based advantages. But moving beyond the minimum of engagement in CSR can provide real operations-based benefits. The obvious one, as we have mentioned before, is that in some ways the interests of CSR and those of the firm very obviously coincide. Energy saving, minimizing transport costs, avoiding reputational risk-laden issues, and so on, are the 'low hanging fruit' of CSR. But beyond this there may be advantages for businesses that regularly monitor the environment (including the business environment) generally and keep in touch with and aware of what is happening in the world. CSR can only encourage this. Finally, it may be that operations that 'push the envelope' of their own processes in order to improve their ethical behaviour also are the ones with the greater process knowledge. In other words, moving beyond the strict minimum of CSR behaviour may be one of the best signs of competent operations management. Reportedly, some stock market analysts believe that examining the excellence of a company's CSR policy may be helpful in assessing the quality of its management more generally.

How can operations managers analyse CSR issues?

It should already be apparent that CSR is both important and yet difficult to analyse. It is an issue on which not everyone holds similar views. It involves an only partially understood relationship between cause and effect. It often involves conflicting short-term and long-term costs and benefits. More than anything else, it is complex, involving operational, strategic, socio-economic and geopolitical aspects. How then can operations managers attempt to understand CSR issues? It will certainly involve operations managers in mastering new skills and analytical techniques. Yet there are existing concepts (some of which are covered in this book) that can be used to enhance our understanding of CSR. Here we have space to look at only two of them – trade-off theory and risk management.

Trade-offs and CSR

In Chapter 3 we introduce the idea of trade-offs and how the concept of the 'efficient frontier' could help with an understanding of operations strategy. It can also help with an understanding of CSR. Figure 21.5 illustrates the idea of trade-offs between the financial and the ethical performance of any operations. The first point to make is that there are relatively extreme positions on both financial and ethical performance. On the side of those who believe that CSR is essentially a distraction for business, the most famous quote comes from Milton Freeman, the famous economist, who said:

> *'The business of business is business. A society that puts equality before freedom will get neither. A society that puts freedom before equality will get a high degree of both.'*

In the opposite corner, representing those who believe that business should only exist in the context of a broader set of social responsibilities, is the founder of Body Shop – Anita Roddick. She said:

> *'In terms of power and influence . . . there is no more powerful institution in society than business . . . The business of business should not be about money, it should be about responsibility. It should be about public good, not private greed.'*

In between these two positions, most businesses try and reach some degree of compromise. In this sense they are 'repositioning' themselves on an efficient frontier as in Figure 21.5(a). As pointed out in Chapter 3, repositioning an operation on the efficient frontier is sometimes necessary as the demands of the market (or environment) change. Also, as we pointed out in Chapter 3, it is possible either to adopt an extreme position at either end of the efficient frontier (that is, designing a focused operation) or to try and break through the efficient frontier through operations improvement activities. In this case, it is increasingly difficult to focus exclusively on either financial or ethical performance. Societal pressure and issues of reputational risk are defining minimum ethical standards while tough market conditions and stockholder expectations are defining minimum financial standards. Thus exercising improvement creativity to try and become better at financial and ethical performance simultaneously could be argued to be the only realistic option for most businesses, see Figure 21.5(b).

Risk management

Although treating CSR as risk management is frowned on by some experts, it is likely that, in practice, many companies, while doing their best to adopt ethical standards, are certainly influenced by the reputational risks of unethical behaviour. Look at this quotation from one report on the subject. *'Most of the rhetoric on CSR may be about doing the right thing and trumping competitors, but much of the reality is plain risk management. It involves limiting the damage to the brand and the bottom line that can be inflicted by a bad press and consumer boycotts, as well as dealing with the threat of legal action.'*[16] Given this, it is worth reminding

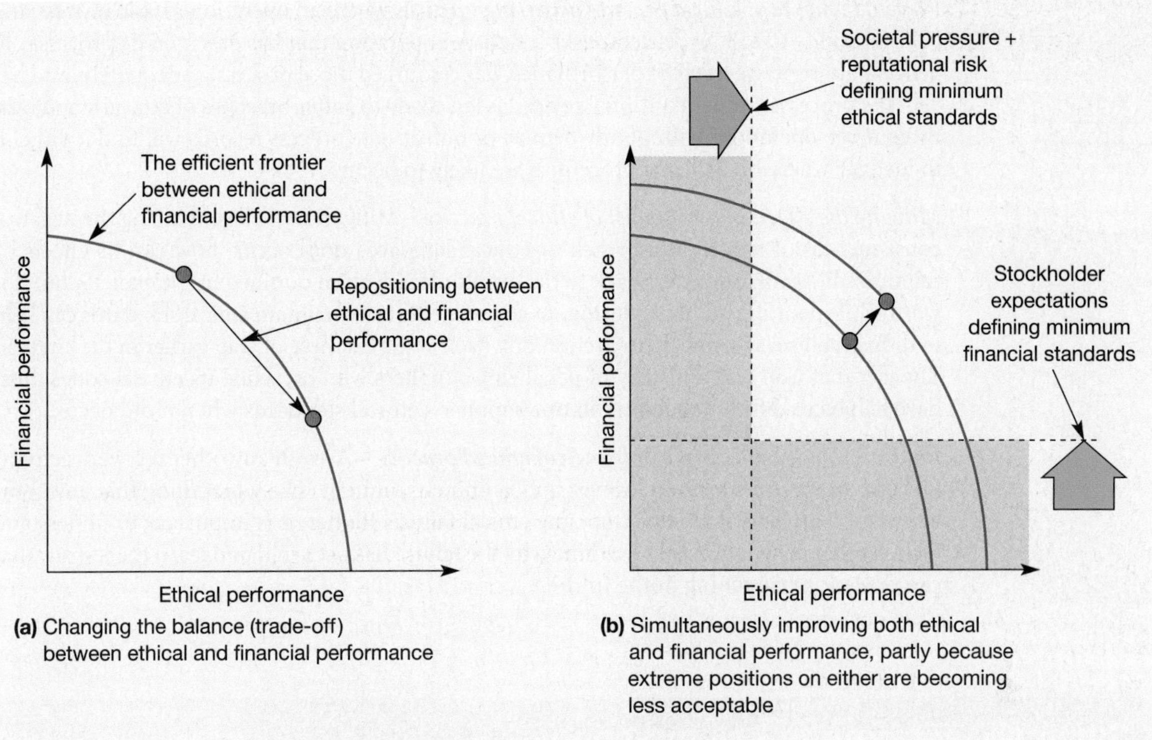

Figure 21.5 To what extent do ethical and financial performance trade off?

ourselves of how we described risk management in Chapter 19. Figure 21.6 summarizes an operations view of risk management as it could be applied to CSR. Essentially it involves thinking through and planning for four steps.

Assess the potential causes of and risks from any breach of ethical practice – The first stage in any risk management is to look at what could go wrong. In this case, exactly what could the operation do that would fall short of sound ethical practice? One of the main problems here is that different stakeholders will judge what sound ethical practice is differently.

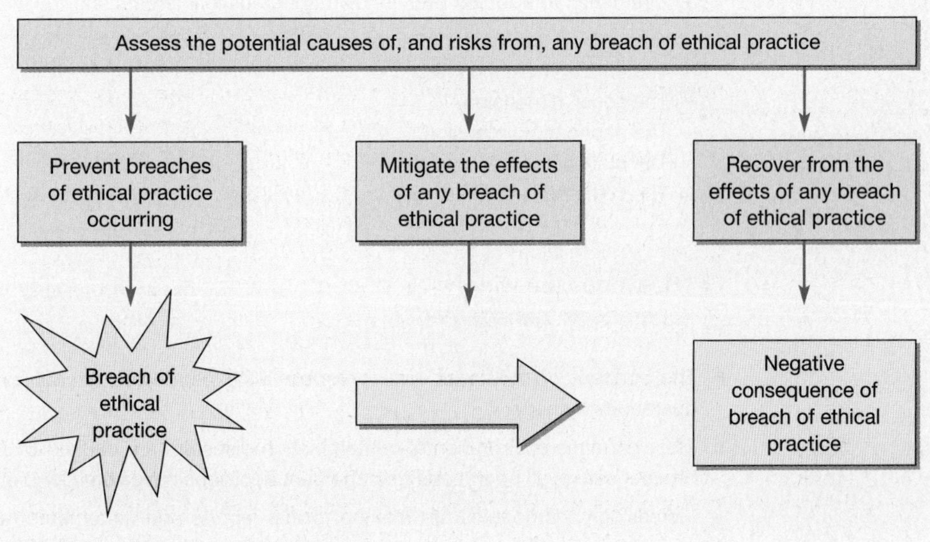

Figure 21.6 CSR as risk management

Prevent breaches of ethical practice occurring – This is where an operation's basic process and cultural ability to follow procedures is tested. An operation that has designed its processes to delivery appropriate levels of performance, has resourced those processes adequately, and has kept the processes under continual review, is less likely to suffer breaches of ethical standards. By contrast, operations with poorly defined or out-of-date process records will find it difficult to identify where breaches of procedure are likely to occur.

Mitigate the effects of any breach of ethical practice – Mitigation means reducing the negative consequences of failure. If a breach of ethical standards does occur, how can its effects be minimized? Again, one refers back to the details of mitigation outlined in Chapter 19, but it is worthwhile pointing out that a history of genuine efforts to maintain ethical standards can help to diffuse failures when they do occur. Look back at the example of Gap earlier in the chapter. The fact that Gap had a history of penalizing suppliers who breached its ethical codes must have helped to diffuse the failure in one supplier's ethical standards when it did occur.

Recover from the effects of any breach of ethical practice – As with any other recovery activity, it is important to be prompt, honest and genuinely penitent. The worst thing that any company could do is try and 'cover up' any ethical failure. Rather, it is important to understand what has happened, honestly examine why the failure has occurred and learn the lessons that can prevent it happening in the future.

Summary answers to key questions

*Check and improve your understanding of this chapter using self assessment questions and a personalised study plan, audio and video downloads, and an eBook – all at **www.myomlab.com**.*

➤ What is corporate social responsibility (CSR)?

- CSR is about how business takes account of its economic, social and environmental impacts in the way it operates – maximizing the benefits and minimizing the downsides. It is the voluntary actions that business can take, over and above compliance with minimum legal requirements, to address both its own competitive interests and the interests of wider society.
- Although there are many definitions of CSR, they usually include five 'dimensions':
  - The environmental dimension
  - The social dimension
  - The economic dimension
  - The stakeholder dimension
  - The voluntariness dimension.

➤ How does the wider view of corporate social responsibility influence operations management?

- The concept of corporate social responsibility permeates almost every decision taken by operations managers.
- Most dramatic environmental contamination disasters are caused by operational failure. In a broader sense, all operations management decisions have some kind of environmental impact.
- Increasingly, companies are making formal reports and statements relating to their environmental practice. Operations managers are often responsible for providing the basic information for these reports. The environmental management system ISO 14000 is being adopted by a wide range of organizations. Operations managers will often have to implement these standards.

- Corporate social responsibility includes understanding the effects of operations management decisions on all stakeholder groups.
- Although globalization is an emotive issue, operations managers are affected in all the decision areas by aspects of globalization.
- Operations managers are at the forefront of trying to balance any costs of CSR with any benefits. This means attempting to understand where extra expenditure will be necessary in order to adopt socially responsible practices against the savings and/or benefits that will accrue from these same practices.
- Groups that are affected by ethical management practice include the organization, the customers, staff, suppliers, the wider community and the organization's shareholders.
- Some authorities claim that CSR is meaningless if it involves nothing more than what is required by legislation, or even simple good management.

➤ How can operations managers analyse CSR issues?

- Analysing CSR issues in difficult in the context of operations management decisions, partly because of the complexity of those issues. Two models that were introduced in earlier chapters, and can be used to understand how to approach CSR, are trade-off analysis (including the idea of the efficient frontier) and risk management.

Case study
CSR as it is presented

The following are extracts from the corporate social responsibility corporate web sites of four reputable companies.

Source: Corbis

HSBR (bank)

For HSBC, . . . 'CSR' means addressing the expectations of our customers, shareholders, employees and other stakeholders in managing our business responsibly and sensitively for long-term success. . . . [this involves] . . . Listening to our stakeholders . . . [which] . . . helps us to develop our business in ways that will continue to appeal to customers, investors, employees and other stakeholders. . . . We believe the world is a rich and diverse place. The better our workforce reflects this diversity, the better we can anticipate and meet our customers' needs. . . . Involving our employees in the community brings many benefits. Our employees gain in understanding, confidence and self-esteem. And being recognised in the community as good corporate citizens and employers helps HSBC to attract great people who in turn can provide great service to our customers.

Orange (mobile telecoms operator)

As part of our commitment to corporate social responsibility and to the communities we operate in, Orange have developed a framework in the UK called community futures, which is about enabling people to participate more fully in society. It provides a co-ordinated approach to our corporate community involvement, bringing together all activities undertaken by our employees and the company. Community futures covers three core areas – charity, community futures awards and education. Many people with sensory disabilities find it difficult to participate fully in society. Communication is clearly key to improving lives and we believe our expertise in this area can make a real

difference. Therefore, we have chosen sensory disability, with a focus on the visually and hearing impaired, as the single issue for national campaigning in the UK. Orange support local projects around the country that are working to make a difference to people with sensory disabilities. Through the provision of awards, Orange seek to recognise and reward innovative community projects that use communication to enable people with sensory disabilities to participate more fully in society. Education plays a key role in any community, bringing it together. It helps people participate more fully in society by improving the ability to communicate.

John Lewis Partnership (retailer)
The Partnership was ahead of its time in recognising that commercial success depended on showing the highest level of good citizenship in its behaviour within the community. Today we are best known for the fact that our business is owned for the benefit of our employees, but we know that to cut our way through tough competitive conditions, we have to continue to prize sound relationships with our customers and suppliers, and sustain a keen sense of civic responsibility.

Starbucks (coffee shops)
Giving back to communities and the environment. Treating people with respect and dignity. Serving the world's best coffee. Every day, we demonstrate our beliefs in the guiding principles of our mission statement in the way we do business. In fact, corporate social responsibility at Starbucks runs deeply throughout our company. Here are some of the commitments we've made to do business in a socially responsible manner. (a) By making investments that benefit coffee producers, their families and communities, and the natural environment, Starbucks is helping to promote a sustainable model for the worldwide production and trade of high-quality coffee. (b) From promoting conservation in coffee-growing countries to in-store 'Green Teams' and recycling programs, Starbucks has established high standards for environmental responsibility. (c) We strive to be a responsible neighbour and active contributor in the communities where our partners and customers live, work and play. (d) At Starbucks, we believe in treating people with respect and dignity. This is especially true of the way we treat the people who work for Starbucks – our partners.

Questions

1 What are the similarities and differences between these statements?

2 Why do large companies like these go to so much trouble to invest in CSR?

3 Of these companies, two, HSBC and Starbucks, have been the target of anti-globalization violence. Why these two?

Problems and application

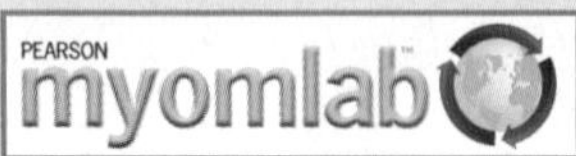

*These problems and applications will help to improve your analysis of operations. You can find more practice problems as well as worked examples and guided solutions on MyOMLab at **www.myomlab.com**.*

Try debating the following points:

- Business ethics is a contradiction in terms.
- For-profit companies have a primary responsibility to their shareholders; social responsibility therefore only makes sense when it is in the commercial interests of companies.
- Life would be considerably simpler if we went back to serving our own national markets rather than global ones.
- Anti-capitalist globalization protesters are basically conservatives who are frightened by the modern world. Throughout history there have been people like this.
- Soon all organizations will be global organizations. The Internet will see to that.
- The modern corporation cannot separate itself from the society in which it operates. We are entering the mature age of capitalism, where business objectives must reflect the interests of all their stakeholders.
- The only way to get firms to be environmentally responsible is by taxing them for the environmental damage they do.
- The best way to encourage firms to be environmentally responsible is by educating customers only to buy products and services from environmentally responsible companies.
- How can operations managers ever be creative in their response to CSR? To do their job well, they have to be dull, technologically obsessed and sad. They ought to get a life.

Selected further reading

Harvard Business Review (2003) *Harvard Business Review on Corporate Responsibility*, Harvard Business School Press, Boston.

Kotler, P. and Lee, N. (2005) *Corporate Social Responsibility: Doing the Most Good for Your Company and Your Cause*, John Wiley & Sons Inc.

McWilliams, A. and Siegel, D. (2001) Corporate social responsibility: a theory of the firm perspective, *Academy of Management Review*, vol. 26, no. 1, 117–27. Discusses the 'ideal' level of CSR, which managers can determine using cost–benefit analysis.

Useful web sites

www.imf.org The International Monetary Fund web site. Not a neutral in the globalization debate, but some well-argued commentary.

www.ifg.org Site of the International Forum on Globalization (IFG), an 'alliance of sixty leading activists, scholars, economists, researchers and writers formed to stimulate new thinking, joint activity, and public education in response to economic globalization'. They don't like it, but their discussions are interesting.

www.sustainable-development.gov.uk/ The UK government's site.

www.technologyreview.com/ MIT's online technology review. Full of interesting stuff (if you like technology, that is).

www.kmmagazine.com/ A knowledge management journal with articles and links.

Now that you have finished reading this chapter, why not visit MyOMLab at ***www.myomlab.com*** *where you'll find more learning resources to help you make the most of your studies and get a better grade?*

Notes on chapters

Chapter 1

1 Sources include: company web site (2009), Baraldi, E. (2008) Strategy in industrial networks: experiences from IKEA, *California Management Review*, vol. 50, no. 4, IKEA plans to end stressful shopping, London *Evening Standard*, 24 April 2006, Walley, P. and Hart, K. (1993) *IKEA (UK) Ltd*, Loughborough University Business School.
2 We are grateful to Simon Topman of Acme Whistles for his assistance.
3 Source: Oxfam web site (2009).
4 Source: Discussion with company staff.
5 Quote from Chairman of the British Medical Association, speech from the Annual Conference, 2002.
6 An earlier version of this case appeared in Johnston, R., Chambers, S., Harland, C. Harrison, A. and Slack, N. (2003) *Cases in Operations Management*, 3rd edn, Financial Times Prentice Hall, Harlow.

Chapter 2

1 Sources include: BBC web site, BA managers leave after T5 fiasco, 15 April 2008; Browning, A., How do you clear a bags backlog? BBC web site, 19 April 2008; Fran Yeoman and Nico Hines, Heathrow T5 disruption to continue over weekend, Times Online, 28 March 2008; Kevin Done, BA to cancel hundreds more flights from T5, *Financial Times*, 30 March 2008; Kevin Done, Long haul to restore BA's reputation, *Financial Times*, 28 March 2008; David Robertson Why Heathrow's T5 disaster provide a lesson for Dubai's T3, *The Times*, 29 November 2008.
2 Jensen, M.C. (2001) Value maximization, stakeholder theory, and the corporate objective function, *Journal of Applied Corporate Finance*, vol. 14, no. 3, 7–21.
3 Source: Catherine Pyne and Nick Fuge, Lower Hurst Farm.
4. Sources include: Marlinson, C., The golden hour, *Sunday Times*, 21 Sept. 2006.
5 Sources include: Dabbawala web site (2009) www.mydabbawala.com; *The Economist*, The cult of the dabbawala, 10 Jul 2008; Ashling O'Connor, Big business learns a thing or two from the humble dabbawalas, *The Times* (of London), 21 April 2007.
6 Source: Fiona Rennie, Discussions with the News Team at the BBC.
7 Source: John Hendry-Pickup of Aldi.
8 Hon Hai web site, www.foxconn.com.
9 Source: Miles, A. and Baldwin, T., Spidergram to check on police forces, *The Times*, 10 July 2002.
10 Skinner, W. (1985) *Manufacturing: The Formidable Competitive Weapon*, John Wiley.
11 We are grateful to the management of the Penang Mutiara for permission to use this example.

Chapter 3

1 Sources include: press releases, Ryanair; Keenan, S., How Ryanair put its passengers in their place, *The Times*, 19 June 2002; Flextronics web site.
2 Hayes, R.H. and Wheelwright, S.C. (1984) *Restoring our Competitive Edge*, John Wiley.
3 For a more thorough explanation, *see* Slack, N. and Lewis, M. (2008) *Operations Strategy*, 2nd edn, Financial Times Prentice Hall, Harlow.
4 Mintzberg, H. and Waters, J.A. (1995) Of strategies: deliberate and emergent, *Strategic Management Journal*, July/Sept.
5 Also called 'critical success factors' by some authors.
6 Hill, T. (1993) *Manufacturing Strategy*, 2nd edn, Macmillan.
7 There is a vast literature which describes the resource-based view of the firm. For example, *see* Barney, J. (1991) The resource-based model of the firm: origins, implications and prospect, *Journal of Management*, vol. 17, no. 1; or Teece, D.J. and Pisano, G. (1994) The dynamic capabilities of firms: an introduction, *Industrial and Corporate Change*, vol. 3, no. 3.
8 Source: Lifting the bonnet, *Economist*, 7 October 2006.
9 Weick, K.E. (1990) Cartographic myths in organizations, in A. Huff (ed.) *Managing Strategic Thought*, Wiley, London.
10 This case was written by Shirley Johnston, 2009. It is based on a real organization and all names and places have been changed.

Chapter 4

1 Source Horovitz, A., Fast food world says drive-through is the way to go, *USA Today*, 3 April, 2002.
2 Source: Genes, R. (2002) Smart ecology, *The Manufacturing Engineer*, April.
3 Hayes, R.H. and Wheelwright, S.C. (1984) *Restoring our Competitive Edge*, John Wiley.
4 Hayes, R.H. and Wheelwright, S.C. *op. cit.*
5 The Workflow Management Coalition (2009) www.wfmc.org
6 *The Economist*, A new departure for London's airports, 21 Aug 2008.

Chapter 5

1 Sources include: *The Times*, Timeline – Airbus A380 superjumbo, 26 October 2006; BBC news web site, Q&A: A380 delays, Monday, 30 October 2006; BBC news web site, Q&A: Airbus job cuts, 28 February 2007; Peggy Hollinger and Gerrit Wiesmann, Airbus is hampered by cultural differences, The *Financial Times*, 15 July 2008; *The Economist*, Airbus Marathon man, 17 Jul 2008; *The Economist*, Boeing and Airbus – swings and roundabouts, 27 Nov 2008.
2 The Design Council web site.

3 Sources include: Doran, J., Hoover heading for sell-off as Dyson cleans up in America, *The Times*, 4 February, 2006.

4 Sources: many thanks to Mark Taber and his site www.takelifeeasy.com; *The Economist*, Open, but not as usual, 16 Mar 2006; Ralph Kisiel, BMW wants joint effort to develop open-source in-vehicle platform, *Automotive News Europe*, 23 October 2008.

5 Sources include: Square fruit stuns Japanese shoppers, BBC web site, Friday, 15 June 2001; S. Poulter, Square melons on the way, *Daily Mail*, 3rd August 2006; we would also like to thank our colleague, Paul Walley, who first found this example for us.

6 With thanks to George Northwood, Manager of Daniel Hersheson's Mayfair salon.

7 Source: Think local, *The Economist*, 13 April 2002.

8 For more information on QFD for products and services *see*, for example: Behara, R.S. and Chase, R.B. (1993) Service quality deployment: quality service by design *in* Sarin, R.V. (ed.), *Perspectives in Operations Management: Essays in Honor of Elwood S. Buffa*, Kluwer Academic Publishers; Evans, J.R. and Lindsay, W.M. (1993) *The Management and Control of Quality* (2nd edn), West Publishing, Minneapolis; Fitzsimmons, J.A. and Fitzsimmons, M.J. (1994) *Service Management for Competitive Advantage*, McGraw-Hill; Meredith, J.R. (1992) *The Management of Operations* (4th edn), John Wiley.

9 Taguchi, G. and Clausing, D. (1990) 'Robust quality', *Harvard Business Review*, vol. 68, no. 1, 65–75.

10 Bennis, W. and Biederman, P.W., *Organizing Genius: The Secrets of Creative Collaboration*, Addison-Wesley, 1997; new edn, Nicholas Brealey, 1998.

11 Hayes, R.H., Wheelwright, S.C. and Clarke, K.B. (1988) *Dynamic Manufacturing*, The Free Press.

Chapter 6

1 Source: For whom the Dell tolls, *Economist*, 13 May 2006; Rory Cellan-Jones, Dell aims to reclaim global lead, BBC Business, 14 April 2008.

2 Brandenburger, A.M. and Nalebuff, B.J. (1996) *Co-opetition*, Doubleday, New York.

3 Hayes, R.H. and Wheelwright, S.C. (1994) *Restoring our Competitive Edge*, John Wiley.

4 Sources: Einhorn, B. and Zegels, T.M., The underdog nipping at Quanta's heels, *Business Week*, 21 October 2002; *Economist*, His hi-tech highness, 13 July 2002.

5 Bacon, G., Machan, I. and Dnyse, J. (2008) Offshore challenges, Manufacturing, The Institute of Electrical Engineers, January.

6 Sources include: Devendra Damle; *Economist*, Nano wars, 28 August 2008; *Economist*, The one-lakh car, 10 January 2008; *Economist*, A new home for the Nano, 9 October 2008.

7 Sources include: www.tescoplc.com, www.investorcentre.tescoplc.com/plc, www.tescolotus.net and discussions with managers at Tesco.

8 Source: 2003 Cedep Working paper, Paris.

9 Sources: Einhorn, B., Hi-tech in China, *Business Week*, 28 October 2002; Kripalani, M., Calling Bangalore, *Business Week*, 11 November 2002.

10 This case was prepared using published sources of information. It does not reflect the views of the Walt Disney Company, which should not be held responsible for the accuracy or interpretation of any of the information or views contained in the case. It is not intended to illustrate either good or bad management practice.

Supplement to Chapter 6

1 Linstone, H.A. and Turoof, M. (1975) *The Delphi Method: Techniques and Applications*, Addison-Wesley.

2 Hogarth, R.M. and Makridakis, S. (1981) Forecasting and planning: an evaluation, *Management Science*, vol. 27, 115–38.

3 Hogarth, R.M. and Makridakis, S., *op. cit.*

4 Armstrong, J.S. and Grohman, M.C. (1972) A comparative study of methods for long-range market forecasting, *Management Science*, vol. 19, no. 2, 211–21.

Chapter 7

1 Sources: Paul Walley, our colleague in the Operations Management Group at Warwick Business School, Irisys web site (2009) www.irisys.co.uk, Martin, P., How supermarkets make a meal of you, *Sunday Times*, 4 November 2000.

2 Jonathon Carr-Brown, French factory surgeon cuts NHS queues, *Sunday Times*, 23 October 2005.

3 Sources: Interviews with company staff and Johnston, R., Chambers, S., Harland, C., Harrison, A. and Slack, N. (2003) *Cases in Operations Management*, 3rd edn, Financial Times Prentice Hall, Harlow.

4 Francis, Richard L. and White, John A. (1974) *Facilities Layout and Location*, Prentice-Hall, Englewood Cliffs, NJ.

5 There are many different methods of balancing. See, for example, Kilbridge, K. and Wester, L. (1961), A heuristic method of assembly line balancing, *Journal of Industrial Engineering*, vol. 57, no. 4; or Steyn, P.G. (1977) Scheduling multi-model production lines, *Business Management*, vol. 8, no. 1.

Chapter 8

1 *Economist*, Help! There's nobody in the cockpit, 21 December 2002.

2 Sources: *Financial Times*, Rise of the robots, 3 April 2009; *The Times*, When robots do the really dangerous jobs, 14 August 2006.

3 Sources: Company web site and George, R., Mr Sushi-Go-Round, *The Independent on Sunday*, 30 December 2001.

4 Source: IBM company web site.

5 Source: Booz Allen and Hamilton data quoted in de Jacquelot, P. (1999) Ups and downs of Internet banking, *Connections*, Issue 1, *Financial Times*.

6 Based on A. Gunasekaran, H.B. Marri, R.E. McGaughey and M.D. Nebhwani (2002) E-commerce and its impact on operations management, *International Journal of Production Economics*, 75, 185–97.

7 Tiwari, Rajnish and Buse, Stephan (2007) *The Mobile Commerce Prospects: A Strategic Analysis of Opportunities in the Banking Sector*, Hamburg University Press.

8 Adapted from Jayaraman, V. and Srivastara, R. (1996) 'Export systems in Production and Operations Management', International Journal of Operations and Production Management, vol. 16, no. 12.
9 Brown, D., Mechanical milkman allows farmer a lie in, *Daily Telegraph*, 11 Sept. 1993.
10 Loh Den (2008) My New Favorite Barber: QB House, denniland.com, 25 June.
11 Walley, P. and Amin, V. (1994) 'Automation in a Customer Contact Environment', *International Journal of Operations and Production Management*, vol. 14, no. 5, 86–100.
12 Details courtesy of Johan Lindén, S.V.T. and Pär Åhlström, Chalmers University.
13 Dosi, G., Teece, D. and Winter, S.G. (1992) 'Towards a theory of corporate coherence', in Dosi, G., Giametti, R. and Toninelli, P.A. (eds) Technology and Enterprise in a Historical Perspective, Oxford University Press.
14 Chew, W.B., Leonard-Barton, D. and Bohn, R.E. (1991) Beating Murphy's Law, Sloan Management Review, vol. 5, Spring.

Chapter 9

1 Sources include: company web site; The Sunday Times Best Companies to work for, W.L. Gore & Associates (UK), *The Sunday Times*, 8 March 2009; Simon Caulkin, Gore-Tex gets made without managers, *The Observer*, Sunday 2 November 2008; Nick Smith, Profile: W.L. Gore, The Institution of Engineering and Technology Knowledge network, 21 October 2008.
2 Accenture web site, www.accenture.com.
3 Ulrich, D. (1997) *Human Resource Champions: The Next Agenda for Adding Value and Delivering Results*, Harvard Business School Press, Boston.
4 Source: Fuzzy maths, *The Economist*, 13 May 2006.
5 The Health and Safety Executive (HSE) of the UK government, www.hse.gov.uk/stress.
6 Based on work from the Advisory, Conciliation and Arbitration Service, ACAS.
7 Morgan describes these and other metaphors in Gareth Morgan (1986) *Images of Organization*, Sage.
8 Hoxie, R.F. (1915) *Scientific Management and Labour*, D. Appleton, Washington, DC.
9 Hackman, J.R. and Oldham, G. (1975) A new strategy for job enrichment, *California Management Review*, vol. 17, no. 3.
10 Bowen, D.E. and Lawler, E.E. (1992) The empowerment of service workers: what, why, how and when, *Sloan Management Review*, vol. 33, no. 3, 31–9.
11 Sources include: company web site; The Times Best 100 Companies, www.thetimes100.co.uk.
12 Kobrick, J.L. and Fine, B.J. (1983) Climate and human performance' *in* Osborne, D.J. and Gruneberg, M.M. (eds) *The Physical Environment and Work*, John Wiley.
13 This case was written by Dr Ran Bhamra, Lecturer in Engineering Management, Loughborough University. It is based on a real situation, but names have been changed for reasons of commercial confidentiality.

Chapter 10

1 Source: Interview with Joanne Cheung, Steve Deeley and other staff at Godfrey Hall, BMW Dealership, Coventry.
2 Sources: Jean Farman (1999) 'Les Coulisses du Vol', Air France. Talk presented by Richard, E. Stone, Northwest Airlines at the IMA Industrial Problems Seminar, 1998.
3 The concept of *P*:*D* ratios comes originally from Shingo, S. (1981) *Study of Toyota Production Systems*, Japan Management Association; and was extended by Mather, K. (1988) *Competitive Manufacturing*, Prentice-Hall.
4 Source: Walley, P. (2009) MBA Course Notes, Warwick University, UK.
5 Johnson, S.M. (1954) Optimal two-stage and three-stage production schedules, *Naval Logistics Quarterly*, vol. 1, no. 1.
6 We are grateful to our colleague Paul Walley for this section.
7 Source: Thanks to Lawrence Wilkins for this example.
8 Goldratt, E.Y. and Cox, J. (1984) *The Goal*, North River Press, Great Barrington, Mass.
9 These are described in Betts, A. and Slack, N. (1999) Control, knowledge and learning in process development, *Internal Report*, University of Warwick Business School. The original four dimensions are based on Hofstede, G. (1981) Management control in public and not for profit activities, *Accounting Organization and Society*, vol. 6, no. 3.
10 Source: Company website.

Chapter 11

1 With thanks to Alistair Brandon-Jones of Bath Business School and staff at Britvic National Distribution Centre.
2 Sources: Ashworth, J., 'Met Office brings sunshine to the shops, *The Times*, 17 August 2002; *The Economist*, And now here is the health forecast, 3 August 2002; Jackson, H., Weather derivates are hot, *Wall Street Journal Europe*, 13 February 2002.
3 With special thanks to Philip Godfrey and Cormac Campbell of OEE Consulting Ltd. (www.oeeconsulting.com).
4 Sources: Lynch, P. (1991) Making time for productivity, *Personnel Management*, March; and Pickard, J. (1991) Annual hours: a year of living dangerously, *Personnel Management*, Aug.
5 Kimes, S. (1989) Yield management: a tool for capacity-constrained service firms, *Journal of Operations Management*, vol. 8, no. 4.
6 Sources include Robinette, S. (2001) Get emotional, *Harvard Business Review*, May.
7 Maister, D. (1983) The psychology of waiting lines, *Harvard Business Review*, Jan–Feb.

Chapter 12

1 Source: NBS web site and discussions with NBS staff.
2 With special thanks to John Mathews, Howard Smith Paper Group.

Chapter 13

1 This example was prepared by Carsten Dittrich of the University of Southern Denmark. Siemens case back-

ground data: © Siemens Archives 2007. Sources include Siemens Homepage web-source: http://w1.siemens.com/entry/cc/en/. Special thanks to Dr. Christian Frühwald, Partner – Supply Chain Consulting, Siemens Procurement & Logistics Services.

2 Source: Grant, J., A cautionary tale of roof racks and widgets, *Financial Times*, 4 November 2002.

3 Definition from the UK Government Purchasing Agency.

4 Source: Grad, C., A network of supplies to be woven into the web, *Financial Times*, 9 February 2000.

5 Garcia-Dastugue, S.J. and Lambert, D.M. (2003) Internet-enabled coordination in the supply chain, *Industrial Marketing Management*, vol. 3, no. 32.

6 Wheatley, C., How to know if e-procurement is right for you, *CIO Magazine*, 15 June 2003.

7 Minahan, T., Global sourcing: what you need to know to make it work. CIO.com, 11 August 2003.

8 Source: www.levistrauss.com/responsibility/conduct/guidelines.

9 Source: Interview with David Garman, September 2006.

10 This short case was written by Richard Small. Sources include: Helia Ebrahimi, Hedge funds put Gate Gourmet in the departure lounge, *Daily Telegraph*, 6 Dec. 2008; Maggie Urry, Northern Foods wins BA contract, *Financial Times*, 5 December 2008.

11 Parkhe, A. (1993) Strategic alliance structuring, *Academy of Management Journal*, vol. 36, 794–829.

12 Fisher, M.L. (1997) What is the right supply chain for your product, *Harvard Business Review*, March–April.

13 Basu, A. and Siems, F. (2004) The impact of e-business technologies on supply chain operations, Working Paper 0404, The Reserve Bank of Dallas, November.

14 Source: Lee, H.L. and Whang, S. (2001) Demand chain excellent: a tale of two retailers, *Supply Chain Management Review*, 3 January.

15 Towill, D.R. (1996) Time compression and supply chain management – a guided tour, *Supply Chain Management*, vol. 1, no. 1.

16 Christopher, M. (2002) Business is failing to manage supply chain vulnerability, *Odyssey*, Issue 16, June.

17 All information taken from each company's web site.

Chapter 14

1 With thanks to Julian Goulder, Director, Logistics Processes and IT, Rolls-Royce.

2 Wight, O. (1984) *Manufacturing Resource Planning: MRP II*, Oliver Wight Ltd.

3 Christopher Koch and Thomas Wailgum (2007) ERP definition and solutions, www.cio.com.

4 Source: Company web site www.sap.com.

5 Source: Thanks to Lawrence Wilkins for this example.

6 Satyam press release, Satyam to Implement SAP at Vijay Dairy & Farm Products (P) Ltd, Satyam Computer Services Ltd, 23 March 2009.

7 Based on a review of the research in this area by Sherry Finney and Martin Corbett (2007) ERP implementation: a compilation and analysis of critical success factors, *Business Process Management Journal*, vol. 13, no. 3, 329–47.

8 Chris Kanaracus, Waste Management sues SAP over ERP implementation, *InfoWorld*, 27 March 2008.

9 Turbit, N. (2005) ERP Implementation – The Traps, The Project Perfect White Paper Collection, www.projectperfect.com.au.

Chapter 15

1 Spear, S. and Bowen, H.K. (1999) Decoding the DNA of the Toyota production system, *Harvard Business Review*, Sept–Oct.

2 Harrison, A. (1992) *Just-in-time Manufacturing in Perspective*, Prentice Hall.

3 Kamata, S. (1983) *Japan in the Passing Lane: An Insider's Account of Life in a Japanese Auto Factory*, Allen and Unwin.

4 Based on an example in Womack, J.P. and Jones, D.T. (1996) *Lean Thinking*, Simon and Shuster, New York.

5 Source: Mathieson, S.A., NHS should embrace lean times, *The Guardian*, Thursday 8 June 2006.

6 Quoted in: Schonberger, R. (1982) *Japanese Manufacturing Techniques*, The Free Press.

7 Yamashina, H. Reducing set-up times makes your company flexible and more competitive, unpublished, quoted in Harrison A., *op. cit.*

8 This great metaphor seems to have originated from the consultancy '2think', www.2think.biz/index.htm.

9 Staats, B. and Upton, D. (2007) Lean principles and software production: evidence from Indian software services, Harvard Working Paper, Harvard Business School.

10 Goldratt, E.M. and Cox, J. (1986) *The Goal*, North River Press.

11 Goldratt, E.M. (1990) *What Is This Thing Called Theory of Constraints and How Should It Be Implemented?* The North River Press, Great Barrington, Mass.

12 Based on: Sergio Rattner (2009) What Is the Theory of Constraints, and How Does it Compare to Lean Thinking? The Lean Enterprise Institute, at www.leanvs.com/TOCvsLeanThinking.pdf.

13 Voss, C.A. and Harrison, A. (1987) Strategies for implementing JIT, *in* Voss, C.A. (ed.) *Just-in-time Manufacture*, IFS/Springer-Verlag.

Chapter 16

1 Source: Slack, A., Popping the Millau Cork, Translated and adapted from Le Figaro Entreprises, Wednesday, 15 December 2004.

2 From Nicholas, J.M. (1990) *Managing Business and Engineering Projects: Concepts and Implementation*, Prentice-Hall.

3 Based on Pinto, J.K. and Slevin, D.P. (1987) Critical success factors in successful project implementation, *IEEE Transactions on Engineering Management*, vol. 34, no. 1.

4 Weiss, J.W. and Wysocki, R.K. (1992) *Five-Phase Project Management: A Practical Planning and Implementation Guide*, Addison-Wesley.

5 Source: Interview with Leigh Rix, Project Manager, The Workhouse.

6 Barnes, M. (1985) Project management framework, *International Project Management Yearbook*, Butterworth Scientific.
7 Lock, D. (1996) *Project Management*, 6th edn, Gower.
8 Lock, D. *ibid*.
9 Source: Organization web site.

Chapter 17

1 Source: Interview with Michael Purtill, the General Manager of the Four Seasons Hotel Canary Wharf in London. We are grateful for Michael's cooperation (and for the great quality of service at his hotel!).
2 Based on Gummesson, E. (1993) Service productivity, service quality and profitability, *Proceedings of the 8th International Conference of the Operations Management Association*, Warwick, UK.
3 Parasuraman, A., Zeithaml, V.A. and Berry, L.L. (1985) A conceptual model of service quality and implications for future research, *Journal of Marketing*, vol. 49, Fall, 41–50; and Gummesson, E. (1987) Lip service: a neglected area in services marketing, *Journal of Services Marketing*, vol. 1, no. 1, 19–23.
4 Haywood-Farmer, J. and Nollet, J. (1991) *Services Plus: Effective Service Management*, Morin, Vancouver.
5 Berry, L.L. and Parasuraman, A. (1991) *Marketing Services: Competing through Quality*, The Free Press.
6 Mechling, L., Get ready for a storm in a tea shop, *The Independent*, 8 March 2002 and company web site.
7 Based on Parasuraman, A., *op. cit.*
8 Sources include: Company web site (2009); Best Factory Awards, End of day harvest extends shelf life (2005); Clarkson, G.J.J., Rothwell, S.D. and Taylor, G. (2005), *Hortscience*, vol. 40, 1431–5.
9 Source: Scan avoids needless appendectomy, *The Sunday Times*, 23 Feb 1997.
10 Feigenbaum, A.V. (1986) *Total Quality Control*, McGraw-Hill, New York.
11 Matsushito, K. (1985) Why the west will lose, *Industrial Participation*, Spring.
12 For more details of the Taguchi approach, *see* Stuart, G. (1993) *Taguchi Methods: A Hands-on Approach*, Addison-Wesley.

Chapter 18

1 Source: Deaves, M. (2002) Bottoms up! *Manufacturing Engineer*, Dec.
2 Lewis Carroll (1871) *Alice through the Looking Glass.*
3 Imai, M. (1986) *Kaizen – The Key to Japan's Competitive Success*, McGraw-Hill.
4 International Standards Organization, *ISO 8402*, 1986.
5 Dale, B.G. (1994) Quality management systems, *in* Dale, B.G. (ed.) *Managing Quality*, Prentice Hall.
6 Sources include: Company web site, The Best Factory Awards (2006).
7 Ohno, T. (1988) *Toyota Production System: Beyond Large-scale Production*, Productivity Press, Portland, Ore.
8 Davenport, T. (1995) Reengineering – the fad that forgot people, *Fast Company*, November.
9 Johansson, H.J. (1993) *Business Process Reengineering: Break Point Strategies for Market Dominance*, Wiley, New York.
10 Based on an example in Kruse, G. (1995) Fundamental innovation, *Manufacturing Engineer*, Feb.
11 For example, Davenport, T. (1995) op. cit.
12 Source: Discussion with staff at Xchanging.

Chapter 19

1 Sources include: Michael Herman and Dearbail Jordan (2007) Cadbury fined £1 million over salmonella outbreak, Times Online, 16 July, and Valerie Elliott, Cadbury admits hygiene failures over salmonella in chocolate bars, *The Times*, 16 June 2007.
2 The Institute of Risk Management, www.theirm.org/.
3 Quoted in The Risk Management Infokit (2009) Published by JISC Infonet, available at www.jiscinfonet.ac.uk.
4 Christopher, M. (2002) Business is failing to manage supply chain vulnerability, Odyssey, Issue 16, June.
5 Source: BBC News site (2008), Pilot arrested over alcohol fears, http://news.bbc.co.uk/, published 2008/10/20.
6 Sources include: Naughton, J. The typing error that gave us thirty years of spam, *The Observer*, Sunday 4 May 2008; *The Economist*, The etiquette of telecommunications: a parable of manners from Victorian dentists to modern airlines, 13 Dec 2007.
7 Information for this section is based partly on a private communication from Ben Betts of ht2.com.
8 Raynor, C., Airport security, BBC news web site, 25 July 2005.
9 Nahajima, S. (1988), Total productive maintenance, Productivity Press.
10 Source: Otis web site.
11 Armistead, C.G. and Clark, G. (1992) *Customer Service and Support*, Prentice Hall.
12 Judge, E., Instant replacements to make it business as usual – from new offices to key staff, *The Times*, 15 February 2003.
13 Based on information from Read, P.P. (1994) *Ablaze: The Story of Chernobyl*, Secker and Warburg; and Reason, J. (1987) The Chernobyl errors, *Bulletin of the British Psychological Society*, vol. 4, 201–6.

Chapter 20

1 Source: the EFQM web site, www.efqm.org.
2 Deming, W.E. (1982) *Quality, Productivity and Competitive Position*, MIT Center for Advanced Engineering Study.
3 Deming, W.E. (1986) *Out of Crisis*, MIT Center for Advanced Engineering Study.
4 Based on Neely, A. (1993) *Performance Measurement System Design – Theory and Practice*, Manufacturing Engineering Group, Cambridge University, April.
5 Kaplan, R.S. and Norton, D.P. (1993) *The Balanced Scorecard*, Harvard Business School Press, Boston, M.A.
6 Bourne, M., Franco, M. and Wilkes, J. (2003). Corporate performance management, *Measuring Business Excellence*, vol. 7, no. 3, 15.
7 Based on Slack, N. (1994) The importance–performance matrix as a determinant of improvement priorities, *Inter-*

national Journal of Operations and Production Management*, vol. 14, no. 5, 59–75.

8 Ferdows, K. and de Meyer, A. (1990) Lasting improvement in manufacturing, *Journal of Operations Management*, vol. 9, no. 2.

9 Schein, E.H. (2004) *Organizational Culture and Leadership*, 3rd edn, Jossey-Bass.

10 Johnson, G. (1988) Rethinking incrementalism, *Strategic Management Journal*, vol. 9, 75–91.

11 Bessant, J. and Caffyn, S. (1997) High involvement innovation, *International Journal of Technology Management*, vol. 14, no. 1.

12 Argyris, C. and Schon, D. (1978) *Organizational Learning*, Addison-Wesley, Reading, MA.

13 Deaves, M. (2002) Bottoms-up, *Manufacturing Engineer*, December.

14 For further details of this approach, see Schaninger, W.S., Harris, S.G. and Niebuhr, R.L. (2000) Adapting General Electric's Workout for Use in Other Organizations: A Template, www.isixsigma.com; Quinn, J. (1994) What a workout! *Sales and Marketing Management*, Performance Supplement, Nov., 58–63; Stewart, T. (1991) GE keeps those ideas coming, *Fortune*, 124 (4), 40–5.

15 The authors gratefully acknowledge the valuable assistance of Teo Yi Wen, Department of Industrial and Systems Engineering, NUS. The authors would like to thank the interviewees for their participation in this project and Johnson Paul and Sharon Foo for facilitating the research. All Rights Reserved, National Library Board Singapore and the Authors, 2009.

Chapter 21

1 World Business Council for Sustainable Development, at www.wbcsd.org.

2 Marks and Spencers, retailer, at www.marksandspencer.com.

3 CSR Asia at www.csr-asia.com.

4 BAA, airport operator, at www.baa.com.

5 Mallen Baker, a writer, speaker and strategic adviser on CSR, www.mallenbaker.net.

6 International Finance Corporation.

7 European Commission.

8 Dahlsrud, A. (2006) How corporate social responsibility is defined: an analysis of 37 definitions, *Corporate Social Responsibility and Environmental Management*, vol. 12, no. 2.

9 Ehrlich, P. and Commoner, B., as quoted in Hart, S.L. (1997), Strategies for a sustainable world, *Harvard Business Review*, Jan–Feb.

10 Meadows, D., Our footprints are treading too much earth, *Charleston (SC) Gazette*, 1 April 1996.

11 *The Economist*, Just good business, 17 Jan 2008.

12 Traidcraft Exchange (2001) EU Corporate Social Responsibility: a Green Paper, at www.traidcraft.co.uk/.

13 Source: company web site.

14 Based on Kolk, A. (2000) *The Economics of Environmental Management*, Financial Times Prentice Hall, Harlow. Also see www.globalreporting.org.

15 McDougall, D., Gap child labour shame, *The Observer*, 28 October 2007.

16 Economist Intelligence Unit (2008) Why CSR?

Glossary

ABC inventory control: an approach to inventory control that classes inventory by its usage value and varies the approach to managing it accordingly.

Acceptance sampling: a technique of quality sampling that is used to decide whether to accept a whole batch of products (and occasionally services) on the basis of a sample; it is based on the operation's willingness to risk rejecting a 'good' batch and accepting a 'bad' batch.

Active interaction technology: customer processing technology with which a customer interacts directly, for example, cash machines.

Activity: as used in project management, it is an identifiable and defined task, together with event activities form network planning diagrams.

Aggregated planning and control: a term used to indicate medium-term capacity planning that aggregates different products and services together in order to get a broad view of demand and capacity.

Agility: the ability of an operation to respond quickly and at low cost as market requirements change.

Allowances: term used in work study to indicate the extra time allowed for rest, relaxation and personal needs.

Andon: a light above a workstation that indicates its state, whether working, waiting for work, broken down, etc.; Andon lights may be used to stop the whole line when one station stops.

Annual hours: a type of flexitime working that controls the amount of time worked by individuals on an annual rather than a shorter basis.

Anthropometric data: data that relate to people's size, shape and other physical abilities, used in the design of jobs and physical facilities.

Anticipation inventory: inventory that is accumulated to cope with expected future demand or interruptions in supply.

Appraisal costs: those costs associated with checking, monitoring and controlling quality to see if problems or errors have occurred, an element within quality-related costs.

Attributes of quality: measures of quality that can take one of two states, for example, right or wrong, works or does not work, etc.

Auto-ID: abbreviation for automated identification; a device incorporating a memory chip into which is embedded a unique 95-bits-long electronic product code (ePC) that uniquely identifies an individual part or product, it enables the exact state and location of a part or component to be tracked through its life.

Automated guided vehicles (AGVs): small, independently powered vehicles that move material to and from value-adding operations.

Back-office: the low-visibility part of an operation.

Backward scheduling: starting jobs at a time when they should be finished exactly when they are due, as opposed to forward scheduling.

Balancing loss: the quantification of the lack of balance in a production line, defined as the percentage of time not used for productive purposes with the total time invested in making a product.

Bar code: a unique product code that enables a part or product type to be identified when read by a bar-code scanner.

Basic time: the time taken to do a job without any extra allowances for recovery.

Batch processes: processes that treat batches of products together, and where each batch has its own process route.

Bath-tub curve: a curve that describes the failure probabilty of a product, service or process that indicates relatively high probabilities of failure at the beginning and at the end of the life cycle.

Behavioural job design: an approach to job design that takes into account individuals' desire to fulfil their needs for self-esteem and personal development.

Benchmarking: the activity of comparing methods and/or performance with other processes in order to learn from them and/or assess performance.

Bill of materials (BOM): a list of the component parts required to make up the total package for a product or service together with information regarding their level in the product or component structure and the quantities of each component required.

Blueprinting: a term often used in service design to mean process mapping.

Bottleneck: the capacity-constraining stage in a process; it governs the output of the whole process.

Bottom-up: the influence of operational experience on operations decisions.

Brainstorming: an improvement technique where small groups of people put forward ideas in a creative free-form manner.

Break-even analysis: the technique of comparing revenues and costs at increasing levels of output in order to establish the point at which revenue exceeds cost, that is the point at which it 'breaks even'.

Breakthrough improvement: an approach to improving operations performance that implies major and dramatic change in the way an operation works, for example, business process re-engineering (BPR) is often associated with this type of improvement, also known as innovation-based improvement, contrasted with continuous improvement.

Broad definition of operations: all the activities necessary for the fulfilment of customer requests.

Broad responsibilities of operations management: the wider, long-term, ethical and strategic activities involved in producing products and services.

Buffer inventory: an inventory that compensates for unexpected fluctuations in supply and demand, can also be called safety inventory.

Bullwhip effect: the tendency of supply chains to amplify relatively small changes at the demand side of a supply chain such that the disruption at the supply end of the chain is much greater.

Business process outsourcing (BPO): the term that is applied to the outsourcing of whole business processes; this need not mean a change in location of the process, sometimes it involves an outside company taking over the management of processes that remain in the same location.

Business process re-engineering (BPR): the philosophy that recommends the redesign of processes to fulfil defined external customer needs.

Business strategy: the strategic positioning of a business in relation to its customers, markets and competitors, a subset of corporate strategy.

Capacity: the maximum level of value-added activity that an operation, or process, or facility is capable of over a period of time.

Capacity lagging: the strategy of planning capacity levels such that they are always less than or equal to forecast demand.

Capacity leading: the strategy of planning capacity levels such that they are always greater or equal to forecast demand.

Cause–effect diagrams: a technique for searching out the root cause of problems, it is a systematic questioning technique, also known as Ishikawa diagrams.

Cell layout: locating transforming resources with a common purpose such as processing the same types of product, serving similar types of customer, etc., together in close proximity (a cell).

Centre-of-gravity method of location: a technique that uses the physical analogy of balance to determine the geographical location that balances the weighted importance of the other operations with which the one being located has a direct relationship.

Chase demand: an approach to medium-term capacity management that attempts to adjust output and/or capacity to reflect fluctuations in demand.

Cluster analysis: a technique used in the design of cell layouts to find which process groups fit naturally together.

Combinatorial complexity: the idea that many different ways of processing products and services at many different locations or points in time combine to result in an exceptionally large number of feasible options; the term is often used in facilities layout and scheduling to justify non-optimal solutions (because there are too many options to explore).

Commonality: the degree to which a range of products or services incorporate identical components (also called 'parts commonality').

Community factors: those factors that are influential in the location decision that relate to the social, political and economic environment of the geographical position.

Competitive factors: the factors such as delivery time, product or service specification, price, etc. that define customers' requirements.

Component structure: *see* 'Product structure'.

Computer-aided design (CAD): a system that provides the computer ability to create and modify product, service or process drawings.

Computer-integrated manufacturing (CIM): a term used to describe the integration of computer-based monitoring and control of all aspects of a manufacturing process, often using a common database and communicating via some form of computer network.

Computer numerically controlled (CNC): machines that use a computer to control their activities, as opposed to those controlled directly through human intervention.

Concept generation: a stage in the product and service design process that formalizes the underlying idea behind a product or service.

Concurrent engineering: *see* 'Simultaneous development'.

Condition-based maintenance: an approach to maintenance management that monitors the condition of process equipment and performs work on equipment only when it is required.

Content of strategy: the set of specific decisions and actions that shape the strategy.

Continuous improvement: an approach to operations improvement that assumes many, relatively small, incremental, improvements in performance, stress the momentum of improvement rather than the rate of improvement; also known as 'kaizen', often contrasted with breakthrough improvement.

Continuous processes: processes that are high-volume and low-variety; usually products made on a continuous process are produced in an endless flow, such as petrochemicals or electricity.

Continuous review: an approach to managing inventory that makes inventory-related decisions when inventory reaches a particular level, as opposed to period review.

Control: the process of monitoring operations activity and coping with any deviations from the plan; usually involves elements of replanning.

Control charts: the charts used within statistical process control to record process performance.

Control limits: the lines on a control chart used in statistical process control that indicate the extent of natural or common-cause variations; any points lying outside these control limits are deemed to indicate that the process is likely to be out of control.

Core functions: the functions that manage the three core processes of any business: marketing, product/service development and operations.

Corporate social responsibility: how business takes account of its economic, social and environmental impacts.

Corporate strategy: the strategic positioning of a corporation and the businesses with it.

Cost-to-function analysis: an analysis of how much of the cost of a product or service is devoted to its primary and secondary functions.

CRAFT: Computerized Relative Allocation of Facilities Technique, a heuristic technique for developing good, but non-optimal, solutions.

Crashing: a term used in project management to mean reducing the time spent on critical path activities so as to shorten the whole project.

Create-to-order: *see* 'Make-to-order'.

Critical path: the longest sequence of activities through a project network, it is called the critical path because any delay in any of its activities will delay the whole project.

Critical path method (CPM): a technique of network analysis.

Customer contact skills: the skills and knowledge that operations staff need to meet customer expectations.

Customization: the variation in product or service design to suit the specific need of individual customers or customer groups.

Cycle inventory: inventory that occurs when one stage in a process cannot supply all the items it produces simultaneously and so has to build up inventory of one item while it processes the others.

Cycle time: the average time between units of output emerging from a process.

Decision support system (DSS): a management information system that aids or supports managerial decision-making; it may include both databases and sophisticated analytical models.

De-coupling inventory: the inventory that is used to allow work centres or processes to operate relatively independently.

Delivery flexibility: the operation's ability to change the timing of the delivery of its services or products.

Demand management: an approach to medium-term capacity management that attempts to change or influence demand to fit available capacity.

Demand side: the chains of customers, customers' customers, etc. that receive the products and services produced by an operation.

Dependability: delivering, or making available, products or services when they were promised to the customer.

Dependent demand: demand that is relatively predictable because it is derived from some other known factor.

Design acceptability: the attractiveness to the operation of a process, product or service.

Design capacity: the capacity of a process or facility as it is designed to be, often greater than effective capacity.

Design concept: the set of expected benefits to the customer encapsulated in a product or service design.

Design feasibility: the ability of an operation to produce a process, product or service.

Design funnel: a model that depicts the design process as the progressive reduction of design options from many alternatives down to the final design.

Design package: the component products, services and parts within a product or service design that provide the benefits to the customer.

Design screening: the evaluation of alternative designs with the purpose of reducing the number of design options being considered.

Design vulnerability: the risks taken by the operation in adopting a process, product or service.

Direct responsibilities of operations management: the activities that produce and deliver products and services.

Diseconomies of scale: a term used to describe the extra costs that are incurred in running an operation as it gets larger.

Disintermediation: the emergence of an operation in a supply network that separates two operations that were previously in direct contact.

Disruptive technologies: technologies which in the short term cannot match the performance required by customers but may improve faster than existing technology to make that existing technology redundant.

Distributed processing: a term used in information technology to indicate the use of smaller computers distributed around an operation and linked together so that they can communicate with each other, the opposite of centralized information processing.

Division of labour: an approach to job design that involves dividing a task down into relatively small parts, each of which is accomplished by a single person.

DMAIC cycle: increasingly used improvement cycle model, popularized by the Six Sigma approach to operations improvement.

Do or buy: the term applied to the decision on whether to own a process that contributes to a product or service, or, alternatively, outsource the activity performed by the process to another operation.

Downstream: the other operations in a supply chain between the operation being considered and the end customer.

Drum, buffer, rope: an approach to operations control that comes from the theory of constraints (TOC) and uses the bottleneck stage in a process to control materials movement.

Earned-value control: a method of assessing performance in project management by combining the costs and times achieved in the project with the original plan.

E-business: the use of internet-based technologies either to support existing business processes or to create entirely new business opportunities.

E-commerce: the use of the internet to facilitate buying and selling activities.

Economic batch quantity (EBQ): the amount of items to be produced by a machine or process that supposedly minimizes the costs associated with production and inventory holding.

Economic order quantity (EOQ): the quantity of items to order that supposedly minimizes the total cost of inventory management, derived from various EOQ formulae.

Economy of scale: the manner in which the costs of running an operation decrease as it gets larger.

Effective capacity: the useful capacity of a process or operation after maintenance, changeover and other stoppages and loading has been accounted for.

EFQM excellence model: a model that identifies the categories of activity that supposedly ensure high levels of quality; now used by many companies to examine their own quality-related procedures.

Electronic point of sale (EPOS): technology that records sales and payment transactions as and when they happen.

Emergent strategy: a strategy that is gradually shaped over time and based on experience rather than theoretical positioning.

Empowerment: a term used in job design to indicate increasing the authority given to people to make decisions within the job or changes to the job itself.

End-to-end business processes: processes that totally fulfil a defined external customer need.

Enterprise project management (EPM): software that integrates all the common activities in project management.

Enterprise resource planning (ERP): the integration of all significant resource planning systems in an organization that, in an operations context, integrates planning and control with the other functions of the business.

Environmental protection: activities and decisions in operations management that minimize the negative impact of processes, products and services on the environment.

E-procurement: the use of the internet to organize purchasing, this may include identifying potential suppliers and auctions as well as the administrative tasks of issuing orders etc.

Ergonomics: a branch of job design that is primarily concerned with the physiological aspects of job design, with how the human body fits with process facilities and the environment; can also be referred to as human factors, or human factors engineering.

Ethernet: a technology that facilitates local-area networks that allows any device attached to a single cable to communicate with any other devices attached to the same cable; also now used for wireless communication that allows mobile devices to connect to a local-area network.

European Quality Award (EQA): a quality award organized by the European Foundation for Quality Management (EFQM), it is based on the EFQM excellence model.

Events: points in time within a project plan; together with activities, they form network planning diagrams.

Expert systems (ES): computer-based problem-solving systems that, to some degree, mimic human problem-solving logic.

External failure costs: those costs that are associated with an error or failure reaching a customer, an element within quality-related costs.

Extranets: computer networks that link organizations together and connect with each organization's internal network.

Facilitating products: products that are produced by an operation to support its services.

Facilitating services: services that are produced by an operation to support its products.

Fail-safeing: building in, often simple, devices that make it difficult to make the mistakes that could lead to failure; also known by the Japanese term 'poka-yoke'.

Failure analysis: the use of techniques to uncover the root cause of failures; techniques may include accident investigation, complaint analysis, etc.

Failure mode and effect analysis (FMEA): a technique used to identify the product, service or process features that are crucial in determining the effects of failure.

Failure rate: a measure of failure that is defined as the number of failures over a period of time.

Fault tree analysis: a logical procedure starts with a failure or potential failure and works backwards to identify its origins.

Finite loading: an approach to planning and control that only allocates work to a work centre up to a set limit (usually its useful capacity).

First-tier: the description applied to suppliers and customers that are in immediate relationships with an operation with no intermediary operations.

Fixed cost break: the volumes of output at which it is necessary to invest in operations facilities that bear a fixed cost.

Fixed-position layout: locating the position of a product or service such that it remains largely stationary, while transforming resources are moved to and from it.

Flexibility: the degree to which an operation's process can change what it does, how it is doing it, or when it is doing it.

Flexible manufacturing systems (FMS): manufacturing systems that bring together several technologies into a coherent system, such as metal cutting and material handling technologies, usually their activities are controlled by a single governing computer.

Flexi-time working: increasing the possibility of individuals varying the time during which they work.

Flow record chart: a diagram used in layout to record the flow of products or services between facilities.

Focus group: a group of potential product or service users, chosen to be typical of its target market who are formed to test their reaction to alternative designs.

Forward scheduling: loading work onto work centres as soon as it is practical to do so, as opposed to backward scheduling.

Four-stage model of operations contribution: model devised by Hayes and Wheelwright that categorizes the degree to which operations management has a positive influence on overall strategy.

Front-office: the high-visibility part of an operation.

Functional strategy: the overall direction and role of a function within the business; a subset of business strategy.

Gantt chart: a scheduling device that represents time as a bar or channel on which activities can be marked.

Globalization: the extension of operations' supply chain to cover the whole world.

Heijunka: *see* 'Levelled scheduling'.

Heuristics: 'rules of thumb' or simple reasoning short cuts that are developed to provide good but non-optimal solutions, usually to operations decisions that involve combinatorial complexity.

Hierarchy of operations: the idea that all operations processes are made up of smaller operations processes.

High-level process mapping: an aggregated process map that shows broad activities rather than detailed activities (sometimes called an 'outline process map').

Hill methodology: an approach to formulating operations strategy, most often used in manufacturing operations.

Hire and fire: a (usually pejorative) term used in medium-term capacity management to indicate varying the size of the workforce through employment policy.

House of quality: *see* 'Quality function deployment'.

Human factors engineering: an alternative term for ergonomics.

Immediate supply network: the suppliers and customers that have direct contact with an operation.

Importance–performance matrix: a technique that brings together scores that indicate the relative importance and relative performance of different competitive factors in order to prioritize them as candidates for improvement.

Improvement cycles: the practice of conceptualizing problem solving as used in performance improvement in terms of a never-ending cyclical model, for example, the PDCA cycle or the DMAIC cycle.

Independent demand: demand that is not obviously or directly dependent on the demand for another product or service.

Indirect process technology: technology that assists in the management of processes rather than directly contributes to the creation of products and services, for example, information technology that schedules activities.

Indirect responsibilities of operations management: the activities of collaborating with other functions of the organization.

Infinite loading: an approach to planning and control that allocates work to work centres irrespective of any capacity or other limits.

Information technology (IT): any device, or collection of devices, that collects, manipulates, stores or distributes information, nearly always used to mean computer-based devices.

Infrastructural decisions: the decisions that concern the operation's systems, methods and procedures and shape its overall culture.

Input resources: the transforming and transformed resources that form the input to operations.

Intangible resources: the resources within an operation that are not immediately evident or tangible, such as relationships with suppliers and customers, process knowledge, new product and service development.

Interactive design: the idea that the design of products and services on one hand, and the processes that create them on the other, should be integrated.

Internal customers: processes or individuals within an operation that are the customers for other internal processes or individuals' outputs.

Internal failure costs: the costs associated with errors and failures that are dealt with inside an operation but yet cause disruption; an element within quality-related costs.

Internal suppliers: processes or individuals within an operation that supply products or services to other processes or individuals within the operation.

Internet: the network of networks that allows electronic data interchange over a wide geographical area.

Inventory: also known as stock, the stored accumulation of transformed resources in a process; usually applies to material resources but may also be used for inventories of information; inventories of customers or customers of customers are usually queues.

ISO 9000: a set of worldwide standards that established the requirements for companies' quality management systems, last revised in 2000, there are several sets of standards.

ISO 14000: an international standard that guides environmental management systems and covers initial planning, implementation and objective assessment.

Job design: the way in which we structure the content and environment of individual staff members' jobs within the workplace and the interface with the technology or facilities that they use.

Job enlargement: a term used in job design to indicate increasing the amount of work given to individuals in order to make the job less monotonous.

Job enrichment: a term used in job design to indicate increasing the variety and number of tasks within an individual's job, this may include increased decision-making and autonomy.

Job rotation: the practice of encouraging the movement of individuals between different aspects of a job in order to increase motivation.

Jobbing processes: processes that deal with high variety and low volumes, although there may be some repetition of flow and activities.

Just-in-time (JIT): a method of planning and control and an operations philosophy that aims to meet demand instantaneously with perfect quality and no waste.

Kaizen: Japanese term for continuous improvement.

Kanban: Japanese term for card or signal; it is a simple controlling device that is used to authorize the release of materials in pull control systems such as those used in JIT.

Keiretsu: a Japanese term used to describe a coalition of companies which form a supply network around a large manufacturer and can include service companies such as banks as well as conventional suppliers.

Lead-time usage: the amount of inventory that will be used between ordering replenishment and the inventory arriving, usually described by a probability distribution to account for uncertainty in demand and lead time.

Lean: an approach to operations management that emphasizes the continual elimination of waste of all types, often used interchangeably with just-in-time (JIT); it is more an overall philosophy whereas JIT is usually used to indicate an approach to planning and control that adopts lean principles.

Less important factors: competitive factors that are neither order-winning nor qualifying, performance in them does not significantly affect the competitive position of an operation.

Level capacity plan: an approach to medium-term capacity management that attempts to keep output from an operation or its capacity, constant, irrespective of demand.

Levelled scheduling: the idea that the mix and volume of activity should even out over time so as to make output routine and regular, sometimes known by the Japanese term 'heijunka'.

Life cycle analysis: a technique that analyses all the production inputs, life cycle use of a product and its final disposal in terms of total energy used and wastes emitted.

Line balancing: the activity of attempting to equalize the load on each station or part of a line layout or mass process.

Line layout: a more descriptive term for what is technically a product layout.

Little's law: the mathematical relationship between throughput time, work-in-process and cycle time (throughput time equals work-in-process × cycle time).

Loading: the amount of work that is allocated to a work centre.

Local-area network (LAN): a communications network that operates, usually over a limited distance, to connect devices such as PCs, servers, etc.

Location: the geographical position of an operation or process.

Logistics: a term in supply chain management broadly analogous to physical distribution management.

Long-term capacity management: the set of decisions that determine the level of physical capacity of an operation in whatever the operation considers to be long-term; this will vary between industries, but is usually in excess of one year.

Long thin process: a process designed to have many sequential stages, each performing a relatively small part of the total task, the opposite of short fat process.

Maintenance: the activity of caring for physical facilities so as to avoid or minimize the chance of those facilities failing.

Make-to-order: operations that produce products only when they are demanded by specific customers.

Make-to-stock: operations that produce products prior to their being demanded by specific customers.

Management information systems (MIS): information systems that manipulate information so that it can be used in managing an organization.

Manufacturing resource planning (MRP II): an expansion of materials requirement planning to include greater integration with information in other parts of the organization and often greater sophistication in scheduling calculations.

Market requirements: the performance objectives that reflect the market position of an operation's products or services, also a perspective on operations strategy.

Mass customization: the ability to produce products or services in high volume, yet vary their specification to the needs of individual customers or types of customer.

Mass processes: processes that produce goods in high volume and relatively low variety.

Mass services: service processes that have a high number of transactions, often involving limited customization, for example mass transportation services, call centres, etc.

Master production schedule (MPS): the important schedule that forms the main input to material requirements planning, it contains a statement of the volume and timing of the end products to be made.

Materials requirement planning (MRP): a set of calculations embedded in a system that helps operations make volume and timing calculations for planning and control purposes.

Mean time between failures (MTBF): operating time divided by the number of failures; the reciprocal of failure rate.

Merchandising: a term used to describe a role in retail operations management that often combines inventory management and purchasing with organizing the layout of the shop floor.

Method study: the analytical study of methods of doing jobs with the aim of finding the 'best' or an improved job method.

Micro-detailed process map: a process map that shows each single motion or small element of an activity.

Milestones: term used in project management to denote important events at which specific reviews of time, cost and quality can be made.

Mix flexibility: the operation's ability to produce a wide range of products and services.

Modular design: the use of standardized sub-components of a product or service that can be put together in different ways to create a high degree of variety.

MRP netting process: the process of calculating net requirements using the master production schedule and the bills of material.

Multi-skilling: increasing the range of skills of individuals in order to increase motivation and/or improve flexibility.

Multi-sourcing: the practice of obtaining the same type of product, component, or service from more than one supplier in order to maintain market bargaining power or continuity of supply.

Network analysis: overall term for the use of network-based techniques for the analysis and management of projects, for example, includes critical path method (CPM) and programme evaluation and review technique (PERT).

Open sourcing: products or services developed by an open community, including users.

Operational efficiency: helps improve supply chain performance.

Operations function: the arrangement of resources that are devoted to the production and delivery of products and services.

Operations management: the activities, decisions and responsibilities of managing the production and delivery of products and services.

Operations managers: the staff of the organization who have particular responsibility for managing some or all of the resources which compose the operation's function.

Operations resource capabilities: the inherent ability of operations processes and resources; also a perspective on operations strategy.

Operations strategy: the overall direction and contribution of the operation's function with the business; the way in which market requirements and operations resource capabilities are reconciled within the operation.

Optimized production technology (OPT): software and concept originated by Eliyahu Goldratt to exploit his theory of constraints (TOC).

Order fulfilment: all the activities involved in supplying a customer's order, often used in e-retailing but now also used in other types of operation.

Order-winners: the competitive factors that directly and significantly contribute to winning business.

Outline process map: *see* 'High-level process mapping'.

Outsourcing: the practice of contracting out to a supplier work previously done within the operation.

Overall equipment effectiveness (OEE): a method of judging the effectiveness of how operations equipment is used.

Pareto law: a general law found to operate in many situations that indicates that 20 per cent of something causes 80 per cent of something else, often used in inventory management (20 per cent of products produce 80 per cent of sales value) and improvement activities (20 per cent of types of problems produce 80 per cent of disruption).

Partnership: a type of relationship in supply chains that encourages relatively enduring cooperative agreements for the joint accomplishment of business goals.

Parts commonality: *see* 'Commonality'.

Parts family coding: the use of multi-digit codes to indicate the relative similarity between different parts, often used to determine the process route that a part takes through a manufacturing operation.

Passive interaction technology: customer-processing technology over which a customer has no, or very limited, control, for example, cinemas and moving walkways.

PDCA cycle: stands for Plan, Do, Check, Act cycle, perhaps the best known of all improvement cycle models.

***P*:*D* ratio:** a ratio that contrasts the total length of time customers have to wait between asking for a product or service and receiving it (D) and the total throughput time to produce the product or service (P).

Performance measurement: the activity of measuring and assessing the various aspects of a process or whole operation's performance.

Performance objectives: the generic set of performance indicators that can be used to set the objectives or judge the performance of any type of operation, although there are alternative lists proposed by different authorities, the five performance objectives as used in this book are quality, speed, dependability, flexibility and cost.

Performance standards: a defined level of performance against which an operation's actual performance is compared; performance standard can be based on historical performance, some arbitrary target performance, the performance of competitors, etc.

Periodic review: an approach to making inventory decisions that defines points in time for examining inventory levels and then makes decisions accordingly, as opposed to continuous review.

Perpetual inventory principle: a principle used in inventory control that inventory records should be automatically updated every time items are received or taken out of stock.

Physical distribution management: organizing the integrated movement and storage of materials.

Pipeline inventory: the inventory that exists because material cannot be transported instantaneously.

Planning: the formalization of what is intended to happen at some time in the future.

Plant-within-a-plant: a similar term to a cell layout but sometimes used to indicate a larger clustering of resources, *see also* 'Shop-within-a-shop'.

Poka-yoke: Japanese term for fail-safeing.

Polar diagram: a diagram that uses axes, all of which originate from the same central point, to represent different aspects of operations performance.

Predetermined motion–time systems (PMTS): a work measurement technique where standard elemental times obtained from published tables are used to construct a time estimate for a whole job.

Preliminary design: the initial design of a product or service that sets out its main components and functions, but does not include many specific details.

Prevention costs: those costs that are incurred in trying to prevent quality problems and errors occurring, an element within quality-related costs.

Preventive maintenance: an approach to maintenance management that performs work on machines or facilities at regular intervals in an attempt to prevent them breaking down.

Principles of motion economy: a checklist used to develop new methods in work study that is intended to eliminate elements of the job, combine elements together, simplify the activity or change the sequence of events so as to improve efficiency.

Processes: an arrangement of resources that produces some mixture of products and services.

Process capability: an arithmetic measure of the acceptability of the variation of a process.

Process design: the overall configuration of a process that determines the sequence of activities and the flow of transformed resources between them.

Process layout: locating similar transforming resources together so that different products or services with different processing needs will take different routes through the operation.

Process mapping: describing processes in terms of how the activities within the process relate to each other (may also be called 'process blueprinting' or 'process analysis').

Process mapping symbols: the symbols that are used to classify different types of activity; they usually derive either from scientific management or information-systems flow-charting.

Process of strategy: the way in which strategies are formulated.

Process outputs: the mixture of goods and services produced by processes.

Process technology: the machines and devices that create and/or deliver goods and services.

Process types: terms that are used to describe a particular general approach to managing processes; in manufacturing these are generally held to be project, jobbing, batch, mass and continuous processes; in services they are held to be professional services, service shops and mass services.

Production flow analysis (PFA): a technique that examines product requirements and process grouping simultaneously to allocate tasks and machines to cells in cell layout.

Productivity: the ration of what is produced by an operation or process to what is required to produce it, that is, the output from the operation divided by the input to the operation.

Product layout: locating transforming resources in a sequence defined by the processing needs of a product or service.

Product–process matrix: a model derived by Hayes and Wheelwright that demonstrates that natural fit between volume and variety of products and services produced by an operation on one hand, and the process type used to produce products and services on the other.

Product/service flexibility: the operation's ability to introduce new or modified products and services.

Product/service life cycle: a generalized model of the behaviour of both customers and competitors during the life of a product or service:; it is generally held to have four stages: introduction, growth, maturity and decline.

Product structure: diagram that shows the constituent component parts of a product or service package and the order in which the component parts are brought together (often called components structure).

Product technology: the embedded technology within a product or service, as distinct from process technology.

Professional services: service processes that are devoted to producing knowledge-based or advice-based services, usually involving high customer contact and high customization, examples include management consultants, lawyers, architects, etc.

Programme: as used in project management, it is generally taken to mean an ongoing process of change comprising individual projects.

Programme evaluation and review technique (PERT): a method of network planning that uses probabilistic time estimates.

Project: a set of activities with a defined start point and a defined end state which pursue a defined goal using a defined set of resources.

Project manager: competent project managers are vital for project success.

Project processes: processes that deal with discrete, usually highly customized, products.

Prototyping: an initial design of a product or service devised with the aim of further evaluating a design option.

Pull control: a term used in planning and control to indicate that a workstation requests work from the previous station only when it is required, one of the fundamental principles of just-in-time planning and control.

Purchasing: the organizational function, often part of the operations function, that forms contracts with suppliers to buy in materials and services.

Push control: a term used in planning and control to indicate that work is being sent forward to workstations as soon as it is finished on the previous workstation.

Qualified worker: term used in work study to denote a person who is accepted as having the necessary physical attributes, intelligence, skill, education and knowledge to perform the task.

Qualifiers: the competitive factors that have a minimum level of performance (the qualifying level) below which customers are unlikely to consider an operations performance satisfactory.

Quality: there are many different approaches to defining this. We define it as consistent conformance to customers' expectations.

Quality characteristics: the various elements within the concept of quality, such as functionality, appearance, reliability, durability, recovery, etc.

Quality function deployment (QFD): a technique used to ensure that the eventual design of a product or service actually meets the needs of its customers (sometimes called 'house of quality').

Quality loss function (QLF): a mathematical function devised by Genichi Taguchi that includes all the costs of deviating from a target performance.

Quality-related costs: an attempt to capture the broad cost categories that are affected by, or affect, quality, usually categorized as prevention costs, appraisal costs, internal failure costs and external failure costs.

Quality sampling: the practice of inspecting only a sample of products or services produced rather than every single one.

Quality variables: measures of quality that can be measured on a continuously variable scale, for example, length, weight, etc.

Queuing theory: a mathematical approach that models random arrival and processing activities in order to predict the behaviour of queuing systems (also called 'waiting line theory').

Rating: a work study technique that attempts to assess a worker's rate of working relative to the observer's concept of standard performance – controversial and now accepted as being an ambiguous process.

Received variety: the variety that occurs because the process is not designed to prevent it.

Recovery: the activity (usually a predetermined process) of minimizing the effects of an operation's failure.

Redundancy: the extent to which a process, product or service has systems or components that are used only when other systems or components fail.

Relationship chart: a diagram used in layout to summarize the relative desirability of facilities to be close to each other.

Reliability: when applied to operations performance, it can be used interchangeably with 'dependability', when used as a measure of failure it means the ability of a system, product or service to perform as expected over time, this is usually measured in terms of the probability of it performing as expected over time.

Reliability-centred maintenance: an approach to maintenance management that uses different types of maintenance for different parts of a process depending on their pattern of failure.

Remainder cell: the cell that has to cope with all the products that do not conveniently fit into other cells.

Re-order level: the level of inventory at which more items are ordered, usually calculated to ensure that inventory does not run out before the next batch of inventory arrives.

Re-order point: the point in time at which more items are ordered, usually calculated to ensure that inventory does not run out before the next batch of inventory arrives.

Repeatability: the extent to which an activity does not vary.

Repetitive strain injury (RSI): damage to the body because of repetition of activities.

Research and development (R&D): the function in the organization that develops new knowledge and ideas and operationalizes the ideas to form the underlying knowledge on which product, service and process design are based.

Resource-based view (RBV): the perspective on strategy that stresses the importance of capabilities (sometimes known as core competences) in determining sustainable competitive advantage.

Resource-to-order: operations that buy-in resources and produce only when they are demanded by specific customers.

Reverse engineering: the taking apart or deconstruction of a product or service in order to understand how it has been produced (often by a competing organization).

Robots: automatic manipulators of transformed resources whose movement can be programmed and reprogrammed.

Rostering: a term used in planning and control, usually to indicate staff scheduling, the allocation of working times to individuals so as to adjust the capacity of an operation.

Run-to-breakdown maintenance: an approach to maintenance management that only repairs a machine or facility when it breaks down.

SAP: a German company which is the market leader in supplying ERP software, systems and training.

Scheduling: a term used in planning and control to indicate the detailed timetable of what work should be done, when it should be done and where it should be done.

Scientific management: a school of management theory dating from the early twentieth century; more analytical and systematic than 'scientific' as such, sometimes referred to (pejoratively) as Taylorism, after Frederick Taylor who was influential in founding its principles.

Second-tier: the description applied to suppliers and customers who are separated from the operation only by first-tier suppliers and customers.

Sequencing: the activity within planning and control that decides on the order in which work is to be performed.

Service-level agreements (SLAs): formal definitions of the dimensions and levels of service that should be provided by one process or operation to another.

Service shops: service processes that are positioned between professional services and mass services, usually with medium levels of volume and customization.

Set-up reduction: the process of reducing the time taken to changeover a process from one activity to the next; also called 'single-minute exchange of dies' (SMED) after its origins in the metal pressing industry.

Shop-within-a-shop: an operations layout that groups facilities that have a common purpose together; the term was originally used in retail operations but is now sometimes used in other industries, very similar to the idea of a cell layout.

Short fat processes: processes designed with relatively few sequential stages, each of which performs a relatively large part of the total task, the opposite of long thin processes.

Simulation: the use of a model of a process, product or service to explore its characteristics before the process, product or service is created.

Simultaneous development: overlapping these stages in the design process so that one stage in the design activity can start before the preceding stage is finished, the intention being to shorten time to market and save design cost (also called 'simultaneous engineering' or 'concurrent engineering').

Single-minute exchange of dies (SMED): alternative term for set-up reduction.

Single-sourcing: the practice of obtaining all of one type of input product, component, or service from a single supplier, as opposed to multi-sourcing.

Six Sigma: an approach to improvement and quality management that originated in the Motorola Company but which was widely popularized by its adoption in the GE Company in America. Although based on traditional statistical process control, it is now a far broader 'philosophy of improvement' that recommends a particular approach to measuring, improving and managing quality and operations performance generally.

Skunkworks: a small, focused development team who are taken out of their normal working environment.

Social responsibility: the incorporation of the operation's impact on its stakeholders into operations management decisions.

Spatially variable costs: the costs that are significant in the location decision that vary with geographical position.

Speed: the elapsed time between customers' requesting products or services and their receiving them.

Stakeholders: the people and groups of people who have an interest in the operation and who may be influenced by, or influence, the operation's activities.

Standardization: the degree to which processes, products or services are prevented from varying over time.

Standard performance: term used in work measurement to indicate the rate of output that qualified workers will achieve without over-exertion as an average over the working day provided they are motivated to apply themselves, now generally accepted as a very vague concept.

Standard time: a term used in work measurement indicating the time taken to do a job and including allowances for recovery and relaxation.

Statistical process control (SPC): a technique that monitors processes as they produce products or services and attempts to distinguish between normal or natural variation in process performance and unusual or 'assignable' causes of variation.

Stock: alternative term for inventory.

Strategic decisions: those which are widespread in their effect, define the position of the organization relative to its environment and move the organization closer to its long-term goals.

Structural decisions: the strategic decisions which determine the operation's physical shape and configuration, such as those concerned with buildings, capacity, technology, etc.

Subcontracting: when used in medium-term capacity management, it indicates the temporary use of other operations to perform some tasks, or even produce whole products or services, during times of high demand.

Supplier quality assurance (SQA): the activity of monitoring and improving levels of quality of the products and services delivered by suppliers, also used to assess supply capability when choosing between alternative suppliers.

Supply chain: a linkage or strand of operations that provides goods and services through to end-customers; within a supply network several supply chains will cross through an individual operation.

Supply chain dynamics: the study of the behaviour of supply chains, especially the level of activity and inventory levels at different points in the chain; its best known finding is the bull-whip effect.

Supply chain risk: a study of the vulnerability of supply chains to disruption.

Supply network: the network of supplier and customer operations that have relationships with an operation.

Supply side: the chains of suppliers, suppliers' suppliers, etc. that provide parts, information or services to an operation.

Support functions: the functions that facilitate the working of the core functions, for example, accounting and finance, human resources, etc.

Synthesis from elemental data: work measurement technique for building up a time from previously timed elements.

Systemization: the extent to which standard procedures are made explicit.

Taguchi method: a design technique that uses design combinations to test the robustness of a design.

Tangibility: the main characteristic that distinguishes products (usually tangible) from services (usually intangible).

Teleworking: the ability to work from home using telecommunications and/or computer technology.

Theory of constraints (TOC): philosophy of operations management that focused attention on capacity constraints or bottleneck parts of an operation; uses software known as 'optimized production technology' (OPT).

Throughput time: the time for a unit to move through a process.

Time study: a term used in work measurement to indicate the process of timing (usually with a stopwatch) and rating jobs; it involves observing times, adjusting or normalizing each observed time (rating) and averaging the adjusted times.

Time to market (TTM): the elapsed time taken for the whole design activity, from concept through to market introduction.

Top-down: the influence of the corporate or business strategy on operations decisions.

Total productive maintenance (TPM): an approach to maintenance management that adopts a similar holistic approach to total quality management (TQM).

Total quality management (TQM): a holistic approach to the management of quality that emphasizes the role of all parts of an organization and all people within an organization to influence and improve quality; heavily influenced by various quality 'gurus', it reached its peak of popularity in the 1980s and 1990s.

Total supply network: all the suppliers and customers who are involved in supply chains that 'pass through' an operation.

Trade-off theory: the idea that the improvement in one aspect of operations performance comes at the expense of deterioration in another aspect of performance, now substantially modified to include the possibility that in the long term different aspects of operations performance can be improved simultaneously.

Transformation process model: model that describes operations in terms of their input resources, transforming processes and outputs of goods and services.

Transformed resources: the resources that are treated, transformed or converted in a process, usually a mixture of materials, information and customers.

Transforming resources: the resources that act upon the transformed resources, usually classified as facilities (the buildings, equipment and plant of an operation) and staff (the people who operate, maintain and manage the operation).

Two-handed process chart: a type of micro-detailed process map that shows the motion of each hand used in an activity on a common timescale.

Upstream: the other operations in a supply chain that are towards the supply side of the operation.

Usage value: a term used in inventory control to indicate the quantity of items used or sold multiplied by their value or price.

Utilization: the ratio of the actual output from a process or facility to its design capacity.

Valuable operating time: the amount of time at a piece of equipment or work centre that is available for productive working after stoppages and inefficiencies have been accounted for.

Value engineering: an approach to cost reduction in product design that examines the purpose of a product or service, its basic functions and its secondary functions.

Variation: the degree to which the rate or level of output varies from a process over time, a key characteristic in determining process behaviour.

Variety: the range of different products and services produced by a process, a key characteristic that determines process behaviour.

Vertical integration: the extent to which an operation chooses to own the network of processes that produce a product or service, the term is often associated with the 'do or buy' decision.

Virtual operation: an operation that performs few, if any, value-adding activities itself, rather it organizes a network of supplier operations, seen as the ultimate in outsourcing.

Virtual prototype: a computer-based model of a product, process or service that can be tested for its characteristics before the actual process, product or service is produced.

Visibility: the amount of value-added activity that takes place in the presence (in reality or virtually) of the customer, also called 'customer contact'.

Volume: the level or rate of output from a process, a key characteristic that determines process behaviour.

Volume flexibility: the operation's ability to change its level of output or activity to produce different quantities or volumes of products and services over time.

Waiting line theory: an alternative term for queuing theory.

Web-integrated ERP: enterprise resource planning that is extended to include the ERP-type systems of other organizations such as customers and suppliers.

Weighted-score method of location: a technique for comparing the attractiveness of alternative locations that allocates a score to the factors that are significant in the decision and weights each score by the significance of the factor.

Wide-area networks (WANs): similar to local-area networks (LANs) but with a greater reach, usually involving elements outside a single operation.

Work breakdown structure: the definition of, and the relationship between, the individual work packages in project management, each work package can be allocated its own objectives that fit in with the overall work breakdown structure.

Work content: the total amount of work required to produce a unit of output, usually measured in standard times.

Workflow: process of design of information-based processes.

Work-in-progess (WIP): the number of units within a process waiting to be processed further (also called 'work-in-process').

Work measurement: a branch of work study that is concerned with measuring the time that should be taken for performing jobs.

Work study: the term generally used to encompass method study and work measurement, derives from the scientific management school.

World Wide Web (WWW): the protocols and standards that are used on the internet for formatting, retrieving, storing and displaying information.

Yield management: a collection of methods that can be used to ensure that an operation (usually with a fixed capacity) maximizes its potential to generate profit.

Zero defect: the idea that quality management should strive for perfection as its ultimate objective even though in practice this will never be reached.

Index

Page numbers in **bold** refer to entries in the Glossary